IBSEN

IBSEN

A BIOGRAPHY

MICHAEL MEYER

DOUBLEDAY & COMPANY, INC.

GARDEN CITY, NEW YORK

1971

Library of Congress Catalog Card Number 78–150906

Note

All translations of passages from languages other than English are original, unless otherwise indicated.

Acknowledgments

Excerpts from Volume IV of THE COLLECTED PAPERS OF SIGMUND FREUD, edited by Ernest Jones, M.D., Basic Books, Inc., Publishers, New York, 1959.

Excerpts from MY LIFE IN ART by Constantin Stanislavski, translated by J. J. Robbins, republished with the permission of its publishers, Theatre Arts Books, New York, Copyright 1924 by Little, Brown & Company, Copyright 1948 for the Stanislavski Estate by Elizabeth Reynolds Hapgood.

Selection from THE NOTEBOOKS OF MALTE LAURIDS BRIGGE by Rainer Maria Rilke. Translated by M.D. Herter Norton. Copyright, 1949, by W. W. Norton & Company, Inc. Used with the permission of the publisher.

Excerpts from THE CRITICAL WRITINGS OF JAMES JOYCE edited by Ellsworth Mason and Richard Ellmann. Copyright © 1959 by Harriet Weaver and F. Lionel Monro, as administrators c.t.a. of the Estate of James Joyce. Reprinted by permission of The Viking Press, Inc.

Letter dated March, 1901 to Henrik Ibsen from LETTERS OF JAMES JOYCE edited by Stuart Gilbert. Copyright © 1957, 1966 by The Viking Press, Inc. Reprinted by permission of The Viking Press, Inc.

"The Trembling of the Veil" from THE AUTOBIOGRAPHY OF WILLIAM BUTLER YEATS by William Butler Yeats. Copyright © 1965 by The Macmillan Company. Used with the permission of the publisher.

Excerpt from "Sour Land," by Sidney Keyes from THE COLLECTED POEMS OF SIDNEY KEYES, edited by Michael Meyer. Copyright © 1945 by Routledge & Kegan Paul Ltd.

To Nora, with love

Contents

List of Illustrations

Introduction

Over forty years have elapsed since the publication in 1928 of Halvdan Koht's monumental two-volume biography of Ibsen (though a revised and partly rewritten edition appeared in 1954). Koht was acquainted with Ibsen's work as few other men have been, and was able to tap the memories of the dramatist's family and acquaintances. He was, too, an historian of distinction, and his book must be the foundation stone for any new study of Ibsen.

But for all its many and admirable qualities, Koht's biography has long been regarded as not wholly satisfactory. It is written from a narrowly nationalistic standpoint; Koht himself grew up as a young man during the period of Norway's struggle for political independence, and this theme frequently occupies the centre of his biography, with Ibsen reduced to the status of a foreground, sometimes even of a background figure. Ibsen's attitude towards his country's political problems was that of an independent observer rather than a committed patriot, and Koht could not always forgive him for not, on certain occasions, having behaved and written like Bjørnson. Koht, too, was not a man of the theatre, and Ibsen interested him more as a writer for the printed page than as a dramatist who was exploring and revolutionising the business of stagecraft. And Koht was born in 1873, only thirteen years after Chekhov, and his judgments are those of his generation. They are not necessarily the less correct for that, but a writer of Ibsen's stature means something different to every generation, and requires re-examination in every age.

Most importantly, however, Koht omits much vital and interesting factual information and leaves certain central questions unanswered. There is much that a student of Ibsen needs to know and cannot find there, yet which is in fact available, widely scattered in memoirs, letters, theses and newspaper reports; for example, Ibsen's years as director of the ill-starred Norwegian Theatre in Christiania between 1857 and 1862; his life in Rome while he was writing *Brand* and *Peer Gynt;* those seemingly rather barren but (like so many seemingly barren periods in writers' lives) powerfully formative years in Dresden from 1868 to 1875; the truth of his relationship with Suzannah and with the young girls he loved, or became infatuated with, in his old age; and the reaction to his work of his great contemporaries such as Tolstoy, Strindberg, Freud, Chekhov, Zola, Hardy, Henry James, Yeats, Rilke and Joyce. Such questions the present biography seeks to answer, or at any rate to provide the information from which the reader may hazard his own answer.

At the same time, I have tried to reconsider Ibsen's development as a man and as a writer; to reassess his work, both intrinsically and historically; to portray the changing theatrical world of his time, and to show the impact of his achievements on various countries. For even when, as in *Brand* and *Peer Gynt,* he was writing not for the stage but for a private theatre of the imagination, Ibsen was restlessly testing and expanding his craft, as explosive an international force in his field as Darwin or Marx or Freud in theirs.

Of the many people who have helped me in my work, I must especially thank the poet's grandson, Mr. Tancred Ibsen; Professor Francis Bull, whose knowledge of the subject is encyclopædic; Mr. Øyvind Anker, the librarian of Oslo University, and his ever-patient staff; and the staffs of Oslo Bymuseum, the University Library of Bergen, the University Library of Stockholm, the Royal Library of Stockholm, the Library of University College, London, the British Museum, the British Drama League, and the Victoria and Albert Museum, London. Professor Bull and Dr. Elia Bredsdorff kindly read my first volume in typescript and made numerous valuable suggestions. Mr. Nils Lie, Mr. Odd-Stein Andersson, and Mr. Jo Ørjasæter, who between them translated the three volumes into Norwegian, also drew my attention to various errors; and I must thank Dr. Einar Østvedt, Mr. Gordon Hølmebakk, and Mr. Rodney Blumer for their advice and encouragement.

This book rests heavily, not merely on Koht's biography, but on the great Centenary Edition of Ibsen's work edited by Koht, Professor Bull, and the late Professor Didrik Arup Seip, and published by Gyldendal of Oslo. Errors have been found in its twenty-one volumes, as in any work of such dimensions; they do not diminish it. My indebtedness to these three scholars' introductions to the plays and to the rest of Ibsen's work needs no underlining. I also pay respectful homage to Ibsen's earlier biographers: Paul Botten Hansen (1863), Henrik Jæger (1888), J. B. Halvorsen (1892), Edmund Gosse (1907), Gerhard Gran (1918), and A. E. Zucker (1929). My debt to other sources is acknowledged in the footnotes and bibliography.

I must thank Mrs. Reginald Orcutt for permission to quote from her father Basil King's articles, "Ibsen and Emilie Bardach," published in the *Century Magazine* in October and November 1923 including his translations of Emilie's diary and Ibsen's letters to her. The late Richard Graves and Mr. James Maxwell helped me with the translation of part of the Ger-

man correspondence between Ibsen and Emilie Bardach. All other translations of foreign passages, including Ibsen's letters, speeches, and articles, are
my own, except where otherwise specified.

My thanks are due also to the following for permission to reproduce
the various paintings, caricatures, photographs and manuscripts used in
the illustrations: Nasjonalmuséet, Oslo (cover portrait of Ibsen by Erik
Werenskiold); Nationalmuséet, Stockholm (Severin Falkman's drawing of
Carl Snoilsky); Drottningholms Teatermusée, Stockholm (still from 1883
production of *Ghosts*); Kungl. Biblioteket, Copenhagen (photographs of
Magdalene Thoresen, Georg Brandes, Frederik Hegel, Clemens Petersen,
Hans Christian Andersen and Laura Kieler); Municipal Gallery of Modern
Art, Dublin (Max Beerbohm's caricature, *Henrik Ibsen receiving Mr.
William Archer in audience*); Dominic and the National Theatre, London
(photograph of Maggie Smith as Hedda Gabler); Fru Viola Wahlstedt-
Guillemaut (photograph of Rosa Fitinghoff). All other illustrations are
reproduced by kind courtesy of Universitetsbiblioteket, Oslo, and Gylden-
dal Norsk Forlag, Oslo.

Finally, I owe, and gratefully admit, a debt of a different kind to Mr.
Casper Wrede and Mr. Michael Elliott, who between them taught me
whatever theatrical insight into Ibsen's work I may have acquired. From
them I learned to consider Ibsen as a man writing for the theatre rather
than for the printed page, and it is primarily from that viewpoint that I
have written this book.

London, 1970.   MICHAEL MEYER

IBSEN

Anyone who wishes to understand me fully must know Norway. The spectacular but severe landscape which people have around them in the north, and the lonely, shut-off life—the houses often lie miles from each other—force them not to bother about other people, but only their own concerns, so that they become reflective and serious, they brood and doubt and often despair. In Norway every second man is a philosopher. And those dark winters, with the thick mists outside—ah, they long for the sun!

Ibsen in conversation, quoted by Felix Philippi,
"Mein Verkehr mit Henrik Ibsen," in *Neue Freie Presse,* Vienna, 27 October 1902

We can see horribly clear in the works of such a man his whole life, as if we were God's spies.

John Keats, writing of Robert Burns to John Hamilton Reynolds

The Making of a Dramatist

1

Ancestry and Childhood

1828-1843

Henrik Johan Ibsen was born on 20 March 1828 in the small trading town of Skien on the east coast of Norway, a hundred miles south of the capital Christiania (now Oslo). He was the second child of a merchant, Knud Ibsen, and his wife Marichen, *née* Altenburg.

Ibsen is a Danish name (Ib is an old Danish form for Jacob), and in later years when he felt more than usually ill-disposed towards his native country, Henrik Ibsen was wont to assert that he had not a drop of Norwegian blood in his veins. In fact, thirteen of his sixteen great-great-grandparents were Norwegian, and as far as can be calculated he was approximately two-thirds Norwegian, one-sixth Danish and a little less than one-sixth German, with a slight admixture of Scottish. Apart from his father, his paternal ancestors had for over two hundred years been sea-captains; and towards the end of his life Henrik Ibsen is said to have looked, and walked, more and more like a sea-captain himself.

The earliest of his ancestors to have been traced was one Simen Ibsen-Holst, who was born in Bergen in the 1570's and obtained his captain's certificate there in 1604. He often travelled to Stege on the Danish island of Møen, and there, in due course, he married a wife and settled. His son Rasmus dropped the Holst from the family name; he, too, was a skipper, combining this activity with those of merchant and farmer. In about 1720 three of Rasmus Ibsen's sons went to live in their grandfather's birthplace of Bergen, where they married the three daughters of an émigré merchant named Heinrich Holtermann. In 1726 the youngest of the three sons, Peter, and his wife Birgitta had a son whom they named, after his German grandfather, Henrich.

This Henrich Ibsen, the dramatist's great-grandfather, married a girl named Wenche Dishington, whose ancestors had, at least four generations previously, come to Norway from Scotland. He was also of course a skipper and died in 1765 aged thirty-nine. Soon after his death Wenche bore a son whom, in memory of his father, she christened Henrich Petersen. A little later she remarried with a clergyman, Jacob von der Lippe. In 1771 he was appointed to a living at Solum, near Skien; thus the family moved from western to eastern Norway.

Henrich Petersen Ibsen, the dramatist's grandfather, was remembered as "a witty, clear-minded man, with many lively and eager interests; of a sanguine temperament, always full of jests and pranks."[1] On 22 November 1797, when he was thirty-two, the vessel of which he was both owner and captain went down with all hands off Hesnæs, near Grimstad, a tiny port a hundred miles south of Skien where, half a century later, his grandson was to write his first play. Only a few fragments of the wreck, including one bearing the name of the ship, drifted to land to tell the tale. Two years earlier he had married the daughter of a local merchant, Johanne Cathrine Plesner. Both her grandfathers were Danish and, like her husband, she also had German blood; she is said to have been "a cultivated woman, by the standards of the day; she took an eager interest in contemporary movements, her character was strict and earnest, and she is reported to have been deeply religious, which was not general in circles such as hers."[2] She gave her husband two sons before he died. Their firstborn, Jacob von der Lippe Ibsen, died in 1805 as a child of nine; their second, born in 1797, they called Knud Plesner Ibsen after his maternal grandfather.

The year after her husband's death, Johanne Ibsen married again, with a shipmaster named Ole Paus. She bore him eight children, four boys and four girls. Two of her sisters had married into rich merchant circles, so that she considerably raised the social standing of the Ibsens, and young Knud grew up with his eight half-brothers and half-sisters at a house in the parish of Gjerpen, just outside Skien, in an atmosphere of greater pretension than any earlier Ibsen had known.

On 1 December 1825, Knud Plesner Ibsen married Marichen Cornelia Martine Altenburg; he was twenty-eight, she twenty-six. She was also of Danish and German as well as Norwegian blood, and was an excellent match. Her father, Johan Andreas Altenburg, who had died the previous year, had been a wealthy shipmaster, and also, later, a merchant; in 1804–5 he is known to have been worth twenty to thirty thousand specie-dollars, or over five thousand pounds,[3] a considerable fortune in the Norway of those days. Little is recorded of Johan Altenburg's character; there is a tradition in Skien that the dramatist had him in mind when he wrote of Rasmus Gynt, that thrifty grandfather of Peer Gynt whose son Jon so wastefully squandered his inheritance. A girl who was brought up in

---

[1] Henrik Jæger, *Henrik Ibsen: et livsbillede* (Christiania, 1888, p. 5.
[2] *Ibid.*, p. 4.
[3] With the English pound then the equivalent of $4.8667, about $24,375. The specie-dollar may be reckoned as roughly the equivalent of the contemporary U.S. dollar, the Norwegian crown as about 25 cents.

the house remembered Hedevig Christine Altenburg many years later as "an authoritative woman, strict with children; clever and thrifty, keeping her house in exemplary order."[4] She was the sister of Knud Ibsen's step-father Ole Paus, and Knud had frequently visited the Altenburg house as a child, so that he and Marichen had virtually grown up together.

Knud and Marichen Ibsen had their first child, a boy, Johan Altenburg Ibsen, on 3 October 1826, but he died at the age of eighteen months on 14 April 1828. Three and a half weeks before this unhappy event, on 20 March, a second son was born. They named him Henrik Johan, after his two grandfathers. He was baptised at home on 28 March, which suggests that he may have been weakly, and again in church on 10 June. Three citizens of substance stood as godfathers: Ulrich Cudrio, merchant and shipmaster, Jacob Bakke, sea-captain, and J. Stenersen, sea-captain; also a humbler figure, Jacob Boyssen, storekeeper at a works, probably a member of the church committee. Marichen Ibsen herself and Knud's half-sister Mariane Paus were registered as the child's godmothers. Knud and Marichen Ibsen had four more children during the next seven years, all of whom survived into adulthood: Johan Andreas Altenburg, Hedvig Cathrine, Nicolai Alexander, and Ole Paus. Henrik Ibsen thus grew up as the eldest of five.

The house in which he was born stood in the main square of Skien and was named Stockmannsgaarden. It no longer stands, having been destroyed, like most of the other houses in the centre of the town, by the great fire of 1886. A contemporary water-colour portrays it as a pleasing wooden edifice of two storeys with tall windows divided into tiny panes. When Henrik was two, his father bought his widowed mother-in-law's house, Altenburggaarden, a larger and more opulent building with its own paddock, just around the corner in Prindsensgade (now Henrik Ibsens gate), and they moved there in the following year, 1831.

Ibsen's first biographer, Henrik Jæger, writing in 1888, described the Skien of Ibsen's childhood as being "a homely little timber town, containing scarcely three thousand inhabitants. But, small as it was, it was the scene of much busy life and a not unimportant centre of trade."[5] The town had made considerable economic progress since the turn of the century; many shipmasters and captains had earned useful fortunes during the Napoleonic Wars and the export of timber to England had also proved rewarding. Edmund Gosse compared it to "a kind of Poole or Dartmouth . . . existing solely for purposes of marine merchandise, and depending for prosperity, and life itself, on the sea."[6] It possessed a flourishing timber trade and in the eighteen-twenties boasted four spectacular weirs and some forty sawmills. Many years later, in 1895, Ibsen

[4] Oskar Mosfjeld, *Henrik Ibsen og Skien* (Oslo, 1949), p. 17.
[5] Jæger, p. 6.
[6] Edmund Gosse, *Ibsen* (London, 1907), p. 2.

described it as "the town of the storming, soughing, seething waters. Over the whole town there is, as it were, a song in the air from all the weirs. So at least I remember it. . . . It is not for nothing," he added, "that I was born in the town of rushing waters."[7]

The natives of Telemark, the province in which Skien lies, are, temperamentally, a race apart from their fellow-countrymen. Foreigners who know Norway only through Oslo, the west coast, and the northern and central ski resorts have written of Ibsen as an untypical Norwegian. He was by no means an untypical native of Telemark. "They appear sanguine but are often melancholic," a Norwegian historian has written. "They analyse and pass judgment on themselves."[8] Another, speaking of the people of Skien in particular, observes: "They are proud and stiff, combative when anyone threatens their interest, dislike being told. They are reserved and cautious towards strangers, do not easily accept their friendship, and are not very forthcoming even towards their own kin. Strangers who go to live there often feel isolated. The people of Skien are afraid openly to surrender to a mood, or let themselves be carried away; this apparent lack of spontaneity is what Ibsen calls the 'shyness of the soul.' They have an alert critical sense, but their criticism is not mercilessly direct and honest such as, for example, one finds in the people of Bergen. The citizens of Skien prefer to express theirs in quiet, ironical observations, in subtle satire, in mimicry. An unlucky and thoughtless utterance can easily be remembered so long that it becomes a proverb."[9]

Apart from a few weeks in 1814, and we must remember this when considering Ibsen's early artistic and spiritual problems, Norway had not known true independence for nearly 450 years. This proudest of people had come under Danish rule in 1387, when the crown had passed to a member of the Danish royal house, and had remained thus, an Ireland to Denmark's England, until in 1814 the Treaty of Kiel at last freed her from this unwilling union. She at once tried to assert her independence by setting up a constitution, which still stands; but the Great Powers, led by England and Russia, promptly handed her over to Sweden as a reward for the latter country's support of their cause against Napoleon. The Norwegians took up arms in defence of their liberty, but the new king-elect of Sweden, Napoleon's long-nosed former marshal Bernadotte, shortly to become Carl XIV Johan,[10] defeated them in a brief campaign and forced them into yet another unwilling union; although he permitted them to keep their constitution and retained only a suspensive, not an absolute veto on the decisions of the Storthing, the Norwegian Parliament. Norway

[7] Letter to Hildur Andersen, 29 July 1895.

[8] Vetle Vislie in *Norge, 1814–1914,* ed. N. Rolfsen and E. Werenskiold, II (Christiania, 1914), 164.

[9] Mosfjeld, p. 57.

[10] The old king, Carl XIII, was childless, and the Swedish Parliament had chosen Bernadotte to succeed him.

had thus merely exchanged the Danish yoke for a Swedish one. Politically, she was a province of Sweden; culturally, she remained a province of Denmark. Her citizens read Danish novels, or Danish translations from the English and French; even the written Norwegian language, *riksmaal*, was virtually indistinguishable from written Danish, though a movement was afoot to utilise the natural rhythms and idiomatic richness of the country dialects—a situation very similar, linguistically as politically, to that which was to exist in Ireland half a century later.

Unlike Ireland, however, Norway had virtually no literature to boast of: only one writer of international standing, the eighteenth-century dramatist Ludvig Holberg (1684–1754)—and he, though born in Norway, had done all his writing in Denmark for Danish readers—and in the nineteenth century two distinctive and interesting poets, Henrik Wergeland and J. S. Welhaven. Otherwise, there were only the old ballads and folk tales, which were now being reclaimed as, in the previous century, scholars such as Bishop Percy had reclaimed the Old English and Scottish ballads and, more recently, the brothers Grimm the folk tales of Germany. The Icelandic Sagas, written six centuries earlier by Norwegian emigrants to Iceland, were no more intelligible to nineteenth-century Norwegians than the Anglo-Saxon Chronicles are to modern Englishmen.

At the time of Ibsen's birth, Norway was still a very primitive country. Many of the houses in the remoter rural areas were windowless, as they had been in the Middle Ages, with only a hole in the roof to let out the smoke. Farming methods were extraordinarily antiquated; "the cattle," we learn, "wintered in stalls built without light or standing-room, so as to give the maximum of warmth, from which they were lifted out as living skeletons when spring came; the accumulated muck was then shovelled out on to the fields."[11] Fishermen still used the line instead of the costlier but far more effective net; and as late as the middle of the nineteenth century, leprosy was still to be found along the west coast, in some areas affecting as high a proportion as 1 per cent of the population. The towns were tiny. Even the capital Christiania (which had been Oslo until 1624, but was not to regain its old name until 1925) boasted less than 30,000 inhabitants. The country possessed no coal. Little of her mountainous soil was cultivable (even today the figure is less than 3 per cent), and a quarter was covered by forests. Her people depended largely upon the sea for their livelihood and for their communications; Ibsen was a grown man before the first railway was seen in Norway.

In 1881 Ibsen jotted down some childhood memories, the only extended fragment of autobiography to which he ever committed himself:

When a few years ago the streets in my birthplace of Skien came to be named, or perhaps I should say re-named, I had the honour to have one

[11] T. K. Derry, *A Short History of Norway* (London, 1957), p. 142.

street called after me. Or so at any rate the newspapers have reported, and I have also heard it from reliable travellers.[12] They tell me that this street stretches from the main square down towards the harbour, or *muddringen*.[13]

But if this news is correct, I cannot think on what grounds the street came to bear my name; for I was not born in it, and have never lived in it. I was born in a house in the main square, Stockmannsgaarden, as it was then called. This house stood directly opposite the front of the church, with its steep steps and lofty tower. To the right of the church stood the town pillory, and to the left the town hall, with is cell for delinquents and "lunatic-box." The fourth side of the square was occupied by the Grammar School and Lower School. The church stands isolated in the centre.

This prospect was accordingly the first sight of the world that greeted my eyes. Only buildings; nothing green; no rural, open landscape. But above this square of stone and timber the air was filled all day long with the softly booming whisper of Langefoss and Klosterfoss and the many other weirs; and through their watery roar there penetrated, from morning to dusk, something resembling the sharp cries of women, now shrieking, now moaning. It was the hundreds of sawblades working out on the weirs. When later I read of the guillotine, I always thought of those saw-blades.

The church was of course the town's most imposing building. When one Christmas Eve towards the end of the last century, thanks to the care-lessness of a servant-girl, Skien was burned down, the old church was burned too. The servant-girl was, not surprisingly, executed. But the town, which was rebuilt with broad and regular streets covering its hills and hol-lows, gained thereby a new church, of which the citizens used to claim with a certain pride that it was of yellow Dutch clinker, had been raised by a Copenhagen master builder, and exactly resembled the church at Konigs-berg. These merits I understood at that time insufficiently to appreciate them; but what inscribed itself powerfully in my memory was a large, white, heavy-limbed angel which on weekdays hovered high up under the vaulting with a bowl in its hands, but on Sundays, when a child was to be baptised, descended softly among us.

Almost more than the white angel, however, another resident of the church excited my imagination; the black poodle, which dwelt at the top of the tower where the watchman called the hours at night. It had glowing eyes, but was not often seen; indeed, as far I know it only showed itself once. It was a New Year's Eve, just as the watchman shouted "One!" through the window in the front of the tower. Then the black poodle came up out of the staircase behind him, stood still, just looked at him with its glowing eyes, that was all; but the watchman fell through the window on to his head in the square, where they saw him lying dead, all the good people who walked that New Year's morning early to matins. Since that night, the watchman never shouts "One" through *that* window in the church at Skien.

---

[12] Ibsen had, at the time of writing, been resident in Italy and Germany for seven-teen years.

[13] Derived from *mudre,* to dredge.

This business with the watchman and the poodle happened long before my time, and I have since heard tell that similar events occurred in olden times in several other Norwegian churches. But that same tower window held for me, when I was a child, an especial significance, in that it was there that I received the first conscious impression that has remained with me. My nursemaid carried me one day up into the tower and let me sit alone in the open window, safely held from behind, of course, by her faithful arms. I remember clearly how impressed I was at being able to see the crowns of people's hats; I looked down into our own rooms, saw the window frames, saw the curtains, saw my mother standing down there in one of the windows; yes, I could see over the rooftop and down into the courtyard, where our brown horse stood tied to the stable door swishing its tail. On the stable wall I remember there hung a pail. But then there was a hubbub, and a crowd of people, and a waving upwards from down there in the doorway, and the maid pulled me hurriedly away and ran down with me. I don't remember the rest; but afterwards they often told me how my mother had caught sight of me in the window of the tower, had shrieked, had fainted, as people did then, and later, having got me back, had wept and kissed and petted me. As a boy I never afterwards crossed the square without looking up at the window in the tower. I felt that that window belonged to me and the church poodle.

I have kept only one other memory from those earliest years. As a christening gift I had been given, among other things, a large silver coin with a man's head on it. The man had a high forehead, a big hooked nose and a protruding underlip; he was, moreover, bare-necked, which I found strange. The nursemaid taught me that the man on the coin was "King Fredrik Rex," and once I tried to bowl it along the floor, with the unfortunate result that the coin rolled down into a crack. I think my parents interpreted this as an unlucky omen, it being a christening gift. The floor was taken up and they searched and dug around assiduously, but King Fredrik Rex never saw the light of day again. For a long time afterwards I could not help regarding myself as a wicked felon, and when I saw the town constable, Peter the German, emerge from the town hall and make his way towards our door, I ran as fast as I could into the nursery and hid myself beneath the bed.

As things turned out we did not live long in the house on the square. My father bought a bigger house, into which we moved when I must have been about four [sic] years old. This new home of mine was a corner house, sited a little higher up in the town, just at the foot of Hundevad Hill, so called after an old German-speaking doctor whose majestic wife drove around in something we called "the glass coach," which in winter was used as a sleigh. This house had many large rooms, both downstairs and upstairs, and much entertaining went on. But we boys did not spend much time indoors. The main square, where the two biggest schools stood, was the natural meeting-place and battlefield for the youth of the town. The Grammar School was at that time ruled by the eminent and exceedingly lovable old Dr. Ørn; while in the Lower School the principal authority was, I believe, the janitor Iver Flasrud, an equally impressive old man who also acted as the town barber. Between the boys of these two schools many a violent battle was waged around the church; but I, being a pupil of neither, was for the most part merely an attendant spectator. In any event I was as a child not, as a rule, combatively inclined.[14] For me there resided a far more potent attraction in the aforementioned pillory and in the town hall with all its presumably sinister secrets. The pillory was a reddish-brown post of about the height of a man; above, it had a big round knob which had originally been painted black. By now this knob looked like a friendly and inviting human face, cocked slightly askew. On the front of the post hung an iron chain and from this an open hoop, which seemed to me like two small arms waiting gleefully to fasten themselves around my throat. This had not been used for many years; but I remember well that it stood there all the time I was in Skien. Whether it still stands I do not know.

Then there was the town hall. Like the church, it had a steep flight of steps. Beneath were the cells, with barred windows looking on to the square. Behind those bars I have seen many pale and sinister faces. One room deep down in the cellars was known as the "lunatic box" and must in fact, improbable as it now seems to me, have been used in its time to confine lunatics. This room had barred windows like the others; but behind the bars the whole of the small window space was filled with a massive iron screen, bored with innumerable tiny holes so that it resembled a colander. This place was also said to have served as residence for a famous criminal of the time known as Brandeis, because he had been branded; and I believe it was, too, once occupied by an escaped slave who had been recaptured and was flogged up in Li Square. Of this last fellow eye-witnesses told how he had danced as they led him to his place of punishment, but that when the time came for him to return to prison he had to be carried in a cart.

Skien was, in the years of my childhood, an unusually gay and sociable town, very much the opposite of what it was later to become. Many highly cultivated, esteemed and prosperous families lived there then, either in the town itself or on the great estates outside. Most of these families were either closely or distantly related, and balls, dinner parties and musical gatherings followed each other in rapid succession, winter and summer. Many travellers also visited the town and, since there were then no proper hotels, they stayed with friends or relations. We almost always had people staying in our large and roomy house, which at Christmas and Fair-time would be full, an open table being kept from morning to night. Skien Fair was held in February, and was an especially happy occasion for all us boys; a full six months ahead we would begin to save our pennies so as to be able to watch the jugglers and the rope-dancers and the "equine artists," and buy gingerbread in the market stalls. Whether this Fair greatly contributed to the commercial prosperity of the town I do not know; I remember it

[14] He was one of those children who seem old.
Lacking the will to join his wild companions
In their free play, he but looks quietly on,
Sufficient to himself.
                              Epic version of *Brand,* 1865

principally as a great popular feast which lasted for something like a whole week on end.[15]

The 17th of May[16] was not in those days an occasion of particular festivity in Skien. A few young people fired off popguns out on Bleaching Hill, or let off fireworks, but that was about all.[17] I think this reserve in our otherwise ebullient town arose mainly from respect to a certain worthy gentleman whose ancestral home lay in the neighbourhood and whom for various reasons people were reluctant to offend.

But we made up for this on Midsummer Eve. This was not communally celebrated, but the boys and young men of the town would divide up into five or six groups, each devoted to gathering material for its own bonfire. As early as Whitsuntide we would start going around in packs to the shipyards and shops to "beg" empty tar-barrels. One curious custom had survived from time immemorial. What was not freely given us we stole, without either the owner or the police ever considering laying a complaint against such outrageous behaviour. A group would thus gradually assemble a whole pile of empty tar-barrels. We enjoyed the same time-honoured right over old boats. Should we happen to come upon any of these drawn up on land, and succeed in dragging one or another of them away undetected and keeping

[15] These February fairs were revived in 1835 after having been dropped for about fifty years. They were held down by the wharfs, and seem to have been mainly for the sale of hides; many people came from all over Telemark, and even foreigners. The local newspapers, *Bratsberg Amtstidende* and *Ugebladet,* tell us some of the entertainers who appeared, and whom Ibsen may have seen. In 1841 and 1842, for example, there was Balabrega, whose *kunstcabinet* contained "mechanical artifices, a collection of illuminations, and all the Swedish Kings and ruling Queens from Gustav I to the Present Monarch"; Guidotti with his Cabinet of Extraordinary Waxworks; Alexander and his Equestrian Artists. G. Francke announced that he would send up two hydrogen-filled "Acrostatic Figures," namely, "An Observation Balloon with the Norwegian Tricolour" and "A Turk, Life-Size, with a Globe in his Hand"; P. Dahl and Company advertised a great display of "Gymnastics, Equilibrianism, Rope-Dancing, Indian and Malabara Conjuring, and Feats of Strength"; and the Norwegian sprinter and clown Hermann offered to race "The Town's Horsemen" for a wager. In March 1844 a big circus came to Skien, Gautier's Equestrian Company, boasting no less than fifty-two performers and forty horses; they marched into the town from the quay with instruments playing, like the circus performers in *The Pillars of Society.* (Mosfjeld, p. 47.)

[16] The anniversary of the promulgation of the Norwegian Constitution in 1814.

[17] The 17th of May does not always seem to have been as dull as Ibsen suggests. In 1842 *Bratsberg Amtstidende* describes the scene at Skien as follows: "At around six o'clock signs of life began to appear in the streets, and a crowd such as our town seldom offers to the eye gathered in the vicinity of the square. To the accompaniment of music and with the beautiful tricolour flag at their head hundreds of people set forth across the bridges to the Abbey Wood, whither many had already repaired, to celebrate the Day of Liberation in God's blessed nature. Here all the people now mingled, and a general dance began, in which rank and social distinctions were for some hours laid aside. As well as the modern dances, our nimble mountain lads aroused lively interest by their smartness and agility in the Halling and the Leap. The Song of Liberation was frequently heard from the enthusiastic multitude. The whole ended with a grand firework display and the sending aloft of an Air Balloon, a rare occurrence in this parish." (Mosfjeld, p. 55.)

our prize safely hidden, then our right of ownership was thereby conceded, or was anyway never challenged by anyone. Then, the day before Midsummer Eve, the boat would be carried in triumph through the streets to the place of our bonfire. Up in the boat would sit a fiddler. I have on several occasions witnessed a procession of this nature, and once myself took part in one.

Here Ibsen tantalisingly concludes his reminiscences. When he was seven, his childhood suddenly became clouded by misfortune and disgrace, and even in old age he evidently had no desire to commit his later memories to print.

Knud Ibsen ran a *bondehandel,* a general store which sold practically everything: groceries, dairy produce, glass, hardware, ice cream, wine and schnapps. This last commodity he distilled himself; indeed, his was the second largest distillery in town. He also acted as a general importer, and the customs records indicate the extent of his trade. From Bordeaux he imported wine, grape brandy and groceries; from Flensburg, dolls, pewter, ivory combs, glassware, hardware and catgut; from London, woollen and cotton goods; from Altona, aniseed, coriander and fennel seed, presumably for schnapps-making; from Hamburg, woollen goods; and from Newcastle, malt mustard, stone goods and whetstones.[18] He did well; in the year 1833-34, only sixteen private individuals in the district had a higher income, and around the middle of 1833, anxious no doubt to keep pace with his relatives and friends, he indulged in the luxury of buying a small country house with forty acres of land at Venstøp in the parish of Gjerpen, a couple of miles outside Skien, for 1,650 specie-dollars (about £410).

No photograph or portrait of Knud Ibsen exists. He is remembered as having been "under medium height, slight-limbed, oval-faced, with a rather long and slightly crooked nose and a small mouth; narrow between the eyes, with a somewhat sly expression; fair and rather long hair,"[19] and as "a wag, a satirist, and very foxy."[20] Another witness who met him as an old man found him "a trivial little fellow of the most ordinary kind with no distinguishing characteristics, who, however much he talked, never said anything of the faintest interest";[21] but that was when he was nearly eighty and the years of failure, poverty and drink had taken their toll. In his youth he seems to have been a good raconteur with a large stock of funny stories and a quickly inventive tongue. He loved trotting and was a great hunter (there were many wolves in the district then). In his last years he "came every morning at eleven o'clock to a baker whose shop stood next to the old school. In the back room of the bakery was a little café, where Knud Ibsen would take a schnapps and a glass of beer.

[18] Skien customs records, quoted by Mosfjeld, p. 62.
[19] J. A. Schneider, *Fra det gamle Skien,* III (Skien, 1924), 249.
[20] Mosfjeld, p. 23.
[21] *Ibid.,* pp. 23-24.

As he sat there enjoying himself, the boys from the school would often come and bang on the window and shout abuse to annoy him. Then he would become raging mad and rail at them furiously, but at the same time so wittily that the words fairly crackled. It was like a firework display."[22] His son was to paint three different but equally recognisable portraits of him in his plays: as Jon Gynt in *Peer Gynt,* Daniel Hejre in *The League of Youth,* and Old Ekdal in *The Wild Duck.*

Knud Ibsen's wife Marichen (pronounced Marken) is said to have been very beautiful. A silhouette of her as a young girl (the only likeness we have) shows a pleasing profile with a *retroussé* nose. As a young girl she was keen on drawing and painting (some water-colours by her which have survived show a not negligible talent); and she was, then, merry and gay, and worried her family by her passionate interest in the theatre. Evening after evening she would slip away to the performances that travelling Danish players gave in the town. Her parents were also disturbed by her fondness, even when she was a grown girl, for playing with dolls; an expression, it has been suggested, of her frustrated theatrical passion. She played the piano and sang, was lively and spontaneous, small and dark-haired, with deep and sensitive eyes.

Such were Henrik Ibsen's parents for the first seven years of his life: a gay and prosperous couple, keeping open house. But in 1834, when Henrik was six, his father's troubles began. On 10 June of that year the authorities closed his schnapps distillery, and he was distrained for thirteen dalers for tax arrears. This was less than a year after he had had the seventeenth largest private income in the town. During the latter half of 1834, most of 1835 and part of 1836 he was forced to mortgage or sell most of his possessions. The newspaper *Ugebladet* contains repeated advertisements of forthcoming auctions to this end. In January 1835 his domestic animals, six cows, four horses and four pigs, were put up for sale; on 2 May, the proud Altenburg mansion, to meet the bills of the Hamburg house of Kragelius; on 9 June, the furnishings thereof, including "bedclothes, two rare carpets and two large mirrors"; and in August, two boat-houses. His creditors did not, as has been supposed, bankrupt him, for his name remained on the list of citizens entitled to vote, from which bankrupts were excluded. They left him his small country house at Venstøp, and to this, probably early in June 1835, Knud and Marichen retired with their four children, and a fifth on the way.

Financial ruin has been known to alter a man's character for the better. It was not so with Knud Ibsen. He became combative, sarcastic and bitter towards those who were not his friends and also very litigious. The legal archives of Skien are full of petty suits which he brought against this person and that, including even his servants. Oskar Mosfjeld, who interviewed several people who had known Knud Ibsen, or whose parents had

[22] *Ibid.,* p. 23.

known him, comments: "He wanted to dominate everyone . . . and if people did not bow to his wishes he became coarse and uncontrolled, especially when he had a little drink inside him. One can imagine what bitterness the sense of social degradation must have unleashed in a man of his temperament, how difficult it must have been for him to accept the fact that no one any longer looked up to him. He found people unjust and ungrateful, and struck at them with the only weapon he had left: his sharp tongue. When misery got the better of him, he sought refuge in the bottle and dreamed of the day when he should regain the social position which befitted him. He lacked balance and did not understand how to accept his downfall with dignity. Had he done so, things might in some measure have righted themselves, for his half-brothers were well-to-do and amiably disposed towards him, and he had every opportunity to have worked his way up again had he set his mind to it. But such now were his state of mind and his conduct that many felt embarrassed at being called friends of Knud Ibsen; and when his acquaintances one after another turned away from him, the reason was not, as he supposed, that they despised him for being poor, but because his less fortunate characteristics had come to the surface and made him disagreeable company. At home he felt no inhibitions to his passion for dominance, which at times bordered on brutality. Here he took his revenge for all the frustration which he encountered elsewhere, and made his wife and children pay for it. He could still be polite in company and sociable at home when he chose. But he was moody and incalculable and, when the inclination took him, he gave his touchiness full rein."[23]

Marichen Ibsen, too, became a different person. The gay young woman with a passion for the theatre developed into a withdrawn and melancholy recluse. We are told that she hardly dared to speak to people after her husband's degradation, but hid herself away so as to attract as little notice as possible. "Knud Ibsen scared the wits out of her," an old lady told Mosfjeld, "so that in the end she became like a changeling";[24] and other witnesses confirmed that throughout the years at Venstøp she was silent and withdrawn. But she remained loyal to Knud Ibsen. Her daughter Hedvig, many years later, described her as "a quiet, lovable woman, the soul of the house, everything for her husband and children. She always sacrificed herself; bitterness and fault-finding were unknown to her."[25]

To the disgrace of his father's financial ruin and social degradation was added another source of embarrassment which must profoundly have affected Henrik Ibsen's childhood. It was openly rumoured that Henrik was not Knud Ibsen's son, but that of an old admirer of his mother named Tormod Knudsen. Marichen had met Knudsen in 1825, shortly before her marriage, when he had come to work as a clerk in the local sheriff's office, and although she was then already engaged, there is a

[23] *Ibid.*, pp. 20–21.
[24] *Ibid.*, p. 27.
[25] Letter to Henrik Jæger, p. 5.

strong tradition in Telemark that she and Knudsen were lovers. This tradition furthermore asserted that the affair continued after her marriage, and that Tormod not only was Henrik's father, but even claimed to be. Knudsen's legitimate son, Knut Knudsen, knew of this rumour years later, and believed it.[26] An old lady who lived on in Skien until the nineteen-thirties told Mosfjeld that she knew something "terrible" about Marichen Ibsen, but had sworn never to reveal it; and Mosfjeld adds that this informant "was by no means of the sensation-mongering type, but on the contrary exceedingly reliable, sober and truthful."[27] Henrik Ibsen himself knew of these rumours. His friend Christopher Due recorded that once at Grimstad, when Ibsen was in his late 'teens and drunk, he blurted out his suspicions to Due and to their friend Ole Schulerud. "As he spoke," writes Due, "he gradually became very excited, said in plain words that there were irregularities connected with his birth and bluntly named Tormod Knudsen." Due adds that he never liked to press Ibsen on the subject, and that Ibsen never mentioned it again.[28]

Whether this rumour was true we shall never know. But one important piece of evidence is against it. Henrik Ibsen never remotely resembled Knudsen, whom photographs show as having a long face with a pointed jaw and a protruding underlip; but he very closely resembled Knud Ibsen. Professor Francis Bull states that people in Skien used to say of Henrik Ibsen in his later years that "it was like seeing old Ibsen [i.e., Knud] resurrected."[29] J. A. Schneider quotes persons who knew both Knud and Henrik Ibsen as saying that they had something in common in "appearance, character and habits";[30] and J. Borchsenius writes that Knud Ibsen in old age wore that same peculiarly tight expression around the mouth that we see in Henrik Ibsen's photographs.[31] Against all this we have only rumour. Knudsen's own claim to have been the father means little. Men who covet another man's wife and are known or thought to have been intimate with her before marriage often claim to be the father of one of her children, especially if they are as vain as Tormod Knudsen is reputed to have been. But "an unlucky and thoughtless utterance can be remembered so long that it becomes a proverb," and the rumour reached Henrik Ibsen's ears when he was a child, probably from other children who had heard it from their parents. He believed it, as would most children who heard rumours of their illegitimacy if, like Ibsen, they had no respect for their father, and it was something from which he was never

[26] Mosfjeld, p. 32.

[27] *Ibid.*, p. 33.

[28] Albert Bœck, "Små randgloser til Ibsens biografer," in *Nordisk Tidskrift*, Stockholm, 1940.

[29] Ibsen, *Samlede verker, hundreårsutgave,* XX (Oslo, 1930), 8. This source will henceforth be referred to as "C.E." (Centenary Edition).

[30] Schneider, III, 243.

[31] J. Borchsenius, *Skien før branden 1886* (Oslo, 1934), p. 85.

to escape. Bankruptcy and illegitimacy recur spectre-like throughout his work. Hardly a play he wrote, from *The Pretenders* to *Rosmersholm,* but has its illegitimate or supposedly illegitimate child: Haakon and Peter in *The Pretenders,* Gerd in *Brand,* the Ugly Brat in *Peer Gynt,* Regina in *Ghosts,* Hedvig in *The Wild Duck,* Rebecca West in *Rosmersholm.*

Such was the background against which Henrik Ibsen spent the next eight years of his childhood, from seven to fifteen. We know little about his early education. He began to read the Bible at the age of six or seven, and it was to remain his favourite book, though he was never a practising Christian. He may possibly have gone to a primary school in Skien before the move to Venstøp; after that, he may, as would seem logical, have been a pupil at a school near the Ibsen house which existed primarily for the benefit of employees at a local factory, but which other children were also permitted to attend. If so, he was fortunate. The headmaster was a young man of thirty-seven named Hans Isaksen who had travelled abroad, knew several languages and was celebrated for the beauty of his handwriting. Alternatively, he may have been educated by one Sexton Lund, who was a good friend of Knud Ibsen and had an excellent private school not far away, much patronised by children from Skien. Lund is known to have said of Ibsen as a child that he would become "a great man," possibly from having known him in the classroom.[32]

The house at Venstøp had been somewhat ramshackle when Knud Ibsen bought it, having stood unoccupied for two years; the previous owner, a seaman's widow, had died in 1831. Her husband, a certain Niels Jørgen Hirscholm, had lived a romantic and dangerous life. Among other adventures, he had been a convict in England and a slave in the Barbary States, and had acquired the nickname of "The Flying Dutchman." He had died in 1828, the year of Henrik Ibsen's birth. Many of his books remained in the large loft at Venstøp and, although a lot were in English and therefore unintelligible to him, the young Ibsen gained much of his early knowledge from reading them. They included an old illustrated edition of *Harrison's History of London,* that book which was so to excite Hedvig Ekdal's imagination in *The Wild Duck.* "There's a great big book called *Harryson's* [sic] *History of London*—I should think it must be a hundred years old—and it's got heaps and heaps of pictures in it. On the front there's a picture of Death with an hour-glass, and a girl. That's horrid, I think. But then there are lots of other pictures of churches and castles and streets and great ships sailing on the sea. . . . There was an old sea captain who used to live here once and he brought them home. They called

---

[32] Sexton Lund's daughter, who was at school with Ibsen (either at her father's establishment or at Fossum) recalled three-quarters of a century later that Ibsen as a small boy sometimes used to go to school in a red woollen cap, and that when there was snow on the ground the top of his cap could be seen over the wall of a bridge he had to cross well before he himself, being small, came into sight. (J. Brunsvig, "Ibsen-huset på Snipetorp," in *Ibsen-årbok* 1953 [Skien, 1954], p. 70).

him The Flying Dutchman. It's funny, because he wasn't a Dutchman.
. . . In the end he got lost at sea and left all these things behind."

Ibsen as a boy resembled his father, with the same short build and
strong nose, though he had his mother's dark colouring. Apart from
painting and reading, his chief passion seems to have been clothes. Old
Mr. Lund, the father of the aforementioned sexton, was something of a
Beau Brummell, and had a special uniform which he used to don on
festive occasions comprising velvet breeches, a waistcoat of brown and
yellow striped silk, a brown broadcloth coat, a starched cravat and buckled
shoes. Ibsen loved to be allowed to come while the old man put all this
on. He liked also to paint people in fine clothes and glue them on to bits
of wood. He amassed a collection of these, and would arrange them in
groups as though in conversation, as in a puppet theatre. No one else was
allowed to touch them. Sometimes, as he looked at them, he would "sit
laughing silently to himself, so that he shook." He would also arrange
living tableaux, a pastime in vogue then, and enjoyed joining in when they
went *på julebuk,* going from house to house at Christmas to collect
money like carol singers. Then he would "dress up grandly, and cut the
finest figure of them all."[33]

By the entrance to the kitchen at Venstøp (the house still stands, a spacious and agreeable wooden building of two storeys, with a fine view across
the valley), one may see the little porch with the closet where Henrik
Ibsen as a child used to lock himself in with his books, dolls and drawings.
Soon he started his own puppet theatre. An old lady, Benedikte Paulsen,
who saw these puppet shows as a small girl in 1841 or 1842, has described
them:

In the early eighteen-forties Henrik Ibsen ran a puppet theatre at Venstøp.
The house had an extension to the north which incorporated the wash-house,
the servants' quarters, a storehouse and various other rooms. The storehouse
served as a theatre. At one end a raised platform had been built, consisting
of several broad table-tops, behind which was a gallery hidden by a curtain.
From this gallery the movement of the puppets was controlled with the
assistance of strings. Henrik himself was responsible for this, abetted by a
trusty assistant, usually Theodor Eckstorm from Grini. It cost a halfpenny
to attend the performance. But some people got in free. People came a long
way to see these performances. Some of the boys came to make fun of the
proceedings.

Of the female puppets the star attraction was Isabella of Spain. How
splendid she was! Coal-black ringlets, a crinoline of rose-red silk. She moved
elegantly across the boards, to the delight of the little girls. Then Fernando
came riding on to the stage. Feathered hat, scarlet costume laced with gold.
He moved slowly and aristocratically towards Isabella. Then, alack, there
suddenly appears, swift as lightning, a blackamoor, who seizes her and makes
to carry her off. But Don Fernando buffets him so heartily that he falls

[33] Interview in *Nationen,* 4 August 1920.

to the ground and stays there, whereupon Fernando and Isabella bow to the audience. Such was the play. But one spring day, when a gala performance had been advertised at Venstøp and the stage decorated with blue anemones, there was an unexpected *denouement*. Ole Paulsen from Gulset and Peder Lund Pedersen from Limi cut the strings. Then Henrik became really angry. He went for Ole, though the latter was much bigger. Peder had to go to his friend Ole's help for, though Henrik was small, he was tough. The young audience yelled and screamed, and the din was fearful. Then a voice was heard which drowned them all: "What's all this?" It was Knud Ibsen, Henrik's father. When he saw the combatants, he grasped the situation at once, for he said: "Can't you leave Henrik and his dolls in peace?"

Henrik did not lose heart, but got new strings for his puppets. His mother said she could well understand why she ran so short of clothes lines. Midsummer Night that year the performance was repeated. Then they lit bonfires on Venstøp Hill, and a large crowd attended, adults as well as children. Henrik exploited the occasion to make a lot of money for his theatre.[34]

Ibsen also learned some skill as a conjuror: how to make a watch disappear from someone's pocket and replace it there unseen, or pound a watch in a mortar and restore it whole; and other tricks, including ventriloquism, with the aid of his young brother Nicolai concealed in a box. "Often on a Sunday evening," his sister Hedvig wrote to Henrik Jæger, "he obtained leave to give a performance in one of the sitting-rooms, and the neighbours were invited to come and watch. I can see him now in his round jacket, standing behind a large chest, which was brought in and dusted for the occasion; and he would perform miracles which to the astonished onlookers seemed truly magical. None of them, of course, knew that Henrik's younger brother was sitting in the chest, having been well paid to do so; for otherwise he threatened to make a scandal and, since that was the worst Henrik could imagine, he always promised whatever the boy asked." He also made a little money by constructing small painted cardboard houses and so forth, which an old woman named Maren Mela sold at her fruit stall in the market square. He had inherited something of his father's satirical turn of mind; once, when he had been asked to paint a nice face on a doll for his sister, she found him working on it and laughing unpleasantly to himself. She ran to her mother, crying: "Oh, now he's laughing again!" But when asked why, he replied that he was merely thinking of the face he *could* have painted. He loved to draw caricatures, and would occasionally harangue his brothers and sisters, standing on a barrel.

At the age of thirteen, Ibsen was enrolled at a small private school started that year (1841) by two young men with theological degrees, Johan Hansen and W. F. Stockfleth. This lay in Skien itself, on Telemarksgaten, not far from Ibsen's birthplace. It had only twenty pupils, but appears to have been well thought of, as at least one distinguished local worthy sent

---

[34] Mosfjeld, pp. 106–7.

his son there. Ibsen attended this school for two years. His favourite subjects were history, especially that of classical antiquity, and religion, when he would sit for hours looking up the passages in the Bible to which references were given.[35] He also learned German, and had private lessons in Latin from Hansen, whom he later praised highly as a teacher, adding that he had "a mild, amiable temper, like that of a child."[36] When Hansen died in 1865, Ibsen mourned him; he was practically the only person connected with his childhood, apart from his sister, for whom he retained any affectionate sentiment. The local sexton (not Lund), who helped with the lessons, recalled the young Ibsen as "a quiet boy with a remarkable pair of eyes, but with no particular cleverness apart from an unusual gift for drawing."[37] One of his fellow-pupils remembered him as "a little hasty of temper, sharp-tongued, and of a satirical bent, but at the same time friendly and sociable,"[38] adding "I remember too, how one day the whole class sat dead silent while Ibsen read us a composition of his own, in which he related the following dream:

While wandering across the mountains we were surprised, confused and weary, by the darkness of night. Like Jacob of old we lay down to rest with stones beneath our heads. My companions soon slumbered; I could not sleep. At length weariness overcame me; then in a dream I saw an angel standing over me saying: "Arise, and follow me." "Whither wilt thou lead me in this darkness?" I asked. "Come," he replied. "I will show thee a spectacle, human life in its reality and truth." So I followed, afraid, and we descended as though down huge steps till the mountains bowed over us in mighty vaults and there before us lay a great city of the dead with every dreadful mark of death and corruption; a whole world turned to corpses, all fallen under the stroke of death, its glory faded, withered, quenched. Over the whole hung a weak twilight, sad as that which church walls and whitened crosses cast over a churchyard, yet brighter than anything it could impart to the bleached rows of bones which filled the dark void in endless rows. The sight cast an icy horror over me as I stood there by the angel's side: "Here seest thou, all is vanity." Then there came a murmur like the first weak mutterings of an approaching storm, as though of a thousand melancholy sighs, rising to a shrieking blast so that the dead moved and stretched out their arms towards me . . . and with a scream I awoke, wet with the cold dew of night.

"On being questioned," continues the reminiscence, "Ibsen wrote that he well remembers having written this composition, which resulted in a coolness between him and the master who taught us our mother-tongue, of

[35] Jæger, p. 20.

[36] J. B. Halvorsen, *Norsk forfatter-lexicon, 1814–80,* III (Christiania, 1892), 3, footnote.

[37] *Ibid.,* p. 3.

[38] Provst B. Ording, quoted by Halvorsen, p. 3.

whom, however, he speaks as an otherwise admirable and cultivated man. The master had, in fact, taken it into his head that the boy had copied his theme out of some book, and when he put forward this hypothesis in class, 'I rejected it,' says Ibsen, 'with more energy than he approved of.' "[39]

Ibsen took art lessons from a painter named Mikkel Mandt and painted local scenes and romantic subjects, including some based on illustrations in the Flying Dutchman's books. If his father had continued on his earlier, prosperous career, Henrik Ibsen might well have chosen to become a painter. But fortunately for posterity, in those days any Norwegian painter with serious intentions had to go abroad for the necessary technical training, usually either to Dresden, where the great Norwegian landscape artist J. C. Dahl lived (and where he was to act as cicerone to Ibsen when the latter visited the city in 1852 to study theatre) or to Düsseldorf. So that career was closed to him.

He was not interested in any kind of sport, except fishing, swimming and, perhaps surprisingly, dancing, though he was physically tough and resilient. "Withdrawn" is the word used again and again to describe him at this time, as throughout his life. His sister records that when she and their four brothers were romping together out of doors, he would retire into a little room by the kitchen entrance and bolt himself in. "He was never a sociable companion," she told Henrik Jæger,[40] "and we always tried our best to disturb him by throwing stones or snowballs at the wall or door. We wanted him to play with us, and when he couldn't stand our taunts any longer, he would rush out and drive us away—but since he had no talent for any kind of athletic exercise, and violence was foreign to his character, nothing further ever came of it. When he had chased us far enough, he would go back into his room."

His more boisterous companions found him self-important, a judgment which, again, is confirmed by almost everyone who knew him at this period. He seems to have reacted to the family's plunge into poverty, as so often happens in such cases, by standing on his dignity; he was unwilling to accept the country lads who were his neighbours as his social equals, and is even said to have given them money so that they would not accompany him to school. When he finally left for Grimstad, the local children shouted after him: "Good riddance, ugly mug! (*Reis med dig styggen!*)"[41] Several of these early traits—withdrawnness, social formality, obsessive interest in dress—he was to retain until his death.

With the other sex, in general, he got on better. Two old ladies interviewed in 1910 remembered him as "nice, quiet, reticent, neat, not shy exactly, but unassuming and withdrawn. But you couldn't call him constrained; he was never at a loss for an answer. His fellows didn't care for him; they thought him pompous." "Yes, and they gave him a good hiding

39 Halvorsen, p. 5, footnote.
40 Jæger, pp. 19–20.
41 Brunsvig, p. 70.

for it at least once," said Fru B. "And," she added, "I think he was a bit uppish." "But," said Fru A., "we girls liked him. He was nice looking and well set up. When he came and asked us to dance, we regarded it as a great honour." "Yes," said Fru B., "we were highly flattered. And he was a great ball-goer. He loved dancing, and was good fun at parties. And once he had started dancing with a girl he would dance the rest of the evening with her, every single dance. . . . Occasionally he joined in the other boys' games, as when they went round the houses dressed up at Christmas, and then he cut the best figure of them all. He liked to dress up grand." "Whom was he closest to?" "His sister Hedvig. She was very quiet too, and resembled him in many ways. His brothers were more boisterous, though they were nice children. His mother was taciturn and became more and more withdrawn and melancholic. Henrik loved her very much. But I think there was less understanding between him and his father. His economic position was one cause of Henrik's bitterness. But his father was a clever, sharp man. Henrik inherited his talents from him. And his father was very fond of Henrik and always gave him the best possible clothes. . . . Knud Ibsen was strict in his own house but generally speaking he was a merry, lively man, and a great one for parties. He could be fun too. When he lived at Venstøp I remember he came to my home one day and we small girls got him to do a solo dance for us. That was the kind of man he was."[42]

Knud Ibsen never succeeded in reinstating himself financially, and seems to have lived the last years of his life largely on the charity of his relatives. He applied repeatedly for a post in the customs—in 1836, 1837, 1838, 1842 and 1843. His application in 1838 reads sadly: "To return to my former business has proved impossible; my possessions, having been mortgaged for debts which I was unable to pay, were sold; my home likewise was sold at the behest of a trading company in Hamburg, my distillery at the behest of the Bank, and my three warehouses to pay the residue of my excise duty and other taxes; and my other taxes are unhappily so great that I see no possibility of satisfying my creditors, nor does the financial position of my relatives hold out any hope of a solution, that of my old parents being especially precarious. For they are dependent upon their children, I myself having contributed to their support while my business prospered; so that through no fault of my own I am come into most unfortunate straits."[43] Repeatedly in his applications he stresses that his financial troubles have occurred through no fault of his. Local worthies wrote in his support, praising his conscientiousness and meticulous attention to detail, characteristics which his dramatist son was to inherit to a marked degree. In his old age Knud Ibsen ran a chicken farm, and the pedantic detail with which

---

[42] Interview in *Nationen,* 4 August 1920. This interview actually took place in 1910, but the two old ladies who were questioned asked that it should not be published until after the death of Ibsen's sister, Hedvig.

[43] Mosfjeld, p. 83.

he recorded his daily output of eggs is very similar to that with which Henrik Ibsen was to keep the account books of the Bergen Theatre and, later, his own.

Knud Ibsen failed to obtain any of the customs posts for which he applied. He took on a variety of minor odd jobs, still, apparently, keeping himself largely by borrowing. In 1849, when the America fever was at its height, he acted as agent for ships carrying passengers across the Atlantic. In 1850, we find him named as enlistment officer and inspector of pilots, and also as agent for Danes selling grain and dairy produce and Dutchmen selling glazed tiles, onions and tobacco. But during the four years from 1848 to 1852, he had to appear no less then seventeen times before the commissioners to answer for unpaid debts. For a brief while he held a minor post at the Savings Bank; but before long he was categorised in the tax records of Skien as a "pauper," from whom no tax was required, and for the last twenty years of his long life (he lived to be eighty) he appears to have had no regular work, doing the odd job, making a little from his chickens, borrowing (mainly from his half-brothers, the Pauses) and sustaining himself with schnapps and daydreams. As Oskar Mosfjeld has observed: "He had long since ceased to play the role of Jon Gynt, and was henceforth to alternate between the roles of Daniel Hejre, Old Ekdal and John Gabriel Borkman."

How much theatre Ibsen saw during his childhood at Skien we do not know; but he had ample opportunities. The town was visited during the eighteen-thirties and -forties by a variety of touring companies, mostly Danish, and the advertisement columns of the local newspaper, *Bratsberg Amtstidende*, give us some idea of the fare offered. In 1838, Messrs. Olsen and Miller announced eleven performances, comprising a total of eighteen items, mostly contemporary French comedy and romantic melodrama: *Le Jeune Mari*, a comedy in three acts by Mazère; *Le Mort de Napoleon*, a historical drama in three acts by Dupeuty and Regnier; *Valeur et Compagnie*, a comedy in one act after Bayard and Devorne; Scribe's *La Lune de Miel* and *Les Premières Amours*, etc. In 1839, their repertoire included two more plays by Scribe, *Le Budget d'un Jeune Ménage* and *Etre aimé ou Mourir*, and Kotzebue's comedy *Blackmail*. In 1840, G. W. Selmer's company performed Goldsmith's *She Stoops to Conquer*, Oehlenschläger's five-act tragedy *Axel and Valborg*, and no less than six Scribes: *Les Premières Amours* (again), *La Pensionnaire Mariée, La Somnambule, Yelva, Le Quaker et la Danseuse*, and *Une Fante*. In 1843, the fare offered by Carl Petersen's company included Scribe's *Clermont, Une Verre d'Eau* and a repeat of *Le Quaker et la Danseuse*, and fictitious introductions to the greatest English actor and actress of recent times, the elder Dumas's five-act play *Kean, l'Acteur Anglais*, and a drama of unnamed authorship entitled *Mistress Siddons, the English Actress.* The list is interesting, for it coincides to a remarkable degree with the repertoire that Ibsen was to find himself compelled to stage as a theatre director in Bergen and Christiania ten and even twenty years later. The titles give a frightening picture of the theatrical taste of the time; and it must not be supposed that this list had been tailored to suit provincial palates, for most of the plays were taken from the repertoire of the Royal Theatre at Copenhagen, Det Kongelige, one of the most accomplished and enlightened theatres then to be found in Europe.

Ibsen left school in the spring of 1843, shortly after his fifteenth birthday, and on 1 October of that year he was confirmed with several other boys in the church at Gjerpen. The order of the candidates was arranged strictly according to their social standing, and Ibsen was placed third, behind Theodor Eckstorm and Peder Lund Pedersen, the boy who had cut the puppets' strings. Knud Ibsen regarded this as a considerable social humiliation and groused about it for years; the only reason he could find was that the parents of the other two boys had given the pastor a fine joint of veal, while he had not been able to afford any such gift. The humiliations of life have a different effect on different people. They drove Knud Ibsen to drink and illusions, and turned his son into a dramatist.

That October, Knud and Marichen Ibsen moved from Venstøp to a house at Snipetorp, in the outskirts of Skien. Set on a slight hill away from the heart of the town, this building, two-storeyed like Stockmannsgaarden and likewise of wood, escaped the conflagration of 1886 and stands today. It was to be the family home for over twenty years, until 1865, but Henrik Ibsen was to live there for only a few weeks, during which time he decorated some of the door panels with large painted caricatures of his brothers and sister as animals; Johan as a monkey, Hedvig as a bear, Ole as a fox, and Nicolai as something that has never been satisfactorily identified.[44]

Now that Ibsen was nearly sixteen, it was time for him to seek a living; and he cannot have been sorry to go. There was constant strife between his parents, his mother was withdrawing more and more into herself, and food was so short that the main meal of the day often consisted only of potatoes. Moreover, many people were emigrating across the Atlantic from the Telemark district, and the local newspapers of those years contain frequent letters from Norwegians who had made their homes in America, mostly in Wisconsin, Minnesota and Dakota, praising the conditions of freedom and opportunity which they had found in the New World. The windows of Snipetorp faced towards the harbour, and from his room the young Ibsen could watch the emigrants embark. In that unhappy house, he must surely have felt the longing to set out, like those hungry families, "towards the

---

[44] These paintings have survived, and may be seen in the Folk Museum at Skien.

new, towards the unknown, towards the strange shore and the saga that is to come."[45] A friend of his father's, a travelling salesman, undertook to look out for a post for him, and found him one as assistant to an apothecary at Grimstad, a tiny huddle of houses around a harbour a hundred miles to the south.[46] Two days after Christmas, on 27 December 1843, he departed from Skien in a tiny sailing ship appropriately named *Lykkens Prøve*, the *Lucky Chance*.

Those eight years between the ages of seven and fifteen left a scar that was never wholly to be healed. In his last years, according to his niece Anna, he often spoke of returning to his birthplace, but could never bring himself to do so. He would, she records, shake his head slowly, and say: "It is not easy to go to Skien."[47]

[45] *The Pretenders*, Act Four.

[46] Fru Mülertz, whose husband had bought half the Venstøp estate in 1837, owned an apothecary's shop in Skien called the Swan, and it has been suggested that Ibsen may have helped there after leaving school and so gained some knowledge of the work.

[47] Mosfjeld, p. 59.

2

The Apothecary's Apprentice

1844–1850

Ibsen arrived at Grimstad on 3 January 1844, two months short of his sixteenth birthday. He was to remain there for six and a quarter years.

Grimstad is a town that has been much maligned by Ibsen's biographers. Edmund Gosse dismissed it as "a small, isolated, melancholy place, connected with nothing at all, visitable only by steamer. Featureless hills surround it, and it looks out into the east wind, over a dark bay dotted with naked rocks. No industry, no objects of interest in the vicinity, a perfect uniformity of little red houses where nobody seems to be doing anything."[1] Simple it certainly was, and is; but, visiting it on a sunny winter's day in 1965, I found it a pleasing cluster of wooden houses, many of them dating from Ibsen's time, attractively situated on its inlet. The surrounding landscape, less rugged than that around Skien, is of a gentle and unpretentious charm.

Similarly, Gosse, like Halvdan Koht after him, assumed that Ibsen's years there, spent in extreme poverty, formed a particularly unhappy period of his life. But the evidence of those who knew him at this time suggests precisely the contrary, as does a letter which Ibsen wrote four months after his arrival to a friend at Skien named Poul Lieungh:[2]

Dear Poul,
    You must please forgive me for not answering your letter before, but I have had so much to do that I haven't been able to do so earlier, and even now I can't for lack of time write a long letter. Hedevall will already have left by now, and I am sure he will find things to his liking, I at any rate am very happy here and have never regretted coming,

[1] Gosse, pp. 11–12.
[2] Lieungh was a year senior to Ibsen, and the two families were old friends; Knud Ibsen was Poul Lieungh's godfather.

as Reimann is very good to me and does everything possible to make
me keen on this chemistry work, which I wasn't very at first. With his
wife, on the other hand, I don't get on nearly so well, and we often
quarrel, since it's impossible to do anything right in her eyes. Reimann
is also the postmaster, so you can tell my brother Johan to enclose your
letters in his, by which means you will be saving postage. I must tell
you that Grimstad, and the surrounding countryside especially, is extremely beautiful, and the ladies, though not as *galante* as those of
Skien, are also very acceptable, and you can be sure I do everything to
win their favour, which is quite easy to obtain. Since the steamer calls
at Grimstad twice weekly I hope to make a trip with it to Skien, if no
obstacle arises, which I don't think will. I have several questions to ask
you, which you must answer by the next post. First and foremost you
must tell me how J.J. took the news of her sweetheart's death, and
who is the lucky man who has taken his place; for I know her too well
to suppose she is still mourning for him. Then you must tell me
whether Carl Aamodt is still writing poetry, and if so please don't
forget to ask him to send a short specimen so that I can see if he has
made any progress. Though I have more to tell you I must stop now
for lack of time, but you may rest assured that my next letter will be
longer. Will you please send the copy of *William Tell* which Hedevall
borrowed back to our house, as it isn't mine? Good luck, and best
wishes to all my good friends, from your affectionate

Henrik J. Ibsen

Please don't let anyone see this, as I have scribbled it in great haste.

With its eight hundred inhabitants, Grimstad was no smaller than many a
Norwegian coastal town then. At first sight, it appeared something of a
backwater. Christopher Due, who came there eighteen months after Ibsen,
and who well into the present century in extreme old age set down some
of the most valuable reminiscences of the early Ibsen that we possess, recorded: "When I arrived one dark autumn evening in 1845, I at once
received the impression of a primitive and impecunious place. There was
no street lighting whatever. The feeble light from such windows (by no
means few in number) as had no curtains, so that even in the so-called
main street one could see families seated around tables illuminated by only
a single tallow candle, merely served to make the street darker, and it
was not undangerous to walk there because of the gutters down the middle."[3] Grimstad had no church of its own until December 1849, a few
months before Ibsen's departure, and, more regrettably for posterity, no
newspaper of its own until 1856 when *Grimstads Adressetidende* was

[3] Christopher Due, *Erindringer fra Henrik Ibsens ungdomsaar* (Copenhagen, 1909),
p. 13.

founded. Nor does it seem to have had any good school, for the better families sent their children away to be educated.

But it was not a sleepy town. On the contrary, with its fine natural harbour and amply accessible timber it was, despite its smallness, a bustling and prosperous centre of shipbuilding. "In every inlet," noted Due, "and there are many inlets in or near the town, one saw a hull on the stocks and, as soon as this had been launched, the frame was erected for its successor. . . . Everyone who had any savings, or could manage to borrow some, bought shares in a ship. The priest, the doctor, the justice, not to speak of the seamen and tradespeople, the artisans and even the servant maids, were all, in greater or less degree, shipowners. . . . To own a share in a ship was reckoned as safe as, and much more profitable than, investing one's money in the Savings Bank. It not seldom happened that, freight rates being what they were then, a ship repaid the cost of its construction in two or three voyages. The greater part of the male population went to sea immediately after confirmation, and thereafter spent only the winter months at home. . . . The people were frugal, undemanding and, above all, peaceably inclined, living out their quiet and modest lives within their narrow circle."[4]

Hans Eitrem, who in about 1909 spoke to several survivors from Ibsen's time there, concluded that Grimstad was, for its period, a tolerant and friendly little town.[5] The pietism that was to dominate it, like so many other Norwegian towns, later in the eighteen-fifties had not yet taken root; the local pastor, who bore the unChristian-sounding name of Pharo, was a worldly and eccentric figure. There was a billiards hall, where you could sit with a toddy; dances were held, sometimes masked, and "excursions with dance" were a popular diversion. In the early forties at least there were amateur theatricals, and the plays performed included Beaumarchais's *The Marriage of Figaro* and works by Ludvig Holberg, Kotzebue, and J. L. Heiberg;[6] in 1909 Eitrem reported that whole chests were still to be found full of scripts. Troupes of wandering players also visited the town, as they did Skien, living from hand to mouth; and when the summer came and the citizens no longer wished to spend their evenings indoors (and the tallow candles which formed the only source of stage illumination could no longer fight the sunlight), they eked out their precarious existence as dancing and fencing masters until the autumn dusk began to close in. Ibsen was to recall these amateur groups and strolling players when, thirty years later, he wrote *The Pillars of Society*, a play that is full of Grimstad memories.

In a town that lived on its shipping, Ibsen must, through his work, have

[4] *Ibid.*, pp. 14–15.

[5] Hans Eitrem, *Ibsen og Grimstad*, written in or around 1911 but not published until 1940 (Oslo), pp. 41–46.

[6] See pp. 90–91.

mixed a lot with sailors. There still lived in Grimstad several men who had been in prison in England during the Napoleonic Wars (in which Norway and Denmark sided with France), and others who had been prisoners in Gothenburg during the brief war against Sweden in 1814. Many foreign ships took refuge from storms in the harbour; the references to American sailors in *The Pillars of Society* make it clear that the inhabitants were well used to having such aliens in their midst. In Christmas 1847 an Italian ship destined for St. Petersburg took refuge in Grimstad because of ice in the Baltic, got frozen in and had to stay until the following May; the sailors' band marched through the streets of the little town with banners flying, singing "O bella Napoli."[7]

Reimann, the apothecary to whom Ibsen was apprenticed, was an amiable but unpractical man of thirty-nine whose business was on the slide. His shop lay in a poor quarter of the town, occupying part of "a small and exceedingly humbly furnished house, with small-paned windows in both of its two low storeys."[8] The remainder of the house (i.e., that part not taken up by the shop) served as accommodation for the Reimanns, their numerous children, their two maids and their new apprentice. Everyone slept upstairs in three rooms. The inmost was occupied by the Reimanns and the smallest children, the second and central room by Ibsen and the three elder sons, and the third by the two maids. Only the last of these had direct access to the staircase, so that when, as happened frequently, anyone came with urgent requirements in the night, Ibsen had to go through the maids' room with his candle to answer the door.[9]

The ground floor comprised the shop, a tiny waiting room and the kitchen. When Ibsen had to prepare anything that required heating, he had to do it over the open fire in the kitchen, often with one of the maids cooking a meal beside him. "When he came to the kitchen fire with his pots and pans, and wanted all the room, we had words," one of these maids, Marie Thomsen, told Eitrem sixty-five years later.[10] Christopher Due, as a very old man, vividly recalled the background against which he saw Ibsen for the first time:

> As I passed [the shop] one day with a friend, the latter asked me if I had seen the apothecary's apprentice, remarking that there was something odd about him. I should explain that long after his arrival there were many people who had not set eyes on him unless they had had any business with the apothecary, since Ibsen was never to be seen outside, at any rate in daytime. Curious to inspect him I soon went into the shop. This comprised a tiny room, so low that I could almost touch the ceiling with my hand, and extremely shabby—undusted, dark and displeasing. As an apothecary's it was

---

[7] Eitrem, pp. 52–53.
[8] Due, p. 18.
[9] Marie Thomsen to Eitrem, *op. cit.,* p. 19.
[10] *Ibid.,* p. 20.

primitively equipped in every respect. . . . There was no one to be seen, nor any sound to suggest that anyone was present, so I had ample time to make these observations; but on banging upon the counter, I perceived some movement behind the so-called prescription cabinet, and soon afterwards there emerged somewhat abruptly a small young man with an attractively vital face. I should here mention that Ibsen in his youth wore a handsome full brown beard, unusually well developed for one so young, which gave his face an energetic and at the same time harmonious expression. . . . The total impression was that of a handsome young man with a good, shapely figure.[11]

Since Reimann, according to Marie Thomsen, "spent most of the time walking outside and did little work,"[12] Ibsen had to see to practically everything. He was perpetually boiling and compounding, breaking off only to serve a customer or to deal with the town's post, for which, as Ibsen explained in his letter to Lieungh, Reimann was officially responsible. He had desperately little free time ("You never saw him in the streets of a weekday," another informant told Eitrem[13]), earned the most miserable of salaries, and did not have enough to eat.[14] Nevertheless, by stinting himself of sleep, he managed to pack far more into each twenty-four hours than most youths of his age. He painted a great deal, drew caricatures of the local citizens, wrote lampoons about them, and serious poetry as well. He also read much; he had brought a whole box of books with him from Skien, and among the authors he devoured were Dickens, Scott, Holberg, Voltaire (whom he especially admired), the contemporary Swedish novelist Fredrika Bremer and the Danish novelist Fru Gyllembourg. Reimann was a member of a reading circle, and allowed Ibsen to borrow books through him.[15]

Not content with such general reading, he studied at night for his matriculation, in the hope that he might eventually qualify to go to the University; and this, as we shall see, was to provide him with the inspiration for his first play. On the infrequent occasions on which he found himself free in the daytime, he took long solitary Wordsworthian walks, often armed with a paintbox, and would occasionally go for a row.

Jørgen Peder Eriksen, who had known Ibsen from the time of the latter's

---

[11] Due, pp. 18–20.

[12] Eitrem, p. 22.

[13] Loc. cit.

[14] Fru Staff told Eitrem (op. cit., p. 135) that even Reimann's own children hardly had any butter on their bread.

[15] A læseselskab, or book club, had been formed in 1835 with twenty-seven members; Reimann and his successor, Nielsen, both belonged, and Ibsen, who could not afford the eight crowns subscription, borrowed books through them. It possessed in Ibsen's time over six hundred volumes, including (in translation) such foreign authors as, in addition to those mentioned above, Dumas, Victor Hugo, Bulwer-Lytton, Fenimore Cooper and Captain Marryat; also that World History of Becker which Peer Gynt intended to consult. (Eitrem, p. 44.)

arrival in Grimstad, was still alive, a vigorous old man of eighty-four, when Eitrem visited the town in 1909. "Yes, of course I remember the lad," he told Eitrem. "He was always wanting to do handgrips and wrestle . . . and we used to lift weights to see who was the strongest. He looked strong, too; he was well built, but small." Eriksen well recalled Ibsen's arrival at the apothecary's: "He came in a candle-snuffer [i.e., a coat fitting tightly at the waist, a novelty in Grimstad then, though it was the fashion in the capital]. He wasn't at all sullen; very talkative, and mixed a lot with the other local youths. But he looked so old; he had a coarse face, full of pimples." Eriksen's sister, Marthe, recalled that "he used to lie on the hill and toboggan with the young girls. With every one of them. There wasn't such a difference between boys and girls then. They were mostly the daughters of sailors and woodcutters."[16] Jørgen Eriksen also remembered that Ibsen was often to be seen reading or painting on Vestre Varden, a high crag above the town.[17]

Another portrait of Ibsen during his first two years at Grimstad comes from a schoolmaster, H. Terland, who in 1900 delivered a lecture to the Christiania Philological Society which was printed in the newspaper *Eidsvold*.[18] "Quiet and withdrawn as he was, he made no effort to gain an acquaintance with the families of the town. Nor, certainly, could he be regarded as an acquisition to the social circles of Grimstad, being a mere boy and of a very unprepossessing exterior. Small and thin, but squarely built, of swarthy complexion, with a dark lock of hair hanging down over his forehead, and a shy glance which he continually averted—thus do old inhabitants of Grimstad depict the young Ibsen's appearance. . . . He was certainly no beauty, and when one recalls that he also had a curious introspective, old-mannish face, and an enclosed personality, it is not in the least surprising that people regarded the sixteen- or seventeen-year-old boy as a queer fish. . . . He was taciturn and withdrawn, didn't say much, but wrote short poems with extraordinary facility, always in rhyme. . . . One must remember that Ibsen was still in the hobbledehoy stage, and the need that boys have then to poke fun at the world and play-act found expression in him through this medium."

The apparent contradiction between Terland's account and that of the Eriksens and others need not trouble us. It is evident that Ibsen was one person when in the company of simple people, with whom he had no sense of social inferiority, and another when with ladies and gentlemen of "good family."

Ibsen does not appear to have made any close friends at Grimstad during

[16] Another old lady who as a girl had known Ibsen in Grimstad recalled how he liked to pull their plaits. (*Selskab for Grimstad bys vels medlemsskrift*, nr. 22, 1956.)

[17] Eitrem, p. 18.

[18] *Eidsvold*, 8 October 1900.

his first couple of years there (he probably did not meet Due until some time in 1846). Then, two and a half years after his arrival, the thing that he could least afford happened.

One of the maids at the Reimanns was named Else Sofie Jensdatter. She was ten years older than Ibsen, having been born on 11 January 1818 in Børkedalen in Vestre Moland. Else was not, as many commentators have taken for granted, a kitchen slut; her ancestors had been gentlemen farmers, and the family had become impoverished in an honourable cause. Her grandfather, Christian Lofthuus, had led a rebellion of the Norwegian peasants against their Danish overlords in the previous century, as punishment for which his farm had been burned, his property declared forfeit, and he himself chained to a block in the fortress of Akershus, where, ten years later, he died.

Else was one of the two servant girls who slept in that outer room through which Ibsen had to pass on his way to answer the night bell. She was, moreover, his *husmor,* which means that it fell to her to see to his personal needs, such as mending. She attended to other needs too. On 9 October 1846, when she was twenty-eight and Ibsen was eighteen and a half, she bore him a son. The birth did not take place in Grimstad; she returned for the occasion to her parents in Børkedalen, so that the affair did not receive the full local publicity which would otherwise have been accorded it. But Ibsen had, out of his almost non-existent salary, to pay paternity costs towards the child's upbringing until he reached the age of fourteen.

Else named her son Hans Jacob Henriksen; and we may turn aside briefly from the story of Ibsen's own life to summarise the unhappy history of his illegitimate son and the latter's descendants. Hans Jacob lived with his mother at Børkedalen, east of Lillesand, until he was twenty-nine, eking out a hard living as a blacksmith. They were very poor; his mother seems to have been unable to do any kind of work, and there is an unconfirmed tradition that she went blind. When, finally, her parents' house was taken from them, Hans Jacob scrawled on a rock the grim word *Sultefjell* —Starvation Hill. Else moved to a "small, grey hut" on a hillside at Tyttebærmœn, west of Lillesand, and died there, a pauper, on 5 June 1892, aged seventy-four. Hans Jacob became, according to one who remembered him late in his life, "a very interesting man, who read a great deal, taking especial pleasure in history, geography and travel books. He was also a bit of a fiddler and fiddle-maker, in general a well appointed man; but unhappily he was a victim of drink." In fact, he became an alcoholic and ne'er-do-well. He married three times and had seven children, but their fate, too, makes sad reading. Six died young; the fate of the seventh is unknown. We have no record of what happened to the eldest, Jens, born out of wedlock in 1876. Hans Jacob married the mother, Mathilde Andreasdotter, but she died five years later of tuberculosis. The following year, 1882, he married one Trine Marie Gunvaldsen; she bore him a daughter, Marie, two months afterwards, but the child lived only a fortnight and the mother died nine days later. In 1883 Hans Jacob made his third and final marriage, with Ida Gurine Olsdatter, who bore him five children. Ole (born 9 April 1884) died as a baby. Isak (born 9 March 1885) died on 7 April 1888, aged three. Inge (born 10 August 1888) was drowned off Rockall in the *Norge* on 28 June 1904, on her way to America, aged fifteen. Gunda (born 24 April 1892) died on 17 September 1896, aged four. The fifth and last child, Jenny, (born 8 March 1895) seemed likely to break this tragic sequence; she lived to the age of twenty-seven, working as a seamstress, but died on 22 September 1922 of tuberculosis shortly before she was due to be married. Hans Jacob himself lived on until 20 October 1916; he had no contact with his famous father until he saw him for the first time, briefly and dramatically, towards the end of the latter's life.[19]

Shortly before the birth of Ibsen's illegitimate son, the unfortunate Reimann's debts at last caught up with him, and in August 1846, at the demand of a fellow-apothecary in Christiania to whom he owed nearly thirteen thousand crowns (about £650), his business was put up for auction and bought by one O. A. Haanshus. Early the next year Haanshus resold it to a former apprentice of Reimann named Lars Nielsen, the twenty-three-year-old bachelor son of a well-to-do local shipmaster. Nielsen transferred the shop from Storgaden 75 to a better locale at Østergade 13, a house owned by a stone-deaf and eccentric widow named Geelmuyden, who spent her whole day in a chair, occupied solely with her snuff-box.[20] Here, Nielsen leased two decent-sized rooms on the ground floor. The outer room, into which the front door opened, was the shop; the inner room, to the rear, served as waiting room, laboratory, parlour, dining-room and bedroom for the young apothecary and his "qualified assistant" (*examinerade medhjelper*), for Nielsen raised Ibsen to this status from his previous one of apprentice and increased his salary. Reimann had given him an excellent reference, saying that he was unusually skilful at his work, conscientious and industrious. The building at Østergade 13 still stands, a pleasant wooden house of two storeys a stone's throw from the sea, and the two rooms are preserved much as they must have been in Ibsen's time, except that then the walls of the parlour were hung with Ibsen's own paintings, few of which have survived. In the shop itself perched a large

[19] For the information contained in this paragraph I am indebted to Fru Ingeborg Björklund-Bexell, who included it in her unpublished thesis, "Ibsens Vildanden, en studie," written in 1962. Her informant who remembered Hans Jacob Henriksen at Lillesand was J. Ager-Hansen.

[20] Fru Geelmuyden's maid, Sofie Høglund, who came to her in 1847 at the age of seventeen and stayed two years, told Eitrem that Ibsen as a lodger was "nice, a really nice person, never complained."

stuffed owl, which had been shot in the tree outside Ibsen's window and which figures in one of his early poems.

A portrait of Ibsen at work as an apothecary comes to us from the other of the Reimanns' two maids, Marie Thomsen. She remembered him as "very quiet; badly dressed; his clothes were as shiny as that stove; you could tell from them that he was hard at it all day." There was an old man called Svend Fjeldmand (Svend the Hillman), who used to wash up and do odd jobs in the shop; he and Ibsen became friends and often took a walk together on Sundays to Fjære churchyard half an hour away. Svend died shortly before Ibsen left Grimstad and Marie recalled that Ibsen painted a picture and put it on Svend's grave at Fjære "with something he'd written." He did a lot of paintings; Marie and the Eriksens were agreed on this. At work he was perpetually boiling and mixing, breaking off only to attend a customer. He was neat at his packaging. Sometimes, in the kitchen, he would get bad-tempered and stump off into the shop. But "a moment later he'd come out again, and the mood would have left him. 'Feel better now?' I'd ask him. I could put him in the right humor, I could. . . . 'If you grow up and get married you'll plague the life out of your wife,' I told him. 'I bet he was a terror in his own house?' she asked suddenly." But when Eitrem replied that he was very nice, she didn't find it surprising. "No, he didn't say much; but he wasn't surly or miserable. He was fun really. He liked playing jokes. . . . That Henrik was a terrible one for reading. He had a whole box bursting with books—but no clothes. He spent nearly the whole night writing and reading. Never in bed before two. Light? Yes, he had a tallow candle—I never heard them refuse him one. Sometimes I'd open the door and say: 'You go to bed now, lad. You'll get fuddle-headed with all this reading.' . . . More than once he said: 'I'll never live to see the day when I get on the right shelf.' He never said what kind of a shelf that might be. We never knew what was going on in his mind, and didn't ask. . . . Most of his spare time he spent drawing and painting. The whole house was full of his pictures. Oh yes, they let him hang them up. No frames on them, though. He painted quick as lightning. Sometimes he'd paint in the shop, sometimes in the storehouse. I don't know whether he painted the shop sign outside [of a swan]. It was certainly done while he was there. He used pencils too. Drew us all—in our working clothes—as we stood washing ourselves and looking dreadful. Old Pharo, the father of the priest at Fjære, he did a drawing of him. He was the one who always went past the window with a finger through a hole in his coat. And he drew people who came to the shop. When he'd drawn anyone he'd come out to us in the kitchen and show it to us."[21]

She confirmed that he liked climbing the hills around Grimstad, and rowing, and denied that he was miserable; the apothecary (Reimann), she

[21] Eitrem, pp. 18 ff.

said, made much of him. "If he'd been father to the boy he couldn't have been kinder to him. A fine man, the apothecary. Not at all bossy, nor was his wife really, only she was always so poorly. One Christmas they hadn't a bite to eat. My mother went down to Crawfurd's shop and got food from the English lady. The apothecary became angry when he heard this and wouldn't take it. 'Well, if you want your family to starve, that's your business,' I said. But in the end he let us keep it. Quite untrue that Ibsen starved—that's a lie. But he [Reimann] drank too much. Ibsen was quick in his movements, silent and quick as an owl."[22]

With the children, he was not always so popular. J. Schulerud, whose brother Ole was to become one of Ibsen's few really close friends, recalled: "We small boys didn't like him, he was always so sour. When we went to the apothecary's to buy liquorice, he gave us miserably little for our half-pennies. Old Reimann gave us much more." Schulerud added that he only once heard Ibsen laugh "good and heartily, like other human beings."[23]

Nielsen, Ibsen's new employer, was a quiet and *soigné* young man, very different from Reimann. He ate all his meals at his parents' house a few minutes away, and at his suggestion Ibsen took lunch with them and had his breakfast and supper brought up to the shop. When they had visitors in the evening, they often invited Ibsen, leaving the maid Sofie to look after the shop and run down to fetch Ibsen if anyone should call. Old Nielsen, the apothecary's father, was a jovial man with a good stock of travellers' yarns. Among his ships was one named *The Palm Tree*, which was to figure, like so many other Grimstad memories, in *The Pillars of Society*. Fru Nielsen was a different type, pious and narrow-minded, and she disapproved of the radical opinions to which Ibsen sometimes gave expression. One of her friends, Fru Damsgaard, once said to her: "I don't know why you talk to that horrid Ibsen, he's so coarse and ill-mannered he isn't worth answering." But Fru Nielsen, to her credit, replied that she believed that he didn't speak thus to offend but because he had a doubting and enquiring mind, and liked to hear other people's opinions.[24]

No real friendship sprang up between Ibsen and his young employer. Ibsen used to refer disrespectfully to him in his absence as "the animal," and when he borrowed Nielsen's galoshes called them "the animal's hind footwear"; he was also heard to utter remarks about "empty heads and full pockets."[25] Ibsen himself later wrote of Nielsen that he was "good and clever, but entirely preoccupied with his work"[26] (which included being cashier at the local Savings Bank, a task which took up more of his time than the shop). Like Reimann, he left the preparation of medicines

[22] *Loc. cit.*
[23] Interview in *Verdens Gang*, 23 and 24 June 1910.
[24] Family tradition quoted by Eitrem, p. 38.
[25] Due, p. 39.
[26] Preface to the second edition of *Catiline*, Copenhagen, 1875.

and the reception of customers almost entirely to Ibsen. A thrifty man, he died in 1865 aged forty, leaving a sizable fortune.

Among the people Ibsen met at the Nielsens was an old Scottish lady named Georgiana Crawfurd. Her brother Thomas, an engineer from Carron in Stirlingshire, had settled in Grimstad in 1822, and she had joined him. She was known in the town as *Tanten,* the old maid, but was a much respected figure, and one of the few people in the town to have a good private library. She took a liking to the abrupt and awkward young newcomer with his radical views, and her nephew, Jens, told Eitrem sixty years later how, as a boy of fourteen, "I often took books from my old aunt to Ibsen."[27] He remembered that she owned Kierkegaard's *Either-Or,* published only a few years earlier in 1843, and she may well have provided Ibsen with his first introduction to Kierkegaard's work.[28]

It may also have been through Miss Crawfurd that Ibsen first discovered the plays of Adam Oehlenschläger, the great Danish poet then approaching the end of his career. Oehlenschläger, as a dramatist, lay somewhere between Corneille and Schiller, the latter being his idol; his plays, like theirs, are written in distinguished, dignified and sometimes eloquent verse, but to a modern reader seem static and declamatory, the kind of theatre that has been unkindly described as grand opera without the music. But we must remember that Ibsen, at this time, could read neither English nor French, and German only with difficulty, and he can have gained little from the poor Scandinavian translations then available of Shakespeare and other foreign dramatists; nor, until he went to Copenhagen in 1852, did he have the chance to see any great tragedy on the stage. Oehlenschläger's poetic dramas, mostly set in Scandinavia during the heroic age (*Earl Haakon the Mighty, The Vikings in Byzantium,* and so forth), were Ibsen's first glimpse of theatrical tragedy; and Oehlenschläger was to be his first model, though he was quickly to discard him, as he was to discard his other influences.

Jens Crawfurd also remembered that his aunt possessed the poetical works of Henrik Wergeland, the Norwegian poet of freedom (1808–45) of whom it has well been said that "few theological students of any university have figured so frequently in the police court" and that "it is a little bit as though Shelley had also been Cobbett."[29] Wergeland was a great admirer of Shakespeare, and revered England as the home of the liberty that he was perpetually preaching. Christopher Due told Eitrem that he read Wergeland's enormous 720-page poem, *Creation, Man and Messiah,* with Ibsen in Grimstad.[30] The earliest poems that we possess by Ibsen, dating

[27] Hans Eitrem, *Maal og Minne* (Oslo, 1910), p. 47. Some reference books mistakenly call Miss Crawfurd Elizabeth, the name of Thomas Crawfurd's wife.

[28] On the possible influence of Kierkegaard on Ibsen, see pp. 175–76.

[29] Derry, p. 149.

[30] Eitrem, *Maal og Minne,* p. 47.

from 1847 and 1848, are very much in the Wergeland manner; carrying titles such as "Resignation," "By the Sea," and "Doubt and Hope," they are, in content, the usual adolescent mixture of eagerness and suicidal melancholy, and are interesting only for an unusual technical maturity, especially in the rhyming. Ibsen's extraordinary facility for writing verse, especially rhymed verse, in practically any metre was to dominate his early play-writing to its disadvantage. In his first ten plays, he is almost always at his best when subjecting himself to the tougher discipline of prose.

Ibsen gave some of his poems to old Miss Crawfurd as he wrote them, and on returning to her home after a Sunday at the Nielsens she would read them. She died in 1865 at the age of eighty-seven, late enough to learn of his success the previous year with *The Pretenders*, though unhappily just too early to hear of his greater triumph with *Brand*.

By the end of 1847, Ibsen was reading hard for his matriculation. The subjects in which he had to prepare himself included Latin and Greek; these, and other subjects, he read with two theological students who visited the shop, S. C. Monrad and Emil Bie. He also wrote Norwegian compositions for a tutor in Christiania, some of which have survived. One, dated 3 February 1848, dealt with a theme which was to preoccupy him throughout his life: *On the Importance of Self-Knowledge*. It is written in a remarkably lucid and mature style for one whose schooling had been so brief.

"Of all the branches of thought [*it begins*] the investigation of our own nature is among those in which the sharpest observation and impartiality are necessary if one is to arrive at that which is the goal of every enquiry, namely, the truth. Self-knowledge demands the most careful study of ourselves, our inclinations and actions, and only by the results of such an analysis is it possible for a human being to reach a clear and truthful understanding of what he really is." He concludes: "Even if a man, by acquiring this self-knowledge, gets to know his worst characteristics and thereby finds himself required to humble himself in his own eyes, such humiliation can in no way impair his self-respect, since it provides evidence of a strong will and an honest quest for what should be man's goal in life—the development of his spiritual gifts and a care for his temporal well-being."

By now, much to his delight and profit, Ibsen was seeing more of Christopher Due, and a close bond sprang up between the two. Due writes:

I felt more and more strongly drawn to him. His intelligence and bubbling humour fascinated me all the more because these characteristics were lacking in my other acquaintances. Gradually I became a daily visitor to the shop, mostly in the evenings, when Ibsen would be sitting peacefully in his room. I used to look forward all day to these meetings. It was a new and entrancing experience to listen to his witty utterances, those independent and, to me, largely new views of life, somewhat audacious, to be sure, as they seemed

to me, and full of paradoxes, but always interesting. And he found in me a
grateful listener, enthusiastically following him in his occasionally somewhat
wild flight from the prosaic material situation in which he lived and which,
by this means, he, as it were, cast off, to our mutual advantage. As is usual
among young persons, we discussed everything between heaven and earth, not
least marriage. Among Ibsen's extravagant caprices I remember that he
contended with a curious ardour that he and his wife, if he ever acquired one,
would have to live on separate floors, see each other at meal-times, and
not address each other as "Du." This was at that time his ideal of marriage. . . . Gradually people began to notice this intelligent and witty young
man, and the waiting room of the apothecary's shop soon became, especially
on Sundays and of an evening, a favourite meeting-place, to which new friends
were continually introduced. It was always fun, with Ibsen as the centre-point
of the grateful circle, for he bubbled with humour and, admittedly, with
sarcasm too, and despite the poverty of his circumstances he was always in
an excellent temper. One never got any feeling that he was depressed. He
possessed to a high degree the elasticity of youth.[31]

Due goes on to confirm that Ibsen often indulged his wit in the form of
sharply satirical poems and caricatures. "He had an astonishing talent for
writing fluent verses, and was a very talented artist. His pencil swiftly and
surely made its point." Due quotes a kind of comic strip which Ibsen composed about a man and his horse, the horse eventually proving far more
cunning than the man. He also wrote "an excellent poem in rhyme" about
a local youth, fitted to the melody of a popular Danish vaudeville of the
time from which the youth in question was always singing extracts. Ibsen
then got the subject of the poem to sing it to a gathering of friends, all of
whom, except the singer, knew that it referred unflatteringly to the latter.

To see Ibsen's pleasure at the merriment which reigned among us when
we persuaded the object of our banter to sing the verses of which he was
himself the comic hero was indescribable. Ibsen's eyes glittered like fire. . . .
In addition to such amusements, we occasionally held a card party of an
evening in Ibsen's room. Only the more trustworthy among us were selected
for these occasions, men who could keep silence about such enormities as
that we drank punch from ointment pots which, should we be surprised by
some suspicious intruder, were swiftly emptied and stuffed into our pockets.
As midnight approached, one of the more thoughtful among us might suggest
that Ibsen needed some peace, since we all knew that he used part of the night
in studying for his examination, but he always assured us that there was
still plenty of time left for both study and sleep.

Ibsen's capacity for work and physical resilience [continues Due] were
phenomenal. Apart from a very few hours he literally worked throughout
the day and night. Most of his day was of course taken up with the business
of the shop. Since there was then only this one apothecary's business between
Kristiansand and Arendal, a matter of some seventy kilometres, there was

[31] Due, pp. 21–22.

obviously a deal to do, and since the apothecary himself was much occupied with his duties as cashier and book-keeper at the local savings bank and was moreover in uncertain health, the result was that Ibsen did most of the work at the shop. This was, like the older shop [*i.e., Reimann's*], even by the humble standards of those days, very inadequately equipped. For example, there was no special room set aside as a laboratory. When any complicated potions had to be prepared, resort was made to the kitchen belonging to the lady who owned the house. She lived in one half of the ground floor of the little house while the apothecary's shop and waiting room occupied the other half. I have actually seen Ibsen in the kitchen over an open fireplace, without even a stove, busy preparing medicines next to Madame Geelmuyden's cooking pots. For smaller preparations a small spirit lamp in the shop served. In those days there was no such thing as a petroleum apparatus. With such primitive equipment the work of the shop was naturally extremely arduous and took a disproportionately long time, to Ibsen's chagrin, since it meant that he could spend less time on what most interested him. . . .

It was quite incredible how much Ibsen got through in each twenty-four hours. Apart from his work in the shop, which as stated took up most of the daytime, he had his matriculation studies, which he had to pursue largely without assistance. . . . These caused him considerable worry and trouble. Then, from a natural inner compulsion, he felt urged to spend part of the day or night writing, which more and more obsessed his thoughts. And yet he also found time to employ his talent as an artist in many directions. Not only was his pencil continually active, he also painted landscapes. . . . When one remembers that visits from his friends occupied part of each day too, it will be appreciated that there was little time left for sleep or rest. But I never heard Ibsen complain of being tired. His health was always exemplary. He must have been uncommonly tough physically. For example, his financial situation compelled him to exercise the strictest imaginable economy, to the point of having to manage without underpants and even, later, without socks. Since there was among the many female charmers of Grimstad a young lady towards whom he was inclined, I jestingly told him that he was acting *Love without Stockings*.[32] We had a good laugh over this. Ibsen was always ready to take a humorous view of his painful circumstances. These sartorial experiments of his succeeded even in winter, when he had, moreover, no overcoat, for I never knew him to catch cold, or suffer from any physical ailment.[33]

One day Grimstad was surprised by the arrival of a young "student" (i.e., someone who had passed the matriculation examination). "A *student* was a rare sight in those parts," comments Due. "Among the natives of the town, for many years there had only been two. One looked up to an *akademiker* with a kind of involuntary respect." This newcomer was Ole Carelius Schulerud, born 1827. Due, who knew Schulerud's father, quickly introduced him to Ibsen, and the three soon became firm friends. "Apart

[32] A parody of neo-classical French tragedy by J. H. Wessel (1742–85), set to music by Paolo Scalabrini.
[33] Due, pp. 29–35.

from our mutual sympathy and literary interests—in those days one eagerly studied Søren Kierkegaard's books, *Either-Or, The Works of Love,* etc., and not least Oehlenschläger's tragedies, and *Clara Raphael's Letters*[34]— we were, all three, in contrast to our other comrades, 'as poor as church mice.' One of us had, for economic reasons, to do without lunch, the second could manage both board and lodging but seldom found the pocket money for a cigar, and the third, Ibsen, had from his pitiful salary to buy clothes and books, pay his matriculation tutor, and even, as 'apothecary's journeyman' (for thus, to his rage, he was described in the tax register), contribute to the town rates. Most of our fellows had, in varying degrees, shares in ships, and were therefore comfortably off. They could afford many things that we three had to deny ourselves. Their situation provided a marked contrast to that of the 'Triumvirate,' with our humble get-togethers, and created, not least in Ibsen, a bitter resentment against 'empty brains with full wallets.' . . . There were a few families where a more intelligent life was carried on, but Ibsen never moved in their circles."[35]

In so small and conservative a community as Grimstad, respectable citizens had begun to notice and shake their heads at the young radical, with his atheistic and republican views. For Ibsen was already a heretic in such matters as marriage, love, morality and religion. He had broken away from his early religious teaching, and was unwilling to believe in a God, except in generalised and agnostic terms. He had, as we know, studied Voltaire, and Due tells how "he championed the latter's Deism and Pantheism. . . . He denied the existence of a personal God. In this he met strong opposition from one or two of us, and we tried our best to move him from his position of complete religious disbelief, but in vain."[36]

To so restless and questioning a soul, it was natural that the idea of republicanism should appeal, especially in a Norway which, for over thirty years, after the briefest period of independence from her old Danish yoke, had languished discontentedly under the suzerainty of a Swedish king and his appointed Norwegian cabinet. When therefore, in February 1848, the people of Paris rose against their king and, on the second day of the street fighting, 24 February, Louis Philippe abdicated and bolted to a villa in Surrey, and France proclaimed herself a republic, the effect on the young Ibsen, a fortnight short of his twentieth birthday, was explosive. According to Edmund Gosse, who once met and talked to Ibsen, this proclamation was "the first political event that really interested him." There was much more of the same kind to interest him in that tumultuous year. During the spring, revolution spread through Italy, touching Rome, Turin, Leghorn, Pisa, Florence and Milan. Even the mighty Austrian Empire was affected.

[34] One of the first calls for female emancipation.
[35] Due, pp. 38–39.
[36] *Ibid.,* p. 40.

On 13 March, a single day's rioting overthrew Metternich, a figure seemingly as impregnable as the Pope, if not more so, and gave Vienna to the people. At this news, even Venice bestirred herself and declared a republic. Later the same month there was rioting and bloodshed in Berlin as a result of Frederick William IV's delay in granting reform, and he was forced to permit the formation of a parliament. In May the Lombards rose and expelled their Austrian garrison. Nearer home, in response to the revolutionary feeling in Germany, the twin duchies of Schleswig and Holstein were up in arms.[37] To the young Ibsen, as to the young Wordsworth in 1789, it must have seemed that a new and glorious dawn was breaking for mankind.

Under the influence of these events, relates Due, Ibsen "gradually became a full-blooded Republican. With him as inspiration social gatherings were arranged at which there was much jollification and speeches were made, with the ideals of republicanism as the leading theme. After the French pattern, we arranged a so-called 'Reform Banquet,' at which Ibsen made a fiery oration against all emperors and kings, the vermin of society, and in defence of republicanism, the 'only possible' form of government."[38]

It was in this exalted mood that Ibsen, during the summer of 1848, paid a short visit to his family in Skien—possibly his first since he had left them four and a half years before.[39] We need not read any particular significance into his not visiting them during this period; he may well have had no holidays, and in any case probably could not afford the journey. We know nothing of what he found or felt on seeing his family again, nor how long he stayed. While he was there, however, the hopes that had been raised in him, as in so many others, by the revolutions of the spring began to be dashed one by one. In June there was civil war in the Paris streets, and Prince Windischgrätz turned his guns on Prague to crush the Bohemian rebellion. On 30 October, after Ibsen's return to Grimstad, the reactionary Jellačić defeated a Hungarian army marching to relieve Vienna against Windischgrätz on the plain of Schwechat. There was to be no more democracy in Vienna for nearly three-quarters of a century. In November,

---

[37] Holstein was within, Schleswig without the confines of the German Confederation, but both had been governed by the King of Denmark continuously since 1490. The Danes were, in 1848, planning to incorporate Schleswig in their monarchy and sever its connection, long deemed insoluble, with Holstein. German opinion was united in holding that the two Duchies must be subject to a single ruler. Confused and indeterminate fighting was ended by the intervention of the Powers only in 1852. King Frederik VII of Denmark had no male issue and by the Treaty of London that year it was decided that on his death Christian of Glucksburg should succeed him and rule in Denmark and the Duchies. This settled the matter until Frederik died in 1863, when the whole trouble flared up afresh.

[38] Due, p. 42.

[39] One of Reimann's sons, with whom Ibsen shared a bedroom at the old shop on Storgaden, told Eitrem that Ibsen had once brought him back toys from a visit to Skien; but this could have been in 1848, when he may still have been in touch with the children.

Frederick William IV dispersed the Berlin Parliament; in April of the following year he ruthlessly stamped out revolt in Saxony, Baden and Hanover; in June the French crushed Mazzini's Roman republic, despite a courageous defence by Garibaldi, recently returned from a nomadic existence in South America; and on 24 October, the Venetian republic also fell. Before long Louis Bonaparte was to stage a *coup d'état,* dissolve the Paris Chamber and make himself master of France.

Twenty-seven years later, Ibsen described his reaction to this volcanic upheaval in Europe. "It was a momentous era. The February revolution, the risings in Hungary and elsewhere, the Schleswig war—all this had a powerful and maturing effect on my development, long though it took for that process to unfold. I wrote resounding poems to the Magyars exhorting them in the name of freedom and humanity to continue steadfastly in the struggle against 'the tyrants.' I wrote a long sequence of sonnets to King Oscar [of Sweden and Norway], mainly, as far as I can recall, entreating him to put aside all petty scruples and straightway, at the head of his army, to rally our brothers to defend the furthermost frontiers of Schleswig. Since I now, unlike then, doubt whether my winged appeals would markedly have assisted the cause either of the Magyars or of Scandinavia, it is probably fortunate that they remained in the semi-privacy of manuscript. But, my motives being so lofty, I could not refrain from expressing myself in a passionate manner, as befitted the mood of my poems, which, however, brought me but doubtful reward both from my friends and from those less amiably disposed towards me, being hailed by the former as demonstrating a bent for the unconsciously ridiculous, while the latter deemed it remarkable that a young person in my humble position should take it on himself to debate matters on which even they themselves did not presume to hold an opinion. I must in truth add that my conduct in more than one respect held out no great hope that society might count on any accession in me of civil virtues, the less so since I had, by reason of certain epigrams and caricatures, fallen out with individuals who deserved better of me and whose friendship I in fact valued. To sum up, while a great age thundered outside I found myself in a state of war with the little community within which, by the circumstances of my work, I sat imprisoned. Such was the situation when, preparing for my examination, I read Sallust's *Catiline,* and Cicero's speeches against the latter."[40]

The sonnets to King Oscar have, perhaps fortunately, disappeared, but two of Ibsen's exhortatory poems have survived, "To Hungary," in which he comforts the Magyars with the assurance that, in years to come, their name will serve as a battle-cry for the new generation that will "topple the pillars of tyranny," and "Awake, Scandinavians!" a similarly unremarkable though lively piece, like inferior Kipling. Where, however, these contemporary rebels failed to inspire Ibsen to any uncommon literary

[40] Preface to the 1875 edition of *Catiline.*

achievement, the rebel who had died two millennia previously, and had been condemned by historians as an arrogant and misguided felon, succeeded. François Mauriac has written that a sinner is closer to a saint than are the vast majority of harmless, middle-of-the-way mortals, because the requisite zeal and passion, and often even the selflessness, are there; it is simply that, perhaps through no fault of the individual, they are misdirected. The figure of the misguided reformer was one that was to fascinate Ibsen throughout his life, and the line of mighty, twisted figures that includes Brand, Julian the Apostate in *Emperor and Galilean,* Gregers Werle and John Gabriel Borkman began, in the ante-room of the apothecary's shop at Grimstad, with *Catiline.*

In his preface to the second edition published in 1875 Ibsen explained:

> My play was written at night. From my employer, a good and able man who, however, had no interests outside his work, I had virtually to steal free time in which to study, and from these purloined hours I thieved further moments in which to write. So I had little time left to me but the hours of night. I think this must be the unconscious reason why almost the whole action of the play takes place at night. . . . As may be seen, I did not share the two old Roman authors' opinion of Catiline's character and conduct, and I still incline to the view that there must have been something great, or at any rate noteworthy, about a man with whom so indefatigable and esteemed an advocate as Cicero did not dare to cross swords until events had taken such a turn that he could do so without fear of the consequences. It should also be remembered that there are few historical personages whose posthumous reputations have been more entirely dictated by their enemies than Catiline.

He wrote the play in the first three months of 1849, in blank verse, with occasional excursions into the rather unusual metre of rhymed trochees. Catiline, as portrayed by Ibsen, has a guilty secret; he once seduced a woman, who, in despair, drowned herself. Disillusioned with the corrupt rulers of Rome, he dreams of "greatness, power and eternal fame." His gentle wife, Aurelia, tries to dissuade him from mixing in politics, so that he can retire with her to a peaceful life in the country; but her influence is defeated by that of Furia, the first of those domineering and destructive women whom Ibsen was to portray at intervals throughout his work: Margit in *The Feast at Solhaug,* Hjørdis in *The Vikings at Helgeland,* Rebecca West, Hedda Gabler, Hilde Wangel, Rita Allmers. She urges him to rebellion:

> I am your genius.
> I must lead you whithersoever you go.
> I am an image out of your own soul.

Furia then betrays his conspiracy, revealing herself to be the sister of the drowned woman. Finally, Catiline kills himself.

When in his later years Ibsen was asked what books he had read in his youth and which authors had influenced him, he tended to shy away from the question almost pathologically. Two of the few influences to whom he admitted were Ludvig Holberg and Oehlenschläger, and in 1880 he told Henrik Jæger that, as far as he could recall, they were the only two dramatists he had read when he wrote *Catiline*. Structurally, it is difficult to see what the play owes to either: it has nothing in common with the swift-moving, short-scene, colloquial comedies of Holberg, or with the static and ponderous tragedies of Oehlenschläger, though the latter may have served as a model poetically. The dramatist to whom the play seems to owe an obvious debt is one with whose work Ibsen can hardly have been totally unfamiliar even at that early stage in his career: Shakespeare. The character of Catiline himself has much in common with that of Brutus in *Julius Cæsar*, and the scenes between Catiline and his fellow-conspirators, and that of his final suicide after his defeat in battle, seem plainly indebted to the same play. He could of course have learned Shakespeare's technique at second-hand, through the works of Schiller or, for that matter, through Oehlenschläger. But Miss Crawfurd, who guided Ibsen's reading so helpfully at this time, can surely not have omitted to draw Ibsen's attention to at least this fellow-countryman of hers; and although Ibsen's English, if it existed at all at this time, would certainly not have been good enough to read Shakespeare in the original, he would have had no difficulty in obtaining him in Danish translation.[41]

Nevertheless, *Catiline* is far from being a mere pastiche. Apart from the considerable skill of the verse, a signpost to the flexible and muscular dramatic poetry that was to come in *Love's Comedy, Brand,* and *Peer Gynt,* the sharpness of the characterisation, the continuous movement of the plot and, rarest of talents in a playwright, the ability to construct and develop not merely a character but a human relationship, are all evidence of uncommon maturity in a largely self-educated youth approaching his twenty-first birthday. Ibsen has rather touchingly described the emotions with which he re-read the play after a lapse of a quarter of a century. "I

[41] Edmund Gosse thought that Sallust's account of the Catiline conspiracy, which Ibsen had been studying for his matriculation examination, had a considerable effect on both the style and viewpoint of Ibsen's play. "If we seek for the master-mind that started Ibsen," wrote Gosse in his 1907 biography, "it is not to be found among the writers of his age or of his language. The real master of Ibsen was Sallust. There can be no doubt that the cold and bitter strength of Sallust; his unflinching method of building up his edifice of invective, stone by stone; his close, unidealistic, dry penetration into character; his clinical attitude, unmoved at the death-bed of a reputation; that all these qualities were directly operative on the mind and intellectual character of Ibsen, and went a long way to mould it while moulding was still possible." Gosse, steeped in the British nineteenth-century passion for the ancient classical writers, probably overstates his case; but it is a theory not to be dismissed.

Gosse also remarks that in October 1848, only a few weeks before Ibsen began his play, a new drama about Catiline by Alexandre Dumas *père* had been staged in Paris, and that although Ibsen could not have read it he may well have seen a mention of it in a newspaper, perhaps in connection with the political events then taking place in France.

had almost forgotten the content, or anyway the details; but on reading it afresh, I found that it contained a good deal that I was still able to acknowledge, especially when one considers that it was my maiden play. Much that my later work has dealt with—the conflict between aspiration and capacity, between will and ability, the overlapping of tragedy and comedy, whether on a general or an individual scale—is already mistily indicated here."[42]

If, as has been argued, everything we write mirrors our internal conflict at the time we wrote it, it is possible to draw certain parallels between the content of *Catiline* and Ibsen's position at Grimstad during that winter of 1849. Like his hero, Ibsen must have been nagged by a sense of being insufficiently appreciated and an ambition for higher things; also, no doubt, by the consciousness of having shrugged off his responsibility towards a woman with whom he had had an affair. Perhaps, as some critics have suggested, the two women who contended for the possession of Catiline represented the conflict that takes place in every artist between settling for a peaceful life and the danger and uncertainty of an artist's career.

In this same preface to the second edition of *Catiline,* Ibsen recalled the enthusiasm with which Due and Schulerud received the news that he had written a play, and the efforts they made to launch it:

An occupation as incomprehensible to my associates as playwriting had of course to be kept dark; but a twenty-year-old poet cannot easily continue without confidants, and I therefore entrusted my guilty secret to two friends of my own age. We three built great hopes on *Catiline* once it was completed. First and most important, it had to be fair-copied so that, over a pseudonym, it might be submitted to the theatre in Christiania; after which it was to be offered to the public in print. One of my loyal disciples [Due] took it upon himself to produce a handsome and legible copy of my rough and uncorrected draft, a task which he performed so conscientiously that he did not omit a single one of the innumerable dashes which, in the heat of composition, I had employed whenever the appropriate expression had not immediately occurred to me. The other friend, whom I take leave to name since he is no longer among the living—Ole Schulerud, then a student, later a lawyer—went with this copy to Christiania. I still remember one of his letters, in which he tells me that *Catiline* has now been delivered to the theatre; that it will soon be performed, of that there can be no possible doubt, since the directorate of the theatre is composed of highly perceptive gentlemen; equally, it is beyond question that all the booksellers of the capital will compete for the honour of paying a good round honorarium for the first edition; the only problem, in his view, being to ascertain which will make the worthiest offer.

After a long and hopeful period of waiting, however, certain difficulties began to reveal themselves. The theatre returned the play to my friend with an exceedingly courteous but none the less conclusive letter of rejection. He then took the manuscript from bookshop to bookshop; but they, with one

42 Preface to the 1875 edition of *Catiline.*

voice, all expressed the same opinion as the directors of the theatre. The best he could get was an offer to print the play for such and such a sum without any question of any money being paid to the author.

All this, however, far from dispelled my friend's confidence in ultimate victory. On the contrary, he wrote to me that what had happened was for the best; I would myself step forward into the limelight as publisher of my own drama; he would advance me the necessary money; the proceeds we would share, in anticipation of which he would take charge of all the business side—apart from the proof-reading, which he thought would be unnecessary, since the printer would have so beautiful and clear a manuscript to work from. In a later letter he declared that with such promising prospects in view he was thinking of giving up his studies entirely in order to devote himself wholly to the publication of my works; he thought I should have no difficulty in composing two or three plays a year, and by a sober reckoning the profit must in a short while enable us to make the journey we had so often agreed on, or at any rate discussed, across Europe to the Orient.

This was in October 1849. The previous month, an important and encouraging event had occurred for Ibsen; for the first time, a work of his appeared in print. It was a poem entitled "In Autumn," and its publication was entirely thanks to Due who, on hearing Ibsen read the poem aloud, sent it to the *Christiania Post,* for which he acted as local correspondent. It was published as being by "Brynjolf Bjarme," a pseudonym which Ibsen was to use for some time (*Catiline* was also to appear under it). When Due received the issue of 28 September containing the poem, he relates: "I was very impatient for evening to come, when the shop would be quiet and I could show Ibsen the newspaper. Enthusiastically, and with a certain triumph at my friend's success, I displayed to him his first 'poem in print.' At first Ibsen turned quite pale with emotion, but soon a flush of joy streamed over his face."[43] In 1858 he was to recall the occasion in his poem "Building Plans."[44]

Three letters which Ibsen wrote from Grimstad to Schulerud while the latter was trying to sell *Catiline* in Christiania have survived. The first, dated 15 October 1849, was evidently written as an apology for an impatient and suspicious earlier letter of the kind which Ibsen was often to pen in his maturer years, and which Schulerud, in obedience to Ibsen's expressed wish, must be presumed to have destroyed:

My dear friend!

Your last letter made me doubly happy, firstly because it promises a speedy outcome of our project, but even more because you have hereby proved yourself a true friend, by regarding my letter to you as a mere expression of impulse and over-enthusiasm. Such forbearance leads me to hope that you have imagined yourself in my position and realised how everything must have seemed to me. I am sure you

[43] Due, pp. 26–27.
[44] See pp. 157–58.

will have guessed the frustration with which I have awaited every post-day, and how this put me in an unpleasant humour. Not being on the spot, I could not guess what was happening, and this uncertainty inevitably aroused a thousand doubts, all the more distressing because I could not in my heart believe that they could have any foundation.

Your letter has stilled every doubt I might have had concerning your conduct, and I should not be worthy of your friendship if I did not unreservedly withdraw anything I may have written which could cast doubt on the honesty of your intentions. I therefore beg you to forget the whole matter as something which can have no influence upon our future friendly relations, and I await an assurance of this in your next letter.

I have no time today to write more—Due asks me to thank you for the guitar, which he looks forward to receiving. I am equally grateful for the trousers—I had forgotten about them and thought they had slipped your memory too, but they are very welcome, as just now I have to save all I can. I have almost finished the first act of *Olaf Tr*. I think it will turn out really well, and hope this play will cause us less trouble than *C*.

Best wishes,
Your affectionate friend,
Henr. Ibsen

P.S. Do me the favour of consigning my last letter to the flames. I hate to think of your having it.

Olaf Tr. was probably to be about Olaf Tryggvason, a king of Norway (*c*. 995–1000) who was bred in Russia, became a Viking chieftain, led an invasion of England in 991 and, on the conclusion of peace, became a Christian and had the doubtful honour of being adopted godson by King Ethelred II. He spread Christianity throughout Norway, by force where necessary, and even into Iceland and Greenland, before being killed in a battle against the Danes. He seems a promising subject for a play, and one would like to know what Ibsen would have made of him, especially in view of Ibsen's hostile attitude at this time towards state-established religions; but he never completed the work, and the fragment has not survived.

Twelve weeks later, on 5 January 1850, Ibsen again wrote to Schulerud:

My dear friend!

Your last letter contained news of *Catiline's* death sentence—it grieves me, but there is no use losing courage. You are perfectly right when you say that this apparent defeat must not be regarded as such. *C*. was only intended as a forerunner of the plans we agreed

on in this field, and it may yet fulfil its purpose. I am absolutely of
your opinion that it is wisest to sell the play, and I think its rejection,
to judge from the theatre's reply, may turn out to our advantage
rather than to our disadvantage, since it seems that it was not for
any integral reason that it was not accepted. You must of course
arrange the sale of the play at your own discretion; I would merely
observe that it seems to me better to sell the publishing rights rather
than have it printed at our own expense, since in the latter event
we should have to pay a lot of money to cover the printing and,
besides, would only gradually get any return from it, whereas in the
former event we would receive an honorarium. However, you must
do as circumstances suggest.

Now a little about my literary activity. As I think I told you, the
first act of *Olaf T.* is more or less ready; the little one-act play
The Norsemen[45] has been revised, or rather will be—I am busy with
it at the moment—and will in its new form deal with a broader
theme than I had originally envisaged. I have used a few stories
and descriptions from Telemark to write some short poems, adapted
to fit well-known folk melodies, and have thus had a shot at nationalistic writing. I have, too, half-completed a longish, perhaps rather
over-dramatic poem entitled "Memories of a Ball," which owed its
existence to my supposed infatuation of last summer. But my most
important work since you left has been a national-historical *nouvelle*
which I have entitled *The Prisoner at Akershus,* and which treats
of the sad fate of Christian Lofthuus. [A long paragraph follows
telling Lofthuus's story].[46]

I think we should preface *Catiline* with some introductory remarks,
and I therefore beg you to copy and insert the following:

FOREWORD

This play was originally intended for the stage, but the directorate
of the theatre found it unsuitable for this purpose. Although the
Author has grounds for supposing that the play's rejection does not
stem from any integral defects, it is nevertheless not without a certain
anxiety that he sets his essay before the public, from whom however he anticipates the forbearance for which a beginner may not
unreasonably hope on his maiden appearance.

N.B. Please don't let any printing errors creep in. I should like to
have the manuscript back, and should be grateful if you would let
me have two copies of the play when it is ready . . .

Best wishes,
Your affectionate
Henr. Ibsen

---

[45] Later adapted into *The Warrior's Barrow.*
[46] See p. 3.

The "supposed infatuation of last summer" probably refers to a girl of nineteen named Clara Ebbell, to whom he had dedicated a poem that year entitled "To the Star." Neither it nor the longer "Memories of a Ball" have much to recommend them beyond a technical facility; they are conventional adolescent poems of hopeless adoration, which rather suggest that Clara, a religious girl who disapproved of his free-thinking, did not reciprocate his feelings, at any rate with much passion. He remained in contact with her, however, sending her poems from Christiania the following year, so that she cannot have rebuffed him completely.

Ibsen seems to have been somewhat timid as a suitor. "He seldom expressed passion," records Due. "It was as though his spiritual life found expression exclusively, or at any rate essentially, through imagination and thought. . . . I got the impression that there was in his nature a deep-seated reluctance to lay bare his feelings. In particular, he had a notable talent for concealing his wants, so that they did not appear to bother him. Thus his acquaintances never found any cause to pity him, the less so since few of them fully comprehended his true circumstances. I, who was for a time his only confidant, sympathised with him deeply, and found it difficult to understand how, in his situation, he could be as merry and vital as he was."[47]

This timidity in relation to physical matters was to remain a feature of Ibsen's character. One of Reimann's sons who shared a room with him told Eitrem that he well remembered Ibsen going off in a sleigh "at a spanking pace" to take some kind of apothecary's examination in Arendal. The man who gave him the lift could remember only one thing from the trip—"the little chap was so scared, so dead scared, that he, the driver, had to laugh. They rode over some water. The ice boomed, as often happens in cold weather. But Ibsen got frightened and jumped out of the sleigh and ran for the shore. He wouldn't get back into the sleigh until it had crossed the ice."[48]

Occasionally Due seems to have succeeded in persuading Ibsen to indulge in the lighter side of life. "Now and then," he tells, "we arranged dance parties. Grimstad had no adequate locale for such entertainments, but we tackled the problem practically and shamelessly in the following manner. The moving spirits among us young people would approach in turn the good gentlemen who owned the largest houses and bluntly ask if we might hold a dance there. The kindly citizens of Grimstad usually granted permission, and with the assistance of two violins and a flute, home-mixed punch and negus, coffee or tea, and cakes, our ball was ready. Several times I had exhorted Ibsen to partake in these festivities, but important considerations had compelled him to decline. The fact was that he had no evening coat and, what was worse, had never danced and

[47] Due, p. 36.
[48] Eitrem, *Ibsen og Grimstad*, p. 27.

did not dare to make his debut at a ball. The sartorial problem, however, was solved by one of those with "full wallets and empty heads" giving him credit. This at first amazed Ibsen, but then he decided that this confirmed his judgment of them, and when at the end of the year he was presented with a bill for the garment, he merely regarded this as providing further confirmation, saying in his humorous way: 'First he is fool enough to give me credit, then he's fool enough to expect me to pay the bill.' I can, though, reveal that this debt of Ibsen's was fully honoured.

"So now he was equipped to play the gallant, but the business of inviting a partner and taking his place among the ranks of dancers he found intimidating. . . . We sought, however, to instil courage into Ibsen, and with the assistance of his lady and other well-wishers succeeded in getting the couple launched into a brisk gallop, not admittedly without its hazards in the early stages, but with no sensational disasters; and soon it went sweepingly, so that the situation was saved. Later he tried his hand at other dances, with fair success."[49]

It is interesting that Ibsen should have pretended that he had never danced, since we know that, as a boy at Skien, he had in fact been a keen dancer.[50] Due adds: "Ibsen was not musical. When we had a sing-song, he would join in, but incorrectly, since he had no ear."[51]

Of the projected *nouvelle, The Prisoner at Akershus,* referred to in Ibsen's last letter to Schulerud, a little over a chapter has survived; this appears to have been all that he wrote of it. The opening is Dickensian (and may indeed have been influenced by Dickens, some of whose works we know were in the book club to which Reimann and Nielsen had allowed Ibsen access). "In a corner of Christ Church cemetery in Christiania," runs the first sentence, "there is a small area which is used as burial place for criminals who have died at the fortress of Akershus, and which is consequently known as 'Criminals' Corner.'" Each day a woman in mourning visits this place, briefly and obscurely does something or other to a grave that is marked with a nameless cross, and departs. When the narrator, Brynjolf, tells his uncle Bjarme of this occurrence, the latter replies thoughtfully that it is a pity he didn't know about this thirty years ago when he was occupied with his "headache"—"a work that unhappily lies uncompleted in my desk, because I lacked the end of the story." But he promises his nephew that he will show him the manuscript that evening, "because I think in this story of the woman I have discovered how it all ended." The narrator then tells us that "that good soul has now gone to his rest, but he has left me his manuscripts, the only things in my life that I have ever inherited or am likely to inherit." The contents of this manuscript he will now relate. But unfortunately the

[49] Due, pp. 42–44.
[50] See p. 21.
[51] Due, p. 44.

second chapter goes no further than the heading: "Chapter Two. In which the Reader makes the acquaintance of Fru Justitia, as she appeared in the previous Century," and a description of the Lofthuus farm. "All this is now gone. Only on a small hillock a little way above the house stands an old oak tree, which affords a fine view of the neighbourhood, and was, in consequence, the then owner's favourite spot. The local people still refer to it as Christian Lofthuus's Oak."

Here, tantalisingly, the fragment ends. Did some re-kindled flicker of affection for Else Sofie Jensdatter impel him to begin this work in, we must presume, praise of her grandfather, and did some stronger feeling of guilt and rejected responsibility stay his hand? It seems curious that he should have abandoned so exciting a theme after so promising a beginning. This fragment of *The Prisoner at Akershus* is, in fact, the best thing Ibsen wrote at Grimstad, matched only by perhaps a couple of scenes in *Catiline*. But when a writer is twenty-one, poetry often seems a more attractive medium than prose, and a fortnight after he had mentioned *The Prisoner at Akershus* so excitedly to Schulerud ("my most important work"), we find him turning aside to compose an elegy in memory of his admired Adam Oehlenchläger, who had just died at the age of seventy-one. He sent this to Schulerud, explaining that he had composed it "in melancholy ardour," and asking him to "arrange to have it inserted in the *Christiania Post* as soon as possible." It was printed there, rather belatedly, on 16 February.

The time had now come for Ibsen to make the final preparations for his matriculation examination, which would involve spending a term at a crammer's in Christiania. After six and a quarter years of boiling medicines and preparing plasters, he was to devote himself entirely to reading, painting and writing, and that exchange of ideas through discussion and debate which has always been the most valuable part of a university education. On 12 April 1850, at the request of a young lady named Sofie Holst, he wrote his last poem at Grimstad, "Moonlight Wandering after a Ball."

Hush! How still! No longer echo sounds of music and delight.
Now no voice, no violin breaks the soft silence of the night.

Westwards soon across the earth the moon her last still glance shall throw;
Earth that dreams in white oblivion 'neath the lilies of the snow.

Dance is ended; yet my eyes still see the dancers as they lead,
And are led in their sharp patterns swaying in a light sylphide.

Soon the moon will seek her valley, hands of sleep will close my eyes.
And the sea of dreams my soul will wander, winged with memories.

The same day, he wrote a farewell note in Christopher Due's album:

If friendship depended on constant companionship, ours would cease, but if it consists of mutual sympathy and the soaring of spirits in the same sphere, then our friendship can never die.

Your affectionate friend,
Henrik Ibsen

It was the custom for anyone leaving a job to burn his name and the date of his departure on some object. Such a branded inscription may be seen today on a cork drawer in the counter of the apothecary's at Grimstad (now the Ibsen Museum); it bears the statement like an epitaph: *Henr. J. Ibsen, 15-4-50.* The fifteenth was the day on which he officially terminated his employment; but it happened to be a Monday, and there is no record of any ship sailing eastwards from Grimstad that day. On Saturday 13 April, however, the *Prins Carl* left Grimstad early in the morning, and among the passengers whom it deposited at Brevik, not far from Skien, at 11:30 A.M. the same day, we find, in the list printed in the local newspaper *Adresse-Tidende for Brevik,* the name "Ipsen." He would have reached Skien by road the same afternoon or evening.

Ibsen had originally intended to proceed direct to Christiania from Grimstad without seeing his family, but before leaving he had received a letter from his sister Hedvig begging him to visit them en route. Ibsen at once agreed. "He says," Hedvig explained in a letter to her cousin Hanna Stenersen, "that he had always very much wanted to come here first, but didn't like to mention it because he didn't know if Father would approve."[52] What lay behind these last seven words no one has ever been able to explain.

Ibsen stayed a fortnight with his family. They were one fewer than when he had left; Johan, the second son, had emigrated to California to seek his fortune in the goldfields. His letters home were to cease this year, and no more was ever heard from him; his family presumed him dead. Nicolai, the third son, had been dropped on the floor when a child, and the injury had affected him, making him abnormally shy and withdrawn. He, too, after failing in business, was to emigrate to, and die in, America. Ole, the youngest, was not yet fifteen, and the only member of Ibsen's family with whom he could make any real contact was his sister Hedvig, three years his junior. During this stay, as she was to recall over half a century later, Ibsen took a long walk with her to Bratsberg and told her of his dreams. He wanted, he said, to achieve nothing less than complete fulfilment "in greatness and in love." "And when you have done that?" she asked. "Then," he replied, "I want to die."

52 Quoted by O. Mosfjeld in *A-Magazinet,* 9 August 1928. Hedvig refers thrice in her letters to Hanna around this time to letters from Ibsen, so he seems to have been corresponding with them at least fairly regularly up to the time of his departure from Grimstad. The break came later.

On 27 April he journeyed down to Brevik and sailed thence, with his schoolfriend Boye Ording, for Christiania, again in the *Prins Carl*. Not only did he never see his parents or any of his brothers again; he even ceased to write home. There has been much loose and unnecessary speculation as to the reason; Ibsen explained it clearly enough in a letter he wrote to his uncle Christian Paus in 1877 on Knud Ibsen's death. "To uncomprehending eyes," he stated, "I know it looks as though I had voluntarily and deliberately cut myself off from my family, or at any rate permanently set a distance between myself and them; but I think I may say that impossible circumstances from a very early stage were the principal cause. . . . That I so seldom wrote home during those years of struggle was chiefly because I could not be of any assistance or support to my parents. I thought it vain to write when I could do nothing practical to help them; I stood in constant hope that my circumstances might improve, but that happened very late and not long ago. . . . I also felt a strong reluctance to come into close contact with certain spiritual trends then prevalent, with which I could feel no sympathy and a collision with which could easily have provoked unpleasantness, or at any rate an atmosphere of discord, which I wished to avoid."

The "spiritual trends" were a reference to a priest named G. A Lammers, who had become pastor at Skien in 1849. Lammers was a fervent evangelist who had become dissatisfied with the established state church, and by the following year he had decided to form a breakaway group. Only three days before Ibsen's arrival in Skien, on 10 April 1850, *Adresse-Tidende for Brevik* carried an announcement that Lammers was gathering money towards the erection of a prayer-house in the vicarage grounds for "mission meetings and other godly assemblies." Ibsen's mother, sister and youngest brother, Ole, had all fallen under Lammers's spell and become strict pietists. To the free-thinking disciple of Voltaire such an atmosphere must have seemed peculiarly intolerable. His sister's defection appears particularly to have disturbed him. Nearly seventy years later, she wrote: "When as a youngish girl I became gripped by the Lammers movement and became a dissenter, he greatly disapproved of this step. I think it was partly because of this that he never came back here."[53] Although she occasionally wrote to him over the next thirty years, it was only in old age that a close and warm friendship was renewed between them.

But no man can escape the roots of childhood. Skien remained strongly in Ibsen's mind. *Brand*, which he wrote in 1865, is full of memories of his birthplace; in 1869 he was to refer in a letter to Hedvig to "the old home,

---

[53] Interview in *Fremskridt*, 19 November 1917. But sectarianism was nothing new in Skien; as early as 1784, B. H. Løvenskiold, in his *Beskrivelse over Bradsbierg Amt* (p. 226) had noted that the town "had become famous for the number of its inhabitants who have become addicted to so-called Pietism." (Mosfjeld, p. 57.)

to which I still cling fast by so many roots"; and when, in 1875, he sat down to write a preface to the second edition of *Catiline* and began to reminisce about Grimstad, Skien, too, came back to him and for the first time for over a quarter of a century he wrote a letter to his aged father. The letter is lost, but Knud Ibsen's reply has survived, with its pathetic expression of joy at hearing at last from his famous son: "for I have not heard or seen anything of you, as you yourself say, for twenty-five years." Unhappy memories have a more lasting influence than happy ones, and when Ibsen disembarked at Christiania from the *Prins Carl* on 28 April 1850 it must have been with a very firm resolve to renounce the past. He was not then to know, though it later became part of his philosophy, that whatever you turn your back on gets you in the end.

3

Ibsen at University
1850–1851

The Christiania which greeted Ibsen as a twenty-two-year-old student in 1850 was a small and, by any but the most humble standards, unimpressive town. Eighty years previously, at the time of the first official census in 1769, it had contained no more than seven and a half thousand inhabitants, and even now they numbered only thirty thousand. Few of the buildings stood higher than two storeys. There were no rail[1] nor telegraphic communications, and no gas lighting in the streets, although pipes for the last-named amenity were just being laid. (London had known street gaslighting for nearly forty years.) As late as 1855 a correspondent to *Morgenbladet* was to complain that the first sight to greet a visitor entering the city over the New Bridge was a vast dunghill, that the sewers were so inefficient that the filth in the streets reached to the edge of his galoshes, and that many gutters lay full, untouched and stinking throughout the summer. Between Piperviksstranden and Munkedamsveien lay a large swamp that, in warm weather, "polluted the air with its foul water."[2]

The city contained few buildings of distinction. A handful remained from the eighteenth century, such as the military school, but these did not

---

[1] Except in the public gardens, where, in 1849, so an English traveller tells us, "a train of imitative railway carriages had been constructed to which a miniature locomotive was attached. These revolved on a platform, something after the fashion of a roundabout at a country fair. But the engine was innocent of fire and smoke, except such as proceeded from the pipes of some of the worthy citizens who selected it as their favourite post, and appeared to perform the functions of stoker and engineer, the train being really propelled by machinery under the platform." (Thomas Forester, *Norway in 1848 and 1849* [London, 1850], p. 448.)

[2] For the information contained in this and the succeeding paragraph, see S. C. Hammer, *Kristianias historie*, IV (Christiania, 1923), 408–11.

appeal to contemporary taste, which preferred the neo-classical, with pediments and pilasters—a style new to Norway, and exemplified in the new palace, started in 1823 and completed in 1848 on a hill a quarter of a mile outside the western limits of the city. Near the foot of this hill, the finishing touches were being applied to the university, the members of which were still in temporary housing on Prindsensgade. Fires had been so frequent that, by a recent ordinance, new buildings in the centre of the city had to be of brick; only in the outskirts could wooden houses be erected in the traditional style. But within the city limits, rebuilding was proceeding apace. Public edifices of varying degrees of hideousness were beginning to rise: St. Olaf's Church, Holy Trinity Church (Trefoldigheds-kirken), Oskarshal pleasure palace, a fire station, a new prison and, ugliest of all, the eagerly awaited Parliament building, though this last was not to be completed until 1866. Constables had only recently replaced the old-fashioned watchmen, and foreign travellers were amazed to see iron-col-lared convicts from Akershus, where Christian Lofthuus had died, working in chain-gangs side by side with ordinary labourers.

Socially, the pattern was the same as in Stockholm and Copenhagen. There was a small aristocratic upper stratum. A German traveller, Theodor Mügge, writes of wealthy young ladies in feathered hats riding English thoroughbreds, their houses filled with English carpets and French damask; and he notes that they spent a good deal of each year abroad.[3] Titles of nobility had, however, been abolished in 1821, and the rising merchant class was beginning to marry into the grand families. The poor were very poor indeed. Eilert Sundt, who in 1858 published the results of in-vestigations he had carried out in 1855, records that of 285 families he visited in the city that year, 233 lived in one room, and that among the working-class each room contained an average of 4.9 people. Barely half the families had their own kitchen; and in 1851 and 1852, 1,800 people, representing over 6 per cent of the city's population, received poor relief.[4]

On his arrival in the capital, Ibsen took lodgings with his friend Ole Schulerud in a house owned by an old lady called Mother Sæter at the corner of Vinkelgaden and Filosofgangen, and enlisted at a celebrated crammer's affectionately known as Heltberg's *studentfabrik*, or student factory, to prepare for his matriculation examination the following August. Many distinguished men passed through the doors of this remarkable establishment, to have the rough edges rubbed off their knowledge of logarithms and Latin grammar; and great was the variety of its occupants, "a medley of human beings from all corners of the land and every stratum of society, from failed merchants and lamed cadets to middle-aged farmers and seamen whose love of adventure had driven them, first on long

[3] *Ibid.*, pp. 370–72.
[4] Eilert Sundt, *Om Piperviken og Ruseløkbakken—Undersøgelser om arbeidsklas-sens kaar og sæder i Kristiania* (Christiania, 1858), quoted by Hammer, IV, 414 ff.

voyages to far-off lands, and then, when they did not find what they sought there, on a new long voyage to the golden shores of knowledge."[5] Heltberg himself, though by now crippled by gout and strangled by asthma, was a splendidly witty and original teacher in his dogskin breeches and fur boots; he is sympathetically remembered in many novels and books of reminiscences.[6]

Of more immediate importance to Ibsen than his matriculation, however, was the fate of *Catiline,* which, after the various vicissitudes described above, had at length been published on 12 April, the day before Ibsen left Grimstad. This had been entirely due to the generosity of Schulerud who, having received a small legacy, had devoted it, with extraordinary faith, entirely to the publication of his friend's supposed masterpiece. *Catiline* was issued by a bookseller named P. F. Steensballe, on commission; and its appearance should have been something of an event in the Norwegian literary world, for, improbable as it may seem, it was the first Norwegian play to have been published since Henrik Wergeland's *The Venetians* seven years previously. The point underlines a state of affairs that was to dominate the next thirteen years of Ibsen's life, the fact that the Norwegian theatre was, at this time, totally dependent upon foreign plays, mainly Danish, French and German.

On the day after publication, a favourable notice of *Catiline* appeared in the handwritten student magazine *Samfundsbladet.* This review was written by the editor, a lively young man with few pretensions to original creative talent, but an unusually perceptive and widely read critic. His name was Paul Botten Hansen; he was three years older than Ibsen, and was to become a close friend—one of the few, apart from Due and Schulerud, that he was ever to know. Botten Hansen wrote that it was a pleasure to read a young poet who did not seek to pander to fashion. He discovered in the play "a certain Shakespearean strength and earnestness," and especially praised the author for bringing about his hero's destruction as the result of inward spiritual conflict rather than of external circumstances.

A couple of weeks after Ibsen's arrival in Christiania, on 16 May, was printed the first, and indeed the only, review of *Catiline* to appear in any general newspaper: the *Christiania Post,* which had published the two poems "In Autumn" and "Elegy for Adam Oehlenschläger." The reviewer was a classical philologist named F. L. Vibe, and he found much to criticise. The poet, he noted with regret, had departed from the historical facts and indulged in forced pathos, too often reminding one of *Love without Stockings,* that parody of neo-classical French tragedy by J. H. Wessel reference to which recurs with such curious frequency in the articles and reminiscences of the time. However, he found the work not

[5] Erik Lindseth in *Ny Illustreret Tidende,* 13 August 1882.

[6] Notably Bjørnson's poem "Gamle Heltberg" and Arne Garborg's novel *Bondestudentar.*

altogether lacking in merit. "The author," he concluded, "has an unusual talent for raising himself to a tragic height and power, together with a rare gift for allowing the passions to emerge in full strength, and his language is of a purity such as we have seldom encountered."

These were the only reviews of *Catiline* to appear before October, when the leading literary periodical, *Norsk Tidsskrift for Videnskab og Litteratur,* noticed it. Again the reviewer was a classical philologist, a species with which the Scandinavian countries are heavily burdened: Carl Müller. He was much less sympathetic, listing with relish the "absurd contradictions in the characters"; the best he could find to say was that there were a few redeeming glimpses of a "comprehension of formal requirements" which suggested that Herr Bjarme might some day "give us something more accomplished."

Even this tart review was not without an accompanying consolation, for in the same issue the editor, Professor M. J. Monrad, a brother of the theological student S. C. Monrad who had been one of Ibsen's tutors in Grimstad, and an important figure in the university as well as in Norwegian cultural life,[7] added a few words of personal encouragement. While regretting that the young author had so little grasp of form (a criticism which, whatever may be the other shortcomings of *Catiline,* seems curiously unjustified), he rejoiced that the play was firmly based on a central idea, and that this idea was "both clear and beautiful," namely, the conflict between the instinct for good and duty and "the individual's dark longing for independence." He concluded by expressing the opinion that a poet with so striking an imagination must ultimately succeed in finding the form he required.

All this was considerably encouraging. Unfortunately, not only did the play remain unperformed; hardly anyone bothered to buy it. Of the edition of two hundred and fifty copies, only forty had been sold by the end of the year. Eventually, Ibsen and Schulerud resigned themselves to the book's failure. "I remember," wrote Ibsen in his preface to the second edition, "that one evening, when our mutual household finances posed seemingly insuperable problems, we degraded this pile of print to the category of waste paper, and were fortunate enough to dispose of it to a pedlar. For the next few days we lacked none of the primary necessities of life."

The failure of the play is not surprising. However much *Catiline* may have been in tune with the spirit of Europe in 1850, it was out of tune with the prevailing spirit in Norway. "Norwegian spiritual life," comments a literary historian of the country, "underwent an idyllic period during the eighteen-forties. Contemporary life was poor and lacking in impulse, all was peace, no danger threatened, people buried themselves in memories,

---

[7] He was Professor of Philosophy at Christiania for fifty-two years, from 1845 until his death in 1897.

and began for the first time to study their own history, their folk traditions, their national origins. Literature was a quiet lake, cut off from the oceans of the world, barely touched by the storms that raged outside. Welhaven, the leading poet of the age, has only tired and peevish words for the Paris rebels of 1848 who disturbed him in his contemplation, and Andreas Munch rubs his hands in bourgeois glee at our country escaping the upheavals of Europe. *Catiline* is the only Norwegian work through whose pages there glows something of the tumultuous unrest and spirit of rebellion that gripped the world outside Norway in 1848."[8]

Meanwhile Ibsen was, for the first time in his life, meeting people of his own age who knew more about literature than he did and who were, themselves, writers. One such was Paul Botten Hansen. A gifted linguist with an immense range of reading, he was already beginning to acquire what was, during the next decade, to become one of the largest private libraries in the country. He had an extensive knowledge of European culture, and the following year was to write a long thesis on *The Young Germany*. What Coleridge was to Wordsworth, Botten Hansen was to Ibsen, opening up new horizons of thought and literature for him. Ibsen was to recall him affectionately as "a man whose appreciation has always been precious and important to me, and to whom I hereby express my renewed gratitude."[9]

Another stimulating companion was a farmer's son from Telemark whom he met at Heltberg's student factory, Aasmund Vinje. Ten years older than Ibsen, and as heavily bearded, Vinje had a sharply satirical turn of mind and was a brilliant talker. Gerhard Gran has described him as "a conversationalist such as we have never had [in Norway] before or since"[10] —and Norway is a country where good conversation is as common as in Ireland. At this early stage in his career, Vinje's powers were far from fully developed; he was inhibited by having to write in *riksmaal,* the formal language used for writing which was based on Danish and was far removed from Norwegian conversational rhythms. *Landsmaal,* the language spoken by country people such as himself, was not yet accepted as a written form, though Vinje was to do much during the next few years to champion its use. This gap between the spoken and written tongues was a handicap to Norwegian writers which few foreigners can appreciate; to comprehend it, one must imagine a J. M. Synge or a Sean O'Casey forced to write in the language of Disraeli or Oscar Wilde. If one compares the characters of Walter Scott who speak English with those, so incomparably more alive and richer, who talk in Scots, one may, likewise, perceive the dilemma.

Vinje was full of undigested knowledge, but he was a lively and exciting companion for Ibsen, whose radical opinions he shared to an

[8] Gerhard Gran, *Henrik Ibsen: liv og verker* (Christiania, 1918), I, 20–21.
[9] Preface to the 1875 edition of *Catiline.*
[10] Gran, I, 28.

even stronger degree. Another still more radical young man happened by chance to be living at Mother Sæter's, Theodor Abildgaard. Abildgaard was closely and vigorously associated with the workers' movement which Marcus Thrane had recently founded. Thrane, following a visit to Paris (where he had been imprisoned for two months as "having no visible means of support") and to the London of the Chartist manifesto, had been infected by the English Christian Socialists' enthusiasm for the co-operative movement, and in eighteen months he had established no fewer than 273 workers' associations in Norway, with 20,854 members, demanding among other things shorter hours of labour, the abolition of trade monopolies and the provision of small-holdings to reduce the competition for employment. Abildgaard found a ready disciple in Ibsen, and only a month after the latter's arrival in Christiania, on 29 May 1850, he and Vinje persuaded Ibsen to join them in a political demonstration.

A German from Schleswig named Harro Harring, who had fought for both the Greeks in their war of liberation against the Turks, and the Poles in their rebellion against the Russians, had come to Norway in 1849 to seek refuge in his old age. There he founded and edited a radical paper, *The Voice of the People,* and at the beginning of 1850 he had published a play entitled *The American Testament* which the authorities decided outstepped the limits of the freedom of the press. An order was issued for his deportation, and on the morning of 29 May the police entered his house and escorted him on board a ship, where he was held prisoner until it sailed. The news of this spread rapidly through the town, and a protest was drawn up, signed by a hundred and forty names, of which Ibsen's was one. This document having been presented to the senior member of the cabinet, the assembly made its way to the quay, where a deputation went on board the steamer and addressed a few words to Harring, who then appeared on deck and was hailed with three times three cheers, followed by a cheer for Norway and freedom. Ibsen, we are told, "was from first to last an eager participator in this affair."[11] It was the only political demonstration in which he was ever to take part.

In addition to Botten Hansen, Vinje, and Abildgaard, there was a fourth student whom Ibsen met during these first weeks in Christiania and who was, in the future, to have a more important impact on his life than any of them: Bjørnstjerne Bjørnson. Bjørnson was younger than the others, only eighteen, the son of a country clergyman; but he attended Heltberg's only occasionally that spring, and it was some little time before he and Ibsen became closely acquainted (though he was among those who signed the Harring protest). In his poem "Old Heltberg" (1873), Bjørnson remembered his young fellow-pupil:

> Thin and intense, with a face pale as gypsum
> Behind an immense coal-black beard, *Henrik Ibsen.*

11 Jæger, p. 67.

Some remembered his hair and beard as brown, some as black; presumably it was of that very dark shade of brown which is often mistaken for black; but all are agreed as to its bushiness.

It was important for Ibsen that he should have come thus early into contact with people of his own generation whose horizons were European and who were, moreover, of a critical and satirical turn of mind instead of, like so many of their contemporaries, being carried along on the popular wave of national romanticism. Where others, such as Andreas Munch and Welhaven, dwelt on the past, Botten Hansen, Vinje, and Abildgaard were absorbed with the present. Vinje was much influenced by the Danish writer and journalist Meïr Aron Goldschmidt, who had founded a provocative magazine in Copenhagen named *The Corsair;* he learned from Goldschmidt to think of the age as one of doubt and contradiction, as "a hovering between yes and no, or rather a combination of the two," so that "behind the most serious truth one glimpses the parody peeping through her curtain, and beneath a light jest one hears the bell-note of seriousness."[12] This dual vision, this satirical touch, was something that Bjørnson, the patriot and romanticist par excellence, was never to acquire, any more than he was to escape the narrowness of nationalism.

During the Whitsun vacation Ibsen settled down to rework the one-act play *The Norsemen* which he had begun at Grimstad. Botten Hansen, in his favourable review of *Catiline,* had expressed regret that Ibsen had not chosen a national-historical theme instead of setting his play in Ancient Rome. Ibsen himself appears to have had divided feelings at this time on the question of nationalistic literature. On the one hand, it was less than a year since he had written the passionate "Sonnets to King Oscar" and "Awake, Scandinavians!" But in his subsequent "Elegy for Adam Oehlenschläger," while declaring that by the latter's death the Norse gods had lost their spokesman on earth, he at the same time expressed the hope that literature would now strike out on new roads, since poetry that sings of "the enshrined past" could not answer the demands of the new age. None the less, *The Norsemen,* or, as he now re-entitled it, *The Warrior's Barrow,* turned out to be a dramatic poem very much in the mould of Oehlenschläger's historical tragedies.

The action takes place on the coast of Normandy "shortly before the introduction of Christianity into the North." An old Norse warrior, Bernhard, and his foster-daughter, Blanka, live there; she tends the burial mound, or barrow, of a warrior who has been killed in the past by marauding Vikings. Both she and Bernhard are Christians. Norsemen now arrive, worshippers of the old gods, led by their king, Gandalf, and bent on avenging the death of his father Audun who had been killed on a raid here. He meets Blanka; they fall in love at first sight; she tries to

[12] Gran, I, 29.

persuade him to turn from paganism to Christianity (as, coincidentally or not, Clara Ebbell at Grimstad had tried to convert Ibsen from atheism). Bernhard now tells Gandalf that the burial mound is in fact Audun's and that he, Bernhard, killed him. The Vikings demand that Gandalf carry out his oath either to kill his father's murderer or to die himself. Rather than kill Blanka's foster-father, he decides to kill himself. She tries to persuade him that an oath to the Norse gods need not, and should not, be obeyed. At this crisis Bernhard reveals himself as Audun; wounded in the battle, he had been found and tended by Blanka, and had become a Christian; the mound contains only, symbolically, his Viking sword and armour. Gandalf, converted, takes Blanka back to the north to be his bride; Audun and the Vikings' bard, Hemming, remain behind.

Such is the banal plot of this short play, and there is no pretending that, dramatically, it has any but the most meagre merits. Even the idea of the Viking who turns Christian to end his days in peace on a southern shore is a blatant crib from Oehlenschläger's *The Vikings in Byzantium,* where an ancient Syrian hermit is revealed to be the great warrior Olaf Tryggvason (about whom Ibsen had begun a play while at Grimstad). Bernhard-Audun's conduct, in particular, is quite inadequately motivated, and none of the characters has any real individuality. Such virtues as the play possesses are poetic rather than dramatic; like *Catiline,* it moves with considerable skill from rhymed to unrhymed verse, and contains several fine passages, notably those in which Gandalf proclaims his faith in the heathen gods.

It often happens, however, that a dramatist's inferior second play is accepted where his more original first effort has been rejected. Although patently less good than *Catiline, The Warrior's Barrow* was more in tune with the current fashion of romantic nationalism, and the Christiania Theatre, which had turned down the earlier play, accepted this one for production that autumn. Ibsen had submitted it under the same pseudonym as before, Brynjolf Bjarme.

Encouraged by this, he started work almost immediately on a third play, in blank verse, again with a romantic-nationalistic theme, entitled *The Ptarmigan of Justedal.* In Andreas Faye's *Norwegian Tales* he must have read the story about a little girl who had been the only person in her valley to survive the Black Death; when, years later, people discovered her, she had become "shy and wild as a bird," so that she came to be called the Ptarmigan of Justedal. In Ibsen's dramatisation of the story, a young farmer's son, Bjørn, and an old hunter, Paal, are walking in the mountains. They begin to speak of the "little people"; Paal tells how, recently, he took aim at a ptarmigan

> But in a trice the bird was gone
> And in its place a sprite crouched on the bough.

He asks Bjørn where he has been lately, and Bjørn replies that he has been exploring in Justedal. "God forgive you!" cries Paal.

> No man has set foot there for many a year.
> It has lain desolate since the Black Death.
> Men say ghosts walk there, and the unburied dead
> Haunt its harsh hillsides.

Paal goes into the hut, and Bjørn, left alone, recalls sadly how

> She called me from her bough, winding her horn,
> Since when I have felt drawn towards that valley
> By some invisible power.

As he speaks, he hears the ptarmigan girl, Alfhild, singing.

Scene Two is in Bjørn's home. His father, a fierce old farmer named Bengt, has autocratically decided that Bjørn shall marry his foster-daughter, Mereta, though neither loves the other. To settle the matter he has summoned Mogens, a bibulous and pedantic priest, the forerunner of those other unsympathetic clerics whom Ibsen was to create: Pastor Strawman in *Love's Comedy*, the Provost in *Brand*, Pastor Manders in *Ghosts*, and the drunken Molvik in *The Wild Duck*. An old minstrel, Knud, appears, but Bengt drives him irritably away; when he tells Paal and Bjørn they are alarmed, for this Knud is a famous bard:

> He brings good luck to those who hearken to him.
> But if a man should drive him from his gate,
> His house is cursed.

Bjørn hears that his father plans to match him with Mereta, but will have none of it. He can only think of the ptarmigan who has bewitched him, and creeps secretly off to the unlucky valley of Justedal to find her.

In Act Two he meets her. Meanwhile, in Bengt's house, Mereta and a young friend of Bjørn's, Einar, pledge their love to each other. Old Bengt surprises them and warns Einar off.

At this point, halfway through the second act (the title page tell us that it was to consist of four), Ibsen abandoned the play; though he was to take it up again six years later and rewrite it as *Olaf Liljekrans*. *The Ptarmigan of Justedal* (like *Olaf Liljekrans*) has been over-readily dismissed by such few critics as have bothered to consider it; as far as it goes, in characterisation and plot development, it was patently the best thing that Ibsen had yet done. The old people especially, Bengt the farmer, Paal the hunter, Mogens the priest, and Knud the minstrel, are splendidly drawn in brief, swift strokes, as is the atmosphere of sick enchantment. Why Ibsen stopped writing it we do not know; it may have been simply that, with his examination approaching, he felt he could no longer afford to spend time away from his studies.

Some time during the summer, Ibsen and Schulerud moved from Mother Sæter's to a Fru Holt on Møllergaden. Living mainly on Schulerud's small allowance, they at first managed almost luxuriously, for it seems they were able to afford not merely dinners provided by their landlady, but even a servant. The latter, however, did not last long; and soon they had to drop the dinners too. Since it would have damaged their reputation, to say nothing of their credit, for it to be known that they could not afford a square meal, they made a habit of going out around dinner time and returning an hour or so later so that the other lodgers and the servants would imagine they were eating in town. They would then make do with coffee and sandwiches of cheese and sausage-meat. Botten Hansen tells that, although he saw Ibsen almost daily at this period, he had no inkling of the extreme poverty in which the latter lived;[13] as at Grimstad, Ibsen's pride forbade him to reveal his circumstances to his friends. It was presumably during this summer or autumn that Ibsen and Schulerud took the desperate measure of selling their remaining copies of Catiline as waste paper.

Ole Schulerud's young brother Johan (the boy to whom Ibsen had, in Grimstad, been stingy with the liquorice) was staying with them now. The three inhabited a tiny room with space for only two beds, one of which the Schuleruds had to share. Johan remembered the three of them, Ole's tiny legacy having been exhausted on the publication of Catiline, as being "permanently poor," and Ibsen as "dark and unapproachable. I didn't like him, and I could see no evidence that he liked me. Small of stature, with an unattractive, square face." Occasionally, Johan recalled, they would have parties with boston[14] and toddy, at which Botten Hansen and Abildgaard were frequent guests, and on these occasions Ibsen would be "much more talkative and agreeable than at other times."[15]

However, a young man's first year at university is often spent in circumstances of comparative want, and that summer of 1850 must, in the main, have been a happy one for Ibsen, rejoicing in his new friends, the liberating atmosphere of university life and the knowledge that a work of his was to be presented at the country's leading theatre. Not many youthful playwrights have been able to claim the honour of seeing their first play printed and their second accepted for production shortly after their twenty-second birthday. Admittedly there came a slight setback in August; Ibsen failed his matriculation. His tutor at the crammer's, Theodor J. Lie, wrote him a good reference, saying that he had a "right faithful and retentive memory, assisted by happy natural gifts," but in no subject did he get the maximum mark of 1, and in only one, German, did he even succeed in achieving 2, or "Very Good." In most subjects, including

13 *Illustreret Nyhedsblad,* 19 July 1863.
14 A kind of whist.
15 Interview with Johan Schulerud in *Verdens Gang,* 23 and 24 June 1910.

Norwegian composition, he scored a moderate 3; on the three Latin papers he got 3, 4, and 5 respectively; and in both Greek and mathematics he failed with 6, so that his average over the whole examination was no more than 3.67. But his creative writing must already have seemed to him more important than his university studies, for he never bothered to attempt the Greek or mathematics papers again, although in view of the papers which he had passed he was entitled to style himself *Student* Ibsen. He continued to attend lectures, but medicine, which he had originally intended to follow, had apparently lost its interest for him; he now studied only literature and aesthetics. He joined the student literary club which had been founded the previous year, and made the required inaugural speech, prefacing it with a recital of seven of his own sonnets.

One would like to know what Ibsen was reading at this time, but neither he nor his friends have left any record of this. He may, as many have assumed, have continued to read Kierkegaard, but it is by no means certain that he did. Such evidence as there is of Kierkegaard's possible influence on Ibsen's writing does not appear until over ten years later. It has, similarly, been asserted that Ibsen probably studied Hegel at this time, because Hegelian philosophy was now sweeping Europe and the new professor of philosophy at the university, M. J. Monrad (the author of the kind editorial note about *Catiline*) was a disciple of Hegel; but we have no evidence that Ibsen ever read a line of Hegel, and if he did, he may well, like Kierkegaard (cf. the latter's journal for 1843) have found Hegel "merely comic" with his "eternal hinting and deceiving." One author who did make an impact on him, however, was the Danish poet, philosopher, critic and dramatist Johan Ludvig Heiberg (1791–1860), whom Ibsen was to meet in Copenhagen the following year and who was one of the very few writers from whom Ibsen, in later life, confessed to having learned something. Heiberg's influence was at its height in Scandinavia in 1850, and he was much discussed in the circles in which Ibsen moved; moreover, there is clear evidence in the drama criticisms which Ibsen was shortly to write that he was well acquainted with Heiberg's little book *On Vaudeville*.[16] But, like so many young men who find themselves during their first year at university in stimulating company after years of forced reading, Ibsen may not have devoted overmuch time to books, and in any case he seems, in common with many dramatists and novelists, not greatly to have enjoyed or comprehended the abstractions of philosophy.

That summer and autumn he also wrote a number of poems. Twelve of these he copied neatly on to light blue paper in the scratchy, difficult, sharply slanted handwriting which we find in his early letters and manuscripts (and which contrasts so remarkably with the lucid bold copperplate

[16] Heiberg's probable influence on Ibsen's dramatic criticisms has been well analysed by Professor Sigmund Skard in *A. O. Vinje og antikken* (Oslo, 1938), pp. 124–25.

of his maturity), and posted to Clara Ebbell at Grimstad. "In sending you the enclosed writings," he wrote stiffly in the short note which accompanied them, "it is my hope that the mood which evoked these poems may serve as an excuse for the observations expressed therein, which might partly be misinterpreted by others and by you. I beg you to forgive me for not being able to refrain from adding these words, probably the last that I shall ever address to you."[17]

The poems included the sonnet sequence which Ibsen had read as a preface to his inaugural speech at the Students' Union, and three romantic trifles entitled "In the Night" (which dates from Grimstad), "Youthful Dreams" and "Among the Ruins." Of these, "In the Night" and "Among the Ruins" are conventional lyrics, and "Youthful Dreams," although skilfully composed in rhymed stanzas, contains no original thought or idea. The sonnets, however, were much the best and most complex poems that Ibsen had written up to that time. On the lake of life, he says, there glide two ships, sailing in opposite directions. One, a merchantman laden to the waterline, rows slowly but safely in the lee of the shore; the other, all sails set, entrusts itself to the winds and tosses perilously upon the waves. Each of us must choose to which ship he will entrust his life. If we choose the second, the ideal instead of the material, our voyage will be hard and uncertain, and our reward will probably come late; but it is better to be like the swan, which discovers the joy of song only in its last moments, than to find those joys early and then lose our way, "and wander lost across life's burning sands." Over the next fifty years, Ibsen was to return again and again in his work to this theme, of the choice that faces man between idealism and compromise.[18]

Of still greater interest are the two other poems which Ibsen sent to Clara Ebbell: "The Miner" and "The Bird and the Trapper." They were the only two poems of this group which Ibsen retained for inclusion in the volume of collected verse that he published as his farewell to that medium in 1871. With the sonnets, they represent an important departure for Ibsen as a poet. Hitherto, his poems had been lyrical—except for the inferior, Kiplingesque exhortations inspired by the political events of 1848. But the sonnets, "The Miner," and "The Bird and the Trapper" are all dramatic poems, in the sense that the poet, instead of merely recording his emotions, dramatises them, as one dramatises an idea for a play; unlike his earlier, lyrical poems, they create strong visual images. The English poet whom Ibsen, in his shorter pieces, most closely resembles is Thomas Hardy (a writer with whom he had, of course, much in common when he turned to prose). Like Hardy, Ibsen was an accomplished lyricist but at his best as a poet when writing dramatic verse, whether in the

[17] In fact he wrote to her once more, the following February, enclosing a poem, "To a Troubadour." Shortly afterwards she married a wealthy man twice her age.

[18] The subject for debate at the Students' Union on the evening when Ibsen read these sonnets was "Realism v. Idealism."

form of dramatic monologues or of sharply told anecdotes. "The Miner"
is an example of the first category, "The Bird and the Trapper" of the
second.

Barely half a mile from Ibsen's childhood home at Venstøp was an iron
mine, only just below ground surface. The noise from it must, when the
wind was right, have been audible at the house, and as a child he must
surely have gone and watched the men working there. The subject of the
miner had attracted other poets; Oehlenschläger had written a poem on
the theme, and so, in 1811, had the Swedish poet Erik Gustaf Geijer; but
where Oehlenschläger had been attracted by the mystery of the darkness,
and Geijer by the peace, Ibsen had been fascinated by the hard and
remorseless toil. All of us who write poems, however badly, write at least
one in adolescence or early manhood which foretells our future, and with
Ibsen that poem was "The Miner":

> Groan and thunder, mountain wall,
> Before my heavy hammer blow.
> Downwards I must carve my way
> Till I hear the iron ore sing.
>
> Deep in the mountain's lonely night
> The rich treasure beckons me.
> Diamonds and precious stones
> Among the red branches of the gold.
>
> Here in the darkness there is peace,
> Peace and rest for eternity.
> Heavy hammer, break me the way
> To the heart-chamber of what lies hidden there . . .
>
> When I first entered here
> I thought in my innocence:
> "The spirits of the dark will solve for me
> Life's obscure riddles."
>
> No spirit has yet taught me that strange answer.
> No sun shines from the depths.
>
> Was I wrong? Does this path
> Not lead to the light?
> But the light blinds my eyes
> If I seek it in the mountains.
>
> No, I must go down into the dark.
> Eternal peace lies there.
> Heavy hammer, break me the way
> To the heart-chamber of what lies hidden there.

So blow follows blow
Till he sinks weak and tired.
No ray of morning shines.
No sun of hope rises.

"The Bird and the Trapper" anticipates, to English ears, the manner of
a poet with whom, again, Ibsen had more in common than might at first
appear—D. H. Lawrence:

Once when I was little
I was running in my father's garden.
The bird was singing its morning song
From its high branch and picket fence.

And I cut from the pine-branch
An ingenious bird-trap.
Before I can count ten
The bird sits there inside it!

And I carried with cruel delight,
Quickly, the trap into the house.
Frightened the bird with my angry
Glance, with my cries and threats.

When I had thus amused myself
And sated my cruelty,
I put the cage on the table;
Cautiously opened the door.

O, how it uses its wings!
It is offered life and freedom.
It would soar high to the light
But—crushes itself against the window pane.

You are revenged, cruelly revenged.
Now a power has trapped me
In a cage, where I can only flutter crazily.

And an eye stares at me
Coldly and scornfully through the bars.
This glance confuses my soul.
Fear makes my body shake.

And when I think I see
The path that leads to freedom,
I sink with broken wings
From my dreamed soaring.

Henrik Jæger tells that Ibsen planned during this first year in Christiania to publish a volume of verse, but gradually rejected poem after poem from his Grimstad days until there was hardly anything left.[19] He no longer wanted to write poems of mood, but poems of ideas; and it was upon the latter kind, beginning with those quoted above, that he was to concentrate during the remainder of his time in Christiania.

On 26 September 1850 came the eagerly awaited production at the Christiania Theatre of *The Warrior's Barrow*. The part of Blanka was performed by a young actress named Laura Svendsen; later, under her married name of Laura Gundersen, she was to become one of Norway's most famous actresses and was to create several of Ibsen's greatest roles, including Ellida in *The Lady from the Sea* and Gunhild Borkman. Ibsen, extremely nervous, hid himself, we are told, in the darkest corner of the theatre; but the play, surprisingly, was well received, and was repeated twice that autumn.

Ibsen's enthusiastic friend, Ole Schulerud, whether from altruistic motives or in the faint hope of retrieving a little of his lost legacy, at once set about trying to get *The Warrior's Barrow* published. He approached Steensballe, the bookseller who had issued *Catiline* on commission, and a contract was signed under which Ibsen was actually to receive an advance of twenty-five specie-dollars:

> I, the undersigned Bookseller Steensballe, hereby acknowledge that I have contracted with Student Schulerud regarding the purchase of Brynjolf Bjarme's manuscript of "The Warrior's Barrow," dramatic poem in one act, and "The Gold Harp," epic poem, on the following terms:
>
> 1. Steensballe shall have the right to print 1, one, edition of 4–500 copies.
> 2. Steensballe shall pay, in return for the rights of this 1st edition, 25, twenty-five, specie-dollars, of which 10, ten, specie-dollars shall be paid forthwith, the remainder when 250, two hundred and fifty, copies have been sold. Christiania 19 December 1850.
>
> I hereby acknowledge receipt from Herr Steensballe of 10, ten, specie-dollars as instalment on the above sum.
>
> Ole Schulerud

For some unknown reason, however, the play was not printed, and this, the original version of *The Warrior's Barrow,* was not published until 1902 (though a revised version, on the occasion of its performance at Bergen in 1854, was serialised in four parts in a local newspaper). Ibsen quickly recognised the play's limitations, and it was one of the only two plays of his which, when a collected edition of his works was planned towards the end of his life, he decided to omit. (The other was *St. John's*

[19] Jæger, p. 239. Halvorsen (p. 8, footnote) denies on Ibsen's authority that such a volume was contemplated; but Ibsen's memory, where his early years are concerned, frequently proved false, and Jæger's statement at least deserves to remain on record.

Night.) No trace has ever been discovered of the planned "epic poem," "The Gold Harp," and it is not known whether Ibsen ever began it.

1850, then, had been a year of poetry. 1851 was to be primarily a year of journalism. Ibsen continued, naturally, to write poetry, as an undergraduate should; but he needed another medium as outlet for the combativeness which was so important a part of his character. An opportunity arose when, in the New Year, he found himself chosen by the Students' Union to become editor of their handwritten magazine, *Samfundsbladet,* in succession to Paul Botten Hansen, probably through the latter's influence.

Ibsen edited *Samfundsbladet* for nine months, but with decreasing assiduousness; in the first quarter of the year he produced three numbers, in the second quarter only one, and in the third quarter none at all. The reason for this was that his energies gradually became absorbed in a more exciting project which Botten Hansen and Vinje had just started, a new, independent literary and political weekly of their own. Their inspiration and model for this was the Danish magazine *The Corsair,* which Meïr Aron Goldschmidt had founded in Copenhagen; Vinje was a great admirer of that neurotic, battling controversialist who, like Vinje himself, despised all party ties and smote around at everyone and everything (among his targets had been such respected figures as Heiberg and Kierkegaard). An advertisement issued in Christiania on 5 March 1851 announced that the new magazine would contain, among other delights, "Poems by Brynjolf Bjarme"; and since, following the production of *The Warrior's Barrow,* Ibsen was now allowed free tickets to the Christiania Theatre, he was also to write the drama criticisms. The magazine had no name. In place of a title, it carried on the front page of the first issue a picture of the main square of Christiania, Stortorvet, with a man in several grotesque postures, on foot and on horseback, eyeing the world satirically. Subsequently the same man was shown in the Storthing gallery alertly listening to the parliamentary debates and taking notes. As a result the magazine came to be known as *Manden,* "The Man."

For the next nine months, Ibsen busied himself with drama criticism and political and topical commentaries, as well as with editorial and subeditorial work and an occasional, and by no means unskilful, caricature. His first drama criticism to be published, on 12 January in *Samfundsbladet,* was a brief and rather flat notice of a production of Holberg's comedy *The Political Tinker;* and on 15 February he contributed a dutiful and dullish survey of the history of the Students' Union. The same issue, however, included a lively piece by him on the old question of the desirability of the country having a Norwegian theatre. The Christiania Theatre had refused to let the Students' Union give a public performance there instead of in their own inadequate premises, and Ibsen took up the cudgels. "It has often been stated in the Students' Union," he declared, "that it is from us that any Norwegian Theatre must originate. . . . The preparatory work is up to us, it is we who must accustom the people to hearing Norwegian spoken from the stage; but the theatre-going public of the capital is not the people. To travel the country preaching theatrical reform is hardly practicable; so why not seize the opportunity to scatter the good seed as widely as possible, and Fair Week is ideally suited to this." (At Fair Week the capital was filled with people from the countryside.)

On 1 March he reviewed, again in *Samfundsbladet,* a student vaudeville in one act entitled *The Asylum in Greenland,* defending the decision to give it a second performance after the first one had been ill received. The review tells us nothing interesting except, by implication, that Ibsen had read J. L. Heiberg's *On Vaudeville,* several undigested gobbets of which may be found floating in Ibsen's prose. Then, on 23 March, in *The Man,* he took the bold step of publicly criticising his own professor's lectures. J. S. Welhaven was not only professor of aesthetics but also the leading Norwegian poet now that Henrik Wergeland was dead. Unlike the gifted but naïve Wergeland, Welhaven was a scholarly, elegant and dignified versifier somewhat in the Matthew Arnold mould. Welhaven had attacked the fashion which had arisen in the eighteenth century of re-telling ancient Greek and Roman myths; taking his text from Holberg, who had satirised this cult, he condemned the contemporary Danish poet Frederik Paludan-Müller for indulging in similar re-tellings, as in his poem *Tithonus* (a subject which Tennyson was to treat more memorably ten years later). Ibsen, with some percipience, suggested that Welhaven was wrong in identifying Paludan-Müller's efforts with those of the previous century. Although Paludan-Müller might have failed in this particular instance, Ibsen asserted, "it in no way follows that the Myth is unsuited to be used in our time as the basis for a poem of ideas. . . . In myth, the content of popular consciousness is a blending of history and imagination. . . . Since the subject-matter of myth is timeless, its validity in time can never be so limited as to disqualify an author from laying another stone upon that mythical foundation. We no longer voyage the seas like Columbus to discover a new country, but rather to study the nature of that country whose existence we accept. So it is with mythical poetry. . . . To draw it up from its resting-place on the ocean bed and consider it anew from a fresh and imaginative standpoint is no violation of the sacredness of myth, nor any perversion of its quintessential nature, but rather a necessary step in its logical development." That last sentence might almost serve as a preface to *Peer Gynt.*

Ibsen was now finding his feet as a journalist, and on 13 April *The Man* printed a review by him of a modern German play, Karl Gutzkow's *Zopf und Schwert,* which is interesting on two grounds. Firstly, it underlines how inadequate he found even at this early stage in his career the trivia of Eugène Scribe, the most popular and esteemed playwright of the day;[20] and secondly, it shows that he was already aware of the possibilities of drama written to be read rather than staged, the genre of which Alfred de Musset was the contemporary master. Fifteen years later Ibsen, like de Musset, was temporarily to abandon stageable drama for the drama of the study and in so doing was to write what many people regard as his two greatest and most theatrically exciting plays. The review, for all its occasional *longueurs,* is worth quoting *in extenso,* if only because it reveals the perplexities amongst which the young dramatist was groping:

Our theatrical repertory having long been recruited exclusively from France and Copenhagen, a play of the new German school was recently shown. The public seemed not to find this modification of their normal diet much to their taste. Far be it from me to seek the cause of this in the public's fastidiousness, for God knows if there is one thing our audiences are not, it is fastidious. The true reason is not hard to find. When a public has grown accustomed, as ours has, year in and year out, to the dramatic candy-floss (*slikkerier*) of Scribe & Co., cautiously seasoned with a suitable admixture of various poetical substitutes, it is very understandable that the solider German fare must strike even the ostrich stomachs of our theatre-goers as somewhat indigestible.

Between modern French and modern German drama there are essential differences. The French drama (using the word drama in its true sense, as covering spectacles in general) makes contact with life only through the medium of actors; only thus is it born into existence. For drama, as it leaves the hand of a French playwright, is still embryonic, and only answers to its name when it achieves reality through actual performance. For a Frenchman, the new drama has no title to be regarded as literature for reading, any more than our mountain peasants would regard a sheet of music as such. The German dramatist, on the other hand, writes his play without specifically envisaging it in performance. If it can be staged in the form in which it leaves his pen, well and good; if not, it can be read, and he regards it as thus equally satisfying the requirements of drama, for in Germany the claim of drama to be regarded as reading literature is one with its claim to be regarded as dramatic literature.

From this it naturally follows that the German, when he writes a play for the stage, has other considerations in mind than when writing without thought of performance. But this conflict between his general view of drama, and the demands which he has to face on such isolated occasions, reveals itself in his work and destroys the unity without which art cannot exist. In order, as he supposes, to achieve reality, he paints characters and situations with a broad brush, but thereby defeats his purpose, since he thus oversteps the boundaries of drama. Thus the German drama is to the French as a *tableau vivant* is to

[20] Ibsen told Henrik Jæger in 1887 that "he of course saw much Scribe in his youth, but that, dramatically, he then rated the elder Dumas higher." (Jæger's notes for his biography of Ibsen, first printed in H. Midbøe's *Streiflys over Ibsen* [Oslo, 1960], p. 162.)

a painting; in the former, figures exist in their natural dimensions and colours, in the latter they merely *appear* thus. . . .

This is not to say that the French drama has no advantages over the German; it is a question of how far it meets the demands which it has set itself. If literal reality has no place in art, neither does a work that does not contain the germ of reality within it; and herein lies the weakness of the French drama. In it characters too often appear as pure abstractions; to portray contrast (the hobby-horse of French drama) they are usually painted as either angels or devils, seldom as people. Whereas when the German aims at reality, which is not in general his hunting ground, he does it with a vengeance, portraying not just human beings as such but only the most trivial kind of everyday people as we daily see and hear them. Yet the character of an everyday person is, from an artist's standpoint, by no means trivial; it is as interesting to him as any other.

The play under review is as typically German in its faults as in its virtues. It is essentially a play of situations, for it is the situation that develops; the characters do not.

After outlining the absurd plot, which takes place at the Prussian court, and delivering himself of some comments on the characters ("Sir Hotham is the complete Englishman, ready to help his friend without ever losing sight of his country's material interests"), the dramatic faults of the play ("When the Princess is arrested she addresses a thunderous speech to the Dragoons, stopping at frequent intervals to let her lady-in-waiting have her say, which strikes us as unnatural"), and the performances, which he praises rather uncritically, Ibsen continues:

> But now a little about our public's reaction to the play. Were it not the fashion just now to attack the theatre and the "Danish" players, this might have seemed a good opportunity for them to express their indebtedness to both without imperilling their artistic conscience. But by no means! The play was greeted with scarcely any applause, except for those moments when the author moves into burlesque, as when the Dragoons march in with the soup tureen and the woollen stockings, and the King appears without coat or trousers. And what was it, in the last-named instance, that pleased our ingenuous public? Not the fact of the King of Prussia receiving the Prince of Bayreuth in his underpants, though the situation is artistically comic, but the joy of seeing Herr Jørgensen appear thus clad upon the stage— that was the great joke. . . . And this is the public that clamours for a National Theatre! In truth, should this and other demands currently being made by this public be met, then "Goodnight, ye Muses!" But with our prospects of a National Theatre we shall deal more closely in a later article.

After a dutiful piece in *Samfundsbladet* later the same month on the inadequacies of the Union library, we find Ibsen, on 4 May, trying his hand at opera criticism. The subject was Rossini's *William Tell,* and he had sharp words to say about the libretto. "It is regrettable that this splendid music should be shackled with so mediocre a text. It consists merely of loose fragments torn from Schiller's tragedy of the same name and lumped together without the librettist achieving any real unity or coherence. The effect of the music is unquestionably much reduced in consequence." In the same article, Ibsen noticed revivals of two plays by Scribe, *La Famille Riquebourg* and *Une Chaumière et sa Cœur,* the latter being a collaboration with Robert Alphonse. In view of the hoary myth, which one may still hear repeated, that Ibsen was a disciple of Scribe, it is worth noting that he described these efforts as "two old plays that ought long ago to have been regarded as dead and buried."

The following week, again in *The Man,* we find Ibsen attacking an anonymous French vaudeville, *Un Homme Blasé,* for its complete lack of realism and structural incompetence:

> One naturally expects that the hero's character will reveal itself through dramatic action; but our author is of another opinion. Instead of letting his hero do things, he makes him *tell* the audience about his *ennui,* how life has lost its sparkle and everything seems an interminable misery. That this lengthy narrative should interest the good friends to whom he addresses it seems scarcely likely; for he says nothing that they cannot already know. What the cause of all this boredom is we are not informed; the hero merely assures us that he is bored, and we must take him at his word. . . . At last one of his friends has an idea. He must get married. It seems curious that this not impossibly out of the way notion has not occurred to him before; however, our author will have it so, and we must accept it. But this idea comes to nothing, and so the first act ends. But then the blasé gentleman meets a young peasant girl and is soon head over heels in love with her. Unfortunately all this takes place behind the curtain during the interval between acts one and two, so that we have to be satisfied with an account of the affair which the hero is kind enough to give us. . . .
>
> The fact that the public whistled must be taken as a happy sign that there are, after all, a few among us who can distinguish truth from falsehood. The few who clapped we must bear with; their demonstration can hardly have been on behalf of the play, and if it was aimed at the acting it was fully justified. . . . The directors of the theatre can, however, scarcely be censured for presenting this piece. The public is always complaining that it is offered nothing but warmed-up leftovers, so something new must be offered. We ourselves write nothing, neither do the Danes, Scribe has been done to death, and what is there left? Besides, it is good for us now and then to be given a really clear picture of what a play ought not to be.

From May until August, Vinje was away on holiday, and in his absence Ibsen took over the political commentary of *The Man,* which the editors now decided to rename *Andhrimner,* after the cook who prepared the food for the gods in Valhalla. On 18 May he reported a debate in the Storthing on the repeal of the usury law, which allowed money lenders to fix their own rates of interest for short-term loans without security. Ibsen singled out for especial scorn A. B. Stabell, the member for Akershus and editor of the then Liberal newspaper[21] *Morgenbladet,* who that year had left the opposition party and joined the government, and had delivered himself of the unfortunate remark that "it would be improper for educated men to listen to the clamour of the rabble and allow themselves to be influenced by it." "These words," commented Ibsen, "were uttered in this year of grace 1851 by Herr Stabell, that same Stabell who for so many years has reiterated his faith in the infallibility of popular opinion; who has set himself up as the standard bearer of 'the nine-tenths,' and has delivered resounding assurances of the political authority wielded by the common man, listening for his opinions like a conscientious actor cocking an attentive ear towards the prompter's box. . . . Stabell's conduct reminds one of that resilient English priest who set his mind on dying, as he had lived, the guardian of his parishioners' souls, forswearing Catholicism under Henry VIII, re-embracing it under Mary, re-forswearing it under Elizabeth, re-embracing it yet again under James, and thus achieving his ambition." Ibsen accompanied this article with an excellent caricature showing an unfortunate debtor being relieved of his clothes by two smiling usurers.

The next week, on 25 May, he contributed to *Andhrimner* a general theatrical article on a theme he had already touched upon in his review of Rossini's *William Tell:* the tendency to underrate the importance of libretti in opera. Ibsen never had much ear for or appreciation of music except in its simplest forms, such as folk song, and liked opera mainly for its dramatic quality, so that a bad libretto offended him more than it would musically minded spectators—"who regard opera as a combination of two separate entities, music and text, of which, in their view, the one can make its effect even if the other is less successful. . . . The most complete harmony must exist between the music and the text; the music is the soul of the opera, the text the concrete form holding it. . . . When music lovers declare that they prefer to close their eyes during a performance so as not to be disturbed in their enjoyment of the music, this is either an affectation or else is grounded on a total misunderstanding of the purpose of opera music. In a concert hall, it is permissible, since there the words are inessential and the music is everything and sufficient unto itself; but this is not the case in opera, where the music is a content first perceptible through the plastic form that is its setting."

The occasion of these observations was Bellini's opera *Norma,* about a Roman pro-consul, Severus, who, after seducing a priestess, Norma, and giving her two sons, deceives her with a temple maiden named Adalgisa. Ibsen saw it performed on 20 May, and within ten days wrote a parody, also entitled *Norma,* in which the characters were members of the Nor-

---

[21] It was to go Conservative in 1859, largely because of the foundation that year of a "Reform Club" which it feared might be used for revolutionary ends.

wegian Storthing. Some ten pages long, it was published anonymously in *Andhrimner* in two instalments, on 1 and 8 June, with the following prefatory explanation:

> The other day I found myself in the parliamentary gallery. The subject under discussion was of the usual kind, and I cannot, therefore, remember what it was about. When Schytz rose to speak, and I consequently had nothing upon which to fix my attention, I allowed my imagination to roam, and reasoned thus. In these 106 heads, some wigged, some not, may be found the essence of all the finest talents that old Norway has to offer . . . wisdom, eloquence, patriotism, liberalism. . . . I let my thoughts wander thus for some hours until Schytz stopped speaking and the peace of my reflections was abruptly disturbed. The same evening I saw *Norma,* and suddenly the revelation struck me: "Our Storthing is really a gifted company of actors! . . . The more I considered the matter, the clearer it became. Holmbœ is the noble and respected father in the comedy, Motzfeldt, Lange and Harris are the peevish old uncle who has lost his feeling for the poetry of life but is useful to have around in the background, however much his prosaic worldly wisdom may seem to throw water on the fiery plans, and castles in the air, of the young lovers. The opposition is a kind of corporate coquette, whom every young hothead eagerly courts but, in the end, decides not to marry (especially when her rival in his affections dangles a tempting dowry). Stabell is of course the hero of the play. He is one of those genuinely dramatic characters of whom Heiberg says "one must guess at rather than fully comprehend their nature," and at the end of the play they are in the situation in which, at the beginning, one would least have expected to see them.
>
> Such were the reflections that moved me to pen this opera, *Norma, or a Politician's Love,* the text of which follows, and which I hereby offer to our Storthing for performance on any festive occasion of their choice. The music they must find themselves, but since they have at their command virtuosos on every thinkable instrument from trumpet to bassoon and drum, I think they will find no difficulty there.

Ibsen's parody opens with a chorus of Druids (members of Parliament) worshipping at the shrine of Freedom, which they have sworn to guard. Severus (Stabell) enters as they leave, and begins an eloquent speech in praise of Freedom; then he finds he is alone, and says he could have spared all that rubbish. Adalgisa his present love (the Government) enters, and accuses him of still secretly loving Norma (the Opposition). Severus replies that she was merely a youthful passion, a foolish dream, of whom he is now well cured. Norma now enters with her two children by Severus (votes of "No confidence"[22] in the Government); abandoned by their

---

[22] Alarmed by the growing strength of the workers' movement under Marcus Thrane, Stabell had, when in opposition, dropped the vote of no confidence which he had been generally expected to move, and which would almost certainly have been carried. Ibsen believed, probably correctly, that Stabell was putting personal ambition before political integrity.

father, she laments, they seem certain to die. Severus enters to her; she up-braids him, and he begs the stage manager, for decency's sake, to lower the curtain. When it rises again, the Druids are asleep, although the day is well advanced, "since, as is well known" (the stage direction informs us), "they are always somewhat behind the time." Norma raises her dagger to kill Severus, but the Prime Minister "appears in the form of an angel and transforms Severus into a demi-god, or, as the modern term is, a minister of the crown." So all ends happily.

Norma was not intended to be performed, nor does it ever appear to have been; yet it is not without significance in any study of Ibsen's work. Written in brilliantly rhymed verse, rather reminiscent, to an English reader, of the best of R. H. Barham's *Ingoldsby Legends,* it was, if we ex-cept the Grimstad lampoons, Ibsen's first essay at satirical verse, and was a pointer to what was to come. Of his next ten plays, four (*St. John's Night, Love's Comedy, Peer Gynt,* and *The League of Youth*) were conceived as satires, and a fifth, *Brand,* was primarily regarded as such when it first appeared, although to modern readers (as with *Peer Gynt*) the satire has dwindled and the tragedy remains.

On 8 June, in the issue that contained the final instalment of *Norma,* Ibsen contributed two further parliamentary commentaries, the second of which he illustrated with another admirable caricature, of a man trying to push a pig towards its trough while the pig resists, indignantly com-plaining: "Leave me alone, I can find my own way!" These commentaries, like his theatre articles, are uncommonly lively and pungent pieces, and leave one to reflect how fortunate it was that no newspaper editor had the imagination to offer the young writer a position on his staff. The delights of journalism often seem more attractive to an undergraduate than those of creative writing, especially when he is near the starvation line, and, as we shall see, Ibsen was to snatch eagerly at the first salaried post that was offered to him. But *The Man* and its successor, *Andhrimner,* aroused an astonishing lack of interest among the students and citizens of Christiania (they never achieved even a hundred subscribers), so that it is quite possible that no newspaper editor in Christiania even read it; and subordinate journalists in a small town have their own mouths to think of without recommending lively young fellows who might jump ahead of them. In any event, journalism was poorly developed in Norway at this time; even the Christiania dailies such as *Morgenbladet* contained only four pages, including one of advertisements, and read like the more unprepossessing kind of provincial news-sheet.

Later that month the thorny problem of nationalistic drama raised its head again, when *The Goblin's Home,* an "original play in three acts with music and chorus" by P. A. Jensen, was performed. This seems to have been a particularly unhappy example of rustic whimsy, and Ibsen, after a blistering summary of the plot, concluded his notice:

Such is the basic content of this national drama, *The Goblin's Home*. One does not need to dig deeply to find that such nationalism as it contains is merely a tacked-on embellishment and has no organic connection with the play. Among such tinsel we may enumerate a quarterstaff duel, a country dance, a few rustic swear words and some fragments of *patois* which may dazzle the ignorant but which, critically investigated, reveal themselves in all their hollowness and triviality. What does this shell contain? A theme which is anything but national; or is it a feature of our national life that old hunters wander around farmyards leaving behind infant daughters who, after a lapse of sixteen or seventeen years, are then reclaimed by their rightful guardian? (I use the word "guardian" because the parson says that Astrid is his niece, but with every respect for the worthy cleric I must add that I strongly suspect him to have been something of a bounder in his youth, and to be more closely related to the young lady than he is prepared to admit.) Nor can the secret wedding be described as typically national, nor the parson's efforts to test and strengthen Gutorm's Christian faith. In other words, our national dramatic literature is no better off than it was before the performance of *The Goblin's Home*. Nor can it be as long as our authors fail to distinguish between the demands of reality and the demands of art, and lack the taste to polish the rough surface of reality so that it may qualify to be admitted into the realm of art. Then they may realise that nationalism in art does not consist merely of the trivial copying of scenes from everyday life, and will see that a national author is one who understands how to give his work those undertones which call to us from mountain and valley, from meadow and shore, but above all from within our own soul.

How could Ibsen know that he would, in nine years, find himself compelled to stage this wretched piece himself at the theatre of which he was, at least nominally, artistic director?

All these articles were unsigned; but before June was out, the name of Henrik Ibsen appeared in print for the first time, beneath two songs written for the gathering of students from the various Scandinavian countries which took place in Christiania that month. They are lively and agreeable lyrics of an undemanding kind, which stood up well to those composed for the occasion by established poets such as Welhaven, Munch and Jørgen Moe, and attracted favourable attention. The following month, July 1851, the pseudonym Brynjolf Bjarme was printed for the last time, over a long ballad (of a hundred and seventeen verses!) entitled "Helge Hundingsbane," published in *Andhrimner*. From now on, Ibsen was to use his own name.

"Helge Hundingsbane" appeared in three parts, on 6, 13, and 20 July, and the day after the publication of the first instalment (though the events were unconnected) Ibsen found himself in trouble. In addition to his work for *The Man, Andhrimner,* and *Samfundsbladet,* Ibsen had been contributing to the radical newspaper *Arbejderforeningernes Blad,* which had been edited since the beginning of the year by his friend Theodor

Abildgaard. Unfortunately we do not know which of the articles in this newspaper were written by Ibsen, since all contributions were unsigned and no manuscripts have survived.[23] He had also been helping Abildgaard with a local workers' Sunday school, presumably, since he was a free-thinker, in general rather than religious subjects. On 7 July the police raided the newspaper office, arrested Abildgaard and Marcus Thrane, the workers' leader, and took away as many manuscript articles as they could lay hands on in order to identify and act against the authors. Ibsen was saved only by the quick thinking of the compositor, who crumpled up a number of manuscripts and threw them on the floor, where the police rather indolently took them to be waste paper. These included all of Ibsen's unprinted contributions and, whether for lack of evidence or because they were only interested in the big fish, the authorities took no action against him. Thrane and Abildgaard spent three years in prison awaiting trial, and then served four-year sentences; by the time they were released, in 1858, their movement lay in ruins. Thrane's downfall bears a resemblance to that of his predecessor among Norwegian champions of liberty, Christian Lofthuus, and it is ironical that Ibsen, who was himself to become a famous champion of liberty, should have had such humiliating connection with them, fathering an illegitimate child on to the grand-daughter of the one and, as it were, denying the other. A bolder spirit than Ibsen might have declared himself and accompanied his friends to prison; but Ibsen's courage, throughout his life, was limited to the written word. He was, as the man who gave him the lift from Grimstad across the ice had noticed, timid of physical danger.

The Sunday school closed, as a rather pathetic announcement informed the pupils, "since Stud. Ibsen does not feel able to conduct it unassisted." When it restarted in October, Ibsen was turning to other fields of activity, and Vinje took his place. Thus ended Ibsen's brief career as a Sunday school teacher.

During July and August the theatre was closed for the summer, and Ibsen, despite the fright he had been given, concentrated on political commentaries. The most forceful of these pieces was an attack on the servility of the Swedish press. The Swedish newspaper *Morgonbladet* (not to be confused with Stabell's *Morgenbladet*) had complained that Sweden was being insulted by "the little people of Norway, a small country that has for centuries been nothing more than a province of Denmark." Ibsen retorted: "It would be sad indeed if this yelp were to be taken as an expression of the feelings of the Swedish people. Whence does it arise? Not from the Swedish people, but from the mildewed Swedish aristocracy. . . . Norway, with its liberal institutions, has always been a thorn in the flesh of these anachronistic relics; their party has always feared lest the

---

[23] Ibsen told Halvorsen (*op. cit.*, p. 8, footnote) that his contributions to *Arbejder-foreningernes Blad* were "merely insignificant"; but he may have been referring to their quality rather than their frequency.

Swedes might learn from Norway how a people that has matured towards independence roots out such obsolete institutions as have ceased to justify their existence. . . . The Swedish people is too clear-sighted, too enlightened, to let itself be blinded, and *Morgonbladet* must not hope that it can arouse nationalistic hatred as a barrier to divide Norwegian from Swede, any more than it can close the eyes of the Swedish nation to the inexorable necessity of certain reforms within their own frontiers."

On 28 September 1851 *Andhrimner* folded, after thirty-nine issues. Despite the vigour and vitality of its contributions, it had steadily lost money, and eventually the publisher, Axelsen, decided that he could not afford to continue. Ibsen, who had a long memory, was to caricature him unkindly in *The League of Youth* in 1869, thinly disguised as Printer Aslaksen, a figure whom he also introduced into *An Enemy of the People* in 1881. The little magazine reads excellently, even at this distance of time, and it is a sad comment on the apathy of the Christiania students that it should never have succeeded in mustering even a hundred regular subscribers.

Ibsen now found himself at a period in life when three or four careers seemed to beckon to him, none of them very enticingly. He had given up his early ideas of becoming a doctor or a painter. He had completed two plays, but although one had been published and the other performed, neither had achieved any real success. The theatre as such does not appear particularly to have excited him. His dramatic reviews of 1851 hardly ever say anything interesting or constructive about the actual staging or performances, which usually receive only a short paragraph of conventional and uncritical praise. In the ordinary course of events he would probably have continued with his studies for another three, four, or even five years in the leisurely Scandinavian manner, or perhaps, if he could not make the necessary money on the side, have sought a job in journalism. He had written few poems during the nine months he had been working on *Samfundsbladet*, *The Man*, *Andhrimner*, and *Arbejderforeningernes Blad;* only half a dozen are known to have come from his hand during this time, most of those that appeared in print dating from the previous year. He had left *Olaf Tryggvason* and *The Ptarmigan of Justedal* both uncompleted. Play-writing can hardly have seemed to hold out any possibilities of a livelihood in a country where nearly all the actors were Danish, and where the capital itself was so small that even a successful serious play could hardly hope to achieve more than half a dozen performances. It was chance, not inner compulsion, that at this particular juncture determined that Ibsen's career was to be in the theatre.

The man singled out by fate to be her instrument in this operation was a forty-one-year-old composer and violinist named Ole Bull. Born in Bergen in 1810, Bull had attended university at Christiania, ostensibly to study theology, but had devoted most of his time there to music and political agitation. Then, during a visit to Paris, he heard Paganini play, and immediately, with the impulsiveness which characterised his whole life, conceived the ambition of becoming a great violinist. He could afford little in the way of tuition, far less the expense of studying in a foreign conservatoire; nevertheless, despite being virtually self-taught, he developed a brilliant technique and, while still a young man, achieved international fame, not least through performances of his own works and arrangements. From 1843 to 1845 he spent two years in the United States, where his talents were particularly admired.

In the summer of 1849 Bull returned to his native Bergen and gave a series of concerts there. During this visit he learned that the citizens, infected by the widespread desire in Norway to develop a specifically national culture, were considering the project of founding a Norwegian National Theatre in their town; and they asked Bull, as their most famous living citizen, to lend his support. Bull, an erratic, attractive, ebullient character with a passion for idealistic causes (in 1848 he had waited on Alphonse Lamartine, with a Norwegian flag in his hand, to express the sympathy of the Norwegian people with the new Republic), at once agreed. The town already possessed a charming theatre, built in 1799 by the then flourishing local amateur dramatic society[24] on a patch of raised ground overlooking the water, and capable of holding eight to nine hundred people. Bull, acting on behalf of his sponsors, leased it for the winter of 1849–50, and on 23 July 1849 he inserted an advertisement in the local newspaper *Bergenske Blade* inviting applications from anyone who wished to join as an actor, or to contribute in any other way. "Those Ladies and Gentlemen," the advertisement stated, "who number among their accomplishments singing, instrumental music, acting, or national dancing, will be considered for engagement. Original dramatic and musical works are invited, and will be rewarded as circumstances permit."

Lorentz Dietrichson, later to become a close friend, and also an enemy, of Ibsen, was a boy in Bergen at the time, and has described the response. "From crofts and respectable villas, from factories and from the street itself, they came milling forth, labourers, kitchen-maids, errand-boys and crones. . . . Every scullery girl who could sing a note, every artisan who could recite a poem, sang, declaimed or acted, each convinced that he or she was destined to become a classical stage lover or a prima donna."[25]

[24] In 1800, the year the theatre was opened, this society numbered no less than 600 members, of whom, astonishingly, 400 were women. They presented six or seven plays a year until the society was wound up in 1828. In 1835 they reconstituted themselves and hired a permanent Danish company to give performances to its members; but as this company was free to hold public performances also, and in fact mainly subsisted on these, the dramatic society had, by 1849, lost all real importance. (Cf. T. Blanc, *Norges første nationale scene* [Christiania, 1884], pp. 8–10).

[25] Lorentz Dietrichson, *Svundne tider*, I (Christiania, 1894), 147–48.

Even an old aunt of Dietrichson's applied, and was accepted, despite the fact that the absence of a front tooth rendered her speech somewhat indistinct; the theatre generously acquired a tooth for her and, when her engagement was terminated, less generously demanded the tooth back. Dietrichson recalled how he and his fellow schoolboys would wait for Bull outside the theatre and follow him cheering to his home where, never the man to miss an opportunity for a speech, he would address them from a first-floor window, promising "to offer everything he possessed for the Norwegian Theatre, and vowing that as long as he had a farthing in his pocket and a drop of blood in his heart, he would consecreate them to the Theatre and to Old Norway—speeches full of bombast and rant, but, at the time, most assuredly uttered from the heart. That a short while later he declared himself prepared to consecrate his last farthing and drop of blood to Oleana on the other side of the globe did not abate our enthusiasm for him."[26]

From all these applicants Bull selected a company whose inexperience was matched only by their willingness to learn, and on 21 November 1849 they gave their first performance before an invited audience. The bill, a lengthy and varied one typical of the theatrical fare of those days in any European country, comprised five items. The curtain rose, appropriately, on a play by Ludvig Holberg, the most famous author (in fact, the only internationally famous author) whom Norway had yet produced, and a native of Bergen; the piece chosen was his charming comedy *Henrik and Pernilla* (1724). There followed Mozart's Jupiter Symphony, now heard for the first time in Bergen; a monologue, "The Man from Paradise"; then, eagerly awaited, a performance by Bull of his own composition *Et Sætersbesøg (Visit to a Mountain Farm)*; and, finally, a comic sketch in the Bergen dialect entitled *The Shoemaker*. Bull described the reception in a letter to his wife (30 November 1849): "During the past week I have tested public reaction by inviting the theatre's patrons and some other people to attend a trial performance. The result was astounding! Even our opponents declared themselves not merely dumbfounded, but even convinced that here are talents of so superior a kind that their like has never previously been seen in Bergen. . . . I am having a machine constructed which will heat the whole theatre." This last was an important innovation, for previously there had been no heating of any kind, and spectators had been accustomed to watch performances in their overcoats, "which," T. Blanc, the historian of the Bergen Theatre, records, "were not always of the most distinguished quality."[27] *Bergenske Blade*

[26] *Ibid.*, p. 151. On the subject of Oleana, see p. 87.

[27] Blanc, p. 22, footnote. A member of the company recalled that on the rise of the curtain the players were commonly greeted with an overwhelming odour of drying clothes and *gammelost,* an excellent but pungent Norwegian cheese with which the citizens of Bergen sustained themselves during the long performances. (Marie Bull, *Minder fra Bergens første nationale scene* [Bergen, 1905], pp. 91–92.)

complimented Bull on the "pure language, good diction, rounded gestures and fluid movement" to which he had trained his company.

On 2 January 1850, the Norwegian Theatre held its first public performance. The main item was another Holberg comedy, *The Woman of Whims,* supported by various musical items. During the next five months, before the theatre closed for the summer on 2 June, twenty-seven performances were given, comprising sixteen different plays, eight of one act and eight of two or more acts. The enthusiasm in the town remained great; as early as 22 December 1849, before the season had even opened, Bull wrote to his wife that all seats had been taken for the twenty performances so far planned.

However, as was so inevitable in so small a town (Bergen then contained only 25,000 inhabitants), no bill could be played for more than two or at the most three performances, and the income from the sale of seats proved insufficient to cover expenses. In September 1851, accordingly, Ole Bull went to Christiania to petition the Storthing to give the National Theatre in Bergen a monetary grant. His request was turned down. This refusal sparked off a violent debate throughout the country, and nowhere were the pros and cons of the matter more hotly argued than among the students of Christiania. The last issue of *Andhrimner* to appear, on 28 September, included a violent indictment of the government's parsimony by Paul Botten Hansen, and Vinje wrote an open verse letter to Bull which was printed in *Morgenbladet.*

More importantly for posterity, the matter was the subject of a particularly vehement debate in the University Literary Society. It must not be supposed that even intelligent opinion was unanimously behind Bull. While it was agreed that Norway ought to have a national drama of its own and not be dependent on Danish, French, and German plays, it was not generally accepted that Norwegian plays ought necessarily to be written in the vernacular *landsmaal* instead of in the (virtually Danish) *riksmaal* used for formal writing. Ibsen himself, as we have seen from the dramatic criticisms he wrote earlier in the year, had clearly seen the dangers inherent in too chauvinistic an approach to the problem.

But when the University Literary Society debated the issue, a poet named Andreas Borchgrevink read a scornful paper on "A Visit to the National Theatre at Bergen" in which he poked fun at the limitations and inexperience of Bull's company. When he had concluded, Ibsen rose and delivered an eloquent speech in Bull's defence. His words are unfortunately not recorded, but an eye-witness has stated that "his countenance spoke the unmistakable language of anger." It was almost certainly this speech that first brought the young Ibsen to Ole Bull's notice. The student supporters of the Norwegian Theatre promptly took further action. As a protest against the Storthing's decision, a motion was put before the Students' Union that a "musical evening" be arranged to raise funds for the new enterprise. After a fiery debate the proposal was carried by a large majority.

On 15 October 1851, accordingly, a grand concert was held in Christiania. The house was full, over a thousand people somehow managing to fight their way in; many had to be turned away. Ole Bull, naturally, performed, and songs were sung by Emma Dahl, a famous operatic artiste of the day, and by the three choral societies of the capital, representing the students, the mercantile class, and the manual workers respectively. Ibsen contributed two pieces, a prologue in nicely rhymed pentameters, read, according to *Morgenbladet*, "with deep feeling and natural freshness" by Laura Svendsen, the young actress who had played Blanka in *The Warrior's Barrow*, and a choral piece, which the three choirs sang together to "a powerful and impressive setting by Ole Bull." Both of Ibsen's compositions were praised in the press, and down in Telemark the *Skien Correspondent* proudly reported the success of the local boy, not forgetting to add that "Herr Ibsen is a son of Knud Ibsen, merchant of this town."

The tickets were evidently very cheap, for the net takings amounted to no more than 300 specie-dollars; but even that was an appreciable contribution to the Norwegian Theatre's resources. The occasion was, though, to have a much further-reaching effect. Bull met Ibsen, was impressed by him, and offered him a job. The salary was humble indeed: five pounds a month. But the prospect of being able to abandon Greek and mathematics (the two subjects which he still had to pass in order to matriculate), and of actually being paid to write, must have seemed irresistible. Barely a week after the concert, he said goodbye to Botten Hansen and Vinje, packed his few belongings and departed by steamer for Bergen. On 26 October *Bergenske Blade* listed, under the heading NEW ARRIVALS IN THE CITY, the name of "Stud. H. Ibsen, c/o Sontum." The minute book of the Bergen Theatre takes up the tale:

> On 6 November, Student Henrik Ibsen was engaged, having signified his willingness, to assist the Theatre as dramatic author, for which a monthly honorarium of twenty specie-dollars is to be paid him as from 1 October.

He was to spend six years there, years of poverty, bitterness, and failure, learning the alphabet of his craft.

4

The Unholy Trade

1851–1854

"It is a most unholy trade"—Henry James, on the theatre, to William Heinemann

Bergen is, today, a much more attractive city than Oslo, and it must have been so then, perhaps to an even greater degree. Despite the great fire of 1830 it was, as contemporary photographs show, still essentially of the eighteenth century, with "whitewashed wooden houses with pantiled red roofs, steep steps leading from the front doors to the street and, outside every house, the traditional water-butt and bench where the whole family would sit in the mild and humid summer evenings . . . receiving visits from friends and neighbours, the father in his dressing gown, nightcap and slippers, with a long pipe in his mouth, the mother with her knitting and her sons and daughters about her." Thus Lorentz Dietrichson,[1] who was a schoolboy when Ibsen arrived in Bergen, and other witnesses amplify the picture. "The number of streets is very limited," observed a Professor of German from London University, "and they are so narrow that there is hardly space sufficient to admit of the passage of two vehicles. . . . The houses are huddled together, but they have about their exterior an air of cleanliness and comfort, and the interior is commodiously arranged, though not much embellished. . . . The quantity of butcher's meat consumed in the town is but small, as the middle and lower classes live almost exclusively on fish, which is very abundant. . . . The greatest inconvenience the inhabitants are subject to is the want of timber, and even of firewood, which two articles must be brought from great distances, and are consequently very dear." The harbour, he noted, "very rarely freezes, although nearly half a degree nearer to the Pole than St. Petersburg, whose harbour is closed up by ice for four months and longer every winter"; and the

[1] Dietrichson, I, 16–17.

inhabitants struck him as being more cosmopolitan than those of other Norwegian towns.[2]

The climate was (and is) very rainy. Every baby in Bergen was popularly supposed to be born with an umbrella; but the setting on the fjord, with its seven surrounding hills, was idyllic, even when, as was usually the case, the peaks of these were shrouded in cloud. "Delectable, merry, earnest and peaceful," Dietrichson apostrophised his birthplace, "with all your strangeness, your rain and mist, your fresh beauty and your eternal youth."[3]

Fishing was the principal industry, and the principal topic of conversation; Bergen was not a place where the arts or any intellectual interest flourished. "The habit of buying books," Dietrichson tells us, "had not yet become widespread, and only four or five houses boasted anything that could be called a library. . . . Apart from its theatre, the town possessed few sources of public entertainment."[4] These he enumerates. A Madame Davidsen challenged all comers, of whichever sex, to foot-races on Sunday afternoons; Rippo performed feats of strength, juggled, and walked a tightrope; there was a ventriloquist named Professor Bill, and a magician named Olivo who showed "Cosmoramas"; and occasional visits were paid by a troupe of horseback artists. Café life was virtually unknown, and a billiards saloon which had been opened in the late forties was regarded with suspicion. Two music societies existed, and an art society; and on Saturday afternoons in the summer one might see "countless groups of both sexes, belonging to the lower middle class, singing their way into the countryside, with their baskets of food and drink . . . always with a fiddler or a clarinettist at their head, the melody of whose instruments would last long into the bright summer night."[5] The citizens, Dietrichson concludes, were "a curious mixture of calculation and idealism, provincialism and poetry."[6]

Ibsen was fortunate in his first landlady in Bergen—though landlady, to judge from the account of an English traveller who lodged with her a couple of years before Ibsen, is scarcely a dignified enough description. "There are besides the hotels," wrote Thomas Forester,[7] "several private establishments at Bergen where travellers are entertained with the advantages of more quiet and comfort than at the hotels. We considered ourselves fortunate in having been directed to that of Mrs. Sontum. Well connected, and allied to persons of great consideration, circumstances having induced her to embark in her present undertaking, she is indefatigable in her endeavours to promote the comfort of her guests. Her house is the favourite

[2] Wilhelm Wittich, *A Visit to the Western Coast of Norway* (London, 1848, pp. 89–93.

[3] Dietrichson, I, 21.

[4] *Ibid.,* p. 125.

[5] *Ibid.,* p. 128.

[6] *Ibid.,* p. 144.

[7] Forester, *Norway in 1848 and 1849,* pp. 232–34.

resort of English travellers, and abundantly merits the preference given to it. . . . Nor must I omit the daughters of our hostess. . . . Two sorts of fish (trout and fried cod), besides lobsters and cutlets, with dishes of strawberries, wild and cultivated, were served for breakfast. The dinners were excellent. We had salmon, and more varieties of fish than I can name; and some national dishes which we thought admirable . . . We had good Bordeaux wine at one and eightpence a bottle. . . . But the evening reunion was the most agreeable part of the day, when we assembled round the supper-table, spread with cold meat, lobsters, tarts and cakes, tea being served à l'Anglaise."

Nor was Fru Helene Sontum (as some might infer from the above account) a snob; on the contrary, all reports of her agree that she was a kindly lady who mothered her guests.[8] Even if Ibsen did not get the full treatment accorded to Mr. Forester, things must have seemed an extraordinary improvement on conditions at Mother Sæter's or Fru Holt's. Within five days of his arrival, he was writing an epithalamium for the wedding of Fru Sontum's son, Nicolai, a conventional but agreeable and deftly turned poem, which we must assume earned him, if he had not already received it, an invitation to the marriage feast.

During the six years he was to spend in Bergen, Ibsen performed practically every task associated with theatrical production except that of acting; he is one of the very few playwrights who seems never to have performed on any stage, not even as an amateur. But, in addition to writing plays and prologues to other people's plays, he directed, coached in movement and speech, designed sets and costumes, ran the business side and saw to the accounts. Evidence of all this activity is to be found in the archives of the theatre, now in Bergen University Library: the account books, most neatly kept (his experience at the apothecary's must have served him well here); and, an endless source of fascination, his prompt books, with his stage plots for various plays, the movements of the characters carefully traced in dotted lines, and his set and costume designs, extremely detailed (as one would expect, remembering his early interest in dress), and coloured with paint or crayon. His handwriting in these prompt books, as in his manuscripts and correspondence of this period, is small and crabbed; as he grew older and more famous his handwriting became, in contrast to the general rule, neater, not only in his correspondence but even, blessedly for his editors, in his rough drafts.

Ibsen's first official assignment at Bergen, appropriately enough, was to write a prologue for an entertainment which the theatre, in return for the support which the Christiania Students had given, performed on 17 November in aid of the Students' Union Building Fund. It was spoken by the most talented of the theatre's young actresses, Louise Brun; Ibsen's

[8] E.g., Victor Smith's interview with Fru Henrikke Holst-Tresselt (Rikke Holst) in Lørdagskvelden, 22 December 1923.

name, surprisingly considering that he was now a member of the company, is not mentioned in the programme. His next task was one which he must particularly have relished. The policy and performance of the Bergen Theatre had been attacked in one of the two town newspapers, *Bergenske Blade,* by a local worthy boasting the unfortunate name of Poul Stub, who, by coincidence, had acted as one of Ibsen's correspondence tutors when Ibsen was preparing in Grimstad for his matriculation. Stub had corrected Ibsen's Norwegian essays. Apparently the newspaper had received no free tickets since the opening performance, presumably because the entire season had been over-subscribed by the public, and this neglect seems to have influenced Stub's attitude, for he poked fun at the inexperienced actors in a pedantically spiteful and unnecessary way. Ibsen replied to Stub's remarks point by point in the rival paper, *Bergens Stiftstidende,* on 30 November, attacking Stub particularly for the negativeness of his criticisms. "If a critic is to pose as an actor's mentor," suggested Ibsen, "he must explain to him how a role *should* be played, never mind how it should *not*"—a remark that might profitably be pinned up above many a critic's desk. He continued the assault on Stub in three further articles on 4, 18, and 21 December, with a zest that makes one wonder whether he had not perhaps personally experienced the sharpness of Stub's pen at the expense of his Norwegian compositions. Like Ibsen's dramatic and political articles in Christiania, these essays are excellent examples of polemical writing, clearly reasoned and precisely worded, and reading them a century later one is again grateful for the fate that allowed him no opportunity at this period of his life of taking up journalism as a career.

Ole Bull had by now left Bergen; it had never been the intention that he should do more than launch the theatre. He had given two years to the schemes and the financial sacrifice to himself, in loss of earnings, must have been considerable. He had in fact planned to leave at the end of October 1851, but had stayed a few weeks longer; now, in November, he returned to the United States, there to embrace an even more idealistic and improbable cause. Bull was an admirer of the Welsh philanthropist Robert Owen, who at the beginning of the century had set up a model factory at New Lanark in Scotland, in which he refused to employ young children, provided further education for the older children whom he did employ, limited the working hours of his adult workers and established a co-operative store. In describing his experiment Owen had, in 1817, been the first recorded man in Britain to use the word "socialist," and between 1825 and 1829 he had tried, vainly, to found a socialistic community in America at New Harmony, Indiana. Bull, seeking to succeed where Owen had failed, bought 125,000 acres in Potter County, Pennsylvania, to start a socialistic Norwegian community which, immodestly, was to be named Oleana; but his title to the land turned out to be faulty, and the scheme ended in disaster. (Ibsen was later to commemorate this unfortunate project in *Peer Gynt*, where Peer speaks of founding a new community to be called Gyntiana.)

From the time of Bull's departure, things began to go less well for the Bergen Theatre. The first play of the new year, 1852, a Norwegian work entitled *The Christmas Guest*, by C. P. Riis, was a fiasco; on the second night there was so thin a house that the reviewer of *Theatervennen* commented: "We can hardly remember having seen so few spectators in a theatre." They had better luck with Ponsard's *Charlotte Corday*, in which the young Louise Brun created an excellent impression in the title role and a new actor, Andreas Isachsen (with whom Ibsen was to have a long running feud, extending beyond his stay at Bergen) gave a fine performance as Marat. Isachsen was the first *student* to join the company (i.e., the first to have passed his matriculation, then, as now, an important status symbol in Scandinavia), and the advent of so qualified an intellectual into the theatrical profession created something of a sensation in the town. *Charlotte Corday* opened on 1 February, and five days later a topical new play, entitled *The First Jew*, also proved successful. The entry of Jews into Norway for residential purposes had been forbidden until 1851, and the play dealt with the problems encountered by an early immigrant. The author's name was kept secret, but it was generally supposed to be the local Recorder, a lawyer of literary learnings named C. R. Hansson.

Although Ibsen's contract had specified that he was to "assist the theatre as dramatic author," it was also intended that he should help with the work of instructing the actors and the rest of what would nowadays be called production. The theatre, however, already possessed an artistic instructor, a local schoolmaster named Herman Laading. Laading, at thirty-eight, was fifteen years older than Ibsen, and was quite a considerable person in Bergen. Peter Blytt, a timber merchant and board member of the theatre, shortly to become its chairman, describes Laading as "a cultured and educated man with a natural elegance of manner . . . and a vast and encyclopædic knowledge." At Christiania University the subjects which he had read included law, medicine, theology and even mineralogy, all, apparently, to some effect. He was also a fine fencer and an excellent shot, and knew several languages. Blytt further describes him as amiable but very quick-tempered, and a "master-conversationalist," adding that he was often, but wrongly, thought to be affected.[9] Laading had started his own school in Bergen in 1837, and continued to run it while working at the theatre; indeed, he ran it for fifty years, until his retirement in 1887. The Scandinavian theatres have always displayed what to other countries sometimes seems an exaggerated respect for the academic mind; however, in this instance the choice may have been justified, since the members of the company had, for the most part, scarcely any education at all, and in

[9] Peter Blytt, *Minder fra den første norske scene i Bergen* (Bergen, 1894), pp. 13–14.

the performance of historical plays especially some kind of general background knowledge was plainly desirable.

The board soon realised that the precise duties of Laading and Ibsen must be clarified, and on 10 February 1852 wrote to them suggesting that the instructional work be divided into two: "either, the one instructor to study roles with the actors and the other to take charge of the scenic arrangements, or the one to instruct the actors and the other to instruct and educate the pupils."[10] The former arrangement seems to have been agreed upon as the less unworkable of the two. Meanwhile, both Laading and Ibsen were given a formal three months notice, that they might then be appointed to their new posts.

The directors of the theatre were finding considerable difficulty in choosing plays that lay within the capabilities of their company and were suited to the taste of their audience. The French conversation pieces popular in Christiania made demands which the untrained actors of Bergen could not meet. (By one of the more chauvinistic of the Bergen Theatre's regulations not only the actors and instructors, but even the prompter, had to be of Norwegian birth.) The great classics were even more obviously outside the company's range; attempts that season to stage Calderon's *El Alcade de Zalamea,* Oehlenschläger's tragedy *Axel and Valborg,* and Garrick and Colman's *The Jealous Wife* all failed completely. In an enterprising effort to meet the situation, the board decided to send their new "dramatic author," together with the two most talented younger members of the company, Johannes and Louise Brun, abroad, to study foreign theatrical methods and obtain new and suitable plays; and on 13 April 1852 Ibsen was given a new contract which included a travel grant of 200 specie-dollars "to visit, over a period of three months, certain foreign theatres, notably in Copenhagen, Berlin, Dresden and Hamburg, in order to acquire such knowledge and experience as may equip him to fill a position at the theatre as instructor, the work to include, in addition to the instruction of the actors, responsibility for everything pertaining to the furnishing, equipment and decoration of the stage, the actors' costumes, etc."[11] On return, he was to occupy this post for five years at an annual salary of 300 specie-dollars, which was not bad by the Norwegian standards of those days; it was the same as the older and more experienced Laading was to receive, and represented an increase of 25 per cent on Ibsen's original salary. The board must have felt satisfied with and confident in their new recruit. Paris was not included in the itinerary, presumably because neither Ibsen nor the Bruns knew French.

On 15 April 1852, accordingly, Ibsen sailed from Bergen to see, for the first time, what the world looked like outside Norway. There was no direct

[10] A. M. Wiesener, *Henrik Ibsen og det norske theater i Bergen, 1851–1857,* (Bergen, 1928), pp. 9–10.

[11] Bergen Theatre archives quoted by Wiesener, pp. 11–12.

route by ship to Copenhagen, so they travelled via Hamburg, which was linked with Bergen by a regular fortnightly service. Ibsen's companions were even younger than he was; Johannes Brun was twenty, his wife, whom he had married the previous year, twenty-one. They were two deeply contrasted characters. Johannes Brun, Blytt tells us,[12] was merry and spontaneous and, like Ibsen, extremely clothes-conscious and elegant in appearance. Louise, on the other hand, was rather reserved and formal, "not handsome," and careless in her dress "almost to the point of slovenliness." Both were destined to reach the heights of their profession and to die while still in their prime, she at thirty-five, he at fifty-eight. Johannes Brun, indeed, was to become perhaps the most famous of all of Norway's actors, and to create several of Ibsen's most famous character roles, including the Old Man of the Mountains in *Peer Gynt,* Daniel Hejre in *The League of Youth,* and Ulric Brendel in *Rosmersholm.* His statue stands outside the National Theatre in Oslo only a few yards from that of Ibsen.

After a brief pause in Hamburg, of which Ibsen vexatiously records no impression, they reached Copenhagen on 20 April. The Danish capital still had oil lighting in the streets and watchmen shouting the hours, but its cosmopolitanism and elegance, and architectural pleasures, must, to the young provincial from Norway, have been a revelation. It possessed, moreover, in the Royal Theatre, Det Kongelige, one of the great theatres of Europe, with a fully international repertoire and actors and actresses comparable to the best of France and Germany, and better than those of England, where Macready had finished his career the previous year (though he was to live for another twenty-two, surely the longest time that any great actor has spent in unenforced retirement), and Irving was a boy of fourteen. Ibsen's first task was to look for a room, and he found what he wanted, central and agreeable. An advertisement in the newspaper *Adresseavisen* on the day of his arrival, which presumably led him to it, gives us details. "For a polite gentleman (*en galant Herre*), a large, bright, handsomely decorated room, with three windows to the street in a genteel house, to be let, immediately or from the 1st, at Reverentsgaden 205, 2nd floor, adjacent to Kongens Nytorv." It sounds much better than what he had been used to in Norway, but he must have wanted to live a little more grandly if possible, as official representative of Norway's first national theatre.

C. R. Hansson, the literary-minded Recorder of Bergen, had given Ibsen a letter of introduction to the director of the Royal Theatre, Johan Ludvig Heiberg, and this proved of great value. Heiberg, besides being a scholar, was a considerable poet and dramatist, and one of the very few authors whom Ibsen, in his maturity, admitted to admiring. Born in 1791,

[12] Blytt, pp. 23–24.

the son of a woman who later, as the Baroness Gyllembourg-Ehrensværd, was to achieve fame as a kind of Danish Mrs. Gaskell, Heiberg had been elected to a lectureship in Danish at Kiel University at the age of thirty-one; but creative writing attracted him more than academic life, and three years later he returned to Copenhagen with the expressed intention of introducing vaudeville to the Danish stage. Vaudeville then meant not, as now, music hall, but comedies with music, with the characters, at climactic moments, breaking into songs consisting of new lyrics set to familiar tunes. Heiberg wrote a great many of these, based on French models but with Danish settings and topical Danish themes; Ibsen was to stage several of them in both Bergen and Christiania. The author of a number of comedies and straight plays, of which the best are perhaps *The Day of the Seven Sleepers* and *A Soul after Death*, Heiberg was also a poet, and a vigorous critic; and in 1847, five years before Ibsen met him, he had been appointed to his present position as director of the Royal Theatre. Since Oehlenschläger's death two years previously he was regarded as the most eminent man of letters not merely in Denmark, but in Scandinavia, more so than his juniors Hans Christian Andersen and Søren Kierkegaard. In many ways he must have seemed a pattern of what the young Ibsen might have hoped to become; his fields of activity and his critical, nonconformist standpoint were very much Ibsen's own.

Heiberg had now virtually retired from authorship and had become a formidable pundit. "Standing in the centre of his office in the Royal Theatre," we are told, "he would hold audience with his hands clasped behind his back, his legs parted, the upper half of his body swaying from side to side, as he fastened his stare, as cold as water, upon his unfortunate visitor, who as often as not would become confused and lose the thread of his discourse under the impact of that superior and ironic smile."[13] Hansson had, however, with lawyer's cunning, couched his introductory letter in terms highly flattering to Heiberg, describing Ibsen as "a bright and gifted young man of more than common poetical talent" whom he had come to like, since he had "found in him the same passionate admiration of you that formed one of the worthiest emotions of my youth."[14]

Hansson's letter seems to have had the required effect, for Heiberg immediately granted Ibsen and the Bruns free entry to the theatre each evening; disappointingly, however, he advised them not to bother to attend any rehearsals since, the season being so far advanced, nothing of interest was in preparation. He commanded his chief instructor, Thomas Overskou, who was also a playwright and translator of some repute, to show Ibsen round the theatre, drawing his attention in particular to the stage machinery,

[13] O. Zinck and W. Kolling, reported by Robert Neiiendam in *Mennesker bag masker* (Copenhagen, 1931), p. 117.

[14] *Ibid.*, p. 118.

which was far in advance of anything that Ibsen had seen in Christiania or Bergen. Overskou, writing to his daughter at this time, described Ibsen as "a little clenched (*sammenbidt*) Norwegian with alert eyes."[15]

Overskou was not, as a stage instructor, the best of models for a young man; even by the standards of those days, he was coming to be regarded as somewhat old-fashioned. However, he proved a friendly and helpful guide, as Ibsen's letters to his directors in Bergen (the first we have from his hand since those which he had written to Schulerud from Grimstad) show.

> I am happy to be able to tell you [*he wrote on 25 April 1852*] that . . . both Heiberg and Herr Overskou have received us with exceptional kindness, and through the latter I shall easily obtain all the information I require concerning the internal organisation of the theatre. As regards the other matters you have instructed me to investigate, such as the procuring of a dancing teacher for Brun and his wife, etc., I have not yet managed to arrange this, but hope to do so within the course of the next week.

Three weeks later, on 16 May, he wrote his employers a long and informative letter; he had a good deal to report.

> As dancing teacher for H. Nielsen [*another actor from Bergen who had joined them in Copenhagen*], and for Brun and his wife, I have engaged Herr Hoppe, solo dancer at the Royal Theatre, reckoned to be the best they have and, a point on which I assured myself before approaching him, their most experienced instructor. The main subject of instruction is to be the Minuet, and anything else that will assist in the learning of elegance of movement upon the stage.

The man who could have told Ibsen most about dancing he had, alas, met only briefly.

> As regards the projected engagement of a dancer to instruct the other members of the company in Bergen, I have the following to report. *Balletmeister* Bournonville left for Christiania soon after my arrival here, and I was able to discuss the subject with him only in general terms the evening before his departure; at the end of the month, most of the other dancers here will go up to join him. Herr Gade, another leading dancer, who will be remaining here, might possibly not be averse to sailing to Bergen this summer, but you would in such an event have to provide a guarantee that he would be able to undertake the journey without sustaining any financial loss. . . . As regards the internal appointments of the Theatre, Herr Overskou has under-

15 *Loc. cit.*

taken to acquaint me with them, as also with the methods of stage management, machinery, etc. Books on costume I have not been able to obtain, but Herr Overskou is going to let me know what there is and where I may get hold of them; so I shall be able to purchase these before my journey is finished. . . . I have bought only one play, *Ten Years Ago*, by Carl Bernhard;[16] but for this item of expenditure, too, I must crave a small extra allowance, since I shall probably happen in Germany upon something which might be worth buying. . . . Regarding my grant for this journey, I greatly fear that it will not suffice. During my stay in Hamburg I had a foretaste of what it means to be a tourist in Germany; and Brun, too, would have been considerably embarrassed if our fellow traveller, Dr. Hofmann, had not helped him and made it possible for him to continue to Copenhagen. I therefore beg that I may be advanced the sum of 48 specie-dollars from my salary which, together with the 12 specie-dollars which I applied for as I left, and which I hope you have approved, could be subtracted from my salary at the rate of 5 specie-dollars per month.

Ibsen goes on to report on the plays he has seen.

We have been very fortunate with the repertory. We have seen *Hamlet,* and several other plays by Shakespeare, and by Holberg— also *La Bataille des Dames, A Sunday at Amager, The Kinsmen,* etc.[17] I need hardly add that we acquainted ourselves with everything that might be of artistic interest. The Danes have in all respects shown us the utmost courtesy and good will and, so far from feeling any annoyance at our seeking to liberate ourselves from their influence upon our theatre, they only wonder that this has not happened long ago. I have made the acquaintance of H. C. Andersen; he advises me strongly, when I have finished in Dresden, to go on to Vienna to see the Burgtheater; he may be there himself then, in which case he will act as my guide; if not, I hope Professor Dahl may be able to assist me.

Hans Andersen was then forty-seven, and five years previously had paid a famous visit to Charles Dickens in London; but unfortunately, the directors of the Bergen Theatre decided that they could not afford to extend their young apprentice's tour beyond Dresden, so that the fascinating prospect of Hans Andersen showing Ibsen around Vienna never materialised. "We feel," wrote the Bergen board on 28 May, "that it will be much more

---

16 This comedy was not in fact by Bernhard (the pseudonym of A. N. de Saint Aubin) but by his nephew Andreas Buntzen. It was performed at Bergen in October 1852.

17 *La Bataille des Dames* was a comedy by Scribe and Legouvé; *A Sunday at Amager* a vaudeville by Heiberg's wife, Johanne Luise Heiberg; and *The Kinsmen* a vaudeville by Henriette Nielsen. All three were subsequently performed at Bergen.

rewarding for you to stay longer at a place such as Dresden than to move on from town to town." They also warned him that "we know from experience that living in Germany is very cheap, so that if you do not manage on your 200 specie-dollars we shall be forced to conclude that you have not arranged your economy wisely," and at first refused to refund him the 24 specie-dollars he had paid to Hoppe for dancing lessons, telling him that he and the Bruns were expected to pay for this out of their grants. Since neither he nor they could afford this, Ibsen had to write another begging letter to his board; not the last example he was to encounter of the parsimony of committees.

But these irritations must have been more than compensated for by the new horizons that were being opened for him theatrically and æstheti-cally. He was indeed, as he had told his board, "very fortunate with the repertory." During his six weeks in Copenhagen that spring he, who had never previously seen a Shakespeare play on the stage, saw four—*Hamlet, King Lear, Romeo and Juliet,* and *As You Like It.* He also saw four of Holberg's best comedies, *The Lying-In Room, Henrik and Pernilla, Pernilla's Brief Mistress-ship,* and *The Woman of Whims;* three Oehlen-schläger tragedies, *Queen Margareta, The Vikings at Byzantium,* and *Earl Haakon the Mighty;* Mozart's opera *Don Giovanni;* two of Heiberg's own works, including his best and most famous vaudeville, *No;* and two plays by a popular second-rate Danish dramatist named Henrik Hertz, *Sheikh Hassan* and *King René's Daughter,* the latter of which had already been translated into English no less than thrice and become popular throughout the English theatre (sufficient proof, the English theatre being what it then was, of its, and the author's, mediocrity). The actors, too, were far superior to any he had seen in Norway. The great tragedian Michael Wiehe was then at his peak, and a generation later Ibsen was to name him as still the finest actor he had seen. "When I recall his per-formances," he said, "it is as though I were walking through a gallery filled with ancient statues. Pure *plastik!* Pure beauty!"[18] He was also fortunate enough to witness, for the first time, a major actress demonstrating her art: Johanne Luise Heiberg, whom he saw in one of her most famous parts as Lucretia (the title role) in Holberg's *The Woman of Whims,* a lady so moody and changeable that her two lovers, ecstatically describing their mistresses to each other, do not realize that they are speaking of the same person. Fru Heiberg was to become a close friend of Ibsen in later years, and he was to address to her one of his most delicate poems.

In contrast to Wiehe, there was the young Fredrik Høedt, who was to be the founder of a new school of acting, more realistic and analytical, less inclined to the grand manner and subtler in his appreciation of psycho-logical nuances. Ibsen saw Høedt as *Hamlet,* but admired him more as the

---

[18] Laura Kieler, *Silhouetter* (Odense, 1887), pp. 8–9. Wiehe was only thirty-two when Ibsen saw him. He died at the age of forty-four in 1864.

young lover, Grignon, in Scribe's *La Bataille des Dames*.[19] When one remembers the wretched plays that Ibsen had seen in Christiania and, reading between the lines of his dramatic criticisms, the moderate talents of the actors there (to say nothing of Bergen, where even the Bruns were still raw beginners), one realizes what a revelation to him these evenings in the theatre at Copenhagen must have been. The actors, he reported wonderingly to his directors in Bergen, knew their parts before rehearsals of a play began.

His experiences in Copenhagen were not limited to the Royal Theatre. He also visited the Casino Theatre on Amaliegade (which twenty-five years later was to stage the first performance of Strindberg's *The Father*), and the Royal Court Theatre at Christiansborg (now the Theatre Museum). At the latter, he watched a performance by the University Drama Society attended by King Frederik VII. At the former he saw a romantic comedy by Jens Christian Hostrup called *Master and Pupil* which interested him enough to make him call on Hostrup at the latter's home to discuss the play, which he subsequently directed at Bergen. Hostrup later remembered Ibsen from this visit as "a quiet, withdrawn personality."

Finally, and by no means least, it was probably during his stay in Copenhagen that Ibsen happened upon a short book written by a young German professor at Jena and published only that year which was to have a considerable influence upon his writing. It has rather glibly been assumed that Ibsen discovered Herman Hettner's *Das moderne Drama* after his arrival in Dresden; but as avid a reader of advertisements as Ibsen always was can hardly have missed noticing, in the columns of the leading Danish magazine of the day, *Fædrelandet,* a large advertisement drawing the attention of the public to a newly opened "Newspaper Salon" on the corner of Kjøbmagergade and Silkegade where books and papers might be perused on payment of an entrance fee of eight skillings (about four cents), refundable on purchase of refreshments." As Ibsen's purpose in Copenhagen was to study modern trends in European drama, it seems likely that he would have availed himself of this inexpensive means of reading a book that, we know, was much discussed in the city that spring.

Two aspects in particular of Hettner's book must have interested him: the sections dealing with historical drama and with *Märchenlustspiel,* or romantic fairy-tale comedy. Hettner asserted that historical plays should be written so as to be psychologically relevant to modern times; human character had not changed fundamentally over the centuries, nor, *mutatis mutandis,* had the issues of human conflict. Historical drama, in other words, should be written as psychological character-conflicts, and not, like Oehlenschläger's plays, as grand opera without music. Nor was there any place in serious drama, whether historical or modern, for the paraphernalia of coincidence with which (as in Scribe's plays) it was commonly cluttered:

[19] Midbøe, p. 163.

overheard conversations, intercepted letters, mistaken identities and the like. Such things were all very well in comedy; but in serious drama, what mattered (Hettner asserted) was conflict of, and development of, character. The lesson of Shakespeare had been largely forgotten; Hettner held up *Coriolanus* as a model.

As regards *Märchenlustspiel,* the important thing about this genre, it seemed to Hettner, was the fact that it dealt with two opposite worlds, that of everyday reality and that of fantasy; in the best plays of this kind, these two worlds are constantly being juxtaposed in such a way that the world of dreams is shown as a source of truth and wisdom, while that of everyday reality is made to seem comic and unrealistic. As a prime example of this type of play, Hettner instances Shakespeare's *A Midsummer Night's Dream.* It is a genre that has always seemed to hold an especial appeal for Scandinavians—Oehlenschläger, Heiberg, and Hostrup had all experimented in it, and so, in plays as well as in stories, had Hans Andersen. Ibsen's next five plays were to be either historical dramas or *Märchenlustspiel,* and in each of them he was to follow, or try to follow, Hettner's precepts—though here again, as with Kierkegaard, we must beware of assuming that Hettner did more than crystallize ideas that were already present in Ibsen's mind. Another demand which Hettner made, that dramatists should stick closely to historical facts, Ibsen was, like Shakespeare, to ignore.

Hettner also drew Ibsen's attention to a recent play by a young German dramatist, Friedrich Hebbel's *Maria Magdalena,* written nine years previously in 1843. Hettner thought this powerful melodrama, written in highflown prose about ordinary village people, worthy to stand beside Sophocles's *Electra* and Goethe's *Faust* as an outstanding specimen of the tragedy of ideas, and as an example of how *bürgerliche Tragödie* need not be trivial, but may be both profound and poetic. Several witnesses, such as John Paulsen and Gunnar Heiberg, have testified to Ibsen's later admiration of *Maria Magdalena,*[20] and it seems probable that it stemmed from this period; after reading Hettner's praise, he is hardly likely to have missed the chance of studying it. Hettner did not know of Alexander Ostrovsky's experiments in the same field (his play *The Bankrupt,* though written in 1849, had been banned, and although he was to become known in Russia in 1853 through *The Poor Bride,* it was to be many years before his fame spread to western Europe). Nor did Hettner know of Gogol or Turgenev, both of whom, like Ostrovsky, would have supported his faith in the

---

[20] "The best evidence of how unforgettable an impression *Maria Magdalena* made on him is the meticulous *précis* he dramatically gave us of the plot. I saw the various scenes come alive before me, and heard not without emotion the old father's last, despairing cry: *'Ich verstehe die Welt nicht mer!'* ['I understand the world no longer!']—a sentence which had long haunted Ibsen." (John Paulsen, *Mine Erindringer* [Copenhagen, 1900], pp. 162–63.) Gunnar Heiberg also records that Ibsen advised him to read Hebbel (*Salt og sukker* [Christiania, 1924], p. 44).

potentialities of *bürgerliche Tragödie*. Their examples would have been useful to Ibsen; in the event, ignorant of their experiments, he was, in his own good time, to follow the path that they had trod, and go far beyond them.

Shortly before Ibsen left Copenhagen, Heiberg honoured him with an invitation to dinner at his house; but the occasion proved something of an anticlimax. To Ibsen's disappointment, the great man discoursed on neither literature, the theatre nor even politics, but solely on questions of gastronomic interest; and he never saw Heiberg again before the latter died in 1860, embittered at the constant sniping he had had to undergo from his fellow-countrymen during his last years. Ibsen (although Heiberg had by then rejected *The Vikings at Helgeland*) wrote a handsome elegy in his honour. "He lit a torch in the land. You used it to burn his brow. He taught you to wield a sword. You pressed it against his heart. Boldly he fought the trolls of his day. You crushed him between your shields." The situation of the prophet who is without honour in his own country had, by 1860, already become familiar to Ibsen.

On 6 June, the Bruns having returned to Norway, Ibsen departed alone for Dresden. Here he found a helpful guide in a celebrated fellow-countryman, the old Norwegian painter J. C. Dahl, to whom (Dahl noted in his diary) Ibsen handed his letter of introduction on 11 June, having settled in an apartment at Topfergasse 13. He was not able to obtain free tickets to the theatre, as he had done at Copenhagen, but he was lucky enough to see, and compare, two exciting actors of contrasting styles. One was Emil Devrient, a fine performer in the traditional classical manner (and son of the mighty Ludwig Devrient, who frequently collapsed in an epileptic fit while playing Lear); the other was an exciting young Polish actor, Boguwil Dawison, whose more modern approach, with its realism and subtlety of characterisation, resembled that of Fredrik Høedt. Ibsen saw Dawison play Hamlet, and much preferred it to Høedt's performance in the role which he had seen in Copenhagen the previous month.[21]

He studied the stage machinery at the Hofoper, where three years earlier the young Richard Wagner had been *Kapellmeister,* and spent many hours in the Dresden art galleries and museums. In those days photography was in its infancy, and until one saw the original works of a painter one knew of them, if at all, only by engravings or verbal description; the effect of the great galleries of Dresden on one who still cherished ambitions of his own in the field of painting can be imagined. (When, a dozen years later, he visited Italy, it was the paintings and sculptures, more than anything else, that excited him.) Remembering that one of his tasks on this trip was to

[21] Midbøe, p. 163. The repertory also included, while he was there, *A Midsummer Night's Dream*, *Richard III*, Goethe's *Egmont*, and Lessing's *Emilia Galotti*, but we do not know how many of these he saw; probably, as will appear, at least the first-named.

obtain books of costume design to assist the Bergen Theatre in its staging of foreign plays, he reported to his directors on 24 June the discovery of two such volumes which impressed him: "Bonnard's *Costumes from the 13th to 18th Centuries,* and a *Collection of Spanish Folk Costumes* which has recently been published here." Unfortunately, the theatre informed him that they had already ordered some costume books from Paris, and refused him authority to buy them.

Ibsen stayed in Dresden for about a month, returning to Norway some time in July. Ships sailed from Hamburg to Bergen on 15 and 29 July that year, and Dahl noted in his diary that Ibsen took leave of him on 2 July, which suggests that he travelled by the earlier ship. Paul Botten Hansen, in his short biography of Ibsen printed in *Illustreret Nyhedsblad* in 1863, writes, presumably with Ibsen as his source, that Dahl "despite certain outbursts of his customary harshness, on the whole treated him [i.e., Ibsen] with much kindness and courtesy." He had hoped to see Berlin on his way home, and also to spend a short while in Hamburg, both cities with an old tradition of fine theatre. His biographers have generally assumed that he did neither, on no evidence that I can discover; if, as we may assume, he left Dresden shortly after saying goodbye to Dahl, how else did he spend his time until the boat sailed on, at the earliest, 15 July? But if he visited Berlin or Hamburg, or anywhere else, he left no record of it.

During his three months abroad, probably while he was in Dresden, Ibsen completed a play which he may have begun at Bergen in the spring: *Sancthansnatten* (*St. John's Night,* i.e., Midsummer Night). This is unique among Ibsen's plays in being the only one which he refused to allow to be printed in his lifetime. When, in 1897, his German editor (and, later, executor) Julius Elias asked permission to include it in the German collected edition of his works, Ibsen angrily replied (19 September 1897): "I neither will nor *can* permit the play *St. John's Night* to appear in any collection of *my* works. The play is a miserable thing which is not really by *my* hand. It is founded on a rough mess of a draft which I was given by a student acquaintance, re-worked, and put my name to, but which I cannot now possibly acknowledge as being mine. . . . Far from illuminating the rest of my work it stands totally outside of and unconnected with it; I have therefore for many years regarded it as unwritten and non-existent."

This statement may be true; but ten years earlier he had told Henrik Jæger, his first biographer,[22] that, after agreeing to co-operate with this student acquaintance (one Theodor Bernhoft, the nineteen-year-old son of a poet and bookseller) he had himself written a draft and sent it to Bernhoft, who replied that he was now otherwise occupied and no longer

[22] If we exclude the 2,500-word "profile" which Paul Botten Hansen wrote for *Illustreret Nyhedsblad* in 1863. For the information about the authorship of *St. John's Night,* see Jæger's notes on his conversations with Ibsen in 1887 (Midbøe, p. 143).

interested. Certainly when *St. John's Night* came to be performed at Bergen the following year, and again when he applied for a civil list pension eleven years later, Ibsen felt no qualms about naming it as his own unaided work. However, in accordance with his wishes it was not printed until after his death, in 1909, and has been dismissed by most commentators as negligible. It is in fact a curiously engaging work, considerably superior to *The Warrior's Barrow* and *The Feast at Solhaug*, both of which he allowed to be printed, and one imagines that his rejection of it stemmed not from any lack of merit so much as from the almost pathological horror which he showed throughout his life at any suggestion that anything he had written owed anything to any other author, living or dead. He was, indeed, probably less influenced by other writers than any other great dramatist, but not as little as he made out.

He called the play an *eventyrkomedie*. *Eventyr* means, roughly, fairy tale, so that *eventyrkomedie* is the Norwegian equivalent of *Märchenlustspiel*. Four young people are gathered in a house on Midsummer Night: Johannes and Juliane, who are engaged but do not love each other; Julian Poulsen, a student friend of Johannes; and Anne, Juliane's step-sister, whose freshness and innocence contrast with the sophisticated artificiality of the other three, and whom they regard as "fey." A *nisse*, or goblin, lives in the loft; Anne accepts his presence, sensing no difference between natural and supernatural things; only she can see him. This goblin, a kind of Puck, puts a potion into the bowl of punch which the young people are about to drink; then, in a charming scene, they go up to the hilltop where the midsummer pyre is dying, and catch a glimpse of the other-world of the supernatural. But only those with poetic souls, Anne and Johannes, see and understand; to the two blinded by intellect, Julian and Juliane, it is an obscure and incomprehensible vision. Under the influence of the magic night, all four declare themselves to the ones they truly love, Johannes to Anne and Julian to Juliane. Next morning, they realise they are betrothed to the wrong people. At first, they resign themselves fatalistically to the apparently unavoidable; in the end, however, each gets his or her true partner.

St. John's Night is written mainly in prose, with occasional excursions (as when the goblin speaks) into rhymed verse. It is very much in the romantic fairy-tale tradition which was popular in Scandinavia then— Oehlenschläger had written a comedy entitled *A Midsummer Night's Play*, and Heiberg a similar one, *The Day of the Seven Sleepers;* Hans Andersen had exercised himself in the genre and, as stated, Ibsen had seen Jens Christian Hostrup's *Master and Pupil* while in Copenhagen.[23] Ibsen's

[23] The action of these three plays by Oehlenschläger, Heiberg, and Hostrup takes place, as does *St. John's Night,* on a summer night when the supernatural world reveals its secrets: and Heiberg, like Ibsen, suggests that only those whose souls are genuinely poetic can see that world.

St. John's Night, however, like Strindberg's later and remarkable essay in the same genre, *The Virgin Crown,* has a wit and individuality which lift it far above the rest of its kind; in this, his first essay in prose drama, he shows himself already able to write excellent colloquial dialogue, to create satirical characters, and to keep a complicated structure of plot and sub-plot continuously ticking. Julian Poulsen, quoting undigested gobbets of Heiberg and Kierkegaard, is the first of those pretentious charmers, vain, romanticising and self-pitying, who were to become a feature of Ibsen's work, the forerunner of Falk in *Love's Comedy,* Peer Gynt, Stens-gaard in *The League of Youth,* Hilmar Tønnesen in *The Pillars of Society,* Hjalmar Ekdal in *The Wild Duck,* and Ulric Brendel in *Rosmersholm.* Through Julian, Ibsen ridiculed that exaggerated passion for all things national which had made it fashionable to admire everything rustic simply because it was, or seemed to be, untainted by Danish or Swedish influence, just as later, in other countries, it was to become fashionable to admire any literary work that was, or appeared to be, working-class. The attempt to create a new language (*landsmaal*) based on the country dialects became the subject of a questioning eyebrow, not for the last time in Ibsen's work; so, too, did the kind of bogus aestheticism which W. S. Gilbert was to caricature a generation later in *Patience. St. John's Night* is too topical in its allusions, and too reminiscent of *A Midsummer Night's Dream* in cer-tain phases of its plot, to stand much chance of proving more than an interesting curiosity if it were staged today; but the ridiculer of contempo-rary poses who was to hold an unflattering mirror up to his countrymen in *Love's Comedy, Brand, Peer Gynt, The League of Youth,* and *An Enemy of the People* is more clearly distinguishable in *St. John's Night* than in any of the other plays of Ibsen's immaturity. And Julian, towards the end of the play, makes a point which Ibsen was to stress more sharply in *Love's Comedy,* and which was especially to enrage contemporary opinion: the necessity of qualifying one's ideal of love when one gets married.

On Ibsen's return to Bergen, the board got down to the problem of defining his duties in his new post of instructor and distinguishing them from those of Laading. On 30 August 1852, these were finally clarified. Laading was to be *rolleinstruktør,* Ibsen *sceneinstruktør.* Laading was "to be at the theatre every day from 9 to 12 to direct reading rehearsals, using the rest of the time for special study of the roles and general educa-tion of the actors." Among other things, it was specified that he was to pay especial attention to "giving the actors the necessary historical information and ensuring correct interpretation of the roles, seeing that their diction is correct, and stressing that they memorise their roles painstakingly and accurately, so that they can attend the opening rehearsals without books or papers." Ibsen, as *sceneinstruktør,* was "to be present at the theatre for as many hours each day, holidays included, as may be required for complete and painstaking instruction on the stage, that each play may be ready for public performance at the time laid down by the board. In other words, he is, when he has found the players sufficiently prepared, to continue the instruction from the point reached at the last reading rehearsals. . . . He may, if necessary, send the players back for further reading rehearsals. The *sceneinstruktør* shall also be responsible for (1) supervising the scenic arrangements for each play (costumes and decor included), and for the general staging (groupings, entries, exits, etc.); (2) supervising in detail each actor's gestures and mime, so that all physical expressions shall fit the words of the character represented; (3) ensuring that the players play together, and indicating to each of them the role that he or she has to play in the plot as the situation changes." It was further laid down that the two instructors should, before any new play went into rehearsal, confer so as to reach agreement on the interpretation of the various characters, "the board to decide, in the event of disagreement" on this or any other point.[24]

The duties of the two instructors were thus inconveniently divided; the equivalent in a modern production would be as though a new director were to take over halfway. Amazingly enough, the theatre archives, which record evidence of disagreements and complaints, suggest that there was in fact little serious conflict between the two. On 30 November 1852 Laading asked to be relieved of his post, but this appears not to have been the result of dissatisfaction with his working conditions but merely because he found it difficult to combine so responsible a duty with that of running his own school. In the event, he was persuaded to stay.[25] This lack of disagreement between Laading and Ibsen is the more surprising in that their attitudes towards acting seem to have been almost diametrically opposed. Whereas Ibsen liked his players to be naturalistic, Laading, according to an actress who worked under him, "was of the old school, and liked the conventional French style of acting with all its affectations. He wanted us to *act*, not to be natural."[26]

A letter which Ibsen wrote to Laading twenty years later suggests that it was the difference between the two men in age and maturity, coupled with Ibsen's shyness, which prevented them from quarrelling. "Yes," wrote Ibsen (10 March 1875), "those years in Bergen were certainly my years of schooling! I found myself at that time in a state of fermentation, which did not permit me to open myself completely to anyone. I did not really understand myself, and this must explain, if not excuse, many follies and so forth that I committed. You, on the other hand, were already a mature man, and this created a distance between us. But you often showed me a friendliness which closed the gap, and I was grateful to you for this, without being able to give this feeling proper expression."

24 Wiesener, pp. 28–31.
25 *Ibid.*, pp. 33–34.
26 Sophie Monsen, interviewed in *Bergens Tidende*, 13 January 1913.

One of Ibsen's jobs at Bergen was to provide a new play to be performed each year on the anniversary of the opening of the theatre, 2 January, and that autumn of 1852 he offered as his contribution for the coming anniversary *St. John's Night*. It was accepted, and thus became the second of Ibsen's plays to appear on the stage. Anticipation in the little town was great; the theatre-goers of Bergen were eager to see what their young "dramatic author" could do. New decor, a luxury that the theatre could scarcely afford, was prepared, so that the play would not be seen in the familiar standard sets; it would not be quite true to say that no expense was spared to make the evening a success, but at least the few pennies that the theatre could disburse were freely given. The opening performance was sold out in advance, and many people were turned away without tickets. Alas, the occasion turned out a fearful failure. The first night audience so disliked the play that they whistled and hissed it; and at the second performance not merely seats but whole rows were empty. Word spread fast in a town that size. *Bergenske Blade* dismissed it as "a somewhat unfortunate piece, though it contains some pretty fancies." The management accepted the verdict of the public and withdrew the play, replacing it, ironically, with P. A. Jensen's *The Goblin's Home,* that tedious essay in rustic romanticism which Ibsen had condemned so severely in Christiania, and exactly the kind of play for which *St. John's Night* had been intended to ring the death knell.

Why was it such a failure? Was it because of integral defects in the play, inadequacy of performance—or did the subject matter offend? Did the public dislike seeing a nationalistic ideal held up to ridicule? Did the chauvinistic extravagances of Julian Poulsen suggest an implied criticism of the affectionately remembered utterances of the town's idol, Ole Bull? We do not know. Perhaps Peter Blytt, of the theatre board, reflects the general reaction when he says in his memoirs that the play struck him as "a curious, rather obscure mixture of romance and reality."[27] Time and again in Bergen, and later in Christiania, Ibsen was to find that his audiences disliked any play that did not fit into an established and recognisable category. Whatever the reason, *St. John's Night* died and remained forgotten for over half a century until its posthumous publication.

This failure must have been a bitter disappointment to the young dramatist, not merely in itself but in its implications. The Bergen public had shown that it preferred banal melodramas, superficial comedies, and mock-rustic folk tales to anything critical, novel, and unusual. Seldom can the prospects for experiment have seemed as unpromising to any writer as to the young Ibsen in Bergen. Even at this early stage of his career we find him challenging and experimenting; but he had neither the actors to carry out his wishes nor the public to appreciate them. It is not

[27] Blytt, p. 11.

hard to imagine with what feelings he must have turned to the direction of the plays that formed the rest of the season, a list that makes the programme of the humblest modern provincial theatre or stock company appear almost astral by comparison. The best of the bunch that winter and spring, apart from a solitary Holberg, *Jacob von Thyboe* (the first Holberg that Ibsen was to direct), were Henrik Hertz's *King René's Daughter,* the elder Dumas's *Katharine Howard,* and Scribe's *Babiol et Jablot,* and even these, though reasonably competent in their stagecraft, were trumpery and meretricious rubbish.

It was an exceptionally bad period for the drama throughout Europe. During the half-century that had elapsed since the death of Schiller in 1805, a gap had opened between the theatre and the serious playwright. A number of interesting plays had been written, but most of them remained unperformed even in their own countries, let alone in so theatrically backward a land as Norway. The two most exciting, Georg Büchner's *Danton's Death* and *Woyzeck,* both composed in the eighteen-thirties before Büchner died of typhoid at the age of twenty-three, were to remain for many years unknown to anyone; neither play was staged anywhere before the twentieth century. Nor, in Norway, was anything to be seen before 1900 of either of those other brilliant but tragically-fated young German dramatists of the period, Friedrich Hebbel,[28] whose *Maria Magdalena* Ibsen had discovered through Hettner, or Christian Dietrich-Grabbe (1801–36), the author of that eccentric but remarkable play *Comedy, Satire, Irony and Deeper Meaning;* nor anything by Heinrich von Kleist, who had committed suicide in 1811 at the age of thirty-four, except *Kätchen von Heilbronn,* and that not until 1868. The Russian realists, Gogol, Turgenev, and Ostrovsky, had equally long to wait. Neither *The Government Inspector* (1836), nor *A Month in the Country* (1850) reached Norway before 1890, nor anything by Ostrovsky until the present century. Alfred de Musset's comedies of the eighteen-thirties were unperformed in Norway until the sixties, when Ibsen himself directed *Un Caprice.* It is a commentary on the theatrical taste of the period that the only contemporary plays in the general European repertoire which have survived are the farces of Eugène Labiche, such as *An Italian Straw Hat* (1851). Zola was not to start writing for the stage till the seventies, Becque till the eighties.

Nor, in Bergen, did Ibsen have the opportunity, which he would have found in, say, Copenhagen or Stockholm, to work on classical plays. No Greeks, no Shakespeare, no Molière; even the few English Restoration playwrights who reached him, and there were not many, did so in botched adaptations hideously translated, and shorn of the elegance of their prose

---

[28] Though Hebbel was slightly known in Denmark, where Adam Oehlenschläger had looked after him in Copenhagen in 1842, the winter before he wrote *Maria Magdalena.*

they must have seemed pretty poor stuff. Only Holberg and Heiberg can have had anything to teach him that he did not already know about construction and characterisation. From Scribe he could have learned no virtue that was not better exemplified in both these writers; and whatever Ibsen's admiration for Oehlenschläger as a poet, he can hardly have been blind to his limitations as a dramatist.

Neither could the circumstances under which Ibsen worked as a director have been much less fortunately arranged. His duties were confined to deciding the decor and costumes and arranging the movements; the interpretation of the roles and the speaking of the lines were Laading's business. Not that this was an uncommon arrangement in those days. Even at the Royal Theatre in Copenhagen, Thomas Overskou limited his advice to visual matters, not bothering about the psychology of the characters, their relationships, or the way the actors spoke their lines. Such subtleties were not then regarded as necessary to a theatrical perform- ance, any more than until very recently they were regarded as necessary in opera. Tragedy was, to repeat, a kind of grand opera without music, interesting only in so far as it afforded opportunities for sonorous dec- lamations, spectacular outbursts, and striking visual effects; comedy was merely an excuse for individual inventiveness. Nobody except a very few innovators, such as Fredrik Høedt and Boguwil Dawison, expected a play to reflect real life, any more than they would have expected an opera to do so; what people wanted to see on the stage, in tragedy as in opera or musical comedy, was a world of fantasy. There was no such thing as what we today would call a straight play; there was tragedy, comedy, farce, and melodrama, with or without music. Comedy might be in prose, but tragedy had to be in verse; the idea that a tragedy could be written in prose, or could be about people of humble birth and of ordinary human dimensions like the lower-paying members of the audience, would have struck both actor and public as absurd. (Even a play such as Hebbel's *Maria Magdalena* was in a high-flown prose, to modern ears uncomfortably close to the language of *Maria Marten*.) Such few attempts as there had been to break this rule had failed, which seemed to confirm its general validity. Büchner had succeeded, but nobody knew about Büchner; *Dan- ton's Death* had been published in 1835, but in a version vulgarised almost beyond recognition, and the confused manuscript of *Woyzeck* was not to be discovered until 1879, the year in which, by a strange coincidence, Ibsen won international fame with *A Doll's House*, achieving, in his own way, what Büchner had sought to achieve forty years earlier—the writing of a major serious play in simple prose, employing characters who were not kings and princesses, nor even Capulets and Montagues, but ordinary people called Mr and Mrs, such as might live next door.

The actual stage conditions under which Ibsen operated at Bergen were some fifty years behind the times, and resembled those commonly to be found on the Continent and in England during the eighteenth century. The sets had no side walls, but a painted backcloth and a sequence of painted wings, with borders (i.e., hanging strips of cloth) overhead. The wings were mounted on wheels which rested in a kind of tramline, and were moved by a cranking device beneath the stage. Spectators sitting in the side seats could see through the gaps between the wings. The backcloth had to be rolled up like a home cinema screen before being hoisted into the flies to make way for another. The lighting consisted of chandeliers above the stage and auditorium, footlights, and lamps vertically arranged behind the various wings to give a primitive kind of side illumination. Gas was not introduced at the Bergen Theatre until 1856, the year before Ibsen left; until then, chandeliers, footlights and wing lamps worked on candles or petroleum. Little variation was possible, and such as there was was obtained by the use of movable coloured shades. Light and shadow were often painted on the decor. The front of the stage received the most light, thanks to the footlights and the extra illumination from the lamps and candles in the auditorium, and all dialogue scenes (as opposed to crowd scenes, mime, dances, etc.) were accordingly played downstage. In any case, words spoken upstage tended to get lost in the wings. The smoke, melted wax, and spilt oil inevitably gave the decor, and especially the wing cloths, a soiled appearance. When, in 1848, the management had tried winching the main auditorium chandelier up to the roof, so as to give more effect to the stage lights, spectators complained that it was no longer possible to "enjoy the diversion of looking at the audience when the plays or the performance were such that a broader field of view might prove less exhausting to the limbs and spirit than if eye and mind should be directed uninterruptedly towards the stage."[29]

New decor, when the theatre could afford it, which was not often, and then only in the case of a new Norwegian play such as *St. John's Night,* usually consisted simply of one or more new backcloths. The wing sets were seldom changed, and included standard representations of *a street, a park, a church, winter, a grotto, a pillared hall,* etc. A French visitor to Bergen in 1841 had satirically enquired why the theatre's painter employed his talents on the faces of the actresses instead of on the scenery.

Doors, windows, furniture, vases of flowers, mirrors and so on were, as in other countries, normally painted on the wings and backcloth. Even in England and on the Continent it was not until well into the second half of the century that real furniture was used; as late as 1888 we find Strindberg, in his preface to *Miss Julie,* complaining that "stage doors are

[29] *Bergens Stiftstidende,* 31 January 1848. A useful study of stage conditions at Bergen in the eighteen-fifties has been made by Roderick Rudler: see his "Scenebilledkunsten i Norge for 100 år siden" in *Kunst og kultur,* Oslo, 1961, and his "Ibsens teaterid i Bergen" in *Bergens Tidende,* 7 November 1864.

made of canvas and flap at the slightest touch," and pleading that "even if the walls have to be made of canvas it is surely time to stop painting them with shelves and kitchen utensils."[30]

The normal number of rehearsals judged necessary for a production when Ibsen was at Bergen was three to five. Such properties as could not be painted on the decor (chairs, tankards, etc.) were borrowed from well-wishers in the town; these even included eighteenth-century clothes, of which the citizens of Bergen, already famous for their thrift, had a surprising number in their family wardrobes. These were especially welcome when, as occurred once or twice a season, a play by Holberg entered the repertory.

The normal placing of actors at Bergen was in a horizontal bow, with its tips in the downstage corners and everyone facing the audience, even when they were meant to be speaking to each other. Ibsen's sketches in his prompt books show that he tried to get away from this convention; and when the company visited Trondhjem in 1856, his direction elicited some interesting praise from local critics. "It deserves to be remarked," wrote one, "that the actors have abandoned the stiff and unnatural old-fash-ioned custom of running right down to the footlights or turning to the audience whenever they have anything to say." It was also noticed that "the actors keep quite far upstage," and, amazingly, "turn towards each other when conversing." This was eye-opening stuff indeed for the pro-vincial theatre-goers of Norway, and one assumes that it was one of the fruits of Ibsen's study trip to Copenhagen and Dresden.

But although Ibsen was a visually imaginative director, as befitted one whose early ambition had been to become a painter, and although he was in advance of his time in his meticulous attention (when the theatre could afford it) to costume detail, all reports agree that he was not a good instructor of actors. He was far too timid. Peter Blytt relates: "There was not much about him to suggest the creative genius which he was later to display. This quiet, reticent, not very prepossessing, unassuming young man, with a glance that was usually half-veiled and seldom lit up, and then only briefly, rather gave the impression of being an exceedingly withdrawn and shy person. One knew he had a quick and fertile poetic

---

[30] Nor were things much better in Christiania. Rudler relates that when Schiller's *Mary Stuart* received its premiere there in 1841, a critic complained that "Queen Elizabeth's residence consisted of the Pompeian room which is familiar to us from every performance that we have been offered of the new French drama, and which is now almost worn out." When *Macbeth* was performed for the first time in Norway in 1844, the same periodical (*Den Constitutionelle*) remarked that "the room in Macbeth's castle into which Duncan enters was the inevitable Pillared Hall, the back-cloth of which is by now completely indistinguishable." Things were different in Germany, where the scenic designer was so highly regarded that his name was printed on the bills together with those of the actors, and he would be called on to the stage during a performance to take a bow whenever his handiwork elicited the plaudits of the public.

talent . . . but no one would have guessed that this pale, fully bearded face, with its tightly closed lips, concealed a mind of such quality. . . . He moved quietly, almost soundlessly, about the wings at rehearsals. . . . He not infrequently manifested a certain helplessness, and appeared embarrassed when forced directly to address any actor or, worse still, actress, in order to rebuke or even to correct them. . . . He carried the director's books without in the true sense of the word being a *director*. . . . He struck me as a naturally withdrawn personality who had difficulty, and even reluctance, in forming a close and intimate relationship with anyone. He preferred to wander around alone and unnoticed. . . .

"It became repeatedly evident," Blytt continues, "that economic calculations and estimates, which were naturally an essential part of his work, lay somewhat outside his range. But no one doubted his good will. Undemanding and retiring, he aroused in that easily emotional and often passionate theatrical world no enmity—though one might now and then perceive in him a certain indolence, doubtless the consequence of his quickly fermenting talent. . . . He was regarded with a certain shy veneration, and when, as stated, he moved soundlessly or, as the company sometimes put it, mooched [*tussede*] around in the wings in his curious, capacious, and somewhat worn cloak, he was respected but won little sympathy. He made scarcely any intimate friends . . . but he made no enemies either. He preferred to go his own way, taciturn, enclosed, little understood. . . . He did not often interrupt with instructions at rehearsals, and delivered no harangues, but when he did intervene his comments were perceptive, illuminating, and to the point. His suggestions were brief, clear, precise, and helpful."[31]

H. Wiers-Jenssen, the author of the play *Anne Pedersdotter* (known in England as *The Witch,* and brilliantly filmed by Carl Dreyer as *Day of Wrath* in 1943) records that an actress who had worked with Ibsen at Bergen, whom he does not name, told him how Ibsen would rehearse his actors either mooching soundlessly in the wings (she uses the same word as Blytt) or sitting far back in the auditorium "pulling at his beard and edging back if anyone came near. He would sometimes approach some young and as yet unintimidating beginner who happened to be sitting near him and, referring to the actress speaking on the stage, would say: 'Don't you hear how falsely she said that line? And how untrue and unnecessary that movement was?' 'But, Herr Ibsen, why don't you tell her?' 'No, *you* tell her, Frøken Nielsen.'" They thought of him, she told Wiers-Jenssen, as someone who "wouldn't frighten a cat."[32]

Another actress, Lucie Wolf, who worked under Ibsen in both Bergen and Christiania, recalled in her memoirs: "I remember him as a silent, surprisingly shy man, who I always found kept himself very remote from

[31] Blytt, p. 10.
[32] *Aftenposten,* 24 December 1912.

us, and whose personality in no way encouraged one to speak privately or confidentially with him. He was always amiable and courteous, but in a way that made me get very quickly through whatever it was I needed to ask him. There was no question of his ever giving us instruction as Bjørnson did. I, at any rate, was afraid of him. He always went around wrapped in a great cloak, and if one approached him he shrank back and hid himself like a snail in its shell. I remember someone once asked me to speak to him about a rehearsal we were going to have. 'No, thank you!' I said. 'Go and ask him yourself! Don't you see how he creeps back into his cloak? And how it bristles all over? That's all the great thoughts he's pregnant with; they're sitting in there ready to burst his cloak and fly out into the world!' His great brain was boiling and seething; his powerful spirit could find no place among us and all the pettinesses we had to battle with when everything was just beginning. That mighty world-shaker could not but feel crushed and bound by the monotonous daily routine of narrow Bergen."[33]

During the spring of 1853 Ibsen left Fru Sontum's and moved into an apartment in the rear annex of the theatre, where, the theatre archives tell us, he was provided with "a complete [!] bed and such furniture as may be necessary for the two rooms which have been placed at Ibsen's disposal." An inventory is given of this furniture: "1 bedstead plus necessary bedclothes, including 4 sheets, 4 pillow-cases, and 2 blankets, also mattresses and bolsters, 8 curtains and 8 curtain-holders, 6 birch chairs with covers, 1 birch table and 1 smaller ditto, 1 japanned washstand with mug and bowl."[34] He was looked after by the theatre's "restauratrice," an old lady named Frøken l'Abbée "with a red face and grey curls beneath her cap,"[35] who cooked him two meals a day. Many years later, Ibsen remembered the excellence of her cooking. "Her fried cod," he told John Paulsen, "was a masterpiece."[36] Sophie Monsen recalled that he "always ate his meals by himself in his rooms in the rear annexe—and when he needed anything he would go across the courtyard to the woman who cooked for him rather than ring for and disturb the servant, who would then be eating himself. He was very thoughtful."[37]

The winter of 1852–53 had been a depressing one for Ibsen, with the failure of St. John's Night and the dull and dismal list of plays. Spring, however, occasionally brings consolations to the professionally unsuccessful,

[33] Lucie Wolf, Mine livserindringer (Christiania, 1898), pp. 182–83.

[34] Wiesener, pp. 35–36.

[35] John Paulsen, Samliv med Ibsen, I (Copenhagen and Christiania, 1906), 100.

[36] Loc. cit. Let no one whose experience of cod is confined to England or the United States sneer. The cod of Bergen, properly prepared, is a masterpiece.

[37] Interview in Bergens Tidende, 13 January 1913. Sophie Monsen had begun as an actress at Bergen, at the age of fifteen, at a salary of 12 specie-dollars a month. She emigrated to America, and played Margit in The Feast at Solhaug in San Francisco shortly before the great earthquake of 1906.

and it now did for Ibsen. He fell in love. At Fru Sontum's, shortly before
he moved into the theatre annexe, he met a young girl named Rikke
(i.e., Henrikke) Holst. She was only fifteen, ten years younger than Ibsen,
and not yet confirmed, the niece, indeed, of that Sofie Holst for whom he
had written his last Grimstad poem, "Moonlight Wandering after a Ball."
Rikke is reputed to have drawn his attention to her by pertly throwing a
posy of flowers in his face. Ibsen bought her cakes, sent her flowers, and
went for walks with her; she was a merry, extrovert girl and seems to have
enjoyed his company. He wrote her several charming poems, including
one entitled "Earth Flowers and Potted Plants," in which he contrasts her
freshness with the sophistication of other young ladies, as a wild flower
contrasts with a cultivated plant in a window.

Rikke seems to have reciprocated his love, and he spent a happy spring.
On Whit Sunday, 15 May, he climbed with a group of young people up to
Ulrikken, and declaimed a poem in two parts which he had written for the
occasion. It began with a lyric:

> As swans that long for the south
> Soar into the white clouds,
> So our desires took joyful wing.
> Our spring dreams rose and flew.

and was followed by a "Prospect of Bergen," in which he affectionately
apostrophised the city. Rikke recalled the occasion thirty-six years later:
how, when they had reached the top, they unpacked their picnic baskets,
the musicians began to play, and Ibsen suddenly leaped to his feet and,
standing there on the mountainside, declaimed an apparently spontaneous "Ode to Joy." "He could be like that sometimes," she remembered.
"But there were other times when he did not wish to be seen even by his
friends, but would hide himself away completely. . . . When anything
annoyed him," she continued, "he could leap up suddenly and in swift
and bitter outbursts tell his hostess all the truths he had guessed. And
that didn't win him friends. . . . When he was alone with you he could
suddenly start to talk in a frenzied, ruthless torrent of words—paradoxes
and wild truths, so that one walked bewitched beside the little man as he
exploded savagely against all conventions. He sometimes said that he was a
lonely person, would always be a lonely person, whom no one believed
in and no one, no one in the world, cared about. But there were other times
when he would be quite silent and spend long periods shut up like a book.
He was usually melancholy."[38]

Two days after the Whit Sunday excursion, he joined in the 17th of
May celebrations, when the young actors of the theatre (the ladies were
not allowed to partake in this ceremony) walked in procession through

[38] Fru Henrikke Holst-Tresselt interviewed by Herman Bang in *Af Dagens Krønike*,
a Danish monthly magazine (Copenhagen, 1889), pp. 340–44.

the town wearing the Hungarian *luva* of grey-green cloth with a tassel, to demonstrate their support of Kossuth's new uprising. Rikke remembered how he "descended from the mountain . . . and delivered an eloquent speech about how Norway still lay in her swaddling-clothes; but development was near, and must surely come. This aroused great enthusiasm and he was greeted with joyful demonstrations. . . . It made him happy in those days occasionally to stand face to face with a crowd and feel that he had tamed it and was able to control it. . . . Even his friends sometimes felt it was embarrassing to walk with him across the street, for there was something strange about him, even the way he dressed. But once he began to talk, you forgot everything and were caught up by the fire that burned in him."[39]

On 6 June he wrote a new poem to her, entitled simply "To R. H.," as romantic and adolescent as anything he had composed at Grimstad: "O, I know a fair land, Distant as the stars of night. . . . There I whisper many a song To the goddess of my soul." He ends, like any lovestruck youth, by asking: "Must my love be but a memory, and I lost and without hope, or shall I find my richest treasure in life's reality?" Better than this was a charming poem which he addressed to a rose that he sent her, asking its pardon for ending its life. When the theatre season ended, and some of the company went on a walking tour to Voss and Hardanger, he wrote a buoyant song for them to sing as they walked and climbed. Whether he accompanied them, we do not know; he loved walking tours,[40] but may have chosen to remain in Bergen to be near Rikke.

Early that June he asked her to marry him. But her father refused to countenance any engagement before she was confirmed; furthermore, he forbade her to continue seeing this young poet, who was poor, of uncertain prospects, had failed his matriculation, held radical political views, and must altogether have seemed, to any respectable citizen, a singularly unpromising match. Despite this edict, they continued to meet, with her five-year-old brother as chaperon and a girl friend of hers as look-out, and plighted their troth in a time-honoured and romantic manner by joining their rings on a key-ring and throwing them linked into the fjord. Thus, according to an ancient tradition, the sea had joined them as surely as any priest. Unhappily, one day her father surprised them together. Many years later Rikke's little brother, then an old man, remembered the occasion: a clenched fist raised threateningly in the long avenue of trees, and his father's face "green with anger." A bolder lover might have braved it out; but Ibsen turned tail and fled. That was the end of things

[39] *Loc. cit.*

[40] Marcus Grønvold recalls Ibsen telling him that as a young man at Bergen he had taken great walks in the countryside, once hiking with Andreas Isachsen to Hardanger. On the way, he took a plunge in water that had melted from the snow, and then, in the Russian manner, rolled naked in the snow. "It didn't feel especially cold," he commented. (*Fra Ulrikken til Alperne* [Oslo, 1925], p. 140.)

between Ibsen and Rikke Holst. Thirty years afterwards, when revisiting Bergen, he called on her; she was by now a comfortably married *hausfrau* with many children. The old warmth, we are told, rose again in him, and he asked wonderingly: "I wonder why nothing ever came of our relationship?" She laughed as in the old days, and said: "But, my dear Ibsen, don't you remember? You ran away!" "Yes, yes," he replied. "I never was a brave man face to face."[41]

It is tempting to exaggerate the effect of the Rikke Holst affair on Ibsen's life. Most of us have loved and lost in our early twenties; it is an essential part of any artist's education; and at least his love had been reciprocated. He wrote a sad little lyric mourning his loss:

> One fine spring day
> We walked the avenue.
> Enticing as a riddle
> Was the forbidden place.
>
> And the west wind whispered
> And the sky was blue.
> A bird sat in the lime tree
> And sang to her young.
>
> I painted poems for you
> In darting colour-play.
> Two brown eyes shone
> And laughed and listened.
>
> Above us we can hear
> Whispering and laughter.
> But we, we said a soft farewell
> And never met again.
>
> Now when alone I wander
> Along the avenue
> Those little feathered dwarfs
> Give me no peace.
>
> That sparrow sat and listened
> As we walked hand in hand,
> And made a song about us
> And set it to a tune.
>
> Now every bird has learned it,
> And in the leafy eaves
> Each tiny beak sings crooningly
> Of that fair day, now gone.

41 Paulsen, *Samliv med Ibsen*, I, 107–27; Halvdan Koht, *Henrik Ibsen: eit diktarliv* (rev. edn., Oslo, 1954), I, 98.

It was probably at this time, too, that he wrote at any rate the first draft of the long, brilliant and bitter poem, "In the Picture Gallery":

> There dwells an ugly demon in my breast
> Who sometimes visits me in evil hours;
> In loneliness, or when life's joys are best,
> As when I dream, or, rhyming, sense my powers . . .

> "Will you not realise," it whispers, gloating,
> "How meaningless it is, your life's short span?
> Have you not lost your faith in God and man?

> Can you not understand, your hopes are nothing?
> Your ideals but a distant candle are;
> Your goal a meteor, and not a star?" . . .

> Outside my window stood an apple tree,
> Its branches filled with flowers and with fragrance.
> There a small bird sang for my ear alone,
> Singing of life's great glory and abundance.

> Now those bright flowers rot black against the roots.
> The once-green leaf rustles against the stone.
> A tempest snatched them from the stage of life,
> And the sweet singer of the spring has flown.

> Now autumn reigns within me and without.
> I press my forehead to the window, where
> The frost makes foolish patterns on the pane.

> What proof have I that once I saw the spring?
> A withered leaf, a stump of memory;
> That is the sum and total of life's gain!

Not surprisingly, his work at the theatre suffered, and on 30 July the board felt constrained to send him a letter demanding that he apply himself more actively to his duties:

> It has come to the notice of the board that some of the responsibilities connected with your work have been postponed and subsequently overlooked, while others have not always been carried out in the most desirable manner. . . . It would be to the advantage of all parties if you could be more active in the theatre, both as *regissør* and as *instruktør*. The board believes, however, that this neglect of duty stems rather from lack of experience than from any want of ability or willingness to perform your duties.

The kindly tone of this rebuke suggests that Ibsen's directors liked and appreciated him, an impression that is reinforced by Peter Blytt in his memoirs. On 4 August, Ibsen replied somewhat plaintively to the above letter: "That there is much in the matter of scenic arrangements, decor, etc., that could be otherwise, there can be no doubt. The question is whether the board is willing to agree to the outlay required to supplement the grievous deficiencies now existing. . . . I most readily admit that my work as *regissør* is still not all that it might be, but I assumed that it would be obvious to anyone with knowledge of the theatre that what a *regissør* requires above all else is experience, and I know only too well that it has not been possible for me adequately to achieve this when limited to a mere three to five rehearsals per play." This excuse, plausibly as it reads, did not strike the board as sufficient; they acknowledged his letter, but did "not feel required to retract anything that they had written in their communication of 30 July."[42]

Ibsen should have written a new play that autumn for the coming anniversary of the theatre's opening but, although he wrote to Paul Botten Hansen on 5 August that he was "pretty productive, as you will discover before the winter is out," he in fact did no more than revise *The Warrior's Barrow*, individualising the characters more sharply, improving the motivation, reducing the mythological apparatus (rather to the play's detriment), and generally polishing the verse. In this new form *The Warrior's Barrow* accordingly received its second production, at the Bergen Theatre on 2 January 1854. Perhaps it was not unreasonable of Ibsen to wish it to be performed again; after all, it had been sympathetically received in Christiania. But at Bergen it failed, even more calamitously than *St. John's Night,* for it was dropped after a single performance. The local press did not notice it at all. Coming on top of the break-up of his affair with Rikke, this must have been a particularly painful disappointment to him; though there was some faint consolation in that *Bergenske Blade* decided to serialise it, in four instalments. *The Warrior's Barrow* thus became the second of Ibsen's plays to appear in print; it was not published in book form until over forty years later, when Ibsen allowed it to be included in the German collected edition of his works published in 1898 to celebrate his seventieth birthday. "I find, on reading it through," he wrote to Julius Elias, on 7 September 1897, "that there is, after all, some merit in this youthful trifle, and am very grateful to you for making me include it"; but it is difficult to see what merit so austerely self-critical a writer as Ibsen could have discovered there. It seems blatantly inferior to *St. John's Night,* which he refused to allow to be printed in his lifetime. *The Warrior's Barrow* is nearer to being worthless than any other play he wrote.

[42] Wiesener, pp. 36–39.

5

Kid Gloves in Bergen

1854–1857

The effect of the failure of *The Warrior's Barrow* upon Ibsen's self-confidence can be measured by the fact that he offered his next play to the Bergen Theatre anonymously. In September 1854 Peter Blytt became chairman of the board; at thirty-one, he was only five years older than Ibsen. In his memoirs he records that a few weeks after his appointment to this post, Ibsen came to see him with a quarto notebook under his arm. "I was immediately struck," notes Blytt, "by the fact that he seemed more than usually ill at ease that day. After a few confused preliminary remarks he handed me the book, saying that it was a manuscript that had been sent him by a friend in Christiania, a historical drama or, if one preferred, a tragedy, which the author in question, who wished to remain anonymous, would like to be performed at the Bergen Theatre, should it be deemed worthy of acceptance. But before submitting it to the board he—Ibsen—desired me to read it through and give him my opinion."[1]

The play was entitled *Lady Inger of Østraat*. Blytt guessed from Ibsen's demeanour that he was probably the author; he read the play, liked it, and quickly put it into rehearsal. It was only a few days before the opening performance that Ibsen admitted to its authorship. Blytt tells us that at a rehearsal Ibsen, in his capacity as *sceneinstruktør*, suddenly rushed on to the stage, interrupted one of the actors in the middle of a long speech, and showed him with unusual feeling how it ought to be spoken. Blytt noticed that Ibsen did this without referring to the prompt book, and this confirmed what, one imagines, he must in any case have suspected. Nevertheless, Ibsen remained adamant in refusing to allow his name to appear as the author on either the posters or the programme.

H. Wiers-Jenssen, quoting an actress who was in the company at the time, confirms this story with some interesting additional details. The

[1] Blytt, p. 11.

speech about which Ibsen felt so strongly was the one in Act Three in which Nils Lykke says to Lady Inger's daughter, Eline: "How often have you not sat here at Østraat, alone, your brain in a whirl . . . longing to get away, to flee far away, you know not whither? How often have you not wandered alone along the fjord, and a gilded ship with knights and ladies aboard, with harps and singers, has glided by, far from the shore; a faint echo of mighty deeds has floated to your ear; and you have felt a longing in your breast, an irresistible longing to know what exists on the other side of the sea? . . . When you dreamed of the many-coloured life out there in the wide world—when you dreamed of tourneys and merry feastings—did you never see in your dreams a knight standing with a smile on his lips and grief in his heart in the midst of the tumult—a knight who had once dreamed, as fairly as you, of a woman, noble and virtuous, and whom he had sought in vain among all those who surrounded him?"

When (Wiers-Jenssen tells) Ibsen had sprung on to the stage and delivered this speech with a passion which astonished the actors standing silently around, he fell silent for a moment and then said to the actor who was playing the part: "Well—you know—something along those lines —I think the speech will sound best if you say it that way—But if you don't feel—of course—then—it's you who are acting it—yes." And he shuffled back into the wings.[2]

Lady Inger of Østraat is set in Norway in 1528. Like *The Warrior's Barrow* and *St. John's Night* (and, for that matter, his next two plays, *The Feast at Solhaug* and *Olaf Liljekrans*), it conforms to Aristotle's demand for unity of time, place, and action, for the entire story takes place during a single night in Lady Inger's castle. The plot is extremely complicated. Lady Inger, a rich and powerful noblewoman, is under persuasion to lead a Norwegian uprising against the Danish overlords. A Norwegian patriot, Olaf Skaktavl, tells her that a stranger will come to her castle that night; he is the son of a Swedish rebel murdered by the Danes, Sten Sture, and is preparing a rebellion which Olaf begs Lady Inger to support. Sure enough, a stranger arrives; but he is not Sten Sture's son, but a Danish intriguer, Nils Lykke, who has got wind of Sten Sturesson's plans and has come to intercept and kill him. Lady Inger, however, supposes him to be Sturesson. A sub-plot, beautifully worked into the main action, is that Lady Inger's eldest daughter Lucia had, some years before, been seduced by Nils Lykke, and had killed herself; but Lady Inger has never seen Lykke, and does not recognise him. She has a surviving daughter, Eline, whose ambition is to discover and revenge herself upon her sister's seducer; but she knows his face no more than her mother does, and she, like her sister, is seduced by him that night. Then a second stranger arrives at the castle, so late that everyone has gone to bed except Nils Lykke, who is waiting to murder him. But this second stranger is

[2] *Aftenposten*, 24 December 1912.

not, as he had expected, Sten Sturesson, but his half-brother Sten Steens-son, an illegitimate son of Sten Sture born to him long before by Lady Inger herself. Lady Inger, who has not seen him since childhood, supposes him to be his legitimate half-brother and thinks that if she can kill him she may pave the way for her own son to be king; herself unable to rule because of her sex, she has cherished a secret ambition to become the mother of a king. She has him killed, only to discover that he is her own son. At the same time, Eline discovers that her lover, Nils Lykke, is her sister's seducer. Lady Inger dies by her son's coffin, and Nils Lykke walks quietly out, his mission accomplished. Evil has triumphed.

Lady Inger of Østraat was the first of Ibsen's plays to be written entirely in prose; it is also the first that would stand up to performance today. In 1857, even after he had had a public success with *The Feast at Solhaug,* Ibsen, writing to Paul Botten Hansen, twice referred to *Lady Inger* as "my best play." It is indeed, despite its obvious faults, a remarkably mature and powerful work. Not that it is to be regarded as a harbinger of the new drama; it is rather a brilliant essay in the old tradition. In it, Ibsen has retained, as yet without question, much of the old paraphernalia of plot which was still then supposed to be indigenous to tragedy, as to comedy—mistaken identities, intercepted letters, overheard conversations, lengthy monologues, and frequent asides (which last can be deleted from *Lady Inger* without in any way obscuring the action). The language, too, is often stiff, though of considerable quality and precisely phrased. But the characterisation is much more searching than anything he had achieved previously, and the action moves towards its climax with that inevitability which we associate with his later and more famous works. Here, too, for the first time, we hear that tone of controlled yet searching self-analysis which we shall later come to recognise as the authentic Ibsen music. In particular, Lady Inger's con-flict of courage and cowardice, her desire to act and her doubts that hold her back, was a theme to which Ibsen was to return again and again in his plays; it is the dilemma of Skule in *The Pretenders,* Mrs. Alving in *Ghosts,* Ellida in *The Lady from the Sea,* Rebecca West in *Rosmersholm,* and Hedda Gabler.

It has been suggested that *Lady Inger of Østraat* was technically in-fluenced by Scribe's historical drama *Les Contes de la Reine de Navarre,* which Ibsen had helped to direct that autumn, in October 1854. The rapid succession of short scenes, it is argued, and the various coincidences vital to the plot, are typical of Scribe. Have the critics who make such assertions never read Shakespeare? Mistaken identities, intercepted letters, overheard conversations, monologues and asides are all to be found in both *Hamlet* and *King Lear,* which we know Ibsen had seen in Copen-hagen, and which he had almost certainly read; indeed, off-hand, it is difficult to think of a Shakespeare play that does not contain them. And anyone who has ever acted in, or been associated with, a Shakespeare production knows how, with the free Elizabethan method of staging, Shakespeare was addicted to the frequent use of the short scene. Even if Ibsen had not learned all this from Shakespeare, he would have done so from Holberg. In any event, Blytt tells us that Ibsen offered him the play "a few weeks" after he had become chairman of the board, which we know to have been on 9 September, and *Les Contes de la Reine de Navarre* was not performed until October. Are we to suppose that Ibsen wrote this long and very complex play in a few days? One repeats that the myth of Ibsen's debt to Scribe, of whom he never recorded a good word, needs to be exploded. Scribe, if shallow in characterisation, was a skilful theatrical craftsman, but there is no evidence that he ever exerted the slightest influence upon Ibsen.

Sixteen years later, in a letter to Peter Hansen (28 October 1870), Ibsen stated that *Lady Inger of Østraat* stemmed "from a sudden love affair, violently broken off, which you will also find treated in several short poems, such as 'Earth Flowers and Potted Plants,' 'A Birdcage,' etc." This reference to the Rikke Holst interlude has evoked a quantity of obtuse speculation from commentators who have sought to identify Rikke with Eline, and have even suggested that, since there is no relationship in the play which resembles that between Ibsen and Rikke, he must, in a moment of aberration, have been mistakenly referring to some other drama. Surely it is obvious that it is the tragic and nihilistic mood of the play which stemmed from the unhappiness of that summer. Again and again in his later years Ibsen was to remind questioners, unhappily with little effect, that he distilled his experiences into his plays, and did not, except in very rare instances, mirror them directly.

Lady Inger of Østraat might, if its reception had been different, have proved the first major turning-point in Ibsen's career as a dramatist; it was his first step on that road of high tragedy which he was ultimately to extend into previously uncharted country. As fate decreed, however, he was thrown smartly off that road, and it was to be another decade before he ventured to return to it. For *Lady Inger* was as big a failure with the Bergen public as *St. John's Night* and *The Warrior's Barrow* had been. They received it so poorly at its first performance on 2 January 1855 that it was repeated only once; and even when, the following year, Ibsen had a success with *The Feast at Solhaug* and tried to persuade them to revive *Lady Inger*, the board refused.[3] It is possible, of course, that it may, like

[3] This may, however, have stemmed not so much from a poor regard for the play as from the inability of the Bergen actors to cope with tragedy. Peter Blytt writes that when, in the winter of 1854–55, they tried to do Victor Hugo's *Angelo, Tyran de Padron*, the board had to call off the production after the final dress rehearsal because the play was "obviously far outside the company's range." (Blytt, p. 128.) On 12 July 1855 *Bergens-Posten* printed a late notice of *Lady Inger*: "If he can only raise pillars of shame, then let them rest, the poor shadows."

so many plays that have failed critically and publicly, have won him the admiration of a discriminating few, but we have no evidence for this.

He does not seem to have found any replacement for Rikke Holst; those who knew him at this period say that he was preternaturally shy and had few friends. As far as we know it was to be almost three years before he again formed any close association with a girl, and then it was to be the one he was to marry. The over-all picture we have of Ibsen at this time is very different from that which Christopher Due paints of him at Grimstad only five years earlier, when he had, apparently, become infatuated fairly often. No love poems have survived from the years 1854 and 1855. But this, again, is not so inexplicable a phenomenon as some critics and biographers have tried to make out. Some young men fall in love at the drop of a handkerchief, others rarely and with difficulty, and it is not uncommon for a young man to change in his twenties from one type to the other. Nor should we be surprised that he, who had made several close friends in Christiania, found none in Bergen. Although the two towns were roughly similar in size, Bergen had no university and, as Lorentz Dietrichson has told us, little culture. Ibsen was not the first man who, on leaving a university city for a small provincial town, has found himself isolated and friendless and sought in vain for someone to love.

Outwardly, too, and especially sartorially, Ibsen was very different from the shabby apprentice, lacking socks and overcoat, whom Due had known at Grimstad. True to the child who, at Venstøp, had admired the sexton's father as he arrayed himself in his fine clothes, Ibsen used what must have been a largish proportion of his salary to dress elegantly. Magdalene Thoresen, seeing Ibsen around 1870 in a velvet coat, "was reminded of an earlier attempt at the elegant which he once made in Bergen when, very smart, he swung round a corner wearing light yellow kid gloves. In Bergen!" she added uncharitably.[4] Herman Bang, writing in 1889, quotes a description given him by someone who had known Ibsen at Bergen: "He was so soigné, almost precise and finicky, in his dress. He wore elegant frilled poet's cuffs, with lace edges extending over his hands. And on the street he carried a short little cane. People thought he looked unimpressive, and he suffered from the consciousness of being small—but those who dismissed him as insignificant had never seen his eyes. They could catch fire and throw a glance that pierced you, so that you remembered it long afterwards."[5] Bang's informant may have been Rikke Holst, for John Paulsen, who interviewed Rikke when she was an old woman, records that she described him in almost identical terms: "Ibsen was at that time very soigné, even pedantic, in his dress. For example, his coat had sleeves which were very broad at the wrist, *engageant* sleeves as they were then

---

[4] From an interview first printed in *Juleroser* (Copenhagen, 1901), subsequently in Karl Larsen's edition of *Henrik Ibsens episke* Brand (Copenhagen and Christiania, 1907).

[5] Article in *Af Dagens Krønike* (Copenhagen, 1889), p. 341.

called, and these were adorned with curious long lace cuffs, a fashion which the other men did not affect. He always wore frilled shirts. . . . The same precise order ruled in his rooms. There was never a speck of dust on the furniture, and elegant vases of flowers stood in the windows. . . . His physical appearance, with its brown complexion and black hair and full black beard, was interesting rather than handsome."[6] And Lorentz Dietrichson mainly remembered, from this time, "his full dark brown beard, covering the whole chin, which was then still quite unusual, his grey cloak, his lively eyes, and his quick gait."[7]

That February, 1855, he wrote a pleasant epithalamium to celebrate the marriage of another of his former landlady's sons, Edvard Sontum: it is the only poem from Ibsen's pen that has survived from this year, apart from those which he was to insert into his new play. The same month, he directed one of the few good plays (apart from Holberg's and his own) which came his way at Bergen: Eugène Labiche's farce An Italian Straw Hat. Otherwise, the repertory made the usual dismal reading: Scribe, Bayard, Mélesville, Hertz, with German, Danish, and (occasionally) Norwegian pieces of equal triviality and, usually, less expertise.

That others besides himself were dissatisfied with such dramatic fare Ibsen would have learned from a drama criticism by Bjørnson which appeared in Aftenbladet on 1 February that year. The starting-point of the article was a new French play, Le Gendre de M. Poirier, by a thirty-four-year-old dramatist named Emile Augier, which had been produced in Paris the previous year. Bjørnson wrote admiringly of "the economy of the dialogue, the careful unfolding of character, so that even in the fourth act the author has new aspects of personality with which to surprise us," and of "the perspective which is opened . . . by the dialogue never illuminating the character directly but . . . as it were, merely allowing it to be distantly glimpsed." This new naturalism is generally agreed to have dated, as far as the French theatre is concerned, from the production of Musset's Un Caprice at the Comédie-Française in 1847 (though in the novel it can be traced back at least twenty-five years, to Balzac's Le Peau de Chagrin [1830] and Stendhal's Le Rouge et le Noir [1831], and was to reach its peak in Flaubert's Madame Bovary in 1856). Bjørnson, praising the psychological advance which Augier had made on Scribe, expressed the hope that the new movement might help "to reform the taste of our time for characterless drama."

Later that year, in Morgenbladet on 9 December, Bjørnson developed his demand for realism in the drama at greater length. Again contrasting the work of Musset, Augier and Dumas fils with the artificialities of Scribe, he

---

[6] Paulsen, Samliv med Ibsen, I, 120–21. It is interesting that Rikke, unlike other witnesses, remembers his complexion as brown. They were together in the spring and summer only, when he had evidently caught the sun.

[7] Dietrichson, I, 331.

wrote: "In a time such as ours, one cannot be content with mere hints of character. People are delving more deeply into human nature from every angle, in science as well as in art; we investigate each minutest trait, we dissect and analyse . . . the smallest flower, the least insect. . . . And in art this current of naturalism reveals itself in a striving for truth rather than beauty, manifesting itself in theatrical terms in a strong demand for individualisation." In a piece such as Felicien Mallefille's *Le Cœur et la Dot,* Bjørnson continues, "it is no longer a question of revealing merely that aspect of a person's character for which one happens to have use; no, one puts the whole person into the play, with all his social roots." The danger is that, in ill-written works, "he [the character] occupies so much space that he halts the action and destroys the interest." What playwrights must do is "to let his [i.e., Scribe's] dramatic machinery and their more detailed characterisation merge to their mutual advantage"; the plot must be the result of "the characters' own development." Two years later (in March 1858), Bjørnson was to write in *Bergens-Posten* that "Scribean comedy is now finished in France," and that the characters now being created there "are no longer marionettes moved by invisible strings but human beings, men and women with the pain of life in their faces."[8]

But Ibsen was unable to read Augier because of his ignorance of French, and some time during the spring or summer of 1855 he made a literary discovery which excited him much more: the Icelandic Sagas. They were the first literature that had excited him for several years, since his discovery in his teens of Voltaire, Oehlenschläger, Holberg, and Heiberg, and the Shakespeare he had seen in Copenhagen and Dresden; and they were to be virtually the last. Once Ibsen had thrown off the not very inspiring influence of Oehlenschläger and had absorbed what he could of Shakespeare from seeing him and reading him in bad translations, he was never again to be seriously influenced by any writer, dead or alive. He would sometimes pick up a thought from Kierkegaard or Brandes, or a hint by Bjørnson, and develop it; but he was, as Edmund Gosse observed, one of the very few great writers who worked without a library. For the last half of his life indeed, if not longer, Ibsen read little but newspapers and the Bible (the latter, he would hasten to point out, for the language only); but he read them, and the newspapers especially, most minutely; his last twelve great prose plays, from which the whole of modern prose drama stems, are like fragments of newspapers written by some all-seeing editor.

The sagas, however, fascinated him. It is remarkable that he had not discovered them before; even such knowledge of the Viking Age as he had required when writing *The Warrior's Barrow* had been gleaned from Oehlenschläger. It was not that no good translations of the sagas were available in Norwegian or Danish, for N. M. Petersen had produced four

---

[8] Quoted by Christen Collin in *Bjørnstjerne Bjørnson, hans barndom og ungdom,* II (Christiania, 1907), 436.

excellent volumes between 1839 and 1844. But somehow Ibsen had missed them. They excited him as the literature and history of the Middle Ages, which he had studied when preparing *Lady Inger of Østraat*, had failed to do.

At the same time, groping back into the literature of the remote past, he happened upon another form that proved a revelation to him: the mediæval folk tale. Ibsen had a better excuse for his ignorance of this rich field, for the rediscovery of it in Norway was still barely under way. The pioneer in this had been Jørgen Moe, a farmer's son who was later to become a bishop. He had begun to collect folk tales from his fellow-peasants as early as 1834, when a youth of twenty-one. A few years later he was joined in his researches by another enthusiast, Peter Christian Asbjørnsen, and in 1841 they published their first collection; their full edition of 1856 was to create among Norwegian writers something like the sensation which Thomas Percy (likewise destined to become a bishop) had aroused in England in 1765 with the publication of his *Reliques of English Poetry*, which were to inspire so much of the literature of the Romantic Movement. Other Norwegians besides Moe and Asbjørnsen were digging up the literary past in the eighteen-fifties; in 1853, M. B. Landstad had published the first of his collections of folk ballads, while from 1853 to 1859 L. M. Lindeman brought out, in instalments, the peasant melodies of Norway. All this fitted well with the nationalistic movement that was afoot in Norway, in literature as in politics; here was a literature that was neither Danish nor Swedish, but truly Norwegian.

Twenty-eight years later, in a foreword which he wrote to *The Feast at Solhaug* in 1883, Ibsen recalled the effect which the discovery of this ancient literature had had upon him at the time:

The year before [*The Feast at Solhaug*] I had written *Lady Inger of Østraat*. The preparation of this drama had necessitated my delving into the history and literature of the Middle Ages, particularly the later stages of that period. I tried, as well as I could, to live myself back into the habits and customs of those times, the emotional life, the ways of thought and speech. The period is, however, not especially attractive to dwell in for any length of time; nor does it provide material particularly suited to dramatic treatment. I soon, therefore, turned to the saga age. But the sagas of the kings, and the strict historical traditions of that remote time, did not grip me; I found myself unable, then, to make any creative dramatic use of the strifes between kings and chieftains, factions and families. That was to come later.

On the other hand, in the Icelandic *family* sagas I found in rich measure what I required in the way of human clothing for the thoughts, moods, and ideas which at that time were filling, or anyway running around in, my head. Hitherto I had been ignorant of these Old Norse contributions to the personal history of our saga age, had indeed scarcely heard of them. By chance N. M. Petersen's excellent translation (excellent, at least, as regards the feel of the language) came into my hands. In these family chronicles, with their varied relationships and confrontations between man and man, woman and woman, above all between human being and human being, I discovered a rich, vital, and personal life; and from my encounter with all these intensely rounded and individual men and women there arose in my mind the first rough and misty outline of *The Vikings at Helgeland*. . . . But then something intervened. This was principally and decisively of a personal nature; but I think it was not without significance that I had at that time begun to study Landstad's collection of Norwegian folk ballads which had been published a few years previously. The mood in which I then found myself fitted better with the literary romanticism of the Middle Ages than with the deeds of the sagas, better with verse than prose, better with the linguistic music of the folk ballad than with the characterisation of the sagas. So it happened that the shapeless, embryonic idea of *The Vikings at Helgeland* gradually transformed itself into the lyrical drama *The Feast at Solhaug*.

Ibsen wrote *The Feast at Solhaug* during the summer of 1855. It is partly in rhymed verse, partly in prose, and is set in the fourteenth century. The plot must be given briefly. Margit is the bored young wife of a rich and tedious old landowner named Bengt. She has a younger sister, Signe. The king's officer, Knut Gæsling, is on a visit to them, with a dual purpose; he intends to propose to Signe, and is also on the lookout for a former friend of theirs, Gudmund Alfson, who is suspected of treason. This Gudmund now turns up at Solhaug, protesting his innocence; and, in an improbably romantic manner, he declares that he is in love with someone at the house without naming her. Margit and Signe have both been in love with him, in each case (again somewhat improbably) without the other suspecting, and each now assumes herself to be the one he loves. Margit believes that, if she had not been so foolish as to marry Bengt, Gudmund would long ago have married her; she therefore decides to poison her husband. Meanwhile, Knut has been rejected by Signe and, hearing that she loves Gudmund, sees a double reason for killing him as soon as the day is over (it would offend against the laws of hospitality if he were to murder a fellow-guest during a feast). Bengt now gets drunk, fights Knut to avenge a supposed insult, and is killed by him; whereupon the servants overpower and bind Knut, so that he is now in Gudmund's power. Gudmund chivalrously spares him. News now arrives that the king has discovered that Gudmund is not after all guilty of treason. Knut is freed, Gudmund is now also free, he marries Signe, and all ends happily for everyone except Margit.

The Feast at Solhaug is, except possibly for *The Warrior's Barrow*, the worst play that Ibsen ever wrote. The plot and characterisation are both extremely banal, and the only merit lies in some of the lyrical writing. The influence of the folk ballad is very apparent; both the style and the atmosphere of the play are full of echoes from Landstad's collection, and so are the characterisation and motivation. Professor Francis Bull has remarked that examples of this are to be found on "almost every page" of the play; *inter alia,* Landstad contains songs about characters named Margit, Gudmund, and Signelita who have much in common with Ibsen's Margit, Gudmund, and Signe. If Ibsen had any illusions about its quality at the time, he soon abandoned them; writing to Peter Hansen in 1870 he dismissed it as "a trifle that I no longer wish to acknowledge."

But even the worst of plays may serve a purpose, and *The Feast at Solhaug,* as Ibsen was to discover when it was staged the following January, was to prove extremely important to him, for two reasons.

Meanwhile, he continued with his work as *sceneinstruktør.* In June of that year (1855) the board, for some unexplained reason, proposed that Laading and Ibsen should switch jobs. Both protested. "Three full seasons have now elapsed since Herr Ibsen took over the *sceneinstruktion,"* wrote Laading to the board, "so he has all the details at his finger tips far more than I. . . . Whether Ibsen will be able to fill my place as reading supervisor and rest content that the experience which he has gained of stage management should lie unused, he must himself inform you."[9] The board dropped the idea.

On 30 September 1855, Ibsen, for the first and last time in his career, directed a Shakespeare play—*As You Like It,* adapted by a Frøken S. Beyer and re-entitled *Livet i skoven,* or *Life in the Forest.* The Bergen public did not appreciate it, and it was dropped after two performances. T. Blanc, the historian of the Bergen Theatre, comments: "The play seems to have proved too difficult for the company's talents."[10]

That autumn, however, Ibsen had the honour of being elected to a fairly exclusive club, the 22 December Society. The name had no political significance, but arose merely from the fact that on 22 December 1845 twenty-five citizens had met in Bergen to found a literary society which was to meet every fortnight during the winter for lectures and readings; the playing of cards was to be strictly forbidden. Peter Blytt, the chairman of the theatre board, had become president of this society in 1855, and during the autumn he proposed Ibsen as a new member. He was elected unanimously. The records of the society inform us that on 27 November 1855 "Instruktør Ibsen gave a lecture on W. Shackspear [*sic*] and his influence on Scandinavian Art." Exasperatingly, the manuscript of this talk has not survived, and we have no record of anything that Ibsen said in it. One would give a lot to know. It seems, at any rate, to have interested the members, for the following month, to celebrate the tenth

[9] Wiesener, pp. 41–44.
[10] Blanc, p. 206.

anniversary of their founding, Johannes Brun was invited to give a dramatic reading of the Falstaff scenes from *Henry IV*.[11] Ibsen wrote a song for the occasion, and also for the following anniversary in 1856, by which time the society had over eighty members. Neither song is of much poetic value.

On 2 January 1856, *The Feast at Solhaug* was performed, under Ibsen's direction, at the Bergen Theatre and, thanks to the debased taste of the public, was a success: the first, apart from the very limited praise accorded to *The Warrior's Barrow* in Christiania, that Ibsen had known. As much as the play itself, people admired the apparently authentic mediaeval peasant costumes and furniture, and the new decor which, like the costumes, Ibsen had designed, or at any rate co-operated on. In his 1883 foreword to the play, Ibsen described the first night reception:

> I was at the time employed as stage instructor at the Bergen Theatre, and so personally supervised the rehearsals of my play. The performance was admirable, and of a rare warmth; acted with joy and devotion, it was received in the same spirit. . . . The performance ended with repeated calls for the author and cast. Later that evening the orchestra, accompanied by a large part of the audience, serenaded me outside my windows. I am not sure that I did not permit myself to be so carried away as to deliver a kind of address to the gathering. I know, at any rate, that I felt profoundly happy.

When, after a subsequent performance, one of the actors made a speech in his honour, Ibsen thanked them for "the recognition that will strengthen me in my pursuit of the goal towards which I am striving, and which I *shall* achieve." Later, he said it was the only really happy day he ever spent in Bergen.[12]

The Feast at Solhaug was repeated five times during the next few months, a record previously achieved at the theatre only by C. P. Riis's rustic "dramatic idyll" *Til sæters* [*At a Mountain Farm*]. Ibsen was by now nearly twenty-eight, and he badly needed some kind of success; a poet or a novelist can work unrecognised, but hardly a playwright. The occasion had, though, a side effect which in the long run was to prove vastly more important to his writing.

Among the audience at the Bergen Theatre that January evening in 1856 was a thirty-six-year-old authoress named Magdalene Thoresen. Danish by birth, she had fled from her native country to escape from a love affair with an Icelandic poet, and had married a twice widowed clergyman seventeen years her senior, Hans Conrad Thoresen, the Dean of Bergen. She was a beautiful and remarkable woman, who had already

---

[11] See the article by Professor Francis Bull in *Edda*, 1919. He says "from *Henry V*," but there are, of course, no Falstaff scenes in that play. The 22 December Society folded in the autumn of 1861.

[12] Koht, I, 117.

achieved recognition as a novelist and short story writer, and had both
written and translated plays for the Bergen Theatre, so that she had already met Ibsen several times. Now that he was acclaimed as a successful
playwright, she invited him to a literary evening at her house, and he paid
his first visit there five days after the premiere of *The Feast at Solhaug*,
on 7 January 1856.

Dean Thoresen has been described as "a greatly gifted man, witty and
eloquent, with a voice like the clearest bell, able to do in an hour what
another man could not achieve in a week";[13] and as "a quiet, sedate,
and lovable man" who "never went out but was immensely proud of his
beautiful wife."[14] His first wife, Sara, had died in 1841, aged thirty-five,
leaving him two daughters, Suzannah and Marie. Suzannah, in 1856, was
nineteen, eight years younger than Ibsen. Her closest friend was a girl of the
same age named Karoline Reimers; they "subscribed to the same lending
library, and often sat back to back on a sofa reading novels. They
promised each other that if the one should have a son and the other a
daughter, the two should marry; and so it turned out."[15] Karoline Reimers
was destined to become the wife of Bjørnstjerne Bjørnson; she lived into
her ninety-ninth year, and gave her daughter, Bergliot, a vivid description of Suzannah at that time, which Bergliot recorded nearly a century
later:

> The Dean's study was lined with books, and Magdalene Thoresen, being
> an authoress, gave the house an added literary atmosphere. But Suzannah
> Thoresen was not just generally interested in literature; she was a bookworm,
> with a voracious appetite. . . . She was especially interested in the drama,
> being herself of a dramatic temperament. Her descriptive power was on
> occasion so imaginative that both her sister Marie and her mother would
> burst into laughter; but then she would laugh herself, for she had a great
> sense of humour. But what was most deep-rooted in her nature was, and
> remained, her sense of the epic in life, her feeling for everything that was
> intense and powerful like herself, her understanding of the monumental and
> the tragic. No wonder that both her sister Marie and her friend Karoline
> began to whisper that the young dramatist at the city theatre, Henrik Ibsen,
> was the man for Suzannah.[16]

Bergliot herself remembered Suzannah only as "an old woman, crippled
by gout, sitting motionless in a chair, sharp of feature and dim of eye."[17]
But a photograph of her in her early thirties, fifteen years after Ibsen met
her, shows a lively face, not classically beautiful but attractive and well-

[13] Marcus Grønvold, p. 144, quoting his father.
[14] Bergliot Ibsen, *De Tre* (Oslo, 1948), p. 13, presumably quoting either her
mother or her mother-in-law.
[15] *Loc. cit.*
[16] *Ibid.*, pp. 13–14.
[17] *Ibid.*, p. 17.

proportioned, with unusually fine eyes. She was famous for the beauty of her hair. "Everyone in Bergen talked about it," writes Bergliot Ibsen. "Once it was even weighed on a festive occasion in the town; and it was so long that it stretched right down to her feet like a cloak, chestnut brown and splendidly wavy. Her figure had always been somewhat full, but the taste of the time was different from ours. Her sister Marie was the prettier, but Suzannah's face acquired a beauty from the strength and vitality that coursed through her."[18]

Suzannah's views on most matters were, partly no doubt thanks to the influence of her stepmother, advanced to the point of radicalism, and she was probably the first "new woman," apart from Magdalene herself, whom Ibsen had ever met. It is easy to imagine the effect she must have made on the lonely and restless young poet; less easy to guess whether Magdalene, never averse to the admiration of young men (she was later to have a celebrated passion for Georg Brandes, twenty-two years her junior), was pleased to note this, or a little jealous. Ibsen, at any rate, was immediately attracted by Suzannah, and she by him. Their second and decisive meeting took place later that month at a ball in Bergen given by the local Philharmonic Society. Here, Bergliot tells us (and her mother and both parents-in-law were present on the occasion) "he did not dance, and neither did she. They talked together deep into the night; and that same night he wrote to her that if she would join her destiny to his, he could become something great in the world." Later he was to re-create the atmosphere of that evening in an exquisite love poem, entitled "To the Only One."[19]

Ibsen now became a constant visitor to the Thoresen household; which, as Bergliot Ibsen observed, presumably on her mother's information, "must surely have both astonished and vexed the admired Magdalene Thoresen, to see the young Ibsen paying court to her stepdaughter and not to herself."[20] Before the end of the month he sought formal permission to ask for Suzannah's hand. Halvdan Koht, who knew both Ibsen and Suzannah and presumably had the story from one or other of them, or perhaps from Karoline Reimers-Bjørnson, tells what followed:

> He went in his best clothes to receive an answer, and was shown into an empty room to wait for her. Time passed, and she did not come. He paced to and fro, sat down, got up, became more and more restless. Finally, in despair, he moved towards the door. Then he heard a laugh from beneath

18 *Loc. cit.*

19 It has sometimes been stated that he sent her this poem that same night as a form of proposal, but this seems rather doubtful. He wrote several other poems to Suzannah during their courtship, but only one other has survived; she destroyed the rest, and also, it seems, all his early letters to her, shortly before her death. "Our relationship," she said, "concerns no one but ourselves." She was, to the last, the most formidably inflexible of women.

20 Bergliot Ibsen, p. 18.

the sofa, and a head peeped out; she had been hiding there all the time. She gave him her answer, and they became engaged.[21]

His position and prospects were, however, not yet adequate to support a wife, and it was to be two and a half years before they could marry.

Magdalene Thoresen commented briefly: "The engagement went off very quietly, and gave not the slightest occasion for strong outbursts of emotion."[22] Her attitude towards her future stepson-in-law remained, throughout her long life, curiously ambivalent. "Henrik Ibsen," she continues in the same memoir, recorded in 1871, "was a silent, withdrawn person whom no one got closer to than he, Ibsen, wished. This strong reserve became the weapon with which he kept clear the ground about him. . . . Even in one of his more inspired moods, when he would be caught up in a swift exchange of conversation and ideas, his personality was on guard, and the famous 'three steps from life' were never crossed. . . . Even with the woman who approached him willingly and admiringly he seemed to lack the abandon to yield to her power of enchantment. As a young man he had a certain awkwardness about him, as though groping for a foothold, which in most people would have suggested a mental confusion. But his clear glance was so firm and sure that no one could doubt that this man knew where he was going. Yet one couldn't help smiling at him."

"Even with the woman who approached him willingly and admiringly . . ." It is difficult not to believe that Magdalene was speaking here from personal experience. Ibsen, after all, was eight years her junior; and Bjørnson, who was to succeed Ibsen at Bergen the following year, was four years younger than Ibsen. "I know immediately," she recorded later, "if I make an impression on people and gain power over them. It happened with Bjørnson. We two understood each other at once, we shared the same instincts. . . . I was born anew, I understood myself, it was then that I first really became a writer. No one has been as spiritually akin to me as he was, he is in truth my spiritual father. I had to love him."[23] The pattern was to be repeated with the yet younger Georg Brandes.

Magdalene, in the same memoir, goes on to make an interesting comparison between Ibsen and another writer of genius whom she had met in her own country of Denmark. "One couldn't restrain an involuntary smile—and that awoke a memory. As a young girl I had once met Søren Kierkegaard. It now occurs to me that there was a striking similarity between these two great spirits. Outwardly the resemblance was small;

[21] Koht, I, 125.

[22] Interview with G. Knudtzon on 28 April 1871, checked and added to by Magdalene, first printed in *Juleroser* (Copenhagen, 1901), and reprinted with comments in Karl Larsen's introduction to his edition of the epic version of *Brand*.

[23] *Breve fra Magdalene Thoresen, 1855–1901*, ed. J. Clausen and P. F. Rist (Copenhagen, 1919), p. 43.

Søren Kierkegaard was long-striding and gangling, while Ibsen took short paces and had the squat build of a miner. What similarity there was must, therefore, have lain deeper; and so it was. I have never seen in any other two persons, male or female, so marked a compulsion to be alone with themselves."

That spring of 1856 was a good one for Ibsen. On 13 March *The Feast at Solhaug* was produced in Christiania, and received a considerable ovation. Six days later it was published there by Christian Tønsberg— the first book by Ibsen to appear since *Catiline,* and the first to carry his name on the title page.[24] Critical opinion, admittedly, was less favourable than the reception by the first night audience had been; he was accused of having plagiarised both Henrik Hertz's *Svend Dyring's House,* an inferior melodrama written ten years earlier (and which Ibsen had directed on 24 February 1856 in Bergen), and Heinrich von Kleist's *Kätchen von Heilbronn*—a charge which the Danish press later repeated, and which Ibsen was angrily to rebut in his 1883 foreword to *The Feast at Solhaug,* concluding his assault on the critics by expressing the hope that "people may in the future allow to each of us three Henriks un-disputed possession of what rightly belongs to him." One of the few critics to praise the play in print was Bjørnson who, we must remember, had at this time scarcely met Ibsen, and who wrote a dynamic notice of the work in *Morgenbladet.* "It was," commented Ibsen in the same forword, "not in the real sense a review or a criticism, but rather a brilliant free fantasy, a poetic improvisation on the subject of the play and its performance." *The Feast at Solhaug* was repeated five times in Christiania that season, a sign of fair success for a comparatively serious work.

While all this was happening in Christiania, Ibsen was far to the north in Trondhjem where, under his supervision, the Bergen company had just arrived to play a short season. He wrote four business-like reports to his board that March; practical matters kept him very busy. "I am pleased to inform you," he told them on 3 March, "that we all arrived here in good order on Sunday afternoon. During Monday and Tuesday we obtained the permission of the local authorities to hold performances, engaged orchestral players, singers, walk-ons, a property master, etc. Subscription lists were issued and circulated in the town. I have succeeded in agreeing inexpensive terms for the hire and improvement of the more essential items of decor. . . . Yesterday (Wednesday) we presented *Bureaucracy*[25] and *The Monkey.*[26] Fru Isachsen has still lost her voice, so I gave her role (in the first-named play) to Frøken Jensen, who acquitted herself well. . . . The takings at yesterday's performance amounted to 122 specie-dollars which must be reckoned good, especially considering the dreadful

[24] It sold poorly, however; it took fifteen years to exhaust the small edition.

[25] A comedy by F. L. Høedt based on Jean François Bayard's *Un Château des Cartes.*

[26] A vaudeville by Johanne Luise Heiberg.

weather and the choice of plays; *Bureaucracy* has a poor reputation here, having been twice very ill played by Danish actors (and whistled), while *The Monkey* has been acted here innumerable times. But . . . both plays were greeted with loud and sustained applause. Interest in our theatre is great. . . . The gas lighting is calculated to cost roughly 3 specie-dollars per performance, rehearsals included."

Having got the Trondhjem season safely launched, he sought permission to come home before the rest of the company. "Although actual theatrical matters occupy only a small part of my time during our stay here in Trondhjem," he wrote to the board on 31 March, "daily trivialities prevent me from concentrating in peace on a task which it is essential that I complete as soon as possible; I therefore beg your permission to return to Bergen by the next steamer." He was not, as far as we know, working on any new play at the time, but the company was due to stay in Trondhjem for a further two months, and three months, especially in the Scandinavian spring, is a dangerously long time to leave a self-willed young lady without an escort. The board, whether or not they knew the real reason for his restlessness (and in a town as small as Bergen, one suspects that they did), agreed to his request and sent Laading up to replace him. A month later *The Feast at Solhaug* was added to the repertory there, and on 26 May Laading reported that it was a success. "After the performance," he added, "we gathered on the stage and drank Ibsen's health on the house. After the dessert the bride and bridegroom [*sic*] were toasted, and H. Nielsen was authorised to convey to Ibsen and his chosen one the good wishes of the entire company."

That summer the theatre at Bergen was honoured, and nearly bankrupted, by two royal visits. In July Crown Prince Carl, soon to become King Carl XV, announced his intention of descending on the town, together with the young Prince of Orange. The theatre was redecorated for the occasion, an expense which could ill be afforded; and a grand banquet was laid on, including, so Peter Blytt (who, as chairman of the board, was principally responsible) tells us, "every wine of the choicest vintage." The two princes were expected in the early afternoon, and the reception committee, together with the garrison, a band, and most of the populace, assembled at three o'clock to welcome them. They waited; hour after hour passed; but no prince appeared. Evening came, and still there was no sign. Eventually, at midnight, the royal vessel was sighted, and anchored a mile offshore. The Crown Prince had enjoyed the ale and, no doubt, the other attractions provided for him at Hardanger so much that he had refused to leave, "despite repeated reminders from his distinguished entourage." Now, however, he was here, and would soon surely be rowed ashore in the royal barge by the pick of Bergen's oarsmen, who had joined the ship at Hardanger for this purpose. But no barge was to be seen, and it was not until nearly one o'clock in the morning that the princes finally landed, ten hours late, from a small dinghy. The Bergen oarsmen had, shameful to relate, regaled themselves over-merrily like their master, and had smashed the barge against the buoy.

The royal visitors stepped ashore amid huzzas, but there were further worries in store. The Crown Prince's equerry asked what play was to be performed on the morrow and, when informed that it was to be a new musical comedy "with witty songs" by Jens Christian Hostrup entitled *Fun in the Army,* declared that under no circumstances could this be shown, since the Crown Prince regarded one of the characters as an insult to Sweden. At a few hours notice, therefore, the theatre had to substitute J. L. Heiberg's vaudeville *No,* which passed without offence. Even then, their troubles were not over. When, at the banquet, the Crown Prince was asked what he would like to drink, he graciously enquired what they had. "I think," said Blytt proudly, "we can say we have anything that your Royal Highness could demand." The Crown Prince replied that if this was so, he would like nothing better than a glass of Hardanger ale, which he had sampled the previous day for the first time and thought the best beer he had ever tasted. This was, of course, the one thing that the organisers had not thought of, and Blytt had to keep the Crown Prince engaged in what must have been a thirsty conversation while emissaries hastened into the town to knock up the more discriminating beer-drinkers and ask if they could supply the need. But none of the ale could be found, and "their Royal Highnesses had to slake their thirst with other beverages, which Orange, who was scarcely more than seventeen or eighteen, did so thoroughly that H.R.H. became quite unsteady."[27]

That was awkward enough for everyone concerned with the theatre, but it was nothing to what followed. On the afternoon of Saturday, 23 August, Prince Napoleon, the son of King Jerome Napoleon and nephew to Napoleon I, landed completely unannounced in the city, asked if it contained a theatre and, on learning that it did, "thrice expressed the wish to see a performance" on the following day, before departing on the Monday. The theatre was by now closed for the summer recess, the actors were all holidaying out of town, and the Prince's request did not reach Peter Blytt until ten o'clock that Saturday night, when he was in bed with a painful attack of gout, and had to go to be presented to the Prince wearing one shoe and one galosh, the afflicted foot being too swollen to take any more elaborate form of footwear. Blytt did not quite see how the company could be reassembled and re-rehearsed in what was, after all, less than twenty-four hours; however, he said he would see what could be done, and sent a message to Ibsen telling him to come and see him at once.

Ibsen, who had also gone to bed, in due course appeared, "evidently in no good humour," and told the board that what they were asking was quite impossible. Blytt asked whether, since most of the company, in-

27 This anecdote and the one which follows are related in detail by Blytt, pp. 88 ff.

cluding the leading players, were known to be together at Kolstien just outside town, a messenger could not be sent to summon them back. Reluctantly Ibsen wrote a letter, asking them to return first thing in the morning; then, after it had been despatched, "became more abrupt and unforthcoming than usual. He spoke only when directly addressed, and made no suggestions as to how the various difficulties might be overcome. Suddenly he jumped up and said with vehement irritability: 'No, it's no good—I've just remembered. We have no orchestra. All the wind instruments have been commandeered for tomorrow by the steamer *Patriot* for its cruise to Hardanger. I'd forgotten.'"

Blytt said that this could surely be countermanded. Ibsen still shook his head. Then Blytt had a brilliant idea. "It would be a pity if we had to cancel the performance," he said, "for the play we had in mind to show His Royal Highness was *The Feast at Solhaug*. It is as Norwegian as anything in our repertory—Norwegian author, Norwegian subject, Norwegian costumes—all of which unfamiliar material cannot but enrapture Prince Napoleon." At this, Blytt tells, "a marked change became noticeable in Ibsen. He suddenly became transformed into a bundle of energy and vitality, and looked interested, happy, and hopeful. The difficulties began to vanish." Ibsen promised to conduct a rehearsal at eight the next morning. The wives of the board, plus Magdalene Thoresen, were bidden to prepare a supper of, indigestible as it sounds, "ice cream, cakes, fruit, confectionery and champagne," and to lend their best china and silver, "there being no hotel in the town then." Real gold and silver cups for use on stage in the performance were to be borrowed from local goldsmiths, and posters were to be run off by a relative of one member of the board who fortunately happened to be a printer, so that the citizens might be informed and a full audience assembled.

Early the next morning Blytt received a note from Ibsen telling him that "the company had arrived early and in the best of spirits, delighted at the honour of being asked to play before Prince Napoleon." And at seven o'clock that Sunday evening the performance took place. Prince Napoleon, who knew no Norwegian, had asked for a written synopsis of the play in French; but the few French and French-speaking people in the city were all engaged in the preparations for the banquet, except for the local barber who was regarded as unsuitable. Blytt, however, knew German and, on enquiring whether the prince understood that language, and finding that he did, having, surprisingly, taught it once in Alsace ("the reader of these lines may shake his head in doubt, but I can swear on my honour and conscience that Prince Napoleon actually told me this"), stood behind him throughout the performance, despite his gout (and still clad in a galosh?), giving the prince and his suite, which included Ernest Renan, a brief résumé before each act of what was to come.

During the second interval the author and his company were presented, whereupon "Ibsen offered the prince a handwritten copy of the play bound in red Morocco. He received it graciously, took wine with Ibsen, and promised that he would see that the play was translated into French and performed at the Imperial private theatre at St. Cloud.[28] He also ordered a copy, exactly similar in colour and cut, to be made of the costume that Louise Brun had worn [as Margit], which, executed in silk and velvet, he proposed to present to the Empress Eugénie. This, before being despatched, was exhibited in Bergen, and aroused much admiration." The prince enjoyed his visit so much that he postponed his departure by a day, and attended a special ball hastily arranged by some local bigwigs, to which Ibsen and several of the company but, to Blytt's rage, on account of some private quarrel, none of the board were invited.

Some time during that summer or autumn Ibsen settled down, no doubt with greatly increased confidence, to write another play for the next January anniversary. After the success of *The Feast at Solhaug* it seemed obvious to attempt another comedy in the balladic manner; and he bethought himself of the theme on which he had begun to work during his first year at Christiania in 1850, and raked out the unfinished manuscript of *The Ptarmigan of Justedal*.

To complete this in its original metre would have meant abandoning the style which had served him so well in *The Feast at Solhaug*, for *The Ptarmigan of Justedal* was, so far as it went, written in unrhymed blank verse, and Ibsen wished to use again a mixture of prose and rhymed verse of varying rhythms as found in the ballads. He therefore rewrote it completely, retaining only the original idea of a girl (still named Alfhild) who was the sole survivor in a valley devastated by the Black Death, and thus lived a wild, bird-like existence uncontaminated by the materialism of civilisation; and also the character of the wandering singer. Apart from this he kept nothing. Not a single line of *The Ptarmigan of Justedal* is carried over.

He found the theme for his new play in a ballad in Landstad's collection about a character named Olaf Liljekrans who, while out riding the evening before his wedding, is killed by fairies because he will not let them seduce him into joining them. Ibsen set his drama in the Middle Ages, in a village in the Norwegian mountains. Two families have waged a vendetta for generations; now their two present heads, Arne of Guldvik and Dame Kirsten Liljekrans, have decided to end the quarrel and merge their fortunes by marrying Dame Kirsten's son Olaf to Arne's daughter Ingeborg. In a spirited opening scene, Arne and his followers, on their way to the wedding, are met by Dame Kirsten in a state of great confusion; Olaf has disappeared. Wandering in the mountains, he has met the strange, half-elfin girl Alfhild, and has been bewitched by her innocence (as Johannes, in *St. John's Night*, was bewitched by the innocence of the unworldly Anne). Arne suspects trickery, and his daughter, Ingeborg, is furious; she is in any case half-infatuated with her father's servant, Hemming. However,

[28] Neither of which things happened.

Olaf and Alfhild are now discovered, and are persuaded to come down to the village; Dame Kirsten thinks she can settle things by marrying off Alfhild to one of her servants.

Alfhild is told that a wedding will be arranged for her, and assumes in her innocence that her husband is to be Olaf. He, meanwhile, back among civilised people, weakly agrees to marry Ingeborg. When Alfhild discovers the truth, she bars the doors and windows of the house, sets fire to it and flees back into the mountains. The guests manage to get out, and Ingeborg runs away with Hemming, also into the mountains; she no longer wishes to marry a man who does not love her. Dame Kirsten, Arne and their followers pursue Alfhild and capture her; then, on the mountain-side, Dame Kirsten, as is her right under feudal law, sentences Alfhild to be thrown to her death unless any man can be found willing to marry her. She proclaims this twice, and no one answers; at the third and final proclamation, however, Olaf claims her as his. Dame Kirsten has no alternative but to accept the situation, and Arne reluctantly has to agree to his daughter, Ingeborg, marrying his servant Hemming (being much more worried at the prospect of losing his best servant than at his daughter marrying beneath her).

Olaf Liljekrans was immediately accepted by the theatre for production the following January. During the last three months of 1856, before he got down to directing it, Ibsen found himself staging several worthwhile plays of a much better class than had usually fallen to his lot—none of them, needless to say, new. In October he produced two of Holberg's best comedies, *The Scatterbrain* and *Erasmus Montanus;* in November, Oehlenschläger's *The Vikings in Byzantium;* and in December, Scribe's best comedy, and perhaps the only play by him that stands revival today, *Une Verre d'Eau,* which is set at the court of Queen Anne and has as its main characters the Queen, Bolingbroke and the Duchess of Marlborough. (What with this play, Dumas's *Katharine Howard,* and two comedies by Alexandre Duval called *La Jeunnesse d'Henri V* and *Edouard en Ecosse, ou La Nuit d'un Proscrit,* which he had directed earlier, Ibsen was learning a lot of bad English history.) He also busied himself with preparing a lecture on The Heroic Ballad and Its Significance to Modern Poetry which he was due to deliver to the 22 December Society the following February, and which he later expanded into a lengthy essay.

After the success of *The Feast at Solhaug,* there was a great rush for seats for *Olaf Liljekrans* when it was announced for 2 January 1857. According to *Bergens Tidende,* "the demand was so great that only the stronger succeeded in forcing their way to the box office, under the present somewhat unfortunate arrangements for the sale of tickets." It was quite cordially received at its first performance, and the board rewarded Ibsen with an honorarium of 100 specie-dollars, a large sum when one considers his salary; but after his previous play expectations had been high, and among the public, and even more so among the critics, there was a feeling of disappointment. Peter Blytt noted that it was "little understood, and was not a success; the audience which had filled the theatre, hugely expectant, left in a cool mood."[29] Ibsen took a curtain call, and Marcus Grønvold, who was present, remembered him many years later "pale, thin, and with a full black beard."[30] *Bergens Tidende* admired the "pretty versification and often beautiful and poetic images," but plainly thought little of the plot, which it summarised disparagingly; and the correspondent of the Christiania *Aftenbladet* expressed himself bewildered by "all the confusion" of the action. (Ibsen reacted to the latter criticism with a sharp letter demanding that the reviewer justify his "mischievous and irresponsible" remarks, but received no reply). The play was repeated only once, on 4 January, and was never performed again in Ibsen's lifetime; nor was it published until shortly before his death, over forty years later. Ibsen himself rejected it as completely as *St. John's Night*. When writing to Julius Elias in 1897 about his various early works, he deliberately omitted all mention of it, and subsequent commentators have rather slavishly accepted his judgment.

In fact, *Olaf Liljekrans* is by modern standards a much better play than *The Feast at Solhaug*, or indeed than any other play that Ibsen had yet written except *Lady Inger of Østraat*. The principal characters are all sharply drawn: Olaf and Alfhild, confused and unhappy poetic creatures in a materialistic world; the crusty and avaricious Arne, the domineering Dame Kirsten, the spoiled, self-willed Ingeborg, and the proud, lonely minstrel Thorgejr, who acts as a kind of chorus to the action. The plot, which so confused the critic of *Aftenbladet*, is more complex than that of *The Feast at Solhaug*, which one would have thought a trifle uncomplicated even for the Bergen public, but it is less unravellable than that of *Lady Inger;* to a modern eye its complexity, yet lack of obscurity, is one of its virtues. The rhymed verse anticipates *Peer Gynt* in the freedom with which it changes from one rhythm to another; and here and there one perceives motifs which were to be echoed more strongly in his later, maturer work. The contrast between the purity of life on the mountain and the corruption in the valley was one on which Ibsen was to dwell in his long poem "On the Heights," in *Brand* and, forty years later, in *When We Dead Awaken*. The reference to Alfhild's mother Ingrid, who was stolen by the minstrel Thorgejr on her wedding night and carried by him up into the mountain, is a clear anticipation of what was to happen to that other Ingrid in *Peer Gynt*. Moreover, Ingeborg's and Hemming's discovery in the last act that life on the mountain is not as idyllic as they had supposed, and that to feed and clothe oneself are practical problems that even the most romantic among us must face, shows that Ibsen, unlike some of his contemporaries who were attempting the same kind of play, had no illusions about the supposedly idyllic life of the countryside.

The main difficulty to a modern reader, and one which would probably

[29] Blytt, p. 12.
[30] Marcus Grønvold, p. 140.

prove insuperable upon the stage, lies in Alfhild herself. Two types of character are notoriously difficult to make convincing in the theatre, mad people and peasants, and a mad peasant-girl offers a formidable challenge to any actress and audience. Gerd, in *Brand,* can be made acceptable because she appears only in three brief scenes; but Alfhild is the leading character in *Olaf Liljekrans,* and Ibsen has, it must be admitted, put a deal of rather mawkish dialogue into her mouth. The play, depending as it does so much upon the lyrical quality and subtle rhyming of the dialogue, would be monstrously difficult to translate, and will probably never be adequately translated; but it is not to be dismissed as negligible.[31]

One curious relic of *Olaf Liljekrans* has survived in the form of six coloured drawings from Ibsen's hand. They have the appearance of costume designs; all are of characters in mediæval rustic dress. Two, which are similar, show a young man in national costume, confused and distraught, his fists clenched; the others, respectively, are of an oldish man with a staff, a stern middle-aged woman with arms akimbo and a threatening expression, and two young girls, both wearing bridal crowns, the one shy and innocent, the other sharp-eyed and purposeful. We have no direct evidence that these represent the characters in *Olaf Liljekrans,* but they correspond precisely to Olaf, Arne of Kildal (or possibly Thorgejr), Dame Kirsten, Alfhild, and Ingeborg.

On 2 February 1857 Ibsen delivered his lecture on The Heroic Ballad and Its Significance to Modern Poetry to the 22 December Society. On 17 April he sent an expanded version of this to Paul Botten Hansen in Christiania, hoping that the latter might accept it for publication in *Illustreret Nyhedsblad,* a literary periodical which he was now editing. The letter which accompanied this essay is, apart from business reports and requests to the board of the Bergen Theatre, a note to the publisher of *The Feast at Solhaug,* the brief letter to Botten Hansen in 1853 which has already been referred to, and a line of thanks to a lady in Bergen for praising *The Feast at Solhaug,* the first letter that we have from Ibsen's hand since that which he wrote to Ole Schulerud from Grimstad seven years previously, enclosing his elegy on the death of Oehlenschläger:

Bergen, 17 April 1857

My dear old friend!

I send you herewith, first and foremost, my warmest greetings, and secondly, some observations on the Heroic Ballad, in the hope that they may be found worthy of acceptance in your paper. Should you be willing to make use of the article, I beg that you print it in as large

---

[31] The prose, too, bears the marked and not altogether fortunate influence of the Icelandic Sagas (or Petersen's translation of them) in the frequent inversion of the natural word order—"Little shall it boot you . . . ," etc. The unnaturalness of verse works in the theatre; unnatural prose seldom does, except in comedy. But the discovery of this fact, and its corollary, that high tragedy could be written in ordinary colloquial prose, still lay many years ahead.

instalments as possible, and above all that you break it where most appropriate, and finally, that you pay particular care to correcting any errors of spelling or punctuation that you may find; for as I have, as you will see, had the manuscript fair-copied by someone else, and have only managed to glance through it.

I have often meant to write to you, but have always put it off. I once thought of sending you some travel articles, but nothing came of that either—however, this summer I intend to go on a long tour, and then perhaps I shall be able to send something which you can use.

Of my life here I can think of nothing of interest to tell you, except that last year I became—engaged to a daughter of Dean Thoresen here in Bergen (her stepmother is the authoress of *A Witness* and one or two other things which you have at various times reviewed in *Nyhedsbladet*).

I must thank you most warmly for your notice of *The Feast at Solhaug;* I sent my new play, *Olaf Liljekrans,* to the Christiania Theatre a couple of months ago, but Borgaard is not one of those who hurry about anything. My best play, *Lady Inger of Østraat,* he has refused to include in his repertory unless I make several changes, which I wasn't prepared to agree to; around the New Year I sent it to Chr. Tønsberg in the hope that he might publish it, which he couldn't for the time being, and since it is extremely important for me to get this, my best play, published, I beg you to take the matter in hand and do what you can for me. The play is with Tønsberg, read it through and—find me a publisher! I don't mind on what terms—I'll gladly forego payment if you can only get it printed—I'm sure that if you could be so kind as to try to do this for me, we'd succeed. It has occurred to me that it might possibly be published in aid of the Students' Union Building Fund—I would gladly preface the play with a short prologue dedicated to the youth of our three countries and the future of Scandinavianism. Dear friend! please help me—I give you a free hand with *Lady Inger,* bully a publisher till he gives in!!

Please send me a line as quickly as possible! Let me know how everything is with you and with our mutual friends in Christiania.

Best wishes,
Your affectionate
Henr: Ibsen

Eleven days later he wrote again to Botten Hansen:

Bergen, 28 April 1857

Dear friend!

A brief line only, since the post is about to leave. Call my article, if you agree: "On the Heroic Ballad and Its Significance to Modern Poetry." I cannot immediately think of any title which more accurately describes its content—"A Note on . . . etc." might not be bad—I could have written at ten times the length on this subject—but since the expression smacks of Ole Vig[32]—forget it!

Your suggestion of printing *Lady Inger* in *Nyhedsbladet,* and then doing an offprint, I think absolutely splendid. But the play won't possibly fit into two numbers; the best thing would be if each issue could contain one act. I trust that the offprint will be tastefully and attractively done, and give you full authority to handle the play as though it were your own property, and in particular to recover the manuscript which I previously offered to Hr. Tønsberg, for which purpose I enclose the necessary authorisation.

I should dearly like to see *Olaf Liljekrans* published in a similar manner as soon as it has been acted at the Christiania Theatre; but I still haven't heard a word from Borgaard about this. I feel strongly inclined to start a campaign against him about his refusal to stage *Lady Inger* in its present form. According to his letters he finds the play "poetic, full of good characterisations and powerful dramatic moments"—and yet—well, you'll be able to understand his motives when you read the play.

As regards payment, etc., I beg you to arrange everything as you think best, I shall be happy with whatever you decide. One thing more: in *Lady Inger* I have once or twice referred to the Lady's dead husband as Lord High Steward Henrik Gyldenløve, but I have since found that he was called "Niels Henrikson Gyldenløve"—but since there are already two Nielses among the characters apart from him, will you please just call him "Lord High Steward Gyldenløve" (with no Christian name). If you could drop me a line and tell me what you think of the play as soon as you have read it, I should be particularly grateful.

If you meet O. Schulerud, give him my regards. Abildgaard—yes, how are things with him? Why don't you make a trip to these parts? You'd find it rewarding; the landscape is magnificent; quite something apart.

Best wishes for now—I know you will do whatever is best for me.

Yours affectionately,

Henr. Ibsen

I am already working on a new play; it will be rather different from my previous works, in both tone and content.

H.I.

This "new play" was *The Vikings at Helgeland,* which he had begun to write in verse, but was to complete in prose in Christiania during the

[32] A Norwegian author whose death Ibsen was to commemorate with an elegy two years later.

autumn.[33] His contract at Bergen had expired on 1 April, and on 11 April he had signed for one more year; but in the event he was to stay in Bergen only for another five months.

Ibsen's article on The Heroic Ballad appeared in *Illustreret Nyhedsblad* on 10 and 17 May 1857, in two instalments each of about 3,500 words. It is a skilfully reasoned defence of his use of the ballad style in *The Feast at Solhaug* and *Olaf Liljekrans*. "The time will come," he wrote, "when our national poetry will return to the ballad as to an inexhaustible gold-mine; cleansed, renewed to its original purity, and elevated through art, it will then once again strike root in the people." He also made the interesting point that "it must some day surely be admitted that the iambic pentameter is far from being the most suitable metre for the treatment of ancient Scandinavian themes. This verse form is completely foreign to our national prosody, and only through a national *form* can full justice be done to national subjects. . . . The flexible metre of the ballad allows many liberties that are of great importance to dramatic dialogue, and there can be little doubt that this poetic source will sooner or later be used by poets who will exploit it to build upon the foundation laid by Oehlenschläger; for it is surely clear that his work can only be regarded as a foundation, and by this I imply no denigration of his talent, since it is a characteristic of whatever is good and beautiful that it is not a complete end in itself but contains within it the germs of a more absolute fulfilment."

Ibsen then goes on to make the point that the ancient ballad succeeds as no modern form does in reconciling the two worlds of the natural and the supernatural. "The Asa-worshipper, who was ignorant of the power of faith, created for himself a world in which the laws of reason were completely suspended; in this, the supernatural became *All,* and consequently *Nothing,* and thus he found a *modus vivendi,* thus he succeeded in reconciling faith with reason. The romantic view of life, on the other hand, follows another course, it pays homage to Shakespeare's thesis that 'there are more things in heaven and earth than are dreamed of in our [*sic*] philosophy'; it concedes the power and validity of reason, but together with, surrounding and permeating this is the Mystery, the riddling, the inexplicable, the Christian if one wishes so to call it, since Christianity is itself a mystery; it preaches faith in those things 'which are beyond comprehension.' This is where the mythical saga differs essentially from the ballad; the one is to the other as an ordinary story is to a fairy tale; the ordinary story does not embrace the miraculous, the fairy tale is rooted therein. It is this world, where the natural and supernatural co-exist, that the ballad reveals to us."

Hettner's teaching is apparent here; and the problem of reconciling the

---

[33] According to Henrik Jæger's notes of his conversations with Ibsen on 2 September 1887 (Midbøe, p. 143), Ibsen told Jæger that he finished the first two acts of *The Vikings at Helgeland* before leaving Bergen.

best of heathenism with the best of Christianity was one that he was to consider in *The Vikings at Helgeland* and to explore more deeply in *Emperor and Galilean*.

We know, disappointingly, virtually nothing of Ibsen's activities during this, his last summer in Bergen. He must have felt that the little town had nothing more to offer him, artistically or materially. He could not marry Suzannah on any salary that the Bergen Theatre seemed likely to pay him in the foreseeable future; he badly needed the security of married life, they had already been engaged for a year and a half, and he must have felt that if this delay were to continue indefinitely, he might well lose her. Nor can the apparently unending prospect of directing Scribe and his followers have offered any incentive to remain.

Suddenly an avenue of escape appeared. He got leave from 9 July until the end of August, and on 17 July he wrote to Botten Hansen in the capital:

My dear friend,

Tomorrow I leave on a three weeks visit to Christiania. Should you by any chance know how one acquires a decent room for such a period, you would be doing me a great service. I hope this letter will find you in town—I am trusting to *Nyhedsbladet* to keep you there—even now when everyone is moving out into the country—for the chief purpose of my trip is to enjoy myself and see old friends again. In great haste—

Your affectionate
Henr. Ibsen

He arrived in Christiania on 21 July. Two days later he wrote the following letter:

Christiania, 23 July 1857

To the Directors of the Norwegian Theatre at Bergen:

On my arrival in Christiania I saw in the newspapers a report which has probably by now also reached Bergen, and which I should accordingly like to correct. It asserts that the directors of the Norwegian Theatre in Christiania have entered into negotiations with me with a view to my taking over the post of artistic director at the Norwegian Theatre, recently vacated by Cronborg.

The facts are as follows. Some time before my departure from Bergen G. Krohn[34] received a letter from Engineer-Lieutenant Lund in which the head of the Norwegian Theatre enquired whether he knew of anyone in Bergen who might be willing to accept the aforesaid

---

[34] An actor at the Bergen Theatre. He later joined Ibsen at the Christiania Norwegian Theatre.

post. Krohn disclosed to me the contents of this letter (which was confidential), and I told him that if I could obtain release from my contract with the Bergen Theatre, and if the terms proposed by Christiania should prove acceptable, I might not be unwilling to accept such an offer. Krohn replied to them on these lines, and on the day I left Bergen I received from Lieut. Lund, on behalf of his directors, an offer to take over the aforesaid post at an annual salary of 600 specie-dollars, with the promise of a gratuity and an increase in salary as soon as the theatre could afford it.

The reason, gentlemen, that I did not inform you of this situation lay simply in the uncertainty which I felt about the whole matter; I felt I had to come and assure myself at first-hand of the theatre's circumstances and prospects, etc. This I have now done, and I am now satisfied that the Christiania Theatre is as securely established as that of Bergen, and that here, as there, there is a chance that something may be achieved. I need not stress the advantages there would be to me in living in the capital; they are overwhelming and, painful as it would be to me to leave Bergen and the Bergen Theatre, I cannot but question whether it would not be indefensible of me to reject the opportunity which now presents itself of taking up a not unrewarding post. I speak in terms of salary and material advantages, but I am, please believe me, not merely being mercenary, or ungrateful. I shall never forget the debt I owe to the Bergen Theatre, but I also have duties towards myself, and I have long found working conditions at the Bergen Theatre oppressive; every way in which I might achieve anything has been barred to me, my hands have never been free, and I have as a result felt daily frustrated by the consciousness of having to work without being able to accomplish what I desired. In now addressing myself to you and asking whether, in the event of my agreeing terms with the Christiania Theatre, I may be released from my duties at Bergen, and how soon—I regard myself as appealing not merely to my superiors, but also to benevolent counsellors who will not refuse to look at the situation from what is, to me, its most important aspect. Should I be released from the remainder of my contract, I should naturally feel bound to refund my last month's salary, which has been paid in full. I need scarcely add that, offered equal conditions, I should prefer to remain at the Bergen Theatre, where I regard myself as having grown up, but I know that the theatre cannot stretch its resources further than has already been done, and I feel sure you will not be surprised that I feel compelled to seize this opportunity of a securer future. I await your reply eagerly.

Your obedient servant,

Henr. Ibsen

During the days of waiting to know their decision, he renewed his acquaintance with Bjørnstjerne Bjørnson, whom he had met occasionally during his student period in Christiania and who was just completing *Synnøve Solbakken,* the peasant novel that was to make him famous. "Ibsen has come from Bergen—read his *Feast at Solhaug!*" wrote Bjørnson to the Danish critic Clemens Petersen on 2 August; adding: "I love him!!" On 4 August Herman Laading replied to Ibsen on behalf of the Bergen directors "regretting that your application should come at a time when, as you must know, any reduction in the number of our instructors will be especially felt, since with the departure of Brun [in April] practically the whole of our repertory has been dislocated; but the board feel that the obvious advantages which must ensue to you from your new appointment and from living in the capital must override other considerations. We therefore release you from your contract with the Bergen Theatre, and wish you every luck in your work for your new theatre, whose goal is our own."

On 11 August 1857 Ibsen signed a contract with the Norwegian Theatre of Christiania. On 21 August *Morgenbladet* announced: "Hr. Ibsen's appointment as stage instructor and artistic director at the Christiania Norwegian Theatre has now been confirmed. His salary is to comprise 7½ per cent of the theatre's gross takings against a guaranteed minimum salary of 600 specie-dollars per year. He has, as is well known, worked for five years at the Bergen Theatre, whither he has now returned to make preparations for his final removal. He is expected here at the end of the month."

Ibsen left Bergen as unheralded as he had arrived—indeed, more so, for no newspaper thought it worth while to inform its readers of his departure, the date of which remains unknown. He said farewell to his fiancée and on 3 September took up his new post in Christiania.

He had, including his study trip to Copenhagen and Dresden, spent five years and ten months in Bergen. They had, after the first excitement, been extremely frustrating. As a director, his hands had been tied; as an author, he had repeatedly seen every attempt he had made to experiment and diverge from either the antiquated conventions of static verse tragedy, or the banalities of nationalistic rustic comedy, derided. His voyage abroad had opened his eyes to the potentialities of theatrical art; he had seen *Hamlet* and *King Lear,* met Heiberg and Hans Andersen, seen Michael Wiehe and N. P. Nielsen, Johanne Luise Heiberg and Frederik Høedt, Emil Devrient and Boguwil Dawison act. Bergen must have seemed more than usually provincial to him after that, and he must have been hideously aware of the inadequacy of the performances which he directed, whether of his own plays or of others.

Nevertheless, it is easy to over-stress his depression. He may well have felt that, in spite of everything, he had developed his powers not unprofitably during those five years. He had written four full-length plays in that time, and re-written a fifth; admittedly, all but one had failed, but there is some evidence that even the "failures" were admired by a discerning minority. Some writers and artists, particularly if they are restless experimentalists, as Ibsen was to be all his life, are content with such recognition; conscious of the power and quality of their work, they know with the certainty of religionists that they are right and other people wrong. What they normally need is one other person who shares their faith in themselves; and this he had now found. As he packed his bags that August day in Bergen, Ibsen may well have felt that his time of fulfilment and recognition was at hand. If so, he was to be unpleasantly disillusioned. The six and a half years he was to spend in Christiania were to be far more chilling to his spirit than anything he had experienced in Bergen, or Grimstad, or Skien.

6

The Chicken Ladder

1857–1859

The Norwegian Theatre of Christiania, of which Ibsen in the autumn of
1857 found himself artistic director, was a more recent enterprise than
its counterpart in Bergen. At first a drama school, it had been founded in
1852 as an angry reaction by a few extreme patriots against what they
regarded as the failure of the Bergen Theatre to live up to its expressed
ideals.

The previous year, 1851, some working-class amateurs had given a few
performances in the vernacular at a Christiania theatre owned by Benedict
Klingenberg to raise money for such of their fellows as had been arrested
for supporting Marcus Thrane's socialist agitations. These performances
had increased the demand, already strong in the capital, for a theatre to
express the growing tide of nationalistic enthusiasm. Klingenberg had accordingly visited Bergen, and had been badly disillusioned by what he saw.
Not only were very few of the plays in the repertory Norwegian, and the
near-Danish *riksmaal* as much in evidence as the vernacular; worse, many
of the actors adopted a deliberately Danish intonation. On his return to
Christiania he formed a committee of three (the other two members, oddly
enough, both being Danes) to establish, as they proclaimed in turgid
language, "a training school for Norwegians who might have a talent for,
and wish to pursue, a dramatic career, but who lack the opportunity to
acquire sufficient education to enter the [Danish-controlled] Christiania
Theatre, where, in any event, the essentially foreign character of the
organisation proffers many obstacles to the advancement of those of native
birth."

This training school had opened in Møllergaden on 11 October 1852
with eleven pupils, mostly working-class and ill-educated. Cronborg, one
of the two Danish committee members and a former instructor at the
Christiania Theatre, was appointed general instructor and, since one of the

declared aims of the school was to preserve and encourage the Norwegian language, a celebrated champion of the vernacular, a pernickety linguist named Knud Knudsen, was engaged as "language teacher." Public performances were given; and the committee was so encouraged by the results that two years later, in the autumn of 1854, they dropped the description of "school" and proudly re-titled their foundation the Norwegian Christiania Theatre.

The idea of a Norwegian theatre had by no means been received with unqualified enthusiasm in the capital. Knud Knudsen tells in his memoirs how indignant the higher stratum of Christiania society, "more Danish than the Danes themselves," was to find actors in the theatre at Møllergaden speaking in the accent and idiom which Norwegians used, indeed, in private conversation, but regarded as unsuitable for public occasions; just as, a century earlier in Copenhagen, before Holberg had begun to write, we learn that the Danish language was never heard in a gentleman's house, and that polite Danes were wont to say that a man wrote Latin to his friends, talked French to the ladies, called his dogs in German, and used Danish only for swearing at his servants. Particular offence was caused by the fact that many of the actors at Møllergaden were from the eastern country districts of Norway and spoke in the despised "eastland" dialect. Bergenese was just acceptable, but eastland dialect, no. This contempt of the educated public had a damaging effect on the Norwegian company, who soon realised that if they were to progress in their career they would have, sooner or later, to perform elsewhere in Danish, however fervent their patriotism might be. Nor did the unfashionable situation of the new theatre help. Møllergaden was an ugly and dirty street, full of doubtful inns where drunken individuals engaged in horse-coping and similar ungenteel transactions. When the young Laura Svendsen (later Laura Gundersen) was asked by a relative why she did not perform at the Norwegian Theatre, she replied that she would sooner beg in the gutter.

The Christiania Theatre (such being the official title of the "Danish" Theatre at Bankpladsen) not surprisingly gave little encouragement to its new rival. An application from Knudsen and his committee for free tickets for their actors to the performances at Bankpladsen was refused; and whenever a promising player appeared at Møllergaden, the Christiania Theatre immediately tried to seduce him or her away with the carrot of higher pay. From the state, the new theatre received no more help than Bull had. Requests for financial support were repeatedly refused, the most recent appeal, only three months before Ibsen took up his post, having been rather unluckily rejected in the Storthing by 57 votes to 49, a majority of eight.

The Christiania Norwegian Theatre soon found, as the Bergen Theatre had, that to fulfil the ideals of experimentalism is easier in theory than in practice. Such new Norwegian plays as came their way were naïve and either undramatic or melodramatic. Nor could they follow the common practice of experimental theatres today when new plays fail, by taking refuge in the classics, firstly because the classics could not be translated into *landsmaal,* and secondly because the inexperienced actors were totally incapable of the heights demanded by classical tragedy or of the technique required for classical comedy. The translations, too, were mainly of poor quality, conveying little poetry or wit. Soon the directors found themselves compelled, like their fellows at Bergen, to fall back upon the staple diet of Danish vaudeville and French farce and musical comedy, so that it came to be said that a good singing voice was more likely to get an actor a leading part than acting ability. The usual evening bill consisted of two or three short pieces varied with songs, declamations, and *tableaux vivants.* After five years of activity no new authors had been discovered and neither the repertory nor the talents of the company had been noticeably broadened. By the spring of 1857 things were so bad that the committee considered winding up the whole project; but they decided to continue, and it was to remedy matters that they imported Ibsen to replace Cronborg as artistic instructor. Cronborg, apart from being a Dane, had been an actor very much in the traditional manner. They had appointed him because no qualified Norwegian existed; now that, in Ibsen, one had arisen, they gave him the job.

The reputation of the Norwegian Christiania Theatre when Ibsen arrived to take over on 3 September 1857 was, then, very low. Even those who sympathised with its aims found it difficult to give their whole-hearted approval. Lorentz Dietrichson, by now a student at Christiania University, recalled: "It did not stand very high in our favour when Henrik Ibsen became director, however nationalistically fervid we might be. The lesson that mediocre Norwegian art was better for us than good Danish art did not altogether strike home. . . . The pronounced eastland accent of the Møllergaden players, the amateurish new plays that were presented there, and above all the desperate attempts at neology with which the theatre diverted itself . . . failed to win our unqualified assent. This language movement made in all a dry and desiccating impression, frequently seeming to sacrifice drama to grammar. The public decided that it did not visit the theatre in order to learn grammar."[1] The newspapers, however, showed good will. During the summer of 1857, when the theatre was at its lowest ebb, both *Morgenbladet* and *Christiania-Posten* exhorted their readers to support it; and *Aftenbladet,* encouraging its subscribers to. attend Cronborg's benefit performance on 10 August and a farewell evening for him on 13 August, concluded: "Nor should it be forgotten that the theatre must now be regarded as having taken a step closer to its ultimate goal by appointing a native Norwegian as artistic director." One can understand how, to Ibsen, it must have seemed a promising field for activity.

[1] Dietrichson, I, 269–72.

Ibsen took lodgings in a house at the corner of Akersgaden and Carl Johansgade, and got down to work at once. Only a fortnight after his arrival, on 18 September, a double bill of two Norwegian plays was performed under his direction. Both were familiar works, by writers who had died ten to fifteen years previously: Henrik Bjerregaard's musical, *A Tale of the Mountains,* and Henrik Wergeland's sequel to that play. Ibsen contributed a rhymed prologue in praise of the two dead dramatists, and *Morgenbladet* remarked that "the stage management showed evidence of considerable care, and augurs well for Herr Ibsen's direction of the theatre." *A Tale of the Mountains* proved a public success, and was performed twenty-two times that season.

Most of the repertory that autumn consisted of revivals of plays produced in previous seasons—a fact that has surprised some commentators, but which is simply explained in Ibsen's report to his board two years later, on 2 July 1859. "Nothing had been prepared . . . and there was nothing new to begin with." The titles read dismally. *Cousin Lotta,* a vaudeville by C. M. Wengel; *The Cobbler and the Countess,* a musical by Ibsen's mentor in Copenhagen, Thomas Overskou, based on a French piece named *Riquiqui; A Foolish Girl,* a vaudeville by Erik Bøgh, adapted from a French comedy which had in turn been adapted from a play by Calderón (*Casa con dos puertos mala es de guardar*); and J. H. Wessel's old musical parody, *Love without Stockings.* The only three new additions to the repertory before Christmas were on the same level: R. Benedix's comedy *Die Lügnerin,* which had to be withdrawn after one performance; *Lazarilla,* an operetta based on Scribe's comic opera *La Chanteuse Voilée,* which was a success and achieved sixteen performances before the summer closure; and Alexandre Duval's comedy, *La Jeunesse d'Henri V,* which Ibsen had already directed in Bergen, and which managed nine performances. A revival of Holberg's *Jeppe of the Hill,* an old favourite about a peasant who finds himself rich for an afternoon, was the only play of genuine distinction to be produced that season.

Not that the quality of the repertory at the Danish-controlled Christiania Theatre was any different, or any better. This was clearly what the public wanted. Ibsen, in addition to his work at the Møllergaden theatre, wrote occasional reviews for Botten Hansen's *Illustreret Nyhedsblad* of the productions at Bankpladsen, an arrangement which strikes a modern reader as somewhat unprofessional but which does not appear to have caused any surprise or offence then. On 11 October 1857, less than six weeks after his arrival in Christiania, we find him castigating the theatre-goers of the capital for their lack of taste. The play under review was Hans Andersen's *A Country Tale,* adapted from Salomon Mosenthal's *Der Sonnenwendhof;* and Ibsen warned his readers that it could hardly expect a long run, since "its quality is essentially poetic. This is the age," he continued, "of transparencies, of clever technical effects. Technique, in the most superficial meaning of the word, is the only thing the public is capable of appreciating, and the theatre is perfectly justified, from a financial standpoint, in continuing as hitherto to present the more recent French works which have for so long constituted the basic diet of our repertory. These plays commonly display a skilled technique, which the public likes, and, which is probably even more to their taste, they have nothing whatever to do with poetry." Ibsen goes on to express sentiments which may surprise those, still, sadly, a majority, who think of him principally as a social realist on the strength of a few plays which he wrote in the middle of his career. Many people, he writes, "will regard this play as both untrue and unwholesome, because it does not bear a photographic resemblance to reality. . . . People demand reality, no more and no less. That art should elevate is not a popular conception." The only limitation of photography, he concludes ironically, is that it cannot, except in an abstract kind of way, reproduce colour; but this, doubtless, will soon be remedied, and an even greater realism will result, a tendency which art and poetry will doubtless follow in their quest for further popularity.

Two months later, in a tribute to the actor Anton Wilhelm Wiehe published in *Illustreret Nyhedsblad* on 13 December, Ibsen returned to the attack on modern French drama and photographic realism. Denouncing the former as "lacy weavings," which "so sadly flaunt virtuosity at the expense of art," and "can only degrade art into the vulgar emptiness of 'effect,'" he praises Wiehe for his "spirited pursuit, not of banal realism, but of truth, that loftier, symbolic representation of life which is the only thing artistically worth fighting for, yet the existence of which is acknowledged by so few"—a bitter comment from one who, during his six years at Bergen, had seen ridiculed every attempt he had made to rise above the contemporary level of taste, and only his one exercise in banality, *The Feast at Solhaug,* applauded. He was, over the next six years, to find the taste of the Christiania public as inflexibly wedded as that of Bergen to the mediocre and the trivial. The former, however proudly it might boast itself to be the country's capital, remained as determinedly provincial as the latter.

A further insight into Ibsen's feelings at this time concerning the proper purpose of drama is given in a long review by him, amounting to over seven thousand words, which appeared in the next two issues of *Illustreret Nyhedsblad* on 20 and 27 December 1857. The subject in question was a historical drama, *Lord William Russell,* by Andreas Munch (1811–84), a reputable Norwegian writer who had sat with Ibsen and Bjørnson in the author's box at the premiere of the latter's *Between the Battles* the previous month. Lord William Russell was an English Catholic who was executed in 1683 for supposed complicity in the Rye House Plot to assassinate King Charles II, and it is apparent from Ibsen's very favourable review that both the theme and Munch's treatment of it had considerably excited him. Attacking "the traditional demands which are made of tragedy in general," he writes: "It has become customary to expect from tragic characters a loftiness, a purification, a greatness of thought and expression, will and action, that shall fulfil the function of the Greek cothurn—namely, to give us the feeling that we are outside the realm of everyday life. But this achieves the exact opposite of its purpose; the world portrayed by the dramatist is rendered completely foreign to the spectator, no bond exists between us and the protagonist as he struggles and is defeated, and so he cannot fully engage our sympathy." One of the great virtues of Munch's play, Ibsen says, is that whereas "traditional tragedy presents minor gods, A. Munch's work presents great mortal men." Sixteen years later he was to explain his final abandonment of poetry as a dramatic medium in similar words.[2]

Ibsen then expatiates briefly on the proper treatment of symbolism, in a paragraph which should be compulsory reading for the many commentators who have written ignorantly about this aspect of Ibsen's work. "Every notable human being," he writes, "is symbolic, both in his career and in his relationship to history. But bad writers, misconstruing the theory that the significant phenomena of life should be intensified in art, make this symbolism conscious. . . . Instead of it existing hidden in the work, like a vein of silver ore in a mountain, it is continually being dragged into the light of day." One of the virtues of Munch's play, says Ibsen, is that "he has allowed the symbolism to stand there without commentary like a runic inscription, leaving it to each member of the audience to interpret it according to his or her individual needs. . . . It is no conscious battle of ideas that enacts itself before us, any more than that ever happens in reality; what we see is human conflicts, behind which, yet interwoven with them, ideas conflict and conquer or are vanquished. And the play does not end at the fall of the curtain on the fifth act. The true end lies beyond; the poet indicates the direction in which we may seek; it is now up to each one of us to find his or her own way there."

These two ideas, that tragedy should present recognisable human beings rather than superhuman creatures, and that symbolism should be integral rather than overt, were, in time, to become two of his principal dogmas as a dramatist. At this early stage of his dramatic career, however, cut off by his ignorance of all foreign languages except German from practically all great specimens of drama, save in clumsy translations and adaptations, and blinded by the claims of the nationalistic movement and his excitement at the discovery of ancient Scandinavian literature, he was still groping inexpertly towards a satisfactory form. This isolation from the main tradition of classical tragedy was, eventually, to prove his strength, compelling him to strike out hugely on his own. But the confusion and uncertainty in which he now, at the age of twenty-nine, found himself are clearly

[2] "What I sought to depict was human beings, and therefore I would not let them talk 'the language of the gods'" (Letter to Edmund Gosse, 15 January 1874).

shown in the play which he had completed a few weeks before writing the *Lord William Russell* review, *The Vikings at Helgeland.*

As explained, Ibsen had conceived this tragedy two years earlier in Bergen, as a result of reading N. M. Petersen's translation of the Icelandic Sagas, but had turned aside, under the influence of the folk ballad, to write *The Feast at Solhaug.* When he returned to it, during the spring of 1857 ("a new play . . . rather different from my previous works, in both tone and content," as he had explained to Botten Hansen on 28 April of that year), he began to write in verse, but abandoned that medium in favour of a prose based on the Homerically simple yet formalised language of the sagas. That Ibsen was aware of the difficulties of dramatising saga material is evident from certain passages in the essay on the Heroic Ballad which he had sent to *Illustreret Nyhedsblad* on 17 April 1857, when he was already working on the play. "The saga," he had written, "is huge, cold, remote, self-sufficient, epic, quintessentially objective. . . . We cannot see the saga age except in this cold, epic light. . . . If a writer is to create a dramatic work out of this epic material, he must inevitably introduce a foreign element. . . . The age and the milieu which had originally been offered us in an abstract and plastic form he now presents as a painting, with colours, light and shadows. . . . This dramatic treatment brings the saga age closer to reality, but that is exactly what should not happen. The statue does not gain by acquiring natural skin tints and real hair and eyes."

This incompatibility between saga material and dramatic form was a problem which Ibsen found himself unable to solve. The ancient Greek dramatists had solved it, but Ibsen knew no Greek and had very possibly never read a Greek play, even in bad translation; nor was the Norwegian theatre of the nineteenth century a medium remotely suited to epic presentation. *The Vikings at Helgeland* is a remarkable literary pastiche, and contains, buried in the impossible form of this pastiche, the kernel of what, over thirty years later, in a very different setting, was to become one of his greatest plays. It was the closest he had yet come to writing a great play; the construction, the consistency and development of the characterisation, and the sense of an inevitable working out of destiny evolving directly from given characters in given situations, are for the first time in his work under mature and successful control. Only the remoteness of these ancient, heroic figures, and, more especially, of the conventions which governed their lives, defeated him.

The Vikings at Helgeland is set in northern Norway during the tenth century. As in *The Feast at Solhaug* (and, earlier, *Catiline*), the two principal women are diametrically contrasted characters: Hjørdis is a ruthless and formidable visionary, Dagny gentle, uxorious, and practical. Each is married to a man who is her own opposite: Hjørdis to the peaceful Gunnar, Dagny to a great warrior, Sigurd, Gunnar's foster-brother. Hjørdis despises her husband for his gentleness; only one thing binds her to him. As a girl in Iceland she had, in a splendid symbol, been guarded in her room by a huge white bear "of the strength of twenty men"; no man might win her until he had killed this monster. One night, Gunnar had done this, and so she had become his wife; but their marriage has not been happy. She admires Sigurd, and he her, but he remains faithful to Dagny. During a feast, Hjørdis tries to start a quarrel between her husband and Sigurd; this so enrages Dagny that she reveals what Sigurd has told her, that it was he, and not Gunnar, who killed the white bear, in order that his foster-brother might win the woman he loved. Then, in the most effective, because it is psychologically the most modern scene in the play, Hjørdis and Sigurd, left alone, reveal their love for each other; neither has been happy in marriage; their good and gentle partners have not been what they wanted, and needed. Hjørdis tries to tempt Sigurd to kill Gunnar; but instead, he challenges Gunnar to single combat, knowing that, if he wins, the ancient laws of vendetta will compel Hjørdis to kill him. In the final act Hjørdis, believing that she and Sigurd can only be united in death, shoots him with her bow; but before he dies, he reveals to her that now they can never be together, since he, unknown to her, has embraced the Christian faith, and Christians and heathens can never meet after death. Hjørdis then kills herself in despair.

Thus bleakly outlined, *The Vikings at Helgeland* may seem little, if at all, superior to the static Viking dramas of Oehlenschläger; and the remoteness of the setting, the deliberate pastiche of the prose, and the Homeric simplicity of the characters make it unlikely that it could ever successfully be staged before a modern and sophisticated audience. In its own century it was to prove the most successful of Ibsen's early plays; the audiences who admired the Devrients and Frédéric Lemaître, Sarah Bernhardt and Henry Irving, liked their heroes and heroines to be huger than life, and *The Vikings at Helgeland* was to be performed more often in Christiania before 1900 than any of even his mature works. But for a play to work today one must be able to some extent at least to identify oneself with the characters; and the ethics and motivations of these mighty archetypal figures are wholly foreign to our own.

Nevertheless, *The Vikings at Helgeland* is of extraordinary interest to anyone who reads it with a knowledge of what Ibsen was later to write. Beneath the formalised characters of this ancient world with their strange conceptions of honour lies the story of Hedda Gabler. Hedda, like Hjørdis, dreamed romantically of heroes, was guarded against them by a "white bear" (in Hedda's case, a horror of things physical), married a gentle and unheroic man, was jealous of the tender and uxorious girl to whom her hero attached himself, and, in her frustration, sent him to his death and took her own life. There is even a scene in the second act of *The Vikings at Helgeland* in which Hjørdis passionately seizes her rival, Dagny, and

clasps her tightly, at which Dagny cries: "Let me go! I don't want to listen
to you!" just as Thea Elvsted, when passionately clasped by Hedda in the
second act of that play, cries: "Let me go! I'm frightened of you!" And
the great scene in the third act when Hjørdis and Sigurd sit down quietly
together and reveal to each other for the first time their mutual love that
can never find fulfilment, carries strong anticipatory echoes of that famous
scene when Hedda and Eilert Løvborg pretend to peruse the photograph
album. The sense, too, of fate spinning her inflexible web around men,
and of evil spirits ruling their world—"but their power is small unless they
find willing helpers within our hearts, and happiness is granted to him
who has the strength to fight against fate" (as Hjørdis tells Sigurd)—is
something with which we shall become familiar in every mature play of
Ibsen's from *The Pretenders* to *When We Dead Awaken*. Structurally, too,
The Vikings at Helgeland shows an important advance on his previous
plays in two important respects. It is blessedly free from the coincidences
and improbabilities of *Lady Inger* and *The Feast at Solhaug;* and it does
not contain a single monologue (though Ibsen was to revert to the monologue, with calculated effect, for a period later).

Ibsen's first months in Christiania during that autumn of 1857 must have
seemed full of encouragement. Apart from the relief of directing a theatre
without having to share the work with a *dramaturge* of superior upbringing
and education, other irons were beginning to glow in the fire. On 4 November *The Feast at Solhaug* was performed at the Royal Dramatic Theatre in Stockholm, the first time any of his plays had been staged outside
Norway, and it was well received. The same month, *The Vikings at Helgeland* was accepted by the directors of the Danish-controlled Christiania
Theatre for production the following spring. He had offered the play to
them rather than to his own theatre on the assumption, rightly as it turned
out, that his own actors at the Norwegian Theatre were as incapable of
high tragedy as the actors at Bergen had been. And as though his work at
the theatre were not sufficient to occupy him fully, he applied on 13 November for a university bursary in Scandinavian literature of 260 specie-
dollars a year (largely, one imagines, on the strength of his essay on the
Heroic Ballad). In his letter to the authorities he admitted that he "has
indeed not much to plead in support of his application, but ventures to
nominate himself since he has good grounds for supposing that other applicants find themselves similarly placed." Two months later, however, on
13 January 1858, he withdrew his application, having presumably decided
that the reorganisation and direction of the Norwegian Theatre was not,
after all, a part-time job.

The newspapers, meanwhile, were taking notice of the improved standard
of production at the Norwegian Theatre. That February a correspondent
in *Aftenbladet,* after complaining at the way in which the gallery is allowed
to dominate the style of performance, so that "inconceivable exaggerations,

vulgarities, and untruthfulness" evoke "hysterical applause," praised the "more faithful, if less technically skilled, interpretation of the author's ideas . . . than is often the case at the other, the Danish Theatre, despite the larger size and superior experience of the company at the latter." If only, the writer continued, critics would give a lead, the unfortunate public interruptions during performance, which are at present in danger of destroying the good work of the new artistic director, might cease. "However, Herr Ibsen will surely, being a man of creative power and sensibility, be able to guard against the effect of this repeated caterwauling on his sense of theatrical vocation; yet it needs to be remarked that at present he stands virtually alone, and alone in his vision; and it should not be so." It was to remain so for longer than the anonymous author of these lines could have guessed.

Another article at about the same time in *Christiania-Posten* gives an interesting picture of the difference between the new Norwegian Theatre and the Danish-controlled one at Bankpladsen. The audience of the one, we learn, comes in "working clothes," the other in "going-out dress." In the Danish Theatre the main purpose is to see and be seen, especially since it has acquired a new chandelier. "In the Norwegian Theatre the lighting is not quite so bright; there are no boxes to underline differences of class and wealth, and the short jacket of the hill peasant may be seen side by side with a coat of the most elegant cut. Yet if one of the regular Thursday patrons of the Christiania Theatre were to visit Møllergaden *incognito* he might find to his surprise that the acting was not so bad nor the audience so obtuse as he had confidently imagined." By and large the repertories of the two companies were very similar,[3] since both depended mostly on

[3] During Ibsen's five years at the Norwegian Theatre, the Christiania Theatre at Bankpladsen presented the following classics, mostly in clumsy and unfaithful adaptations: Sheridan's *The Rivals* (September 1857); Shakespeare's *All's Well that Ends Well* (December 1857) and *The Taming of the Shrew* (March 1858); Colman's and Garrick's *The Jealous Wife* (October 1858); Goldsmith's *She Stoops to Conquer* (November 1858); Molière's *L'Ecole des Femmes* (September 1859); Sheridan's *The School for Scandal* (October 1859); Shakespeare's *Much Ado about Nothing* (January 1860); Molière's *Le Médecin Malgré Lui* (April 1860); Shakespeare's *Twelfth Night* (November 1860), *The Merchant of Venice* (September 1861), and *As You Like It* (January 1863). In other words, the Danish Theatre presented on an average only two classics a year; otherwise the repertories were similar. (*Hamlet*, astonishingly, was not staged in Christiania until as late as 1870, apart from a single performance of Act 3 only in 1830.) During Ibsen's five and a half years of directorship, from 1857–63, the Norwegian Theatre, while not attempting Shakespeare, presented two Molières, one Musset, one Goldoni, one Calderon, and nine Holbergs. For the record, they also, during this period, presented nine Scribes, fourteen plays by Erik Bøgh, ten by Mélesville, eight by J. F. Bayard, four Heibergs, four Hans Andersens, three Labiches, one Sardou, one Kotzebue and one Dumas *père*. Cf. Øyvind Anker's *Kristiania Norske Theaters Repertoire, 1852–1863* (Oslo, 1956), to which, together with Audhild Lund's *Henrik Ibsen og Kristiania Norske Theater, 1857–1863* (Oslo, 1925), this and the following chapter are much indebted.

Danish adaptations of contemporary French and, occasionally, German comedies, musical or not. In anything requiring singing the Norwegian Theatre seems to have had a slight edge over its rival; moreover, the playing there was in general brisker, and so, we are told, was the scene-changing.

An interesting portrait of Ibsen at this juncture in his career is provided for us by Bjørnstjerne Bjørnson, who had recently returned from a year in Denmark and of whom, for the first time, Ibsen had begun to see a good deal. At the premiere on 27 October of Bjørnson's first play, *Between the Battles* (a fine one-acter, set in a moment of peace during a bloody civil war, and vitiated only by a certain glibness of climax which was to be one of Bjørnson's besetting faults as a dramatist), Ibsen had sat beside him in the author's box; and in a letter that November (which Bjørnson, as so often, forgot or did not bother to date) to the young but influential Danish critic Clemens Petersen, Bjørnson, who had evidently read *The Vikings at Helgeland* in manuscript, gives his impressions of his fellow-playwright. He found Ibsen, for his tastes, too derivative. "I'm afraid," he wrote to Petersen, "he must find a new and a different road before I can have any faith in him. In *The Feast at Solhaug* he has so buried himself in the heroic ballad that he ended up by becoming a ballad incarnate. To the point where he made the language his own. Then he moved on to the saga, and now he's emerging from that with all its expressions, its language, word for word, its least nuance and its dead poetry. He is a greater virtuoso than Ole Bull, let alone Henrik Hertz. He has a curiously dreamy personality which can't immerse itself in life but only in dead poetry. . . . In *The Vikings at Helgeland* he has recreated Sigurd Dragon's-Bane and the whole of that vast song-cycle and the legends which belong to it. He has pastiched it and dramatised it absolutely. That I must grant, and praise him for it, and yet I find myself fuming with indignation, just because he's so good and trusting that I can't bring myself to speak out. If it weren't that he's not big enough to believe me free from envy I'd have told him the truth all the same, in a quiet moment, if possible while I was pressing his hand. . . . Ibsen is making every ordinary human being who lived in Erik Bloodaxe's time just like Sigurd Dragon's-Bane. I can't believe that people who lived then were superhuman and godlike. No, damn it, they were human!"

It is scarcely possible to imagine two more contrasted characters than Ibsen and Bjørnson. Even Dickens and Thackeray were less dissimilar. Ibsen was small, gauche, self-distrustful, shy of women, physically unattractive and, artistically, a slow developer. Bjørnson was tall, powerfully built, self-confident, gregarious, an intensive and successful womaniser, and a brilliant public speaker, who achieved literary fame in his middle twenties. For half a century a violent and extraordinary love-hatred relationship was to exist between them, harsh words and condemnations alternating bewilderingly with protestations of admiration and devotion. The wonder is, not that their friendship was so perpetually troubled, but that somehow, in defiance of all probability, it eventually managed to survive.

We have disappointingly few letters from Ibsen's hand during the six and a half years that he was now to spend in Christiania. He must, lamentable correspondent though he was, have written at least occasionally to Suzannah in Bergen during the nine months they were separated (from September 1857 to June 1858), but she apparently destroyed his early letters as she did his early poems. "Our relationship concerns no one but ourselves." The only letter of interest which we have during this period is one dated 30 January 1858 to a friend seven years younger than himself, one Carl Johan Anker, who was now serving in the Norwegian Guard in Stockholm and with whom he had gone on a walking tour from Bergen to Hardanger and back in the summer of 1856. After the usual apology for silence, with which so many of his letters were to begin, he recalled their excursion affectionately, and continued: "I have often wondered what you must have thought of me then, whether you didn't find me walled about with a kind of off-putting coldness which makes any close relationship with me difficult. And yet I found it incomparably easier to make contact with you than with anyone else, for I found in you a spiritual youthfulness, a joy in life, a chivalry of outlook which warmed my heart. Keep all this! Believe me, it is not pleasant to see the world from an October standpoint; though, strangely, there was once a time when I wanted nothing more. I have passionately longed for, yes, almost *prayed* for, a great grief which might fill my existence, give content to my life. It was foolish, and I have fought my way out of that state of mind—but the memory of it will always remain." This is a very different Ibsen from the "merry and vital" young man whom Christopher Due remembered from Grimstad. Yet we should not, as some commentators have done, be unduly surprised at this. The shyest people often have one or two friends from youth, usually (as Due seems to have been) simple and warm-hearted extroverts, who remember them as open almost to the point of ebullience.

The first months in Christiania had been full of promise; the New Year (1858) was to bring two sharp disappointments. In February J. L. Heiberg refused *The Vikings at Helgeland* for the Royal Theatre at Copenhagen. "The Icelandic Sagas," he wrote, "have so markedly epic a character that they can only be mutilated by dramatisation. The wildness and crudity that they depict are palliated in the original by the epic method of presentation. But the moment one dramatises them one is merely left with the subject-matter in all its rawness." This judgment of Heiberg's has been condemned as dogmatic; but it is one with which most modern critics would surely agree (though one might think that a theatre director who

regarded the trivia of Hertz as worth staging could have taken a chance
with so patently more talented a play). A worse blow was, however, to
follow. On 9 March Ibsen learned that Carl Borgaard, the head of the
Danish-controlled Christiania Theatre, who had accepted *The Vikings at
Helgeland* for production that spring, was proposing to postpone production for a year "since the economic position of the theatre and its
immediate prospects do not permit of the payment of honoraria for original
works during the current season."

Ibsen reacted promptly and furiously. The day after he heard the news,
on 10 March, he published a violent attack on the Christiania Theatre in
Aftenbladet. Ever since its inception, he declared, the theatre had jealously
clung to everything Danish. The establishment of a Norwegian theatre in
the capital had now resulted in their deciding to leave the production of
all Norwegian plays to their rival, although they well knew that certain
works, especially those written in the mould of classical tragedy, could
be adequately performed only by trained actors such as the Danish, but
not the Norwegian Theatre possessed. The unofficial truce which had
existed between the two Christiania theatres must, he said, now be ended.
"The time has come," he wrote, "when the peace of our theatrical world
must and shall be broken. Either we must have a Norwegian Theatre which
understands, and has the power to work for, our national artistic interests,
or we must all pledge our allegiance to our so-called principal theatre, we
must all stream towards its doors even when it regales us thrice weekly
with translations scrabbled together from the four corners of the earth.
. . . And yet," he concluded sadly, "the time has now come when a worth-
while national theatre could be established. If the Danish Theatre with its
foreign tendencies and anti-nationalism did not block the path, one could
from the best Norwegian talent at the three theatres [i.e., including that at
Bergen] create a company which would realise the dream of a national
theatre, a theatre which would work hand in hand with our blossoming
literature." On 14 March, Botten Hansen wrote in *Illustreret Nyhedsblad*
supporting Ibsen, pointing out that the Danish Theatre's main success of
the past few months had in fact been a Norwegian play, Munch's *Lord
William Russell*, and that their excuse of not being able to pay for original
works rang thin in view of the fact that they had only recently raised the
salaries of several of their company.

A reply to Ibsen's accusation appeared in *Christiania-Posten* from the
pen of one Richard Petersen, a civil servant who later, not inappropriately,
became a prison governor. In a bitter personal attack on Ibsen, Petersen
dismissed him as "a small-time poet," with no right to set himself up as
spokesman for the nationalistic cause in literature. Ridiculing him for
"identifying himself with all native dramatic literature," he concluded:
"Herr Ibsen is a playwright of gigantic insignificance, about whom our

nation cannot with any enthusiasm plant a protective palisade. *The Feast at Solhaug* is altogether too lacking in originality to encourage any hopes for his future, and his next [*sic*] stage work, *Lady Inger of Østraat,* is devoid of idealism and poetry to a degree which can only be described as astounding. Every character in this play bears the stamp of baseness. . . . Under the circumstances Herr Ibsen should surely appreciate that the public no longer awaits his *Vikings* with any excitement, and that the present is not the most appropriate time to present a play of probably mediocre quality."

Ibsen plunged back into the fray with two further articles in *Aftenposten,* but a more effective, because independent, championship of his cause came from Bjørnson, who had in November succeeded Ibsen as *sceneinstruktør* at the Bergen Theatre. *The Vikings at Helgeland,* wrote Bjørnson in *Bergens-Posten* (28 March 1858), was "the best play that has yet been written in Norway. When it is staged, it will reveal itself as endowed with a scenic power unmatched by anything previous in Norwegian drama."[4] Bjørnson also wrote to *Aftenbladet* asserting that the Danish Christiania Theatre had now served its purpose, praising Ibsen and *The Vikings* in particular, and concluding: "If any feeling of decency exists in this country, we must put a stop to this scandalous maltreatment of Norwegian authors, and especially to the tendency to tread them into the mud merely to sustain the crumbling foundations of a Danish theatre."

On 25 April 1857, *The Vikings at Helgeland* was published as a special supplement to *Illustreret Nyhedsblad.* Twenty-two hundred copies were printed; which, since the magazine had, at that time, some thirteen to fourteen hundred subscribers, meant that about eight hundred copies were available for sale in the shops. The reviews were mixed, but in general the reception was favourable rather than otherwise—*Morgenbladet* hailed it as "a true national drama"—and the good notices were the first praise that Ibsen had received for any new work since the staging of *The Feast at Solhaug* in Bergen over two years before.

During all this controversy, Ibsen had been directing the usual succession of appalling plays at the Norwegian Theatre: Thomas Overskou's *A Chapter of Misunderstandings; Uncle,* a musical comedy by R. Benedix; *Clifford le Voleur,* a drama by Mélesville and Dubetrier; and a French musical entitled *The Day before the Battle of Marengo.* Scribe had, naturally, been represented, by three works, *Les Premières Amours, La Marraine,* and *La Chanteuse Voilée,* the last-named, with its sixteen performances, proving the principal success of the season. Nothing of any quality had been performed since Christmas except Holberg's comedy

---

[4] This is hardly the opinion of the play which he had expressed to Clemens Petersen; but Bjørnson, like Walt Whitman, regarded self-contradiction as a sign of mental flexibility. ("I contradict myself?" wrote Whitman. "Very well then. I contradict myself.")

Henrik and Pernilla, and that had been a revival of an earlier production. The only plays by living Norwegian authors had been Rolf Olsen's *Anna Kolbjørnsdatter,* and revivals of two old vaudeville successes, C. P. Riis's *To the Mountains* and H. Ø. Blom's *Tordenskiold.*

This lack of new plays, and in particular of new Norwegian plays, was noted by the board of the Norwegian Theatre at its annual general meeting that summer, and they instructed Ibsen to try to introduce more fresh material into the repertory for the coming season. A prize of 100 specie-dollars had in fact been offered on 22 November 1857 for "a full length drama (at least three acts), preferably a musical, the subject matter to be taken from our own history and the piece suited to the talents of the company"; but only three entries had been submitted, and none had been adjudged worthy of production. Nevertheless, the season had proved, on the whole, not unsuccessful. The takings, which totalled some 9,000 specie-dollars, had been higher than in the preceding year, and the theatre had more or less paid its way.

Preoccupied as he was with the practicalities of direction (he had somehow managed to get forty-four plays of varying lengths on to the stage during the season, sixteen of them being new productions), Ibsen had had little time for writing poetry. During January he published three occasional pieces in *Illustreret Nyhedsblad,* an elegy for the author Ole Vig, a "Festal Song" and an "Ode to the Memory of Carl Johan," all echoing his nationalistic work at the theatre and devoid of serious merit. These, as far as we know, were the only new poems he wrote during his first year in Christiania, though he published for the first time (also in *Illustreret Nyhedsblad*) several poems which he had written in Bergen, including "A Bird's Song," "Earth Flowers and Potted Plants," and "Building Plans," the original version of which (though he was to alter it significantly when preparing his collected poems in 1871) runs thus:

I remember as well as if it had happened today
The time I saw in the paper my first poem in print.
I sat there in my room puffing my pipe,
Exuding smoke in blest complacency.

I hummed and I read for surely the twentieth time
That paper, finding it strangely interesting.
And imagination played its restless game—
Well, what is life without a little madness?

I built a dream castle. The work went swiftly and well.
I set myself two aims, one little and one great.
The great aim was to become an immortal man.
The small, to own a lovely water-lily.

I thought it a noble and harmonious plan,
But then confusion entered into it.
As I grew sane, the whole plan went quite crazy.
The great aim shrank to nothing. The other was all that mattered.[5]

In June, a few days before the season at the Norwegian Theatre ended, Ibsen went to Bergen to marry Suzannah Thoresen. The wedding was celebrated quietly on 18 June 1858, under melancholy circumstances, for only seven days previously her father, the Dean, had died at the age of fifty-two. His death cannot have been unexpected, for the obituary notice in *Bergens Adressecontoirs Efterretninger* speaks of "grievous physical suffering." No eyewitness account of the wedding ceremony has come down to us; small loss probably, for who ever reported anything interesting about a wedding? Ibsen took Suzannah back to share his life in Christiania, taking the opportunity as the steamer touched at Grimstad to introduce her to his old friend Christopher Due. Magdalene Thoresen, before very long, returned to her native Denmark, where the sorrows of widowhood do not seem greatly to have inhibited her.

On 23 August the new season began at the Norwegian Theatre. Both it and the Christiania Theatre had decided on a policy of more new plays, to the pleasure of the newspapers; and the open quarrel between Ibsen and Borgaard seems to have had a good publicity effect, for both theatres found themselves playing to increased business. Every week, we learn, the Norwegian Theatre presented something new, if only a one-acter. On 1 October Ibsen was praised by a critic in *Morgenbladet*, who pointed out that he was answerable not only for the staging of the plays but also for the coaching of the younger and less talented of his players, "and has therefore much more responsibility than his Danish counterpart." Such

[5] A note accompanying this poem, "A Bird Song," and "Earth Flowers and Potted Plants," when the three were first printed in *Illustreret Nyhedsblad* on 14 March 1858, states that they "belong to an earlier period in his life." It has generally, and I think rightly, been assumed that "Building Plans," like the other two, was written either during or shortly after Ibsen's short-lived association with Rikke Holst in 1853. When Ibsen revised the poem in 1871 he rewrote it as follows:

> I remember as well as if it were yesterday
> That evening when, in the paper, I saw my first poem in print.
> I sat there in my garret puffing my pipe
> And dreaming dreams of blest complacency.
>
> "I shall build a cloud-castle. It shall shine over the North.
> Two wings shall it have; one little and one great.
> The great wing shall shelter an immortal poet.
> The small wing shall be a young girl's bower."
>
> I thought it a noble and harmonious plan,
> But then confusion entered into it.
> As the master grew sane, the castle went all crazy.
> The great wing shrank; the small fell into ruins.

productivity, declared the writer, can only be the result of "a harmonious co-operation between the director and his company, and a ceaseless striving towards a mutual goal." So extensive a repertory, the article concluded, might be supposed deleterious to the actors; but this was not the case. The plays were well rehearsed "and the roles well memorised." It is evident that Ibsen was, at this stage, pursuing his task with energy; and the public, too, was well pleased.

Yet the plays themselves were little more exciting than before. The staple fare continued to consist of light comedy, musicals, and vaudevilles, mainly Danish adaptations from the French. Thus, one of the chief successes of the new season was *Zoë, ou l'Amant Prêté,* by Scribe and Mélesville, of which a critic wrote that "the presentation was uncommonly agreeable and the instruction excellent." Madame Døvle, he declared, gave a "handsome and lively" performance in the title role, and her marked progress was attributed to "Herr Ibsen's talent for using her abilities, and those of the rest of the company, in the best manner." Another success was *Seven Girls in Uniform,* an adaptation by J. L. Heiberg of a German adaptation of a French comedy by Francis, Dartois, and Théaulon entitled *Les Jolis Soldats;* on 30 October *Aftenbladet* wrote that "one cannot praise too highly Herr Ibsen's energy in arranging so excellent a repertory and one must admit that he has been highly successful in choosing plays that suit the talents of his company."

Ibsen now decided to risk his company in *The Vikings at Helgeland,* rather than wait a year in the uncertain hope of the more experienced Danish players performing it. *Morgenbladet* (1 October) doubted the wisdom of attempting so difficult a play on so small a stage and with a company virtually devoid of experience outside comedy and vaudeville. However, in one of his letters to the press complaining of Borgaard's rejection of the play, Ibsen had observed that "only by seeing their plays performed can dramatists discover their faults and learn for the future," and Botten Hansen took the opportunity to remind readers of *Illustreret Nyhedsblad* how warmly the play had, when printed, been received outside Norway. Public interest was excited, and when *The Vikings at Helgeland* received its premiere at the Norwegian Theatre on 24 November 1858 the house was full and people had to be turned away.

The production, amazingly, proved a success. "That this uncommonly imaginative work, long known to readers, should succeed on the stage in its own right," wrote *Morgenbladet,* "was to be expected. What was not expected was that the Norwegian Theatre would give so worthy a performance. . . . The whole presentation is virtually free from serious criticism, something that seldom occurs in our theatres when a tragedy with so large a cast is staged." The management had gone to the expense of new decor and costumes, spending as much as 500 specie-dollars on the production. At the final curtain there was loud cheering, and "the

author, Herr Ibsen, was called for, and was thunderously applauded."
Aftenbladet remarked that the production was the first essay that the
Norwegian Theatre had attempted in "the higher dramatic art," and that
the result exceeded all expectations. "No effort had been spared by the
actors to see that the play should succeed, and encouraging outbursts of
applause occurred not infrequently. It did one good to hear the powerful
language of the play spoken in the homely accents of our mother tongue.
The diction was clear and none of the play's content was lost. . . . The
winter decor with the open, turbulent sea in the background was beautiful, and the scenic arrangements were generally successful." Botten Hansen
in *Illustreret Nyhedsblad* noted the significance of "a national play being
presented with every technical advantage that stage management can
provide," and took the opportunity to quote a laudatory comment upon
the play by a German critic.

The evening had, in fact, been a triumph for Ibsen, the last that he was
to know for over five years. Both the play and his production of it had been
acclaimed almost unanimously. Admittedly, a supporter of the rival theatre
wrote an article in *Aftenbladet* on 11 December accusing Ibsen of plagiarising the work of "a younger and more talented fellow-countryman" (a
reference to Bjørnson's *Between the Battles*),[6] and condemning the performance as "destroying the image one has hitherto cherished of the
characters in the Sagas"; but this evoked an eloquent retort in *Morgenbladet* on 16 December, and a party was arranged to celebrate Ibsen's
success as both dramatist and director, at which a speech of congratulation
was delivered by Professor M. J. Monrad. The first four performances were
well attended, with takings totalling 460 specie-dollars, a quarter of which
was allotted to Ibsen as honorarium.

But in spite of the excellent reviews and the attractions of the new
decor and costumes, the play proved to have a limited appeal. There
was not the same public in Christiania for a tragedy as for a comedy or a
vaudeville, and only four more performances were given that season,
compared with twenty-one of *Les Jolis Soldats*.

Nevertheless, by the end of 1858 the hopes with which Ibsen had come to
Christiania must still have been high. He had written a few poems for
special occasions during the autumn—for the fiftieth anniversary of a
society, for the inauguration of new school buildings in Lillehammer, for a
student ballet performance, receiving as payment now a silver mug, now
a punch bowl with matching glasses—and the tone of these is vigorous

---

[6] Ibsen had almost certainly read *Between the Battles* before writing *The Vikings
at Helgeland*, since Bjørnson had unsuccessfully offered the former to the Bergen
Theatre in the winter of 1856–57, not long before Ibsen began his play. But *The
Vikings at Helgeland* is no more imitative of *Between the Battles* than Shakespeare's
Richard II is imitative of Marlowe's *Edward II*. Hartvig Lassen, the author of the
article in *Aftenbladet*, was not the first critic to confuse imitation with the receiving
of stimulus.

and optimistic, almost Kiplingesque in its naïve nationalism. In December he wrote a more interesting poem in the same mood, "Gull Cry." The Danes were objecting that the Norwegians, by their chauvinism, were isolating themselves from the rest of Scandinavia and obstructing a closer union between the four countries. Ibsen, in his poem, retorts that the cry of the Norwegian gull is not beautiful, but that it makes that sound because it must; it is its nature. In passing, he rebuked the Danes for allowing their culture to fall so deeply under German influence. The language of this poem is deliberately very Norwegian, using several words and forms with which a Danish reader would be unfamiliar. One is reminded of the young James Joyce, fifty years later, similarly caught up in the toils of a nationalism which diverted his genius, and who, likewise, was not to fulfil himself until he had escaped from it into a self-imposed exile.

In January of the New Year (1859) Ibsen revived two Holberg comedies, *Jeppe of the Hill* and *The Peasant in Pawn,* and in March he produced, for the first time at the theatre, a Molière, *Les Fourberies de Scapin;* but, characteristically, none of these proved as popular as a slight vaudeville by Erik Bøgh called *All Possible Parts,* based on a French original but set locally at "the Hotel Nord in Christiania." Then, emboldened by the reception of *The Vikings at Helgeland* (which had also been staged at Trondhjem on 10 February and at Bergen on 4 March, the latter production being directed by Bjørnson, though with no great success[7]), Ibsen decided to see what his company could do with *Lady Inger of Østraat.*

Unfortunately, *Lady Inger* defeated the talents of the Christiania actors as completely as it had those of the company at Bergen. More than any other of Ibsen's early plays, *Lady Inger* requires, especially in the title role, the kind of acting between and against the lines that he was to demand in the prose plays of his maturity. This was something to which the inexperienced players of the Christiania Norwegian Theatre were not equal without the kind of forceful instruction which Ibsen was too shy to give them. Neither the press nor the public liked *Lady Inger* when it was

[7] "The play hasn't succeeded, though it may seem from a distance to have. . . . Ibsen has a little clique of admirers headed by *Nyhedsbladet*. But every time he has to face the general public everything goes wrong and I've had to go to his aid twice, because Ibsen despite his aberrations *is* a poet. And I hope some day to get him to be himself and turn away from all this damned pastiche. The day Ibsen admits *he is small* he'll become a perfectly enchanting poet. I've told him as much pretty plainly, but the result is, he's jealous. He's done all sorts of little things to annoy me, and does still. He's angry that I haven't put *The Vikings at Helgeland* into my repertory. . . . I haven't read his poem, 'Gull Cry'; I've heard it's rather affected stuff, and was written largely because a Danish monthly said he was a lesser writer than me. Now that's exactly the kind of thing that always distracts Ibsen from what he ought to be and do. The point is, he's a rather small and gnomish little chap, with no chest or rump, so he feels that as he has no other gifts he has to strain most frightfully when he writes. And so he doesn't write what he'd really like to, and could." (Bjørnson to Clemens Petersen, Bergen, 5 March 1859.)

presented on 11 April 1859, and the second performance, two evenings later, was so poorly attended that it was withdrawn and never revived. From the reviews of the play we learn among other things that contemporary Norwegian taste found it difficult to stomach what we would nowadays regard as a typical Ibsen ending; they wanted a play to conclude in calm and reconciliation. To remedy the financial loss incurred by this failure, the theatre engaged two English dancers, a pair of sisters named Agnes and Christine Healey, who filled the theatre night after night.

The success of the Norwegian Theatre caused the directors of the Danish Theatre to rethink their policy. On 13 January 1859 *Aftenbladet* had declared that a milestone had been reached in Norwegian theatrical history, in that the directors of the Christiania Theatre had decided "to convert our country's leading theatre into an entirely Norwegian organisation, emancipating it from Danish influence and . . . henceforth to make every effort to recruit Norwegian actors, and not in the immediate future to engage any more Danish staff." *Morgenbladet* took this information with a pinch of salt, observing (on 19 January) that it was excellent news "if this pronouncement is true," but warning the Norwegian Theatre not to place too much trust in these "magnificent promises." This scepticism proved to be justified, for the Christiania Theatre, when it came to the crunch, decided against dismissing their experienced players, and the feud continued.

At the annual general meeting of the Norwegian Theatre on 2 July 1859, Ibsen presented his report, which was fully quoted in *Christiania-Posten* (on 4 July). Surprisingly neglected by his earlier biographers, it gives us a detailed insight into his feelings at this time about his work as a theatre director. At the close of the previous year, he reminded his committee, he had been called upon to present more new plays; during the season just completed, he has staged no less than thirty-one, and now people are saying that he has gone too far in this direction. But it is not merely the number of new productions that matters.

> A theatre can be as active in a year in which it presents ten new plays as in one in which it presents thirty. The question is whether one wishes to see plays that have been adequately or inadequately rehearsed. . . . In the theatre one learns to be practical, to admit the power of circumstance and, when absolutely necessary, to abandon one's higher ideals. . . . This necessity arises, alas, all too often in a theatre such as ours, which has no means of support other than its daily takings, and where every possible economy must be exercised in every possible direction. It is this consideration that has guided my policy during the past year. Under the continual strain of three or four performances a week, the company has been forced practically throughout the season to start rehearsing a new play each Wednesday for performance the following Wednesday; so that it is understandable enough if the first performances of plays presented under such circumstances should prove more

satisfactory financially than æsthetically. The physical conditions under which we perform add to our difficulties. In a large auditorium one may aim at a general effect, but in one as cramped as ours an actor must concentrate more upon detail, and this demands a lengthier preparation and more thorough study if the result is to please.

While therefore all possible credit must be paid to the company for their enthusiasm and endurance, the ceaseless activity of the past year should not, from the theatre's viewpoint, be a matter for unqualified praise. One may accept it as necessary; but everyone who does not regard æsthetic considerations as irrelevant must, not merely for the company's sake but for the sake of our theatre, hope that this state of affairs will prove to be transitory. To express unqualified approval would be as irrational as was last year's allegation of insufficient activity because, it was said, too few new plays were being presented. I must therefore disassociate myself from the view that those allegations caused me to alter my policy. I was, even before my arrival here, too experienced in practical theatrical matters not to have determined the principles I had to follow.

Ibsen then recapitulates the conditions under which he took up his post.

I arrived here just as the season was about to begin. Nothing was prepared, and anyone who knows anything about such matters must realise that no theatre director can prepare a repertory for a company of whose capacities he is ignorant. If the selection of a repertory consisted merely of assembling a casual miscellany of plays and putting them on one after the other, the problem would be easy. But that is not the case. One must, as I say, know the material with which one is to work; one must also, regrettably, to some degree take into account public taste; one must seek a suitable balance between different types of play (so many with music, so many without, so many full-length, so many short, etc.); ideally, moreover, different schools of literature and different periods should be represented; and, finally, the parts must be fairly shared among the various members of the company. All this should of course have been prepared during the course of the summer, at least in outline; but I was not and could not have been prepared. The season began, and there was nothing new to begin with. I must therefore refute the accusations made at the last annual general meeting. . . .

Ibsen concluded his report by stressing the need for enlarging and improving the theatre.[8] Economically as well as artistically, he explained, this would prove advantageous, "since it is an accepted rule that a larger theatre attracts a larger public, and through a larger public, and only thus, can we expand our technical resources so as to achieve the artistic result towards which we must hope to strive."

[8] *Morgenbladet*, on 16 October 1859, commented on a production of Holberg's *Jean de France* that the stage was so small that four people seemed a crowd, while anyone who stood alone in the wings "looks a Goliath."

But if the results of the season had not satisfied Ibsen's "higher ideals," they had, financially, proved highly successful.[9] The one hundred and thirty-one performances given had produced takings of just over 11,000 specie-dollars, a much larger figure than in any previous year since the theatre had opened. Admittedly, this had resulted in a loss on the year of 1,048 specie-dollars, but this was partly accounted for by the rebuilding of the stage machinery and various expenses inseparable from new pro-ductions, such as fees to authors and translators, new decor and costumes (on occasion), and the cost of gas for the many extra rehearsals. The main item of expense, however, was the rent. The committee had been offered the freehold of the theatre for 15,000 specie-dollars, and on 12 April they had announced in the press a "national subscription" to help raise the money. An upper limit of 5 specie-dollars per person had been set, and by 12 June, 2,000 specie-dollars had been contributed.

That summer, after the season at the Norwegian Theatre had ended, Ibsen paid a brief visit to Skien, not to see his family but to ask for financial help from his half-uncle, and most prosperous relative, Christo-pher Blom Paus, a merchant in the town. Hanna Olsen, at that time a maidservant of Paus, recalled to J. Brunsvig[10] nearly seventy years later how Ibsen had arrived in a top hat and frock coat. "He looked sad and dispirited; his clothes were somewhat worn, but neat and well cared for, so that one did not immediately notice that they were far from new. In his whole demeanour there was a suggestion of suffering which we servants could not but mark. We realised that things were going hardly for him, and pitied him. When he left we stood in the window watching him go." She added that he did not sleep at his uncle's, but ate his dinners there, and took many walks in and around the town, out to Venstøp and up to Bratsberg. He did not, she said, visit his parents; he had stayed in the neighbourhood about a week, and his uncle had suggested that he should come and work in his shop, but Ibsen had refused. "As he walked through the streets, he kept to himself, seemingly deep in thought. It was as though he knew no one and no one knew him. But people turned and looked at him; for he stood out from the generality with his neat clothes and shrewd and learned mien."

Ibsen himself never referred to this visit; in a letter to his sister Hedvig in 1891 he refers to having last been "at home in Skien" in 1850 (on his way from Grimstad to Christiania). Halvdan Koht[11] rejects Hanna Olsen's evidence on the strength of this statement, and the fact that Ibsen and Hedvig, and his father and another uncle, Christian Paus, several times

[9] They were, in fact, doing better than the Bergen Theatre under Bjørnson, whom we find complaining in *Bergens-Posten* on 8 March 1859: "Talent and enthusiasm have been wasted the whole winter on houses a half, a quarter, an eighth and even less full; the actors and the directors are losing heart."

[10] *Fremskridts Ibsen-nummer*, 17 March 1928.

[11] Koht, "Data om Henrik Ibsen i Skien," in *Ibsen-årbok 1954*, Skien, 1955.

later write of having last met in 1850. But this proves nothing except that Ibsen did not see them during any visit he may have made, which falls in with Hanna's statement that he did not call on his parents; and Ibsen's letter of 1891 specifically states that 1850 was the last time he was *at home*. Koht, who had been appointed one of Ibsen's literary executors, was inclined to reject, sometimes rather high-handedly, anything that redounded to his old master's discredit. Hanna's account is very detailed, and Oskar Mosfjeld, who met her and was a critical judge of witnesses, found her testimony convincing.[12] She also told him that Christopher Paus visited Ibsen in Christiania later during the year and, on his return to Skien, reported that Ibsen was living in humble circumstances, with a "chicken-ladder" leading up to his room.

12 Mosfjeld, p. 162.

7

The Thousand Beaks

1859–1862

That summer of 1859 marks a turning-point during Ibsen's second sojourn in Christiania. Up to now he had faced the difficulties of trying to run a national theatre with inexperienced actors and no worth-while plays to produce, hopefully. From now on the obstacles became too much for him, and the next three years are a sad story of administrative failure and creative barrenness. He wrote no plays at all between *The Vikings at Helgeland* in 1857 and *Love's Comedy* in 1862, the longest period of inactivity as a dramatist that he was to know until the first of his strokes incapacitated him in 1900, six years before his death.

He staged nothing of interest at the Norwegian Theatre during the autumn after his return from Skien, preferring mainly to revive the light successes of the previous season. For this policy he was attacked in the press. Why, asked *Morgenbladet* on 9 September, did he allow his company to waste their talents on such trivialities as *Le Chevalier des Dames*, a farce by Marc-Michel and Labiche, and *Frontin, Mari, Garçon*, a vaudeville by Scribe and Mélesville? The fact that the public seemed to enjoy them, declared the critic, was no excuse. Thus Ibsen, for the only time in his life, found himself rebuked for truckling to the box-office. The chief new success of the season was *A Caprice*, not Alfred de Musset's comedy of that name (though Ibsen was to direct that two years later), but a "dramatic divertissement with song and dance" by the prolific Erik Bøgh, which had been a triumph in Copenhagen with the Spanish danseuse Pepita d'Oliva,[1] and for which Ibsen engaged a celebrated German per-

---

[1] Pepita had already, in 1852, embarked on a liaison that was to last nineteen years with an English diplomat, Lionel Sackville-West (later the second Lord Sackville). They never married, but she bore him seven children before dying at the age of forty in 1871. One of her granddaughters, Victoria Sackville-West, wrote a delightful book about her: *Pepita*, London, 1937.

former called Bianca Bills. This ran for the unprecedented number of twenty-four performances before the end of December, and for a further eleven in the spring. Its reception encouraged Ibsen to present a similar entertainment in November, *The Two Comets,* a vaudeville by Hans Peter Holst, in which Fräulein Bills was joined by another dancer with the even more exotic name of Dobsen St. Louis. This achieved eleven performances.

It was especially ironical that Bøgh's play should have revived the fortunes of the Norwegian Theatre, for it poked considerable fun at the extravagances of nationalism: one of the characters was a Norwegian balletmaster who spoke broad *pipersvik* dialect and whom the other characters consequently found difficulty in understanding. But it is characteristic of Ibsen that he should have encouraged a parody of what he himself had been preaching, as though warning against the dangers of extremism; just as a quarter of a century later he was to underline, in *The Wild Duck,* the dangers of that "claim of the ideal" which was seemingly the cornerstone of his teaching. The implications of *A Caprice* bitterly offended Bjørnson, who had by now left the Bergen Theatre, after two tumultuous years as Ibsen's successor, and had returned to Christiania as co-editor of *Aftenbladet,* living for a while in the same house as the Ibsens on Akersgaden. Never a man to tolerate mockery of his convictions, Bjørnson published a sharp attack on the Norwegian Theatre's policy. "This theatre," he wrote, "which but lately was going cap in hand around the country with the appearance of being about to drop dead from starvation . . . has, in the space of a month, not merely raised itself to its feet but has even found the strength to dance. . . . In the process it has cast overboard the heavy burden of honest nationalistic intent with which, last year, it seemed likely to throttle itself, and has hired a pair of foreign dancers who have achieved a thunderous success. . . . In short, it is dancing away its youth." *Morgenbladet* joined in the attack, suggesting on 18 September that if Ibsen regarded his company as inadequate for better plays he might consider trying to recruit some actors from Bergen where, especially since Bjørnson's departure, economic conditions were now so bad that they might well be glad to move to Christiania. The article concluded, somewhat unethically one might feel, by advising Ibsen to exploit his friendship with the Bergen players and use "a little personal persuasion."

These newspaper attacks continued throughout the autumn. On 9 October *Morgenbladet* declared that "the so-called Norwegian Theatre no longer exists," and that the public was attending "in blind devotion to the cause which the Norwegian Theatre is supposed to be advancing, but which it no longer raises a finger to support. . . . It is declining into a kind of amusement ground for the lower classes. . . . We are amazed that the theatre should be allowed to slide lazily and without apparent resistance on to the well-greased chute of Danish mediocrity—under the guidance of a *Norwegian* poet."

Ibsen retorted to these criticisms by producing, on 12 October, Holberg's five-act comedy *Jean de France;* but this was the only play of any quality that he staged before the end of the year, and the newspaper attacks were soon renewed. Bjørnson defended him, with his usual eloquence, on 26 November in *Aftenbladet;* on 7 December, however, the most vituperative attack yet on the Norwegian Theatre appeared in the form of a poem in *Morgenbladet* by one H. Ø. Blom[2] (ostensibly a farewell tribute to the Danish actor Anton Wilhelm Wiehe, who was leaving the Christiania Theatre). Ibsen replied in *Aftenbladet* three days later, likewise in rhymed verse; whereupon Blom came back at him with another poem, of twenty-two strophes, using his seniority to deliver the magisterial rebuke:

> But here's the difference. I am H. Ø. Blom,
> And you are Henrik Ibsen, nothing more.

Blom had himself been at school at Skien, and may have been hitting at Ibsen's being the son of a virtual bankrupt; the lines quoted suggest a sense of more than literary superiority. Ibsen's reply was so violent that Bjørnson thought it best not to print it.

This undignified controversy had, however, one concrete result. Ibsen told Henrik Jæger in 1887 that when he took his reply to Blom's first attack to the *Aftenbladet* office (presumably on 9 December, since it was printed the following day), he, Bjørnson and Bjørnson's co-editor, Richter, had a conversation in which "the view was expressed that the time was ripe for the establishment of a group to work for nationalistic aims."[3] Within a few days, Bjørnson and Ibsen, with the former as prime mover, had established Det Norske Selskab (The Norwegian Society). At first its aims were purely artistic. A special committee was set up, with Ibsen as a member, to try to assemble a national team of the best Norwegian actors from the three theatres in Christiania and Bergen to give a series of special performances in the capital during the summer (when the three

---

[2] Blom was a great admirer of Scribe, whom he had declared (in *Morgenbladet* on 1 November 1859) to be "the prince of playwrights," deprecating the current "Scribophobia" in Christiania.

[3] Midbøe, p. 150. Bjørnson recorded (in *Aftenbladet,* 28 December 1859) that he had been thinking of founding some such society during his last year in Bergen, but that when he came to Christiania he found the atmosphere so different from what he had expected that he had lost interest, and that nothing would have happened "had not Herr Ibsen been of the opinion that the mere act of founding such a society would start a movement that would achieve several desirable ends. . . . He took all the necessary measures, and to him must all the honour be given." An older Norwegian Society had been formed in Copenhagen in 1772, with the writer J. H. Wessel as its leading figure, and this had moved to Christiania after the break with Denmark in 1814; but, according to Vinje in *Dølen,* it was now only "an excuse for social get-togethers with food, drink and cards."

theatres would normally be closed). Another of the Society's vaguely stated aims was to tempt all Norwegian actors who worked at the Bankpladsen Theatre to leave, though no one seems to have had any clear idea how this was to be done. Opposition was also expressed to the so-called Düsseldorf school of painting. It was still the custom for Norwegian painters of any talent to emigrate to Düsseldorf, where J. C. Dahl, who had helped Ibsen in Dresden, held sway, and where, so Bjørnson and other purists felt, they came too much under foreign influence! The absurdity of this view deterred several moderate minds from joining, Botten Hansen among them.

Under Bjørnson's energetic leadership, however, the Society soon acquired a hundred members, artists, scientists, journalists and, before long, politicians, including Ole Bull (who was giving a series of concerts in Christiania and who, naturally, played at the first meeting), Vinje, J. E. Sars, Johan Sverdrup and, surprisingly, Ibsen's enemy H. Ø. Blom. They met on Tuesday evenings, ate, drank punch, made speeches and, as always seems to happen in Norway at even the most esoteric gatherings, invariably ended up singing. Ludvig Daæ, later to become an eminent scholar as well as an active politician, found the meetings ridiculous and thought that Ibsen and one other member, a Dr. Bidenkap, were "the only people who talked any sense."[4] Gradually, as more and more members of the Storthing joined, the Norwegian Society acquired a more political aspect, and Ibsen began to lose interest in its proceedings.

He was beginning, like so many writers before and after him, to find nationalism cramping to his talent. The occasional poems which he wrote during these first years in Christiania, with their naïve exhortations, ring somewhat hollow. An extreme point was reached the month after the founding of the Norwegian Society, in January 1860, when he wrote a poem called "Life in the Mountains" to be spoken on the stage of the Norwegian Theatre as an accompaniment to a *tableau vivant* "in which," a contemporary tells us, "several of the city's most feted ladies appeared."[5] Ibsen couched this poem in such extremely Norwegian language that, according to Yngvar Nielsen,[6] the eminent Danish actor Anton Wilhelm Wiehe refused to read it, saying that he could not understand many of the words, and Laura Gundersen had to take his place. From about the beginning of 1860 Ibsen seems to have begun to grow sceptical about nationalism; but it was to be some time before he grew finally disillusioned

[4] W. S. Dahl, the biographer of Johan Sverdrup, describes Ibsen at these meetings as "quietly in attendance, listening to every word spoken but himself scarcely uttering a syllable"; and another member of the Society, O. Hansen, recalled over fifty years later that Ibsen "never made any speech but listened, and walked to and fro, smiling slightly." (Collin, II, 482 and 487.)

[5] Yngvar Nielsen, *En Kristianiensers erindringer fra 1850- og 1860-aarene* (Christiania and Copenhagen, 1910), p. 315.

[6] *Loc. cit.*

with it, and with no other job in sight he was in no position to give up his job at the Norwegian Theatre because of a lack of faith in its ideals.

Of Ibsen's private life at this time, we know virtually nothing; it remained, as it was always to remain, a closed book to the outside world. Such scanty evidence as we have suggests that, now as later, Suzannah was a source of extraordinary strength to him. "She is just the kind of character I need," he wrote to Peter Hansen in 1870, "illogical, but with a strong poetical intuition, a bigness of outlook, and an almost violent hatred of all things petty. My fellow-countrymen understood nothing of all this." And their son was to declare: "It is probably true, as has been suggested, that he sometimes rebelled against her will and wished himself far away so that he could lose himself in his daydreams. I am thinking particularly of their first years together. But if he had lost her for good he would have been inconsolable; he would have been miserable had she withdrawn her will. He was the genius, she was the character. His character. And he knew it, though he would not willingly have admitted it until towards the end. But she knew it the whole time, and so was unconcerned by what people said, and by the criticisms of friends and acquaintances. She knew what fate had entrusted to her care, and she regarded it as her life's task. Let them call her a kill-joy when bad friends, in my father's younger days, wanted to drag him out with them—or self-willed, when she was old, and kept the fire still burning in him. She knew that ultimately, her will was his will."[7]

This son was born to them on 23 December 1859. They called him Sigurd, after the hero of *The Vikings at Helgeland*, and Bjørnson stood as godfather. Bjørnson's wife Karoline asserted to numerous acquaintances during the next three-quarters of a century (she died in 1934, in her ninety-ninth year) that, as they were returning from the christening, she heard Suzannah loudly declare that she would never have another child —a statement which, at that time, as Fru Bjørnson never failed to point out to her listeners, was taken to mean that a woman had decided to cease sexual relations with her husband. But there is no record that Fru Bjørnson began to spread this story until much later, when her dislike of Suzannah and jealousy of Ibsen had become marked; and her relish in the telling of disparaging stories about them once Ibsen's fame had begun to surpass that of her husband makes her not the most credible of witnesses. "Anyone who has ever done me any wrong," wrote Bjørnson of her on 5 March 1859 to Clemens Petersen, "is immediately, and for ever, her most implacable enemy." Whatever Suzannah Ibsen's faults may have been, disloyalty to her husband was never one of them, and it seems extraordinarily unlikely that, if she had decided to give up sleeping with her husband, she would have said so out loud in public, particularly with Karoline Bjørnson around.

Much more to Ibsen's liking than the Norwegian Society was a group

---

[7] Bergliot Ibsen, p. 185.

which Paul Botten Hansen had gathered round him, and which Ibsen, during this same winter of 1859–60, began to frequent. Botten Hansen was a passionate bibliophile, who had already amassed a fine library when Ibsen had first met him in 1850; he had had to sell it all the following year to pay his debts, but in the eight years since, by assiduous attendance at book auctions, he had built up another, of no less than fourteen thousand volumes.[8] With his "pale, angular face and irregular gait," as Ludvig Daæ[9] describes him, he had a remarkable flair for discovering rare and often valuable books in the most unlikely places; it used to be said that the most obscure provincial could not die owning one worthwhile book without Botten Hansen hearing of and acquiring it. "Damn that Dutchman, he has his spies everywhere!" said Ludvig Daæ of him, quoting Holberg. The name caught. Botten Hansen came to be known as "the Dutchman," and his circle as "The Learned Holland."

The aims of The Learned Holland were almost diametrically opposed to those of the Norwegian Society. Its members were, in the main, critics and scholars rather than creative writers. A kind of cross between the Bloomsbury Set and the Fabian Society, they distrusted naïve plans for the future, and submitted them to sceptical analysis. They strongly opposed some of the Norwegian Society's more cherished and chauvinistic aims, especially in the field of language: such as Bjørnson's passion for injecting Norwegian words and turns of style into the established *riksmaal* (a habit with which, as we have seen, Ibsen also had become infected), and Vinje's attempts to establish a Norwegian *landsmaal*. Mutual admiration was frowned on; criticism was the purpose of the gatherings, which took place on Monday evenings. They would assemble at Botten Hansen's apartment, Raadhusgaden 28 (known as Pipersgaarden, "probably the oldest three-storey house in Christiania"),[10] where he had two large rooms on the second floor, with books everywhere, including the hall and passages; even the bed was in an alcove of bookshelves. From there they would proceed to one or another café: Nibbe's, the Hotel Angleterre, Engebret Christoffersen's at the corner of Raadhusgaden and Kirkegaten, Peter's Restaurant, which they facetiously nicknamed St. Peter's, or, most often, L'Orsa's, a small Swiss café with a convenient back parlour.

Here Ibsen met rising young scholars, such as J. E. Sars and his own wife's cousin, Ludvig Daæ, both later to become eminent historians; Asbjørnsen, the collector of folk lore; his old professor, the poet J. S. Welhaven; and other lively minds, such as Jakob Løkke, Michael Birkeland, and Olof Rygh. Vinje, though they stood for everything that he did not, occasionally attended, for old friendship's sake; so, even, did Bjørnson,

[8] His landlord forbade him to bring in any more books lest the floor should give way, and he had to smuggle them in when the landlord was out (Ludvig Daae, "Paul Botten Hansen," in *Vidar* [Copenhagen, 1888], p. 339 note).

[9] *Ibid.*, p. 335.

[10] *Ibid.*, p. 342.

who found the sceptical mood of the gatherings by no means to his liking. Another promising new author to be seen there was the young Jonas Lie, a Charles Lamb-like figure with whom Ibsen soon struck up a lasting friendship. Lie later recalled Ibsen at these Holland meetings "in that dark, closed cape and felt hat, his face framed by an outlandishly dark head of hair and beard. . . . Apart from those moments when, in a fit of euphoria, he would hold forth, there was something knotted about him."[11]

Holberg, the supreme iconoclast, was, not surprisingly, the principal idol of the Holland group. Some of the members knew his comedies almost by heart, and his style and vocabulary influenced their conversation, so that they would often talk a kind of Holberg pastiche. They gave each other nicknames taken from his characters, and Ibsen became known as Gert Westphaler, after the talkative barber in the play of that name. This does not seem to have been applied to him in sarcasm; Christopher Due, Jonas Lie and Lorentz Dietrichson have all testified that, when the mood took him, he could, like many depressives, hold forth with passionate eloquence. He loved, at these gatherings, to quote hypothetical paradoxes; imagine, he would say, an owl afraid of the dark, or a fish intolerant of water; being at the earth's centre, and not knowing the difference between up and down; and whether two and two would make four on, say, Sirius. Six years later, in *Brand,* he was to recall this mood:

> When I was a boy, I remember,
> Two thoughts kept occurring to me, and made me laugh.
> An owl frightened by darkness, and a fish
> Afraid of water. Why did I think of them?
> Because I felt, dimly, the difference
> Between what is and what should be; between
> Having to endure and finding one's burden
> Unendurable.
> > Every man
> Is such an owl and such a fish, created
> To work in darkness, to live in the deep;
> And yet he is afraid. He splashes
> In anguish towards the shore, stares at the bright
> Vault of heaven, and screams: "Give me air
> And the blaze of day!"

One of Ibsen's early biographers, Gerhard Gran, half a generation younger than the Hollanders, knew most of them well and has left an interesting comment upon them. "They were," he writes, "almost without exception, distinguished for learning rather than for original ideas, for intelligence rather than energy or vitality, for critical ability rather than

[11] *Henrik Ibsen: festskrift i anledning of hans 70de fødselsdag,* edited by Gerhard Gran (Bergen, Stockholm, and Copenhagen, 1898), pp. 15–16.

creative fertility. The ideals they worshipped were old and dying ideals; they clung tightly to the old Danish traditions, from which others were seeking to emancipate themselves, they abased themselves before the classical education which even then was beginning to show cracks in its seams, they worshipped the concept of Scandinavianism, which was soon to be proved bankrupt. The river of progress passed them by, and, clinging to the past, they watched it glide—each according to his temperament, some in hopeless surrender, others bitterly resentful—certain that their country was moving swiftly towards perdition." No wonder that Bjørnson hated them; but Ibsen, as Gran says, "felt at home in this atmosphere which Bjørnson found poisonous. Ibsen had no reason to look on life with a hopeful eye; the iron had, not unnaturally, entered deep into his soul, he had little faith left, and he was, like so many of those others, cynical; he shared readily in their causticity. There was in Ibsen's highly complex make-up a strong measure of conservatism . . . radical as he was in matters of the spirit and in his championship of individuality, he was indifferent, even antagonistic towards anyone with a bombastic passion for external reforms. He, who was so shy and silent, was by nature suspicious of facile enthusiasm and loud-mouthedness. . . . Eloquence was to him an empty jingle, a politician synonymous with a self-seeker, a patriot with a screeching monkey; he hated nothing so much as silken phrases. One can easily understand why such a man found himself at home among the Hollanders. . . . He shared their antipathies, at any rate to a degree. He found in their circle an echo of his contempt for the poverty of Norwegian political and cultural life."[12]

Ibsen's preference for the Holland group over the Norwegian Society is confirmation of his growing disillusionment with nationalism. Under the circumstances, it is hardly surprising that his work at the theatre was soon to deteriorate; a man can hardly be a good theatre director if he has doubts about its policy.

Ibsen's associates in "Holland" and the Norwegian Society were in the main acquaintances rather than friends; he did not make friends easily, and that autumn he lost one of the few he had. Ole Schulerud, who had published *Catiline* at his own expense and shared his small means with Ibsen in their student days, died in October at the age of thirty-one. He was one of the few people with whom Ibsen had been, or was ever to be, really intimate, and Ibsen composed a simple and moving little poem to be sung at his graveside. Eleven years later, on 9 June 1870, he wrote Schulerud's widow a long and, for him, unusually personal letter recalling the debt he owed to her husband:

   . . . He was a true friend to me, unstinting, unqualified, and loyal. When I look back, there was no one so closely bound up with my

[12] Gran, *Henrik Ibsen: liv og verker*, I, 103–6.

youthful development as he. And amid the successes which I have since achieved it has been a great grief to me that he could not be here among us and share my joy with me. He was the friend I needed in the days when one had to make certain renunciations and prepare oneself for the future; and how few such one has in times like those! There are plenty of people who take note of one when things go well; but the likelihood of failure was every bit as great as that of success when he joined his fortunes to mine with all his loyal and noble heart. Then our lives parted; we seldom wrote to each other; we didn't seem to need to; now that I think back, we never really exchanged a word about friendship or anything like that. What existed between us arose quite spontaneously and developed into something completely unforced, and it never occurred to us to think it could be otherwise. And then, when we met again, our time together was so sadly brief.

But a loss has it exaltation, as it has its grief. The sharpened memory, the inward truth, remain; what parting robs us of is inessential. . . . I should deeply love to have a portrait of Ole, if you can spare one; I have none . . .

In warmest friendship,
Henrik Ibsen[13]

The picture we have of Ibsen at this stage in his career, when he was approaching his thirty-second birthday, is of a writer distracted. At the age when an author is commonly at his most fertile, if not at his best, he found his creative energies diverted by the claims of two ideals which he was gradually finding to be false: the ideal of nationalism, and the ideal of creating a worth-while theatre. Both demanded something that he lacked, and that Bjørnson revelled in: gregariousness, the love of being with and working with other people. To Ibsen, torn between his ideals and his daily work on the one hand, and his instincts and nature on the other, the problem was especially tormenting; and during the last months of 1859 he managed, heaven knows how, to find the leisure to write a long poem of three hundred and eighty-four lines in which he dramatised his dilemma. He called it "On the Heights," and it is perhaps the finest of his non-dramatic works.

The narrator, a young man, leaves his mother "with scrip on back and gun in hand" to seek solitude in the mountains. On the way he sees a girl, spends the night with her, and promises to return and marry her. But once in the mountains, he feels different:

[13] This letter is unexplainedly omitted from C.E., XVI (Oslo, 1946), though it had been printed in Sigurd Høst's *Ibsens diktning og Ibsen selv* (Oslo, 1927) nineteen years previously.

> All passions dark, all wild desires
> Are driven from my thoughts.
> I'm born anew. Up here I stand
> Near to myself and God.

Among the peaks he meets a stranger. "Tears play in his laughter. His lips, when silent, speak." His eyes are like the mountain lake, born of, and caged by, the glacier. He teaches the young man a "new wisdom"; the old desires and longings lose their power over him. On Christmas Night he looks down and sees his home burn, with his mother in it; but the stranger, by his side, views the scene through his hollowed hand and points out the beauty of the red flames in the moonlight. He loses all desire to return to the life of the valley below. Finally, at midsummer, he sees the girl he loves riding to church to marry another man, and shades his eyes with his hand, like the stranger, better to appreciate the aesthetic effect of the gay clothes against the white birch trees. He is now freed from all foolish emotional ties, and senses in his heart "full evidence of petrifaction." The poem ends:

> I am steeled. I am done with the lowland life.
> Up here on the heights are freedom and God.
> Men do but grope in the valley.

"On the Heights" is one of Ibsen's most personal poems; and again, as with so many of his best, the English poet whom it most calls to mind is Thomas Hardy, with its changing rhythms, frequent use of dactylic metres, strong dramatisation, economy of narration, and extreme simplicity of statement that trembles on, yet never quite oversteps, the cliff-edge of banality. The problem of whether an artist should plunge into life or withdraw from it had been exhaustively and comparatively recently examined by Kierkegaard in (among other works) *Either-Or;* yet this temptation of total withdrawal is one that has confronted writers in every age, whether as Aestheticism (Kierkegaard), Apollonianism (Nietzsche), the Ivory Tower (Yeats) or, in our own time, non-commitment. At the same time, Kierkegaard was one of those thinkers whose ideas were certainly discussed in the Holland circle, and Ibsen may well, as at other times, have been infected by them at second-hand. The dilemma of commitment or non-commitment remained with him, as it had to while he continued with his grind at the theatre; and he now, in the first month of 1860, began to plan a play on the theme—*Love's Comedy*, which, however, he was not to finish until 1862.[14]

This question of Kierkegaard's influence on Ibsen is one that no student

----

[14] "Not until I married," wrote Ibsen to Peter Hansen on 28 October 1870, "did my life achieve a weightier content. The first fruits of this was a longish poem, 'On the Heights.' But the demand for freedom which runs throughout this poem did not find full expression until I wrote *Love's Comedy*."

of either writer can sidestep. On the one hand, it has undoubtedly been exaggerated by critics who seem ignorant of the frequency with which authors distrustful of and hostile to each other's work have followed parallel paths to the same goal; and Ibsen, as we have seen, when questioned in later life as to this influence, replied testily that he had "read little of Kierkegaard and understood less." This statement was probably true, for Ibsen was never much interested in philosophical writing. On the other hand, he shares with Kierkegaard such striking similarities not merely of thought but of phrasing that the matter cannot be allowed to rest there.

Ibsen, though a free-thinker from a very early age, had, like Kierkegaard, been brought up in an atmosphere of deep pietism and, again like Kierkegaard, regarded the Christian doctrine with a mixture of fear and admiration. Julian the Apostate, in *Emperor and Galilean,* was to voice this duality: "Whoever has once been in His power can never completely free himself from it." Ibsen must often have felt, as Kierkegaard did, that he could never fight his way out of the stranglehold which the Galilean system of ethics had put on him; and Kierkegaard's stern conception of Christianity, contempt for the established church, and insistence that religion was a matter for the individual soul must have appealed very strongly to him. The two men had, moreover, much in common psychologically. Both were ugly, and shy of close human relationships. Kierkegaard had written (in his journal for 1841): "The curse which rests on me is never to be allowed to let anyone join themselves to me deeply and inwardly," just as Ibsen had apologised to C. J. Anker in 1858 for being "walled about with a kind of off-putting coldness which makes any close relationship with me difficult." Both despised the masses, and were suspicious of so-called liberalism and all party lines; both tended to ask questions rather than give answers; both were oddly addicted to reading newspaper advertisements. Many ideas receive almost identical expression in their writings: Kierkegaard's "Truth is in the minority" and Dr. Stockmann's "The minority is always right"; Kierkegaard's "The great thing is not to be this or the other, but to be oneself, and of that every human being is capable if only he wills it," and Brand's:

> To be wholly oneself! But how,
> With the weight of one's inheritance of sin? . . .
> It is not by spectacular achievements
> That man can be transformed, but by will.
> It is man's will that acquits or condemns him.

Kierkegaard had stressed, as Ibsen was frequently to do, the necessity of self-liberation as opposed to liberation from without, and the need for an artist to experience sorrow (though Keats had also stressed this, and he had died when Kierkegaard was eight). And Kierkegaard had stated, in "A Seducer's Diary" (in *Either-Or*) that: "When two people fall in love and decide that they are destined for each other, then they must have the courage to break it off. For to continue is to lose everything and win nothing"; which was to be precisely the theme of *Love's Comedy*.

Such similarities could be coincidental; Strindberg and Freud share as many, yet Strindberg almost certainly never read a word of Freud,[15] and Freud came to his conclusions without Strindberg's help. (As Coleridge remarked when Hazlitt accused him of plagiarising Shakespeare: "Is there no such thing as two men's having similar thoughts on similar occasions?"). But many of Ibsen's friends were ardent Kierkegaardians. In June 1857, towards the end of Ibsen's stay in Bergen, Magdalene Thoresen wrote to a friend that she read Kierkegaard "unceasingly," so that Ibsen can hardly have avoided hearing a lot of him through her. Kierkegaard was also much discussed by Ibsen's friends in the "Holland" circle; and the young priest Christopher Bruun, with whom Ibsen was to have close contact during his first year in Rome, was another enthusiastic disciple. In short, Kierkegaard's ideas were everywhere in the air around Ibsen during the latter's formative years and, bored and puzzled as he may have been by Kierkegaard's philosophical processes, he must have found many of his own half-formed thoughts crystallised there.

Meanwhile, now that he had written "On the Heights," the Norwegian Theatre continued to occupy most of his time and energy. He had, as we have seen, been under fire from the press; but towards the end of 1859 the repertory began to show signs of improvement. On 11 December, the day after he published his long verse counter-attack on H. Ø. Blom (how on earth did he find the time for that during the last days of rehearsing a new production?), he staged Holberg's full-length comedy, *Jacob von Thybœ* (about a boastful soldier), and followed it ten days later with a new Danish one-acter, Carit Etlar's *When the Sun Goes Down*. On 3 February 1860 he directed *Ole Shut-Eye,* a comedy by Hans Andersen requiring elaborate staging and scenery, and this proved a popular as well as a critical success, being performed thirteen times that month and nineteen in all before the end of the season. Another new play, Thomas Overskou's *The Devil's Master* (after Mélesville's *Le Fils de la Vierge*) followed in March, and this, too, was a success; the critics went out of their way to praise the production, which included several tableaux of "witchcraft," with "Bengal

---

[15] There is no mention of Freud in Strindberg's twenty thousand surviving letters, which are full of references to what he was reading, nor is there any work of Freud's in Strindberg's library; and he always bought rather than borrowed books, even when he could least afford them. Freud's *The Interpretation of Dreams* was scarcely reviewed at all when it appeared in 1900, and took eight years to sell its first edition of 600 copies, so that Strindberg, though he did not die till 1912, had probably never heard of Freud's name.

candles." "The acting in general," wrote *Aftenbladet* (on 10 March) surveying the theatre's recent productions, "bears witness to such conscientious instruction that the performances give considerable satisfaction." Dumas *père's Les Demoiselles de St. Cyr*, in April, achieved only two performances, as did Joseph Bouchardy's *Le Sonneur de St. Paul* the following month. No one could now complain that the theatre was not presenting new works, even if disappointingly few of the required quality were being written by native dramatists.

On 18 May the Storthing rejected another appeal from the theatre for a state grant. Some time during the summer Ibsen had again to humiliate himself by asking his uncle, Christopher Blom Paus, for money.[16] He visited the latter at his country estate, Buslaaten, in Gjerpen, just outside Skien. We do not know whether he succeeded in his mission, and he does not seem to have visited his family on this occasion either. That summer there were floods in Skien which caused widespread destruction, and the last memory he took away of his native town (for he was never to visit it again) may have been of the great waters pouring through the streets. No wonder he later remembered Skien as "the town of the storming, soughing, seething waters." There is also a local tradition that at about this time he applied to the Skien town council for help;[17] but many of the council papers were destroyed in the fire of 1886, so that this cannot be confirmed or denied.

On 1 July he wrote a song for the winners at the summer festival of a rifle club to which he belonged in Christiania; this was published in *Illustreret Nyhedsblad* on 8 July. On 6 August he applied, together with Bjørnson and Vinje, for state travel grants. Ibsen's application reads pathetically:

To the King!

Henrik Johan Ibsen most humbly begs that he may be granted a sum of 400 (four hundred) specie-dollars from the fund set aside for artists and scholars for foreign travel, for a six months journey to London, Paris, the larger German cities, Copenhagen and Stockholm, to study dramatic art and literature.

During ten years of literary activity, and an earlier period of preparation for this work, the study of dramatic art and literature, its principles, system, and histories, has absorbed the greater part of my time and constituted my main occupation. The criticisms of my dramatic works which have during this period been published by foreign as well as native judges may, I trust, present sufficient testimony that these efforts have not been fruitless; as the sympathy with which the

[16] According to Hanna Olsen, Paus's maid, who, as a very old woman, gave the information to Oskar Mosfjeld (*op. cit*, p. 162).

[17] *Ibid.*, pp. 162–63.

public has received my various plays, several of which have also
been performed in Sweden and Denmark, may testify to a talent for
the vocation which I have chosen. . . .

Your Majesty's most humble servant,
Henr. Ibsen

The Akademiske Kollegium, to whom the applications of the three
writers were referred, at first rejected them all. The head of the Ministry
for Ecclesiastical and Educational Affairs, Christian Birch-Reichenwald,
persuaded them to reconsider their decision in the cases of Bjørnson and
Vinje, though each received only half the amount applied for (Bjørnson
500 specie-dollars instead of 1,000, and Vinje 250 instead of 500). But they
steadfastly refused to make any grant to Ibsen, whose application had been
the most modest of the three. It is interesting to speculate on the influence
that a visit to London and Paris might have had on Ibsen at this stage of
his career. The London theatre was undergoing a particularly lean period;
Harley Granville Barker has described its state during the fifties and
sixties as one of "slovenly chaos."[18] There were no good playwrights;
Ibsen would have been just too early for the "realistic" plays of T. W.
Robertson (who was to write *Caste* in 1867) and for W. S. Gilbert, whose
first play, *Dulcamara*, would be produced in 1866; he would have seen
nothing more interesting in the way of new plays than the comedies
of H. J. Byron and J. R. Planché, which were no better than the trivia
he had been directing at home. Nor was it a great period for English
acting. Macready had recently ended his career and Henry Irving, though
he had just started on his, did not play in London in either 1860 or
1861.[19] The best that Ibsen could have seen would have been Charles
Kean, J. L. Toole, Samuel Phelps, Helen Faucit, and Dion Boucicault,
none of them major talents. Nor would Paris have had much more to offer.
Rachel had died in 1858, and Sarah Bernhardt was not to make her début
until August 1862. Frédéric Lemaître, now aged sixty, had gone into
decline. Of the French dramatists, Ibsen already knew about Dumas *père*
and Victorien Sardou; he had produced several plays by the former, and
was to stage the latter's *Pattes de Mouche* later that year. He might have
seen in Paris a revival of the younger Dumas's *La Dame aux Camélias*,
which had been first produced in 1852 (but was not to reach Christiania until 1899). What would most have interested him, however, would
have been the plays of Emile Augier. Augier's plays, with their contemporary themes and settings, such as *Gabrielle*, *Le Gendre de M. Poirier*, *Le Fils
de Giboyer*, and *Lions et Renards*, today seem scarcely more "realistic"
than *La Dame aux Camélias*, or *Caste*, or *The Second Mrs. Tanqueray*.

[18] See his essay in *The Eighteen-Sixties*, edited by John Drinkwater, London,
1932.
[19] See Laurence Irving, *Henry Irving* (London, 1951), pp. 98–110.

The characters seem shallow, the plots melodramatic. But they dealt, however superficially, with current problems; they castigated contemporary morals, and even introduced contemporary politics. No doubt Ibsen, even without any French, would have been delighted to see such things on the stage. But since he himself was to do exactly these things in his next play, *Love's Comedy,* and since his dramatic technique was already much superior to Augier's, it is difficult to imagine that seeing the latter's plays acted would have had much, if any, influence on him.

As things turned out, Ibsen was never to visit England; nor, although he was to live for twenty-seven years in Italy and Germany, was he to enter France, except to pass briefly through in 1869 on his way to and from the opening of the Suez Canal.

So he stayed in Norway, and on 17 August that year, 1860, we find him again in the role of hack poet, writing a song to greet visiting members of the Swedish Parliament. A week later, on 25 August, J. L. Heiberg died, and Ibsen wrote a moving elegy[20] to the memory of the man who had received him courteously in Copenhagen eight years before, and whose plays had been among the few that it can have given him any pleasure to direct. Ibsen retained his admiration for Heiberg, and for his actress wife, all his life.[21] He also, in the role of unofficial local laureate which he so curiously filled, wrote a poem to be spoken on the day of the new King Carl XV's coronation, and yet another greeting to the Swedish M.P.'s, this time to a deputation from them which was visiting Trondhjem. All of these pieces, except the Heiberg elegy, are naïvely, even (to an outsider) embarrassingly patriotic, with frequent exhortations to "Men of Norway" and "Norway's Heroes." Needless to say, they delighted most of his contemporaries. "Thank Ibsen for his poems!" wrote Vinje to Botten Hansen (who had published three of the worst of them in *Illustreret Nyhedsblad*) on 8 September. "They are the most Norwegian of all!"

On 29 September Ibsen presented his annual report to the board of the Norwegian Theatre. It is very defensive in tone, and consists largely of an attempt to answer criticisms of the repertory during the early part of the season. "Fräulein Bills's engagement," he stated, "was entered into in September with an especial eye to the presentation of the one-act plays, *A Caprice* and *The Two Comets*. These two plays, which were performed (as they had to be) continuously over the next two months, since her contract did not extend beyond that period, had naturally to be accompanied by pieces which would not occupy a whole evening. The repertory during this period had therefore to consist mainly of short works, a state of affairs which could not be remedied except by the already remarked concentration of full-length plays towards the end of the season." Ibsen concluded by admitting that some of the new plays could have been

[20] See p. 97 above.
[21] *Cf.* e.g. John Paulsen, *Samliv med Ibsen,* I, 46.

better performed, but pleaded as an excuse various sicknesses within the company.

Despite the criticisms, the season had proved financially the most successful that the theatre had known. The takings had amounted to some 12,000 specie-dollars, about 860 specie-dollars more than in the preceding year. Expenses, however, had exceeded income by 2,000 specie-dollars, which meant dipping into the 3,500 specie-dollars raised by the national appeal.

Ibsen seems, however, around this time to have become apathetic about his work at the theatre. That summer the theatre was being rebuilt, at considerable expense, and Knud Knudsen, the language instructor who was also on the board, records that Ibsen showed little interest in the theatre's affairs, was lazy during August and September in rehearsing new plays for the coming season (which did not open until the rebuilding was completed in October), and frequently absented himself from board meetings "for no other reason than that he knew he would be asked what he had done since the last meeting. I remember we once found ourselves holding a board meeting in a rear room at L'Orsa's café in Prindsensgade, because we had heard that he happened to be there." He recalled that at one board meeting this year he "gave Ibsen a real dressing-down, the like of which he can never have experienced before or since"; and that Joachim Garborg, another board member, had told him (Knudsen) that he had treated Ibsen "like a truant schoolboy." But, says Knudsen, "Ibsen took what I gave him without saying a word"; and he adds that Ole Bull, now back from Oleana, who himself had spoken severely to Ibsen at the same meeting, told him: "You've got to be tough with Ibsen if you're to get anywhere."[22]

Evidence of Ibsen's apathy can be found in the fact that he chose as his second production of the new season that tedious nationalistic drama, *The Goblin's Home,* by P. A. Jensen, which he had condemned in such violent terms as a student back in 1851. He may have thought his cynicism justified when the production received enthusiastic reviews and ran for ten performances. The enlarged stage[23] and more elaborate scenic effects that could consequently be achieved were doubtless partly responsible; on 30

[22] Knudsen did not publish his memoirs, but D. A. Seip noted extracts from them in the inaugural issue of *Edda,* Christiania, 1914.

[23] A description of the improved arrangements appears in *Christiania-Posten* (nr. 286). Conditions, we are told, are now "much more comfortable and agreeable for the audience. In the stalls, as in the amphitheatre and the first tier of boxes, every spectator has an individual seat with arms; where, previously, the seating was cramped and displeasing, there is now plenty of room, and although the auditorium has now been sunk into the basement, by which arrangement it has been possible to incorporate a second tier of boxes, the total capacity has not significantly been increased. . . . The theatre is handsomely decorated, the white colours harmonising agreeably with the gilded embellishments; and the new curtain, representing a mountain landscape traversed by a stream, makes a gratifying impression."

October, *Morgenbladet* noted with pleasure that it was no longer necessary for "one step to signify four, or for lovers to crowd and buffet each other incongruously for lack of space."

On 25 October Ibsen addressed yet another appeal for assistance to the Storthing on behalf of the theatre. Comparing its circumstances to that of theatres in other countries, he expresses the hope that those who have done so much to encourage the other arts will not neglect that of the stage. No art, he suggests, has "so active and meaningful an influence on the development of a people" as the dramatic; and he begs for support, that they may not be "driven by oppressive circumstances to strike a false path. . . . Under such conditions a theatre is all too often compelled to *follow* public opinion instead of *guiding* it, to be dragged down by current and often depraved taste instead of controlling it. If our theatre possessed greater resources," he continues, "it would also be in a position to increase and improve its acting strength, and to give it a more thorough preparation and training. It would be able to discriminate more in its choice of plays and in the performing of them, to reward original writing and thus assist our dramatic literature, and, in general, to work in a more artistic and national spirit than has hitherto been possible."

Needless to say, the appeal was rejected.

In November Ibsen revived another play which he had seen as an undergraduate in 1851, a five-act German historical drama by Karl Gutzkow entitled *Zopf und Schwert* (Pigtail and Sword), set in the court of Frederick William I. It had been badly received then, but he had admired and defended it: "When one has, like our public, inured oneself year in and year out to the dramatic candy-floss of Scribe & Co., cautiously seasoned with a ration of bogus poetry, it is not to be wondered at that this more solid German fare should prove indigestible even to the ostrich stomachs of Christiania audiences." The play was newly translated, by Suzannah Ibsen, and was sympathetically reviewed; but the public liked it no better than they had in 1851, and it was withdrawn after four performances.

No wonder Ibsen was feeling apathetic towards his work. The public had made it clear that it had little appetite for serious drama, and that what it wanted, and what the theatre needed if it was to remain solvent, was a virtually unbroken diet of comedy, preferably with music and dancing. Even Sardou's *Pattes de Mouche,* being without music, proved too much and ran for only three performances that November; and *The Foster Brothers,* an adaptation by J. L. Heiberg of a comedy by Karl Töpfer based on an adaptation by J. R. Planché of William Rowley's 1632 comedy. *A New Wonder, A Woman Never Vext* (the list of credits underlines the kind of material with which Ibsen had to work, even when the original was of some quality) managed only four in January. A reviewer of the Sardou complained that the actors seemed to "lack instruction," to which

Ibsen replied in *Aftenbladet* (5 December) that "under me, no debutant has appeared on the stage without sufficient preparation. It is another thing for beginners to show lack of experience, which your reviewer has confused with lack of instruction." On 22 November, meanwhile, he had learned that his application for a travel grant had been rejected.

During the autumn of 1860 the theatre had, greatly daring, started a ballet school, and on New Year's Day 1861 a "dance divertissement" was presented. *Morgenbladet* (3 January) complained that the performers "have not yet acquired the first rudiments of dancing. . . . Granted that the performance found its public; a storm of applause was heard from the gallery when the curtain fell, and the dancers appeared with happy faces. . . . But we would ask the artistic director to consider whether the Norwegian Theatre and the superior public that it has lately acquired are not somewhat beyond 'dance divertissements' of this quality."

Bowing to the public taste, Ibsen presented in February a "folk comedy" entitled *The Builders,* an adaptation of a French piece by Théodore Cogniard and L. F. N. Clairville, *Les Compagnons de la Truelle.* The play, as adapted, was set locally in Christiania, and this caused the greatest excitement. The public, we learn, were amazed and delighted to see "their own windows" on the stage, and the presentation of Frederiksberg and the Klingenberg gardens with their famous Apollo *salon* evoked "a storm of spontaneous enthusiasm." There was a scene in Storgaden "at eventide," another against the background of the fortress of Akershus and, the grand climax, a bird's-eye view of the whole city. *Morgenbladet,* which seems to have acquired a new and caustic reviewer at the beginning of this year, complained that this was merely "the photographic language of reality . . . as if one were to present masons with chalk dust on their faces or a blacksmith with dirty fingers"; a reminder that every age has its critics who object to what they regard as excessive realism. The same gentleman also felt that the humble diction of the actors was unsuited to the representation of upper-class Christiania society, though he appears to have accepted it in the portrayal of foreign royalty and aristocrats. But the public liked the show, and it ran for twelve performances that season.

This was, however, almost the only success of the New Year. *Erasmus Montanus,* another of Holberg's best comedies, achieved only three performances, and H. P. Holst's adaptation of Charlotte Birch-Pfeiffer's *Das Glücksind* four. Ibsen fell back on farces and vaudevilles, but attendances at the theatre declined badly throughout that winter and spring. This was partly because the Christiania Theatre had engaged the toast of Copenhagen, Pepita d'Oliva, and was presenting her in Bøgh's *A Caprice,* in the role in which she had taken the Danish capital by storm. Even the re-engagement by Ibsen of the two English dancers, the Healey Sisters, could not compete with this.

Throughout this winter and spring of 1861 Ibsen was violently and repeatedly attacked in the press for his conduct of the Norwegian Theatre. His new enemy in *Morgenbladet* was particularly to the fore. "Amid all the joy and enthusiasm which the Spanish Sennora [*sic*] is spreading over Christiania," he wrote, "the lesser theatre stands forgotten, thanks to the very bad plays which the artistic director thinks fit to present week after week. A visit to the Norwegian Theatre is like a kind of æsthetic visit to a hospital; to wander down the long empty corridors to the empty rows of stalls and boxes is 'a journey through the abodes of misery and the vales of sorrow.' Things could scarcely be worse if the artistic director strove his utmost to make the repertory as unattractive as possible."

At the beginning of March Ibsen wrote a series of four articles for *Aftenbladet* under the general title "The Two Theatres of Christiania." Asking whether the Danish-controlled Christiania Theatre was equipped "to fulfil the Norwegian people's justifiable demand for a national dramatic art form" (it is as wordy as that in the original), he critically examined its repertory, its artistic achievements, and its attitude towards nationalistic sentiment. Concluding his final article, Ibsen indicated that he might, at some future date, continue with these criticisms; to which the rival newspaper *Morgenbladet* reacted by printing a triple headline in heavy type repeating thrice the request: HERR IBSEN! MORE THEATRE ARTICLES, PLEASE! followed by a short piece demanding that he justify the criticisms he had made. Ibsen did not reply, and his silence was the signal for further attacks on him. On 28 May, *Christiania-Posten* joined in the fray. "Lucky the man," declared this newspaper, "who has a beautiful idea to fight for, and when that idea is a whole people's, and the people have chosen this man to carry their idea towards fulfilment, then that man must be adjudged doubly lucky. Herr Theaterdirektør Ibsen has such an idea to fight for, the Norwegian people have made him controller of their national theatre; *he* is to have charge of this youthful cultural centre, he is, as best he can, to create a national art and elevate our dramatic literature. Such, surely, was the original plan, such surely the principles on which a Norwegian Theatre was to be organised?" But when the rebuilt theatre opened, "one lacked any sense of over-all direction, the theatre stood tottering, the acting was bad, the repertory bad." After castigating the unnecessary expenditure on redecorating and redesigning the interior of the theatre, the writer contrasts "the Herr Ibsen who writes in *Aftenbladet* with the Herr Ibsen who presides in the Norwegian Theatre, the Norwegian Theatre Herr Ibsen describes in the newspaper with the Norwegian Theatre which Herr Ibsen directs," and ends by concluding that "Herr Ibsen is not the man to direct our theatre."

The author of these words continued his attack in two further articles. Ibsen defended himself in *Aftenbladet* on 1 June, listing the Norwegian plays, the classics (such as Holberg), and the new foreign plays that he had presented. His anonymous opponent, however, wrote three more lengthy articles in *Christiania-Posten* that month, the first of which began: "There is a kind of person who supposes that merely by showing himself, merely by stepping forward with an avowal of good conscience and saying *"Hier bin ich,"* he will fell his adversary to the ground. Such a person is Herr Ibsen. He thinks that simply by writing a string of articles in *Aftenbladet* he can get people to believe, not merely that he understands about such things, but that he cherishes a living interest in our theatre."

Ibsen replied in *Aftenbladet* on 12 June, but the feeling that he had neglected his duties was evidently fairly widespread. Knudsen records in his memoirs that on 14 May Ibsen had been rebuked by the board for holding no rehearsals at all between 29 April and 10 May; and a correspondent in *Morgenbladet* asked what Herr Ibsen had done with two new Norwegian plays, J. L. Sundt's *Niels Lykke* (a new treatment of one of the chief characters in *Lady Inger of Østraat*) and a drama entitled *From the Fjord,* both of which had been submitted to him as long ago as 1859 and which he had promised would be performed that season. "Herr Ibsen has thus repeatedly discouraged his authors, flaunted his committee, and vexed his public. One cannot but ask whether such behaviour is becoming in Herr Ibsen, who recently took such offence because the directors of the Christiania Theatre found themselves compelled to postpone for a few months the production of his own play, *The Vikings at Helgeland."* An even more damaging attack, however, came in the form, not of an article, but of a lecture by a member of his own company named Døvle.[24] While the five unpaid members of the board, asserted Døvle, had done all that could reasonably be expected of them, this could not be said of the sixth, paid, member, who was receiving a salary of approaching 1,000 [*sic*] specie-dollars a year, and whose direction of the theatre during the season had been "somewhat negligent." Another correspondent in *Morgenbladet,* in an article carrying the headlines BRING BJØRNSON HOME! demanded that Ibsen be ejected from a post which he seemed to regard as a sinecure and that Bjørnson be put in his place. The news of this campaign, when it reached Bjørnson in Ariccia, did not please him. "Colonel Bassøe," he wrote to Ditmar Meidell, one of the co-editors of *Aftenbladet,* that summer (the letter is again, maddeningly, undated), "says that Ibsen is running the theatre badly. That's ill news indeed."

To these last attacks Ibsen remained silent, and it fell to his old friend Paul Botten Hansen, in *Illustreret Nyhedsblad,* to speak out in his defence. He made the interesting assertion that, apart from Døvle's lecture, all the attacks on Ibsen, while purporting to come from different sources, were in fact being written by the same pen, and declared that "people are destroying the good name of the press by pretending to speak with a multitude

24 Reported in *Morgenbladet,* 30 May 1861.

of voices from selfish political motives." The public, he went on, should not forget the difficulties under which Ibsen has had to work: "box office considerations, ideals, artistic considerations and unsuitable material all make their own special powerful demands." He admits that Ibsen might perhaps show a little more energy; but, whatever Ibsen may or may not have achieved for the Norwegian Theatre, he is not "a man whom any schoolboy may treat as an equal, even if the wind of opinion should be blowing against him." By writing such works as *The Vikings at Helgeland,* and others, Ibsen has laid claim to "a position in our literature which demands a modicum of reason from his opponents, whether they be members of his own company or whether they be undergraduates." Botten Hansen concluded: "These vulgarians of art and letters who have spoken so scornfully of Ibsen should have sufficient insight into the future and sufficient sense of their own poverty of talent to realise that this man, so viciously attacked by them, will live in Norwegian literature long after moss and grass have grown over their own graves and nettles over their literary reputations."

Nevertheless, even if all the newspaper attacks were, as Botten Hansen claimed, written by the same pen, it seems likely that they were at least in part justified. It must have been more than a mere difference of opinion that caused Døvle to speak out; Ibsen told Henrik Jæger that Døvle was angry because "his wife was not getting enough to do,"[25] but one notes that no other member of the company raised his or her voice in public to contradict him. And Ibsen had, as we have seen, been rebuked by his board. Moreover, he was now drinking heavily. At least once students returning to their rooms at night saw his bearded figure lying senseless in the gutter.[26]

If it was any comfort, the Christiania Theatre had been doing little better. It was clear that so small a town as Christiania then was could not profitably support two theatres. Indeed, the previous autumn (1860), when things at the Christiania Theatre were especially bad, a feeler had been put out to the Norwegian Theatre concerning the possibility of a merger. This had happened, however, when the Norwegian Theatre was in the middle of its rebuilding operations, which the board hoped would solve their problems; besides which, they feared that a merger would simply result in their being swallowed by the larger organisation. So the Danish offer was rejected. But as the season had progressed, and neither

25 Midbøe, p. 161.

26 Told by H. Koht (whose father saw Ibsen thus) to A. E. Zucker, and recorded by the latter in *Ibsen, The Master Builder* (London, 1929), pp. 94 and 310-11 note. Professor Francis Bull writes: "I realised how Ibsen was regarded by the bourgeoisie of Christiania in the eighteen-sixties when generalkonsul Andresen Butenschøn told me that as a young man, in 1864, he had been encouraged by his uncle to subscribe to a fund so that 'the drunken poet Henrik Ibsen' might go abroad and be rescued from his misery." (*Tradisjoner og minner,* 3rd edn. [Oslo, 1963], p. 100.)

theatre had prospered, there had been a good deal of unofficial testing of opinion from both camps. The possibility remained in everyone's mind as they broke for the summer vacation.

During the summer, Ibsen started trying to rewrite *Olaf Liljekrans* as an opera libretto, and on 18 July he sent the first scenes to the composer M. A. Udbye in Trondhjem. The pages that have survived show that he had worked on the text to make the language as "Norwegian" as possible; he was still evidently under the influence of the nationalistic movement. But Ibsen, with his poor ear for music, had little idea, despite his earlier youthful article on the subject, of the problems of libretto writing, and despite Udbye's encouragement he left the project unfinished. He wrote only one poem that summer, a completely worthless exhortatory piece to be sung on 17 May (Independence Day), which opens "We are a people, our land is free," and gets no better.

The new season at the Norwegian Theatre opened on 14 August, and Ibsen seems to have taken some at least of the criticisms to heart, for the repertory for the first few weeks contained several new plays; but their reception was hardly propitious. The first, a French comedy by P. Dinaux and G. Lemoine, *La Dotte de Suzette,* was described by *Morgenbladet* as "one of those mediocre products which unfortunately seem to constitute the principal diet of our capital's theatres, and which, even more regrettably, appear to attract the public."

It didn't, for it ran for only three performances. On 13 September the long awaited *Niels Lykke* was at last performed, and proved a disaster. The critics annihilated it (*Morgenbladet* called it "an example of how not to write a play"), and it, too, was withdrawn after three performances. On 25 September Ibsen presented a third play new to Christiania, Gustav Freytag's five-act drama *Count Waldemar,* which had been successfully performed at practically every theatre in Germany. Suzannah Ibsen translated it, the critics welcomed it and praised Ibsen for having had the enterprise to produce it; but the public again showed its distaste for anything remotely serious by staying away, and it, too, lasted for only three performances. The experiences of this month alone underline, if any underlining were needed, the impossibility of Ibsen's position. He was abused for not presenting new plays, or plays of sufficient quality; when he tried to do so, they emptied the theatre. It was a situation with which other directors of experimental theatres over the next hundred years were to become increasingly familiar.

At the annual general meeting of the Norwegian Theatre on 19 September 1861, Ibsen presented his report in what must have been an uncomfortable atmosphere. Owing to the fact, he says, that his new actors were not engaged until the end of September, he was unable to plan his repertory ahead, since this was dependent upon what players he might have at his disposal. The departure of several members of the old company had meant that, whereas previously he had a repertory of about a hundred plays which he could revive at short notice, he was now left with only one which would not require recasting and, consequently, protracted rehearsals. Then, the old decor did not fit the new stage, and had to be "enlarged and repainted," and was not ready until after it was needed. The company, with so many new members, was unused to playing together, and there had been a number of illnesses, as a result of which five performances had had to be cancelled and seven replanned.[27] Despite all this, the theatre had presented more new plays during this seven-and-a-half-month season than in the previous season of nine months. As regards complaints about the economic situation, he presented figures to remind the board that takings had considerably increased since he had taken over the artistic directorship.

Ibsen's defence does not read altogether convincingly at this distance of time. One cannot help feeling, and no doubt the board felt, that, while the difficulties had been considerable, they were of the kind with which a theatre director must more or less expect to be faced, and that a more energetic and resourceful man might have overcome them more successfully. Bjørnson's achievements during his two years as Ibsen's successor at Bergen had become a legend, fostered, we may be sure, by those actors who had recently joined Ibsen's company from there, and that newspaper headline BRING BJØRNSON HOME! must have been in the mind's eye of many a person present. The chairman of the board, Judge Hansteen, expressed his opinion that "the artistic director has not shown the zeal that might have been wished for."

Undeterred by the failure of the three new plays with which he had opened the season, Ibsen presented on 9 October Bjørnson's latest work, *King Sverre,* a three act historical drama written the previous spring. The Christiania Theatre had thought of staging it, but had renounced their rights, and were probably congratulating themselves; to confront the Christiania public with another historical play after the failure of *Niels Lykke* and *Count Waldemar* must have seemed like asking for trouble.

However, the evening after the premiere of *King Sverre,* a gala performance was given to celebrate the laying of the foundation stone of the new Storthing building. The cabinet and members of the Storthing were invited, the house was full, and the evening was a triumph. When the final curtain fell, Johan Sverdrup, the Liberal leader, led three cheers for Bjørnson from the stalls. "It is refreshing to see this kind of dramatic writing as a change from the welter of comedies," commented *Aftenbladet.*

[27] To make matters worse, though Ibsen did not mention this, the cost of rebuilding and redecorating the theatre had so exceeded the original calculations that in February the board had found themselves compelled to summon a meeting of all the actors and staff and announce a reduction of salaries by one-sixth for the next four months; if necessary, they were prepared to postpone this reduction until 1 April, to avoid hardship, but the actors and staff agreed to accept it forthwith.

The acting, as well as the play, was praised, though no one bothered to mention the direction. *King Sverre* was played six times during the season which, if nothing compared to the runs of comedies and musicals, was reckoned good for a serious play. Bjørnson, now in Rome, must have felt grateful to Ibsen. Advising Clemens Petersen on the arrangements for the unveiling of a statue to Oehlenschläger, he wrote: "Ibsen can't make a speech, but if he comes, you get hold of him. Believe me, that man can *think.*"

On 30 October Ibsen, continuing his policy of new plays, staged Alfred de Musset's *Un Caprice* (translated into Norwegian as *En Fantasie,* so as not to be confused with Erik Bøgh's *En Kaprice,* which had been such a success during the two previous seasons). This delicate conversation piece, requiring high comedy acting of the most skilled order, was a bold choice, and the newspapers, to give them credit, praised Ibsen for attempting it. But the public, not surprisingly, found it lacking in action, and four performances were all that it could muster. Financially, the new season was proving a disaster. The mediocre Bøgh, however, came to the rescue with a musical adaptation of Victor Hugo's *The Hunchback of Notre Dame* entitled *Esmeralda.* Ibsen provided an elaborate production, with processions and choirs, and the play ran for thirteen performances. A new Norwegian play, *The Brothers,* by H. O. Hansen, achieved only three, but *Don César de Bazan,* a five act drama by Philippe Dumanoir and Eugène Dennery, paid its way with six, and both productions were praised for their careful acting. Indeed, the newspapers were being as favourable to the productions at the Norwegian Theatre as they had been critical the previous year; perhaps Ibsen's enemy on *Morgenbladet* (and on *Christiania-Posten* too, if we are to believe Botten Hansen) had got the sack. *Aftenbladet* called on the Christiania Theatre to note "how neatly and attractively costumed their colleagues at the impecunious Norwegian Theatre always appear," and *Christiania-Posten* remarked: "If one has censured the Norwegian Theatre in previous years for lack of enterprise, it has certainly shown during the current season energy which fully deserves the appreciation and encouragement which the public by its regular attendance [!] has given it. During the few months since the opening, it has, apart from revivals, presented a number of plays that are either new or at least new to Christiania—and no one can say that the Theatre has shrunk from the demands that this policy has involved, or from the obstacles that have had to be overcome."

But the strain was beginning to tell on Ibsen. On 5 December a notice appeared in the press that the artistic director was ill and therefore unable to perform his duties. "Ibsen is sick, I see?" wrote Vinje to Botten Hansen on 13 December. Magdalene Thoresen, as an old woman in the next century, recalled his illness in her novelettish style:

He had a violent attack of nervous fever. He, who had hitherto possessed a body of granite, resistant to all the buffets of fate, found himself for once in a situation in which he required care and nursing. He was now a married man with a home, so that all the help he needed was to hand. But he absolutely refused to accept any. . . . He left his home each morning and wandered around in the winter air, planless, alone, dazed with fever. And he came through. The sickness gradually left him. But when, after this test of strength with the enemy of life [*Magdalene had grown Ouida-like in her old age*] he had become himself again, it was as though he had covered a part of his journey as a writer underground, and had come up into the daylight again in another place. Henceforth Henrik Ibsen was to steer a new course. It is no longer in the open pages of history that he seeks his themes; from now on he follows a personal path, and strides forth as a cleanser, with a scourge in his hand.[28]

Magdalene always, even as a young woman, preferred the melodramatic to the prosaic explanation. Ever since his teens, Ibsen had been intensely interested in contemporary problems, whether political, social, or personal. It was the tide of nationalism, plus the convention that high tragedy usually concerned the dead, that had caused him to seek his themes in the pages of history; and in any event, it was to be another twelve years before he finally turned his back on historical drama. He had always been by nature a cleanser; it was simply that from now on, he was to use the drama instead of journalism as his medium for this.

The first work that he wrote after his illness,[29] though, was as uncontemporary as it could be: a long, patriotic historical poem entitled "Terje Vigen." Set during the Napoleonic Wars, when Norway was blockaded by the Allies, it tells how a wild youth of that name was changed by the birth of a daughter into a responsible citizen. To save his wife and child from starvation, he tries to run the blockade in a rowboat, but is intercepted by an English man-of-war (the poem is studded with English words, such as "Stop!", "Mylord" [*sic*], etc.), and spends five years in prison. When he is freed, he returns to Norway and finds that his wife and child have starved to death. He becomes a pilot; and one night an English yacht is shipwrecked. Terje, by now grizzled, rows out to save the occupants, and who should they be but the English "Mylord" who had arrested him, with his "Mylady" and child. Conscience and the desire for revenge struggle within him; conscience wins, and he brings them safely to

[28] Magdalene Thoresen, "Om Henrik Ibsen og hans hustru," published in *Juleroser* (Copenhagen, 1901). According to Julius Elias, who had it from Suzannah and Lorentz Dietrichson, Ibsen meditated suicide during this illness (Elias, "Christiania-Fahrt," in *Die Neue Rundschau* XVII [1906], 1464); how seriously is not known.

[29] Though he may have written it just before. It was published on 23 February 1862, as a rather belated New Year's supplement for *Illustreret Nyhedsblad*'s subscribers, but the exact date of its composition is unknown. Ibsen told Halvorsen that he wrote it at the end of 1860, but this must be an error; cf. Koht, II, 303.

land, for, as he explains, "the little one's sake." If, without knowing, one were asked to guess the author of this curiously sentimental and conventional ballad, the last name that would come to mind would be Ibsen's; yet the poem, perhaps because it is one of the few tolerable patriotic works that he wrote, is held in Norway in extraordinary affection. Victor Sjöström, one of the pioneers of the silent cinema, made a film of it in 1916, only ten years after Ibsen's death.[30]

In the New Year of 1862, Ibsen presented several more new productions at the Norwegian Theatre: Mélesville's comedy *Sullivan*, Emile de Najac's *Une Croix à la Cheminée*, *More than Pearls and Gold* (a romantic comedy freely adapted by Hans Andersen from both F. Raimund's *Der Diamant des Geisterkönigs* and *The Thousand and One Nights*), and two new Danish plays, J. C. Hostrup's *A Night in the Mountains* and Meïr Aron Goldschmidt's *Rabbi Eliezer*. *More than Pearls and Gold* ran for seven performances, *Sullivan* for six; the others for only two, four and two performances respectively. Bjørnson's historical verse drama, *Lame Hulda*, in April, managed only three.

On 14 March, Ibsen applied to the Akademiske Kollegium for a stipend of 120 specie-dollars "to make a journey during two of the summer months through outer Hardanger and the districts around the Sognefjord, northwards to Molde and back through Romsdal, to collect and annotate such folk songs and tales, old and new, as may still be extant. On 24 May this application was granted, though the college cheeseparingly knocked 10 specie-dollars off the amount asked.

The economic position of the Norwegian Theatre was by now critical. On 18 March the board had to ask the actors to renounce their holiday pay during the summer, in return for being allowed to lease the theatre free during these months and share the proceeds. In April the orchestra announced that they would not perform until their wages had been paid. That catastrophe was averted; but Ibsen himself was being dunned by creditors, and on 14 May he wrote to J. B. Klingenberg, the treasurer:

If, as promised, you have met any members of the board or would be willing to act on your own account, you would do me the greatest possible service if you could possibly send me by messenger some of the money that is due me. A warrant of distraint has been served on me for last year's tax (11–12 specie-dollars), and I am threatened with the removal of my possessions. This is more than hard, since I am owed a considerable part of my salary, and I therefore place my trust in you as the only person to whom I can turn.

Your obedient servant,
Henr. Ibsen

[30] Sjöström lived long enough to act the leading role in Ingmar Bergman's film, *Wild Strawberries*, in 1957.

A sad note by Klingenberg that same day in the record books of the theatre shows that they had no more than 53 specie-dollars in the till. "Last week," concludes Klingenberg's note, "I had to pay 126 specie-dollars from my own pocket to settle salaries and other essential debts concerned with the running of the theatre."[31]

But by now the Norwegian Theatre had reached the point of no return. The rebuilding operations, on which they had embarked with such hopes, had crippled them, and they now found themselves with debts amounting to 28,000 specie-dollars. The board approached the Christiania Theatre to reopen the question of a merger. Among the conditions they proposed were (1) that the artistic director of the combined venture "shall never be a Dane or other foreigner," (2) that "the standing rule that only Norwegian actors and actresses may be engaged shall not be broken." The Christiania Theatre replied recalling that they had themselves suggested a merger in 1860, but that "although this proposal appeared to have been favourably received, the directors of the Norwegian Theatre withdrew from further negotiations, so that the opportunity of uniting without either side incurring an impossible financial debt was lost." The Christiania Theatre (the letter continued) felt unable to take over the very considerable debt now owed by the Norwegian Theatre; if, however, the latter should succeed in selling its building for some non-theatrical purpose, and could arrange for its debt to be paid off in annual instalments of 1,500 specie-dollars, agreement might possibly be reached.

These terms, especially in view of the high-handed manner in which they were worded, the Norwegian Theatre found unacceptable. It was decided to file a petition of bankruptcy, and Ibsen and his company were given notice as from 1 June. The actors, however, decided to remain together and lease the theatre as an independent concern for the coming season for a payment of 18 specie-dollars per performance.

So Ibsen's career as a theatre director ended. If his six years at Bergen had been hard, these five years at Christiania had been harder. For him, of all people, so fastidious in his tastes and so shy of human contact, to produce this succession of featherweight farces and musicals with an inexperienced company, contemptible rehearsal time, and hopelessly inadequate financial and technical resources, abused in the press, attacked from within his own company and condemned by his board, it must indeed have been a protracted nightmare. His own dramatic talent, instead of flowering as he had hoped, had gone barren; and now, with a wife and son to support and no private means, he was without a job.

Moreover, he was now being blamed in some quarters for the theatre's failure. Knud Knudsen, in his unpublished memoirs, makes no bones

[31] Øyvind Anker, "Ibseniana og Bjørnsoniana fra Kristiania-teatrene," in *Edda*, 1956.

about the matter. They should, he said, have got rid of Ibsen much earlier, and had only not done so "because (1) we had no one else to turn to (2) we always hoped that the pressure exerted by the board must some time take effect (3) he undeniably *understood* the work better than anyone else we could possibly hope to get (4) we were unwilling to make a man, in other respects so deserving, jobless. . . . People would hardly credit that an author who could create so strong-willed a character as Brand could have been so slack and lethargical in practical matters."

Knudsen's condemnation probably goes too far. We know that he and Ibsen had disagreed violently from the beginning about how far the theatre could go in being "Norwegian"; Knudsen was a fanatic on this subject, and there is evidence that, in common with a curiously high proportion of linguists, he tended to become paranoiacally hostile to anyone who opposed him on his pet subject. If one peruses the newspaper reactions to the hundreds of productions which Ibsen presented at the Norwegian Theatre, one finds him praised more often than blamed; frequently we read that the scenic arrangements are "especially handsome and tasteful," the ensemble playing excellent, the costumes attractive (he was always especially meticulous about other people's clothes as well as his own). Not only the standard of acting and production, but also the box-office takings improved markedly during his tenure of office, except during his last season, and the falling-off then was almost certainly directly due to his pursuing a policy of new plays on the orders of his committee. Under his direction, the Norwegian Theatre soon found itself able to compete on equal terms with, and sometimes even surpass, the Christiania Theatre, which had a better building and stage, a smarter position, much more experienced actors, and an established audience. When Ibsen arrived, the annual takings at the Norwegian Theatre had averaged 7,000 specie-dollars; during his first year this rose to 9,000 and over the next few years it rose to 12,000—an increase of more than 70 per cent. If the board had not over-reached themselves by their decision to rebuild, and so saddled themselves with a debt they could never hope to pay off, they would probably still, eventually, have had to merge with the Christiania Theatre, because the city could not support two theatres running roughly similar repertories; but Ibsen would at least have been recognised as having done the job he had been appointed to do, namely, to raise the Norwegian Theatre to the same level as the Christiania Theatre. He was not the first nor the last theatre director to become a scapegoat for the failings of his committee and the preferences of his audience for light entertainment rather than serious drama.

Nowhere, probably, in Europe could he have found a less inspiring town to work in. "Christiania during the late eighteen-fifties and early eighteen-sixties," wrote Gerhard Gran, "must have been a sadly jejune place. . . . All observers from this time agree in their condemnation of its spiritual indifference."[32] J. E. Sars called it "a temple of puritanism and narrow-mindedness, a community of the old, granting youth no rights whatever."[33] Henrik Jæger, writing in 1887–88, noted: "It is significant that none of our living Norwegian authors choose to live in the capital. They have arranged to live in the country . . . or have buried themselves in a small town. And usually they have chosen to exile themselves for a shorter or longer period."[34] The most eloquent condemnation of nineteenth-century Christiania, however, comes from one of Norway's most distinguished novelists, Henrik Wergeland's sister, Camilla Collett:

> O great and little city! What a cold and surly sky broods over you! You are great enough, with your thousand beaks! great enough slowly to peck to death the man who no longer diverts you, or against whom you bear a grudge. But not so great that one of these unhappy creatures can find a corner in which to hide. . . . You have all the consuming passions, yearnings and pretensions of a great city; and yet you are so small, and so petty, that you cannot gratify one of them. . . . We, your children, must live off one another, feed on one another . . . [*The Judge's Daughters*, 1854–55].

In the long run, however, we must be grateful that things happened as they did. If Ibsen had been successful and happy in his work in Christiania he might, with his lifelong dislike of travel, never have uprooted himself from Norway and spent the greater part of his working life abroad; and, as with so many creative writers, it was only when he transplanted himself to foreign soil that his genius really began to flower.

---

[32] Gran, I, 86–87.

[33] Quoted by Gran, I, 87. He does not specify where in Sars's writings this reference occurs, nor have I succeeded in tracing it.

[34] Jæger, p. 163.

8

Out of the Tunnel

1862 – 1864

On 20 June 1862 Ibsen signed a contract with Jonas Lie, who by now had taken over the ownership of *Illustreret Nyhedsblad* (though Botten Hansen was still its editor) for the publication of a new play, his first in five years; and on 29 June the magazine announced that "a modern verse comedy in three acts by Henrik Ibsen" would constitute its New Year supplement. The idea for this play had first come to Ibsen as early as 1858, and in 1860 he had begun to write it under the title of *Svanhild* (the name of the heroine). About sixteen pages of this draft have survived; apart from a song which opens it, a solo with choruses, it is in prose, a modern satirical comedy set just outside Christiania. But during 1860 he had been overwhelmed by a general feeling of apathy towards his work, and had abandoned the project. Now, during either the spring or, more probably, the early summer of 1862, he had taken it up again, this time writing it in verse which, one can scarcely repeat too often, came to him as a young man more easily than prose, not least in the composing of dialogue. It has usually been assumed, on no evidence that I can find, that he had completed the first draft by the time he signed his contract. But that spring had been a particularly hectic time at the Norwegian Theatre, and it seems likelier that he merely showed Lie and Botten Hansen the draft of *Svanhild,* or a few pages of verse rewrite, and that they, knowing his past achievements and perhaps wishing to give him an additional incentive, commissioned the play, which he eventually re-titled *Love's Comedy.*[1]

[1] Ibsen only just got the final version ready in time for it to be published on 31 December; after he had handed in the first two acts, he was so long over the third that Lie only managed to extract it from him by threatening: "If I don't get it now, I'll write it myself." Now this final version differs very little from the first verse draft, and the only substantial changes occur in Act One. Ibsen had nothing else to occupy him after his return to Christiania in early August except a little casual journalism, and it seems more probable that he spent those next five months completing his

On 24 June, he left Christiania on his trip northwards to gather folklore, for which the Akademiske Kollegium had granted him a stipend. He travelled partly by coach, partly on foot, partly by fjord steamer, and partly by rowboat. A brief diary which he kept during the first three weeks, barely a thousand words all told, was discovered as late as 1932, and enables us to follow him, in the company of a newly-engaged young law student and a stern Catholic priest, to Lillehammer, along the valley of Gudbrandsdal and across the Sogne mountains; thence he voyaged along the Sognefjord, northwards through the spectacular landscape of Sunnfjord and Nordfjord, over the mountains from Breim to Sunnylven, by steamer to Søholt, on to Vestnes in Romsdal, and back through Gudbrandsdal to Christiania. The harshness of life in the remoter areas astonished him. He came to one valley where the parsonage had been destroyed by an avalanche. The wife, who had just given birth to a child, occupied a screened-off corner, while the husband transacted the business of the parish in the rest of the room. Another house lay at the foot of a precipice so sheer that the inhabitants had no fear of avalanches; the stones, they told him, always fell at a slight angle so that, hugging the rock, the house was safe. From the Jotunfjeld he looked straight down on a steeple hundreds of feet below, and could see no possible way of descent; but there turned out to be a path cut in the face of the precipice, and he descended this with his Catholic priest and a sick woman tied to a horse. He mistook two Swedish fellow-travellers in succession for the young Swedish poet Carl Snoilsky, who that year had published his first book of poems (and who was to become his close friend a quarter of a century later); was depressed by the heavy rain which followed him everywhere; commented on the varying quality of his lodgings; took showers when he could, bathed, fished, and collected stories.

Some of these he dismissed as fabrications, such as the sea-serpent caught in Lysterfjord and sold for 300 specie-dollars to an Englishman, who got his money back; "for" (records Ibsen), "he knew where the sea-serpent hides in its belly all costly objects of gold and silver which it swallows, and slit it open and took them." But others seemed more authentic; and he found two especially rewarding informants. One was a free-thinking peasant known as Steins-Knut, whom Ibsen described as "the wisest countryman he had ever met"; the other, at Solnær, was a local historian named Peder Fylling, to whom Ibsen was introduced by his wife's cousin, Ludvig Daæ. From Fylling he scribbled down over a hundred pages of legendary anecdotes, most of them dealing with supernatural visitations. Many of these centred on an eighteenth-century priest named Peter Strøm; he had

---

first draft and then revising it than that he devoted them purely to the revisionary work, which we know to be slight. Moreover, the announcement in *Illustreret Nyhedsblad* on 29 June gives no title, which suggests that at that stage it was merely begun or projected.

studied the "Black Book" at Wittenberg, as was common among churchmen of those days, for the ability to perform seemingly impossible tricks enabled them to impress and convert otherwise sceptical peasants. Thus, Ibsen learned, Peder once sank an unbeliever in the earth up to his shoulders and freed him only when he had promised to follow the true faith. He terrified the local witches by telling them that, if they were in league with the Devil, blood would run from their butter when he cut it with his knife; "and those present saw a new sight, for the blood not only ran from the butter but drenched the whole table." Then there was the story of St. Olav's pig; the saint left it with a peasant, and at first the animal thrived, "but as the rumour spread that the saint was dead, the pig began to pine, and finally so sickened that it turned into stone, and so it may still be seen standing there today." There was the witch who, as they took her to the stake, swore that no living thing would grow for as far as she could see as she burned, "wherefore they deemed it expedient to bandage her eyes"; and the ignorant charcoal-burner whose one desire was to become a priest, though he could neither read nor write. By a trick played on the king, he managed to obtain a living, but his ignorance was so patent that the parishioners petitioned the bishop to remove him. Knowing the bishop to be a lecher, he feigned death, having bidden his wife to sit alone with the bishop watching over his coffin. Then, as the bishop began to fondle her, the charcoal-burner rose from his coffin and denounced him, as a result of which "the bishop had to let him remain as priest, although he could not read the Book."

In addition to these notes, Ibsen made drawings of the landscape, and when he returned to Christiania in early August, four of these (two of Gudbrandsdal, one of Vestnes, and one of Nordfjord) were published in *Illustreret Nyhedsblad*—the only time, so far as we know, that he ever received payment for any artistic work. They are excellent realistic studies; Ibsen had continued with his painting[2] all the time he had been in Christiania, even, when he could ill afford it, taking lessons from a feckless painter named Magnus Bagge who was to be one of the models (there were several, for it is a common enough Norwegian type) for Hjalmar Ekdal in *The Wild Duck*. He accompanied these drawings with stiff little descriptive sketches, of the kind expected from nineteenth-century travellers. He also wrote up for *Illustreret Nyhedsblad* four of the stories that Peder Fylling had told him, and on 17 November signed a contract with the bookseller and publisher Johan Dahl to make a book of them, of two hundred and fifty pages, for an honorarium of 160 specie-dollars—a project which (surprisingly, in view of his need for cash) he never completed. Now that the Norwegian Theatre had closed he was without a job, and had to support his wife and son by casual journalism, plus whatever he may have saved from his travel stipend. There cannot

[2] Dietrichson recalled seeing a landscape on an easel in Ibsen's room in the summer of 1861 (I, 332).

have been much left from the 110 specie-dollars; but Ibsen (and Suzannah, too) were, all their lives, the thriftiest of people, and they seem to have managed somehow.

Ibsen wrote eight long articles for *Illustreret Nyhedsblad, Aftenbladet,* and even *Morgenbladet* (which had been so hostile towards him) before the end of the year. The first two, on "The Crisis in the Theatre" (that perennial subject) included, in addition to an indictment of the public for indifference, a bitter attack on the complacency of actors. "Our players," he wrote, "have not as yet experienced the blessing of privation, which no man escapes with impunity. The man of ideas who lacks the opportunity to starve or suffer is thereby deprived of *one* way of becoming great." He went on to express his personal faith in a vivid image. "When Vesuvius erupted and destroyed Pompeii with earthquake and ash, a Roman soldier stood guard at the temple. Slaves and anyone, anything that could flee, fled past him; but the soldier remained at his post, bound by his duty, guarding his trust. The rain of ash rose and rose around him, inch by inch, and rose so high that it buried him; he could not flee, for *he had not been dismissed!* Such action is spiritual, it is a revelation of the spirit that should rule in art as in the army or the Church . . . to remain at one's post and guard one's trust."[3] He was, though he did not know it, about to be given a further opportunity to test the strength of his belief in his calling.

On 31 December 1862 *Love's Comedy* was published, as *Illustreret Nyhedsblad*'s special New Year supplement for their subscribers. Ibsen received 100 specie-dollars, "at that time a goodish fee," noted Henrik Jæger.[4] Apart from *St. John's Night,* it was the first play he had written with a modern setting.

The action takes place in the garden of a villa just outside Christiania, owned by Mrs. Halm, the widow of a civil servant. She has married off seven nieces from this house, and is anxious to do the same for her two daughters, Anna and Svanhild; which ambition seems about to be fulfilled, for they are being courted by her lively young student lodgers, Lind and Falk. Falk, however, believes that marriage and love are incompatible; marriage, he declares, is "a galley of chains and thralldom," and as though to prove his point the local Pastor Strawman enters with his wife and eight of their twelve children. Once he had been a burning young idealist like Falk; now he has faded into dullness and conventionality, and the girl he loved has become a plump housewife. "Everything's burned out, dead!" cries Falk. "Where's the green joy of life?" He calls on Svanhild to join her life to his, but without the bond of marriage. "If you must die, live first! Be mine, in God's green spring!" With her to inspire him, he knows he could become a great poet. Like the falcon whose name he bears:

---

[3] *Aftenbladet,* 31 August 1862.
[4] Midbøe, p. 164.

> I must fly against the wind to reach the heights,
> And you're the gust to carry me . . .
> Be mine, be mine, until the world shall claim you!
> And when our tree grows bare, why, then we'll part.

SVANHILD. You think of me as a reed that a child cuts
> Into a flute to play on for an hour,
> Then casts away.

FALK. Better that than to stagnate in the marsh
> Till autumn comes and chokes you with grey fog.

But she, the first of those imaginative yet realistic girls whom Ibsen was to create, the predecessor of Agnes in *Brand,* Solveig in *Peer Gynt,* Dina Dorf in *The Pillars of Society,* Nora when the scales have fallen from her eyes, replies:

> You called yourself a falcon . . .
> Another image came into my mind.
> I saw you as no falcon, but a kite,
> A poet's kite of paper, that is nothing
> Without its string . . . impotently beseeching:
> "Send me aloft, that the strong winds may bear me!"

She leaves him; and impulsively he decides that he must, after all, marry her.

But in the second act his disillusionment returns. His friend Lind, whom Anna has by now accepted, begins to show the marks of domesticity; and Pastor Strawman does not help by descanting on the joys of marriage. Falk, in exasperation, denounces marriage to the assembled company. Love, he says, anticipating T. S. Eliot, has to cross the desert; to marry is to turn one's back on that desert. Marriage is to love "as is a potted plant to fresh field flowers." The company is scandalised and departs into the house; only Svanhild remains, awed by his fury as Agnes was to be by Brand's, and says that, if he still wants her, she will go with him. He tells her that they will show the world that there is a love which marriage need not destroy, takes off his ring and puts it on her finger.

This is where most dramatists of the age would have ended the play; but Ibsen, even this early in his career, had something up his sleeve for the final act. Pastor Strawman, hitherto merely a figure of fun, tells Falk that the latter's denunciation of marriage has reminded him of his own lost ideals, and begs him, somehow, to give him (Strawman) back his faith. Falk says he cannot. But now Guldstad, a rich but kindly business man, and himself an admirer of Svanhild, steps in. He reminds Falk of what the latter had said yesterday, about the incompatibility of marriage and love; has he really changed his views? The only possible foundation for a happy marriage, says Guldstad, is the kind of love that is based on other

things than passion; it is not inferior to passionate love, and it grows where
the other fades. He leaves Falk and Svanhild alone to make their decision.
Svanhild asks Falk if he would not still cherish her if and when his love
died; to which he replies: "No. When my love died, all else would die
too." She asks whether he can promise her that he will love her for ever;
he answers: "For a long time." She says that the kind of love she and
Falk bear for each other can only survive if the lovers part when it is at
its full, and keep it as a memory. This memory will do more for Falk as a
poet than if they should stay together and their love fade. She kisses his
ring, throws it into the fjord, and tells Guldstad that she will marry him;
and is left sadly seated as the others congratulate her, while Falk, free as he
has always longed to be, goes off into the mountains with his illusions.

Love's Comedy was, both structurally and in the depth of its characterisation, by far the best play that Ibsen had yet written. Why is it never
acted today, in Scandinavia any more than elsewhere? The reason lies in
the form which Ibsen employed. It is written throughout in rhymed
verse, of remarkable concentration and ingenuity, but of an extreme
formalism, as though by a modern Alexander Pope. Admittedly, Ibsen was
to use rhyme throughout both *Brand* and *Peer Gynt*, but in both those plays
he employed it far more flexibly than in *Love's Comedy*. In them the
characters speak dialogue, in *Love's Comedy* they deliver set pieces
packed with epigrams. To work on a modern stage, the play would have to
be translated into free verse; and even then, the effect of set pieces would
remain. Attempts to revive it in this century have never proved successful,
and are never likely to; it remains a brilliant dramatic poem rather than a
poetic play. It is crippled by the untheatricality of its form, just as *Olaf
Liljekrans* is crippled by the untheatricality of the ballad form and *The
Vikings at Helgeland* by that of the saga style.

The day after *Love's Comedy* was published, on 1 January 1863, Ibsen
took up a part-time employment as *æsthetisk konsulent* to the Christiania
Theatre, which had decided to bow to public opinion and go Norwegian.
The Danish manager, Carl Borgaard, had been dismissed, and negotiations
were in progress for the services of the actors of the Norwegian Theatre
who, since that body had declared itself bankrupt, had been giving per-
fórmances at the Møllergaden theatre as an independent company. Most
of them were to move to Bankpladsen in the summer. Ibsen's duties in his
new post included, as well as literary advice, supervision of the historical
accuracy of the decor and costumes, and, when required, stage direction.
His salary was pathetically small, 25 specie-dollars per month, and since
even this small sum was dependent on the box-office takings exceeding a
certain figure, he in fact received only a fraction of it.

On 8 January he offered *Love's Comedy* to the theatre at Trondhjem
for the modest honorarium of 60 specie-dollars, and while he was awaiting
their reply a notice appeared in *Illustreret Nyhedsblad*, on 25 January, to

the effect that the play was shortly to be staged at the Christiania Theatre. But during February and March reviews of the most unfavourable nature began to appear in the press. Professor M. J. Monrad, who had welcomed the appearance of *Catiline* thirteen years earlier, warned Ibsen in *Morgenbladet* that he would destroy himself if he became "a mouthpiece for the loose thinking and debilitating nihilism that is now fashionable." The play, he asserted, was "an offence against human decency. . . . The underlying theme, that marriage and love are irreconcilable opposites, is not merely basically untrue and, in the loftier sense of the word, immoral, in that it denigrates both love and marriage; it is also unpoetical, as any viewpoint must be which claims that idealism and reality are incompatible."

In *Aftenbladet*, Ditmar Meidell called *Love's Comedy* "a wretched specimen of literary dilettantism," and said that Ibsen had "abandoned himself to a wild pursuit of effects, not shunning the most fanciful and tasteless paradoxes to achieve his goal." Ibsen, he continued, "does not possess genius, but merely talent. . . . He could develop into a pleasing poet, since he has a facility for modelling himself on good masters and an ear for verbal music," but "he sets out deliberately to portray marriage and family life as the darker side of human existence, nay, as the very cause of all the misery that this world contains, since the state of marriage, in his view, extinguishes true love and closes men's eyes permanently to all ideals." Botten Hansen, as always, attempted to defend his friend in *Illustreret Nyhedsblad*,[5] but the public was left in no doubt that *Love's Comedy* was an immoral work (just as, eighteen years later, they were to receive a like warning about *Ghosts*). The Christiania Theatre, never (then or later) renowned for flying in the face of public sentiment, decided that they dare not perform it.

Ibsen never forgot the abuse with which his compatriots had received *Love's Comedy* and the effect it had had on him. When, three years later, following the success of *Brand, Love's Comedy* came to be reprinted, he decided to hit back at his attackers in a preface. "I made the mistake," he wrote, "of publishing it in Norway. Both the time and the place were ill chosen. The play aroused a storm of hostility, more violent and widespread than most books could boast of having evoked in a community the vast majority of whose members commonly regard matters of literature as being of small concern. This reception did not really surprise me. . . . When, in my comedy, as best I could, I cracked the whip over the problem of love and marriage, it was only natural that the majority should rush shrieking to the defence of those institutions. Not many of our critics and readers have acquired the intellectual discipline and training which enable a man to

[5] A caricature in the weekly magazine *Vikingen* (7 March 1863) shows Botten Hansen, pierced with arrows and quill pens, using *Illustreret Nyhedsblad* as a shield to defend Ibsen against the attacks of *Aftenbladet*.

recognise delusions." In a letter to Peter Hansen on 28 October 1870, he recalled: "People brought my personal affairs into the discussion, and my reputation suffered considerably. The only person who approved of the play was my wife. . . . I was excommunicated. Everyone was against me."[6] Perhaps partly because of the hostility of its reception, he retained a particular fondness for the play. "Structurally," he wrote to Hartvig Lassen on 24 October 1872,[7] "I am more than ever convinced that it cannot be faulted, and has not in this respect been bettered in any of my other plays. All in all, I reckon *Love's Comedy* to be among the best things that I have done"—and this was after he had written *Brand* and *Peer Gynt*.

Ibsen admitted that his wife had been the model for Svanhild. "Illogical, but with a strong poetic intuition, a bigness of outlook, and an almost vehement hatred of all petty scruples" was how he was to describe Suzannah (in the letter to Peter Hansen quoted above); and the description would apply equally to Svanhild. Similarly, he declared Suzannah to have been the model for Hjørdis in *The Vikings at Helgeland*, because Suzannah, like Hjørdis, thought that the highest thing that a woman could do was to accompany her loved one into battle and "set his vision aflame." He may have taken the name Svanhild from the Volsungasaga, one of his main sources for *The Vikings at Helgeland*; in that, there is an innocent young girl named Svanhild who has to suffer a tragic fate because of the crimes of her family, just as Ibsen's Svanhild was to suffer because everyone around her had sinned against the true concept of love.

Ibsen's finances were now at rock bottom. They had, as we know, been bad enough when he was receiving 50 specie-dollars a month from the Norwegian Theatre; now he was forced to resort to money-lenders, and to making further applications for grants and stipends. On 6 March he applied to the Akademiske Kollegium for a renewal of the stipend allowed him the previous year for the collection of folk lore. He asked 120 specie-dollars and was granted 100. Four days later he addressed a petition to the king: "Henrik Ibsen," it begins, "most humbly begs . . . that he be granted an annual pension of 400 (four hundred) specie-dollars, to enable him to continue his literary activity."

The document makes sad reading. Ibsen describes his career up to this point: how he had started work at fifteen, "my parents being in needy circumstances"; how he had prepared himself for his matriculation; and

---

[6] "They began, as is customary in such cases, to search into Ibsen's private life and investigate the nature of his own marriage. As Ibsen once put it to me: the printed criticism of the comedy might have been borne at a pinch, but the oral and private criticism was absolutely unbearable." Georg Brandes, *Henrik Ibsen* (Copenhagen, 1898), pp. 57–58—Muir-Archer translation.

[7] This letter is not in the Centenary Edition, but was printed by Øyvind Anker in his article "Kjærlighedens Komedie på Christiania Theater," in *Edda* (1961), pp. 59–81.

then lists his publications and the plays which he has had staged, naming the various salaries he has enjoyed.

My salary at the Bergen Theatre amounted to 300 specie-dollars annually, and I was compelled to leave the city in debt. My appointment at the Norwegian Theatre of Christiania carried with it an annual salary of about 600 specie-dollars, but the theatre's bankruptcy involved me in a loss of over 150 specie-dollars, together with all permanency of occupation. At the Christiania Theatre I have been allotted a nominal salary of 25 specie-dollars per month, but the payment of this is dependent upon higher takings than the theatre has achieved during the current winter. My financially most successful work, *The Vikings at Helgeland,* which occupied me for nearly a year, brought me in all 277 specie-dollars. Under the circumstances I have incurred debts of some 500 specie-dollars, and since I have been unable to envisage any prospect of improving my financial situation in this country, I have felt compelled to make the necessary preliminary arrangements to emigrate this spring to Denmark. To leave my native land and abandon a career which I have hitherto regarded, and still regard, as my true vocation, is, however, a step which I find inexpressibly distressing, and it is in the hope of avoiding this step that I now, as a last resort, most humbly beseech that a proposal signed by Your Majesty be laid before the present Parliament granting me an annual pension of 400 specie-dollars, whereby I may be enabled to continue a career in the service of letters which I have reason to believe that the public would not wish to see brought to an end.

Your Majesty's most humble servant,
Henrik Ibsen

This appeal was rejected; not, as some biographers have suggested, because of *Love's Comedy* (though one member of the grants board, a cleric named Riddervold, declared that the man who could have written such a play deserved not a grant but a thrashing). The records of the Department of Education (who had, after all, granted his folk lore application the previous year) show that in their report they admitted that "the applicant's literary achievements must be agreed to be of no small importance to our literature, and would have wished that Ibsen could be granted support to enable him to continue his work under more favourable circumstances; but, since we must hesitate before recommending new grants that are not of immediate urgency, Parliament having been assembled for so long, we cannot feel that there is the same urgency to make such a recommendation as in that of the grant for Bjørnstjerne Bjørnson," who had applied simultaneously. The memorandum added a reminder that Ibsen's request in 1860 for a travel grant had not been acceded to, and concluded: "We feel it is probable that he will be favourably considered at the next allocation of stipendia, though this statement naturally cannot be regarded as binding."[8]

On 27 May he made a further application, this time for a grant of 600 specie-dollars "to spend a year, principally in Paris and Rome, studying art, art history, and literature." The petition continues: "The many and great difficulties with which an author has to contend in this country are increased still further by the almost total absence of opportunity to obtain the necessary grounding in general culture which everywhere else is regarded as an essential condition for the successful and profitable continuation of the work which I believe to be my vocation. I venture to observe that travel grants of this nature have been granted to every Norwegian writer who has devoted himself exclusively to authorship except myself, and I therefore most humbly beseech that I may be allotted six hundred specie-dollars from the Fund for Foreign Travel in the Pursuit of Art and Science."

"Ibsen can rely on a bigger grant than Bjørnson, surely!" wrote Vinje to Botten Hansen on 11 June; but he was wrong. Although, on 12 September, the Akademiske Kollegium at last acceded to his request, they did so as grudgingly as possible, giving him the last place on their list and recommending that the award be reduced to 250 specie-dollars. This sum struck even the Department of Education as miserly, and they recommended that it be increased to 400 specie-dollars "which, though considerably less than the amount applied for, may be regarded as sufficient to ensure some satisfactory return, which can scarcely be said of so small a sum as that suggested by the Kollegium."[9]

The result of this latest application was not made known to Ibsen until mid-September, and he existed that summer, we must suppose, largely on the 100 specie-dollars which he had been granted to continue his study of folk lore, and which he in fact never used for that purpose. O. Arvesen describes how Ibsen could be seen in his shabby clothes entering L'Orsa's café punctually at two o'clock each afternoon to drink coffee and read the foreign newspapers, and adds: "That this man with the threadbare coat, old, soft mormon hat and profoundly unassuming mien would become one of Norway's and Scandinavia's greatest men was an unimaginable thought."[10]

The tide was, however, about to turn.

In June Ibsen received an invitation from students to attend a choral festival at Bergen, at which over a thousand singers were to gather from

[8] Statssekretariatets Arkiv, quoted by Halvorsen, p. 13.
[9] Loc. cit.
[10] O. Arvesen, Oplevelser og erindringer (Christiania, 1921), pp. 128–29.

various parts of Norway. He accepted, and wrote a song which the three choral groups from Christiania learned for the occasion. The news of Ibsen's imminent return aroused no enthusiasm in Bergen. A list of those requiring accommodation was posted in the town; those willing to offer hospitality were asked to sign against visitors whom they would like to have, and, we are told, Ibsen's was the last name to be taken up. Ignorant of this, he left Christiania with the three choirs by ship on 12 June, and reached Bergen two days later.

The voyage in the company of these people, and the festival itself (which lasted four days) had a remarkable effect on him. For the first time in his life, he was lionised. The critics, especially of late, had been hostile to his works, the cultural authorities had repeatedly negatived his applications, and, living, as he did now, a comparatively solitary life, he can seldom have heard a word of praise except from those he knew well, and that one never quite believes. But now, forced into the company of this largely youthful gathering, he, who had previously felt isolated and rejected, found himself surrounded by sympathy, friendship, and spontaneous admiration. One incident especially moved him. At a banquet in Bergen on 16 June, Bjørnson paid him a most generous public tribute, speaking out handsomely in praise of his writing and denouncing those people who had tried, as critics will in every age that contains writers of comparable stature, to turn them into adversaries. "Have I not experienced," cried Bjørnson, "that my friend Ibsen has been held up against me for the purpose of disparaging me, and I against him, to disparage him?" His speech was followed by the song which Ibsen had written for the occasion, dealing, it so happened, with the importance of naturally dissimilar people living together in harmony—a coincidence which Ibsen, no more than anyone else, can hardly have missed. Four days after his return to Christiania, on 25 June, he wrote to his host at Bergen, a shipping agent named Randolph Nilsen:

It is eight days to the hour since we said goodbye, and, God be praised, I still carry within me the spirit of the festival, and I hope I shall long keep it. My hearty thanks to you and your good wife for all the indescribable warmth and friendliness you showed me. The festival up there, and the many dear and unforgettable people whom I met, are working on me like a good visit to church, and I sincerely hope that this mood will not pass. Everyone was so kind to me in Bergen. It is not so here, where there are many people who seek to hurt and wound me at every opportunity. This powerful feeling of elevation, of being ennobled and purified in all one's thoughts, must I think have been common to all who attended the choral festival, and he would indeed have something hard and evil in his soul who could remain insensitive to such an atmosphere.

Further encouraging things were to happen that summer. On 18 July, the young Danish critic Clemens Petersen published a long review of *Love's Comedy* in the Copenhagen magazine *Fædrelandet*. It occupied half the issue, and was by no means altogether favourable; indeed, it summed the play itself up as "a failure." Petersen praised the skill of the verse, but thought, rightly, that there was too much virtuoso rhyming, and that the reasoning was sometimes glib. He also asserted, one would think less correctly, that Ibsen wrote well only when he wrote "in the shadow of some accepted prototype," saying that he was "unsure and hit-or-miss" when left to his own resources; he thought that Ibsen had striven to compete with Bjørnson, at the same time imitating him and trying to do the opposite to him. What Ibsen ought to do, concluded Petersen, "with his fine eye for a prototype and his rich talent for carrying on where others have left off" was to unite the old traditions with the new. Although, therefore, Petersen ultimately came down against *Love's Comedy*, his review made it clear that he regarded Ibsen as a writer of both accomplishment and promise, to be taken seriously; and this, from the most influential critic in Scandinavia, must have seemed praise indeed compared with the kind of criticisms which Ibsen had been getting in Norway.

The following day, 19 July, a long "profile" of Ibsen was published in *Illustreret Nyhedsblad*. These weekly profiles were a feature of the magazine; notabilities thus honoured that summer included Lamartine, Liszt, and Stonewall Jackson, so that to appear in the series was something of a distinction. Paul Botten Hansen was the author, and the piece, some twenty-five hundred words in length, was accompanied by the first likeness of Ibsen to be printed, a clumsy linocut "after a photograph by Petersen," not easily distinguishable from one of Vinje, similarly bearded and melancholy, which was published in the next issue, and much inferior to a large illustration of Princess Alexandra of Denmark's arrival in London for her wedding with the Prince of Wales which appeared in the same issue as Ibsen's profile. Pointing out that Ibsen now had no fixed income other than his uncertain salary as *aesthetisk konsulent* to the Christiania Theatre, Botten Hansen continued: "He is consequently mainly dependent on such honoraria as his writing may bring him. But this, Ibsen being the kind of author he is, can never prove a rich source, for he is one of those individuals whom external circumstances, and even privation, cannot readily incite, except as the expression of a temporary inspiration. The reason for this is a self-criticism which often rejects not merely long-matured plans, drafts and works already commenced, but even completed *œuvres* which, when he considers them coldly and at a distance, no longer satisfy him." Botten Hansen went on to compare Ibsen's lyrics with those of Heine, but said that his dramatic works were his most important, and concluded with the information that Ibsen "is at present busied with a new saga-play set in Norway in the Middle Ages."

A further reference to this latest project occurs in a letter which Ibsen wrote on 10 August to Clemens Petersen, thanking him for his notice of *Love's Comedy:*

> Mr. Clemens Petersen.
>
> I don't like writing letters, largely because I suspect that the criticisms which you make, rather harshly I feel, of my prose in general may justly be levelled against my efforts in this field. However, I must write briefly to thank you warmly and sincerely for your review of my book. I thank you both for what I agree with (which isn't only the flattering bits) and for what, if I ever have the good fortune to meet you, I shall at any rate *try* to dispute. I am especially grateful to see that you are not in general as opposed to my work as I had instinctively imagined; this has for me an importance which is perhaps difficult for you to understand who do not know how frighteningly alone, in a spiritual sense, I feel up here. My "friends'" opinion of me doesn't hurt; in matters where I myself am concerned, I see far more clearly than all my friends—and the result is far from flattering. I am now engaged on a historical drama in five acts—but in prose, I *cannot* write it in verse. You do me a little injustice when you suggest that I have tried to imitate Bjørnson; *Lady Inger of Østraat* and *The Vikings at Helgeland* were written before Bjørnson had composed a line. (N.B. It is possible that *Between the Battles* was in existence by the time I wrote *The Vikings*, but I did not and could not have read it.) As regards *Love's Comedy*, I can assure you that if ever an author had to get a mood and a subject off his chest, it was the case when I sat down to write that. I shall follow your kind advice to offer *Lady Inger* to the Royal Theatre [*at Copenhagen*]; please heaven I handle the matter in the right way, and it comes off. I feel compelled to send you these lines of thanks because I feel most warmly and sincerely that you have done me a great kindness in not putting my book aside in silence.
>
> Yours gratefully,
> Henr. Ibsen

This "historical drama," or, as Botten Hansen had described it, "saga-play" on which Ibsen was now engaged was his first really major dramatic work: *The Pretenders.*

He had begun to plan this work as early as five years previously, in the summer of 1858. The idea seems to have come to him then through reading the third volume of P. A. Munch's *History of the Norwegian People,* which had been published the previous year, and which dealt with the civil wars between 1177 (the date of accession of King Sverre, the hero of Bjørnson's play of that name) and 1240, when the chief character of *The Pretenders,* King Skule, died. According to a letter which Ibsen wrote to J. B. Halvorsen (18 June 1889), he had also worked on it during 1860. But he had put the project aside, and it needed the tonic effect of the Bergen Festival, and his meetings there with Bjørnson, to get him into the mood to write it. He seems to have begun it almost immediately on his return to Christiania from Bergen towards the end of June (1863), and he completed it in six to eight weeks. It was published by the Christiania bookseller Johan Dahl towards the end of October (though, by an error, the date 1864 appears on the title page of the first edition). In a letter (12 February 1870) to his later publisher, Frederik Hegel of Gyldendal, Ibsen described how this publication came about:

> One day early in September 1863, with the fair copy of *The Pretenders* under my arm, I met Johan Dahl on the street in Christiania, told him I had written a new historical play, and offered it to him for publication. Dahl immediately expressed his willingness, and agreed without demur to my request for an honorarium of 150 specie-dollars for the first edition. Dahl took the manuscript, the printing began forthwith, and on 15 September I signed the contract in Dahl's bookshop. . . . I later heard . . . that 1,750 copies of the book were printed.[11]

The Pretenders is set in Norway during the first half of the thirteenth century. The King, Inge, has just died leaving no legal heir, and there are several claimants to the throne. Of these, the two strongest are Earl Skule, brother to the dead King, a famous warrior and a skilled statesman, and Haakon Haakonsson, a boy still in his teens who claims to be the dead King's illegitimate son. The Grand Council votes Haakon king; he, to win Skule's friendship, takes Skule's daughter to be his Queen, and gives Skule a third of his kingdom. But the villainous Bishop Nicholas, whom sexual impotence has twisted into evil, and who is anxious that "there must be no giants in Norway, for I was never one," sows discord between them. He incites Skule to rebel against Haakon, hoping that they will destroy each other. Skule proclaims himself King, and civil war breaks out. At first, things go Skule's way. He is the more experienced soldier and statesman. But he has one fatal defect, and Haakon one supreme advantage. Skule has, when it comes to the crunch, no real belief in himself; he lacks single-mindedness. Haakon, on the other hand, never has a

[11] In fact 1,250 copies were printed. It sold poorly, and six years later Dahl still had 200 copies on his hands.

moment's doubt that "he is the one whom God has chosen." It has been Skule's fate, throughout his life, to vacillate when success was within his grasp; and so it is now. He is defeated and killed. Haakon is left King of, for the first time in its history, a united Norway.

Such is a brief outline of the plot, but it gives little idea of the richness and complexity of the play, of its intense poetic imagination (though it is written in prose) and epic sweep, working remorselessly towards the superb climax in the abbey, where Skule has taken sanctuary with Haakon's baby son as hostage and the peasants are waiting outside to lynch him. It contains, in Skule, Haakon, and Bishop Nicholas, three characters comparable in stature with any that he was to create later, and a dozen splendidly drawn minor parts: Peter, Skule's illegitimate son, a former priest whom blind belief in his father has turned into a ruthless killer; the lonely bard, Jatgeir; the young Queen, Margaret, torn between love of her husband and of her father; Ingeborg, Skule's former mistress and Peter's mother; and the Cassandra-like figure of Skule's sister, Sigrid. Ibsen's previous plays, from *Catiline* to *Love's Comedy*, had been rangefinders; *The Pretenders* is the first of the great epic quartet that was to embrace *Brand*, *Peer Gynt*, and *Emperor and Galilean*.

Stylistically, too, it marks an important stage in Ibsen's development as a dramatist. Of his previous nine plays, four (*Catiline*, *The Warrior's Barrow*, *Norma*, and *Love's Comedy*) had been written in verse, and three (*St. John's Night*, *Lady Inger of Østraat*, and *The Vikings at Helgeland*) in prose (apart from songs, etc.), while *The Feast at Solhaug* and *Olaf Liljekrans* had been composed in a mixture of the two. Although he had managed here and there to achieve a colloquial prose, he had limited it to his peasants and lower class characters; his princes and chieftains had spoken a formal dialogue, and in *The Vikings at Helgeland* he had, as stated, deliberately imitated the antique language of the sagas. Bjørnson had disapproved of this experiment, and Ibsen himself, in a review of Bjørnson's historical drama *Sigurd Slembe* published in *Illustreret Nyhedsblad* on 21 December 1862, had expressed his conviction that the language of a historical play should be living and colloquial, whoever might be speaking. In *The Pretenders* he attempted to create such a dialogue, retaining formal language only when the characters use a deliberately formal mode of address—as in the opening exchange between Haakon and Skule—and occasionally for special effect. He succeeded, not indeed completely, but to a considerable degree.[12] The play is full of terse, colloquial statements that we do not find in *Lady Inger* or *The Vikings*, and that shock by their unexpectedness; as in the exchange between Skule, when his fortunes are at their height, and the bard Jatgeir:

[12] Not least in the delightfully easy rhymed verse given to the Bishop's ghost in Act Five, and dismissed by some critics as "doggerel." If this is doggerel, so is much of *Peer Gynt*.

SKULE. There seem to dwell two men in you, Icelander. When you sit among the warriors at a feast, you draw cap and cloak over every thought. But when a man is alone with you, you seem the kind of man one would choose to have as a friend. Why is this?

JATGEIR. When you go to swim in the river, my lord, you do not undress where the people walk to church. You seek out a lonely place.

SKULE. Of course.

JATGEIR. My soul is shy. So I do not bare it when the hall is full.

SKULE. Hm. (*Short pause*). Tell me, Jatgeir, how did you come to be a singer? From whom did your learn your art?

JATGEIR. The art of song cannot be learned, my lord.

SKULE. Then how did you acquire it?

JATGEIR. I received the gift of sorrow, and found myself a singer.

SKULE. Is that what a singer needs?

JATGEIR. I needed sorrow. Others may need faith—or joy—or doubt—

SKULE. Doubt too?

JATGEIR. Yes. But then he who doubts must be strong.

SKULE. And whom would you call a weak doubter?

JATGEIR. He who doubts his own doubt.

SKULE (*slowly*). That sounds to me like death.

JATGEIR. It is worse. It is twilight.

. . . SKULE (*grips him by the arm*). What gift do I need to become King?

JATGEIR. Not the gift of doubt, or you would not have asked.

SKULE. What gift do I need?

JATGEIR. My lord, you *are* King.

SKULE. Are you always sure that you are a poet?

JATGEIR (*looks at him silently for a moment, then asks*). Have you never loved?

SKULE. Yes, once. Passionately, beautifully; sinfully.

JATGEIR. You have a wife.

SKULE. I took her because I wanted a son.

JATGEIR. But you have a daughter, my lord. A gentle and noble daughter.

SKULE. If my daughter had been a son, I would not have asked you what gift I needed. (*Passionately.*) I must have someone by me who will obey me instinctively, believe in me unflinchingly, stand close by me through good days and evil, live only to give light and warmth to my life—someone who, when I fall, must die! What shall I do, Jatgeir?

JATGEIR. Buy a dog, my lord.

In a sense, that last line of Jatgeir's is the beginning of modern prose drama.

The Pretenders is one of Ibsen's most personal plays; there can be little doubt that the conflict between Skule and Haakon reflects Ibsen's sense of bitterness at the contrast between his failure (at the time he wrote it) and the younger, less gifted but utterly self-confident Bjørnson's success. This contrast must have seemed especially painful in that summer of 1862, when his fortunes were at their lowest, and he portrayed it very recognisably in *The Pretenders,* in which a man of great gifts invalidated by self-distrust is worsted by a potentially lesser man who possesses the supreme virtue of believing in himself. Bjørnson was very much the model for Haakon (whom, incidentally, he had praised in a speech at Bergen as "Norway's best king"), and Ibsen put much of himself into Skule and also, by his own admission, into the bard Jatgeir. "I know I have the fault," he was to write to Bjørnson from Rome on 16 September 1864, echoing the words he had used earlier to Carl Johan Anker, "that I can't make close contact with those people who demand that one should give oneself freely and unreservedly. I am rather like the bard Jatgeir in *The Pretenders,* I can never bring myself to strip completely. I have the feeling that, where personal relationships are concerned, I can only give false expression to what I feel deep down inside, to my true self, and that is why I prefer to shut it up within me, and why we have sometimes stood as it were observing each other from a distance." And to Peter Hansen, on 28 October 1870, he wrote: "The fact that everyone was against me, that there was no un-committed person who could be said to believe in me, could not but give rise to the strain of feeling which found utterance in *The Pretenders."*

The Pretenders received mixed reviews when it was published in October 1863, including a disappointing one from Clemens Petersen; but the Christiania Theatre accepted it for production the following January. It was presumably this last turn of events which caused Ibsen to delay his departure for the south; on 8 October he had asked for an advance of 100 specie-dollars from his pension to send his wife and son to Copenhagen, to stay with Magdalene Thoresen, and on 27 October he applied for a further 300 specie-dollars, "since it is my intention to leave during the next few weeks by steamer for Hamburg." But a production of his new play was something which he could not afford to miss.

Ibsen directed the production himself—the last time that he was ever to direct a play of his own or anyone else's—and it received its first performance at the Christiania Theatre on 17 January 1864. Halvdan Koht has described the premiere. "It was not a really integrated per-formance. The young Sigvard Gundersen had not yet the strength or assurance to give King Haakon the assurance of victory that is begotten of genius. The Danish actor Wolf played Duke Skule better than any role he had previously attempted . . . but in general it was the strong hero that he presented rather than the soul-sick doubter. . . ." Neverthe-less the play gripped the public. Although it lasted for nearly five hours—later they managed to reduce the playing time to four—we are told that "from start to finish it was followed with excited attention" and that "after the fall of the curtain there was a general cry for the author who, when he appeared, was rewarded with thunderous applause." In less than two months [adds Koht] *The Pretenders* was performed eight times, a success unique for a play as long and serious as this in a town as small as the Christiania of those days. . . . Now for the first time he rested in a full and free confidence in his own ability to write, and in his calling as a poet."[13]

Between the writing of *The Pretenders* and its production, however, larger and more far-reaching issues had arisen to occupy Ibsen's mind.

On 15 November 1863 King Frederik VII of Denmark had died without male issue, and been succeeded by a collateral member of the family, Christian IX. The old and grisly problem of the Duchies of Schleswig and Holstein now reared its head. They disputed Christian's claim to be their ruler, since they had always accepted the Salic Law and denied claims through females. The German states, who had long resented the Danish suzerainty over the Duchies, maintained that the rightful ruler of them was now the Duke of Augustenburg, and Bismarck, supported by Austria, championed the German cause. In December the armies of the German League attacked Holstein; in mid-January the Prussians issued an ultimatum to Denmark; and on 1 February the Prussian forces invaded Schleswig. It was the first testing of Bismarck's new army, which Lord Palmerston had recently scorned ("all military men who have seen it at its annual reviews of late years have unequivocally declared that the French could walk over it and get without difficulty to Berlin"),[14] and which Franz Josef and Napoleon III were similarly, and more disastrously, to under-rate.

The young king of Sweden and Norway, Carl XV, and his foreign minister, Count Manderström, had continuously and openly professed support for Denmark in this matter of the Duchies, and Manderström had made several pronouncements, notably one in July, which left no doubt in most Scandinavian minds, including Ibsen's, that, if Danish independence were threatened, Sweden and Norway would come to her aid. A few days after Manderström's July statement, Carl XV offered Denmark a military alliance. But, not for the last time in Swedish history, strong forces within the government advocated a policy of isolationism, and the king found his hands bound. The Norwegian students held a big meeting on 12 December, at which they sent a declaration to the Swedish students asserting that all

---

13 Koht, I, 214–16.

14 Sir Spencer Walpole, *History of England from the Conclusion of the Great War in 1815,* rev. edn. (London, 1890), II, 388, note 1). The campaign was planned and finished off by the great Moltke who might, had he chosen differently forty years earlier, have been fighting on the other side. His father, a Mecklenburger, had become a Danish subject, and he himself was educated in Holstein and Denmark, became a page at the Danish court and entered the Danish army in 1818. But three years later, unfortunately for millions of unborn Europeans, he transferred to the Prussian army.

Scandinavians must now regard the Danish cause as their own, and a week later a gathering of three thousand citizens in Christiania sent the king a message of support for any military action he might take in support of the Danish cause. But the Storthing would go no further than to make a promise of financial aid to Denmark, and that conditional on one of the great western powers joining the alliance. Palmerston had declared in the House of Commons that autumn that any nation which challenged the rights of Denmark "would find in the result that it would not be Denmark alone with which they would have to contend," but for any effective intervention the co-operation of France was essential, and Palmerston could not face the prospect of a French conquest of Prussia. When the crisis came, Denmark found herself alone.

Ibsen's feelings towards his countrymen, already strained, became considerably aggravated by this, as he thought, chicanery. He had had hard things to say about Denmark in the cultural field in recent years, but this example of aggression against a small neighbour by a bullying power angered him as much as that similar situation had done in 1848, when, as now, the Swedes and Norwegians had uttered professions of sympathy but had sent no help. On 13 December, the day after the student meeting in Christiania, Ibsen published in *Illustreret Nyhedsblad* a furious indictment of his fellow-countrymen. He called the poem simply "To Norway."

> Those generous words that seemed to gush
> From bold hearts swelling high
> Were but a flood of empty gush,
> And now their stream is dry!
> The tree, that buds of promise bore
> Beneath the banquet's light
> Stands stripped and smitten to its core,
> A graveyard cross upon the shore
> That's ravaged in a night.
>
> 'Twas but a lie in festal song,
> A kiss that Judas gave,
> When Norway's sons sang loud and long
> Beside the Danish wave.[15]

The poem continued in such vehement terms that Botten Hansen, who wished to print it in *Illustreret Nyhedsblad,* asked Ibsen to tone it down; and a comparison of the Norwegian people to Cain was modified, as was a suggestion that they would do well in the future to deny their nationality since the stigma attached to the word "Norwegian" would be such that even the country's flag would be shunned like a plague pennant. Ibsen has sometimes been condemned for compromising in this fashion,

[15] Edmund Gosse's translation.

especially since his next play after *The Pretenders, Brand,* was largely an indictment of compromise; but in that tiny community it was fairly certain that no one but Botten Hansen would have published the poem in any form, and it was presumably a question of getting it printed in a modified version or not at all. And Botten Hansen, himself no coward, may have been right in thinking that the poem would be more effective if it made Norwegians ashamed rather than angry. It appeared in *Illustreret Nyhedsblad* on 13 December 1863, and shortly afterwards Ibsen wrote an elegy to King Frederik VII which developed into a moving expression of sympathy with the beleaguered Danes. This was sung at a meeting in the Christiania Students' Union on 13 January 1864, and printed in *Illustreret Nyhedsblad* four days later on the day of the premiere of *The Pretenders.*

Christiania was icebound that winter until early April, so that Ibsen had to kick his heels for ten weeks, separated from his wife and son, before starting on his journey. He occupied part of his time in planning a new historical drama to succeed *The Pretenders;* some notes have survived which he copied from history books about Magnus Heineson, a sixteenth-century freebooter from the Faroe Islands who ended his life on the executioner's block. But he never completed or, as far as we know, even began this work, though he was still talking about it as late as 1870.[16] Meanwhile, Bjørnson, who had returned to Christiania the previous autumn, had, with characteristically impulsive generosity, set about raising a fund to augment Ibsen's small grant and, we may suppose, to help pay off his outstanding debts in Norway. He used his powers of eloquence to such effect that he managed to gather 700 specie-dollars, and thus more than double Ibsen's finances. Johan Sverdrup, the future Prime Minister, was among the subscribers.

On 2 April The Learned Holland Group gave a banquet at the Hotel Nord, partly to celebrate Paul Botten Hansen's recent appointment (on 7 March) as university librarian, and partly to say farewell to Ibsen. Of this surely interesting occasion there is, infuriatingly, no record whatever. Three days later, in the early morning of Tuesday 5 April 1864, Ibsen left Christiania with Botten Hansen in the first southbound steamer of the year. The next day he joined his wife and son in Copenhagen; it was to be ten years before he set foot in Norway again, and a further seventeen before he returned to live there.

On 17 April Ibsen wrote from Copenhagen to Bernhard Dunker, a lawyer who had helped Bjørnson to organise the fund for him,[17] thank-

[16] P. A. Rosenberg remembered Ibsen speaking of the Magnus Heineson project at his (Rosenberg's) father's house in Copenhagen during the summer of 1870. Rosenberg, then a boy of twelve, asked who Heineson was. "Ibsen looked at me, and I noticed that one of his eyes was larger than the other. Slowly and weightily he replied: 'He was a great scoundrel' " (*Nationaltidende,* Copenhagen, 28 July 1926).

[17] He had been Marcus Thrane's defending counsel.

ing him for the money and adding: "On Wednesday I leave for Lübeck, and shall proceed thence to Trieste. I have gained much pleasure and profit from my stay here; as soon as I reach Rome I shall work on a new five act play, which I hope to have ready by the end of the summer." This, presumably, was the abortive project about Magnus Heineson.

The next day the Prussians stormed Dybbøl, and the brave Danish resistance was ended. Two days later, on 20 April, Ibsen sailed to Lübeck, leaving Suzannah and Sigurd to follow him later, and continued on to Berlin. There, on 4 May, he saw the Danish cannon captured at Dybbøl led in triumph through the streets while Germans lining the route spat at them. "It was for me," he wrote a year later, "a sign that, some day, history would spit in the eyes of Sweden and Norway for their part in this affair": [18] and the idea for a new play, unlike anything that he had hitherto written, grew in him "like a fœtus."

From Berlin he took the railway to Vienna, and thence southwards across the Alps. Thirty-four years later, in a speech in Copenhagen on 1 April 1898, he was to recall his first sight of Italy. "I . . . crossed the Alps on 9 May. Over the high mountains the clouds hung like great, dark curtains, and beneath these we drove through the tunnel and, suddenly, found ourselves at Mira Mara, where that marvellously bright light which is the beauty of the south suddenly revealed itself to me, gleaming like white marble. It was to affect all my later work, even if the content thereof was not always beautiful." He described his emotion at that moment as "a feeling of being released from the darkness into light, emerging from mists through a tunnel into the sunshine." He travelled on through Trieste, Venice, Milan, Piacenza, Parma, Bologna, and Florence; what impression these cities made on him we do not know, apart from the fact that he admired Milan Cathedral. Otherwise, of these six weeks in May and early June of 1864, when Europe was opening itself before him, no record exists; the letters which he must have written to Suzannah were, like all his early letters to her, destroyed. "Our relationship concerns no one but ourselves." At last, in the middle of June, he reached Rome.

[18] Letter to Magdalene Thoresen, 3 December 1865.

PART TWO

Italian Spring

9

The New Michelangelo

1864 – 1866

The Italy which greeted Ibsen in the summer of 1864 was a country rejoicing in new-found unification and liberty. Here, if nowhere else in Europe, the hopes of 1848, that year of revolutions and disillusionments, had at last been fulfilled. In 1859, five years before Ibsen's arrival, Napoleon III had helped the Italians to drive their Austrian overlords out of Milan and Lombardy, and although, to the anger of his allies, he had then made peace with the young Emperor Franz Josef and left him in possession of Venice, the fires of rebellion had been ignited. One by one the little kingdoms of Modena, Parma, and Tuscany had risen against and ejected their tyrants. In 1860 Garibaldi had liberated Sicily, taken Naples, and been dissuaded from marching on Rome only by the fear of provoking a clash with Napoleon; after which, in surely the most remarkable gesture that any conqueror has made, he accepted the sovereignty of the young King Victor Emmanuel of Piedmont-Sardinia and sailed away with a little borrowed money to a life of hard work, poverty, and meditation on the island of Caprera. So Rome, when Ibsen entered it that June, was still an independent state under the once liberal but now reactionary Pope Pius IX, garrisoned and protected by French troops. It and Venice were the only parts of Italy that remained outside the new kingdom, of which Florence was the capital, and into which they, too, were to find themselves incorporated within four years.

Rome, which then contained some two hundred thousand inhabitants, was, more than Paris, the cynosure of contemporary writers and artists, and to Scandinavians especially it was the promised city. Its influence had been a decisive turning-point in the lives of Oehlenschläger, Thorvaldsen, Hans Andersen, Ole Bull, and many others, as it was to be in Ibsen's. An Englishman who was a boy there at the time described Rome in the eighteen-sixties as "changed but little from the Rome of the eighteenth

century . . . still lit at night by oil-lamps, with streets mostly innocent
of sidewalks, but gay with the coloured hoods of the wine-carts and
the coaches of the Cardinals with their big black horses and red trappings. . . . Only the uniforms of the French army of occupation struck a
rather anomalous note."[1] The old ghetto still existed near the Cenci
Palace, though its walls had been pulled down in 1848. Another Englishman
visiting the city in 1866–67 noted the narrowness of the streets ("there
are few, if any, in which three friends can walk arm in arm"); even
the Corso was "a very long, narrow and dirty lane with many turnings."[2]
Compared with Florence, it was an evil-smelling city. "The streets of Rome,
the houses of Rome—to the very palaces and museums—reek with such
horrible odours that you are very soon led to conjecture that the ever-
quoted malaria from the Pontine Marshes has been made responsible for
a great deal of which it is quite innocent, and that one of the chief
predisposing causes of the Roman fever is the inconceivable filthiness of
the people and their dwellings."[3] George Augustus Sala was not ex-
aggerating, for Ibsen later recalled how "the inhabitants were permitted
to perform their necessary functions, for want of other arrangements, in
the courtyards of the ancient palaces."[4] Nor did the method of supplying
dairy products contribute to the general cleanliness, for the streets in the
early mornings were commonly full of goats which would be milked
outside any restaurant that needed that luxury, and were even led up
two or three flights of stairs to individual customers.[5]

Up to five years previously, visitors from the north had travelled the
final stages of their journey by coach, keeping a sharp watch for bandits,
and had ridden romantically in through the Porta del Popolo; but in
1861 the railway had been completed, so Ibsen arrived soberly by train
—doubtless to his relief, for the bandits still flourished, and tourists un-
wise enough to stray outside the city after dark were liable to be kidnapped
and held to ransom.

Ibsen lost no time in acquainting himself with the Norwegian consul,
a hook-nosed old Holstein Jew named Johan Bravo. Born in the previous
century, he had lived in Rome since 1827 and was to prove a good friend
and counsellor to Ibsen over the next two decades. Early on the morning
of 19 June, presumably the day of or the day after Ibsen's arrival, Bravo
took him along to the Circolo Scandinavico, or Scandinavian Club, a
lively meeting-place with impressive quarters in the Palazzo Correa, which
had been built into the remains of the Mausoleum of Augustus. Bravo's
young secretary, Lorentz Dietrichson, was librarian of the club, and lodged

[1] Sir Rennell Rodd, *Rome of the Renaissance and Today* (London, 1932), p. 24.
[2] George Augustus Sala, *Rome and Venice, with Other Wanderings in Italy*
(London, 1869), pp. 443 and 446.
[3] *Ibid.*, p. 448.
[4] John Paulsen, *Samliv med Ibsen, II* (Copenhagen and Christiania, 1913), 111.
[5] Dietrichson, III, 29.

there. He was in bed when his visitors arrived, but Bravo roused him with a series of oaths and commanded him to take the newcomer on a tour of the city.

Dietrichson, who was six years younger than Ibsen, was a native of Bergen, where he had been a childhood friend of Suzannah, and had known Ibsen slightly in Christiania. After studying at the university, he had worked for a while under Paul Botten Hansen on *Illustreret Nyheds-blad*, and had then lectured for two years on Scandinavian literature at Upsala University, where he had scandalised the Swedes by denouncing their modern poets as sterile and backward-looking and, worse, by bidding them turn to the tougher and more realistic work being produced in Norway by such as Ibsen and Bjørnson. He had now been in Rome for two years, studying art history, a subject in which he was later to become professor at Christiania University, and he proved an excellent and sympathetic guide. It was a fine, hot Sunday, and, after witnessing High Mass at St. Peter's—almost the only recorded instance of Ibsen attending a church service, except at weddings and funerals—they walked to the Forum and examined its ruins. Then they crossed the Tiber into the working-class quarter of Trastevere and climbed the Janiculum Hill, where Garibaldi had made his stand for the republic against the papal troops in 1849, and whence they enjoyed a magnificent panoramic view of the city. On the way down, they passed the oak tree where Tasso was reputed to have found the inspiration for his epic *Jerusalem* and, when evening came, sat down to dine in a little garden restaurant by the Tiber named Fornarina, after the baker's daughter of that name whom Raphael loved and whom he was reputed to have first seen there.

Forty years later, Dietrichson recalled in his florid style the impression that Ibsen had made on him that first evening in Rome. He found him, to his surprise, "quite another person than the withdrawn and bitter man I had left three years earlier. He had of course been deeply shaken by the latest events in Scandinavia, and expressed himself with burning indignation on the deceitful policies which had been adopted towards Denmark and how, with suppressed anger, he had seen the Prussians enter Berlin with their trophies from the Schleswig campaign. But at the same time it was as though, on his arrival into *la bella Italia* and *la Roma eterna,* he had put all this behind him, and now wished only to live as intensively as possible for his writing. . . . Now he was able to laugh at all the dust which *Love's Comedy* had raised, and which had embittered his life in Norway—now he was able doubly to rejoice in the ten [*sic*] full houses which *The Pretenders* had achieved before he had left. And when the sun went down and we felt the gentle air of the Italian evening shimmer through the little garden where we sat beneath the vine leaves in our pergola with a *foglietta* of Roman wine before us—while the natives of Trastevere came to enjoy the cool of the river flowing beneath the garden wall, and the small dwarf improvised to his mandolin beneath the vines that hung out over the river—while the lamps burned on the garden tables and the lights on the far bank in the Palazzo Farnese and around the great and ancient city mirrored themselves in the water—yes, then, for a moment, we were two young men happy in the certainty that life was rich and beautiful and that its finest fruits were beckoning to us from the future. . . . With the aid of our *fogliettas* we built our dream castles in the little garden, and when night fell we wandered home in the soft Mediterranean moonlight."[6]

Ibsen spent the next few days in further sightseeing, spending much time, as befitted a painter, in the museums and galleries, where he formed impressions quite out of fashion with prevalent taste. Yet while he wandered the streets and hills of Rome, unembarrassed by the smells and enjoying the unaccustomed heat in which, like so many Scandinavians, he was always to revel, the indignation which was so inescapable a part of his character seethed unabated; and it was not long before it found expression. The Scandinavian community was about to break up and go into the countryside to avoid the worst of the summer heat, and they held a farewell party at Raphael's Vigne on the Aquiline Hill, on the then still completely rural Via Merulana between S. Maria Maggiore and the Lateran. Dietrichson describes the scene, "on an open loggia, where we ate our frugal dinner and drank a glass of wine under the sky. It was the first evening for some while that Ibsen had spent among Scandinavians, and he began to speak of the painful and disturbing impressions of recent events in the war which he had received on his journey. Gradually, and almost imperceptibly, his talk took on the character of an improvised speech; all the bitterness which had so long been stored up within him, all the fiery indignation and passion for the Scandinavian cause which he had bottled up for so long, found an outlet. His voice began to ring, and in the evening dusk one saw only his burning eyes. When he had finished, no one cried Bravo or raised his glass, but I think we all felt that that evening the Marseillaise of the North had rung out into the Roman night air."[7]

According to another listener, Ibsen concluded his speech by banging on the table "so that all the wine-glasses rattled," and vowing that "never should his son set foot on Norwegian soil before Norway had expiated the wrong that she had done to Denmark."[8]

Dietrichson and his family had taken a villa at Genzano on Lake Nemi, and Ibsen decided to join them there. After watching the illumination of St. Peter's and the fireworks on Monte Pincio on St. Peter's and St. Paul's Day, 29 June, he rode out to Genzano with the Finnish sculptor Walter Runeburg (son of the famous poet J. L. Runeburg) and took

6 *Ibid.*, I, 330, 333–34.
7 *Ibid.*, pp. 334–35.
8 Koht, I, 236, quoting the Danish painter Frederik Lund.

lodgings with the village *caffettiere,* who leased them a room in the billiards saloon. To protect himself against the sun Ibsen had purchased a broad-brimmed soft hat with a sky-blue lining, which earned him among the locals the nickname of *capellone* (big hat). "Here," records Dietrichson, "we spent the summer in a delightful *far niente.*"[9]

Also living at Genzano that summer was a Norwegian lady named Lina Bruun, with her artist son Peter and her daughter Thea, both suffering from tuberculosis, from which they were both to die within eighteen months. Her other son Christopher, a theological student, had accompanied them to Rome the previous year, but had returned north to fight with the Danes against their Prussian invaders; he was to become a lifelong friend of Ibsen, and was to provide one of the chief inspirations for his next play. Ibsen saw a good deal of Lina, Thea, and Peter Bruun at Genzano, and on 4 July Lina wrote to Christopher conveying her distaste for their new acquaintance. Ibsen, she wrote, aroused "evil feelings" in her; five days previously (i.e., within twenty-four hours of Ibsen's arrival), they had had a set-to; his genius, she explained, needed something to censure and chastise, and he had continually to be seeking targets for his wrath. However, they got on better than she had anticipated. On 5 August she wrote again to Christopher about Ibsen: "So dual a character it is difficult to imagine. To meet day by day he is the most sociable, cheerful, and friendly man you could conceive." But sometimes, she added, his eyes glitter cruelly, and then all he wants is to play the devil. She added a note on his drinking habits. "He likes to take a glass of wine, because it heightens his animal spirits, and, since they are already lively, it is easy to get a false impression. . . . But when he is writing, he drinks tea."[10] Ibsen assured Lina Bruun that if Christopher fell in the war he would raise a memorial to him in poetry. Christopher Bruun did not fall, but returned to point the finger of judgment at Ibsen, who raised a poetic memorial to him none the less.

Dietrichson tells how Ibsen and he spent their days in Genzano. "In the morning we worked. At noon we gathered to eat in a wine cellar, literally a cellar, an almost pitch-dark room filled with wine barrels and a huge basket containing a bitch with her litter. There was only one tiny window and when, as frequently happened, one of the village donkeys stopped outside to scratch itself against the wall, Ibsen or one of us had to run out and chase it away so that we could see to eat." In the afternoon they lay reading or chatting under the trees on one of the hills overlooking Lake Nemi. "I remember especially" writes Dietrichson, "that one day I was lying there reading Ammianus Marcellinus's account of Julian the Apostate's campaigns, and Ibsen became much interested in this. We began to talk of Julian, and I know that the idea of writing about this subject took root in his mind that day. At any rate, when I had finished reading, he said he

[9] Dietrichson, I, 336.
[10] Francis Bull, *Nordisk kunsterliv i Rom* (Oslo, 1960), pp. 163–64.

hoped no one would write about it before he did. . . . Towards evening we either walked across the hill to Lake Nemi or descended to the lake, strolled along it and climbed up to Nemi through the bushes. There, many an evening, we good friends emptied a glass of Nemi wine on a pretty verandah with a splendid view across the lake, the village of Genzano, the *campagna,* and the sea, or inside in the little *locanda* where the cat rubbed itself against the foot of the old woman at her spinning-wheel and Piux IX smiled benignly down on us from a fearful painting on the wall, while the tiny Roman lamp was lit and the landscape outside with its lake, woods, and *campagna* grew dim in the magic dusk of evening, which swiftly turned into the blackest night. And as we walked home we would usually meet the natives singing as they moved from Madonna portrait to Madonna portrait with their devout songs in the warm, dark summer night, while the lamps gleamed in the niches of the saints along the roadside and at street corners."[11]

One day they heard that the Pope, whom Ibsen had not yet seen, was to pass in formal procession through the nearby village of Castelgandolfo on his way to his summer residence there, and they decided to have a look at him. "We acquired two donkeys," related Dietrichson, "and rode cheerfully off. As we approached the village we saw that its single long street was filled with people waiting to watch the procession and receive his blessing; they thronged the street on either side. . . . We had no choice but to ride with as good a face as we could muster through the town gate and, like two *matti inglesi,* run the gantlet of the laughing lines of people. For a few moments all went well, but then the donkeys broke into a violent gallop, and suddenly first one of them, then the other, were flat on their bellies in the middle of the street with us standing above them. The jubilation was immense. At that moment, the papal procession arrived. The donkeys were dragged out of the way, braying and protesting, and the Pope made his entry undisturbed by the Norwegian poet and his squire; nor did he withhold from us the blessing which he extended to his loyal disciples."[12] Which was just as well, for Pius IX was supposed to have the evil eye, to counter which many a peasant would hold a finger pointed towards him, in the cover of his pocket.

That summer at Genzano, Ibsen began to write a play in prose;[13] but he encountered a "block," technical or psychological, and began to rework it as a long epic poem. This was the work the theme of which had been growing in him "like a foetus" ever since that day in April when he had seen the Danish cannon captured at Dybbøl drawn in triumph through the Berlin streets and spat on by the watching crowds. He

[11] Dietrichson, I, 336–37.

[12] *Loc. cit.*

[13] So states Martin Schneekloth in his diary for 6 February 1867, printed in Peter Schindler's moving memoir of Schneekloth, *En Ungdom* (Copenhagen, 1942), pp. 120–22.

composed this poem in eight-line stanzas of rhymed pentameters, and clearly planned it as an indictment of his countrymen for their lassitude and materialism, as particularly manifested in their non-assistance of the Danes. The opening section, "To the Accomplices," states the theme:

> My people, my fair land, my northern home . . .
> I'll sing you a sad song. Perhaps my last
> As Norway's bard. For no bard sings again
> Who has bemoaned the passing of his people.
> And the sickness has begun. I see a corpse
> Huge as a giant's, poisoning field and fjord.
> Deck it with Norway's flags and sink it deep . . .
> What is dead can't be lied back to life.
> What is dead must go down into the dark.
> The dead have only one task; to provide
> Soil and nourishment for the new-sown seed.

The second section shows two boys lying on a Norwegian hillside. One is "the kind that looks bright-eyed upon the world"; the other "faces north, his back towards the sun." The former, looking down into the valley, speaks of his happy home; the other speaks of his, and tells how, when his father died, he had dreamed he had seen his mother creep in and strike her husband's corpse. Soon after this point the section breaks off, apparently unfinished. The third section, entitled "Across the Mountain," shows the happier of the two boys, Ejnar, now a painter, with his fiancée, Agnes, taking farewell of friends at a betrothal feast in the mountains. As they leave, they meet the "northward-facing boy, Koll (later altered to Brand), who is now a priest. From this point until the fragment ends, the action closely corresponds to that of the play which Ibsen was shortly to write. Brand denounces Ejnar's lazy and self-indulgent hedonism as typical of their countrymen, continues alone on his way, and comes to the village where he was born. As he looks down into the valley with its cramped church, a crazed peasant girl sees him and says: "Come to my church," and leads him up the mountain to a huge natural cave hollowed into the rock which local people call the "Ice Church." Brand ponders the contrast between this awe-inspiring God-made church and the mean building below. He descends to the village, where there is famine. The mayor is doling out meagre rations to the people; he appeals to Brand to give food or money, but Brand tells them that the famine is God's judgment on them for their materialism and lack of spirituality. The poem breaks off in the middle of his sermon.

It measures, to this point, just over two hundred stanzas, or sixteen hundred lines. With its splendidly Byronic opening denouncing his compatriots, its fine descriptions of natural scenery and the powerful rhetoric of Brand's condemnation of Ejnar and, later, of the villagers, it was certainly the most powerful and exciting poem that Ibsen had yet written. Yet it made painful progress; he was at one of those critical stages in a writer's career when he realizes, slowly and unwillingly, that he is writing in the wrong medium. The composition of these two hundred stanzas took him over a year before he finally abandoned the work in its epic form and began to rewrite it as dialogue.

Meanwhile, as a distraction during that summer of 1864, he composed three short poems, all in something approaching his best manner. "In Time of Dybbøl" tells how, on the ship from Norway to Denmark the previous spring, the passengers had begun to talk of the Dano-Prussian war, and one old lady had said with a calm smile: "I do not fear for my son." Ibsen admired her courage until he learned the reason for it; her son was a soldier in the Norwegian army, and so stood in no danger of being involved in the fighting. "The Power of Memory" describes how an animal trainer teaches a bear to dance; he ties it in a copper which he heats, and then, as it begins to burn the bear's feet, plays a tune on his barrel organ. The bear dances with pain; afterwards, by association, it dances whenever that tune is played. So, continues the poem, I too must dance whenever I hear the tune that reminds me of the time when "more than my skin was burned." The final verse runs:

> Whenever I hear an echo from that time
> It is as though I were bound in a burning copper.
> It pierces me like a needle under my nails
> And makes me dance in verse.

The third poem was a lyric of twelve lines entitled "Gone," and is traditionally supposed to have been written for Thea Bruun:

> We followed the last
> Guest to the gate.
> The night wind stole
> The syllables of farewell.
>
> The garden and house
> Where sweetest sounds
> Had drugged my senses
> Lay deserted.
>
> It was but a feast
> Before the black night.
> She was but a guest
> And now she is gone.

In Genzano that July, Ibsen received a letter from Richard Petersen, the chairman of the Christiania Theatre who six years earlier had publicly denounced him as "a playwright of gigantic insignificance," inviting him to become the theatre's artistic director. The post had been offered to Bjørnson, but he had demanded powers the board regarded as too sweeping. The temptation to Ibsen must have been considerable, for, cheap as life was in Italy, his grant was insufficient to provide him with more than the barest necessities. But he had had enough of the "daily abortion" of running a theatre, and Italy had given him a peace he had not previously known and was not prepared to surrender. He declined the offer.

In September Ibsen returned, like the other Scandinavians, to Rome, and on the 16th of that month he wrote a long and revealing letter to Bjørnson in Christiania, the first we have from his hand since his arrival in Italy. Bjørnson had learned of the Christiania Theatre's offer to Ibsen, and, not unreasonably, had written to Dietrichson asking for clarification. Ibsen, to whom Dietrichson had passed on the message, explained that Petersen had assured him that negotiations with Bjørnson had broken down, and had urged: "since *you* would not take the job, I *must*. . . . I rejected the offer, rejected it totally and unreservedly, and without implying that any change of circumstances could ever alter my position. . . . So you see, my dear Bjørnson, that in this matter you have done me an injustice by nurturing the mistrust which is apparent in your letter to Dietrichson. . . . I cannot, though, deny that I can think of an explanation for this mistrust, and that I blame you less than myself for it." He then allowed himself a rare moment of self-revelation, which has been quoted earlier but bears repeating in its original context. "I know I have the fault that I cannot make close contact with people who demand that one should give oneself freely and unreservedly. I am rather like the bard in *The Pretenders:* I can never bring myself to strip completely, I have the feeling that, where personal relationships are concerned, I can give only false expression to what I feel deep down inside, to my true self, and that is why I prefer to shut it up within me, and why we have sometimes stood as it were observing each other from a distance." The letter continues:

Please accept my thanks for all the beauty I have drunk in on my journey; I can tell you, it has done me good. Here in Rome especially much has been revealed to me; though I can't yet get to terms with classical art, I don't really understand its relevance to our time, I lack the illusion, and above all, the sense of personal and individual expression in the subject as in the artist, and I cannot help often seeing (as yet, anyway) mere conventions where others postulate laws. It seems to me that the classical plastic works of art are, like our heroic ballads, the products of their age rather than of this or that master; which may perhaps be a reason why so many of our modern sculptors fail when they persist, today, in trying to create heroic ballads in clay and marble. Michelangelo, Bernini and his school I understand better; those fellows had the courage to commit a madness now and then.

The architecture has impressed me more, but neither the classical style nor its later offsprings attract me as much as the Gothic; to me, the cathedral in Milan is the most overwhelming thing I can imagine in this field; the man who could conceive such a work must have been capable, in his spare moments, of creating a moon and tossing it into the heavens. I know you won't agree with much of what I have loosely indicated here, but I think it is consistent with my general standpoint, and that my appreciation of art will develop along these lines.

Here in Rome there is blessed peace for writing; I am now working on a longish poem, and am planning a tragedy, *Julian the Apostate,* a task which I embrace with inordinate enthusiasm and which I think will bring me joy. My wife and small son will be coming here this autumn; I hope you approve of this arrangement. . . . Dietrichson will be leaving Rome in the New Year, and I shall be taking over his job [as librarian of the Scandinavian Club], which will mean free furnished lodgings and a small salary too; I can live a year in Rome on 400 specie-dollars.

Political events at home have grieved me sadly, and have much clouded my happiness. So it was all lies and dreams. These recent happenings will have a considerable effect on me. We must now draw a line through our ancient history; the Norwegians of today clearly have no more connection with their past than the Greek pirates have with the race that sailed to Troy and fought beside the gods. . . .

Ibsen's first reaction to classical art closely reflects his feelings about drama—the need to get away from the generalized and the heroic towards the human and the individual. The ancient Greek statues in Rome must have seemed to him like the characters in Oehlenschläger's plays, devoid of personality; he preferred, as Shelley had done half a century earlier, the Roman busts, which portrayed recognisable human beings. For the same reason, he was disappointed in the paintings of Raphael, whom his fellow-Scandinavians idolized. In Michelangelo, on the other hand, then fashionably regarded as extravagant and barbaric, rather as Shakespeare had been during the previous century, he must have recognised a kindred spirit, one of those bleak and lonely artists who tower above their age like a snow-capped mountain, as Dante, Milton, and Wordsworth had done, and as Ibsen himself was to do. During his visit to Florence on his journey south, Ibsen can scarcely have missed seeing Michelangelo's unfinished statues, then in the Boboli Gardens, and those mighty figures straining to free themselves from the imprisoning marble must have seemed to him a mirror of his own struggle as an artist. In the plays to come, from *Brand* to *When We Dead Awaken,* he was to create similar gigantic and tormented prisoners. More than any writer, Michelangelo was to be Ibsen's master; the one was to create in words what the other had created in stone.

Ibsen's equally unfashionable admiration of the Gothic (Milan Cathedral) and the Baroque (Bernini) was also logical in the man who was shortly to write *Peer Gynt*.

When Suzannah and Sigurd arrived, Ibsen moved into an apartment at 55, Via Capo le Case, a house (now demolished) on the corner of the Via Due Macelli. The hoped-for librarianship, with its free lodgings, did not materialize, and they remained in the Via Capo le Case until they left Rome four years later. Dietrichson relates that for several days before the arrival of his wife and son Ibsen was "restless with excitement," and that when they finally met, an occasion at which Dietrichson was present, few words were exchanged, but no one could have doubted that "these two highly individual people belonged intensely to one another. And I said to myself: 'She and no one else is the wife for him; the only one. Only someone like her, with her strong, masculine love of truth and her deep, feminine devotion, can guide him to fulfilment.' "[14]

By October Ibsen had exhausted his grant, and only a timely draft of 100 specie-dollars from Bjørnson, tireless as ever in whipping up money for worthy causes, saw him through the last ten weeks of the year. He was earning nothing, and his expenses in Rome came to 40 scudi (40 specie-dollars) a month.[15] Bjørnson's letter of 5 October enclosing the money contained a few home truths:

> Your whole life has been such that the sun never reached it, and under such circumstances plants absorb more water than light and acquire more mud than colour. What you lacked was affection, love, a calm view of essentials. Now, God be praised, you have all that, and we shall have the fruits! . . . . There are many goblins in your head which I think you ought to placate. But, as I'm sure I have often told you, they are a dangerous army to have around; they're like the Prætorians and mediæval mercenaries; after routing their enemies, they turn on their masters and plunder them. . . . I understand your admiration for the Gothic; but you'll see it differently when you get home. . . . As regards classical art, I think you'll soon perceive the individualism behind the convention; but it's true, our senses have to be attuned first. . . . Here . . . the theatre has stood empty for six weeks and is expected to go bankrupt, which would be the best thing for everyone. . . . I enclose 100 specie-dollars. When you want more, you must tell me.[16]

Ibsen did not acknowledge this gift for two months, a delay which seems ungracious even for him. To make matters worse, his letter went astray and was never delivered.

Ibsen led a gregarious life that autumn and winter in Rome, as indeed he was to do during the whole of his stay there. But he limited himself to

---

14 Dietrichson, IV, 398.
15 Letter to Bjørnson, 28 January 1865.
16 Bjørnstjerne Bjørnson, *Gro-tid* (*brev fra aarene 1857–1870*), ed. Halvdan Koht (Christiania, 1912), II, 142–46.

his fellow-Scandinavians; he does not seem to have made any Italian friends, nor did he meet any of the foreign celebrities living there, such as Franz Liszt, or the aged English consul Joseph Severn, in whose arms John Keats had died nearly half a century before. He became a regular habitué of the Scandinavian Club, which had an excellent library; it had just received a big grant of books from the university library in Christiania and possessed six thousand volumes. The register shows that Ibsen borrowed, among others, the following books during these four years in Rome—and although the list gives no positive clue to his reading, since most were probably taken out for Suzannah, a far more avid reader than he, at least we can be sure that she would have discussed them with him: 1864, Becker's *World History,* and several volumes of Goethe, including *Wilhelm Meister;* 1865, more Goethe, including *Faust,* several of Scott's novels, including *The Heart of Midlothian, Waverley,* and *The Bride of Lammermoor,* Dante's *The Divine Comedy* in Danish (in May, borrowed again in October), two volumes of Goldoni's comedies, and Garibaldi's autobiography; 1866, Aristophanes' *The Birds,* a book about Euripides by Christian Wilster, novels by George Sand, Dickens, Dumas, and Maria Edgeworth, and *Faust* again; 1867, more Goethe, Eckermann's *Conversations with Goethe,* two volumes of Shakespeare, *Don Quixote,* and *David Copperfield.* At various times he also borrowed several volumes of Ludvig Holberg's plays.[17]

Ibsen's name appears frequently in the Club's suggestion book, demanding that the lamps be cleaned, that a packet of glue be removed from the pedestal of a bust of a dancer, that "the dancer's big left toe be restored," that a map of the papal state be procured and hung, and that the newspaper *Osservatore Romano* be provided. On 6 December he was elected a member of the newspaper committee; on 20 January 1865 he proposed "That Germans be not permitted entry into the Club," a motion which was rejected at an extraordinary general meeting on 6 February with only two votes in its favour; and on 13 February he was put in charge of the library accounts (why he was not, as he had hoped, appointed librarian is not clear). He was invited to serve on the general committee, but refused, explaining: "I must belong to the opposition."[18] He was not the most clubbable of members. One of his fellows recalled how, in his "single

---

[17] Cf. Øyvind Anker, "Ibsen og den skandinaviska forening i Rom" in *Edda,* 1956, and C.E., XIX, 130–34.

Ibsen seems to have visited Italian theatres at least occasionally during this stay, for in 1877 he remarked to Didrik Grønvold that Italian actresses swooned realistically "whereas in his time in Norway actresses always swooned according to fixed rules, always on the left of the stage and always with a handkerchief in their left hand." (Cf. Didrik Grønvold, *Diktere og musikere* [Oslo, 1945], p. 16.)

[18] Though when the committee decided to revise the rules, Ibsen "moved, with statesmanlike dexterity, behind the chairs, dropping a word here and there which seemed to have its effect." (Frederik G. Knudtzon, *Ungdomsdage* [Copenhagen, 1927], p. 165.)

suit of shabby leek-green cloth, he used to stalk sullenly up and down . . .
not speaking a word to anyone until supper-time, when he would empty a
flask of thin red wine and slowly brighten up, not into geniality exactly,
but into loquacity, and dart the scathing bolts of his sarcasm ruthlessly
in all directions."[19] One day, finding in an illustrated magazine a portrait
of Count Manderström, the Swedish foreign minister and an advocate of
non-intervention, he drew a halter round the count's neck; when, at the next
meeting of the Club, the offender was challenged to reveal himself, Ibsen
silently rose from his chair.[20]

He often dined with his fellow-Scandinavians at an *osteria*, the Cucina
Tedesca, or "Deutsche Küche," a very humble place at the junction of the
Via Felice and the Via del Tritone, which in addition to the usual Italian
dishes served sauerkraut and pancakes; Lepre, on the corner of the Via
Condotti and the Via Mario dei Fiori, where the wine waiter, Marco, had
been a famous bandit; Mangani, outside the Porta Pia; and, especially, Il
Genio in the Due Macelli. The wine waiter here, Evangelista, had been
one of Garibaldi's thousand, and they had a table permanently reserved
for them in the far left-hand corner. A meal with half a *foglietta* of wine
at any of these places cost 1½ paolo, or about 60 øre (15¢); or you
could buy your own food from shops and stalls, washing your vegetables
in the nearest fountain, and the *osteria* would provide salt, pepper, and
oil, and, most importantly, wine, and cook what needed to be cooked. A
Danish acquaintance of Ibsen who came to Rome the following year describes one such shopping expedition in detail. "You saw a *pizzicarolo*
and went in and bought a sardine—1 soldo[21]—or, better still, tunnyfish
(3 or 4 soldi)—and cheese (1 or 2 soldi). Then the butcher, who for
5 soldi would sell you a veal chop, and the greengrocer, where you could
get a lettuce head for 1 soldo. At the entrance to the *osteria* sat a man
crying, *'Uova dure! Uova toste! Un soldo l'uno!,'* so you bought an egg.
Another man would be sitting in the doorway working a machine, specially
designed for the purpose, which, disagreeable as it sounds, treated arti-
chokes with lard so that they absorbed it completely. He cried: *'Carciofi
romani!,'* and sold you one for a soldo. Then you entered the front room
of the *osteria*. Behind a counter stood a handsome, blonde, Junoesque
creature. You gave her your salad to prepare and your chop to fry. To
the right a door led into a larger room, where a long room table was reserved for the Scandinavians. You ordered *mezza foglietta, bianco*. . . .
With the wine arrived two glazed clay plates, one bearing the fried chop,
the other the salad; also a tin fork, its thin teeth splayed in all directions,
a knife, and a napkin of unbleached linen. One now had a splendid
dinner: *entrée,* sardine or tunnyfish; *pièce de resistance,* chop with salad,

[19] Edmund Gosse, *Two Visits to Denmark, 1872, 1874* (London, 1911), pp. 174–
75, quoting the Danish writer Christian Molbech.
[20] Kristofer Janson, *Hvad jeg har oplevet* (Christiania, 1913), p. 77.
[21] A soldo was worth less than one cent.

including egg; vegetable, artichoke; and, finally, cheese—stracchino, gorgonzola, or parmigiano. The preparation of the salad cost 1 soldo, the frying of the chop the same, and the wine 6–7 soldi."[22] They usually dined between seven and eight, and took their coffee at the century-old Café Greco in the Via Condotti, as Oehlenschläger, Thorvaldsen, and Hans Andersen had done, smoking long pipes or bad papal cigars.

As always, Ibsen took many long walks, alone or in the company of Suzannah and Sigurd, the latter often carried upon Walter Runeburg's shoulders, "walks," recalled Dietrichson, "that usually ended in some rustic *osteria* on the Ponte Molle or in the Moletta at the foot of the Palatine Hill."[23] Among the other writers and artists whose acquaintance he now made were the shy and lonely Jens Adolph Jerichau, the leading sculptor in Denmark since Thorvaldsen's death; the Danish painter Carl Bloch (whom Bjørnson, a few years earlier, had described in a letter to his wife as "big, handsome, childlike, lazy, nice");[24] and, most importantly, the young Swedish poet Carl Snoilsky, who had arrived in Rome that September and with whom Ibsen was later to enjoy a close friendship. Aged twenty-three, and in appearance not unlike Robert Louis Stevenson, Snoilsky had already won himself a reputation as one of the most gifted poets in Scandinavia, and as a romantic and successful lover.

Bloch, Snoilsky and Walter Runeburg were all ten or so years younger than Ibsen who, living up to his Learned Holland nickname of Gert Westphaler, the Talkative Barber, would sit at the centre of the table as they dined, wearing his broad-brimmed hat and leading the discussions in Socratic vein, pressing the arguments of the others to their often uncomfortable conclusions, challenging and bantering. Once when someone, galled by this insistent cross-examination, declared that the truth was as clear as that two and two make four, Ibsen asked whether one could in fact be sure that two and two would make four on, say, Jupiter? One question to which he obsessively returned was how far an artist ought to reject the demands of society and live according to his own creed and morality; he enjoyed citing the example of the English poet Thomas Chatterton, who had starved to death, swallowing (according to legend) even his doorkey, rather than take an ordinary breadwinning job. Ibsen declared that Chatterton had been right, and that he himself would choose the same course; it is ironical to reflect that, unknown to him, his friends in Christiania were at this time trying unsuccessfully to get him an assistant librarianship and, of all things, a post in the customs, the latter of which professions a writer of Ibsen's own temperament and stature on the other side of the world, Herman Melville, was shortly to embrace (and to remain

[22] Knudtzon, pp. 125–26. Extra information from Dietrichson, III, 29 ff.

[23] Dietrichson, I, 343.

[24] Bjørnstjerne Bjørnson, *Breve til Karoline, 1858–1907,* ed. Dagny Bjørnson-Sautreau (Oslo, 1957), p. 49.

in for nineteen years). Snoilsky remembered Ibsen at these dinners, "the lightning flashing from beneath the enormous hat."[25]

The topic which obsessed Ibsen most, however, was still the old question of the Dano-Prussian war, and the failure of Norway and Sweden to help their neighbour. Again and again in his letters and recorded utterances he returns to the subject. "The significant and decisive thing for me," he wrote to Magdalene Thoresen (3 December 1865), "has been that I have got far enough away from our country to see the hollowness behind all the self-created lies in our so-called public life. . . . How often do we not hear people in Norway speak with intense complacency of our Norwegian 'good sense,' which really means nothing but a tepidity of spirit which makes it impossible for those honest souls to commit a madness [the phrase is the one he had used in praise of Michelangelo and Bernini]. . . . Down here, I assure you, it is different!" In a Norwegian paper he had read of a boy who had cut off a finger to avoid military service. "I know mothers in Piedmont, in Genoa, Novara, Alessandria, who took their fourteen-year-old sons from school that they might join Garibaldi's adventure in Palermo; it was not so much a question of liberating their country as of realising an idea. How many of our politicians do you suppose will do likewise when the Russians invade Finnmark? . . . I was in Berlin at the time of the triumphal entry, I saw the people spit on the cannon from Dybbøl, and it was to me a sign that history will spit in the eyes of Sweden and Norway for their part in that affair. Here in Rome I find every kind of spiritual squalidity among the Scandinavians. What do you think of the fact that during the war Danish men and women sat on Sundays among the Germans in the chapel of the Prussian embassy and listened piously while the Prussian priest prayed from his pulpit for victory for the Prussian armies in their just war against the enemy? But I have raged and scourged, believe me; for down here, I fear nothing; at home I was afraid when I stood in that clammy crowd and sensed their ugly smiles behind me. . . . I had to get away from all that swinishness up there to become cleansed. Up there I could never achieve any coherent inner life; so that I was one thing in my work and another outside it; and so that my work, too, never achieved any real entity."

Yet as Ibsen mocked his fellow-Scandinavians for their cowardice under the Italian sky, there was one man who did not quail before his onslaughts, and whose presence must have nagged Ibsen like a Banquo—the young theological student Christopher Bruun, newly returned to Rome that autumn from the Danish war, having made the journey through Europe on foot. At a meeting of the Christiania Students' Union three days before Ibsen left Norway, which Ibsen did not attend, being otherwise occupied with his Learned Holland friends, Bruun had exhorted his fellow-country-

25 "Til Henrik Ibsen," a poem contributed by Snoilsky to *Henrik Ibsen: festskrift i anledning af hans 70de fødselsdag,* ed. Gerhard Gran, pp. 5–7.

men to volunteer with him and thereby "testify by action that idealism, truth, and justice are not mere subjects for speeches on festive occasions, but things for which a man should be prepared to live, fight and, if necessary, die."[26] He had been much disillusioned with the Danish army, finding little idealism or patriotism, but mainly a desire to return safely home; on one occasion he had been warned not to shoot lest he "irritate the enemy." He had signed off from the war, and had arrived in Rome a deeply disappointed man, very different from the idealist who had set forth from Christiania.[27] One day when Ibsen brought the Danish war up for discussion Bruun asked him why, if he felt so strongly, he had not volunteered. "We poets have other tasks to perform," Ibsen replied, but a doubt remained in his mind. He wondered whether he had been right to compromise, and with this doubt was linked another. Was he right to believe so inflexibly in his calling and thus, in all probability, condemn his wife and child to continued poverty?

So this breakaway year of 1864 ended in a mood of, if possible, more than usual doubt. The new year was ushered in by a buoyant letter from Bjørnson who, notwithstanding his earlier protestations, had finally accepted the directorship of the Christiania Theatre and had forgiven Ibsen the latter's apparent failure to acknowledge his previous letter and draft. "How often I long for you, Ibsen!" he declared (19 January). "I always do when I am parted from you, even when you were in Bergen and I was here—but when we meet, things go wrong. Why? . . . Stay down there as long as you can, and go to Naples and Sorrento as soon as you can manage after Easter." He added a suggestion which was to have far-reaching and beneficial consequences for Ibsen. "Let me put you under Hegel's wing! He'll gladly send you an advance, which I shall guarantee on your behalf."[28]

Frederik Hegel, the first great Scandinavian publisher, had been born the illegitimate son of a servant-girl and her employer's son, Frederik V. Mansa, later to become a well-known doctor and medical historian. One of Mansa's patients was a certain Jacob Deichmann, the head of a small Copenhagen publishing house named Gyldendal, and at Mansa's suggestion Deichmann took Hegel into his employ when the latter was fifteen. In 1850, at the age of thirty-three, Hegel became head of the firm, and within fifteen years had transformed it from its modest beginnings into the distinguished house which it has since remained. Bjørnson had lately become one of his authors, and had found him a wise and generous counsellor; an opinion which Ibsen, after an unfortunate preliminary misunderstanding, was

[26] Francis Bull, "Henrik Ibsen," in *Norsk litteratur-historie*, ed. Francis Bull, Fredrik Paasche, A. H. Winsnes and Philip Houm, IV (Oslo, 1960), 344.

[27] Cf. Eivind Berggrav and Francis Bull, *Ibsens sjelelige krise* (Oslo, 1937), pp. 37 ff.

[28] *Gro-tid*, II, 150–51.

permanently to share. His association with Hegel, on whose advice he came to rely not merely in literary but also in financial matters, was to give him that feeling of trust in his publisher which can be, as it was with Ibsen, such a stabilising influence on an author's career.

This last letter of Bjørnson crossed with one which Ibsen wrote to him on 28 January confirming Bjørnson's prediction that his senses would gradually become attuned to classical art and sculpture. Its beauty, Ibsen confessed, "grows more and more on me, as you said it would. It comes in flashes, but a single flash throws light over whole vistas. Do you remember the 'Tragic Muse' which stands outside the hall in the Rotunda in the Vatican? No sculpture here has yet been such a revelation to me. I may even say that it is through this that I have understood what Greek tragedy was. The indescribably calm, noble and exalted joy in the expression of the face, the richly laurelled head containing within it something supernaturally luxuriant and bacchantic, the eyes that look both inwards and at the same time through and far beyond the object of their gaze—such was Greek tragedy. The statue of Demosthenes in the Lateran, the Faun in the Villa Borghese, and the Faun (of Praxiteles) in the Vatican (*bracchio nuovo*), have also opened great windows for me into Greek life and the Greek character, and have enabled me to understand what imperishability in beauty really is. Pray heaven I may be able to use this understanding for my own work. Michelangelo's Moses in S. Pietro in Vincoli I had not seen when I last wrote to you; but I had read about it and built up an expectation which has not quite been fulfilled—however, I have only seen it once.

"How glorious the landscape is down here; in both forms and colours there is an indescribable harmony. I often spend half the day lying out among the graves on the Via Latina or the old Via Appia, and think it an idleness but no waste of time. Caracalla's Baths are another place which holds some especial attraction for me . . ."

On 25 March he applied to the Royal Norwegian Society for Knowledge at Trondhjem for a grant of 500 specie-dollars to extend his stay in Italy, explaining that he was "preparing a long dramatic work based on material from Roman history." Bjørnson, who had himself received a grant from them, supported Ibsen's application with an ingenious letter to the Society, pleading that "a poetical work does not, indeed, strictly come under the heading of knowledge, but . . . the circumstances under which it springs into existence, and the sum of experience, knowledge and mood from which it is born, demand a very special protection. If this is not forthcoming, the wine ferments—and Henrik Ibsen has always been particularly vulnerable to this danger" (not perhaps the happiest of metaphors to use about one who was well known recently to have been an alcoholic). "His work," concluded Bjørnson's letter, "is more strictly akin to knowledge

than my own, since he has a greater talent than I for abstract thought."[29]
But the application arrived too late, the Society having already made all its
allocations for the next six months.

That spring of 1865 Ibsen struggled with three projects: *Brand* (as
an epic poem), *Emperor and Galilean* (as a prose drama), and another
epic poem set against the background of a Seventeenth of May celebration in Norway. He read Dietrichson a song from the last of these which,
however, he abandoned and rewrote four years later as a prose play,
The League of Youth. The two other projects, likewise, made painful
progress. The relaxing atmosphere of Rome, "its ideal peace, the carefree companionship of the artistic world, an existence comparable only
to that of Shakespeare's *As You Like It*," as he was later to describe
it,[30] was totally different to the conditions which had stimulated his
writing in Norway, and it took time for him to assimilate it. *Emperor
and Galilean* he was already finding too big a theme to fit into the span
of a normal play. "Why can't one write a drama in ten acts?" he asked
Dietrichson one day. "I can't find room in five."[31] *Emperor and Galilean*
was in fact to occupy ten acts and to take him eight more years to
complete; the malaise of contemporary Europe, and of Norway in particular, obsessed him too much for him to concentrate on the problems
of Julian the Apostate. The subject uppermost in his mind, as with those
two other exiles half a century later, James Joyce and D. H. Lawrence,
was the complacency and narrowness of his fellow-countrymen, with their
failure to support the Danes as the indelible symbol. Yet his own failure
to have acted may have been responsible for the writer's block which he
now experienced.

On Good Friday, 14 April, John Wilkes Booth fired a pistol into a
box at Ford's Theatre in Washington, and the event roused Ibsen to
compose a striking poem, one indeed of his finest, "The Murder of
Abraham Lincoln." Characteristically, he directed his indignation not, like
the rest of the world, at Booth, but at what he regarded as the hypocrisy
of human reaction. Why such anger now? he asks. Was this worse than
the Prussian action at Dybbøl, the Russian rape of Poland, England's
bombardment of Copenhagen in 1801 and 1807? These broken promises
and betrayals have "manured the soil of history"; could anyone expect
a sweeter harvest? But, the poem ends, I shall not cry woe over every
poisoned blossom that opens on time's tree. Let the worm gnaw; there
can be no rebirth till the skull is clean. Let the mockery of our system
be exposed. Nemesis will the sooner sit in judgment on our hypocrisy.

The same month (the letter is undated) Bjørnson wrote that he was

---

[29] *Gro-tid*, II, 159–61.
[30] Letter to Peter Hansen, 28 October 1870.
[31] Dietrichson, I, 339.

thinking of reviving the Norwegian Theatre in Møllergaden and running it in harness with the Christiania Theatre, and asked Ibsen to come home in six or twelve months to help him. "I am willing to share the salary, the work, and the responsibility with you. Let me know."[32] He promised also to write to Consul Bravo and ask him to advance Ibsen 50 specie-dollars to see him over the next month. One wonders how Ibsen would have survived that first year and a half in Italy without Bjørnson.

In late June Ibsen left Rome for the countryside, this time to Ariccia, fifteen miles to the southeast in the Alban mountains. Ariccia was, and still is, an idyllic little town, containing several fine works by Bernini, including the main piazza, its two fountains and the magnificent Chigi Palace. The Ibsens lived, as Suzannah later described it to her daughter-in-law, "not just humbly, but like paupers. . . . Sigurd can tell you how he used to go each afternoon and buy three soldi-worth of bread and three soldi-worth of Caceotto cheese; this, with half a carafe of red wine, was our dinner."[33] The work continued to go painfully, and Ibsen needed all the encouragement that Bjørnson could give him:

Copenhagen, 25 July 1865

Why the devil don't you write? You don't need to frank them. . . . From Trondhjem a provisional "No," i.e., you applied too late as always, they had made their allocations, but I've spoken to one of them, written again, and something'll happen soon, so don't lose heart if it comes a bit late. . . .
Your prospects now are:

What you can earn yourself
What I can raise (*very* little)
300 from Trondhjem Society (am of course asking 500)
400 from Storthing
A performance at the theatre (if Dunker agrees)
Whatever you get when you come home from the theatre or the university library (I'm trying to get you something there whether you like it or not) . . .

But the problem is, you need money *now*. . . . Can't you start sending the MS for printing? Then you can ask a bigger advance. If you can't do that yet I'll have to resort to murder. . . . Don't lose heart, don't lose faith in your friends, or in your admirers—but, my dear Ibsen, why all these gloomy words? Hasn't everything gone splendidly for you (a few misfortunes apart, which were your own fault partly) since you came to Christiania [!]—you are now regarded as one of the leading poets in Scandinavia, respected, your work eagerly anticipated, you are in Italy, you are liked down there (I hear that

[32] *Gro-tid*, II, 156–59.
[33] Bergliot Ibsen, p. 29.

from Bloch), you have a handsome and assured future (assured both by the State and by your own dramatic talent), you have young people around you, and you have me!

Your most affectionate
Bjørnstjerne

P.S. Stay in Rome and Italy till everything is settled here, the Storthing, Trondhjem, maybe the library or the theatre too, if you'd prefer that. If you'd like to *run* the theatre, that too; I'll soon have had enough. But my advice is: don't, or at most for a limited period like me. . . . I'll tell them it's a question of money or life—"A poet is dying!" Though you won't b——— die, you're tough, brave, lazy—such people never die.[34]

But by the time this letter reached Ibsen, the longed-for breakthrough had come. Ibsen described it in his reply to Bjørnson:

Ariccia, 12 September 1865

My dear Bjørnson!

Your letter and the draft from Hegel came at a good time. Thank you, my dear, blessed friend, for both! But affectionate and kind as your letter was—indeed, all the more therefore—I have read it with self-reproach because of the worry and anxiety you have endured on my account. Thank you for this too! It all adds up to one thing, by far the most important thing for me and for my calling in life—the fact that I have met and really found you—this I can never repay except by a devotion which neither my friends nor your enemies will ever be able to alter. I know you will understand that it is not Bjørnson the fund-raiser whom I have in mind. Well, more of this when we meet; now I can speak openly to you, I could never do so before. Everything is going well for me now, and has really been so the whole time, except for isolated periods when I didn't know which way to turn, not only as regards money, but because my work would not progress. Then one day I went into St. Peter's—I had gone into Rome on some business—and suddenly everything I wanted to say appeared to me in a strong and clear light. Now I have thrown overboard the work with which I had been torturing myself for a year without getting anywhere, and in the middle of July I started working on something new which has been making such progress as no other work of mine has ever done. New, I mean, in the sense that I only then began to write it, but the matter and mood have been weighing on me like a nightmare ever since those many distasteful happenings at home which forced me to look into myself and our life there and think seriously about things which had previously passed me by and about which I didn't seriously bother. It is a dramatic poem,

[34] *Gro-tid*, II, 166–69.

of serious content; contemporary theme; five acts in rhymed verse (but no *Love's Comedy*). The fourth act is almost finished, and I feel I shall be able to complete the fifth in a week. I work both morning and afternoon, which I have never been able to do before. It is blessedly peaceful out here; no one I know; I read nothing but the Bible—it is powerful and strong!

If I were to name the most important result of my coming here, I should say that it was that I have rid myself of that aesthetic attitude, that forcing of oneself into isolation and self-sufficiency, that formerly held sway over me. Aestheticism in this sense now seems to me as great a curse to writing as theology is to religion. You have never been troubled by aestheticism in this sense, you have never looked at things through the hollow of your hand. Is it not an indescribable joy to be able to write? But it carries with it a great responsibility, and I now have sufficient earnestness to realize this and be stern with myself. A Copenhagen aesthete once said when I was there: "Whatever else one may feel about him, Christ was the most interesting phenomenon in the history of the world." The aesthete relished him as the gourmet relishes the sight of an oyster. I have always had the strength not to become that kind of cartilaginous animal, but God knows what all those spiritual asses might not have made of me if they had had me to themselves, and what prevented them from having me, my dear Bjørnson, was you . . .

You say the Storthing will approve my grant. Do you think so? I have a suspicion that my new work will not dispose the members more charitably towards me, but may God punish me if, for that reason, I cut a single line, whatever those pygmy souls may feel. Let me rather be a beggar all my life. If I cannot be myself in what I write, then my work would be nothing but lies and humbug, and our country has had enough of that without handing out grants for more . . .

I don't think the theatre could stage my play—if I were on the board I would have to vote against it. But if you can use it, that's another matter; it's dramatic all right; but whether it is performable on other grounds you must judge for yourself . . .

> Our warmest regards to you and yours,
> Your affectionate
> Henr: Ibsen

The new version of *Brand* was in the form of a poetic drama and, as the above letter indicates, Ibsen wrote it at an extraordinary speed. We do not know the exact date of his visit to St. Peter's, but even if it took place within a week of his leaving Rome it means that he composed nearly three and a half thousand lines of rhymed octosyllabics in, at the most, ten weeks, a rate of fifty lines a day, and it is a measure of his new-found confidence that he was expecting to complete the fifth act in a week. In the end it took him longer, for it extended to seventeen hundred lines, or one-third of the play, but he wrote it at the same rate, finishing it in a little over a month.

Dietrichson has described Ibsen's working routine at Ariccia. "He liked to rise at 4 A.M. and take a stroll in the woods or the great Chigi park before the day grew hot. As the sun rose higher in the heavens he sat down at his desk, where he would work more or less uninterruptedly until the day ended; and in the evening he liked to sit and enjoy the cool on the big flight of steps in front of the church."[35] "I was," Ibsen wrote to Bjørnson the following March, "despite my poverty and tribulation, so indescribably happy, I felt such a crusading joy within me, that I do not know the thing I would have lacked the courage to tilt at." On another occasion he used a less Bunyanesque image to describe his mood of that summer. "At the time I was writing *Brand* I had on my table a scorpion in an empty beer glass. From time to time the brute would ail; then I would throw a piece of ripe fruit in to it, on which it would cast itself in a rage and eject its poison into it; then it was well again."[36] Ibsen's euphoria and venom both found vent; the play is at the same time an exultation and an indictment.

Brand marks an extraordinary leap forward in Ibsen's development as a dramatist, and the chief reason is clear. He was not writing for performance, and was thus able to work uninhibited by the limitations of practical staging (and we have seen how severe these were in the middle of the nineteenth century). He wrote it, as Alfred de Musset and Turgenev had written their plays (even *A Month in the Country*), and as Thomas Hardy was to write *The Dynasts,* to be read, and so was able to include, *inter alia,* a storm at sea and an avalanche. But there are other reasons for the immensity of *Brand* compared with any of his previous works. The distance and relaxation he had found in Italy offered ideal circumstances for the expression of that *sæva indignatio* from which his poetry welled; and his first sight of Italian Renaissance art and, more particularly, sculpture and architecture, especially that of Michelangelo, had given him a new standard at which to aim. His former masters, one must remember, had been Oehlenschläger, Holberg, Heiberg, the sagas and ballads, and Shakespeare glimpsed through the mist of dull translation; now he had Michelangelo. It is significant that his revelation of how the play should shape itself had come to him in St. Peter's, under Michelangelo's dome. *Brand* is a mighty cathedral of a play, and Brand's God, "young and strong like Hercules," is an exact description of Christ

---

[35] Dietrichson, I, 345.
[36] Letter to Peter Hansen, 28 October 1870.

as painted by Michelangelo in the Sistine Chapel. The same taste that disparaged Michelangelo and Milan Cathedral and admired Raphael dominated Scandinavian taste in drama; it was the dogma of æstheticism which Heiberg had laid down and which no critic had yet authoritatively challenged, though Georg Brandes was shortly to do so. No wonder Ibsen had told Bjørnson that he regarded ridding himself of his æstheticism as the most important result of his coming to Italy. Michelangelo, Bernini and the unknown architect of Milan Cathedral had what Ibsen recognized as "the courage to commit a madness now and then," and *Brand* is the direct result of their influence. Its power is not static but dynamic; each scene, superb in itself, moves irresistibly on to the next, culminating in what is arguably the greatest final act that any dramatist had written since *King Lear*.

The story of the play is that of the epic Ibsen had left unfinished, lopped of its introductory section about the boys on the hillside, and carried to its terrifying logical conclusion. Brand, the young priest, walking in the mountains, meets (as in the poem) his old schoolfriend Ejnar with the latter's fiancée, Agnes. He denounces their materialistic hedonism in words that uninhibitedly reflected Ibsen's opinion of his countrymen:

> You separate
> Faith from doctrine. You do not want
> To live your faith. For that you need a God
> Who'll keep one eye shut. That God is getting feeble
> Like the generation that worships him.
> Mine is a storm where yours is a gentle wind,
> Inflexible where yours is deaf, all-loving
> Not all-doting. And he is young
> And strong like Hercules. His is the voice
> That spoke in thunder when he stood
> Bright before Moses in the burning bush,
> A giant before the dwarf of dwarfs. In the valley
> Of Gideon he stayed the sun, and worked
> Miracles without number—and would work
> Them still, if people were not dead, like you. . . .

EJNAR (*waves him away*). Turn the world upside down.
    I still have faith in my God.
BRAND.   Good. But paint him
    With crutches. I go to lay him in his grave.

Brand goes on his way and meets the mad girl Gerd, who is pursued in her imagination by a hawk that is for ever diving and clawing at her. She tries to lead him to her Ice Church among the peaks:

> Come with me!
> Up there, cataract and avalanche sing Mass.
> The wind preaches along the wall of the glacier
> And the hawk can't get in. He swoops down
> On to the Black Peak and sits there
> On my church steeple like an ugly weathercock.

He descends instead to the village where he was born, which is gripped by famine, and tells the people that their plight is God's judgment on their lack of faith. Agnes, inspired by his words, and by his courage in sailing across the storm-tossed fjord to shrive a dying man, leaves Ejnar and joins him. Brand warns her what life with him will mean:

> Young woman, think carefully before you decide.
> Locked between mountains, shadowed by crag and peak,
> Shut in the twilight of this ravine
> My life will flow like a sad October evening.

AGNES. The darkness no longer frightens me. A star
Pierces through the night.

BRAND.   Remember, I am stern
In my demands. I require All or Nothing.
No half-measures. There is no forgiveness
For failure. It may not be enough
To offer your life. Your death may be required also.

EJNAR. Stop this mad game, leave this man of dark law.
Live the life you know you can.

BRAND. Choose. You stand at the parting of the ways.

She marries Brand, and he remains in the village as priest. They have a child who, the doctor warns them, will die if they stay in this cold place which "the sun never warms." Brand sees this as a temptation to abandon his calling; he stays and the child dies; as a result, Agnes dies too. Then Brand sees his whole life as a failure and leads the villagers up into the mountains to find God (as Lammers the revivalist had done with the people of Skien). There they lose heart, revile and, finally, stone him. Abandoned, he is joined by the mad girl Gerd who, seeing the blood on him, thinks he is the Saviour and kneels down and worships him.

GERD. Priest, you're limping. Your foot's hurt.
How did that happen?

BRAND. The people hunted me.

GERD   (goes closer). Your forehead is red.

BRAND. The people stoned me.

GERD. Your voice used to be clear as song.
Now it creaks like leaves in autumn.
BRAND. Everything—everyone—
GERD. What?
BRAND. Betrayed me.
GERD (*stares at him*). Ah! Now I know who you are!
I thought you were the priest.
Fie upon him and all the others!
You're the Big Man. The Biggest of all.
BRAND. I used to think I was.
GERD. Let me see your hands.
BRAND. My hands?
GERD. They're scarred with nails. There's blood in your hair.
The thorn's teeth have cut your forehead.
You've been on the cross. My father told me
It happened long ago and far away.
But now I see he was deceiving me.
I know you. You're the Saviour Man!
BRAND. Get away from me!
GERD. Shall I fall down at your feet and pray?
BRAND. Go!
GERD. You gave the blood that will save us all.
There are nail holes in your hands. You are the Chosen One.
You are the Greatest of all.
BRAND. I am the meanest thing that crawls on earth.

As the sun rises, Brand sees that they are standing in the Ice Church, symbol of the cold and grandiose emptiness of his life. Gerd fires her rifle at the imaginary hawk which she still thinks pursues her, and this brings down the Ice Church in an avalanche, killing them both. As it engulfs them, Brand cries in despair:

Answer me, God, in the moment of death!
If not by will, how shall Man be redeemed?

And a voice replies through the thunder:

He is the God of love.

The character of Brand himself, while probably owing something to hearsay memories of Lammers at Skien,[37] was, by Ibsen's own admission,

[37] So Ibsen told both William Archer ("Ibsen as I Knew Him," in *Monthly Review* [June 1906], p. 8), and Henrik Jæger (Midbøe, p. 147). Arnt Delhi, Ibsen's masseur during his last years, says that Ibsen denied this (interview in *Aftenposten*,

largely based on Christopher Bruun, whose deep religious feeling, distrust of the established Church and contempt for compromise, had made so profound an impression on Ibsen during the past months in Rome. Bishop Eivind Berggrav, who knew Bruun well, wrote of him that "behind Bruun's cold mask burned an intense flame, and also great goodness," but that he *"appeared* hard and cold. . . . He could not find the right harmony between loving and chastising. . . . This was Bruun's tragedy, an unholy gulf between the warmth of the love that was in him and the coldness of his character; they should have balanced and harmonised each other, but could not be reconciled."[38] Another friend of Bruun reveals that Bruun himself admitted that his greatest defect was his inability to love.[39] Ibsen, however, confessed that he had put a good deal of himself into the part. "Brand," he once remarked, "is myself in my best moments."[40] He later told Georg Brandes that he could as easily have made Brand a sculptor or a politician, or even Galileo—"except that then of course he would have had to have held strongly to his beliefs, and not pretended that the earth stood still."[41] It is also worth noting that in the spring of 1865, when he was wrestling with *Brand,* Ibsen had found "joy and strength"[42] in reading Bjørnson's play *Mary Stuart in Scotland,* one of the central characters of which is the Calvinist preacher John Knox, a figure with whom Brand has much in common.

Another historical figure who probably contributed to the portrait of Brand was Garibaldi, who, when he led the last forlorn hope out of Rome in 1849 to continue his resistance in the Italian mountains, had said to his followers: "I offer neither pay, nor quarters, nor provisions. I offer hunger, thirst, forced marches, battle and death"—words markedly similar to those used by Brand to his parishioners on the mountain in Act Five—and we know that Ibsen borrowed Garibaldi's autobiography from the Scandinavian Club library during the year he wrote *Brand.*

Agnes he based at least partly on Bruun's sister Thea, the pretty girl whom he had known in Genzano and who had by now returned to Norway to die. She is perhaps the most tenderly drawn of all Ibsen's heroines. Walter Runeburg, the gay young Finnish sculptor who loved Thea, is traditionally supposed to have been the original of Ejnar who, one suspects, also represented Ibsen's idea of himself in his worst moments, æstheticism pushed to its extreme, like the hero of "On the Heights."

---

14 March 1928); but Ibsen often contradicted himself, and his earlier assurances seem the more trustworthy; Delhi knew him only when he was very old and had been weakened by strokes. He told both Jæger and Delhi that Thea Bruun had been the part-original of Agnes.

38 Berggrav and Bull, pp. 37 ff.

39 *Ibid.,* p. 39.

40 Letter to Peter Hansen, 28 October 1870.

41 Letter to Georg Brandes, 26 June 1869.

42 Letter to Bjørnson, 12 September 1865.

The idea for Gerd probably came from a half-mad peasant girl he had met at Hellesylt on his folklore trip in 1862; and a hard old peasant woman whom he heard of at Graffer on the same trip may have contributed towards the portrait of Brand's mother. Many of the descriptions of natural scenery stem from that journey; among other things, he had heard of a priest who earlier that year had been killed by an avalanche.

Ibsen wrote the play in rhymed four-beat verse, using both iambics and trochees, iambics mainly for colloquial or argumentative dialogue, trochees for scenes of passion, poetry, or vision. "I wanted a metre," he told William Archer, "in which I could career where I would, as on horseback,"[43] and he achieved a marvellous flexibility, moving without incongruity between colloquialism and high poetry. Archer perceptively observed of *Brand* that it contained "the prophetic fire of Carlyle fused with the genial verve and intellectual athleticism of Browning, and expressed by aid of a dramatic facility to parallel which we must go two centuries backwards."

A great deal has been written about the symbolism of *Brand,* and the different significances that might be attached to the hawk, the Ice Church, and so on. Dr. Arne Duve, in his stimulating book *Symbolikken i Henrik Ibsens skuespill,* suggests that the hawk represents the life of the emotions, or love, and that it is Brand's fear of the powers of life and light that make him, in Act Five, dismiss the hawk contemptuously as "the spirit of compromise." The Ice Church, thinks Dr. Duve, represents the opposite of the hawk, the negation of love. Gerd, like Brand, fears and distrusts love (like him, she is the child of a loveless marriage), and Brand's negation of love finally leads him, too, to the terrible citadel of the Ice Church; what Ibsen, thirty years later in *John Gabriel Borkman,* was to term "the coldness of the heart." The Ice Church finally killed Brand, just as the coldness of the heart killed John Gabriel Borkman.

Michael Elliott, who directed the justly-celebrated production of *Brand* in 1959 in London, has expressed the view that the hawk represents nothing as specific as love but rather, in a general way, "whatever one rejects," just as Room 101 in George Orwell's *1984* contained "the worst thing in the world," whatever that might be for each individual. I agree with this theory, and believe that the Ice Church stands for the false citadel that each of us builds in his own imagination as a refuge from his particular hawk.

On 30 September, while he was still engaged on Act Five of *Brand,* Ibsen returned to Rome where, in the beginning of November, he posted off his fair copy of the first four acts to his new publisher, Frederik Hegel

---

[43] William Archer, "Ibsen as I Knew Him," p. 7.

in Copenhagen, promising that the remainder of the play would shortly follow. There now ensued an extraordinary chapter of misunderstandings.

Bjørnson, in recommending Ibsen to Hegel earlier in the year, had informed him that Ibsen's next work was to be "a play set in the time of Christian IV" (i.e., the drama about Magnus Heineson). Hegel, on receipt of the parcel containing the first four acts of *Brand,* assumed it to be the play Bjørnson had spoken of and, anxious to get it out in time for the Christmas sales, somewhat rashly sent it straight to the printers without bothering to read it. At the same time he wrote to Ibsen promising to have the play published by Christmas provided he received the rest of the manuscript before the end of the month and offering to print 1,250 copies against an honorarium of 30 Danish riksdollars (15 Norwegian speciedollars) per signature of sixteen pages, which worked out at just over £50 for the edition. Ibsen immediately accepted this offer and posted the remaining pages on 15 November, the day after he received Hegel's letter. Only when the proofs began to appear from the press did Hegel discover that he was going to publish, not a drama of Danish history, but an immense dramatic poem indicting the modern Norwegian attitude towards almost everything in life. He thereupon (23 November) wrote nervously to Ibsen expressing the fear that *"possibly,* despite its many beauties, it may not be comprehended by the mass of readers, and the demand may not be such as to justify printing so large an impression as 1,250 copies. I hasten therefore to inform you that I propose to print half that number, viz. 625 copies, and accordingly offer 15 riksdollars per signature. . . . I sincerely hope, for your sake, that my fears may prove groundless." He added that should Ibsen not feel able to accept these terms, and prefer to offer the book to another publisher, "I shall, despite the value I place on becoming your publisher, and despite the fact that much of the book is already printed, be willing to withdraw."

Ibsen was deeply disappointed at this information. However, he could not afford to be grand, and on 2 December he replied accepting Hegel's conditions. But this letter got lost in the post, with the result that Christmas and the New Year came and went, and *Brand* remained one-third unprinted. In February Hegel wrote a puzzled note to Bjørnson: "I don't understand Ibsen. I should be very sad if I have unwittingly offended him."[44] At the beginning of March he wrote again to Bjørnson: "It is strange that Ibsen has sent me no word. But now we are already into March, and in all conscience I dare not let his book stand unpublished any longer. I shall issue it in a week, and shall print in accordance with the terms originally agreed."

Meanwhile, as can be imagined, Ibsen in Rome was getting more and more worried at the non-appearance of his play, searching the Danish

[44] L. C. Nielsen, *Frederik V. Hegel: et Mindeskrift* (Copenhagen, 1909), I, 218.

newspapers as they arrived, a week late, in the hope of seeing a review, or at least an advertisement. On 4 March he wrote a very depressed letter to Bjørnson: "You call Hegel a high-minded man, and so does Fru Thoresen. . . . I have had a thousand difficulties with him, and have agreed to everything so as to have my book out by Christmas, but it hasn't appeared. . . . You can well imagine my state of mind, eaten up with worry and tension, waiting for the book and maybe all manner of controversies, attacks, etc., arising from it, unable to start work on a new project which I have in my head waiting to be written. Well, enough of that. Dear Bjørnson, I feel that I am, by some huge and inexorable fate, cut off from both God and man. . . . There is nothing so enervating as this accursed waiting. Well, it can only be temporary, I must and shall conquer some day. If Fate has so willed it as to set me in this world and make me the man I am, she must accept the consequences. But no more of this. . . . You are the only friend I have. You do not know what it means to have only one friend. . . . P.S. I am availing myself of your offer not to frank my mail. I do this from necessity, not from choice."

Three days later he wrote to Hegel beseeching him for news of *Brand* and asking him to send the balance of his fee "to be regarded as an advance on future works, should there be no second edition. . . . My new work," he added rather pathetically, "is a historical drama from the early years of Christian IV and is being written with a view to performance. I also have material for a collection of poems. . . . Please debit the postage of this letter to my account with you."

Brand was published in Copenhagen on 15 March 1866, but Ibsen did not hear of this until the actual day of its appearance, when he received a letter from Hegel dated 5 March which at last put him in the picture. "I hope," he replied on 16 March, "that all misunderstandings are now dispelled, and that in the future I may have the honour and pleasure of being associated with you as an author, just as it is my intention to associate myself as closely as possible with Denmark. Norwegians and Swedes have a terrible debt of blood to expiate with you, and I feel it is my calling to use the talents which God has given me to wake my compatriots from their sloth and make them realize what are the important issues in life."

In the event, the miseries and frustrations of this winter were soon forgotten, for Hegel's fears as to the reception of *Brand* proved totally false. Throughout Scandinavia it created an immediate and widespread sensation. As he was so often to do in the future, Ibsen had touched his contemporaries on their most sensitive spot; the movement towards liberalism and individualism was just approaching its climax, and the call to follow one's private conscience, avoid compromise, and "be oneself" answered a general and unspoken need. *Brand* established Ibsen in Scandinavia as the pioneer of revolt against dead thought and tradition.

It had the same explosive effect in Norway, Sweden, and Denmark which, eleven years later, *The Pillars of Society* was to have on German audiences and, later still, *A Doll's House* on thinking people throughout the western world.

To modern readers *Brand* is a mighty, Lear-like poetic tragedy of a lonely, misguided, and tormented spirit. To the Scandinavia of 1866 it was before all else a gantlet thrown down to authority, an attack on complacency and conventionality, whether in the field of religion, of patriotism, or of human relationships. Orthodox Christianity, as preached by the established church, was of course a prime target (in this respect, the play did for Scandinavians what the new scientific teaching and Bible criticism were doing in England), but unthinking humanism, as represented by Ejnar and to some extent by the Mayor, also came under fire. Truth, the play stressed, was something which every man must find out for himself, and every woman too. One could no longer accept the sum of human wisdom garnered through the ages. Another target important to his contemporaries, and one which, again, Ibsen was further to indict in so many of his later plays, was the narrowness of small community life, that parochialism which still besets the Scandinavian countries more than their bigger neighbours, and which no writer had so eloquently condemned before. Finally, the character of Brand himself—narrow, intolerant, harsh to his wife and child as to his flock and himself—was a new kind of hero, new at any rate since *Coriolanus,* and as unfamiliar and refreshing to readers in the eighteen-sixties as another kind of anti-hero was to be to European theatre audiences ninety years later.

Illustreret Nyhedsblad of 29 April 1866 quoted *Morgenbladet*'s Copenhagen correspondent on the book's reception in Denmark: "Of the new literary works that have lately appeared, *Brand* takes a pre-eminence which few poetic works have previously been able to claim. It is read with the greatest interest, its praise is in all men's mouths, and its powerful words in all men's thoughts." Paul Botten Hansen added an editorial comment: "That this picture is not exaggerated is confirmed by private information from Denmark. Wherever people meet, the talk is only of *Brand.* . . . The interest in *Brand* has also led men of letters to read Ibsen's earlier works, such as *Love's Comedy,* and they have marvelled greatly that such a book managed to create so little effect up here as to pass virtually unnoticed." In Sweden it was the same. The writer Gustaf af Geijerstam recalled: "It would be vain for me to attempt to describe the passion with which we young men read and discussed the great poet." The reading of Ibsen, he explains, became a bond of unity between friends and lovers. "No more sacred gift could be offered to anyone than *Brand.*"[45] Axel

---

[45] Gustaf af Geijerstam, "Två minnen om Ibsen," in *Ord och Bild* (Stockholm, 1898), pp. 116-17.

Lundegård remembered how the play had "hypnotised us all with its rigorous pietism. . . . That dark fanatic who set out to slay the obsolete God of the time has been the pennant-bearer of our younger generation."[46] And August Strindberg, who was seventeen when *Brand* appeared and twenty when he read it belatedly in 1869 (and wrote a play that year, *The Freethinker*, which bears evident signs of its influence), described it as "the voice of a Savonarola."[47]

So controversial a work naturally excited some opposition. The disciples of J. L. Heiberg's doctrine of æstheticism found it contrary to their beliefs (though Heiberg's widow sent Ibsen a letter of admiration), and Clemens Petersen, while finding much to praise in it ("This remarkable poem," began his front-page review in *Fædrelandet*), declared that so violently committed a work "could not be called poetry."[48] "He is no poet," Petersen wrote privately to Bjørnson that March, "but a critic. His imagination breeds reflection, not human beings; he can perceive ideas, but not create them. . . . *Brand* . . . is essentially criticism, and not poetry"[49]—a statement typical of the æsthetic viewpoint which was always to find Ibsen's work unsatisfying. Similarly: "The Devil is in that man," wrote the Danish art historian Julius Lange of Ibsen when he met him in Rome a couple of years later. "If I had the curing of him, I'd prescribe Greek literature or art, first in small doses so he wouldn't spit them out, then in larger and larger quantities until his sense of form and purpose was restored to health."[50] Lange defined the quality that offended him as "spiritual overstrain," reminding one of early critical reaction in England to Shelley and Keats.

It is curious for a modern reader to find Ibsen condemned as a romantic. Yet this reaction against the supposed extravagances of *Brand* was echoed by the man who most of all might have been expected to welcome them, the young Georg Brandes. But Brandes, in 1866, was only twenty-four and had not yet found himself as a critic; he, too, was still under the sway of that "æsthetic" attitude towards life and literature which Ibsen was

[46] Axel Lundegård, *Röde Prinsen* (Stockholm, 1889), p. 219.

[47] August Strindberg, *Den litterära reaktionen i Sverige sedan 1865*, a lecture given in Paris on 25 November 1885 and printed in the Copenhagen monthly, *Tilskueren*, in May 1886 (p. 393).

[48] Ibsen had written to Petersen on 4 December 1865 expressing the hope that Petersen would review *Brand* when it appeared: "Your criticism will have a decisive effect on how my compatriots receive the book. . . . Should you have anything to say to me for which you cannot find space in your review, which I await confidently and with anticipation, I should be most grateful for a few lines. I have an intolerably oppressive sensation of standing alone." There is no record of whether Petersen bothered to send Ibsen a letter—probably not, judging from his remarks to Bjørnson.

[49] Cf. Kari Hamre, *Clemens Petersen og hans forhold til norsk litteratur i aarene 1856–1869* (Oslo, 1945), pp. 160–61.

[50] *Brev fra Julius Lange*, ed. P. Købke (Copenhagen, 1902), pp. 29–30.

congratulating himself on having escaped from.[51] Brandes's response to
Brand was confused. He admired the work as literature but disapproved of it
on doctrinaire grounds; he believed that poetry should move and calm
the reader, not enflame or disturb him. "One cannot but admire," he
wrote in the Danish newspaper *Dagbladet* on 23 May 1866, "the versifying
skill and command of language which enable him to compose so long a
poem from start to finish in short lines of sometimes triple or even
quadruple rhymes . . . but . . . they rush forward at a speed so im-
petuous that the Muse might almost be wearing the red shoes of Andersen's
story; one stumbles now on a tastelessness of language, now on an ill-
chosen image, now on an expression which imperfectly clothes the thought;
and one's only consolation is that one very quickly finds one's feet again.
. . . As in general his pen flows too freely, so too does his indignation."

Brandes also found the characters (Brand himself and even Gerd) in-
consistent; he seems, like so many contemporary critics of Ibsen, to have
been unable to accept that a character could be divided. And yet, he
admitted, "it is a poem which will leave no reader cold. Every receptive
and unblunted mind must feel, on closing the book, a penetrating, nay,
an overwhelming impression of having stood face to face with a great
and indignant genius, before whose piercing glance weakness feels compelled to cast down its eyes. What makes the impression less definite,
namely, the fact that this mastermind is not quite clear and transparent,
renders it, on the other hand, all the more fascinating."[52]

"From the critics in Norway," Ibsen wrote to Bjørnson on 4 March,
"I expect no understanding. I know they will attack me." He was right.
By far the most vehement opposition to *Brand* came from his fellow-
countrymen. Professor M. J. Monrad, by now well behind the times,
wrote four long articles in *Morgenbladet* to prove that the play was both

---

[51] Brandes's attention had first been drawn to Ibsen works in 1863–64, probably
through Clemens Petersen's not very understanding reviews in *Fædrelandet* of *Love's
Comedy* and *The Pretenders* and Carl Rosenberg's more sympathetic article on *The
Pretenders* in *Dansk Maanedsskrift,* February 1864. He really got to know Ibsen
as a dramatist in November 1864 when, according to his diary, he read five of the
plays in five days, admiring especially *The Pretenders,* which he thought "magnificent,
remarkable." Ibsen, on his side, first became interested in Brandes early in 1866
through a mutual friend in Rome, Ludvig David, as we know from the latter's letters
to Brandes. When David died in tragic circumstances that March Ibsen wrote to
Brandes informing him of the details—the first direct contact between the two. But at
that time he knew of Brandes as a writer only through the latter's polemics against
Professor Rasmus Nielsen on the question of faith in a scientific age which had
appeared in *Fædrelandet.* Brandes had not yet published any literary criticism except
a reprint of some lectures on Paludan-Müller. Eighteen months later he was to write
a much more favourable consideration of *Brand* in *Dansk Maanedsskrift,* November
1867. (Cf. Henning Fenger, "Ibsen og Georg Brandes indtil 1872," in *Edda* [1964],
pp. 169–208, and Francis Bull's introduction to *Georg og Edvard Brandes Brevveksling
med nordiske Forfattere og Videnskæbsmænd,* IV [Copenhagen, 1939], xxvi ff.)

[52] William Archer's translation.

morally and politically misguided, asserting that in fact the only true form of self-sacrifice lay in compromise. Nor did he approve of it on æsthetic grounds. "The author," he declared (5 April 1866), "has not spared his colours, and they are perhaps in some places employed with a trifle too much boldness"; and he could not understand why "a man who knows so well how to achieve the pure music of language chooses to employ such discords." A priest named O. T. Krohg attacked the play later in *Morgenbladet* (nr. 324) as immoral; amazingly for one of his profession, he thought that when Agnes, in the boat, says: "We are three on board" (the third, of course, being God), it signified that she was pregnant with Ejnar's child, and protested, equally surprisingly, that it was against Christian ethics that Brand, knowing this, should marry her. Johan Vibe in *Norge* dismissed it as "brilliant lunacy."

Bjørnson detested it for what seemed to him its nihilism. "I'll tell you my opinion of Henrik Ibsen's *Brand,*" he wrote to Clemens Petersen on 30 March, a fortnight after the play's publication. "It is no poem, and Ibsen is not really a poet. He has been, for he has possessed the talent to a great degree, if only he wouldn't destroy it by doubt and sophistry. . . . The truths come out fighting, screaming, racketing, *à la* Kierkegaard, but are elementary enough; they've never had any flesh and blood of their own. . . . The whole thing's no more than an abstract experiment. . . . The book so bored me that I still haven't been able to read it properly through, I've skimmed to the end, unable to manage more than a few pages a day. Apart from everything else, it's so badly constructed. . . . The book is only . . . a furious outburst against religion. . . . Grant that he's achieved the sensationalism which seems to be his only goal (you can't call this a crusade), but I beg you, help us to go on building and working for a healthy society. . . . What *is* Ibsen? First in *Catiline* he imitates Victor Hugo or whoever it was, then Hertz, then the sagas and me, then Paludan-Müller and Byron—then off he hops of a sudden to the negative philosophy of the Germans and comes back with their dregs. . . . That any poet should help such charlatans [i.e., negative philosophers] I never thought possible in so positive a people as that of Scandinavia." Bjørnson was not unique among authors in confusing his own limitations with that of a work that repelled him.[53]

Yet even in Norway such condemnation was not universal. There were men and women, especially among the young, for whom *Brand* said things that had long needed saying. An anonymous correspondent (possibly the young philosopher G. V. Lyng) replied to Monrad's criticisms in *Morgenbladet* pointing out that Ibsen had not put Brand forward as a model of conduct but as a tragic and misguided figure striving blindly for truth.

---

[53] Though, to give him his due, he recanted his condemnation twelve years later. "I understand *Brand* better now," he wrote to Georg Brandes on 29 April 1878. "I didn't understand it before. You'll see, that book will come again! For the first time I am deeply grateful to Ibsen for it." (*Gro-tid,* II, 189–92.)

"The poem," he declared, "has had a powerful and elevating effect on hundreds of our countrymen." Ditmar Meidell in *Aftenbladet* (7 April 1866), while doubting the dramatic merits of the play,[54] praised it highly as literature, admiring "the sonorous tone and beauty which one expects from an Ibsen poem. Here and there the language is marred by violent word formations, just as the expression is now and then bold to the point of looseness. Nevertheless, despite these and other weaknesses which one might note, it is distinguished by such daring imagination and such strength of execution that one may safely assert, not merely that it is its talented author's most significant work, but that it will claim for itself a lasting and influential place in our national literature." And Ibsen's old friend Vinje, although as a fervent nationalist he was upset by some of the hits at the Norwegian character, compared it favourably with the much more fashionable plays of Bjørnson. "Ibsen's bright knife with its cutting edge," he wrote in *Dølen* (8 April 1866), "is more to my taste than Bjørnson's bland smile. Ibsen can cast bolts of lightning, and in *Brand* there are many. . . . And Ibsen knows better how to construct a play." He concluded by declaring *Brand* to be "a satirical masterpiece, comparable with Pope's *Dunciad*. . . . It is acid, biting, witty, and poetic."

Brand was, in short, discussed and debated as no previous book had ever been in Scandinavia—including Kierkegaard, for *Brand* was written in more accessible and less abstract language. Sermons were preached about it; more importantly for Ibsen, it sold. Within two months Hegel ordered a reprint of five hundred copies; a third edition followed in August, and a fourth in December. Yet nobody dared to stage it. Act Four was performed at the Christiania Theatre on 26 June 1867 (after an amateur performance at the Students' Union), and was successful enough to take its place in the general repertory; but it was to be nineteen years before the play was presented in its entirety. But Ibsen, who had not written it for the theatre, cannot have been surprised or disappointed at this.

Together with the critical and popular success of the book came relief from financial worry. Bjørnson, despite his feelings about *Brand,* had not relaxed his efforts to raise money for Ibsen; indeed, he decided with his usual naïvety that a sense of security was the most likely thing to give Ibsen "that clear and moving view of life which alone makes a man a poet."[55] He asked Riddervold, the minister in charge of the ecclesiastical department which administered grants to authors, to give Ibsen the same civil list pension which he himself had received; but Riddervold, perhaps

---

[54] "This poem can only be called dramatic insofar as it is written in the form of dialogue. . . . The thread which runs through the main personage's various utterances and holds them together is sometimes so thinly spun that, at a first reading at least, it is difficult to follow. . . . The play on which the curtain here rises belongs only to the theatre of the imagination."

[55] *Gro-tid,* II, 193.

remembering *Love's Comedy,* refused. Undeterred, Bjørnson approached friends in the Storthing, and together they collected twenty-eight signatures to a motion demanding that a pension be allotted "which, by assuring Ibsen of future means, will surely honour and reward us as much as it will him."

The sponsors of this motion were not sanguine as to its chances, but by good fortune Riddervold fell ill and his place in charge of the ecclesiastical department was taken by another parliamentarian, Frederik Stang, who let it be known that he would treat any application relating to Ibsen sympathetically. On 19 April Ibsen's friend Michael Birkeland, now the state archivist, sent Stang a formal plea on Ibsen's behalf signed by three others of the Learned Holland Circle, O. A. Bachke, Jakob Løkke and Paul Botten Hansen. This was approved within two days and forwarded to the king in Stockholm for ratification. Birkeland had already telegraphed Ibsen advising him to write personally to the king, and on 15 April, four days before Birkeland formally handed his appeal to Stang, Ibsen posted his petition to Carl XV. "I am," he wrote, "not fighting for a sinecure existence, but for the calling which I inflexibly believe and know that God has given me—the calling which I believe to be the most important for a Norwegian, namely, to wake the people and make them think big. . . . It rests in Your Majesty's royal hands whether I must remain silent and bow to the bitterest deprivation that can wound a man's soul—the deprivation of having to abandon one's calling in life, of having to yield when I know I have been granted the spiritual armoury to fight, and this would be tenfold grievous to me; for to this day I have never yielded."

His request was modest: an annual pension of 400 specie-dollars. On 12 May this proposal was put before the Storthing and was approved with only four dissenting votes. A few days earlier the Trondhjem Society for Knowledge had allotted him a single grant of 100 specie-dollars, and on 28 July the government gave him a new travel stipened of 350 specie-dollars—a total of 850 specie-dollars. The first edition of *Brand* had brought him 200 specie-dollars, so that he, who for the past year had lived on loans, now found himself with 1,050 specie-dollars to his credit, a sum so far in excess of his modest requirements that on 21 May he wrote Hegel that he did not need to avail himself of the latter's offer of an advance on the second edition.

A letter which Ibsen addressed to Michael Birkeland on 4 May thanking him for organizing the petition expresses the euphoria he now felt. "I had not expected," he wrote, "that my book would be so favourably received. I have been sent many expressions of admiration and good will from Denmark . . . also various invitations, etc., which make me happy, since I am thinking of making Copenhagen my future home. . . . I have such a lust for work, such strength, that I could strangle bears. I went round wrestling with that play of mine for a year before it took shape, but once I had it I wrote from morning till evening and finished it in under three months. About Rome it's impossible to write, especially when one knows it inside out as I do. I have wandered through most of the Papal States at various times, on foot with a knapsack on my back. The brigand situation isn't as dangerous as people at home imagine. . . . Inwardly I think I am in certain respects much changed; yet I feel I am more myself than ever before. Outwardly I've grown thin, which I shall prove with a photograph."

This new security and euphoria found visible expression. During the months of nervous waiting for the publication of *Brand* he had, as in those months of despair in Christiania, neglected his dress and appearance, and walked around with untrimmed beard, shoes worn to their uppers and holes in his leek-green coat. When the Norwegian colony in Rome held a vote for the worst-dressed member among them, they unanimously elected Ibsen.[56] The first thing he did when he learned of the money that was coming to him was to reform his dress to the smartness for which he had been noted in Bergen. One day in May of 1866 he set out with friends on a walking tour in the mountains around Rome, but at the first *osteria* at which they halted a mood came over him, he decided to go no farther, and they proceeded without him, leaving him unkempt, shaggy, and silent over a *foglietta* of wine. When they returned a few days later they found him elegantly clothed, shod and barbered—as a photograph taken that year, probably identical to the one promised to Birkeland, bears witness. Another piece of evidence exists in the form of a clothes list written in Ibsen's hand on the back of a letter to him from Consul Bravo:[57]

8 shirts	16 scudi	
8 pairs socks	3	
1 pair boots	3	
2 woollen vests	3	
1 frock coat	14	
2 waistcoats	4	
1 pr. black trousers	6	
1 pr. coloured ditto	6	
1 overcoat	14	
1 hat	3	
2 cravats	1	
cuff-links	3	
watch	10	
lorgnette	2	
	88 scudi	

[56] Bergliot Ibsen, p. 33.
[57] In the possession of Mr. Tancred Ibsen.

His son Sigurd later remembered that when the advance for *Brand* arrived, his parents were so overwhelmed by the "enormous sum" that they did not know what they would do with it all.[58] And Kristofer Janson (later to be the partial model for Hjalmar Ekdal) records that, finding himself short of money that summer, he asked Ibsen for a loan, and Ibsen opened a drawer, took out a sock, and gave Janson some silver from it, explaining that "this was the fruit of *Brand,* and that he was so well off that he had been able to put some in the bank."[59]

In such a mood Ibsen felt disinclined to rest on his newly won laurels. "I will let you know shortly which work I shall be embarking on next," he wrote to Hegel on 21 May. "I feel more and more inclined to get down in earnest to *Emperor Julian,* which I have been thinking about for two years." Magnus Heineson, the sixteenth-century freebooter, had been pushed into the background. But as things turned out the Emperor Julian was to join him there. A new and hitherto unmeditated theme began to preoccupy Ibsen's mind.

[58] Bergliot Ibsen, p. 33.
[59] Janson, p. 75.

10

Peer Gynt

1866–1868

Early in June 1866 Ibsen left Rome to spend the summer in Frascati, a few miles to the southeast. "I live out here among the mountains, see no newspapers, and know nothing of what is happening outside," he wrote to Hegel on 9 June. "It is miraculously beautiful." A week later he, who had written so many letters begging for help, received one himself. Edvard Grieg, not yet twenty-three, had spent five months in Rome that winter and spring; like Ibsen, he claimed, and was proud of, Scottish ancestry, which in his case was less remote, his grandfather having emigrated after the battle of Culloden in 1746. Ibsen and Grieg had got on well (they had even considered collaborating on an operatic version of *Olaf Liljekrans*), and now, on 10 June, Grieg wrote to Ibsen from Christiania asking him to recommend him for the job of *Kapellmeister* at the Christiania Theatre. Would Ibsen drop a line to the artistic director, Bjørnson, who had not answered Grieg's application of six weeks previously?

"He may not be able to stand me, I may be being stupid about the matter, but I hope you will be able to put things right. . . . I have read your splendid *Brand;* it's a strange thing about truth, people can take it in poetry, it doesn't go too near the knuckle, whereas in plain prose, as Kierkegaard has said, it's too close, too cheeky. How else explain the tremendous furore *Brand* has created, the huge numbers who daily gulp it down?"[1]

Ibsen tried to help, but Grieg never got the job; instead, he became *Kapellmeister* at the Philharmonien. But he remained grateful for Ibsen's assistance and encouragement ("Don't say your whole future depends on this," Ibsen wrote to him on 24 August. "No, my dear Grieg, your future will be bigger and better than a musical directorship."), and a decade

[1] Grieg's letter was first published in Bergliot Ibsen, pp. 57–58.

later their friendship was to ripen into a successful if mutually uncomprehending partnership.

Ibsen enjoyed Frascati. "We live in an old palace of the nobility, the Palazzo Gratiosi, inexpensively and in splendour," he wrote to Paul Botten Hansen on 22 July. "Frascati lies below ancient Tusculum where, as you know, Cicero had his great villa and wrote his Tusculan letters; the ruins of the villa are still standing; his little theatre, probably the same as what he called his *schola,* where he used to give lectures to a chosen circle of guests, remains almost intact. It is indescribably beautiful to sit up here of an evening, two thousand feet above sea level, with a view far out over the Mediterranean, the *campagna,* and Rome; eastwards the whole mountainous Sabine country, with the Apennines, and southwards the Volscian mountains rising on the Neapolitan frontier. From the windows of my study I can see in the farthest distance Mount Soracte towering in solitary splendour across the limitless plain. In short, whichever way one turns it is as if one were surveying the battlefield where the Goddess of History staged her greatest events. Soon, now, I shall write in earnest; I am still wrestling with the material, but soon, I know, I shall have the beast under me, and then the rest will glide forwards of its own volition." He was still undecided whether to stay away from Norway. "When I shall return I can't say; I am already known, and feel at home, here; but I must go back some time. I can live on my pension here, since life is very cheap, and the climate suits us all well."

Whether the "beast" referred to was *Emperor and Galilean* or the old Magnus Heineson project we do not know, but whichever it was it continued to resist him, and on 22 August he had to tell Hegel that he was doubtful whether it would be ready by the autumn, suggesting instead a re-issue of *Love's Comedy* "as a Christmas book," and hopefully observing, as a bait, that "it may be regarded as a forerunner of *Brand.*" Hegel accepted the idea, and Ibsen spent the next five weeks revising the play and removing some of the more specifically Norwegian words so as to make it more palatable to Danish readers (and thereby, it has been suggested, indirectly indicating his contempt for the campaign in his own country to purge the Norwegian language of its foreign influences, a campaign which he was shortly to castigate in a more outspoken and vehement fashion).

In the first week in October he returned to Rome; and his financial position was now so secure that he was able to ask Hegel (5 October) "not to send me the honorarium for *Love's Comedy* when it falls due, but to hold it over till next summer, or such time as I shall need more than serves my ordinary purposes." He was planning to use this money, he informed Michael Birkeland the same day, "to pay a visit next summer to Paris, and then to Greece"—the latter perhaps to gather background material for *Emperor and Galilean,* part of which is set there (though as things turned out, when the summer arrived he found himself writing a different play, and he never to the end of his life visited Greece, a country which would surely have excited him). He also decided to risk a little gentle speculation and requested Hegel to buy him some tickets for the Copenhagen lottery: "I hold no hope of winning, but there is an excitement in it which I enjoy." He was in fact to win two small prizes within the year.

The following month came disagreeable news; a Christiania solicitor named Nandrup, who had lent Ibsen money in 1862, had obtained a warrant of distraint on such few of Ibsen's possessions as remained in Norway, and had sold them by auction. "I don't," he wrote to Bjørnson,[2] "mourn the loss of my furniture, etc., but to know that my private letters, papers, drafts, etc., may be in anyone's hands is a most vexatious thought, not to speak of the loss of many things which had a more than material value for me. You were not told the truth when they said the auction was held because I had not surrendered possession of my lodgings; it was because Nandrup, from the time I left, was discourteously rebuffed at Dunker's[3] office—I won't bother you with the details." In the same letter he hinted for the first time that his stay in the south might be more than temporary. "In a year or two I plan to come north, but scarcely farther than Copenhagen. If I can now and then make a summer trip to Norway, I think that will be the best arrangement."

On 2 November he told Hegel he was still meditating the Magnus Heineson play, but added a rider: "Whether this work will be the *first* I shall complete I am not yet certain. I have a couple of other themes in my head; but this very division of interest means that none of them has yet sufficiently matured; however, I feel sure this will soon happen, and hope to be able to send you the completed manuscript during the spring." As the three themes jostled for precedence in his head that November and December, he completed his revisions for *Love's Comedy* and, painfully, composed the foreword.

That December a young Dane named Frederik G. Knudtzon, later to become a distinguished publisher, visited Rome, and his memoirs, published long after his death, give a vivid picture of Ibsen in his new role of established author in exile, a picture which interestingly contrasts with that left by Lorentz Dietrichson of those first eighteen months of struggling poverty. Recalling that Ibsen once described these years as his *"Sturm-und-Drang* period,"[4] Knudtzon continues: "There was so much

---

[2] This letter, uncharacteristically undated by Ibsen, was originally dated October by Halvdan Koht in the Centenary Edition of Ibsen's works; but Koht later (C.E., XIX, 487) re-dated it November, on the evidence of an item in Ibsen's account books.

[3] Bernhard Dunker, who had several times helped Ibsen with money, was acting as his lawyer in Norway.

[4] Letter to Lorentz Dietrichson, 2 March, 1871.

conflict within him that he could never appear a harmonious person. His high ideals, his extraordinary narrow-mindedness in social matters, his joy in Italy and in art, his residue of bitterness towards Norway, the financial difficulties which he had only recently overcome, and his secret need to keep a strict discipline—all this and much more that simmered within him meant that he was liable to explode to this side or that, and he moved among the Scandinavians like a lion of whom most of them were terrified. There was a *noli me tangere* quality about his personality, as about his dress; a long, buttoned tail coat, an elegant cravat—everything impeccable. The previous year, I was told, he had walked around with holes under his arms, as though indifferent to such trivia."[5]

The character of the Scandinavian Club had changed somewhat during the past year; several of the livelier members, including Bruun and Snoilsky, had returned home, and memories of the Danish war had receded. Even Ibsen seemed to have got a good deal of it out of his system with *Brand*. A few days after Knudtzon's arrival in Rome he attended a Christmas party at the Club with Ibsen present, and has left a pleasant record of the occasion. "It was the custom for every guest to bring a little gift for the Christmas tree. When the dance round the tree was finished, the gifts were shared out, so that everyone went home with something other than what he had brought. . . . We ate rice porridge, and duck had to serve for the goose we would have enjoyed at home. . . . In the absence of a fir, a laurel had to serve as Christmas tree."[6] Then Consul Bravo, the badness of whose Danish was a perpetual source of joy to the members, rose as he had done for years to propose the health of "the three Norwegian kingdoms." What he meant was the three Scandinavian kingdoms, but he had (surprisingly, considering his position as consul) never mastered the difference between *nordisk* (Scandinavian) and *norsk* (Norwegian), and it had long been agreed that no one should spoil this annual delight by telling him.[7]

During the dinner, however, there was trouble. The new arrivals included Kristofer Janson, the young novelist to whom Ibsen had lent money from his sock. Janson was a fervent devotee of the *landsmaal* movement, of which Ibsen was an equally fervent opponent, and he announced to the gathering that after the meal he proposed to read one of his stories in *landsmaal* aloud; at which Ibsen declared that if Janson did this he, Ibsen, would leave. Janson saved the situation by reciting a poem by

[5] Knudtzon, pp. 161–62.

[6] *Ibid.*, p. 127.

[7] "He talked no language quite correctly," recalled Bjørn Bjørnson of Bravo. "He was, as it were, born a foreigner." Bjørn's father used him as the model for Harald Gille in his play *Sigurd Slembe*. Bravo prided himself greatly on the perfection of his teeth, and once put Johanne Luise Heiberg's fingers into his mouth to feel them, which much offended her. (Bjørn Bjørnson, *Fra barndommens dage* [Christiania, 1922], pp. 201–2.)

Bjørnson; not, one might think, the most tactful alternative, but one that passed off without ado.[8]

Knudtzon gives several further examples of Ibsen's pepperiness that winter. One evening in the Club some well-meaning member proposed a toast to the two members who had chosen the food and wine, Ibsen and an old Danish painter named Lars Hansen. "Hansen rose, ready to drink. But Ibsen suddenly stood up, stamped his foot, and said: 'No one is going to drink my health as a member of the food committee.'"[9] On another occasion a Swedish nobleman, Count von Rosen, entered the Club with an effeminate young guest whom he introduced as Herr Sverdrup. When the two had left, Jerichau, the sculptor, remarked that the guest was evidently a girl. Most of the members, writes Knudtzon, thought this a fair joke, but "Ibsen felt deeply offended on behalf of the fair sex. . . . He declared to all and sundry that the Scandinavian Club should not tolerate such behaviour; ladies were not admitted into the Club except on special occasions; Rosen and Sverdrup should be banned. Ibsen felt that the insult touched him most deeply as a *paterfamilias*—he was worried more on Fru Ibsen's account than on that of the Scandinavian ladies in general. He lived at the time in a state of permanent anxiety at not being sufficiently appreciated *qua familie*."[10] It turned out that Rosen's companion was indeed a girl, named Emma Toll, and Ibsen started a campaign to get her and Rosen excluded, writing letter after letter to Consul Bravo, and then to a Docent Landmanson who was acting on Rosen's behalf. Landmanson diplomatically managed to delay the explosion until Rosen and Emma had left Rome, and Ibsen was very annoyed with the Norwegians and Danes for their lack of co-operation.

Then the German Club in Rome decided to hold a banquet and told Dietrichson's successor as librarian at the Scandinavian Club, Otto Mourier, that any of their members who wished to come would be welcome. Mourier wrote letters to the four Scandinavian families which contained young ladies who would need to bring dresses suitable for dancing, and informed the rest of the members by means of a notice on the Club board. "Every sensible person," comments Knudtzon, "had to agree that Mourier had acted correctly and with discretion. But there was one member who felt otherwise and regarded himself as having been disgracefully insulted, and that was Henrik Ibsen. Mourier's failure to send him and his wife a special invitation like the other four families had been an insult to his house, and he attacked the unfortunate librarian with reproaches and accusations—more, he demanded that he be dismissed from his post. Ibsen's anger and vehemence could hardly have found a more inappropriate target than Mourier, who was everyone's favourite.

[8] Knudtzon, pp. 128–29.
[9] *Ibid.*, p. 166.
[10] *Ibid.*, p. 168.

. . . It naturally followed that Ibsen's violent attack on him and his absurd demand that he be dismissed resulted in everyone rallying to Mourier's defence, and the most active of these was Vilhelm Bergsøe [a Danish novelist of whom Ibsen was to see a good deal more that year]. Bergsøe pleaded Mourier's case against Ibsen before us and easily out-manœuvred his more heavily armed adversary. His task was simple, for Fru Ibsen, who was not in her first youth and was, besides, very stout, could scarcely be thought of as a *baldame,* and to have issued her with a special invitation might almost have been taken for a saucy jest. Ibsen's defeat was absolute."

Knudtzon continues: "Most people must wonder that Ibsen could have become so furious and have felt so deeply insulted over so comparatively trivial a matter. But this was Ibsen's most vulnerable point: not receiving sufficient respect as a *paterfamilias.* Ever since his youth in Bergen and Christiania he had felt most painfully that he was not accepted in the best society, and until this was put right, during his visit to Cophenhagen in 1870,[11] this remained a tender point with him—he longed not to be excluded from what was best in high society. The visit to Fru Heiberg and his "Rhymed Letter" to her[12] reveal his enjoyment of and gratitude for some of the happiest moments of his life."[13]

These memoirs of Knudtzon are the earliest record we have of a trait which Ibsen appears to have developed after achieving fame, and which was to remain his most unappealing characteristic. Throughout the rest of his life he maintained a monarchical sensitivity in matters of protocol. Amazingly for one who so despised convention, and who was to bring such enlightenment to his contemporaries, he was, in his contacts with other human beings, to remain always a *nouveau riche* (or anyway a *nouveau* well-to-do, for his capital was never to exceed eleven thousand pounds) of the most aggressive and hypersensitive kind. The root lay deeper in time than Knudtzon knew, in his father's bankruptcy and the rumours of his own illegitimacy, those twin themes which haunt his plays so obsessively. Kristofer Janson noted: "As long as one took care not to touch on those old and hated memories, Ibsen was friendly and amiable. But [he adds, and it is a point which others were to make] you had to be alone with him."[14]

Ibsen spent the last weeks of 1866 completing his foreword[15] to the new edition of *Love's Comedy,* which he posted to Hegel on 5 January 1867, complaining that "these few lines have caused me a bigger headache than the whole play. I have rewritten it innumerable times and finally settled for the first version." He had, though, more important news. "At

[11] More correctly, his visit to Stockholm in 1869.
[12] See pp. 339–40.
[13] Knudtzon, pp. 213–20.
[14] Janson, p. 75.
[15] See p. 201.

last I can tell you that my new work is well under way and will, if nothing untoward happens, be ready early in the summer. It will be a long dramatic poem, having as its principal a part-legendary, part-fictional character from Norwegian folklore during *recent* times. It will bear no resemblance to *Brand,* and will contain no direct polemics or anything of that kind. I have long been pondering the theme;[16] now I have the whole plan worked out and on paper, and have begun the first act. It grows as I work on it and I am confident that you will be satisfied with the result. Please keep this secret for the time being."

This new play was *Peer Gynt;* though, if we are to believe the dates inscribed by Ibsen on his manuscript, he did not in fact begin it until 14 January, nine days after his letter to Hegel. He had a tendency, not unique among authors, to tell white lies to his publisher. He composed it, as he had composed *Brand,* in rhymed verse, but of a far greater variety, in both octosyllabics and decasyllabics, not merely iambic and trochaic ($-\smile$), but dactylic ($-\smile\smile$) and anapæstic ($\smile\smile-$) too, and even, for those interested in these things, amphibrachs ($\smile-\smile$). He completed Act One in six weeks, on 25 February. Six days later, on 3 March, he started on Act Two. On 8 March he wrote Hegel what must have been another slight untruth, that he had "now reached the middle of the second act," adding: "it will comprise five [acts] and as far as I can calculate will occupy about 250 pages. If you wish, I shall be able to send you the manuscript as early as July."

The play continued to make good progress, for on 27 March he was able to tell Hegel that he had finished Act Two. Then there was something of a hold-up, for by 2 May he had no further progress to report than that "the plan for the rest of the play is completely clarified and worked out. Here in Rome," he added, "I scarcely think I shall be able to manage any more on it; for I feel a restlessness in my blood and, still more, the need for greater isolation."

A week after Ibsen wrote this letter, the "restlessness" to which he referred manifested itself in an unpleasant incident which showed him at his ugliest. Knudtzon tells that on 10 May the Scandinavians were having a party at an *osteria,* and a young painter named August Lorange, who suffered from tuberculosis (he was to die of it eight years later), was helping old Lars Hansen to add up the bill. "Ibsen suddenly stood up and began a speech which gradually turned into a brutal attack on Lorange. He was irritated partly because Lorange was helping to add up the bill, partly because he was generally hostile to the young man both as an artist and as a person; he was a poor painter, very untalented and

---

[16] As early as 16 March 1866, the day after the publication of *Brand,* he had written to Anton Klubien: "In the summer I shall go to Sorrento, where I plan to write a new play; I must be near the sea to get the right air into it." And as things turned out he was (thanks to an earthquake) to write the last two acts of *Peer Gynt* there. This letter is not in the Centenary Edition, and was first printed in *Ibsen-Arbok 1953,* p. 100.

unstable. He was (thus Ibsen concluded his speech) 'not worthy to walk on two feet, but ought to crawl on four.' We were all left speechless at such an attack on an unoffending and defenceless man, an unfortunate consumptive who had enough to contend with without being banged on the head by Ibsen. But then Vilhelm Bissen[17] intervened and told Ibsen it was wrong to suggest that Lorange had interfered about the bill, since he himself had heard Hansen ask Lorange to help him. Ibsen became a little calmer; but the insult to Lorange had been delivered and could not be withdrawn. And the worst of the matter was that most of what Ibsen had said about Lorange both as an artist and as a person was true—though clearly it should not have been said so brutally, least of all to an unfortunate invalid. When Ibsen had been silent for a while, he rose again, and now, after the storm, the gentleness in his nature found expression. He proposed a toast to a young man who was an example of the best kind of artist, Ludvig Abelin Schou [a Danish painter]. In handsome and well-chosen words he praised Schou's talent, his truthfulness and industry, and we emptied our glasses to his future."

When the party broke up, several of the diners went off with Lorange to console him, and Ibsen, Knudtzon, and a journalist named Jørgen Meincke were the last to rise. "But alas! It now became apparent that Ibsen could not steer his own course. So Jørgen took him by the right arm and I by the left, and we started on our way home. This afternoon walk with the great poet was not of the shortest. On the road a few remarks passed, but not many. At Ibsen's door I asked him to give me his key so that I could let him in. This he did; but when we made to accompany him up the stairs to his apartment he resisted violently. Beyond doubt Ibsen's brain was functioning much better than his legs. He pondered, made up his mind, and gravely expressed his thanks to us."[18]

Ibsen was evidently (there are other witnesses to the fact) one of that not uncommon tribe who, when drunk, become cruel, lose the use of their legs, yet remain mentally clear. It was not until Ibsen attempted to walk that Knudtzon realized he was drunk; perhaps that was why he remained at table till most of the others had left.

Eleven days after this incident, on 21 May, Ibsen left Rome with Suzannah and Sigurd for the island of Ischia, where he lived for three months in the little town of Casamicciola on the northern side of the island, near the extinct volcano of Epomeo. The weather was exceptionally hot, even for the natives, but Ibsen seemed to revel in it; he completed Act Three in as little as two and a half weeks, on 2 July. Vilhelm Bergsøe was his companion throughout his stay, and noted his routine. He rose early, took a walk, drank coffee and wrote from ten till two. Then

---

[17] A sculptor who executed a bust of Ibsen around this time—as did Walter Runeburg. The two worked simultaneously in Bissen's studio.

[18] Knudtzon, pp. 172 ff.

he had a siesta and, in the late afternoon, read through what he had
written and fair-copied it. For relaxation he went on long, silent walks
with Bergsøe, often saying nothing. He wrote, as the speed of his composition confirms, at intense pressure; he told Bergsøe that he felt "like a
rearing stallion about to leap,"[19] and later recalled to William Archer
that his head was so full of verses that he would sometimes rise in his
nightshirt to write them down—though, as so often happens in such
cases, these sometimes turned out in the morning to be "the veriest nonsense."[20]

In the beginning of July the sirocco arrived, and lasted ten days, tear-
ing the roofs off houses, scattering the chairs and tables, and leaving,
when it departed, the air filled with a fine yellow dust through which the
sun glowed dully, casting no rays. They scattered ice on the stone floor
to give a little cool as it melted, but Ibsen continued to work uninterruptedly. One day, while walking with Bergsøe, Ibsen suddenly asked:
"Can one put a man on the stage running around with a casting-ladle?"
"Yes, why not?" "But it will have to be a big ladle—big enough to recast
human beings in." "It'll look rather strange," Bergsøe ventured, to which
Ibsen replied, "Yes, I think so too, but I don't think the play's for
acting."[21]

Bergsøe's portrait of Ibsen during these months on Ischia is vivid and
detailed. He cites several examples of that physical cowardice which has
already been remarked. "He had a curious fear of anything that might
bring death or misadventure. This fear was not grounded in the thought
of losing his life, but in a terror lest he might not achieve the artistic goal
he had set himself."[22] Once Bergsøe took him to a crevasse named *valle
del tamburro*. "As one penetrates more deeply the crevasse changes character, the vegetation becomes sparse, the walls narrow, the light fades and
. . . finally one has to walk on the big stones that lie in the hot water.
When we reached this point Ibsen exclaimed in alarm: 'Where are you
taking me, do you want me inside the mountain? I won't go any farther.
It might close over us.' When I said this was impossible he cried: 'But a
rock might fall and crush us! I want to get out, I want to go home!'
Ignoring my assurances, he hastened off, and that afternoon I saw him no
more."

A similar thing happened when they climbed Punto Imperatore, a hill
with a fine view over the sea. "The last part of the way I had almost to
drag Ibsen with me, for he repeatedly asserted that the cliff might fall,
and when I objected that we were in proportion to the cliff as a fly to a
tower he made the curious observation that even a fly could bring down a

[19] Vilhelm Bergsøe, *Henrik Ibsen på Ischia og 'Fra Piazza del Popolo'* (Copenhagen, 1907), p. 160.
[20] William Archer, "Ibsen as I Knew Him," p. 18.
[21] Bergsøe, p. 212.
[22] This anecdote and those which follow are from Bergsøe, pp. 159–79.

tower if it were on the point of falling." Unable to persuade him further, Bergsøe climbed alone to the cliff's edge and surveyed the view. "Now and then I seemed to hear Ibsen's voice, but because of the roar of the sea I could not distinguish what he was saying. When I finally turned around, I saw him lying with his face to the ground, clasping a rock with both hands. 'You will kill me!' he cried furiously. 'Why didn't you come when I called? I shall never go on one of your so-called nature walks again!' "

Even now their troubles were not over, for on their way down they found their path barred by a large dog. "There is a dog," said Ibsen, and stopped. Bergsøe assured him that it had no hostile intentions. "You cannot know," replied Ibsen. "I am not going near it." Bergsøe said there was no danger so long as Ibsen did not appear afraid. "I am not afraid," said Ibsen angrily, but moved over to the other side. "So we walked briskly towards the dog, which stood there calmly enough; but just as we were about to pass it Ibsen made a movement as though about to break into a run, and immediately the dog jumped at him and bit him in the hand. A well-aimed blow from my stick sent it yelping off, but Ibsen went as white as a corpse and stared at his hand. I looked at it and found only a tiny scratch, but Ibsen cried: 'The dog is mad, it must be shot, otherwise I shall go mad too.' In vain I explained to him that there was no evidence that the dog was mad, and that it was a groundless superstition that a human being could catch hydrophobia if, long after biting him, a dog developed the disease. He was foaming with rage, and it was several days before his fear departed."

Bergsøe noted (as Knudtzon did) Ibsen's habit of interlarding his conversation with phrases from Holberg, especially from *Jeppe of the Hill*— "Hej, Jakob Skomager! Er Du opstaaen? Lukk op, Jakob! Hej, Jakob Skomager, nu ska vi mare have os en Dram! [Ho, Jacob Cobbler! Are you up? Open up, Jacob! Ho, Jacob Cobbler, let's have a dram!]"—and the meticulous care with which he recorded even the smallest purchases. Once he bought two cheap local cigars, took out his notebook, and carefully wrote down their price. " 'Do you make a note of things like that?' I asked in amazement. 'Yes,' he replied, 'I have to keep a very careful account of my expenses now I am married. I didn't when I was young.' "[23] Sometimes he would behave in an unexpectedly schoolboy fashion. When a copy of *Fædrelandet* arrived with a hostile criticism of Bergsøe's work in it, Ibsen astonished the townspeople by rolling it into a trumpet and hooting through it as he trotted across the square. On the subject of his mother country he was very haughty. "I shall not go back to Norway," he told Bergsøe, "until Norway calls me."

[23] Similarly, John Paulsen saw the accounts Ibsen had kept at Ariccia while working on *Brand*, and noted that one item read: "Bought an orange, 1 bajoc [a cent]. To a beggar, 1 bajoc. A glass of lemonade, 2 bajoc." (Paulsen, *Samliv med Ibsen*, II, 221.)

At the beginning of August the sirocco returned even worse than before, and the temperature rose to no less than 37° Reaumur or 115° Fahrenheit [46° Centigrade], making it almost impossible to breathe. Nevertheless, on 8 August Ibsen was able to write to Hegel: "I have today sent you, via Consul-General Danchertsen in Naples, the manuscript of the first three acts of my new work, entitled *Peer Gynt*, a dramatic poem. This section will come to around 120 printed pages, and the remainder will add up to about the same. I hope to be able to send you Act Four towards the end of the month, and the rest not long afterwards. In case it should interest you, Peer Gynt was a real person who lived in Gudbrandsdal, probably around the end of the last century or the beginning of this. His name is still famous among the people up there, but not much more is known about his life than what is to be found in Asbjørnsen's *Norwegian Fairy Tales* (in the section entitled "Stories from the Mountain"). So I haven't had much on which to base my poem, but that has meant that I have had all the more freedom with which to work on it."

On the night of 14 August there was a slight earthquake on Ischia. The next day Ibsen and Bergsøe walked down to the church in Casamicciola, where a crack broad enough for a man's hand to enter had opened in the tower. Ibsen put his hand in the crack, looked at it, looked at Bergsøe and left the island next day for Sorrento.[24] Here he remained for two months, writing the last two acts. There was no earthquake to trouble him, but in nearby Naples there was an outbreak of cholera, and at one time he thought Suzannah had caught it; but this fear proved to be unfounded. We do not know when he began the long fourth (African) act, but he completed it on 15 September and posted the fair copy to Hegel three days later, adding: "If the printing of the *dramatis personae* could be delayed until I have sent you the rest of the play, I should be grateful, since I might possibly wish to add a few minor ones; but this isn't important." The next day, 19 September, he began the great final act, which he completed, amazingly, in twenty-five days on 14 October—over a thousand lines of rhymed verse, at the rate of forty a day. Four days later he posted the fair copy of this to Hegel—"and may luck attend it!"

The Ibsens spent a week relaxing in Sorrento; then, towards the end of the month, left for Pompeii, where they stayed two days. From there they moved on to Naples, now free of the cholera. Bergsøe tried to persuade Ibsen to take a trip with him in a fishing boat to Capri, but Ibsen refused. "I won't go out with these Neapolitans. If there's a storm they lie flat in the boat and pray to the Virgin Mary instead of reefing the sails." Bergsøe adds, however, that Ibsen's fear in this context was, again, not without foundation, since a boat with a young girl in it had recently

---

[24] For once Ibsen's fears were to prove not altogether groundless. Sixteen years later Casamicciola was destroyed by an earthquake.

3. Grimstad. Water colour by Ibsen of the town and harbour, 1849.

4. The interior of the apothecary's where Ibsen worked from 1847 to 1850. "I have actually seen Ibsen in the kitchen over an open fireplace . . . busy preparing medicine next to Mme. Geelmuyden's cooking pots."

5. Christiania. Carl Johansgade, approaching the palace. Lithograph
by I. Loos, c. 1850.

6. Bergen. Oil painting by Frederik Collett, 1875.

7. The Norwegian Theatre in Møllergaden, Christiania. Engraving by
L. Kleiser, c. 1860.

8. Costume design in water colours by Ibsen, probably for the character of Olaf Liljekrans.

9. Page from Ibsen's prompt book. His sketch plan for Act One of *Un Mariage sous Louis XV,* by Dumas *père,* Adolphe Leuven and L. L. Brunswick.

10. Three caricatures by Ibsen published in *Andhrimner* in 1851.

11. Tormud Knudsen. "Ibsen . . . said there were irregularities connected with his birth and bluntly named Tormud Knudsen."

12. Ole Schulerud. "He was the friend I needed."

13. Paul Botten Hansen. "What Coleridge was to Wordsworth, Botten Hansen was to Ibsen."

14. Ole Bull, c. 1850. "Erratic, ebullient . . . with a passion for idealistic causes."

15. Bjørnstjerne Bjørnson, c. 1860. "For half a century a violent and extraordinary love-hatred relationship was to exist between them."

16. Rikke Holst. "What proof have I that once I saw the spring?"

17. Magdalene Thoresen. "Her attitude towards Ibsen remained, throughout her long life, curiously ambivalent."

overturned in the bay—"whereupon the fisherman swam ashore, and the young girl was found drowned the following evening."[25]

At the end of October they set out from Naples for Rome. But politics intervened; a week previously Garibaldi had invaded the Papal States, fighting was in full progress, the railway was cut, and the Ibsens and Bergsøe found themselves stuck at San Germano, a few miles short of the Papal frontier. For a professed champion of liberty, Ibsen showed a disappointing lack of enthusiasm for his hero's cause, very different from his mood of two years earlier. "Damn all war!" he wrote to Consul Bravo in Rome from San Germano on 4 November, two days after Garibaldi had been defeated at Mentana by the French and Papal forces. "We have been sitting here, a few miles from the Papal frontier, since Wednesday, in the continued but as yet vain hope of being able to proceed to Rome."[26] At length, on 8 November, the trains started running again and he was able to return.

Rome presented a strangely changed appearance. "The corso," writes Bergsøe, "was almost empty, and the few people I met were foreigners. Many of the great palazzos seemed deserted, there was quiet in the small streets, and instead of the conversing groups usually to be found on the Piazza Colonna one now saw bivouacking soldiers, their rifles piled in pyramids, guarded by sentry posts at each corner of the square. Patrols moved ceaselessly through the streets; but when the French bugles sounded, the Romans stared at the red-breeched troops with a mixture of hatred and contempt, remembering that it had been a French general who had defeated Garibaldi at Mentana." At night "numerous patrols roamed in long grey coats and with rifles over their shoulders. When an Orsini bomb exploded they placed themselves back to back and fired at random in all directions, regardless of where the shots might land."[27]

On 14 November 1867, six days after Ibsen had returned to Rome and less than four weeks after Hegel had received the final section of the manuscript, *Peer Gynt* appeared in the Scandinavian bookshops. Ibsen was delighted at its being out in time to catch the Christmas sales. "Let us hope the critics will be kind to us," he wrote to Hegel on 23 November. "I think the book will be much read in Norway."

Peer Gynt, however—the tale of a man the exact opposite of Brand, a compromiser who thinks only of himself, shuns work and suffering, and

---

25 Bergsøe, p. 248.

26 Edmund Gosse (*Ibsen*, p. 121) rightly observes that in his attitude of passive appreciation Ibsen resembled Walter Savage Landor rather than those other illustrious exiles such as Stendhal, Lamartine, Ruskin, and the Brownings, who had "spent nights of insomnia dreaming of Italian liberty." Landor had died in Florence three months after Ibsen's first arrival in Rome.

27 Bergsøe, pp. 271–72. Felice Orsini had tried to assassinate Napoleon III by throwing a bomb (made in Birmingham) at his carriage in 1858, and had been executed.

(it is hinted) typifies the most common Norwegian failings—had a mixed reception in Scandinavia. The first omens were good; Hegel sent word that the first edition of 1,250 copies had sold out almost at once, and that a second edition of 2,000 was in the press. Three days after publication Bjørnson, that most patriotic of poets who more than most might have been expected to take offence at the fun poked at Norwegian nationalism, especially since Peer was the exact opposite of Bjørnson's own romanticised peasant heroes, wrote Ibsen a letter full of admiration: "I love your spleen, I love the courage with which it has armed you, I love your strength, I love your recklessness—oh, it turned all my thoughts to laughter, like the smell of the sea after the closed air of a sickroom," and ending: "This is a love letter, and nothing else. . . . *Peer Gynt* is magnificent, Ibsen! Only Norwegians can see how good it is!"[28] He reviewed the book in *Norsk Folkeblad* on 23 November, describing it as "a satire on Norwegian egotism, narrowness, and self-sufficiency, so executed as to have made me not only again and again laugh till I was sore, but again and again give thanks to the author in my heart, as I do here in public,"[29] and dispraising nothing but the over-exuberance of detail and certain aspects of the versification. He especially admired the threadball scene.

F. Bætzmann wrote a long and favourable review in *Aftenbladet* (30 November and 4 December), noting that "the kind of free dramatic writing to which *Peer Gynt* belongs . . . [means] that the author need not bother about the many cramping considerations to which one must pay regard when writing for stage performance." He complained, however, that the "happy" ending was banal "and a little absurd," questioned whether "the genre in which [in *Love's Comedy, Brand,* and *Peer Gynt*] Ibsen has shown increasing mastery is really a good genre and answers to the demands which our society and age make of literature," and concluded by expressing the hope that "as eminent a talent as Ibsen's might give us less of polemics and nihilism and more that is beautiful and æsthetically satisfying than he has in his last three wide-ranging dramas." An anonymous reviewer in *Morgenbladet* (29 November), although complaining that the play stopped before the end of Act Four [!] and that Act Five was stationary and therefore dramatically bad, ended by praising it as "a work which takes a very pre-eminent place in our literature . . . giving the most striking evidence of the originality of [Ibsen's] views and the strength and depth of his imagination . . . an expression of a great spirit's battle for truth and beauty in life."

So far, so good; but the most influential critic in Scandinavia was Clemens Petersen, and his long notice in *Fædrelandet* (30 November), though granting the play some merits and admitting its "often surprising brilliance," ultimately rejected it on doctrinaire philosophical grounds.

[28] *Gro-tid,* II, 244–46.
[29] William Archer's translation.

The article, a formidable specimen of woolly-mindedness and dogmaticism, condemned *Peer Gynt* as lacking in idealism, objected that the characters were not fully rounded or alive and that the play contained "riddles which are insoluble because they are empty," dismissed Peer's identification of the Sphinx with the Boyg as "an intellectual swindle," and ended by categorizing the play as political journalism, declaring that "it is not poetry, because in the transmutation of reality into art it fails to meet the demands of either art or reality."

Hostility to *Peer Gynt,* it gradually became apparent, was widespread. Hans Andersen hated it. "Ibsen is repellent to him," wrote Edvard Grieg to Bjørnson, "and *Peer Gynt* the worst that he has read." Camilla Collett, the pioneer of women's independence in Norway, was offended by the passivity of Solveig's character, declaring that a more forceful female would have shown Peer the error of his ways much earlier. Kristofer Janson, in *Aftenbladet,* denounced the attack (through the character of Huhu) on the language reformers, of whom he was one. A reviewer in *Nordisk Tidskrift* thought the play had "too much thought"; another, in the Danish newspaper *Berlingske Tidende,* thought it "not truly æsthetic." Even Georg Brandes, in his notice in the Copenhagen *Dagbladet* on 16 December, joined in the condemnation. While granting Ibsen's "incredible gift for versification" and "wonderful command of language," he found the theme and its treatment ethically offensive. "What great and noble powers are wasted on this thankless material! . . . It would be unjust to deny that the book contains great beauties, or that it tells us all, and Norwegians in particular, some important truths; but beauties and truths are of far less value than Beauty and Truth in the singular, and Ibsen's poem is neither beautiful nor true. Contempt for humanity and self-hatred make a bad foundation on which to build a poetic work. What an unlovely and distorting view of life this is! What acrid pleasure can a poet find in thus sullying human nature?"[30] And in a second review, in *Illustreret Tidende* on 29 December, Brandes complained: "The more polemical and tendentious Ibsen's satire, the greater is the danger of its proving short-lived. . . . There is a lack of harmony and to some extent of clarity. . . . In conclusion, one wishes that this man would give himself time and peace to work out particulars which have not flowed perfectly from his pen and which he has all too carelessly allowed to stand."

On 30 December *Morgenbladet* printed a letter from its Copenhagen correspondent summarising critical reaction in Denmark: "The verdict on this remarkable work, which was at first uncertain and much divided, now seems more or less agreed that a writer of such great gifts, mastery of form

---

[30] Archer's translation. It is much to Ibsen's credit that he did not let these adverse reviews spoil the friendship which was shortly to develop between him and Brandes. He recognized the difference in quality between Brandes's mind and Petersen's. Brandes was later to recant his condemnation of *Peer Gynt,* except concerning Act Four.

and intellectual depth, ought to abandon the moralising and polemising in which he has indulged in his latest works and serve with a larger sense of beauty and discrimination the Muse of Poetry who has elected to bless him with her patronage."

Petersen's review, from which Ibsen had hoped so much, drove him into a fury, not merely because it was hostile (Brandes's was almost equally so), but because it represented just that kind of pompous mental rigidity which he most detested and which he was to spend his life castigating. He received a copy of the notice just as he had composed a letter of thanks to Bjørnson for the latter's praise of the play, and was so enraged that he tore this letter up and wrote another. His redrafted letter reveals that manic side of his character which he rarely allowed to appear in his writing but which, as we have seen, not infrequently emerged in social intercourse. "Dear Bjørnson," he wrote on 9 December. "What is this curse that at every juncture interposes itself between us? It is as though the Devil came in person to cast his shadow over us. . . . An hour ago, I read Hr. Clemens Petersen's review in *Fædrelandet*. . . . If I were in Copenhagen and anyone stood as near to me as Clemens Petersen does to you, I would have struck him senseless before allowing him to commit so calculated an offence against Truth and Justice. . . . My book *is* poetry; and if it isn't, it will become such. The conception of poetry in our country, in Norway, shall shape itself according to this book. . . . However, I am glad that this injustice has been flung at me; it is a sign of divine aid and dispensation; anger increases my strength. If there is to be war, then let there be war! If I am not a poet, what have I to lose? I shall try my hand as a photographer, I shall deal with my contemporaries up there, each and all of them, one by one, as I have dealt with these language reformers; I shall not spare the child in its mother's womb, nor any thought nor feeling that may have motivated the actions of any man who shall merit the honour of being my victim. . . . Do you know that all my life I have turned my back on my parents, on my whole family, because I could not bear to continue a relationship based on imperfect understanding?"

He did not post the letter at once, but added a postscript the following day: "I have slept on these words and read them again in cold blood. The mood they express is that of yesterday; I shall send them, nevertheless." After another hysterical outburst ("Do not underrate my friends and supporters in Norway; the party whose paper has allowed its pages to carry an injustice against me shall realize that I do not stand alone. . . . My enemies shall learn that if I cannot build I have at least strength enough to destroy"), he ended on a scarcely appeasing note: "I reproach you merely with inactivity. It was not good of you to permit, by doing nothing, such an attempt to be made in my absence to put my reputation under the auctioneer's hammer."

Bjørnson accepted this abuse calmly, and wrote Ibsen a letter (16 December) of splendid generosity and exhortation, begging him to "be just towards us and have faith in yourself." He told Ibsen that he had misread Petersen's article and (which was scarcely true) that Petersen had disliked it only from a philosophical standpoint; added that "they are thinking of 'decorating' us—shouldn't we reject this?" (a question which was to remain a lifelong bone of contention between them), and ended by summarising the critical reaction to the play. "Don't rely too much on Brandes, there's something misleading about anyone who doesn't believe in God. . . . Brandes has written in *Dagbladet* about *Peer Gynt*, like Petersen, but more severely . . . Erik Bøgh has written excellently, wittily, full of praise. . . . Bætzmann cleverly in *Aftenbladet*. . . . Petersen was here just now; he wants to answer you himself; expect a letter which will be plain-spoken but will do it decently"[31]

Bjørnson's letter, which ran to 3,500 words, reached Ibsen on Christmas Day and so mollified him that in his reply, of 28 December, he actually asked Bjørnson to give Petersen his regards. But his old feeling of resentment soon returned, and it was to be ten years before he wrote to Bjørnson again.

After his first outburst of fury, Ibsen accepted the criticisms calmly. "How goes it with *Peer Gynt?*" he asked Hegel on 24 February 1868. "In Sweden, as far as I can tell from the newspaper reviews, it has been very well received; but has it sold accordingly? In Norway I gather the book has caused a great rumpus; which bothers me not in the least; but both there and in Denmark, people have discovered much more satire than I intended. Why can't people read the thing as a work of fiction? That is how I wrote it. The satirical sections are pretty isolated. But if, as seems to be the case, the Modern Norwegian recognizes himself in Peer Gynt, that is those good gentlemen's own funeral."

Surprisingly, in view of the controversy surrounding it, *Peer Gynt* did not sell particularly well; the second edition, printed immediately after publication, was not exhausted until 1874, by which time *Brand* had entered its seventh edition. It was nine years before anyone staged it, and thirteen years before Ibsen received a request for translation rights.

Like *Brand*, Alfred de Musset's comedies, Turgenev's *A Month in the Country* and (probably, for Büchner's exact intention regarding his plays is unknown) *Woyzeck* and *Danton's Death*, *Peer Gynt* was written with no thought of performance; and the consequent rejection of the accepted limitations of stagecraft proved, as with *Brand*, tremendously liberating. It was not merely that Ibsen felt free to move uninhibitedly in time and

[31] *Gro-tid*, II, 256–67.

space (*Peer Gynt* contains forty scenes). He had done that in *Brand*. More importantly, he felt free to ignore other frontiers, the frontiers between reality and fantasy, between (as we should now say) the conscious and the unconscious. Nobody, one hopes, any longer takes the last act of *Peer Gynt* at its face value, as the return of an old man to his youthful love; such an ending would have been, for Ibsen, most untypically banal and sentimental, two adjectives which recur frequently in contemporary criticisms of it. Whether one regards Peer as having died in the madhouse at the end of Act Four, or in the shipwreck at the beginning of Act Five, we must surely take that fifth act as representing either the unreeling of his past life in his mind at the moment of death or (which is perhaps the same thing) as the wandering of his soul in purgatory, *"limbo patrum,* nigh to hell." Viewed thus, the last hour of the play is Peer's life seen in a distorting mirror, just as the troll scene in Act Three is the wedding party and Peer's hopes and fears concerning it dreamed by a drunken and confused man: the desirable yet (once he has got her) repulsive girl, the wrathful vengeance-seeking father, the conflict between lust and conscience. To present *Peer Gynt* on a purely realistic level, as still, alas, occasionally happens, is to reduce it to an amiable and confused pantomime with a facile ending, an interpretation to which Grieg's music, for all its intrinsic merits, has lent authority. Ibsen was not Freud's darling playwright, and Joyce's, for nothing; he understood, as few of their predecessors did, the power of the unconscious, the truth behind dreams and nightmares, the higher reality of what most of his contemporaries dismissed as unreality; and *Peer Gynt* may be regarded as the first prolonged exploration, whether deliberate or unconscious, of this field, to which, nearly twenty years later, he was to return with such effect in *Rosmersholm, The Lady from the Sea,* and the powerful and, to his contemporaries, scarcely intelligible plays which followed. *Peer Gynt* is the direct ancestor of Strindberg's *A Dream Play.* But at the time of its appearance, as Ibsen complained, it was regarded mainly as a satire.

Yet in one sense at least Ibsen's critics came nearer the truth than some of the play's later admirers. They were right to find it disturbing, discordant, and offensive. It is one of the most upsetting and uncomfortable plays ever written. Trolls, properly understood, are not mere goblins but, as Professor Francis Bull has written: "the evil forces of Nature . . . embodying and symbolizing those powers of evil, hidden in the soul of man, which may at times suppress his conscious will and dominate his actions. . . . By ever pandering to his evil instincts and desires they have come to be really his rulers—mysterious powers that make him afraid of himself."[32] This is what *Peer Gynt* is really about—the struggle between the divine purpose and our undermining passions and egocentricities, between man's deeper self

[32] Taylorian Lecture at Oxford, 1954, published in the catalogue to the Oslo University Library Ibsen memorial exhibition of 1956 (p. 12).

and his animal, or troll, self; in Stekel's phrase "how the soul, oppressed by the primal passions, struggles to escape the hell of the instincts."[33] The Boyg, the Greenclad One, and the Strange Passenger are, like the Thin Person, lackeys of the Enemy; as is Peer himself, apart from the image of him which Solveig keeps

> With the mark of destiny on his brow
> As he sprang forth in the mind of God.

The Strange Passenger has been the subject of several extraordinary theories. Michael Elliott, who directed the 1962 production of the play at the Old Vic, suggests, and I agree, that he, like the hawk in *Brand*, represents the thing that destroys you because you reject and exclude it, and that the turning-point in Peer's quest for salvation is that moment of despair when he sees the star fall, because the moment of despair is the moment of hope.

Ibsen himself thought *Peer Gynt* too Norwegian ever to be appreciated abroad, much as Synge felt about *The Playboy of the Western World* (a character who has much in common with Peer, as the styles of the two plays have much in common, with their ebullient rhythms and extravagant imagery). "Of all my books," Ibsen wrote to a would-be German translator, Ludwig Passarge (19 May 1880), "I regard *Peer Gynt* as the least likely to be understood outside Scandinavia. . . . You know the people and the personalities one finds up there. But is not all this necessary if one is to find any real flavour in the poem?" Ibsen's doubts were to prove unfounded, for *Peer Gynt* has become the best known of his works outside as well as inside Scandinavia. Peer himself has everywhere been accepted as a national prototype; a Japanese critic has described him as "typically Japanese";[34] as Bernard Shaw wrote: "The universality of Ibsen makes his plays come home to all nations."[35]

In a later letter (16 June 1880) to Passarge, who, despite the warning, had translated the play, Ibsen made it clear, if any confirmation were needed, that *Peter Gynt* is a self-analysis. Referring specifically to this play, he stated: "Everything that I have written is most minutely connected with what I have lived through, if not personally experienced; every new work has had for me the object of serving as a process of spiritual liberation and catharsis; for every man shares the responsibility

---

[33] Wilhelm Stekel, "Analytic Notes on Peer Gynt" in *Compulsion and Doubt* (London, 1950), II, 599–600.

[34] Bull, "Taylorian Lecture, 1954," p. 23.

[35] *Saturday Review*, London, 22 November 1896. But there is some evidence that Ibsen in later years rather took against *Peer Gynt*. P. G. la Chesnais tells that, to a French visitor who began to praise the play in 1900, Ibsen replied (I quote la Chesnais's version; Ibsen would not have said it in French): "Bah! Une oeuvre de jeunesse! Ce fut mon Manfred. Qui sait s'il n'a pas persisté en moi un byronien attardé?" (*Oeuvres complètes d'Henrik Ibsen, traduites par* P. G. la Chesnais [Paris, 1914–45], VIII, 94.)

and the guilt of the society to which he belongs. That is why I once inscribed in a copy of one of my books the following dedicatory lines:

> To live is to war with trolls in heart and soul.
> To write is to sit in judgment on oneself."[36]

If, as Ibsen once remarked, Brand was "myself, in my best moments," Peer was the other side of the medallion.

Ibsen's letters from Rome during the last months of 1867 show him toying with the idea of returning to Scandinavia. Several times he hints that Copenhagen may be the answer; Norway still seemed out of the question. "I can never make out how you endure it up there," he wrote to Magdalene Thoresen on 15 October. "Life up there, as I now see it, seems boring beyond description. It bores the soul from one's body, it bores the marrow from one's will; that's the damnable thing about petty surroundings, they make a man's soul petty!" And in his last letter to Bjørnson on 28 December he had said: "Where we shall spend next winter, I don't know. I only know it won't be in Norway. If I went home now, one of two things would happen. Either I'd make an enemy of everyone within a month, or I'd bury my head in the sand again and become a lie to myself and others." After warning Bjørnson not to continue in theatre management ("Working in the theatre is for a writer, a daily repeated abortion . . ."), he exhorted him: "No, come abroad, *carissimo!* Both because distance gives one a broader perspective, and because one is out of people's sight." In a similar mood at this time he told Frederik Knudtzon: "One should live down here and rule them all."[37]

But his son was now eight, and there was his schooling to consider; for all his hatred of Norway, Ibsen was unwilling that Sigurd should be educated as a foreigner. He did not know enough Italian, anyway, to go to an ordinary local school, and such foreign schools as there were in Rome at this time could not take a child who was fluent only in Norwegian; so on 24 February 1868 we find Ibsen asking Hegel to send him "a geography book, a general world history, an arithmetic book, and books containing the elements of religious instruction, all suitable for an eight-year-old child. . . . My little boy has read a lot, especially history (both general and biblical), but as yet quite unsystematically, and it must not continue so." By the spring he was beginning to accept that, if for this reason only, he would have to return to Norway. "What it will be like to live outside Italy, and above all what it will be like to live in Christiania," he wrote to Magdalene Thoresen on 31 March, "I can scarcely imagine. However, I suppose I shall have to. But one will have to isolate oneself

---

[36] William Archer's translation.
[37] Knudtzon, pp. 165–66.

totally up there (I shall, anyway), if I am not to make an enemy of everyone. . . . The best that could happen to our country would be a great national calamity. If one can't survive that one has no right to live. I have witnessed sacrifices down here which make me draw comparisons from which our country does not emerge with honour."

Early in 1868 Ibsen had resumed work on *Emperor and Galilean,* but after *Brand* and *Peer Gynt* he found himself wanting to write for the theatre again, as opposed to the printed page, and on 28 February he told Hegel: "My next work will probably be a play for the stage, and I hope it will not be long before I begin to work seriously on it." Another plan had occurred to him. "I have been thinking of making a collection of my various unpublished poems, but I can't do that down here, as they must be ferreted out of various newspapers, etc. But some time I shall have to come north again, and I suppose make a detour to Christiania, in which case I could start things moving."

That spring, Ibsen seems to have been in an unusually prickly mood. His marriage may have entered upon a difficult phase. Martin Schneekloth, a young Dane whom Ibsen found sympathetic and who, like so many of those young Scandinavians in Rome, was shortly to die of consumption, noted in his diary, which was to remain unpublished for three-quarters of a century:

> To find that one does not really love the woman one has married, that one's requirements for a happy co-existence are so opposed to one's wife's that no reconciliation is possible, must be a desperate situation for a man, and that is Ibsen's. He is a domineering character, egocentric and unbending, with a passionate masculinity and a curious admixture of personal cowardice, compulsively idealistic yet totally indifferent to expressing these ideals in his daily life, restlessly questing, confused, yet striving for clarity. *She* is un-womanly, tactless, *but* a stable, hard character, a mixture of intelligence and stupidity, not deficient in feeling but lacking humility and feminine love. They cannot find peace through love, so they wage war on each other, ruthlessly, coldly, and yet she loves him, if only through their son, their poor son, whose fate is the saddest that could befall any child, to see divided what should be reconciled in him. Whose is the fault if not the man's? He took her from her father's house, led her out into the strange world, and instead of devoting his life to finding some form of reconciliation he gives all his mind and passion to a demonic pursuit of literary fame. It is disturbing to hear him describe his plans to send his wife and child home so that he may work in peace abroad. He lacks the courage to pursue his career without abandoning his domestic responsibilities, to face up to the consequences of his ambition, to work incessantly to give her life fulfilment, to suffer and strive to educate his son. Thus he, who so loudly and brilliantly condemns the cravenness of our age, who in mighty poems proclaims the strength of human will, is himself a craven, a vacillating weakling.

This formidable indictment is reinforced by a later entry for the same month:

> Does Ibsen love his wife? I don't know, but she loves him, but is not happy in her love. Ibsen himself is so obsessed with his work that the proverb "humanity first, art second" has practically been reversed. I think his love for his wife has long vanished, and been replaced by a mood of resignation, if such is possible in so restless a character. His crime now is that he cannot discipline himself to correct the situation, but rather asserts his moody and despotic nature over both her and their poor, spiritually warped, terrified son.[38]

Schneekloth might almost have been prophetically describing the marriages of the Master Builder, John Gabriel Borkman, or Arnold and Maja Rubek in *When We Dead Awaken;* and the theme of at any rate the last two plays is indeed "humanity first, art (or ambition) second." Yet Schneekloth's account, though probably accurate, gives only half the picture, the surface half which so many other acquaintances of the Ibsens were to record. Unlike Solness, Borkman, and Rubek, Ibsen was dependent on and devoted to his wife, as the statements of their son and daughter-in-law, and the frequent references in his own letters, show. Ibsen was, like Milton, Dickens, Tolstoy, Dostœvsky, Shelley, Carlyle, D. H. Lawrence and Joyce (to say nothing of numberless great painters and composers), monstrously egocentric and frequently cruel; yet if he had survived Suzannah and recorded his private thoughts about her, it is difficult to imagine that they would have greatly differed from those of Thomas Carlyle about his Jane, another couple whom their contemporaries supposed to live in a state of permanent mutual torment.

Frederik Knudtzon recounts an anecdote from this spring of 1868 which vividly illustrates the duality of Ibsen's nature, and the suddenness with which he would switch from one mood to another. One Sunday afternoon, while accompanying the sculptor Frederik Strambœ to the latter's studio, Knudtzon saw Ibsen on the other pavement in the Via Felice, together with Lars Hansen and the Norwegian sculptor Ole Fladager.

> As soon as Ibsen caught sight of us he crossed the street towards us and cried: *"Ih, mare,*[39] Knudtzon! You must come out with us to La Baracca." "But I've promised Strambœ I'd go to his studio." That could be done tomorrow, said Ibsen; we must join him; it would be a delightful walk. So we turned round, introduced ourselves to his companions and joined them. It soon became apparent that Ibsen had been lunching with them and had come straight from the table. We arrived at the Piazza Barberina. There were several cabs there, and Ibsen made straight for them. As he seized on the

[38] Schindler, pp. 120–22.

[39] An exclamation much used by Jeppe of the Hill in Holberg's play of that name, roughly equivalent to "What cheer?"

first, Fru Ibsen announced that she would not accompany us. Ibsen protested at this, but she maintained that she would not come. "Get up into the cab!" thundered Ibsen with all his might, if somewhat indistinctly. It was very disagreeable for the four of us to listen to. But the moment the words were out of his mouth Fru Ibsen climbed up and took her seat in the cab. Ibsen and Fladager followed, we three others jumped hastily into another cab, and the two vehicles rolled off. After a quarter of an hour we trundled into the spacious courtyard of La Baracca, with its splendid view towards the blue Alban mountains. Our little Sunday symposium was about to begin; but the violent scene in the Piazza Barberina had undeniably given us the feeling that there was thunder in the air.

Under the great tree where we usually sat there was ample room. I came first to the table, and as the Bodega simultaneously presented himself I ordered *un mezzo*, but Ibsen was just behind me, and when he heard my order he shouted in a leave-this-to-me voice: *"Due mezzi!"* This meant three *mezzi*, i.e. six *fogliette*, which if equally divided would mean a whole *foglietta* each. . . . However, we drank and chatted and the wine effected a considerable change in the atmosphere. Ibsen seemed from the start to have some worm of indignation in the depths of his soul, an indignation which grew as the tempo heightened under the influence of the wine and the general euphoria increased. This indignation weighed on him and demanded an outlet. It may have been connected with Ibsen's sense of responsibility and calling as a poet; he once told me he saw his ideal of a poet in the Old Testament prophets. Perhaps . . . his prophetic indignation had built up until it could find vent only through an explosion.

However, as we sat under the great tree looking now at each other, now at the blue Alban mountains, everything still went agreeably. I think we emptied most of the three *mezzi*, and as darkness fell we prepared to leave. But now the same happened as the previous year; Ibsen's brain was found to be functioning better than his legs. Had we been wise we would have sent for a carriage. But we failed to take that precaution. We moved off, Fru Ibsen going ahead with old Hansen and Fladager. Ibsen followed some distance behind, with Strambœ and myself on either side; we kept a good hold of him under the arms and started to walk slowly and carefully. But when we had come about a third of the way, something on the other side of the road caught Ibsen's attention. Behind an iron gate in a wall surrounding one of the big villas we saw a huge dog, which barked angrily at us. Ibsen quickened his pace—he had to go over to it, in other words, *we* had to go over, and soon the three of us were standing at the gate. Ibsen had a stick in his hand, which he now began to poke at the dog, one of those gigantic brutes that resemble small lions. It came closer, and Ibsen poked and struck at it, trying in every way to madden it, and succeeding. It rushed at the gate, Ibsen prodded and struck it anew, and worked it into such a rage that without doubt, had not the solid iron gate stood between it and us, it would have torn us apart. This, I realized, was the explosion of violence which resulted from the enjoyment of the wine, and which had been the cause of the attack on Lorange. But it lasted longer. Ibsen must have stood teasing the dog for six to eight minutes. At length he grew bored with the sport. Then his eye chanced on two Italian children who, attracted by the furious barking, were standing by his side, two enchanting children in national dress with fresh, red cheeks, a sight in complete contrast to the raging dog. Ibsen looked down at them, and with an astonishing glow of kindness and gentleness in his eyes took between two of his fingers a little pinch of each child's cheek, and released it—a gesture of love that was expressive of both human kindness and the need to protect. It was an *adagio* after the storm, like the speech to Ludvig Abelin Schou after the outburst against Lorange. Now both his prophetic indignation and his benevolence had found expression, and we continued on our way.[40]

People still occasionally write about Ibsen as though he were a figure of Olympian calm and detachment. It cannot be over-emphasized that, while his writing was indeed detached, in the sense of being supremely objective, it was a detachment born of a fearful discipline exercised over a manic depressive temperament. Ibsen never spoke more truly than when he likened himself to an Old Testament prophet. Isaiah, dressed in a tall hat and morning coat, would surely have looked and talked like Ibsen.[41]

On 9 May 1868 Ibsen, Suzannah, and Sigurd left Rome, "to spend the summer," as he informed Hegel on 27 April, "in northern Italy or the Tyrol," probably with the intention of proceeding to Christiania in the autumn. For the time being, at any rate, on account of Sigurd's schooling, they had put Italy behind them. They spent eight days in Florence, two in Bologna, eight in Venice and eight in Botzen (now Bolzano) in the Tyrol. In the middle of June, riding in an old-fashioned coach with the postilion blowing his bugle, they reached the little Bavarian resort of Berchtesgaden, where they settled for the summer (and to which they were frequently to return). "I don't know if you are familiar with this place," Ibsen wrote to Consul Bravo on 22 June. "If not, it is worth discovering. It is the most beautiful country I have seen north of the Alps, cheap, easy of access, pleasant in every way. . . . I have started a new work, which I hope to complete here. . . . When we shall return to our home in Rome is still uncertain; but some time we shall come back, or anyway I shall, life and health permitting." On 28 July he wrote to Hegel: "We shall spend the winter in Munich and Dresden, and shall then probably come home. I have not yet got down seriously to anything big, but I shall soon. . . . The landscape here is splendid, but the weather changeable; I miss my beloved Italy in more respects than one." He visited Salzburg, and in August spent eight days walking to Gastein and

---

[40] Knudtzon, pp. 215–18.

[41] The Swedish writer Ola Hansson once remarked that Ibsen always had "something of Moses on Sinai with the tablets of the law in his hand." (Quoted by Paulsen, *Samliv med Ibsen*, II, 233.) Cf. also Ibsen's own insistence that he was a passionate writer, p. 533 below.

back. By this time, his new play was beginning to mature in his mind. "My new dramatic work (written for the theatre, and wholly realistic, influenced no doubt by the heavy German air) occupies all my thoughts," he told Hegel on 20 August.

At the end of August they left Berchtesgaden and proceeded to Munich. They stayed there a month, in an apartment at Maximilianplatz 13, "the whole time under a blessedly Italian sky, rejoicing in the city's wonderful art treasures and in the local populace's hatred of all things Prussian."[42] In the first days of October they arrived in Dresden, where they were to spend the next six and a half years.

[42] Letter to Hegel, 22 September 1868.

PART THREE

German Seed-Time

11

Dresden: *The League of Youth*

1868–1869

A century earlier the poet Johann Gottfried von Herder, fresh from introducing the young Goethe to the beauties of Shakespeare and Gothic
architecture, had described Dresden as "the German Florence," and the
compliment, if not strictly accurate, was still reasonably deserved. Surrounded by blue hills, and traversed by the curving Elbe with its ancient bridges and terraces, the city greeted the traveller with a picturesque skyline of green copper roofs, spires, and cupolas. In 1868
Dresden was still, despite the bombardment it had suffered in 1760,
largely of the seventeenth and eighteenth century, with many fine mediæval
buildings in the Altstadt or Old Town, which Canaletto had so admired.
It was a favourite resort of foreigners, partly for the splendour of
its art collections and historic buildings, and partly, for those with
children, on account of the famed excellence of its educational facilities—
an important consideration for Ibsen, whose movements in Europe over
the next decade and a half were largely to be dictated by the needs of his
son.

He took furnished lodgings in a small two-roomed apartment on the
first floor at An der Frauenkirche 6, shown in contemporary photographs
as a pleasant, tall house, and settled down to complete his plans for
his new play. On 10 October, less than a week after his arrival, he asked
Hegel to send him regular copies of the Danish newspaper *Dagbladet*,
"not to satisfy an idle curiosity for news . . . but because I shall thereby
be drawn more closely and intensively into life in Norway, and thus feel
strengthened for my work." He was determined to make his play nothing if
not realistic.

He began his first draft on 21 October, and completed Act One in
five days. On the last of the month he was able to report happily to Hegel
that "the play makes swift progress. All this summer I have been turning

it over in my mind without actually writing; now the whole draft is ready
and on paper, Act One is finished, Act Two will be in a week, and I hope
the whole play will be completed by the end of the year. It will be in
prose, and written entirely with the stage in mind. The title of the play
is *The League of Youth,* or *Our Lord & Co;* a comedy in five acts. It
deals with frictions and currents in modern life. I find myself in a calm
and happy frame of mind, and write accordingly." He added a request
for further reading matter. "Will you please send me a copy of Brandes's
Aesthetic Studies and debit it to my account? While I was in Rome I
heard that he was writing an essay on comedy, a subject on the theory of
which I must confess to having no very clear ideas, and about which I
should greatly like to be informed, especially by Brandes." Lacking introductions, and cut off by his shyness from striking up acquaintances in
cafés as Bjørnson would have done, he added a sad little plea. "Do you
know of no Dane who might stop off in Dresden this winter? I long much
for Scandinavians. There may be some here already, but I haven't met any,
and the consul knows nothing." However, he was finding Dresden "very
pleasant and very cheap," and concluded: "I go much to the theatre. It
is one of the best in Germany, but is far, far behind that of Copenhagen
in taste and accomplishment. But that is so everywhere in Germany"—an
opinion which Hans Andersen had expressed twenty years earlier. One would
like to know which plays Ibsen saw but, unhelpful as so often, he names
none.

Hegel sent him a copy of *Aesthetic Studies,* a solid book of 318 pages.
It comprised a section on "The Nature of Tragedy" (the introduction to a
thesis which had won Brandes the Copenhagen University Gold Medal in
1862–63); two essays on "The Theory of Comedy"; five studies of modern
Scandinavian writers (Christian Rickardt, Frederik Paludan-Müller, Emil
Aarestrup, Henrik Hertz and Ibsen himself); and three short pieces on
individual plays, Oehlenschläger's *The Little Herdsman,* Heiberg's *The
Inseparables,* and Molière's *L'Ecole des femmes.* The sections on tragedy
and comedy read rather dully today and are the kind of abstract theorising
Ibsen was accustomed to find particularly indigestible; but the studies
of the individual writers sparkle with good sense, perception, and breadth
of outlook. To read them side by side with the cloudy utterances of Clemens
Petersen, that feared pundit, is like comparing the essays of Matthew
Arnold (the first volume of which had appeared three years previously)
with those of the executioners of the *Edinburgh* and *Quarterly* reviews. Ibsen devoured the book with delight, even, apparently, the abstract sections.
"It has," he informed Hegel on 22 December, "been a veritable gold
mine for me. . . . Brandes is a remarkable man for seeing clearly, deeply
and cohesively." He must have been gratified to find that the essay on
himself, of fifty-five pages, was more than twice as long as any of the
others about individual authors.

Hegel had expressed doubts about the propriety of Ibsen's suggested subtitle for his new play; he feared that some might think *Our Lord & Co* blasphemous, and Ibsen agreed to alter it. "I was myself half of the same opinion," he told Hegel in the same letter, "though the expression would not have offended anyone *once they had read the play*. It contains no word on religious matters; but people can't know that in advance, and the subtitle might well cause offence; so, away with it! The play will be the most artistically finished work I have yet written. . . . I hope to send you the fair copy in February." He was less good than his word; he did not complete even his first draft until 28 February. "It is a blessed feeling," he wrote to Hegel that day, "to be done with something which for a whole year now has never for a single day been out of my thoughts."

The fair-copying of his manuscript took him a further nine weeks, a long time, one might think, even allowing for a certain amount of re-writing. A more cogent reason for this apparent dilatoriness, however, may have been his reluctance to return (as he would then have had to have done) to the heart-searching labour of *Emperor and Galilean,* that burden which had for so long been on his back. Replying on 23 March to Martin Schneekloth, the young Dane who had so sharply observed his marriage, and who had enquired about the progress of the Roman play, Ibsen wrote: "I am not thinking about 'Julian' for the moment, and don't want to bother about him in the near future; to be honest, I shrink from both the man and the theme. . . . We visit the theatre regularly. . . . Life is fabulously cheap here. In the New Year Sigurd became a pupil at Dr. Holbe's famous school, which is principally attended by foreigners, Americans, English, Russians, Poles, etc. . . . We shall stay here at least a year."

Sigurd later recalled to his wife Bergliot[1] how poor his parents were during those first months in Dresden. He himself was looked down on by his schoolmates because he was so ill-dressed; Suzannah made his clothes out of his father's old ones, and cut them big enough to allow for growth. His trousers were too long, and the boys in the street used to run after him shouting: *"Du tretst in deine Hosen! Du tretst in deine Hosen!* [You're treading on your trousers!]." Once, when Ibsen suggested that Sigurd should bring some of his schoolfriends home, he told his father that he "didn't want to," ashamed that they should see how humbly his parents lived; at which his father gave him "a long, wounded, and questioning look" which left such an impression on him that "I would have given years of my life to have unsaid it." The neighbours' children mocked him too, and he had to make up fantastic tales to impress them, such as that his mother (who had been ill for some weeks, and had left the shopping to him) was a negress who never went out of the house, and that he had a brother whom his parents kept in a box. Suzannah

brought him up austerely, continually drumming into him the importance
of duty; once when he had cut his head so that it bled and he was running
a fever, Suzannah simply bandaged it and sent him to school as usual.

When there was some occasion for celebration, such as the anniversary
of their wedding, or Suzannah's or Sigurd's birthday, Ibsen would design
an imitation banknote for a certain sum, to be cashed when sufficient funds
should be in hand. Several of these banknotes have survived, the earliest
from 1867 when he was on Ischia writing *Peer Gynt,* and continuing as
late as 1875, after the move to Munich. Most of them contain drawings
of either a cat or an eagle—both nicknames that he had affectionately coined
for Suzannah. (His own nickname in the family was "The Tiger" or "The
Bear.") He also on occasion awarded them medals, often copied from real
medals, and sometimes amused himself by sketching these in the margins
of his manuscripts.

Each week, Sigurd received a tiny amount of pocket money, which he
never spent but kept in a money-box; this he opened three times a year,
at Christmas and on his parents' birthdays, to buy presents for them. Every
evening, after he had finished his homework, Ibsen would play cards
with him, and always let him win. One evening Ibsen won, and
Sigurd was so upset that he threw the cards on the floor; thereafter,
they never played cards, but always chess, which they continued to do for
many years. They had a small music-box which played the "Tyrolienne"
from Offenbach's *La Vie Parisienne,* Gounod's "Faust-Walzer" and
"Klosterglocken"; Suzannah still liked to play it forty years later as an
old woman. Sigurd remembered what a great reader his mother was,
ploughing through the year's books and recommending to Ibsen what he
should read. From the age of four Sigurd was regularly sent to the
library with a basket to change the books; the first thing they always
did when they came to a new town was to find the library. And
whenever Ibsen had finished a new play he would read it to Suzannah
and Sigurd; he had done this at least as early as *Peer Gynt,* when Sigurd,
on hearing the speech in Act One in which Aase scolds Peer, cried:
"Why, that's just like mother!" This habit, too, continued all their
lives; when Sigurd married, Ibsen, on finishing a play, said to his
daughter-in-law: "Bergliot, you mustn't take it ill if I don't ask you
to listen with us. I'm used just to reading to Sigurd and his mother."

Sigurd remembered too how Suzannah used to force Ibsen to write,
when the mood was not on him. Gradually he realized that she was
right. "When you are not in the mood to write," he told Sigurd many
years later, "you must nevertheless sit down calmly at your desk, and
the inspiration will come of itself." Bergliot (who recorded her husband's memories) adds an interesting note on Suzannah which needs
to be measured against the detractions of casual observers. "From the
very beginning of their marriage she tried to keep away friends or

acquaintances who might distract him. . . . She let nothing and no one disturb him. . . . Nor could anyone give him enthusiasm as she could. When he was depressed she knew how to ignite his courage. One needs to have personally heard her proclaim her fanatical faith to understand the strength she gave him through the years. When hostile criticism depressed him she did not lose courage. Her eyes blazed and she said: 'With your genius, what should you care what this rabble writes?' And it always ended with his walking calmly into his study."[2]

He still, even after he had come to Dresden, hankered after painting, and it cost Suzannah much effort to dissuade him from pursuing it seriously. "I had to fight with him," she told Sigurd, who commented to Bergliot, "The world can thank my mother that it has one bad painter the fewer and got a great writer instead."[3]

About this time, Ibsen spotted an item of news in the Danish press which must surely have caused those tight lips to allow themselves the luxury of a small smile. To few authors is it granted to see a hostile critic of their work publicly humiliated; but in March Clemens Petersen, whose review of Peer Gynt had so enraged Ibsen, became involved in a homosexual scandal concerning some boys at a school where he had been lecturing, and had to leave hurriedly for the United States, where for the next thirty-five years he devoted himself to religious journalism among the Scandinavian-Americans, a fate which even Ibsen himself might have hesitated to wish on a leading literary critic. "This is a dreadful business about Clemens Petersen," he wrote to Hegel on 7 April. "I have always had strong suspicions about his character; but such a thing—!" Petersen's passionate admiration of Bjørnson, which may have had a sexual element in it (not that Bjørnson would have approved of or been likely to perceive that), was probably partly responsible for his denigration of Ibsen's work; Ibsen may well have appeared to him principally as a challenger to his idol. As soon as he left Denmark, Petersen's name became taboo and his influence ceased. His friends subscribed to bring him home in 1904, and he died ten years later at the age of eighty-four, almost forgotten.

During 1869 the rift between Ibsen and Bjørnson gradually widened. They had not corresponded since the end of 1867, and their letters to third parties show that a mutual distrust had developed. "From Ibsen," wrote Bjørnson to Hegel on 25 February, "I've heard nothing but a discourtesy which he sent me through someone else. Whether I have deserved it, I don't know, nor care; for now I'm tired; he must sail his own moody sea."[4] And on 15 July Ibsen cynically observed to Brandes, with whom Bjørnson had likewise recently quarrelled: "For him [Bjørnson] there exist only two kinds of men, those whom he might

[2] Bergliot Ibsen, pp. 41–42.
[3] Ibid., p. 41.
[4] Gro-tid, II, 298.

use and those who embarrass him"—an ungrateful and untrue remark.
More accurately, he added: "However good Bjørnson may be at analysing
his own characters, he is a poor psychologist when it comes to dealing with
real people."

The exact cause of their alienation remains unknown; but that it
should have happened when the two were separated by half Europe
is hardly surprising. Both were sharp-tongued, free in their condemnation
of other human beings, inordinately sensitive to any kind of criticism
and, as such men are, more than usually ready to believe gossip. Even
if they did not say caustic things about each other, and they pretty
certainly did, we may be sure that rumours of such remarks reached
both pairs of ears. "Have I not experienced," Bjørnson had publicly
declared at Bergen six years earlier, "that my friend Ibsen has been
held up against me for the purpose of disparaging me, and I against
him to disparage him?" If they had been able to meet, the differences
might have been resolved, as they were when, many years later, they did
at last see one another. But Ibsen's suspicions were intensified by something, whether true or false we do not know, which his old Holland
acquaintance Jakob Løkke told him in Stockholm later that summer.
Bjørnson tried to mend things by writing Ibsen a friendly letter in September, ten days before the publication of *The League of Youth,* saying
that he was looking forward to reading the play; but the implied
insult to him contained in the character of Stensgaard, and the continued success of the play on the stage, widened the gap impossibly;
and although Ibsen told Hegel in December that he would like a reconciliation, it was to be eight years before they corresponded again and
fifteen before they met.

Hegel held *The League of Youth* over until the autumn, when the
publication of the play and its stage premiere would conveniently coincide,
and Ibsen spent the summer relaxing. "I lead a pleasant and carefree
life," he wrote to Lorentz Dietrichson on 28 May, "and plan to get
down to 'Julian' in the autumn." Asking Dietrichson to write a brief
biographical sketch of him to preface a German translation of *Brand*
which was to be published that autumn,[5] he exhorted him to "forget
the starving poet stuff; tell rather how the government and Storthing
have granted me a pension, how I travel, am happy in *dem grossen
Vaterlande,* etc." Dietrichson has recorded how, on receiving this letter,
he failed to recognize the neat, elegant handwriting, so unlike the scratchy
script of Ibsen's earlier correspondence; and a photograph which followed

---

[5] As things turned out, although the translator, P. F. Siebold, a travelling salesman
from Kassel, completed his translation that autumn, he did not succeed in getting it
published until 1872, when it marked the first appearance of any of Ibsen's plays in
a non-Scandinavian language. John Grieg, the brother of Edvard Grieg, had translated *The Pretenders* into German as early as 1866, but never managed to find a
publisher.

three weeks later, with the words: "I enclose the requested likeness of my phiz; I don't know whether you will recognize me from my bearded period," surprised him equally with its trimly barbered head, mutton-chop whiskers and assured expression in the eyes. Ibsen's letter included a defensive note on *The League of Youth:* "The play is a pure comedy and nothing else. People in Norway may say that I have portrayed specific persons and circumstances, but this is untrue; though I have used models, which is as necessary for a writer of comedy as for a painter or sculptor."

On 26 June Ibsen wrote to Georg Brandes to thank him for the essay on him in *Aesthetic Studies.* "You have written illuminatingly of my work as no one else has done. Please accept my warmest thanks. . . . I have read it sixteen times and sixteen times again. . . . But now I am very excited to hear what you will say of my new work. It is written in prose and, consequently, with a strongly realistic emphasis. I have paid particular attention to the form, and *inter alia* have been artful enough to manage without a single monologue, or even an 'aside.' " He then, however, began to have doubts whether Brandes would approve of *The League of Youth,* and on 15 July he wrote: "I begin to feel that perhaps I should not have asked you to read my new comedy. On reflection, I think that what really interests you in a work is the tragedies or comedies that are played out inside each individual, and that you care little or nothing about factual circumstances, whether they be political or not. In which case you may well ask, when faced with my play 'What's Hecuba to me?' But this once I didn't want to write anything but what this play is about, and it must be judged accordingly. . . . As regards certain aspects of *Peer Gynt,* I cannot agree with you. I do, of course, accept the laws of beauty, but I don't bother about its conventions. You mention Michelangelo; to my mind, no one has contravened the laws of beauty more than he; yet everything he has created is beautiful because it is *individual.* Raphael's art I have never really warmed to; his figures are from before the Fall; and in general, the southerner has a different æsthetic attitude from us; he likes things to be formally beautiful; for us, that which is not formally beautiful can be beautiful by reason of the truth that lies in it. But it is no use arguing about this with pen and ink; we must meet."

Brandes's "illuminating" essay on Ibsen was an expansion of an article he had published in *Dansk Maanedsskrift* in November 1867, surveying Ibsen's career only as far as *Brand,* which he had disparaged at the expense of *The Pretenders. Peer Gynt* had not yet appeared when Brandes wrote this, so for the essay in *Aesthetic Studies* he added the review of *Peer* which he had written for *Dagbladet* the following month, modifying, however, some of his fiercer objections to Ibsen's supposed offences against the "laws of beauty." At first sight, it is a little surprising that Ibsen should have shown such enthusiasm about this article, which is a curious

mixture of penetration and insensitivity. The main body of it, which
deals with the early plays up to and including *Brand* (but excluding
The Warrior's Barrow, St. John's Night and *Olaf Liljekrans,* none of
which had been published), is a remarkable piece of writing for a young
man of barely twenty-five. "It is the destiny of truth and beauty," declared
Brandes, "only to shine forth for a moment, like meteors which are
extinguished as soon as they touch the earth. . . . There is . . . something combative, rebellious, violent, and melancholy deep down in [Ibsen's]
being that is reflected in his works, and darkens even his love of the
light. . . . He makes start after start, each, as it were, the run before
the leap that is to carry him into the promised land. But for a long
time it seemed as though this leap would never be taken. His genius
cannot come to rest; it tosses about like a sick, restless child; now it
searches within among its dreams and thoughts, but does not find them
clear or strong enough to be able to step forth in vigorous nudity; now it
searches without, finds a delicate, spotless drapery, wraps itself in it
so as to become almost unrecognizable, seeks for a style, nay, more, a
language; then it throws away what it has found, realizes at length
that all borrowing is pure loss, and labours until at last it finds its
true self. . . . Strength of will is, to him, the really sublime."[6] The
individual plays are finely analysed, especially *The Pretenders,* and Brandes
makes the valid criticism that Ibsen "has not infrequently marred his
works by speeches which seem to come from a spectator rather than an
actor . . . letting the characters utter sentences that are far too general,
self-conscious and suitable to a thousand occasions, when one would
expect them to be exclusively taken up with what is happening to
themselves personally, to them alone, in this particular situation." Brandes
observes, too, that Ibsen is "especially successful in his female figures. . . .
One is tempted to exclaim 'Have you been a woman in some other life,
that you thus know a woman's heart?'"

The study of *Peer Gynt* which concludes Brandes's essay, however, was
(with slight modifications) the indictment which he had published in
Dagbladet, and remembering Ibsen's reaction to Clemens Petersen's scarcely
more hostile review one can only suppose that Ibsen regarded these
five pages of disapproval as a fair price to pay for the preceding fifty
pages of brilliant sympathy. "It is clear to me," Ibsen had written to
Jonas Collin on 21 October 1867 after reading Brandes's attack on the
philosopher Rasmus Nielsen in the name of free thought, "that this man
will play a big role in the cultural and spiritual life of the north." A
modern Danish critic has shrewdly observed that Ibsen's intuition probably
told him that "a man who was ideologically progressive could not long

---

[6] The Jesse Muir translation, revised by William Archer and doubtless owing much
of its quality to him. Whatever Archer's limitations in the rendering of dialogue, he
is incomparable as a translator of narrative or critical prose.

hold to an antiquated æsthetic standpoint," that Brandes felt attracted by Ibsen's poetic genius and powerful personality, but at the same time repelled by the works in which that genius and personality manifested themselves," and that after Petersen's review of *Peer Gynt* Brandes took over the position of friend and ally which had previously been occupied by Bjørnson.[7] Ibsen wrote to Hegel on 10 June asking where Brandes was proposing to travel that summer and saying that if he was going to be in Germany he, Ibsen, would gladly go out of his way to meet him.

Brandes was much excited by Ibsen's letter of 26 June. "I prize it," he wrote to his old tutor, Hans Brøchner, on 25 July, "because Ibsen is not, like Andersen, a man who praises everyone who praises him."[8] He told Ibsen of his own recent quarrel with Bjørnson, which must have endeared him further, and Ibsen, in his letter to Brandes of 15 July, expressed great joy at this new-found friendship. "It is a great blessing to have discovered an integrated personality," he declared, and expressed the hope that, since Brandes had no immediate plans to come to Germany, they might perhaps be able to meet in Copenhagen, to speak "not merely about all the literary matters on which we disagree, but also about many human matters on which we stand closer together." Later that year he told Hegel that he hoped Brandes would review *The League of Youth,* since "nobody could do it as he could, and I feel he is a true friend to me,"[9] and that "there is something in both his praise and censure which indescribably pleases me; the fact of being understood."[10]

During the spring of 1869 Ibsen had applied to the Norwegian government for a stipend of 300 specie-dollars to enable him to spend a year in Sweden studying the art, literature, and other aspects of that country's cultural life. This was granted him; meanwhile he received an invitation to take part in an orthographic conference in Stockholm, convened in order to agree on a unified spelling for the three Scandinavian countries (a purpose in which it failed signally). After changing his lodgings in Dresden to a first-floor apartment at Königsbrücker-Strasse 33, he departed for Stockholm on 20 July.

Stockholm was then, apart from its impressive public buildings, still largely a town of small wooden houses; a piped water system had only just been introduced, and men and girls with buckets on yokes could still be seen selling water from the wells. Citizens were awakened at night by the collectors of night-soil, thumping on the door with their long poles. As the closets were usually in the attic, the soil was commonly thrown out of the windows into, or at, the carts; foreign travellers compared Stockholm to Constantinople for its combination of beauty and filth.

Ibsen took lodgings at Herkulesgatan 5, a narrow street just across

[7] Fenger, "Ibsen og Georg Brandes indtil 1872," pp. 180–81.
[8] *Brandes Brevveksling,* I, 69.
[9] 22 September 1869.
[10] 14 December 1869.

the bridge from the royal palace, and was regally entertained. "I live here," he wrote to his brother-in-law, J. H. Thoresen, on 2 August, "in an endless round of festivities. I have not had a single day when I have not been invited to dinner or something." The other delegates to the conference included Knud Knudsen, his old enemy from the Norwegian Christiania Theatre, and Jakob Løkke of the Learned Holland circle, who widened the rift between Ibsen and Bjørnson by telling the former of some unkind things the latter had reputedly said of him. He saw a good deal of Lorentz Dietrichson, and renewed his acquaintance with Count Snoilsky, to whom he apologized for the halter incident in Rome. He had, he said, changed his mind about Manderström, who was Snoilsky's uncle, and had come to the conclusion that he was not really to blame. "Then we are still as far apart as ever on this subject," replied Snoilsky, "for I have come to the conclusion that he was." Ibsen spent several days with a family named Limnell, who had a villa on Lake Mälaren. Herr Limnell held a high position in the railways, and his wife, the widow of a famous newspaper editor, was the centre of a literary circle; Ibsen was to thank her for her hospitality in one of his best longer poems. He met writers, actors, and politicians, one of whom, a lively young liberal named Adolf Hedin, rebuked him for his conservatism—an incident which was later to provoke another interesting poetic declaration.

Ibsen's appearance and demeanour caused astonishment. "People had expected the author of *Brand*," writes Dietrichson, "to be an earnest, severe old ascetic, and there appeared an elegant, youngish man in a velvet coat, refined, lively and likeable. People could not reconcile *Brand* with its author,[11] and several people openly expressed their amazement, amounting in some cases to downright disappointment; but soon he had taken them all by storm, especially the ladies."[12] On 22 September, two months after his arrival, he told Hegel: "My stay in Sweden has been, and still is, one long festivity. From all sides I meet a courtesy and friendliness which cannot be described. . . . I have plenty of plans for new works; but to get down to them I must find solitude again; I cannot write here."

Thus Ibsen, for the first time in his life, found himself lionized; and the experience was not distasteful. King Carl XV, who, in his enjoyment

[11] August Strindberg, who in 1869 was twenty and had just failed his medical exams and concluded his brief and calamitous career as a professional actor, did not meet Ibsen (then or ever), but eight years later he recalled the impression Ibsen made in Sweden: "Who does not remember the famous poet's appearance when he visited Stockholm a few years back? Dressed in a velvet jacket, a white waistcoat with black buttons, and a cape of the latest fashion, with an elegant cane in his hand and a protective self-mocking curl to his lip, he went his way, avoiding all deep subjects of conversation." (August Strindberg, "Konstakademiens utställning, 1877," in *Kulturhistoriske studier* [Stockholm, 1881], p. 125.)

[12] Dietrichson, I, 350.

of the company of writers, artists, and pretty women, much resembled England's Charles II, invited him several times to the palace, where (he later told John Paulsen), he spent "unforgettable" and highly informal evenings, continuing long after midnight, with champagne and merry stories, "not always for dainty ears."[13]

Shortly before he left, the director and actors of the Royal Theatre held a farewell dinner for him and Dietrichson (who was leaving at the same time) at the Hôtel du Nord in Carl XII's Torg. The actor Daniel Hwasser, proposing Ibsen's health, recited a poem in Swedish which Ibsen only gradually recognized as a very free translation of one of his own songs from *Love's Comedy*. "It was very droll," recalled Dietrichson, "to see Ibsen's expression as, towards the conclusion of the first verse, he recognized his own child."[14] Dietrichson wrote an article about him in the leading Swedish illustrated weekly, *Ny Illustrerad Tidning*, describing him as "one of the greatest poets of our time, if not absolutely the greatest"; and so considerable was the impact Ibsen made on Stockholm that someone advised the king to recommend that he be chosen to represent his country that autumn at the official opening of the Suez Canal. Ibsen received the invitation with unmixed delight. "I get everything free," he wrote happily to J. H. Thoresen on 24 September, "the trip from Paris and back included." And on his last evening in Stockholm, Carl XV invited him to the palace and personally invested him with the Order of Vasa, the first of those many medals he was to receive and in which he took so curious and childlike a pride.

These weeks of lionizing in Stockholm left Ibsen with an affection for Sweden he was never to lose. He had received the homage, not merely of his fellow-artists but of society; and the latter, considering his gnawing sense of social inferiority, may well have seemed at the time the more important. His previous feelings towards Sweden had been almost entirely hostile. Vilhelm Bergsøe records an occasion in Sorrento in 1867 when Suzannah had begun to praise that country. "For some time Ibsen endured her talk in silence, but when she began to speak of the Swedish war heroes, Gustaf Adolf and Carl XII, he exclaimed violently, 'Stuff and nonsense! What are these fellows now? Still tramping around in Carl XII's boots, but they haven't any shoes to run in when it comes to the point!' Fru Ibsen tried to qualify this unreasonable verdict of Ibsen's, but when she praised the Swedish warriors afresh, he shouted, 'Keep quiet! I won't listen, you make me sick!' And he hit the table a thump so that the bottle trembled. Little Sigurd, who had sat and listened to our conversation with big eyes, suddenly said: 'Father can't stand the Swedes.' "[15] Ibsen had

[13] Paulsen, *Samliv med Ibsen*, I, 51–52.

[14] Dietrichson, I, 353.

[15] Bergsøe, pp. 237–38. Cf. also Ibsen's letter to Anton Klubien of 20 October 1865, not in the Centenary Edition but printed in *Ibsen-Årbok 1953*, p. 98: "Some

caricatured the nation unkindly in *Peer Gynt* through the character of the pompous Herr Trumpeterstraale; but the charm and elegance (and perhaps the snobbery) of Stockholm society had won him over.[16]

On 26 September, two days before he left Stockholm, Ibsen wrote a letter which must have been on his conscience for a long time. On 3 June his mother had died in Skien, at the age of seventy-one, and his sister, Hedvig, now married to a ship's captain, Hans Jacob Stousland, had sent him the news. Only now, three and a half months later, did he reply. It was, as far as we know, the first contact between Ibsen and his immediate family since he had paid his brief visit to them on the way from Grimstad to Christiania nineteen and a half years before:

Dear Hedvig!

It is months since I received your letter, and I have not replied. But there is so much that stands between us, between me and home; understand this, and do not think that my silence during these long years and now this summer is the result of indifference. I cannot write letters; I must be near someone and give myself completely. You are different; you can write; do so often! I will answer—at the least with a loving greeting, or with news which I hope will not sadden you.

I look inwards into myself; there is my battleground, where I now conquer, now suffer defeat. But I cannot write about all this in a letter. Do not try to change me. I want to be true to myself. What will be, will be.

So our dear old mother is dead. Thank you for so lovingly carrying the burden for us all. You are indeed the best of mortals.

I wander around much in the world. Who knows if I may not come to Norway next summer, in which case I should like to see our old home, to which I am still held fast by so many roots. Give Father all my love; explain to him about me; you understand so well, he perhaps does not . . .

I enclose my photograph; if you have one of your husband and children, please send it to me. I wish you knew my wife; she is exactly the right one for me, and sends her love. Our address in Dresden is: Königsbrucker-Strasse, no. 33.

This letter is short and I have passed over much that you must have wished that I should speak of. It cannot, for the present, be

---

wretched Swedes come and go, but I don't bother with them. . . . I wanted to annoy the Swedish dogs who were present [at the club]."

[16] John Paulsen remarked (*Samliv med Ibsen*, II, 224) that Ibsen liked the formality and aristocratic elegance of Swedes in contrast to what he regarded as the boorishness and provincialism of Norwegian manners—just as so many Irish exiles (Goldsmith, Burke, Wilde, Shaw, Yeats) preferred London society to that of Dublin.

otherwise; but do not think I lack that warmth of heart which must, above all else, be present if a person is to enjoy a true and healthy spiritual life . . .

Hedvig had always been the only member of his family with whom he had been able to feel any real affinity, and she was the only one for whom he retained any affection. A non-conformist in religion like himself, she needed, unlike him, to belong to a religious movement, and had joined a sect roughly corresponding to the Quakers. Her Paus relatives, shocked at this, had tried to exert pressure on her by threatening to discharge her husband from their employ; she resisted, and he got the sack. Ibsen was to remember this episode when, twelve years later, he wrote *An Enemy of the People,* in which Captain Horster is likewise sacked for befriending Dr. Stockmann.[17]

His mother's death was not the only bereavement that Ibsen suffered that summer. On 7 July his old friend Paul Botten Hansen, who had published so many of his poems and given him such wise encouragement, had died of pleurisy at the age of forty-four. "A less self-seeking man would be hard to find," wrote Ludwig Daæ of him in an obituary memoir, "and if any man was free from vanity, he was."[18] To give some support to his four children, the city of Bergen bought his fine book collection for three thousand crowns, and established it as a free public library.

On 29 September Ibsen left Stockholm for Dresden. The next day, while he was en route, *The League of Youth* was published in Copenhagen.

The importance of *The League of Youth* to a modern reader lies in the fact that it was Ibsen's first attempt to write a play entirely in modern colloquial dialogue. The plot must be briefly summarised, since the play is little known, though its complexity is such that any summary must seem bewildering. The scene is a market town in south Norway, generally thought to have been modelled on Skien. Stensgaard, an ambitious young liberal politician, in a burst of enthusiasm at an Independence Day celebration, founds an anti-capitalist party which he christens the League of Youth. In the course of his speech he delivers an eloquent attack on the local ironmaster, Brattsberg; he does not name him, however, and Brattsberg thinks he is referring to a landowner named Monsen, whose daughter, Ragna, Stensgaard has been courting. Fickle in love as in all else, Stensgaard now takes a fancy to Brattsberg's daughter, Thora, and to restore himself to favour makes a public apology to her father, who shows him the door in a fury. Then Stensgaard learns that Brattsberg's son, Erik, has forged a bill, realizes that Brattsberg may be

[17] Zucker, pp. 238–39. His informant was Hedvig's son, Captain John Ibsen Stousland.

[18] *Vidar* (Copenhagen, 1888), p. 354.

disgraced too, and turns his attentions back to Ragna Monsen. But he hears that Monsen may likewise be involved in the scandal, so proposes to a rich tradesman's widow named Mrs. Rundholmen. Then he finds that Monsen was involved but not Brattsberg, and renews his interest in Thora. She no longer wants him; in despair, he announces his engagement to Mrs. Rundholmen; but she has accepted someone else, and he is left with nobody. Yet his future is by no means gloomy. "Mark my words," says someone at the end of the play. "In ten or fifteen years Stensgaard will be in Parliament or the Privy Council"; and another character adds a quotation from Napoleon: "Double-dealing is the stuff of which politicians are made."

Ibsen had for some time sensed that the dialogue of drama must move towards a greater colloquialism, as the novel had been doing, and Bjørnson had shown him the way four years earlier in a two-act comedy called *The Newly Wedded Couple*, a slight piece about a young wife bound to her parents of which Ibsen, on reading it, is said to have remarked: "This is how we must write modern drama." He tried, in *The League of Youth*, to escape as far as possible from all the old conventions of artificial drama (as witness his proud claim to Georg Brandes that he had completed it "without a single monologue or aside"). Having raised poetic drama to its finest peak since Shakespeare (for *Brand* and *Peer Gynt* are greater *plays* than anything by Racine, Gœthe, or Schiller, none of whose works is tolerable in the theatre if performed in any language but its own), he had set himself to cultivate, as he was later to phrase it, "the much more difficult art of writing the genuine, plain language spoken in life."[19] As William Archer observed: "Having now outgrown his youthful romanticism, and laid down, in *Brand* and *Peer Gynt*, the fundamental positions of his criticism of life, he felt that, to carry that criticism into detail, he must come to closer quarters with reality; and to that end he required a suppler instrument than verse."[20]

Over the next thirty years *The League of Youth* was to prove the most popular (if judged by the number of performances given) of all Ibsen's plays in Norway. Since 1900, however, it has been staged less often than any other of his established plays, there as elsewhere. Edmund Gosse dismissed it as "the most provincial of all Ibsen's mature works," an adjective that was often later to be aimed at Ibsen by his denigrators. In fact, *The League of Youth* is no more provincial than *The Pillars of Society* or *An Enemy of the People,* which likewise have as their themes the petty-mindedness which prevails in small communities; and anyway the word "provincial" has ceased to be pejorative when applied to drama. The real reason for posterity's lack of interest in the play lies, despite Ibsen's professed aim in writing it, in the outdatedness of its technique. The synopsis

[19] Letter to Lucie Wolf, 25 May 1883.
[20] Introduction to *The League of Youth* (London, 1907), p. viii.

given above is much simplified; it omits (otherwise it would have been as unravellable as those verbal cats'-cradles which confront us in opera programmes) a mesh of sub-plots which depend for their working on the old-fashioned machinery of misdirected letters, overheard conversations and the like which Ibsen had inherited from Holberg and which commentators have so often mistakenly attributed to his supposed admiration for Scribe. Holberg's plays, Ibsen wrote to Lorentz Dietrichson on 28 May 1869, shortly after sending the last pages of *The League of Youth* to the printers, were "almost the only book I never tire of reading"; but the conventions of mannered comedy, amusing in their proper context, are destructive to any play that sets out to impress by its realism. They did not bother nineteenth-century audiences, but they bother us. To keep a tightly knit plot (as opposed to the looser, freer and more modern structures of *Brand* and *Peer Gynt*) running was something that Ibsen was not yet able to manage without recourse to the rusty starting-handle of coincidence.[21] The play is, moreover, full of topical references which were a source of delight and fury to Ibsen's contemporaries, but which would be lost on a modern audience. As Archer remarked, it was essentially an experimental, transitional work; and by the time Ibsen became known abroad, ten years later, its technique was already outdated.

With all its faults, however, it was an advance on the technique of the day. The plot never stops moving—something that can scarcely be said of any other comedy of the period, apart from the farces of Labiche—and, like every other play Ibsen had written since *St. John's Night*, it contains a galaxy of minutely observed characters. Unlike Strindberg, who was often perfunctory in his drawing of secondary personages, Ibsen never, in his maturity, created the smallest role that was not worth the playing. Stensgaard, the leading character, has been well summed up as "Peer Gynt as a politician"; an "inescapably split personality," as Dr. Fjeldbo describes him in the play, he is another in the long line of self-deceivers which began with Julian Poulsen in *St. John's Night* (or even with Severus in *Norma*), and was to continue through Karsten Bernick, Torvald Helmer, Hjalmar Ekdal, and Ulric Brendel to its culmination in John Gabriel Borkman and Arnold Rubek. Ibsen once admitted that Stensgaard contained a good deal of himself, a curious confession, one might think, from the writer who, above all others, has come to be associated with a hatred of self-deception. But Brand, we must remember, Ibsen had declared to be himself "in his best moments," and Stensgaard, like Peer Gynt, presumably represented those qualities in himself of which he was ashamed and which he sought, not always successfully, to subdue—

21 " 'It is much easier,' he said, 'to write a piece like *Brand* or *Peer Gynt*, in which you can bring in a little of everything, than to carry through a severely logical scheme, like that of *John Gabriel Borkman*, for example.' " (William Archer, "Ibsen as I Knew Him," p. 18.)

cowardice, readiness to compromise when faced with unpleasant realities, and facile eloquence. Bjørnson, while possessing many qualities which Ibsen envied, at the same time personified one of the subtlest snares that can destroy a writer: the temptation to give full rein to those gifts which bring the easiest and most immediate success; and in this sense Ibsen may have been speaking honestly when, later, he asserted that Stensgaard was not (as his contemporaries assumed) a portrayal of Bjørnson, Johan Sverdrup, or any other specific individual. The real model for Stensgaard, as for Peer Gynt, was any Norwegian with charm and eloquence, which in practice meant, then as now, almost any Norwegian, including Ibsen himself.

Of the other characters, Daniel Hejre, a clever and malicious man who has lost his money but retained his wit, is generally accepted as being a portrait of the dramatist's father; and Aslaksen, a timid and bibulous printer who was to re-appear, still timid but now a teetotaller, in *An Enemy of the People,* seems to have been based on N. F. Axelsen, the publisher of the student magazine *Andhrimner,* who, like Aslaken, apparently disapproved of provocative young writers. The most important character for Ibsen's future and the future of drama, however, was the minor figure of Selma Brattsberg, the ironmaster's young daughter-in-law who, chafing against the bonds of marriage, complains to her husband: "You dressed me up like a doll; you played with me as one plays with a child." When Georg Brandes read the play he suggested in his review[22] that she, or a character like her, might make a good central figure for a later work, a suggestion which ten years later was to bring forth remarkable fruit.

The League of Youth received mixed notices in the Scandinavian press. Georg Brandes, as Ibsen had feared, disliked it. He complained that "it lacks something of what characterises Ibsen's work, the *'Dieu dans l'âme, le diable au corps,'*" and that Stensgaard "grows ever smaller and smaller, becomes more and more a simple blackguard and gradually loses any suggestion of significance. . . . Ultimately one wearies of being present at the downfall of so feeble a wretch. . . . And what we have said of the main character is true of most of the minor ones; they are too mean for us not, in the long run, to grow sick of their company. . . . In the absence of any genuinely mirthful comedy one sighs for some beauty; one hopes to find at any rate one or two of Ibsen's pretty female characters in this *monkey-house;* but alas, they are not to be found"—though Brandes made a grudging exception of Selma. He granted that the play showed an advance in character drawing—"the author's characterisation in previous plays has been somewhat unsure and loose[!]," but found that the absence of monologues and asides made the plot somewhat difficult to follow. "While admitting the great technical facility to which Ibsen has attained,

[22] *Illustreret Tidende,* 10 October 1869. "She is a new figure, and a whole play might be written about her relationship with her family."

one must point out that the monologue is not in itself an incomprehensible dramatic device, and that it is far better to be wholly comprehensible with the aid of an observation confined to the audience than to be unclear because of over-economy." Brandes, lacking any practical experience in the theatre, was never to become a good dramatic critic; all his life, he was to judge plays as literature and for their moral and philosophical content; but his remarks are frighteningly revealing of the kind of mental conservatism with which Ibsen had to contend in his readers and audiences.

An anonymous critic in the newly-founded *Dagbladet* (20 October)[23] objected to the play on the usual æsthetic grounds. "The main impression one gains from a reading of Ibsen's later work is neither calm nor harmonious . . . [but rather] of discord . . . coarse and brutal characters. . . . Idealism does appear but has no active part in the unfolding of the play . . . [it is] regrettable that the ingenious and carefully finished dialogue should be wasted on such insignificant material." But another anonymous critic, writing in *Morgenbladet* (17 October) saw what Ibsen was trying to do: "This latest work marks a new and significant phase in the author's artistic development, a step forward. . . . He places us slap in the midst of real life, where we meet people who are unquestionably of flesh and blood, people such as we unfortunately meet every day." The reviewer concluded: "It is inevitable in our small community that when a writer presents the contemporary scene on the stage through typical characters he will meet the same criticism as was levelled at Ludvig Holberg in former days; even though the figures be types, people will point to this or that living person and say: 'It is meant to be him, it is he to the life.' So it was with Holberg. . . . It would be no less ridiculous to demand of a modern writer that he should abstain from presenting contemporary life on the stage. But if this should happen, Henrik Ibsen need not be ashamed to share such a fate with Ludvig Holberg."

Further support for Ibsen came from a somewhat unexpected quarter. Erik Bøgh, the fashionable and successful Danish playwright whose vaudevilles had so often figured in Ibsen's repertory at the Bergen and Christiania theatres, might, one would think, have resented the work of this disturbing newcomer. In fact he saw more clearly than most of his contemporaries what Ibsen was really getting at, and his reviews of Ibsen's plays as they appeared from the press were (except in the case of *Ghosts*) remarkably sympathetic and penetrating, much more so than Brandes's. He found *The League of Youth* "like all Ibsen's plays, an outstandingly powerful and fertile work, so original that it must in most respects be called unique in its genre." The many Danish admirers of *Brand* and

---

23 An independent left-wing daily established that year in Christiania. There had long been a Danish newspaper of the same name (cf. p. 250 above, etc.).

Peer Gynt, he continues, must wonder why such a master of dialogue has not written for the stage, and Bøgh tells them of Ibsen's earlier works which, we must remember, were still unknown to most Danes, none of his plays yet having been performed in that country. The only disadvantage of *The League of Youth* from a theatrical point of view (Bøgh concluded) was that the plethora of excellent minor characters would make the play "almost as long as [Bjørnson's] *Mary Stuart in Scotland,* and will demand more skilful actors than most theatres will be able to provide." Bøgh ended by exhorting the public, as they read the play, to imagine the lines being spoken with a Norwegian accent.[24]

Ibsen's old friend Aasmund Vinje probably summed up the general feeling when he wrote in *Dølen* (24 October): "Those who think that they or their friends are portrayed in the play complain and find it bad; but those who enjoy seeing these people so caricatured are happy, and find it a good piece." As one of the former, he compared Ibsen to Don Quixote, expressed indignation at Ibsen's mockery of his country, and hoped that he would soon get bored with "acting Brand."

Ibsen, however, saw none of these reviews until several weeks after they had appeared, for on his return to Dresden at the beginning of October he had departed almost immediately by train for Paris on the first stage of his journey to Suez. What impression did Paris make on him? We do not know, for of this, as of his first sighting of Venice and Florence in 1864, he has left no word. With the other delegates from northern Europe he entrained for Marseilles, and thence, on 9 October, he sailed on the SS *Moeris* for Alexandria.

[24] *Folkets Avis,* 29 October 1869. The review is reprinted in *Dit og Dat fra 1869* (Copenhagen, 1870), pp. 200–6.

12

Egypt

1869

They were eighty-six guests of the Khedive aboard the *Moeris:* Frenchmen, Germans, Dutchmen, Spaniards and Scandinavians, but no Englishmen; they followed with the Russians and others in another ship the next day. Surprisingly few of the names of Ibsen's fellow-travellers mean anything today; one exception was Théophile Gautier, who fell down the steps to the dining saloon on the first morning, dislocated a shoulder and spent the rest of the voyage with his arm in a sling. Ibsen's ignorance of French prevented him from holding any conversation with him. The only other Norwegian delegate was an Egyptologist, Professor J. D. C. Lieblein, who had condemned *Brand* as an insane work, but got on with its author well. Lorentz Dietrichson should have accompanied them, but was prevented by illness. Ibsen, as usual, kept mainly to his fellow-Scandinavians throughout his holiday. These included a pleasant young Danish literary historian, Peter Hansen (later to become director of the Royal Theatre in Copenhagen), and a Swedish army captain, Oscar von Knorring, who had served as a volunteer in the first (1849) Schleswig-Holstein war, was something of a composer, and later published a naïve but readable account of his visit to Suez. He noted as his first impression of Ibsen that he had "elegant manners and an agreeable social tone."[1]

The voyage across the Mediterranean was rough, and Lieblein, who sent regular and lively despatches back to *Morgenbladet*, reported on the second day that "there has been some distress among the bulk of the passengers."[2] They sailed between Sardinia and Corsica, the high mountains of which reminded Lieblein, and doubtless Ibsen too, of the Norwegian

[1] Oscar von Knorring, *Två månader i Egypten* (Stockholm, 1873), p. 14.

[2] *Morgenbladet,* 21 October 1869. Except where otherwise specified, all quoted references to the Egyptian journey are from Lieblein's despatches to *Morgenbladet*, printed on 21 October, 6, 14 and 24 November, and 5, 17 and 23 December 1869.

coast; then, the next day, they passed close to Caprera, where Garibaldi was living in retirement, and wondered which of the buildings there was "the home of the great adventurer and republican." They skirted Sicily, and admired Stromboli; the Plough sank towards the horizon and the moon rose higher towards her zenith as they proceeded south. The weather remained rough all the way, so that "several of the party were unable to take full advantage of the Khedive's hospitality," which included four meals a day. At last, on 13 October, after four days at sea, they reached Alexandria.

Ferdinand de Lesseps, the creator of the Canal, was there in person to greet them, and they were escorted to the Hôtel d'Europe, where "the best rooms and carriages with dragomans" were placed at their disposal. Lieblein gives the menu of one of their dinners there:

> 1 potage varié
> 1 relevé de poisson
> 1 relevé de viande de boucherie
> 1 entrée chaude
> 1 entrée froide
> 1 rôti de volaille, soit dinde, soit gibier
> 1 salade verte
> 1 entrée de legumes
> 1 entremêts de patisserie
> 4 desserts divers assortis
> fromage
> café noir et liqueurs assortis
>
> vin ordinaire Medoc
> Madeira
> vin de Bourgogne
> Ch. Lafite
> Champagne

This must have been by some way the best meal Ibsen had ever eaten, even allowing for the hospitality he had received in Stockholm (unless something comparable had been provided in Paris and Marseilles); and, eating habits being what they were in those days, it was followed by "a supper at midnight."

They spent two days in Alexandria, visiting among other memorabilia Pompey's Pillar and Cleopatra's Needles (not yet removed to the Thames Embankment and New York's Central Park) and were banqueted in the Khedive's garden, where they were entertained with European military music and "somewhat monotonous Arab melodies." At eight in the morning of 17 October they left Alexandria, and five hours later, arrived in Cairo.

The guests stayed five days in the Egyptian capital, luxuriously accommodated at the Hôtel de l'Orient, where von Knorring notes that he and Ibsen "spent many hours under palm trees on a terrace. I take this opportunity," he added, "publicly to record my gratitude for the many interesting and delightful moments which the amiable and truly cultivated Henrik Ibsen's company afforded me during both my journey to Egypt and our passage up the Nile."[3] They walked through the bazaars, "streets too narrow for any vehicle to enter," were shown the mosques and the citadel, from which they could distantly glimpse the Pyramids, and made expeditions to the museum at Bulak, old Cairo, where they saw the tombs of the Mamelukes, and Heliopolis, whence Ibsen sent Suzannah some flowers. The day after their arrival, the Khedive, "a little, fat, powerfully built man in European dress," received them at his palace, Kasr-el-Nil; he was "friendly, and talked with everyone . . . in fairly fluent French," which must have been lost on Ibsen. Von Knorring had an introduction to de Lesseps, who gave him a signed photograph; whether Ibsen accompanied him on his visit to the great man he does not say.

Not content with paying his guests' passages from Paris and back ("Who will finally foot the bill for all this hospitality may be questioned," reflected Lieblein. "Probably the unfortunate fellah, who is already poor enough without our coming and eating his last sheep"), the Khedive, Ismael Pasha, had arranged a three-week expedition for them up the Nile under the guidance of his conservator, the French Egyptologist Mariette Bey, who eighteen years earlier had discovered the subterranean catacombs of the Apis bulls. On the morning of 22 October they set off in three steamers, each towing a *dahaby,* or barge, covered by an awning for the greater comfort of the passengers. Ibsen and von Knorring shared a cabin on the SS *Ferus,* which also carried Lieblein, a Swiss, a Dutchman, and seventeen Germans, whose behaviour was to earn them a derogatory simile in a poem which Ibsen later wrote about the trip and which was to involve him in a controversy in the German press. They tried to insist that the German flag be hoisted on the ship, " 'Scandinavians, Dutchmen, and Swiss being of course pure Germans'; but this was luckily prevented, and we still sail under the crescent of Turkey, whose guests we are. The Germans are frightened lest the French hear of their failure, but the secret is already abroad. . . . The French and German guests are on very uneasy terms." Lieblein found the Prussians "more overbearing than ever after their military exploits of recent years"; only nine months were to elapse before the outbreak of the Franco-Prussian War.

Several of the places they had hoped to visit en route were unfortunately rendered inaccessible by heavy floods, including Gizeh, so that Ibsen, who had written about the Sphinx in *Peer Gynt,* glimpsed it only from afar; also Memphis, Sakkara, the tombs at Beni-Hasan, and the ruins of Abydos. On the second day von Knorring and Ibsen intervened to save an aged

[3] Von Knorring, p. 69.

Arab from being flogged by the ship's dragoman for idleness, an action which earned them the good will of the crew for the remainder of the expedition. One imagines that Captain von Knorring did most of the intervening. That same day they were surprised by a visit from Coptic monks from a monastery, who swam out to them, "climbed up on the stern and asked for *baksheesh*. . . . Since they presented themselves to the passengers in a state of the utmost primitiveness, they had nothing to put the money in but stuffed it all, silver and copper alike, into their mouths."

On the third day they stopped at Roda, where they were shown round a sugar factory employing five thousand workers by the English manager, "with great courtesy." At Assiut they inspected the great tombs. As Ibsen and Lieblein were returning, they "walked along the river bank and came to a great white brick house. Outside the entrance sat two distinguished-looking Arabs. They seemed glad to see us, offered us chairs, and had us served with coffee." One of the Arabs spoke fluent French and explained that this was a school and they the teachers; they invited Lieblein and Ibsen in, and the pupils demonstrated their skill in French and mathematics. Lieblein wrote a message of thanks on the blackboard. Upstairs they were shown a dormitory with a hundred and fifty beds; the pupils wore a kind of military uniform after the French pattern.

In the evening the travellers were entertained, on sofas, to a "Fantasia by Torchlight," songs and dances performed by five expensively dressed and bejewelled girls. "Since this was . . . enacted in the open air," comments Lieblein prudishly, "the dance was reasonably decent, though certain wild Frenchmen did everything to persuade the performers into the licentiousness with which such dances customarily end."

The heat grew intense as they approached the 26th parallel, reaching 28° Reaumur (95° Fahrenheit). The natives hereabouts wore nothing but fig leaves, "a fashion which the Europeans observed with envy, making a few, admittedly incomplete, attempts to imitate it." They visited Kena, where there was more torchlight dancing, and the Hathor Temple at Dendera, and spent the last three days of October in Thebes. Here Ibsen and his companions walked round the twin cities, the Temple City on the east bank and the City of the Dead on the west; they saw the huge statue of Rameses the Great, eleven times lifesize, the Temple of Amon Ra with its one hundred and thirty-four pillars, the Temple of Rameses III at Medinet Habu, the Memnon statue of which Ibsen had written in *Peer Gynt*, and the great tombs. Arabs offered them pieces of mummy for sale, and Ibsen "bought a little woman's hand with a scarab ring. It must have come from a grand lady, perhaps from one of the ancient noble houses of Egypt, and now her hand was being sold for a shilling."[4]

On the third day, 31 October, the Empress Eugénie arrived at Thebes

[4] Conversation with Ibsen recorded by Nordahl Rolfsen in the latter's *Læsebog for folkeskolen*, Part III (Christiania, 1894), and reprinted in C.E., XIX, 191.

amid spectacular ceremony. "It was towards sunset," Ibsen recalled twenty-four years later. "Far in the distance a pillar of smoke approached, rising from the polished river. A handsome great Nile ship glided towards us. This must be the empress. But she was not there. Far, far away, a new pillar of smoke. An even larger ship, white, with silken banners. This *must* be she. No. A new Nile ship, bigger than the others, rose-pink. *Here* she sits, clothed in white, beautiful as Cleopatra, while the setting sun casts its gold over the banners and carpets and silken tents of the ship. Before a year had passed, she would be no mightier than the kings we had just visited."[5]

She was greeted by a firework display and, at six o'clock, a banquet in a specially erected tent which all the guests attended, while the crews and servants were given sheep to roast. They left Thebes the next day, and continued as far as the great cataract, pausing at Esna, Edfu, Gebel Silfilis, Kom Ombo and Assuan, whence they rode on donkeys a short way into Nubia, through the desert to the Isle of Philae, in a temperature of over 100° Fahrenheit. At last, on 6 November, they turned back towards Cairo.

From Assuan to Cairo, with the following current, they travelled "almost with the speed of a railway." The floods had by now subsided sufficiently for them to be able to visit some of the places they had missed on the outward trip, including Luxor and Girgeh, where they had another donkey-ride, this time to inspect the ruins of Abydos. They stopped at Beni-Hasan and Gizeh, where they spent their last night aboard the *Ferus;* next morning, they visited the Great Pyramids and Sakkara, the necropolis of Memphis, to see the Step Pyramid, the oldest of them all. At last, on the evening of 13 November, after twenty-three days on the river, they returned to Cairo.

Ibsen kept a diary of his Egyptian experiences, which has not survived, but on his return to Dresden he began to write an account of his trip. He abandoned this after completing some four thousand words, apparently restless with the medium of direct narrative prose, and a year later summarised his impressions more succinctly in a long poem, "Balloon Letter to a Swedish Lady"—further evidence of the fact that he wrote most comfortably in verse or dialogue. The Egyptian prose fragment—which, apart from the prefaces to *Catiline* and *The Feast at Solhaug*, a few speeches, and his unfinished childhood memoirs, was to be the last prose article that Ibsen would write—is especially interesting for the rare evidence it provides of Ibsen's sharp eye as an observer of landscape:

A kind of soundless peace rules over the landscape of the Nile valley. It possesses something of the Sphinx's dumbness. Today there was no breath of air to be felt save that caused by the ship's progress.

[5] *Loc. cit.*

The river flowed broad and swelling between its double banks of palm groves. Behind them the land rises on both sides towards distant lines of mountains, and everything that the Nile cannot touch, all the yellow limitless waste which glitters and throws its reflection into the air, is the desert: westwards the Libyan, eastwards the Arabian.

On the mudbank, which the falling river reveals, stands here and there a solitary maribou on two stiff legs, drooping its beak and bald head on to its breast with a very human air of melancholy. Herons stalk and pelicans scrabble in the mud, and ibis birds rise from the *durrah* like a flock of white doves.

Within an hour we have sighted the slender minarets of Girgeh before us; but it takes time for the ship to reach them, for the river is full of bends. At last, towards noon, we swing round and lay to. The three other steamers, which travelled more slowly, and had therefore been brought up from Quenneh the previous evening, lay with their *dahabies* or towed barges moored outside the town.

It was a motley picture that now unfolded before us; Europe and the East in a picturesque composition. Directly in front of us stood a minaret, erect and sparkling in the sunlight. Beside it lay the ruin of a Coptic monastery, the whole front of which had collapsed into the river. For the rest, Arab huts, mounds of gravel, palms and sycamores. Inside the ruins of the monastery an Egyptian coffee-house proprietor had established himself; the coffee-room itself lay outside beneath a roof of withered palm branches. Here we see a great concourse; long beards and long pipes are dominant; long Eastern silence and, too, long European chatter. And familiar faces. That handsome, brown-eyed man, who at a distance so strikingly resembles Abdul Kader, and who cannot be acquitted of playing the coquette a little in his elegant silk *koffie* and white-striped Beduin *burnous,* is the archæologist Lenormant. Beside him, alert and friendly, with red fez and sky-blue flannel shirt, sits Dr. Lambert, the Murray and Bædeker of Egypt in one person. That distinguished little white-haired man, with no parasol and his felt hat pulled down like Kilian in *Ulysses von Ithaca,* is the chemist Ballard. Out on the farthest slope of the shore stands Dr. Bertholet, short, robust and jovial, with a thousand items of news to shout to us. A lady glitters, the sole representative of her sex in the party; her dress is European, her proportions oriental. She is of course Madame Collet, the Parisian *literatrice.* For the moment her attention is taken up with her diary, in which our arrival is noted, that the information may be transmitted to an important French magazine. A score of baying dogs send us the usual greeting from the housetops. In doors and corners stand Arab women, staring motionlessly from behind their long black veils, and up the high

gravel mounds hasten the humbler members of the populace, the
fellahs, amid laughter and cries, pursued by policemen who, with
the aid of long palm staves, seek to persuade them to lend us a hand
with the mooring of the ship.

On the voyage up the Nile, I felt for the first time that to belong
to a small nation can have its advantages. Europeans bring bickering
with them wherever they go, and so it is here. The Germans and
French were, however, kind enough to take care of that, so that the
rest of us had our time, and peace of mind, undisturbed. As things
turned out, a few hours of intrigue and counter-intrigue ensured that
our departure to Abydos should be postponed until the following
morning. Only a rebellious minority of seven or eight broke away
during the evening to spend the night among the ruins.

As soon as lunch and its consequent siesta were over I went ashore
to look round the town. Girgeh was in olden times the capital of
Greater Egypt, and is still said to have about thirty thousand inhabitants. It takes its name from St. Girgis, or George, to whose memory
the aforementioned monastery is consecrated. In its time it is reputed
to have been extremely wealthy, and at its peak housed over two
thousand monks. By far the greater part of the population consists,
naturally, of Arabs.

If one can imagine the sites of many burned houses packed together,
everything grey against grey, ramshackle, filthy, chaotic, buried in
dirt and with narrow twisting lanes between, that is a fair picture
of a south Egyptian town. Girgeh is no exception. I wandered among
the bazaars, which were most humbly provided. A few tin and copper
objects, a little pottery of the simplest kind, tobacco, millet, woollen
goods, that was about all. Nor was there any detectable sign of
family life; no friendliness between one human being and another.
The Oriental associates only with his superior or his inferior, never
with his equal; his mind appears bewitched by the same silence and
dumbness which paralyses the landscape. A torpid, dreaming apology
for life seems to veil him. I doubt whether coffee, tobacco, or opium
transport him into any abnormal state of mind; they appear rather to
extend his natural form of existence.

If this is the case, one may easily appreciate what an immense task
faces the government which is attempting to establish an over-all
civilization in this country. The main problem here is not to introduce
temporary improvements into the existing state of things so much as to
recreate the whole spiritual *habitus* of the people, to break down the
prejudices of millennia, even, to some degree, to violate the national
character. Only an uninhibited autocracy could achieve such a trans-
formation. A democratic parliament on the European model would
merely get lost in gentle arguments over human rights; it would, like

the river Nile, swell into an all-obliterating flood, though the resultant mud would scarcely fertilize any field save that of oratory. . . .

A couple of stark naked *fellah* children followed me faithfully on my
saunter, never wearying of repeating: *"Baksheesh!"* A *"Rue!"* or a
"Mafish!" sent them away for a moment; but at the next corner,
there they were again. I walked on through the maize markets outside the town, and beyond them into the desert plain. The sun was
sinking behind a cluster of palm trees, the long shadows of which it
cast towards me on the yellow stretch of sand. Never have I felt
the peace of sunset as here in Egypt. At home, I always found it
oppressive; it made my spirit melancholy and impelled me to seek
company. Here, where the philosophy of the hermit first found expression, one understands this philosophy, just as in Italy one learns
to understand how a man can enter a monastery and be happy there.

At a turning in the road I found a high sandbank between me and
the western sky. On top of it perched several vultures, gnawing the
carrion of a camel. They looked magnificent, sharply outlined against
the background pregnant with light. Further off an Arab woman was
driving her buffalo home; a calf capered behind; on the cow's back
sat a naked brown Arab boy; his young brother was riding on the
woman's shoulder.

The road led back to the Nile. There, all was life and merriment.
The Levantines in our crew were playing leapfrog, while the natives
stood around in great droves, watching; seriousness and decorum
were cast aside as one salvo of laughter followed another. During
all this, night fell, and long lines of pitch torches were lit in honour
of us foreigners. On board, the signal was sounded to announce
that our evening meal was ready.

The night that followed was miraculous; its beauty grew and grew.
The stars leaped forth, full and round on the transparent blue-black
sky. A flat mist lay over the Nile valley, and redesigned the landscape
into a gigantic bay, bounded on the south by mighty mountains.
Now and then a barge glided past with the current. A paper lantern
glowed large and red on the prow; the monotonous rhythmical song
of the crew was borne to us and died away far down the river. We
Scandinavians had gathered in silence; I am sure our thoughts
were in the north. In such an hour one wishes to be reconciled
with all mortals, and asks oneself: "How have you deserved to witness
all this beauty?" I felt that they stood before me, all those many
at home who annually perform their silent task—all those who have
a need and craving for what lies outside their sphere, but who must
renounce that craving and tread the millwheel of their days to the
end. Well, it was not long before I had to admit that we, too, had
our cross to bear; for it was after midnight, and time to grope

our way down into our torture chamber with its mosquitoes and its policemen snoring against the threshold.

At 4:30 the next morning the reveille sounded. Two negroes, our servants' servants, ran round the ship creating a fearful din with fire-tongs and frying-pans. Swiftly we performed our toilet and ate our breakfast. It was still dark, but with a faint shimmer of daylight in the east. On the shore could be discerned a confused throng of asses, horses, camels and Arabs, who had been organized to escort us to Abydos. Each of us selected a beast and driver, and the company broke up singly or into small groups. I had acquired a well-saddled donkey with an Arab attendant who had managed to learn some words of *lingua franca*, and to whom I could therefore, with the occasional assistance of Italian, make myself understood.

We rode southwards, with the Nile on our left, and within a few minutes were outside the town. A dry stony plain lay before us; clumps of palm trees could be indistinctly glimpsed in the morning mist, and the stars grew even fainter. After half an hour's ride we came to a canal, which had been dug right across the plain, and across which, by means of a ferry of the most primitive kind, expecting every moment to sink and in the most perilous confusion, we were shipped to the farther bank. Here we continued our way along an endless dyke, beside another canal at a right angle to the first. The landscape was very monotonous. Great plains of maize stretched on the other side of the water as far as the eye could see; a solitary sycamore or a clump of palm trees stood here and there upon the plain, and at the field's edge a native family had erected its brown woollen tent, with a pack of dogs baying at the entrance. On the slope of the dyke clambered a flock of goats. Yellow-grey, with narrow faces and shoulders, and long ears hanging down like corkscrews, they bore a striking resemblance to English lady travellers. A native woman ferried herself across the canal in a strange vessel, woven of branches and resembling a large inverted bottle-basket; it was filled with empty clay pots to give buoyancy, and was hauled to and fro by means of two fibre ropes.

The dyke on which our road lay stretched in a straight line as far as the eye could see. The sun came up over the splendid mountains on the other side of the Nile. The innumerable birds of Egypt began to stir; suddenly they were flying in all directions, but quite soundlessly: no cries, no song, no twitter.

Our caravan made an imposing procession. Warriors with drawn sabres mounted on Arab horses sped back and forth, as though some calamity were imminent. In the centre of our line rode the leader of our expedition, the famous Egyptologist Lepsius, with his Jovian head of youthful white curls, on a handsome ass with red velvet saddle hangings, surrounded by officials from Girgeh. "Leps, Leps!" whispered the natives as he rode past; everyone knew him from his three-year sojourn here, just as the scientific world knows him from his twelve-volume work on those travels and discoveries. His young and very tall Swiss colleague, Herr Naville, bore himself impressively on an almost unnaturally large thoroughbred, sent him by a rich Copt of these parts. The native herdsmen drove their buffalo away from the dyke and out into the canal; others stood motionless on the verge of the road, staring after us, leaning on their long palm staves.

After an hour's ride we came on several hundred natives, mostly children, who had been driven in from the surrounding villages to improve the road and, especially, to render a collapsed bridge passable. It undeniably looked somewhat fragile as they built it before our eyes of branches and Nile mud, with of course no handrails; and I do not think I was the only person who felt a certain queasiness at the prospect of crossing it on ass-back. But all went well, and we emerged on to a richly fertile and well-tended plain with newly planted avenues and numberless groves of unusually luxuriant trees. A pleasant village lay on our right hand, surrounded by a ditch, where a crowd of natives slaked their thirst and washed their legs amid sociable chatter. Farther out in the plain lay the town of Bardies, the newly whitewashed houses of which, half-overgrown with a wonderful abundance of creepers, gave it the appearance of an immense floral display. A place I would happily have settled in! The inhabitants, evidently instructed, lined their houses and garden walls and greeted us civilly as we rode by. At every fork in the road guards were posted. Everything here suggested an unusually well-ordered communal life; many Copts live in the area.

We came to another huge Nile dyke, and were soon riding as though on a mole in the middle of a huge bay. Admittedly the floods were subsiding, but they were still considerable enough to give one an idea of how they must be at their peak. Here, as elsewhere, one no longer wonders at the information that the Nile annually emits into the sea a volume of water five times that of the Danube.

Suddenly we noticed that our outriders had halted, and as we came up with them we stood there in a tight group, unable to proceed farther. To allow the flood waters free access to the plain the dyke had been breached to a width of about a hundred yards, and there below us lay two Nile barges making their humble preparations to ferry us over. It was an indescribable scene, all noise and confusion; everyone wanted to be first into the boats, the horses reared and kicked as they were driven aboard with sticks, the donkeys were literally thrown down into the vessels, the Europeans swore and the natives shrieked at each other like madmen. The water swirled through the gap in the dyke, and the boats swung across, aided by a tattered rope. A similar scene ensued when we landed; first one saw riderless donkeys and horses, then riders with nothing to ride; for some of the attendants were still waiting to embark, and we had no choice but to give chase to our long-eared mounts, which had straightway set forth along the dyke at a steady trot.

Gradually the terrain began to rise, the arable soil ceased, and we rode into the desert, which stretched for miles towards the western range of mountains. A solitary Arab hut stood in the sea of sand; by its wall stood a water trough; it was an old sarcophagus. On the roof stood a dog and a camel was tethered a short way from the house, standing there motionless with its back to the sun. Its eyes squinted after us as we rode by; otherwise it did not move.

The desert is not completely flat. Here and there it rises in gentle waves, and on these the sand is driven together in sharp crests, like the snow with us. One cannot of course traverse these, but must find a way round. But one seldom encounters this problem, as the drivers know instinctively which route to follow.

Thus we rode on, singly or in long lines; sun and sand trembled hotly against each other, as one might imagine a sea of molten metal. Our parasols gave scant protection, and gradually we gave one article of clothing after another to our drivers' keeping. Far to the south several dark mounds protruded into the air, and all our eyes were directed towards these; for they were the burial mounds, which over several millennia had gathered height so that they towered over ancient Abydos.

As is known, in olden times several places were named Abydos. The name arose here as the result of a Greek corruption of the Egyptian word *Ebot;* now the Arabs who live in the area call it *el matfun,* which means "the buried place." And burials there are, with a vengeance. A gathering of sand dunes sixty to eighty feet high adorn this immense city, which ancient authors described as the mightiest in Egypt after Thebes; when it is excavated, it will be that country's Pompeii.

Abydos seems, like other Egyptian cities, to have been a necropolis, a place of burial as well as a city for the living. Here was discovered the grave of Osiris, and accordingly for thousands of years all rich Egyptians had themselves buried here that they might rest with their god and king in the earth he had sanctified. Many grave writings bear witness to this, and several of these date right back to the sixteenth dynasty, that is to say, 3,700 years ago.

A stream had cut its course through the desert immediately below the town; here we rode along a poor strip of grass beneath sycamores and acacias. The mounds became more and more frequent, especially on our left. Here the *fellahs* were engaged in the famous excavations under the guidance of Mariette Bey, the Khedive's principal Egyptologist and the supervisor of all antiquities in the Nile valley. To the uninitiated, the work which this man is doing seems strange . . .

There, as tantalisingly as with his unfinished childhood memoirs, the fragment ends. Ibsen was able to write sharp and sensitive narrative prose; one can only surmise that it bored him, and that—which was his strength as a dramatist—he disliked writing in the first person, except under the mask of verse.

After returning to Cairo, the Khedive's guests rested for thirty-six hours before leaving by train for Alexandria, early on the morning of 15 November. There, trouble awaited them. A hundred guests needed transport to Port Said, where the Canal was to be ceremonially opened, and the steamer was found to have room for only fifty. No extra ship could be organized before the following day, so Lieblein and some others, including Ibsen, persuaded the authorities to lay on a special train to take them overland to Ismailia. It arrived there in oriental style six hours behind schedule, but by sailing up the still officially unopened Canal they managed to arrive at Port Said in time for the beginning of the festivities on 16 November. These were inaugurated with a double religious service, Catholic and Muslim, attended by the Empress Eugénie and the Emperor Franz Josef of Austria. The following day, Wednesday, 17 November, the Suez Canal was declared open.

At nine in the morning the procession of ships began to enter the Canal, led by the Empress in *L'Aigle*. The Scandinavians travelled in the Danish corvette *Nordstjernen;* this should have gone with the second group of ships, but to their annoyance they had to wait while the third, fourth and fifth groups steamed past, "doubtless," comments Lieblein, "because the small nations have to stand aside for the big." They did not get started until the next day, when further trouble awaited them, for the Egyptian ship in front of them went aground twice, so that the journey to Ismailia, which should have taken seven to eight hours, occupied three days. Determined not to miss the celebrations at Ismailia, the Scandinavians abandoned the Danish vessel and transferred to a barge towed by a small steamer, which, proceeding at "the pace of a tortoise,"[6] got them there just in time.

Lieblein describes the scene at Ismailia as being "like a story from the Thousand and One Nights," a phrase which Ibsen was later to borrow. "The whole town and harbour [writes Lieblein] glittered with light and colour. Ships, quays and the town were brilliantly illuminated, fireworks were exploded, and everything was decked with the flags of all the nations." Tents had been erected everywhere; the huge crowds included people of "every race and country"; there were carriages, camels, donkeys, European brass bands, orchestras playing dance music, and Asian flutes and pipes. In the evening a great ball was held in a palace especially built by the Khedive for the occasion; some of the furnishings had evidently arrived only just in time, for the huge wall mirrors from Europe

---

[6] Ibsen to Nordahl Rolfsen, C.E., XIX, 192.

were "still uncleaned and bearing the makers' labels." The dancing continued until three in the morning.

All this must have been heady stuff for Ibsen; and shortly before he had left Port Said to sail down the Canal, a letter had been handed to him on the quayside which, in that setting at that moment, must more than ever have underlined the narrowness and pettiness of life back home in Norway.

A month earlier, on 18 October, the day after Ibsen had first arrived in Cairo, *The League of Youth* had received its first performance at the Christiania Theatre. The political implications of the play, which by then had been in the bookshops for nearly three weeks, were already one of the chief talking points in the capital. Ibsen was later to protest that his characters were not meant to represent specific individuals ("There is a big difference between using someone as a model and directly portraying them"), but it had become a parlour game in Christiania to try to identify the models, and it was of little comfort to those selected that traits of other politicians were to be found in the same character. Stensgaard's facile eloquence, his readiness to make a patriotic speech at the drop of a hat, and his repeated invocation of the Almighty, were irresistibly reminiscent of Bjørnson; and his penchant for proposing to rich ladies was a well-known characteristic of another of the liberal leaders, Ole Richter. Johan Sverdrup, who shared Bjørnson's love of speechifying, was declared by others to be the original of Stensgaard; and Lundestad, the rich farmer, was generally assumed to be a caricature of Ueland, the leader of the Peasants' faction in the liberal party.

The play, in short, as William Archer observed, offended the entire progressive front.[7] Ten days before its publication Bjørnson had broken his silence towards Ibsen by writing to him to tell him how much he was looking forward to reading it; but when he did, it struck him, not unnaturally, as a stab in the back for freedom. *"The League of Youth,"* he declared later, "tried to paint our young freedom-loving party as a mob of speculating mountebanks." "Ibsen's play," he wrote to Rudolf Schmidt on 30 November, "seems to assert that the young Norway is an intriguing and self-seeking society which abuses the name of freedom to satisfy its own ambition and covetousness"; and he expressed his resentment to Sverdrup in an eloquent verse:

> If poesy's sacred grove be made
> The assassin's hiding-place, if this
> The new poetic fashion is
> Then I for one renounce its shade.[8]

Twelve years later, in 1881, Bjørnson explained what he meant by this term. "It was not the portrayal of contemporary life and known personages

---

[7] Introduction to *The League of Youth* (London, 1907), p. x.

[8] Edmund Gosse's translation.

that I called assassination. It was the fact that *The League of Youth* sought to represent our young liberal party as a gang of ambitious speculators, whose patriotism was as empty as their phraseology; and particularly, that prominent men were at first rendered recognizable, and then had false hearts and shady characters foisted on them."[9]

Ibsen later told Henrik Jæger that Stensgaard was not specifically based on Bjørnson, Richter, or Sverdrup, but that "in the Norwegian Society he had had the opportunity to study the liberal jargon of the time. There was then a group of not very talented people in Christiania who were Bjørnson's sworn admirers and who caricatured his mode of expression."[10] And he protested to Hegel that the play was an attack, not upon true liberalism, but on demagogy: "Bjørnson . . . must surely realize that it isn't he but his damnable and lie-steeped clique that have served me as models."[11] But (to quote Archer again), "it is difficult to see how Ibsen can have expected Bjørnson to distinguish very clearly between an attack on his 'lie-steeped' clique and a lampoon on himself. . . . The case, in fact, seems to have been very like that of the portraiture of Leigh Hunt in Harold Skimpole [in *Bleak House*]. Both Dickens and Ibsen had unconsciously taken more from their respective models than they intended. They imagined, perhaps, that the features which did not belong to the original would conceal the likeness; whereas their actual effect was only to render the portraits libellous."[12]

Ibsen's apparent betrayal of the progressive cause seemed all the more ungrateful when it was recalled that Bjørnson had organized the fund for Ibsen five years earlier, and that both Richter and Sverdrup had been among the subscribers, as well as signing the petition for him to be awarded a Civil List pension. To quote Archer a third time, the cleavage between the right and the left was now at its sharpest in Norway, not merely in politics but also in religion, literature and even art; no one was regarded as an independent, and so Ibsen, to his embarrassment, found himself hailed as a champion of conservatism, a charge which had also (as we have seen) been levelled against him in Stockholm. As a consequence, the atmosphere on the opening night resembled that of a political meeting. This is how Suzannah described it in the letter which Ibsen received on the quayside at Port Said:

Dresden, 29 October 1869

Dear Ibsen,

I have received your letters, from which I see that you are having the best possible time. Sigurd says it is that thought which comforts him, and I say the same, take and enjoy everything which is offered you, one is not a king's guest every day.

---

[9] Archer's translation (introduction to *The League of Youth*, p. x).
[10] Midbøe, p. 151.
[11] Letter to Hegel, 14 December 1869.
[12] Archer, introduction to *The League of Youth*, pp. x–xi.

But while you are enjoying the splendour of the south, there is a terrible storm in Christiania over *The League of Youth*. The first evening the first three acts were greeted with loud applause, but in the fourth act when Bastian says his line about what the nation is,[13] the gallery started to whistle, led by a few students who are fighting for the new language. What do you think of that?

According to *Morgenbladet* the evening went brilliantly, Krohn's and Isachsen's performances[14] were works of art, all the company were called, *Morgenbladet* printed several excellent reports. The evening ended with thunderous applause.

But then came the second evening, your benefit performance. They had already decided in advance that things were going to start now; the house was sold out, as soon as Lundestad finished his first speech the whistles began, time after time they were drowned by applause, but they would not stop. The curtain had to come down. The director had to come forward and ask for quiet so that the play could continue, and the commotion so grew that after the performance was over the lights had to be put out. . . . But your play has not suffered . . .[15]

Indeed it had not. Within ten days of the premiere, the sales of the book had been such that Hegel had already brought out a second edition; and so heavy was the demand for tickets at the theatre that seats were even sold in the space normally reserved for the orchestra. The violent demonstrations continued, however; the atmosphere in the theatre was that of an angry debating-chamber. Ibsen's later plays were to arouse far more widespread debate than *The League of Youth*, but none was to provoke audiences to such immediate and noisy hostility. Ibsen carefully kept every hostile criticism. "My enemies have helped me so much," he is said to have remarked. "They protested so much that in the end people wanted to know who this man was whom everyone was always abusing."[16] On his return to Dresden, he recorded his reaction to these events in a poem, "At Port Said":

> The eastern dawn
> Rose on the harbour.
> The flags of the nations
> Hung from the masts.
> The sound of music
> Preceded the hymn;
> A thousand cannon
> Baptised the Canal.

[13] "The people who have nothing and are nothing, who lie in chains."

[14] Krohn played Lundestad, Isachsen, Aslaksen. Johannes Brun was Daniel Hejre, Laura Gundersen Selma, Arnoldus Reimers Stensgaard, and Lucie Wolf Mrs. Rundholmen.

[15] Cf. Bergliot Ibsen, pp. 44-45.

[16] *Ibid.*, p. 42.

The steamers moved
Past the obelisk.
Whispers reached me
In my mother tongue.
The mirror I had polished
For male coquettes
Had been dirtied there
By a shower of saliva.

The gadfly bit me;
Memories stirred.
Bright star, I thank thee!
My home hasn't changed.
We hailed the frigate
From our small deck.
I waved my hand
And saluted the flag.

To the feasting, on!
Though the snake spit venom.
A chosen guest
Through the Bitter Lakes.
As the day dies, quenched,
Dreaming I slumber
Where Pharaoh drowned
And Moses passed over.

By the time he reached Ismailia, Ibsen had had enough of Egypt. Leaving Lieblein and von Knorring to enjoy another month of the Khedive's hospitality, he returned to Cairo, took the train to Alexandria and embarked for Marseilles. By the end of November he was back in Paris, where he stayed for a fortnight at his own expense. These two weeks provide another infuriating lacuna in our knowledge of Ibsen's life. No letters from him while he was there have survived; we know only that he spent much time visiting art galleries and exhibitions. What did he see? He was five years too early for the first Impressionist exhibition, but he might possibly have noticed the odd painting by Manet or Monet, who had begun to exhibit in 1861 and 1865 respectively; and one would like to think that he may have wandered in for a drink at the Café Guerbois on the Avenue de Clichy, where the future Impressionists (the name had not yet been coined) habitually gathered that year. But art galleries and exhibitions close soon after dark; how did he spend his later hours? Did he (we must remember his almost total ignorance of French) go to the theatre? Did he visit other, less decorous, places of entertainment? We do not know. He told no one; or if he did, they have not told us. In the middle of December he rejoined Suzannah and Sigurd in Dresden.

13

Doubts and Hesitations

1870

Whatever the limitations of Ibsen's physical courage may have been, he revelled in hostile criticism. "The reception of *The League of Youth*," he wrote to Frederik Hegel on 14 December 1869, shortly after his return to Dresden, "delights me. I was prepared for opposition to it, and would have been disappointed had there been none. . . . I will write to him [Bjørnson] today or tomorrow, and hope the affair will, despite all our differences, end in a reconciliation." But he does not seem to have written any such letter, and it is difficult to imagine that by this time it would have had any effect, except to add fuel to the flames. He was already meditating a successor to *The League of Youth:* "I am planning a new, serious, contemporary drama in three acts; I expect to start work on it in the very near future." Of his visit to Egypt he had little to say. "I had a pleasant journey. I got right down into Nubia and the Red Sea, underwent many experiences and met many interesting people. But it is best to sit quietly at home and look back on it all."

"I shall probably come up to Christiania in the summer," he informed his brother-in-law, Johan Thoresen, on 17 December. Year after year he toyed with the idea of revisiting Norway, without bringing himself to take the plunge. The reaction to *The League of Youth* must have confirmed his conviction that a writer did best to study his subject matter from a distance. "From the attacks that I read," he wrote to Jonas Collin on 4 January 1870, "it seems that in Norway people regard empty phrase-making, hollowness and mean-mindedness as national characteristics which are therefore sacrosanct. But none of this bothers me in the least."

Ibsen was not the only foreign writer who was studying his subject matter from a distance in Dresden that year. One wonders whether he ever noticed a short, bearded Russian, even smaller than himself,[1] who

[1] Dostœvsky stood five feet six inches, Ibsen about five feet seven and a half.

haunted the art galleries and theatres (which he found poor), and consumed in the cafés great quantities of ice cream, for which he had a passion. From August 1869 until July 1871 Fyodor Dostœvsky was living in Dresden, at Viktoria-Strasse in the English quarter, not very far from Ibsen, writing *The Possessed* and heartily disliking both the city and its inhabitants, who were for ever short-changing him in the shops and restaurants and misdirecting him in the streets. "Dresden is a very dull place," he complained to a friend in December 1869, the month Ibsen returned from Egypt. "I can't bear these Germans." His working routine was very different from Ibsen's, though equally rigid. "I get up at one o'clock in the afternoon because I do my work at night. I work from 3 to 5 P.M., then go for half an hour's walk to the post office and back through the Royal Gardens—always the same route. We dine at home and then I go out for another walk and back home through the Royal Gardens again. At home I have tea and at half-past ten sit down to work and usually work till five o'clock in the morning. Then I go to bed and punctually on the stroke of six fall asleep. That is my life."[2]

Since Ibsen, too, liked to walk in the Gardens, and both men frequented the cafés on the Brühl Terrace, the two must surely have seen each other; but Dostœvsky would not, any more than most other non-Scandinavians, have heard of Ibsen, and although Ibsen must at least have heard of Dostœvsky, who had already published *Crime and Punishment* and *The Idiot,* the latter's presence in Dresden seems to have been known to very few. Nearly thirty years later Ibsen was to name *Crime and Punishment* as the Russian novel which attracted him most[3]—and he was a great admirer of the Russian novelists, especially of Turgenev and even (despite Tolstoy's hatred of him) of *Anna Karenina.* But we do not know whether he had yet read Dostœvsky when they were neighbours in Dresden.

The "contemporary drama" referred to in Ibsen's letter to Hegel of 14 December must have been *The Pillars of Society,* for his first notes for that play date from this year. "The main theme," he recorded, "must be how women sit modestly in the background while the men busily pursue their petty aims with an assurance that at once infuriates and impresses." But he found unusual difficulty in (as he had written in another context) "getting the beast under him." On 25 January he informed Hegel that he hoped to have it ready by the following October, but two and a half months later he had to tell him that it had not yet got beyond the draft "and since I have to put my travel notes in order it looks like being delayed for some time." (He had promised articles on Egypt to both *Morgenbladet* and *Dansk Tidsskrift,* but never completed

[2] David Magarshack, *Dostœvsky* (London, 1962), p. 405. For other information on Dostœvsky's life in Dresden, see *The Diary of Dostœvsky's Wife* (London, 1928), pp. 35-172.

[3] Interview with Hans Tostrup in *Ørebladet,* 19 March 1898, reprinted in C.E., XIX, 211-15. For Tolstoy's opinion of Ibsen, see pp. 600-1.

them.) When October arrived, so far from having the play ready he could only tell Hegel that it had "sufficiently developed in my mind for me to hope that any day now I may be able to start writing it."

It was in fact to be a further seven years before he completed this next work, an extraordinary period of silence for one who had written three successful plays in five years and who was to be so prolific for the remainder of his life. Nor can it be explained away by the stumbling-block of *Emperor and Galilean*. This long gestation has been much debated by commentators; *The League of Youth*, it has been argued, shows that he had already and painlessly made the decision to abandon poetic drama for prose. Yet the reason is surely plain to see, and Georg Brandes, whose entry into Ibsen's life at this period was to be so important to both of them, stated it. Ibsen's artistic instincts, Brandes wrote in his autobiography, "were unconsciously leading him in the direction of modern prose drama. He was to remain silent for several years while these new efforts were taking shape within him. Admittedly he had written the sharply modern satire, *The League of Youth*, in 1869, but without the intent of striking out a new path; which was why he straightway turned back to the distant past (in *Emperor and Galilean*)."[4]

The key word here is *unconsciously*. Commentators may argue whether *The League of Youth* is the first of Ibsen's "new" dramas, or a bridge between the old and the new. The point is that Ibsen himself did not yet know in which direction he was moving. He had not yet taken the decision to abandon poetry for prose; he was to arrive at that standpoint slowly and agonizingly over the next few years, and the long gestation of *The Pillars of Society*, the gathering, revision and publication of his poems, and the unusually flawed quality of *Emperor and Galilean*, are all evidence of the struggle within him, and of the hesitation with which he took that momentous step. Abandoning poetry, in which he felt so free, for prose, in which he felt so constricted, was for Ibsen like abandoning the Mediterranean to return to Norway. Georg Brandes was to remark that "some time during the battle of life, a lyrical Pegasus must have been killed under him."[5] It would be truer to say that he shot it himself, and that from this action, much as we may regret that *Brand* and *Peer Gynt* were to have no successors, the whole of modern prose drama was to stem.

Ibsen's shortage of acquaintances in Dresden, which had chafed him during his first months there, seemed now not to bother him. On 6 March 1870 he addressed a few words of fatherly advice on the subject to Georg Brandes, now being reviled in Copenhagen for his open liaison with Caroline David, a lady who had left her husband (and whose daughter Marie, twenty-one years later, was to be accused by Strindberg, probably for once justifiably, of having a Lesbian affair with the latter's wife Siri).

[4] Georg Brandes, *Levned*, II (Copenhagen, 1907), p. 103.
[5] Georg Brandes, *Henrik Ibsen*, p. 64. (Muir-Archer translation).

Brandes's letters to Ibsen have, like so many others which Ibsen received, disappeared, but he had evidently pictured himself as a kind of Ishmael.

"You say you have no friends at home," wrote Ibsen. "I have often supposed this to be the case with you. When one stands, as you do, in so intensely personal a relationship to one's life-work, one cannot really expect to keep one's friends. But I think it is, in the long run, good for you that you are setting out[6] without leaving any friends behind. Friends are an expensive luxury; and when one invests one's capital in a calling or mission in this life, one cannot afford to have friends. The expensive thing about friends is not what one does for them but what, out of consideration for them, one leaves undone. Many spiritual ambitions have been crippled thus. I have been through this, and that is why I had to wait for several years before I succeeded in being myself."

He returned to this theme in other letters that spring and summer, and the unusual emotion with which he, normally so uncommunicative a correspondent, expatiated on it seems further evidence of the split which was beginning to widen in his creative personality. On 29 May he warned Magdalene Thoresen (from whose clutches Brandes had only recently escaped, and who was now unsuccessfully refocussing her attentions on Bjørnson) against being over-sensitive to criticism. "Most critical objections," he assured her, "boil down to a reproach against the writer for being himself, thinking, feeling, seeing and writing as himself, instead of seeing and writing as the critic would have done, had he been able. The essential thing is to protect one's essential self, to keep it pure and free of all intrusive elements, and to draw a clear distinction between what one has merely experienced and what one has spiritually *lived through;* for only the latter is proper matter for creative writing."

During the spring, a young Norwegian girl named Laura Petersen had published an emotional contribution to the debate on women's rights in the form of an imaginary sequel to *Brand* entitled *Brand's Daughters.* She sent Ibsen a copy, which one would have expected him to ignore or, at best, formally acknowledge; but young girls sometimes brought out the cavalier in him, or anyway the father-figure, and on 11 June he wrote her a long and kindly reply. "Are you thinking of continuing to write?" he enquired. "Much more is needed than mere talent. One must have something to create from, some geniune experience. If one lacks that, one doesn't write in the true sense, one just makes books. . . . Intellectually, man is a long-sighted animal; we see most clearly from a distance; details distract; one must remove oneself from what one wishes to judge; one describes the summer best on a winter's day. . . . The main thing is to be true and faithful to oneself. It is not a question of willing to go in this

[6] Brandes was about to embark on a long and fruitful European tour, which was to bring him the friendship of Taine, Renan and, especially, John Stuart Mill.

direction or that, but of willing what one absolutely must, because one is oneself and cannot do otherwise. The rest is only lies."

To be true and faithful to oneself, to will what one must; this, more perhaps than anything, was to be the theme of all Ibsen's future work. Nora gave herself at any rate a chance of salvation by following her own convictions; Mrs. Alving was destroyed because she did not follow hers, but stayed with the husband she despised. Yet Ibsen, even this early in his career, knew that to follow one's convictions may end in self-destruction; Julian the Apostate and Rebecca West destroyed themselves thus, and who knows whether Nora's life ended more happily than Mrs. Alving's? To write in verse for the printed page, as in *Brand* and *Peer Gynt*, which had brought him fame with a comparative minimum of controversy, or to write in prose for performance, which had stirred up a hornets' nest about his head? To remain in exile or to return home? The easy course would have been to continue in the medium of verse drama for reading, but in artistic matters Ibsen was never to take the easy course, any more than he was ever to take the easy way out of a fifth act. He was never to write the same play twice, never to repeat a success; he was to remain for ever the most restless of experimentalists.

The problem of whether or not to return to Norway crops up as frequently in Ibsen's letters of this period as the importance of being oneself, a question of which, in Ibsen's case, it was of course part. He knew well that he could never deny the Norwegian in him, or turn his back, as other self-exiled writers had done, on the country that had at first rejected and now at last acclaimed him.[7] "I long to come northwards," he wrote to Ole Schulerud's widow on 9 June (in the letter already partly quoted),[8] "if only for a short while—I have grave doubts about settling permanently up there. I fear it would cramp my activity. . . . Everything that is irrelevant or transitory acquires undeserved significance when one stands in the midst of the tumult; or so I have always felt. I have wandered widely since we parted. I have lived and travelled in Italy for about five years; then two years in various places in Germany. I have, as you may perhaps know, also been in Egypt; have travelled all the way down into Nubia; have sat by the Red Sea and looked across to Sinai. Yet I feel more Norwegian in my soul than ever before; you must not believe, as so many do, that I feel hostile towards my native land. It is the excrescences on our social existence which I hate; but

---

[7] He retained, like so many exiles, a nostalgic longing for the simple food of his homeland. Several times in his letters he begs friends to send him *gammelost*, the pungent Norwegian cheese, and on 22 January 1871, complaining of the lack of fresh fish in Dresden, he asked a chemist acquaintance in Trondhjem to send him a cask of a north Norwegian speciality: "a very delicate fish called redfish, rosefish, rose-perch or some such name."

[8] See pp. 173–74.

they are not organic to it." And he concluded his letter to Laura Petersen: "Sooner or later I shall come to Norway. . . . You must not think
me so ill-disposed towards my countrymen as many assert; and in any
case I can assure you that I am no more tolerant towards myself than
towards others. . . ."

If Ibsen was getting nothing written that spring and summer of 1870,
at least *The League of Youth* was being more widely performed
than any of his previous plays. On 11 December it had been staged in
Stockholm, at the Royal Theatre, and had been a success, for Sweden
too had its Stensgaards in political life. In Copenhagen it at first seemed
no more likely to get produced than anything else he had written. The
censor of the Royal Theatre, old Carsten Hauch, an early befriender of
Brandes but somewhat conservative in his literary judgments, reported
to his board that the author had "adopted an unfortunately fragmentary
style which constantly, as it were, chops the dialogue into pieces," complained that "one has to know about all the humbug which can be performed with false bills of hand, and the mysteries of fraud, to be able to
follow the action and fully comprehend it," and concluded: "The play is
totally unsuited to the theatre." But the board, doubtless mindful of the full
houses the play was attracting in Christiania, asked Hauch to think again,
whereupon he grudgingly admitted that, despite the "chaotic obscurity and
formlessness from which the play, in my view, so sadly suffers," since
the board felt that "the play must possess some significance as a political
satire which it lacks æsthetically," he would not oppose its production.[9]
Johanne Luise Heiberg herself directed it, and it received its premiere
in Copenhagen on 16 February 1870, the first Ibsen play to be performed
in Denmark; and here, as in Christiania and Stockholm, despite some
critical disapproval, it proved a success.

Ibsen spent the spring in a leisurely revision of *The Pretenders* for
republication by Gyldendal, a task which principally involved amending the
spelling so as to conform with the recommendations of the Stockholm
orthographic conference. He also altered a few phrases to read more
particularly and less generally, in deference to the objection Brandes had
made on that score. When July came he packed Suzannah and Sigurd
off for a holiday in Teplitz and, doubtless encouraged by his reception in
Stockholm the previous summer and by the success of *The League of
Youth* in Denmark, went off to be lionized in Copenhagen. He sailed
from Lübeck on 19 July, a momentous day for Europe, for it marked
the outbreak of the Franco-Prussian War. Brandes, unfortunately, was in
England, being horrified by the poverty, disappointed with Oxford and
with the theatres and ladies of London, enjoying the Zoo and Kew Gardens
and talking French (since his English was poor) with John Stuart Mill at

---

[9] Edvard Agerholm, "Henrik Ibsen og Det Kgl. Teater," in *Gads Danske Magasin*
(Copenhagen, 1910–11), p. 278.

Blackheath. But Ibsen met his publisher, Frederik Hegel, for the first time, and renewed two acquaintances which he had fleetingly made on his study visit eighteen years before, with Johanne Luise Heiberg and Hans Christian Andersen.

Hegel had received a neurotic letter from Bjørnson warning him about his guest and concluding: "Beware of Ibsen! He is ungrateful, and a man who is that is capable of anything!"[10] But he had by now doubtless learned to discount whatever the two writers said about each other, and he took excellent care of Ibsen throughout the latter's stay, though he never, during their long friendship, managed to penetrate Ibsen's reserve. "Ibsen is an extremely courteous man and pleasant to do business with," he wrote eleven years later, "but very cautious and withdrawn, and I have the feeling that I haven't got any closer to him now than in 1866 when I had the honour to publish *Brand* for the first time—and that saddens me."[11]

Hans Andersen[12] was eager to meet the new dramatist, having apparently forgotten their brief encounter in 1852. On 11 August he noted in his diary: "Fru Melchior told me that the poet Ibsen was dining today with Carl Bloch, and expressed surprise that I had not been invited. I was put in a bad humour by the thought of how little attention B. had paid to me."[13] "I wasn't there," he wrote the next day to Henriette Collin, "but would have liked to have been invited, to see at last this Norwegian poet who doesn't like the Norwegians."[14] A week later he got his wish, when Moritz Gerson Melchior, a politician in whose eighteenth-century house overlooking the Sound Andersen had, by a generous arrangement, a permanent suite of three or four rooms, gave a party for the two writers. Andersen tried to prepare himself for the meeting with a little homework, and the result depressed him. "Read *Peer Gynt*," he noted in his diary for 18 August, "which is written by a mad poet. One goes crazy oneself reading this book. The poetry isn't good either, there

[10] *Gro-tid,* II, 356.

[11] Nielsen, I, 297.

[12] Edmund Gosse, who met Andersen at the Melchiors two years later, recorded a vivid impression of him: "a very tall, elderly gentleman, dressed in a complete suit of brown, and in a curly wig of the same shade of snuff-colour. I was almost painfully struck, at the first moment, by the grotesque ugliness of his face and hands, and by his enormously long and swinging arms; but this impression passed away as soon as he began to speak. . . . Gentleness and ingenuousness breathed from everything he said. . . . He had but to speak, almost to smile, and the man of genius stood revealed." Andersen read a story to Gosse but lost his voice during the conversation that ensued and had to be "conducted to his bed with infinite precautions." Gosse especially remembered his "amazingly long and bony hand—a great brown hand, almost like that of a man of the wood—grasping my shoulder as he read to me." (*Two Visits to Denmark,* pp. 97–100.)

[13] *H. C. Andersens Brevveksling med Edvard og Henriette Collin,* ed. C. Behrend and H. Topsøe-Jensen (Copenhagen, 1933–37), IV, 163.

[14] *Loc. cit.*

is something sick and distraught about the whole thing. Am sorry I read it, as Ibsen is coming here this evening for the first time. I've never seen him; he's said to be taciturn and gloomy."[15] But the occasion passed off unexpectedly well, for the diary continues: "After dinner he arrived with Bloch, and made a good impression. . . . He talked well and amiably. We all liked him."

Andersen's diary conceals how close the evening came to being a disaster. According to John Paulsen, who had the story from Ibsen himself:

Many of the city's most notable personages were among the guests. Everyone had arrived and was ready to sit down, but no Andersen descended from his rooms upstairs. A quarter of an hour passed, half an hour; a nervous restlessness settled on the company, and the hostess looked unhappy. Message after message was sent up, but he still did not appear. The hostess quietly went upstairs, but returned with a more worried expression than before. He would not come down. No one said anything to the guest of honour, but Ibsen sensed what was afoot. Andersen did not like to be with people of whose sympathy he was not sure. When people mentioned strange authors he would naïvely ask: "Does he admire me?" The atmosphere grew more embarrassed. It was now three-quarters of an hour past the appointed time for supper. The host and hostess were at a loss what to do. Were they to sit down without Andersen?

Then Ibsen saved the situation. He took his host aside and asked to be allowed to go up to Andersen's room and speak with him. The host nodded and showed him the way. A minute later, to the joyful surprise of the company, the two great writers entered the room arm in arm, Andersen evidently deeply moved, smiling through his tears. He was like a small child who has got his way.

"But what happened between you and Andersen in his room?" I asked Ibsen. Ibsen smiled at the memory. "I embraced him and paid him a casual compliment. He was moved and, as he returned my embrace, asked, 'Then you really like me?'" Ibsen added: "It was one of the pleasantest evenings I have ever known. Andersen could be lovable and entertaining as few other men when he wanted to be."[16]

Andersen was delighted with his new acquaintance. He wrote to a friend that he had found Ibsen "very amiable, unassuming and pleasant. I like him a lot, but *Peer Gynt* not at all."[17]

Johanne Luise Heiberg, whose acting had been such a revelation to

---

[15] *H. C. Andersens Dagbøger og Breve, 1868–1875,* ed. Jonas Collin (Copenhagen, 1906), p. 64.

[16] Paulsen, *Samliv med Ibsen,* I, 39–40.

[17] Letter to Henriette Collin, 26 August 1870. She replied agreeing that Ibsen was "odd and likable, but why do you read *Peer Gynt?* Put it away and read *Brand* and *The Pretenders.*" (*H. C. Andersens Brevveksling med Edvard og Henriette Collin,* IV, 164–65.)

Ibsen on his previous visit, invited him to dine with her at her home, the beautiful seaside villa (not far from the Melchiors') where her husband's conversation had so disappointed Ibsen in 1852, and where he now, in turn, disappointed her by his taciturnity, a fault for which he was to make handsome amends in a poem the following year. Sadly for him, she had retired from the stage, and of the other actors whom he had admired then Michael Wiehe and N. P. Nielsen (whom he had seen as Lear) were both dead; but there was an exciting new talent to enjoy in Emil Poulsen. Fru Heiberg arranged a special performance of *The League of Youth* in Ibsen's honour. Stensgaard was played by Anton Wilhelm Wiehe, whom Ibsen had known and respected in Christiania—an unexpected but shrewd piece of casting, for Wiehe specialised in strong romantic roles, such as Oehlenschläger's heroes, and, as Edvard Brandes observed, "all his faults as well as his virtues helped him in the part"[18] of Ibsen's narcissistic hypocrite.

The documentation of these weeks is scanty. The only letters of Ibsen which have survived, apart from a brief note thanking Wiehe for his interpretation, are two which one would be happy to do without, revealing as they do one of the quirkiest and least attractive aspects of his character. Addressed (9 and 12 September) to a Danish lawyer named Anton Klubien whom he had known in Rome, they ask him to use his influence to obtain for the writer the Order of Dannebrog which, Ibsen reminds his correspondent, had been awarded to his fellow-countrymen Welhaven and Andreas Munch. "I must tell you," runs the first of these embarrassing documents, "that I am greedy for any recognition that I can receive from Denmark. You have no conception of the effect this kind of thing has in Norway. . . . A Danish decoration would much strengthen my standing there. . . . Seriously—the matter is important to me." One might have thought that the success of *The Pretenders, Brand, Peer Gynt* and *The League of Youth,* his selection as delegate to Suez and the Swedish Order of Vasa would have been enough. But medals were always to hold some especial significance for Ibsen.

While he was in Copenhagen Ibsen received two letters from Suzannah in Dresden. The first of these, undated, is worth recording if only to underline the genuineness of the affection which bound this remarkable and difficult couple, and which many casual acquaintances (such as Martin Schneekloth) and envious gossips failed to appreciate:

Dear Ibsen!
We returned here on Thursday evening, and found your letter. I was very happy, for I had been longing to hear from you.
I would have replied at once but I have had such bad pains that I have

[18] Edvard Brandes, *Om Teater* (Copenhagen, 1947), pp. 146–47.

not been able to hold a pen for four days. I am glad to learn that you are so happy, but you must go to Norway too, my dear Ibsen! Do not put it off for another year! It will look like indifference, and I am afraid may do you harm. You can make it a short visit, but overcome your reluctance and go there. Once you are there I am sure it will do you good.

We had a very nice time in Bohemia. Each day we received an excellent Viennese newspaper which was filled with nothing but telegrams about the war, as much about France as Germany. Here it is quite different, as you can imagine, everything from one side, France, its emperor, empress and prince all mocked in the most common lampoons, caricatures of them in the windows, that is what one sees here. In Bohemia everyone's sympathies were with the French. The people hate the Prussians, there was *great* sorrow when the news came of France's defeat.

The woman we lived with was quite fanatical, she said she could not sleep night or day; and she and Sigurd argued so, it was a delight to hear them. He is all for the French, and champions his cause each day with his fists at school, he is a real war-hero, there is no room for hesitation in this matter, he says.

The boys told Herr Elbe that Sigurd was for the French. "Das ist nicht gut, mein lieber Sigurd." "Aber Norwegen-Schweden hält auch mit den Franzosen, und ich will keine Ausnahme machen," the boy replied.

This is now your son's creed, I am myself horribly depressed by what is happening. The city is filled with wounded. Many Frenchmen. Otherwise, flags, cannon, victory celebrations. I have before me a special edition of a newspaper dealing with the victory at Metz; in a few days they will be in Paris, I cannot think of it, it hurts me so. The way is now open for the Prussians to take what they want.

Dear Ibsen, your long letter made me so happy, and I often long deeply for you, but of course it is much more important that you are where you are now.

Give my best greetings to Mother. . . . After paying Herr Berger I still have sixty thalers left.

Be happy, my dear Ibsen. Warmest greetings from

Your affectionate
Suzannah Ibsen[19]

Another letter from her tells how Sigurd had been beaten up daily for a fortnight "because he would not declare himself pro-German." She had complained to the headmaster, who had promised to see that the bullies were punished. "It would look bad for his school, where over half the pupils are foreign, if such treatment were permitted; so now we have peace. . . . Herr Elbe is quite mad; instead of religion he talks only politics and the wickedness of the French. The French teacher could not stick it, so they have had to engage an Italian. . . . Last Saturday was a sad day for us. At eight in the morning we received telegrams announcing the fall of Napoleon. Huge crowds gathered, and

[19] Bergliot Ibsen, pp. 46–48.

there were horrible scenes, cheering and hooting. Marie and I were quite frightened to speak on the street, as all foreign tongues jar in their ears. All their flags made me quite sick. You cannot imagine what it is like to live here among such a coarse bawling mob."[20] Dostœvsky was suffering similarly a few streets away. "Even the German shopkeepers," he recalled a year later in his *Writer's Diary,* "when talking to a Russian customer, invariably put in the remark: 'Now that we've finished with the French, we're going to start on you.'"[21]

Ibsen returned to Dresden towards the end of September. "I had intended," he wrote to Johan Thoresen on 3 October, "to visit Norway too, but the war made things so uncertain that I feared I might not be able to get back here, and when things were all right again the autumn was so far advanced that I decided to postpone my visit until next spring." The excuse rings rather feebly; despite Suzannah's exhortations, he was still reluctant to see Norway again, and four more years were to pass before he did. "Life here just now," the letter continues, "is anything but pleasant. The city is full of prisoners and wounded, and the atmosphere feverish and oppressive." A week later (10 October) he informed Hegel:

"The city is filled with sick and wounded; at any hour of the day one can be sure of encountering a military funeral, or waggons filled with new patients for the hospitals. We have, besides, several thousand French prisoners; some of them walk around freely, enjoy good treatment and seem contented enough. There is no sign of enthusiasm for the war; what the papers say about this is completely untrue.[22] The country is suffering dreadfully; half-grown boys and middle-aged fathers are called to the colours and sent to France; almost every family wears mourning for someone; many have lost all their relatives; all this despite the fact that no casualty lists have been published for the past six weeks. As I say, it is horrible living here. . . ."

On 28 October he wrote a long letter to Peter Hansen, his companion in Egypt, supplying information for a short biographical note which the latter was writing for a book entitled *Scandinavian Writers of the Present Century,* due to appear that Christmas. Most of the matter in this letter has already been quoted,[23] but two passages especially reflect the mood of this year of 1870. "Everything I have written," runs the first paragraph of the autobiographical section, "has had its origin in a mood and situation in which I found myself; I have never written anything because I had, as the saying goes, 'found a good subject.'" And

---

[20] *Ibid.,* pp. 48–50.

[21] Magarshack, p. 419.

[22] Ibsen's impression here is curiously at variance with that expressed by Suzannah in her letters to him; though, since Saxony had fought against Prussia in the Austro-Prussian War of 1866, any absence of enthusiasm would hardly have been surprising.

[23] See p. 117, etc.

the section concludes: "The locality in which one writes has a great influence on the form through which the imagination works. May I not, like Christoff in [Holberg's] *Jacob von Thyboe,* point at *Brand* and *Peer Gynt* and say, 'Such are the effects of wine'? And is there not in *The League of Youth* something which smacks of *knackwurst* and beer? I don't mean thereby to rate the play lower; I mean that my standpoint is different because I live here in a society well-ordered to the point of tedium. What will happen when I finally come home? I will have to seek peace in distance, and then I intend to get down to *Emperor Julian.*" The letter also contains those words on Suzannah which bear repeating: "She is just the kind of character I need, illogical but with a strong poetical intuition, a bigness of outlook and an almost violent hatred of all things petty."

The contemporary drama which Ibsen was planning still eluded him. On 6 November he wrote Hegel that he felt a "strong inclination" to write an opera libretto for the Danish composer Peter Heise, based on the saga of Sigurd Jorsalfar. He got as far as completing a draft synopsis, from which it appears that among other things it was to deal with the difference between the northern and southern temperaments, the one dominated by a sense of duty, the other by *livsglæde,* the joy of life. But he abandoned the idea (though coincidentally Bjørnson wrote a play about the same character the following year).[24] In a desultory way he began to think again about preparing a collection of his shorter poems; the appearance in 1870 of such a collection by Bjørnson, plus his lack of inspiration for any larger project, encouraged him to pursue the idea to the extent of asking Jacob Løkke to get hold of and copy as many of his poems as the latter could find in Norwegian newspapers and periodicals. His own copies had disappeared during the auction of his goods in Christiania and, surprisingly, he seems to have taken none to Italy.

The question of medals cropped up again that autumn. On 23 November Ibsen addressed a supplicatory letter on the subject to a shadowy character in Stockholm named Ohan Demirgian, an Armenian who had brought some Berber horses as a gift from the Khedive of Egypt to Carl XV, won that genial king's favour, and landed the job of royal stable-master (but evidently made enemies somewhere along the line, for he was sacked as soon as the king died in 1872). The letter is couched in similar terms to the one written to Klubien; after stating that he had learned while in Egypt that he was to receive a decoration, Ibsen continues: "This honour was in the highest degree flattering to

[24] Cf. Hans Andersen's glum letter to Edvard Brandes, 1 July 1871: "Bjørnson is writing a new work, *Sigurd Jorsalfar.* I hear Ibsen is writing one on exactly the same subject. I am writing nothing, and wish I had never written anything!" (*H. C. Andersens Brevveksling med Edvard og Henriette Collin,* IV, 181.)

me, *as too it would be of the greatest help to my literary standing in Norway.* It would likewise have been a consolation to me for the neglect I have endured at home, where the Order of St. Olaf has been given to several artists, painters and musicians, while I have been passed over—and that despite the fact that I faithfully support the government, with my pen and all my talents. . . . The [Egyptian] decoration would have been regarded in my country as proof of the favour of my king and would have been doubly precious to me."

Of all the begging letters addressed to patrons from Grub Street (and a list of signatories would include most of the great writers of the world up to that date), this is one of the least appetising. A man may be forgiven for humbling himself to obtain money, but not in order to get a medal, and a foreign one at that. It is not easy to see how the award of an Egyptian or Turkish medal (in the end it turned out to be Turkish, since Egypt was still part of the Ottoman empire, and the delay was due to the fact that the matter had to be referred to Constantinople) could have been regarded in Norway as "proof of the favour of my king." What is particularly nauseating is Ibsen's statement that "I faithfully support the government," not because the supporting of governments is necessarily wrong but because it was untrue. Ibsen supported the government no more than he did the opposition; his political position was one of genuine independence, and one would have expected him to be proud of it. This passion for medals and willingness to demean himself in order to acquire a further specimen is a trait in Ibsen's character with which it is difficult to feel any sympathy.

Ibsen, however, felt no qualms about his position, and defended it eloquently in another poem stemming from his Swedish visit, which he addressed to a young liberal politician he had met there, Adolf Hedin. Hedin, a gifted and imaginative statesman who should have become his country's prime minister, but was kept out of office by the personal animosity of Carl XV's successor, Oscar II, had accused Ibsen of becoming reactionary. Ibsen entitled his reply "To My Friend Who Talks of Revolutions":

> You say I've become a conservative.
> I am what I have been all my life.
>
> I've never been one for shifting pawns.
> Blow the board to glory—*then* I'm your man!
>
> I can only recall one revolution
> That wasn't scamped half-heartedly.
>
> It makes all subsequent lettings of blood
> Seem small—I refer of course to the Flood.

> Though even then Satan was left the poorer;
> It was Noah who ended up as Führer.
>
> All right, let's do it again, my friends!
> But let's not scamp to achieve our ends.
>
> You unleash the waters to make your mark.
> I set a torpedo under the Ark.

The last verse summarises the attitude Ibsen was to hold towards reform for the rest of his life: that it was a writer's duty to aim at a bigger and more basic explosion than politicians could dare to envisage. He believed that politicians, once they had achieved power, invariably compromised with their ideals, and that the only way to avoid doing the same was to keep oneself free from all party loyalties. Such compromise might be permissible in a politician if he were to achieve practical reforms, but for a writer it was not permissible; he must be totally independent and never sacrifice his integrity. It was an attitude which, seventy years later, George Orwell was to adopt, and which Ibsen himself was to epitomise in a phrase which is less un-Orwellian than might at first sight appear: "The minority is always right." At this early stage of its development he elaborated the theory in a letter dated 20 December 1870 (three months before the explosion of the Paris Commune) to Georg Brandes, then in hospital in Rome recovering from typhus:

> That glorious yearning for liberty—that is now past. I must confess that the only thing I love about liberty is the fight for it; for the possession of it, I care not. . . . The old France of illusions is broken in pieces; and now, too, the new pragmatic Prussia is in pieces, so that suddenly we find ourselves at the start of a new era. How the ideas tumble about us now! And indeed it is time. All that we have been living on until now is but scraps from the table of the last century's revolution, and that gristle has been chewed and re-chewed for long enough. The ideas need to be scoured and re-interpreted. Liberty, equality, and fraternity are no longer the same as they were in the days of the lamented guillotine. That is what the politicians refuse to understand, and that is why I hate them. These fellows only want individual revolutions, external revolutions, political, etc. But all that is just small change. What matters is the revolution of the spirit, and you must be one of those who march in the van.

"The revolution of the spirit"—the phrase epitomises what Ibsen was striving to achieve and, more perhaps than any man of his century except Karl Marx, was to achieve. And it is worth noting that Ibsen's distinction between freedoms and Freedom was one which Marx (whose first volume of *Das Kapital* had appeared in 1867, the year of *Peer Gynt*) was also to make.

Ibsen's restlessness with Bismarck's Prussia expresses itself in a letter he wrote the same day as the one to Brandes, to his old friend Consul Bravo. "My wife and I both long deeply for our beloved Rome, and we shall probably be taking up residence there again. The only thing which makes me hesitate is whether there is any good Protestant school in Rome." The answer was apparently no; once again, the question of Sigurd's education was to determine the residence of his parents.

That December the Christiania Theatre mooted the possibility of a stage production of *Peer Gynt*, and Ibsen wrote to Johan Thoresen, who was now managing his affairs in Norway, suggesting as terms the net takings of the first performance, with a minimum guarantee of 150 specie-dollars. But the project fell through, and *Peer Gynt* was not staged until 1876.

In 1870 Ibsen had begun to keep an account book, in which he meticulously noted (in careful copperplate) details of his income and investments. He continued to do this until his first stroke in 1900, and these two black books, now in the possession of his grandson, Mr. Tancred Ibsen, provide fascinating statistics. For the year 1870 Ibsen's earnings were as follows:

	specie-dollars	
Fee for *The League of Youth* at Christiania Theatre	301	
Fee for *The League of Youth* at Royal Theatre, Copenhagen	600	
Fee for 2nd edn. of *The Pretenders*	200	
	1,101	£308

In addition to this, there was his Civil List pension of 400 specie-dollars and a balance of 100 specie-dollars which he had apparently managed to save from his Swedish travel grant. He had a balance of 282 specie-dollars to his credit with Hegel from previous years, and he notes that at the beginning of the year he had 74 specie-dollars in his *huskasse*, or domestic money-box. It is a measure of how cheaply he lived that he was able to ask his publisher to hold money for him; as he built up a small reserve, he was to invest all that he could possibly spare in the soberest and least speculative securities. He had no intention that he and his family should ever be faced with the spectre of bankruptcy as his father had been. Once, later, when Sigurd asked his father whether they could not occasionally eat a little less frugally, Ibsen replied, "It is better to sleep well and not eat well, than to eat well and not sleep well."[25]

[25] Information from Mr. Tancred Ibsen.

14

The Farewell to Poetry

1871

The New Year brought a change of heart about the Danish medal, and on 8 January Ibsen wrote to Anton Klubien asking him to forget about it. The circumlocution of the language is evidence of Ibsen's embarrassment at the importunity he had previously shown.

My dear Klubien,

There is nothing for it; I must write you while there is still time.

When I was in Copenhagen this summer, so close to my own country, it seemed to me so pre-eminently desirable to be able to return home under conditions which I regarded as essential that I expressed a wish which, could a calmer mood have prevailed, I would have left unsaid.

I now see clearly that I cannot explain this matter to you in any way which will acquit me of the charge of unpardonable vanity. Nor, consequently, will you have been able to evoke any other reaction in the people you would have had to approach.

This has troubled me since; I have felt as though I were walking unwashed on the street.

This I cannot bear; I must restore my self-respect. I therefore entreat you to forget the whole matter, and to strive your utmost to restore my standing in the eyes of those people whose respect I feel I cannot do without. All other considerations must, compared with this, be regarded as secondary.

Thank you for all the friendship and proofs thereof which you showed me in Copenhagen! And when *The Pretenders* is staged, write me a long letter and tell me how it went. I have lately written a longish poem, entitled "Balloon Letter" to a Swedish lady; it will

probably be in today's *Morgenbladet*. Read it; it will tell you something about my attitude towards present-day problems.

There! Now I feel better. Remember me once more as your old
Roman *carissimo* and devoted friend

Henrik Ibsen

Ibsen's change of heart came too late to affect the issue, however, for
Klubien had talked to Fru Heiberg who had talked to the Minister
of Justice who had talked to the Minister of Culture, and the machinery,
as Ibsen was shortly to discover, had already been set in motion.

On 11 January the Royal Theatre in Copenhagen, encouraged by
the success of *The League of Youth*, staged *The Pretenders*, and this,
too, was well received. "The audiences have not poured in to admire the
brilliant acting of Mr. A. or Miss B.," reported Johanne Luise Heiberg,
who had directed it, to Ibsen on 25 April. "It is the great play itself
that has excited their wonder. . . . Not since 1807, when [Oehlen-
schläger's] *Earl Haakon* received its premiere, has any tragic drama
gripped audiences as *The Pretenders* has done."[1] Edvard Brandes thought
she had cast it badly, with Wiehe too open and uncomplicated for
Skule and Jens Nyrup a poor Haakon; but the young Emil Poulsen
gave a memorable performance as Bishop Nicholas.[2] Hans Andersen
went, and quite enjoyed himself, though he, like Brandes, had doubts
about the production. "There was too much music," he wrote in his
diary that evening, "so that it became almost melodramatic. It's a rambling
piece, but with some splendid lines. It's the best thing I know of
Ibsen's."[3]

The "Balloon Letter to a Swedish Lady"[4] mentioned by Ibsen in his
letter to Klubien was a belated expression of thanks to Fru Fredrika
Limnell for the hospitality she had shown him in Stockholm. Outside
his plays, it is Ibsen's longest poem—four hundred and forty-four lines
of rhymed octosyllabics, with an occasional septisyllabic—and one of his
best. Apart from its technical accomplishment, it is of considerable psychological interest, for it crystallises (as he had found himself unable to
do in prose) his impressions of the confused events of the past eighteen

---

[1] In the same letter, she asked permission to cut the final line of the play ("Skule
Baardsson was God's unwanted child on earth"), since she felt it blasphemous to suggest that God had any unwanted children. (She had made some cuts in Bjørnson's
Mary Stuart in Scotland on similar grounds.) No reply by Ibsen has survived, but a
sentence in Fru Heiberg's memoirs (*Et Liv gjenoplevet i Erindringer*, III [Copen-
hagen, 1892], 192) suggests that he acceded to her request. Cf. Herleiv Dahl, "Ibsen
og Johanne Luise Heiberg," in *Ibsen-Arbok 1954*, pp. 102–6.

[2] Edvard Brandes, *Om Teater*, p. 148.

[3] *H. C. Andersens Dagbøger og Breve, 1868–1875*, p. 79.

[4] Paris was being besieged by the Germans when Ibsen wrote this poem, in
December 1870, and the Parisians were sending messages by balloon.

months—the accusations of conservatism, the Egyptian visit, the lionising in Stockholm, Egypt and Copenhagen, and the Franco-Prussian War.

The poem opens (like so many of his prose letters, but with a grace seldom apparent in them) with an apology for not having written sooner. He has entitled this a balloon letter, he explains, because

> I have no doves. Doves are the birds of hope.
> In this cramped grave but owls and ravens build,
> No messengers for a lady.

He tells her of his Egyptian journey, comparing his fellow-travellers to various birds and animals:

> Eleven cocks from France, four Spanish stallions . . .
> A kind of ram from Switzerland . . . and, of course,
> A herd of German wild pigs, almost tamed.

—which last remark was to cause great offence in Germany. After narrating how they voyaged up the Nile, Ibsen describes the still life of the desert:

> Wading through endless streets where living nature
> Is wedded to death, transformed by time
> Into a mad architecture of stone.
> Ribs, femurs, spines, poke up like shattered plinths,
> And camels' skulls like fallen capitals.

What especially remained with him from his Egyptian visit, continues Ibsen—and it is typical that he should have referred so little to this in his letters, and have resorted to poetry to say what really mattered to him—was the total deadness of Egyptian religion. The gods of Greece, he writes, still live today; Zeus still moves in the Capitol. But

> Where is Horus? Where is Hathor?
> No trace exists, no memory.

The reason, he suggests, is easy to find, and in stating it he stated the essential difference between his plays and the nineteenth-century conception of drama against which he was rebelling—the greater urgency, as he saw it, of the individual as opposed to the idealised, that same contrast which he had remarked in Italy between Roman and Greek sculpture, between Michelangelo and Raphael:

> Where personality is lacking,
> Where there is neither hatred, indignation
> Nor joy, no beat of pulse nor flush of blood,
> Glory is but a dry rattle of bones.
> Who has not seen Juno in his mind's eye,
> Pale in her wrath as she surprised her lord? . . .

But the Egyptian gods were otherwise.
Static, they never, like the gods of Greece
And men, sinned, groped, and raised themselves from sin.
And so this culture, four millennia old,
Lies like a bloodless mummy in a crypt.

A parallel, Ibsen suggests, is to be found today. Bismarck's Germany
is as ossified as the Pharaohs' Egypt. Gustaf Adolf and Carl XII were poets
of action, but Moltke has "killed the poetry of war." The poem concludes
on a note of Apollonian detachment:

Our age craves beauty.
But that's a kingdom outside Bismarck's range.
Shall we go to the feast, madame? Who knows when the dove
Will descend with the invitation? We must wait.
Meanwhile, I pace my room, kid-gloved. Till then
I shall seek peace, tracing my words on vellum.
This will anger the mob. They will doubtless
Brand me a heathen. But I shrink from the mob.
I have no wish to be clasped to their hot bosom.
I shall await whatever time may bring
In a well-pressed morning coat.

The "Balloon Letter" was (as Ibsen had told Klubien) printed in
Morgenbladet on 8 January, and received praise from an unexpected
quarter—Count Manderström, he of the halter, who, so Georg Sibbern,
the Norwegian Minister in Stockholm, told Ibsen, was "enchanted."
"The old man," commented Ibsen to Hegel (16 February), "is truly
heaping coals of fire upon my head!"
Early that January Ibsen had received the copies of his lost poems
which he had been awaiting from Jakob Løkke. "They make a thick
book," he informed Hegel on 8 January. "But I am throwing out three-
fourths of them and rewriting the rest." Løkke had collected fifty-two
poems—eight from the student magazine *Andhrimner,* five from *Aftenbladet,* three from *Morgenbladet* and no less than thirty-six from Botten
Hansen's *Illustreret Nyhedsblad.* Ibsen set to work on them at once, as
though happy to get away from the play that was tormenting him, and
on 21 January he sent Hegel the first batch, promising to post "a
similar batch each week" (an undertaking which, for once, he kept).
Further instalments followed on 31 January and 8 February, with requests
concerning the typography. "I earnestly beg [31 January] that the printer
see carefully to it that the verses lie in the centre of the page, with no
greater a margin on one side than the other; this is not always done,
and the appearance suffers. And I greatly love the big French type-
faces; I have never seen anything more beautiful for poetry; and, what

is most important, they seem to me to match exactly the character of my poems. Printed thus they will be twice as good!"

He seems to have kept no copies even of the poems (or some of them) which he had written in Rome, for he had to ask Hegel to get hold of the elegy on Abraham Lincoln "which appeared in *Fædrelandet* in either March or April 1865," the drinking song from *Love's Comedy* "since I don't have the book," and a dirge from *The Vikings at Helgeland* which he appears not to have had either. Has any other poet, major or minor, when preparing a collection of his own work for the press, been so dependent on friends to supply him with the material?

On 16 February he sent two more poems, which "I supposed lost, and couldn't remember[!]; finally I found them among my travel papers." Both were unusually personal statements (which some would say was a cause of his supposing them lost and being unable to remember them). One was a confession of the bond he still felt with Norway. He called it "Burned Ships":

> He turned his ship's
> Prow from the north,
> Seeking the trail
> Of brighter gods.
>
> The snow-land's beacons
> Quenched in the sea.
> The fauns of the seashore
> Stilled his longing.
>
> He burned his ships.
> Blue smoke drifted
> Like a bridge's span
> Towards the north.
>
> To those snow-capped huts
> From the hills of the south
> There rides a rider
> Every night.

He placed this poem last in the book, as though to remind his compatriots that, whatever thunderbolts he might send from the south, his roots remained fast in the country which had rejected him. The other new poem, for Suzannah, he entitled simply "Thanks":

> Her grief was the sorrows
> That cobbled my path.
> Her joy the spirits
> That lifted me o'er them.

Her home lies here
On Freedom's sea
Where the poet's ship
Finds its mirror.

Her children are
The shifting figures
Who glide, waving
Flags in my song.

Her goal is to fan
My vision's embers
So that none knows
Whence the fire cometh.

And because she asks
And expects no thanks,
I give her now
Thanks in a song.

The task of revising his earlier poems proved much more arduous than Ibsen had imagined. Never the man to skimp a job, he went through every poem he had decided to include, cutting away anything that now struck him as conventionally poetic or self-indulgent, making the language more natural and less redolent of Wergeland and Welhaven, his two earliest influences, and sometimes deleting whole sections of a poem which one is rather sorry to lose. The twenty-three sonnets which comprise "In the Picture Gallery," for example, he omitted altogether, though he used five of them as the bases for new poems.[5] Among these was the Hardyesque "In the Gallery," the mood and language of which were near-perfectly caught by a Victorian translator, F. E. Garrett:

With palette laden,
She sat, as I passed her,
A dainty maiden
Before an Old Master.

What mountain-top is
She bent upon? Ah,
She neatly copies
Murillo's *Madonna*.

But rapt and brimming
The eyes' full chalice says
The heart builds dreaming
Its fairy palaces.

[5] "The Ravine," "A Swan," "Fear of the Light," "In the Gallery" and "My Young Vine" are, as Didrik Arup Seip has pointed out (C.E., XIV, 491) based on sonnets 2, 3, 14, 17, and 21 of the earlier sequence.

The eighteenth year rolled
By, ere returning,
I greeted the dear old
Scenes with yearning.

With palette laden
She sat as I passed her,
A faded maiden
Before an Old Master.

But what is she doing?
The same thing still—lo,
Hotly pursuing
That very Murillo!

Her wrist never falters;
It keeps her, that poor wrist,
With panels for altars
And daubs for the tourist.

And so she has painted
Through years unbrightened,
Till hopes have fainted
And hair has whitened.

But rapt and brimming
The eyes' full chalice says
The heart builds dreaming
Its fairy palaces.

On 13 February Ibsen received "an exceedingly beautiful document" announcing that he had been made a Knight of Dannebrog. The chain of action started by that word to Klubien in Copenhagen had had its effect, and his qualms seem to have vanished. "Now," he assured Hegel on 16 February, "my compatriots will think my poems twice as good as they would otherwise have done!"

"Since Christmas," he wrote the next day to Georg Brandes, who was still in the hospital in Rome, "I have been occupied practically day and night preparing this collection. It has been a damnable job to relive all those attitudes which I long since left behind. But together they form a kind of whole." He returned to the obsessive question of freedom and its true meaning. "I shall never agree to identify Freedom with political freedom. What you call Freedom I call freedoms, and what I call the battle for Freedom is nothing but the continuous pursuit of the idea of Freedom. He who possesses Freedom otherwise than as something to be striven for possesses something dead and meaningless, for by its very definition Freedom perpetually expands as one seeks to embrace it, so that if, during the quest, anyone stops and says: "Now I have it!" he shows thereby that he has lost it." Ibsen found Brandes's suggestions for political reform inadequate, as he had found Adolf Hedin's, and was now (he, the most ordered of men!) suggesting that the only solution was anarchy. "The state must be abolished!" he concluded in the same letter. "*There's* a revolution to which I will gladly lend my shoulder. Abolish the conception of the state, establish the principle of free will and all that is spiritually akin to it as the one prerequisite for a universal brotherhood—*there* is the beginning of a Freedom that is worth something!"

This was a bit much even for Brandes. "His radicalism really exceeds all conceivable bounds," he wrote to a friend on 22 February. "My head grows dizzy with reading of all he wishes to revolutionize. I am afraid that had he power commensurate to his genius, or had he lived in another era, he would have been regarded as a greater radical than Marat in one field, Proudhon in another. Not only does he reject the established concepts of religion and morality, he even rejects the concept of the state."[6] Ibsen's ideas as expressed in this letter are so close to those of Proudhon, who had died only six years earlier ("Government of man by man in every form is oppression," Proudhon had written. "The highest perfection of society is found in the union of order and anarchy") that one wonders whether Ibsen may not have been reading him, or anyway had Suzannah read him and pass on the gist; but such ideas were, like those of Kierkegaard, so much a part of everyday conversation among thinking people then that he would have been a dull and out-of-touch fellow who had not absorbed something of them.

In that same letter of 14 February to Brandes, Ibsen cited the Jews as an example of the advantages of abolishing the state. "How is it they have kept their place apart, their political halo, amid surroundings of coarse cruelty?" he asked. "By having no state to burden them. Had they remained in Palestine, they would long ago have lost their individuality in the process of the state's construction, like other nations."[7] He referred to the Jews as "the aristocracy of the human race." This need for an aristocracy, not of birth but spiritual, was something that Ibsen was increasingly to stress, notably in *An Enemy of the People*, and it made him many enemies among Scandinavian liberals. Even today (as this writer knows from experience) Dr. Stockmann's demand for this kind of aristocracy upsets many a liberally inclined director and actor working on the play.

On 25 February Ibsen sent the (as he thought) last pages of his poems to Hegel, but as late as Easter week he composed a long and, again, technically intricate piece, "Rhymed Letter to Fru Heiberg," which Georg Brandes, a quarter of a century later[8] was to describe as Ibsen's most

6 Fenger, "Ibsen og Georg Brandes indtil 1872," p. 189.

7 I quote William Archer's incomparable translation of this difficult passage, printed on p. 59 of the English edition of Brandes's *Henrik Ibsen* (London, 1899).

8 *Henrik Ibsen: festskrift i anledning af hans 70de fødselsdag*, p. 25.

artistically accomplished poem. In this exquisite work, two hundred and eighty-two lines of astonishing variety, Ibsen stated his attitude towards the rival media of verse and prose in a sentence that anticipated his imminent abandonment of the former for the latter. "Prose is for ideas, verse for visions. The joys and sorrows of the soul, grief that snows upon my head, indignation's lightning bolt—these I endow most fully with life, and express most freely, in the bonds of verse." The renunciation of this medium, in which he moved so easily, was to be a continuation of the austere process which he had begun with the astringent revision of his poems.

The "Letter to Fru Heiberg" ends with an expression of faith, unfashionable for the period, that things created in the theatre may perhaps last longer than works which never leave the printed page. Ibsen intended this as a compliment to the great actress now living in retirement, but it plainly expresses a conviction which he himself possessed, and which is a little surprising when we remember that his two triumphs, *Brand* and *Peer Gynt*, were still both commonly regarded as unstageable. "Some say," runs the poem, "that the art of the theatre, born for and bound to the moment, must, like a soap bubble or nocturnal meteor, dazzle, then burst to leave no trace. Free yourself from this dark thought! The very fact that your art is a child of fragrance, of the spirit, of a mood, of personality and imagination, and not something of wood or stone, or even a thought fixed fast in black on white, but a sprite for ever swinging free on beauty's vine, the fact that it lacks tangible form, renders it immune to the gnawing of time's worm. And," he concludes, "that is what life truly means: to live in memory, to rest in people's minds free of the mildew and rust of age . . . and this lot has been granted you."

Ibsen's *Poems* were published on 3 May 1871. The edition was a large one, 4,000 copies (the equivalent, counting Norway and Denmark as one, of something approaching 200,000 in modern America). The reviews were generally most favourable. An anonymous critic in *Bergens Tidende* complained that "he seems to look down at everything from a poetic iceberg," but found in the "Balloon Letter" hope that Ibsen, "in addition to his latest brilliant but ugly works, will also give us something brilliant and beautiful." The Danish poet Otto Borchsenius, writing in *Bergens-Posten,* praised Ibsen for omitting his early poems, wished he had omitted some others (including, surprisingly, the "Elegy to J. L. Heiberg"), regretted the absence of the Priest's sermon in *Peer Gynt*, and feared that the lines about the "well-pressed morning coat" (in the "Balloon Letter") might imply an intent to withdraw from the battle. He hoped Ibsen might "gradually mellow this half-ironical, half-melancholy view of life, people and their actions," but admitted that "the age needs a disciplinarian, and we should be sorry to see Herr Ibsen withdraw from the battle as long as he can still wield his sword."

Rudolf Schmidt, in *Fædrelandet*, compared the volume with Bjørnson's recent collection; he found Bjørnson's poems "certainly the richer and weightier," and complained that: "Behind all doubt there must lie a conviction which must be equally strong, so that doubt strikes out in scorn and indignation. But sometimes with Henrik Ibsen this expresses itself rather as hesitation, as though doubt had struck inwards and quenched the spark of inner wisdom." Bjørnson himself, predictably, disliked the book. "I have now read Ibsen's poems," he wrote to his wife Karoline on 14 May. "Except for the old ones and one to his wife and a few others, and apart from an almost too virtuoso style in some, such as the one to Fru Heiberg, I find nothing noteworthy about the collection. As with almost everything by Ibsen I am left so empty afterwards. His standing vis-à-vis his country is becoming almost comic, and his poem to the king, praising him for not daring to do anything in 1864, seems to me criminal."[9]

The man about whose opinion Ibsen was most anxious had mixed reactions. "I was so uncontrollably delighted with Ibsen's book when it arrived," Brandes wrote to Hegel, "that the reading of the poems put me in a most violent state of nervous emotion. It went through me like a storm through an Aeolian harp. . . . But later my critical sense asserted itself, and my judgment on these poems is that only a few of them are good, and those the ones already known. Most of them are *obscure* to the point of incomprehensibility, many are clumsy, and the humour is nearly always unsuccessful. It's nearly all doggerel. But there are things in the book which carry me away, and despite everything I *was* greatly carried away."[10] Writing to his family a month later, he declared: "I was tremendously moved by "Terje Vigen." It is a true masterpiece, a real classic. . . . The only pity is that there is so much rubbish in the book"[11]—a not altogether unfair comment, for a number of the poems fall far below Ibsen's best standard. He was much more uneven as a poet than as a dramatist. Brandes did not review the book until the autumn, by which time he had met Ibsen, and his review was to reflect that meeting.

That first fortnight in May was a good one for Ibsen, for on 9 May, six days after the publication of his *Poems*, he at last received his longed-for Medjidje Order, "a handsome object," he informed Hegel the same day, "together with a large and unintelligible diploma from the Grand Turk himself." With unusual (on this subject) candour he admitted that the main reason for his getting the decoration was that "we brought a lot of Swedish and Norwegian decorations for Egyptian bigwigs, and this courtesy was merely being reciprocated."

[9] *Breve til Karoline, 1858–1907*, p. 174.
[10] Fenger, "Ibsen og Georg Brandes indtil 1872," p. 190.
[11] *Loc. cit.*

Down in Rome, Georg Brandes had at last left hospital after five months, his attack of typhus having been followed by a blood clot in the leg. Brandes's sense of kinship[12] with Ibsen had been deepened by their correspondence; from his sickbed earlier in the year he had written a poem entitled "To Henrik Ibsen," describing his lonely struggle and his longing for a comrade in arms:

> Brother! I found thee. What care I
> That thou art a matchless chieftain, I
> But an armourer? Our souls are kin.
> We shall sound a spiritual call to arms.[13]

Ibsen reciprocated the younger man's feeling; and so, as Brandes's biographer has put it, "these two lonely men joined hands."[14] None, alas, of Brandes's letters to Ibsen has survived, but Ibsen's side of the correspondence is proof of the warmth which already existed between them:

> Dresden, 18 May 1871
>
> My dear Brandes!
>
> . . . Well, I never really believed you were in danger; one doesn't die in the first act;[15] the great world *dramaturge* needs you for a leading role in his *Haupt- und Staatsaction*[16] which He is now doubtless preparing for our respected public.
>
> Warmest thanks for your portrait! . . . I always like to have a physical likeness to hang my conception on. I shan't rest till I have met you, when I think we shall prove to have more in common than a liking for velvet jackets.
>
> During this somewhat long interval I have managed to persuade myself not to write to you. I sensed from your last letter that you were a little angry with me, and since my poems were about to

[12] The previous autumn Brandes had told a friend that he felt "spiritually akin" to Ibsen, though he regarded himself as "incomparably less gifted." Ibsen, he declared, "has quite overwhelmed me with his sympathy. Does not this arise from a kind of kinship?" (Letter to Emil Petersen, 15 October 1870, quoted by Fenger, "Ibsen og Georg Brandes indtil 1872," p. 187.)

[13] Brandes wrote the poem on the night of 9–10 January 1871, but felt diffident about sending it to Ibsen and did not post it until 11 February.

[14] Henning Fenger, *Georg Brandes Læreår* (Copenhagen, 1955), p. 341.

[15] A reference to the Strange Passenger's cold comfort to Peer Gynt: "One doesn't die in the middle of the fifth act."

[16] "A type of entertainment popular in Germany in the seventeenth and eighteenth centuries, consisting of a chronicle play, improvised farce and spectacular effects. The chronicle play presented the extravagant and absurd adventures of an emperor or general over a period of many years." (*Ibsen's Letters and Speeches,* ed. Evert Sprinchorn [New York, 1964], p. 111.)

be published I didn't want to do anything which might look like an attempt to conciliate you before you should read them. I know you would not let this affect your judgment, but a kind of diffidence bade me avoid even the appearance of having supposed any such thing. My dear friend, you will understand what I mean.

I trust you will long since have received the book from Hegel. It contains both old and new material, and much that I no longer set much store by; but it all belongs to the story of my development. So tell me what you think of it; I attach the greatest importance to your judgment.

And what are you up to now, down there in beautiful, warm Italy? Your illness will perhaps have had one good result, I mean, that you may have to spend a summer there. I think of you daily; sometimes I see you in Frascati, sometimes Albano or Ariccia. Which is right? And what new work are you preparing down there for our spiritual enlightenment? I am sure something must have matured during your long sickness. One of the blessings of being ill is that it gives a kind of purity and stature to so much which otherwise would not blossom. I have only once been really ill; but that may be another way of saying that I have never, perhaps, been totally well. *Chi lo sa!*

Is it not wretched of the Paris Commune to have gone and spoiled my excellent theory of the State—or rather, of the No-State? Now the idea is ruined for ages; I cannot even decently write a poem about it. But the idea is sound, of that I am sure, and some time it will be achieved without caricature.

I have often thought about what you once wrote, that I had not taken up the standpoint of modern scientific knowledge. How could I overcome this failing? But is not each generation born with the prejudices of its time? Have you never noticed in a painting of a group from some previous century a curious kind of family likeness between people of the same period? So it is in the field of intellect too. What we profane creatures lack in knowledge I think we possess, to a certain degree, in intuition or instinct. And a writer's task is essentially to *see,* not to mirror; I am conscious of a particular danger to myself in indulging the latter tendency.

Dear Brandes—it is always a relief for me to talk to you, and a great, great joy to hear you talk, if only on paper. So give me that pleasure again soon.

Your affectionate
Henrik Ibsen

Brandes was overwhelmed. "I received an extremely charming and flattering letter from Henrik Ibsen," he informed his family on 26 May, "almost too flattering for me to believe that he was being completely honest."[17] Visiting Walter Runeburg's studio in Rome he was interested to see the latter's "remarkable bust of Ibsen, fiery yet overcast."[18]

Meanwhile, Ibsen had at last broken the creative block that had been tormenting him. "I have now begun my big play, *Emperor Julian*," he wrote to Johan Thoresen on 26 June, "and hope to have it ready by Christmas. . . . I work blazingly fast, but only for a few hours[!] each day." On 12 July he told Frederik Hegel: "I am well into *Emperor Julian*. This book will be my masterpiece, and occupies all my thoughts and all my time. The positive view of things which the critics have so long demanded of me they will find here."

At last, on 14 July 1871, Ibsen and Brandes met. Brandes had arranged his homeward journey to Copehagen so as to pass through Dresden, and had arrived there the previous night. His autobiography contains a vivid account of his first sight of Ibsen:

> As I approached the house, which lay in an avenue, Dippoldiswaldær-strasse, I saw him, easily recognizable from his portrait, leaning out of the window in his shirtsleeves. But when I entered he had put on a velvet jacket. He hugged me to his breast, almost suffocating me. I found him handsome (*smuk*), with an incomparable forehead, clear eyes, long curled hair. I was surprised how handsome I found him.

They talked for two or three hours, "partly of his work, partly of conditions at home, much of me." Ibsen was wearing an order ribbon in his buttonhole, which slightly disturbed Brandes.[19] Later that day Brandes returned, and Ibsen took him to the Waldschlösslein "where we ate and drank beer. . . . Ibsen told me how Bjørnson had tried to persuade him to avoid all contact with me, and promised to show me letters the following day. He told me how they had demanded, in the most shameless manner, that he should become co-editor of [the literary magazine] *Idea and Reality*, demanded it of him as his *duty*. . . . He had replied that he felt no inclination to occupy a seat that was still warm from Clemens Petersen." They discussed Danish writers. Brandes asked Ibsen if there was any one he cared about. "After letting me guess for some while in vain, he answered: 'Once upon a time, somewhere in Zealand, there walked behind his plough an old man in a smock frock who had looked upon men and things until he was wroth at heart. That is a man I like." They

---

[17] Fenger, "Ibsen og Georg Brandes indtil 1872," p. 190.

[18] Edvard and Georg Brandes, *Brevveksling med nordiske Forfattere og Videnskabsmænd,* ed. Morten Borup, Francis Bull, and John Landquist (Copenhagen, 1939–42), IV, xxxi. (These eight volumes are henceforth referred to as *Brandes Brevveksling.*)

[19] "I often regret that I so thoughtlessly repeated to you the impression I got last year from that trifle in his buttonhole. Ibsen no longer wears his decoration at home. But I have only now, for the first time, really got to know him." (Letter from Brandes to Hans Brøchner, 29 September 1872; *Brandes Brevveksling,* I, 172.)

agreed in their admiration of Heiberg and shared a feeling that Scandinavia was sadly backwards in its cultural development. "Ibsen was full of plans and hopes, and overflowing with the spirit of battle. 'You needle the Danes, I'll needle the Norwegians!' were the last words he smilingly addressed to me."[20]

Brandes, no doubt, told Ibsen of the exciting actors and actresses he had seen in Paris the previous summer—Ristori as Lady Macbeth, Mounet-Sully as Hernani, Coquelin in Ponsard's *Gringoire,* the young Sarah Bernhardt in George Sand's *L'Autre;* no doubt, too, they argued about John Stuart Mill, whom Brandes so revered and whom Ibsen found tedious. Ibsen left no record of their meeting, but a vivid impression of how Brandes looked and behaved at around this time survives from a young Englishman who made his acquaintance three years later, Edmund Gosse. Gosse found Brandes

> a tall, thin young man . . . gentle and even mild in appearance, pale, with a great thatch of hair arched over a wide forehead. . . . I never met anyone more impatient than Brandes, and this probably had something to do with the atmosphere of anger and suspicion which he had created around him in Copenhagen. He not merely did not hear fools gladly, but he was easily driven to distraction, and to the visible stamping of feet, by those who were not, even in his own measure, fools, but merely less arrowy in their mental movements than himself. Thus I immediately fell under his ban because I spoke Danish so slowly. . . . Brandes went pacing, infuriated, between the sofa and the door, and snapped his long tapering fingers.[21]

Gosse's account of the distrust with which Brandes was regarded by his fellow-countrymen helps us to understand why he and Ibsen, two difficult men whose views on literature and other matters often differed so widely, were drawn to each other. Brandes was, writes Gosse, "the only man in Denmark who represented the spirit of modern Europe in *belles-lettres,*" and the Danes were angered by his cultivation of friendships with German authors such as Paul Heyse—hostility towards Germany still being fierce in Denmark—and his attempts to impose their writings on Danish readers.

> It was difficult to account for the repulsion and even terror of Georg Brandes which I heard expressed around me whenever his name came up in the course of general conversation. . . . Brandes was a Jew,[22] an illuminated specimen of a race little known at that time in Scandinavia, and much

---

[20] For the information contained in this and the preceding paragraph, cf. Brandes's *Levned,* II, 55 ff.; Henning Fenger's "Ibsen og Georg Brandes indtil 1872," pp. 191–93; and Brandes's *Henrik Ibsen,* p. 90 (Muir-Archer translation). The poet-ploughman was Christian Hviid Bredahl (1784–1860).

[21] Edmund Gosse, *Two Visits to Denmark,* pp. 167–68.

[22] His father had been born Cohen, but the family name was changed to Brandes when Georg's grandmother remarried with a man of that name.

dreaded and suspected. That a scion of this hated people, so long excluded from citizenship, should come forward with a loud message of defiance to the exquisite and effete civilization of Denmark was in itself an outrage. . . . The tone of Copenhagen was graceful, romantic, orthodox; there was a wide appreciation of literary speculation of a certain kind, kept within the bounds of good taste, reverently attached to the tradition of their elders. This, too, was markedly national. It was part of the political isolation of Denmark, of the pride which her two European wars had fostered, to be intellectually self-sufficient. It was orthodox to believe that the poetry and philosophy and science of the national writers was all that Danes needed to know of a modern kind. Here, then, was an angry Jew, with something of the swashbuckler about him, shouting that mental salvation was impossible without a knowledge of "foreign devils" like Taine and John Stuart Mill and Schopenhauer. . . . There was something exasperating, too, in the lofty tone which Brandes adopted. He did not spare the susceptibilities of his countrymen. . . . "How these Christians hate me!" he could not help saying. He belonged to the race of iconoclasts, like Heine before him, like Nietzsche after him, and he was expected to disturb all the convictions of his contemporaries. In religion a deist, in politics a republican, in ethics an extreme individualist, Brandes seemed at that time prepared to upset every part of the settled and convenient order of things.[23]

In other words, Brandes was, as a critic, doing for Denmark what Ibsen, as a creative writer, was doing for Norway, and what August Strindberg, now a twenty-two-year-old student at Upsala, was shortly to do for Sweden: in Ibsen's own phrase, to "wake the people and make them think big."

The meeting with Ibsen had given Brandes the stimulation he had been hoping for, and the next months were for him a time of violent fermentation, as his diaries for August and September show. On 20 September he noted: "Towards 2 A.M. I wrote a long, violent and ardent letter to Ibsen. Surely this will inflame him? Thought him worth more." Doubtless he compared Ibsen with John Stuart Mill, whom he was to describe in his autobiography as "the incarnation of the ideal I had drawn for myself of the great man. . . . His boldness was not of the merely theoretic kind; he wished to interfere and remodel."[24] Ibsen was in fact to interfere and remodel contemporary thought at least as much as Mill; what must have disappointed Brandes was Ibsen's lack of inflexibility and his willingness (like Schopenhauer) to compromise in his private life. Brandes's letter to Ibsen of 20 September has disappeared, but we have Ibsen's answer, from which it is evident that Brandes had tried to persuade him to play a less detached and more active and committed role.

---

[23] Gosse, *Two Visits to Denmark,* pp. 156–57, 164–66, 288.

[24] *Recollections of My Childhood and Youth* (London, 1906), pp. 270–71. The excellent and vigorous translation is anonymous.

Dresden, 24 September 1871

Dear Brandes!

It is always with curiously mixed emotions that I read your letters. They are more poems than letters; they come to me like a cry for help from a solitary survivor in some immense and lifeless desert. I cannot but rejoice and thank you for addressing this cry to me. Yet it worries me, for I ask myself: "To what will such a mood lead?" I can only comfort myself with the hope that it is merely transitional. It seems to me that you now find yourself in the same crisis that I was in when I wrote *Brand,* and I am sure you too will find the medicine to drive the sickness from your body. Energetic creation is an excellent remedy. Above all, I would wish you a full-blooded egotism, to persuade you for a while to rate yourself and your thoughts as the only things that have any value or significance and everything else as non-existent. Do not regard this as a sign of brutality in me! You cannot serve your community better than by minting this metal which lies within you. I have never really had any strong liking for solidarity; I have always regarded it as just another traditional dogma—and if one had the courage completely to disregard it one might perhaps be rid of the ballast which weighs heaviest on a man's individuality. There are times when the whole history of the world seems to me but a mighty shipwreck, and the only sane course to save oneself. I hope for nothing from isolated reforms. The whole human race is on the wrong track; that is the situation. Is there really any hope in the present state of affairs, with these unattainable ideals, etc.? Human history seems to me like a young man who has left his work-bench and gone to the theatre. We have made a fiasco of everything, both as lovers and as heroes; the only role for which we have shown a faint talent has been that of the fool; and with our increasing sophistication we shall no longer be able to play that. Nor do I think things are better arranged in other countries; the masses, whether at home or abroad, have no understanding of higher things.

And so I am to try to raise a banner? Alas, my dear friend, that would be like Louis Napoleon's arrival at Boulogne with an eagle on his head. When his hour of destiny eventually struck, he needed no eagle. Working on *Julian* has made me something of a fatalist; but this play will be a kind of banner. Don't fear, however, that this will be a tendentious work; I explore the characters, their conflicting plans, their story, and do not try to seek a moral—always remembering that one must not confuse the moral of a story with its philosophy; for it is inevitable that a philosophy must emerge as the final judgment on the conflict and the victory. But all this can be illustrated only in practice. . . .

I have received your book [*Criticisms and Portraits*]. I can only say
that it is something to which I return again and again. Yes, my dear,
splendid Brandes, I cannot understand how *you* can be despondent.
You have received a spiritual summons as clearly and unmistakably
as is granted to few people. So why this gloom? Have you a right to
feel thus? Though don't imagine that I don't fully understand you . . .

Finally, hearty thanks for the visit you paid me in Dresden; those
were festive hours for me. Good luck, courage, good health and good
everything!

Your affectionate
Henrik Ibsen

We have no record of Brandes's reaction to this letter, but his diaries
of the period show how continuously Ibsen was in his thoughts. On
21 September, presumably just after he had sent his letter, Brandes
noted: "If only Ibsen would write me a powerfully *poetic* reply! Were
he a ready and fertile writer he could hardly not do so." And the next
day: "Is it I who am to raise the battle cry, is it really I who am the
sole chieftain of the young? I feel like Moses and Jonah when the Lord
chose them and they prayed for strength. . . . Ought I to hold a lecture
in the Students' Union to sound a trumpet call for the young? I think I
must, I think it my duty." On 30 September: "Still no letter from H. Ibsen.
I am hurt and indignant." The same day he began to write a review of
Ibsen's volume of poems, and a day or two later he received Ibsen's
reply of 24 September which must have struck him as disappointingly
evasive, and which inspired him to the deeply personal statement which
that review, published in *Illustreret Tidende* on 22 October, represents—a
wonderfully mature assessment which repays quoting *in extenso*. After
apologizing for writing about the volume so long after its appearance,
Brandes continues:

"The book is in no way very rich, and does not contain many poems
that broaden the soul . . . but . . . it brings us a message from a spirit
who has the rare characteristic of being a warrior, in the fields of both
artistic and human endeavour. . . . Despite its faults, it is so passionate
that it contains passion, and one likes to write about something by which
one has been powerfully moved." Ibsen's poetry is "the poetry of loneliness,
portraying the lonely need, the lonely strife, and the lonely protest"; as
examples, Brandes names "The Miner," "The Murder of Lincoln" and "On
the Heights." "It is out of isolation that Ibsen writes. It is irrelevant
that he isolated himself partly out of discontent as not being able to carry
the public with him. It was loneliness that first drove Ibsen to become a
poet, and this collection of poems mirrors in microcosm the whole development of Ibsen's life, beginning as it does with a series of works of no
marked individuality." There are those who attain to self-knowledge and

originality almost at their first contact with the world, with its society and personalities so different to their own. "But others, the lonely ones, achieve this only by the gradual rejection of bonds and scruples, as being ever more weighty and useless ballast. I remember I once heard a man of this ilk say: 'It is good to be without friends. Friends are an expensive luxury, and when one invests one's capital in a mission, a calling in this life, one cannot afford to keep friends.' . . . Ibsen is like this man; he became himself by becoming a solitary."

One of the tasks of poets, continues Brandes, is to give the lead in ideas to the young—not that the young do not know what their password must be, "but they wish to hear it uttered, for the first time, by inspired lips. If the poet does not, at the right moment, give the answer that is awaited from him, it forms itself without his help in the mouths of the young, and then it is the poet himself who is challenged and asked if he knows the password; if he does not, the young will strike him down and proceed. But where scattered yearnings do not work towards a single goal and seek a central point, no rallying cry can be expected, and then the poet withdraws into himself. Ibsen's character fits such a situation and draws strength from it. His strength depends on the night-stillness around him, on the calm darkness in which alone he can freely breathe. Not the twelve fair hours of the day but the dark hours of the night stand godparents to his poetry. Alone, he divides more than he unites. He shows each man the way back to the powers which he may discover within himself when, without fear or scruple, he follows his own nature and his own star. But a star shines only in the night. It is useless to ask Ibsen to raise a banner. He writes only for himself and for those who are created like him; to them he offers not a banner but an example. . . . He, the enemy of apathy and sloth, is alarmed and indignant at seeing his people sit out the sword-dance, retreat like Peer Gynt, turn their backs on the opportunity to be tested, and this mood has called forth a string of his most notable works." As examples, Brandes cites *Brand* and *Peer Gynt*, "The Murder of Lincoln" and "A Brother in Need," even the poem to Carl XV which Bjørnson had mocked, "To One Unnamed." "In such protests the poet's genius stands forth in its full strength, the axe glints, the torch glitters in his hand. The axe and the torch! These are his emblems. One recalls those words of Hippocrates which Schiller set on the title page of *The Robbers:* 'What medicine cannot cure, the iron will heal; what the iron cannot heal, will be cured by fire.' Can this lonely and passionate spirit seriously be regarded as one who delights in annihilation and renunciation?"

Wise readers, explains Brandes, find this kind of destroyer easy to understand, and such an instinct, Ibsen's character being what it is, natural. He quotes the anecdote from Lamartine's *Jocelyn* about the travellers who, desiring to cross a river, in flood, laid their axes to the trees under which they had just rested, to the amazement and consternation of the birds and beasts of the forest; but by destroying these trees they were able to build a bridge, cross the river, and continue their journey. "Thus the human spirit fells what had once sheltered it, and thus it progresses over the corpses of what it has destroyed."

Regarding Ibsen's supposed lack of faith, Brandes asserts that: "Faith consists in believing in truth though untruth reign and lies triumph and drug men's minds. In believing in justice though injustice inflict one defeat after another, in believing in the future despite the present." There are, he concludes, two kinds of unbelievers. On the one hand, there are those who regard themselves as believers, but whose ideals lie "not before them, but behind them, like some physical, tangible object of the past. . . . While mankind strives forward, these men, calling themselves philanthropists, liberals, men of the future, cling on with all their might to protect what has fallen, shore up what is crumbling, curse the presumption of those who demolish and deny, lend all their strength to reaction. In contrast to these, those whose highest ideals lie not behind them but ahead of them, in the future which they are preparing, build bridges over the abyss from the trees which they have felled and, in the darkest night, believe, with all the passion with which they have demolished and denied, in the dawn and the sunrise."

The poet of loneliness, of iron and fire, the divider not the uniter, the believer in truth and justice who "shows each man the way back to the powers he may discover within himself"—has any critic in the century since Brandes penned these words more penetratingly epitomised what Ibsen stood for, even though the judgment was delivered before Ibsen had written most of the work on which his fame rests? No wonder that, however fallible Brandes's judgment may have been concerning individual plays, not only Ibsen, but Strindberg also, regarded him as the one contemporary critic whose opinion they could respect.

That autumn, Ibsen got involved in a public row with H. J. Jensen, formerly the publisher of *Illustreret Nyhedsblad,* who claimed the right, since *Lady Inger of Østraat* and *The Vikings at Helgeland* had first appeared in his periodical, to reprint the two plays in book form. Ibsen protested; Jensen defended his claim in the newspapers; Ibsen's friends, Ludvig Daae and O. A. Bachke, entered the controversy on Ibsen's side, and Ibsen himself published two open letters on the subject in the Danish newspaper *Dagbladet.* Jensen, undeterred, brought out his pirated edition of *The Vikings,* whereupon Ibsen sued him. When the case finally reached the courts, four years later after Dickensian delays, Jensen was fined and ordered to pay compensation, and the edition was confiscated. Ibsen's letters of September and October 1871 are scattered with neurotic references to the matter. On 28 October, writing to Michael Birkeland, he hysterically blamed Norway in general for the publisher's action, declaring: "This business will leave its scar on me if I should live to be a hundred. . . . From now on I must regard myself as completely homeless. I know that certain of my friends would not mind this—I know some people think I can do my bulldog act in their interests better abroad than at home, and that therefore they do not want me home. Now they have achieved their wishes." The same day he wrote to Bachke: "The law protects the salmon in our rivers and the deer on the mountains, but authors seem to be classed with birds of prey; they do their best to smoke us out."

Simultaneously, he had become embroiled in an equally tedious controversy in the German press as a result of his uncomplimentary references to Germans in his Balloon poem. "The newspaper *Im neuen Reich,*" he informed Hegel on 27 December, "which is published in Leipzig under the editorship of Alfred Dove and Gustav Freytag, has attacked me for some of the things I have said in verse about the Germans. The battle has also been taken up in the *Constitutionelle Zeitung,* and several other papers of less import. I have of course been compelled to reply." Fortunately, these petty distractions did not hinder his work on *Emperor and Galilean.* "My new play," he told Hegel in the same letter, "goes forward unceasingly. Part One, 'Julian and the Friends of Wisdom,' comprising three acts, is already finished and *fair-copied.* . . . I am now busily engaged on Part Two, and this will go more quickly and be much shorter. Part Three will, though, be somewhat longer; the whole thing will probably run to between 280–300 pages, all in prose, in a style mainly approximating to that of *The Pretenders.*" Camilla Collett, the novelist champion of women's rights, was now in Dresden.[25] "She is thinking of proceeding to Rome," Ibsen told Hegel, "but I doubt if she will get any farther, for she has no idea how to arrange a journey." She was hopelessly unpractical and kept her gold coins in a matchbox. She and Ibsen met often and indulged in many lively debates; she was scandalized at what she regarded as the old-fashionedness of his ideas about woman's place in society. Her forthrightly expressed views on the subject were to have a considerable influence on him.

1871 had been another thin year financially, even worse than 1870. *Poems* had earned him 562 specie-dollars; a sixth edition of *Brand* had brought a welcome 212 specie-dollars; and *Morgenbladet* had paid him

---

[25] Edmund Gosse, who met her in Copenhagen three years later, got on less well with her than Ibsen did. "This lady, whom I found singularly unpleasing, had an air of affectation based, apparently, on her familiarity with Hamburg and Rome, but still more with Paris, where she seemed to have made a lengthy residence. She detested England and the English, and she stirred up Andreas Munch to satirical outbursts against us. . . . 'You belong, sir, to a nation of shopkeepers,' Camilla Collett remarked to me across the dinner table. The hackneyed impertinence was applauded by the host." (*Two Visits to Denmark,* p. 315.) But Gosse was always less happy with women than with men.

25 specie-dollars for the "Balloon Letter"—a total of 799 specie-dollars. His only other source of income had been his pension of 400 specie-dollars. But this was enough for his very modest requirements. "Everything has become dreadfully expensive here in Germany since the recent war," he wrote to Consul Bravo on 16 February 1872. "Luckily my income has risen proportionally, so that we can live without worry; new editions of my books are appearing regularly[!] and I am always busy with something new." He was miserly with his money, but not for selfish reasons. "The little capital which I have succeeded in amassing during these years," he told Johan Thoresen on 22 February, "must be further increased, if Suzannah and Sigurd are to be reasonably secured against all eventualities. This consideration precedes all others, as far as I am concerned. Nor can I be certain that my literary talents may not decline with time; I cannot rely on new editions of my books being printed every year." He badly needed to complete *Emperor and Galilean* during the next twelve months; in the event, he didn't, and 1872 was to prove, financially, a lean year indeed.

15

An English Admirer; and a New Friendship

1872–1873

On 24 February 1872 Ibsen made a fresh monetary application to the Ecclesiastical Department in Christiania, this time for a stipend of 450 specie-dollars to enable him "by comprehensive research in the Berlin Museum of Egyptology to complete my knowledge of Egyptian architecture and sculpture, and their connection with corresponding ancient forms of art in Europe. Next year family considerations will compel me to return home. I had planned to do so this year, but a big new work on which I am engaged makes this impossible. The mental disturbance inseparable from a change of residence and a re-entry into an environment which, after an absence of more than eight years, has in many respects become foreign to me, could not but leave an unfortunate mark on an uncompleted work." What these "family considerations" were is not clear, unless Sigurd's independence of outlook had been running him into further trouble at school. In any case, Ibsen's application was refused.

That month P. F. Siebold's German translation of *Brand* was at last published, the first foreign version of any of Ibsen's plays to be thus honoured. It was rapidly followed by German translations of *The Pretenders* and *The League of Youth;* and before they appeared, on 3 March, his name was printed for the first time in English.[1] The periodical was

[1] At any rate in England. But some time in 1872 (I have not been able to ascertain the month) a native of Bergen named Johan A. Dahl published there his own English translations of *Norwegian and Swedish Poems,* including (together with items by Wergeland, Welhaven, Andreas Munch, J. L. Runeberg, Esaias Tegnér, the National Anthem and a prose story by Bjørnson) "Terje Vigen." This brave effort is not always successful; for example:

> The sea rushed in thro' the opening broad,
> In two feet of water it sunk.
> And gone was the precious barley-load
> But not so our hero's spunk.

This volume is sometimes stated to have been published in 1874, but the title-page and preface are both dated 1872.

The Spectator, the article a review of Ibsen's *Poems,* and the author a twenty-three-year-old member of the cataloguing department at the British Museum. While on a visit to Norway two years previously, Edmund Gosse, who then knew no Norwegian, had gone into a bookshop at Trondhjem to buy an English novel, entered into conversation with the manager, H. L. Brækstad, and asked him whether Norway had any poets. Brækstad (who later became Norwegian vice-consul in London and translated Hans Andersen into English) showed Gosse a copy of Ibsen's *Poems* newly arrived that day from Copenhagen. "I put the small green volume in my pocket and left the shop. Of course I could not understand one word, but I could see that the versification was singular and good, and altogether felt much attracted to the unknown poet."[2]

That winter, at the suggestion of a colleague in the British Museum, W. R. S. Ralston, Gosse began a systematic study of the Dano-Norwegian language. Ralston probably thought it would be useful to have someone on the staff who could deal with Scandinavian literature; and Gosse had been told by the editor of *The Spectator,* R. H. Hutton: "The reason you get articles refused is because you write about the great familiar classics. Choose something out of the way, Scandinavian literature for instance, and you will get a hearing."[3] That was probably one reason why Gosse had gone to Norway, and indeed a travel article about the Lofoten Islands which he wrote on his return was the first thing he ever got published (in *Fraser's Magazine* in November 1871).

There was no Danish or Norwegian grammar or reader available in English then, and Gosse taught himself by going through a Danish novel with an English crib. He then managed to work his way through the book of poems he had bought in Trondhjem, and wrote a review which Hutton accepted. As well as dealing with the poems, the article naturally referred to Ibsen's dramatic achievements; and Gosse, always an assiduous cultivator of the great, sent a copy, with an accompanying letter, to Ibsen in Dresden, and received a gratifying reply:

Dresden, 2 April 1872

Most honoured sir!

Some days ago I had the great pleasure to receive your very flattering letter, accompanied by your kind review in "The spectator."

My knowledge of the English language is unfortunately not such that I dare attempt to write it, so I hope you will forgive me if I use

---

[2] From an autobiographical sketch written by Gosse in 1875 for a "profile" of him by K. A. Winter-Hjelm which appeared in *Ny Illustreret Tidende* on 14 February 1875. The sketch is quoted in full from the manuscript on pp. 82–85 of Elias Bredsdorff's *Sir Edmund Gosse's Correspondence with Scandinavian Writers* (Copenhagen, 1960), which gives (pp. 24–55 *et passim*) an excellent account of the development of Gosse's acquaintance with Ibsen, to which this chapter is much indebted.

[3] Bredsdorff, p. 2.

my native tongue to express my deepest and most heartfelt thanks for the generous way in which you have written of my work.

I could not wish to be introduced to a foreign public better or more sympathetically than in your excellent article; nor is there any public by whom I should be prouder to be read than the English. Should this, thanks to your kind and perceptive assistance, come about, I shall feel boundlessly and permanently indebted to you. . . .

The English people are so close to us Scandinavians spiritually, intellectually and emotionally—for which reason it has been especially painful to me that language should set a barrier between my writing and the whole of this great related world. So you will appreciate the pleasure you have given me by the prospect of removing this barrier.

Here in Germany several editions of my books are in preparation. A translation of *Brand* has been published in Cassel, but I am not satisfied with it. Another translation of the same play is announced in Berlin. Also in Berlin there have appeared German versions of *The Pretenders* and *The League of Youth,* both excellently rendered by Dr. Adolf Strodtmann, the admirable translator of Byron and Tennyson. Dr. Strodtmann is currently engaged in translating my shorter poems.

To be introduced to the English reading public is, though, my chief concern, and the sooner this could happen the happier I should be. . . .

Your most respectful and obliged
Henrik Ibsen

Gosse's reply is not extant, but he must have explained that his contribution to the campaign would mainly be in the form of articles and reviews, for on 11 April Ibsen informed Michael Birkeland: "The translations are to be executed by various hands, and Mr. Gosse, though in charge of the enterprise, is not likely to be most active in this side of the work, but will do his utmost to advance the cause by placing articles in the English newspaper." Gosse kept one-half of his promise,[4] for he published a review of *Peer Gynt* in *The Spectator* on 7 July, another

---

[4] Not without difficulty. "I had an introduction to the *Saturday Review*, so I submitted a longish article on *Peer Gynt.* Mr. Harwood, who was then the editor, said that I had used terms of so warm an eulogy that he could not publish the article unless I could find some other witness to the merit of this strange piece by an unknown foreign writer. But no sponsor for Ibsen's poetic respectability was forthcoming, and the review did not appear. A little later on I tried the same editor with an article on *The Young Men's League,* which was tartly rejected. . . . I wrote more articles, which were rejected. . . . Mr. Archer is the host, and his guests and dances; but it was I who swept the floor and lighted the candles." (An article by Gosse congratulating Ibsen on his seventieth birthday, printed in *The Sketch,* 23 March 1898, and quoted by Bredsdorff, p. 184.)

of *The Pretenders* in the *Academy* on 1 August, an article on "Norwegian Poetry since 1814" in the October issue of *Fraser's Magazine*, and, in January 1873, a long article in the *Fortnightly Review* entitled "Ibsen, the Norwegian Satirist." But in his attempts to arrange translations, he was less successful. He completed a blank verse version of *Love's Comedy* in the spring of 1873, but failed to find a publisher, and (not surprisingly, considering how few English people knew Norwegian, and the indifference shown to his own single effort) does not seem to have found any willing collaborators.[5] No English version of an Ibsen play was to appear before Catherine Ray's translation of *Emperor and Galilean* in 1876.

While Gosse was learning Norwegian in London and introducing Ibsen's name to a tiny section of the English public, Ibsen's Danish champion had been running into trouble in Copenhagen. On his return there the previous summer after the meeting in Dresden, Georg Brandes had applied for a position at Copenhagen University, where it was obvious that a successor would soon be needed to the octogenarian Carsten Hauch as Professor of Aesthetics. Hauch himself had been an early champion of Brandes, and the latter was asked to give a series of lectures to show his qualifications. He chose as his subject *Main Currents in Nineteenth-Century Literature,* and delivered his first lecture on 3 November 1871.

The hall was filled, one-third of the audience consisting of women; not only was Brandes the translator of Mill's *The Subjection of Women,* he was also known to have been the lover of a married woman with six children.[6] The lectures were a tremendous turning-point in Scandinavian culture. Brandes declared that Danish thinking was half a century behind the times, that it was reactionary and divorced from reality instead of, like French literature (which Brandes, fresh from his meetings with Taine and Renan, took as his model) dealing with contemporary social problems. Danish literature, he asserted, lived in the past; it was the duty of writers to live in the present and the future. Harmless as these sentiments appear today, they infuriated the powerful conservative element in Danish society and its press organs. In November Brandes wrote a satirical piece about a modern Red Riding Hood, a free-thinking girl who is gobbled up by the *opposition* press (he despised the official opposition party in Denmark as much as Ibsen did its counterpart in Norway). For this he was violently attacked in *Fædrelandet;* it and the other newspapers of the capital closed their columns to him, and to reply to the attack he had to insert a paid advertisement. When the first volume of Brandes's lectures was published

[5] Gosse also translated "The Poet's Song" from *Love's Comedy* and "Agnes" from *Brand,* and included them in his own collection of poems, *On Viol and Flute,* published in London in 1873.

[6] On these lectures, cf. Evert Sprinchorn's excellent note in his edition of *Ibsen's Letters and Speeches,* pp. 120–21. I do not like Mr. Sprinchorn's translation of the letters, except where it follows the Maurvik-Morison version of 1905, but his notes are informed and illuminating.

in February 1872 it, too, was violently abused in every Danish newspaper; and when Carsten Hauch died in March, his recommendation that Brandes should be his successor was ignored, and Brandes was not given a position at the university until thirty years later—the penalty of following Ibsen's advice about "needling the Danes." He wrote to Ibsen, pouring out his troubles; the letter has perished, but we have Ibsen's reply, the rough comfort of a battle-scarred veteran to a subaltern enduring his first experience of shellfire:

Dresden, 4 April 1872[7]

Dear Brandes!

I have this moment received your letter, and am replying immediately.

But what unbelievable news you tell me! And I imagined you revelling in success and triumph. Surely, though, you must have an army behind you. Remember that these are but recruits whom you are leading into battle. The first time, they will retreat; the second time, stand their ground; and after that they will follow you to victory.

So the liberal press has closed its doors to you. But of course! I once expressed to you my contempt for political freedom. You thought me wrong on that occasion. From your story of *The Red Hat* I see you have gained some experience. My dear friend, the liberals are the worst enemies of Freedom. Spiritual and intellectual freedom flourish best under absolutism; that was proved in France, then in Germany and it is now being proved in Russia.

But I must turn to what for these past weeks has continually filled my thoughts and disturbed my nightly rest. I have read your lectures.

A more dangerous book could never fall into the hands of a pregnant writer. It is one of those books which set a yawning gulf between yesterday and today. When I was in Italy I could not understand how I had managed to exist before I went there. In twenty years people will not understand how anyone managed to live spiritually in Scandinavia before these lectures. . . . Your book is not literary history in the accepted meaning, neither is it cultural history; what it is, I shall not attempt to describe. It is to me as the goldfields of California were to those who discovered them; they either made men millionaires or ruined them. Now, is our spiritual constitution in the North strong enough to survive this shock? I don't know; but it doesn't matter. Whatever cannot sustain these new ideas must fall.

You say everyone in the faculty of philosophy is against you.

[7] Ibsen misdated the letter 1871 (cf. Halvdan Koht's note in C.E., XIX, 497).

My dear Brandes, would you have it otherwise? Are you not fighting to destroy the philosophy of that faculty? A war such as yours cannot be waged by a crown servant. If they did not bar the door against you, it would show that you had failed to frighten them.

As regards this agitation which is being worked up against you, all these lies and calumnies and so forth, let me give you a word of advice which I know from experience to be sovereign. Be an aristocrat! Aristocracy of the spirit is the only weapon against this kind of thing. Appear indifferent; never write a word of reply in the newspapers; if you polemise in your writings, never direct your polemic against this or that specific attack; never write a single word which could make it seem as though your enemies had found their mark; in short, act as though you had no idea that anyone was opposed to you. What power of survival do you suppose your enemies' attacks will have? In the old days when I read an attack on me in the morning, I used to think: "Now I am finished, I shall never be able to hold up my head again!" But I did; no one any longer remembers what was written, and even I myself have long forgotten it. So, don't cheapen yourself by getting involved in mud-slinging. Start a new series of lectures, unperturbed, unmoved, maddeningly indifferent, cheerfully contemptuous of everything that is crumbling around you. Do you think that what is rotten to the core has any powers of resistance?

How this mortal combat between two epochs will end, I do not know; but anything is preferable to the *status quo*—of that I am certain. I do not promise myself that victory will result in any permanent improvement; every historical development has been but a lurch from one delusion to another. But the battle itself is good, healthy and invigorating; your revolt is a mighty and emancipating declaration of genius. When these old men complain that you mock God, they should reflect that they themselves are the mockers. The Great Aforesaid created you for a purpose.

I hear you have founded a society. Do not rely implicitly on everyone who joins you; what matters is whether they do so for the right reason. Nor am I sure that this will strengthen your position; my own conviction is that the strongest man is he who stands most alone. But I sit here outside it all while you stand there in the midst of the storm; that makes a big difference.

Au revoir, my dear Brandes! Keep a friendly place in your heart for me and mine, next to what must henceforth be the only important thing to you, because it is your own child in spirit and in truth.

Forgive the haste and incoherence of this letter!

Your affectionate
Henrik Ibsen

No wonder that Ibsen was so excited by *Main Currents,* which still reads wonderfully well today. The theme, as stated in Brandes's introduction, is "the revolution waged by the first decades of the nineteenth century against the literature of the eighteenth, and the victory of that revolution," as reflected in French, English and German literature up to 1848; in other words, the gradual conquest of liberal ideas through such writers as Byron, Hugo, Lamartine and Heine. It is easy to realize what a revelation this brilliant survey of Ibsen's spiritual ancestors must have been to one ever conscious of his imperfect education and inability to read French and English.

Meanwhile, *Emperor and Galilean* was grinding slowly on, for ever falling further behind schedule. On 19 January he had told Hegel that he hoped to have the whole play finished by June; on 24 April he was still optimistic enough to write: "I shall soon be ready with Part Two of *Julian.* The third and final section will go easily. The spring has now arrived here, and I always work best in warm weather." He was not in fact to complete even Part Two until August, nor the whole play until the following February. "We have had the pleasure of seeing several Danish travellers," continued this last letter to Hegel. "H. C. Andersen is now here." Andersen and Ibsen met on 22 April, and evidently got on well again, for Andersen (though he continued to spell his new friend Ipsen)[8] sent him a copy of the final volume of his *New Tales and Stories,* which had appeared that year. An undated letter from Ibsen, or rather a fragment of it, has survived: "Thank you for your visit to Dresden; thank you for the book; thank you for everything else. . . ." The rest of the letter has been cut away.[9]

On 7 July Edmund Gosse's review of *Peer Gynt* appeared in *The Spectator.* Not unnaturally, the play had considerably bewildered him, but much of the article still reads respectably. "The dramatic power displayed in this poem," Gosse declared, "quite raises it out of any mere local interest, and gives it a claim to be judged at a European tribunal." Like so many Scandinavian critics, however, he was disturbed by the jagged and discordant quality of the work; indeed, his criticisms almost suspiciously resemble Brandes's. "The book is not without marks of haste, and there is a general sense of incongruity and disjointedness . . . mixture of brilliant and crude elements; one is alternately delighted and scandalized. It is to be hoped that Ibsen will not be so led away in future by the perilous sweetness of the Lynean god as to neglect to give his work its due elaboration and polish." English critics were saying very much the same kind of thing about Robert Browning.

Some time early in July Ibsen moved from Dippoldiswaldær-Strasse to a new apartment at Grosse Plauensche Strasse 9, and on the fifteenth he

[8] Cf. Andersen's letter to Martin Henriques, 20 April 1872. (*H. C. Andersens Dagbøger og Breve, 1868–75,* p. 118.)

[9] C.E., XVII, 46.

took Suzannah and Sigurd for a holiday to Berchtesgaden, where they had enjoyed themselves four years previously. There he received a request from Brandes to help him and his brother Edvard in a new magazine they were planning, to be named *The Nineteenth Century* and to be published by Gyldendal. Ibsen replied (23 July) that he was thinking of writing some more rhymed epistles on the lines of the "Balloon Letter" and the "Letter to Fru Heiberg," "concerning our position, and that of our age in general, vis-à-vis politics, literature, etc. They would be a kind of declaration of faith." But he refused to associate himself more actively with Brandes's project. "They would be of no direct help to you and your cause; but, my dear Brandes, this is all I can do for you. I must confine myself within my own chosen sphere; here, all my thoughts are concentrated. Its range is not wide, but I exploit it as best I can. Please don't regard this as evidence of egotism! How soon I can begin these epistles for you, I don't know; the monster Julian still has so firm a hold on me that I cannot get away from him. But we can discuss this in more detail later, preferably when we meet. I do not in the least fear being regarded as holding partisan sympathies," he concluded surprisingly. "I cannot understand why people now regard me as having no party allegiances." Presumably he meant by this last sentence that his criticisms of the faults of the left did not imply that his sympathies lay elsewhere, and that one could owe allegiance to a party without toeing the line, just as a man can regard himself as a good Catholic while retaining the right to independent criticism.

On 18 July Norway celebrated her thousand years as a kingdom, and Ibsen wrote a special poem for the occasion which the university library in Christiania printed on the day. It contained one of the most disturbing messages of thanks that any country or individual can ever have received. Edmund Gosse was not always the most accurate of translators, but his rendering of the first two verses of this poem will hardly be bettered:

> My countrymen, who filled for me deep bowls
> Of wholesome bitter medicine, such as gave
> The poet, on the margin of his grave,
> Fresh strength to fight where broken twilight rolls—
> My countrymen, who sped me o'er the wave—
> An exile, with my griefs for pilgrim-souls,
> My fears for burdens, doubts for staffs, to roam—
> From the wide world I send you greeting home.
>
> I send you thanks for gifts that help and harden,
> Thanks for each hour of purifying pain;
> Each plant that prospers in my poet's garden
> Is rooted where your harshness poured its rain;
> Each shoot in which it blooms and burgeons forth

> It owes to that grey weather from the north;
> The sun's fire loosens, but the fog secures!
> My country, thanks! My life's best gifts were yours.[10]

He worked hard on *Julian* in Berchtesgaden, and on 8 August he was able to write joyfully to Hegel that he had completed Part Two and assure him that the third and final part "is so clear in my mind that it will go very much quicker than the others." On 30 August he left for Dresden where, a fortnight later, he was joined by Georg Brandes. This time, Brandes stayed a month, during which period he saw Ibsen almost daily, and his autobiography contains some vivid reminiscences of their meetings:[11]

Each day I walked from the small, very bad hotel which he had recommended to me nearby, and collected him for a walk, often broken by a visit to an inn, where the waiters were impressed by the barbaric splendour of his buttonhole, but invariably ending with tea at his apartment. I received a new impression after the year that had passed since I had last seen him. Not very tall, but handsome, athletically built, with a mighty head, big neck, powerful shoulders—he looked as though one would need a club to overpower him. He spoke, in general, little, though he was communicative to me; but the curious thing about his speech was its calm and slowness, and the fact that he never smiled except when the person to whom he was talking smiled first. This sometimes had an effect that was almost of timidity. Yet if one had to choose a single adjective to describe him, it would be menacing. He could look terrifying, as he sat with his watchful eyes. Then he resembled a judge. He looked a man who was accustomed, in intercourse with other men, to occupy the standpoint of a schoolmaster confronting his pupils, and to instil fear. For all his hostility towards the Norwegians he was, in essence, very Norwegian.

There lay stored within him twenty-four years of bitterness and hatred; his contempt for humanity knew no limits. He was an aristocrat to his fingertips, with all that that implied. It was an article of faith with him that all politicians—parliamentary politicians, that is, not men such as Bismarck—were hypocrites, liars, drivellers, dogs. . . . His hatred for false freedom movements was supplanting his interest in genuine ones. . . . The true freedom was social freedom, spiritual freedom, freedom of thought, freedom of conscience. . . . He hated the liberals of Norway,[12] and regarded most Nor-

[10] The Christiania magazine *Vikingen* printed a cartoon showing Ibsen standing in front of a magic mirror flanked by a beer-mug and a money-bag marked "Poet's Pension 400 [specie-dollars]," the objects being reflected in the mirror as a pilgrim's staff and a glass marked "wholesome bitter medicine."

[11] *Levned*, II, 99 ff. Cf. also Brandes's letter to Hans Brøchner, 29 September 1872; *Brandes Brevveksling*, I, 171–73.

[12] "In political matters he is very conservative, or rather absolutist. . . . The political liberals are almost illiberal in intellectual matters, and he says it is better to be under the rule of one big tyrant than several little ones." (Letter from Brandes to Hans Brøchner, 29 September 1872; *Brandes Brevveksling*, I, 172.)

wegian peasants as sordid and self-seeking. . . . He laughed at Bjørnson's rustic tales: he chortled over the space that love occupied in them, saying that nothing bothered the Norwegian peasant less, unless one used the word "love" in its crudest sense. A youth of twenty would gladly marry a woman of sixty if she were well-to-do. Let Bjørnson but continue till his hero Arne got into Parliament, and we should see that fellow in his true colours. Many years later I learned from Ibsen's letters that he at times felt friendly towards Bjørnson, even infatuated. But on this occasion, and others, I heard him name Bjørnson only with the most vehement distaste and contempt. The violence of his fanaticism struck me one day when in an angry outburst he decried Magdalene Thoresen's writings, damned their language, called them artificial and false, and then broke off to remark: "Mind you, she has more talent than that Bjørnson." One must, however, add that, as Christian Rickardt once rightly observed, Ibsen never spoke as disparagingly of Bjørnson as the latter did of him.

Walking out towards Plauenscher Grund he said: "Scandinavia lies outside the cultural mainstream. The unhappy consequence is that we never get anywhere until the rest of Europe has moved on. . . . It is as though one were to introduce astronomy into Madagascar and begin with the Ptolemaic system. . . ." He spoke of the importance of written work having "an intense connection with the author's spiritual life," and thought the major advance of the age was that poetry was becoming more and more psychological, and not merely poetry but all literature. "What will ensure your latest book a future life is that it reveals how *you* have regarded things. If you want objectivity, then go to the objects. Read me so as to get to know *me!*" He thought that this was the great literary revolution that he was attempting.[13]

Of *Emperor and Galilean,* Brandes recalled: "At first he could not be persuaded to read a line of it to me. When he wanted to rewrite a scene to refine the dialogue, he would not let me see its first, inferior form. He said: 'I never write a line without asking myself: "What will G.B. think of this?" So how could I let you see it in the rough?' However, he shortly afterwards read me long extracts, including the scene between Julian and the mystic Maximos. His quiet voice lent itself well to the expression of what was powerful and disturbing." He took Brandes to more than one meeting of the Dresden Literary Society (where, says Brandes, Ibsen regularly attended lectures); among other subjects, they heard a talk on Tieck's essay on the monologues in *Hamlet,* "of which, strangely enough," comments Brandes, "I was the only person present who had foreknowledge."

Another Danish visitor to Dresden that month was Meïr Aron Goldschmidt, founder of *The Corsair,* the magazine on which, twenty years earlier, Botten Hansen and Vinje had modelled *The Man,* to give Ibsen his

---

[13] Another example of Ibsen's imperfect acquaintance with literary history. "Read me so as to know *me*" had been one of the principles of the Romantic movement throughout Europe at the beginning of the century, as one would have expected him to know from his acquaintance with Byron's work.

first opening in journalism. Goldschmidt invited Ibsen and Brandes to dinner at the Hotel Berlin. The conversation turned to religion. Goldschmidt denied that Voltaire was an atheist, and suddenly asked Ibsen if he believed in God. Ibsen "replied in astonishment at this inquisition: 'Certainly.' 'Then I don't see how you can associate with someone like Brandes who doesn't believe in any God. . . .' Ibsen replied in rising displeasure: 'I have no idea what Brandes believes in or doesn't believe in. I have never discussed it with him, and feel no cause to.' "[14]

They talked of Brandes's plans for a new magazine, and Ibsen wrote to Hegel to try to persuade him to back it. "If *you* will publish it," he wrote on 15 September, "I think, nay, I feel sure, that it will succeed and be able to survive with profit for some considerable time. In my experience an enterprise of this kind depends almost totally on its publisher. I need hardly add that, once assured of this, I shall gladly associate myself with the project as closely or distantly as you may think fit. I long for a regular secondary occupation and had indeed thought of contacting one or another of our public media when Dr. Brandes and subsequently yourself mentioned this project, which attracts me more than any other. Hegel agreed, and the result was *Det Nittende Aarhundrede (The Nineteenth Century)*, edited by Georg Brandes and his brother Edvard, which set a new standard for critical journalism in Scandinavia.

Ibsen does not record what Brandes said to him during these meetings in Dresden; but some things, at least, we can guess at, and if we are correct, they were to bear importantly on Ibsen's future work. As Dr. Henning Fenger, the distinguished Brandes scholar, points out, Brandes had that spring followed up his lectures of the preceding winter with a series of six on the development of French drama from Beaumarchais to Dumas *fils*. In these lectures, Brandes had shown especial interest in the connection between money and morality—the way French dramatists regarded money as playing a vital role in determining human destinies, the way false share dealings are brought to light, and so forth. This interlocking of money with morality was something that was to feature strongly in *The Pillars of Society* and *A Doll's House*. Moreover, from these unpublished lectures Dr. Fenger quotes Brandes's description of the new type of woman who was threatening to replace the traditional romantic heroines:

> This young girl is no longer ignorant of life and the world. She walks forth into it self-possessed and sceptical. She does not throw herself at the first man who asks her. Even in extreme youth, she has a character of her own. She has a man's seriousness, power of decision, and will.

These words exactly describe the "heroines" (did anyone then, in conversation if not in print, ever refer to them as anti-heroines?) whom Ibsen

[14] Georg Brandes, *Levned*, II, 107.

was henceforth to create, beginning with Dina Dorf, Nora and Petra Stockmann, and of whom Selma in *The League of Youth* was, as we have seen, in a small way (for she has very few lines) the forerunner.

Brandes also, in his lectures, praised Dumas *fils* for his realism and "physiological, clinical view of human nature . . . a directness, a brutality, but at the same time a truthfulness of expression hitherto unparalleled."[15] One must assume that Brandes expatiated on this to Ibsen during their Dresden walks; and any writer knows how immensely stimulating and strengthening it is when, apparently ploughing a lonely furrow, he meets someone who can crystallize in clear language his own unstated intuitions.

Most importantly, perhaps, Brandes had demanded in his lectures that the Scandinavian dramatists should employ "careful and truthful study of human character" in the service of liberal thought—in other words, not stand objectively and ironically aloof, as Ibsen had done in *The League of Youth*, but use the drama as a pulpit for preaching the ideals of the new age. Dr. Fenger rightly comments that to Ibsen this uncompromising demand that he should commit himself must have come as manna from heaven. "Here was the answer to the problems he had wrestled with in 1869–70. . . . A whole-hearted commitment to the ideals of the new age was something that would lift and animate the most realistic portrait of actuality."[16] Remembering that these lectures of Brandes were (and were to remain) unpublished, the conversations that Ibsen had with him in Dresden that September may well have been vital in stimulating Ibsen to make the leap from the uncommittedness of *The League of Youth* to the committed progressiveness of *The Pillars of Society* and its great successors.

In England, Edmund Gosse's review of *Peer Gynt* had been followed by another of *The Pretenders,* published in the *Academy* of 1 August. Gosse sent copies of both articles to Ibsen as they appeared, from Denmark where he was holidaying, but Ibsen does not seem to have replied, or even to have acknowledged them. Undeterred, Gosse sent Ibsen another article early in October, on the subject of "Norwegian Poetry since 1814," which had appeared in *Fraser's Magazine* of that month; and this, at last, elicited a response from Ibsen, the warmth of which must have consoled Gosse for the months of silence. "A better, clearer or kinder interpretation of my poem I could not wish for," wrote Ibsen (14 October) of the review of *Peer Gynt*. "I only wish that the praise you extend to my work were fully justified; the objections you make are reasonable enough; I can partly see the faults myself, now that time has set me at a sufficient distance to be able to consider it as though it were by another hand." After praising the

[15] It is interesting that, according to the French scholar P. G. la Chesnais (*Oeuvres Complètes d'Henrik Ibsen,* XI, 409), Dumas *fils* was probably partly responsible for the first (private) staging in France of *A Doll's House* in 1891.
[16] "Ibsen og Georg Brandes indtil 1872," pp. 207–8.

other two articles, Ibsen continued: "I am working daily on *Julian the Apostate* and hope to have the whole play ready by the end of the year. As soon as the book is printed I will send you a copy, and can only hope it will win your approval. I have put a good deal of my own spiritual life into this book; I have myself lived through what I portray, in other forms; and the historical theme I have chosen has a closer connection with our own time than people might suppose before reading it. This I regard as an indispensable prerequisite to any modern treatment of material so remote in time, if it is to arouse interest as an original work."

That autumn a new artistic director, Hartvig Lassen, had been appointed at the Christiania Theatre, and on 24 October Ibsen wrote to him suggesting that he consider staging *Love's Comedy*. "The fears I once had regarding the presentation of this play," he explained, "have long since disappeared. I have for various reasons become convinced that the public now realizes that this is, in essence, a deeply moral work; and artistically, I am more than ever sure that it is irreproachable, and at any event not bettered by anything else I have written. All in all, I rate *Love's Comedy* among my best efforts. I think my standing in Scandinavian literature gives me a certain right to make this friendly request, which would be superfluous for an author similarly placed in any other country."

He enclosed a suggested cast list, adding: "If Johannes Brun could, without damage to things generally, be kept out of it, it would in some ways ease my mind. . . . As a fee I should require the gross receipts from the premiere against a guaranteed minimum of 300 specie-dollars." Lassen replied promptly, on 2 November, saying that he had only hesitated about staging *Love's Comedy* because he had feared his company was inadequate to the demands of the play; Ibsen's letter had, however, dispelled his fears, and he would present it as worthily as his resources would allow. Ibsen wrote again on 14 November with further casting suggestions, and explaining his doubts about Brun. "Is Herr Brun capable nowadays of learning a part properly? Can he be persuaded to subject himself to the inconvenience? . . . If he plays it for comedy, Svanhild's decision, the trickiest thing in the play, may easily seem too crude; and if he plays it seriously, without comedy, he will be in a field foreign to him. Might it not be appropriate to approach Herr Reimers? Herr R. is an intelligent man, and if he can play the part I think he will act it in such a way that Svanhild's abandonment of Falk for the tradesman may not seem impossible, which would be a great gain."[17]

Ibsen evidently assumed from Lassen's letter that the play would be put on that season, for the next week he told Hegel that it would be staged "in the very near future"; but changes were made at the theatre and Lassen

[17] These two letters to Lassen were not discovered until 1960, and are not in the Centenary Edition. Øyvind Anker published them in his article "Kjærlighedens Komedie på Christiania Theater" in *Edda* (1961), pp. 59–81.

was reduced to the position of artistic consultant (the post Ibsen himself had held briefly a decade earlier). The direction of the theatre was entrusted to a Swede, Ludvig Josephson—much to Ibsen's subsequent advantage—and *Love's Comedy* had to be postponed until the following autumn.

Some time during November Ibsen moved for the second time that year, from Grosse Plauensche Strasse to a first-floor apartment at Wettiner-Strasse 22. Thence on 20 November he assured Hegel that "I definitely hope to have my new play finished by the end of the year. . . . During the summer I plan to give *Lady Inger* a thorough going-over with the Royal Danish Theatre in mind, after which, if all goes well, I am thinking of writing a longish comedy, the plan of which is already pretty well matured." This last project may have been *The Pillars of Society,* or (which is very possible) it may have been some other plan which never came to fruition.

Ibsen had a welcome visitor that month in Lorentz Dietrichson, whom he had not seen since his visit to Stockholm three years earlier. Dietrichson, like Brandes, enjoyed the unusual pleasure of hearing Ibsen read Part One of *Julian,* and remembered the disappointment of the thirteen-year-old Sigurd at being ordered into another room to do his divinity homework instead of being allowed to listen. "I think there's as much divinity in father's play as in my homework," he pleaded, but in vain. "Although Ibsen has no outstanding talent for reading [writes Dietrichson], it was a rare and exquisite delight to hear him read his drama in his pleasant voice and noble, totally unaffected diction." It was nearly midnight before Ibsen read the final line: "For Thine is the Kingdom, the Power and the Glory"; and Dietrichson walked home "quite shaken, and convinced that I had heard one of the most remarkable tragedies written since the time of Shakespeare. Its mighty figures haunted me even in my dreams."[18]

Dietrichson (again like Brandes) was amazed that Ibsen had not made the acquaintance of Hermann Hettner, whose *Das moderne Drama* had so excited the dramatist twenty years earlier, and who was now living in Dresden. "I tried to bring them together, but did not succeed in the few days I could spend in Dresden. Hettner knew Ibsen's name well, indeed, almost everyone I met in Dresden was aware that a great Norwegian writer was dwelling in their midst; but very few then knew his work, and those who had read his *Brand* in Siebold's translation . . . could not really get a grip on the work; they could of course sense the grandeur of its scope, but found its full meaning, to put it mildly, obscure."[19]

Ibsen's avoidance of Hettner may have been conscious; as we have

[18] Dietrichson, I, 354–55.
[19] *Ibid.,* p. 354.

seen, he had a neurotic fear of admitting that he owed a debt to anyone, a feeling which is perhaps tied up with his obsession about bankruptcy. He may, too, have felt that he had outgrown Hettner's teaching and would gain little from a meeting, for Hettner had written nothing very interesting since (though Brandes had met him several times and found him rewarding). The other fact which Dietrichson mentions, that Ibsen's German literary acquaintances had to take his reputation on trust—in the next five years, only *The Vikings at Helgeland* and *Lady Inger of Østraat* were to be translated, in addition to the three plays published earlier that year, and of his best work, *Brand* was most inadequately translated and *Peer Gynt* not at all—no doubt helped to increase his already formidable reserve.

Ibsen spent the last months of 1872 combining Parts One and Two of his *Julian* trilogy into a single part of five acts, and beginning the draft of his final section (the ultimate Part Two).[20] The great work was at last approaching its end; indeed, it was urgent that it should, as Ibsen must have realized when making up his balance sheet for the year. His total earnings for 1872 were the two hundred specie-dollars which he had received for the third edition of *The Pretenders*. And this was five years after the publication of *Peer Gynt*.

[20] Cf. J. W. McFarlane's note in *The Oxford Ibsen*, IV (London, 1963), 560.

16

The End of Several Phases

1873–1875

1873 opened propitiously for Ibsen, in several respects. On New Year's Day the *Fortnightly Review* in London published a long article by Edmund Gosse entitled "Ibsen, the Norwegian Satirist," the first full assessment of Ibsen in English. "Where shall we look for a young great poet among the continental nations?" asked Gosse. "It is my firm belief that in the Norwegian, Henrik Ibsen, the representative of a land unknown in the literary annals of Europe, such a poet is found. . . . Ibsen has many golden arrows in his quiver, and he stands, cold and serene, between the dawn and the darkness, shooting them one by one into the valley below, each truly aimed at some folly, some affectation, of the everyday life we lead." After surveying Ibsen's life and development, Gosse passed on to a discussion of "his three great satires," *Love's Comedy*, *Brand* and *Peer Gynt*, quoting long extracts of the first and third plays in his own translation. The article concluded: "*Love's Comedy*, *Brand* and *Peer Gynt*, despite their varied plots, form a great satiric trilogy—perhaps for sustained vigour of expression, for affluence of execution, and for brilliance of dialogue, the greatest of modern times. They form, at present, Ibsen's principal and foremost claim to immortality; their influence over thought in the North has been boundless and, sooner or later, they will win for their author the homage of Europe. It was a white day with me when I first took *Brand* into my hands in the languor of a summer's day at Trondhjem, and I may trust that some competent translator will one day set these books before my countrymen in an English dress."

News also arrived from Hegel that reprints were in hand of both *Brand* and *Love's Comedy;* and Ibsen himself had good tidings to send in reply. "I have the great joy," he wrote on 6 February, "to be able to inform you that my great work is finished, and more happily so than anything I have previously written. The book is entitled *Emperor and*

Galilean; A World Drama in Two Parts. It contains: Part One: Cæsar's Apostasy, a play in five acts (170 pages). Part Two: Emperor Julian, a play in five acts (252 pages). Do not let the description "World Drama" frighten you! I shall begin fair-copying the play in a week and shall send you a weekly batch of 48 pages. . . . This has been a Herculean labour for me; not the work itself, that has gone easily, but the pain it has cost me to live myself freshly and vividly into so distant and alien an age." The letter ended with a request for money. "I have in my credit account with you and in the savings bank about 49 riks-dollars. Will you advance me as much as, added to this sum, will make 150 Prussian thaler, and send it to me? The Christiania Theatre's procrastination concerning *Love's Comedy* leaves me financially embarrassed, and I need money." He explained his plans for the summer: "I shall completely rewrite *Lady Inger of Østraat,* and it will be one of my best books."

Ibsen at first kept pretty well to his timetable for the fair-copying; he posted batches of forty-eight pages to Hegel on 22 February, 1 March, and 9 March. Then there was a gap until 22 April, but further instalments followed on 30 April, 9 May, and finally 24 May. "There is much self-anatomy in this book," he told Edmund Gosse, who used the information to publish a brief note about its imminent appearance in the *Academy* on 1 April; and to Ludvig Daae, who was helping him with the spelling of the Greek names, he wrote: "The play deals with a conflict between two irreconcilable powers in human life which will always be repeated, and that is why I call it 'A World-Historical Drama.'" It would, he assured Daæ, "be my masterpiece."

Even the Dresden Literary Society began to take notice of him, thanks to Strodtmann's translations of *The Pretenders* and *The League of Youth,* and his praise of Ibsen in a series of articles in the *Hamburg Correspondent.* The articles especially, he told Strodtmann (20 March) "have added immeasurably to my standing here. They have been the subject of three separate lectures in the Literary Society, together with the two plays you translated. This has put me back into a good humour with my surroundings, so that I now feel happy again in Dresden—the only home I can imagine for myself north of the Alps." Yet he concluded his letter: "I stand unspeakably alone, today—which happens to be my birthday— more than ever."

He tried to read Georg Brandes's translation of Mill's *Utilitarianism,* but found it, like most theoretical writing (apart from Brandes's own), unsatisfying. "I don't know," he wrote to Brandes on 30 April, "whether I dare express an opinion on a subject on which I have no professional expertise. When, however, I reflect that there are writers who lay down the law about philosophy without any knowledge of Hegel or German thought in general, it seems to me that anything is allowed. So I must honestly tell you that I cannot see any hope of progress, or any future at all, in the way Stuart Mill prescribes. I don't see why you have bothered to translate this book, the philistine sophistry of which harks back to Cicero or Seneca. I am convinced you could have written a ten times better book yourself in half the time it must have taken you to translate it. . . . Come here soon! I long to see you, despite our many differences of opinion." Brandes, he must have felt, was the only person who could relieve his loneliness.

While he was awaiting the publication of *Emperor and Galilean,* a pleasant diversion offered itself. He was invited to attend the International Exhibition in Vienna as representative for Denmark and Norway on the jury which was to award the prizes in the painting and sculpture sections. The Exhibition opened on 1 May, but Ibsen's services were not required until the following month. He left Dresden by train on the evening of 12 June, and the day after his arrival in Vienna he wrote to Suzannah. It is the earliest of his letters to her that has survived:

Vienna, 14 June 1873

Dear Suzannah!

A few hasty words, just to put you in the picture. I arrived here yesterday morning at nine o'clock, and was met at the station by Thomas,[1] who brought me word from Tobias Møller that I could have a room next to his, which he strongly recommended. I could not have done better! The house, which is near the Exhibition, only fifteen minutes' walk or five minutes' ride for five *kreutzer,* is an excellent and respectable hotel in the most elegant part of the city. The first floor, which I have rented, overlooking the street, or avenue, belongs to a baroness, who has left town and instructed her *Wirthschafterin,* or housekeeper, to rent out the room for the summer. She is an absolute pearl of amiability, honesty and helpfulness. Hildur[2] is enthusiastic about her, and rightly. For my room, with service, cleaning and valeting, errands within the city, etc., I pay 80 *gulden* a month, i.e., about 2½ *gulden* a day. She brings me coffee when I require it, with rolls and butter for breakfast, all for 30 *kreutzer* or 6 *groschen.* I ate breakfast here this morning, beautifully served on a silver tray with a cloth and napkin, a whole small pot of coffee, lots of milk, bread, butter, and sugar, all of the best quality, and delicious.

I visited the Exhibition yesterday, but cannot of course yet venture any opinion on it. I live next to the Møllers. Our admirable landlady lives quite alone in the house and sees to everything herself.

Møller and I have to go out now to pay our official respects. It is

---

[1] The elder of Magdalene's two sons by Dean Thoresen. They both died at the age of thirty, Thomas (who was a successful writer of vaudevilles) in 1876, Axel in 1881.

[2] The daughter of Randolph Nilsen, with whom he had stayed at Bergen in 1863.

said to be expensive here, but I have found that I can manage economically for lunch, etc.

This must be all for today. Be patient in my absence and write soon to

Your affectionate
Henrik Ibsen

When you write you can until further notice use the address I gave you. My lodging is: Augarten Allée-Strasse no. 23, first floor.

Suzannah's birthday fell on 26 June, and Ibsen dutifully remembered it:

Vienna, 25 June 1873

Dear Suzannah!

Now that the good time approaches when there will be roasting and frying for three days on end, and the coffee-pot will simmer unceasingly from early morning, I write you a few words to wish you many happy returns of the day. The only handsome present that I can offer you for the moment is the enclosed banknote, which I beg that you will not disdain, and which you will be able to change immediately into Prussian currency. Had Thomas not been inaccessible these past days, I would have sent some small thing with him. But he remained invisible, and left without saying goodbye. So you must be patient, dear cattttt!

The jury work has now started in earnest, so you must not expect long letters from me for a while. I have become a juror for both painting and sculpture, and have therefore double duties. My timetable is as follows: in the morning I rise at 6, and by 8 have completed my toilet, eaten breakfast, read the newspaper and smoked my morning pipe. Then I go out to the Exhibition, where the painting jury meets from 9 to 12. As soon as this is finished, I go to a restaurant nearby, where I eat a good meat dish, with admirable beer. At 2 the sculpture jury's meetings begin, and these last till 4:30 or 5. These meetings are, however, not always confined to the table; for example, these last days we have been walking round the huge Exhibition buildings studying the works of art. There has of course been no question of any midday siesta since I arrived in Vienna. When the jury meetings are finished I am, as you can imagine, tired. Then I sit down in one of the many open-air restaurants in the Prater and look at the thousands of people driving along the avenue while I eat my evening meal, comprising bread and cheese, with excellent beer. At 9 I go home and, immediately, to bed. I greatly enjoy this life here. They have not yet begun to offer hospitality to the jurymen, though I hear this is to come later.

Thank you for your letter and the *strilen*'s [Marie's]. Yes, I have received *Lady Inger*. Dietrichson is expected here. Each day I find myself in the company of many notables, and all the officials at the Exhibition have instructions to show us the greatest respect.

Write again soon. I shall only be able to send our dear young student[3] my visiting card today. I shall celebrate tomorrow by indulging in some luxury.

Happy birthday!
Your affectionate
Henrik Ibsen

Ibsen stayed in Vienna until the end of July. One of his fellow-jurors was a Swede, Fritz von Dardel, a gifted caricaturist (and much besides) whose diaries are an endless source of fascination to anyone interested in the Scandinavia of those years. In addition to a lively drawing of Ibsen, Dardel (to whom, almost alone among his fellow-jurors, Ibsen's name was known) noted in his diary:

> The black clothes and white cravat which he always wore, and the searching, penetrating glance which issued from behind his spectacles, gave him the appearance of a French notary rather than an artist. Throughout all our meetings he remained completely silent, spoke to no one and avoided all opportunity of making the acquaintance of his fellows, who were mostly eminent persons. When the rest of us went to take lunch together in the restaurant, Ibsen retired to the beer-hall, where he sat quite alone emptying his tankards. I joined him there a couple of times, and found much interest in his conversation. My fellow-jurors were amazed when I told them that their supposed notary was a famous dramatist.[4]

On 8 July the jurors were presented to the Emperor Franz Josef, whom Ibsen had seen from a distance at the Suez opening; and four days later, they were taken by train to Murz to be dined by Baron Schwarz-Senborn, the director of the Exhibition. "At every station where the train halted," the *Illustrated London News* of 19 July 1873 reported, "troops of little children came running up with baskets of wild strawberries, bouquets of Alpine flowers, and jugs full of fresh, cool water from the mountain springs. . . . At the repast which followed the greatest conviviality prevailed." Six days later Ibsen was awarded another medal to add to his collection. On 18 May the new King of Sweden and Norway, Oscar II (the younger brother of Carl XV, who had died of syphilis without legitimate male issue), having been crowned in Stockholm in

---

[3] Koht (C.E., XIX, 554) takes this to refer to Thomas Thoresen's younger brother Axel, but Bergliot Ibsen (p. 52) states that the phrase was one which Ibsen used affectionately of his fourteen-year-old son; presumably he enclosed a short note on a visiting card to Sigurd as an apology for not writing him a letter.

[4] Fritz von Dardel, *Dagboksanteckningar, 1873–1876* (Stockholm, 1916), pp. 28–29.

May, was crowned again before his Norwegian subjects in Trondhjem. In the ensuing welter of decorating Ibsen received the coveted Order of St. Olaf. On 26 July the jurors were invited on a trip to Budapest along the Danube, but Ibsen, surprisingly, seems not to have gone; at any rate there is no mention of it in his letters. It is possible that he had, by then, already left; the date of his departure from Vienna is not known.

He wrote a short report on the Exhibition for *Morgenbladet,* which that newspaper published on 30 August. What impressed Ibsen most were the entries from Eastern Europe. The Exhibition, he writes, "will dispel certain prejudices which have hitherto existed; I refer especially to the outdated superstition that the Slav peoples have little or nothing to contribute to the great common task of civilization. The acquaintance which Europe has made in recent years with Russian writing should have ended such an attitude; but I have no doubt that the Vienna Exhibition will lead to a quite different and juster appraisal. It teaches us that in every sphere of graphic art Russia stands among the leaders of our age." Ibsen concluded by asserting that Russia possessed "a school of painters fully comparable with those of France, Germany, or any other country"—a judgment hardly confirmed by posterity—and suggested that young Norwegian artists should be given grants to enable them to visit Vienna.

Ibsen's taste in painting was less discriminating than his taste in literature; for, explaining that "medals could only be awarded to living artists and then only for works completed since 1867, a condition to which several countries, notably England, paid scant attention," he adds: "Thus the English exhibits, though almost exclusively comprising masterpieces, gained comparatively few medals." What were these "masterpieces" provided by England? Ibsen does not name them, but a list is given in the *Official Catalogue of the British Section at the Vienna Universal Exhibition, 1873* (London, 1873). Turner, who had been dead for over twenty years, was represented by "Walton Bridges," Whistler by six etchings, and Cruikshank by five. Otherwise, there was W. P. Frith's "Ramsgate Sands" and "Lord Foppington Relating His Adventures" (from Vanbrugh's play, *The Relapse*); Millais's "Portrait of Miss Nina Lehmann" and "The Sisters"; G. F. Watts's "Portrait of Robert Browning" and "The Angel of Death"; Landseer's "The Sanctuary" (lent by Queen Victoria) and "The Arab Tent" and "Self-Portrait" (both lent by the Prince of Wales); and Thomas Woolner's bust of Charles Darwin, lent by the subject. Also in the oils section were Mrs. E. M. Ward's "The Tower, Aye, the Tower" and "The Last Sleep of Argyll"; W. B. Richmond's "The Lament of Ariadne"; George A. Storey's "The Shy Pupil"; C. V. Cope's "Othello Relating His Adventures to Desdemona"; John Pettie's "Touchstone and Audrey"; and Sir G. Harvey's "School Dismissing."

It is a melancholy comment on Ibsen's taste in painting, which was always to remain curiously conservative (to the end of his life there is no record of his taking any interest in Impressionism[5]), that he should have described this collection as "almost exclusively comprising master-pieces"; nor could they even be defended on the ground of realism; they were the visual equivalent of exactly the kind of sentimental melo-drama that he was trying to lead the theatre away from. A seventeen-year-old Scot, also in Vienna that August, making his journalistic debut as a roving correspondent for the *Alloa Advertiser*, condemned the whole of the English art section as "glaringly inferior." But the two men did not meet; William Archer had not yet heard of Ibsen.

Nor, one supposes, had a young Jew who left school in Vienna that summer and was likewise to become a passionate admirer. Sigmund Freud was then just seventeen, and in some ways his and Ibsen's lives and personalities were curiously similar. "I could tell you about my long years of honourable, but painful, loneliness that began for me as soon as I got the first glimpse into the new world; of the lack of interest and understanding on the part of my nearest friends; of the anxious moments when I myself believed I was in error and wondered how it was going to be possible to follow such unconventional paths and yet support my family . . . and of the calm certainty which bade me wait until a voice from beyond my ken would respond." That is Freud writing to Jung in 1910, but the words could have been Ibsen's; and in a few years Ibsen might have echoed: "I understood that from now onward I belong to those who have 'troubled the sleep of the world,' as Hebbel says, and that I could not reckon upon objectivity and tolerance." To Freud too, as to Ibsen, Rome "became the symbol for a number of warmly cherished wishes," and a source of "great happiness and even exaltation . . . expe-rienced on every visit." And one suspects that Ibsen, like Freud, had a "confessed need for periodic experiences of intense love and hate."[6]

One interesting relic of Ibsen's stay in Vienna has survived in the form of a photograph of the art and sculpture jury, twenty-five formidably bearded and whiskered figures. Ibsen, looking much the youngest (as, at forty-five, he probably was) is seated noticeably apart from the others,

---

[5] Ibsen's apparent indifference to Impressionism is the odder when one recalls that Naturalism, as Mr. Walter Allen has observed, "was the literary equivalent of Impressionism in painting; just as the Impressionists painted objects seen in certain conditions of light and atmosphere, so the Naturalists depicted human beings in terms of their environment. . . . It is part of Zola's strength, for instance, that in his novels he often sets out to describe a scene as nearly as possible as Manet might have painted it." (Walter Allen, *The English Novel*, [London, 1954], pp. 282–83.) One would have supposed that the author of *The Lady from the Sea* and *The Wild Duck* must have admired the Impressionists, especially as he himself was painted by Edvard Munch.

[6] Ernest Jones, *The Life and Work of Sigmund Freud*, Pelican edn. (London, 1964), pp. 226, 238, 318, 384.

neatly barbered, in frock coat and spats, an order in his buttonhole, a top hat on his knee, and a rolled umbrella between his legs.[7]

There was an outbreak of cholera in Dresden that July, so on leaving Vienna Ibsen spent a few weeks at Pillnitz, an hour from Dresden by steamer. Suzannah and Sigurd joined him there, and he had two other visitors. Lorentz Dietrichson, who had missed him in Vienna, dropped in on his way north, and found him more grandly dressed than when they had last met in Stockholm. "His outward appearance had undergone a change; instead of his smart short velvet jacket he was now wearing a long black coat that reached beneath his knees, of a very severe character."[8] Dietrichson was not suprised when Ibsen told him that during their summer in the Tyrol the local children had kissed his hand and asked for his blessing, taking him for a Catholic priest.

Ibsen's other caller at Pillnitz was Ludvig Josephson, the young Swede who had succeeded Hartvig Lassen as artistic director of the Christiania Theatre. In Stockholm, Josephson had enjoyed considerable success as a dramatist, and had been director of both the Royal Theatre and the Opera, but had had to leave because the Swedish actors disliked being ordered about by a Jew.[9] In Christiania he had an equally rough baptism; as he tells in his memoirs, "one director after another had been forced to resign because of the savage press criticisms and public hostility,"[10] and there was additional feeling against Josephson because he was (in addition to being a Jew) a Swede. The premiere of his first production that February had been repeatedly interrupted with boos, hisses, and cries of "Out with the foreigner!" and the police had to be called to restore order. One of the ringleaders was the son of Johan Sverdrup, the president of the Storthing. Bjørnson was rumoured to be behind the demonstration; Josephson, who had directed several of Bjørnson's plays in Sweden and whose relations with him had hitherto been cordial, disbelieved this and went to Bjørnson to ask his help, but found him so hostile that he feared the rumour might be true.[11] He stuck to his post, however, and during his four years there raised the artistic standard of the theatre to a height it had never previously attained, as the list of plays that he presented bears witness.[12] Josephson may be ranked as the earliest of those

[7] See illustration no. 31.

[8] Dietrichson, I, 357.

[9] Per Lindberg, *August Lindberg* (Stockholm, 1943), p. 26.

[10] Ludvig Josephson, *Ett och annat om Henrik Ibsen och Kristiania Teater* (Stockholm, 1898), p. 12.

[11] *Ibid.*, pp. 16 ff.

[12] They included: 1873, the first production in Norway of *The Merry Wives of Windsor* (with Johannes Brun as Falstaff), Molière's *Le malade imaginaire*, Schiller's *Joan of Arc*, Bjørnson's *The Newly-Wedded Couple*, *Between the Battles* and *Mary Stuart in Scotland*, Holberg's *Jeppe of the Hill*, and Ibsen's *The Pretenders* and *Love's Comedy*. 1874: *Coriolanus*, *A Winter's Tale*, *The Merchant of Venice*, Molière's *Tartuffe*, Sheridan's *The School for Scandal*, Musset's *Il faut qu'une porte*

imaginative young directors, after Duke Georg of Saxe-Meiningen and his lieutenant Ludwig Chronegk, who saw in Ibsen's plays the dawn of a new era in the theatre. He was the forerunner of August Lindberg, André Antoine, Otto Brahm, Aurélien Lugné-Poe, Konstantin Stanislavsky, and J. T. Grein.

Josephson was anxious to make the acquaintance of the author of *Love's Comedy,* which was on the theatre's schedule for the coming season, and wrote diffidently to ask if he might visit him. Ibsen assented; and "as the steamer approached the humble jetty, I saw a solitary figure walking to and fro on the shore, dressed in black with medal ribbons in his lapel, kid gloves, and a tall black hat—a costume which suited neither the season nor the shabby surroundings. . . . I recognized him immediately from the portraits I had seen. My astonishment at his dress and the formality of his manner (a weakness which never left him once he had gone abroad) vanished as soon as we had exchanged preliminary courtesies. Soon the total unpretentiousness of the man became clear to me beneath the formal surface, and I found him the most friendly, kind and unpretentious [Josephson repeats the word, *anspråkslös*] great man that I had ever met among famous authors. I have often since wondered at this curious passion of Ibsen's for appearing, if I may say so, dressed up. The appearance he chose for himself was more suited to a rich merchant or banker than to a philosopher and a poet."[13]

Josephson accompanied Ibsen back to Dresden at the beginning of September, and they spent a good deal of time together, both in the cafés and at Ibsen's home. Josephson noted with curiosity the relationship between father and son. He found Sigurd "handsome and elegant" but "very strange, withdrawn, and brooding. . . . I observed with surprise that the young Ibsen would at mealtimes make his entry at the last moment, bow deeply like a stranger to his parents, and seat himself silently at table. In that house, where everything happened silently, scarcely a word was ever exchanged between father and son in a stranger's presence, and when the father or mother did speak, the son always replied in a very few words, very slowly and formally. . . . After eating, the young man retired immediately with the same stiff ceremonious bow. . . . We were happiest when we sat over our coffee and in the evening, when he had a great glass jug of ale brought in, which stood beside him on the floor and from which he himself filled our glasses . . . But I never saw

---

soit ouverte ou fermée, and Holberg's *The Scatterbrain* and *The Lying-In Room.* 1875: *Hamlet,* Gœthe's *Egmont,* Molière's *L'Avare,* Marivaux's *Le jeu d'amour et du hasard,* Holberg's *The Political Potter,* Bjørnson's *A Bankrupt,* Ibsen's *Lady Inger of Østraat.* 1876: Calderón's *Life is a Dream, Peer Gynt* (then, on 15 January 1877, the theatre was badly damaged by fire, which curtailed the season). 1877: *Richard III, The Vikings at Helgeland,* Musset's *On ne badine pas avec l'amour.*

[13] Josephson, pp. 38 ff.

his study . . . and I don't think many of his visitors were more favoured than I in this respect." His favourite cafés, Josephson remembered, were those on the Brühl Terrace, the restaurants near the Wildsrufferplatz, and the Café Français in the Old Town, where there were Scandinavian newspapers available.[14]

Ibsen liked the young Swede. On the whole, dare one say, he got on better with Swedes than with his own countrymen; the Swedish formality suited him, and he felt free of the reproach, unspoken or expressed, of being a "bad Norwegian."

He restlessly awaited the publication of *Emperor and Galilean*. "I hear from Norway," he wrote to Georg Brandes on 8 September, "that Bjørnson, although he can know nothing of the book, declares it to be 'Atheism,' and says it was inevitable that I should come to that." Bjørnson's hostility towards Ibsen had doubtless been sharpened by the latter's acceptance of the Order of St. Olaf, and although he was in Dresden that autumn he did not contact Ibsen.

On 2 October Hegel wrote that "the orders for your new book have been so large that I have had to have no less than eight hundred copies bound," and that as an honorarium he had credited Ibsen's account with 3,200 riksdollars.[15] Ibsen replied on 6 October asking Hegel to invest the whole sum in gilt-edged securities "giving an interest of at least 4%." His letter ended with a reference to "new literary plans which have begun to stir in me." These, again, probably (though not certainly) refer to *The Pillars of Society*, though it was to be four painful years before he completed it; its gestations was to be almost as difficult as that of *Emperor and Galilean*. A few days later he learned from Hegel that, despite the first printing of four thousand copies (twice that of *The League of Youth*), a second edition was already being prepared; he greeted this good news soberly by asking Hegel to use the new advance to buy Swedish railway shares, adding: "More profitable shares are nothing to have if one is disinclined to speculate."

Emperor and Galilean was published on 16 October 1873. "The booksellers were so interested in this work," Hegel informed Bjørnson, who cannot have been overjoyed at the news, "that the large edition . . . was almost entirely subscribed, and the rest were taken by the Copenhagen booksellers on the day of publication."[16]

Of all Ibsen's plays, including even *When We Dead Awaken*, *Emperor and Galilean* is the one most under-rated by posterity; indeed, it is unique among his major works in having been admired less by posterity than by his contemporaries. Ibsen himself several times referred to it as his

[14] *Ibid.*, pp. 92–93 and 96–98.
[15] Nielsen, II, 313–14.
[16] *Ibid.*, pp. 51–52.

masterpiece;[17] most subsequent commentators have rejected it as a worthy failure. But few Ibsen commentators can have seen it, and fewer still seem able to read a play as a play, mentally excising (as a director of Shakespeare must) what on the stage would be tedious and superfluous —for we must remember that *Emperor and Galilean,* like *Brand* and *Peer Gynt,* was written not for the spectator but for the reader. *Brand* was regarded as unactable in England until 1959, *When We Dead Awaken* until 1968; in some countries they are still regarded as such, awaiting the director who can reveal their profound and exciting theatricality. The same is true of *Emperor and Galilean.* It has longueurs, especially in the first half of Part Two, but so have *Brand* and *Peer Gynt;* once one has stripped away the superfluous detail, a play is revealed which is a worthy successor to those two great dramas.

The action of *Emperor and Galilean* covers twelve years, from A.D. 351 to 363. Julian, who is nineteen when the play opens, and his brother Gallus live in terror of the mad Emperor Constantius, their cousin, who has already had their parents and nine other kinsmen murdered. Julian, like the Emperor, is a Christian, but is restless in his faith; under the influence of the philosopher Libanius ("There is a whole glorious world to which you Christians are blind") he goes to Athens to study the pagan religion. But in Athens he becomes equally disillusioned with paganism and longs for a vision to show him his way. He hears of a mystic, Maximus, who claims to have power over ghosts and spirits, and visits him in Ephesus. There, Maximus expounds his philosophy to Julian: "First, there is the kingdom founded on the Tree of Knowledge. Then the kingdom founded on the Tree of the Cross. The third kingdom is the kingdom of the great mystery, which shall be founded on both the Tree of Knowledge and the Tree of the Cross. . . . Its life-spring has its source beneath Adam's grove and Golgotha." In other words, Julian must combine the wisdom of Christianity and the wisdom of paganism.

Now Maximus summons up the spirits of three men who, as unconscious instruments of the world-will, most altered the course of history: Cain, Judas Iscariot, and—but the third does not appear. Then Maximus realizes that this third is either Julian or himself; which, he does not know. Julian believes that he could alter the course of history, granted the companionship of a "pure woman." Then he hears that the Emperor has offered him his sister Helena as wife. This seems to him a further sign that he has been chosen by destiny.

The Emperor sends Julian to Gaul to quell a rebellion. His brother Gallus has been executed at the Emperor's orders, so that now Julian is the last of his line. He knows he is being spied on, and that the Emperor has

[17] Witness e.g., William Archer's introduction to the English translation of the play (London, 1907), p. xvi, and the report by Arnt Delhi printed in *Aftenposten,* 14 March 1928.

sent him to Gaul so that if he fails at least the Emperor will be rid of
him. When he defeats the rebels, a tribune comes from the Emperor to
arrest him, lest he should march on Rome. Helena is pregnant; the
tribune brings her a gift of peaches from the Emperor; she eats them and
is poisoned—the Emperor's precaution lest she should bear Julian an heir.
In her delirium before she dies, she reveals that the child she is carrying is
not Julian's. This extra disillusionment dispels Julian's last scruples; he
decides to lead his army against Rome; but before doing so, he denies
Christ, and under the guidance of Maximus, embraces paganism and
appears before his soldiers smeared with the blood of the sacrifice. Here
Part One ends.

In Part Two, Julian is Emperor, Constantius having died before Julian
reached Rome. He proclaims a regime of tolerance; although he himself
is a pagan, the Christians will be granted freedom of worship. But the
Christians will not permit a return to paganism; they destroy the temples,
and Julian is forced to take repressive measures against them. He becomes
a worse tyrant than Constantius, because on a wider scale. He leads an
army against the Persians, and is killed in the desert by a Christian who
had been his friend but who now sees him as anti-Christ. As he dies he
realizes that by his tyranny he has roused the Christians from their apathy
and advanced their cause. Like Cain and Judas he has unwittingly, and
in the opposite direction to which he intended, altered the course of history.

Emperor and Galilean is full of extraordinary scenes: the opening in
Constantinople, with Julian and his brother waiting for the mad Emperor's
hand to fall on them as on their eleven murdered kinsmen; Julian's confrontation with the philosopher Libanius, who tempts him to forsake the
church for the debating-halls; Maximus's evocation of the ghosts of the
"corner-stones" of history, and Julian's sudden realization that he himself
is to be the third of these; Helena's revelation that she is pregnant by
another man, and Julian's order to the doctor not to save her; and the
great climax to Part One, when Helena's body lies in the church and the
army outside grows mutinous while Julian hesitates to lead them against
Rome until he has taken the final step of renouncing Christianity; he
learns that Helena's body is working miracles because she was "the pure
woman" and, maddened by the falsity of this, he makes the sacrifice and
appears with the blood of the beast on his forehead. The first three acts of
Part Two mark a certain slackening of tension, and are over-weighted with
grubbed-up knowledge which Ibsen does not carry very lightly; in any
production, they would profit most by cutting. But the last two acts are
of the quality of the whole of Part One; Julian's gradual submission to the
force on which he has turned his back but which he cannot evade is as
powerful and moving in its inevitability as the final acts of *Brand, Peer
Gynt,* or any of the great prose plays.

Emperor and Galilean marks a vital turning-point in Ibsen's development as a dramatist. Although it is on an epic scale like *Brand* and *Peer Gynt*, he wrote it in prose; it is both the last play of one period and the first of another. The conviction which had been growing in him for several years that he must abandon the poetic medium in which he had gained his greatest triumphs found expression in a letter he wrote on 15 January 1874 to Edmund Gosse. Gosse, in a review of the play published in *The Spectator* on 27 December 1873, had regretted Ibsen's abandonment of verse; and we must be grateful to Gosse that he wrote as he did, for his remarks stimulated Ibsen to a clear statement of his new policy in play-writing.

"The illusion I wanted to produce," he informed Gosse, "is that of reality. I wished to produce the impression on the reader that what he was reading was something that had really happened. If I had employed verse, I should have counteracted my own intention, and prevented the accomplishment of the task I had set myself. The many ordinary and insignificant characters whom I have introduced into the play would have become indistinct, and indistinguishable from one another, if I had allowed all of them to speak in one and the same rhythmical measure. We are no longer living in the age of Shakespeare. Among sculptors, there is already talk of painting statues in the natural colours. Much can be said both for and against this. I have no desire to see the Venus de Milo painted, but I would rather see the head of a Negro executed in black rather than white marble. Speaking generally, the style must conform to the degree of ideality which pervades the representation. My new drama is no tragedy in the ancient acceptation; what I desired to depict were human beings, and therefore I would not let them talk in 'the language of the gods.'"[18]

In other words, *Emperor and Galilean* is at the same time Ibsen's farewell to the epic drama (at any rate until the final act of *John Gabriel Borkman* and *When We Dead Awaken*), and the forerunner of those naturalistic prose plays which were shortly to explode upon the nineteenth century like a series of bombs.

Despite the seeming remoteness of its theme, *Emperor and Galilean* is one of Ibsen's most personal statements, as self-analytical as *The Pretenders, Brand, The Master Builder,* or *When We Dead Awaken*. Somewhat unexpectedly, he took pains to establish this fact. "I have put a good deal of my own inner life into the play," he had written to Gosse on 14 October 1872, and again to Gosse on 20 February 1873: "There is much self-anatomy in this book." Three days later he told Ludvig Daae that it contained "more of my own personal experience than I would publicly admit." The problem that baffled and finally destroyed Julian was one that was always at the back of Ibsen's mind, though he seldom if ever mentioned it; where to find a faith to replace the Christianity of his up-

18 Edmund Gosse's translation.

bringing. The third quarter of the nineteenth century was, more than preceding ages, a time of revolt against conventional religious thinking, with Bible criticism and natural science marching hand in hand, and *Emperor and Galilean,* in its search for a "third kingdom" (a phrase which had not yet acquired a sinister significance), was as much a book of its era as *The Origin of Species,* Renan's *Life of Jesus,* and *Das Kapital.* "He who has once been under Him [Christ] can never be free," says Julian, and they are words that Ibsen himself, and many of his contemporaries, might have spoken.

It is a cliché that man is attracted by the qualities he lacks, and Ibsen's plays are permeated by a longing for what, in *Ghosts,* he was to term *livsglæde,* the joy of life. He deplored its absence in contemporary Christian teaching, which he probably (and with reason) blamed for his own inability to experience that joy; Brand and Pastor Manders, and those daunting lay preachers Rørlund, Gregers Werle, and Kroll, denounce it as a sin; Bishop Nicholas and John Rosmer would like to enjoy it but cannot, as though castrated by their own church upbringing. To find a religion which would combine Christian ethics with the joy of life is a problem that has troubled many a piously educated man and woman; it was a problem which Ibsen personally was never to solve and it is the central theme of *Emperor and Galilean* as it was to be the theme (or part-theme) of so many of his plays, whether explicitly as in *Ghosts* and *Rosmersholm,* or implicitly, as in *The Master Builder, John Gabriel Borkman* and *When We Dead Awaken.*

When Ibsen said that *Emperor and Galilean* contained "more of my own personal experience than I would care to admit," I do not think there is much doubt that he was referring to the emotional strait-jacket in which he found himself confined, and from which, like his childhood Christianity, he could never escape. It is relevant to add here a remark that Professor Francis Bull once made to this writer: that his father, Edvard Bull, who was Ibsen's doctor during his last years, once told his son that Ibsen was preternaturally shy about exposing his sexual organs even during medical examination. There was, indeed, much of Hedda Gabler in her creator.

Critical reaction to *Emperor and Galilean* was generally favourable, though somewhat bewildered. *Dagbladet* (25 October 1873) and *Morgenbladet* (13–16 November) both sat on the fence and contented themselves with discussing the theological and ethical implications of the play. Kristian Elster in *Aftenbladet* (19 November) praised it highly; Part Two, he thought, lacked the dramatic tension of Part One, but "if this latter half makes a lesser impression . . . there is no doubt that its subject matter demands even greater skill than the earlier play. . . . It contains such a wealth of reflection, is written with such imaginative power and worked out with so rare an art that it nowhere essentially falls below the level of *Caesar's Apostasy*. . . . Both plays comprise a masterpiece of high rank."

Arne Garborg published a long pamphlet on the play before the year was out, and it is an interesting example of the kind of grudging admiration with which so many of Ibsen's contemporaries regarded him. "He is read with interest, even greedily," Garborg admitted. "His books are gutted with an eagerness otherwise unknown in our literary circles. As soon as the rumour spreads that a new work is expected from his pen, the public gets worked up into an anticipation which sometimes reaches fever pitch, and once it has been published and read it is discussed to the exclusion of all else for a long time afterwards in the circles where such interests hold sway."[19] Yet with all this, continues Garborg, Ibsen is not the usual idea of a "popular" author. He only asks, he gives no answer, he is but a seeker, and so people call him negative. "Ibsen has somewhere said that the 'gift of doubt,' too, can make a man a poet. But this is unhappily where Ibsen is wrong. Doubt is not a gift, it is a standpoint—nay, more, it is only a temporary standpoint. As long as a soul doubts it is not yet fully developed, not free, and however mighty its talent it will stand impotent before its calling. Ibsen is an example of this. He has received the gift of creativeness in the richest measure, but doubt destroys his song. His poetry . . . cannot achieve full beauty because it is bounded by obscurity and darkness, and lacks reconciliation and harmony. This is the main reason why people are reluctant to acknowledge him. They are conscious of the sickness which lies at the heart of his work."[20] Similar objections were to be raised against Ibsen's plays as they gradually came to be translated and staged in other countries.

Yet Garborg, though not realizing that Ibsen's strength lay precisely in this power of arousing unease in people's consciences and forcing them to self-analysis, admitted his creative power ("Brand, Peer Gynt, Stensgaard, with what splendid strength do these figures not live in everyone's mind!"[21]), and granted that his lack of inner peace and harmony made him a true spokesman of his time—"for a lack of peace and harmony is the essential characteristic of our age."[22] At the same time: "It is with *Emperor and Galilean* as with all of Ibsen's works. One lays them down with a disagreeable feeling of dissatisfaction. . . . With each book Ibsen merely throws a new *problem* at the world—a new problem which always turns out to be the same old one. Ibsen's misfortune is that he cannot, like so many others, rest content with a half answer, and from the standpoint he occupies he will never find the whole answer."[23] However, the pam-

[19] Arne Garborg, *Henrik Ibsens* Keiser og Galilæer: *en kritisk studie* (Christiania, 1873), pp. 3–4.

[20] *Ibid.*, p. 5.

[21] *Ibid.*, p. 8.

[22] *Ibid.*, pp. 16–17.

[23] *Ibid.*, pp. 55–56.

phlet concluded generously: "Viewed as a whole, it must be admitted that *Emperor and Galilean* is in many ways a truly monumental work, possibly without equal in any literature. It has its weaknesses, of course. But these weaknesses are mainly non-æsthetic, and the virtues of the book are so numerous and so important that one is inclined to excuse its philosophical shortcomings. All in all, our literature has good ground to be proud of it."[24]

Erik Bøgh no doubt summed up many people's reaction when he stated in the Danish newspaper *Folkets Avis* (4 November) that, while *Emperor and Galilean* was "an interesting work" with "certain scenes of great power," it was so unlike what one had expected that "many of his friends and the friends of his muse will surely lay it down sighing: 'Thank God Henrik Ibsen has finished *that!*'" Ibsen's fellow-authors were less respectful than the critics. J. P. Jacobsen, the Danish novelist whom Rilke so revered, disliked it: "There's no pace in the play, it's cold, the characters are without character."[25] So did Bjørnson. "I've read Ibsen's *Emperor and Galilean*," he wrote to H. E. Schirmer from Florence on 19 November. "It was a great disappointment." But he added a perceptive prophecy: "I think he's finished with *Brand*-style writing . . . and that we shall henceforth have what he will be a master at—plays of plot. We need them!"[26] Georg Brandes did not at first like it. "I am sitting in agony over Ibsen's *Julian*," he wrote to his mother soon after the book's publication. "I can't really bear the play, though of course there's a good deal in it."[27] He did not review it until the following year, when he and his brother had founded *The Nineteenth Century,* and although his matured verdict was kinder, he still, as usual where Ibsen's work was concerned, found himself divided. He found the dialogue "full of dramatic strength and fire," and felt that in the best scenes "Ibsen had never written with greater effect, perhaps never as greatly." But he, like Garborg, questioned Ibsen's metaphysics: "His strength and originality lie in psychological insight, and not in the solution of metaphysical problems. . . . The sum impression of Ibsen's great new work seems to me then to be approximately the same as that of *Peer Gynt*. It is full of splendid things, in the highest sense profound and poetic. . . . Had Part One been published first as a separate volume one would have praised it to the skies. A weaker section in Part Two has in some wise damaged the powerful effect of the earlier play." But he ended by declaring that the work confirmed one's hopes for Ibsen's future, and that "never previously has he understood and portrayed history as he has here." With few of these judgments would one disagree.

Ibsen was delighted with the reception of *Emperor and Galilean*. "I was

---

[24] *Ibid.,* p. 69.

[25] Letter to Edvard Brandes, 7 August 1884; *Brandes Brevveksling*, II, 261.

[26] Bjørnstjerne Bjørnson, *Brytnings-aar* (*brev fra aarene 1871–1878*), ed. Halvdan Koht (Christiania, 1921), I, 168.

[27] *Brandes Brevveksling*, IV, xxxv.

especially pleased to hear that the first edition of the book has sold out so
quickly," he wrote to Hegel on 13 November. "And I am happy that the
second edition can be expected so soon; for should the bookshops be without it any longer, every day would have reduced the advantage which we
both might have had from its publication. I know my countrymen; they
will save their money by borrowing it, and then not buy it. But this can't
be helped; for who would have supposed that the whole large first edition
would so soon disappear? From many letters from Norway I gather that
none of my previous books has aroused such a stir up there. It has established itself in circles not normally concerned with literature." Yet
despite its (one would have thought) obvious dramatic possibilities, *Emperor and Galilean* was not to be performed even in part until 1896, when
an adaptation was staged at the Leipzig Stadttheater. The first attempt
to stage any of it in Norway was in 1903, when Part One was produced
at the National Theatre in Christiania.

Ibsen had a row that November with Andreas Isachsen, the actor who
had been the first "student" to join the Bergen company, and who had
witnessed Ibsen's rolling in the snow during their walk to Hardanger.
Without asking Ibsen's, or indeed anyone's permission, Isachsen gave a
public reading of *Emperor and Galilean* in Christiania, in two parts, on
1 and 8 November. Ibsen read an advertisement of this event in a newspaper, and on 4 November he penned Isachsen a furious letter. "You will
doubtless recall," he reminded him, "that I have repeatedly impressed on
you the need of foreign travel. Being abroad does not merely develop one's
artistic outlook; it also teaches one the requirements needful to behave like
a gentleman. . . . I have made it indubitably plain to you that I am
wholly opposed to your interposing yourself between me and my public. I
wish my books to come direct from me to my readers, and I cannot see
what right you have to obstruct my wishes. Nor can I understand how
you can find it in your conscience to make money from a work of art
which you have had no share in creating. For you can scarcely deny that
every penny you get from publicly reading my book you take from my
pocket; and I cannot spare one of these; for I need money to live decently.
Moreover, the fact of your choosing a new work for your performance
shows that you have no idea what the purpose of a reading is. A work
that is to be read publicly should be one with which everyone is familiar;
otherwise what people will come to hear will be the work itself, and not
the manner of its reading. And what is one to say to your presuming after
so few days to seek to interpret by a public reading a work such as my
latest? I can assure you that you need longer to get to the bottom of it."

Morgenbladet devoted a leader to the matter on 18 November; Isachsen
replied four days later that he had asked Ibsen a year or two back if he
could give a public reading of some new work of his, and that Ibsen had,
by implication, given him permission: "His time was exclusively occupied

with a big work, a trilogy, but once this was published I would find sufficient material there, which I took to be sufficient permission." The author
of the leader retorted with justice on 30 November that there was a difference between reading bits of a play and the whole of it. The incident,
trivial in itself, underlines a problem which Ibsen was to face for the
whole of his career: lack of copyright protection. Ibsen's letter to Isachsen
is scarcely pricklier than what a modern playwright would write under
similar circumstances to someone who had given an unauthorised performance of his work, and modern playwrights are not, as Ibsen then was,
dependent on book sales for the bulk of their income.

That same month, on 24 November, *Love's Comedy* received its first
performance, eleven years after publication. This, again, was thanks to
Ludvig Josephson, the new director of the Christiania Theatre, who had
just opened his second season that September with a revival of *The Pretenders*. There was much curiosity to see how *Love's Comedy* would act,
the general opinion being (not unreasonably) that it was "scarcely suited
to the stage";[28] but the result exceeded all expectations, even though
Sigvard and Laura Gundersen, as Falk and Svanhild, "lacked the youth
that these two roles demand."[29] Johannes Brun, however, was excellent
as Pastor Strawman, and so, despite his strained relations with Ibsen, was
Isachsen as Guldstad. The play at once became a regular item in the
theatre's repertory, and in the next twenty-five years was performed there
seventy-seven times.

As the year drew to its close, Ibsen heard from Johan Thoresen that his
debts in Norway had finally been paid off. "I am particularly happy," he
wrote to Thoresen on 12 December, "that the business with Nandrup[30]
has at last been settled. I am clear of debt and have several thousand
crowns invested in the public funds, which Hegel has arranged for me
over the years, and which steadily increase in value, so that I look forward
to the not too distant time when we shall be able to live exclusively on my
interest and my pension." When he came to make up his accounts for the
year, he found it had been by a long way his best yet:

	crowns	
3rd edn. of *Love's Comedy*	645	
1st edn. of *Emperor and Galilean*	6,400	
1st edn. (supplementary fee)	640	
2nd edn. of *Emperor and Galilean*	3,200	
2nd edn. of *The Vikings at Helgeland*	609	
3rd edn. of *The Vikings at Helgeland*	609	
Fee for performances of *Love's Comedy* in Christiania	1,200	
	13,303	£739

[28] T. Blanc, *Christiania theaters historie, 1827–1877* (Christiania, 1899), p. 281.
[29] Josephson, p. 36.
[30] See p. 258 above.

With his pension of 400 specie-dollars, a grant of 100 specie-dollars which he had received for his trip to Vienna, and interest on his Danish and Swedish shares of 107 specie-dollars, Ibsen's total income for the year amounted to £908. This was excellent by the average standard of Norwegian salaries. In 1870, a Professor ordinarius in Christiania received a basic salary of £250, rising to a ceiling of £333; a headmaster earned £300. At the same time, it was pathetically little compared with what leading authors of a stature comparable to Ibsen's were getting in the larger European countries. Anthony Trollope, for example, earned at his peak £4,500 annually. John Ruskin averaged £4,000 from his book royalties during his later years. George Eliot had refused £10,000 for the copyright of *Romola* in 1862, and *Middlemarch* brought her £9,000 in seven years. Ibsen only started to earn one thousand pounds a year regularly when he was well into his sixties, long after he had become world famous; and, as we shall see, he often, thanks partly to his refusal ever to repeat the pattern of a success, made barely half that amount, sometimes less. Although he lived most parsimoniously until his death and sold his copyrights outright, he left only a fractional sum compared with his peers abroad. Yet so humble was the rate of earning in Norway that the myth that he was a rich man has survived there to this day.

Still, "This has been a good year for me," he was able to tell Hegel on 30 December, adding: "I have something new in my head and it grows clearer all the time, so that I think it cannot be long before I begin to write."

The success of *Love's Comedy* on the stage stimulated Ibsen to think afresh about the possibility of a production of *Peer Gynt,* and on 23 January 1874 he wrote to Edvard Grieg asking him if he would consider providing a musical accompaniment and suggesting cuts, some of them surprising:

Act One should be retained in its entirety apart from some thinning out of the dialogue. . . . The wedding scene on p. 28 can be made much more of, with the help of ballet, than appears in the text. . . . In Act Two the incident with the three peasant girls on pp. 57–60 should receive whatever musical treatment you feel appropriate; but there must be devilry in it! . . . There will have to be some kind of musical accompaniment to the scene in the troll palace, though here too the dialogue must be considerably thinned out. The scene with the Boyg, also, which should remain uncut, must have music; the Bird Voices to be sung, the church bells and psalm singing to be heard in the distance. . . . Pretty well the whole of Act Four will be omitted in performance. In its place I thought we might have a great musical tone-picture to suggest Peer Gynt's wanderings in the wide world, with American, English, and French melodies interwoven as changing and disappearing *motifs*. . . . Act Five must be shortened considerably. . . . The scenes on the upturned boat and in the churchyard will have to go. . . . The scenes with the Button Moulder and the Old Man of the Mountains must be trimmed down. On p. 254 the churchgoers sing on the forest path; church bells and distant psalm singing should be indicated in the music during the dialogue which follows until Solveig's song concludes the play, at which point the curtain will descend while the psalm singing is heard again clearer and louder. That is roughly how I have imagined it. . . . If you agree to come in with me on this, I shall immediately approach the management of the Christiania Theatre, send them an acting script and ensure that the play is guaranteed a production. As a fee I propose to ask 400 specie-dollars to be shared equally between the two of us. I think it certain that we can also reckon on the play being performed in Copenhagen and Stockholm.

Grieg accepted the invitation, though not with unmixed delight. "It's a dreadfully intractable subject," he wrote to his friend Frantz Beyer that August, "except for certain passages—e.g., the part where Solveig sings— I've done that all right. And I've made something of the Old Man's palace in the mountains, which I literally can't bear to listen to, it stinks so of cow dung and Norwegian insularity and self-sufficiency! But I think people will sense the irony behind it." On 12 September Grieg complained to Bjørnson, who had told him that he was wasting his time: "I can't but admire the way from start to finish it [*Peer Gynt*] splutters with wit and venom; but it will never win my sympathy. Though I think it the best thing Ibsen has written. Am I not right? But you don't imagine I had a free choice in the matter! I got the offer from Ibsen last year [*sic*], and naturally baulked at the prospect of putting music to this most unmusical of subjects. But I thought of the 200 [specie-dollars] and of the voyage, and made the sacrifice. The whole thing sits on me like a nightmare."

Grieg continued to grouse privately about the task, and it was not until eighteen months after he had accepted the commission, in August 1875, that he finished the music. Ludvig Josephson, on the other hand, to whom Ibsen broached the project in a letter on 6 February after having received an affirmative answer from Grieg, reacted enthusiastically to the proposal, begging him only not to omit the whole of Act Four, and suggesting instead several extra cuts, to which Ibsen agreed.

It was in fact only by the chance of a lost manuscript that Grieg was invited to compose the music for *Peer Gynt*. Ludvig Josephson tells in his memoirs how a gifted Swedish composer, August Söderman, "had so fallen in love with *Peer Gynt* that, soon after its publication, he began to compose music for the play; and I still happily remember the many occasions when, sitting at the piano beside him, I went through scene after scene to the accompaniment of Söderman's personal performance of all the accompaniments he had provided to Ibsen's masterpiece. Unfortunately this composition could not be found at Söderman's death. It is known that in his lifetime he lent this work to various people, but when, later, *Peer Gynt* came to be staged, Söderman was dead and no one knew where his music was. So it fell to Edvard Grieg to set his great compatriot's ideas to music."[31]

Admittedly Ibsen offered the idea of a stage production to Josephson on the basis of Grieg's promise to write the music; but the idea of a performance was already on the Christiania files when Josephson took over, and I think there is little doubt that had Söderman's score been available Josephson, being familiar with and enthusiastic for it, would have suggested a production before Ibsen did. And even after getting Ibsen's letter, he would probably have succeeded in persuading the unenthusiastic Grieg to withdraw from the project had a good score already been available.

Meanwhile, another continent was beginning to show a flicker of interest in the new dramatist. "I am especially glad," Ibsen wrote to Hegel on 10 February, "that a new market had been opened up for us in America. I think that *Brand, Peer Gynt* and *The League of Youth* will all, for different reasons, appeal to the taste of American Scandinavians. The only pity is that the sending of books there will involve so much extra expense." The interest seems, however, to have been limited to those Americans who were able to read Ibsen in his own language (of whom there were already several thousand, after the large-scale immigrations of the past two decades). There was to be no American translation or performance of Ibsen for several years to come.[32]

That spring and summer of 1874 Ibsen worked on the rewriting of *Lady Inger of Østraat*. He asked Ludvig Daæ if the latter had any comments on it as history, but Daæ's reply, to the effect that it was historically very false and erred on the side of chauvinism, convinced Ibsen that to bring the play into line with the facts would involve too sweeping changes. So he limited himself to cutting asides, breaking up the longer monologues and sharpening the characterization and dialogue.[33]

[31] Josephson, p. 9.

[32] This same year, according to Koht (II, 74), there appeared the first French article on Ibsen, by a Mlle. Leo Quesnel; but Koht gives no further details.

[33] P. F. D. Tennant (*Ibsen's Dramatic Technique* [Cambridge, 1948], p. 104) points out that of the fifty-nine asides in the original version of *Lady Inger*, Ibsen cut twenty-three in revision. Another thirty-one he replaced by stage whispers and thinking aloud; though what the difference is between them and an aside is not easy to see. Evidently it had some significance, for when revising *The Feast at Solhaug* in 1883 he replaced nineteen asides by stage whispers and thinking aloud. It is not until *Ghosts* that Ibsen dispenses with them and with monologues.

Georg Brandes visited Ibsen for a couple of days in June and was disturbed at what seemed to him Ibsen's eccentric and conservative opinions. The gap between the two men had begun to widen. "Kind though Ibsen was to me, as always," Brandes wrote to his mother on 18 June, "I am too superior to him in education to get any use from long conversations from him"[34]—an astonishingly vain and foolish judgment, which Brandes was later to retract. Three days later he described their meeting to a biologist friend in Copenhagen, Professor C. J. Salomonsen, as "a visit on which I look back with a certain sense of despondency, though he received me most warmly. The man sits there producing very little, unable to draw intellectual nourishment from the world around him because he lacks the organs to do so, and is rigidly set in all kinds of prejudices and eccentricities. He has a sure eye for only one thing, namely, the prejudices of his homeland, everything that is obsolete in Norway and Denmark; but the lack of any kind of systematic education makes him desperately limited. Fancy—he seriously believes in a time when 'the intelligent minority' in these countries 'will be forced to enlist the aid of chemistry and medicine in poisoning the proletariat' to save themselves from being politically overwhelmed by the majority. And this universal poisoning is what he wants. The Germans, too, among whom he has lived for so long (without getting to know a single intelligent one and without reading more than one or two books a year—literally), the Germans too he knows very incompletely, and his acquaintance with one or two crazy Catholics has led him to throw in his sympathy with the Catholic faction, the while he calls himself a Freethinker. In short, he is lost in an endless chaos of characterlessness."[35]

As a further example of Ibsen's eccentricity, Brandes recalled (eight years later, but referring to this same visit) that he was "loud in his praise of Russia. 'A splendid country,' he said with a smile. 'Think of all the grand oppression they have.' 'How do you mean?' 'Only think of the glorious love of liberty it engenders. Russia is one of the few countries in the world where men still love liberty and make sacrifices for it. That is why she holds so high a place in poetry and art. Remember that they possess a writer such as Turgenev; and they have Turgenevs too among their painters, only we don't know them; but I have seen their pictures in Vienna.' "[36]

Brandes thought that one reason for Ibsen's partiality for Russia lay in the fact that the country had no parliament. "Ibsen's whole character presupposes a distrust of and ill-will towards parliamentarianism. He believes in the individual, in the single great personality; the individual,

[34] *Brandes Brevveksling*, IV, xxxv.
[35] *Ibid.*, I, 313.
[36] From Brandes's "Second Impression" of Ibsen, written in 1882 and reprinted in his book *Henrik Ibsen*, pp. 79–80. Muir-Archer translation.

and he alone, can accomplish everything. Such a body as a parliament is, in Ibsen's eyes, a mere assembly of orators and dilettanti."[37] Like so many liberals who were working actively against conservatism in literature and politics, Brandes felt that Ibsen, by his contempt for practical politics, was not helping their cause; and it explains that growing coolness towards Ibsen which has already been noted. A couple of months after their meeting he was to describe Ibsen to a friend as "remarkably receptive to every kind of reactionary influence."[38] One can sympathize with Brandes's distress; ironical paradoxes of the kind with which Ibsen had loved to taunt his companions in Rome are infuriating to the earnestly committed. But that summer Ibsen was to undergo a series of experiences which were to alter his course sharply from the conservatism to which, as Brandes had observed, he was beginning to lean.

He had at last, under the influence of Suzannah's constant urging, taken the decision to do what he had been planning, and putting off, for so many years: to revisit Norway. He made the journey with the utmost trepidation; as he sailed up the fjord, he was to recall ten years later, "I literally felt my chest tighten with a feeling of sickness and unease."[39] It was ten years and one hundred and five days since he had last set foot on native soil when, at six o'clock in the evening of Sunday 19 July 1874, he disembarked with Suzannah and Sigurd in Christiania from the SS *Aarhus*.

They lodged modestly at a pension in Pilestrædet, in the centre of town, and stayed two and a half months, apparently spending the whole time in Christiania apart from a week in Stockholm during August to attend an archæological congress. The experience left him with, if possible, even more confused feelings towards his country than before. The people of whose friendship he had felt surest had, he found, become remote; and those about whose feelings towards him he had least evidence, and perhaps cared most, acclaimed him as a champion.

The first to seek him out were, naturally, his old friends from the Learned Holland Circle, Michael Birkeland, Olof Rygh, Jacob Løkke (who had helped him with the poems), and Jonas Lie. But the decade that had elapsed since he had last seen them had separated their viewpoints, and he found himself much less in sympathy with them than before. Their cynicism, which he had previously found stimulating, now seemed to him to have stiffened into an extreme conservatism which he found distasteful. Moreover, he found that, thanks to *The League of Youth*, he was now hailed by those right-wing elements which ten years earlier had scorned and excommunicated him as a champion of the established order. The medals which he had sought so assiduously in the hope that

---

[37] *Ibid.*, p. 81.

[38] Letter to Hans Brøchner, 10 August 1874 (*Brandes Brevveksling*, I, 203).

[39] Letter to Bjørnson, 29 September 1884.

they would give him a position in Norwegian eyes had had their effect, and he found the result not altogether to his liking. Ibsen had no desire to be regarded as a pillar of society. The experience must surely have reminded him that, although he had mocked the pretensions of the left in *The League of Youth,* and stood aloof from the liberal party, his political sympathies still lay to the left of centre, and with the young rather than with the old; and when he read in the right-wing newspaper *Morgenbladet* an editorial demand that a candidate for a professorship at the university should be rejected on the ground that he was a free-thinker, he seized the opportunity to advertise his independence. He withdrew his subscription to *Morgenbladet* and changed to the left-wing newspaper *Dagbladet.* The uneasiness of the conservatives on hearing this would have been considerably increased if they had known what he was preparing for them.

This distant attitude towards his old friends was, by some at least of them, reciprocated. "Ibsen is in town," wrote Jonas Lie to Bjørnson on 4 September. ". . . [He] has become a somewhat elderly gentleman with fixed opinions and personality," and he went on to describe Ibsen as "Bismarckian."[40]

But if Ibsen's old friends in Norway greeted him with reserve, the general public did not. The Christiania Theatre put on special performances of *Love's Comedy,* which Ibsen had not seen before, and *The League of Youth.* He attended on both occasions, and was loudly cheered in the theatre which had so repeatedly humiliated him as a young man. After the performance (appropriately) of *The League of Youth* on 10 September, the Students' Union and Choral Society honoured him with a torchlight procession. They sang a song for him and thrice cried: "Welcome home!" words which ten years earlier he can hardly have expected ever to hear in Christiania. In reply he delivered a cryptic yet, if one reads between the lines, revealing speech of thanks, in which he squarely identified himself with the young against the old:

Gentlemen!

When, during the latter years of my residence abroad, it became more and more clear to me that the time had now come when I must revisit my homeland, I will not conceal that it was with a certain unease and doubt that I prepared to return. My stay here was indeed to be but brief, but I felt that, however brief it might be, it might yet be long enough to shatter an illusion with which I wished to go on living.

I asked myself: in what kind of spirit will my countrymen receive me? The sympathetic reception accorded to the books I had sent home

40 Carl Nærup, *Jonas Lie og hans samtidige* (Christiania, 1915), p. 94.

could not wholly reassure me; for the question always remained—what is my *personal* relationship with my countrymen?

It would be idle to deny that at several points a suspicion has prevailed. As far as I have been able to make out, the complaints against me have been twofold. People have felt that I regarded my personal and private relationship with my country with undue bitterness, and have accused me of attacking certain things in our national life which in the view of many demanded other treatment than that of scorn.

I do not think I can use this, to me, so flattering and joyous a day better than by making a statement and a confession.

I have never made my private relationships the direct subject of any work. These relationships were of much less consequence to me in those hard and early days than I have ever been able to explain to myself afterwards. When the eider bird's nest was plundered once, twice and thrice, it was of illusions and hopes that it was plundered. When, on festive occasions, I have reacted to reminders like a bear in the hands of its trainer, it has been chiefly because I shared the guilt of an age which drowned a beautiful ideal in songs and rhetoric.

Well, what does it mean—to write? I realized late that to write is essentially to *see,* but—mark well—to see in such a way that the object seen becomes the possession of the reader in precisely the form in which the writer saw it. But only what one has *lived through* can be seen and possessed thus. And this business of living through what one writes about is precisely the secret of modern literature. Everything that I have written in the past ten years I have spiritually lived through. But no writer lives through anything in isolation. What he lives through, his contemporary fellow-countrymen also live through, together with him. If it were not so, what would become of the bridge of understanding between the writer and his audience?

And what is it, then, that I have lived through and written of? The range has been wide. On the one hand, I have written of those visions of greatness and beauty which have stirred me in rare glimpses, in my best hours. I have written of what, so to speak, rose above my ordinary daily self, and I wrote of it in order to set it permanently before me and in my heart.

But I have also written of the opposite—of what, when one looks inwards, one sees as the slag and sediment of one's personality. In this context writing has to me been like a bath, from which I felt myself to emerge cleaner, healthier, and freer. Yes, gentlemen, no man can portray in his writing anything for which he does not, to some degree and at least on occasion, find the model in himself. And where is the man among us who has not now and then sensed and admitted in himself a contradiction between word and deed, between will and duty, above all between life and doctrine? Or who is there among us who has not at any rate now and then been self-sufficient in a selfish and egotistical sense and, half-unconsciously, half in good faith, attempted to extenuate this state of mind both to others and to himself?

I believe that in saying this to you, who are students, I am addressing these words to their rightful audience. You will understand them as they are meant to be understood; for the student has essentially the same task as the poet, to clarify for himself, and thereby for others, those topical and timeless questions which are being asked in the age and the society to which he belongs.

In this respect I dare claim for myself that during my exile I have striven to be a good student. A writer is by nature long-sighted. I have never seen my country, and the living heart of my country, so clearly or so closely as when absent and afar.

And now, my dear countrymen, a few words in conclusion which also relate to an experience which I have lived through. When Emperor Julian stands at the end of his road and everything is crashing about him, there is nothing which saddens him so much as the thought that all that he has achieved has been to be remembered with respectful homage by clear, cold minds, while his adversaries remained deeply loved in warm and living human hearts. This conclusion I have reached through deep personal experience; it has its origin in a question which I have sometimes asked myself down there in my solitude. Now the youth of Norway has come to me here this evening and given me my answer in words and song, an answer so warm and full as I had never expected to hear. I shall take this answer back with me as the richest fruits of my visit to my countrymen and my home; and it is my hope and my belief that what I am experiencing here this evening is an experience which will some day be mirrored in some future work. And if this should be, if I should some day send such a book home, then I beg that you students will accept it as a handshake and an expression of thanks for this meeting; I beg you to receive it as fellow-authors.

Ibsen made one friendship during this visit to Christiania which, two decades later, was to have much meaning for him. Annette Sontum, the daughter of his old landlady at Bergen, had married an engineer named O. M. Andersen; he struck up an acquaintance with them and he enjoyed their company, and, too, that of their ten-year-old daughter Hildur, who already showed signs of becoming a talented musician. When he returned to Norway for good seventeen years later, Hildur was to become a considerable factor in his life.

"I have," he wrote to Hegel on 16 September, shortly before he left, "been received with extraordinary friendliness by everyone. All earlier unpleasantness is now past. I am thinking of exploiting these good times by indulging in a little property speculation. Several of my friends have become well-to-do by this means, and I think things might turn out well for me too."[41] But this did not mean that he was thinking of settling there himself. Ludvig Josephson, who saw Ibsen several times during his stay, recalls that he "sensed that Ibsen did not yet really feel at home or at ease in his native capital, nor, to speak plainly, that he was happy. I and his wife had unceasingly sought to persuade him to return to Norway for good, but he disliked having the matter raised, and was disinclined to consider it, the more so since this visit had failed to convince him that the move would bring him pleasure, fertilize his imagination, or help him to reflect and meditate as he loved to do."[42] Josephson adds that he thought Ibsen would have missed the art galleries and ancient buildings of Germany and Italy.

Ten years later, Ibsen confirmed Josephson's impression. In the letter to Bjørnson already quoted in which he told how, on his journey up the fjord, he felt his chest tighten with sickness and unease, Ibsen contined: "I had the same sensation during the whole of my stay there; I was no longer myself with all those cold and uncomprehending Norwegian eyes staring at me from the windows and pavements." While his country had to some degree atoned for the neglect and contempt with which it had treated him during the first half of his life, he had not felt totally accepted there, in the way he had been in Stockholm and Copenhagen. He was to continue his voluntary exile. Some hard truths remained to be uttered, and Ibsen preferred to ponder and utter them from a distance.

On his return to Dresden at the end of September, Ibsen settled down to his rewriting of *Lady Inger,* interrupting it briefly to compose an epithalamium for the wedding of Hegel's son Jakob on 9 October. On 22 October he posted the final instalment of *Lady Inger* to Gyldendals, and Hegel published the play in November in an edition of four thousand copies, together with a new edition of *The League of Youth.* Both were virtually fully subscribed before publication; and Hegel had the further good news for him that both *Catiline* and *Poems* were to be reprinted early in the new year.

But the happiness of the Ibsen household was tempered by sad tidings. Suzannah's sister Marie, who had been spending a good deal of time with them in Dresden, and to whom they were both much devoted, fell seriously ill in Copenhagen, where she was living with her stepmother

---

[41] In the end he decided against it, and instead bought 1,000 specie-dollars worth of shares in the new Christiania railway company.

[42] Josephson, pp. 54–55.

Magdalene. Suzannah went to visit her and found her dying. Ibsen, who now found himself looking after not only Sigurd but also his nephew Thomas, with the aid of only a single servant, wrote a characteristic letter to Suzannah on 13 November:

Dear Suzannah!

I received your last letter the day before yesterday, but have not replied before because Sigurd has not had time to write. Don't worry, I am looking after him. We walk home together from our dining rooms. Towards 5 we go out for a walk and return at 6:30. He gets up to far too many pranks when he is alone for me to dare to leave him by himself. So of course I never manage to get to the Literary Society. But he works hard and does his homework without my having to remind him.

I seem unable to do anything for Thomas just now. The humble food that I have to offer him does not seem to attract him, and he seldom comes here. He is working on a translation for the Christiania Theatre, and that may perhaps be another reason why he doesn't come here more often. He does not find the food good enough at the place where we eat dinner, so now he goes elsewhere. I don't think anyone would know he was ill; but when he has attacks he stays at home, and I have no time to visit him.

There is a lot of cleaning going on, as the winter windows have to be put in. But the cold weather has eased and it is very fine. The people of the house do everything for me excellently, and Lina [the maid] is very helpful.

I had intended to write some new poems for the second edition of my collection; but I cannot think about that while I have all the household affairs to bother about. We don't spend much; we have not had any extra expenses; in the evening we eat only bread and butter; we have not bought cheese, sausage, or anything like that. Sigurd has received a very nice winter coat from my Roman woman, and it only cost 2 thalers 15 groschen.

I must strongly insist that you fortify yourself with wine and nourishing food of the best quality; to stint on this could easily be a false economy.

Greet poor Marie from me, of course. You and she will know that I think of her with heartfelt sympathy.

I must stand by what I said in my previous letter about Herr and Fru Ludvigsen [Marie's sister and brother-in-law]. You say that Sara has been good to Marie. Yes, the kind of goodness one shows to a sick servant. If Marie had been in Bergen the Baars [her other in-laws] would not have sent her to hospital but would have kept her at home with them. Likewise in Christiania; and so of course would we have done. Don't let yourself be fooled by such hysterical nonsense. But enough of that for today.

I received the enclosed letter a moment ago. It must be from either Frøken Holck or the French Frøken Pradez; for it is postmarked Kallundborg and Count Lerche lives there. If it is anything that concerns me, keep it. If it is from Frøken Holck, tell her that I have written to her in Copenhagen and that it may not yet have reached her. She is one of our true friends, and a true sympathiser unlike certain others, despite all their forced empty phrases and protestations. Thomas very seldom remembers to ask after Marie. When he was in Copenhagen he did not visit her, although he knew he would never see her again. He says Sara told him it would disturb Marie to see him. Ask her if this is true; I should like to know.

Now it is getting towards dinner-time and I must meet Sigurd at the dining rooms. Write soon and let me know in detail how you are; for I don't really know at all. If anything critical happens you must telegraph.

> Your affectionate
> Henrik Ibsen

Two days later he had occasion to write again:

> Dresden, 15 November 1874

Dear Suzannah,

Yesterday afternoon we received your letter with the sad news of our dear Marie's death. So she is no longer with us; but we will cherish her in fond memory.

Sigurd has told her closest friends here in Dresden of the event; Thomas came to see us last night and learned then.

Now it is your task to make the last arrangements with composure and serenity. You do not say in your letter when you expect to be finished in Copenhagen. The *Titania* leaves on Wednesday. If you travel in her, drop me a line ahead. But if you feel too tired you must not leave so soon.

I hope you will have received my previous letter today, Sunday. I am addressing this, likewise, to the hospital, though I don't know if you are still living there; but anyway you will have left your new address with them.

You will of course see that the letters, etc., that Marie has left do not come into strange hands; in which category I include her Danish relatives.

Make sure you have enough money and clothes for the homeward journey. It will be bitterly cold on the way south. Travel in a second-class ladies' compartment, and take among other things a bottle of good port wine with you. I have described your best route in an earlier letter.

I am writing this on Sunday morning. Sigurd is at Thomas's. If possible, let me know the time of your departure from Copenhagen. Whether we shall be able to meet you at the station I do not know, since we cannot be sure which train you will be taking.

Who will send the news to Marie's family and friends in Norway? I strongly urge that this should not be left to your mother, as I am sure you will agree.

Your affectionate
Henrik Ibsen

Suzannah, with typical single-mindedness, had, on discovering that her sister had been taken to die in a public hospital, installed herself there so as to be with her day and night. "Suzannah Ibsen came here from Dresden," wrote Magdalene to Lorentz Dietrichson on 1 December, "and tended her and watched over her with a splendid devotion. You know Fru Ibsen. What she does she does with all her soul—nothing by halves."[43]

Suzannah's enforced trip to Copenhagen placed an additional burden on Ibsen's already strained finances. Already on 22 October, after their return from Norway, he had written to Hegel: "This has been an expensive year for me. I am almost frightened to look at my account books." For the financial promise of the previous year had not been fulfilled. This year, he had earned less than half as much:

	specie-dollars	
7th edn. of *Brand*	255	
3rd edn. of *Peer Gynt*	247½	
3rd edn. of *The League of Youth*	215½	
2nd edn. of *Lady Inger of Østraat*	568	
Extra royalties from Christiania Theatre	200	
	1,486	£413

With his state pension, dividends from his gilt-edged and railway shares, and a win of £5 in the Danish state lottery, Ibsen's total income for 1874 had been £576; not much for a man approaching his forty-seventh birthday who was the most talked-of writer in Scandinavia and one of its best-sellers.

On 27 January 1875 Ibsen posted Hegel his foreword to the forthcoming reprint of *Catiline*. "On reading through it [the play]," he explained, "I clearly recalled my original conception and realized that the

---

[43] Dietrichson, "En Ibsen-myte," in *Samtiden* (1907), p. 97.

form hardly anywhere achieved a full expression of what I had intended. I therefore decided to rewrite this youthful poem as I think I could have done even then, had I had the time and had circumstances been more favourable. But the ideas, conception, and general development of the play I have not tampered with. The book remains as it was, save that it now appears in a fulfilled and completed form. These things remembered, I beg that it may be accepted by my friends in Scandinavia and elsewhere, I beg that they will accept it as a greeting from me at the end of an era which has been, for me, rich in change and contrasts. Much of what I dreamed of twenty-five years ago has come true, if not always in the way I then hoped, or as quickly as I had hoped. But I think it was best for me thus; I would not wish that anything that has happened should not have happened, and when I look back on my experiences as a whole, I do so with a sense of gratitude for everything that happened and to everyone who was involved."

That winter Ibsen made up his mind to leave Dresden, for several reasons. One was, again, Sigurd's education. "The school which Sigurd has been attending here," he wrote to Ludvig Daæ on 4 February, "has done away with its two senior *gymnasialklasser,* and the state schools of the city seem to me, in their general method and organization, unsuitable for foreign pupils. Besides, I have again begun to feel the wanderlust, and during this past year more and more foreigners have been leaving Dresden. My move will, I fear, take me somewhat farther from home; but as compensation for that I shall be a little nearer Italy, and shall moreover have the pleasure of living among Catholics, who in Germany are un-questionably preferable to the Protestants."[44] A further reason was that of economy. "Dresden, when I first went to live there in 1868," he told Jonas Lie (25 May 1879), "was a cheap place to live in; but after the war, rents and all other necessities so rose that in the last years we were there, up to the spring of 1875, we spent twice as much as when we first came"; and to Johan Thoresen, on 20 February, he complained: "Dresden has now become the most expensive place to live in in all Germany." He added: "I have recently drafted the plan for a new five-act modern drama, which I hope to complete during the summer. I much look forward to getting down to this work, which has long been fermenting in my mind and has at last matured."

The day before he wrote to Thoresen, on 19 February, *The Vikings at Helgeland* received its first performance in Denmark, at the Royal Theatre in Copenhagen, and proved such a success that the theatre, on

[44] "I think spiritual and intellectual life find fuller and more agreeable expression down there [in Munich] than here in North Germany, where the state has dragooned every power into its service and sequestered every interest," he wrote to Edmund Gosse on 10 March 1875. This letter is not in the Centenary Edition, but is printed in Bredsdorff, p. 36.

their own initiative, doubled Ibsen's original honorarium of 1,000 crowns.[45] On 20 March, Ibsen's forty-seventh birthday, the new edition of *Catiline* was published, to celebrate his twenty-five years of authorship, and, as a further act of homage, *Lady Inger of Østraat* was performed in its revised form at the Christiania Theatre, where the play had never been acted before.[46]

For some reason, a few weeks earlier, Ibsen had felt impelled to write to his father, for the first time in a quarter of a century. It may have been that, as he implied in his preface to *Catiline,* he now wished to forgive all that had happened and reconcile himself with the past. His letter has not survived, for Knud Ibsen was so overjoyed at receiving it that he always thereafter carried it around on his person, showing it to all and sundry, until it fell to pieces. But we have the old man's reply (in Gothic script); it was one of the few personal letters that Ibsen kept:

Skien, 1875

My dear Son,

It gave me great joy to receive your welcome letter of 25 February, it was in truth unexpected, as I have neither heard nor seen anything of you, as you yourself say in your letter, for 25 years, none the less I have heard from you in your writings, *Brand, Peer Gynt, Love's Comedy, The League of Youth,* have all been given me. *Emperor and Galilean* I have received from Brøndlund, but I don't know if I may keep it.

It is a trial for me to write a letter, I wrote pretty well in my youth, but now age bothers me, for think I am 80 years old all but a couple of years, so writing tires me, so I have lived my best years and I only await my end. You will come to Norway this summer and then I hope we in Skien will hear from you, it will make me very happy. I expect Hedvig will have told you in her last letter about the family, so I will not repeat it as nothing has changed.

But I have one piece of news for you, and that is this, that Peder Lund Pedersen, who was confirmed with you, married a few weeks ago. He was previously engaged to a forester's daughter, but she would not marry him and he wanted to marry, so he had to make do with something terrible, one of his servants. Well now I must stop my prattling for I am boring my learned son with this nonsense. I wanted to read over this letter but couldn't

[45] Encouraged by its acceptance, Ibsen had, on 1 December, submitted another play which had been rejected when first offered, *Lady Inger of Østraat;* but the theatre's censor, Christian Molbech, reported that "the picture this play presents is from first to last so gloomy and despairing that a stage performance would not elevate the audience but would have a saddening and depressive effect. . . . Poetry should not merely show death and defeat, it should also thereby proclaim life and resurrection" (Agerholm, pp. 276–80). The board agreed, and *Lady Inger* was never performed at the Royal Theatre.

[46] But it was not a great success. "This youthful and sombre work did not succeed in arousing any very great excitement, partly because none of the main roles, except Lady Inger . . . was quite adequately performed" (T. Blanc, *Christiania Theaters historie, 1827–1877,* p. 289).

decipher it, which made me very ashamed, so I must just end with a friendly greeting to you, your wife and son from

Your old and affectionate father
Knud Ibsen[47]

It was the last contact between father and son; they neither met nor corresponded again before Knud Ibsen died two years later.

On 13 April, Henrik, Suzannah, and Sigurd Ibsen left Dresden. The seven years he had spent there had not, on the surface, been particularly fruitful compared with his four years in Italy: two plays (one of them, admittedly, of double length), and a handful of poems. *The League of Youth* and *Emperor and Galilean* had both been successes, and his earlier plays were being steadily reprinted; but his reputation still rested principally on *Brand* and *Peer Gynt*, and many of his admirers must have felt, like Edmund Gosse, that the brilliant achievement of those two plays had not quite been followed up. At forty-seven his prospects must have appeared, possibly even to himself, not quite so glittering as they had been at forty, and if it had been known that he would never again write a poetic drama he might well have been written off as having passed his seemingly brief peak. But the apparently barren years of a writer's life are often, when viewed in retrospect, the most fruitful. *Brand* and *Peer Gynt* may, in themselves, be Ibsen's greatest plays, but his main contribution to the future of drama still lay ahead of him. Neither *Brand* nor *Peer Gynt* was to inspire many notable successors; whereas the "contemporary" drama which he had been brooding on for nearly five years and was now, at last, about to write was, though it is seldom performed today, to be the foundation-stone of most of the plays that anyone has written since.

On 1 May 1875, after a fortnight's house-hunting in Munich, the Ibsens moved into a ground-floor apartment at Schönfeldt-Strasse 17, yet another corner-house, gloomy and barrack-like to judge from a contemporary photograph. The same day, in Christiania, the Storthing rejected by 54 votes to 42 a motion to increase his state pension.

[47] Bergliot Ibsen. pp. 73–74.

PART FOUR

The Critic of Society

17

Munich and Gossensass

1875 – 1876

Ibsen found Munich much to his liking. "Many Norwegians live here," he reported to Johan Thoresen on 21 May (how that recommendation would have surprised his countrymen!), "and I find the air much fresher and more invigorating than in Dresden, a natural result of the proximity of the Alps." Ibsen had an almost English passion for fresh air, as visitors to his apartment occasionally discovered to their discomfort. "He needs good air in quantity," an acquaintance was to note twelve years later. "Lofty, airy rooms are an absolute necessity to him."[1] He was a great one for leaving windows open.

Soon after his arrival, two unexpected windfalls came his way. *The League of Youth* in Stockholm and *The Vikings at Helgeland* in Copenhagen had both proved so successful that both theatres sent him an extra honorarium, and he found himself with an extra 500 specie-dollars to his credit. Thanks to this he was able to contribute to a wedding present for Edmund Gosse, for which a whip-round was being organized among Scandinavian writers. He also learned (through reading about it in *Morgenbladet*) that as an additional commemoration of his twenty-five years of authorship he had been awarded a special gold medal by King Oscar, from whom, on his last day in Dresden, Ibsen had received "a very friendly letter in his own hand." Moreover, Sigurd, he was able proudly to inform Thoresen, had, "after an exhaustive examination," been accepted into the top form but one of the Royal Maximilian Gymnasium, "although all acceptances should have been closed by last October." Altogether, it was a good month.

Ibsen's fondness for versification was dying hard, and he wrote three poems that spring. He had been invited to attend a meeting of students from the various Scandinavian countries at Upsala, and although he re-

[1] Midbøe, p. 160.

fused he sent them, to excuse his absence, an "Ode to Sweden"—a conventional piece stressing the importance of looking forwards and not backwards, and declaring his belief that a new age was dawning. This was not much better than the hack celebratory poems he had turned out during his lean years in Christiania; on reflection, the sentiments he had expressed struck him as hollow, and he considered the subject more cynically in the first of the intended series of "rhymed letters" he had proposed to Brandes for the *Nineteenth Century:* thirty couplets of iambics and anapæsts entitled "A Distant View" (*Langt Borte*). Hopes similar to those at Upsala, he recalls, had recently been voiced in Italy and Germany, but "the ghosts of old grey men" had appeared to quench them. Nevertheless, the young men of these countries had eventually triumphed; "they *willed* their dream," and so Europe grew up. We in the north, Ibsen concluded, must learn these hard lessons.

He posted this poem to Brandes on 8 June, promising to send a further poem each month "unless unforeseen obstacles prevent me" (which they did). The following month, however, he developed the same theme in a longer poem simply entitled "A Letter in Rhyme," which, he told Brandes, had occupied him "exclusively for four weeks." Why, the poem begins, does modern man seem oppressed by restlessness and apathy, so that he is incapable of either true joy or true grief? As so often in his work, Ibsen chose as his central symbol a voyaging ship, but a ship with a difference. Sometimes, he says, a vessel will set forth, and all seems well. Then, suddenly, in mid-ocean, a blackness settles on her and on all aboard her; the sail falls slack, even the sea-birds' cry seems to bode ill. When this happens, sailors have a saying that "there is a corpse in the cargo." So, suggests Ibsen, it is with us today. A voice has whispered in his ear: "I think we're sailing with a corpse in the cargo."

> I only ask. My task is not to answer.

—a line that his enemies were often to use against him, apparently unaware that great writers very rarely answer the questions they ask, unless it be to preach resignation. In fact, however, Ibsen was to state clearly and repeatedly what he believed the corpse to be: a willingness to let oneself be dominated by one's past. The idea that we can only become ourselves, true individuals, if we slough off the past was a theme he was to develop throughout his final twelve plays from *The Pillars of Society* to *When We Dead Awaken,* finding its fullest and most vivid expression in *Ghosts* and *Rosmersholm.*

This "Letter in Rhyme" was not merely the last of Ibsen's promised contributions to the *Nineteenth Century.* It was to be the last poem of any length which he was ever to write.

Another event that summer of 1875 strengthened Ibsen's conviction that prose was the path which he must now follow. The previous year Bjørnson, in Rome, had completed two new plays, *A Bankrupt* and *The Editor,* both written in prose on contemporary themes (he had begun *A Bankrupt* first, but finished it after *The Editor*). Both had been printed in the summer of 1874, but their publication had been held back to coincide with their production, an event which turned out to be considerably delayed. The Christiania Theatre refused to stage *The Editor* on the ground that the main character, a ruthless journalist who comes to a bad end, too obviously represented the then editor of *Morgenbladet,* Christian Friele, and indeed it was not performed in Norway until 1917, seven years after Bjørnson's death. Indignant at this censorship, Bjørnson offered the two plays to Nya Teater in Stockholm, which accepted them, performing *A Bankrupt* in January 1875 and *The Editor* in February. Georg Brandes was greatly excited, and wrote: "At last it seems as though we of the north, too, are to have plays in which those two great forces, the present and reality, demand respect and enter into their right." He noted, correctly, that Ibsen had sketched both an editor and a bankrupt in *The League of Youth,* but thought that Bjørnson's were the first genuinely modern realistic dramas; and Strindberg (then twenty-six) later described them as "signal rockets."

Neither *The Editor* nor *A Bankrupt* reads very well today. *The Editor* is impossibly melodramatic and is hardly ever performed even in Norway; *A Bankrupt* works reasonably until the last act, when it declines into one of those facile happy endings to which Bjørnson was so fatally prone. (He defended it on the ground that "it is good for people to know that a man can raise himself up again," and that "it shows a true family life, good, happy people,"[2] confusing, as he so often did, art with morality.) Ibsen had treated contemporary problems far more profoundly in *Love's Comedy* and *Brand,* but these had been in verse; and although *The League of Youth* nowadays strikes one as both more serious and more penetrating than *A Bankrupt,* it was, ostensibly at any rate, a comedy, and comedies were expected to be in prose. *A Bankrupt* and *The Editor* dealt with contemporary problems seriously and in everyday prose, and as such represented, at the time of their writing, an important breakthrough not merely in Scandinavian but in European drama.

Brandes's claim on behalf of the plays needs some qualification. Gogol and Ostrovsky had both written plays at least as modern and realistic as Bjørnson's; but these were as unknown in western Europe as *Woyzeck* and *Danton's Death.* And in 1873, the year before *The Editor* and *A Bankrupt,* Emile Zola had written *Thérèse Raquin,* so often named by historians as the first proletarian stage tragedy. Zola was indeed fully

[2] Letter to Edvard Stjernström, 25 May 1874; *Bjørnstjerne Bjørnsons brevveksling med svenske, 1858–1909,* ed. Øyvind Anker, Francis Bull, and Örjan Lindberger (Oslo and Stockholm, 1960–61), I, 150–51.

conscious of the need to do away with the artificially "well-made" play. "I have no taste for watchmaking, and a great taste for truth," he had written as early as 1865, two years after the Goncourt brothers had written *Henriette Maréchal*, which Zola himself regarded as the first naturalistic play. But although *Thérèse Raquin* represented a considerable step forward from the old Scribean dramas of intrigue, its language was highly melodramatic, running directly counter to Zola's demand that actors should not act but *live* before the audience (a theory which André Antoine was to put into practice at his Théâtre Libre a decade later). Zola wanted the drama to do what the naturalistic novel had done, as in Flaubert's *Madame Bovary* and his own works. But, unlike Bjørnson, Zola did not know much about writing plays; his own dramas, *Thérèse Raquin* included, are much less interesting than his prefaces and programme notes.[3]

The success of *A Bankrupt* in Scandinavia quickly spread to Germany, where before the end of the year it was performed in practically every town that boasted a theatre. Bjørnson was never to have another success to equal it in that country. Ibsen asked Hegel to send him a copy when it at last got published in 1875, and in June he saw it acted in Munich. Its success gave him the stimulus he had been needing to get his own new play off the ground. On 22 August he was able at last to write to Hegel from Kitzbühel in the Alps, where he had gone to escape the city heat: "I have now completed my plan for the new five-act play about contemporary life which I have long been thinking of writing, and which, if nothing unforeseen happens, I shall finish during the winter." The block that had obstructed him for so long seemed to have been broken. "My new work is progressing swiftly," he wrote Hegel on 23 October from Munich. "In a few days I shall have completed the first act, which I always find the most difficult part. The title will be *The Pillars of Society*, a play in five acts. In a way it can be regarded as a counterblast to *The League of Youth*, and will touch on several of the more important questions of our time." On 25 November he wrote: "Act 1 of my new play is finished and fair-copied; I am now working on Act 2," and by 10 December he was "working at it daily and am now doubly anxious to get the manuscript to you as quickly as possible."

So 1875 ended on a hopeful note. He was busy with, and excited about, his new play; a new production of *The Vikings at Helgeland* had opened in Stockholm on 3 November, and in Christiania preparations were under way for the first stage production of *Peer Gynt*, Edvard Grieg having finished the music that July. Moreover, the first complete book about him had appeared: *Henryk Ibsen, poeta norwegski*, published in Warsaw,

[3] Of the other early realistic prose dramas which have survived, Henri Becque's masterpiece, *Les Corbeaux*, was to be completed in 1876 but remained unperformed until 1882. Tolstoy's *The Power of Darkness* was written in 1886, and Strindberg's first effective modern play *The Robbers* (later rewritten as *The Comrades*) in 1886–87.

and written by Count Lars von Engeström, a Pole of Swedish descent. And the first days of 1876 were to see the first publication of an Ibsen play in English—Catherine Ray's translation of *Emperor and Galilean*. It created little stir; of the three reviews which appeared, one was signed by Edmund Gosse and the other two, which appeared anonymously, were probably also by him;[4] still, it was a beginning.

When Ibsen totted up his earnings for 1875, they were as follows:

	spd.
Fee for *The Vikings at Helgeland* at Royal Theatre, Copenhagen	250
2nd edn. of *Catiline*	328½
Fee for *Lady Inger of Østraat* at Christiania Theatre	300
Fee for *The League of Youth* at Royal Theatre, Stockholm	250
Fee from *Nineteenth Century* for "A Distant View"	25
Extra fee from Royal Theatre, Copenhagen, for *The Vikings at Helgeland*	125½
Fee from *Nineteenth Century* for "A Letter in Rhyme"	25
4th edn. of *The Pretenders*	281¼
4th edn. of *The Vikings at Helgeland*	150
2nd edn. of *Poems*	243¼
	1,978½ £548

This, though better than the previous year, was nothing like as good as 1873. His stocks and shares at the end of this year amounted to over £1,300, but this was the result of considerable parsimony; his *huskassebeholdning,* or money in hand, was only 25 specie-dollars, a little under £7.

Posterity must be grateful that Ibsen was never able, like his more fortunate fellow-dramatists in countries where there was copyright protection, to rest on the laurels of his past successes. He could not afford either to slow down his production or to let his quality decline. It was plainly necessary that he should complete his new play with all possible speed. Asking Hegel to advance him the 400 crowns due to him as interest on his investments, he explained (10 December): "You will think that I have become a spendthrift or that life is very dear in Munich, since I am spending so much money here. But neither is the case; the fact is that we have been compelled to part-furnish our present apartment, which we have now done, so that in future we shall live more cheaply. But this has been an expensive year for me." He ended the letter on a nostalgic note. "This time ten years ago I was uneasily awaiting the

---

[4] Cf. Bredsdorff, p. 27. The signed review was in the *Academy* on 10 June, the anonymous ones in the *Examiner* on 29 January and the *Athenæum* on 12 February.

publication of *Brand*. Thank you for all that has happened since! No one has contributed as much as you to the difference between my situation as it was then and as it is now. Be sure that I shall never forget this." Nor did he.

By now Ibsen was making friends among the local Germans, something he seems never to have done in Dresden. "I have begun to mix in a large literary group," he informed Johan Thoresen on 6 February 1876, "where I have been greeted with exceptional kindness and courtesy." This group was known as the Crocodile, and its members included several well-known German literary figures: the poets Hermann Lingg and Karl Streler, the comic writer Ferdinand Bom, Franz Grandaur, dramaturge and director of opera at the Munich Hoftheater, and, the most talented among them, the novelist and short story writer Paul Heyse, who had recently published two acclaimed novels, *Kinder der Welt* and *Im Paradiese*, the latter being a *roman à clef* about writers and artists in Munich. (It is a pity Ibsen did not come to Munich a year earlier, or he might well have appeared in it.) Heyse was also a prolific dramatist (though he was less successful in this field), a fluent linguist (ultimately he even learned Norwegian), and a distinguished translator of, among others, Shakespeare and Leopardi. "Visit him often," Ibsen was to advise a young fellow-Norwegian. "You will always learn something from this excellent and artistic writer."[5] Two years younger than Ibsen almost to the day, Heyse was (though he disapproved violently of *Ghosts*) to maintain a long friendship with him—and he was to achieve one literary feat which Ibsen never did, for in 1914 he received the Nobel Prize for Literature, although, as with so many recipients of that prize, posterity has not confirmed the verdict of the Swedish Academy.

Among the younger members of the Crocodile was a writer named Paul Lindau, who forty years later recalled their meetings. He remembered that Ibsen looked much older than his years and that he combed his hair frequently and never tired of looking at himself in mirrors. In the street he would stop before every mirror and comb his hair back from his forehead. Although Ibsen enjoyed jokes, he disapproved (surprisingly, for so ostentatious a free-thinker) of any jests concerning religion. Once when Lindau made such a jest, Ibsen became very tight-lipped, snapped: "There are some things one doesn't make fun of," and left the table. Lindau also recalled that Ibsen once told him that every time he finished a play he felt it was the last he would write, because he had said in it everything that he had to say.[6]

The Crocodile used to meet daily at noon, first at the Café Probst,

---

[5] Paulsen, *Samliv med Ibsen*, II, 43.

[6] Paul Lindau, *Nur Erinnerungen* (Stuttgart and Berlin, 1917), pp. 369, 374–76, 383.

subsequently at their favourite rendezvous, the café of the Hotel Achatz in the Maximilianplatz. Another member was a young Norwegian painter named Marcus Grønvold, whom Ibsen liked and who has left an interesting account of him at this period. According to Grønvold, Ibsen at first attended these gatherings regularly, and even stood a couple of parties himself at a restaurant—"but since he was afraid that his work might suffer and social life gain the upper hand, he later began to attend less regularly."[7]

Grønvold describes Ibsen's routine. He would breakfast simply on a small cup of black coffee and a roll, and would then work till one. After lunch he would rest, and then walk in the streets,

> his sharp eyes perceiving everything, however buried in his own thoughts he might seem. People, shop windows, even dogs, were the objects of his attention. Sometimes he pondered what he would put on paper the following morning. On winter evenings his figure would appear like a phantom in the dark arcades of the Hofgarten. On these walks Ibsen did not like to be disturbed; he was as scant of speech then as, at other times, he could be communicative. When he returned home he again usually remained silent, and after his evening meal would walk up and down the room, smoking his pipe and listening to the conversation. But he listened carefully, taking pleasure in it, and sometimes partaking greedily, especially when eccentric characters whom he had known in his youth, gifted wrecks, were mentioned—characters such as he was to create in the persons of Ulric Brendel and Ejlert Løvborg. He once referred to such a man as "an ex-human being."

As in the old days in Rome, Ibsen loved to start an argument, but when he got bored with it he would break it off curtly, saying: "Well, there are two sides to every question." He loved to question people about their jobs, "but if he saw that they had come to study him or were expecting witty or Sphinx-like utterances, he withdrew into his shell." He enjoyed stories and anecdotes, especially risqué ones; "he regretted that one could not use such stories and events in one's writing, since they were usually the best" (a pleasant corrective to the customary picture of Ibsen as a puritan). He also once remarked to Grønvold how difficult it was to finish a play when the spiritual process was already completed and other ideas were beginning to crop up. "It demands so much self-discipline *properly* to complete a work," he said, "for interest ceases at a comparatively early stage." He added: "At the moment of conception one must be on fire, but at the time of writing, cold."

Like so many of those who knew Ibsen well, as opposed to his casual acquaintances, Grønvold speaks very highly of Suzannah. He calls her

[7] For this and the following quotations from Grønvold, cf. his *Fra Ulrikken til Alperne*, pp. 137 ff.

"understanding, warm-hearted and moreover . . . free from all pettiness and narrow-mindedness, intellectually independent . . . a woman of aristocratic intelligence."[8]

On 24 February *Peer Gynt* was at last staged, at the Christiania Theatre. It was the most expensive production hitherto attempted in Norway, and proved a tremendous success. The reception at the premiere, recorded Ludvig Josephson, who directed it, was "such as I have rarely experienced."[9] The play seems to have been produced with the accent on the lyrical rather than the satirical aspects (as it was to be for many years to come and, sadly, still often is). Few musical scores can have so softened an author's intentions as Grieg's *Peer Gynt* suite, which turns the play into a jolly Hans Andersen fairy tale; but Ibsen was too unmusical to perceive this, and was delighted with the result, though he might have been less so had he seen it. "Thank you for *Peer Gynt!*" he wrote to Josephson on 5 March. "The outcome of this bold enterprise by your theatre has exceeded all my expectations."[10] The play was performed thirty-seven times during the next ten and a half months, an unprecedented number for so serious a work, when one remembers that *The Pretenders* was reckoned to have done creditably with eight. It would have continued longer had not a fire destroyed the expensive scenery and costumes the following January.

Munich theatrical circles had, meanwhile, begun to take note of the foreign dramatist in their midst, and on 10 April the Hoftheater (thanks perhaps to its dramaturge's acquaintance with Ibsen in the Crocodile) staged *The Vikings at Helgeland,* the first performance of an Ibsen play outside Scandinavia. "The house was virtually full," Ibsen reported to Hegel the following day, "and the play was received with a storm of applause. I watched the performance from the wings, and was called on to the stage five times. After the performance the writers of Munich [presumably his colleagues in the Crocodile] improvised a party for me, which continued long into the night." He even received a congratulatory letter from that passionate theatre lover Ludwig II, the mad King of Bavaria, Richard Wagner's friend, who was to kill himself (and his doctor) ten years later.

The success of *The Vikings* was good enough, but better was to follow. "I have this moment," Ibsen informed Hegel on 30 May, "received an invitation from the Duke of Meiningen to go to Berlin, where on Saturday his company is to act *The Pretenders* for the first time. . . . The story that a Danish paper printed about the play being acted in Meiningen and receiving no applause is untrue. It was only a trial performance without the new decor and without any cuts." To appear suitably dressed at so

---

[8] *Ibid.*, p. 145.

[9] Josephson, p. 62.

[10] But Ibsen seems to have had second thoughts about Grieg's score (see p. 739 below).

18. Ibsen in 1874. Photograph by J. Lindegaard, Christiania.

19. Ibsen's home-made bank-notes. "To be cashed when sufficient funds were in the bank." "Cat" and "Eagle" were Ibsen's nicknames for Suzannah.

20. Sigurd, 1879. Portrait by H. Olrik. "Very strange, withdrawn and brooding."

21. Suzannah Ibsen, 1876. "She is exactly the right one for me."

22. Ibsen, 1877. The portrait by Julius Kronborg of which Strindberg
wrote, "The face is Brand's: the high brow of the fanatic . . . so repellent, so attractive!"

23. Clemens Petersen. Involved
in a homosexual scandal.

24. An Italian osteria in 1830. Painting by Luigi Fioroni. "With the aid
of our fogliette we built our dream-castles."

25. Carl Snoilsky, 1864. Drawing by Severin Falkman. The Swedish poet on whom Ibsen based John Rosmer in *Rosmersholm*.

26. Laura Kieler, the model for Nora in *A Doll's House*. "He called her his 'skylark.' "

27. Manuscript extracts from Ibsen's drafts of *Peer Gynt*. Above, Act One, Scene I. Below, Act Five (Threadballs scene).

important an occasion required more money than Ibsen had to hand, and he begged Hegel to send 450 reichsmarks (£22) to him in Berlin and a like sum to Suzannah in Munich. This was hardly a loan, for Hegel had 400 crowns to Ibsen's credit from the Stockholm production of *The Vikings,* and the interest on his shares was due in June. Hegel obliged as always, and so Ibsen saw for the first time the greatest theatrical company of his age.

The influence of the "Meiningers" on the technique of stage production was almost as great as that of Ibsen on the technique of dramatic writing, and we may pause for a moment to consider it. André Antoine, who saw them in Brussels in 1888, and Konstantin Stanislavsky, who spent a year with them, have both described how the Meininger productions opened their eyes to the possibility of a theatrical realism of which they had never dreamed. Stanislavsky, indeed, recalled that it was their appearance in St. Petersburg which first fired him to enter the theatre. The company was the creation of the new ruler of Saxe-Meiningen, Duke Georg II. Meiningen itself was a tiny town of only seven thousand inhabitants, but Duke Georg was no dilettante; the great Viennese actor, Josef Levinsky, described him as "the finest theatrical director Germany has ever known," adding significantly: "His deep understanding of dramatists' intentions is far more important than any amount of splendid decor."[11]

Many of the innovations which we today accept as a natural prerequisite of any good production, and which are commonly attributed to Antoine, Stanislavsky, Reinhardt, and Granville Barker, were introduced by Duke Georg in the eighteen-seventies. Ensemble acting; the conception of decor as an integral and imaginative part of the production instead of a mere background; intelligent and searching characterization, instead of the kind of theatricality that used the text as a trampoline; and above all, the treatment of crowds as so many individuals and not as a dumb and uncomprehending collection of extras—these were the innovations (or rather, since nothing is wholly new in the theatre, the recreations) of Duke Georg which astonished and excited his contemporaries. What these methods meant to an imaginative man of the theatre may be best evoked by quoting the reactions of Antoine and William Archer on seeing them for the first time. Here is Antoine writing to the critic Francisque Sarcey after seeing the Meiningers in Brussels in 1888:

> They showed us things absolutely new and very instructive. Their crowds are not like ours, composed of elements picked haphazard, working men hired for dress rehearsals, badly clothed, and unaccustomed to wearing strange and uncomfortable costumes, especially when they are exact. Immobility is almost always required of the crowds on our stage, whereas the supernumeraries of the Meininger crowds must act and mime their characters. Don't understand by that that they force the note and that the attention is

[11] Bjørn Bjørnson, *Bare ungdom* (Oslo, 1934), p. 153.

distracted from the protagonists. No, the tableau is complete, and in whatever direction you may look, you fix your eyes on a detail in the situation or character. At certain moments, its power is incomparable.

The troupe of the Meininger company contains about seventy actors of both sexes. All those who do not take a part are expected to figure in the play, and every evening too. If there are twenty actors occupied, the fifty others, without a single exception, even in the case of the leading players, appear on the stage in the tableaux, and each leading actor is the chief, the corporal, of a group of real supernumeraries, whom he directs and watches as long as the company is under the eye of the public. This obligation is such that the wife of Hans von Bülow,[12] one of the stars of the Meininger, having refused to perform this service, which she considered beneath her talent, was dismissed, although her husband had the title and functions of *Kapell-meister* to the Duke of Saxony. In this way they obtain ensembles that are extraordinarily true to life. . . . Mlle. Lindner, their star, playing in *A Winter's Tale,* took a silent part in the tableau of the seat of Justice, and mimed a woman of the people as conscientiously and as carefully as she interpreted on the following evening the important role of Hermione in the same piece.[13]

William Archer covered the company's visit to London in June and July, 1881, as a young critic of twenty-five for the *London Figaro* (4 June and subsequent issues). Of their opening production, *Julius Caesar* (in which Bjørnson's son, Bjørn, the only non-German member of the group, acted Casca), Archer noted: "In the first scene already, a peculiarity of stage management is noticeable. The crowd does not remain *au deuxième plan,* acting as a background to the tribunes. On the contrary, Flavius and Marullus mix with it and elbow with it, sometimes almost hidden in its midst. It has all the uncertain fluctuations of an actual crowd. Its splendid drill produces the effect of absolute freedom from drill." Of the scene when Antony addresses the crowd in the Forum, Archer wrote that the actor, Ludwig Barnay, "did not address himself to the imagination of the audience, but to the living and moving populace before him. . . . It is rather by inference than by personal sensation or intuition that we recognize the power of Mark Antony's oratory. We see how it moves the crowd, and by an act of judgment we decide that it should and must be so moved. . . . The scene is presented in a manner far surpassing anything of the kind as yet attempted in England. Indeed, I search my memory in vain for anything with which to compare it even for an instant."

Of their decor, Archer wrote: "They take the trouble to distinguish between tree and tree, whereas our scene-painters have one recipe for every species of foliage, varied only by a dash of red-brown when an

[12] Marie Schanzer. Bülow's first wife, Cosima, had left him to become the mistress, and later the wife, of Richard Wagner.

[13] S. M. Waxman, *Antoine and the Théâtre Libre* (Harvard, 1926), pp. 95–96.

autumn landscape has to be depicted. Their handling of tree-stems and bark struck me as particularly admirable." In their production of *William Tell* ("a marvellously fine and thoughtful presentation"), he noted the effect of rain which they achieved by "a peculiar arrangement of light, and some motion in the backcloth"; the use of steam to represent dust when the Swiss tear down the Austrian castle; the small boys with beards on scaffolding at the back of the stage to give the effect of perspective; their presentation of the figure of Time as a young girl; and the care and individuality of their make-up. And they were far in advance of other European companies in their treatment of comedy; Archer thought that their *Malade imaginaire* "need not shrink from comparison with the Comédie-Française itself," though he had seen Coquelin in the part.[14] Henry Irving saw them during their visit, and admired, and was influenced by, their crowd work and lighting.

The Meininger production of *The Pretenders* in Berlin was a great success; how one would love to have seen what Duke Georg did with the crowd scenes in which the play abounds, and especially his treatment of the battle scenes. Writing to Ludvig Josephson on 14 June, Ibsen described the performance as "brilliant and spectacular. The play was received with great applause, and I was repeatedly called. I don't think this much pleased the Berlin critics, most of whom are themselves play-wrights. However, the play has run for nine successive performances, and would have continued longer had the Meiningers not been scheduled to end their season on the 15th. After the opening performance I was invited by the duke to visit him at his summer palace at Liebenstein in Meiningen, where I have been staying until I came back here [to Munich] the day before yesterday." And as if that was not enough: "On my departure he decorated me with the Knight Cross of the Saxon-Ernestine Order, First Class. *The Pretenders* is to be given in Schwerin too, and *The Vikings* has been accepted by the Burgtheater in Vienna, where Charlotte Wolter is to play Hjørdis." Ibsen got on well with monarchs, and the duke, who plainly liked Ibsen, as Carl XV and Oscar II had done, invited him to come back in the winter. Indeed, the time was to come when Ibsen had to give up visiting a certain resort be-

---

[14] Irrelevantly but interestingly, one may mention that in his column of 4 June Archer quotes an American paper as reporting that "the adoption of a revolving stage, such as is seen in Japanese playhouses, is contemplated by several European theatres," and that on 13 July, reviewing a production of *Romeo and Juliet* by the Oxford Agamemnon Company, he observed with pleasure that "Shakespeare's original text was followed throughout, instead of the ordinary acting version." Archer's criticisms during his six years with *London Figaro* and his twenty-one years with *The World* are a fascinating mine of theatrical history.

Bjørn Bjørnson records that when they acted in Meiningen itself the duke used real soldiers from his own army for the crowd scenes, and that when they played in big theatres they would have five or six hundred people on the stage. (*Bare ungdom,* p. 176.)

cause Duke Georg, who had a place in the vicinity, so pestered him with invitations as to make it impossible for him to work.

Did the Meininger methods influence Ibsen's future writing? It is possible; the realism of that production of *The Pretenders* may well have had its effect on *The Pillars of Society,* which he was at last to complete during the following year. Mr. Peter Tennant suggests: "The setting and detail of the stage directions, with their references to gesture and expression, could almost have been taken out of a Meiningen producer's manuscript, and the detailed realism of the play strikes one as a reminiscence of the Meiningers and an exploitation of Meininger methods in the interest of modern social drama. The influence of the Meininger Company on Ibsen's technique cannot be proved, but circumstantial evidence goes to show that it was a factor."[15] In fact, Ibsen had already, by the time he saw the Meiningers, completed his first draft of Act One and part of Act Two, with stage directions almost as detailed as in the final draft; but their methods must have given him the assurance that a technique of production and acting was developing which might eventually be equal to the demands on them he was planning to make.

On 5 August Ibsen took Suzannah and Sigurd for their usual holiday in the mountains, but this year, instead of Berchtesgaden, they tried somewhere new. "We shall be staying," he informed Edvard Grieg, who was in Bayreuth for the opening of the Festspielhaus with the first complete performance of Wagner's *Ring,* "at Gossensass, a country town near the Brenner railway, between Brenner and Sterzing. You must come via Munich, Rosenheim and Innsbruck, it being only three or four hours by rail from the last-named town to Gossensass. We shall probably be lodging at the Brauhaus Inn—in any case, you will find out where we are even if you don't warn us of your arrival. You will be most warmly welcome, and I hope you won't make too brief a stay. After the exhausting pleasures of Bayreuth you will need fresh mountain air, and you will find it up there."

Grieg duly arrived in Gossensass, bringing with him a young writer from Bergen named John Paulsen, who had accompanied him to Bayreuth. Paulsen, then twenty-five, had published a few things, including some poems which Grieg had set to music, and he was to become a prolific, if not greatly talented, novelist and playwright. His poems and novels are scarcely read today, and his plays will never be performed again, but in a series of memoirs he was to leave one of the most vivid and intimate pictures of Ibsen that we possess. He was inclined to romance when reporting from hearsay, but his first-hand observation was perceptive and lively.

Paulsen had his first sight of Ibsen as he and Grieg walked from the station into the little town. They had not warned Ibsen of their arrival, and chanced on him as he was taking a walk.

[15] Tennant, p. 54–55.

Ibsen . . . reminded me of a bridegroom going in his best clothes to meet his beloved. The black tail coat with order ribbons, the dazzlingly white linen, the elegantly knotted cravat, the black, correct silk hat, the precise movements, the reserved expression, all put me in mind of his poem:

> I shrink from the mob.
> I have no wish to be clasped to their hot bosom.
> I shall await whatever time may bring
> In a well-pressed morning coat.

Grieg introduced me. The conventional courtesies were exchanged. Ibsen's face expressed neither joy nor displeasure at seeing us. Gradually I studied his remarkable physiognomy—the small, blue-grey eyes behind the gold spectacles, the high, unusually broad brow, seemingly gnarled with thought, the long grizzled whiskers, the fine, pursed mouth, thin as a knife-blade. . . . I stood before a closed mountain-wall, an impenetrable riddle.[16]

Paulsen could not help contrasting this figure with the poet in his Christiania days as described to him by an unnamed friend who had known Ibsen then: "seated alone at one of the humbler cafés, his cheek resting on his hand and a careworn expression round his mouth, his beard allowed to grow unchecked, his hair an unkempt mane, on his head an old slouch hat."[17]

Each evening they ate together in the Brauhaus, "the cosy little room with the Madonna painting on the wall, the friendly young Tyrolean landlord who knew Latin and Italian . . . the meal, which usually consisted of ham and fried eggs, with home-brewed beer or *vin ordinaire,* and a bunch of grapes for dessert, the itinerant zither-player who occasionally appeared to my delight and Grieg's distress. . . . All day Ibsen would be silent and unapproachable. He often invited me to accompany him on his walks, but never uttered a word. . . . Yet when we parted he never failed to thank me for my 'pleasant company.' . . . In the evenings he usually thawed and became communicative and cheerful." Grieg, adds Paulsen, had "a particular talent for getting him going."[18]

Lorentz Dietrichson joined them at Gossensass, with his wife and daughters; he too (noted Paulsen) was good at "getting Ibsen going." One morning the four men left the ladies and went for a walk; but a flurry of snow caused them to seek shelter in a small wooden pavilion. Paulsen slipped back to the hotel to fetch some brandy, hot water, sugar, and glasses, and they sat in the pavilion drinking toddy and telling stories. Paulsen was surprised to discover (as Marcus Grønvold had done) that Ibsen enjoyed slightly *risqué* anecdotes, which he would acknowledge with "silent, chuckling laughter."[19] Ibsen himself told one

[16] Paulsen, *Mine Erindringer* I, 10–11.
[17] *Ibid.*, p. 15
[18] *Ibid.*, pp. 16–17.
[19] Paulsen, *Samliv med Ibsen,* I, 183–84.

about an unnamed author, then much admired, "one of those hyper-
æsthetic characters whom Germany possesses in such abundance, who
would like to forget that we humans, for all our spiritual qualities, share
certain needs with animals." Once, while travelling by rail (related Ibsen),
this gentleman was afflicted with a painful stomach-ache and, unhappily,
the train possessed no W.C. In addition to the hat he was wearing he
had in his trunk a *chapeau-bas* "which, since he was fortunately alone
in the compartment, was now pressed into service." It having served its
purpose, the man threw it out of the window; but he had unluckily forgotten that the hat carried his visiting-card in the inside band. The train
was a slow local, and when it reached the station of the tiny town where
he lived, and of which he was the leading inhabitant, the station-master
ran up as the great man emerged with dignity on to the platform and
proffered the hat with a respectful bow, it having been found on the line
and rushed to its famous owner. The author was furious, at first denied
that the hat was his, and ended by throwing it in the station-master's
face.[20]

Ibsen told another story about an old man from Skien whom, to his
surprise, he once met in Christiania, dressed like an undertaker in a white
cravat and old black gloves. When Ibsen asked what he was doing in
the capital, the old man replied: "Herr Ibsen, my only joy in life is
following corpses and being present at burials, but I have little opportunity to do these things in Skien, where people live to too great an age
and refuse to die. So I have now sold my little house there and moved
to Christiania, where people pass on like flies and, the Good Lord be
praised, I can follow corpses almost every day of the year."

Grieg talked of Wagner and Liszt, whom he had seen at Bayreuth,
especially of Liszt, whose warm testimonial had been largely instrumental
in Grieg's receiving a civil list pension from the Storthing. He also surely
(though Paulsen does not mention it) told Ibsen of Wagner's experiments
in staging at Bayreuth, such as his plunging the auditorium into total
darkness throughout the performance, something that had not been done
in the theatre before (though the Meiningers were to follow suit), and
his concealment of the orchestra, so that the audience was separated
from the stage by a "mystical abyss." But even the shortest concert
bored Ibsen, and he never visited Bayreuth.

From Liszt, the conversation moved on to Ole Bull. Grieg told how
the young Queen Isabella of Spain, who was "more interested in love
than politics," conceived a passion for the handsome Norwegian violinist
and commanded him to play privately for her at the palace. He obeyed;
no other person was present at the recital. Afterwards he received a
Spanish medal carrying the inscription: *Pour le vertu*. When he came to
Stockholm old Queen Desirée, who in her youth had been the fiancée

[20] For this and the following anecdotes, *ibid.*, pp. 10 ff.

of Napoleon Bonaparte, asked Bull what he had got this medal for, and he replied: *"Pour le vertu, votre majesté."*

They discussed German women, and Ibsen remarked that "a German lady in *grande toilette* always reminds me of a prize cow with gilt trappings and paper flowers between its horns." He added that he thought animals realised that such decorations were a token of praise, since they resisted when anyone tried to remove them. On the subject of Bjørnson he observed: "Bjørnson and I are not enemies, as many people believe. It is our disciples who are enemies." At this interesting stage in the conversation the ladies surprised them over their glasses, and the three famous husbands were led back to the hotel "with their tails between their legs."

Grieg said that he was looking for a new subject for an opera. Ibsen suggested *Olaf Liljerkrans,* but this did not appeal to Grieg, who suggested that Ibsen should write something new for him; but Ibsen said he was too preoccupied with his new play.

In September Ibsen and his companions moved south from Gossensass to the little town of Kaltern on the Italian border, where the Ibsens lodged with the burgomaster. They several times went fishing in a boat. "Ibsen," writes Paulsen, "turned out to be a passionate fisherman, and had miraculous luck. Every time he casually, and as though absent-mindedly, cast his line, a big fish immediately bit at the hook. In the space of half an hour he had caught a dozen. . . . This put him in an excellent humour. His success as a sportsman pleased him more than if he had achieved some great artistic triumph."[21]

Meanwhile, the success of *The Vikings* in Munich and of *The Pretenders* in Berlin had led to a rapid and widening increase in performances of Ibsen's work in the theatres. On 15 September he reported to Hegel: *"The Vikings* is to be staged at the Burgtheater in Vienna in October; I have received an official invitation to attend, as also in Schwerin, where *The Pretenders* is to be done in November. *The Vikings* is to be performed at the Dresden Hoftheater in a few weeks; the same play is also in rehearsal at the Stadttheater in Leipzig, and is now being acted again with great success in Munich. From all of these theatres I receive ten per cent of the gross takings from all performances during my lifetime, and my heirs for a further fifteen years. This is undeniably a great deal better than what Herr Berner thinks proper to offer me, and people will now understand why I regard it as pre-eminently important to make my work profitable here. A German translation of *Lady Inger* is already completed in manuscript, and will be performed, for a start, in Meiningen and Munich. My preoccupation with all these matters has necessitated my postponing the completion of my new play; but on my return to Munich at the beginning of next month I intend to get it finished, although it is not very tempting to write for the theatres at home. . . . I

[21] Paulsen, *Mine Erindringer,* p. 35.

have long been waiting to see the new edition of *Peer Gynt* advertised; I hope it will soon appear. And perhaps there might be a call for a new edition at Christmas of one of my other books? I should be very happy if this were possible; for I need money, and theatre royalties down here are only paid quarterly or half-yearly. May I therefore, notwithstanding my debt to you, ask you to be so kind as to send me 450 reichsmarks [80 specie-dollars] at the above address? You would be doing me a great service, and I sincerely hope it will not be long before my account with you is balanced."

Ibsen's reference to the lack of temptation to "write for the theatres at home," and to the importance of making his work "profitable" for the German theatres, may partly explain the apathy he had been showing towards *The Pillars of Society*, on which he had been working with such enthusiasm the previous autumn and winter. His successes in Germany had been with sweeping historical plays in the grand manner (*The Vikings at Helgeland* and *The Pretenders*) and, despite the success of Bjørnson's *A Bankrupt*, *The Pillars of Society*, with its very parochial and Norwegian atmosphere, must have struck Ibsen as unlikely to appeal either to German theatrical taste or to that country's traditional style of acting. It was with reluctance and doubt that he was to finish *The Pillars of Society;* but his fears were to prove totally unfounded, and it was to set the style for all his future work. Not only was he always thereafter to write in prose and on contemporary themes; he was never to set any more of his plays outside Norway, though he took good care to give his characters names that could easily be pronounced by foreigners.

Ibsen left Kaltern at the end of September; apart from other considerations, Sigurd had to be back at school in Munich by 1 October. Paulsen accompanied them back to Munich; as the train drew in, Paulsen exclaimed: "What a big city!" and Ibsen surprised him by replying: "One can't live anywhere smaller."[21]

Ibsen's letters during the last three months of 1876 contain, significantly, no reference to *The Pillars of Society*. Even when writing to Hegel he avoided the subject. In October *The Vikings at Helgeland* was performed in Vienna and Dresden, and also in Bergen. The director of his old theatre there annoyed him by suggesting that he should public-spiritedly allow them to stage it without payment, to which he replied (30 September): "It should be the task of rich men, not authors, to bear the cost of such experiments. . . . It has long vexed me to see how at every possible opportunity people at home try to put the burden on to artists and writers. For the restoration of Haakon's Hall [in Bergen] artists were blackmailed into presenting paintings each of which is worth 600–800 specie-dollars. I should be interested to know what the merchants of Bergen have con-

[22] *Ibid.*, p. 36.

tributed."[23] In November *The Vikings* was revived at the Royal Theatre, Copenhagen. A fourth edition of *Peer Gynt* appeared this autumn; German translations of *Lady Inger* and *Brand* (the third German version of that work, this time by Baron Alfred von Wolzogen) were promised for the winter, and Ibsen was able to report to Hegel that the German edition of *The Vikings* was almost sold out. The inexpensiveness of book production in Germany amazed him; the first thousand copies of *The Vikings,* printed on "very handsome paper," cost only 325 reichsmark. Unfortunately, such fees as he might expect from all this lay in the future, and he had to ask Hegel to advance him another 400 crowns.

Paulsen stayed in Munich until December, and recorded some further perceptive notes about Ibsen's routine in that city. In some respects his habits had changed since the early days in Dresden. He never now went to the theatre, unless to see one of his own plays; such as *The Vikings,* to which he took Paulsen, who found the production "exciting and spectacular," especially "a grand snowstorm."[24] The picture galleries which had attracted him as a young man he no longer visited, nor the studios of the numerous Norwegian painters who were in Munich at that time (and who included such distinguished artists as Erik Werenskiold, Eilif Peterssen, Christian Skredsvig and Gerhard Munthe).[25] He isolated himself more and more, and was now even reluctant to accept invitations to dinner in other people's houses.[26] "Social life does not merely steal one's time," he

[23] Eventually, by a contract signed on 28 October, it was agreed that he should receive 100 specie-dollars for the first performance of each new play staged at the Bergen Theatre, 10 specie-dollars for each of the next five performances and 5 specie-dollars for each subsequent performance—except for *Catiline* and *The Feast at Solhaug,* which it was reckoned would each occupy only half an evening, and for which he was to receive half the above fees.

[24] Paulsen, *Samliv med Ibsen,* II, 27.

[25] But he had already given up visiting picture galleries during his time in Dresden. John Paulsen (*Samliv med Ibsen,* I, 152) quotes Julius Lange: "I had to promise Ibsen yesterday that I would go with him to the gallery one day, since he, who has lived here two years, is so ignorant of its contents that it's a disgrace. It is amazing how incapable he is of really appreciating a work of art, and how little inclination he has for looking at anything of that kind."

[26] This had not always been so; Lorentz Dietrichson, who spent a year in Munich from Christmas 1875 to February 1877, records that "Ibsen entertained an unusual amount at this time. . . . How many travellers must there be who retain grateful memories of the Ibsens' apartment, and especially Fru Ibsen's untiring kindness towards young and lonely compatriots of either sex during their stay in the Bavarian capital" (*Svundne Tider,* I, 356–57). Bergliot Ibsen (who presumably had it from her husband, Sigurd) confirms this, with an embarrassing rider which explains Ibsen's subsequent unwillingness to accept invitations. "At first they offered much hospitality. Once a week they held open house for the Norwegians in the city. But after a time Ibsen heard that the Norwegian guests found the fare offered not good enough, with the result that the Ibsens closed their doors to them." She adds: "It is curious to reflect on the kind of criticism which the Ibsens have always encountered

told Paulsen. "It stultifies. An author who wants to achieve anything must isolate himself. Live alone in his thoughts and for his work." He remarked of a Norwegian novelist (unnamed) who always allowed himself to be taken to dinner: "When does that man write? I wonder he manages to accomplish anything." But unwilling as he was to partake in social life, he was very curious to know what went on there. When Paulsen had attended any such dinner, Ibsen would question him minutely about everything that happened—what topics had been discussed, what the hostess had worn, even how much people had tipped the footman.[27]

Arriving punctually at his fixed hour at the Café Maximilian, he would (Paulsen noted) always seat himself opposite a large mirror which reflected the door.

> Here, without needing to turn his head, he could observe everything in the mirror, and sat there behind his big newspaper like some fiction detective. Nothing escaped his sharp eyes. He noticed, not merely people's appearance and habits . . . but picked up bits of their private conversations,[28] and noted characteristics which were peculiar to them and which he had not perceived elsewhere. . . . He also learned much from the newspapers. There he found the answers to so many of his unuttered questions about the people among whom he lived. . . . From a small article or advertisement which other readers overlooked he could learn more than they from years of study. . . . But Ibsen was no ordinary newspaper reader. He read the advertisements minutely, and remarked that they were not the least informative section of the paper. He began reading from the title at the top of page one and read right through to the names of the printer and publishers at the foot of the final page.[29]

Paulsen was surprised to find that Ibsen liked to do as many domestic tasks as possible himself. If a button came loose on his trousers, he would "go into his room, close the door firmly and, after various preparations as humorous as they were unnecessary, would sew on the button with the same care with which he would fair-copy a new play." One of Ibsen's convictions was that "women never know how to sew on a button so that

---

from Norwegian sources. Even now, more than forty years after his death, people write disparagingly of the food Fru Ibsen cooked. . . . When after his parents' death Sigurd presented his father's furniture etc. to the nation the newspapers expressed nothing but contempt for Ibsen's bad taste." She sums up: "Ibsen hated people's perpetual scrutiny of his private life and especially the incessant nagging about his modest circumstances. That was one extra reason why they kept themselves more and more withdrawn. . . . The first time Sigurd encountered this meanness of spirit was probably with the Norwegian guests at Munich" (*De Tre,* pp. 62–64).

[27] Paulsen, *Samliv med Ibsen,* II, 42.

[28] "Ibsen listened all his life, though he often seemed to be otherwise preoccupied." Lugné-Poe, *Ibsen* (Paris, 1936), p. 74.

[29] Paulsen, *Samliv med Ibsen,* I, 31–33.

it stays, whereas when he sewed one on himself it remained fast for ever." Suzannah, however, told Paulsen that after Ibsen had sewed on a button she would stitch it, "which Ibsen always forgets, and which is the most important thing. But let him go on believing it, it makes him so happy."[30]

On the other hand, Ibsen hated seeing his wife doing anything manual such as knitting, and Paulsen says he never saw Suzannah thus occupied because she knew her husband's aversion to such things.[31] This business of independence Ibsen carried to unexpected lengths. One morning he startled Paulsen by asking him "with an earnest and worried expression" whether he polished his own boots. Paulsen confessed that he did not. Ibsen said: "But you must. . . . One should never let another person do for one what one can do for oneself." He was even, unexpectedly, something of a cook, and especially liked making soups."[32]

As Paulsen had discovered at Gossensass, Ibsen could, when the mood took him, be an excellent raconteur. But despite his enjoyment of risqué anecdotes, "Ibsen, with a bashfulness unusual among writers, avoided all sexual topics."[33] On this subject he was evidently inhibited to a degree unusual even for the nineteenth century. Paulsen reflects:

> And yet this man, according to his fellow students, had been in his youth soft, emotional, almost sentimental, as . . . letters and poems from that time confirm. But the same cold hand that closed his eloquent lips laid itself early, like a frost, over his emotional life too. . . . Lest the world should cause him further pain he built a shell of satire over everything in him that was tender and vulnerable. . . . His heart gradually died, and with its his dreams of personal happiness. The door to the world of love and friendship was slammed shut.[34]

Ibsen once astonished Paulsen by declaring that there were three things that meant nothing to him: flowers, music, and children.[35] The last part of this claim is contradicted by several witness, such as Johanne Lie and Bolette Sontum,[36] who have testified to the kindness and affection he showed them when they were small. His indifference to music has already been remarked; I do not know of any other evidence of his feeling for or against flowers. What is perhaps most interesting about Ibsen's claim, however, is not whether it is true, but that he should have made it. It is very much the statement of a man who has turned his back on all things of the heart.

[30] *Ibid.,* pp. 33–35.

[31] Cf. Helmer's lines in *A Doll's House:* "Knitting—that's an ugly business—can't help it. Look—arms all huddled up—great clumsy needles going up and down—makes you look like a damned Chinaman."

[32] Paulsen, *Samliv med Ibsen,* II, 220.

[33] Paulsen, *Mine Erindringer,* p. 18.

[34] *Ibid.,* p. 19.

[35] Paulsen, *Samliv med Ibsen,* I, 36.

[36] Cf. pp. 469 and 683, below.

Ibsen was almost theatrically fortunate in being permitted to witness the humiliation of former enemies. Clemens Petersen's fate has been related; and one day after dinner in Munich, Paulsen was standing at the window with Ibsen looking out into the street when they noticed a curious old man dressed like a priest in black with a white cravat slouch past. "Did you ever meet him in Bergen?" Ibsen asked. He had identified him as Poul Stub, the pedant who had corrected Ibsen's Norwegian essays when he was studying in Grimstad, and had attacked the policy and inexperience of the Bergen company shortly after Ibsen's arrival there in 1851. "I looked long at the old, bowed schoolmaster, once Ibsen's merciless critic, now pensioned and, for economical reasons, compelled to live in Munich because of its cheapness. I thought how differently their lives had shaped themselves since their clash in Bergen. Ibsen sat there, a famous man in an elegant home, while Poul Stub was—still Poul Stub."[37]

Paulsen noted, as Vilhelm Bergsøe had on Ischia, Ibsen's physical timidity. "In windy weather he was always apprehensive lest a tile might fall on his head, and it always amused me to see how he glanced up over his gold spectacles at the threatening rooftops. His fear of dogs was also marked; he moved quickly aside if a bulldog approached."[38] Paulsen comments that in this respect, as in the contrast between the conventionality of his life and the unconventionality of his thought, Ibsen resembled Gœthe. Another weakness was his unwillingness that strangers should know of his liking for a nap after lunch. "When Fru Ibsen once mentioned his long afternoon sleep, he got angry and declared: 'It isn't true. I merely lie on the sofa and reflect.' 'How can you say such a thing, my dear Ibsen?' said Suzannah. 'You sleep so heavily that we can hear your snores in the living-room.' At this Ibsen left the room without speaking, evidently insulted."[39] Suzannah also confided in Paulsen that Ibsen "likes us to have maids who look pretty; he can't stand old, ugly ones," adding: "Though he never looks at them—that is, he looks at them, but only æsthetically, as one looks at a statue or a painting."[40] One is reminded of Irene's accusation of Rubek in *When We Dead Awaken*.

Ibsen had an extraordinary dislike of using Christian names, even with his close friends; Suzannah told Paulsen that Ibsen had addressed her as "De" (the Norwegian equivalent of *vous*) throughout their engagement, "which caused much amazement in the circles in which the young couple moved."[41] He used affectionately to address Suzannah as "the cat" or "the eagle," the latter name having been given her long ago by her brothers and sisters because of her bold character (hence his drawings of

[37] Paulsen, *Samliv med Ibsen*, II, 37–38.

[38] *Ibid.*, p. 41.

[39] *Ibid.*, p. 37.

[40] *Ibid.*, p. 39.

[41] *Ibid.*, p. 221 note.

these creatures on the family's home-made banknotes). Sigurd he called "the old one";[42] and he amused Paulsen by exhorting him not to disturb the boy at work, for Paulsen knew that "Sigurd's 'studies' just then consisted of smoking cigarettes and reading a novel by Zola, which on his father's approach he would hastily conceal behind a large dictionary."[43]

As regards Ibsen's method of work, Paulsen relates that he would (like so many writers) break off at an appointed hour even if in the heat of composition or in the middle of a scene, since "instead of the mood evaporating it would carry over to the following day, when he would find the inspiration still fresh and could continue immediately without having to search for the central thread."[44] He once surprised Paulsen by declaring that "the creative function operates exactly like the stomach. One receives certain material from without, digests it, and excretes it—*voilà tout!*"[45] Nevertheless, Suzannah told Paulsen that Ibsen "always approached his desk like a sanctuary, *soigné,* in a 'well-pressed morning coat.' "[46]

In December, Paulsen departed for Rome. "Promise me you won't write a line the first year you are in Italy," was Ibsen's advice to him as they said farewell. "Just take in impressions."[47]

Considering that he had not completed any new work during the year, 1876 had, thanks mainly to the continued success of *The Vikings at Helgeland,* the Christiania production of *Peer Gynt,* and the reprints of *Peer Gynt* and *Brand,* been financially fair:

	crowns[48]	
Fee for *The Vikings at Helgeland* at Royal Theatre, Stockholm	1,000	
Fee for *The Vikings at Helgeland* in Bergen	100	
Fee for *Peer Gynt* in Christiania	2,024	
Royalties from *The Vikings at Helgeland* at Munich Hoftheater	344	
Extra fee for *The Vikings at Helgeland* in Copenhagen	500	
4th edn. of *Peer Gynt*	1,650	
Extra fee for *The Vikings at Helgeland* in Bergen	400	
Extra fee for *Peer Gynt* in Christiania	843½	
8th edn. of *Brand*	1,700	
	8,561½	£474

[42] *Ibid.,* p. 220.
[43] *Ibid.,* pp. 39–40.
[44] Paulsen, *Nye Erindringer* (Copenhagen, 1901), p. 137.
[45] Paulsen, *Samliv med Ibsen,* II, 217.
[46] Paulsen, *Nye Erindringer,* p. 135.
[47] Paulsen, *Samliv med Ibsen,* II, 28–29.
[48] From 1876 Ibsen recorded his income in crowns instead of specie-dollars. At the contemporary rate of exchange, a crown was worth about 25 cents.

18

The Pillars of Society

1877–1878

Ibsen opened the new year, 1877, with an eloquent appeal on 4 February to Johan Sverdrup, as President of the Storthing, for an increase in his pension, and his letter again underlines the disadvantage he suffered through Norway and Denmark not having copyright agreements with other European countries:

As a result, our books can be translated without let or hindrance anywhere and by anyone. And this is happening all the time. In England the whole of *Emperor and Galilean* was translated and published last year; I had not at that time the money available to arrange this at my own expense; now the translator and publisher take the profits; I take nothing. In Berlin, A. Strodtmann has taken my poems from me, as well as my plays *The Pretenders* and *The League of Youth*. Now these works are being widely read and performed in Germany, which brings money to the translator but not to me. The same has happened with *Brand,* of which three separate German translations now exist without providing me with a penny. Even in Sweden the situation is the same for us; we have no legal right to payment either from the theatres or from the publishers who have us translated. One Swedish translation of *The Vikings at Helgeland* has already appeared and another is in the press. All I have managed to keep for myself has been the editions I commissioned personally of *The Vikings at Helgeland* and *Lady Inger of Østraat,* but these editions cost me a considerable outlay which I can expect to regain only gradually over the years.

I appreciate that the Norwegian government cannot consider entering into cultural agreements with the great countries of literature. The advantage to us of the present anarchic situation is so evident that none of us, out of respect to our general reading public, would wish it altered. Should free access to foreign literary works be denied us, the source of intellectual progress and freedom in virtually every walk of life would be blocked, or at any rate rendered less accessible to us. Of that there must be no thought. But, Mr.

President, I appeal to your sense of justice whether it is fair that the financial loss resulting from such an arrangement should be borne by us four or five writers? Give each of us an extra 200 specie-dollars supplement to our pensions as compensation for what we lose on the majority's behalf. With this extra help we could at least save some of our works from falling into the hands of foreign translators; we could keep them for our own benefit, and thereby also ensure that our literature is presented to foreign readers in a more correct form than is now commonly the case.

Eleven days later Sverdrup moved in the Storthing that all pensions of composers and authors should be raised by a total sum aggregating 800 crowns. This modest proposal was rejected. Ibsen's finances were now so low that on 27 February he had to ask Hegel to advance him the honorarium due on the forthcoming reprint of *Love's Comedy,* and Hegel generously obliged with 1,000 specie-dollars. With this, plus a windfall of 400 crowns from the Bergen Theatre for *The League of Youth,* which had opened there on 25 February, Ibsen was able to look round for new lodgings "where I can work undisturbed, my present apartment leaving much to be desired in this respect."[1] On 1 May he moved to a first-floor flat at Schellingstrasse 30.

Meanwhile he had at last begun to make progress with *The Pillars of Society.* "I shall have it ready during the summer," he told Hegel, who must have received the news with scepticism. But by 20 April it was "moving rapidly towards its conclusion," and on 24 June, for once on schedule, he was able to report: "Today I take advantage of a free moment to tell you that on the 15th inst. I completed my new play and am now going ahead with the fair-copying." He posted the fair copy to Hegel in five instalments between 29 July and 20 August.

While he was engaged on the copying, Georg Brandes visited him for one evening, accompanied by his wife; for the previous summer he had married Gerda Strodtmann, the ex-wife of Ibsen's German translator. The hostility towards Brandes in his native country had reached such proportions that he had decided, as Ibsen had done, and as Strindberg was shortly to do, to go into exile—though in his case (unlike theirs) his departure was regretted, for forty-five eminent Danes published a joint letter thanking him for what he had done, and even Bjørnson, who had quarrelled so deeply with him, added his thanks in an article in a Danish newspaper. Brandes was struck by the impersonality of Ibsen's living conditions, an impression which other observers were to record of his various dwellings. "Since 1864," Brandes was to write five years later, "he has not had his feet under his own mahogany, nor slept in his own bed. . . . He has lived as though in a tent, among pieces of hired furniture, which could be sent back on the day appointed for his departure. . . . When I last visited him [*on this occasion in 1877*], on my asking whether nothing

[1] Letter to Hegel, 27 February 1877.

at all in the apartment belonged to him, he pointed to a row of paintings on the wall. They were the only things that were his own. . . . He feels no longing to possess a house and a home, still less a farm and lands like Bjørnson."[2]

This unhomeliness which was always so characteristic of Ibsen's apartments is especially curious in a writer whose plays are so often permeated by a deep sense of home. Fifty years ago Gunnar Heiberg (a distinguished director of Ibsen's plays) pointed out how important it is when staging *A Doll's House* that the audience should have the feeling that a *home* is being broken up,[3] and the same is true of *An Enemy of the People* and *The Wild Duck*. Unless Dr. Stockmann's house is given the feeling of a home, the effect of the last act when we see it with the windows broken is greatly minimised. And one has seen productions of *The Wild Duck* ruined by a failure to present the four Ekdals as a closely knit family. By contrast, there are other plays, such as *Ghosts, The Master Builder* and *When We Dead Awaken,* in which the characters sadly remark on the fact that the house they live in is not in the fullest sense a home (as is also implied in *Hedda Gabler, Little Eyolf* and *John Gabriel Borkman*). Neither Ibsen nor Suzannah, for all their strong sense of family, seems to have had the gift of making the place they lived in homely—which need cost very little, as anyone who has lived in a bed-sitting room can testify. One remembers Ibsen's admission of his indifference to flowers.

Another visitor to Ibsen that summer was Ole Bull, making what proved to be his last concert tour. They spent an evening together reminiscing over old times, and Marcus Grønvold, who was present, noted Ibsen's amusement that Bull expressed such pleasure in *Peer Gynt,* for which he himself had been the part-model.[4]

A week after he had sent the final instalment of *The Pillars of Society* to Hegel, Ibsen left for Sweden, having borrowed 600 crowns from his ever-willing publisher to pay for the ticket. The cause of his visit was an agreeable one; Upsala University, the oldest in Scandinavia, was celebrating its four hundredth anniversary, the occasion was to be marked by festivities, including the awarding of honorary degrees, and Ibsen was to be made a doctor of letters. (For this he had to thank Lorentz Dietrichson, who had been informed that he was to receive a doctorate and suggested that Ibsen should be similarly honoured). Suzannah took the opportunity to pay a visit to Norway, taking Sigurd with her and leaving Ibsen to fend

[2] An article written in 1882 and reprinted (as "Second Impression") in Brandes's *Henrik Ibsen,* p. 59; Muir-Archer translation. The young Danish novelist Herman Bang, visiting Ibsen around this time, received the same impression, of a man "curiously homeless amid a mass of rented furniture." (Bang, *Ti Aar* [Copenhagen, 1891], p. 185.)

[3] Gunnar Heiberg, *Ibsen og Bjørnson på scenen* (Christiania, 1918), pp. 5–6.

[4] Marcus Grønvold, p. 138.

for himself for ten days in Munich before leaving—which, in his way, he managed to do, as appears from the following letter:[5]

Munich, 21 August 1877

Dear Suzannah!

As soon as I received your letter and Sigurd's yesterday I telegraphed that everything was all right here, and I hope the telegram reached you safely. I am glad the sea trip went so well, and I hear from Sigurd that you praised your own dress at the dinner table![6]

The whole manuscript is now despatched, and I am making preparations for my departure, which will probably be on Monday. I don't expect to be away longer than strictly necessary, i.e. about a fortnight. Here everything is as usual. Helene is very good, makes good coffee and does all her work very punctually and exactly the way she has seen that I want it. I usually dine at Schleich's, which is better than the Museum and not wickedly dearer. For 1.75 [about 35¢] I get an excellent soup, fish, two meat dishes with all kinds of vegetables, and a compote, followed by pastries, cheese, bread and butter. This is pretty well my only meal, for I always stay at home in the evenings and then eat only a sandwich. Vullum has also been eating at Schleich's till yesterday, when he left. I have been with Grønvold once or twice and intend to invite him to dinner, since his brother has been so kind to you in Bergen.

I hope you are enjoying yourselves up there; but don't run any risks, and take good care of Sigurd and of your money and don't let the locals rob you.

I will write again from Sweden and hope to receive another letter from you there. No more for today. Enjoy yourselves.

Your

Henrik Ibsen

He enclosed a Polonius-like letter to Sigurd, exhorting him to "be sure to be careful both ashore and at sea; the least carelessness can bring consequences. . . . Don't go out too much on the water, and not in a sailing boat!"

[5] Suzannah had written him from Bergen that all the people "were as though taken from *The Pillars of Society,* portrayed to the life, even Rørlund [the puritanical schoolmaster]. Sigurd said he couldn't understand how you could know how everything was." Her old family home, she found, had become a coffee-shop. "I think of you every day," she concluded. "It seems so long since I left you, yet it is only five days." (Bergliot Ibsen, pp. 64–65.)

[6] Forgetting that she was among Scandinavians, Suzannah had said at dinner the first day aboard the ship: "I think my dress is much smarter than the other ladies." (*Ibid.,* p. 65.)

Ibsen spent a fortnight in Sweden. After a few days in Stockholm, he accompanied the other guests to Upsala, fifty miles north of the capital, on 4 September. "The aquavit will begin to flow," he wrote to Grønvold, "and I don't expect to get any peace for letter-writing during the next few days." The festivities in Upsala began on the 5th with a dinner. On the 6th the honorary degrees were handed out, and Ibsen had a laurel wreath placed on his head by the archbishop. That afternoon a banquet was given in the Botanical Gardens, attended by fifteen hundred people, the doctors still wearing their laurel wreaths; in the evening there was a firework display and a torchlight procession, and the finance minister, Hans Forssell, who was also a distinguished man of letters, gave a party attended by several of the leading Swedish writers of the day, including Snoilsky, Victor Rydberg, and Zacharias Topelius. "Within five minutes," says Dietrichson, who was there, "it was Ibsen who led the conversation and made it interesting. How Ibsen has acquired the reputation of being so excessively silent I have never been able to understand."[7]

The following evening there was a ball in the Botanical Gardens in a specially created building, looking (to judge from an engraving in *Ny Illustrerad Tidning*) remarkably like Paddington Station. During these days at Upsala, Ibsen had several meetings with King Oscar II, who had already shown him several marks of his favour, and got on with that bluff but prickly giant nearly as well as he had with his much more open and attractive brother, Carl XV.

When the Upsala celebrations had ended, the king gave a farewell banquet for the guests at his palace at Drottningholm, just outside Stockholm, with illuminations in the park; and the Royal Theatre honoured Ibsen with a special performance of *The Vikings at Helgeland* (how antiquated that play, now twenty years old, must have seemed to the man who had just written *The Pillars of Society!*). Such a week, one might think, would have moved even Ibsen to write a spirited description to his wife, but she received only the following:

Stockholm, 12 September 1877

Dear Suzannah!

You will have read in the papers of the tremendous festivities in Upsala, which are now over. On Monday *The Vikings at Helgeland* was performed; full house; the author repeatedly called, amid the greatest enthusiasm. I will tell you all about this when we meet. Throughout my whole stay in Sweden I have received only *one* letter from you and Sigurd, i.e., that in which you tell me of your visit to Folgefonden; I hope to find a letter awaiting me in Copenhagen— I leave for there today. I am tired now and long to be back in Munich; here there have been invitations and receptions every day.

[7] Dietrichson, I, 360.

In Upsala I spoke with the king every day and was at once received by him in the friendliest manner. This is just to let you know that all is well with me; let me soon hear the same from you . . .

Ibsen spent a couple of days in Copenhagen, where Hegel put him up in style at the Hotel d'Angleterre opposite the Royal Theatre, refused to let him pay for anything, and gave a party in his honour at his villa. Unwittingly, however, Ibsen offended Georg Brandes by not contacting him, having been wrongly informed that Brandes was out of town. Brandes, as touchy as any of the many touchy persons in this narrative, was mortally offended. "Ibsen and I," he wrote to Bjørnson the following June, "have been good friends for so many years that I am unwilling to say any hard or unfriendly words about him. He seems to me to be an enclosed, shy person who has difficulty in finding words, is reluctant to open himself, and is full of suspicion and distrust, even to those who have never done him anything but good" (another case of the pot calling the kettle black). Amazingly, Ibsen seems to have been unaware of Brandes's change of attitude towards him; a year and a half later, on 18 February 1879, thanking Hegel for Brandes's book on Disraeli, he was to praise it as an "absolute masterpiece" and to ask Hegel to convey to Brandes his admiration and best wishes. But he did not write direct to Brandes for four years, from 1877 to 1881 (for which the blame must largely rest with Brandes; their correspondence had always in the main been a case of Ibsen replying to Brandes's letters); and this silence unwittingly fed Brandes's suspicions that Ibsen's feelings towards him had cooled.[8] So there was another friendship down the drain.

By 20 September Ibsen was back in Munich, whence three days later he again wrote characteristically to Suzannah:

. . . You must have read in the newspapers how hugely I was feted in Upsala. The Danish papers say I was the most feted of all the guests in Upsala, and this was indeed the case. But now I am content to be at peace again, although things are not very comfortable; it is tiresome to have to eat out every day, the food does not suit me, the evenings are long, cold, and gloomy. I sit here alone since Grønvold is in the country. . . . If you could find the time to buy me six pairs of gloves in Copenhagen, I should be grateful; they must be of fine, thin leather, preferably dark brown, size 8½; I bought a pair there for 1 kr. 70 øre (45¢) in a shop on the corner of Østergade and Kongens Nytorv. Perhaps Sara [Suzannah's sister] could help you with this; but pack them deep in your trunk, for the customs inspection.

[8] Cf. *Brandes Brevveksling*, IV, xxxvi.

As he awaited the appearance of *The Pillars of Society,* Ibsen learned to his annoyance that John Paulsen had passed on to a Norwegian journalist a few facts about the play which Ibsen had confided to him, and that the journalist had printed these, getting many of the details wrong. Among other errors, the title of the play was given as *Samfundets Piller* (*piller* is an archaic word for "pillars," but more commonly means "pills"). Didrik Grønvold (the brother of Marcus) visited Ibsen at Schellingstrasse just after he had discovered this, and found him "walking up and down his room like a lion in its cage, sparking with anger, not so much at the leak of information as at the multilated title."[9]

Ibsen had been painted that summer by Julius Kronborg, wearing his new doctor's cloak—a portrait which Ibsen kept until his death. Strindberg, a much better painter and judge of painting than Ibsen, saw this portrait at an exhibition in Stockholm, and wrote an eloquent description: "The face is Brand's; the high, broad brow of the fanatic, the strong mouth of the witness whose lips have never uttered the truths that his hand has penned, the cold, determined look that never wavered when it stared 'the spirit of compromise' in the face; that is Ibsen, the fanatical sceptic . . . so impressive and terrifying, so repellent, so attractive!"[10]

On 11 October 1877 *The Pillars of Society* was at last published, and achieved an immediate and widespread success. The first edition of 6,000 copies sold out within seven weeks, and a further 4,000 had to be printed. A German translation appeared before the end of November.

Since *The Pillars of Society* is an indictment of a particular kind of right-wing figure, contemporary opinion naturally varied according to the political views of the reader; the liberals and radicals hailed it with the same delight with which the conservatives had greeted *The League of Youth.* Curiously, the Christiania papers scarcely noticed it at all; it was reviewed less in the capital than any play Ibsen had written since he had left Norway in 1864;[11] not only the right-wing *Morgenbladet* but (inexplicably) the liberal *Dagbladet* ignored it. Indeed, only three Christiania publications printed reviews, and two of these were disparaging. Ditmar Meidell in *Aftenbladet* (3 November), though granting the play certain virtues, dismissed it as "one of Ibsen's weaker works," and Arne Garborg, in *Fedraheimen* (27 October), after complaining that Ibsen, having mocked the peasants in *Brand,* the language reformers in *Peer Gynt,* and the liberals in *The League of Youth,* "has no sympathy with those who believe in a future for Norway," continued, *"The Pillars of Society* gives me the impression that Ibsen is on the downward path. It lacks the fire and bounce of his earlier works. . . . Its structural virtues are but tame

---

[9] Didrik Grønvold, pp. 8–9.

[10] August Strindberg, *Konstakademiens utställning, 1877,* p. 124.

[11] Halvorsen, *Norsk forfatter-lexicon, 1814–1880,* III, 58.

routine. . . . He could never write really badly . . . but the blaze and spark of his best work seem here to have been quenched. . . . Ibsen . . . seems burned out."

The provincial newspapers were more perceptive. An anonymous critic in *Bergens Tidende* (27 October and 3 November) wrote: "He has satisfied the demands of the stage to a degree which as far as we know has not been equalled in Germanic literature since the English Renaissance"; and, comparing the play favourably with Bjørnson's *A Bankrupt,* rightly remarked that the probable reason why Bjørnson had not brought his dramatic talent to full flower in the same measure as Ibsen was that Ibsen had concentrated on drama and not dissipated his efforts on novels and short stories (and, he might have added, journalism and political agitation). And Nordahl Rolfsen, in the first of four articles in *Bergens-Posten* (24, 26, and 28 October and 4 November), which Ibsen praised as "saying everything I should most like to be said about the play," was shrewd enough to see (24 October) that *The Pillars of Society* was more than a mere political salvo: "It will help," he wrote, "to dispel the idea that Ibsen is primarily a polemical writer. The real targets of Ibsen's indignation are mean-mindedness and pettiness, wherever they may be found. He does not position the sheep and goats so that all the goats are to be found on one side and all the sheep on the other." He also shrewdly observed that the "lack of harmony" for which Ibsen was so continuously condemned was the source of the intensity of his satire. In his final article (4 November), Rolfsen quoted a *Punch* cartoon of the siege of Sebastopol, showing a room with the door blown in by a bomb and a man in bed crying: "I'm a little deaf. Did someone knock? Come in!" Rolfsen comments:

> Ibsen believes our society is like the man at Sebastopol. People will not say "Come in" until a bomb has blown open the door. . . . In this his latest play [as compared with *Brand* and *Peer Gynt*] Ibsen's satire has changed its form. It is no longer a Homeric spread, a broad stream of mocking words to accompany each sword-thrust; it is a quiet duel to the death, with no rattle of harness nor clash of blades; one watches, in a deathly silence, the elegant fencer's sure and piercing passes. His satire has gained in objectivity without losing in strength. . . . Many may prefer the lyrical beauty and kaleidoscopic display of epigrams [in his earlier work] to this dramatic astringency —the beauty of the youth to that of the man. To us it seems that scarcely one of Ibsen's earlier satires can be compared to *The Pillars of Society* in the way the action reveals the characters and the dialogue naturally reflects the personality not of the author but of the speaker.

The Danish reviews were all good, apart from an anonymous complaint in *Fædrelandet* (19 November) that "one hears too seldom the beating of

12 Letter to B. E. Bendixen, 21 December 1877 (C.E., XIX, 252–53).

a great and warm heart." The writer of light vaudevilles, Erik Bøgh, again generously acclaimed the new dramatist whose fame was so far exceeding his own:

> It is a mighty test of strength that Henrik Ibsen has essayed in trying a fall with one of "The Pillars of Society." . . . He has gone about it like a Samson, and even if his shaking has not brought about the upheaval which levelled the Temple of Dagon, several Philistine hearts must surely have trembled as it groaned to its foundations in his mighty grip. . . . Ibsen does not suffer from the Danish malaise of never doing anything whole-heartedly [a disease which Ibsen had in fact condemned in *Brand* as being peculiarly Norwegian]. If falsehood is to be stripped bare, he will work at it till its fine feathers cling protectively to the wearer's skin like the shirt of Nessus. If necessary, he will remove the skin too, and should a little flesh be adhering to the skin, that will not deter him.

Like Rolfsen, Bøgh compared the play favourably with Bjørnson's *A Bankrupt* ("Ibsen never perpetrates a fifth act showing his hero restored to prosperity and converted as Bjørnson did"), and concluded with a shrewd criticism: "there are too many speeches which delay the fall of the curtain after the action is finished and the play is over." It was an error which (except in *An Enemy of the People*) Ibsen was never to commit again; anyone who has tried to cut one of his plays (for television, for instance) knows that, while a good deal of the exposition can usually be thinned out from the first act, and a certain amount from the middle, there is scarcely a line in any other of his last acts from *A Doll's House* onwards that will bear removal.

Surprisingly, especially for men of their political leanings, neither of the Brandes brothers liked it (which may be the reason why neither reviewed it). "Ibsen is so anxious to provoke," wrote Edvard to Georg on 30 November, "that there is nothing *big* about his play. It's a big problem seen small and treated small."[13] And Georg wrote to J. P. Jacobsen on 16 December, "Ibsen's play is technically fine, but it taught me nothing."[14]

The Pillars of Society is not often performed today on the professional stage, though in England, at least, it pops up frequently in the drama schools. The reason in both cases is the same: the size of the cast. There are nineteen characters, not including the crowd at the end, an advantage to students and amateurs but an expensive obstacle to any unsubsidized company. *Peer Gynt* needs as many actors, but *Peer Gynt*, like Shakespeare, can usually be sure of an audience. This neglect of *The Pillars of Society* is sad, for until the last five minutes it holds the stage splendidly, quick-moving, strongly plotted, sharply characterized, and full of feline wit.

[13] *Brandes Brevveksling,* II, 6.
[14] *Ibid.,* III, 132.

Were it not for those last minutes—but since the play is generally little known, one must pause briefly to outline its plot (a procedure which will not invariably be inflicted on the reader when more famous plays come to be discussed).

It is set in a small port. The chief character, Karsten Bernick, a wealthy shipowner, has (like John Gabriel Borkman) married a woman he does not love, to further his career. His life has been a series of successes founded on double-dealing, sometimes above the law, sometimes not. Caught in an actress's bedroom while still engaged (fifteen years before the play opens), he allowed his fiancée's brother Johan to take the blame. Planning a railway to the town, he has secretly bought up all the land through which the line will pass. When Johan returns from America and threatens to expose him, Bernick lets him go to sea in a ship he knows is rotten and must sink—only to find, seemingly too late, that his own son has stowed aboard. In the unconvincing ending, the ship is discovered not to have sailed, and Bernick in his relief confesses his crimes and is left not only unpunished but rather better off than he was before.

Such a summary omits the various sub-plots and several of the play's best characters: Lona Hessel, Bernick's former love, returning robustly (with a knapsack on her back) from America to let fresh air into the closed society of the little town; the narrow-minded schoolmaster, Dr. Rørlund; Dina Dorf, the young orphan daughter of Bernick's former mistress, and his ward; Aune, the shipyard foreman, fearful of the unemployment that new machines may bring; Hilmar Tønnessen, Mrs. Bernick's cousin, an indolent æsthete; Martha, Bernick's sister, who has loved Johan and waited for his return only to find that he has no eyes for her, but only for Dina who is half her age; and Bernick's three shifty capitalist associates and their gossiping wives. The pettiness of provincial life, which was one of the things Ibsen hated most about Norway (in its capital no less than in its small towns) is mercilessly detailed; and in two important respects the play marks a notable advance over *The League of Youth*.

One is the clarity with which the sub-plots are interwoven with the main plot, instead of the play being a Congrevian maze; the other is the sharpness with which individual modes of speech are differentiated, something which was to be one of Ibsen's supreme strengths, and one of his main contributions to the technique of prose drama. Lona Hessel, for example, fresh from America, has a breezy, slangy way of speaking which contrasts markedly with the prim speech of the local stay-at-homes; and Hilmar Tønnessen talks in an extraordinary, fanciful manner, over-loaded with adjectives and ridiculous flights of imagination, like Hjalmar Ekdal in *The Wild Duck*. Ibsen was a wonderfully minute observer of the way people talked (as of the way they looked and dressed), even to noting that we speak differently at different times of the day, and that women phrase their sentences differently from men. Other playwrights, such as Bjørnson, had attempted to differentiate the speech of their characters, but their efforts are crude compared with Ibsen's. These different modes of speech are one of the most difficult problems that face a translator; if one fails, one deprives the actor of his subtlest weapon.

The Pillars of Society is full of memories of Grimstad, the little port where Ibsen had spent six years as a chemist's apprentice (just as *The League of Youth* is full of memories of Skien). *The Palm Tree* (a ship which appears importantly in the play) was the name of a Grimstad ship. An actress belonging to a touring theatrical company had returned there in Ibsen's time after being involved in a scandal, and had tried to keep herself by taking in washing and sewing like Dina Dorf's mother, but had been shooed out of town by local gossips. Foreign ships came in for repairs, and foreign visitors turned the place upside down, like the American crew of whom the citizens in the play complain. In the autumn of 1849, six months before Ibsen left for Christiania, the socialist Marcus Thrane had come to Grimstad and founded a Workers' Association, like the one Aune the foreman belongs to. And the Bernicks had their origin in a family named Smith Petersen. Morten Smith Petersen, the original of Karsten Bernick, returned to Grimstad from abroad in the eighteen-forties, and ran his aged mother's business for a while, but finally had to close it down. He then started his own shipyard and an insurance company; he had died in 1872, but his sister Margrethe Petersen survived. She was an elementary schoolteacher and the original of Martha Bernick.

The play dealt with two problems of especial topicality for the eighteen-seventies. One was the question of women's rights; the other, that of "floating coffins." Controversy over the former problem had reached its height in Norway (as elsewhere) during the seventies; in 1876 Asta Hansteen, a great champion of the cause, began a series of lectures on the subject, but was so furiously assailed that in 1880 she emigrated to America. She was the original of Lona Hessel (Ibsen at first gave the character the surname of Hassel, but changed it, presumably so as to avoid too direct an identification with Hansteen). Camilla Collett, the novelist, another doughty warrior, had probably exerted a good deal of influence on him when they had met in Dresden in 1871 and in Munich in 1877, when he was writing the play and they had many arguments about marriage and other female problems; and Suzannah, too, had long felt strongly about these things. Ibsen had already touched tentatively on the subject in *The League of Youth,* and he was to deal with it more minutely in his next play. His original intention in *The Pillars of Society* had been to be even more outspoken than he finally was, for in his first draft Dina announces her decision to go off with her lover, Johan, without marrying him; but he evidently doubted whether the theatres would stage a play which suggested anything quite so daring, and legalized their relationship.

The question of the "floating coffins" was first forced upon Ibsen's

28. Manuscript extracts. Above, the opening page of Ibsen's rough draft for *The League of Youth*. Below, from Ibsen's preliminary notes for *Ghosts*.

29. Georg Brandes, c. 1867. "How these Christians hate me!"

30. Edmund Gosse, 1874. "It was I who swept the floor and lighted the candles."

31. The jury at the Vienna International Exhibition, 1873. Ibsen is on the extreme right, "seated noticeably apart, trimly barbered, in frock coat and spats."

32. Frederik Hegel, Ibsen's publisher and counsellor.

33. Hans Christian Andersen, c. 1870. "I like Ibsen a lot, but *Peer Gynt* not at all."

34. Edvard Grieg, 1876. ". . . had a particular talent for getting Ibsen going."

35. *A Doll's House,* Christiania, 1880. Sketch of the tarantella scene in Act Two by the designer of the first Norwegian production, Olaf Jørgenssen.

36. *An Enemy of the People,* Christiania, 1883. Arnoldus Reimers and Henrik Klausen as Dr. Stockmann and Morten Kiil in the first Norwegian production.

37. *Ghosts,* Hälsingborg, 1883. August Lindberg and Hedvig Charlotte Winter-Hjelm in the first European production.

38. Henrik Ibsen as disciplinarian. Caricature in *Vikingen,* 1882. Ibsen belabours the left in *The League of Youth* and is applauded by the right; belabours the right in *The Pillars of Society* and is cheered by the left; and finally indicts all political parties in *An Enemy of the People* and antagonizes everyone.

attention by an English Member of Parliament. In 1868 Samuel Plimsoll had sought in the House of Commons to have the state interfere against the cold-blooded and unscrupulous sacrifice of human life by sending men to sea in rotten ships. In 1873 he succeeded in getting a law passed to enforce seaworthiness; but this proved too slack. On 22 July 1875 he created a tremendous commotion in Parliament by a boldly outspoken attack on the people responsible for such a policy; he called the owners of such ships murderers and the politicians who supported them scoundrels. This so roused the conscience of the nation that a temporary bill went through in a few days, and its principles were made permanent by the Merchant Shipping Act of the following year. Plimsoll's protest echoed throughout the world, and in a seafaring country such as Norway it rang especially loudly. A particularly scandalous case had occurred in Christiania during Ibsen's visit there in 1874. On 2 September of that year, at the annual general meeting of the shipping insurance company Norske Veritas, which had been founded by that same Morten Smith Petersen, questions were asked about a ship which, after having been declared seaworthy, sprang a leak while at sea and was shown to be completely rotten. At the annual general meeting a year later two similar cases were mentioned, and a storm of indignation was aroused. The matter was reported in detail in the newspapers, and Ibsen can hardly have failed to read about it.

The presentation in a dramatic form of problems that were urgent and topical rather than eternal was not unprecedented; it was the depth and subtlety of Ibsen's characterization, his psychological insight and ability to strip respected people and institutions of their masks, that made The Pillars of Society a revelation to its contemporaries, especially the young, in a way in which The Editor and A Bankrupt, La Dame aux Camélias and Thérèse Raquin, for all their theatrical effectiveness, had never been. Two of the rising stars of the German theatre, then both in their early twenties, have recorded the effect that the play had on them.

"Our young eyes," recalled Paul Schlenther, "were opened to the false tinsel of the theatre that was being offered to us. We thrilled with joy. We returned incessantly to the theatre where it was being played; when it was full, we read the play in Wilhelm Lange's terrible translation. Until then, Ibsen had been but an empty name to us. It was this play that taught us to love him, a love that lasted for life. I can testify on behalf of many of my generation that under the influence of this example of modern realism there was implanted in us, at that formative age, an orientation of taste which was to be decisive for the whole of our lives."[15]

And Otto Brahm, at twenty-two a year younger than Schlenther, wrote: "It was there that we gained the first inkling of a new world of creative

[15] Henrik Ibsens sämtliche Werke in deutscher Sprache, ed. Georg Brandes, Julias Elias, and Paul Schlenther (Berlin, 1898 ff.), VI, xvii–xviii.

art, first felt ourselves face to face with people of our time, in whom we could believe, and with a criticism which embraced the whole society of our time."[16] In a few years Schlenther and Brahm were to be leading spirits in the founding of the Freie Bühne, which was to do for the German theatre what Antoine's Théâtre Libre was to do for the French.

So exciting and new were the qualites of *The Pillars of Society* that Ibsen's contemporaries as a whole (political opponents and the Brandes brothers excepted) forgave the weakness of the last act; but it is a weakness we find less easy to forgive. It has been suggested[17] that this ending possesses "ironic potential"; that Ibsen, by showing how a double-dealer can survive exposure and remain at the helm, underlined the danger that such men are to the society they control. The idea may indeed have been at the back of his mind; and if it was, and if he betrayed his real belief by settling for a happy ending, this may explain why that ending is so unconvincing. Erik Bøgh, in the review quoted above, wrote: "Ibsen never perpetrates a fifth act showing his hero restored to prosperity and converted, as Bjørnson did [in *A Bankrupt*]," but this in fact is exactly what Ibsen did in *The Pillars of Society*, and it is a fault that no amount of sophistry or skilful acting can conceal. Yet the rest of the play is so fine that with a good production we forgive this unlikely ending, as we forgive the equally unlikely ending of (for example) *A Winter's Tale*.

The Pillars of Society was not (as it is sometimes claimed to be) the first realistic prose play. Nor was it even the first that Ibsen had written in colloquial prose; he had done that in *The League of Youth* (and to some extent in *Emperor and Galilean*). But it can be fairly claimed to have been the first (always excepting Büchner and Gogol) to combine the three elements of colloquial dialogue, objectivity, and tightness of plot which are the requirements and characteristics of modern prose drama. And it is the first in which we can identify several of those elements which we nowadays instinctively associate with Ibsen's name—a marriage founded on a lie, passionate women stunted and inhibited by the conventions of their time, and an arrogant man of high intellectual and practical gifts who destroys, or nearly destroys, the happiness of those nearest to him. It also exhibits, unlike his earlier plays, what Henry James admiringly described as "the operation of talent without glamour . . . the ugly interior on which his curtain inexorably rises and which, to be honest, I like for the queer associations it has taught us to respect: the hideous carpet and wallpaper (one may answer for them), the conspicuous stove, the lonely central table, the 'lamps with green shades' . . . the pervasive air of small interests

---

[16] Otto Brahm, *Kritische Schriften über Drama and Theater* (Berlin, 1913) pp. 447 ff.

[17] J. W. McFarlane, "Meaning and Evidence in Ibsen's Drama," in *Contemporary Approaches to Ibsen* (Oslo, 1966), pp. 38–39.

and standards, the sign of limited local life."[18] Above all, *The Pillars of Society* has, despite its overtones of comedy, that peculiarly Ibsenish quality of austerity which contrasts so sharply with the exuberant cornucopia of his earlier work; what Henry James, on another occasion, described as "the hard compulsion of his strangely inscrutable art."[19] No wonder, when we remember the technical problems imposed by this new form, that *The Pillars of Society* took Ibsen longer to write than any of his other plays except the triple-length *Emperor and Galilean*. As *Peer Gynt* had been a farewell to the old drama, so *The Pillars of Society* was the harbinger of the new.

By the end of 1877, *The Pillars of Society* had received three separate productions, at the Royal Theatre in Copenhagen[20] on 18 November, at the Bergen Theatre on 30 November, and at the Royal Theatre in Stockholm on 13 December. The Christiania Theatre, however, had incurred Ibsen's wrath by permitting a performance that June of Act Four of *Brand* without reference to him and, worse, forcing the resignation of Ludvig Josephson, who had done so much for him (and for the theatre) over the past four years. "The board would have acted more in the interests of the theatre if . . . they had sacked themselves," Ibsen wrote to Hartvig Lassen on 2 November. ". . . And what kind of a successor have you appointed! This successor was here in Munich last summer, and talked about his job like a five-year-old child. How long do you suppose this miserable and totally useless fellow will survive? He won't last the season." Ibsen added sadly that Josephson had had plans to stage a shortened version of *Brand,* and Part One of *Emperor and Galilean*. Not only did Ibsen allow the Bergen Theatre to give the first Norwegian production of *The Pillars of Society;* he rubbed in the lesson a year later by permitting a Swedish company to act it in Swedish at the

[18] Henry James, "On the Occasion of *Hedda Gabler*" (*New Review*, June 1891), reprinted in *The Scenic Art: Notes on Acting and the Drama, 1872–1901* (London, 1949), p. 249.

[19] Henry James, "On the Occasion of *The Master Builder*" (*Pall Mall Gazette,* 17 February 1893), reprinted in *The Scenic Art,* p. 258.

[20] The Royal Theatre's new censor, Christian Molbech, had reported to his board that the play possessed considerable merit: "although here, as in several of the author's works, the ideal is sadly out-shadowed by the real, and the satire is sharper and more intense than the sympathy, the over-all impression is a healthy and attractive view of life, leaving a satisfying impression." The production achieved twenty-one performances that season. (Agerholm, pp. 276–80.) Johanne Luise Heiberg (according to John Paulsen) remarked that Lona Hessel would have been a part for her ("I never got roles of that kind when I acted. The writers of that time hadn't enough sense of reality"). Paulsen was amazed that she, who had specialized in romantic queens and princesses, should have hankered after playing an emancipated woman who washed her hands at the town pump (*Samliv med Ibsen,* I, 43).

old Møllergaden theatre in Christiania (on 6 November 1878), and it was not performed in the capital in Norwegian until the following March, seventeen months after publication.[21]

Ibsen marked the appearance of *The Pillars of Society* by sending a copy of it to Bjørnson with a brief but affectionate note, the first contact between the two for eight years. The chief reason for this olive branch was, ironically, Bjørnson's public declaration of thanks to Georg Brandes, whom Ibsen, though he did not realize it, had himself now mortally offended. "This one step [of Bjørnson's]," Ibsen wrote to Hegel on 28 October, "in my eyes greatly expiates much else; it was a noble action. I should now like to bring about a closing of the gap between him and me, and therefore beg you to send him the enclosed note with a copy of *The Pillars of Society.*" The note read:

Munich, 28 October 1877

To Bjørnstjerne Bjørnson!

Your utterance on the occasion of G. Brandes's departure has delighted and deeply moved me. This is the true you. Will you be so good as to accept the enclosed book from me and give it to your wife?

H.I.

The olive branch was rejected. "He has sent me a warm message of thanks and his last book because of what I wrote about you in D.F.," Bjørnson informed Brandes on 10 June 1878. "I didn't answer him, for I find his conduct towards me shabby. I think he's a pipsqueak with his titles and decorations and nauseating letters to every little person who praises him in the tiniest newspaper. . . . People excuse Ibsen because he comes from 'simple folk' [*sic*]. He needs it for his self-esteem. Well, well!"[22]

That autumn, on 24 October, Ibsen's father died, and as though to reconcile himself with the past and blot out old quarrels, he penned a letter to his uncle, Christian Paus, in Skien, the circumlocution and stiltedness of which mirror the guilt and embarrassment underlying the awkward words:

[21] And when Ibsen did at last grant the Christiania Theatre permission to stage *The Pillars of Society*, he stipulated that the "miserable and totally useless fellow," Johan Vibe, should have nothing to do with the casting, that he himself should have a veto on the casting, and that he should receive a lump payment of either 2,000 crowns for twenty-five performances or 2,500 crowns for forty performances; thereafter, 2½ per cent of the gross takings. They agreed to the former alternative, the biggest fee they had yet paid to any author. (Cf. Ibsen's letter to Harald Holst, 2 November 1878, printed in Øyvind Anker's *Henrik Ibsens brevveksling med Christiania Theater, 1878–1899* [Oslo, 1965], pp. 11–18). Ibsen was not far wrong in his assessment of Vibe, who lasted only two years in the job.
[22] *Brandes Brevveksling*, IV, 57–58.

Munich, 18 November 1877

Dear Uncle Christian!

Although one of your closest relatives, I fear you must almost, and with good ground, regard these lines from afar as coming from a stranger. To uncomprehending eyes I know it must look as though I had voluntarily and deliberately cut myself off from my family, or at any rate permanently set a distance between me and them; but I think I may say that impossible circumstances from a very early stage were the principal cause.

You will of course guess the reason why I am writing to you today. From foreign newspapers, and also through a letter from Hedvig, I learn that my old father has passed away, and I feel a need to express my most grateful thanks to all you members of the family who have so lovingly helped to ease so many years of his life, and have thereby taken upon yourselves on my behalf, or in my stead, a task which, until very recently, I felt in no position to fulfil.

From my fourteenth [sic] year I was sent away to care for myself. I have for many long years been compelled to fight hard to make my way and achieve my present position. That I so seldom wrote home during all these years of struggle was chiefly because I was unable to be of assistance or to support my parents. I thought it vain to write when I could do nothing practical to help them; I stood in constant hope that my circumstances might improve, but that happened very late and not long ago.

It was therefore a great consolation to me to know that my parents, especially in recent years my old father, were surrounded by loving relatives. And when I express my thanks to all those who have stretched out a loving hand to him who is now gone, these thanks also incorporate the help and relief that I have thereby found on my journey through life. Yes, my dear Uncle, I say to you, and please tell this to my other relatives, that the portion of my duty and my love that they have taken on their shoulders has to a considerable degree sustained me during my longings and strivings, and has contributed to the fulfilment of what I have accomplished in the world.

During my last visit to Norway I felt a strong inclination to visit Skien and, especially, my family; but I felt also a strong reluctance to come into close contact with certain spiritual truths, then prevalent, with which I could feel no sympathy and a collision with which could easily have provoked unpleasantness, or at any rate an atmosphere of discord, which I wished to avoid. I have, nevertheless, not abandoned the thought that I may some day see again my old childhood home. In a year my son will matriculate here, and then we shall be able to live anywhere we choose. We shall probably first pay a short visit to Italy and then take an apartment in Christiania, although I fear I could not in the long run be happy or work in Norway. The context in which I live here is far more advantageous; I mean, the intellectual freedom and broad view of life which a cosmopolitan way of living inculcates. Though to live thus demands certain sacrifices of various kinds.

I enclose my photograph. It is now twenty-seven years since we saw each other, and you will of course not recognize me; but I hope we shall see the day when the family will have the opportunity personally to decide whether or not the portrait is a good likeness.

And with this, my dear Uncle, I shall close. Warmest regards to yourself and the family from

> Your grateful and affectionate nephew
> Henrik Ibsen

When, at the end of 1877, Ibsen reckoned up his accounts, he had reason to feel satisfied:

	crowns	
Royalties from *The Vikings at Helgeland* at Munich Hoftheater	250	
Royalties from *The Vikings at Helgeland* at Dresden Hoftheater	92	
Royalties from *The Vikings at Helgeland* at Wien Burgtheater	960	
Fee for *The League of Youth* at Bergen Theatre	400	
4th edn. of *Love's Comedy*	1,000	
Extra fees from Bergen Theatre	360	
Miscellaneous fees from German Society of Dramatists	67	
1st edn. of *The Pillars of Society*	4,637½	
Advance for *The Pillars of Society* from Royal Theatre, Copenhagen	1,000	
Extra fee for *The Vikings at Helgeland* from Royal Theatre, Stockholm	1,000	
Advance on 2nd edn. of *The Pillars of Society*	3,091	
Fee for *The Pillars of Society* at Odense, Denmark	600	
Fee for *The Pillars of Society* at Bergen Theatre	400	
	13,857½	£772

It is noteworthy that despite the number of theatrical productions, nearly two-thirds of this sum was from book sales in Scandinavia. For many years yet, performance rights were to remain a subsidiary source, and foreign translations, as he had complained to Sverdrup when appealing for an increase in his pension, were seldom to bring him anything at all.

This fact was exemplified at the beginning of 1878. The success of *The Pillars of Society* in the three Scandinavian countries did not pass unnoticed in Germany where, in the absence of copyright protection, translators and theatre directors fastened upon the play like vultures. In addition to the translation authorised by Ibsen, two pirate versions appeared before the end of January. One was by a man named Emil Jonas, whom Ibsen described to Hegel (28 January) as "a frightful literary bandit," and to whom, ten days earlier, he had addressed one of those formidable rebukes which he so well knew how to word:

Munich, 18 January 1878

Herr Emil Jonas,
Berlin

In reply to your communication I must remind you of a fact of which you cannot be unaware, namely, that I myself, at the beginning of November last, published with Messrs. Theodor Ackermann a German version of my play, *The Pillars of Society*. A translation from your hand is therefore utterly superfluous, and I must totally disassociate myself from any adaptation such as you envisage.

Your suggestions for cuts in Act One are quite senseless and show that you have totally failed to understand this work which you regard yourself as worthy to adapt. Even to the most ignorant literary hack I should have thought it obvious that in this play no roles can be omitted and not a single line deleted. The play has already been accepted in an unabridged and unbowdlerized form by many German theatres. . . .

If, in spite of me, you permit the proposed monstrosity to be put before the public, you at least owe it to me to clear my name by seeing that the placards outside the theatre carry the caption: "Travestied by Emil Jonas."

Faithfully,
Henrik Ibsen

The extent to which this pirating cut into Ibsen's earnings soon became clear. In February *The Pillars of Society* was performed at five separate theatres in Berlin alone within a fortnight. Before the end of the year, it had been staged at no less than twenty-seven theatres in Germany and Austria. But financially, these productions brought Ibsen little joy. The play was performed almost exclusively in pirated versions. In a letter to the Swedish newspaper *Göteborgs Handels- och Sjöfarts-Tidning* (nr. 60, 1887), Jonas, defending his adaptation by declaring that it "suited German taste," pointed out that it had been accepted for performance by thirty-two German theatres, whereas Ibsen's authorised translation had been played only at the Nationaltheater in Berlin and the Munich Hoftheater. (Even the other pirated version, by Wilhelm Lange, had been performed at four theatres.) Most of Ibsen's German royalties and fees (excluding those from the Munich Hoftheater and one or two other theatres which had honourably offered to deal with him direct) were henceforth collected for him by the German Society of Dramatists, and appear only as unitemized lump sums in his account books; but from these twenty-seven productions, excluding Munich, he earned that year only 626 Norwegian crowns plus another 251 crowns which arrived early the next year. Most of the German theatres do not appear to have paid him anything at all. Georg Brandes reckoned that Ibsen was robbed thus of 15,000 marks (13,284 crowns) which he should have earned from *The Pillars of Society* in this year alone—"and his [German] publisher has lost much, much money, for three [sic] other pirate publishers sold it for 2 groschen while his own publisher was asking 2 marks."[23] How much Emil Jonas made from the play is not on record.

In England, however, he had a new admirer, and one who was to do far more for him than Edmund Gosse, whose interest in Scandinavian literature had rapidly faded.[24] William Archer, now twenty-two, had spent much of his childhood in Norway and had grown up bilingual in English and Norwegian (his grandparents had settled in Larvik in 1825 and spent the rest of their lives there, and one of his uncles, Colin Archer, was to build Nansen's famous ship, the *Fram*). Archer had first made the acquaintance of Ibsen's work in 1873 (the year in which he had, unknowingly, been in Vienna at the same time as Ibsen), and at once became an addict.

> A *chokolade-selskab* [chocolate party] was going on, and I, a boy of seventeen, sat listening to the chatter of a lot of ladies. One of them, whom I never saw before or since, but whose face I remember as though I had seen it yesterday, said: *"Jeg synes Kjærlighedens Komedie er saa glimrende vittig"* ["I think *Love's Comedy* is so brilliantly witty"]. "Hullo," I thought, "have they got anything *glimrende vittig* in Norwegian? I must look into this"— and forthwith went and bought the book. Then I read *Kongsemnerne* [*The Pretenders*], *Hærmænderne* (*The Vikings*), and all that he had written up to that time, with increasing delight.[25]

When *Emperor and Galilean* appeared that autumn of 1873,

> I remember locking myself up in a little bare hutch of a bathing-house by the fjord in order to devour its ten acts in the luxury of unbroken solitude. . . .

[23] Letter from Georg Brandes to V. Pingel, 14 April 1878 (*Brandes Brevveksling*, III, 273–74).

[24] After contributing over twenty essays or reviews concerning Ibsen to English periodicals between March 1872 and March 1878, Gosse was to write nothing about Ibsen for five years. During these years the only two other articles, etc., published in English about Ibsen were an account by Edith Pradez of Ibsen's 1874 visit to Norway in the *Academy*, 10 October 1874, and Archer's review of *The Pillars of Society* in the *St. James's Gazette* in 1878. Cf. Bredsdorff, pp. 38–39 and 175.

[25] Letter to Edmund Gosse, 23 March 1898 (Bredsdorff, pp. 184–85).

I laid in provisions to enable me, if necessary, to stand a siege. Even in those days, you see, Ibsenite and Ishmælite meant much the same thing.[26]

Archer waited impatiently for the publication of Ibsen's next play, and when *The Pillars of Society* at last appeared it so excited him that he made a hurried translation (rather uninspiredly entitled *The Supports of Society*), and on 2 March 1878 published an analysis of the play, with extracts from his translation, in *The Mirror of Literature*. He tried to interest publishers in his translation, but "no publisher would look at"[27] it, and people "used to jeer at my rapture over this incomprehensible Hyperborean."[28] With Scottish resolution, he settled down to prepare another, more careful version which, eighteen months later, was to meet with better luck.

A young Norwegian woman named Laura Kieler, whom Ibsen had met a few times over the past seven years, now re-entered his life, with results which were to prove significant for both of them. As Laura Petersen, a decade previously, she had written a sequel to *Brand* in the form of a novel entitled *Brand's Daughters;* then, in the summer of 1871, she had visited Dresden for a couple of months and had called on him. He must have liked her, for they saw a good deal of each other during her stay; he called her his "skylark," and encouraged her to write more.

She married a Danish schoolmaster named Victor Kieler, and in 1876 visited Ibsen again, in Munich. She now had a sad story to tell him (or rather, she told Suzannah, and Suzannah told Ibsen). Her husband had contracted tuberculosis, and she had been advised that the only way to save his life was to take him for a while to a warmer climate. They lacked the means for this and, since Kieler became neurotically hysterical at any mention of money, she took it on herself secretly to obtain a loan, for which a friend stood security. The trip (to Italy) had been successful, for Kieler, unluckily for Laura, lived for another forty years; but the matter weighed on her mind, and Ibsen noticed sadly that his little skylark "could no longer sing her happy songs."

During the first months of 1878 Suzannah received a letter from Laura enclosing the manuscript of a novel she had written and begging Suzannah to ask Ibsen to recommend it to Hegel. Ibsen found himself embarrassingly placed, for the book struck him as really bad; any writer who has been asked by a friend to pass on a poor manuscript to a publisher will sympathise with his position. He replied in stern but kindly terms, telling her that he could not possibly recommend it. "You speak," he wrote to her on 26 March, "of circumstances which compelled you to write this book under pressure. I do not understand. In a family where the husband is alive it can never be necessary for the wife to

[26] Charles Archer, *William Archer* (London, 1931), p. 37.
[27] *Ibid.*, p. 72.
[28] Letter from Archer to Edmund Gosse, 23 March 1898 (Bredsdorff, p. 185).

sacrifice her heart's blood as you have done. I am amazed that he should permit you to do so. There must be something which you don't tell me and which colours the whole situation; that is my impression after several readings of your letter. . . . It is unthinkable that your husband knows everything; so you must tell him; he must take on his shoulders the sorrows and problems which now torment you. . . . Hegel would never have accepted your manuscript even if I had recommended it. . . . Confide all your troubles to your husband. He is the one who should bear them."

She had, indeed, not told Ibsen the full story; perhaps she feared he might take it as an attempt to touch him for a loan. Repayment had been demanded of the money she had borrowed to take her husband to Italy two years earlier. She did not have it, and dared not tell her husband because of his neurotic attitude towards such matters; worse, the friend who had stood security had himself fallen into straits, and told her he would be ruined if pressed for payment. Laura, who had published a book of sketches and a novel (*Everil*, about an unhappy marriage), had seen no way out but to write another book and hope for an unusually large advance; hence the hasty and unfortunate manuscript. Ibsen's reply (though he can scarcely be blamed) was to have disastrous consequences.[29]

The success of *The Pillars of Society*[30] not surprisingly stimulated Ibsen to think immediately about following it up with another play in the same genre, just as the success of *Brand* had stimulated him to follow that work with another drama-for-reading. On 5 May he informed Hegel: "I have begun to busy myself with plans for a new play with a contemporary setting; it will, like the last, be in four acts. When it will be ready, however, I can as yet have no idea." His own letters of that spring and summer deal exclusively with business matters. He was to ponder his theme for another twelve months before writing the first line of dialogue—a routine he was to adopt with every play he subsequently wrote, with but one exception.

That summer Sigurd took his matriculation, and passed with high honours. He was a far better student and examinee than his father had been; but he had been better taught. Now that the boy's schooling was finished, Ibsen felt free to do what he had been longing to do for several years: to return to Italy. He had enjoyed his three years in Munich, but the Mediterranean beckoned to him, and on 2 August he wrote to Hegel:

[29] B. M. Kinck, "Henrik Ibsen og Laura Kieler," in *Edda* (1935), pp. 504–6.

[30] Not that the conservatives liked it any more in Germany than they had in Norway. Karl Frenzel, the influential critic of *Deutsche Rundschau*, who had written of *The Pretenders* that Ibsen was poor at dramatic construction and did not know how to work out a plot, found *The Pillars of Society* an effective criticism of social conditions but reiterated that Ibsen was "no dramatist." (W. H. Eller, *Ibsen in Germany, 1870–1900* [Boston, 1918], p. 32.)

Towards the middle of this month we shall be leaving for the south; we plan to spend the winter in Rome, where I hope to find time and peace to complete my new work. The weather here has been beastly the whole time, so that we have had no real summer. I greatly long to get across the Alps . . .

Mrs. Laura Kieler has, as you probably know, suffered a sad calamity. Her husband informed us rather curtly that she had been admitted into a mental clinic. Do you know the exact circumstances of this, and whether she is still there? . . . As soon as I have settled in at Florence, where we expect to spend a couple of months, you will hear from me again. Sigurd . . . will probably continue his studies at the university here [in Munich] when we return next autumn.

When the full news of the Kieler affair reached Ibsen, it must have shaken him. On receipt of his letter of 26 March she had burned the manuscript and forged a cheque. The forgery was discovered, and the bank refused payment; whereupon she told her husband the whole story. He, regardless of the fact that she had done it purely for his sake, treated her like a criminal, told her she was unworthy to have charge of their children and, when she in consequence suffered a nervous breakdown, had her committed to a public asylum (where she lived in a ward among lunatics) and demanded a separation so that the children could be removed from her care. After a month she was discharged from the asylum and, for the children's sake, begged her husband to take her back, which he very grudgingly agreed to do.[31]

The story must have seemed especially relevant to a writer whose last play had dwelt upon the unequal position of woman in contemporary society, and Georg Brandes's advice nearly a decade earlier that he should make such a woman the chief character in a play must have come to his mind, if it had not already done so (we do not know how far the news changed Ibsen's plans).

On their way south, the Ibsens visited Gossensass, and remained there for several weeks till the last days of September. Ibsen wrote to Nils Lund on 23 September cancelling the *gammelost* which he had asked the latter to send him as early as 25 March, and which seems to have been a long time coming (not that a few months one way or the other would have made much difference to that particular delicacy). They forsook their original plan to stay in Florence "since I greatly long for familiar surroundings, so as to find peace for work,"[32] and by the end of September, for the first time in ten and a half years, Ibsen was back in Rome.

[31] Kinck, pp. 506 ff.

[32] Letter to Hegel, 8 October 1878. John Paulsen observed that Ibsen seemed to feel the same indifference towards Florence as Goethe, who likewise never stayed long there but always moved on quickly to Rome (*Samliv med Ibsen,* I, 30).

19

A Doll's House

1878–1880

[handwritten: 1. 2. Laura Keilar]

Within three weeks of his arrival in Rome Ibsen, installed in an apartment in a pleasant, five-storied corner house next to a church on the Via Due Macelli, jotted down the following:

Rome, 19. 10. 78

NOTES FOR A MODERN TRAGEDY

There are two kinds of moral laws, two kinds of conscience, one for men and one, quite different, for women. They don't understand each other; but in practical life, woman is judged by masculine law, as though she weren't a woman but a man.

The wife in the play ends by having no idea what is right and what is wrong; natural feelings on the one hand and belief in authority on the other lead her to utter distraction.

A woman cannot be herself in modern society. It is an exclusively male society, with laws made by men and with prosecutors and judges who assess feminine conduct from a masculine standpoint.

She has committed forgery, and is proud of it; for she has done it out of love for her husband, to save his life. But this husband of hers takes his standpoint, conventionally honourable, on the side of the law, and sees the situation with male eyes.

Moral conflict. Weighed down and confused by her trust in authority, she loses faith in her own morality, and in her fitness to bring up her children. Bitterness. A mother in modern society, like certain insects, retires and dies once she has done her duty by propagating the race. Love of life, of home, of husband and children and family. Now and then, as women do, she shrugs off her thoughts. Suddenly anguish and fear return. Everything must be borne alone. The catastrophe approaches, mercilessly, inevitably. Despair, conflict, and defeat.

[handwritten: 3. Quotes from play]

But although he told Hegel on 7 December that he was "concerning myself only with the preparations for my new play," it was to be another six months before he wrote the first line. Meantime, as was his wont, he pondered the theme and characters until he knew them in depth. One day he surprised Suzannah by saying, "Now I've seen Nora. She came right up to me and put her hand on my shoulder." "What was she wearing?" asked Suzannah, as a woman should; to which Ibsen "with great earnestness" replied: "A blue woollen dress."[1]

"A lot of Scandinavians have arrived here, but we have got to know few of them at all well," he wrote to Marcus Grønvold on 30 December. "On the other hand, we have made several acquaintances among German and Italian scholars, artists and writers, whom I meet frequently. Sigurd attends lectures at the university here, and has already pretty well brushed up his old forgotten Italian; he follows the lectures completely and without trouble. We shall stay in Rome until the university holidays begin in June or July; we have made no plans beyond that, but intend to return to Munich in early October."

Lady Inger of Østraat had just received its first German production in Berlin. But when he made up his accounts for 1878, a year in which his most recent play had been performed at over thirty theatres in Scandinavia and Germany, they offered no scope for extravagance. With only one new reprint, and that a small one, the improvement of the last three years had not been maintained:

	crowns	
Fee for *The Pillars of Society* at Nya Teater, Gothenburg	1,000	
Royalties for *The Vikings at Helgeland* at Munich Hoftheater, second half of 1877	122	
Extra fee for *The Pillars of Society* at Royal Theatre, Copenhagen	500	
Extra royalties for *The Pillars of Society* from Royal Theatre, Stockholm	2,425	
Actor Brock's reading of [unspecified] work in Nordhausen	18	
Further extra fee for *The Pillars of Society* from Royal Theatre, Copenhagen	500	
5th edn. of *The Vikings at Helgeland*	720	
Fee for *The Vikings at Helgeland* at Trondhjem	100	
Fee for *The Pillars of Society* at Trondhjem	400	
Fees from Bergen Theatre for eight perfs. of *The Pillars of Society* and 3 perfs. of *The League of Youth*	320	
Royalties from Munich Hoftheater for *The Pillars of Society* and *The Vikings at Helgeland* for first half of 1878	818	
Royalties and fees from German Society of Dramatists	626	
	7,549	£421

[1] Paulsen, *Samliv med Ibsen*, II, 60.

Ibsen was touchy and nervous that winter in Rome. "We live in general pretty quietly," he wrote on 22 January to Marcus Grønvold. "Lunch is brought in to us, and our landlady prepares our breakfast and supper. Everything is much cheaper here than in Munich, and wine especially is to be had for practically nothing this winter, so that in the Sabine villages one can buy excellent wine for 3 soldi [about 3¢] a litre!" Despite his poor earnings for the past year and his habitual economy, he now indulged himself in an unexpected direction. "I am taking the opportunity," he informed Grønvold in the same letter, "to buy old paintings, and have already purchased eleven, all good and valuable and at a comparatively modest price. I intend to buy more, so that I shall be able to furnish my next apartment in Munich solely with works of art. If only I can find somewhere suitable!" These paintings, or most of them, came from the collection of a recently deceased cardinal, and included a supposed Titian. Lorentz Dietrichson, who, as a professor of art history, ought to have known, refers to them as "important pictures, especially by the older Italian masters."[2] One would like to know more about them.

He visited the Scandinavian Club regularly, but mainly to read the newspapers; although he occasionally entered into a conversation, he was evidently in one of those long combative moods which periodically settled on him for weeks on end. Once he got into a violent argument about religion with two Danish theologians after drinking Swedish punch. He attacked the teachings of the orthodox church as being slanted to prop up an antiquated society, got angrier and angrier, and had to be supported home in the small hours by the Danish novelist and botanist J. P. Jacobsen and a young Norwegian named Gunnar Heiberg, later to become one of his country's best theatrical directors and a distinguished playwright. On the way he grew more and more abusive of the human race and its aims and ambitions; and when Heiberg tried to mollify him by suggesting that at any rate Ibsen himself had written some great truths, and started to quote from his "Balloon Letter," Ibsen roared contemptuously: "Verse, verse! Just verse!"[3]

It was in this prickly mood that, on 28 January, he put two proposals before the club: that the post of paid librarian (which he had coveted himself fifteen years earlier) should be thrown open to women, and that women should have the right to vote on all club matters. When these proposals came to be debated on 27 February, he delivered a lengthy and impassioned speech; Sigurd, who was present, tells[4] that he got so worked up that he occasionally abandoned his prepared text and improvised with that eloquence which, when the mood was on him, he knew how to command. Even his written text (which has survived) was fiery enough, if

[2] Dietrichson, I, 361.
[3] Heiberg, *Salt og sukker* pp. 51–52.
[4] C.E., XV, 469.

ill-calculated to gain support from the older members who formed the majority:

Is there anyone in this gathering who dares assert that our ladies are inferior to us in culture, or intelligence, or knowledge, or artistic talent? I don't think many men would dare suggest that. Then what is it men fear? I hear there is a tradition here that women are cunning intriguers, and that therefore we don't want them. Well, I have encountered a good deal of male intrigue in my time, not least recently. . . . Is it perhaps the supposed unpracticality of women in matters of business? Even if women were as unpractical as many an unpractical gentleman would like to suppose, are artists so especially practical in business matters? No, gentlemen, I think not. I hold it to be good and profitable that we should have ladies present at our annual general meeting just as I hold it good and advantageous that we should have young people there, those young people whose presence is now threatened by a proposal that the vote should only be allowed to those who have been resident for a year in Rome. I repeat that I am not afraid of these so-called unpractical women; women have something in common with the true artist, just as young people in general have—something that is a good substitute for worldly understanding. Look at our student societies in Norway! Matters are decided there which are ten times more complicated than ours; yet do not they manage well, although youth, untried, unpractised and unpractical youth, there enjoys an overwhelming majority? And why? Because youth has this instinctive genius which unconsciously hits upon the right answer. And it is precisely this instinct which women share with youth, and with the true artist. And that is why I want us to allow women to vote at our annual general meeting. I fear women, youth and inexperience as little as I fear the true artist. What I do fear is the worldly wisdom of the old; what I fear is men with little ambitions and little thoughts, little scruples and little fears, those men who direct all their thoughts and actions towards achieving certain little advantages for their own little and subservient selves. Should the affairs of this club fall into such hands, I should greatly fear for its survival, at any rate as a society of artists. And that is why I wish to have ladies included at our annual general meeting, so that they, together with the young, may see to it that power is placed into true, and truly artistic, hands.[5]

The first of Ibsen's motions, concerning the librarianship, was accepted; but the second failed by a single vote to get the necessary two-thirds majority. Ibsen was furious.[6] He left the club immediately and sat alone in a café, refusing to speak to anyone who had voted against him. Some days later, however, to the general amazement, he attended a gala evening at the club, and Gunnar Heiberg, who was present, has left a picturesque account of what happened:

[5] C.E., XV, 402–3.

[6] Feelings evidently ran high on both sides, for J. P. Jacobsen, who supported Ibsen's motion (as did the Swedish painter Ernst Josephson), relates that a captain of marines all but challenged Ibsen to a duel on the matter. (*Brandes Brevveksling*, II, 344.)

No one would have guessed it—but Ibsen came. He looked magnificent, in full panoply, with medals to boot. He ran his hand ceaselessly through his rich, grizzled hair, greeting no one in particular, but everyone in general. There was a deep peace in his face, but his eyes were watchful, so watchful. He sat alone. We all thought he had forgiven his fellow mortals, and some even supposed him penitent. This helped the atmosphere to be unusually gay and euphoric. Then, suddenly, he rose and stepped forward to a big table, so that he was facing the whole ballroom with its dancing couples.

"Ladies and gentlemen!" It was a tense and dramatic moment. What was going to happen? Was he about to admit the error of his ways? Surely he was not going to propose a toast? . . . He stroked his hair calmly. Then he began, softly, but with a terrifying earnestness. He had recently wished to do the club a service, he might almost say a great favour, by bringing its members abreast with contemporary ideas. No one could escape these mighty developments. Not even here—in this community—in this duckpond! He did not actually use the word duckpond, but the contempt around his mouth proclaimed it loudly. And how had his offer been received? As a criminal attempt! Rejected by a paltry couple of votes. And how had the women reacted—the women for whom his gift had been intended? They had intrigued and agitated against him. They had thrown his gift into the mud. What kind of women are these? They are worse—worse than the dregs, worse than scum—

Now he was no longer speaking calmly, no longer thoughtfully stroking his hair. He shook his head with its grey mane. He folded his arms across his breast. His eyes shone. His voice shook, his mouth trembled, and he thrust out his underlip. He resembled a lion, nay, more—he resembled that future enemy of the people, Dr. Stockmann. He repeated and repeated: what kind of women are these, what kind of ladies, what kind of a sex, ignorant, in the truest sense ill-bred, immoral, dregs, contemptible—

Thump! A lady, Countess B., fell to the floor. She, like the rest of us, flinched from the unspeakable. So she took time by the forelock and swooned. She was carried out. Ibsen continued. Perhaps slightly more calmly. But eloquently and lucidly, never searching for a word. He intoxicated himself with his rhetoric against the ignorant, contemptible, and rigid resistance that mankind, and especially women, was attempting to offer to these new ideas, whose purpose was to make people bigger, richer, and better. He looked remote, ecstatic. As his voice thundered it was as though he were clarifying his own secret thoughts, as his tongue chastised it was as though his spirit were scouring the darkness in search of his immediate spiritual goal, his play—as though he were personally living out his theories, incarnating his characters. And when he was done, he went out into the hall, took his overcoat, and walked home. Calm and silent.[7]

In February Hegel sent him the good news that fresh editions of both *The Pretenders* and *Poems* were in preparation; the fifth of the former and the third of the latter. Spring arrived. "The almond trees have already blossomed," he wrote to Marcus Grønvold on 9 March. "The cherry trees are in full bloom, and all the fields are covered in fresh green grass

[7] Heiberg, *Salt og sukker*, pp. 68–71.

and violets." Yet something was missing in Rome. He no longer found the same excitement there which had so stimulated him fifteen years earlier. "I have often thought of sending Sigurd back [to Munich] to continue his studies alone," he wrote in the same letter. "But in various respects it is desirable that I should get back into German literary life. Down here one is in most respects too much outside the movements of the times." Was it, he may have wondered, that he was no longer as young as he had been? Edvard Brandes, meeting him this spring, was surprised by the venerability of his appearance. "I spoke a few words with Henrik Ibsen in the street," he wrote to his brother Georg on 1 May. "How old he is! I'd imagined him different, alert."[8]

Old he may have looked; but the following day, he began the first draft of his new play and, as usual, once he had started the work went swiftly. He finished the first act in three weeks. The second act took him six weeks, but was interrupted by a holiday move. "We had at first thought to go to one of the mountain villages around Rome," he told Hegel on 19 June, "but the sanitary conditions there leave much to be desired [he had grown fastidious since the old days at Genzano and Ariccia] and so we have decided to retire to Amalfi, on the coast south of Naples, where there are facilities for sea-bathing."

He left for Amalfi on 5 July, armed with an inscribed copy of Edmund Gosse's *Studies in the Literature of Northern Europe,* published that February, and containing an essay on Ibsen (a revised reprint of Gosse's article in the *Fortnightly* in 1873, plus his reviews of *The Pretenders* and *Emperor and Galilean* and an account of *The League of Youth*). "English causes me some difficulty," he had written to Gosse the previous day. "But when we leave tomorrow . . . your book will be about the only one I shall take with me." At Amalfi they had "two small rooms with three plain iron bedsteads"[9] in the Albergo della Luna, an old monastery converted into a hotel, situated (still) on a cliff overlooking a sheer drop into the sea. Here he was well cossetted by the proprietress, Marietta Barbaro; he had an ante-room where he could write, and the desk at which one of the most influential of all plays came to be written may still be seen there. When not working he bathed in the sea and took long walks in the hills.

Shortly before he finished Act Two, he received a letter from Bjørnson, the first for nine years, seeking to enlist his support in a campaign to remove the mark of union with Sweden from the Norwegian flag. A more unfortunate subject for the reopening of correspondence between the two men could hardly have been chosen. The business of the flag lay very close to Bjørnson's heart, and was exactly the kind of concern that Ibsen regarded as chauvinistic and irrelevant. "I have not much sympathy for

[8] *Brandes Brevveksling,* II, 43.
[9] Bergliot Ibsen, p. 78.

symbols," he replied on 12 July, a remark that many an Ibsen critic might ponder.

Symbols no longer have any meaning except in Norway. Up there people bother so much about symbols and theories and ideas that no practical progress is ever made. . . . I regard it as a sin against our people to make an issue burningly important when it is not. A people can never get seriously concerned about more than one burning issue at a time. . . . We have only one thing which I think worth fighting for, and that is the introduction of an up-to-date education for our people. This embraces all other issues; if it cannot be brought about, what use are all the rest? It is quite immaterial whether our politicians bring about isolated reforms if they do not achieve liberty for the individual. They call Norway a free and independent kingdom; but I don't set much store by this freedom and independence as long as I know that individuals are neither free nor independent. There are in the whole of Norway no more than twenty-five free and independent individuals. They just don't exist. I have tried to acquaint myself with our educational system, school plans, timetables, teaching material, and so forth. It is disturbing to see how much class time, especially in the primary schools, is taken up with old Judaic mythology and saga history and mediæval distortions of a moral code of teaching which in its original form was undoubtedly the purest that has ever been preached. This is the field in which we should all, with one voice, demand a "pure flag." Let the mark of union remain, but take the mark of monkishness from people's minds; take away the mark of prejudice and narrow-mindedness and short-sightedness and subservience and unthinking trust in authority, so that every individual can sail under his own flag. . . . I don't think it is our job to make ourselves reponsible for the liberty and independence of the state, but rather to awake as many individuals as possible to liberty and independence.

Ibsen's dismissal as trivial of this question of the "pure flag" deeply offended Bjørnson, to whom it was a matter of almost religious significance, and the gap between the two men, which had seemed about to close, now became so wide as to be all but unbridgeable. Georg Brandes tells how he found himself next to Karoline Bjørnson at a dinner at Hegel's around this time and asked her if she could not use her friendship with Suzannah to bring her husband and Ibsen together. The next day Bjørnson came to Brandes in a great rage and "rode his hobby-horse, his contempt for decorations; Ibsen had his chest covered with orders, and a whole dog-collar around his neck. Bjørnson thought it disgusting; rather than offer him his hand he would plunge it into a toadstool."[10]

[10] Georg Brandes, *Levned*, II, 350 ff. In fairness to Bjørnson, however, one must remember that the years 1875–85 were a peculiarly frustrating time for him, especially coming as they did just after the success of *A Bankrupt*. Of the plays that he wrote during this decade only one, *Leonarda*, was immediately accepted for production in Christiania. *The New System* had to wait eight years, *A Glove* three, while *The King, Beyond Mortal Power, I* (his finest play) and *The Editor* never got

Having got the matter of the Norwegian flag off his chest, Ibsen returned to the more important business of finishing his play. He started Act Three on 18 July and completed it in less than three weeks, on 3 August. "I cannot recall any work of mine," he informed Hegel on 15 September, enclosing the fair copy, "that has given me more satisfaction in the solving of specific problems." And indeed, the technical advance on *The Pillars of Society* is enormous; no one could complain of *A Doll's House* that it was let down by the final act.

He left Amalfi at the end of September, with the plan for a new play already in his head, and stayed a week in Sorrento, at the Hotel Tramontano. Another guest at the hotel was Ernest Renan, the great French orientalist whom Ibsen had met briefly in 1856, when Renan had visited Bergen as a member of Prince Napoleon's suite. Renan was now working on the final stages of his *Origins of Christianity,* and in view of what Ibsen had just written to Bjørnson about the Church's perversion of Christ's teaching they might have found much common ground; but Ibsen's ignorance of French and shyness of strangers inhibited him from introducing himself (though since Renan was equally shy, conversation might anyway have been difficult). On leaving Sorrento, Ibsen spent a week in Rome, and by 14 October was back in Munich, where he moved with his Italian paintings into a new and larger apartment in an elegant house at Amalienstrasse 50.

That autumn Magdalene Thoresen visited them; and Bjørnson, too, came to Munich. He stayed a stone's throw from the Ibsens, at the Hotel Bambergerhof, and John Paulsen, also back from Rome, tells how Ibsen and Suzannah sat hoping that he would visit them, but in vain. Sigurd, who was Bjørnson's godson and had not set eyes on him since childhood, went along to the Café Probst to see what the great man looked like. When he returned, and Paulsen asked him how Bjørnson looked, Sigurd replied, "An Emperor! An Emperor!"[11] Ibsen's friend Paul Heyse gave a dinner for Bjørnson during his visit, but (according to Georg Brandes) disliked the "missionary and world-improver"[12] in him.

In November an old painter named Knud Både died in Munich, and Ibsen attended the funeral. Paulsen, who was present, noted: "I shall

---

played until the National Theatre opened its doors there with his son as director, in 1899. His plays were similarly rejected in Copenhagen, including even *Leonarda*. He was attacked continuously by the press in Norway, Denmark, and Sweden, suffered from a deep sense of persecution, and around 1880 was in such financial straits that he even tried to sell his beloved home at Aulestad. The success of *The Pillars of Society* and *A Doll's House* must have been galling to him, especially that of the latter, overshadowing as it did *The New System* published only six weeks earlier.

[11] Paulsen, *Samliv med Ibsen,* I, 195–96. Paulsen quotes Bjørnson as later saying: "I now think I was wrong; anyway, I regret that I didn't visit him" (*ibid.,* p. 198, note).

[12] Georg Brandes, *Levned,* II, 353.

never forget the manner in which he approached the open grave and cast a handful of earth on the coffin. He did it with a solemnity and deep intensity which moved us all and brought tears to my eyes. . . . Ibsen must have been a deeply religious person; no one who saw him at this moment could doubt that."[13] His demeanour put Paulsen in mind of Brand. Living painters seemed to concern Ibsen less; when Paulsen took him to the studio of one Nils Hansteen, Ibsen showed less interest in the paintings than in the model of a ship which hung from the ceiling. On the way home he told Paulsen that if he ever returned permanently to Norway he would live in a fjord town smelling of pitch and seaweed where he would be able to see many ships and shipyards, "especially the latter."[14]

On 4 December 1879 *A Doll's House* was published in Copenhagen, in an edition of 8,000 copies, the largest first printing yet of any of Ibsen's works. Its success was immediate and sensational. Despite its size, the first edition sold out within a month; a second edition of 3,000 copies appeared on 4 January, and a third of 2,500 copies on 8 March. Such sales (proportionately equivalent to something around 675,000 in the United States today) were without precedent for a play in Scandinavia; and certainly no play, in Norway or anywhere else, had had quite such an effect. "*A Doll's House,*" recalled Halvdan Koht, who was a child when it appeared, "exploded like a bomb into contemporary life. *The Pillars of Society* . . . though it attacked reigning social conventions, still retained the traditional theatrical happy ending, so that it bit less sharply. But *A Doll's House* knew no mercy; ending not in reconciliation, but in inexorable calamity, it pronounced a death sentence on accepted social ethics."[15]

Several times during that famous last act Ibsen seems about to settle for a happy ending—when Krogstad promises Mrs. Linde to take back his letter, when he returns Helmer's I.O.U., and when, in the closing moments of the play, Helmer remembers and echoes Nora's words: "The miracle of miracles—?" But the terrible offstage slamming of that front door which brings down the curtain resounded through more apartments than Torvald Helmer's. No play had ever before contributed so momentously to the social debate, or been so widely and furiously discussed among people who were not normally interested in theatrical or even artistic matters. Even Strindberg, who disapproved of it as being calculated to encourage just the kind of woman he dreaded most (and was infallibly drawn to), and attacked it in his volume of stories, *Marriage* (1885), admitted in his preface that, thanks to *A Doll's House*, "marriage was revealed as being a far from divine institution, people stopped re-

[13] Paulsen, *Samliv med Ibsen,* II, 40–41.
[14] Paulsen, *Samliv med Ibsen,* I, 152–53.
[15] Koht, II, 107.

garding it as an automatic provider of absolute bliss, and divorce between incompatible parties came at last to be accepted as conceivably
justifiable." What other play has achieved as much?

Many voices were, naturally, raised against it. "Those who were against
revolution," writes Koht, "against social and moral upheaval, against
female emancipation, came to see in Ibsen their greatest and most dangerous enemy."[16] There were æsthetic objections too. Frederik Petersen
spoke for the traditionalists when he complained in *Aftenbladet* (9 January 1880) that "one does not leave this play in the mood of exaltation
which, ever since the days of the Greeks, has been regarded as a *sine
qua non* for every work of art and literature. We have seen something
sorely unbeautiful and retain only the sense of pain which is the inevitable
outcome when no conciliation shows us the final victory of ideals." But
most critics accepted Ibsen's implied thesis that a play need not merely
provide an æsthetic experience, but had a right to upset people and
cause them to re-think. An anonymous reviewer in *Morgenbladet* (10
December) praised his "most profound insight into the essentials of
dramatic art and marvellous technical mastery," and Erik Vullum, in
Dagbladet (6 and 13 December), perceptively noted the absence of
imagery in the writing compared with Ibsen's earlier works. "One can
read the book from first to last page and find scarcely one image. Ibsen
no longer needs them. He has so worked out what he wants to portray
that he no longer needs to resort to any graphic aid to natural dialogue."

So explosive was the message of *A Doll's House*—that a marriage was
not sacrosanct, that a man's authority in his home should not go un-
challenged, and that the prime duty of anyone was to find out who he
or she really was and to become that person—that the technical originality
of the play is often forgotten. It achieved the most powerful and moving
effect by the highly untraditional methods of extreme simplicity and
economy of language—a kind of literary Cubism. Erik Bøgh, perceptive as
usual, spotted this when *A Doll's House* received its first performance,
at the Royal Theatre in Copenhagen on 21 December.[17] "It is long," he
wrote in *Folkets Avis* (24 December), "since any new play was awaited
with such excitement, and even longer since a new play brought so much
that is original to the stage, but it is beyond memory since a play so
simple in its action and so everyday in its dress made such an impression
of artistic mastery. . . . Not a single declamatory phrase, no high dra-
matics, no drop of blood, not even a tear; never for a moment was the
dagger of tragedy raised. . . . Every needless line is cut, every exchange
carries the action a step forward, there is not a superfluous effect in the

---

[16] *Ibid.*, pp. 107–8.

[17] Despite the fact that the Royal Theatre's censor, Christian Molbech, had only
grudgingly recommended it, finding the break-up of the Helmers' marriage "not
merely painful and unsatisfying but psychologically somewhat inexplicable." (Agerholm, p. 279.)

whole play . . . the mere fact that the author succeeded with the help only of these five characters to keep our interest sustained throughout a whole evening is sufficient proof of Ibsen's technical mastery."[18] *The Pillars of Society* had used nineteen characters. And there are other ways in which *A Doll's House* marks a considerable technical advance over *The Pillars of Society.* The characters do not (as occasionally happens in the earlier play) tell each other what the listener already knows for the benefit of the audience; points once made are not drummed home in the manner beloved by politicians; the final curtain is not tediously delayed after the climax has been reached (an elementary fault which every playwright learns reluctantly to avoid, the more reluctantly if he has ever written a novel, in which such rapid wind-ups seem melodramatic). Only in the subplot of Krogstad does a trace of the old melodramatic machinery remain.

Edvard Brandes had mixed feelings about the play. Admitting that "it made a powerful impression on the stage," he complained to his brother Georg on Christmas Day: "I don't really believe in the psychology. Is the marriage of those two very credible?" Then he read it and liked it better. "It is a fine work," he wrote to J. P. Jacobsen three days later. "I hadn't read it when I saw it." But a month later, on 8 February, he wrote to Alexander Kielland: "The play evades the issue. It ends where it ought to begin. . . . If the first scene had shown the relationship between the two as Nora realizes it to be in the last act, and the whole play had dealt with their separation instead of that coming as it does now, like a *Satan ex machina,* the audience wouldn't have clapped but Ibsen's plot . . . would have been clearer and better." (It would in fact have been much more talkative and less explosive.) Yet the play's influence on Edvard Brandes was such that the next year Brandes wrote his first play, and followed it during the next quarter of a century with eleven more, all bearing the clearest signs of Ibsen's influence.[19]

Brandes's correspondents saw the merits of the play more clearly than he did. *"A Doll's House* is really refreshing," Alexander Kielland wrote him on 8 January. "So simple, and spare as a statue—you can positively hear the superfluities clattering away from the slim figure after the merciless hacks with which the Master has for the past two or three years been chiselling away everything unnecessary. I know nothing so perfect."[20] And J. P. Jacobsen, on 14 March 1880, wrote, *"A Doll's House* seems to me

---

[18] Reprinted in *Dit og Dat, 1879* (Copenhagen, 1880), pp. 252–63.

[19] *Brandes Brevveksling,* II, 57 and 342; V, 117. Brandes's doubts following the performance may have been partly due to the fact that (as he later recalled) it was not well acted or directed—he thought Emil Poulsen's Helmer the only really adequate performance—though "this fault was scarcely noticed amid the enormous sensation and controversy which the play aroused." (Edvard Brandes, *Om Teater,* pp. 149–50.)

[20] *Brandes Brevveksling,* V, 112.

decidedly the most important and successful thing Ibsen has ever done."[21] Bjørnson hated the play. "It is technically excellent," he wrote to Sophus Schandorph on 9 January, "but written by a vulgar and evil mind."[22]

It is the tragedy of books carrying a particular message for their times that they tend to be remembered by posterity for the wrong reasons. *A Doll's House* and its successor, *Ghosts,* are particular examples; critics still occasionally write about *A Doll's House* as though it were a play about the hoary problem of women's rights—an attitude largely conditioned by the habit, among British and American critics, of consulting Bernard Shaw's *Quintessence of Ibsenism,* that brilliantly misleading book which should have been called *The Quintessence of Shavianism,* before writing about any Ibsen play. *A Doll's House* is no more about women's rights than Shakespeare's *Richard II* is about the divine right of kings, or *Ghosts* about syphilis, or *An Enemy of the People* about public hygiene. Its theme is the need of every individual to find out the kind of person he or she really is and to strive to become that person. Ibsen knew what Freud and Jung were later to assert, that liberation can only come from within; which was why he had expressed to Georg Brandes his lack of interest in "special revolutions, revolutions in externals," and had declared that "what is really wanted is a revolution of the spirit of man." The effect of *A Doll's House* in the theatre today is less explosive than when it was written, but scarcely less hypnotic, because there is hardly a married woman in the audience who does not sometimes want (or has not at some time wanted) to leave her husband. The unspoken thoughts in the cars and taxis returning from a modern performance of the play cannot vary much from those in the returning carriages of ninety years ago.

One woman to whom *A Doll's House* did not bring joy was Laura Kieler. Her tragedy was known to enough people in Copenhagen for them immediately to realize that Ibsen had based Nora's story very closely upon hers (except for the ending), especially as she had been proud to advertise her friendship with him; and the link soon became common knowledge. It must have made the situation between her and Kieler, which was already bad enough, even less tolerable; and she was also much hurt by the reference in Act Three to the "recklessness and instability" of Nora's father. Yet it is hard to blame Ibsen. The play is an admiring vindication of her conduct, and he may well have supposed that she would be happy to be recognized as the original of so sympathetic and courageous a character, as later Julius Hoffory was proudly (and with much less reason to be proud) to advertise that he was the original of Ejlert Løvborg in *Hedda Gabler.* It is ironical that the play which estab-

[21] *Ibid.,* II, 349.

[22] *Bjørnstjerne Bjørnsons brevveksling med danske, 1875–1910,* ed. Øyvind Anker, Francis Bull, and Torben Nielsen (Copenhagen and Oslo, 1953), I, 175.

lished Ibsen as the champion of women should have been so deeply resented by the woman who had inspired it.

A Doll's House was to make Ibsen internationally famous. But this (contrary to popular supposition) did not happen at once, or even quickly. It was to be two years before the play was performed outside Scandinavia and Germany, and ten years before a recognizably faithful version was seen in England or America, although perverted adaptations were to make brief and unsuccessful appearances.[23] France, even further behind the times, did not see the play until 1894. By the time it took its place in the general European repertoire, Ibsen was over sixty and had moved on to a very different kind of writing.

The success of *A Doll's House* in book form made 1879 a somewhat better year for Ibsen financially, though considering the impact of the play his earnings remained unremarkable:

	crowns	
Royalties and fees from German Society of Dramatists for last quarter of 1878	251	
Royalties from Munich Hoftheater for previous half-year	261	
Fee for *The Pretenders* at Bergen	400	
Fee for *The Pillars of Society* in Christiania	2,000	
Fee for *The Pretenders* in Stockholm	1,000	
5th edn. of *The Pretenders*	1,125	
Miscellaneous fees from Bergen Theatre	360	
3rd edn. of *Poems*	947	
1st edn. of *A Doll's House*	5,288	
Fee for *Love's Comedy* at Bergen	400	
2nd edn. of *A Doll's House*	1,969	
	14,001	£778

1880 opened with what must by now, for Ibsen, have been the familiar mixture of public acclaim and stolen rights. On 8 January the Royal Theatre in Stockholm presented *A Doll's House,* and Christiania and Bergen followed suit within the month. In all three cities the play was a triumph, (though Edvard Brandes, on a visit to the Christiania production, was shocked to hear how the two principals, Johanne Juell and Arnoldus Reimers, "both rephrased in the most shameless manner practically every line"[24]). The Germans, however, were, as usual, treating him badly. Wilhelm Lange's authorised translation was being freely sold in Copenhagen at a lower price than the original—a serious matter in a city where educated people read and spoke German as readily as educated Russians spoke French. "I receive no payment from the publisher," Ibsen

---

[23] It is significant that even Bernard Shaw does not mention Ibsen in his letters before 1889.

[24] Edvard Brandes, *Fremmed Skuespilkunst* (Copenhagen, 1881), p. 27.

complained to Hegel on 22 January. "The translator has to give me such copies as I need for the German theatres, and that is all." Hegel estimated the Danish sales of this German version to be as high as 2,000 copies. However, he was able to comfort Ibsen with two good pieces of news, that a fourth edition of *The League of Youth* and a fifth of *Emperor and Galilean* were in preparation, and that "the last five performances of *A Doll's House* [at the Royal Theatre, Copenhagen] have brought you an honorarium of 2,270.12 [crowns] i.e., 3,904.99 in all. The next five performances will bring you a third of the takings, excluding subscription seats; so far the play has been sold out for every performance."[25]

But far worse than the undercutting of his book sales was what was about to happen to *A Doll's House* on the German stage. A well-known actress of the day, Hedwig Niemann-Raabe, had announced her intention to present the play with herself in the leading role, but she refused to act the final scene as written, on the grounds that "*I* would never leave *my* children!" In the absence of copyright protection, Ibsen's hands were completely tied; and he decided that, as the lesser of two evils, a "happy" ending written by himself would be preferable to one by another hand which could be published and performed at other German theatres. "To forestall any such possibility," he explained in an open letter (17 February 1880) to the Danish newspaper *Nationaltidende*, "I sent my translator and agent for use in an emergency a drafted emendation in which Nora does not leave the house but is forced by Helmer to the doorway of the children's bedroom; here a few lines are exchanged, Nora sinks down by the door and the curtain falls. This emendation I have myself described to my translator as a 'barbaric outrage' on the play. . . . But if any such outrage is threatened, I prefer, on the basis of previous experience, to commit it myself rather than submit my work to the treatment and 'adaptation' of less tender and competent hands."

Frau Niemann-Raabe accepted this distorted version and acted it in February at Flensburg and later in Hamburg, Dresden, Hanover and Berlin. In the last-named city there was a public protest at the perversion (though when, subsequently, the original ending was used, there were further protests on the ground that the play had obviously been shorn of its fourth act!) The "happy ending" was never a success, and eventually Frau Niemann-Raabe reverted to the original text. Meanwhile, on 3 March, an unbowdlerized production took place at the Munich Residenztheater, with Ibsen himself in the audience. John Paulsen accompanied him, and recorded his reactions. Ibsen had attended several rehearsals; the play was, to Paulsen's mind, well acted, and went down excellently with the public. After the premiere, Ibsen thanked everyone who had taken part in the production warmly. But afterwards, at home, he was

[25] Letter from Hegel to Ibsen, 5 February 1880 (Nielsen, II, 343–44).

full of criticisms, not merely of the interpretation of the play and the various roles, but of details such as that Nora had the wrong-sized hands (whether too big or too small Paulsen could not remember), and that the colour of the wallpaper in the Helmers' apartment was wrong and conveyed a false atmosphere. Paulsen wondered that Ibsen had not mentioned at any rate this last point during rehearsals; but the actors later told Paulsen that Ibsen had "neither praised nor blamed, but just remained silent," and that when they asked him if they had fulfilled his intentions, he merely complimented them, which frustrated rather than pleased them "since they knew they were far from perfect."[26] Even now that he was famous, and anything he said would have been obeyed, Ibsen was as reluctant to offer advice as in the old days in Norway. Paulsen recalled that the Norwegian actress Lucie Wolf told him that, when a director in Christiania, Ibsen had "always seemed happy with what we had done, though this was often moderate."[27]

A Doll's House had a mixed reception in the German theatres, and was in general coolly received by the German critics. Karl Frenzel reiterated in Deutsche Rundschau (nr. 26, 1881) that Ibsen was poor at dramatic construction, and added that he seemed to love the repulsive; and Paul Lindau (later to become an admirer and friend of Ibsen) declared in Die Gegenwart (nr. 18, 1880) that the ending as originally written was both illogical and immoral. Georg Brandes sadly commented that Ibsen would never be understood in Germany.[28] But if he was not understood, he was immensely discussed. "Down here," he wrote to Hegel on 14 April, "A Doll's House has excited as much controversy as at home. People have taken sides passionately either for or against the play, and it has hardly ever happened before in Munich that any play has aroused such lively discussion."

One extraordinary version of A Doll's House appeared this year in the form of an English translation by a Danish schoolteacher named T. Weber, published in Copenhagen, surely one of the most sustained specimens of unconscious humour in all literature. The final scene contains the following examples:

NORA. Don't utter such stupid shuffles . . . Doff the shawl . . . From this
    moment it depends no longer on felicity; it depends only on saving the
    rests, remnants, and the appearance.

HELMER. You are first of all a wife and mother.
NORA. . . . I believe that I am first of all a man, I as well as you—
    or at all events, that I am to try to become a man.

[26] Paulsen, Samliv med Ibsen, I, 60–61.
[27] Ibid., p. 58.
[28] Eller, pp. 36–39.

NORA. As I am now, I am no wife for you.
HELMER. I have power to grow another.

HELMER. Change yourself in such a manner that—
NORA.—that cohabitation between you and me might become a matrimony. Goodbye.

Of this last line, Harley Granville Barker wrote that he was "not indisposed to offer a prize at the Royal Academy of Dramatic Art to the student who could manage to speak [it] without making the audience laugh."[29]

During the early months of 1880, Ludwig Passarge asked leave to prepare the first German (or, indeed, foreign) translation of *Peer Gynt*. Ibsen, as we have seen, was dubious about the possibility of the play succeeding with any but a Scandinavian public, but granted permission. In Finland, meanwhile, a young scholar named Valfred Vasenius published the second book to be devoted entirely to a study of Ibsen's work, a not unperceptive doctoral thesis covering the plays up to and including *The Pretenders*. In Sweden, the Gothenburg Theatre acquired the rights to *A Doll's House* (for an outright payment of 500 crowns), and in Stockholm Ludvig Josephson, now doing his best on a shoestring at the little Nya Teater, asked permission to present not merely new productions of *The Vikings at Helgeland* and *The Pretenders,* but also the first Swedish production of *Love's Comedy,* and the first production anywhere of *Catiline*. Ibsen granted him the rights in return for outright payments of 100 crowns (!) for each of the first two plays and 400 crowns for the other two.

Knowing that he would not start on a new play before the following year, and anxious to have a new work in the bookstores by Christmas, Ibsen suggested to Hegel on 31 May that he might prepare "a small volume of 10–12 signatures [160–192 pages] consisting of prefaces to his various plays on the lines of the one he had written for *Catiline*. "For *Lady Inger* and *The Vikings* I could describe my time in Bergen; for *The Pretenders* and *Love's Comedy,* the years that followed in Christiania; my life in Rome while I was writing *Brand* and *Peer Gynt,* etc., etc. . . . I plan to spend the summer doing this, for I don't intend to write another play this year and have nothing else with which to occupy my time." Surprisingly, Hegel dissuaded him from this project:

[29] Harley Granville Barker, "The Coming of Ibsen," in *The Eighteen-Eighties,* ed. Walter de la Mare (Cambridge 1930), p. 196.

Copenhagen, 6 June 1880

Dear Dr. Ibsen!

Since you ask my opinion regarding the plan you propose in your kind letter, I must tell you why I very definitely entreat you not to go ahead with this. A foreword such as that which you wrote to *Catiline* can have, and has, value as relating to a youthful work later revised and reissued by a then fully matured writer. Outside these special circumstances it is in my view a statement of a semi-private character which would scarcely interest the public did it not bear the signature of Henrik Ibsen. But even in this special instance a thing of this nature should appear only once. Repetitions would weaken the effect, and if stretched out to cover a succession of works they would assuredly strike the reading public as the kind of anecdotal writing which should at all costs be avoided.

Your works stand on their own as clear and characteristic entities, the significance of which does not need to be tied to such slight footnotes which would unconsciously work themselves into the consciousness of their readers and introduce a new and distracting element. . . . It would be quite another matter, I feel, if you ever wanted to write an *aus meinem Leben*, in which these fragments would then appear in context and thereby cease to be fragments. But I think you would be wise to postpone writing such a work just yet. . . .[30]

The last paragraph reads like good sense and might tempt one to forgive Hegel. But when, eighteen months later, Ibsen suggested writing just such an autobiography, Hegel again dissuaded him. Ibsen meekly accepted his advice, and the details which he could have given us about the gestation and composition of his plays remained unwritten.

Ludvig Josephson visited Ibsen in Munich that summer, on the way home from seeing the passion play at Oberammergau, and enjoyed the interesting experience of accompanying him on a visit to his tailor, where Ibsen ordered a black velvet coat and amazed Josephson by the minuteness of his instructions to the man. Ibsen, he noted, now usually wore a white cravat and white gloves with his invariable black coat, and a tall, shiny felt hat with a very broad brim, which with his "long dark hair, not yet grizzled or white" gave him rather the appearance of a sectarian minister.[31]

As a companion to Oberammergau Josephson had taken a young Swedish actor-director named August Lindberg, who had just acted a remarkable Hamlet for him at Nya Teater and who was to become one of the foremost interpreters of Ibsen's plays, both as actor and as director. He advised Lindberg, who was returning later than he, to visit Ibsen, warning him that Ibsen was "an odd person, difficult to make conversation with." "Don't talk to him about the theatre," advised Josephson, "nor about plays, his or anyone else's." "As I had just come from Oberammergau,"

[30] Nielsen, II, 347.
[31] Josephson, pp. 40–41.

records Lindberg, "I began to talk of Jesus, Mary and all the apostles in the moving drama I had seen amid the mountains, but it was heavy going, and in the end I sat silent on a rock, and when I left retained only the memory of a pair of spectacles."[32] In three years' time Ibsen was to have cause to be profoundly grateful to Lindberg.

In the beginning of August, Suzannah and Sigurd went to Norway, partly so that Sigurd could investigate the chances of his being able to study law at Christiania without going through the preliminary examinations; and Ibsen, shortly before they left, addressed a letter to King Oscar pleading, unsuccessfully as it turned out, that his son should be granted exemption. While awaiting the royal reply, he made preparations to leave with John Paulsen for a holiday in Berchtesgaden.

The preparations for this excursion, which would have occupied most people for perhaps a couple of hours, caused Ibsen extraordinary distraction. A week before they were due to depart Paulsen chanced to visit him at Amalienstrasse and found him walking up and down in great agitation with an open trunk on the floor. "When Ibsen was going away," Paulsen explains, "he began to pack, not a day or two, but a whole week ahead, and, for fear of arriving late, would come to the station at least an hour before the train was due to leave."[33] When the day came, "although I reached the station in good time, Ibsen was of course waiting, dressed in a new, elegant travelling suit and a big broad-brimmed felt hat which rendered him half unrecognizable." They took the train as far as Salzburg. There, while they awaited the diligence which was to convey them to Berchtesgaden, Ibsen showed Paulsen round the town, "the white houses with their flat roofs and green awnings, the marble buildings, the numerous churches, fountains and palaces, and the archbishop's ancient palace," though not, which seems strange even when one remembers Ibsen's indifference to music, Mozart's house. When they reached Berchtesgaden, they had to share a bedroom for the first night at the Salzburger Hof; but, to Paulsen's surprise and relief, Ibsen "slept as silently as a child."[34]

Living à deux with Ibsen was less difficult than Paulsen had feared. He took an inordinate time to dress in the morning, often an hour or more—"and when he was ready, there was nothing particularly special about his appearance; he was attired like everyone else." He was inclined to be testy during the morning, and did not much like being spoken to before noon. But "later in the day he would begin to talk a little; after lunch he became amenable and friendly, and in the evening warm and lovable." He bought a coloured feather and stuck it in his hat, which caused the local children to stare after him. He was brooding on his next play, and

[32] Per Lindberg, *August Lindberg*, p. 36. Per Lindberg, like his father, was a fine actor and director, and his book is one of the best of theatrical biographies.
[33] Paulsen, *Samliv med Ibsen*, II, 75.
[34] *Ibid.*, pp. 76–79.

once in bad weather, when Paulsen tentatively asked him about it, he replied, "It is a family story as sad and grey as this rainy day."[35]

Paulsen noted with interest the respect which Ibsen showed towards priests, despite the contempt with which he portrayed them in his plays. Whenever a priest passed them on their walks Ibsen would bow respectfully. At the hotel, he got annoyed because another guest kept taking the copy of *Berliner Tageblatt* which was reserved for him; but when he learned that the offender was a priest, Ibsen offered him the newspaper next morning with a deep bow. In contrast to this, he showed little respect for actors. A young German-American actor who was staying at the hotel and was an admirer of Ibsen tried to strike up an acquaintance, but Ibsen ostentatiously avoided him.[36] He enjoyed, however, talking to artisans about their work. One day on their walk he saw a cobbler working outside his house and engaged him in a lengthy conversation. "He took the boot, examined the leather and stitching carefully, and asked in surprise, 'Does one do that now? In my day one did so-and-so.'" When they left, the cobbler bade farewell to Ibsen "with the respect of a fellow-craftsman."[37]

He ate little, but extremely slowly, chewing each mouthful almost as many times as Gladstone.[38] They spoke of literature. Paulsen, while in Paris, had met Turgenev and his platonic mistress, Pauline Garcia-Viardot, and declared his amazement that any woman could have so "demonic an influence" on a man that he could become her slave. This interested Ibsen. "A man is easy to study," he said, "but one never fully understands a woman. They are a sea which none can fathom." He expressed to Paulsen (as he later did to William Archer) his admiration for Turgenev and "the Russian writers" in general;[39] we know from other sources that these included Dostœvsky and Tolstoy, but his opinion on Gogol (whom one would expect him especially to have enjoyed), Pushkin and Ostrovsky is not on record. Of French literature, on the other hand, Paulsen found that Ibsen was largely ignorant. He had read nothing of George Sand, despite Suzannah's admiration of her (she read *Consuelo* almost annually) and the only thing he knew about Madame de Staël was her remark *"Tout comprendre est tout pardonner,"* on which he commented that anyone who had written that must be "an unusual woman."[40] He praised Paul Heyse's work, especially the elegy for his dead child and his stories, *The Last Centaur, Salamander* and *The Widow of Pisa,*[41] and exhorted Paulsen to read Kleist's conte, *Michael Kohlhaas,* "which he averred to be a true mas-

[35] *Ibid.,* pp. 79–80.
[36] *Ibid.,* pp. 104–5.
[37] *Ibid.,* pp. 134–35.
[38] *Ibid.,* p. 108.
[39] *Ibid.,* pp. 93–94.
[40] *Samliv med Ibsen,* I, 171.
[41] *Samliv med Ibsen,* II, 102.

terpiece."[42] But he spoke contemptuously of Heine as a poet for adoles-
cents.[43] Gœthe and Schiller he admired as poets but not as dramatists,
and when anyone spoke, as Germans often did, of Gœthe's *grosse, reine
Liebe* (great pure love), Ibsen would laconically comment, "That d——d
old goat!"[44] As regards Italian authors, Paulsen "gained the impression that
he had in his time studied Dante in translation," but "the modern Italian
writers, such as Verga, Edmondo De Amicis, Fogazzaro, and Gabriele
D'Annunzio were merely names that Ibsen had seen in the newspapers."[45]
English authors he does not seem to have been reading at all. One would
have expected Suzannah to have admired George Eliot (who was to die
this year), and Thomas Hardy, who at forty had already published several
of his finest novels, including *Far from the Madding Crowd* and *The
Return of the Native;* but there is no record of Ibsen ever mentioning
either writer.

On the subject of other Scandinavian authors, Ibsen expressed little
sympathy for Henrik Wergeland, whose early influence he had long since
rejected, but considerable admiration for his old professor J. S. Welhaven,
both as a poet and as a man. He told how once, after a particularly brilliant
lecture by Welhaven in Christiania, he had been surprised, when standing
outside the lecture hall, to hear the great man complain to his wife as he
emerged that his trouser buttons were loose and he had spent the whole
hour wondering if they would fall off. He also related with approval a
story of how Welhaven (who, like Ibsen, could be rude to people who
bored him) once attended a party at which the hostess was a very fat lady
with an enormous double chin and, exhausted by her conversation, put his
finger to the crease between her chins and said, "Couldn't you manage one
little smile?"[46] Of Alexander Kielland, whose proletarian novels Ibsen regarded as meretricious, he remarked, "I have the impression that after a
good dinner he suddenly remembers, over his coffee and Havana cigar,
that there are poor people in the world, takes out a sheet of vellum and
writes with a golden pen of their needs, thus, by the law of opposites,
increasing his gourmet's pleasure in the moment."[47] He praised Carl
Snoilsky's poetry, and also mentioned approvingly Strindberg's novel about
Bohemian life in Stockholm, *The Red Room,* which had appeared the
previous year[48] (and which contains a scene in which the young hero is
struck dumb with admiration on meeting a publisher who has been permitted to address Ibsen as "Du"). This was the book which established
Strindberg's reputation and probably provided Ibsen with his first intro-

[42] *Mine Erindringer*, p. 162.
[43] *Samliv med Ibsen*, II, 226.
[44] *Samliv med Ibsen*, I, 72–73.
[45] *Ibid.*, 29–30.
[46] *Samliv med Ibsen*, II, 211.
[47] *Ibid.*, p. 207.
[48] *Ibid.*, p. 224.

duction to an author whose work, despite Strindberg's oft-declared hostility to him (mainly because of his championship of women), he was to read with continued interest and respect.

On 17 August, Ibsen's old mentor Ole Bull, who had given him his first job in the theatre, died at the age of seventy. He had lived a full life to the last (at the age of fifty-eight he had married an American girl of nineteen, and that was by no means the last of his conquests). Marcus Grønvold relates how, on hearing that Bull, on his death-bed with a sprig of heather in his hand, had thanked God for everything, Ibsen remarked with a quiet smile; "Ah, he thought he'd get away with it all!"[49]

Ibsen often spoke to Paulsen of Sigurd and, when Paulsen remarked on the young man's talent for languages, declared, "He has inherited that from me." "But," ventured Paulsen, "you are poor at languages, Herr Ibsen, you have said so yourself." "Yes," replied Ibsen, "but I flatter myself that I know *our* language minutely—and this feeling which I have toiled to perfect I have passed on to my son." Ibsen related with relish how Sigurd, as a small boy, on being spanked and ordered from the room, had turned on his father and shrieked: "Poet! Poet! All you know is how to tell lies and rubbish!" "Ibsen rubbed his hands as he told this story. It evidently amused him that the title which in the eyes of Europe was a term of honour was used by his small son as a term of abuse."[50]

One day a letter arrived at Berchtesgaden from Sigurd telling his father that there seemed little chance of his being excused the preliminary examinations before being admitted to read law at Christiania University, and that he would probably be required to study there for eighteen months first. Paulsen was with Ibsen when he received this letter. "He sat silent, angry and tight-lipped . . . I scarcely dared to look at him. He refused the food that was brought to him and limited himself, with a martyr's expression, to eating a little bread and salt. I can still hear the rasping sound of the salt crystals as he crushed them with his knife. . . . After a long and indescribably oppressive silence, he said: "But I shall raise a memorial to that black band of theologians who rule in Norway. They shall remember how they have treated me."[51] A foolish priest was to be one of the central characters of the play he was meditating, and was to dominate it to the point of imbalance.

This decision of the Ecclesiastical Department, which controlled matters of education in Norway, affected Ibsen's own future as well as that of his son. Bergliot Ibsen says that had Sigurd been accepted at Christiania

[49] Marcus Grønvold, p. 139.
[50] *Samliv med Ibsen*, II, 98–99.
[51] *Ibid.*, p. 115.

University Ibsen would have settled there himself so as to be near Sigurd.[52] As things were, he was to spend a further eleven years in exile.

"His mood," recalled Paulsen of this summer, "could change like an April day. He could be uncommonly gentle and irrigate one with his calm smile, his good humour and his merry Peer Gynt-like fantasies, but he could also be dark and angry. . . . There were times when the satirist in him awoke and his sharp tongue spared nothing. . . . And he had other, huger moments when, filled with a holy indignation at the meanness and unjustness of humanity, he could thunder like Brand or an Old Testament prophet. By nature he was talkative, but if an unexpected reverse met him which awoke bitter memories of the old days, his mouth shut tight in bitterness as though padlocked, and there emanated from him an icy coldness which silenced everything about him. And once I caught a glimpse of the bird of prey in him, as later portrayed in Solness and Rubek, the falcon questing for a victim, some poor fellow-human whom he could dissect and then throw away."[53] Sometimes he would indulge in a macabre humour. When, for instance, he related the story of a German painter who had tried repeatedly to commit suicide in different ways and had succeeded only at the fourth attempt, "Ibsen told these horrible details with a merry laughter, as though the story were funny rather than tragic. . . . At such moments there emerged a demonic side to Ibsen's character which he normally concealed."[54]

Rather than waste a year and a half on formal and useless studies, Sigurd suggested to his father that he should abandon all thought of trying for a legal degree in Norway and should instead continue his education in Italy. Ibsen telegraphed his approval and followed his telegram with a letter. "Since I received the Ecclesiastical Department's reply," he wrote on 18 September, "I have naturally given much thought to the matter, and have come to the conclusion that you are probably best served by the turn which, thanks to our imbecile and superannuated regulations, events have taken. What would it have profited you to have studied law in Norway? It was not your intention to become a civil servant up there. The only positions which attract you are still within your reach: you can become a professor or enter the diplomatic service without taking any civil service examination; for we have foreign professors at the university. . . . But don't think further ahead than studying abroad; you should wait before deciding whether it would be advantageous to become an Italian citizen."

Ibsen's old fellow-student from Christiania, Jonas Lie, by now a distinguished novelist, was spending the summer in Berchtesgaden with his wife Thomasine (who was also his cousin) and their children. Success

---

[52] Bergliot Ibsen, p. 84.
[53] *Samliv med Ibsen*, II, 116–17.
[54] *Ibid.*, pp. 182–83.

had come late to Lie, as it had to Ibsen; but during the past decade such novels as *The Visionary, The Pilot and His Wife* and *Adam Schrøder* had established him as an imaginative portrayer of human relationships. The Lies were living in a small white house in which Ibsen himself had stayed during his first visit to Berchtesgaden in 1868, and he visited them every Saturday evening, sometimes with Paulsen. Lie's son Erik, then a boy of twelve, recorded his father's memories twenty-eight years later, and added his own in another and equally rewarding book.

Jonas and Thomasine Lie were the kind of warm-hearted, sensitive people with whom Ibsen found it most easy to relax. In their company "he talked away about everything, told anecdotes, enjoyed himself to the full and never left before three in the morning." "I have never seen that closed face which people attribute to Ibsen," Lie once remarked (and he must have been almost the only acquaintance who never did). "When we were together in Berchtesgaden I always had the impression, as we sat together of an evening, of two front teeth which appeared more and more often as time went on—two front teeth with a gap between. And the higher his humour rose, the more he laughed and glowed, till at last he sat there like a good prattling midwife."[55] The observation about the gap between the teeth, surprising at first sight, reminds us that there exists no photograph or portrait of Ibsen with his mouth open. Apart from those Saturday evenings Ibsen and Lie virtually never saw each other, by mutual agreement, since Lie was working on a new novel. But, the latter remembered, "more than once Ibsen walked past the house where we were living, and it was observed that he often paused before the lighted windows on the ground floor and peered tentatively in at the family as we sat at our evening meal."[56]

Ibsen's passion, already remarked, for sewing on his own buttons manifested itself during this holiday. "One morning," recalled Jonas Lie, "Ibsen suddenly appeared and asked to speak to my wife. She was not to disturb me; it was only a trifling matter, to wit, a button. He had brought needle and thread. 'But may I not sew it on for you?' asked Thomasine. No, he wanted to do it himself. 'But what's the matter, then?' 'I wondered if you could help me to thread the needle. I have tried and tried, but I must confess it is a more difficult art than I had imagined.' Fru Lie of course immediately helped him. A week later she asked him if there was nothing else she could help him with. To thread another needle, perhaps? 'No, thank you,' replied Ibsen. 'Once I had the thread in, I took enough to last me the whole summer.' "[57]

The Lies particularly recalled Ibsen on his country walks, "following

[55] Erik Lie, *Jonas Lie, oplevelser, fortalt af Erik Lie* (Christiania and Copenhagen, 1908), p. 256.

[56] *Ibid.*, p. 257.

[57] *Loc. cit.*

the same precise routes along the rustic roads as, later, he was to do down Carl Johan [in Christiania] to the Grand Café." As soon as a cart appeared Ibsen would move off the road until it had passed and the dust had settled. "He would then take out the silk handkerchief which he carried in his left breast-pocket, wipe his spectacles, and carefully refold it . . . and walk on with his small, tripping steps, elegant and finical, despite the green Tyrolean hat which he had acquired soon after his arrival, and into which he had put a cock's feather which nodded at every step." Erik Lie also remembered how Ibsen loved to sit among the village children watching Punch and Judy shows, continuously wiping his spectacles as the puppets killed each other; how he rebuked John Paulsen angrily for making jokes about a dowager duchess; how he once remarked that he would ideally like to live on an island guarded by two hungry bloodhounds; and how little Elizabeth Lie, Jonas's elder daughter, on hearing her parents refer admiringly to Ibsen's *Doll's House*, supposed him to be a toymaker and was bitterly disappointed that he never brought any present for her. The youngest daughter, Johanne, recalled that he was "nice, and very kind to children," and (confirming Paulsen's observation) that he loved to talk with the local cobbler, Jacob Hasenknopf.[58]

Ibsen, as far as we know, did no writing that summer at Berchtesgaden. It was to be the last time he visited the little town; they had recently extended the railway to it, and the seclusion he so prized was gone. At the end of September or the beginning of October he returned to Munich whence, on 25 October, he informed Hegel that "we are now returning to Rome, where he [Sigurd] will complete his legal studies, and then become naturalized." Whether he had in fact taken this decision or whether it was still under discussion, we do not know. Ibsen went on to repeat, almost precisely, the words he had used to Paulsen on first hearing the news of the rejection of Sigurd's petition. "To the black band of theologians who temporarily rule in the Ecclesiastical Department, I shall in due time raise a fitting memorial."[59]

That October Ludwig Passarge's German translation of *Peer Gynt* appeared. On 2 November the Ibsens left Munich, arriving in Rome (the journey took thirty-one hours) on the 4th. They stayed the first week in a hotel, and on the 11th moved into "a very handsome and spacious, but somewhat expensive apartment" at 75, Via Capo le Case, close to where they had lived twelve years earlier. The description occurs in a letter Ibsen wrote to Hegel the next day asking him to send 1,600 crowns, adding, however, that "luckily accommodation is practically the only

---

[58] *Ibid.*, pp. 254 ff.; *Erindringer fra et dikterhjem* (Oslo, 1928), pp. 43 ff.; *Urd, Ibsen-nummer* (Oslo, 1928), p. 150.

[59] The similarity of the phrasing has led some critics to doubt the truth of Paulsen's reminiscence. But Ibsen often used in his letters (and plays) phrases which he is known previously to have used in conversation.

thing which can be called dear down here." He added that he was "turning over new literary plans, which I hope will have sufficiently matured within the next few months for me to begin on the actual writing." Edmund Gosse wrote to him asking permission to translate *A Doll's House* into English, to which Ibsen agreed; but Gosse never translated the play, nor even (as he had Ibsen's earlier works) reviewed it.

Ibsen received evidence that autumn of how his plays could be misinterpreted. A Scandinavian lady appeared in Rome with her lover. Having found her marriage unsatisfactory, she had left her husband and children. The Norwegians in Rome condemned her action as unnatural; and Ibsen, when asked his opinion, said: "It is not unnatural, but it is unusual." When the lady sought out Ibsen at a public function, he treated her rather coolly; and when she complained that she had only behaved as his Nora had done, he replied: "But my Nora went alone."[60]

The English theatre at last paid brief and belated recognition to Ibsen's existence that winter. On the morning of 15 December 1880 William Archer's revised translation of *The Pillars of Society* was given a single performance at the Gaiety Theatre in the Strand, the first in England, amateur or professional, of any Ibsen play—though Ibsen might have had some difficulty in recognizing it as his, for it was much abridged and adapted, and was entitled *Quicksands*. Charles Archer, in his biography of his brother William, describes how the play at last found its way on to the stage:

> Having failed to find a publisher for his translation of *The Pillars of Society,* Archer had set himself, as the only way of bringing Ibsen to the front, to adapt the play for the English stage; for in those days it was unthinkable that a faithful translation, even of a French piece, much more of a play by an unknown Hyperborean dramatist, should ever make its way on to the London boards. By the end of 1878 an "adaptation," which might better have been described as an abridgement, had been accepted by Mr. W. H. Vernon, who was much struck by the part of Consul Bernick. But Mr. Vernon had no theatre at his disposal, and negotiations for a London production dragged on for nearly two years. At last, since no better might be, the piece was produced experimentally at a Gaiety Theatre matinee on 15 December 1880—and fell perfectly flat. The production, as a whole, was inevitably scrambling and ineffective. But the best setting and acting could not have made the play a success with the English critics and audiences of that day. Ibsen's time was not yet come.[61]

The *Athenæum* (24 December) praised the play as "a good and telling story which introduces some novel, if not very powerful, types of character . . . extremely fine comedy . . . we shall be glad to know more

[60] Zucker, p. 182. The story was told to Zucker by Julius Elias's widow.
[61] Charles Archer, p. 82.

of its author's workmanship." *The Theatre* (February 1881) described the performance as "tentatively produced and fairly successful," but felt that "Bernick's cold-blooded villainy appears somewhat inadequately punished." The Danish correspondent of a Copenhagen newspaper reported that at the final curtain the audience called loudly for the author, "a request which was readily met, without any trace of embarrassment or reserve, by Mr. Archer, the English translator."[62] Archer's translation was not published until 1888, and then in a much revised form.

At the end of 1880 Ibsen found that he had, for the first time, earned over a thousand pounds in a single year:

	crowns
Fee for *A Doll's House* in Christiania	2,500
Fee for *A Doll's House* in Gothenburg	500
Fee for *A Doll's House* in Bergen	400
4th edn. of *The League of Youth*	898
Miscellaneous fees for *A Doll's House* from Norwegian touring companies	800
3rd edn. of *A Doll's House*	1,406
Extra fee from Royal Theatre, Copenhagen, for *A Doll's House*	6,103
Extra fee from Gyldendal for *The League of Youth* and *A Doll's House*	177
Fee for *A Doll's House* in Swedish provinces (Åbjörnson)	200
Royalties from Munich Hoftheater, 1st quarter	253
Fee for *A Doll's House* in Swedish provinces (J. F. Smith)	200
3rd edn. of *Emperor and Galilean*	1,600
Extra fee from Royal Theatre, Stockholm, for *A Doll's House* (after 30 perfs.)	2,451
Fee for *A Doll's House* from theatre-director Rylander	100
Royalties from Munich Hoftheater, 2nd quarter	83
Fee for *A Doll's House* at Flensburg and Schleswig	62
Extra fees from Bergen Theatre	620
Royalties from Munich Hoftheater, 3rd quarter	106
Extra fee for *A Doll's House* from Royal Theatre, Copenhagen (16–21 perfs.)	1,966
Extra fee for *A Doll's House* from Royal Theatre (22–26 perfs.)	709
Extra fee for *A Doll's House* from Foght's travelling company in Norway	400
	21,534 £1,196

Several features of this year's accounts are interesting. For once, book sales constituted a minority of his income. Performing rights represented

[62] McFarlane, *The Oxford Ibsen*, V, 434. He does not name his source.

approximately five-sixths of it, and these were almost entirely from a single play, *A Doll's House*. The fees from the Royal Theatre in Copenhagen alone (8,778 crowns) exceeded his total income for many a previous year, and underline how much he lost by not getting similar royalties from all theatres. The German theatres, be it noted, paid him a total of 504 crowns.

But if Ibsen supposed that a period of financial affluence lay ahead of him, he was to be disillusioned. It was to be another ten years before his annual income again reached £1,000. The decade from 1881 to 1890, which was to see the composition of *Ghosts, An Enemy of the People, The Wild Duck, Rosmersholm, The Lady from the Sea* and *Hedda Gabler,* was to bring him a total income of under £6,500—less than playwrights of far inferior stature in larger countries, such as Scribe, W. S. Gilbert and Pinero, would expect to make in a single year.

20

Ghosts

1881 – 1882

Ibsen, as he approached his fifty-fourth birthday, was becoming, if not an international figure, at any rate one of the few Scandinavians whom other countries bothered to consider at all. The January 1881 issue of *Unser Zeit* contained a long essay on him by Eugen Zabel—the first, other than reviews of individual plays, to be devoted to him in a German paper. It was by no means wholly favourable; drawing parallels between Ibsen's philosophy and German pessimism, Zabel thought that both *Brand* and *Peer Gynt* had much in common with Goethe's *Faust,* but declared that Ibsen's imagination, although fertile, was enclosed in a frigid sheath of intellect, and that much of *Peer Gynt* belonged to the realm, not of poetry, but of pathology—an unconsciously penetrating observation.

At the same time, a far shrewder and more balanced assessment of Ibsen's work was placed before the English reading public in the form of two articles by William Archer in the January and February issues of the *St. James's Magazine.* Instead of condemning Ibsen, as so many of his critics were doing, for pessimism, discord, and "lack of idealism," Archer, familar with the novels of George Eliot and Thomas Hardy, recognized that in these supposed defects lay much of Ibsen's strength. "His countrymen," wrote Archer, "admire, fear, and hate him. The lash of the satirist has fallen heavy upon them as a nation. . . . While admitting his greatness, they maintain that the negativeness of his aims detracts from, or almost nullifies it. . . . [But] Ibsen depicts a real world, not the ideal where satisfaction and reconciliation are possible. . . . The old theory that all great work comes from a positive age is rapidly dying away. Ibsen is one of the great negative voices of a negative age which tries in vain, by shrieking in falsetto and thundering in the deepest bass, to convince itself that it is positive."

This was remarkably mature criticism from someone aged barely twenty-four; and before the year was out Archer was to introduce Ibsen's work to a chance acquaintance who was to become, not merely his most influential apologist, but also his most distinguished disciple as a dramatist. "In the winter of 1881–82," Archer recalled, "I used to go almost every day to the British Museum Reading Room in London. I frequently sat next to a man of about my own age who attracted my attention, partly by his peculiar colouring—his pallid skin and bright red hair and beard—partly by the odd combination of authors whom he used to study—for I saw him, day after day, poring over Karl Marx's *Das Kapital* and an orchestral score of Wagner's *Tristan und Isolde*. How we first made acquaintance I have forgotten; but one did not need to meet him twice to be sure that George Bernard Shaw was a personality to be noted and studied. . . . We became fast friends."[1]

Not only did Archer introduce Shaw to Ibsen; he also got Shaw his first critical work, first as a book reviewer, then as art critic and finally as music critic.[2] The debt of English and Irish literature to William Archer is inadequately realized; he was also one of the first people to encourage the young James Joyce.

In America, too, that February, Ibsen's name was praised, the first record of its mention in the New World. The writer was none other than Bjørnson who, having delivered an oration at Ole Bull's funeral in Bergen, had been invited by Bull's young widow to visit her in Boston, and had stayed in the States for seven months. In the course of a long article entitled "Norway's Constitutional Struggle" in *Scribner's Monthly* Bjørnson declared: "I do not hesitate to say that in my opinion Henrik Ibsen possesses the greatest dramatic power of the age. I am so much the more certain of my judgement from the fact that I do not always like his dramas. It is surprising to me that he is not translated in America. He is one whom his contemporaries should know."[3] This was an extraordinarily generous tribute from a man whose own star was sliding into eclipse.

Several of Ibsen's old friends and acquaintances were in Rome that winter, including Lorentz Dietrichson, Camilla Collett and Kristofer Janson; and among the newcomers whom he met was a young Swedish poet, Verner von Heidenstam, later to become a Nobel prizewinner, but at this early stage in his career still regarded as a rich dilettante. John Paulsen, who was there too, records that Ibsen used to go every day to the Café Artisti, where the Scandinavians gathered, to see if anyone new had arrived. He began, too, to hold soirées, "cosmopolitan rather than homely, but very agreeable. One arrived between nine and ten, and an Italian servant offered tea. On the sideboard stood wine, fruit, and cakes,

[1] Charles Archer, p. 119.
[2] *Ibid.*, p. 135.
[3] *Scribner's Monthly Magazine*, XXI (1881), 606.

to which one helped oneself during the course of the evening. Ibsen, dressed in a black frock coat without decorations, received the guests with a calm and impressive dignity."[4]

Paulsen, who was there on a travelling scholarship from the Norwegian government, which he had received largely thanks to Ibsen's recommendation, achieved something of a record on his arrival by becoming, surely, the only man ever suspected of being Suzannah Ibsen's lover. Calling at the Ibsens' apartment, he found them out and asked the Italian maid to tell Suzannah that her *amico* was in Rome and would return in the afternoon. The maid conspiratorially warned Suzannah on her return, knowing that then *il signor commendatore* (a title by which Ibsen was known among the Italians, because he was a Commander of the Medjije Order) might be at home, and adding delightedly: "How rash of the young man!" The incident became, as long as their friendship with Paulsen lasted, a standing joke in the Ibsen household.[5]

Among the other Scandinavians then in Rome was the Swedish painter Georg Pauli, who was amazed one day to see a figure walking towards him down the street wearing medals—"not ribbons, but medals." The two became acquainted, and it was not long before Pauli, like others before him, found himself assisting Ibsen back to his apartment, with the help of the Norwegian painter Christian Meyer Ross. "We supported the great man on either side," Pauli noted in his diary, "and he showed his gratitude by incessantly giving us his confidential opinion of our insignificance. I, he said, was a 'frightful puppy,' and Ross 'a very repulsive character.'" On another occasion Pauli asked Ibsen what books he was reading and was surprised to receive the answer: "I don't read books, I leave them to my wife and Sigurd." But Pauli, like other observers, confirms that Ibsen read the newspapers most minutely. Pauli noted that Sigurd, now twenty-one, was very much his father's son, meticulous in dress and demeanour, reserved, buttoned-up and "seldom ungloved, even on the most informal occasions."[6]

Ibsen's dislike of reading books has disturbed many a man of letters, starting with Edmund Gosse; but it is not surprising that he, whose principal interest was modern people and modern ideas, should have found the newspapers more rewarding. They kept him better abreast of his subject. "He has often seemed to me," wrote Georg Brandes in an essay published the following year, "to stand in a sort of mysterious correspondence with the fermenting, germinating ideas of the day. Once or twice I have even had a distinct impression that new ideas, which were on the point of manifesting themselves publicly but were not yet perceived

---

[4] Paulsen, *Nye erindringer,* pp. 103–4.

[5] *Ibid.,* pp. 87–89.

[6] Georg Pauli, *Mina romerska år* (Stockholm, 1924), pp. 111–20.

by others, had been preoccupying and indeed tormenting him"; and he added in an eloquent phrase that Ibsen possessed the true poet's ear for "the low rumble that tells of ideas undermining the ground . . . for the throb of their inions in the air."[7]

Not long after Ibsen's arrival in Rome the two Swedish princes Oscar and Carl visited the city. The Scandinavian Club gave a fancy-dress ball in their honour, which Ibsen attended, not, sadly, in fancy dress (what could he have gone as but himself?), but in, as the saying was, full gala, with his decorations on his chest and a *chapeau-bas* in his hand. King Oscar had given the princes a letter to Lindstrand, the Swedish minister in Rome, commanding him to introduce them to Ibsen, "from whom they might learn much"; but Lindstrand, instead of inviting Ibsen to the dinner he gave for them, merely asked him to join them for tea afterwards. Ibsen, well able to answer one snub with another, replied by sending his visiting card bearing the brief message: "I do not drink tea."[8]

In fact he liked tea, and often visited Christian Meyer Ross at the latter's studio to drink it of an afternoon, even though it involved listening to music, his unconcealed boredom with which offended a young New England girl married to a Danish diplomat. "There is always a little music," she noted in her diary. "Ibsen sits sullen, silent, and indifferent. This is not, as you may imagine, inspiring to the performers. In fact, merely to look at him takes all the life out of you. He is a veritable wet blanket."[9]

One day John Paulsen risked promulgating some theories about Ibsen's work and received a warning against "looking for obscurities in his work where none existed." Ibsen complained that "critics were eager to find a double meaning, a hidden symbol, in every word or action," a tendency that has not lapsed with the years. He quoted as one example a Swede's assertion that Nora's extravagant tip to the porter of a crown, which he had intended merely to exemplify her carelessness with money, signified her desire to level the relationship between capitalist and worker; and told how another scholar had discovered a deep meaning in his choice of the name Makrina (which in Greek means far-sighted) for a character in *Emperor and Galilean,* whereas he had only used it because he had found the name in an old book and liked it.[10]

He also gave Paulsen some stern advice about writing. "Fixing me with a glance over his gold spectacles, he said, 'You mustn't walk around dream-

---

[7] Georg Brandes, *Henrik Ibsen,* pp. 83 and 94 (Muir-Archer translation).

[8] Paulsen, *Nye Erindringer,* pp. 126–27. The story is confirmed by Fritz von Dardel, who had it from Ibsen himself, and adds that the princes took the hint and invited Ibsen to dinner the following day. (Fritz von Dardel, *Dagboksanteckningar, 1881–1885* [Stockholm, 1920], p. 86).

[9] Madame L. Hegermann-Lindencrone, *The Sunny Side of Diplomatic Life* (New York, 1914), pp. 100–1.

[10] Paulsen, *Samliv med Ibsen,* I, 75–76.

ing. Use your eyes. That is doubly necessary for anyone who wishes to become an author. . . . Tell me,' he asked suddenly, 'what colour is the wallpaper in your room?' " Paulsen had to confess that he did not know. " 'You see!' cried Ibsen triumphantly, as always whenever he discovered anything which confirmed his suspicions. 'I was right. You don't notice anything. Though how a human being with normal senses can live in a room without noticing the colour of the walls. . . . When I enter a strange house I note the tiniest detail, nothing escapes me. Yes,' he added quietly, more to himself than to me, 'I see everything.' "[11]

He gave proof of his visual memory that winter when a Norwegian lady named Fanny Rijs, on being presented to him at one of his own receptions, said, "There is no need to introduce us. We danced together in Bergen." Ibsen replied curtly (and untruthfully), "I have never danced," and walked away into his study. But a few minutes later he emerged, said, "You are right," described precisely what she had been wearing at the dance twenty-five years before, and even sketched a necklace she had been wearing.[12] When she left on 28 February, Ibsen gave her a signed photograph of himself bearing the inscription: "Do not forget Rome."

During the spring of 1881 Ibsen, still smarting under the treatment accorded to Sigurd, seriously pondered giving up his Norwegian citizenship. "He [Sigurd] is intending to become naturalized here," he wrote to Johan Thoresen on 9 March. "He speaks and writes French, German and Italian like a native, is well versed in both politics and economics, and so feels confident that he will be able to make a career without having to resort to Norway. The question is whether I too shall not feel occasioned to expatriate myself. There will be many advantages for me in becoming an Italian or German citizen, and now that the Ecclesiastical Department has dispossessed my son I don't know what further business I have up there. We are exceptionally contented here in Rome." He was never in fact to make so final a break with Norway, thanks largely perhaps to Suzannah's influence; but the mood expressed in this letter was shortly to find dramatic expression.

He had not, hitherto, been lucky in his translators in any country, but he all but acquired what would have been a very interesting one that spring. Ludvig Josephson had, as we have seen, conceived the idea of staging *Love's Comedy* in Stockholm, and he approached no less a person than August Strindberg to translate it. Although Strindberg, then thirty-two, had written eight plays, only one of these, the historical drama *Master Olof*, ranks among his best; his great days as a dramatist still lay ahead of him. Josephson's suggestion tempted him. "I have looked at Ibsen's *Love's Comedy*," he replied on 14 March. "It will be a

[11] *Ibid.*, pp. 21–22.
[12] Information from Professor Francis Bull.

long and expensive job. If you want me to translate it, make me a formal offer and name a deadline, for I daren't risk attempting so big a task for nothing."[13] Unfortunately Josephson could offer very little, and the project lapsed (it was to be eight years before *Love's Comedy* was seen in Sweden). One wonders what Strindberg, whose marriage to Siri von Essen was already beginning to strain at the seams, would have made of this particular play, with its message that love and marriage are incompatible.

On 27 March Ibsen made a further attempt to have his pension increased, addressing his appeal on this occasion to H. E. Berner, editor for the past ten years of *Dagbladet* and now a newly-elected member of the Storthing. The letter, with its detailed documentation of the problems which faced a successful author in a small country a century ago, is worth quoting *in extenso*:

> . . . When some time ago the Storthing granted first Bjørnson and later myself an annual pension of 400 specie-dollars, this was generally regarded as a public recognition of and reward for our literary activity, and was as such gratefully accepted by us. The notion of copyright was then, as now, still largely disregarded in Scandinavia. Neither the government nor the Storthing had taken measures to insure Norwegian authors, least of all dramatists, against the arbitrary pilfering of any outsider who chose to pick up a pen. In other words the law did not permit us, like other citizens, to enjoy the fruits of our labours. The Christiania Theatre's practice was to pay a small fee for the right to perform a play in perpetuity. Thus, for *The Vikings at Helgeland* I received thirty specie-dollars, with an intimation that if I was not satisfied with this sum they proposed to stage the play without paying any fee at all, as the law entitled them to. The other theatres in Norway, and the touring companies, of course paid nothing. The same was true of the smaller theatres in Sweden and Denmark. Even the Royal Theatre in Stockholm once, as you will probably recall, performed a play of Bjørnson without paying a farthing, although the author protested strenuously. Subsequently, perhaps as a result of the notice which that matter attracted, the Royal Theatres of Stockholm and Copenhagen have rewarded us by paying whatever they felt inclined to, a token of progress which we were compelled to accept and be grateful for, since neither the government nor the Storthing had protected our literary interests by signing literary conventions with Sweden and Denmark.
>
> Thus virtually all of Bjørnson's and my plays were taken from us, one after the other, without our being able to enjoy the financial fruits which are permitted without question to authors in other countries.

[13] *August Strindbergs brev*, ed. Torsten Eklund (Stockholm, 1948 ff.), II, 241.

I have only fully realised the extent of our loss since the copyright agreements with Sweden and Denmark were signed.[14] But for Bjørnson and myself these agreements have come too late, because during those earlier anarchic years our works were taken from us for nothing or, at the best, for very small sums.

But this is not all; indeed, for us it is the least of the matter. What has hit us far harder has been the absence of any copyright agreement between Norway and Germany or any other country outside Scandinavia. You know that many of Bjørnson's and my books have been translated in Germany and that many of our plays are performed in the theatres there. But if people assume that this gratifying recognition brings us any considerable, or even trivial, financial reward, they are much mistaken. It is the translators or their publishers who reap the reward, and we Norwegian dramatists can do nothing about it. If we commission translations of our plays at our own expense we can be pretty sure that within a short time another translation, if not several, will appear and supplant our own.

It is, I appreciate, unthinkable that Norway should take steps to initiate a general international copyright agreement; or rather become a party to the agreement which already exists between most other European countries. As a good Norwegian I would not wish such a thing; for such an agreement would enormously increase the cost of every foreign book, scholarly or literary, which we might wish to make available to our public in translation. And this would block many of the sources of enlightenment to which Norway now has free access. Free? Yes, free for Norway, but not for Bjørnson or me. For it is we who, for many years, have paid, as we do today, the bulk of the duty on our country's imports of foreign literature. And this duty amounts to no small sum. I think I could with a good conscience declare that Bjørnson and I are the two most heavily taxed men in Norway. . . .

The money which Bjørnson and I have received from the state bears no relation to the loss we have suffered and shall continue to suffer both at home and abroad. Could not the Storthing consider it both just and inexpensive to grant us reasonable compensation by increasing our pensions? . . . It is noteworthy that in our country edible game has become protected by law before authors. In our dealings with foreign countries we are still classed with beasts of prey. Anyone may hunt us without let or hindrance, and the worst is that we have to pay the cost of their ammunition. . . . I would respectfully call to mind that when Nordenskiöld and Palander discovered the North-

[14] These agreements came into force from 1 January 1878 (Sweden) and 1 January 1880 (Denmark). Similar agreements were made with Italy in 1884 and France in 1893, but Ibsen's copyright remained unprotected in other countries until Norway joined the Berne Convention in 1896.

East Passage[15] the Swedish Parliament granted them each an annual pension of 4,000 crowns. I permit myself to think that Bjørnson and I have, by our literary explorations, discovered something approximating both North-East and North-West Passages, which may in the future be as much used by the Scandinavian peoples as those which Palander and Nordenskiöld have opened. . . .

Berner promised to do his best in the matter, and it came before the Storthing a year later, with what success we shall see.

That spring of 1881 Ibsen spent a couple of days with Lorentz Dietrichson revisiting the country places they had explored together seventeen years earlier. They took the train to Frascati and Tusculum and rode on donkeys, as before, across to Grottaferrata and Castelgandolfo, this time without mishap. They spent a night at Albano and the next morning walked to Genzano, looking in at the café in which Ibsen had lived and strolling down to Lake Nemi. In Olcanda all was unchanged except that the portrait of Pope Pius IX had been replaced by those of Victor Emmanuel, Cavour and Garibaldi. During this trip Ibsen, after bewailing the inability of governments to put big ideas into practice, suddenly broke off and said: "People think I have changed my views as time has passed, but that is quite wrong; my development has been wholly consistent. . . . I am jotting down a few notes which will show the world how precisely similar I am now to what I was when I first discovered myself." Dietrichson comments that this seems to be evidence that Ibsen was already preparing the autobiography from which Hegel was so unfortunately to dissuade him.[16] It may have been of this project that Ibsen informed Hegel on 22 March: "I am writing a new book which will be ready in the summer. . . . This work interests me much, and I feel convinced that it will also be received with interest by the public. But I won't for the moment tell you its theme; later, perhaps." (But it may also have been *An Enemy of the People,* which he completed with unwonted speed the following year and which may already have been in his thoughts.)

Meanwhile, John Paulsen had been running into trouble as an author; his latest novel had been refused by Hegel, and he seems to have become swollen-headed. His relations with Ibsen had taken a marked turn for the worse. "I am not surprised that you do not wish to publish it," Ibsen wrote to Hegel on 21 April. "I am afraid Paulsen is falling more and more into the bad habit of over-rapid and slipshod composition. No properly prepared plan, no rounded, lifelike characters. But I've grown tired of warning him against this path which he has chosen to follow, as I see it bears no fruit and, besides, he takes it amiss. He has an

15 In 1878–80, from the Atlantic to the Pacific.
16 Dietrichson, I, 363.

immense and unmannerly confidence in himself." Ibsen's doubts about Paulsen's character were shortly to receive painful confirmation.

On 18 June Ibsen informed Hegel: "There has been a change in my literary plans for the summer. I have temporarily shelved the work I previously mentioned to you, and early this month embarked on a theme which has long occupied my thoughts and which at length forced itself so insistently upon me that I could no longer ignore it. I hope to be able to send you the manuscript by the middle of October. I'll tell you the title later; for the moment I shall merely say that I describe it as 'a domestic drama in three acts.' I need hardly add that this play has no kind of connection with *A Doll's House*." This last remark was in reply to a letter from Hegel telling him that there was a rumour in Copenhagen that he was working on a sequel to that play.[17]

That month John Paulsen left Rome; he and Ibsen were never to meet again. On 28 June Ibsen moved with Suzannah and Sigurd to Sorrento on the west coast, where they stayed, as they had two years previously, at the Hotel Tramontano and where Dietrichson and his family shortly joined them. The weather was tremendously hot. "My wife suffers more than us from the heat, and especially the sirocco," he wrote to Camilla Collett that August, "but she manages to survive with the help of a daily sea-bathe. I don't think you could have survived the summer down here. To walk is almost out of the question; one must just sit as still as possible." Despite these conditions, he was able to write to Hegel on 30 September: "I take advantage of a free moment to tell you briefly that on the 23rd inst. I finished the first draft of my new play and on the 25th began my fair copy. The play is entitled *Ghosts: A Domestic Drama in Three Acts*. If possible you shall have the whole thing by the end of October."

This "fair copy" in fact took the form of a new draft, and as time was getting short if the book was to catch the Christmas sales Ibsen revised Act One (the draft of which he finished on 4 October) and posted off the fair copy of it to Hegel on 16 October before redrafting Acts Two and Three. "The second act," he assured Hegel, "which will be somewhat shorter, you shall have within fourteen days, and the rest at the beginning of next month, so that the book will I hope be able to be in the bookshops in early December, which was the time *A Doll's House* appeared. . . . I beg that the manuscript shall not be allowed to come into the hands of any unauthorised person." Working feverishly against the clock, he completed the draft of Act Two (which he had begun on 13 October) in seven days, and that of Act Three in four days. On 4 November he posted off the fair copy of Act Two plus the first page of Act Three to Hegel, promising that "the remainder will be sent to you with all speed from Rome, whither we return tomorrow."

[17] Nielsen, II, 576.

On 23 November, writing from Rome, he uttered a mild warning to
Hegel. *"Ghosts* will probably cause alarm in some circles; but that can't
be helped. If it didn't, there would have been no necessity for me to have
written it." He was already, he added in the same letter, "planning a new
four-act comedy which I had thought about before but put aside to make
way for *Ghosts,* which was obsessing me and monopolising my thoughts."

Ghosts—the story of a woman who leaves her husband, is persuaded
by the Pastor (whom she loves) to return home, does so, and bears a son
who turns out to have inherited his father's syphilis—was duly published
by Gyldendal, in an edition of ten thousand copies (two thousand more
than *A Doll's House*) on 13 December 1881, and at once aroused a
consternation and hostility beyond anything Ibsen had envisaged. At first
he accepted this calmly; he knew there were small prospects of its being
performed in either Scandinavia or Germany, but reckoned it would, like
Brand and *Peer Gynt,* make its effect on the reading public. On 22
December he wrote to Ludwig Passarge, "My new play has come out,
and has created a violent commotion in the Scandinavian press. Every
day I receive letters and newspaper articles, some for, some against. A copy
will be sent you very shortly; but I feel it is quite impossible that the play
should be performed in any German theatre at this time; I hardly think
they'll dare to stage it even in Scandinavia for some little while. Incidentally, it has been printed in an edition of 10,000 copies, and there is
every prospect that a new edition will be required soon"—a forecast that
was to prove sadly incorrect, though on the strength of it he had, two
days earlier, asked Hegel to invest almost the whole proceeds of the first
edition, 6,000 crowns, in gilt-edged securities at 4½ per cent.

Replying to a toast at the Scandinavian Club on 20 December, he
remarked that Christmas, which to most people brought joy and peace,
to him usually brought battle, since it was at this season that his books
appeared; but that to him battle was a joy and peace merely a breathing-
space until he could take up the struggle anew. Nevertheless, when he
added up his accounts for 1881, he must have hoped hard for that
second edition, for he had earned barely half as much as in the previous
year:

	crowns	
9th edn. of *Brand*	1,360	
Fees from German League of Dramatists, 1st quarter	29	
Fee from Thalia Theatre, Hamburg, for *"Nora"*	816	
5th edn. of *Peer Gynt*	1,320	
Fees from German League of Dramatists, 2nd quarter	26	
Fees for *"Nora"* in north German Theatres, via E. Lange	1,336	
Fees from Bergen Theatre for various performances	240	
1st edn. of *Ghosts*	6,150	
	11,277	£626

However, on 2 January 1882, he wrote in buoyant mood to Hegel: "The violent criticisms and insane attacks which people are levelling against *Ghosts* don't worry me in the least. I was expecting this. When *Love's Comedy* appeared there was just such an hysterical outcry in Norway as there is now. They moaned about *Peer Gynt* too, and *The Pillars of Society* and *A Doll's House,* just as much. The commotion will die away this time, as it did before." Only as an afterthought did he add: "One thing worries me a little when I think how big an edition you printed. Has all this fuss damaged the sales of the book?"

Hegel replied on 10 January:

Dear Dr. Ibsen,

. . . You ask: has all this to-do damaged the sales of the book? To this I must decidedly answer: Yes.

As you will know from the reviews, *Ghosts* has caused a great sensation and has been the literary event of the winter, like *A Doll's House* two years ago. This is only as one would expect. But, amazingly, there ensued almost at once great indignation at the circumstances which are portrayed in *Ghosts* and which people wish at all costs not to have in family literature. The effect of this became noticeable immediately. Of the large edition a not inconsiderable number of copies had been subscribed in advance, partly to the provinces, partly to Norway and Sweden.

From several of the booksellers outside Copenhagen, notably from Chr-a, Bergen, and Stockholm, where the papers have openly opposed the sale of the book, I have already been informed that they could not find the expected sales for *Ghosts* and have therefore asked me to take back large quantities of the book, not merely those they had on sale or return, but also some that they took on the normal terms and which should not normally be credited. In view of the need to maintain a good relationship with my colleagues I felt it wisest to make them this concession.

Here in Copenhagen the sales of *Ghosts* have been markedly smaller than those of your earlier books. And the whole business has had a damaging effect on *their* sales. I usually sell a not inconsiderable number of your works each Christmas, but this year the figures have been noticeably smaller.

I felt bound, my dear Herr Ibsen, to tell you this plainly . . .

Your most affectionate

Fr. Hegel[18]

August Lindberg has described the scene in Stockholm on the day of publication. "There was a rush to the bookshops. But the excitement vanished in silence. Absolute silence. The newspapers said nothing and the bookshops sent the book back to the publisher. It was contraband. Something which could not decently be discussed."[19] And Alexander Kielland informed Georg Brandes that Cammermeyer, the leading book-

[18] *Ibid.,* 355–56.
[19] Per Lindberg, p. 43.

shop in Christiania, had returned no less than five hundred copies to Gyldendal.[20] *Ghosts,* in short, was not a book to have about the house. It was not merely that it attacked some of the most sacred principles of the age, such as the sanctity of marriage (*A Doll's House* had done that), and the duty of a son to honour his father. Far worse, it referred unmistakably (if not by name) to venereal disease, defended free love, and suggested that under certain circumstances even incest might be justifiable. Even some of Ibsen's strongest supporters were antagonized. When Lindberg asked Ludvig Josephson, who had championed Ibsen's cause so ardently in Christiania, whether he would not consider presenting *Ghosts* at his theatre in Stockholm, Josephson refused point blank. "The play," he told Lindberg, "is one of the filthiest things ever written in Scandinavia."[21] And Erik Bøgh reported to his board at the Royal Theatre, Copenhagen, that *Ghosts* was "a repulsive pathological phenomenon which, by undermining the morality of our social order, threatens its foundations,"[22] and advised its rejection, a recommendation with which the board concurred.

It was, however, in Norway itself that *Ghosts* was attacked most violently. Ibsen had expected the conservative papers to dislike it, but he was shocked to discover that the liberal press denounced it with even greater fervour. The left-wing *Oplandenes Avis* set the tone when it declared (21 December) that "complete silence would, in our opinion, be the most fitting reception for such a work." Despite this recommendation, the reviewer went on to describe it as "the most unpleasant book we have read for a long while," drawing some comfort from the fact that it was "in our humble opinion at least, much worse written than the author's previous works." An anonymous reviewer in *Dagbladet* (14 December) wrote: "It is as though Ibsen had taken enjoyment in saying all the worst things he knew, and in saying them in the most outrageous way he could conceive." The author of these words, Arne Garborg, had, ironically, just published a story entitled "The Freethinker." The ageing Andreas Munch published a poem in *Morgenbladet* called "A Fallen Star," likening Ibsen to a star which has allowed itself to be lured down into "the region of mists," has there turned into a meteor which has buried itself in "the black earth, swollen with corpses," and lies there giving off "an evil stench of corruption." An editorial in the same paper on 18 December concluded: "The book has no place on the Christmas table of any

---

[20] *Brandes Brevveksling,* IV, 336. Kielland added interestingly that he liked *Ghosts* "less for its own sake than for the insight it gives me into this elegant, cautious, decorated, slightly snobbish person who, like Nora, has always had a secret desire to say: 'Damn and blast!' in the midst of all his elegance—and has now acquired the courage."

[21] Lindberg, p. 45.

[22] Agerholm, p. 279.

Christian home." Even such progressive writers as Jonas Lie and Alexander Kielland privately raised their eyebrows; and Henrik Jæger, who six years later was to write an admiring biography of Ibsen, lectured at Christiania University attacking the play, and toured the country repeating his opinions (which he later recanted).

A few bold spirits championed the play. Hans Jæger, later to be imprisoned for writing a supposedly pornographic novel, the young director Gunnar Heiberg, and those two formidable suffragettes Amalie Skram and Camilla Collett, all defended it in *Dagbladet;* so did Bjørnson, who, despite the recent bad friendship between him and Ibsen, praised it as "free, brave and courageous." "That is like him," wrote Ibsen to Olof Skavlan on 24 January 1882. "He has in truth a great imperial spirit, and I shall never forget this." And P. O. Schjøtt, the Professor of Greek at Christiania University, writing a year later in *Nyt Tidsskrift,* compared the play to the ancient Greek dramas:

> When the greatest tragic and comic poets of Athens presented the political, ethical and religious ideas of their age, and even their champions, on the stage, someone no doubt denounced them and called their work tendentious. But posterity saw this as quite normal practice. When the ancient art of dramatic writing stood at its zenith, in that golden age, it was this realism or, if you will, this tendentiousness, which gave it its vitality and character. . . . We generalize thus with particular reference to Ibsen's latest play. . . . For of all the modern dramas we have read, *Ghosts* comes closest to classical tragedy. . . . When the dust of ignorant criticism has subsided, which we trust will happen soon, this play of Ibsen's, with its pure, bold contours, will stand not only as his noblest deed but as the greatest work of art which he, or indeed our whole dramatic literature, has produced.

Schjøtt's last sentence was a reference to a review of the play by Georg Brandes, who, in *Morgenbladet* (the Danish, not the Norwegian newspaper of that name), had declared it to be "not the most perfect play he has written, but the noblest deed in his literary career." Brandes was almost the only Dane to come out in the play's favour; his review delighted Ibsen, and re-established good relations between the two men.

In Rome, Ibsen read the various comments with increasing indignation. "What is one to say of the attitude taken by the so-called liberal press?" he wrote to Brandes on 3 January 1881 (his first letter to Brandes for over five years). "These leaders who talk and write of freedom and progress and at the same time let themselves be the slaves of the supposed opinions of their subscribers?" Three days later he wrote to the Danish writer Sophus Schandorph: "I was prepared for some such commotion. If for nothing else, certain of our Norwegian reviewers have an undeniable talent for completely misunderstanding and misinterpreting the authors whose books they presume to judge." After protesting that the views expressed in *Ghosts* were not necessarily his own ("In none of my plays is the author so totally detached and uncommitted as in this"),[23] he went on to deny that *Ghosts* advocated nihilism. "The play is not concerned with advocating anything. It merely points to the fact that nihilism is fermenting beneath the surface in Norway as everywhere else. It is inevitable. A Pastor Manders will always incite some Mrs. Alving into being. And she, simply because she is a woman, will, once she has started, go to the ultimate extreme."

On 28 January he wrote to another Danish writer, Otto Borchsenius: "It may well be that in certain respects this play is somewhat audacious. But I thought the time had come when a few boundary marks had to be shifted. And it was much easier for me, as an elder writer, to do this than for the many younger writers who might want to do something of the kind. I was prepared for a storm to break over me; but one can't run away from such things. That would have been cowardice. What has most depressed me has been not the attacks themselves, but the lack of guts which has been revealed in the ranks of the so-called liberals in Norway. They are poor stuff with which to man the barricades."

On 8 March he wrote a letter of warm thanks to Bjørnson "for so openly and honourably standing forth in my defence at a time when I have been attacked from so many quarters. It was of course only what I would have expected from your bold warrior spirit. . . . Rest assured that I shall never forget you. I have also noticed that during your stay in America you wrote kind words in my praise. Thank you for that too. . . . I heard you were ill there, and when you were on your way home I read of storms at sea. Then I suddenly and vividly realized how immensely much you mean to me, as to all of us. I felt that if anything should happen to you it would be a great disaster for our land and I should lose all joy in creating."

So far from discouraging him from further writing, the smell of battle stimulated Ibsen. On 16 March he informed Hegel that he was "fully occupied with preparations for a new work. This time it will be a peaceful play, which cabinet ministers and wholesale merchants and their ladies will be able to read, and from which the theatres will not need to shrink. . . . As far as *Ghosts* is concerned, comprehension will seep into the minds of the good people of our country, and that in the not too distant future. But all these fading and decrepit figures who have spat upon this work will one day bring upon their heads the crushing judgement of future literary historians. . . . My book contains the future."

[23] This assertion was denounced by Strindberg in a letter to Edvard Brandes, 18 February 1882 ("Isn't Ibsen cowardly?"). But Strindberg admired the play, telling Brandes to thank his brother for the latter's defence of it, and even in 1884, when he had become violently hostile towards Ibsen, he admitted: "But he has written *Ghosts*. I mustn't hate him." (Letter to Bjørnson, 4 May 1884; *August Strindbergs brev*, II, 353; IV, 146.)

The Christiania Theatre and the Royal Theatre in Stockholm followed the example of the Royal Theatre in Copenhagen and Nya Teater in refusing to stage the play. On 20 May, however, *Ghosts* at last received its world premiere in, of all places, Chicago, where it was presented in the original language at the Aurora Turner Hall before an audience of Scandinavian immigrants with the Danish actress Helga von Bluhme as Mrs. Alving, the other parts being taken by Danish and Norwegian amateurs. This production—the first on record of any Ibsen play in America—subsequently toured Minneapolis and other cities of the Middle West which contained large Scandinavian populations. But it was to be over a year before the play was performed in Europe, and even when the scandal had died down and it was being acted before respectful audiences it was thirteen years before a new edition was required. It remained a book not to be seen about the house.

But if *Ghosts* shocked the literary and theatrical establishment of Scandinavia, it made an immediate and stimulating impact on the young. Herman Bang, then aged twenty-five, and later to become a celebrated Danish novelist and one of Ibsen's most influential pioneers in France, describes how it excited his generation even before it became a subject of scandal.

> The play was distributed to the booksellers towards evening. The keenest buyers ran out in the dark to get it. That evening I visited a young actor who had just read *Ghosts*. . . . "This," he said, "is the greatest play our age will see." The debate had already started by the next morning. An extraordinary number of people seemed to have read the play that night. . . . One or two restless people who had nothing to lose, having no good name to be smeared by associations with *Ghosts*, gave public readings. People flocked to the obscure places where these readings took place, out by the bridges, far into the suburbs. A group of unwanted actors determined to take it on tour. They wanted to act the play in the provinces.[24]

But, Bang adds, "good society knew its duty," and the project had to be abandoned. Nevertheless, it "was performed semi-privately, in I know not what impossible places," and all but achieved a professional production in Copenhagen within weeks of publication, for Theodor Andersen, the head of the Casino Theatre, "read it twenty times before finally rejecting it."[25]

In Germany, once the play had been published (which did not happen until 1884), the same pattern was repeated. Bang was in Germany then and tells of a performance of *A Doll's House* at Meiningen, with the celebrated actress Marie Ramlo as guest artist. The theatre was full of young students.

[24] Herman Bang, *Teatret* (Copenhagen, 1892), pp. 239–40; cf. also Skavlan, p. 105.
[25] Bang, pp. 230–31.

Frau Ramlo was excellent, but it was not she who held their attention. The young people barely heard her. They read when the curtain was down, and they read when the curtain was up. They read furtively and amazed, as though fearful, read, as the book was passed secretly from hand to hand, a little, humble, yellow, paperbound volume of a hundred pages bearing the title *Gespenster* [*Ghosts*]. What a strange evening when all those hundreds of young people read as one the play about the sins of their fathers, and when, as a drama about marriage was being acted behind the footlights, that other drama of parents and their children forced its way up from the auditorium on to the stage. They did not dare to read the book at home, and so they read it secretly here.[26]

Bang adds that young actors and actresses used *Ghosts* as an audition piece long before it was allowed to be played in Germany (in 1886, and then only privately), and that "young beginners acted the play secretly in suburban halls far out on the fringes of civilization, as in Norway."[27]

Ibsen's contemporaries saw *Ghosts* primarily as a play about physical illness, just as they had seen *A Doll's House* primarily as a play about women's rights. With few exceptions, they failed to realize that the true subject of *Ghosts* is the devitalizing effect of a dumb acceptance of convention. As Halvdan Koht has written: "Oswald is branded with disease, not because his father was a beast, but because Mrs. Alving had obeyed the immoral ethics of society"[28]—in other words, *Ghosts* is a play about ethical, not physical debility. The importance of waging war against the past, the need for each individual to find his or her own freedom, the danger of renouncing love in the name of duty—these are the real themes of *Ghosts*, as they are the themes of every play Ibsen wrote from *A Doll's House* onwards. And the targets are the same as those he had attacked in *A Doll's House* and, before that, in *The Pillars of Society*, and which he was to go on attacking until the end of his life—the hollowness of great reputations, provincialism of outlook, the narrow and inhibiting effect of small-town life, the suppression of individual freedom from within as well as from without, and the neglect of the significance of heredity—a problem much discussed among the Scandinavians in Rome, one of whom, the botanist and novelist J. P. Jacobsen, has translated Darwin's *Origin of Species* and *The Descent of Man* into Danish. Zola, of course, had hastened to exploit Darwin's thesis that man, like other animals, must adapt himself to the environment in which he lives; but Ibsen hated

[26] *Ibid.*, p. 240.

[27] *Ibid.*, p. 241.

[28] Koht, II, 118. In view of the oft-repeated complaint that syphilis cannot be inherited from one's father, it is worth pointing out that it can be inherited from one's mother, and that a woman can have syphilis without realizing it or suffering any particular discomfort. In other words, and this is a far more frightening explanation of Oswald's illness than the usual one, Mrs. Alving could have caught syphilis from her husband and passed it on to her son. Dr. Jonathan Miller has pointed out to me that Oswald could also have been infected by smoking his father's pipe. Ibsen knew more about medicine than some of his critics.

being compared with Zola, for whom he had a low regard. "Zola," he once remarked, "descends into the sewer to bathe in it; I, to cleanse it."[29]

How much Ibsen had actually read of Zola is not clear. In 1882 he told William Archer he had read nothing, but in 1898 he informed a Swedish journalist he had "read much of him, though not his great cycle of novels," and described him as "clearly and beyond doubt a great talent." But this was during his seventieth birthday celebrations, when he was being polite about everybody. Zola's opinion of Ibsen seems to have been equally ambiguous. He was largely responsible for the first French production of him in 1891, by reminding Antoine of *Ghosts* (Antoine had thought of doing it, but had dropped the idea; Zola had read an essay by Jacques Saint-Cères in the *Revue de l'Art Dramatique* describing Ibsen as a naturalist, and felt he had found a fellow-warrior).[30] On the other hand, when asked his opinion of the influence of Ibsen on the French stage (and of Tolstoy on the French novel), Zola is said to have "replied that he did not attach much importance to the question, for he held that the ideas which were supposed to rain on Paris from the north were in reality French ones which had been disseminated by French writers and had come back to their place of origin, occasionally crystallized or intensified by the more sombre imagination of Scandinavian or Russian writers."[31] The legend of Ibsen's supposed debt to Scribe, Dumas *fils,* George Sand, and the rest died hard.

Ibsen never liked admitting that any of his plays owed a debt to any other writer, protesting that in any age writers tended to find similar themes. As Professor Francis Bull has remarked,[32] however, the similarities between *Ghosts* and a *conte* entitled "The Daughter" by the Norwegian writer Mauritz Hansen published half a century earlier are so striking that it is difficult not to believe that, consciously or unconsciously, Ibsen must have used the latter as a starting-point. "The Daughter" tells how a dissipated lieutenant-colonel, formidably named Hannibal Hedebrandt, has in his youth had an affair with his maid, Else. Then he meets a lady of his own station but, on discovering that Else is with child, marries her off to a caretaker. Else goes mad and dies, but her daughter Henriette grows up in the Hedebrandt household; she is repelled by her supposed father, the caretaker, who has a wooden leg. It is of course perfectly possible, and I think likely, that Ibsen had read this story in his youth and forgotten it, and that certain details had forced themselves up out of his unconscious—possibly assisted by his memories of his own illegitimate child by a servant-maid likewise named Else.

[29] Erik Lie, *Jonas Lie, en livsskildring* (Oslo, 1933), p. 169, quoting Georg Pauli.

[30] Cf. Antoine's diaries, quoted by H. Gregersen, *Ibsen in Spain* (Cambridge, Mass., 1936), pp. 20–21.

[31] Cf. William Archer, *Ibsen as I Knew Him,* p. 8; Kela Nyholm, "Henrik Ibsen på den franske scene," in *Obsen-Årbok, 1957–1959* (Skien, 1959), p. 26; E. A. Vizetelly, *Emile Zola, Novelist and Reformer* (London, 1904), p. 389.

[32] C.E., IX, 20.

The character of Manders, as has been noted, was immediately motivated by Ibsen's indignation at the Norwegian Ecclesiastical Department's
treatment of his son. Regina was based on a maid whom the Ibsens had
had in Munich; she was of Bavarian birth, but had spent some time in
Paris, and incorporated various French expressions in the high German
she used when speaking to Ibsen and Suzannah, though among her friends
she talked the Bavarian dialect. Mrs. Alving is not unlike a portrait of
what Nora might have become had she decided to stay with her husband
and children, and one wonders whether her creation may not have been
partly inspired by that "happy ending" which Ibsen had found himself
compelled to write for *A Doll's House*. Like Nora, Mrs. Alving is strangled
by convention and a misplaced sense of duty. "I *had* to write *Ghosts*,"
Ibsen told the Swedish Countess Sophie Adlersparre in a letter of 24
June 1882. "I couldn't stop at *A Doll's House;* after Nora, I had to create
Mrs. Alving." Viewed in this context, Oswald's syphilis may be regarded as
a symbol of the dead customs and traditions which stunt and cripple us
and lay waste our life.

Ghosts has been described by many critics, following Schjøtt, as the most
classically constructed of Ibsen's plays, not merely in its obedience to the
Aristotelian unities but in the economy of its construction. That is not
quite true; it is in fact, along with *The Pillars of Society* and *An Enemy
of the People* and, though this may surprise some, *The Wild Duck,* one of
the most cuttable plays he wrote. Manders in particular has a good deal of
superfluous dialogue; his is much the longest part in the play, and
represents one of the very few examples, if not indeed the only one, of
Ibsen allowing his personal feelings to get out of hand to the extent of
unbalancing his composition. It is particularly important in performance
that he should be played straight, not as a caricature, and that he should
be a handsome man; otherwise Mrs. Alving's youthful infatuation with him
becomes hard to believe. Nor should his verbosity and pomposity be
exaggerated; he has not much more of either than many a modern bishop
or politician.

In one important technical respect *Ghosts* anticipates the later plays,
and that is in the density of its dialogue. *The Pillars of Society* and
A Doll's House are both simply written (and comparatively easy to
translate), because for most of the time the characters say what they mean.
But in *Ghosts,* Mrs. Alving and Manders especially spend much of the
time circling round a subject to which they dread referring directly, and
at these moments the dialogue is oblique, sometimes even opaque. This
double-density dialogue, when the characters say one thing and mean
another, was to be one of Ibsen's most important contributions to the
technique of prose drama. He knew that when people talk about something concerning which they feel a sense of guilt, they cease to speak directly
and instead talk evasively and with circumlocution; and actors, when
they are playing these lines, have to speak the text but act the sub-text,

the unspoken thoughts between the lines. One of the greatest problems that faces a translator of Ibsen is to convey this meaning behind the meaning; if this is not indicated (as Ibsen himself indicates it) it is practically impossible for an actor to convey that sense of guilt and evasion from which almost all of Ibsen's major characters suffer, and which is so often at crises the mainspring of their actions, or their failure to act.

Historically, *Ghosts* occupies a position of immense importance. Julius Hoffory remarked in 1888 that much of its effect on Ibsen's contemporaries was due to the fact that here was a play comparable to those of Aeschylus and Sophocles, but about modern people;[33] a fact easily forgotten by us, to whom it is as much a costume play as the *Agamemnon*. *Ghosts* was the first great tragedy written about middle-class people in plain, everyday prose. *Danton's Death* and *Woyzeck* are composed in a high-flown prose which frequently, and splendidly, overlaps the frontier of poetry; and while other playwrights had attempted to do what Ibsen achieved in *Ghosts*, none had succeeded. Time has not dulled its impact (though it sometimes, in England and America at any rate, suffers from being publicised as "the play which shocked our grandfathers"). Indeed, it gains enormously by not having, as so often in the last century, a declamatory and melodramatic Mrs. Alving. Ibsen's plays needed, and helped to nurture, a new kind of player with the strength of restraint, life-size, not Wagnerian. Bernhardt and Henry Irving rejected his works; Duse embraced them.

In March 1934 James Joyce saw a performance of *Ghosts* in Paris. The fact that one of Captain Alving's children was a wreck and the other (Regina) healthy intrigued him, and the following month the problem inspired one of his wittiest poems:

EPILOGUE TO IBSEN'S *Ghosts*

Dear quick, whose conscience buried deep
The grim old grouser has been salving,
Permit one spectre more to peep.
I am the ghost of Captain Alving.

Silenced and smothered by my past
Like the lewd knight in dirty linen
I struggle forth to swell the cast
And air a long-suppressed opinion.

For muddling weddings into wakes
No fool could vie with Pastor Manders.
I, though a dab at ducks and drakes,
Let gooseys serve or sauce their ganders.

[33] *Tilskueren* (Copenhagen, 1888), pp. 61–70.

My spouse bore me a blighted boy,
Our slavey pupped a bouncing bitch.
Paternity, thy name is joy
When the wise sire knows which is which.

Both swear I am that self-same man
By whom their infants were begotten.
Explain, fate, if you care and can
Why one is sound and one is rotten.

Olaf may plod his stony path
And live as chastely as Susanna
Yet pick up in some Turkish bath
His *quantum est* of *Pox Romana*,

While Haakon hikes up primrose way,
Spreeing and gleeing while he goes,
To smirk upon his latter day
Without a pimple on his nose.

I give it up I am afraid
But if I loafed and found it fun
Remember how a coyclad maid
Knows how to take it out of one.

The more I dither on and drink
My midnight bowl of spirit punch
The firmlier I feel and think
Friend Manders came too oft to lunch.

Since scuttling ship Vikings like me
Reck not to whom the blame is laid,
Y.M.C.A., V.D., T.B.,
Or Harbourmaster of Port-Said.

Blame all and none and take to task
The harlot's lure, the swain's desire.
Heal by all means but hardly ask
Did this man sin or did his sire.

The shack's ablaze. That canting scamp,
The carpenter, has dished the parson.
Now had they kept their powder damp
Like me there would have been no arson.

Nay, more, were I not all I was,
Weak, wanton, waster out and out,
There would have been no world's applause
And damn all to write home about.

21

An Enemy of the People

1882

During the winter of 1881–82, when the hubbub about *Ghosts* was at its height, Ibsen met for the first time his energetic new Scottish champion. Young William Archer had been ordered south for his health, and after walking from Cannes to Leghorn he proceeded by train to Rome. One of his first objects there was, naturally, to secure an introduction to the author whose work he so admired, and he described the meeting in a letter to his brother Charles, written in December 1881:

> The great event has come off, satisfactorily, but not in the manner I expected. . . . I had been about a quarter of an hour there [at the Scandinavian Club], and was standing close to the door, when it opened and in walked unmistakably the great Henrik. My photograph is very good as far as the face is concerned, but it gives you the idea of broader shoulders and a fuller chest than he really has. He is of middle height, rather under than over —at any rate in talking to him I feel noticeably taller. [Archer stood around six feet.] . . . He went around for a while talking to different people, and gave you the impression, which I was prepared for, of extreme quietness. The red ribbon which excited young [*sic*] Bjørnson's contempt was very prominent in his buttonhole. After a while I got Professor Ravnkilde [the Danish composer and chairman of the club] to introduce me to him. I saw at once that he did not connect my name with *Samfundets Støtter* [*The Pillars of Society*], so after a little I told him about it. He had heard of the production, but not my name, and took my rather lame excuses for not having got his permission very readily. . . . He invited me to call at his house, which I shall do some day this week; and besides, I shall see him again at the [club], when I hope to get a little more under the surface, if it is at all possible. . . . He does not read any of the French dramatists, and moreover he hardly ever goes to the theatre—and small blame to him in Italy, say I, though he says there are some very good Italian actors, besides the famous ones. Altogether, the interview was a success. Though I can't say that L's description of him as a

spidsborger [*petit bourgeois*] is quite justified, he certainly is not the man you would imagine to have written Aase's death-scene and the fourth act of *Brand* . . . . At first sight there is an absence of anything Titanic about him. . . . However, for the present "the old min's friendly," and that's the main point.[1]

A few weeks later Archer wrote to J. M. Robertson that he was seeing Ibsen "almost every day at a café which he and I both frequent for an afternoon glass of vermouth, and I have a yarn with him occasionally."[2] This was the Café Nazionale at the corner of the Corso and the Via della Mercede. Ibsen must have liked Archer, for he invited him to his home, which Archer found "comfortable, yet comfortless . . . well furnished, but with no air of home about it. . . . His writing room was very bare and painfully orderly."[3] When Archer left Rome on 4 March Ibsen gave him an inscribed photograph; and when he returned in April, "the old min was not only friendly but effusive."[4] Archer wrote an article entitled "Henrik Ibsen at Home in the Via Capo le Case" and offered it to Edmund Yates, the editor of *The World* (a periodical of which Archer was to be the dramatic critic for twenty-one years); but Yates (who had once been the occasion of a quarrel between Dickens and Thackeray) rejected it, it was never published and, sadly, it had not survived among Archer's papers.

A Danish scholar, Harald Høffding, also met Ibsen for the first time that winter. "He looked almost like a boatswain; broad and big-boned, brown in the face, he sat motionless and with half-closed eyes." When he met him again ten years later Høffding received a very different impression, of "an elegant little man." "*À deux,*" he added, "Ibsen was very loquacious, though he avoided any discussion of his writings."[5] Georg Pauli confirms this last point; whenever anyone tried to probe Ibsen about his plays, Pauli says he would reply with a question, such as: "How long have you been in Rome, madam?"—"Did you have a good journey?" etc.[6] And Fritz von Dardel, whom he had met at the Vienna Exhibition and who was now in Rome, confirms Høffding's impression of the new darkness of Ibsen's complexion, though he implies another cause than sun. "He has fattened," noted Dardel in his diary, "and has developed a high facial colour. To any query why he did not have his son educated in Norway, he replied, 'Because he can have a pleasanter life almost anywhere else.' "[7]

On 18 February 1882, Ibsen had written a second letter to H. E. Berner,

---

[1] Charles Archer, pp. 101–2.
[2] *Ibid.*, p. 104.
[3] William Archer, "Ibsen as I Knew Him," p. 7.
[4] Charles Archer, p. 113.
[5] Harald Høffding, *Erindringer* (Copenhagen, 1928), pp. 159–61.
[6] Pauli, pp. 115–16.
[7] Dardel, *Dagboksanteckningar, 1881–1885*, p. 86.

the Member of Parliament whom he had asked the previous March to try to get his and Bjørnson's pensions raised. Berner had replied that April asking for fuller details of the losses Ibsen had incurred through the absence of copyright protection. Ibsen, strangely and, as it turned out, perhaps fatally, delayed replying for ten months; but his letter gives some interesting details and underlines his predicament:

> . . . In Finland many, indeed most of my plays have been translated and played in Swedish as well as in Finnish.
>
> In Russia I know for sure that at any rate *The League of Youth* has been translated and played. I learn from newspaper notices that the same is to be true of *A Doll's House.*[8]
>
> The last-named play has also been translated into Polish and played in Warsaw. Some years ago a translation of my volume of poems appeared there too, but since this was much cut by the Russian censor a completely new edition was arranged, printed and published in Cracow, i.e. on Austrian soil.
>
> *The Vikings at Helgeland* has been translated into and played in Hungarian. I hear the same is true of *A Doll's House,* or anyway a production is being considered.
>
> In England there exist two translations of the last-named play.[9] *The Pillars of Society* has also been translated into English and performed in London.
>
> It can be stated with fair certainty that there exist in various countries translations of my plays which have not come to my knowledge. Naturally I have received nothing for any of the above-mentioned translations and performances.
>
> Regarding my literary affairs in Germany, I shall permit myself the following brief summary.
>
> *The Vikings at Helgeland* was translated at my expense by Emma Klingenfeld, and printed and published likewise at my expense, and without my receiving any payment, by Theodor Ackermann in Munich, who as agent also takes fifty per cent of the income from copies sold. The German booksellers dare not publish Norwegian plays in the normal ways since thanks to the lack of any copyright agreement they cannot be protected against other translations appearing in competition.
>
> *Lady Inger of Østraat* has been translated and published on the same terms as *The Vikings at Helgeland.*
>
> *The Pillars of Society* likewise.

[8] Ibsen's information was out-of-date. Helena Modjeska had already played *A Doll's House* in St. Petersburg (in Polish) the previous November. She played it in Warsaw in February 1882, the month Ibsen wrote this letter.

[9] Weber's unfortunate version and a slightly (but not much) better one by Henrietta Frances Lord, published in London early in 1882.

This play has besides been translated by Wilhelm Lange in Berlin, who on his own account has had it performed at many German theatres and has also published it through Ph. Reclam in Leipzig in his "Universalbibliothek." Lange's translation sells at 2 pfennigs, whereas mine, which is decently produced, costs 2 reichsmarks and therefore enjoys only a small sale. Hr. Emil Jonas has also published an "adaptation" of the play, which likewise is printed in a bargain edition and is played in many places in Germany.

The League of Youth has been translated by Adolf Strodtmann in Berlin and published by Duncker there. This publication has nothing to do with me and of course brings me nothing.

Another translation of this play has been published by W. Lange and similarly brings me nothing.

The Pretenders has been translated by Adolf Strodtmann and published, like the *The League of Youth*. All performing fees for these go exclusively to the translator. . . ."

Moreover, Ibsen adds, many German theatres will not act his plays because he cannot grant them exclusive rights, so that they cannot be sure that it will not be staged simultaneously or even earlier at another theatre in the same town. For the same reason, such theatres as do accept them dare not risk spending as much as they might on decor, etc., because they cannot expect so many performances. As regards Scandinavia, he reckons to have lost 3,000 crowns on *The League of Youth* and *The Vikings at Helgeland* in Sweden, because he got only *ex gratia* payments instead of what he would have received had Norway been a signatory of the copyright pact. By contrast, as a result of the agreement with Denmark, he had received 9,000 crowns from the Royal Theatre in Copenhagen for *A Doll's House,* whereas from *The Pillars of Society* and *The Vikings at Helgeland* he got only 2,000 crowns apiece, and from *The League of Youth* and *The Pretenders* only 1,200 crowns each, although all these four plays had had about as many performances as *A Doll's House.* In all, he reckons to have lost about 21,600 crowns in Danish performing fees alone prior to the signing of the agreement. "Think," he concludes, "what Bjørnson and I could have got had an agreement been in force with Germany, which has a hundred and fifty theatres!"

But his letter was too late. By the time Berner received it he had, on 1 February, put his motion before the Storthing, and they had rejected it.

On 2 June 1882, a fortnight after the Chicago premiere of *Ghosts,* the first American production in English of an Ibsen play took place, though he might have had difficulty in recognizing it as his. The place was Milwaukee and the play *A Doll's House,* re-entitled *The Child Wife,* and freely adapted from the German by a schoolmaster named William M. Lawrence. Lawrence set the play in England, introducing an Irish widow to give the play some humour, and of course using the happy ending. In the second act, one of Nora's (or, as Lawrence called her, Eva's) children sang a pretty song, which the audience enjoyed so much that she had to repeat it. "Love is the theme," noted one reviewer, "yet not a line of the play is impure." Another critic named Lawrence as the author, while a third referred to the *play* as "Henry Ibsen."[10]

Meanwhile, during that spring and early summer of 1882, while the storm over *Ghosts* still raged, Ibsen went ahead with his new play, which progressed with unwonted speed. No working notes or preliminary draft has survived, so we do not know, as we do for most of his plays, how long he took to write each act, or what alterations he made from his original conception; but on 21 June he was able to inform Hegel: "Yesterday I completed my new dramatic work. It is entitled *An Enemy of the People,* and is in five acts. I am still a little uncertain whether to call it a comedy or simply a play; it has much of the character of a comedy, but there is also a serious basic theme." At the beginning of August he left Rome for Gossensass, whence on 9 September he posted the fair copy of the final act to Hegel. "It has been fun," he wrote, "working on this play, and I feel a sense of emptiness and deprivation at being parted from it. Dr. Stockmann and I got on most excellently; we agree about so many things; but the Doctor has a more muddled head on his shoulders than I have, and has besides certain characteristics which will permit people to tolerate things from his lips which they might not accept so readily had they issued from mine. If you have begun to read the manuscript, I think you will share this opinion."

The speed with which Ibsen completed *An Enemy of the People,* without the usual eighteen months of cud-chewing ("He has never been so quick before!" commented Georg Brandes to Alexander Kielland on 30 June),[11] suggests that this must have been the work he had conceived and pondered before putting it aside for *Ghosts,* as described in his letters to Hegel of 12 November 1880 and 22 March 1881. Moreover, Lorentz Dietrichson and Kristofer Janson both record earlier conversations with Ibsen in which he expressed many of the opinions which he was to put into Dr. Stockmann's mouth. On New Year's Eve, 1880, Janson noted in his diary:

> Today Ibsen and I discussed French politics, especially the expulsion of the monks from their monasteries. Ibsen deplored this greatly, and said: "Haven't I always said that you republicans are the worst tyrants of all? You don't respect individual freedom. Republicanism is the form of government in which individual freedom has the least chance of being respected. . . . What is the majority? The ignorant mass. Intelligence always belongs to the minority. How many of the majority do you think are entitled to hold any opinion? The only people I have any real sympathy with are the socialists and nihilists. They want something whole-heartedly and are consistent.[12]

[10] Einar Haugen, "Ibsen i Amerika," in *Edda* (1935), pp. 553 ff.
[11] *Brandes Brevveksling,* IV, 345.
[12] Janson, pp. 78–80.

And Dietrichson recalled: "The ideas which he expressed in *An Enemy of the People* were already fully developed by the spring of 1881 and were aired in almost every conversation we had at that time."[13]

The reception of *Ghosts* in Norway had brought Ibsen's distrust of popular opinion and contemporary liberalism to the boil. "What is one to say of the attitude taken by the so-called liberal press?" he had written to Georg Brandes on 3 January 1882. "These leaders who talk and write of freedom and progress, and at the same time allow themselves to be the slaves of the supposed opinions of their subscribers? I become more and more convinced that there is something demoralizing about involving oneself in politics and attaching oneself to a party. Under no circumstances will I ever link myself with any party which has the majority behind it. Bjørnson says: 'The majority is always right.' As a practising politician I suppose he has to say that. But I say: 'The minority is always right.' I am of course not thinking of the minority of reactionaries who have been left astern by the big central party which we call liberal; I mean the minority which forges ahead in territory which the majority has not yet reached. I believe that he is right who is most closely attuned to the future. . . . For me freedom is the first condition of life, and the highest. At home people don't bother much about freedom but only about freedoms—a few more or a few less, according to the party standpoint. I feel most painfully affected by this vulgarity, this plebeianism in our public attitude. In the course of their undeniably worthy efforts to turn our country into a democratic community, people have unwittingly gone a good way towards turning us into a mob community. The aristocracy of the intellect seems to be in short supply in Norway."[14]

Later the same month (24 January) he had written on similar lines to Olaf Skavlan: "I myself am responsible for what I write, and I alone. I cannot possibly embarrass any party, for I belong to none. I want to act as a lone *franc-tireur* in the outposts, and operate on my own. . . . Is it only in the political field that men are to be allowed to work for freedom in Norway? Is it not first and foremost man's spirit that needs to be set free? Such spiritual slaves as we are cannot even use the freedom we already have. Norway is a free country inhabited by serfs." These words, like those written to Brandes, are precisely in the mood and manner of Dr. Stockmann.

An Enemy of the People tells the story of a doctor at a small spa who

---

[13] Dietrichson, I, 362.

[14] Several of the phrases Ibsen used in this letter recur in *An Enemy of the People*. "When my new play reaches you," he wrote to Brandes on 21 September 1882, shortly after finishing it, "you will perhaps be able to understand what interest and, I may add, fun it has given me to recall the many scattered and casual remarks I have made in my letters to you." Didrik Grønvold recalls that Ibsen had spoken to him of the necessity of having an aristocracy to educate a nation as early as 1877 in Munich (*Diktere og musikere*, p. 12).

discovers that the Baths, on which the livelihood of the town depends, are contaminated. At first the locals praise him as a public benefactor, but when they learn that the baths will have to be closed for several years and their income affected, they turn against him and, when he calls a meeting to put his views to them, brand him as an enemy of the people. In this famous fourth act, Dr. Stockmann utters many of the opinions Ibsen himself had been expressing in Rome:

"I can't stand politicians! I've had all I can take of them! They're like goats in a plantation of young trees! They destroy everything! . . ."

"The most dangerous enemies of truth and freedom are the majority! Yes, the solid, liberal, bloody majority—they're the ones we have to fear! . . . Who form the majority in any country? The wise, or the fools? I think we'd all have to agree that the fools are in a terrifying, overwhelming majority all over the world! But in the name of God it can't be right that the fools should rule the wise! Yes, yes, you can shout me down. But you can't say I'm wrong! The majority has the power, unfortunately—but the majority is not right! The ones who are right are a few isolated individuals like me. The minority is always right! . . ."

"I'm not so forgiving as a certain person. I don't say: 'I forgive ye, for ye know not what ye do!'"

Dr. Stockmann's first reaction as his daughter is sacked, his patients refuse to employ him, and the mob breaks his windows is to take his wife and children away; but he finally decides to stay and try to re-educate the townspeople, beginning with the lowest and poorest:

DR. STOCKMANN. . . . I'm going to experiment with mongrels for once. They've good heads on them sometimes.

EILIF. But what shall we do when we've become free men and aristocrats?

DR. STOCKMANN. Then, my boys, you'll chase all those damned politicians into the Atlantic Ocean!

MRS. STOCKMANN. Let's hope it won't be the politicians who'll chase you out, Thomas.

DR. STOCKMANN. Are you quite mad, Catherine? Chase me out? Now, when I am the strongest man in town?

MRS. STOCKMANN. The strongest—now?

DR. STOCKMANN. Yes! I'll go further! I am one of the strongest men in the whole world. . . . Hush! You mustn't talk about it yet. But I've made a great discovery!

MRS. STOCKMANN. Not again!

DR. STOCKMANN. Yes—yes! (*Gathers them round him and whispers to them.*) The fact is, you see, that the strongest man in the world is he who stands most alone.

The plot of *An Enemy of the People* had its origin in two actual incidents. Alfred Meisner, a young German poet whom Ibsen knew in Munich, had told him how, when his father had been medical officer at the spa of Teiplitz in the eighteen-thirties, there had occurred an outbreak of cholera which the doctor felt it his duty to make known publicly. As a result the season was ruined and the citizens of Teiplitz became so enraged that they stoned the doctor's house and forced him to flee the town.

Then there had been the case in Norway of a chemist named Harald Thaulow. For nearly ten years Thaulow had furiously attacked the Christiania Steam Kitchens for neglecting their duty towards the city's poor. He had delivered a violent speech on the subject in 1874, during Ibsen's visit to Norway; and on 23 February 1881, only a fortnight before he died, Thaulow had attempted to read a prepared speech at the annual general meeting of the Steam Kitchens. The chairman of the meeting tried to prevent him from speaking, and eventually the public forced him, amid commotion, to withdraw. Ibsen read a report of this meeting in *Aftenposten* (24 February), just at the time when his indignation at the reception of *Ghosts* was reaching its climax, and he must have recognized in the eccentric old chemist a spirit very kindred to his own. The newspaper account is worth quoting:

THAULOW. I will not stop, you have no right to stop me, Mr Chairman. (*Continues*). Point number ten—

CONSUL HEFTYE. Mr Thaulow must be stopped!

THAULOW *continues. Several of the public show their displeasure by walking about the hall.* THE CHAIRMAN *asks the meeting whether they recognize his right to bar* MR THAULOW *from the floor. Unanimous "Ayes."* THE CHAIRMAN *again asks* MR THAULOW *to stop reading.*

THAULOW. I will not be silenced.

THE CHAIRMAN. In that case, I shall—

THAULOW. I'll keep it quite short. (*Reads on.*)

CONSUL HEFTYE. Is he to be allowed to continue?

THAULOW (*continues reading*). The glorious achievements of the Christiania Steam Kitchens— I'll soon be through.

CONSUL HEFTYE. If this goes on the meeting can't continue.

CHAIRMAN. I regret that I must interrupt Mr Thaulow. You have not the floor—

THAULOW *reads on.*

CONSUL HEFTYE. Be quiet, or you'll be thrown out.

THAULOW. Oh, very well.

THAULOW *sits down at last. After* THE CHAIRMAN *had read his report for some minutes—*

THAULOW. . . . It's too much. It's no use trying to oppose the mob—

CONSUL HEFTYE. Did the Chairman hear Mr Thaulow refer to us as the mob? . . .

At length MR THAULOW *left the meeting in a rage, saying:* I'll have no more to do with you. I won't cast my pearls into the sand. This is a damned insult being inflicted on a free people in a free society. Now I'll go! Stand in the dunce's corner and be ashamed of yourselves!

As with *The Pillars of Society,* an English Member of Parliament may also have contributed something to the play. Charles Bradlaugh, having narrowly escaped imprisonment for his part in a pamphlet advocating birth control (he had actually been sentenced, but had escaped on appeal), had been elected Radical M.P. for Northampton in 1880, but had been barred from taking his seat on the ground that, since he was a confessed free-thinker, the oath would not bind him. New elections were held in Northampton, and he was returned each time, but was still excluded; in 1881, he was forcibly removed from the house by ten policemen. It was not until 1886 that a new speaker granted him the right to take the oath and sit.

"You should hear Ibsen on Bradlaugh—he has the most vivid sympathy for him," wrote William Archer to his brother Charles on 14 March 1882, when Ibsen was about to start writing *An Enemy of the People;* and Bradlaugh has an obvious deal in common with Dr. Stockmann. So, it has often been pointed out, do Bjørnson and Jonas Lie, both intellectually confused, warm-hearted, eloquent and impatient men, with strong family feelings and an infinite capacity for moral indignation. But, as Ibsen hinted in his letter to Hegel of 9 September 1882, he himself was probably the chief model for the character, at any rate in Act Four; and it is worth remembering that the house in Skien in which Ibsen had been born had been called Stockmannsgaarden.

After posting the final pages to Hegel on 9 September, Ibsen remained for a month in Gossensass, staying, as he was to do on future occasions, at the friendly Gröbner family hotel. While there he received, and granted, a request from America for the right to translate and publish *The Pillars of Society, A Doll's House* and *Ghosts.* The request came from Rasmus B. Anderson, Professor of Scandinavian Languages at the University of Wisconsin, who that year published a review of *Brand* in the *Literary World* and an essay on Ibsen in *The American,* the first articles about him to appear in America apart from Bjørnson's panegyric. Anderson was to supervise the project, and Ibsen, in his reply of 14 September, begged him to see that "the language of the translation be kept as close as possible to ordinary everyday speech; all the turns of phrase and expressions which belong only to books should most carefully be avoided in dramatic works, especially mine, which aim to produce in the reader or spectator a feeling that he is, during the reading or performance, witnessing a slice of real life."

It was advice that many of his translators, recent as well as contemporary, would have done well to heed. But these translations, if completed, never appeared—fortunately, since the translator was that William M. Lawrence who had been responsible for the travestied version of *A Doll's House* produced in Milwaukee. Henrietta Frances Lord's version of *A Doll's House* was published by Dutton's of New York the same year; *The Pillars of Society* and *An Enemy of the People* had to wait until 1888.

On 9 October (the snow must have come later than usual to Gossensass that year) Ibsen left Gossensass and moved south to the little town of Brixen, where he put up at the Hotel Elefant, "the best hotel in the Tyrol," as he described it to Hegel on 28 October. He had intended to stay there only briefly, but heavy floods cut the roads and railways to the south, and it was not until 24 November that he was able to return to Rome.

When he got there he found an unpleasant surprise awaiting him. John Paulsen had published with Gyldendal a novel called *The Pehrsen Family*, and one can only suppose that Frederik Hegel had (as with *Brand*) not read the manuscript before sending it to press or in proof. The book deals with a middle-aged couple and their only son. The father, a self-made tradesman, is short, domineering, emotionally buttoned-up, contemptuous of his country, and obsessed by a secret passion to gain a medal, an end towards which he has done some careful lobbying. He has a drunken old father of whom he is ashamed, and walks with his hands behind his back. As a young man, he had been very poor and taken refuge in alcohol, and there had been a whip-round among his acquaintances to help him out. His wife, an avid novel-reader whose "weak health had been broken in the struggle with this hard man," had seen him through this crisis; the lower he had sunk, the higher she had risen; Paulsen calls her "Murillo's Madonna," the painting named by Ibsen in his poem "In the Gallery." Pehrsen becomes prosperous and tries to be aristocratic (Paulsen uses the adjective *fornem* which had begun to recur somewhat frequently in Ibsen's letters and conversation, and which is held up as an ideal by Dr. Stockmann in *An Enemy of the People*). But the humiliations which he suffered in youth have left him with a feeling of inferiority from which he cannot escape. The son dreams of a diplomatic career, and the family emigrates to Rome (of whose social life Paulsen paints a lively picture). The book has Paulsen's usual virtues and defects; it is extremely readable (even today), written with an eye for detail and a sense of atmosphere, and ends the way his books usually end, in rubbishy and unconvincing melodrama.

It seems inconceivable that Paulsen did not intend to portray the Ibsens, or that he could have been unconscious that his readers would assume them to be the originals; it also seems extraordinary that he could have wished to libel a man whom he genuinely admired and who had been particularly kind to him. Yet perhaps Paulsen was being no more naïve than Ibsen had been in assuming that Bjørnson would not be offended by *The League of Youth*. He wrote Ibsen a letter assuring him that he had intended no harm, to which Ibsen replied with an open card addressed care of the Scandinavian Club and bearing the one word "Scoundrel!" with his signature. And that was the end of that friendship.

An Enemy of the People was published on 28 November 1882, in an edition (despite the calamitous sales of *Ghosts*) of ten thousand copies. Its reception was mixed. Not surprisingly, Dr. Stockmann's hard remarks about political parties offended all the reviewers who belonged to either; a contemporary cartoon (in *Vikingen,* on 9 December) showed Ibsen chastising first the Liberals to the delight of the Tories, then the Tories to the delight of the Liberals, and finally, in the person of Dr. Stockmann, both together. Henrik Jæger, fresh from lecturing against *Ghosts* round the country, declared in *Aftenposten* (4, 5, and 6 December) that *An Enemy of the People* was "personally the most likable, psychologically the most interesting, and æsthetically the weakest of Ibsen's plays." Arne Garborg, in *Nyt Tidsskrift* (1882, pp. 571–81) praised its technique but complained that "there is a great deal of violent swearing," and that the public meeting in Act Four, which evidently nettled him, was "rather detached and distant, almost as though portrayed from some other age but in a modern setting." Erik Vullum in *Dagbladet* (29 and 30 November and 1 December) objected that, just as Bjørnson had been going round the country "and even in America," holding meetings to proclaim his convictions about truth and justice, so "now Ibsen comes and does exactly the same; he holds public meetings from town to town, and the public has to pay to attend them."

Danish liberal circles were very cool. Edvard Brandes, greatly piqued, began his review in *Dansk Morgenbladet* (7 December) by calling it "a disappointment," sharply criticized several of Dr. Stockmann's remarks, and ended by characterising the play as "a mere dramatized newspaper article written in answer to some poor newspaper scribblings [i.e., the attacks upon *Ghosts*] which weren't worth a ha'porth of gunpowder, let alone a literary reply from a great author." Strindberg, whose political feelings were equally fervent, also disliked it. "I begin to hate Ibsen after *An Enemy of the People*," he wrote to Bjørnson on 4 May 1884. "There's something insufferably *æsthetic* about him" (the modern word would be "uncommitted"). Georg Brandes did not review it, though he later described it as "one of his keenest and wittiest plays."[15] Much the most percipient review came from Erik Bøgh who, however wrong he may have been about *Ghosts*, here saw what Ibsen was aiming at. In *Dagens Nyheder*[16] (5 December), Bøgh wrote:

Henrik Ibsen is incontestably the writer who . . . least bothers himself with private causes. He has never pleaded the cause of any social class, any religious faith or any party, political or æsthetic; still less has he, like the

[15] Georg Brandes, *Henrik Ibsen,* p. 144.
[16] Reprinted in *Dit og Dat af 1882* (Copenhagen, 1883), pp. 228–39.

French theatrical advocates, defended any of the Seven Deadly Sins and sought to move hearts and evoke tears on behalf of any penitent Magdalene or interesting criminal. He has other issues on his brief. He is now, once and for all, the attorney of ideas, and this task he performs without pity or mercy, without respect for Right or Left, and with no compliments to the jurors or public gallery. . . . Those who know the play only through newspaper accounts will ask: "But how can an audience's attention be held for an entire evening by a debate which rages for three acts about a drainage system, in the fourth act makes fun of demagogy, and in the fifth is finished?" My answer would be: "It is not possible—for anyone except Ibsen. He has so wrought this masterpiece that no one will deny it, or at any rate no one who knows anything about the theatre." But Heaven preserve us from those who would imitate him without his unique gifts; for the success which this miraculously interesting theatrical debate will have on the stage will certainly result in a multitude of newspaper articles composed in dialogue.

Bøgh also, with a fellow-craftsman's percipience, praised Ibsen's ability to "treat a genuinely tragic theme with no trace of tragic apparatus, no pathos, employing everyday circumstances with everyday people speaking everyday prose . . . presenting his hero not merely without an idealized costume but without any pretence at an idealized personality."

The theatres seized eagerly upon the play. The Christiania Theatre and the Royal Theatres of Copenhagen and Stockholm, all of which had rejected *Ghosts* as unfit for public presentation, immediately acquired production rights of *An Enemy of the People,* apparently unembarrassed by the fact that its theme was the unworthiness of those who "do not dare." Hans Schrøder, the director of the Christiania Theatre, telegraphed Ibsen for permission to give the first public performance of the play, and Ibsen agreed, stinging them for a lump payment of 4,000 crowns; he had let them have *A Doll's House* for 2,500 crowns. During December he wrote Schrøder three letters which have only recently come to light[17] and which are indispensable reading to any director attempting to stage the play:

Rome, 14 December 1882

Permit me to address to you a few lines concerning the forthcoming production of *An Enemy of the People*. It is not my intention or wish to attempt to influence *in absentio* either the staging or the casting; but the expression of certain feelings which I hold regarding various aspects of the play can do no harm.

I trust I may assume that Mrs. Wolf will play Mrs. Stockmann. . . . If for the role of Hovstad you have an otherwise suitable actor of not too heroic build, that is the kind of man you should choose. Hovstad is the son of poor people, has grown up in a dirty home on

[17] Øyvind Anker, *Henrik Ibsens brevveksling med Christiania Theater, 1878–1899,* pp. 25–31.

wretched and inadequate food, has frozen and toiled horribly through-out his childhood and, subsequently, as a poverty-stricken young man, has had to undergo considerable privation. Such living conditions leave their mark not only on a man's spirit but also on his outward appearance. Men of heroic exterior are an exception among the plebs. Whatever the circumstances Hovstad must always wear a depressed appearance, somewhat shrunken and stooping, and uncertain in his movements; all, of course, portrayed with complete naturalism.

Billing's lines are so worded that they require an east-coast and not, e.g., a Bergen dialect. He is, essentially, an east-coast character.

Captain Horster has been ridiculously misunderstood by a Danish critic. He characterizes Horster as an old man, Dr Stockmann's old friend, etc. This is, of course, utterly wrong. Horster is a young man, one of the young people whose healthy appetite delights the doctor, though he is an infrequent visitor at the house because he dislikes the company of Hovstad and Billing. Already in Act One, Horster's interest in Petra must subtly and delicately be indicated, and during the brief exchanges between him and her in Act Five we must sense that they stand at the threshold of a deep and passionate relationship.

Both the boys must be carefully instructed so that the difference in their characters is clearly established. And I must beg that in Act Four every possible actor at your disposal be used. The stage director must here enjoin the greatest possible naturalism and strictly forbid any caricaturing or exaggeration. The more realistic characters you can work into the crowd the better.

Throughout the play the stage director must inexorably insist that none of the players alter his or her lines. They must be spoken exactly as they stand in the text. A lively tempo is desirable. When I was last at the Christiania Theatre the speech seemed to me to be very slow.

But above all, truthfulness to nature—the illusion that everything is real and that one is sitting and watching something that is actually taking place in real life. *An Enemy of the People* is not easy to stage. It demands exceptionally well-drilled ensemble playing, i.e. protracted and meticulously supervised rehearsals. But I rely upon the good-will of all concerned. . . .

Ten days later, on Christmas Eve, Ibsen had occasion to write again to Schrøder:

Morgenbladet has published an announcement about the casting for *An Enemy of the People,* in consequence of which I must further inconvenience you with a few lines. I see that Gundersen is to play the mayor. This actor's appearance hardly suggests a man who cannot

bear to eat hot food in the evening, has a bad stomach and an uncertain digestion, and lives on weak tea. Nor is it well suited to a man
who is characterized as neat, refined, and fastidious. But these shortcomings can partly be countered by the right clothes and make-up.
Mr Gundersen must therefore pay careful attention to these two
points. Nor does Mr Reimers's physique fit such a temperament as
Dr Stockmann's; hot-headed people are in general more slightly built.
The same advice accordingly applies to Mr Reimers as that which I
have suggested for Mr Gundersen. He must make himself as thin and
small as possible.

On 31 December Ibsen wrote again:

I fear I must once again trouble you with a few lines. From your
kind letter which reached me yesterday I gather it is intended to have
both the boys in my play acted by girls. This has somewhat disturbed
me, since it seems to imply that sufficient attention has not been
paid to the spirit in which this play was written and in which it
requires to be staged. To allow boys' parts to be taken by women may
sometimes be excusable in operetta, vaudeville, or the so-called romantic drama; for in these the prime requirement is unqualified illusion; every member of the audience is fully conscious throughout
the evening that he is merely sitting in a theatre and watching a
theatrical performance. But this should not be the case when *An
Enemy of the People* is being acted. The spectator must feel as though
he were invisibly present in Dr Stockmann's living-room; everything
here must seem real; the two boys included. Consequently they cannot be played by actresses dressed up in wigs and stays; their feminine
figures will not be able to be concealed by their costume of shirt and
trousers, and they will never make any spectator believe that he is
looking at real schoolboys from some small town. How in any case
can a grown woman make herself look like a ten-year-old child?
Both parts must therefore be played by children, at worst by a couple
of small girls whose figures are not yet fully developed; and then
damn the corsets and let them have big boys' boots on their legs.
They must also, of course, be taught the way boys behave.

It is stated in the play that at the public meeting Dr Stockmann
is to be dressed in black; but his clothes must not be new or elegant,
and his white cravat should sit a little crooked.

The prospect of increased performance fees, and of a normal sale for the
book, must have comforted Ibsen, for 1882 had been an even worse year
financially than 1881. Apart from Gyldendal's advance on *An Enemy of
the People,* and the reprint of *Poems,* he had earned only 1,130 crowns:

	crowns	
Remainder of fee for *A Doll's House* from August Rasmussen (Danish touring rights)	200	
Royalties for *"Nora"* at Vienna Stadttheater (4th quarter, 1881)	213	
Fee for *Catiline* at Nya Teater, Stockholm	400	
Royalties for *"Nora"* at Munich Hoftheater (3rd and 4th quarters, 1881)	187	
Fees etc. from German League of Dramatists	47	
Further ditto	29	
Unspecified royalties from Munich Hoftheater	54	
4th edn. of *Poems*	975	
1st edn. of *An Enemy of the People*	8,400	
	10,505	£583

Yet, although by the beginning of the year his share holdings had amounted to 66,000 crowns, he nevertheless asked Hegel on 2 December to buy him a further 4,000 crowns worth of securities. Few writers can ever have saved so high a proportion of what they earned.

An Enemy of the People is less frequently performed today than most of Ibsen's mature plays, for two principal reasons. One is, simply, the size of the cast. A crowd costs money, and without a crowd the great fourth act loses much of its impact (and a small crowd is almost worse than no crowd at all). The other problem is ideological. Some of the opinions expressed by Dr. Stockmann, especially his demand for "aristocrats," his contempt for the masses, and his assertion that "the minority is always right," strike an illiberal note in modern ears. On these points Ibsen was in fact expressing a commonly shared attitude; Mill, Tocqueville, Dickens and most liberal thinkers of the time distrusted the tyranny of the common-place majority. "Those whose opinions go by the name of public opinion . . . are always a mass, that is to say, collective mediocrity," wrote Mill in his great essay *On Liberty*. "No government by a democracy or a numerous aristocracy, either in its political acts or in the opinions, qualities, and tone of mind which it fosters, ever did or could rise above mediocrity, except in so far as the sovereign Many have let themselves be guided (which in their best times they always have done) by the counsels and influence of a more highly gifted and instructed One or Few. The initiation of all wise or noble things comes and must come from individuals; generally at first from some one individual." That is precisely Dr. Stockmann's message. But it is an unfashionable viewpoint to put forward in an age of universal suffrage.

The play has, also, suffered worse than most from the dead hand of academic criticism. The kind of commentator that dismisses *Emperor and*

Galilean as "stone-cold," *Brand* as "ambiguous," and *Little Eyolf* as "a falling-off" (to quote from a recent and embarrassing English book intended as a vindication of Ibsen) has tended to reject *An Enemy of the People* as "thin." It lacks, indeed, the extra density and overtones of Ibsen's later works; but there are precious few other plays outside the Greeks, Shakespeare and Chekhov with which it need fear comparison. The truths it expresses have not dated, and are not likely to as long as there are town councils and politicians. Even adequately performed, it is one of the most accessible and compulsive of Ibsen's plays; and Dr. Stockmann is one of the half-dozen greatest male parts he wrote.

Of all the roles that Konstantin Stanislavsky acted, by any author, this was his favourite, and when he acted it in Petrograd in 1905 for the Moscow Arts Theatre it was the scene of a remarkable demonstration. Stanislavsky has described the occasion in his autobiography:

> In that time of political unrest—it was but a little while before the first revolution—the feeling of protest was very strong in all spheres of society. They waited for the hero who could tell the truth strongly and bravely in the very teeth of the government. It is not to be wondered at that the image of Dr Stockmann became popular at once in Moscow, and especially so in Petrograd. *An Enemy of the People* became the favourite play of the revolutionists, notwithstanding the fact that Stockmann himself despised the solid majority and believed in individuals to whom he could entrust the conduct of life. But Stockmann protested, Stockmann told the truth, and that was considered enough.
>
> On the day of the well-known massacre in Kazansky Square, *An Enemy of the People* was on the boards of our theatre. The average run of spectators that night was from the intelligentsia, the professors and learned men of Petrograd. I remember that the stalls were filled almost entirely with grey heads. Thanks to the sad events of the day, the audience was very excited and answered even the slightest hints about liberty in every word of Stockmann's protest. In the most unexpected places in the play the thunder of applause would break in on the performance. . . . The atmosphere in the theatre was such that we expected arrests at any minute and a stop to the performance. Censors, who sat at all the performances of *An Enemy of the People* and saw to it that I, who played Dr Stockmann, should use only the censored text, and raised trouble over every syllable that was not admitted by the censorship, were on this evening even more watchful than on other occasions. I had to be doubly careful. When the text of a role is cut and re-cut many times it is not hard to make a mistake and say too much or too little.
>
> In the last act of the play Dr Stockmann, putting into order his room which has been stoned by the crowd, finds in the general chaos his black coat,[18] in which he appeared at the meeting the day before. Seeing a rent in the cloth, Stockmann says to his wife: "One must never put on a new coat when one goes to fight for freedom and truth."

[18] More accurately, his trousers.

The spectators in the theatre connected this sentence with the massacre in Kazansky Square, when more than one new coat must have been torn in the name of freedom and truth. Unexpectedly, my words aroused such a pandemonium that it was necessary to stop the performance, into which a real mob scene was interpolated by impromptu. There had taken place the unification of the actor and the spectators, who took on themselves the role of chief actor in the theatre, that same mob action of which so much is said by the theoreticians of art. The entire audience rose from its seats and threw itself toward the footlights. Thanks to the fact that the stage was very low and there was no orchestra before it, I saw hundreds of hands stretched towards me, all of which I was forced to shake. The younger people in the audience jumped on to the stage and embraced Dr Stockmann. It was not easy to establish order and to continue with the play. That evening I found out through my own experience what power the theatre could exercise.[19]

There will always, somewhere in the world, be a Kazansky Square;[20] and the historical importance of An Enemy of the People lies, as Erik Bøgh realized, in the fact that it is, except for Danton's Death, which no one then knew about, the first political debate which succeeds in remaining a great play. It possesses, too, a wit and lightness which people do not usually associate with Ibsen, though he had both qualities at his command, as Peer Gynt and The League of Youth bear witness. It is the most Shavian of Ibsen's plays; and the last act is one of his finest. What, one might ask on finishing Act Four, can he write that will not seem an anticlimax after this? Yet when one has read or seen that final act, one wonders how else one could possibly have supposed that he would end the play—the surest test of dramatic inevitability.

Some months after the publication of An Enemy of the People Georg Brandes wrote to Ibsen apparently (the letter is lost) rebuking him for isolationism and not putting his shoulder to the progressive wheel. Ibsen replied (12 June 1883):

> You are of course right when you say that we must all try to spread our opinions. But I firmly believe that an intellectual pioneer can never gather a majority around him. In ten years the majority may have reached the point where Dr. Stockmann stood when the people held their meeting. But during those ten years the doctor has not stood stationary; he is still at least ten years ahead of the others. The

[19] Konstantin Stanislavsky, My Life in Art, translated by J. J. Robbins (London, 1924), pp. 378–79. Stanislavsky based his physical appearance in the role on Rimsky-Korsakov, and borrowed several gestures and characteristics from Gorki.

[20] When it was staged in Paris at the time of the Dreyfus affair everyone identified Stockmann with Emile Zola (cf. Lugné-Pœ, p. 88). Its first performance there became linked with riots in the city (see p. 713 below), and it was deliberately chosen for the first Ibsen production in Spain, at the Teatre de Novetats in Barcelona on 14 April 1893, "to help organized opposition to the established order in government and industry" (Gregersen, pp. 53–54).

majority, the masses, the mob, will never catch him up; he can never rally them behind him. I myself feel a similarly unrelenting compulsion to keep pressing forward. A crowd now stands where I stood when I wrote my earlier books. But I myself am there no longer, I am somewhere else—far ahead of them—or so I hope.

To the end of his literary career, which spanned fifty years, Ibsen was to keep moving relentlessly forward, never repeating the pattern of an earlier success. Just as, fifteen years previously, he had abandoned the epic form of poetic drama which had established him, so now he was to abandon the type of (to use a loose term) sociological drama which was to spread his fame throughout the western world, and with which his name is still principally and misleadingly linked. Having exposed the hollowness of a certain kind of left-wing politician in *The League of Youth,* he had gone on to expose the equal hollowness of their right-wing counterparts in *The Pillars of Society;* having questioned the sanctity of marriage in *A Doll's House,* he had questioned it yet further, together with several other equally sacred cows, in *Ghosts.* Then he had returned to the field of politics, broadening his sights so as to include the ordinary voter in his line of fire. *An Enemy of the People* is an attack, not merely on those who lead people by the nose, but on those who allow themselves to be thus led. These four plays, for all their differences, share one theme: the necessity of discovering who one really is and of trying to become that person. In his next play, he was to question even this belief.

22

The Wild Duck

1883–1884

1883 opened for Ibsen with a series of productions of *An Enemy of the People,* which he had completed the previous June. The premiere took place at Christiania on 13 January; Bergen followed suit on 24 January, Gothenburg and Helsinki in February, and Stockholm and Copenhagen in March. In Germany, strangely considering the success there of *The Pillars of Society* and *A Doll's House,* it had to wait four years before being staged. Its reception was everywhere cordial but nowhere enthusiastic. Carl Georgsson Fleetwood, a young Swedish diplomat, probably hit on the reason for this when, after seeing the Stockholm production, he noted in his diary: "It is a mirror in which our age *could* see itself, but which it does not really understand. The audience tonight did not grasp what the play was really about. . . . From the moment I read it . . . I realized how lonely and uncomprehended a man like Ibsen must be, and tonight confirmed my conviction."[1] Ibsen's main appeal in every country was to the young, to men like Fleetwood, Otto Brahm and Paul Schlenther, Herman Bang, William Archer, Konstantin Stanislavsky and Aurélien Lugné-Poe, and the views of the young, the ones who are about, in Dr. Stockmann's words, to "ginger up the future," are often unreflected in the columns of established reviewers.[2] "Ibsen showed us our problems," recalled a member of the new generation, "our doubts, the injustices of our age, how dead tradition survived in a living shape, our belief in the future, in a just world built upon truth."[3] And another remembered how:

---

[1] Carl Georgsson Fleetwood, *Från studieår och diplomattjänst* (Stockholm, 1968), I, 286.

[2] As witness John Osborne's *Look Back in Anger,* the most influential play of the nineteen-fifties, which, on the occasion of its original production in 1954, was dismissed by nearly all the London critics.

[3] Gurli Linder, *Sällskapsliv i Stockholm under 1880- och 1890-talen* (Stockholm, 1918), p. 160.

Terrified parents well-meaningly tried to exercise a censorship over both the reading and the seeing of his plays, but just as forbidden fruit tastes sweetest, so there lay an indescribable delight, tinged with fear, in sneaking up to the gallery of a theatre against the express commands of parents and school-teachers. . . . Is it to be wondered at that such stage creations as August Lind-berg's Peer Gynt, Hjalmar Ekdal, John Gabriel Borkman, Oswald, etc., were so engraved upon one's memory that they can never be erased?"[4]

An Enemy of the People had scarcely appeared before Ibsen began to think about its successor, for as early as 11 January 1883 he wrote to Hegel that he was "already planning a new drama about contemporary life. It will be in four acts, and I hope to be able to get down to the actual writing within a couple of months at most. The Italian air, and the pleasant way of life down here, greatly increase my eagerness to create. I find it much easier to work here than in Germany." He seems at first to have been projecting another broadside of sociological criticism, for his preliminary notes include caustic observations on marriage ("has set the mark of slavery on everyone"), Christianity ("demoralizes and inhibits both men and women"), modern society ("merely a society of males"), and one splendid aphorism which deserves to figure in any anthology of quo-tations: "Our best thoughts are thought by our worst scoundrels." But in-stead of dashing off this play at once, like *An Enemy of the People,* he returned to his old routine of brooding on it for a year, and by the time he got down to writing the dialogue of *The Wild Duck* social criticism had faded into the background, where it was to remain for the rest of his life.

As a subsidiary occupation and more immediate source of income, he suggested to Hegel that he might revise, and write a preface to, *The Feast at Solhaug.* "The rewriting of this old play," he assured Hegel on 21 February, "will not seriously delay the new work I am planning." Hegel replied on 1 March accepting the idea enthusiastically and suggesting an edition of 4,000 copies against a fee of 225 crowns per signature, or 14 crowns a page. As with his *Poems* thirteen years previously, Ibsen had no copy of his own to work from, in print or in manuscript, and had to ask Hegel to try to obtain one for him from a second-hand book-shop. The work went rapidly (how can he have thought that dull old play worthy of a reprint?), and he posted off the final instalment on 6 April.

Early in May the actress Lucie Wolf, who had worked under him in Bergen and Christiania, asked him to write a verse prologue for a jubilee performance being arranged to celebrate her thirty years on the stage. Any plea to return to poetry touched him on a sensitive nerve, like a plea to

4 Unspecified article by Arne Randel, quoted by Per Lindberg, p. 379.

return to Skien, and he replied on 25 May with a peppery restatement of his position:

. . . If only I could accede to your request! Nothing would be dearer to me. But I cannot; I cannot because of the artistic convictions I hold in this matter. Prologues, epilogues, and everything of the kind should unconditionally be barred from the stage. Only dramatic art belongs there, and declamation is not dramatic art.

Your prologue must naturally be in verse, for such is the accepted convention. But I cannot conspire to keep this convention alive. Poetry has caused dreadful damage to the art of acting. A theatrical artist who seeks his repertoire in contemporary drama should not willingly let a line of verse pass his lips. Poetry will scarcely find any place worth mentioning in the drama of the immediate future; for the creative intentions of the future will certainly not be reconciled with it. So it will die. Artistic forms die out just as inefficient prehistoric animals died out when their time was up.

A tragedy in iambic pentameters is already as rare a phenomenon as the dodo bird, of which only a few specimens survive on an African island.

I myself have during the past seven or eight years hardly written a single verse, but have devoted myself exclusively to the incomparably more difficult art of writing in the consistently true language of reality. It is through this language that you have become the distinguished artist that you are. Slick verse has never helped you to corrupt anyone's judgement.

But this leads me to what I think is the main point. In a prologue all kinds of pleasantries must be addressed to the public. They must be thanked for their indulgence and their guiding judgement; the artist must belittle himself as only the intricacies of rhymed verse will permit. But is there any truth in such a device? You know as well as I do that there is no truth in it. Quite the contrary. You do not stand in the public's debt; it is the public which owes an immense debt to you for your thirty years of loyal service.

I regard it as the duty of any serious artist to maintain this standpoint, both for his own sake and for that of his profession. You will, I am sure, appreciate that, feeling as I do, I cannot with a good conscience agree to compose a prologue for the occasion in question. . . .

But if I cannot serve you in this matter, I hope you will not the less accept the thanks I now send you, thanks for everything that you have been and still are to the art of our theatre, and especially thanks for the distinguished share which you have taken in the presentation of so many of my own dramatic works.

In that hope, and with the heartfelt wish that there may still lie ahead of you a long and brilliant career, I sign myself, in old friendship

Your affectionate
Henrik Ibsen

The new edition of *The Feast at Solhaug* appeared in June, and at the same time Ibsen learned that a sixth edition of *The Pretenders,* one of his steadiest sellers, was in the press. He also heard from Georg Brandes that the latter's most recent essay on him (later published as the "Second Impression" in Brandes's 1898 book on Ibsen) was to appear in Germany, which must have gratified him, since he regarded it as the most penetrating and sympathetic study of his work yet to have appeared.

The Ibsens had now begun to hold weekly soirées, and visitors who had been daunted by tales of their prickliness, and of the Webb-like plainness of the fare they had provided in Munich, were often pleasantly surprised. A young Norwegian named Kristian Glœrsen who attended these gatherings speaks of Suzannah's "always ample and tastefully decorated table, at which a relaxed and witty atmosphere invariably prevailed," and praises both her and Ibsen's excellence as hosts, their attention to even the humblest guests and their skill at arranging congenial little groups within a party, not always a Scandinavian (or for that matter an English) talent. He also refers to Ibsen's "personal amiability," remarking that "despite his withdrawnness, his *noli me tangere,* his often chilly mask and eruptions of vehement bitterness, there appeared frequent glimpses of a warmth of heart and of a fine and noble character, doubly winning because of his anxiety to conceal it."[5] Gunnar Heiberg, too, confirms Ibsen's skill as a host:

> It was an especial pleasure to see Ibsen speak with and entertain the many old or aging ladies who came there. He sat down among them and talked of his experiences, his books, his travels. One evening, I well recall, he spoke in great detail to three old ladies about his trip to Egypt. He gesticulated and talked vividly. He let himself be carried away. It was as though he were describing the events for the first time, as though the words were only this moment forming on his lips. . . . The old ladies' eyes shone with intense gratitude. I remember this sight of Ibsen creeping out of his marble shell in honour of a few old ladies who he thought needed a little sparkle and happiness in their eyes.[6]

Glœrsen, who saw a lot of Ibsen in 1882 and 1883, records how he enjoyed, as of old, to provoke people by the Socratic use of paradox,

[5] Kristian Glœrsen, "Henrik Ibsen: minder fra mit samvær med ham i utlandet," in *Kringsjaa* (Christiania, 1906), xxvii, 342–47.
[6] Gunnar Heiberg, *Salt og sukker,* pp. 55–56.

often pushing his listeners' arguments to the point of absurdity. He "liked to be opposed when he came out with his most audacious paradoxes, which were perhaps directed to that end." Thus, late one night at the Café Nazionale, after a ball at the Scandinavian Club, he declared: "They should guillotine the bourgeoisie as a hundred years ago in France they guillotined the aristocrats." No one in Norway who called himself a liberal or a republican was prepared to make any personal sacrifices. They would give nothing, sacrifice nothing, to enable the poor to be equal with them. If it came to the crunch, none of them would man the barricades. There must be a revolution, everything existing must come down, down. "The Right, did you say? My dear fellow, I want nothing to do with them, one can't count them any longer. They don't belong to the saga of the future. The only useful thing they do is undermine their own position and show us the best way through the ruins. In that respect the reactionaries are our best allies."[7] No wonder the young Bernard Shaw, to whom William Archer was at this time reading Ibsen's plays, translating off the cuff as he went, felt that he had discovered a kindred spirit.

A similar account of Ibsen in provocative mood that year comes from a Dr. Undset, who wrote home to a friend:

Ibsen is interminably radical; I have now got to know him and his opinions better. One evening I went out with him and the writer N.N., who is also here this winter, to a restaurant. Late at night—somewhere around the sixth glass—Ibsen really started talking, and you should have heard him. Poor N.N., who is a Norwegian liberal, a friend of Bjørnson and so forth, has close connections with *Dagbladet* [the liberal daily]; you should have seen him when Ibsen cut loose and started on them! He didn't name B.B[jørnson]. "Sverdrup? The most contemptible sharper that ever lived! *Dagbladet* and *Verdens Gang* [another progressive newspaper]? Cheap, lying, cowardly rags! How can these wretched people not see that to hold power is a very subordinate position?" And so on for more than an hour, I think, to the amazed and terrified N.N.

Ibsen refuses to acknowledge nationalism or anything any more; he is a complete anarchist, wants to wipe everything out—put a torpedo under the ark—mankind must start from the foundations to rebuild the world—and they must begin with the individual! . . . Society and everything else must be wiped out, wherever it in the smallest degree hampers our work; then possibly some kind of insurance companies may be allowed to emerge in place of the present societies and states. Or else—well, that will be society's problem, to decide what is to emerge; the great task of our age is to blow the existing fabric into the air—to destroy. . . . He is remarkable, a titanic character! I mentioned the "sixth glass," but I don't think Ibsen often drinks that much; only, now and then, when he's with someone he likes talking to, he enjoys going into a café and arguing late into the night. But this happens only seldom, and doesn't affect his life or his serious work.[8]

7 Glœrsen, p. 339.
8 Gran, II, 143–45.

Dr. Undset's comment on Ibsen's drinking habits is confirmed by two reliable observers. William Archer wrote: "The oft-repeated stories of his over-indulgence in stimulants were, to the best of my belief, such gross exaggerations as to be practically falsehoods. . . . In Germany, in Denmark, in Norway, I have been with him repeatedly, have seen him evidently pursuing his daily habit in the matter of spirituous liquors, and have always noted the moderation of that habit. On one public occasion when it was afterwards spread abroad that he had conspicuously exceeded, I both walked and talked with him, and can positively assert that there was no truth whatever in the scandal."[9] Bergliot Ibsen confirms this: "I have seen him sit for hours on end sipping at a glass of red wine. In the same way, he used to sip at the famous glass of brandy at the Grand, which people transformed into 'regiment of nips.' People assumed it must always be a new glass, since it always seemed full. When in his old age Ibsen's complexion became ruddy, the gossips found fresh grist for their mill. . . . In fact, Ibsen suffered from a nervous eczema. . . . When he died his physician, Dr. Bull, told me he had never seen a better preserved constitution."[10] The idea that Ibsen was a semi-alcoholic for most of his life is another of the myths that need to be exploded.

Ibsen was sometimes inclined to hold forth on subjects of which he was largely ignorant. Thus, Gunnar Heiberg records, he liked to expatiate on science, although "he was ignorant of the most elementary principles thereof. . . . He talked of flying machines and electricity with a buoyant enthusiasm which deceived us laymen but shocked professionals, or even people with a sound general education. A Danish engineer, unimpressed by Ibsen's literary renown, told him in round terms that he lacked the most elementary knowledge and was talking plain rubbish. Ibsen did not like this, but continued. It often seemed as though he preferred to acquire the rudiments of knowledge in this way rather than by reading, which he did not much enjoy. . . . J. P. Jacobsen often shook his head when Ibsen touched on his particular field of botany; he smiled his wise, gentle smile and said that he knew many small boys who knew more about botany than this ex-apothecary."[11] Heiberg adds, probably correctly, that he felt that "scientific phenomena in themselves interested Ibsen less than how the various people present treated them, the temperament and tempo with which they dismissed them." Glœrsen, too, noted Ibsen's analytical interest in people's ways of speech; he would often ask a question à propos of nothing, directed now to a man, now to a woman, to see how they replied. He once asked Glœrsen: "Have you ever noticed how in conversation a woman usually ends a remark with a word of two or three syllables, a man with a monosyllable?" Glœrsen thought this absurd, but on testing

9 William Archer, "Ibsen as I Knew Him," pp. 9–10.
10 Bergliot Ibsen, pp. 215–16.
11 Gunnar Heiberg, *Salt og sukker*, pp. 46–48.

Ibsen's theory was astonished to find it correct.[12] Ibsen once similarly surprised John Paulsen, before their quarrel, by saying, "Has it ever occurred to you that the lines in a play should sound different according to whether they are said in the morning or the evening?"[13]

Glœrsen noted Ibsen's routine. He liked to take a morning walk up the Via Sistina to Monte Pincio. Between twelve and one he would drop in at the Café Nazionale, where he had a special seat in which he liked to sit, though it was not reserved for him as at the Café Maximilian in Munich and, later, the Grand in Christiania. He was annoyed if he found it occupied. He lunched at two or two-thirty "since he could not reconcile himself to the custom then most followed abroad of two meals a day, lunch at twelve to one, and dinner at seven to eight."[14] He often urged Glœrsen to settle in Rome, since he knew of nowhere else that was so good for writing. "Here I can write a book every year," Ibsen said to him in the euphoric mood of An Enemy of the People. "At home there would be a gap of five years. Why go home and let yourself be buttonholed by hundreds of people, scarcely one per cent of whom you have any use for?"[15] He added that (as he had told Laura Kieler) he preferred to live far from Norway when writing a play with a Norwegian setting. "Life and its phenomena are best viewed by a writer at a distance, in both time and space."[16] He assured Glœrsen that he was quite indifferent to what critics wrote about him, but Suzannah said (in his absence) that this was quite untrue and that he minded a lot.

Sigurd was now in Paris, his father having promised him a holiday there as a reward for having become, the previous summer, at twenty-two and a half, "the youngest Doctor of Law in Rome" (as Ibsen proudly informed Bjørnson on 4 August 1882). It was the first time the young man had gone anywhere alone. He wrote frequent and vivid letters home about his cultural and gastronomic experiences; on 24 May he told his father that he had been to the theatre between twenty-five and thirty times in three months. He saw Sarah Bernhardt in Sardou's Feodora but, as befitted Ibsen's son, had reservations about her performance. "The modern theatre-goer," he wrote, "is somewhat sceptical about daggers and poisoned goblets, disguised spies and swapped letters as the causes of death and catastrophe. It is also possible that Sarah Bernhardt's own personality hinders the illusion, that she is too unusual a person to be convincing as an actress, that she absorbs the role instead of losing herself in it. But her appearance, manner, movement and voice are something so remarkable that no one who has seen her will easily forget her."

[12] Glœrsen, pp. 343–44.
[13] John Paulsen, Samliv med Ibsen, I, 168.
[14] Glœrsen, pp. 337–38.
[15] Ibid., pp. 342–43.
[16] Ibid., p. 347.

The smartness of Paris audiences impressed him; and he relates one sad occasion when Lorentz Dietrichson addressed a gathering of artists and so bored and angered them that "they bombarded him with meatbones and bread, broke his glass so that the wine spilled over his clothes, and called him an idiot . . . so that in the end he had to take his hat and go."[17]

At the end of June, Ibsen left with Suzannah for Gossensass, and while he was there *Ghosts* received its first European performance. The main Scandinavian theatres still fought shy, but August Lindberg, the young Swede who had found Ibsen so taciturn in Munich three years earlier, and had unsuccessfully tried to persuade Ludvig Josephson to stage the play in Stockholm, asked Ibsen's permission to set up a production to tour Sweden, Norway and Denmark. Ibsen agreed, asking 400 crowns for the Swedish provincial rights excluding Stockholm and Gothenburg, another 400 crowns for Stockholm, 500 crowns for Copenhagen and 500 crowns for Christiania, stipulating only that "the play be not staged in Christiania before it has been performed in Stockholm and Copenhagen. The reasons for this I shall not go into." Presumably he thought it more likely to get a fair hearing in the two last-named capitals. He added some advice on the translation, which, though overlapping that given to Rasmus Anderson of Wisconsin the previous year, bears recording. "The language must sound natural and the mode of expression must be distinctive for every character in the play; one human being does not express himself like another. . . . The effect of the play depends greatly on the audience feeling that they are listening to something that is actually happening in real life." He also stressed (a reminder of the immense length of time that nineteenth-century audiences liked to spend in a theatre) that *Ghosts*, "although only three acts, fills a whole evening," and that "nothing else must be acted either before or after the play. I should also like this work of mine to be staged everywhere without the employment of an orchestra, either before the performance or during the intervals."

Ghosts runs (if one allows for two ten-minute intervals) for about two and a half hours, nearly half an hour less than *A Doll's House*, which was itself much shorter than any of his previous plays; one of Ibsen's forgotten contributions to the theatre was to remind audiences of a fact forgotten since the Greeks, that a tragedy need not fill five acts. Strindberg, within the decade, was to prove that it need fill no more than one.

Lindberg coaxed a once-famous actress named Hedvig Charlotte Winter-Hjelm out of retirement to play Mrs. Alving and, to prepare himself for the role of Oswald, visited a hospital in Copenhagen to study children who were insane as the result of inherited syphilis.

Down the steps came a procession of the living dead. Small children, lying in their beds and mechanically playing with a little bell which each held in his or her hand. The procession passed on either side of us. Some were

17 Bergliot Ibsen, pp. 93–98.

carried in nurses' arms, some ran, but most were pushed in their chairs. I bowed to the doctor, ran down the stairs more quickly than I had ascended them, and returned to Hälsingborg. But I never forgot the sight.[18]

The rehearsals had a deeply disturbing effect on the players. Lindberg himself suffered from repeated nightmares, and when he rehearsed with Fru Winter-Hjelm's understudy the scene in which Oswald tells his mother of his illness, the effect was such that she had to leave the stage.

Ghosts opened at Hälsingborg, on the Swedish west coast, on 22 August 1883. The press and audience came expecting to be scandalized; but the play which respectable citizens had refused to have on their shelves proved, in performance, to scandalize no one. Lindberg telegraphed Ludvig Josephson that the atmosphere in the theatre had been like "a new Oberammergau." The Danish newspaper *Dagbladet*'s reporter wrote an ecstatic notice and was rewarded with the sack, the editor being of the opinion that no decent theatre ought to perform the play. Six days later Lindberg's production crossed The Sound and played for ten nights at the Folketeater in Copenhagen, where the effect was the same. "The excitement in the auditorium," Lindberg recalled, "rose as though in small cyclones. Fru Winter-Hjelm whispered at one stage, 'Dare we go on?' " The audiences found themselves unshocked, moved and gripped, and the production played to full houses each night at double the usual prices. "*Ghosts*," wrote Lindberg to Josephson, "is causing an excitement which spreads from house and home, from street and café, to the box office at Folketeater."

Josephson, his fears allayed, signed up the production to visit his theatre in Stockholm in September, where it was so well received that the Royal Theatre, a few hundred yards away, followed with a production of its own within the month. Then, on 17 October, Lindberg's company presented the first performance of *Ghosts* in Norway at, appropriately, the old Møllergaden theatre[19] where, a quarter of a century earlier, Ibsen had, as artistic director, suffered his long series of humiliations. William Archer happened to be in Christiania at the time and attended the premiere.

I was present, and well remember the profound impression it made on the crowded and enthusiastic audience. By this time the reaction in favour of the play had fairly set in. It happened that on the same evening a trivial

[18] For this passage and other details surrounding this production, cf. Per Lindberg, pp. 96–115.

[19] Despite an appeal by Ibsen to Lindberg (19 August 1883) not to stage it there. "The place is so cramped and cluttered, the distance between actors and audience so short, that no full effect will be achievable." One would have supposed such a small theatre to be ideal for *Ghosts;* Ibsen's own bitter memories of Møllergaden may have been the real reason. Lindberg had asked the Christiania Theatre permission to stage it there, but Schrøder refused. The latter went to see the play at Møllergaden, and came away convinced that he had been right. (Carl Just, *Schrøder og Christiania theater* [Oslo, 1948], pp. 184–85, 190–91.)

French farce, *Tête de Linotte* (known in English as *Miss Featherbrain*) was being played at the Christiania Theatre; and the contrast could not but strike people. They saw a masterpiece of Norwegian literature acted by a foreign (Swedish) company at a minor playhouse, while the official theatre of the capital was given over to a piece of Parisian frivolity. The result was that on the following evening, and for some nights afterwards, demonstrations were made at the Christiania Theatre against the policy of the management in rejecting Ibsen's play. . . . Fru Winter-Hjelm's performance of Mrs. Alving was exceedingly powerful, and Lindberg seemed to me an almost ideal Oswald. In his make-up, I remember, there was a strong suggestion of the portraits of Edgar Allan Poe.[20]

Lindberg himself has left an interesting impression of the Christiania premiere as it seemed to someone on the other side of the footlights. "When the curtain was raised, it felt as though the public held its breath. The scenes of the play unfolded in a silence worthy of a spiritual seance. When the final curtain fell, the silence continued for a good while before the ovations started."[21] The Norwegian Gunnar Heiberg commented: "Pastor Manders, Engstrand, Helmer and several other gentlemen had leagued together to prevent *Ghosts* from being staged. . . . A foreigner had to bring us our own play. What the Swede Lindberg did remains one of the great occasions in the history of the Norwegian theatre."[22] And Lindberg himself wrote to Ibsen:

It was high time that *Ghosts* arrived, for the theatres up here have lived for so long on French comedy that we are well on the way to becoming monkeys instead of men. But now we see the truth, and the clowning and smirking are past. Real tears now fall on the stage, and that with no sense of shame. It is something new and splendid to assist in the re-introduction of nature to the stage.[23]

Altogether, Lindberg's company performed *Ghosts* seventy-five times during this tour, and he returned with the production to Christiania several times over the next few years. The following year, a Danish company toured the play through the Norwegian provinces (to give them credit, they and another Danish company had applied for permission to stage *Ghosts* before Lindberg had his premiere),[24] but the main Scandinavian theatres (outside Stockholm) still fought shy, and it was not until 1890, nine years after its publication, that *Ghosts* was acted by a Norwegian company, at the Bergen Theatre. Schrøder, the director of the Christiania Theatre, steadfastly refused to let it be performed there as long as he remained in charge, and it was not played by Norwegians in their own

[20] Archer's introduction to his translation of *Ghosts* (London, 1900), pp. vii–viii.
[21] Per Lindberg, p. 112.
[22] *Ibid.*, pp. 113–14.
[23] *Ibid.*, p. 115.
[24] Cf. Ibsen's letter to Betty Borchsenius, 15 June 1883.

capital until 1900 (when the Christiania Theatre had been replaced by the National Theatre), nor at the Royal Theatre in Copenhagen until 1903. In Germany, police censorship prevented any public performance being given for many years, although a number of private performances took place in various cities from 1886. England and France were not to see the play until the nineties (and no public performance was allowed in England before 1914).

In early October Ibsen left Gossensass for Botzen near the Italian frontier, proceeding to Rome at the end of the month. From Rome, on 30 November, he addressed a final appeal through his old friend O. A. Bachke, to the Norwegian Ecclesiastical Department to admit Sigurd into his country's diplomatic service. The way now lay open, he explained, for Sigurd to make a career in the *Italian* foreign service; "but before this can happen, he will have to be naturalized. And this is the step which we find it so difficult to take. To cut oneself wholly off from one's country—that is a serious matter. I, therefore, on my son's behalf, make this last effort to keep him a Norwegian citizen by asking if you would and could extract a promise from the government that my son will be considered for a post as attaché when one next falls vacant . . . I am reluctant to believe that, as some have suggested, I should be such a *bête noir* to certain members of the government that they will totally refuse to meet me in this matter. I know well what I can expect from the head of the Ecclesiastical Department, but fortunately his voice is not decisive in this case."

The likelihood of any politician doing Ibsen a favour after *An Enemy of the People* must have seemed more than ever remote; but who can foretell the ways of statesmen? Bachke lost his job as Minister of Justice the following spring, so Ibsen approached the Prime Minister, Sverdrup, and when the following summer Sigurd called on Sverdrup in Christiania he so impressed him that Sverdrup pulled the necessary strings. So Sigurd got into the Norwegian consular service and remained a Norwegian. Future prime ministers, unfortunately, were less ready than Sverdrup to appreciate Sigurd's qualities.

So 1883 ended. Thanks mainly to the various productions of *An Enemy of the People,* which brought in 8,704 crowns, it had been a better year:

	crowns
Fee for *An Enemy of the People* in Christiania	4,000
Fee for *An Enemy of the People* in Bergen	800
Fee for *An Enemy of the People* in Gothenburg	500
2nd edn. of *The Feast at Solhaug*	1,575
6th edn. of *The Pretenders*	1,125
Fee for *An Enemy of the People* in Helsinki	250
Fee for *An Enemy of the People* at Royal Theatre, Copenhagen (2nd–10th perfs.)	2,204

	crowns	
Fees from German League of Dramatists	43	
Fee for *An Enemy of the People* at Royal Theatre, Stockholm (2nd–14th perfs.)	950	
Scandinavian provincial rights of *The League of Youth* and *Ghosts* (August Lindberg)	400	
Fee for *Ghosts* in Copenhagen (Lindberg)	500	
Fee for *Ghosts* in Stockholm (Lindberg)	400	
Danish provincial rights for *Ghosts* (Otto Petersen)	500	
Norwegian provincial rights for *Ghosts* (Olaus Olsen)	600	
5th edn. of *The League of Youth*	906	
	14,753	£819

In the same year Henry Arthur Jones, an indifferent English playwright who had just achieved his first success with a melodrama called *The Silver King* (and who that winter was to adapt *A Doll's House* for the English stage), earned £3,398,[25] well over four times as much as Ibsen.

1884 began with a letter from Bjørnson urging Ibsen yet again to return and take over the directorship of the Christiania Theatre. But the offer held even less attraction for him than when it had last been made, and he replied on 9 January:

> My experiences and memories of the theatre in Norway are not such that I feel any inclination to repeat them. I might, it is true, sense some twinge of duty and responsibility in this connection if I thought I could achieve anything of value for our theatre; but of that I have the gravest doubts. Our actors, etc., are demoralized, they will not accept discipline and unqualified obedience, besides which we have a press which is always ready to champion rebels against their leader. This is the main reason why we, unlike other countries where anarchic tendencies are less developed, can never achieve any real ensemble playing. I don't think I could improve matters in this respect; it is too closely tied up with our whole national attitude towards life; and anyway, my liking for the practicalities of theatre work is too small. . . . I am by no means sure how sincerely the Christiania public feels any need for good theatre. The packed houses on which the operettas and equestrian performances at Tivoli can always rely, and the interest with which dilettante productions of students and shop assistants are received there, seem to me to indicate a cultural outlook that is not yet ripe to appreciate genuine dramatic art.

Ibsen's visits to Norway had not mellowed his attitude towards his compatriots.

[25] Doris Arthur Jones, *The Life and Letters of Henry Arthur Jones* (London, 1930), p. 58.

His new play, for which he had laid the first plans over six months earlier, had made negligible progress. "I have had one of those periods," he wrote to Laura Grundtvig on 22 January, "when I can only with the greatest reluctance sit down at my desk. But today I have been out and bought new paper, new ink and new pens in honour of a new play which I have been turning over in my mind." Yet he seems to have done nothing for the next three months but make notes; it was 20 April before he began to write any dialogue.

On 8 February 1884 Ibsen was acted in Russian for the first time (though he had been performed in Russia in Polish and also in Finnish), when *A Doll's House* was staged in St. Petersburg. But the play seems to have made less impact there than in other countries, and it was to be eight years before they staged another of his plays.

That spring Ibsen came as near as he ever did to meeting Strindberg. "Surely I should visit Ibsen in Rome?" wrote Strindberg on 12 February from Ouchy in Switzerland to Bjørnson and Jonas Lie, together in Paris. "Will you be kind enough to ask him to receive me, for if he shows me the door I shall feel hurt. I want to see the angriest man in Europe before I die!" But although Strindberg set off for Italy on 1 March he got no farther than Genoa, where the weather was so bad that he turned in a temper for home. "All water is blue when the sky is blue," he wrote to his friend Carl Larsson on 8 (?) March. "Eva [his children's nursemaid] and I have searched in vain for that damned blue in both sky and water. Humbug, Sir! The olive trees are horribly grey. The landscape like a garden and uglier than the oil paintings. Pine trees are the same everywhere. And the people? Moleskin and slouch hats! Not at all picturesque, old chap! The old houses daubed with red, green and yellow! . . . The whole coast here is occupied by factories and wharves so that one can't get to the beach. The hills covered with villas! Nature is dead here! No walks possible! The roads dusty! Oh, how dusty it is here!" At least it does not seem to have rained much; still, it is a sad thought that had the sun shone in north Italy that week, a meeting would probably have taken place between these two extraordinary men, and one suspects that they might have got on rather well, for Strindberg, when his black mood was not on him, was a tremendous charmer, and he was the kind of emotional individualist (like Brandes) whom Ibsen found stimulating. And when Ibsen liked someone and put his own charm forward, there were few who could resist him. Who but Strindberg would have been unlucky enough to spend a spring week in Italy without seeing the sun? By August, sadly, his hostility towards Ibsen as a champion of feminism had become set, and he was describing the latter's writings as "swinish."[26]

---

[26] Cf. *August Strindbergs brev*, IV, 39, 65 and 302-3. (The words "Humbug, Sir!" are in English; Strindberg, unlike Ibsen, was an accomplished linguist, and mixed up all his languages in his letters).

Meanwhile, on 3 March, Ibsen's name had appeared for the first time (apart from that single matinee of *The Pillars of Society* in 1880) in the West End of London, though scarcely in a manner to cause him joy. Henry Arthur Jones, together with a collaborator named Henry Herman who had helped him with *The Silver King,* had been approached by the Polish actress Helena Modjeska to adapt *A Doll's House* into English. Between them they produced an even freer adaptation than the one seen in America, and re-entitled it

BREAKING A BUTTERFLY

(founded on Ibsen's *Norah*)

and presented it at the Prince's Theatre in Coventry Street (now the Prince of Wales's Theatre). Harley Granville Barker gives an interesting account of their improvements on the text:

> The scene is laid in some English town. Nora becomes Flora and, to her husband, rather terribly, Flossie. He is Humphrey Goddard and we find him gifted with a mother (quite unnecessarily) and a sister (wanted for the piano-playing, *vice* Mrs Linde, who disappears). The morbid Dr Rank is replaced by a Charles-his-friend, called, as if to wipe out every trace of his original, Ben Birdseye! He is not in love with Nora-Flora, of course; that would never do. But Dunkley, alias Krogstad, had loved her as a girl, when Humphrey Goddard stole her young heart from him; so love has turned to hate and revenge is sweet. Observe the certainty with which our operators in the English market fasten on the flawed streak in Ibsen's play and cheapen it still further. The tarantella episode, of course, will be the making of the whole affair (such was many people's judgement then, and now we find it rather marring), and this is left intact. But the third act sees the parent play stood deliberately on its head, and every ounce of Ibsen emptied out of it. Burlesque could do no more. Torvald-Humphrey behaves like the pasteboard hero of Nora's doll's-house dream; he *does* strike his chest and say: "I am the guilty one!" And Nora-Flora cries that she is a poor weak foolish girl, ". . . no wife for a man like you. You are a thousand times too good for me," and never wakes up and walks out of her doll's house at all.[27]

A distinguished cast had been assembled, including Kyrle Bellew as Goddard/Helmer, Beerbohm Tree as Dunkley/Krogstad, and Alice Lingard as Nora/Flora. "The result," noted William Archer, "was a nice little play, standing to *Et Dukkehjem* somewhat in the relation of Mr. Gilbert's *Gretchen* to Gœthe's *Faust;* and even so, it did not succeed."[28]

Such was the introduction of Ibsen to the English theatre—a single matinee of *The Pillars of Society* in 1880, and this scarcely recognizable perversion of *A Doll's House* in 1884, from which, needless to say, Ibsen

[27] Granville Barker, pp. 167–68.
[28] *The Dramatic Review,* 4 April 1885.

did not receive a penny. Apart from an amateur charity performance of *A Doll's House* the following year, there were to be no further productions of Ibsen in England before 1889, when the dramatist was sixty-one. Two years after the Prince's Theatre travesty, however, there was a private reading of *A Doll's House* with, in retrospect, though none of the names meant anything then, a distinguished cast. This, according to Bernard Shaw, took place "on a first floor in a Bloomsbury lodging-house. Karl Marx's youngest daughter played Nora Helmer; and I impersonated Krogstad at her request, with a very vague notion of what it was all about."[29] The date was 15 January 1886 and the place 55 Great Russell Street, opposite the British Museum.[30] One would like to know whether Eleanor Marx-Aveling, shortly to translate (rather badly) *An Enemy of the People* and *The Wild Duck,* ever mentioned Ibsen to her father before he died in 1883.

On 20 April Ibsen began writing *The Wild Duck* and by 28 April (each act of the manuscript is dated) he had completed the first act. On 2 May he began Act Two; but when he was halfway through it he stopped, and started to rewrite the play from the beginning. By 24 May he had completed Acts One and Two in their new form. The last three acts took him less than a week each: 25–30 May, 2–8 June, and 9–13 June—a measure of how carefully he had worked the play out in his mind before putting pen to paper. On 14 June he wrote to Hegel:

> I am glad to be able to tell you that yesterday I completed the draft of my new play. It comprises five acts and will, as far as I can calculate, occupy some 200 printed pages, perhaps a little more. It still remains for me to make the fair copy, and I shall start on that tomorrow. As usual, however, this will involve not just copying the draft but a comprehensive rewriting of the dialogue. So it will take time. Still, unless some unforeseen obstacle presents itself I reckon the whole manuscript should be in your hands by mid-September. The play doesn't touch on political or social problems, or indeed any matters of public import. It takes place entirely within the confines of family life. I dare say it will arouse some discussion; but it can't offend anyone."

As so often, his optimism was to prove unfounded.

This "comprehensive rewriting" he described more precisely in a letter of 27 June to Theodor Caspari, a young poet who had addressed a lyric to him, as "the more energetic individualizing of the characters and of their

[29] Cf. Shaw's preface ("An Aside") to Lillah McCarthy's *Myself and Some Friends* (London, 1933), p. 3.

[30] Chushichi Tsuzuki, *The Life of Eleanor Marx* (Oxford, 1967), p. 165.

modes of expression"—a problem, which, as we have seen, particularly obsessed him. He added a remark which contains the central theme of *The Wild Duck*. Caspari had evidently taken Ibsen up on the latter's abandonment and apparent condemnation of verse, and Ibsen replied:

> You are quite wrong in supposing that I should wish you to break your lyre. . . . I have long ceased to make universal demands of people because I no longer believe that one has any inherent right to pose such demands. I believe that none of us can have any higher aim in life than to realize ourselves in spirit and in truth. That, in my view, is the true meaning of liberalism, and that is why the so-called liberals are in so many ways repugnant to me.

One of the central characters in *The Wild Duck* was to be just such a "so-called liberal," making blind "universal" demands of people and so destroying their illusions and their happiness. Ibsen concluded his letter:

> To find the necessary peace and solitude for this work, I am going in a few days up to Gossensass in the Tyrol. My wife and son will, at the same time, leave for Norway. Would I could have come with them! But it must not be. At my age one must use all one's time for work; one will never finish it all. One "will not find time to finish the last verse";[31] but one wants to get down as much as possible.

Ibsen left Rome on 30 June, and stayed a full four months in Gossensass. It was the longest period he had been separated from Suzannah during the twenty-six years of their marriage, and is consequently the best documented, for he wrote to her and Sigurd almost weekly.

Gossensass, 4 July 1884

Dear Suzannah!

Thank you for your card from Basel, which I received this noon. Your cards from Rome arrived yesterday, together with a couple of newspapers. Of the last-named I have so far received only *one* number of *Dagbladet* direct from Christiania, nothing from *Aftenposten*, though I informed them in good time of my change of address. The scoundrels at *Aftenposten* are of course too conservative to change an address,[32] and from their drunken friends at *Dagbladet* one can expect nothing but chaos and Norwegian slovenliness.

I am happy that you have reached Basel safely, and I trust that by tomorrow, or perhaps even today, you will reach Copenhagen.

---

[31] A quotation from Holberg's *Jacob von Thybœ*, the Cyrano-like hero of which play needs only one word, rhyming with "fool," to finish his letter to his beloved.

[32] *Aftenposten*, originally an unpolitical newspaper, had recently become right-wing, like *Morgenbladet*. *Dagbladet* and *Verdens Gang* represented the left.

As far as I am concerned, all is as it should be. The journey here was as usual; from Modena by night, and as far as Ala I had to keep my overcoat on; thereafter I didn't need it; exceptionally beautiful weather and fresh air all the way up the valley here. The sandwiches proved most useful; they were my only food throughout the journey; I ate the last in Verona, for breakfast, with a cup of black coffee which was brought to me in the compartment; in Florence I had taken only half a bottle of wine, at Ala in the morning nothing; I shall always take sandwiches when I travel; I can eat them with pleasure at any time.

I was heartily welcomed here, but they were much surprised at my arriving alone. I chose the isolated room upstairs in the little annexe, similar to the one Sigurd had downstairs in previous years; no verandah outside, as this room does not stretch so far, and no connecting door with the next room, so that no noise is audible; I am excellently contented here.

Hitherto I have risen at 6:30, breakfasted in my room half an hour later, gone out while they do the room, and then written from 9–1. Then lunch with a ravenous appetite. In the afternoons, too, I have managed to write a little, or at any rate do groundwork. The second act will be ready in five to six days. I am not drinking any beer; which suits me well. But I am drinking milk and a little—not much—white wine, with water. A light evening meal at 7:30. So far I have been in bed each evening by 10, and have been sleeping well.

Quite a lot of visitors have already arrived, and everywhere will soon be full. Of those we know from previous years I have seen only Fru Schlesinger and the Vambergs. Grubhofer has not come yet, but has sent me a card of greeting from Munich. Incidentally, the guests I don't know, who are mostly German ladies, seem to know me, and look very gracious and smiling when we meet. Ravnkilde is expected next week. The three horrors haven't booked yet, so will probably not get in if they come, and will then have to go on to Brennerbad, if they can find anything there.

It feels rather strange to be alone; but my work will keep me occupied for a good while yet. Let me hear from you both some time. You need not write at length. I won't write long letters either; I am busy with my play and there is nothing much of interest here to write about.

But even if I do not write at length or often, I shall be thinking constantly of you and hoping you are having a really good and enjoyable time on your holiday in Norway. Remember of course that you must let me know from time to time where to address my letters. I shall not now repeat my reminders to take care and forethought in everything you do; I hope, though, that you will comply with them as a matter of common sense. . . .

He bade them "profit from the good, nourishing Norwegian food," and to eat much fish especially salmon; and announced that "I have had to give up the white Tyrol wine, which did not suit me, and now drink an excellent Hungarian Carlowitzer which, surprisingly enough, costs exactly the same." Pedantically, he noted his changes of routine:

In the morning I drink tea at seven o'clock precisely; rise each day at six at the latest, often earlier, and find this suits me excellently, though I do not now retire before eleven. For my admirable, isolated and peaceful room I pay this year only 60 kreutzer a day. All my expenses, including tobacco and laundry, come to 50 francs a week. Each Sunday morning I change a 50-lire note, and manage with that until exactly the following Sunday.[33]

His peace was disturbed by a hailstorm, which he describes in this same letter of 20 July:

The hail flew straight through the windows of the dining-room as we sat there; such was their force that they did not smash the panes but made round holes in them of their own size. And what a size! Many were larger than the largest hen's eggs I have ever seen; we collected a lot of them; they were of the hardest ice and polished like glass; I made pencil outlines of two of them. At midnight a new storm burst, and a third at 3 A.M. The church bells rang, incessantly, and most of the guests here stayed up all night; at three I too arose; but then went back to bed. The two following days we had heavy rain and yesterday, Saturday, morning there was a real cloudburst; towards noon the Eisach overflowed its banks . . . and threatened Gossensass where, however, in the end all turned out well. Further down things were worse. You remember the little stream which comes from "Wasserfall" and flows out under the road to Sterzing, just at the curve where there stands a cross to a murdered man. This stream became a mighty, powerful and destructive current, carrying away the highway so that the whole bend is now a great gaping abyss. The railway beneath got covered with mud so that yesterday the trains from the north could not reach here. All the southbound passengers had to seek refuge in our hotel, where a great disturbance resulted.

[33] In 1884 the Austrian gulden (100 kreutzer) was worth 1s. 8d. (40 cents), so that Ibsen's room cost him only 1s. (25 cents) a night. The exchange rate of the French and Swiss francs and the Italian lire was in each case approximately 25.45 to the pound; thus his other expenses (including food) came to under £2 a week.

Young Marcus Grønvold, the painter, had joined him, and his appetite worried Ibsen ("I think he must be suffering from some kind of illness"). An English lady fell and broke her leg, a schoolboy from Berlin cut his hand badly. He warned Suzannah and Sigurd not to bathe ("The water is cold and can easily bring on a fatal attack of cramp"), not to stand behind the horses of Trondhjem "which are well known for their habit of kicking," and, above all, to avoid anyone carrying a gun. "In almost every Norwegian newspaper I read of accidents caused by the careless use of loaded rifles. I shall be exceedingly displeased if you do not keep well away from people carrying such weapons. Should an accident happen I must be informed immediately by telegram." His vanity was gratified by his noticing that "several copies of Passarge's book about me, and of Brandes's essay in *Nord und Süd,* accompanied by an excellent engraving of my likeness, are circulating among the guests. Almost all of them, I suppose, know my plays in German." Ludwig Passarge himself paid a visit with his wife; they "said they only live and breathe in my books." Grønvold's appetite continued to worry him. "It is not just that he eats excessive quantities; everything must be of the best and most expensive, and that for both lunch and dinner; he spends twice as much each day as I do."

Meanwhile, he worked steadily revising *The Wild Duck,* taking about a fortnight over each act. He completed the first two acts in their final form by 12 July, just a month after he had finished his first draft of the play; Act Three took him from 14 July to 29/30 July; Act Four was ready by 17 August. On 27 August he wrote to Sigurd:

My play is now fast nearing its conclusion. In three to four days it will be ready; then I shall read it through carefully and send it off. I take great joy in working on this play; it grows all the time in little details, and I shall miss it when I have to part from it; though at the same time, I shall be glad. The German sculptor Professor Kopf, from Rome, has with him a thirteen-year-old daughter who is the most perfect model for my Hedvig that could be imagined; she is pretty, has a serious face and manner, and is a little greedy.

Three days later, on 30 August, he wrote to Suzannah:

Although I don't know when or where my letters reach you while you continue to move from town to town, I must nevertheless send you the good news that I have just finished my manuscript. The play will be very rich in content, and bigger than any other of my recent works. I have said everything I wanted to say; and I don't think it could easily have been said better. Now to the business of reading it through, which will take two to three days; then off it goes to Hegel.

On 2 September he wrote to Hegel:

> I enclose the manuscript of my new play, *The Wild Duck,* which
> has occupied me daily for the past four months, and from which I
> cannot now part without a certain feeling of loss. The characters in it
> have, despite their many failings, grown dear to me as a result of this
> long daily association. But I cherish the hope that they will also find
> good friends and well-wishers among the great reading public and,
> not least, among theatre people; for they all, without exception, offer
> rewarding opportunities. But the study and representation of them
> will not be easy. . . . This new play occupies, in some ways, a unique
> position among my dramatic works. Its method differs in certain
> respects from that which I have previously employed. However, I
> don't wish to enlarge on that here. The critics will, I trust, see this for
> themselves; they will anyway find something to argue about, something
> to construe. I believe, too, that *The Wild Duck* may possibly tempt
> some of our younger dramatists to explore new territories, and this I
> regard as a desirable thing.

In the middle of Sepember, Ibsen received the letter he had been
awaiting for so many years; an invitation from Bjørnson to visit him and
his wife at Schwaz, where they were holidaying, two or three hours by
rail from Gossensass. Bjørnson had got to know Strindberg in Paris the
previous December, and had spent the spring raising funds for him as
energetically as, twenty years earlier, he had done for Ibsen. Ibsen accepted
his invitation eagerly; so, for the first time in nearly twenty years, these
two old friends and enemies met, and spent three days together. Ibsen
described the occasion in a letter to Suzannah on 17 September:

> I would not for anything have missed this meeting. I will be better
> able to tell you the details when we meet; here I shall merely
> mention a few external circumstances. Bjørnson and his son met me
> at the station; a room was prepared for me at the Gasthaus where they
> are staying; but I preferred to lodge at another hotel where, likewise,
> there awaited me for the occasion an enormous room, very handsome
> and comfortable. At the hotel I of course paid for my board and
> breakfast; but I ate lunch and dinner with the Bjørnsons and was with
> them for almost the whole of the rest of the time; they could not do
> enough for me. Bjørnson has gone grey, but looks strong. Fru B. is
> likewise somewhat greyed, and has grown rather deaf, but in other
> respects is as bright and lively as before and has developed into an
> excellent person. Both their daughters are uncommonly handsome,
> well brought up, unaffected and straightforward; I also much like
> Erling, their son. I did not see Jonas Lie, since he is so far behind

with his novel. But this meant that B. and I were able to talk all the more undisturbed, and this we did, about political, literary, and many other matters. B. was often much struck by my remarks and frequently returned to them. In one respect I have, by my visit, prevented a true misfortune from befalling our country.[34] But I don't want to put anything on paper about this. . . .

Here everything is as usual; many of the summer guests have now departed; but there are still a lot here, and newcomers arrive daily for briefer visits. The weather is now as warm and beautiful as one could wish. . . . Frøken Schirmer from Munich is occupying herself with spiritism [sic], or whatever it is called. She has the power of being able, by touching another person, to make her do what she wishes. Here she found a very ready medium in a Frøken von Pfeuffer, a nervous young lady, with whom she has undertaken a series of the most unlikely experiments, and subsequently with other people; she has now left.

This is the first reference in Ibsen's writings to an interest which was becoming widespread in Europe at this time and which was to manifest itself powerfully in Ibsen's next four plays: the ability of one human being to gain a supernatural power over the mind of another. Sigmund Freud, than a young neurologist of twenty-eight, had already seen hypnotism therapeutically used and probably made his own first experiments with it the following year;[35] and Strindberg was to employ it with terrifying effect in his play *Creditors* three years later.

"Schwaz," continued Ibsen's letter to Suzannah, "is quite a town, with six thousand inhabitants. It was generally known there that I was visiting B., and the locals saluted us when we appeared, whether together or singly. One family sent Fru B. a fine haunch of venison, another game, others had sent excellent Moselle, and yet others old rum and other good things. I saw friendly, contented faces in the doors of the shops and in the windows round about. There has been a lot written about me in the newspapers of Innsbruck and other Tyrolean towns this summer." One of Bjørnson's daughters, Bergliot, aged sixteen, particularly impressed him. When he saw Suzannah he told her: "Now I have seen Sigurd's future wife,"[36] and he was to be proved right.

Bjørnson gave his impressions of their encounter in a letter to Hegel. "Ibsen," he wrote (21 September), "is now a good, well-meaning old gentleman, with whom I disagreed on many points regarding ends and

---

[34] The nature of this national calamity which Ibsen claimed to have averted has never been identified; Halvdan Koht (II, 159) thinks it may have been a projected blind attack on the left-wing government.

[35] Jones, p. 209.

[36] Bergliot Ibsen, p. 115.

means, but with whom it was in the highest degree interesting to exchange views. His intellect, circumspection and wisdom are remarkable. Yet his intelligence is not of the all-round kind, any more than his knowledge."[37] He expanded this last observation in a letter to Jonas Lie. "You and I see more, and we see it better. Our intellectualism is incomparably greater. But he so adjusts himself to his that it gives a pretty good dividend."[38] Bjørnson was not far from the truth; Ibsen's intelligence was, like that of so many creative writers, intuitive and limited; he lacked many of the advantages of a trained mind; on many aspects of life and knowledge he was, as we have seen, almost childishly ignorant. Yet great creative minds are often thus: of Ibsen's contemporaries, Tolstoy, Dickens, Dostœvsky, Herman Melville and Tennyson shared equal areas of ignorance and blindness.

Unfortunately for Bjørnson, no sooner had he become reconciled with Ibsen than he fell out with his new friend Strindberg. Strindberg, who was prosecuted that autumn for alleged blasphemy in his volume of short stories, *Marriage,* resented some fatherly advice Bjørnson chose to offer him, and poked fun at the latter's new play, *A Gauntlet,* for demanding that men should, like women, stay chaste until marriage—a particularly incongruous suggestion from a man hardly famous for marital fidelity. "Be immoral, Bjørnson, as you were when you were young!" Strindberg exhorted him on 14 October 1884. "The virtue which comes when a man is fifty is not worth preaching!"[39] The advice was no better received than Bjørnson's to Strindberg had been.

During their conversations at Schwaz, Bjørnson had yet again attempted to persuade Ibsen to return to Norway and take over the general management of the Christiania Theatre, of which Bjørnson's son Bjørn, fresh from his year's training with the Meiningers, had recently been appointed artistic director. Ibsen was evidently interested enough to leave the question open when they parted, and Bjørnson thought he had persuaded him. "Before I'd been with him a few minutes," Bjørnson wrote to Jonas Lie on 2 October, "I realized he had the most burning desire to go home and take charge of the theatre, and build a new one. . . . He has been playing you up, or you didn't understand him, if you thought he didn't want it. *He has no real interest* now other than to get a good theatre going in a new building in Norway."[40]

But Bjørnson had evidently mistaken Ibsen's desire for a new theatre in a modern building for a willingness to take charge of things himself.

[37] Bjørnstjerne Bjørnson, *Kamp-tid (brev fra aarene 1879–1884)*, ed. Halvdan Koht (Oslo, 1932), II, 245.

[38] *Ibid.,* p. 244.

[39] *August Strindbergs brev,* IV, 355.

[40] *Kamp-tid,* II, 246–47.

Four days earlier Ibsen had in fact written a letter of refusal to Bjørnson, which the latter had not received when he wrote the above lines to Lie:

When one has had to do with theatre managements for as long as I have, and when one has busied oneself as exclusively with play-writing as I have, the inclination to take a practical hand often asserts itself, inevitably and powerfully. The theatre has something siren-like about it, and the two occasions on which you have thrown this idea at me have filled my mind with unrest and longing. Besides, I can't deny that I sometimes feel the need for a fixed occupation with duties attached. So I would have practical grounds for going home and taking over the theatre, were that practicable.

But the tragedy is that for the time being it is absolutely im-practicable. The party which holds power in the theatre is certainly no more favourably inclined towards me than towards you. My wife has just written from up there: "I would have never have believed that we were so much in the black books of the conservatives as has now, by numerous signs, shown itself to be the case." I do not for a moment doubt that her observation is correct. To offer me the leadership of the theatre would therefore be, for the board, to place itself in a position of hostility towards any well-wishing families and individuals whose support they cannot do without. So it will not hap-pen. I shall never become director of the theatre as long as the present board remains in power.

But you will perhaps protest that I could still go home and try in the meantime to work as a private reformer, hasten the building of the new theatre and thereby help to bring about the conditions under which my appointment as director of the theatre might become a possibility. All this might conceivably happen had I sufficient means to live on while this was happening. But I have not. I have still nowhere near saved enough to suffice for me and my family in the event of my abandoning my literary career. And I would have to abandon it if I went to live in Christiania. I am not thinking so much of all the distracting theatre work. No, the fact is I would not be able to write freely and totally uninhibitedly up there. And that is the same as say-ing that I would not be able to write at all. When ten years ago, after a ten years' absence, I sailed up the fjord, I literally felt my chest tighten with a feeling of sickness and unease. I had the same sensation during the whole of my stay there; I was no longer myself with all those cold and uncomprehending Norwegian eyes staring at me from the windows and pavements.

So I must wait another year. If the government and the Storthing decide to raise writers' grants to the extent of making me financially independent, then I might, for the cause of our theatre, reciprocate by leaving one or two dramatic works unwritten until later. . . .

Fortunately, the government remained true to character. It is a dreadful thought that, had they been more generous, *The Lady from the Sea* or *Rosmersholm* might never have been written.

The renewal of acquaintance between Ibsen and Bjørnson did not lead to a complete reconciliation. Karl Konow, who knew them both, was probably right when he wrote: "They respected and venerated each other, they met and talked, but never more than that. . . . Several times I have heard [Bjørnson] express regret that he could not get closer to him, and I think Ibsen felt the same. But the differences were too great. They could talk together, but not feel together. In a way they enjoyed each other's company, but they did not understand each other."[41]

As there was an outbreak of cholera in Italy, Ibsen stayed in Gossensass until the end of October. Suzannah and Sigurd joined him there in the middle of the month ("Should the weather be bad, stormy or foggy when you leave Christiania," he had warned them on 24 September, as neurotic about their safety as he was about his own, "do not take the steamer but go by land via Sweden."). Sigurd had learned on his return to Christiania that his appeal to Sverdrup had been successful, and that he had been appointed to the consular office in Stockholm; he stayed only a few days with his father before returning north. Thoughts of a new play had already begun to crystallize in Ibsen's mind. "I felt pretty nervous and overstrained when I had finished my manuscript," he wrote to Hegel on 18 October, "and decided to rest for a year. But this will not happen. I have already worked out plans for a new play in four acts and hope, before long, when I have settled down in Rome, to be able to start work on it." On 1 November he and Suzannah left Gossensass and, after a few days at Botzen, arrived back in Rome on 13 November.

Two days earlier, *The Wild Duck* had been published, in a printing of 8,000 copies, 2,000 less than *Ghosts* and *An Enemy of the People* (but this was probably due to the fact that there had been a recession in the book trade rather than to any fear that it might prove less popular than its predecessors). The reaction among the critics and the reading public was principally one of bewilderment—which, indeed, was to be the general reaction to his remaining plays. Modern opinion regards these eight final plays as Ibsen's greatest period, or at any rate greater than the middle period of his "social dramas" from *The Pillars of Society* to *An Enemy of the People*. His contemporaries in Scandinavia felt otherwise. From now on, we find him repeatedly accused of being a "riddling Sphinx," of being obscure for obscurity's sake, and of concentrating on

[41] Karl Konow, *Bjørnson og Lie* (Oslo, 1919), p. 72.

the sordid. Only his increasing fame abroad saved his reputation from going into a sharp decline at home.

"The public does not know what to make of it," commented the *Christiania Intelligenssedler* on *The Wild Duck*. "One paper says one thing and the other just the opposite." *Aftenposten* (18 November) complained: "One may study and study to find what Ibsen wants to say and not find it." *Morgenbladet* (16 and 19 November) found the plot "as queer as it is thin. . . . One has an undeniable impression of something artificial and contrived. . . . The total impression can hardly be other than a strong sense of emptiness and unpleasantness." *Bergens Tidende* thought the play proved Ibsen's inferiority to Bjørnson. "He does not speak from his heart as does Bjørnson. He does not make demands of the individual with the same strength, he has no faith in his ability to ennoble humanity by means of his writings. He states the problems excellently as he sees them, but makes no attempt to show the way beyond them; he chastises as one who has authority, but makes no demand for improvement." Bjørnson himself wrote to Hegel on 20 November: "I find Ibsen's new book nauseating."[42] Ditmar Meidell in *Norsk Maanedsskrift for Litteratur* (1884, pp. 569–74) admitted the technical mastery but concluded that: "to read plays in which the characters are total idiots and morally dead . . . is no refinement to the spirit." About the only two Norwegian critics to appreciate the point of the play were Mathilde Schjøtt in *Nyt Tidsskrift* (1884, pp. 616 ff.) who called it a masterpiece, and Irgens Hansen, who, in *Dagbladet* (16 November) recognized that Ibsen "here stands on humanity's ground and speaks humanity's cause, even though it be the cause of a very shabby humanity."

Nor was the play much better appreciated in Sweden or Denmark. Helena Nyblom, writing in *Ny Svensk Tidskrift* (1885, pp. 65–69) complained that "not *every* Norwegian is a good-for-nothing, as Ibsen would have us suppose. . . . Ibsen has only one feeling for human beings, and that is contempt. . . . Once one has slept on them [i.e. Ibsen's plays], one realizes that their effect is merely that of theatrical illusion, and after a few years they can usually not be played again, for only those plays which truthfully reflect life can survive for long." In the same issue (pp. 444–46), Kristofer Randers, writing from Norway, declared: "It is a very old play, a morose play, a tired play. It is moreover a very incomprehensible play . . . It has not made any lasting impression on the reading public. . . . One can only be angry that such a fine technique should be wasted on such ungrateful material." And C. D. af Wirsen, a great admirer of Ibsen's early plays, though he was to hate almost all the later ones, while acknowledging, in *Post och Inrikes-Tidning*, Ibsen's "incomparable technical mastery," thought the play "as cold, hard and implacable as it is gloomy and

[42] Nielsen, II, 136.

pessimistic."[43] Georg Brandes did not review it, but he confidentially told J. P. Jacobsen (23 November 1884) that *"The Wild Duck* was only a half-pleasure," and he never rated it among Ibsen's masterpieces. "Ibsen's [book] made a glum impression on me," he wrote to Alexander Kielland on 13 November. "I thought it rather empty. Why bother exclusively with such totally insignificant people? His contempt for humanity seems perpetually on the increase."[44] Kielland himself wrote to Hegel on 18 November that he found the play "bizarre and archaic . . . these eternal symbols and allusions and heavy underlinings are too crude for me."[45]

Yet a few people appreciated it. An anonymous reviewer in the Stockholm *Ny Illustrerad Tidning* (possibly J. A. Runström) praised it hugely. "Now as always," he wrote (7 February 1885), "[Ibsen] knows how to portray characters so as to excite different opinions, be subjects of argument. And to excite different opinions is just what he wants to do. . . . He can conclude his plays with a question mark, but he never writes a full stop. . . . His work has always opened up new vistas, always contained something other than what one expected." And Edvard Brandes, in *Politiken* (16 November 1884), declared that Ibsen "has no equal in Europe as a master of dialogue" and concluded: "It is plays like this that educate actors and spiritually liberate those who see them." Yet even he, nearly forty years later in 1922, expressed the opinion that *The Wild Duck* "will not survive in the first rank of Ibsen's plays."[46]

Again, however, we must remember that the young, to whom Ibsen principally appealed, were inadequately (if at all) represented among the critics. Carl Georgsson Fleetwood in Stockholm must have been speaking for many of his generation when he noted in his diary on 7 December 1884 that *The Wild Duck* was all the more exciting ("A new book by Ibsen is always an exciting event") because he had heard it described as inferior "by the very people who sing the praise of 'fearless' Ibsen—probably because he has been fearless enough to expose the nakedness of the new gods too!"[47]

Across the North Sea, Ibsen's English admirers were as baffled as their Scandinavian counterparts. Edmund Gosse condemned it four years later in the *Fortnightly Review*[48] as "a strange, melancholy and pessimistic drama, almost without a ray of light from beginning to end. . . . There is really not a character in the book that inspires confidence or liking. . . . There can be no doubt that it is by far the most difficult of Ibsen's dramas to comprehend." William Archer also failed to understand it at

---

[43] C. D. af Wirsen, *Kritiker* (Stockholm, 1901), p. 62.

[44] *Brandes Brevveksling*, IV, 361.

[45] Nielsen, II, 465.

[46] Reprinted in *Om Teater*, p. 116.

[47] Fleetwood, I, 613.

[48] "Ibsen's Social Dramas," in the *Fortnightly Review*, 1 January 1889, pp. 107–21.

first (though he came to admire it greatly once he had seen it staged). Arthur Symons thought it "a play of inferior quality,"[49] and Havelock Ellis dismissed it as "the least remarkable"[50] of Ibsen's recent plays. Almost the only British critic (Ireland being then a part of Britain) to see the point of the play during the next ten years was Bernard Shaw, who devoted to it one of his most penetrating passages in *The Quintessence of Ibsenism:*

> After *An Enemy of the People*, Ibsen . . . left the vulgar ideals for dead and set about the exposure of those of the choicer spirits, beginning with the incorrigible idealists who had idealized his very self, and were becoming known as Ibsenites. His first move in this direction was such a tragi-comic slaughtering of sham Ibsenism that his astonished victims plaintively declared that *The Wild Duck,* as the new play was called, was a satire on his former works; while the pious, whom he had disappointed so severely by his interpretation of *Brand* . . . began to hope that he was coming back repentant to the fold.

Shaw concluded with a remark which strikes surely to the heart of the play: "the busybody [Gregers] finds that people cannot be freed from their failings from without. They must free themselves."

Despite the general bewilderment, however, the book sold remarkably well in Scandinavia. Four days after publication *Dagbladet* announced that the first edition had sold out, and a second impression of two thousand copies was in the shops by early December. The principal Scandinavian theatres wasted no time in buying the performing rights, and productions were already in rehearsal in Christiania, Bergen, Copenhagen, Stockholm and Helsinki. "If there is any living dramatist," reported Erik Bøgh, the censor of the Royal Theatre in Copenhagen, to his board on 17 November, "whose plays the public demand to see performed, whose earlier plays have brought so much honour and profit as to pioneer a path for his successors . . . it must, before all others, be Henrik Ibsen. . . . *The Wild Duck* is in all respects executed with his unique mastery"; and he concluded, unfashionably, by declaring that the play had "a demonstrably healthy moral attitude."[51]

On 14 November Ibsen addressed a letter to Hans Schrøder, of the Christiania Theatre, which, like his letters to the same correspondent about *An Enemy of the People*, is full of sharp practical observations invaluable to any modern director of the play. Foreseeing the danger that whoever acted Hjalmar Ekdal might be tempted to play him as a figure of fun (a temptation which too few actors have resisted, just as too many have played Gregers as spiteful), Ibsen warned Schrøder:

[49] *Universal Review* 3 (1889), 567–74.
[50] Havelock Ellis, *The New Spirit* (London, 1890), p. 166.
[51] Agerholm, p. 280.

Hjalmar must not be acted with any trace of parody. The actor must never for a moment show that he is conscious that there is anything funny in what he says. His voice has, as Relling observes, something endearing about it, and this quality must be clearly brought out. His sentimentality is honest, his melancholy, in its way, attractive; no hint of affectation. Between ourselves, I would suggest you cast your mind towards Kristofer Janson, who still contrives to give an effect of beauty whatever drivel he may be uttering. There is a pointer for whoever plays the part. . . . Where can one find a Hedvig? I don't know. And Mrs. Sørby? She must be beautiful and witty, not vulgar. . . . Gregers is the most difficult part in the play, from the acting point of view. Sometimes I think Hammer would be best, sometimes Bjørn B[jørnson].[52] . . . I hope you will spare me Isachsen, as he always carries on like some strange actor instead of like an ordinary human being.[53] However, I suppose he might possibly make something out of Molvik's few lines. The two servants must not be cast too casually; Petersen might possibly be played by Bucher, and Jensen by Abelsted, if the latter is not required for one of the dinner guests. Yes, those guests! What about them? You can't just use ordinary extras; they'd ruin the whole act. . . . The play demands absolute naturalness and truthfulness both in the ensemble work and in the staging. The lighting, too, is important; it is different for each act, and is calculated to establish the peculiar atmosphere of that act. I just wanted to pass on these random reflections. As regards everything else, please do as you think best.

Wherein does the "method" of *The Wild Duck* differ, as Ibsen told Hegel, from that which he had previously employed? At first sight there is no immediately obvious difference; it seems, like *A Doll's House, Ghosts* and *An Enemy of the People,* to be a realistic play about realistic people, and the method seems to be his old method of raking over apparently dead ashes and exposing the live embers beneath? The symbolism? But Ibsen had used symbolism at least as freely in *Brand*.

[52] Bjørn Bjørnson had joined the Christiania Theatre the previous month. Aged twenty-five, he had acted for a year in the Meiningen company, and had studied music at the Vienna Conservatoire, with Mahler as a fellow-pupil and Bruckner as a teacher. He was to do much towards revivifying the Christiania Theatre, and became chief of the National Theatre when it was founded in 1899. He directed the Christiania premiere of *The Wild Duck*, and records that Johannes Brun, who could imitate any animal or bird, made the sounds of the duck off-stage as well as playing Old Ekdal. (*Fra barndommens dage* [Oslo, 1922], pp. 40–41).

[53] Schrøder ignored Ibsen's plea regarding Isachsen and cast him as Relling, in which role he proved a disaster. "I hear from reliable sources," wrote Ibsen to Schrøder on 30 December 1886, "that by his lunatic conception and dreadful performance . . . he ruined the whole effect of the play." (Anker, *Henrik Ibsens brevveksling med Christiania Theater, 1878–1899,* p. 46.)

Nevertheless, I think there is little doubt that it was the symbolism in *The Wild Duck* to which Ibsen was referring when he spoke of a new method. In *Brand* the symbols are incidental to the play, or at any rate are not fully integrated into it. The Ice Church and the hawk are left deliberately imprecise; there is room for intelligent argument about their meanings; perhaps, indeed, they are intended to mean different things to different people, like the symbols in Kafka. In *The Wild Duck,* however, there is a single and precise symbol, that of the bird itself; and, so far from being incidental to the play, it is the hub and heart of it. *Brand* is a play into which symbols have worked their way; *The Wild Duck* is a play dependent on, and held together by, a symbol; as though the wild duck were a magnet and the characters in the play so many iron filings held together by this centripetal force. This was not a method that Ibsen was to use invariably in his subsequent plays; *Rosmersholm,* for example, and *Hedda Gabler,* have more in common (as regards their symbolism) with *Ghosts* than with *The Wild Duck.* But we find him returning to it in his later plays: the towers and spires of *The Master Builder* and the crutch in *Little Eyolf* serve a similar structural purpose to the wild duck. They are images from which the characters cannot escape, any more than the iron filings can escape the magnet.

Ibsen probably borrowed the image of the wild duck from a poem by Welhaven called "The Sea-Bird" which describes how a wild duck is wounded and dives down to die on the sea-bed; and Professor Francis Bull suggests that he may also have been influenced by Darwin's account in *The Origin of Species* of how wild ducks degenerate in captivity.[54] Some astonishing theories have been advanced as to what the bird is intended to stand for. Surely Ibsen makes it abundantly clear that he intended it as a double symbol with two precise and obvious references. Firstly, it is, like Hedvig, a by-product of Haakon Werle's fondness for sport which has been rejected by him and is now cared for by the Ekdal family (at any rate in Hjalmar's eyes, though we never know any more than Gina does, which of the two men is the father).[55] Secondly, with a more general application, it represents the refusal of most people, once they have been wounded, to go on living and face reality. Both Hjalmar and his father have sought to hide themselves in the deep blue sea of illusion, and Gregers, like the "damned clever dog" trained by his father, hauls them back to the surface. The cynics, Relling and Haakon Werle, watch this operation; so do the two sensible, earthbound women, Gina and Mrs. Sørby. These women,

[54] C.E., X, 23–24.

[55] Gina's answer to Hjalmar in Act Four ("I don't know . . . I—couldn't tell") is open to several interpretations. I take it to mean that she was irregular in her periods, missed one soon after Werle had slept with her, told him, he introduced her to Hjalmar, they slept together at once or almost at once, and so the child could be either man's.

Ibsen seems to imply, offer the only real refuge: love. Mrs. Sørby can save Haakon Werle, despite Gregers's cynicism, just as she could have saved Relling, who had also once loved her; Relling knows this, and it is hinted that the loss of her is partly responsible for his having turned into a drunkard. And Gina, if Gregers had not intervened, could have saved Hjalmar. Yet Ibsen leaves a question mark here: is love simply another illusion, like the Ekdals' loft? And if so, then is not the illusion of the loft justified, just as much as the illusion of love?

At the same time, while the wild duck has these two specific significances within the play, it is possible that, consciously or unconsciously, it reflects Ibsen's impression of himself when he wrote it: one who has forgotten what it means to live wild, and has grown plump and tame and content with his basket, as unlike the author of *Brand* as the duck is unlike the hawk of the earlier play, of which, likewise, the climax is a shot fired at (or supposedly at) a bird by a girl of fourteen. How far, Ibsen must have asked himself—and he was to ask the question again through Allmers in *Little Eyolf* and Rubek in *When We Dead Awaken*—does the artist, like the Ekdals, shut himself off from life? Is his world so very different from their loft with its imitations of reality? Which is the more cowardly refuge, the Ekdals' loft or Brand's Ice Church?

Old Ekdal contains many traits of Ibsen's own father who, too, had been a lieutenant in the militia and a notable huntsman before he had gone bankrupt and brought the family name into disgrace. Hedvig seems to have got her name, and probably some of her character, from Ibsen's sister, the only member of his family for whom he retained any real affection; and the loft was probably a memory of the loft (still to be seen) at Venstøp which, like the Ekdals' loft, contained books left by "The Flying Dutchman," including that book which delighted Hedvig Ekdal as it had delighted the young Ibsen, *Harrison's* (or, as Ibsen spelt it, *Harryson's*) *History of London,* published in 1775. He also borrowed for the play certain details of a trial which had caused a scandal during his student days in Christiania, when an army officer, accused of embezzlement, had, like Old Ekdal, tried unsuccessfully to shoot himself (a source to which he was to return for much of his material for *John Gabriel Borkman*). And, perhaps the most significant echo from his own past, there looms the figure which he had compulsively introduced into *The Pretenders, Brand, Peer Gynt, Emperor and Galilean* and *Ghosts,* of the illegitimate child.

Hjalmar seems to have had several models—Kristofer Janson, the writer whom Ibsen had known in Rome, Edvard Larsen, a photographer with whom Ibsen had lodged in earlier days, Magnus Bagge, a failed artist from whom he had taken drawing lessons around 1860 and who is said to have had a constant longing to lift himself above everyday prose (when he went to live in Germany he called himself von Bagge), and a sculptor in Rome, C. D. Magelssen, who was always talking of a great invention he was about to perfect which would revolutionize the craft of casting in bronze and also, in some strange way, the manufacture of torpedoes.[56] Gregers Werle was at first (as we know from Ibsen's notes for the play) based on the novelist and playwright Alexander Kielland, whose radicalism Ibsen regarded as bogus, but he gradually developed into a kind of *reductio ad absurdum* of Dr. Stockmann, a living illustration of the danger of a single-minded pursuit of truth if not tempered by common sense and an understanding of human limitations. More importantly, Hjalmar and Gregers both represent different aspects of Ibsen himself: on the one hand the evader of reality, on the other the impractical idealist who pesters mankind with his "claims of the ideal" because he has a sick conscience and despises himself. How far, one wonders, did Ibsen identify himself with Gregers in that curious episode when the latter, finding that the stove smokes, throws water on it to put out the fire and only makes the stink worse? He had already portrayed these two conflicting aspects of himself in *Brand* and *Peer Gynt,* and the conflict between Gregers and Hjalmar is as though Brand and Peer Gynt had been brought face to face.

There is one other respect in which the method of *The Wild Duck* was, or seemed, new, and that was the way in which tragedy and comedy tread on each other's heels. This was one of the things about the play which so upset its contemporaries, though it delighted Bernard Shaw—"to look on with horror and pity at a profound tragedy, shaking with laughter all the time at an irresistible comedy," as he wrote of the 1897 London production in the *Saturday Review.* Ibsen instinctively knew what Shakespeare and the Greeks knew, and what Brecht was to remind playgoers of, that if you want to make a tragic event really hurt you must precede it with comedy, a Porter jesting as he leads the night visitors to Duncan's death-chamber, a Grave-Digger who jokes in Ophelia's grave, a Clown to carry the asp to Cleopatra. This was a lesson which had been forgotten by dramatists; and if Ibsen was referring to this when he said it would be easier for him than for younger dramatists to attempt this effect, critical reaction was to prove him right.

As a postscript to *The Wild Duck,* one may remark how, as in almost every play he wrote, Ibsen anticipated one of the main discoveries of modern psychology. "Liberation," he had noted in his preliminary jottings for the play, "consists in securing for individuals the right to free themselves, each according to his particular need." To free *themselves;* how many of Ibsen's contemporaries who regarded themselves as revolutionaries realized that? Ibsen understood that the demand must come from within, and that truth, if it comes from without, is often regarded as an attack on the defensive system which the "life-lie," as Relling called it, represents.

The good book sales of *The Wild Duck* saved 1884 from being one of

[56] Francis Bull, *Vildanden, og andre essays* (Oslo, 1966), pp. 13–14.

Ibsen's worst years financially, for he had made barely £100 from performing rights and had had only one reprint:

	crowns	
Fee from August Lindberg for *Lady Inger*	400	
5th edn. of *Love's Comedy* (2,000 copies)	1,000	
Fee for *The Vikings at Helgeland* at Oldenburg	100	
1st edn. of *The Wild Duck*	7,440	
2nd edn. of *The Wild Duck*	1,860	
Extra fees from Bergen Theatre for various plays	510	
Fee for *Ghosts* in Helsinki	150	
Extra fee for *An Enemy of the People* in Stockholm	182	
Extra fee for *Ghosts* in Stockholm	767	
	12,409	£688

Nevertheless, he asked Hegel (23 November) to buy him "good, sound securities" to the face value of 8,000 crowns, and on 10 January in the New Year gave his agent in Christiania, Nils Lund, instructions that the first 3,000 crowns of the fees due to him from the Bergen and Christiania theatres for *The Wild Duck*, "plus my pension and whatever else may come," should be held and paid out in installments to Sigurd in Stockholm.

PART FIVE

The Explorer of the Unconscious

23

Rosmersholm

1885–1886

Bergen proudly staged the world premiere of *The Wild Duck* on 9 January 1885, Christiania, Helsinki and Stockholm following suit within the month, and Copenhagen in February. The audiences were, for the most part, as bewildered as the critics had been. However unpleasant the messages of *A Doll's House, Ghosts* and *An Enemy of the People* may have been, at least they contained a "hero" or "heroine" with whom one could identify one's sympathy, but the characters of *The Wild Duck,* apart from the child Hedvig, seemed a thoroughly bad lot; and it was difficult to avoid the implication that they mirrored the audience. In Copenhagen the public expressed its disapproval audibly. "Ibsen," commented Edvard Brandes, reviewing the production in *Politiken* on 23 February, "is the finest dramatist writing in Scandinavia and . . . because he punches the Tartuffes of the world in their unctuous phizzes, people hissed him yesterday at the Royal Theatre."

In Stockholm, alone, was the play well received, mainly because August Lindberg, who directed it there, understood the special problems that *The Wild Duck* posed. "With your new play," he wrote to Ibsen before starting rehearsals, "we stand on new and unbroken ground. . . . These are quite new human beings, and what will it avail to use the common approach of actors—people who have lost touch with nature through spending their lives playing boulevard comedy? I realized this with *Ghosts,* and it is the same with *The Wild Duck*." "My mind reels," he confided in a friend. "Such unaccustomed problems for us actors! Never before have we been faced with the like."[1] He cast an unknown actress as Gina and an eighteen-year-old pupil from drama school as Hedvig. At this flouting of the tradition that the best parts went to the most established performers (in Copenhagen Hedvig had been played by Betty Hennings, the

[1] Per Lindberg, pp. 146, 148.

Royal Theatre's leading actress, who was over forty) three of the leading members of the Stockholm company held a press conference to protest.

Lindberg's production of *The Wild Duck* was a landmark in theatrical history, for it anticipated in almost every respect the naturalism which André Antoine was to introduce five years later at his Théâtre Libre in Paris. Lindberg's son tells how his father astonished audiences by making his actors move and talk as though unconscious of the footlights and the audience, not like actors but like human beings such as one might meet outside a theatre, people living in an ordinary room—a room, moreover, which had doors with *handles* that shut with a click instead of the usual canvas flaps, and which even contained a commode. Lindberg's commode became a symbol for this new kind of production, a forerunner of the modern kitchen sink. His own performance as Hjalmar antagonized the conservative critics, probably (reading between the lines of the complaints) because he did not shrink from the contradictions which are so important a part of the character; Gustaf af Geijerstam, praising his performance in *Aftonbladet,* wrote that Lindberg made Hjalmar "a human being of whom one gradually sees new aspects, now comic, now pathetic, just as in life one gets to know a person intimately so that in the end one sees him rounded and whole."[2] He was evidently not afraid, as so many actors have been, of the moments of ridiculousness. Later in his career Lindberg was a famous Gregers; the two roles are closely interlocked, as even Othello and Iago are not, and there can have been few productions of the play when the actors playing them have not at some time felt a compulsive desire to change parts.

Germany had to wait three years before seeing the play (as with *An Enemy of the People*); but Ibsen was about to be introduced to a new and important public, for, as he informed Hegel on 11 February, an "Italian biographer and translator, Alfred Mazza, has made an excellent translation of *A Doll's House,*" and was about to try his hand at *The Wild Duck*. This was to have important results, for although he was never to take Italy by storm as he was to take Germany, England, and (less permanently) France, he was to find there his greatest female interpreter. Further north, he added to Hegel, *A Doll's House* had been revived in Warsaw, "with an actress who is having an extraordinary success in the role [Helena Modjeska]. But of payment to the author there is of course no question."

On 24 March *Brand* was at last staged—in its entirety, moreover—at Ludvig Josephson's Nya Teater in Stockholm, nineteen years almost to the day after the play's publication. Josephson himself directed it, as he had directed the first production of *Peer Gynt*. "It lasted for six and a half hours, until 12.30 A.M.," recalled August Lindberg. "Such ladies as survived to the end lay dozing on their escorts' shoulders, with their corsets and bodices unbuttoned."[3] Yet, "although its length and difficulty pre-

2 *Ibid.,* p. 150.
3 Quoted by Gunnar Ollén in *Ibsens dramatik* (Stockholm, 1955), p. 50.

clude complete success on the stage," wrote *Dagens Nyheter* on 26 March, "it proved always interesting and at certain moments highly effective" and, although demanding "a closer attention on the part of the audience than most modern plays," elicited "frequent and loud applause" from the full house. Ibsen wrote Josephson a grateful letter on 9 April, saying that the event "has at last erased from my mind the impression of all those cold, uncomprehending eyes which you yourself remember from a certain other place in the high north," and expressing the hope that it would not be the last time that he and Josephson would work together "since I still have a whole heap of lunacies in my head out of which I think one might make quite good plays."

The day after the *Brand* premiere, *A Doll's House* received its first English performance in anything approaching the original text. It was not a grand occasion; the performers were an amateur group called the Scribblers, the place the School of Dramatic Art in Argyle Street, London, and it was in aid of the Society for the Prevention of Cruelty to Children. William Archer was there, and wrote about it the following week in the *Dramatic Review:*

> It has been proved of old that amateurs rush in where artists fear to tread, but never was there a more audacious case in point than the late performance of *Et Dukkehjem,* at the School of Dramatic Art. Since I assisted with two or three other barbarians at a Chinese tragedy in San Francisco, I have not seen an audience so hopelessly bewildered as that which stoically sat out Miss Lord's translation of Ibsen's play. The actors themselves had a glimmering idea of the plot and situations, but even this they failed to convey to the spectators; as for the characterization, the tendency, the satire, had the play been in Chinese they could not have been more completely lost on performers and spectators alike. The whole affair reminded me of the memorable performance of the 1603 Quarto of *Hamlet* at the St. George's Hall, with the stage arranged after the Elizabethan manner. Imagine the conception of Shakespeare which a spectator who had never heard of him would have received from this performance of *Hamlet.* As far, or further, from the truth is the conception of Henrik Ibsen conveyed by the Scribblers' travesty to the minds of those who witnessed it. Miss Lord's *Nora* stands in relation to *Et Dukkehjem* somewhat in the relation of the 1603 *Hamlet* to the perfect text, and the Helmer of Mr. Addison was to Emil Poulsen's as Mr. Poel's Hamlet to Mr. Irving's; yet I could not but reflect that the best possible translation of Ibsen's drama, played by the best available English actors, would have been scarcely less bewildering to an average English audience. . . . Miss Lord's translation is clumsy, and though I believe it has attracted attention in one or two narrow circles (the performance at the School of Dramatic Art seems to prove as much), it has been little noticed by the press, and has certainly not reached the general public.

Despite the "cold, uncomprehending eyes" of which Ibsen had complained to Bjørnson, he had begun to dwell with increasing earnestness on the possibility of returning to settle in Norway. Rome had begun to lose its magic; and on 25 April he wrote to Hegel that he felt doubtful whether they would return after their summer holiday. "For several reasons," he explained, "it would be convenient for me to spend another year in Germany, where I could take better care of a deal of literary business than I can from down here." This sounds rather a thin excuse; if he had still been really happy in Rome, he could easily have conducted his correspondence with translators and theatre directors from down there. "Besides," he continued more convincingly, "it will bring me somewhat nearer home, and I have lately begun to think seriously of buying a little villa, or rather a cottage, in the neighbourhood of Christiania, by the fjord, where I could live isolated and exclusively occupied with my work. What I most miss here is the sight of the sea, and this longing increases each year. Besides, I have over the years assembled a not so small collection of works of art, mainly paintings, and all these are now in store in an attic in Munich, without our getting any joy from them." The sea, in Ibsen's work, always stands for the dark, mysterious force within one over which one has no control, and at fifty-seven he was feeling the compulsion, like so many exiles, to spend his old age in the place where he had been born. It is common for writers to react against the place which first spiritually liberated them. The warmth and colour of Italian life and the Italian landscape, which had so excited him as an æsthetically starved man in his middle thirties, seem to have ceased to stimulate him as he approached sixty. He no longer enjoyed presiding over a Socratic symposium at a crowded *osteria*.

He had intended to holiday in the Tyrol or on Lake Constance; but instead, he went to Norway. After a short stop in Copenhagen, he reached Christiania on 6 June. But if he had hoped that his bitter memories would be speedily dispelled, he was to be sharply disillusioned. On 10 June he sat in the gallery of the Storthing to listen to a debate on what came to be known as the "Kielland affair." The immediate issue was whether a civil list pension like his own should be awarded to the novelist Alexander Kielland, but the debate turned into a general discussion of the right of freedom of thought in religious matters. Kielland was a professed freethinker, as Ibsen had been when his application for a pension had been rejected over twenty years earlier; but now, for the first time, there was a liberal government in power headed by a champion of free thought, Johan Sverdrup, and the result would surely be different.

It was not. The government failed to take a decisive stand, the progressives were defeated and Kielland's application was rejected. Ibsen was outraged. The government seemed to him, more forcibly than ever before, to have betrayed its principles, and no longer to represent the true feeling of the left. Next day he took the train north to Trondhjem, and was seen off at the station by Bjørnson's son, Bjørn. "Tell the youth of Norway from me," he said to him, loudly, so that all could hear, "that I will stand with them as the corner-stone of the left. What may seem madness in the young will conquer in the end. Be sure of that."[4]

Three days after his arrival in Trondhjem, on 14 June, the local Workers' Association honoured him with a banner procession, and he used the occasion to deliver a speech demanding a new attitude from those in authority, an attitude which he summed up in that word so beloved of Dr. Stockmann, and as unfashionable in Norway then as it is in most countries now: aristocracy. "There is still much to be done in this country," he declared, "before we can be said to have achieved full freedom. But our present democracy scarcely has the strength to accomplish that task. An element of aristocracy must enter into our political life, our government, our members of parliament and our press. I am of course not thinking of aristocracy of wealth, of learning, or even of ability or talent. I am thinking of aristocracy of character, of mind and of will. That alone can make us free.[5] And this aristocracy, which I hope may be granted to our people, will come to us from two sources, the only two sections of society which have not yet been corrupted by party pressure. It will come to us from our women and from our working men. The reshaping of social conditions which is now being undertaken in Europe is principally concerned with the future status of the workers and of women. That is what I am hoping and waiting for, and what I shall work for with all my might."

Ibsen and Suzannah remained a full month in Trondhjem, where they were joined by Sigurd, on leave from Stockholm. They then moved down the coast to the pretty little town of Molde, where they stayed for two months at the newly-built Hotel Alexandra. Molde was, he wrote Hegel on 11 July, "one of the most beautiful places in the world for panorama. There is a lovely fjord, bounded by an infinity of snow-capped peaks, yet with a rich, almost Mediterranean vegetation. But I would not wish to stay here long; so there will be nothing of my earlier notion of buying a property up here." A newspaper correspondent in the town reported that "he and his wife keep very quietly to themselves, associate with no one and seldom speak to anyone. After meals they return to their rooms." He noted that Ibsen spent hours each day standing on the jetty below the hotel staring down into the water. "He stands there most of the day." When he did talk to anyone he preferred, as at Berchtesgaden and

[4] *Dagbladet,* 11 June 1885, reprinted in C.E., XV, 422.

[5] The question had evidently been on Ibsen's mind much during the past three years. Apart from *An Enemy of the People,* Ibsen had written in his preliminary notes for *The Wild Duck,* jotted down during the winter of 1882–83: "A new aristocracy will arise. It will not be the aristocracy of birth or wealth, of talent or knowledge. The aristocracy of the future will be the aristocracy of the mind and of the will." The thought may not seem particularly relevant to *The Wild Duck,* but it was to be very relevant to *Rosmersholm.*

Gossensass, to chat with the common people rather than the bourgeoisie; and several times he had himself rowed in a boat along the fjord to the open sea.[6]

A fortnight after his arrival, on 24 July, the town held a reception for him; but he noticed that few people who were not of left-wing sympathies attended, and when, the following month, civic receptions were given in honour of the Prince of Wales (26 August) and William Gladstone (27 August), who were independently touring the Norwegian west coast that summer, Ibsen was not invited. He would probably have found little in common with the Prince of Wales, though they could have conversed in German, but one would think that he might have got on well with Gladstone, who loved Norway and found its inhabitants "a small people living happily in a spirit of democracy,"[7] a more charitable verdict than Ibsen would have delivered.

Ibsen's suspicion that he was being ostracized by the conservatives was deepened by a coolness that he discerned, or thought he discerned, in two old friends who were in Molde at the time, Ludvig Daæ and Lorentz Dietrichson. He especially sensed that Dietrichson was being stand-offish towards him, he could only suppose in deference to the latter's fellow-conservatives in the town. Dietrichson denies this, saying that when he met Ibsen there on 12 July he found him "unusually nervous, almost touchy. He had a feeling, which I am sure was exaggerated, of being hated and looked askance at in Norway."[8] He adds that he knew Ibsen was busy with a new work (which he wasn't), and had no wish to disturb him; also, that Ibsen's radical friends had untruthfully told Ibsen that Dietrichson had said harsh things of him.[9] One's instinct is to blame Ibsen's hypersensitivity; but Gerhard Gran, a sober judge in most matters, thinks that Ibsen may have been right in his suspicions. The hatred between conservatives and liberals in Norway then was almost pathological. "A leftwinger," writes Gran, "was not merely a supporter of the ungodly impeachment but also a naturalist, a materialist, an anti-Christian and a moral anarchist."[10]

[6] Per Amdam, "Ibsen og Molde," in *Edda* (1952), pp. 261–77.
[7] Sir Philip Magnus, *Gladstone* (London, 1954), p. 332.
[8] Dietrichson, I, 366.
[9] *Ibid.*, IV, 294.
[10] Gran, II, 183. The "impeachment" the previous year had done more than anything to inflame antagonism between the two parties. The Norwegian cabinet was constitutionally independent of the Storthing and acknowledged responsibility only to the king. This had led to an incongruous situation whereby the Storthing was overwhelmingly Liberal while the Cabinet, chosen by the king, remained Conservative. When the Storthing tried to resolve this situation King Oscar vetoed the bill, whereupon the Storthing took the extreme measure of impeaching the members of the Cabinet before the Supreme Court. One by one they were dismissed and fined. The king selected a new and equally Conservative cabinet; the Storthing dug in its heels;

Still, if Ibsen felt slighted by his political adversaries in Molde, he found ample compensation in the company, from 11 to 15 August, of another old acquaintance from Rome, Count Carl Snoilsky. The two had met again in Stockholm in 1869 and 1877, when Ibsen had been disappointed at Snoilsky's apparent movement towards a more conservative outlook (he had taken a post in the Swedish Foreign Office) and at the withering of his creative talent. In his youth Snoilsky had been a fertile and gifted poet; but after he had married and become a civil servant his creative springs had dried up and for ten years he had found himself scarcely able to write a line. "I have wasted my life," he had noted sadly in 1874, "and it is too late to change things now." But in 1879, at the age of thirty-eight, he had left the Foreign Office, divorced his wife, married one of her relatives, and gone abroad into voluntary exile. At once he had found himself able to write again, and published one volume after another.

But the kind of poetry he was writing now was very different from the charming lyrics that had made his name. He, the refined nobleman, had become absorbed by the class struggle and the spirit of revolution. He longed to enter into contact with the common people; but his own upbringing and aristocratic heritage inhibited him. In 1883, two years before he met Ibsen at Molde, Snoilsky had written: "Certainly creative literature can have an enormous influence, as Ibsen has shown, in the debating of social problems. . . . [But] my powers do not suffice for so lofty a task, and so broad a public. I dare not aim so high. I am, moreover, conscious of my main handicap—that I have not, from childhood, lived the life of the *people*—my education and upbringing in the narrow classical tradition have unfitted me, like the vast majority of our writers, to address the humbler strata of society in a language they understand. Unlike my colleagues, however, I am often painfully conscious of this barrier, this limitation, and do my best to transcend it."[11]

Three years after their divorce Snoilsky's first wife had died of consumption, and many people had blamed him for her death. But Ibsen, during the four days he spent with Snoilsky at Molde, took a great liking both to him and to his new wife; he thought her sensitivity and strength of character largely responsible for Snoilsky's regeneration as a human being. He was deeply interested in Snoilsky's conviction that poetry should not merely deal with the "beautiful" but should be connected with contemporary thought and ideas (he had boldly and outspokenly defended *Ghosts*), and

---

the king refused to yield, and was rumoured to be considering a *coup d'état;* but eventually, on 26 June 1884, he sent for Sverdrup and invited him to form a Liberal ministry. The conflict thus ended in complete victory for the Liberals, but left a legacy of deep and lasting bitterness. For a full account of these happenings, see William Archer's article, "Norway Today," in the *Fortnightly Review,* September 1885.

[11] Cf. Francis Bull's introduction to *Rosmersholm,* C.E., X, 323–26.

in the temperamental difficulty which Snoilsky found in accepting this intellectual conviction. Snoilsky had already expressed this difficulty in a poem, "The White Lady", about the sixteenth-century Duke Carl of Sweden, later King Carl IX, the brother and co-deposer of Erik XIV. Snoilsky portrayed Duke Carl as a man nagged by an uneasy conscience, in contrast to his son, the great Gustav II Adolf, who had no such fear of ghosts. Ibsen, in his youth, had depicted a similar contrast in *The Pretenders*, between Earl Skule and Haakon Haakonsson; and Snoilsky found himself in the same predicament as Earl Skule and Duke Carl— he could not shake off his inherited instincts and identify himself with the people. Gradually, Snoilsky had resigned himself to the idea that he really belonged among the mediæval troubadours rather than among the socially conscious writers of the eighteen-eighties, such as Ibsen and Strindberg. Ibsen was to base the chief character of his new play, John Rosmer, very recognizably on Snoilsky; and Rebecca West in that play bears certain resemblances, though she is not to be identified with her, to Snoilsky's second wife.[12]

Snoilsky found the meeting equally rewarding. "You know how much I admire Ibsen," he wrote to a friend shortly afterwards. "For four days we had the pleasure of his company from morning till evening, and I rejoice to have carried away a warm *personal* memory of the great Sphinx. He was most charming towards us, even forthcoming."[13] Four years later he wrote a poem, "Ibsen at Molde," a pleasant reminder of how Ibsen appeared to the few people whom he liked and in whose company he felt secure:

> I remember an August evening
> With Ibsen in the town of flowers.
> I remember him as a mountain
> Whose crown is swathed in a cloud.
>
> I see the expanse of that mighty brow
> Growing ever more overcast,
> As though sensing some dark storm
> About to eclipse our century's sun.
>
> But to an old friend or acquaintance
> His face could quickly light up,
> And over that grim, closed mouth of his
> The loveliest smile would run.

[12] Ibsen later admitted to Gustaf af Geijerstam the connection between the Snoilskys and *Rosmersholm*, and was alarmed that anyone should have guessed it—though one would think that after Bjørnson and *The League of Youth*, and Laura Kieler and *A Doll's House*, he had learned his lesson.

[13] K. M. Kommandantvold, *Ibsen og Sverige* (Oslo, 1956), p. 18.

I remember that riddling brooder
Among his mountains and his storm-clouds;
But I do not forget how sunnily he smiled
Among the roses in the land of flowers.

A day or two after the Snoilskys left Molde, Ibsen received an un-expected letter from his youngest brother, Ole Paus Ibsen. Ole had been only seven when Ibsen had left home for Grimstad, and they had not met since, except during Ibsen's brief visit home six years later. Ole seems to have inherited both his father's inefficiency and his mother's melancholy ("He is enclosed," wrote his sister to Suzannah nineteen years later, "shy, likes to hide himself away, and is somewhat sad and inclined to look on the dark side of life"). He was also, like Hedvig, deeply religious, and the enormous missive he now penned to Ibsen could scarcely have been more unfortunately conceived as an effort to bridge the gap between them. It opens with words of comfort that would have been more appropriately addressed to Vilhelm Foldal, the unrecognised clerk-dramatist of *John Gabriel Borkman,* than to the author of *Peer Gynt* and *A Doll's House* ("If you live some years longer the day will surely come when you will reap a rich reward for your work"), and continues amid much wild mixing of metaphors into reams of religious cant of the kind that Ibsen most abominated ("What most men lack is Knowledge of God and his ways towards Man").

After rambling on for nearly two and a half thousand words he ended by inviting Ibsen to come and stay with them, on an island at the mouth of the Christiania fjord ("This, I often think to myself, would be the place for Henrik").[14] If Ibsen had cherished any faint inclination to renew contact with his family, this letter must surely have dispelled it; what could those two possibly have found to talk about on Ole's island? Whether he replied to Ole we do not know; yet it signifies something that he, who kept so few letters, kept this one.

On 4 September, the day before Ibsen left Molde, the local Choral Society and Horn Group serenaded him outside his hotel room. Ibsen replied with a brief speech, in which he hinted that the new play he was planning would upset some people since "the things that he found it vitally necessary to say would not please everyone," and asked that "those elements of the community whom it disturbed should respect his views, as he respected theirs." He added that his stay in Molde "with its charming landscape and calm and peaceful inhabitants" might possibly "have some mollifying influence on what he felt compelled to say."[15]

From Molde he sailed down the coast to Bergen. It was his first visit since he had gone there as an alcoholic failure of thirty-five to the Choral

[14] Francis Bull, "Henrik Ibsen og Skien," in *Edda* (1951), pp. 91–96.
[15] *Romsdals Budstikke,* nr. 71, 1885, reprinted in C.E., XV, 422.

Festival twenty-two years earlier, and his first new impression of the town might have been designed by a malicious Providence to revive those melancholy memories. As he came on deck wearing formal dress with decorations, he saw waiting on the quay four of his old drinking companions —two carpenters, a broker, and a sexton—who greeted him with cries of, "Welcome, old Henrik!" Ibsen hastened back to his cabin and did not emerge until assured that they had departed.[16]

Later impressions, however, were more agreeable, and he spent a pleasant week there. His old theatre had arranged a special production of *Lady Inger of Østraat*, which had been such a failure at its premiere there in 1855, and had persuaded Laura Gundersen, the star of the Christiania Theatre, to return to the stage where she had made her debut to play the lead. They wanted to make the premiere a special performance in Ibsen's honour, but for some reason, courteously but firmly, he refused. He astonished them, however, by agreeing to attend a rehearsal and, yet more amazingly (for his unwillingness to involve himself with any production was famous), made several suggestions regarding the placings and the speaking; he also gently remarked on the "improvement" of one of his lines by the young director, Gunnar Heiberg, but allowed it to stand. He came, too, to the dress rehearsal; but when, at the premiere, the audience called for the author, they had to be told that he was not present.[17] And when the artisans' guild wanted to honour him with yet another torchlight procession, he refused—partly, perhaps, to save having to prepare another of those speeches which he so disliked writing and delivering.

Among the acquaintances he renewed in Bergen was one which stirred deep memories. His old love, Rikke Holst, now Fru Henrikke Tresselt, came to see him at his hotel with a bouquet of wild flowers. "I've been gazing at myself all day in the mirror to make sure I looked all right for you," she told him. "I didn't want you to find me too changed." He asked if she had found any trace of her in his writing, and she said she could only think of Fru Strawman and her flock of children in *Love's Comedy* (for Rikke was now the mother of a large family). He asked, "What have you been doing all these years?" and she said, "While you have been writing all these plays that have made you famous I've just been bringing children into the world and mending old pairs of trousers." He took both her hands and said, "You'll never change, Rikke—God bless you!"[18] It was on this occasion that, as recorded earlier,[19] he wondered aloud that nothing had come of their relationship, she reminded him that he had

[16] Paulsen, *Samliv med Ibsen*, I, 122–23.

[17] Skavlan, pp. 147–48; Anker, *Henrik Ibsens brevveksling med Christiania Theater, 1878–1899*, pp. 36–37.

[18] Paulsen, *Samliv med Ibsen*, I, 125–26.

[19] See pp. 110–11.

run away, and he replied: "Yes, yes. I never was a brave man face to face."

Bergen, then, after that unfortunate first episode at the quay, had been a success—though he told a young journalist on the ship to Stavanger that he was sad to find his old theatre in debt, and to hear that the citizens of Bergen were willing to pay 80,000 crowns for a statue of Holberg but not the 2,000 crowns that were required to save the theatre from possible closure.[20] Christiania, to which he now returned, was to revive his sense of being unwanted, and in a way that confirmed his darkest suspicions. At a meeting of the Students' Union on 26 September, Fritz Thaulow[21] (son of that battling chemist on whom Ibsen had partly based Dr. Stockmann) suggested that they should greet Ibsen with (of course) a torchlight procession. The conservatives in the union opposed the idea in a tepid kind of way, but not absolutely; the motion was carried, and Lorentz Dietrichson, as chairman of the union, went with another committee member to inform Ibsen. Ibsen, mindful of Dietrichson's treatment of him in Molde, rejected the proposal, explaining that he had just refused a similar one from the Workers' Association of the city (as he had done in Bergen), and that he disliked public appearances; but he asked Dietrichson to convey his thanks to the students for the idea. The result was to be a dismal and undignified public row from which none of the principals, including Ibsen, emerged with any credit.

While he was in Christiania he met August Lindberg who, after his productions of *Ghosts* and *The Wild Duck*, could claim to be his most distinguished living interpreter. Lindberg found Ibsen more forthcoming than at their previous meeting in Munich, but in a state of great hatred towards Christiania. "His hair was quite white and standing on end. He said: 'Yes, Lindberg, I would give much to see you play Oswald and Hjalmar Ekdal. But not, at any price, in this city.'" Lindberg asked him about the character of the devious Bishop Nicholas, which he was about to rehearse at Nya Teater in Stockholm, but all Ibsen would say was, "Well, you can see him any day here in Norway."[22] The Christiania Theatre might, one would have thought, have arranged a performance of one of his plays during the week he was there; but they did not.

On 29 September Ibsen sailed to Copenhagen, where there were no such problems. The Royal Theatre put on a special performance of *The Wild Duck*, which Ibsen attended, and Frederik Hegel gave a dinner for him at which Georg Brandes delivered the principal speech of welcome. Rasmus B. Anderson, the professor from Wisconsin who had unsuccessfully

[20] P. Rosenkrantz Johnsen, *Om og omkring Henrik Ibsen og Suzannah Ibsen* (Oslo, 1928), p. 16.

[21] Later a distinguished painter who befriended two notable outcasts in Strindberg (during the latter's "Inferno" crisis) and Oscar Wilde.

[22] Per Lindberg, pp. 174 and 178–79.

tried to arrange the publication of Ibsen's plays in America, was present, and was surprised (though one would think he had heard about it) at Ibsen's taciturnity. "No one, not even Brandes, could get him to talk, he was as silent as a sphinx." Brandes concluded his speech by thanking Ibsen "for laying bare our faults so that we may note them and mend them." Anderson continues: "When Brandes sat down all the guests joined in calling for a speech from Ibsen. After much urging he finally rose to state that he was not able to make a speech and so would have to decline; he wished, however, to say in reply to Brandes that it was not the world about him that he had attempted to expose, but that he had only laid himself bare to his readers. Then he sat down."[23]

On a later occasion during this week, however, Anderson found Ibsen far from taciturn. They met at the Hotel d'Angleterre, where Ibsen was staying. Ibsen took Anderson into a small private dining-room and ordered two bottles of champagne and a box of cigars; he did not smoke himself, but offered them to Anderson. "He had evidently had a drink or two before I met him. I let him drink most of the champagne while I did the smoking. This man famous for his taciturnity became very communicative. He talked continuously, telling me over and over again how his books henceforth should become more aggressive. What he had done, he said, was hardly a beginning; but he was going to turn society inside out before he got done with it. He talked of all society as rotten and needing a thorough renovation. He continued talking until far into the small hours of the morning. It must have been about 3 o'clock A.M. [sic] when Mrs. Ibsen came down in her nightrobe, took her husband by the arm, said goodnight to me and to her husband: 'Come with me.' "[24] It is a pity that Ibsen did not unburden himself to a more appreciative listener than Anderson who, though an admirer of Brand, hated all of Ibsen's later works. "Apart from the improprieties and offence against good morals that are found in them," he concludes, "they seem to me mere twaddle."

One meeting during his stay in Copenhagen must have touched Ibsen's conscience. Laura Kieler, now working as a journalist on Morgenbladet, came to interview him, and wrote a disappointingly unoriginal and unrevealing article on him which was reprinted in several Norwegian papers. They met, she recalled years later, "like two strangers who had never known each other."[25] It was not to be their last encounter.

Georg Brandes gave another dinner for him, and persuaded him to attend a meeting on 3 October of the new Radical Students' Union,

[23] Rasmus B. Anderson, My Life Story (Madison, 1915), pp. 495–96. The badness of the English is not due to translation; Anderson wrote his book in English, and his style is as insufferable as his complacency.

[24] Ibid., p. 484.

[25] Kinck, p. 518.

founded three years earlier as a counter to the old union which, like that in Christiania, was controlled by conservatives. Ibsen had already refused an invitation to attend this meeting, and only changed his mind at Brandes's urgent request. But he enjoyed himself, and stayed until after one o'clock in the morning. Brandes made an eloquent speech in honour of "Youth and Henrik Ibsen," calling him "the hammer and the benefactor of the North." Ibsen, in his reply, declared: "I hope to remain a student all my days. When I cease to be one, I shall regard myself as unworthy to live."[26]

That same evening, Ibsen was the central figure of another and far less harmonious occasion, at the Students' Union in Christiania. A Danish student named Ove Rode, later to become a prominent politician, announced that he had a message from Dr. Ibsen to the Union, to the effect that he could not take seriously a greeting conveyed to him by a society whose committee was headed by his old friend, or rather acquaintance, Lorentz Dietrichson, and that if they wanted to please him they should throw out the present committee and elect a new one, in which event he would be happy to accept the Union's greetings. Dietrichson, in the chair, postponed discussion of the matter until the next week's meeting, and wired Ibsen in Copenhagen asking if he had authorized Rode's statement. Ibsen replied that he could indeed not feel sympathy with any body of which Dietrichson was head. It was a petty attitude to take, but rawly sensitive men are often petty when they feel they have been slighted, and Dietrichson's reaction was even less dignified. On 10 October he made a speech at the Christiania Union denouncing Ibsen's attitude and, worse, recited a lampoon which he had written against Ibsen and which the meeting, in a fit of undergraduate high spirits, promptly sang to an extemporized tune.

Next day the story was all over the capital. Dietrichson's speech and lampoon were both published in the conservative newspapers. The left-wing papers retorted by violently attacking the Union and Dietrichson; and the left-wing students staged a protest meeting, to which they invited the townspeople. Seven hundred people attended, and they sent Ibsen an apology and a tribute. The Danish poet Holger Drachmann penned an angry attack on Ibsen, which Dietrichson read out at a later meeting; a prominent Norwegian theologian attacked Ibsen as an example of the danger of free thought; the magazine *Samfundsbladet* declared that it was a straight choice, "Christ or Ibsen." Ibsen, by now in Munich, wrote an immense, neurotic and boring letter to the Union "to be read aloud from the spot from which I was . . . insulted by your chairman," which it was. Dietrichson of course replied at equal length. The result was that two weeks later the left-wing students followed the example

[26] Georg Brandes, *Levned*, III, 146.

of their fellows in Copenhagen by breaking away and forming their own Union, of which they forthwith elected Ibsen an honorary member.[27]

It was the kind of trivial and time-wasting business in which no writer of Ibsen's stature should have got embroiled; yet the affair is significant in that it mirrors the exceptional hatred that existed in Norway just then between the rival political factions. As Gerhard Gran observes, the most extraordinary aspect of the matter is not Ibsen's behaviour but that Dietrichson should, first in Molde and then in Christiania, have risked a friendship of such long standing and of which he was so proud on so minimal an issue. Ibsen was to make the bitterness of this political strife in Norway the background of his next play; that, and his disillusionment with Norway's first liberal government, as particularly exemplified by its conduct in the Kielland affair. "It was a sad moment," he wrote to Georg Brandes on 10 November 1886, "when Johan Sverdrup came to power and got muzzled and handcuffed."

On leaving Scandinavia that autumn Ibsen had re-settled in Munich in a new apartment at Maximilianstrasse 32, "a big corner-house with a bust of mad King Ludwig II as an eighteen-year-old, full of hope, on the stairs." "A maid opens the door," reported a journalist from the Swedish paper *Aftonbladet,* "and we enter a lobby where a great many felt hats and rough natural walking-sticks recall Dr. Stockmann in *An Enemy of the People.* 'Yes, Dr. Ibsen is at home,' says the maid, and one enters a simple living-room, a little stiff and cold, for the rooms are 'furnished.' Ibsen does not want a home. He wants to live as a foreigner in a foreign land." The reporter noted of Ibsen himself that "he has the enquiring, piercing look of a doctor"; his glance reminded the man of "an old seaman I saw one night on a steamer off the north coast near Trondhjem, staring at the rudder, peering out into the night."[28]

Ibsen described his new surroundings rather differently. "We are now living handsomely and spaciously in the smartest and most aristocratic street in Munich," he told Hegel on 26 October, "and yet pay only half the rent we had to pay in Rome." Three weeks later, on 15 November, he informed Gerda Brandes that he was "now starting on a new dramatic work which I hope to have ready during the winter." "We live pleasantly and quietly; almost too quietly," he wrote to Hegel on 4 December. "We wish travelling Scandinavians would visit us a little more often. I have now almost completed my plans for my new play and shall begin to write it in a few days. It will be in four acts and interests me much."

There was excellent news for the family that month. After only nine

[27] Cf. Gran, II, 188 ff., and Fredrik Wallem, *Det norske studentersamfund gjennem hundrede aar, 1813–1913* (Christiania, 1916), II, 840–66. For a right-wing view of the affair, cf. Bredo Morgenstierne's review of Wallem's book in *Aftenposten,* 12 November 1916, reprinted in Dietrichson, IV, 287–93.

[28] *Aftonbladet* (Stockholm), 12–13 January 1887.

months in Stockholm, Sigurd had been appointed attaché to the legation in Washington, and had been awarded a stipend of 7,200 crowns (£400), which he was to receive annually for three years. For the past year he had been working in Stockholm with no salary at all. "It has been an expensive time for me," wrote Ibsen to Hegel on 22 December, and it could hardly have come at a worse juncture. His income that year had consisted almost entirely of fees from performances of *The Wild Duck,* which had not run long anywhere, plus reprints of *Brand, The Vikings at Helgeland* and *Peer Gynt,* and a little from the Stockholm production of *Brand.* It had been his poorest year financially since 1881:

	crowns	
Fee for *The Wild Duck* in Christiania	2,500	
Fee for *The Wild Duck* in Bergen	500	
Fee for *The Wild Duck* in Danish provinces (Julius Petersen)	600	
Fee for *The Wild Duck* in Helsinki	150	
Fee for *The Wild Duck* in Gothenburg and Swedish provinces (L. Lindgren)	400	
Fee for *The Wild Duck* at Royal Theatre, Copenhagen (2nd–10th perfs.)	1,583	
Fee for *The Wild Duck* at Royal Theatre, Stockholm	1,511	
Extra fees for *The Wild Duck* in Swedish provinces	200	
10th edn. of *Brand* (1,500 copies)	1,360	
10th edn. of *Brand* (supplementary fee)	170	
6th edn. of *The Vikings at Helgeland* (1,500 copies)	720	
6th edn. of *Peer Gynt* (1,500 copies)	1,320	
Fee for *Brand* at Nya Teater, Stockholm	400	
Unspecified German fees	356	
	11,770	£652

"I am much happier here than I was last year in Rome," Ibsen wrote to Nils Lund on 16 January 1886. He fell back at once into his old Munich routine. After his frugal breakfast and his morning at his desk, he would spend the afternoons walking the city streets in his tail coat and top hat, umbrella in hand, looking closely at the people and stopping wherever there was any small gathering. Each evening at the same precise hour he would enter the Café Maximilian, in the street where he lived, and seat himself at the second or third table on the right of the entrance, opposite the door and facing a large mirror in which he could see the rest of the room. He would order a cognac and seltzer or a glass of dark Munich beer, arm himself with a stack of newspapers (he especially liked to read the comic ones)[29] and sit there, sometimes glancing at people above his newspaper, sometimes motionless as a marble figure, his lips

[29] Gerard Schjelderup, "Ibsen-anecdoter," in *Morgenbladet,* 17 February 1906.

pursed, his hand as though holding a pen, brooding. After an hour he would silently pay the waitress, take up his silk hat and his ever-present umbrella, and walk out with his short, quick steps.[30]

M. G. Conrad, the editor of *Die Gesellschaft*, who made the above observations, also records a conversation from this period in which Ibsen referred to the necessity of knowing a character fully before starting to write about him or her. "Before I write one word, I must know the character through and through, I must penetrate into the last wrinkle of his soul. I always proceed from the individual; the stage setting, the dramatic ensemble, all of that comes naturally and causes me no worry, as soon as I am certain of the individual in every aspect of his humanity. But I have to have his exterior in mind also, down to the last button, how he stands and walks, how he bears himself, what his voice sounds like. Then I do not let him go until his fate is fulfilled." He added yet another warning against the tendency of critics to find symbols everywhere. "The critics . . . like to symbolize, because they have no respect for reality. And if one really gives them a symbol, then they reduce it to a triviality or they revile the author."[31] No doubt he was thinking of the incomprehension with which they had greeted the simple and clearly explained symbol of the wild duck.

On another occasion, Ibsen explained his method in more detail:

> As a rule, I make three drafts of my plays, which differ greatly from each other—in characterisation, not in plot. When I approach the first working-out of my material, it is as though I knew my characters from a railway journey; one has made a preliminary acquaintance, one has chatted about this and that. At the next draft I already see everything much more clearly, and I know the people roughly as one would after a month spent with them at a spa; I have discovered the fundamentals of their characters and their little peculiarities; but I may still be wrong about certain essentials. Finally, in the last draft, I have reached the limit of my knowledge; I know my characters from close and long acquaintance—they are my intimate friends, who will no longer disappoint me; as I see them now, I shall always see them.[32]

He once remarked that he "liked if possible to plan his day's work in the morning when he awoke, for then he felt his imagination to be at its liveliest; whereas his critical sense was at its least sharp then, in the half-dreaming hour of dawn. This did not fully awake till he was seated at his desk, when it often rejected all the ideas he had hit upon when lying in bed." He also kept small guttapercha devils with

[30] M. G. Conrad, quoted by Zucker, p. 222.
[31] *Ibid.*, pp. 224–25.
[32] Gran, II, 166. He does not quote his source.

red tongues on his desk. "There must be troll in what I write," he said, and in a tone midway between jest and earnest he spoke of his "super-devil." "He only comes out last, when things are really difficult. Then I lock my door and bring him out. No other human eye has seen him, not even my wife. . . . He is a bear playing the violin and beating time with his feet."[33]

Sigurd visited his parents in January en route to his new post in America; it was to be the last time they were to see him for three years. He wrote to them each week, with vivid descriptions of the New World, especially of people he thought might interest his father. Ibsen waited impatiently for these letters; Georg Brandes relates that he was present when one arrived, and that Ibsen's hand was so shaking with excitement that he could scarcely open the envelope. And when, in 1888, Sigurd was transferred to Vienna and came to see his parents at Munich on the way, Ibsen was waiting for him at the station an hour and a half before the train was due.[34]

Henrik Jæger was preparing a biographical study of Ibsen, to commemorate the dramatist's sixtieth birthday in 1888, and Hegel, who was to publish it, wrote to Ibsen asking for information about photographs, paintings and busts of him, and about his own paintings. "The oldest photograph," replied Ibsen on 25 February, "was taken by the author Edvard Larssen [one of the originals of Hjalmar Ekdal] in either 1861 or 1862." He named eight others, four busts ("the oldest are from 1867") and three paintings, none of which (not even the one by Kronborg, which he owned) he thought really good. "My own drawings," he concluded, "have hardly any artistic value. Should they be reproduced, it could only be as curiosities."

In March he heard that yet another edition of *Peer Gynt* (the seventh) was required, although one had been printed only the previous year, and that *Love's Comedy* was to be staged by the Royal Theatre in Copenhagen. He had written to them on 20 February suggesting that they might reconsider this play, which they had twice previously rejected, in 1863 and 1874, and had also asked them to think again about *Ghosts;* but despite the success of the latter play on the stages of Sweden and Norway, they remained (like the Christiania Theatre) adamantly opposed to it. Ludvig Josephson staged *The Pretenders* at Nya Teater in Stockholm, with August Lindberg as Bishop Nicholas; and on Good Friday (of all days), 14 April, Ibsen attended the German premiere of *Ghosts* at Augsburg, where the young poet Felix Philippi had persuaded August Grosse to present it. The police had banned a public performance, so

---

[33] P. A. Rosenberg in *Nationaltidende* (Copenhagen), 28 July 1926, reprinted in C.E., XIX, 217–18. William Archer doubted the existence of these devils, as he never saw them in Ibsen's study. One imagines that when not actually working, Ibsen kept them in a drawer.

[34] Bergliot Ibsen, pp. 116–17.

the play was given in private before an invited audience. The cast was young and keen, and despite certain imperfections the evening was a success. The police ban naturally excited curiosity, and people unable to obtain tickets stormed the bookshops in search of copies.

By now Ibsen was working hard on his new play, to which he had given the provisional title of *The White Horses*. "Ever since my return here," he wrote to Georg Brandes (10 November), "I have been plagued by a new play which absolutely demanded to be written"; and to Carl Snoilsky (14 February) he mentioned that he had "made some close studies for it during my trip to Norway during the summer." As we have seen, he had hoped to complete it during the winter; but it would not come, and on 20 February he had to inform Edvard Fallesen, director of the Royal Theatre in Copenhagen, that "it cannot be expected before the autumn." He had made some brief notes and begun a draft, but had completed less than an act. The notes show that he was basing his two main characters recognizably on the Snoilskys:

WHITE HORSES

He, a refined, aristocratic character, who has switched to a liberal viewpoint and been ostracized by all his former friends and acquaintances. A widower; had been unhappily married to a half-mad melancholic who ended by drowning herself.

She, the governess of his two daughters, emancipated, hot-blooded, somewhat ruthless beneath a refined exterior. Is regarded by their acquaintances as the evil spirit of the house; an object of suspicion and gossip.

There were also, at this stage, to have been two daughters, one "in danger of succumbing to inactivity and loneliness," the other "sharply observant; rich passions beginning to dawn"; but Ibsen eventually removed them from the play and kept them for his next.

But the draft made painful progress, and on 25 May he scrapped it and began an entirely new one. This new draft (still under the title of *The White Horses*) progressed swiftly; he finished the first act by 1 June and the second by 8 June. On 10 June he began the third act; but five days later he scrapped the whole of this second draft and started a third one, re-naming the play *Rosmersholm*—perhaps feeling that *White Horses* was too similar a title to *Ghosts*, especially since Rebecca had been made to say in the second draft that freedom consisted in "getting rid of one's white horses." He completed this third draft in a day over seven weeks; Act One took him from 15–28 June, Act Two from 1–12 July, Act Three from 15–24 July, and Act Four from 26 July to 4 August. Two days later he began his fair copy but, although the third draft is essentially the play as we know it, he made a number of small revisions and did not finish it until 27 September. "It cannot," he told Hegel in a letter of 2 October, "as far as I can surmise, offer grounds for attack from any quarter. I hope, though, that it may provoke a lively debate."

Rosmersholm was published on 23 November 1886, in an edition of 8,000 copies. "Under better conditions," Hegel had written to him on 7 October, "I would have suggested a somewhat larger edition";[35] *The Wild Duck* had, despite its mixed reviews, sold out its first edition of this size very rapidly, but there was a general slump in the book trade in 1886. Even more than *The Wild Duck, Rosmersholm* baffled the critics, and, like *The Wild Duck,* won nothing like the acclaim that had greeted his earlier plays, from *Brand* to *A Doll's House.* Indeed, it got the worst notices of any of his mature plays except *Ghosts. Aftenposten* knocked it twice within a week. "No doubt," observed an anonymous reviewer on 24 November, "*Rosmersholm* will find its admirers, who will acclaim this play as a great masterpiece. But equally surely, many will find it distasteful. These characters are all artificial and totally unwholesome. They would do better to keep their thoughts to themselves." On 30 November in the same paper, Bredo Morgenstierne complained: "What the play is meant to teach us it is impossible to say. . . . Many details of motivation are unintelligible. . . . The sum impression is duller than that of Ibsen's earlier plays." He found the minor characters, apart from Brendel, disappointing, the dramatic tension "not great," and asked: "Is this decadence and decline, or merely an ebb?"

Alfred Sinding-Larsen in *Morgenbladet* (1–2 December) was no more enthusiastic. He too complained of the obscurity, saying that whereas most writers move towards a greater clarity and harmony as they grow older, Ibsen has done the reverse, employing his technical skill "to disturb and depress, leading us not to clarity but to darkness, not to calm contemplation but to the fruitless pondering of unsolved riddles. Ibsen seems more and more to have withdrawn into himself and turned away from life and its realities . . . devoting himself more and more to pessimistic speculation. . . . Will Ibsen ever return to a more wholesome and positive outlook? *Rosmersholm* gives no promise of this." Sinding-Larsen found the two principal characters "sickly, distorted, and lame. . . . Normal people could . . . scarcely act as they do . . . and spiritual abnormalities are no more suited to the theatre than physical abnormalities." He complained that the play was feebly constructed, relying overmuch on reported action and being deficient in true action. "Dramatically, *Rosmersholm* is among the weakest of Ibsen's plays." Even Irgens Hansen in *Dagbladet* (28 November), who as an admirer of Ibsen must have been anxious to champion the play, could be no more than vaguely favourable.

[35] Nielsen, II, 375.

In Sweden and Denmark, however, *Rosmersholm* found admirers. One of his oldest Swedish champions, Urban von Feilitzen (who wrote over the pseudonym of "Robinson") was disappointed; reviewing the book in *Nordisk Tidskrift* (1887, pp. 20–38), he thought that Ibsen was indulging in an excess of symbolism and superfluous lines which destroyed the naturalism of the dialogue. But Georg Nordensvan, in *Ny Illustrerad Tidning* (4 December 1886) found it "shattering, highly characteristic of Ibsen, of his prophetic insight, his restless searching inwards and yet further inwards, his obscurity (here more marked than usual), and his tendency to symbolize, sometimes to the point of unintelligibility." He thought Rebecca one of Ibsen's greatest characters, perceptively observing: "It is his exploration of depths of the human mind which no man has previously sounded that makes him obscure and riddling." Even the reactionary C. D. af Wirsen, after complaining that "scoundrels, rakes, hypocritical boasters, at best clowns, are those who nowadays tread his boards," ended by admitting that "even in the labyrinths into which Ibsen has allowed his writing to stray in these last years, he has retained the gift of magically conjuring forth fascinating figures . . . and sometimes, as here, they have the power terrifyingly to grip the imagination."[36]

Georg Brandes was not particularly impressed after a first reading, but Edvard Brandes loved it. "This profound work", he wrote in *Politiken* on 25 November 1886, "is brilliantly written, and filled with that mixture of love of and contempt for humanity which forms the core of Ibsen's recent plays." He thought that the final scene "equals in tragic imagination the best that Ibsen has written," and that the only modern work with which it could be compared was *Crime and Punishment*. "They are akin, Dostœvsky and Ibsen," he concluded, "and there is something about Rebecca West that reminds one of young Russian girls in their revolutionary struggles. *Rosmersholm* is a masterpiece." "I kneel before *Rosmersholm*," he wrote to Strindberg a few weeks later; and Strindberg himself, despite his increasing hostility towards Ibsen, wrote an appreciation of the play the following spring in an essay entitled "Soul-Murder." In this, he declared that *Rosmersholm* was "unintelligible to the theatre public, mystical to the semi-educated, but crystal-clear to anyone with a knowledge of modern psychology"—one of the very few occasions on which he ever paid public tribute to Ibsen.[37] One can understand the attraction that *Rosmersholm* held for Strindberg, for he, too, was deeply interested in "magnetism" and hypnosis, the ability of one person to gain control over the mind of another. He had treated

---

[36] Wirsen, pp. 67 and 80–81.

[37] Though, with characteristic inconsistency, he seems to have reacted against the play by the summer. On 11 May he sent Edvard Brandes an article in which he asserted that Ibsen had written no true work of art since *The Pretenders*. Brandes thought the article reactionary and stupid and told Strindberg so; and it was never printed.

this theme himself in *The Father,* which he began only two months after *Rosmersholm* had appeared, and was to do so again the following year in *Creditors;* while the degenerating effect of an aristocratic heritage, Rosmer's tragedy, was to be the theme, also the following year, of *Miss Julie.*

The hostile press that *Rosmersholm* received was reflected in its sales, as had not been the case with *The Wild Duck.* "Ibsen's *Rosmersholm* seems unlikely to have the unusually large sale that a new book by him usually has," Hegel wrote to Alexander Kielland on 17 December. *"Morgenbladet's* review seems to have sapped people's desire to read it. It looks as though Lie's novel will be the real Christmas book."[38] Even more damagingly for Ibsen, the Royal Theatre in Copenhagen, which was treating him so generously in the matter of royalties, rejected the play. Nor, as with *Ghosts,* did the play seem more accessible when performed; for years, it was to succeed nowhere. Many even of Ibsen's admirers agreed that the play was hopelessly obscure and that the characters were abstractions rather than human beings.

This reaction is not surprising. If he had been breaking new ground in *The Wild Duck,* Ibsen was breaking much newer and more dangerous ground in *Rosmersholm.* To begin with, the play is about two lovers as potentially passionate as Romeo and Juliet or Antony and Cleopatra; but Rosmer and Rebecca, unlike Shakespeare's couples, are children of the nineteenth century; they are, much as they would like not to be, dominated by bourgeois moral values and, because of forces both outside and within them, they never touch each other until the moment when they clasp hands to walk out and drown themselves. Unless these banked passions are suggested (and how often has one not seen Rebecca played as an intellectual bluestocking and Rosmer as a sexless parson!), there seems no earthly reaon why they should commit suicide. The actors must be able, in Bernard Shaw's words, to "sustain the deep black flood of feeling from the first moment to the last."[39] It is only Rebecca's enemy, Dr. Kroll, who calls her an intellectual. Of course she had an intellect, but that is another thing. Ibsen, like George Eliot, knew well the predicament of the woman of intellect whose passions can find no outlet. Rebecca and Dorothea Brook of *Middlemarch* have a good deal in common.

Moreover, in this play Ibsen was, for the first time not merely in his work but in any play for over two centuries, overtly probing the uncharted waters of the unconscious mind. As already remarked, the problem of how one human being can gain control over the mind of another and persuade him or her to act, not against their will, but according to

[38] Nielsen, II, 484.

[39] Letter to Charles Charrington, 28 January 1890. (George Bernard Shaw, *Collected Letters, 1874–1897,* ed. Dan H. Laurence [London, 1965], p. 240.)

inclinations within them which they repress, was much in the air; yet although we know that it deeply interested Ibsen (his preliminary jottings for *Rosmersholm* contain references to "the sixth sense" and "magnetic influence"), it was not something of which the ordinary theatre-goer was aware, and although readers would have understood it in a novel, where the author can explain and clarify the actions of his characters, they were not sufficiently used to reading between the lines of plays to comprehend what was merely implied (and implied with marvellous subtlety) in the dialogue.

One reader who did understand what *Rosmersholm* was about was Sigmund Freud who, in his essay "Character-Types" which he wrote during the 1914 war, made an extraordinarily penetrating analysis of the play and of the secret motives which impel the characters. In the second section of this essay, sub-titled "Those wrecked by success," Freud deals with the common and disturbing psychological phenomenon of people who, when what they most want at last lies within their grasp, find themselves unable to seize hold of it. After an illuminating consideration of Lady Macbeth, Freud moves on to *Rosmersholm,* and writes of Rebecca:

> Ibsen has made it clear by small touches of masterly subtlety that Rebecca does not actually tell lies but is never entirely straightforward. Just as, in spite of her freedom from prejudice, she has understated her age by a year, so her confession to the two men [Rosmer and Kroll] is incomplete, and as a result of Kroll's insistence it is supplemented on some important points. Hence it is open to us to suppose that her explanation of her renunciation exposes one motive only to conceal another . . . Rosmer's influence may only have been a cloak, which concealed another influence that was operative, and a remarkable indication points in this direction.

When, Freud continues, in the final scene, after her confession about herself and Beata, Rosmer again asks Rebecca to become his wife, by implication forgiving her:

> She does not answer, as she should, that no forgiveness can rid her of the feeling of guilt she has incurred from her malignant deception of poor Beata; but she charges herself with another reproach which affects us as coming strangely from this free-thinking woman, and is far from deserving the importance which Rebecca attaches to it. . . . She has had sexual relations with another man; and we do not fail to observe that these relations, which occurred at a time when she was free and accountable to nobody, seem to her a greater hindrance to the union with Rosmer than her truly criminal behaviour to his wife . . .
>
> After she has learned that she has been the mistress of her own father, she surrenders herself wholly to her now over-mastering sense of guilt. She makes the confession to Rosmer and Kroll which stamps her as a murderess; she rejects for ever the happiness to which she has paved the way by crime, and

prepares for departure. But the true motive of her sense of guilt, which results in her being wrecked by success, remains a secret. As we have seen, it is something quite other than the atmosphere of Rosmersholm and the refining influence of Rosmer. . . .

Rebecca's feeling of guilt has its source in the reproach of incest, even before Kroll, with analytical perspicacity, has made her conscious of it. If we reconstruct her past, expanding and filling in the author's hints, we may feel sure that she cannot have been without some inkling of the intimate relations between her mother and Dr West. It must have made a great impression on her when she became her mother's successor with this man. She stood under the domination of the Oedipus complex, even though she did not know that this universal phantasy had in her case become a reality. When she came to Rosmersholm, the inner force of this first experience drove her into bringing about, by vigorous action, the same situation which had been realized in the original instance through no doing of hers—into getting rid of the wife and mother, so that she might take her place with the husband and father. She describes with a convincing insistence how, against her will, she was obliged to proceed, step by step, to the removal of Beata. . . . Everything that happened to her at Rosmersholm, her falling in love with Rosmer and her hostility to his wife, was from the first a consequence of the Oedipus complex— an inevitable replica of her relations with her mother and Dr West.

And so the sense of guilt which first causes her to reject Rosmer's proposal is at bottom no different from the greater one which drives her to her confession after Kroll has opened her eyes. But just as under the influence of Dr West she had become a freethinker and despiser of religious morality, so she is transformed by her love for Rosmer into a being of conscience and nobility. This much of the mental process within her she understands, and so she is justified in describing Rosmer's influence as the motive for the change—the motive that had become accessible to her.

The practising psycho-analytical physician knows how frequently, or how invariably, a girl who enters a household as servant, companion or governess, will consciously or unconsciously weave a daydream, which derives from the Oedipus complex, of the mistress of the house disappearing and the master taking the newcomer as his wife in her place. *Rosmersholm* is the greatest work of art of the class that treats of this common phantasy in girls. What makes it into a tragic drama is the extra circumstance that the heroine's daydream had been preceded in her childhood by a precisely corresponding reality.[40]

Of all Ibsen's plays, *Rosmersholm* is the most inexhaustible. To a modern reading public or audience, as to Freud, that is cause for admiration and fascination; but can we blame Ibsen's contemporaries for finding it impossibly obscure, when we remember that Freud's own *Interpretation of Dreams,* published fourteen years later, was to take eight years to sell its first edition of six hundred copies?

On the stage, *Rosmersholm* proved even more perplexing than on the

[40] James Strachey's translation.

page. The premiere, at Bergen on 17 January 1887, was coolly received, as was the Christiania production on 12 April, which ran for only ten performances—a particular calamity for Ibsen who, in response to a suggestion from Schrøder, had agreed to take ten per cent of the gross instead of his usual flat fee. No more than six further performances of it were given in Christiania during the next two years, and it was not revived there again before 1900. Its first German production, at Augsburg on 6 April 1887, was a disaster, as was the first English production in 1891. It failed in both Gothenburg (March 1887) and Stockholm (April 1887). The Royal Theatre in Copenhagen, as we have seen, rejected it, and it fell, as so often, to August Lindberg to get to the heart of the play. He toured it through the Swedish provinces and Denmark with himself as Rosmer and with an inadequate Rebecca; and in September 1887 he played in Christiania in the previously unsuccessful production by Bjørn Bjørnson. "Act after act," Lindberg recalled, "I felt the atmosphere tighten, both on the stage and in the audience. . . . The applause rolled up over the stage like waves of heat. The last act is fever and ecstasy. To enter that ecstasy, to feel it rise in one, without losing control over oneself! To feel how Rosmer and Rebecca are gripped by love—it was like being in a trance. It was like exchanging souls. And at last, out from the closed air of that drawing-room, out of human smallness, out to the mill-race."[41] After the performance the Norwegian actress Laura Gundersen told Lindberg that they had never understood the play before.

Before presenting the original Christiania production of *Rosmersholm*, Hans Schrøder, the head of the Christiania Theatre, had written to Ibsen telling him of his plans for casting. Replying on 2 January 1887, Ibsen delivered himself of some pungent comments on Schrøder's taste and some valuable observations on the play:

> You think Fru Gundersen was born to play Rebecca. I don't agree. Fru Gundersen's strength is for the big declamatory line, and there are none of those in my play. How could she manage these seemingly light but extremely pregnant dialogues? Dual personalities, complex characters, are not her forte. Then you want Gundersen to play Rosmer. Permit me to ask what the effect is likely to be when Rebecca tells how she had been gripped by a "a wild and sensual longing" for him? Or when Brendel calls him "my boy," etc.? Or when Dr Kroll hectors and browbeats him? Is G's personality compatible with this and much else? For Rosmer you must choose the most delicate and sensitive personality that your theatre can lay its hands on. . . . That the role of Dr Kroll, that pedagogic autocrat, should be entrusted to Hr [Bjørn] Bjørnson is, I trust, a joke on which I need waste no further ink. Is it, though, conceivable that this monstrous idea is seriously

41 Per Lindberg, p. 210.

being harboured? If the artistic direction of the theatre is so totally lacking in critical and self-critical ability, I can await the production only with the direst misgivings.[42]

Schrøder yielded with a fair grace, and the cast was altered in accordance with Ibsen's wishes. A month later, on 5 February, Ibsen addressed to him some further advice about the characters, including meticulous details regarding their dress:

Dr Kroll is an authoritarian with a passion for domineering, as is so often the case with headmasters. He is of course of good family; Major Rosmer's son married his sister. The Doctor's manner is therefore that of a well-born government official. Despite a certain asperity which now and then manifests itself, his behaviour in general is friendly and agreeable. He can be amiable when he pleases, or when he is with people he likes. But it is to be noted that he only likes those people who share his opinions, The rest irritate him, and with them he easily becomes ruthless and reveals a tendency towards malice. His appearance is distinguished; he is handsomely dressed, in black. Coat almost down to his knees, but no lower. He wears a white cravat, large and old-fashioned, which goes twice round his neck, i.e. no tie. His dress explains why Ulric Brendel at first takes him for Pastor Rosmer and then for a "brother of the cloth." In Act One Rosmer also wears a black coat, but grey trousers and a tie or cravat of the same colour. In Acts Three and Four, however, he is dressed entirely in black.

Rebecca's manner must on no account carry any hint of imperiousness or masculinity. She does not *force* Rosmer forward. She *lures* him. A controlled power, a quiet determination, are of the essence of her character.[43]

During rehearsals for the Christiania production, Constance Bruun, the young actress who had been chosen to replace Laura Gundersen as Rebecca, was taken ill, and the part was given to another young actress, Sofie Reimers. She wrote to Ibsen asking his advice; he gave it briefly (25 March 1887), and it still serves as a general warning to any actor or actress attempting any Ibsen role. "No declamation! No theatricalities! No grand mannerisms! Express every mood in a manner that will seem credible and natural. Never think of this or that actress whom you may have seen. Observe the life that is going on around you, and present a real and living human being." No wonder Sarah Bern-

---

[42] Anker, *Henrik Ibsens brevveksling med Christiania Theater, 1878–1899*, pp. 47–48.

[43] *Ibid.*, pp. 56–57.

hardt and Henry Irving disliked the demands this awkward dramatist made.[44]

Rosmersholm marks Ibsen's final withdrawal as a playwright from the political field. A year after writing it he was to declare (in a speech at Gothenburg) that his political interests were waning and, with them, his eagerness for battle. He may have based the character of Rosmer principally on Snoilsky, but he put a good deal of himself into it too. Although he enjoyed writing and making speeches on controversial subjects, he disliked embroiling himself; and what he had seen of the results of party strife in Norway in 1885 determined him to withdraw still further from the battle. *Rosmersholm* is the last of his plays which introduces national or local politics as a decisive factor in shaping people's characters and destinies. In *The League of Youth, The Pillars of Society, Ghosts* and *An Enemy of the People,* such politics had played an important part; the actions of Stensgaard, Bernick, Manders and Peter Stockmann are, at critical moments, influenced by a fear of offending local political opinion. Gregers Werle in *The Wild Duck* is very much a political animal; and *A Doll's House,* though politics do not enter directly into it, struck at the heart of one of the most controversial issues of the day. But in the six plays which follow *Rosmersholm,* the battle is out of earshot. It is the trolls within, not the trolls without, that determine the destinies of Ellida and Hilde Wangel, Hedda Gabler, Halvard Solness, the Allmers, the Borkmans and Arnold Rubek. They are conscious of strange, sick passions which direct their lives; and *Rosmersholm* provides a link between Ibsen's old method and his new. Rosmer is the last of his characters to be caught up and undermined by local politics; and Rebecca is the first of those passionate but inhibited lovers who dominate the dark plays of his final period.

His disillusionment with politics, arising from his experiences in Norway in 1885, was complete. In his speech in Trondhjem that year he had declared his belief that the present age was the end of an era and that a new age was dawning, a third kingdom in which "current political and social conceptions will cease to exist." As Professor Francis Bull has put it, in Trondhjem in 1885 he had a programme, in Stockholm in 1887 a dream vision; in 1885 he had identified himself with the age, in 1887 and afterwards he cherished only a vague hope for an unguessable future.[45]

---

[44] Irving never acted in Ibsen, though attempts were made to persuade him to play Bishop Nicholas in *The Pretenders* and John Gabriel Borkman, and although Sarah Bernhardt tried herself out as Ellida in *The Lady from the Sea* at Sens in 1904 I can find no record that she played any other of his roles. (Cf. *Aftenposten,* 22 September 1904. The report there says that she acted Hilde Wangel in the play, but even Sarah is unlikely to have tried to portray a teen-age girl when she was approaching fifty-nine.) When Christian Krohg asked Lugné-Poe in the nineties whether Sarah had ever played Ibsen, the latter replied, "She will not. She says contemptuously of him, Strindberg and everything new: *'C'est de la Norderie.'* " (Nyholm, pp. 49–50.)

[45] C.E., X, 318–19.

24

"All the Women Are in Love with Him"

1886–1887

As the Scandinavian theatres perplexedly got down to rehearsing *Ros-mersholm* during the last weeks of 1886, Duke Georg of Saxe-Meiningen was preparing a production of *Ghosts*. Ibsen had fallen sharply out of fashion in Germany since the heady days of *The Pillars of Society* and *A Doll's House;* indeed, apart from the private production of *Ghosts* at Augsburg in April 1886 there does not seem to have been a new production of any of his plays at a German theatre since 1880, a gap of over five years.[1] *Ghosts* was still forbidden by the censors; *An Enemy of the People* had been translated but not performed, and *The Wild Duck* had not even been translated. But if the German establishment had written Ibsen off, the young still believed in him. In November 1886 Otto Brahm, then thirty-one, published an enthusiastic article about him in *Deutsche Rundschau;* and the Meiningen production of *Ghosts,* and that in Berlin which followed, were to convert many people to Brahm's judgment.

The performance (a single one) at Meiningen was fixed for 22 December, and the duke invited Ibsen to stay with him as his guest. He travelled on the 19th, and his reception must have exceeded his most sanguine expectations, as his rather Pooterish letter to Suzannah on the afternoon of the 21st shows:

Dear Suzannah!

I write you in all haste. I reached Würzburg at 1.30 A.M. Left the next afternoon at 1.15. Arrived here at 4.15 and was received at the station by the duke's chamberlain with the ducal coach, and driven to the palace, and here received in the heartiest and most affectionate manner by the duke and his wife, who both accompanied me to the handsome and festively illuminated apartment which has been pre-

[1] According to Eller, pp. 140–41.

pared for me, comprising four immense salons with every possible amenity. A court lackey has been placed at my exclusive service. P. Lindau, R. Voss and Hans Hopfen are also guests here, but they live downstairs and nothing like so magnificently as I. At 5 P.M. dinner was served. Prince Ernst had come from Munich by another train. In the middle of the meal we were all surprised by the appearance of a young couple in travelling clothes. It was the Crown Prince and Princess of Meiningen, who had travelled from Rome to see *Gespenster*. They were then placed at the table. The princess was put beside me, and spoke with great enthusiasm of her journey to the North Cape. She is most amazingly well informed about our literature. After dinner there was a theatrical performance. P. Lindau's translation of a Spanish piece was played. This was a public performance for the paying public, and so will Voss's *Alexandra* be tomorrow. Only *Gespenster* is to be limited to an invited audience this evening. A great many interested people have congregated here from all quarters, especially Berlin, for the occasion. After the performance a grand *soirée* will be given here in the palace. The performance this evening starts at six, in consequence of which dinner has been arranged for two. I am extremely happy here. The atmosphere is as unforced as one could imagine, and the duke and his wife do not know how sufficiently to honour me. I shall be back in Munich on Thursday.

12:30 P.M.

I was interrupted. The duke came to see me, and stayed a long time. I must therefore hasten to finish this letter if it is to catch the train.

I enclose the draft of the telegram for Sigurd, which you must get Lina [their servant] to send on Thursday morning. I may possibly telegraph him from here too.[2]

And how is your eye? I trust it is no worse? Be sure not to worry. It cannot be dangerous. But of course unpleasant. I will try to leave by the morning train on Thursday, if possible. I hope you are no longer suffering any pain or inconvenience from the thing in your mouth, but it is doubly unfortunate that this should happen while I am away. But I hope you are well in other respects! Here there is heavy snow. I am not going out, although I have a carriage at my disposal. The chamberlain has sent his card and I have sent mine to the court functionaries. Personal calls are not required.

Well, I will end here for today. Perhaps I shall hear from you. I feel already as though I had been away for a long time. I am excellently contented; but in the long run I am happiest at home.

Your affectionate
Henrik Ibsen

[2] 23 December was Sigurd's birthday.

The performance, with Maria Berg as Mrs. Alving and Alexander Barthel as Oswald, was a triumph, as great as the same company's production of *The Pretenders* ten and a half years earlier. The following day the duke gave Ibsen another medal to add to his collection: the Saxon-Ernestine Order of Commander, First Class, with star. The citation read *als Zeichen seiner Verehrung und Bewunderung*—"as a token of reverence and admiration." "You mustn't think I tell you this out of vanity" Ibsen wrote to Hegel a fortnight later, on 5 January, "but I can't deny it pleases me when I remember the foolish denunciations of which the play was for so long the object in our countries."

This medal was the occasion of a rare breach of protocol by Ibsen. His fellow-guest at Meiningen, Paul Lindau, tells that on receiving it Ibsen pinned it to his breast next to the Knight Cross that he had previously received from the duke. Lindau pointed out that it was incorrect to wear the two together, "as though a colonel were to wear his lieutenant's pips." But Ibsen replied that the Knight Cross was the first German medal he had been awarded. "It has dear memories for me, and I don't care to be parted from it." Lindau, who seems not to have been the most tactful of men, also offended Ibsen by making some unappreciated joke about the character of Regina; when he apologised, Ibsen said, "One doesn't joke about spiritual matters."[3] Another German guest, a journalist named Gotthelf Weisstein, noted that Ibsen "looks older than his age, with his snow-white hair, and with his stiff silence suggests a small-town German professor, despite his many decorations." He also remarked acidly that Ibsen said the simplest things with an impressive air, "as though he wished to inscribe for ever on the tablets of our memories the fact of his having informed us: 'Tomorrow I shall take the train to Munich.'"[4]

Lindau and Weisstein sound a tedious pair, and Ibsen was never at his best with people who bored him. One is reminded of a remark Georg Brandes once made when a journalist wrote that a conversation he had had with Ibsen had been empty. "The fool, getting nothing out of a conversation with Ibsen! When we were together just for a few minutes it was a complete experience!"[5]

---

[3] Lindau, pp. 373–77.

[4] G. Weisstein, *Meininger Erinnerungen* (Berlin, 1906), quoted by Zucker, p. 227.

[5] *Brandes Brevveksling*, IV, xxxviii. After Ibsen's death Brandes wrote: "Rarely has he been described as he was in daily life. In his younger days he was animated, brilliant and observing, cordial and at the same time caustic, but never what one might call good-natured even when cordial. If alone with one or two friends he was spontaneous, communicative and frank, an excellent listener as well as a remarkable talker; but at social functions or among many people he was silent, easily embarrassed and slightly peevish. It did not take much to put him out of humour or to arouse his suspicion . . . but how many examples have I not of his cordiality, his thoughtfulness, his gentleness!" (*Century Magazine*, New York, February 1917, pp. 544–45). And William Archer ("Ibsen as I Knew Him," p. 9) wrote that he "always found him not only courteous but genial and even communicative."

On his return to Munich, Ibsen made up his accounts for 1886. It had been about the same financially as the two previous years, a little better than the mid-seventies but nothing like as good as the years of *The Pillars of Society* and *A Doll's House*. Performing rights had brought him no more than 2,910 crowns; only the advance on *Rosmersholm* and reprints of *Peer Gynt* and *Poems* had saved it from being a disaster:

	crowns	
Fee for *Peer Gynt* at Dagmars Theatre, Copenhagen	1,500	
Fee from the magazine *Norden* for poem, "Light out of Chaos"[6]	100	
7th edn. of *Peer Gynt*	1,815	
Fee for *The Pretenders* at Nya Teater, Stockholm	400	
Fee for *The Wild Duck* at Royal Theatre, Stockholm (22nd–29th perfs.)	366	
Fee for *The Wild Duck* at Royal Theatre, Copenhagen (11th–13th perfs.)	444	
5th edn. of *Poems*	952	
Single performance of *The Feast at Solhaug* at Dagmars Theatre, Copenhagen	200	
1st edn. of *Rosmersholm*	6,240	
	12,017	£668

However, the interest on his shares for the year came to just over 3,000 crowns, he still, of course, had his pension of 2,000 crowns, and Sigurd was now financially independent—very fortunately, for 1887, thanks to the failure of *Rosmersholm* in the theatres of Europe, was to be Ibsen's worst year financially since 1872.

The Meiningen production of *Ghosts* was such a success that the duke tried to take it to Berlin, as he had done so triumphantly with his production of *The Pretenders* in the previous decade. But *Ghosts* was a different matter. The police censor had not allowed it to be publicly performed anywhere else in Germany and, duke or no duke, he was not now prepared to make an exception. However, the Berlin Dramatic Society gave a private performance of the play on 2 January 1887, and such was the interest aroused by this production that Fritz Wallner of the Berlin Residenztheater determined to follow suit, and managed to obtain permission to present *Ghosts* for a single charity matinee on 9 January. Ibsen travelled up from Munich to see it. "I had scarcely settled

[6] A fine short poem, in theme and manner somewhat anticipating Thomas Hardy's "The Darkling Thrush."

down on my return from Meiningen," he explained to Hegel on 5 January, "and now I must be off again. . . . I would rather have stayed at home; but after the many requests I have received I cannot well not accede to them, especially since *Ghosts* has become a burning literary and theatrical talking-point in Germany. In Berlin I am prepared for some opposition from the conservative press. But this, too, is, for me, an additional reason why I should be present."

Charlotte Frohn played Mrs. Alving, Emmanuel Reicher Manders, and Wallner himself Oswald. The result exceeded all expectations. Wallner recalled: "I have never experienced anything like it. After the first fall of the curtain, silence reigned for several seconds; everyone was held spellbound by the powerful drama. But then a storm, a hurricane, broke forth, such as I had never witnessed in a theatre. The dramatist was acclaimed by all—no one expressed disapproval—and, willingly, drunk with victory, he appeared repeatedly on the stage, tears of joy running down his cheeks."

The conservative critics, as Ibsen had anticipated, rejected the play; but it was an important occasion for those who were dissatisfied with the existing state of the German theatre. Otto Brahm praised "the unconditional truth, the relentless, garish if you like, truth in the portrayal of human character . . . human beings, actual, living men and women, fully and completely observed. . . . If the aim in the development of literature is to absorb more and more of nature into art, to wrest new poetic fields from life, as Faust obtained land from the sea, then no recent dramatist has gone forward more boldly and more magnificently than the author of *Ghosts*." Another member of the audience was the twenty-five-year-old Gerhart Hauptmann, already on the way to becoming Ibsen's most distinguished disciple in Germany. Eugen Sierke, in an article in *Unser Zeit*, states that they could have sold fourteen thousand tickets for the performance,[7] and Julius Hoffory records that the book sold out so completely in the city that five thousand fresh copies had to be ordered from Leipzig.[8]

On 11 January there was a banquet for Ibsen at the Hotel Kaiserhof, with representatives from all walks of life seated at a horseshoe table. Otto Brahm made a speech praising Ibsen as "a great artist who unites a rich and mature technical mastery with the fresh courage of an eternally youthful mind," adding that, just as Lessing had in his day led German literature away from the pattern of French drama by showing them the example of Shakespeare, so "we too have to fight against the renewed preponderance of French drama and turn our eyes to this writer

[7] Eller, pp. 59–61. The translations of the quoted passages are his.
[8] *Tilskueren* (1888), p. 62.

of German [sic] blood to aid and liberate us." The Germans were already claiming Ibsen as a German, as they had claimed Shakespeare.[9] At this banquet Ibsen asked Anton Anno, who had directed the production of *Ghosts*, why they had omitted Mrs. Alving's line about the fabric of Manders's reasoning coming apart because it was machine-sewn. Anno explained that sewing-machines had by now reached such a state of refinement that sewing could not possibly come apart on its own. "You can be sure," replied Ibsen, "that Mrs. Alving still had her old-fashioned sewing machine up at Rosenvold." When people expressed regret that the play was still banned from public performance, Ibsen said, "I can wait. I can wait."[10]

The excitement aroused by these productions of *Ghosts* sharply revived German interest in Ibsen. He informed Hegel on 26 January that *An Enemy of the People* and *Rosmersholm* had both been booked for performance in Berlin that spring, and that two German translations of the latter play were appearing "almost simultaneously." *The Wild Duck*, too, was to be belatedly translated this year. "My visit to Berlin, and everything connected with it," he wrote to Julius Hoffory on 4 February, "I regard as a great and genuine stroke of fortune for me. It has had an amazingly refreshing and rejuvenating effect on me, and will pretty surely leave its mark on my future writing." And indeed, his next play was to approach optimism more closely than anything he had written for years.

Ibsen's new-found success in Germany must have compensated him for the failure of *Rosmersholm* in the Scandinavian theatres. He was particularly annoyed that the Norwegian critics took exception to the portrayal of Kroll and Mortensgaard as representatives of what was narrowest in the conservative and liberal points of view. Writing to Jonas Lie on 27 January of his intention to spend the summer in Denmark, he added: "I shall not, in any event, go as far as Norway. I find little attraction in the happenings, atmosphere, and general tone of things up there. It is in the highest degree painful to see with what a greedy zest they seize on every kind of petty target as if it were an object of the greatest significance."

On 5 March the Ostend Theatre in Berlin presented the German premiere of *An Enemy of the People*. Despite an under-rehearsed opening performance, the production was greeted with a storm of approbation and, although the theatre was situated in an unfashionable part of the city, an hour's carriage ride from the centre, ran for two weeks at a stretch and even succeeded when revived during the hottest part of the summer. On 16 April, *Rosmersholm* was performed at Augsburg; but,

---

[9] Sigurd Høst tells a story of a German officer who, when asked by the Belgian historian Henri Pirenne, then a prisoner of war, to name a single great German since 1870, answered without blinking: "Ibsen." (*Aftenposten*, 14 March 1928).

[10] Hoffory in *Tilskueren* (1888), pp. 64 ff.; Koht, II, 219.

as in Scandinavia, the play bewildered the public. It was evidently a lamentable performance. Ibsen attended the dress rehearsal, and Julius Elias, who was with him, noted his reaction:

> He witnessed the performance with weeping and gnashing of teeth. Seated in the front of the stalls he winced in pain at every word uttered from the stage; with both hands clutching the plush of the orchestra rail, he groaned ceaselessly: "Oh, God! Oh, God!" In the third act John Rosmer conceived the grotesque idea of appearing with elegant *piqué* spats over shining polished calfskin boots. When the man appeared, Ibsen reeled as though struck, and clasped my arm. "Look, look at that!" The Rosmer he had created was wearing bright yellow spats. We were convinced that Ibsen would prohibit the whole performance at the last moment, with some vehement outburst, but then, suddenly, he straightened himself and, with a gesture as though to brush away a bad dream, said, "I must forget my original conception. Then it isn't too bad." And, with quiet resolve, he adopted this attitude. Once he had forgotten his original conception, he found everything satisfactory.[11]

The following month, on 5 May, *Rosmersholm* was much better staged in Berlin, by Anton Anno at the Residenztheater, with Charlotte Frohn and Emmanuel Richer, the team that had been responsible for the triumphant performance of *Ghosts*. The conservative critics greeted it with a fierce broadside. Karl Frenzel, Ibsen's old enemy, was still writing in *Deutsche Rundschau,* and predictably he liked the play no better than he had liked *The Pillars of Society* and *A Doll's House.* He complained that it was never genuine tragic guilt nor a powerful destiny that crushed an Ibsen hero, and that the sickness from which Ibsen and his characters suffered was not life, but Norway. If ever his heroes had had the opportunity to walk down the Unter den Linden, or even the Paris boulevards, they would have been cured of their whims. But if the main purpose of dramatic art was to excite a kind of "moral sea-sickness," then Ibsen was indeed a master of that art.

Another critic, H. von Pilgrim, writing in the *Magazin für die Literatur des Auslandes,* asserted: "Realism . . . is a canker of the time, like the sentimental bias which called forth *Werther* a hundred years ago. At present no physician for the malady is at hand, but I do not for a moment doubt that he will come. . . . Such dramas as those of Henrik Ibsen demonstrate by their vogue how little vitality they contain. It has never been the concern of art to offer the repulsive; symmetry and calm, exalted beauty, are the criterion."[12]

Yet *Rosmersholm*, like *Ghosts,* was appreciated by the young and restless in Germany, and if they were not represented among the professional

---

[11] Julius Elias, "Ibsenminne af hans tyske oversætter," in *Samtiden* (1940), p. 403.
[12] Eller, p. 63 (his translations).

theatre critics, they found outlets to express their admiration. Following up his November article, Otto Brahm published a seventy-page pamphlet on Ibsen that spring. "Ibsen's dramas," he wrote, "are a continued struggle against the lie, and a victory of the spirit of truth. Wherein is their dramatic strength to be found? In the plot? There are hundreds of plays with more significant plots. In the dialogue? More elegant, flowing and perspicacious dialogue is to be found. In their effectfulness? The common effects are avoided with almost puritanical rigour. The victorious strength of the plays lies solely in the idea, in the resolute prosecution of the idea, which is never deflected by bogus effects and ornament, by empty phrases, by superfluous romance. The one idea which constructs the play is so great, so true and staggering, that it carries us away, crushes us—and liberates us."[13] Although Anno's production of *Rosmersholm* had to contend with an unusually hot spring, it played for twenty-three consecutive performances and was withdrawn only because Charlotte Frohn was contracted to appear at another theatre.

Ibsen did no writing that spring or summer of 1887, and at the end of June he left with Suzannah for what turned out to be a three months' holiday in Denmark and Sweden (he ostentatiously avoided Norway). His longing for the sea had by now become almost obsessive. "Both my wife and I," he wrote to Hegel on 12 June, "look forward immensely to seeing the sea again," and he added that they felt a strong inclination to settle permanently in the north—"but it is perhaps best that we should have, at any rate for the present, a fixed point to which we can return outside the boundaries of our homeland."

They had planned to stay in Frederikshavn, near the northern tip of Jutland, but after ten days he moved to the smaller resort of Sæby, farther down the coast. Here he had a visit from William Archer, who described their meeting in a letter dated 25–28 July:

> It was a delightful drive—a perfect summer day, the corn ripe all round, the wild flowers brilliant, and the Cattegat dancing in the sunlight. All the way we could see Sæby Church straight ahead, and at last we rattled over a bridge, past a lovely old watermill, and into the quaint old main street of Sæby—one-storey houses, with great high gables, and all brightly painted or at the very least whitewashed. The moment we were over the bridge, I saw a short, broad figure ahead in an enormously long surtout and a tall hat made of silk looking far too small for his immense head. It was Ibsen, evidently on the lookout for me. I stopped the trap, we greeted each other with effusion, and then he insisted that I should remain in the trap and drive on to the Hotel Harmonien, where he was stopping, he following on foot . . .
>
> We drove into the courtyard of Hotel Harmonien, and by the time I had settled with my fellow-traveller Ibsen had arrived. He took me up into an

13 *Ibid.*, p. 66 (Eller's translation).

39. Ibsen in 1889, at the time of
his meeting with Emilie Bardach.

40. Emilie Bardach. "The May
sun of a September life."

41. Knut Hamsun, 1891. Portrait by Alfred Emil Andersen.

42. August Strindberg. The portrait by Christian Krohg which Ibsen kept on his study wall. He especially liked the "demonic eyes."

43. Helene Raff as an old woman. "A voice within me cries for you."

45. Hildur Andersen. "Here was my Empire and my Crown!"

44. Rosa Fitinghoff, c. 1905. "People do not meet until they have to say goodbye."

46. Ibsen in Christiania, 1901.

47. Ibsen. Caricature by Olaf Gulbransson.

48. Bjørnson. Caricature by Olaf Gulbransson.

49. Ibsen and the English Tourists. Caricature in *Vikingen*, 6 August 1898.

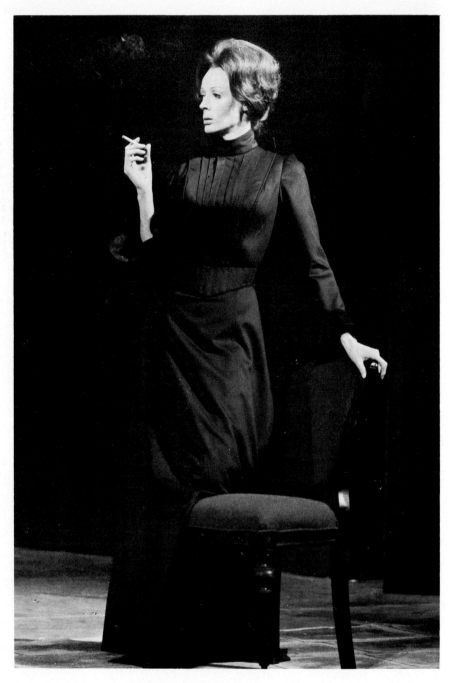

50. Maggie Smith as Hedda Gabler in Ingmar Bergman's production for the National Theatre, London, 1970.

51. Final page of Ibsen's draft manuscript of *Hedda Gabler*.

52. Ibsen's preliminary notes for *When We Dead Awaken*.

53. "Ever Higher." Caricature in *Tyrihans*, 25 January 1895. Ibsen's upward progress from *The Vikings at Helgeland* (with a lapse for *Ghosts*) until, with *Little Eyolf,* he disappears from human view.

54. Henrik Ibsen receiving Mr. William Archer in audience. Caricature by Max Beerbohm. Note the wallpaper.

55. "A dramatist of the first rank." Caricature of Ibsen's birthday banquet in Copenhagen 1 April 1898 in *Blæksprutten*.

56. The mourners of a dramatist. Drawing by an unidentified artist in *Korsaren*, 1906. From left to right: Oswald Alving, Rebecca West, John Rosmer, Halvard Solness, King Skule (of *The Pretenders*), Hedvig Ekdal, Lady Inger of Østraat, Eyolf Allmers, Hedda Gabler, Brand, Catiline, Emperor Julian, Peer Gynt, Hjørdis (of *The Vikings at Helgeland*).

57. Sigurd and Bergliot in 1904.

58. Ibsen with Ellen Sontum at Sandefjord, 1900. Photograph by Bolette Sontum.

59. Ibsen in 1899.

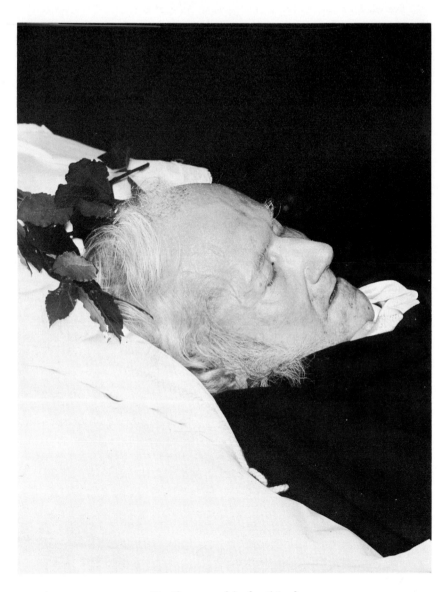

60. Ibsen on his deathbed.

enormous, barely-furnished, uncarpeted room on the first floor, with four if not five windows, and two bedrooms opening off it at the back. This formed his appartement, and here we sat and talked for about an hour, until Fru Ibsen came in from a walk in Sæby forest. . . . After about another hour we had dinner, then coffee and cigars. . . .

Now for a few Ibseniana. I must say in the first place that the old man was really charming throughout—perfectly frank and friendly, without the least assumption of stiffness of any sort. If I only had the art of drawing people out I could have got any amount of ideas out of him. Unfortunately I haven't the art—on the contrary, I have a morbid shrinking from talking to people about their own works; so that our conversation was, on the whole, far too much devoted to mere small talk and (strange to say) politics, Norwegian, Danish and Irish. However, I shall jot down a few of the things that turned up in the course of our talk. He said that Fru Ibsen and he had first come to Frederikshavn, which he himself liked very much—he could knock about all day among the shipping, talking to the sailors and so forth; and besides he found the neighbourhood of the sea favourable to contemplation and constructive thought. Here at Sæby the sea wasn't so come-at-able, but Fru Ibsen didn't like Frederikshavn because of the absence of pleasant walks about it; so Sæby was a sort of compromise between him and her. Fru Ibsen afterwards added that the Norwegian steamers of Frederikshavn were a source of perpetual temptation to her. For the present Ibsen is not writing anything, and hasn't been all last winter, because his time has been greatly taken up with business connected with the production of his plays in Germany. . . . Meanwhile the old man is revolving plans, and hopes to have "noget galskab færdigt til næste aar" [some tomfoolery ready for next year].

I tried to get at the genesis of a piece in his head, but the fear of seeming to cross-examine him prevented me from getting at anything very explicit. [However] it seems that the idea of a piece generally presents itself before the characters and incidents, though when I put this to him flatly he denied it. It seems to follow, however, from his saying that there is a certain stage in the incubation of a play when it might as easily turn into an essay as a drama; and he has to incarnate the ideas, as it were, in character and incident, before the actual work of creation can be said to have fairly commenced. Different plans and ideas, he admits, often flow together, and the play he ultimately produces is often very different from the intention with which he started. He writes and re-writes, scribbles and destroys an enormous amount before he makes the exquisite fair copy he sends to Copenhagen. As to symbolism, he says that life is full of it, and that therefore his plays are full of it, though critics insist on discovering all sorts of esoteric meanings in his work of which he is entirely innocent. He was particularly amused by a sapient person . . . who had discovered that Manders in *Gjengangere* was a symbol for mankind in general, *l'homme moyen* (not especially *sensuel*), and therefore called *Man*ders. . . .

In politics he came out very strong against the "compact majority," but on this point his thinking is scarcely less crude than U.D.'s for example.

This may seem a hard saying, but the fact is I am becoming more and more convinced that as a many-sided thinker, or rather a systematic thinker, Ibsen is nowhere. He is essentially a kindred spirit with Shaw—a paradoxist, a sort of Devil's Advocate, who goes about picking holes in every "well-known fact" as J. would say; or, as Ibsen himself would put it, looking at the teeth of every "normally built truth" and proclaiming it too old to pass any longer. And Ibsen is even worse than Shaw, who (in the main) knows himself for what he is and remembers that the exception proves the rule. To Ibsen, on the other hand, his paradoxes are apt to present themselves as the whole truth, and his general idea is that the exception destroys the rule. To say that the minority is always right, as Ibsen did in so many words, is at least as unphilosophical as to proclaim the infallibility of the majority. But this question of Majority v Minority is really one which can only be treated thoroughly in a scientific, one might almost say in a mathematical essay; whereas the minority-paradox is the very thing for enforcement in dramatic form. The upshot of all this is that if Ibsen were not a great poet he would be a rather poor philosopher—but that is in fact what you can say of all the leading spirits of this century; for example, of Carlyle and Ruskin; George Eliot is the one exception that occurs to me at the moment. But then Ibsen is Ibsen, and I am the last to complain that he is *not* Herbert Spencer. Of course even as a thinker he is on a totally different plane from men like Tennyson and Browning, who only pretend to think and never get any forra'der.

Altogether my day at Sæby was an unforgettable experience. You'd better preserve this letter—it may be useful sometime. . . . A greater than Shelley is here; at least a greater than Shelley ever *was,* though it is hard to say what he might have been but for that white squall in the Gulf of Spezia. It gives one a strange sensation to sit at a man's table and eat and drink and talk with him on equal terms, and then to think every now and then: This is the man who wrote *Peer Gynt* and the fourth act of *Brand,* and *Et Dukkehjem* [*A Doll's House*] and *Gjengangere* [*Ghosts*]. Except Shakespeare . . . I don't know that there is anyone in all literature whom I would care so much to know as Ibsen. Of course one would like to have seen Goethe or Thackeray or George Eliot, but they have not the enigmatic attraction of Ibsen. . . .

I was glad to find Ibsen and his wife warm in praise of [Bjørnson's] *Over Ævne* [*Beyond Mortal Power*], though there is a suggestion of *Brand* about it which a small-minded man, with any ungenerous sense of rivalry, might have turned to Bjørnson's disadvantage. . . ."[14]

"Jutland is a beautiful place to spend the summer in," Ibsen wrote to Hegel on 13 August. "The people are kind and likable; we have the open sea practically under our noses, and the weather is as perfect as one could wish." As at Molde two years earlier, he spent hours each day gazing out to sea. A nineteen-year-old Danish girl named Engelke Wulff, who was also staying there, noticed on the shore "a little broad-shouldered

14 Charles Archer, pp. 152–57.

man with grey side-whiskers and spectacles. He stood staring out across the water, with his hand shading his eyes. He had a stick with him with which he supported himself while he took a book out and wrote something in it. From where I sat and watched him, I supposed him to be drawing the sea." Ibsen saw her, too, as she sat doing her handiwork, and after a time got into conversation with her. She told him of her longing to see the world, and of her love of the theatre, and he promised he would put her into his next play. One thinks immediately of Bolette; but, as we know, he had already conceived Bolette's character in his early plans for *Rosmersholm,* and when they met by chance in a street in Christiania some years later he called Engelke "my Hilde"; so one must assume that some of Hilde's lines in *The Lady from the Sea,* if not her character, stemmed from those conversations on the shore at Sæby.[15]

Another young lady from Sæby imprinted herself on Ibsen's memory, though he never met her, for the good reason that since 1883 she had been lying in the town churchyard. Her name was Adda Ravnkilde; she was a talented young writer who had killed herself at the age of twenty-one, leaving behind her several stories and a novel, which was later published with a foreword by Georg Brandes. One theme recurs throughout her writings: the unsuccessful efforts of a young girl to free herself of her obsession for a man she knows is not worthy of her. Ibsen read her writings, and visited her home and her grave.

Her story must have reminded him of an early and similar adventure which had occurred to his mother-in-law, Magdalene Thoresen. In her own words: "While I was studying in Copenhagen I met a young man, a wild, strange, demented creature. We studied together, and I had to yield before his monstrous and demonic will. With him I could have found passion and fulfilment. I still believe that. . . . So I have lived my life oppressed by a feeling of want and longing." She had fled to Norway to escape from this affair and had married a man nearly twice her age; he "was my friend, my father and my brother, and I was his friend, his child."

And at Molde, two years earlier, the local people had told him two strange legends about the sea, and the power it had over those who lived near it. One was of a Finn who, by means of the troll-power in his eyes, had induced a clergyman's wife to leave husband, children, and home and go away with him. The other was of a seaman who left home and stayed away for many years, so that his family believed him dead; suddenly he returned, and found his wife married to another man. These four tales, with their related themes of the power of the sea and the demon lover, were to form the starting-point of Ibsen's next play. "People in Norway," he said to a German friend the following year,

15 Francis Bull's introduction to *The Lady from the Sea,* C.E., XI, 23–24.

while he was writing *The Lady from the Sea,* "are spiritually under the domination of the sea. I do not believe other people can fully understand this."[16]

At the end of August the Ibsens returned to Frederikshavn, where Henrik Jæger, busy preparing his biography of Ibsen, visited them and stayed for three days. He took detailed notes of their conversations, which remained unpublished until 1960:

Henrik Ibsen's life follows an extraordinarily regular pattern. He rises at 7 in the summer, a little later in the winter; he dresses slowly and carefully, spends an hour at his toilette, then eats a light breakfast. At 9 he sits down at his desk, where he stays till 1. Then he takes a walk before dinner, which in Munich he eats at 3. If anyone wishes to visit him he will be told that he is at home at 2.30. In the afternoon he reads; he takes his evening meal early, at 7. At 9 he drinks a glass of toddy and retires to bed.[17] He eats with a hearty appetite and sleeps well. He spends the winter planning his books, the summer in writing; the summer is his best working time; almost all his books have been written in the summer; of those which he has published since he left Norway in 1864 only two, *The League of Youth* and *Emperor and Galilean,* have been written during the winter. When he begins to write a book he eats and drinks no more than the barest minimum; it inhibits him in his work; a small piece of bread and half a cup of black coffee are all he takes before sitting down to his desk. He smokes a little when working, otherwise not at all.[18] He cannot understand how people who have to work can use stimulants; the only thing he can imagine that might be beneficial is a couple of drops of naphtha on a lump of sugar. In this respect he is like the caterpillar which ceases to take nourishment when it has to spin its cocoon.

In general he is regular to the point of pedantry; his day is divided according to the clock. These three days I have been living in his immediate proximity, dwelt next door to him and eaten at his side, we have lived by the clock from morning to night to a degree I could never tolerate indefinitely. One small example: each day when we have risen from the dinner-table, he has walked over to the window and looked at the thermometer which hangs outside. To do so before sitting down to table, or to ask the servant what the outside temperature is, seems not to occur to him.

He needs good air in quantity; lofty, airy rooms are an absolute necessity to him, he told me yesterday when we were discussing where he might lease an apartment in Munich for the winter. He much praises the air up here in northern Jutland because it is so clean and fresh on account of the unceasing wind. It must be for this reason that he has so often spent his summers in the Gulf of Naples or at Gossensass in the Tyrol. To my question

[16] *Ibid.,* pp. 24–27; Koht, II, 193–94.

[17] It is interesting that Ibsen apparently omitted to mention to Jæger the fact of his daily visit to the Café Maximilian.

[18] This was untrue; several witnesses (William Archer for one) have testified to his liking for a cigar during conversation.

why he chooses to settle in so cold and harsh a climate as Munich he replied that the Munich climate suited his temperament excellently; he said he liked it greatly. Although it is already September here and has been very windy these past few days so that we have had to put double fasteners on the open windows, he has kept two windows open all the time, one in each bay, though his desk is set right next to one bay. Each morning and evening he takes a cold rub down.

Concerning Ibsen's method of work, Jæger noted that "he likes to meditate what he is writing in the fresh air on long walks, and during the time he takes to dress. Works through the whole thing in his head before starting draft. Likes to stop with several lines ready in his head with which he can start the next day, which helps him to begin work. But if he gets stuck he stays put until he has got the thing moving again. Regards first draft as a means of getting to know his characters, outside and in, the way they talk, etc. Then the rewrite, and finally the fair copy.[19] Feels a great sense of relief as he approaches the end of a work, but as he does so new plans start popping up. He has to keep walking when working—he needs three or four rooms to move around in while he is working on his books."

On politics:

He shares the views of the extreme left, but cannot join their party because it is too dishonest; people don't seek truth but only whether it is a "respectable" person who has said something; if one of these respected gentlemen talks nonsense, nobody dares tell him so. . . . Ibsen this evening compared the people at home with tadpoles. Some time they will become fully developed frogs, but they still have black tails hanging down behind, and these black tails which they use to steer their course are obsolete ideas which they ought to have dropped long ago.

Ibsen spoke much to Jæger of his love of the sea. " 'There is something extraordinarily fascinating about the sea,' he said. 'When one stands and stares down into the water it is as though one sees that life that moves on earth, but in another form. Everything is connected; there are resemblances everywhere.' . . . He would have liked to have . . . gone to the west coast of Jutland, where the full force of the North Sea tumbles in; but he gave up that idea because he said that here on the north-east Jutland coast he found the same thing on a slightly smaller scale." He also told Jæger of his hatred of public speaking. "The worst thing he knew was to address a large gathering, and he greatly admired people

[19] Extraordinarily for so meticulous a writer, he never (even after his return to Norway in 1891) read proofs. "I don't bother about proofs," he once remarked, adding: "I have never personally read any of my books. . . . When I have finished a new book I don't look at it again. I begin at once on something new." (Interview with Hans Tostrup in Ørebladet, 13 March 1898, reprinted in C.E., XIX, 212–13.)

who can do it. . . . 'I could never learn to speak publicly,' he said, 'however long and assiduously I might practise.'"[20]

In the second week of September Ibsen crossed the Sound to Sweden, and spent six days in Gothenburg. On his fourth day there, 12 September, he made a speech at a banquet given for him by a literary society, Gnistan, in which he surprised his listeners by saying that his political interests were waning and, with them, his eagerness for battle. He visited the distinguished Valands Club, founded the previous year, and attended a French opera—Massenet's *Don César de Bazan*.[21] On 14 September he left for Stockholm by ship along the Göta Canal.

A handsome blonde of thirty-eight named Anne-Charlotte Leffler accompanied him on the SS *Pallas*. She was well-known as a dramatist and short story writer, and as an outspoken champion of women's rights; three years earlier she had visited England, where she had met (among others) Oscar Wilde, whose mother had just written a book about Scandinavia, Jenny Lind, Karl Marx's daughter Eleanor, and Annie Besant. She had met Ibsen in Gothenburg and had got on excellently with him; the night before their departure, he told her, he had dreamed that he was going on a honeymoon with her, but realized in his dream that this was impossible "for she is married and I am married." Then, still in his dream, he said, "Of course—it is a dramatic honeymoon"; and he added to her, "Perhaps the future will show it to have been so"— which baffled Anne-Charlotte, who assumed it meant that they might co-operate on a play together, but knew he never wrote in collaboration with anyone else. He also spoke cryptically of *The Magic Flute* and the water test which the two characters undergo, and added that "he thought we had done that, and wondered what it would lead to."[22] She was much intrigued by this unfamiliar preoccupation with dreams, and noted in her diary as they sailed along the canal:

> Ibsen is very quiet, but what he says is always interesting. But he is a curiously lonely soul—he seems to read almost nothing—he has certainly read vastly less than I. He associates with almost no one, he just lives and dreams, or lives quietly and looks at life without living it himself. He doesn't work much, years go by when he writes nothing—he hasn't written a line since *Rosmersholm*. Thursday night we spent in the saloon with Robinson, Ibsen's great admirer and commentator, whom we telegraphed to join us at Motala. . . . Ibsen was very amiable to me and told me repeatedly that it was a great pleasure for him to travel with me. They are of course going to fête him tremendously in Stockholm. We must give a dinner for him too.[23]

[20] Cf. Midbøe, pp. 151 ff.; and *Folkebladets julenummer* (Christmas 1887), pp. 23 and 25, reprinted in C.E., XIX, 172–73.

[21] Kommandantvold, pp. 21–22.

[22] Gustav Näsström, "Ibsen på Götakanalen, september 1887," in *Svenska Dagbladet*, 6 April 1969.

[23] Anne-Charlotte Leffler, *En självbiografi* (Stockholm, 1922), pp. 108 ff.

"Robinson" was the pseudonym of the writer Urban von Feilitzen, one of Ibsen's most persistent champions in Sweden (though he had disliked *Rosmersholm*); he described Ibsen after their meeting as a "sensitive hermit devoured by social sympathies, freezing in his austere prophet's cave."[24]

There was another interesting passenger on the *Pallas;* a young Swedish explorer and author named Sven Hedin, who had returned the previous autumn from an adventurous expedition into the heart of Persia. Ibsen invited Hedin to join them, and questioned him closely about Persia; Hedin showed him drawings he had made of Xerxes's palace at Persepolis and other memorabilia, and was surprised to find Ibsen particularly interested in the great ruins at Ctesiphon, which (he later realised) figures in *Emperor and Galilean.* Ibsen asked him the most minute details about this, including the materials of which it was constructed, and Hedin, in turn, questioned him about his trip to Egypt.[25] Hedin, then twenty-two, was to become one of the greatest explorers and orientalists of his time; also, sadly, an enthusiastic Nazi, and a personal friend of Hitler and Himmler. I met him in 1950, shortly before his death, and he expressed to me his amazement that historians were describing these men as cruel. "I knew them both," he said. "They were gentle, humble men." But, as with the Norwegian Nazi, Knut Hamsun, the follies of Hedin's age do not detract from the achievements of his saner years.

Ibsen stayed a week in Stockholm, where reception after reception was given in his honour. The Swedish novelist Gustaf af Geijerstam met him at several of these, and noted his dislike of large gatherings. "I sensed that he was not in his element. He never once spoke so that his voice could be heard throughout the room, and it was noticeable that he only relaxed when he was in a corner talking *à deux.*"[26] On 22 September Anne-Charlotte Leffler and her husband gave a small dinner for him. She wrote to a friend, Adam Hauch:

> He is so inexplicably kind to me, kisses my hand and gives me the warmest assurances of his affection. Yet he is still a closed book to me. I don't understand him. Although I have been together with him quite a lot, and although I usually read people's characters quickly, I couldn't write a character sketch of him. . . . Yesterday I had a very interesting day with Ibsen. Gösta [her husband] gave a stag party. Sonja and I were the only ladies, and it was a select gathering of interesting men, so that Ibsen became quite high-spirited and forthcoming. He isn't anyway nearly as wary and calculating as most people suppose, just a little shy and embarrassed, and needs to be in a special atmosphere to be able to express himself. But he answers quite happily whatever one asks him—how he works, who were his models, etc. . . . Ibsen is no public speaker, but when he replied yes-

[24] Letter to Adolf Noreen, quoted by Näsström.
[25] Sven Hedin, *Stormän och kungar,* I (Stockholm, 1950), 75–79.
[26] Gustaf af Geijerstam, "Två minnen om Henrik Ibsen," in *Ord och Bild* (1898), pp. 115–24.

terday to Gösta's speech he said something very surprising. "Of all my fatherlands," he said, "Sweden is the one where I have found most under- standing. . . ." How angry they would be in Norway if they heard that! . . . He can say terribly crushing, cutting things sometimes, and then a glint appears in those cold steel eyes, which fits well with something he often says, "A writer must never be afraid of a little devilry." He evidently loves devilry before all else. The Devil is his god, like Carducci's in his *Inno Satanico*.[27]

There was in fact a third lady at Anne-Charlotte's party, besides herself and her friend Sonja Kowalewski:[28] a remarkable novelist and short story writer, Victoria Benedictsson, better known under her pseudonym of Ernst Ahlgren, who was to commit suicide the following year (with a razor in front of a looking-glass) at the age of thirty-eight as the result of an unhappy love affair with Georg Brandes. She gave her impressions of Ibsen in a letter to Brandes, then involved in a violent row with Bjørnson as a result of some unkind remarks which he (like Strindberg) had made about Bjørnson's demand for male chastity in *A Gauntlet*.

Ibsen . . . makes so true and human an impression, he doesn't put on a show. He makes one want to confide in him. He looks as though one could talk to him about anything . . . so composed and sealed, so whole. . . .

Ibsen was in a good mood, with little roguish remarks and pats on the shoulder for the ladies, and was treated like God the Father. I was nauseated by this worship and had kept perversely aloof all evening, thinking I could be equally happy whether I'd talked to Ibsen or not. But somehow it happened that he wandered over to a doorway where there was a group of people chatting, including me. Of course the group spread out with our guest of honour as the central point. . . .

"Has anyone been following the row between Georg Brandes and Bjørnson?" the old boy asked without warning.

Some said yes, some no. You can guess how wide my eyes and ears grew! People muttered little hypocrisies. Someone said you had been un- fair to Miss G. and bitter in your attacks—personal.

Then a glint came into those small grey Ibsen eyes.

"He may have been bitter," he said. "And he may have behaved ruthlessly. But one must remember how he has been attacked and how he has been treated. And Denmark ought to know what a man it possesses in him."

There was some talk of propriety and morality, and I couldn't hold my tongue either—people got quite worked up. And then he smiled with that calm, wise smile of his.

"I'll tell you all something," he said. "And you remember it. What one

27 Leffler, pp. 109–12.
28 Sonja Kowalewski was Russian-born, and in 1884 became Professor of Mathe- matics in Stockholm. She wrote a play in collaboration with Anne-Charlotte Leffler, who after Sonja's death wrote a biography of her. Anne-Charlotte herself died shortly afterwards, at the age of forty-three.

must cling to, cling to and defend, is the morality one has within one, within oneself—what the morality of society calls sinful, because it is the new morality, the kind that is germinating and will grow. . . ."

He said more, you can guess what. And they listened, they applauded—they, who all their lives will trample on and stifle everything he talked of, about the individual's inner moral code, the free feeling that in *this* case *this* is right—the individual's development from his own self, his own nature, the fulfilment of his biggest and best potentialities! They applauded; and tomorrow they'll go out and trample on it. . . . Am I being silly again? Are you laughing?[29]

But Ibsen, when the occasion arose three years later, did not defend Brandes publicly, any more than in a few years he was to defend Laura Kieler against a spiteful libel by Brandes himself. On 26 September 1890 Brandes wrote to Jonas Lie that he had been continuously vituperated against in the German press, especially in the Munich newspaper *Allgemeine Zeitung*. "It would only cost Henrik Ibsen," Brandes complained, "who sees this paper every day and is worshipped in Munich as a demi-god, a two-line letter to the editor to end the matter. . . . But you don't for a moment suppose that he'd even turn over in his bed to do any such thing!"[30]

Two days after Anne-Charlotte Leffler's dinner, a grand banquet, of the kind Ibsen disliked most, was given for him at the Grand Hotel. In his reply to the official speech of welcome, Ibsen surprised his listeners by describing himself as an "optimist," declaring that he believed that the world was entering a new epoch in which old differences would be reconciled and humanity would find happiness. August Lindberg was there, but had difficulty in getting near Ibsen because of the press of grand ladies who surrounded him—so many head-plumes, Lindberg noted, as to make Ibsen look as though he were seated in the royal hearse. Lindberg determined, if possible, to give a party for Ibsen where he could meet the young, and especially the young of the theatre, the actors and actresses who had performed in his plays. He and his wife managed at last to get through to Ibsen and asked if he would attend such an informal lunch gathering the next day; and to their delight, he smiled and accepted, "as though he sensed that it was a plot by those who had not been able to get near him during the banquet."[31]

The next day was a Sunday, and they had some difficulty in fixing the food and wine in time; but they managed, and at two o'clock on the dot Ibsen appeared, wearing a top hat but, they were glad to note, no medals or even ribbons.

[29] Letter from Victoria Benedictsson to Georg Brandes, 24 September 1887 (*Brandes Brevveksling*, VI, 247–49).

[30] *Ibid.*, IV, 447–48.

[31] Per Lindberg, p. 211.

It was said that he always liked to sit on a small and uncomfortable chair; he always wanted to appear stiff and correct, and a comfortable chair easily causes a man to hunch himself unattractively. Nevertheless, he was put into a large, high-backed chair with arms, but at least hard, for it was of oak. He did not protest, and even took our one-year-old daughter on his knee. Beside him there stood a bottle of wine, and we saw to it that his glass was always full. "I don't understand," he said. "I keep on drinking, and yet my glass grows no emptier." He enjoyed himself; his old bohemian self emerged from the tightly buttoned coat and he sat and told us about his travels and how *A Doll's House* came to be written. In the end the ladies took hold of him and—chaired him. And he replied kissing each of them on the cheek.[32]

Gustaf af Geijerstam, who was there, adds:

I don't doubt that Ibsen, like other mortals, is capable of feeling pride at being respectfully acclaimed. But this is sure, that he enjoyed it twice as much when the tribute found expression in a style of unforced gaiety, when stiff formalities were banished and merriment reigned, when the great man was allowed to be simply a human being among other human beings. Pehr Staaff in his speech of welcome at this gathering hailed Ibsen as "no pessimist, prepared to sign his name to a declaration of mankind's bankruptcy, but an optimist who believes in the ability of humanity . . . to rise like the Phoenix renewed from its ashes. . . . I give you the health of Henrik Ibsen, optimist!"

It was very strange to see Henrik Ibsen when this tribute was paid to him by a group of young people at a private party. The great man suddenly became communicative, once or twice underlining the speaker's words by murmuring, "Yes! Exactly!"

He had an appointment that evening at the theatre, to see *An Enemy of the People,* and they parted on the warmest terms. Geijerstam continues: "But when I saw Henrik Ibsen later, he was seated in a box surrounded by notabilities, and his face wore something of that expression which commonly appears in his photographs." He concluded:

It is perfectly true to say that Henrik Ibsen can be uncommunicative and off-putting, but it is equally true that no one can be more open-hearted than he, more freely and unforcedly friendly and kind, more susceptible to personal affection. . . . All that is needed to arouse this feeling is that he himself should feel unconstrained and know that he is understood by those with whom he is speaking. That is why Henrik Ibsen is in his heart an enemy to everything official, and why, when lionised by too many people, he can suddenly become enclosed and buttoned-up. . . . Amid all the cheering which echoes around him he searches for a sympathetic and understanding eye to meet his own.[33]

[32] *Ibid.,* p. 212.
[33] Geijerstam, pp. 115–24.

Ibsen's visit to Stockholm had been a triumph. "All the women are in love with him," wrote Anne-Charlotte Leffler to her friend Adam Hauch, "especially Sonja, and one said on Saturday that she wasn't going to wash her hands for a week now that Ibsen had touched them. . . . I was delighted to find that, like almost all men of genius I have met, he fully and firmly believes in a socialistic future." She had been one of Ibsen's companions in the theatre box. "You can't imagine," she continued to Hauch, "how much talk there has been in the press all week about Ibsen's box in the theatre. All the papers have had something to say about us lucky chosen ones, all the scandal sheets have been joking about the 'bouquet of ladies' with whom he surrounded himself . . . I really think it's ladies who get the most out of him. He's a ladies' man like all poets."[34]

On 26 September Ibsen returned to Denmark, and on 5 October he attended a dinner given for him by Hegel. In his address of thanks he said that this summer, in Denmark, he had discovered the sea; that the smooth and pleasant Danish sea, which one could come close to without feeling that mountains cut off the approach, had given his soul rest and peace, and that he was carrying away memories of the sea which would hold significance for his life and his writing.

What were the reasons for this sudden mellowing in Ibsen, as exemplified in his utterances in Gothenburg, Stockholm and Copenhagen? Partly, no doubt, the acclamation he had received in Meiningen and Berlin at the turn of the year; partly, perhaps, his discovery of the sea, though one would guess this to be a reflection rather than a cause of his change of mood. Possibly, too, as Francis Bull has suggested,[35] those conversations with Henrik Jæger at Frederikshavn in September may have had a therapeutic effect. In the course of these conversations, Professor Bull observes, Ibsen had recalled many old memories, to help Jæger with the early chapters of his book. These memories included some which Ibsen had tried to forget; but now, when he dragged them out into the daylight, he found that they no longer had the power to frighten him. Consequently, Ibsen must have felt impelled to ask himself whether it did not lie within a man's power to drive away "ghosts" or "white horses" of whatever kind, provided he had the courage to look his past in the face and make his choice between the past and the present, a choice taken (to quote from the play he was about to write) "in freedom and full responsibility." In *Rosmersholm* a potentially happy relationship between two people is destroyed by the power of the past; in *The Lady from the Sea,* Wangel and Ellida overcome that power, and it may be that Ibsen's conversations with Jæger gave him a new confidence, if only a temporary one, in man's ability to escape from the terror of his own history.

Yet in certain matters he remained as inflexible as ever, and one was

[34] Leffler, pp. 113–14.
[35] Introduction to *The Lady from the Sea,* C.E., XI, 17.

his relationship with his family, always excepting Hedvig. His brother, Ole Paus Ibsen, who seems to have inherited all his father's inability to hold down a job on land, asked Ibsen to support an application he was making for the humble post of lighthouse keeper; this being a state post, Ole, who started his letter "Dear brother Henrik" and described his circumstances as "very bad," begged Ibsen to use his personal influence with the Prime Minister. Ibsen's note to Sverdrup on the subject, dated 3 October 1887 from Copenhagen, is as frosty a reference as one brother can ever have written for another:

> Your Excellency!
> My only surviving brother, Ole Paus Ibsen, domiciled at Tjømø, is applying for a post as lighthouse keeper and asks me to put in a word on his behalf to Your Excellency. May I in this connection ask Your Excellency to be so good as to read the enclosed letters and testimonials. I myself have nothing further to add on the subject.
> I remain Your Excellency's respectful and most obedient servant
> Henrik Ibsen

Ole Paus Ibsen got the job and kept it for seventeen years before retiring for the remainder of his long life (he lived until 1917) to a home for retired seamen.

That month, *Ghosts* was publicly performed in both Berne and Basel, arousing, as it did everywhere, violently conflicting reactions. On the other side of the world the German actor Friedrich Mitterwurzer was touring the play, in English, through America under the title of *Phantoms, or The Sins of the Fathers,* and advertised on the posters as "BANNED IN GERMANY." Clemens Petersen saw it in Chicago and wrote to Bjørnson that it was excellently performed but that the theatre was "disagreeably empty," adding the hope that "Ibsen will write a new *Ghosts* or *Rosmersholm* or the like every year, for then I shall live to see this bubble burst."[36]

Ibsen returned to Munich in the second week of October, and in a letter he wrote on 15 November to a Swedish bookseller named Hans Österling there appears, for the first time in his letters, the name of that former admirer of his to whom his own name was gradually becoming anathema:

> During my visit to Stockholm in September you were so kind as to send me a copy of Strindberg's recently published play *The Father,* and I beg you to accept my sincerest thanks for this most valuable gift.
> One does not read a new work by a writer such as Strindberg

[36] *Bjørnstjerne Bjørnsons brevveksling med danske, 1875–1910* (Copenhagen and Oslo, 1953), I, 280–81.

during the restlessness and changing moods of travelling. I have therefore postponed the perusal and study of this work until now, when I
have returned to the peace of my home.

Strindberg's observations and experiences in the sphere of which
The Father principally treats do not accord with my own. But this
does not prevent me from recognizing and being gripped by the
author's violent strength, in this as in his earlier works.

The Father is soon to be performed in Copenhagen. If it is acted
as it needs to be, with merciless realism, the effect will be shattering.

During the past twelve months, Strindberg's references in his correspondence to Ibsen had become less and less complimentary. In a play
The Robbers, which he wrote in November 1886, he had appealed:
"Give us back joy, you who preach the joy of life! Give us the cheerful
little spirit of compromise, and send the Old Men of the Dovre back to
their caves!" On 10 December 1886, replying to his publisher's offer to
send him the latest works of Ibsen and Alexander Kielland, he declared:
"Ibsen and Kielland have nothing to teach me, two ignorant women's
writers."[37] Apart from Ibsen's championship, or supposed championship,
of the feminist cause, Strindberg disliked him for his praise of aristocrats
(though Strindberg himself was secretly attracted to them), and because
he, Strindberg, always developed a resentment against anyone who had
influenced him. When Edvard Brandes suggested that Strindberg might
address himself directly to Edvard's brother Georg, Strindberg replied
(3 January 1887): "Why don't I write myself? Because I am afraid, afraid
of him as of all fertilising spirits, afraid as I was of Zola, Bjørnson, Ibsen,
of becoming pregnant with other men's seed and bearing other men's
offspring." In *The Father* itself, which he wrote that January, there is
a reference to *Ghosts* ("When I sat in the theatre the other evening and
heard Mrs. Alving orating over her dead husband, I thought to myself:
'What a damned shame the fellow's dead and can't defend himself!'"),
and on 22 January (his thirty-ninth birthday) he wrote to Edvard Brandes,
with reference to his own play *The Robbers,* "That I have portrayed a
mean and dishonourable woman is not more unjust or unæsthetic than
Ibsen's and his sisters' scandalous attacks on men. Woman is, in general,
by nature mean and instinctively dishonest, though we ruttish cocks have
not been able to see it; so, I have portrayed a typical woman."[38]

In May, Strindberg sent Edvard Brandes an article in which he asserted
that Ibsen had written no true work of art since *The Pretenders;* and on
3 June he wrote to August Lindberg, who was preparing to present
Rosmersholm and other Ibsen plays at Dagmars Theatre in Copenhagen,

[37] *August Strindbergs brev,* VI, 123.
[38] *Ibid.,* p. 148. Ibsen's "sisters" were the feminist writers such as Anne-Charlotte
Leffler and Victoria Benedictsson.

that Ibsen was through: ". . . his *genre* is on the way out. You should read the Germans on *Rosmersholm!* Let him go his way, and we ours!"[39] The fact that he himself had, however reluctantly, admired *Rosmersholm* did not prevent him from rejoicing in the Germans' denigration of it. Strindberg knew that all men are full of contradictions, and never bothered about them in himself.

To digress one generation beyond Strindberg, it is interesting to note that a similar resentment towards supposed literary ancestry was displayed by a writer who is often thought of as one of Strindberg's most gifted disciples. "I don't want to write like Galsworthy, nor Ibsen, nor Strindberg, nor any of them, even if I could," wrote D. H. Lawrence to Edward Garnett on 1 February 1913. "We have to hate our immediate predecessors, to get free from their authority." Three months earlier, on 30 October 1912, he had written to Garnett: "I hate Strindberg. He seems unnatural, forced, a bit indecent—a bit wooden, like Ibsen, a bit skin-empty"; and on another occasion earlier that month: "I bet your play will be better than that rotten Strindberg!" But Lawrence's tastes in literature were as unpredictable as Strindberg's. "My God, what a clumsy *olla putrida* James Joyce is!", he wrote to Aldous Huxley and his wife on 15 August 1928. "Nothing but old fags and cabbage-stumps of quotations from the Bible and the rest, steeped in the juice of deliberate, journalistic dirty-mindedness —what old and hard-worked staleness, masquerading as the all-new!"[40]

Ibsen lost a good friend and counsellor that Christmas of 1887; on 27 December Frederik Hegel died at the age of seventy. Their relationship had never been close. But during the two decades of their acquaintance Ibsen had trusted him as he had trusted few people; Hegel had always been ready to advance Ibsen money when he needed it and, although only eleven years older, had been something of a father-figure to Ibsen, as a publisher should be to his authors. His son Jacob, who succeeded him, was a much lesser man—"a decent and well-meaning fellow," wrote Alexander Kielland to his brother, "but . . . I wonder if he isn't really more interested in horses than writers."[41] However, Jacob Hegel had an unusually pretty wife, Julie, and continued his father's tradition of hospitality at Skovgaard. Ibsen's relationship with him remained cordial, and he continued to ask him, as he had asked his father, for advice on investments.

It was not the best time for Ibsen to have lost his publisher, for 1887 had been financially a disastrous year. *Rosmersholm* had failed in the Scandinavian theatres, the flurry of German productions of his plays at the beginning of the year had brought him virtually no money, and he had

---

[39] *Ibid.*, p. 216.

[40] *The Letters of D. H. Lawrence,* ed. Aldous Huxley (London, 1932), pp. 66, 104, 742.

[41] Harald Grieg, *En dansk forlegger og fire norske diktere* (Oslo, 1955), p. 146.

had no reprints. His experiment of taking ten per cent of the gross for the Christiania production had lost him something like 2,000 crowns.

	crowns	
Fee for *Rosmersholm* at Bergen	400	
Fees for various unspecified productions of *"Nora"*	400	
Fee for *Rosmersholm* at Gothenburg	300	
Fee for *An Enemy of the People* at Ostend Theatre, Berlin	228	
Fee for Danish provincial rights of *Rosmersholm* and *A Doll's House* (W. Foght)	400	
Royalties from *A Doll's House* in Munich (last quarter of 1886)	215	
Miscellaneous extra payments from Bergen	320	
Fees for *Rosmersholm* in Berlin and *Ghosts* at Meiningen	305	
Royalties for *Rosmersholm* at Christiania	540	
Royalties for *A Doll's House* at Munich Residenztheater	546	
Royalties for *A Doll's House* at Munich Hoftheater	59	
Unspecified fees from Royal Theatre, Stockholm	950	
	4,663	£259

"Ibsen's plays aren't earning him as much as before," wrote Edvard Brandes (who presumably had the information from someone at Gyldendal) to Jonas Lie on 16 March 1888. "What will he cook up now? Let's hope he doesn't retreat; we'd be in trouble then; we who dabble in the theatre would lose our standard-bearer."[42] And indeed Ibsen might have been forgiven if he had made his next play a straight discussion drama of the kind that had proved so popular, a successor to *The Pillars of Society* and *A Doll's House*. It was typical of his courage and integrity as a writer, however Peer Gynt-like he may have been in his private life, that he followed his own stern bent and wrote a play as difficult and psychologically experimental as the one which had just proved so unpopular.

[42] *Brandes Brevveksling*, V, 283.

25

The Lady from the Sea,
and the Breakthrough in England

1888–1889

Ibsen's sixtieth birthday, on 20 March 1888, was marked by the publication of Henrik Jæger's biography of him, a sober and intelligent appraisal containing some carefully censored biographical matter provided by the subject himself. Among the many telegrams of good wishes was one signed by fifty-four members of the Storthing, one from the actors at the Christiania Theatre, and one from Bjørnson which included the sentence, "Today the world comes to the recluse."[1] Many German writers and artists visited him personally to deliver their greetings. *Aftenposten* printed an anonymous front-page leader (by Professor Bredo Morgenstierne, who disliked and wrote hostile reviews of most of Ibsen's mature plays), paying tribute to "our greatest living writer," stressing how Norwegian he was and declaring that no foreigners could ever more than partially appreciate him, words which must have rung somewhat hollowly in Ibsen's ears. As evidence of his international fame the newspaper proudly published extracts from his early poem "Terje Vigen" in English, German and Polish translation; one would have thought they might have found something more recent. Yet, while the left-wing papers joined in saluting him, the leading Tory paper, *Morgenbladet*, said not a word.

Ibsen's gratitude for the liberals' acclaim of him was tempered by the evidence it gave that he was still the adopted champion of a party in which he no longer had any real confidence. "One of the things that has pained me most in my literary connection with my fatherland," he wrote to Amandus Schibsted, the editor of *Aftenposten*, on 27 March, "is the knowledge that, over a number of years, ever since *The League of Youth* appeared, I have always been claimed as the possession of one or other of

[1] Cf. *Verdens Gang*, 28 March 1888.

the political parties. I, who have never in my life concerned myself with politics, but only social questions! And my presumed opponents refuse to understand this. It is not praise or favour that I ask for, but understanding. Understanding!"

Earlier that month *An Enemy of the People* had been staged at Meiningen, "where [noted William Archer] the fourth act was naturally found to offer a superb opportunity for the Meiningen methods of stage-management."[2] And indeed one would like to have seen what Duke Georg made of that crowd scene, on which so many productions of the play fall down. Max Grübe played Dr. Stockmann; but Ibsen, a little surprisingly, did not attend. "I hardly ever go to the theatre here," he wrote to the Danish playwright Jens Christian Hostrup on 2 April, "though I like to read a play now and then of an evening, and since I have a strong power of imagination for the dramatic . . . the reading serves almost for a performance." No doubt it served much better than most of the performances he saw. Productions of his plays in Munich, however, he could hardly help attending, and he was present when the Residenztheater presented *The Wild Duck* on 4 March, a performance which elicited sixteen curtain calls. There would probably have been more productions to mark his birthday had not the old Kaiser Wilhelm died a few days earlier; but there was scarcely a serious newspaper or periodical which did not commemorate the occasion with a piece about him.

Irgens Hansen wrote a long article on "Ibsen in Germany" which *Dagbladet* in Christiania published in four instalments on 20, 22, 25, and 28 March. In 1880, Hansen recalls, despite the success of *The Pretenders, The Vikings at Helgeland* and *The Pillars of Society,* and the discussion aroused by *A Doll's House,* Ibsen was not on all men's lips in Germany, and was in fact less well known than Bjørnson, thanks to the latter's stories and *A Bankrupt.* Nor had the banning of *Ghosts* helped; but now "what admirers thought impossible in 1886 has become a reality. German actors have dared to perform the play, and German audiences have seen it." So hotly are his plays debated (continues Hansen) that it has even been seriously suggested that "four young Jews have written his entire works," and the recently published translation of *Emperor and Galilean* is to be seen in every bookshop window. Hansen quotes from numerous German newspaper and magazine articles about Ibsen published during the preceding twelve months, but expresses surprise that the German theatres stage his plays for so few performances at a time, for "here is a writer who follows no one and sets sail for unknown shores." The first of the four instalments includes a vivid picture of the dramatist in exile:

In the high rooms at Maximilianstrasse he has hung his beloved paintings. For the third year now one may of an afternoon see his figure, so familiar

[2] Archer's introduction to his translation of *An Enemy of the People* (London, 1901), p. x.

to the citizens of Munich, in his long Ulster and top hat, slowly walking the streets. Behind the spectacles the eyes smile oftener than the severe features would have one suspect; for it amuses him to walk among the crowd. He likes to stop where people throng before a window. He knows everything on his routes and notices every little new thing. For an hour to an hour and a half he walks thus in the city, never in the country—"the country is uninteresting"—and soon after 6:30 one will see him at his regular table at the Café Maximilian. There he sits for half an hour, then returns home. Now and then he spends an evening at the Writers' Club when they have a meeting. Otherwise he is not seen.

Julius Hoffory, the Dane working as a professor in Berlin, wrote a perceptive appraisal of Ibsen's standing in Germany in the Copenhagen magazine *Tilskueren* this year. The critics, he reports, are divided into two factions, "some hailing him as a new leader, others denouncing him as an evil messenger of darkness who strives only to destroy everything that one regards as sacred," contrasting his "gloomy art" with the "bright and beautiful world of Goethe" (a curious comparison, Hoffory comments, remembering that Goethe was the author of *Götz* and *Werther*). The debate cut across party lines; left-wing papers such as *Berliner Tageblatt* and *Volks-Zeitung* were among Ibsen's bitterest opponents, while others such as *Vossische Zeitung* and *Die Nation* championed him in lengthy articles. *Post* and *Deutsches Tageblatt* attacked him; but other right-wing papers such as *Fremdenblatt* and *Börsen-Zeitung* supported him. The government organ *Norddeutsche Allgemeine Zeitung* violently condemned him, while another government publication, *Deutsche Reichs-Anzeiger*, praised his "great art and Titanic strength." Hoffory concludes:

> It must not be forgotten that the attacks on Ibsen contributed just as much as the eulogies to impress the significance of his work on the German public. It can already be claimed without exaggeration that no living German writer is as well known, as widely read, and as earnestly discussed as Henrik Ibsen. In newspapers and books, in brochures and literary magazines, literary historians and essayists, philosophers, lawyers and doctors compete in the interpretation of his work. In the bookshop windows his latest plays are on show by the score, and if one enters, a carefully arranged collection of Ibsen's works is very often the first thing to meet one's eye. His plays are circulated in cheap editions which reach the widest circles and are read and prized by people who are seldom seen with a work of literature in their hand.[3]

Evidence of the continued increase of Ibsen's reputation in Germany over the next few years appears in an article which Georg Brandes contributed to the same magazine two years later. Brandes declared Ibsen to be a more creative influence in German writing than any other living

[3] *Tilskueren* (1888), pp. 61–70.

author, and thought the reason was that he demanded the unusual combination of socialism and individualism—not the individualism of selfishness but the individualism of self-fulfilment. As examples of young German dramatists who were disciples of Ibsen, Brandes cites Richard Voss, Hermann Bahr, Wolfgang Kirchbach (who had been born in London of German parents) and Gerhart Hauptmann who, although only twenty-seven when Brandes was writing, had already completed *Vor Sonnenaufgang*, *Das Friedensfest* and *Die Selicke auf Arno Holz und Johannes Schlef*. All these writers, explained Brandes, admired Ibsen as a realist. "His name has become a banner, and a whole new generation is rallying to this banner in such magazines as *Freie Bühne, Modern Dichtung,* etc." The fact that Ibsen never declared his principles or contributed a line himself to these magazines, concludes Brandes, impressed the Germans hugely; and he was very amiable to his young admirers such as Otto Brahm, Paul Schlenther and Hermann Bahr when he met them or they sent him their work.[4]

A new play was due from Ibsen this year, especially after the poor returns of the previous year, and on 5 June he jotted down his first notes, nearly two and a half thousand words:

> The sea's magnetic power. The longing for the sea. Human beings akin to the sea. Bound by the sea. Dependent on the sea. Must return to it. One species of fish is a vital link in the chain of evolution. Do rudiments of it still reside in the human mind? In the minds of certain people?
>
> Images of the teeming life of the sea and of "what is lost for ever."
>
> The sea operates a power over one's moods, it works like a will. The sea can hypnotize. Nature in general can. . . . She has come from the sea. . . . Because secretly engaged to the young, carefree ship's mate. . . . At heart, in her instincts—he is the one with whom she is living in marriage. . . .

These notes, which include a very detailed synopsis of the first act, provide some interesting revelations of the dramatist's mind at work. At first Ibsen intended to make Wangel, Ellida's husband, a lawyer, "refined, well-born, bitter. His past stained by a rash affair. In consequence, his future career is blocked." But he abandoned this conception, and Wangel became instead a kindly and understanding doctor. His wife first appears as Thora (an echo of Magdalene Thoresen?), but Ibsen changed this to Ellida; in the *Saga of Frithiof the Bold* there is a ship named Ellide which (as Halvdan Koht has pointed out) is like a living person fighting against secret troll-powers that try to drag her down beneath the sea.[5] The young ship's mate does not figure in Ibsen's first cast-list, and Ibsen seems to

[4] *Tilskueren* (1890), pp. 423–50.
[5] Koht, II, 193.

have intended that he should not appear; there is, though, a Strange Passenger, "once a lion in the capital," who "felt a deep attachment to her [Ellida] when she was engaged to the young sailor." Ibsen later changed this character into Arnholm, the schoolmaster, and introduced the young sailor as the Strange Passenger or, as he finally called him, the Stranger. There was also originally to have been "an old married clerk. In his youth wrote a play, which was performed once. Is continually touching it up, and lives in the illusion of getting it published and becoming famous." Ibsen discarded him, but used him four plays later as Vilhelm Foldal in *John Gabriel Borkman,* just as he used here the two young daughters, Bolette and Hilde, whom he had originally conceived as characters for *Rosmersholm.*

Five days after he had made these notes Ibsen began to write Act One, provisionally entitling the play *The Mermaid,* and he completed his first draft in just over seven weeks. Act One is dated 10–16 June; Act Two, 21–28 June; Act Three, 2–7 July; Act Four, 12–22 July; and Act Five, 24–31 July. Early in August he began to revise it, and by 18 August he had corrected the first two acts to his satisfaction. Two days later he began to revise the third act, and on 31 August he started on the fourth. On 25 September he was able to send his fair copy to Jacob Hegel. "The work was finished a little later than I had calculated," he wrote to Hegel the following day, "but I hope it is still in good time, provided the printing can begin at once. May I ask that the title page be printed last and the title kept secret—as, likewise, I trust that the printers will observe the maximum of discretion. . . . I am confident that this play will arouse general interest. In many respects I have struck out in a new direction here."

He was still as bitter as ever about Norway; despite the birthday tributes, his experiences of the previous summer continued to rankle. "It would be totally impossible for me to settle for good in Norway," he wrote to Georg Brandes on 30 October. "There is nowhere where I would feel more homeless than up there. The old conception of a fatherland no longer suffices for anyone intellectually mature. We can no longer rest content with the political community in which we live." He went on to indulge in a little wishful thinking. "I believe that national consciousness is on the way towards dying out, and will be replaced by racial consciousness. I at any rate have undergone this evolution. I began by regarding myself as a Norwegian, developed into a Scandinavian and have now arrived at the general idea of Teutonism." Another of his current preoccupations, his disillusionment with the left, inevitably came in for treatment. "The leaders of the left are wholly lacking in worldly experience and have consequently been cherishing the most unreasonable illusions. They imagined that a leader of the opposition would and could remain the same man after he had achieved power as he had been before"—a note of disenchantment which has been echoed by many a radical voter since.

Continuing the same letter on 4 November, Ibsen added: "I see that that knave John Paulsen has committed another act of literary villainy as thanks for the kindness I showed him." Paulsen had just published a new novel, *Fru Cecilia*, a melodramatic but not altogether contemptible romance about a woman who is wrongly supposed to have had a shady past. The young man who loves her daughter is forbidden by his aristocratic mother to involve himself with such a family; there is an extra complication in that he had admired the mother before he fell in love with the daughter. To clear the young couple's path, Fru Cecilia kills herself. None of the characters could possibly be confused with anyone in the Ibsen household, and the only reference to Ibsen is when the young man says to Fru Cecilia: "I will bring you Ibsen's new play. They say it's full of brilliant paradoxes."[6] It seems a little hard of Ibsen to have regarded this as villainous or ungrateful.

Ibsen indulged in, for him, an unusual amount of correspondence that November, while awaiting the publication of *The Lady from the Sea* (as he had now re-entitled it). Apart from his long letter to Brandes, he wrote a detailed missive to August Larsen, an editor at Gyldendal, dealing with points of spelling and so forth, and adding the (as events were to turn out) surprising remark: "I have never had any doubt that my play will be completely understood outside Norway." He also wrote to Julius Hoffory thanking him for translating the play into German. Henrik Jæger, his biographer, had written from Bergen passing on a suggestion from the theatre there that, instead of paying the usual lump sum, they should give him ten per cent of the gross takings; but this he refused, after his unfortunate experience with *Rosmersholm* in Christiania: "Our impecunious theatres," he replied on 17 November, "would be tempted to perform the plays as seldom as possible; whereas if they have paid the author his whole fee it will be in their own interest to get the money back from performances as quickly as possible. I must therefore stick to the old fixed fee system as the only practicable one as long as the present laws concerning literary copyright persist." He may have sensed that none of his future plays would be popular successes as *The Pillars of Society* and *A Doll's House* had been.

On 20 November he thanked his old Holland friend Ludvig Daæ for a long appreciation of Paul Botten Hansen which Daæ had recently published in the Danish magazine *Vidar*. "It gripped me with an extraordinary power to take myself back again so vividly into those times which exercised so decisive an influence upon my later development and from which I have never really freed myself—never been able or wanted to free myself." (It is interesting that he did not reject the Christiania

[6] John Paulsen, *Fru Cecilia* (Copenhagen, 1888), p. 19.

years of humiliation as he rejected Skien). He ended the letter by asking Daæ to "greet all the survivors" of the Holland circle "from their, and your, affectionate old friend, Henrik Ibsen," a little surprisingly when one remembers how many of that circle had by now retreated into conservatism. This mellow note is repeated in a letter he wrote the following day to Bredo Morgenstierne thanking him (five months late) for his birthday tribute in *Aftenposten* and assuring him that "when I return to Christiania— if that ever happens—I will visit the circle where I feel most at home." And on 25 November, acknowledging to Magdalene Thoresen the repayment of a debt she said she owed him, he wrote that he could not recall having lent her the money and insisted that she take it back. "Use the money on something that will bring you joy. You must in some way or other celebrate your freedom from debt, on which I congratulate you with all my heart. I know from my own experience what such a liberation means"— a reminder, were one needed, of how this particular subject obsessed him.

Jonas Lie visited Ibsen this month on his way to Paris, and, so Lie wrote to Georg Brandes on 26 November, they "had as always an unusually pleasant evening. We've been friends since youth, and although we were so different then he often used to choose me to preach to about his dramatic plans."[7] The next day we find Ibsen expressing an opinion on one of the very few contemporary writers who shared his own stature. Thanking Emmanuel Hansen, a translator who lived in St. Petersburg, for sending him a copy of Tolstoy's play *The Power of Darkness* in Danish, he wrote: "I have read *The Power of Darkness* with much interest. I have no doubt that, carefully and respectfully performed, it must make a considerable effect on the stage. Nevertheless, it seems to me that the author does not possess a complete insight into dramatic technique. The play contains conversations rather than scenes, and the dialogue strikes me in many places as epic rather than dramatic, the work in general as being less of a drama than a narrative in dialogue"—a verdict with which most directors and actors would agree. He added, however, that "the great writer's genius lives and is revealed there."

This was, parenthetically, a more charitable judgment than Tolstoy was to pass on Ibsen, for he found all of the latter's plays (except, oddly enough, *Rosmersholm*) repellent. "Have read *Love's Comedy*," he wrote in his diary on 19 November 1889. "How bad! Clever German sophistry— terrible!" V. L. Nemirovitch-Dantchenko lent him *An Enemy of the People*, but he disliked that too, remarking: "This Dr. Stockmann is much too conceited."[8] On 20 August 1890 he noted; "Have read Ibsen's *Wilde Ente* [*The Wild Duck*]. Not good." (As he called the play by its

---

[7] *Brandes Brevveksling*, IV, 429.

[8] V. L. Nemirovitch-Dantchenko, *My Life in the Russian Theatre*, translated by J. Cournos, 2nd edn. (London, 1968), p. 333.

German title he had presumably read it in that language; it was not translated into Russian until 1892). The next day he noted: "Have read Ibsen's *Rosmer* [*sic*]. . . . So far not bad." But it seems doubtful if he liked the rest of it, for on 14 September 1891 he wrote to Ibsen's Russian translator, P. G. Hansen, that he loved Bjørnson's writing and personality, "but I cannot say the same of Ibsen. I have read all [*sic*] his plays too, and his poem *Brand*, which I was patient enough to read to the end. Everything is contrived, false, and very clumsy, in the sense that none of his characters is consistent and lived-through. His reputation in Europe merely proves the poverty of European creative writing." In his essay *What is Art?*, written in 1898, Tolstoy made particular mockery of *Little Eyolf* and *The Master Builder*; but Ibsen was in good company, for Tolstoy poured equal scorn on Beethoven, Baudelaire, Wagner, Verlaine and Zola. In his diary of 28 October 1900, citing Ibsen as an example of "the poetry and art of the cultural mob," Tolstoy linked his name disparagingly with those of Shakespeare and Dante, finding all three immoral and irreligious and, therefore, bad artists;[9] and, dismissing Chekhov's *The Seagull* as "utterly worthless," he added that it was written "just as Ibsen writes his plays."[10] Chekhov's own attitude towards Ibsen was to be most oddly ambivalent.

On 28 November 1888 *The Lady from the Sea* was published in an edition of 10,000 copies, 2,000 more than *Rosmersholm* or *The Wild Duck*. Ibsen's conviction that the play would be "completely understood outside Norway" proved sadly unfounded; it was not even understood inside Norway. The critics were as bewildered by it as they had been by *Rosmersholm*, and although it got a slightly better press on account of the happy, or seemingly happy ending, such tributes as it received were grudging. "The play is not free from riddles and problems," wrote an anonymous critic in *Morgenbladet* (5, 8, 11, and 12 December), regarding this as a defect, "but wholesomeness emerges victorious. . . . It certainly moves in a cleaner air." At the same time, he complained, Ellida's story "is from first to last a story of sickness, a bizarre psychological case history, the development of which taxes the action of the play. . . . There is no real drama in this." Bredo Morgenstierne, who had been so severe on *The Wild Duck* and *Rosmersholm*, also welcomed (in *Aftenposten*, 5 December) the "cleaner air" of this play, but found little else to praise, and even Irgens Hansen, while praising the truthfulness of the psychology, thought (*Dagbladet*, 30 November) that the subject would have been better treated in a novel. Knut Hamsun dismissed it as an "insanity,"[11] and the historian J. E. Sars doubtless expressed many people's views when he declared: "It seems to me a proof of how modern æsthetics have

---

[9] Cf. Martin Nag, *Ibsen i russisk åndsliv* (Oslo, 1967), pp. 99–103.

[10] David Magarshack, *Chekhov the Dramatist* (New York, 1960), p. 16, quoting Alexey Suvorin's diary for 11 February 1897.

[11] *Samtiden* (1890), p. 8.

strayed that Henr. Ibsen has almost [*sic*] overtaken Bjørnson in public estimation. He is a purely negative spirit. . . . Surely this pessimistic problem writing must by now have reached its limit."[12] Tolstoy would have agreed with that, although it is ironical to reflect that he himself was never to receive the Nobel Prize for Literature, despite the fact that he lived for nine years after its inception, because the Swedish Academy regarded him as insufficiently idealistic.

The Swedish and Danish press were scarcely more favourable. Kristofer Randers, reviewing the play in *Ny Svensk Tidskrift* (1889, pp. 500 ff.), complained that it continued the trend noticeable in Ibsen's work since *The Wild Duck,* in that "an obscure mysticism and a musing symbolism seem more and more to predominate at the expense of the natural and the immediate." C. D. af Wirsen, in *Post och Inrikes-Tidning,* thought it "doubtful whether this curious play will survive long on the stage. Come back, old Shakespeare, with your wholesome humanity, and dispel these eccentricities."[13] (He does not seem to have read *Troilus and Cressida.*) P. A. Rosenberg, a Danish admirer, also found it negative.[14] Edvard Brandes welcomed the play enthusiastically in *Politiken,* but found himself almost alone. "I don't understand," wrote the young Swedish poet Ola Hansson to Strindberg, "how Edvard Brandes can express himself in such superlatives. . . . Of course the end of the play will evoke cries of joy from sheep and rabbits. It might be interpreted as the apotheosis of marital duty." Strindberg replied (7 December) that Ibsen "ought now to be repudiated as moralistic and religious,"[15] though within the decade he was to become both himself. Erik Bøgh advised the Royal Theatre in Copenhagen to reject it, and in a Scandinavian newspaper on the other side of the world a forgotten enemy took up his pen to denounce it. Clemens Petersen gave it a bad review in the Chicago *Nordisk Folkeblad.*[16]

Almost the only critic apart from Edvard Brandes to acclaim *The Lady from the Sea* whole-heartedly was the Swede J. A. Runström, who had recently taken over the dramatic column on the Stockholm weekly *Ny Illustrerad Tidning,* a task which he was to fulfil with considerable distinction. What other critics had condemned in the play, he welcomed. "The psychological," he wrote (15 December), "has always been Ibsen's principal strength and here it is dominant and undistracted by polemical issues. He has put social criticism aside.[17] . . . A play of rare fulfilment.

[12] Letter to John Paulsen, 12 September 1889 (J. E. Sars, *Brev, 1850–1915* [Oslo, 1957], p. 182).

[13] Wirsen, p. 102.

[14] P. A. Rosenberg, *Literatur og Kritik* (Copenhagen, 1888), pp. 444–50.

[15] *August Strindbergs brev,* VII, 196.

[16] Petersen never gave up. As late as 1895 he was still protesting to Bjørnson that Ibsen "is a critic, not a creative writer." (*Bjørnstjerne Bjørnsons brevveksling med danske,* II, 229.)

[17] It is significant that Ibsen, as his notes for the play show, originally intended that Ellida should have broken her engagement with the seaman because of social and

Not only is the characterisation masterly and enthralling; the brilliant assurance with which the plot is conceived and carried through fills one with an admiration which grows the more one ponders it."[18]

It was fortunate for Ibsen that Jacob Hegel did not consider printing a smaller impression of *The Lady from the Sea* following the failure of *Rosmersholm*, for otherwise 1888 had been an even worse year financially than 1887. Not only had there been no reprints of his earlier works; he had received no performance fees from Scandinavia at all, apart from 189 crowns for two performances of *An Enemy of the People* in Stockholm. Luckily for him the German theatres were beginning to pay a little more; even so, his earnings for the year, excluding the advance for *The Lady from the Sea*, totalled only 2,346 crowns (£130).

	crowns	
Fees for *The Wild Duck* in Berlin	195	
Fees for *A Doll's House* in Berlin	300	
Other unspecified fees from Berlin	49	
Fee for 24th and 25th perfs. of *An Enemy of the People* at the Royal Theatre, Stockholm	189	
Fees from Munich Hoftheater for 13 perfs. of *The Pillars of Society* and 1 perf. of *A Doll's House*	1,466	
Fee from Cologne Stadttheater for *The Pillars of Society*	147	
1st edn. of *The Lady from the Sea*	8,550	
	10,896	£605

However, the interest on his investments brought him 3,288 crowns to add to his pension of 2,000 crowns; and so economically did he live that on 11 December and 20 January he asked Hegel to buy him further securities to a total value of 14,000 crowns, which suggests that, with Sigurd now earning a sufficient salary, Ibsen and Suzannah were living on little more than his pension. The fear that he might find himself incapacitated by illness or a stroke (as eventually happened), or that he might lose his public (as now seemed not impossible), was always in his

---

moral prejudices derived from his upbringing; but he discarded this motive, and the conflict between Wangel and the Stranger became instead a struggle to gain control over the subconscious powers of her soul. Cf. Koht, II, 194.

[18] Sadly, Runström used *The Lady from the Sea* as a stick with which to belabour Strindberg's *Miss Julie*, which had appeared almost simultaneously, and which Runström reviewed in the same article. "It goes without saying," he wrote, "that the play *Miss Julie* bears traces of its author's talent, and contains one or two effective scenes, but . . . it treats a subject . . . which, when expressed as nakedly as it is here, makes a most disagreeable impression even upon reading, and will surely nowhere find a public that could endure to see it." In this at least Runström was speaking for his fellow-countrymen, for it was to be sixteen years before *Miss Julie* was staged in Sweden.

mind, and he was determined that he and his wife should never find themselves in the situation in which, half a century earlier, his father had left him.

At last there were signs of a belated breakthough in England. In the closing weeks of 1888, thanks to William Archer's efforts, a publisher bearing the illustrious name of Walter Scott issued a volume, in a series called the Camelot Classics, containing Archer's translation of *The Pillars of Society*, a careful revision by him of Henrietta Frances Lord's version of *A Doll's House*, and a translation by Karl Marx's daughter Eleanor of (as she called it) *An Enemy of Society*. The volume was introduced by a twenty-nine-year-old ex-medical student named Havelock Ellis, then earning a living as editor of the Mermaid Series of Old Dramatists. Ellis expressed his envy of the Scandinavian countries for having a stage on which "the burning issues of the day [may] be scenically resolved," and concluded by declaring that Ibsen's ideas "are of the kind that penetrate men's minds slowly. Yet they penetrate surely, and are proclaimed at length in the market place." Ellis's own first book, *The New Spirit*, which appeared just over a year later, was to contain a forty-three page section on Ibsen. It is a measure of the impact which Ibsen was about to make on the English scene that the little Camelot volume of his plays sold, during the next five years, no fewer than fourteen thousand copies, a quite unprecedented figure for a volume of plays by a living dramatist, and thereby established a new trend which, in due course, Shaw and Galsworthy were profitably to follow.

On New Year's Day, 1889, Edmund Gosse returned to the Ibsen scene after an absence of five years with a long article in the *Fortnightly Review* entitled "Ibsen's Social Dramas," dealing with all the prose plays from *The Pillars of Society* to *The Lady from the Sea*. He welcomed the last-named play as possessing "a glamour of romance, of mystery, of landscape beauty, which has not appeared in Ibsen's work to anything like the same extent since *Peer Gynt*." And before the year was out Ibsen was to enjoy his first success on the London stage. All in all, 1889 was to prove an important year for him abroad.

The Lady from the Sea, however, failed on the stages of Europe as calamitously as *Rosmersholm* had done. It received its premiere on 12 February, simultaneously in Christiania and Weimar.[19] *Aftenposten*, reviewing the Christiania production, dismissed the play as "one of Ibsen's feeblest," and although it managed twenty-one performances that season it was thought worthy of only two the following season. It failed in Weimar and also, four days later, in Copenhagen when, despite Erik Bøgh's rec-

---

[19] According to W. H. Eller (pp. 78–79), four other German theatres applied for the right to stage the first production, but all declined after reading the play.

ommendation to the contrary, the Royal Theatre presented it. There was great public curiosity to see how it would fare on the stage, and the first night's takings were the biggest for any Ibsen play at this theatre during the dramatist's lifetime, but it achieved no more than eleven performances. Edvard Brandes thought it a bad production, and wrongly cast in the leading role; Ibsen had wanted Betty Hennings, but the theatre chose their other leading lady, Josephine Eckhardt. "Who cast the play with such lack of consideration?" asked Brandes in *Politiken* on 20 February. "But one cannot wholly acquit the dramatist of blame, since the aristocratic in- difference with which he treats the Scandinavian theatres extends to his not choosing the casts. . . . They have designed no scenery, but have merely shoved together old pieces. . . . They could have played it success- fully between three bare walls had they played it well." In Stockholm, too, the following month, it failed. J. A. Runström, who had so welcomed it on publication, felt bound to admit (*Ny Illustrerad Tidning*, 30 March) that "the right place for *The Lady from the Sea* is not on the boards. It is a play to be read, and as such is enthralling, but in the theatre it loses a good deal of the magic it exercises on one's imagination. What seems natural and inevitable on the page seems almost unnatural on the stage. . . . The central character is too subtle to withstand the brightness of the limelight. She hovers on the frontier between the world of reality and the world of poetry without appearing to have a true foothold in either."

Like *Rosmersholm*, *The Lady from the Sea* was to fail time and again when staged, with occasional (and memorable) exceptions, and for two reasons. First, like *Rosmersholm*, it delved into depths of the human soul with which both audiences and actors were unfamiliar. Secondly, the part of Ellida needs a very special kind of actress. It is one of those roles, like Lear and Othello, Strindberg's father and Miss Julie, which demand a particular quality of personality, and the most accomplished actress in the world, if she lacks this quality, cannot succeed. She may get excellent notices for her performance, but the play will fail. But with the right actress, the result is one of the rarest experiences that the theatre can offer, like a great Othello. The first to encompass the role was Eleonora Duse. James Agate, in a memorable passage, described her in the part:

> This play is a godsend to a great artist whose forte is not so much doing as suffering that which Fate has done to her. With Duse, speech is silver and silence is golden. . . . The long second act was a symphony for the voice, but to me the scene of greatest marvel was the third act. In this Duse scaled incredible heights. There was one moment when, drawn by every fibre of her being to the unknown irresistible of the Stranger and the sea, she blotted herself behind her husband and took comfort and courage from his hand. Here terror and ecstasy sweep over her face with that curious effect which this actress alone knows—as though this were not present stress,

but havoc remembered of past time. Her features have the placidity of long grief; so many storms have broken over them that nothing can disturb again this sea of calm distress. If there be in acting such a thing as pure passion divorced from the body yet expressed in terms of the body, it is here. Now and again in this strange play Duse would seem to pass beyond our ken, and where she has been there is only a fragrance and a sound in our ears like water flowing under the stars.[20]

Greta Garbo would have been supremely suited to play Ellida; why did nobody think of making a film of it with her? I once saw a young Irish actress, Jean Robinson, make something extraordinary of the part in a fog-filled theatre at Lancaster in 1967.

At the beginning of March there was an Ibsen week in Berlin, with *The Lady from the Sea* at the Schauspielhaus, *The Wild Duck* at the Residenztheater and *A Doll's House* at the Lessingtheater. Ibsen went up for the occasion, staying at the Hotel du Nord, and was feted as enthusiastically as he had been two years earlier. Various banquets were given for him, and he himself invited Otto Brahm, Paul Schlenther, Julius Hoffory and Ove Rode, the young Dane who had led the rebellion in the Students' Union in Christiania, to "a splendid luncheon which lasted almost till evening. . . . It will be good to have some peace again," he wrote to Suzannah on 5 March, after attending a charity matinee of *The Lady from the Sea* the previous day. "I already feel quite tired."[21] But in a letter of thanks on 26 March to Hoffory, whose translation of *The Lady from the Sea* had rapidly gone into a third edition, he described his stay in Berlin as "the most exciting time of my life. When I look back on it, the whole thing seems like a dream. It makes me almost afraid." Before returning to Munich he spent a week in Weimar, where he found the production of *The Lady from the Sea* (he told Hoffory in the same letter) "quite excellent. I could not wish, nor could scarcely imagine, the Stranger better interpreted—a tall, lean figure with a long face, black, staring eyes and a magnificent, deep, subdued voice."

In Munich he found a new edition (the seventh) of *The Pretenders* awaiting him, with the news that an eleventh edition of *Brand* was in the press, and that he now had 17,000 crowns to his credit with Gyldendal, information which he described to Hegel (11 April) as "a great and joyful surprise." The idea of spending any of this windfall on luxuries did not occur to him, or if it did it was firmly rejected, for the next day he wrote Hegel that the whole amount was to be invested in gilt-edged securities, 7,000 crowns' worth of it in Russian railways.

[20] *Sunday Times*, 10 June 1923, reprinted in Agate's *Red Letter Nights* (London, 1944), pp. 71–72.

[21] C.E., XIX, 356. The letter is there dated 1891, but cf. Koht's note on p. 555 of that volume.

The Pillars of Society was revived in April at the Deutsches Theater in Berlin, and the same month he heard from Snoilsky that two of his plays had, at last, been translated into French. The translator was not a Frenchman, any more than Hoffory in Berlin was a German or P. G. Hansen (his Russian translator) a Russian; he was a Lithuanian, Count Moritz Prozor. Married to a niece of Snoilsky, he had, when secretary at the Russian embassy in Stockholm in 1883, seen *Ghosts* performed there; the play had made a deep impression on him, and on moving to the Berne embassy in 1887 he had, with the aid of his wife, turned both *Ghosts* and *A Doll's House* into French. Now, in 1889, he had managed to get both translations published in Paris. (It is typical of the piratical conditions then governing copyright as far as a Norwegian was concerned that Ibsen should not have known even of the translations' existence until after they had appeared in print.) "I have not yet seen it," he wrote to Snoilsky on 19 April, referring to the *Ghosts* translation, "but even if I had read it I would be unable to pass any well-founded judgement, since my knowledge of the French language is very inadequate. I am all the happier that you find the translation very well done." He added that two Frenchmen had been negotiating with his German translators to make versions of his plays from the German, a common practice in several countries up to recent times (one of the most frequently performed "translators" of Ibsen in England during the forties and fifties worked from German texts which were often wildly inaccurate).

On 7 June 1889 Ibsen achieved his first real breakthrough on the English stage. Hitherto, he had been represented only by the single matinee of *The Pillars of Society* in 1880, the dreadful travesty *Breaking a Butterfly* in 1884 and the amateur performance of "Nora" in 1885. Now, however, a young Irish actor-manager named Charles Charrington produced *A Doll's House* in Archer's revised translation at the Novelty Theatre in Kingsway (later the Kingsway Theatre) with his wife, the twenty-five-year-old Janet Achurch, as Nora. Before her premature death in 1916 at the age of fifty-two Janet Achurch was to become one of the great actresses of her generation (in 1907 she was a memorable Mrs. Alving), and this production established her reputation at the same time that it established Ibsen's. William Archer recorded the occasion in the columns of the *World*, of which he had, since 1884, been dramatic critic, starting at a salary of three guineas a week. At the age of thirty-three, he had already proved himself the best English dramatic critic since William Hazlitt:

> The general public [wrote Archer on 19 June,] has risen heroically to the occasion. It has come—nay, more, it has paid—to see *A Doll's House,* and that in larger numbers night by night. . . . So far from having drunk its fill of Ibsen in a single week, it is crying out for more, and the departure of

Miss Achurch and Mr. Charrington for Australia has with difficulty been postponed in answer to that demand. If these things had been prophesied six weeks ago, who would have believed them?

Years later, Archer recalled: "It was this production which really made Ibsen known to the English-speaking peoples. In other words, it marked his second stride towards world-wide, as distinct from merely national renown—if we reckon as the first stride the success of *The Pillars of Society* in Germany. . . . The Ibsen controversy, indeed, did not break out in full virulence until 1891, when *Ghosts* and *Hedda Gabler* were produced in London; but from the date of the Novelty production onwards, Ibsen was generally recognized as a potent factor in the intellectual and artistic life of the day."[22]

Harley Granville Barker, in *The Coming of Ibsen*, noted: "The play was talked of and written about—mainly abusively, it is true—as no play had been for years. The performances were extended from seven to twenty-four. The takings were apt to be between £35 and £45 a night. Charrington lost only £70. This was not bad for an epoch-making venture in the higher drama."[23]

The newspaper criticisms were, as Barker says, generally unfavourable. "I never sat out a play more dreary or illogical as a whole, or in its details more feeble or commonplace," complained the *Sporting and Dramatic News*. "It is as though someone had dramatized the cooking of a Sunday dinner" (no bad subject for a play, one might think nowadays). Bernard Shaw praised it anonymously in the *Manchester Guardian* (8 June); so did R. K. Hervey in *The Theatre* (1 July): "Those who have not read *A Doll's House* or seen it acted can have no conception with what a master hand the characters are drawn." But the same issue contained a violent attack on the play by the editor, Clement Scott: "The atmosphere is hideous . . . it is all self, self, self! . . . a congregation of men and women without one spark of nobility in their nature, men without conscience and women without affection, an unlovable, unlovely and detestable crew." Scott had already written an anonymous attack in the radical organ *Truth* (13 June) on the people who supported this new cult, dismissing them as "a scant audience of egotists and Positivists assembled to see Ibsen . . . and to gloat over the Ibsen theory of woman's degradation and man's unnatural supremacy." Among these despicable characters was W. B. Yeats, then twenty-four, who left an account of the occasion and the impression it made on a young writer in *The Trembling of the Veil*:

> . . . somebody had given me a seat for the gallery. In the middle of the first act, while the heroine was asking for macaroons, a middle-aged washerwoman who sat in front of me stood up and said to the little boy at her

22 Charles Archer, p. 169.
23 Granville Barker, p. 179 note.

side: "Tommy, if you promise to go home straight we will go now"; and at the end of the play, as I wandered through the entrance hall, I heard an elderly critic murmur "A series of conversations terminated by an accident." I was divided in mind. I hated the play; what was it but Carolus Duran, Bastien-Lepage, Huxley and Tindall all over again; I resented being invited to admire dialogue so close to modern educated speech that music and style were impossible. "Art is art because it is not nature," I kept repeating to myself, but how could I take the same side with critic and washerwoman? As time passed Ibsen became in my mind the chosen author of very clever young journalists who, condemned to their treadmill of abstraction, hated music and style; and yet neither I nor my generation could escape him because, though we and he had not the same friends, we had the same enemies."[24]

Archer, in an essay entitled "The Mausoleum of Ibsen" which he contributed to the *Fortnightly Review* in 1893, listed some of the comments of those "enemies" on Charrington's production of *A Doll's House:*

By the new school of theorists the *genre ennuyeux* is assigned a place of distinction; for *A Doll's House* with its almost total lack of dramatic action is certainly not an enlivening spectacle.

The Times

It would be a misfortune were such a morbid and unwholesome play to gain the favour of the public.

Standard

Such a starting point has dramatic possibilities. A Sardou might conceivably turn it to excellent account on the stage. . . . It is simply as a mild picture of domestic life in Christiania that the piece has any interest at all. It is a little bit of genre painting, with here and there an effective touch.

Daily News

Of no use—as far as England's stage is concerned.

Referee

Unnatural, immoral and, in its concluding scene, essentially undramatic."

People

Ibsen . . . is too faddy and too obstinately unsympathetic to please English playgoers.

Sunday Times

Strained deductions, lack of wholesome human nature, pretentious inconclusiveness. . . . Cannot be allowed to pass without a word of protest against the dreary and sterilizing principle which it seeks to embody.

Observer

The works of the Norwegian playwright are not suitable for dramatic representation—at any rate on the English stage.

St. James's Gazette

[24] W. B. Yeats, *Autobiographies* (London, 1955), p. 279.

Among those who made the production possible was, of all people, Henry Irving, who remained until his death in 1906 an implacable opponent of Ibsen. Janet Achurch, relates Irving's grandson, "had asked him for money to sustain her and her husband . . . in a comedy, *Clever Alice*. . . . He had sent her £100, only to discover that she and Eleanor Marx-Aveling were conspiring to produce Ibsen. She asked him to come and see *A Doll's House*. He went. 'If that's the sort of thing she wants to play she'd better play it somewhere else,' was the only comment he made."[25]

Ibsen was delighted with the success of Charrington's production. "The movement in London," he wrote to Archer on 26 June, enclosing a signed photograph for Janet Achurch, "marks a shining epoch in my life, far surpassing anything I had ever dreamed of."[26] The interest in *A Doll's House* stimulated a brief revival of *The Pillars of Society* the following month for a single matinee at the Opera Comique in the Strand. R. K. Hervey, despite his editor's views on the playwright, again wrote enthusiastically in *The Theatre* ("It is impossible in a short article to do justice to this remarkable play"), and Austin Brereton in *The Stage* thought that "the piece . . . would in all probability succeed for a time in an evening bill, more particularly after the excitement and controversy the production of *A Doll's House* created." An American actress named Elizabeth Robins made her first appearance in an Ibsen part, in the role of Martha; she was to do much to pioneer his work on the English stage during the coming decade.

The Charringtons took their production of *A Doll's House* to Australia that year; also to New Zealand and, in due course, to Egypt, India and America. It was well received everywhere except in Sydney, where "an indignant and outraged audience greeted Nora's exodus with howls and hisses."[27]

Ibsen had spent the previous summer in Munich, working on *The Lady from the Sea*, but this year he decided to take a holiday. "In the beginning of next month," he wrote to Nils Lund on 29 June, "we shall be going to the Tyrol to spend the rest of the summer there. We shall probably choose Gossensass, where we have so often stayed before." It was a fateful decision. That summer in Gossensass in 1889 was to throw Ibsen sharply out of the mood of mellow optimism which had found expression in *The Lady from the Sea*, and was to leave its mark on all his future work.

[25] Laurence Irving, *Henry Irving* (London, 1951), p. 535.

[26] Cf. Charles Archer, pp. 183–84, and Bjørn Tysdahl, "Ibsen-brev i Brittisk Museums Archer-samling," in *Edda* (1966), pp. 246–59. Tysdahl notes that the British Museum collection contains seventeen letters written by Ibsen to Archer between 1889 and 1900, only two of which (plus a third not in the British Museum) are printed in the Collected Edition of Ibsen's Works.

[27] Miriam Franc, *Ibsen in England* (Boston, 1919), p. 83.

26

The Summer in Gossensass

1889

It was Ibsen's first visit to Gossensass for five years, since he had spent the summer of 1884 alone there finishing *The Wild Duck*. Sigurd, now transferred from Washington to the embassy in Vienna, joined his parents there; they stayed, as before, at the Gröbner family hotel, and a sister of the proprietor remembered how Ibsen "lived like a clock," just as in Munich. Each day he took a walk along the river Eisach, standing for a long while on the bridge and staring broodingly into the water. The locals, indeed, nicknamed him "Der Wassermann," which might not unfairly be translated as Old Man River. Fräulein Gröbner recalled how *soigné* he was in his dress, even on his country walks, and, from his weekly bills, how simply and modestly he lived.[1]

The little town had decided to celebrate his return by naming his old look-out on the hill the Ibsenplatz, and on 21 July the ceremony took place. There was a grand procession and Ibsen, despite the steep ascent, climbed at the head of it and received with friendliness and dignity the homage accorded him. A concert followed, and after the concert he met a young Viennese girl named Emilie Bardach. As she remembered seventeen years later, this happened at a crowded reception; but if we are to believe an American's transcription of her diary (the original has disappeared),[2] they first really got to know each other when he

[1] Bergliot Ibsen, p. 90.

[2] Basil King printed extracts from Emilie's diary, in English translation, in two articles entitled "Ibsen and Emilie Bardach" in the *Century Magazine*, New York, October 1923, pp. 803–15, and November 1925, pp. 83–92. André Rouveyre published some of the same extracts, in French, in "Le Mémorial inédit d'une amie d'Ibsen," in *Mercure de France*, 15 July 1928, pp. 257–70. There are discrepancies between the two versions and, as Emilie's journal has disappeared, it is impossible to say which is correct. King's daughter, Mrs. Reginald Orcutt, tells me that her father returned the journal to Emilie, and that after her death her effects went to a female

came on her seated alone on a bench, reading a book, in a valley named the Pflerschtal on the outskirts of the town. He seated himself beside her and, questioning her closely as was his wont, learned her age (eighteen), details of her home and family, and the fact that they lived so near each other in Gossensass that his windows looked into hers. A few days later she ran into him at a dull birthday party. "It is a pity," she noted in her journal, "that German gives him so much difficulty, as apart from that we understand each other so well."

She fell ill, and a few days later Ibsen came to see her, climbing over the garden gate to do so. "He remained with me a long while, and was both kind and sympathetic." A little later: "We talk a great deal together. His ardour ought to make me feel proud." He asked her endless questions, and seemed particularly anxious to catch her in a lie.[3] Then:

> Ibsen has begun to talk to me quite seriously about myself. He stayed a long time with me on Saturday, and also again this evening. Our being so much together cannot but have some painful influence over me. He puts such strong feeling into what he says to me. His words often give me a sensation of terror and cold. He talks about the most serious things in life, and believes in me so much. He expects from me much, much, much more than I am afraid he will ever find. Never in his whole life, he says, has he felt so much joy in knowing anyone. He never admired anyone as he admires me. But all in him is truly good and noble! What a pity it is that I cannot remember all his words! He begs me so intensely to talk freely to him, to be absolutely frank with him, so that we may become fellow-workers together.

Next she writes:

> Mamma has just gone out, so that I have the room to myself. At last I am free to put down the incredible things of these recent days. How poor and insufficient are words! Tears say these things better. Passion has come when it cannot lead to anything, when both of us are bound by so many ties. Eternal obstacles! Are they in my will? Or are they in the circumstances? . . . How could I compare anything else that has happened to an outpouring like this? It could never go so far, and yet—!

She swings off to Baron A., the only lover who offered a standard of comparison.

---

cousin, whom I have been unable to trace, and who is now almost certainly dead. Emilie's account of the party meeting occurs in "Meine Freundschaft mit Ibsen," an article she wrote for the Vienna newspaper *Neue Freie Presse*, 31 March 1907. Much fuss has been made about the discrepancy between King's version of her diary and her own reminiscence, but if, in King's translation of her diary extract for 5 August, one substitutes "got to know him" for "made his acquaintance," the problem disappears.

[3] So she told A. E. Zucker in 1927 (Zucker, p. 242).

But how much calmer *he* was, how inarticulate, beside this volcano, so terribly beautiful! Yesterday afternoon, we were alone together at last! Oh, the words! If only they could have stamped themselves on my heart more deeply and distinctly! All that has been offered me before was only the pretence at love. This is the true love, the ideal, he says, to which unknowingly he gave himself in his art. At last he is a true poet through pain and renunciation. And yet he is glad of having known me—the most beautiful! the wonderful! Too late! How small I seem to myself that I cannot spring to him!

Neither Suzannah nor Emilie's mother seem to have suspected what was afoot. But:

The obstacles! How they grow more numerous, the more I think of them! The difference of age!—his wife!—his son!—all that there is to keep us apart! Did this have to happen? Could I have foreseen it? Could I have prevented it? When he talks to me as he does, I often feel that I must go far away from here—far away!—and yet I suffer at the thought of leaving him. I suffer most from his impatience, his restlessness. I begin to feel it now, even when we are in the salon, quite apart from each other. . . .

It all came to me so suddenly! I noticed for the first time how he began to change his regular ways of life, but I didn't know what it meant. Of course I was flattered at his sympathy, and at being distinguished among the many who surround him, eager for a word. . . .

An early snowstorm came, and the guests at Gossensass began to leave. Emilie realized they would soon have to part.

And I have nothing to give him, not even my picture, when he is giving me so much. But we both feel it is best outwardly to remain as strangers. . . . His wife shows me much attention. Yesterday I had a long talk with his son. . . .

I am reading *Love's Comedy,* but if anyone comes I am seen holding Beaconsfield's *Endymion* in my hands. Nearly everyone has gone. The days we have still to spend can now be counted. I don't think about the future. The present is too much. We had a long talk together in the morning, and after lunch he came again and sat with me. What am I to think? He says it is to be my life's aim to work with him. We are to write to each other; but what am I to write?

Ibsen (according to King) confided his feelings to two ladies. One fainted; another described the scene to Emilie as "beautiful and terrible as a thunderstorm. She wonders that I do not lose my head. She says that she herself would have been absolutely overcome. This consoles me. I do not seem so weak."

Did something happen between Ibsen and Emilie on 19 September, and if so was it anything like what Hilde Wangel in *The Master Builder* describes as having happened on another 19 September?

HILDE. . . . Was it just a little detail that I happened to be alone in the room when you came in?

SOLNESS. Were you?

HILDE. You didn't call me a little devil then.

SOLNESS. No, I don't suppose I did.

HILDE. You said I looked beautiful in my white dress. Like a little princess.

SOLNESS. So you did, Miss Wangel. And besides—I felt so happy and free that evening—

HILDE. And then you said that when I grew up, I would be your princess.

SOLNESS (*with a short laugh*). Well, well! Did I say that, too? . . .

HILDE. It sounded as though you were making fun of me.

SOLNESS. I'm sure I didn't mean that.

HILDE. I can well believe you didn't. Considering what you did next—

SOLNESS. And what on earth did I do next? . . .

HILDE. You took me in your arms and kissed me, Mr. Solness.

SOLNESS (*gets up from his chair, his mouth open*). I did?

HILDE. Yes, you did. You took me in both your arms and bent me backwards and kissed me. Many, many times.

SOLNESS. Oh, but my dear, good Miss Wangel—

HILDE (*gets up*). You're not going to deny it?

SOLNESS. I certainly am! . . . All this that you've told me must have been something you've dreamed. . . . No, there's more to it than that . . . I must have thought all this. I must have wanted it—wished it—desired it. So that— Couldn't that be an explanation? . . .

HILDE. Perhaps you've also forgotten what day it was? . . .

SOLNESS. Hm—I've forgotten the actual day, I must confess . . .

HILDE. It was . . . the nineteenth of September.

Nearly forty years later, in 1927, Emilie told A E. Zucker that Ibsen had never kissed her;[4] perhaps with Ibsen, as with Solness, these things only happened in his mind. Next day, 20 September, he wrote in Emilie's album a line from *Faust*: "*Hohes, schmerzliches Glück—um das Unerreichbare zu ringen!* [Oh, high and painful joy—to struggle for the unattainable!]."

The following day, 21 September, another young girl, a German painter named Helene Raff, who was staying at Gossensass and had met Ibsen for the first time four days earlier, wrote in her diary: "The B[ardach] completely crazy about Ibsen"; and the day after, she noted: "Miss B. broken-hearted."[5]

[4] Zucker, p. 242.

[5] Extracts from Helene's diaries are given in C.E., XIX, 173–81, and in the *Oxford Ibsen*, VII, 562 ff.

On 27 September Emilie wrote in her diary:

Our last day at Gossensass. Then nothing but memory will remain. Two weeks ago, memory seemed to Ibsen so beautiful, and now— He says that tomorrow he will stand on the ruins of his happiness. These last two months are more important in his life than anything that has gone before. Am I unnatural in being so terribly quiet and normal? . . . Last evening, when Mamma went to talk to his wife, he came over and sat at our table. We were quite alone. He talked about his plans. I alone am in them—I, and I again. I feel quieter because he is quieter, though yesterday he was terrible.

That night, at 3 A.M., the express from Verona to Vienna passed through Gossensass, and Emilie left on it. A few hours earlier she had confided to her diary:

He means to possess me. That is his absolute will. He intends to overcome all obstacles. I do what I can to keep him from feeling this, and yet I listen as he describes what is to lie before us—going from one country to another—I with him—enjoying his triumphs together. . . . Our parting was easier than I had feared.

Emilie told Zucker in 1927 that Ibsen had, in Gossensass, "spoken to her of the possibility of a divorce and of a subsequent union with her, in the course of which they were to travel widely and see the world."[6] Once back in Munich, however, Ibsen seemed to resign himself to the impossibility of going through with such a plan. Perhaps he feared the scandal; perhaps he felt a duty towards his sickly and aging wife, who had stood so firmly behind him during the long years of failure; perhaps he reflected that the difference of forty-three years between their ages was too great; perhaps, away from Gossensass, he felt old. At any rate, his letters from Munich to Emilie in Vienna are no more than those of an affectionate old man to a charming schoolgirl (though we must bear in mind that he was writing in a foreign language that "gives him . . . much difficulty," that he was always an extremely inhibited letter-writer, and that he must have been very careful not to commit himself on paper):

Munich, Maximilianstrasse 32
7 October 1889

With my whole heart I thank you, my beloved Fräulein, for the dear and delightful letter which I received on the last day of my stay at Gossensass, and have read over and over again.

There the last autumn week was a very sad one, or it was so to me. No more sunshine. Everything—gone. The few remaining guests could give me no compensation for the brief and beautiful end-of-summer life. I went to walk in the Pflerschtal. There there is a bench where two can commune together. But the bench was empty and I

[6] Zucker, p. 292.

went by without sitting down. So, too, the big salon was waste and
desolate . . . Do you remember the big, deep bay-window on the
right from the verandah? What a charming niche! The flowers and
plants are still there, smelling so sweetly—but how empty!—how
lonely!—how forsaken!

We are back here at home—and you in Vienna. You write that you
feel surer of yourself, more independent, happier. How glad I am of
these words! I shall say no more.

A new poem begins to dawn in me. I want to work on it this
winter, transmuting into it the glowing inspiration of the summer.
But the end may be disappointment. I feel it. It is my way. I told
you once that I only corresponded by telegraph. So take this letter
as it is. You will know what it means. A thousand greetings from

Your devoted
H.I.

The "poem" (the Norwegian word *digt* means, like the Greek *poema*,
not merely something in verse but a "thing of creation") may have been
Hedda Gabler, which he was to write the following year, or it may have
been *The Master Builder*, which he did not write until three years later
but may have conceived at this stage and then deliberately put aside
until he could consider it with more detachment.[7] On receiving this
letter, Emilie, the following day, noted in her diary:

> A few words before I go to bed. I have good news. Today, at last, came
> Ibsen's long-expected letter. He wants me to read between the lines. But
> do not the lines themselves say enough? This evening I paid Grandmama
> a quite unpleasant visit. The weather is hot and stuffy and so is Papa's mood.
> In other days, this would have depressed me; but now I have something to
> keep me up.

We do not know how she replied to Ibsen, for he did not preserve
her letter. On 15 October, however, he writes again:

> I receive your letter with a thousand thanks—and have read it,
> and read it again. Here I sit as usual at my desk, and would gladly
> work, but cannot do so.
>
> My imagination is ragingly at work, but is always straying to
> where in working hours it should not. I cannot keep down the
> memories of the summer, neither do I want to. The things we have
> lived through I live again and again—and still again. To make of them
> a poem is for the time being impossible.
>
> For the time being?

[7] Or it may, as Else Høst argues in *Hedda Gabler, en monografi* (Oslo, 1958),
have been a play which never got written.

Shall I ever succeed in the future? And do I really wish that I could and would so succeed?

For the moment, at any rate, I cannot—or so I believe. That I feel—that I know.

And yet it must come. Decidedly it must come. But will it? Or can it?

Ah, dear Fräulein—but forgive me!—you wrote so charmingly in your last—no, no! God forbid! in your *previous* letter you wrote so charmingly "I am not Fräulein for you."—So, dear child—for that you surely are for me—tell me—do you remember that once we talked about Stupidity and Madness—or, more correctly, *I* talked about it—and you took up the role of teacher, and remarked, in your soft, musical voice, and with your far-away look, that there is always a difference between Stupidity and Madness. . . . Well, then, I keep thinking over and over again: Was it a Stupidity or was it Madness that we should have come together? Or was it both Stupidity *and* Madness? Or was it neither?

I believe the last is the only supposition that would stand the test. It was a simple necessity of nature. It was equally our fate . . .

Your always devoted
H.I.

Of this letter, Emilie wrote in her diary:

I left it unopened until I had finished everything, and could read it quietly. But I was not quiet after reading it. Why does he not tell me of something to read which would feed my mind instead of writing in a way to inflame my already excited imagination? I shall answer very soberly.

Before he wrote to her again, he had started up a close acquaintance (it was never to be anything more with any of the young girls who henceforth successively seized and filled his imagination) with his other youthful admirer from Gossensass, Helene Raff. Determined to meet him again when he had no Emilie to dazzle him, Helene spent several days walking up and down Maximilianstrasse until at last, on 19 October, she was successful. The next morning she ran into him again at an art exhibition; and later that day, they saw each other again. Five days later, having meanwhile primed herself by reading Otto Brahm's pamphlet on him, she waylaid Ibsen in Maximilianstrasse, accompanied him to his apartment and spent an hour with him, which she found "very interesting, but rather upsetting." He spoke about hypnosis and the power of the will. "He underlined that women's will in particular tends to remain undeveloped; we dream and wait for something unknown that will give our lives meaning. As a result of this women's emotional lives are unhealthy, and they fall victims to disappointment." The words precisely enshrine the theme of the play he was about to write, *Hedda Gabler*. When Helene left he saw her down to the courtyard, and there they kissed.

They do not seem to have met for a fortnight after this, and in the meantime, on 29 October, four days after that meeting with Helene, he wrote again to Emilie:

I have been meaning every day to write you a few words, but I wanted to enclose the photograph. This is still not ready, and my letter must go off without it . . .

How charmingly you write! Please keep sending me a few lines, whenever you have a half hour not good for anything else.

So you leave my letters unopened till you are alone and quite undisturbed! Dear child! I shall not try to thank you. That would be superfluous. You know what I mean.

Don't be uneasy because just now I cannot work. In the back of my mind I am working all the time. I am dreaming over something which, when it has ripened, will become a poem.

Someone is coming. Can write no further. Next time a longer letter.

Your truly devoted
H.I.

Emilie's diary:

I wrote to him on Monday, very late at night. Though I was tired, I did not want to put off doing so, because I had to thank him for the books I received on Sunday. The same evening I had read *Rosmersholm*, parts of which are very fine. I have had to make so many duty calls, but this and a great many other things I can stand better than I used to. They are only the outward things, my inner world is something very different. Oh, the terror and beauty of having him care about me as he never cared about anyone else! But when he is suffering he calls it *hohes, schmerzliches Glück*—high and painful joy!

Helene noted in her diary for 7 November: "Painted in afternoon, then went in vain to Maximilianstr." But the next day she was luckier, and was "touched by his pleasure at my coming." The day after that: "Visited Frau Ibsen, he also present. Extraordinary situation!" Suzannah told her how at the time of their marriage Ibsen "had an easel and wanted to paint; but I did not like that; I thought a dramatist should not divide himself." Three days later: "Met Ibsen in evening, he wants to visit me—I was much relieved. He accompanied me home; tender parting." It pleased him when she told him she had been educated at home, not at school or in church (her father was a composer).[8] "Well, then," he declared, "you

[8] Joachim Raff, well known in his time. Among other things he was the author of a popular tarantella.

are a little heathen!"; then, becoming serious, he said: "That is the education of the future, without state, school or church," and suddenly seized her hands as though in triumph and cried: "Yes, yes, child, the future is ours!" And then: "Only when one is free of the mass of inherited opinions which school and church hand down can one become outwardly and inwardly strong like you, who are like a child of the forest."

Six days later, on 18 November, he visited her in her studio, bringing a copy of Jæger's biography with him. Helene asked him why he liked her and what he saw in her.

> He replied: "You are youth, child, youth personified—and I need that—for my work, my writing." I was troubled that he used certain phrases which reminded me of what Fräulein Bardach had told me. I asked him not to speak to me as he had to her, to which he naïvely answered: "Oh, that was in the country. In town one is more in earnest."

Helene was clearly displacing Emilie as the object of his affections, for two reasons: she was in Munich while Emilie was in Vienna and (it is a fair assumption) she was less emotionally demanding. He had (in Solness's phrase) offered Emilie a kingdom, and she (like Hilde) did not regard the offer as a joke. Helene, much cooler and harder-headed, seems to have wanted no more from Ibsen than he was giving her, admiration and flattering companionship. The day after this last meeting with Helene he wrote to Emilie in a noticeably cooler (though still affectionate) mood:

> At last I can send you the new picture. I hope you may find it a better likeness than the one you have already. A German sketch of my life will appear within a few days, and you will receive it at once. Read it when you have time. It will tell you my story to the end of last year.
>
> Heartfelt thanks for your dear letter; but what do you think of me for not having answered it earlier? And yet—you know it well—you are always in my thoughts, and will remain there. An active exchange of letters is on my side an impossibility. I have already said so. Take me as I am.
>
> I am greatly preoccupied with the preparations for my new play. Sit tight at my desk the whole day. Go out only towards evening. I dream and remember and write. To dream is fine; but the reality at times can still be finer.
>
> Your most devoted
> H.I.

On the back of the photograph Ibsen had inscribed: *An die Maisonne eines Septemberlebens*—"To the May sun of a September life."

On 28 November Ibsen and Suzannah both visited Helene at her studio; the next day she went to them, and that same evening he wrote her a letter:

Dear Child!

How beautiful, how lovable of you to visit us yesterday. My wife is so deeply fond of you. And I—too. As you sat there in the dusk and spoke to us so sensibly, so understandingly, do you know what I thought and wished? No, you cannot. I wished: Ah, if only I had such a sweet and lovely daughter.

Come and visit us again very soon. But in the meantime keep working hard in your studio. You must not let yourself be distracted.

Blessings on your dear head.

Your devoted

H.I.

Helene was baffled at the way Ibsen was drawing Suzannah into their relationship. When, one evening a couple of weeks later, she hovered on Maximilianstrasse in the hope of seeing him, and was successful, "he towed me off to his wife; I was confused and vexed." Helene did not yet comprehend, any more than Emilie ever would, that, as she phrased it nearly forty years later: "Ibsen's relations with young girls had in them nothing whatever of infidelity in the usual sense of the term, but arose solely from the needs of his imagination; as he himself said, he sought out youth because he needed it for his poetic production."[9]

Some fanciful theories have been advanced to explain Ibsen's unwillingness to attempt to develop any of his infatuations into a full sexual relationship, when his plays show him to have been (to borrow Emilie's metaphor) a volcanically passionate man. But there are many passionate men who are terrified by the reality of sex, even to the point of impotence when offered it, and Dr. Edvard Bull's evidence about Ibsen's unwillingness to expose his sexual organ even during medical examination suggests that this may well have been Ibsen's tragedy. Neither Solness, Borkman nor Rubek, the three most obvious self-portraits among Ibsen's characters, suffered from this inhibition (or did Rubek? He never touched Irene, and his wife was unsatisfied). But John Rosmer and Alfred Allmers (in *Little Eyolf*) were both sexually shy; and so was the chief character of the play which he was now planning, "tight at my desk," and which he might well have sub-titled: *Portrait of the Dramatist as a Young Woman*. "The great tragedy of life," he wrote in his notes for *Hedda Gabler*, "is that so many people have nothing to do but yearn for happiness without ever being able to find it"; and "It is a great delusion that one only loves one person."

[9] Letter from Helene Raff to A. E. Zucker, 8 December 1927, quoted by Zucker, p. 242.

A psychiatrist's view of Ibsen may be noted here. On reading the first section of this biography a distinguished member of that profession, and a distinguished author in his field, Dr. Anthony Storr, wrote to me:

Ibsen appears to have been what psychiatrists call an obsessional character. This type of person is generally meticulous about cleanliness, disturbed by disorder, punctilious, punctual and polite. He is often tied to routine—for example, may feel compelled to take his clothes off and put them on in a particular order. If he becomes neurotic, he may be plagued by irrational thoughts which he cannot banish; parsons fear that swear-words will interrupt their sermons, etc. Ritual cleanliness—compulsive hand-washing, for example—attains a symbolic significance. This kind of character is built upon a fear of letting instincts or emotional forces loose. Emotions must be controlled, for spontaneity is dangerous. Such people find it difficult to "let go" physically or emotionally. They are often constipated and may also have difficulty in reaching orgasm. As a colleague, Dr. Charles Rycroft, has put it in his book *Anxiety and Neurosis;* "the obsessional defence leads to antagonism to emotion as such and feelings come to be regarded as intruders which disturb the orderliness of the world of which the obsessional has made himself master." Creative people of this temperament may be led into creativity because they (a) want to create an imaginary world in which everything can be controlled, and (b) want to avoid the unpredictability and spontaneity of real relationships with real people.

A week after leaving Helene "confused and vexed," on 6 December, Ibsen wrote in a warmer manner than of late to Emilie:

Two dear, dear letters have I had from you, and answered neither till now. What do you think of me? But I cannot find the quiet necessary to writing you anything orderly or straightforward. This evening I must go to the theatre to see *An Enemy of the People.* The mere thought of it is torture. Then, too, I must give up for the time being the hope of getting your photograph. But better so than to have an unfavourable picture. Besides, how vividly your dear, serene features remain with me in my memory! The same enigmatic princess stands behind them. But the enigma itself? One can dream of it, and write about it—and that I do. It is some little compensation for the unattainable—for the unfathomable reality.

In my imagination I always see you wearing the pearls you love so much. In this taste for pearls I see something deeper, something hidden. I often think of it. Sometimes I think I have found the interpretation—and then again not. Next time I shall try to answer some of your questions, but I myself have so many questions to ask you. I am always doing it—inwardly—inaudibly.

Your devoted

H.I.

In her diary, Emilie repeated his words: "It is some little compensation for the unattainable—for the unfathomable reality." She wrote to him and he replied, again warmly and affectionately, on 22 December:

How shall I thank you for your dear and delightful letter? I simply am not able to, at least not as I should like. The writing of letters is always hard for me. I think I have told you so already, and you will in any case have noticed it for yourself.

I read your letter over and over, for through it the voice of the summer awakens so clearly. I see—I experience again—the things we lived together. As a lovely creature of the summer, dear Princess, I have known you, as a being of the season of butterflies and wild flowers. How I should like to see you as you are in winter! I am always with you in spirit. I see you in the Ring Strasse, light, quick, poised like a bird, gracious in velvet and furs. In *soirées,* in society, I also see you, and especially at the theatre, leaning back, a tired look in your mysterious eyes. I should like, too, to see you at home, but here I don't succeed, as I haven't the data. You have told me so little of your home-life—hardly anything definite. As a matter of fact, dear Princess, in many important details we are strangers to each other. . .

More than anything I should like to see you on Christmas night at home, where I suppose you will be. As to what happens to you there, I have no clear idea. I only imagine—to myself.

And then I have a strange feeling that you and Christmas don't go well together. But who knows? Perhaps you do. In any case accept my heartfelt wishes and a thousand greetings.

Your ever devoted
H.I.

That same day, 22 December 1889, Emilie wrote to him from Vienna enclosing at last her photograph. It is one of the only two letters from her which have survived:

Sunday
Here is the photograph—very unlike the original—to wish you a happy Christmas. Are you satisfied with it? Do you think it a good one? I don't think any better picture of me can be expected, but I hope it may give you some small pleasure. Now I must confess that I have had this proof for a fortnight—I kept it back so long in order to send it to you as a Christmas greeting. It was hard to keep it a secret from you for so long, but I wanted to have some little thing to contribute to the lovely holiday. Should I play no role at all in that? It's bad enough that I am not able to do more. In spite of my *"Nicht Rönnaug"* a few weeks ago I painted a trifle for you which would have been altogether pointless if it did not recall Gossensass. I

used to buy little deer bells there, and since I so often met you on my way home from my study trip to the Strassberg ruins I perpetuated the picture on one of these bells. Then I waited for your son to come here as I would have liked to give it to him to take to you—but he didn't come and it seemed too small a thing to make a business of sending it. I will be silent for a while, then I will be able to tell you better about that. How much longer are you going to make me wait? This detailed letter which is to tell me so much—but no—don't think this is a reproach—I don't mean it like that. I will send a Christmas greeting to your wife—I must write a few words just to her.

> Well, once more many tender wishes and regards.
> Sincerely
> Emilie

On Christmas Day Helene paid an afternoon visit to the Ibsens but saw only Suzannah and Sigurd—"she very kind, the son very dull." Four days later she went again to Maximilianstrasse in the hope of seeing him, but "in vain." On New Year's Eve: "With Aunt again to Maximilianstr., where we met Ibsen. . . . He promises I may paint him. To bed contented." The previous day he had written to Emilie:

Your lovely and charming picture, so eloquently like you, has given me a wholly indescribable joy. I thank you for it a thousand times, and straight from the heart. How you have brought back, now in midwinter, those brief, sunny summer days!

So, too, I thank you from the heart for your dear, dear letter. From me you must expect no more than a few words. I lack the time, and the necessary quiet and solitude, to write to you as I should like. . . .

Shortly before Christmas Ibsen fell a victim to the influenza epidemic which swept Europe that winter (this, perhaps, was why Helene did not see him on her Christmas visit to Maximilianstrasse). It was the first time he had been ill for twenty-eight years; but with his iron constitution he threw it off. Emilie, in Vienna, caught it too. "How sorry I am," Ibsen wrote to her on 16 January, "to learn that you, too, have been ill. But what do you think? I had a strong presentiment that it was so. In my imagination I saw you lying in bed, pale, feverish, but sweet and lovely as ever. . . . How thankful I am that I have your charming picture!"

But he had made the decision to break off their correspondence. Her next letter to him has not survived; but on 6 February he wrote to her:

Long, very long, have I left your last, dear letter—read and read again—without an answer. Take today my heartfelt thanks for it, though given in very few words. Henceforth, till we see each other face to face, you will hear little from me, and very seldom. Believe me, it is better so. It is the only right thing. It is a matter of conscience with me to end our correspondence, or at least to limit it. You yourself should have as little to do with me as possible. With your young life you have other aims to follow, other tasks to fulfil. And I—I have told you so already—can never be content with a mere exchange of letters. For me it is only half the thing; it is a false situation. Not to give myself wholly and unreservedly makes me unhappy. It is my nature. I cannot change it. You are so delicately subtle, so instinctively penetrating, that you will easily see what I mean. When we are together again, I shall be able to explain it more fully. Till then, and always, you will be in my thoughts. You will be so even more when we no longer have to stop at this wearisome halfway house of correspondence.

A thousand greetings.

Your
H.I.

"Till we see each other face to face"—"When we are together again" —such words must have excited Emilie's most passionate hopes. And yet he wished to break off their correspondence. She replied to his letter of 6 February the following day:

Please forgive me for writing again so soon. All these days I have been intending to write to you, for it is part of my nature to feel anxious about persons to whom I am deeply attached if I do not hear from them for a longish while. Possibly this is a petty characteristic, but it is impossible to control one's feelings. Nevertheless, I mean to control mine, and since I know how sensitive you are in this respect I came halfway to meet you. Yes, I knew very well that you are an unwilling letter-writer, and from time to time I even felt that you might find my letters a nuisance. All the same, your last letter has shaken me badly, and I have needed all my self-control to conceal my feelings. But I don't want this to prevent you from carrying out your intentions. I certainly do not wish you to write to me frequently, and since you wish it I shall also refrain. However, I cannot allow myself to prescribe the problems and the moods to which, as you say, I should surrender myself in my young life. What I have so often told you remains unaltered and I can never forget it. Unfortunately the fact remains that I cannot surrender myself completely, nor taste unalloyed enjoyment. Forgive me for drawing you into a conflict with fate. That is ungrateful of me, seeing that you have so often said to me that whatever happens we shall remain good friends, and that I must hold fast to that. And is it friendship not to know if the other is ill or well, happy or wretched? And then can I prevent the thought coming to me that *you* want to avoid seeing me again, and anyhow, if you do not write, how am I to know where we can find each other again? Well, I'll be very, very patient; I can wait, but I shall suffer very much if I don't get a line or a book from you from time to time, or some other proof that you think of me. I am not noble enough to dispense with such little proofs of your interest.

Ought I to be ashamed of my frankness? Will you think less of me for not wishing to give up what has made me so happy and more contented through all these months? I know you a little and that is why I understand so much that is in you, but I am sure that *your conscience* should never hinder you from continuing to write to me. By so doing you only show your kindness. I will try to understand all other reasons that may prevent you from writing and certainly I don't want you to act against your feelings. What a multitude of things there are to write about, but you do not wish me to write, even though I should not expect an answer.

Tonight I have an invitation to a ball—with friends; I never go out in public. When I am there I shall allow myself to think a little about you because I often find parties like these extremely uninspiring, unless I have something of my own to fall back on. Anyhow, I mean to go, if I can.

> With love,
> Emilie

Emilie made no entries in her diary for four days after receiving the news that Ibsen wished to break off their correspondence. Then she writes of balls, singing lessons, domestic duties. Then suddenly: "What is my inner life after Ibsen's letter? I wrote at once and henceforth will be silent, silent." Ten days later: "Will he never write any more? I cannot think about it. Who could? And yet, not to do so is in his nature. In his very kindness there is often cruelty."

On 30 December he wrote, again briefly, to thank her for a Christmas present:

I have duly received your dear letter, as well as the bell with the beautiful picture. I thank you for them, straight from the heart. My wife finds the picture very pretty. But I beg you, for the time being, not to write to me again. When conditions have changed, I will let you know. I shall soon send you my new play. Accept it in friendship—but in silence. How I should love to see you and talk with you again! A Happy New Year to you and to Madame your mother.

> Your always devoted
> H.I.

She did not write to him again, nor did the meeting to which they had both looked forward so eagerly ever take place. For seven years there was no contact between them. Then, for his seventieth birthday, she sent him a telegram of congratulation. His letter of reply was the last message that passed between them:

Christiania, 13 March 1898

Herzlich liebes Fräulein!

Accept my most deeply felt thanks for your message. The summer in Gossensass was the happiest, the most beautiful in my whole life.

I scarcely dare to think of it—and yet I must think of it always. Always!

Your truly devoted
H.I.

Only once, as far as is known, did Ibsen ever comment on his relationship with Emilie. The German literary historian Julius Elias (later to become one of Ibsen's executors) writes that in February 1891, less than two months after Ibsen had made the final break with Emilie, he and Ibsen were lunching together in Berlin:

> An expansive mood came over Ibsen and, chuckling over his champagne glass, he said: "Do you know, my next play [*The Master Builder*] is already hovering before me—in general outline, of course. One thing I can see clearly, though—an experience I once had myself—a female character. Very interesting—very interesting." Then he related how he had met in the Tyrol (where she was staying with her mother) a Viennese girl of very remarkable character, who had at once made him her confidant. The gist of it was that she was not interested in the idea of marrying some decently brought-up young man; most likely she would never marry. What tempted, fascinated and delighted her was to lure other women's husbands away from them. She was a demonic little wrecker; she often seemed to him like a little bird of prey, who would gladly have included him among her victims. He had studied her very, very closely. But she had had no great success with him. "She did not get hold of me, but I got hold of her—for my play. Then I fancy she consoled herself with someone else."[10]

This account by Ibsen of his relationship with Emilie is impossible to reconcile, either with Emilie's diary extracts and letters to him, or with his letters to her. It reveals him at his most cowardly; and it came especially ill from one who preached the importance of responsibility. The girl he described to Elias was not Emilie Bardach but the Hilde Wangel he was about to create in *The Master Builder*. But from the time Elias published this account (just after Georg Brandes had published Ibsen's letters to Emilie) people identified the unfortunate Emilie with Hilde, just as they had identified Bjørnson with Stensgaard and Laura Kieler with Nora.

The change which Ibsen's relationship with Emilie wrought on him was immediate and drastic. For years he had deliberately suppressed his

[10] Julius Elias, "Christiania-fahrt: Erinnerungen," in *Neue Deutsche Rundschau,* XVII (1906), 1462.

own emotional life; but his encounter with Emilie had awoken him to the realization that, as Mr. Graham Greene has somewhere remarked, fame is a powerful aphrodisiac. "All the women are in love with him," Anne-Charlotte Leffler had written during his visit to Stockholm in 1887; but it had happened too late for him to gain any joy from it. Throughout his plays he had preached that whatever a man turns his back on gets him in the end; and now the chickens were to come home to roost with a vengeance. In 1887 he had startled his audience in Stockholm by describing himself as an "optimist," and *The Lady from the Sea,* written the following year, had reflected this optimism. "It is in some respects," Edmund Gosse had written on its appearance, "the reverse of *Rosmersholm,* the bitterness of restrained and balked individuality, which ends in death, being contrasted with the sweetness of emancipated and gratified individuality, which leads to health and peace."[11]

But none of his five subsequent plays could by any stretch of the imagination be described as comedies. The mood of *Hedda Gabler, The Master Builder, Little Eyolf, John Gabriel Borkman* and *When We Dead Awaken* is, like that of *Rosmersholm,* "restrained and balked individuality," and I do not think there can be much doubt that this stems from the realization that for various reasons (fear of scandal, sense of duty towards Suzannah, consciousness of old age, perhaps the consciousness or fear of physical impotence), he, who had suppressed his longings for so long, now had the opportunities to fulfil them but was unable to do so. As a result of his meeting with Emilie Bardach a new glory, but also a new darkness, entered into his work.

[11] Edmund Gosse, "Ibsen's Social Dramas," in the *Fortnightly Review,* 1 January 1889, p. 121.

27

Portrait of the Dramatist as a Young Woman

1889–1890

Ibsen's name had come before the readers and audiences of various countries a considerable amount that autumn. In September, August Lindberg, visiting Christiania with his company, gave a special performance of *Ghosts* for members of the city Workers' Association; the play had still not been performed in the capital in Norwegian. On the twenty-ninth of the month Otto Brahm and Paul Schlenther opened their Freie Bühne in Berlin (a private theatre modelled on Antoine's Théâtre Libre in Paris and likewise limited to members in order to escape the shackles of censorship) with a production of *Ghosts*. The cast included a promising young actress named Agnes Sorma as Regina. The Freie Bühne was to last only three seasons, but its effect on the German theatre was incalculable. On 25 October we find Ibsen writing to Moritz Prozor thanking him for his efforts in France, and on 3 November he addressed a similar letter to William Archer, thanking him especially for the "handsome edition" (limited to 115 copies) of *A Doll's House* which Fisher Unwin had brought out, bound in vellum and illustrated with photographs of the Charrington-Achurch production. "I have the book always on my table and it excites the lively admiration of everyone who sees it and who knows anything of the art of typography. I cannot deny that I am somewhat proud that a work of mine should have appeared in great England in such a dress."

The previous day, 2 November, the *Academy* magazine had reported: "Ibsen's vogue seems to be spreading through all parts of the world. A Dutch translation of *The Wild Duck,* one of the least known[!] of Ibsen's plays, has been acted this week in Amsterdam and in the Hague. A Russian version of *The Pillars of Society* is appearing on the stage of one of the St. Petersburg theatres. *A Doll's House, Ghosts* and *The Young Men's League* are all being played in different cities of Germany. An

English version of *The Lady from the Sea* will be published next week by Mr. Fisher Unwin [translated by Eleanor Marx-Aveling with an introduction by Gosse], and we hear of more than one translation of *Rosmersholm* as ready to appear. Finally, there is a rumour of a complete edition of Ibsen's works, to be published first in New York, under the joint supervision of Mr. Archer and Mr Gosse."[1]

A few days earlier there had occurred the first respectable production (in English, at any rate) of Ibsen in the United States. On 30 October, Beatrice Cameron presented *A Doll's House* in Boston, playing Nora herself, and toured it with fair success through several other large cities. But Ibsen's progress in the New World was slow, and it was not until the middle nineties that he was to gain any kind of foothold in the American theatre (and then thanks principally to visiting actors from Europe such as the Charringtons, Gabrielle Réjane and Herbert Beerbohm Tree).

On 7 November *Love's Comedy* received its Swedish premiere, at Gothenburg under August Lindberg's direction, with Lindberg himself as Guldstad and a new star, Julia Håkonsson, as Svanhild. The performance was a splendid success; the audience, Lindberg records, sat "pale with astonishment" as the play, hitherto regarded as a literary pleasantry, turned out to be full of dramatic life.[2] *Göteborgs Handels och Sjöfarts-Tidning* described it as the production of the season; and, as when Lindberg had taken the initiative in staging *Ghosts*, the Royal Theatre in Stockholm, which had twice rejected him as an actor, was quick to seize on the play's success and arrange its own production. Lindberg followed up the success of *Love's Comedy* by reviving *A Doll's House* in Gothenburg, where it went as well as ever.

Sigurd, after his promising start in the diplomatic service, had run into difficulties; he was still prevented from advancing further by the fact of his not having taken the Norwegian law examinations, and his proud assertion of his Norwegianness was a constant source of irritation to his Swedish superiors. Although his Swedish was as good as his Norwegian,

---

[1] This last statement was not quite correct. There were two projects under way. Archer had been negotiating with the London publisher Walter Scott, who, encouraged by the success of the Havelock Ellis volume, agreed to bring out a collection of eleven Ibsen plays in four volumes (later expanded to thirteen plays in five volumes). Archer wrote to Ibsen on 1 November asking his permission, and Ibsen replied on 3 November accepting gratefully—"and I am particularly obliged to you for the terms offered in regard to the author's fee." These terms do not seem to have been very generous, for only very small sums appear in Ibsen's account books and, as stated, the first volume alone sold 14,000 copies in five years. Archer did his work so energetically that the first four volumes appeared within a year, in November 1890. Gosse had meanwhile arranged with the New York house of John W. Lovell to edit a three-volume edition of the plays, which appeared in 1890–91. The only translations common to the series were Archer's versions of *The Pillars of Society, A Doll's House, Ghosts* and *Hedda Gabler*.

[2] Per Lindberg, p. 270.

he wrote his reports from Vienna, which the ambassador had to sign, in Norwegian, and thus they appeared on the Foreign Minister's desk in Stockholm. He caused further vexation by stating that he did not wish to serve in the Swedish Foreign Office; and when it was made clear to him that unless he agreed to do so he would not receive promotion he announced that in such a case he would resign.

On 11 December Ibsen wrote to Emil Stang, who had succeeded Sverdrup as prime minister, asking him to intercede on Sigurd's behalf and reminding him that twenty-five years earlier he (Stang) had acted as intermediary in obtaining for Ibsen the travel stipened which had enabled him to go to Rome. But neither Sigurd nor the Swedes would yield, and that month he implemented his threat, to the considerable annoyance of his by now (in Norwegian eyes) embarrassingly pro-Swedish father. Sigurd's future wife Bergliot notes that this was probably the first time Ibsen and Sigurd had disagreed as adults.[3]

Sigurd returned to Christiania and wrote a series of articles in *Dagbladet* attacking the conditions under which Norwegians serving in the diplomatic service were forced to work, and indicting his fellow-countrymen for their willingness to truckle to the senior partner in the union. Henceforth, he was to be as lone a wolf in the sphere of politics as his father was in the theatre.

Thanks mainly to the productions (albeit unsuccessful) in Christiania, Stockholm and Copenhagen of *The Lady from the Sea,* the reprints of *The Pretenders* and *Brand,* and a number of small German payments, 1889 had been a rather better year financially:

	crowns
Royalties for *The Wild Duck* and *Rosmersholm* at Residenztheater, Berlin, and Thalia Theatre, Hamburg	411
Royalties for *The Pillars of Society* at Cologne Stadttheater	51
Royalties for *The Pillars of Society* at Munich Residenztheater (from 1888)	492
Fee for *The Lady from the Sea* at Christiania Theatre	2,500
Fee for *The Vikings at Helgeland* at Darmstadt (2 perfs.)	116
7th edn. of *The Pretenders*	1,125
Royalties for *The Wild Duck* in Breslau (7 perfs.) and Berlin (1 perf.), and *Rosmersholm* in Hanau (2 perfs.)	117
Royalties for *The Pillars of Society* in Mannheim (4 perfs.)	169
Royalties for *The Pillars of Society* in Munich (1 perf.)	61
Royalties for *The Lady from the Sea* in Kassel, Halle, and Berlin	702
Fee for *Rosmersholm* in Christiania	405
Fees from Royal Theatre, Stockholm, for *The Lady from the Sea* (5 perfs.), *A Doll's House* (5 perfs.) and *The Wild Duck* (3 perfs.)	1,244

[3] Bergliot Ibsen, p. 118.

	crowns	
11th edn. of *Brand*	1,360	
Fees from Bergen for *A Doll's House, The Wild Duck, The*		
Feast at Solhaug and *The League of Youth*	640	
Extra fee for 7th edn. of *The Pretenders*	75	
Fee from Royal Theatre, Copenhagen, for *The Lady from*		
the Sea (1st–11th perfs.)	1,962	
Misc. German royalties	893	
50% of French book sales from Count Prozor	104	
Royalties for *The Pillars of Society, A Doll's House* and		
An Enemy of the People at Munich Hoftheater	607	
Fee for *The Lady from the Sea* at Svenska Teater,		
Helsinki	300	
	13,334	£739

Ibsen had told Emilie, in his letter of 19 November, that he was "greatly preoccupied with the preparations for my new play. Sit tight at my desk the whole day"; but it is unsure whether he was yet working on *Hedda Gabler*. Some notes which would appear to date from that October or November seem to refer to an idea he later abandoned; of two women friends who make a suicide pact, which only one of them carries out. There is a mass of notes and jottings dating (presumably) from this autumn, winter, and spring, some in a notebook,[4] others on odd sheets of paper, a jotting pad and even a visiting card; even the notebook entries may not necessarily have been written in chronological order, and we cannot be sure that he decided definitely on the theme of *Hedda Gabler* before the spring.

Meanwhile, having severed his connection with Emilie, he was seeing even more of Helene, who made avid notes of their conversations. He told her that he needed very little sleep ("four hours is enough for me") and defended his reticence. He warned her: "You must never tell everything to people. . . . To keep things to oneself is the most valuable thing in life. . . . I don't write letters willingly or well, mostly in a shorthand style. I can only speak freely through the mouths of characters in a play." And even plays "are always better while still unwritten than when they have become reality. So one prefers the unwritten to the finished work."

On another occasion he said: "My plays make people uncomfortable because when they see them they have to think, and most people want to be effortlessly entertained, not to be told unpleasant truths. . . . People who are afraid of being alone with themelves, thinking about themselves, go to the theatre as they go to the beach or to parties—they go to be amused. But I find that people's eyes can be opened as well from the stage as from a pulpit. Especially as so many people no longer go to

[4] C.E., XI, 397 ff.; *Oxford Ibsen*, VII, 474 ff.

church." He complained how badly his plays were usually acted, especially by "actresses who declaim instead of speaking," but confessed that he did not interfere at rehearsals. On the subject of fame he said: "I haven't written to become famous. But of course fame has served me in so far as it has created interest in my ideas and my writing."

He inveighed vehemently against indolence, as people who need little sleep often do. Once, he told Helene, on a train journey from Rome to Gossensass, he had shared a compartment with a lady who had slept the whole way without once looking out through the window. Even the memory of her made him angry again. "What a *lazy* woman! To sleep the whole way! How can anyone be so lazy?" On another occasion he remarked: "Most people die without ever having lived. Luckily for them, they don't realize it." He disappointed Helene by his almost (not complete, as John Paulsen and the New England lady in Rome supposed) lack of interest in music; he admitted to her that he had once "positively wallowed" in Hans von Bülow's concerts—"and that says a lot, for music usually only makes me nervous."

He spoke to her of Suzannah; and those who have assumed that, because he loved the company of young girls and longed for what she had never been able to give him, his relationship with his wife was now dead should note his words. He admired (wrote Helene in her diary) Suzannah's "intellectual quickness," and the way she maintained her own individuality. Despite her almost passionate belief in him, she would not hesitate to speak her own mind when her view differed from him. He praised her "inner freedom and completeness of personality," a compliment, he added, which he could not pay to many people. Yet, while he admired strength of character, "strength and subtlety must always go together. Brutal strength is something unbearable."

We have seen how he admired, in Michelangelo, Bernini and the architect of Milan Cathedral, those artists who had the courage to depart from accepted standards of taste, to "commit a madness," as he himself was never afraid to do; and this too, he discussed with Helene. He said he thought it was a longing that everyone possessed, though few yielded to it. As a schoolboy, he remembered, he had often yearned to hit his teacher over the nose with a ruler, without feeling any hatred for the man. "This longing to commit a madness stays with us throughout our lives. Who has not, when standing with someone by an abyss or high up on a tower, had a sudden impulse to push the other over? And how is it that we hurt those we love although we know that remorse will follow?" (a thought that must have been much in his mind at that time). "Our whole being," he added, "is nothing but a fight against the dark forces within ourselves." Those last eight words sum up the theme of *Rosmersholm* and *The Lady from the Sea,* and of the two plays he was to write next, *Hedda Gabler* and *The Master Builder.*

He told her of his dislike and distrust of abstract thought. "Philosophical theories, unless put into practice, seem worthless to me." On the subject of suffering, he remarked: "It is not what we experience that matters, but how we understand it." He spoke much of the importance of will-power. "To me will is always the most important thing. Few people have strong wills. It always strikes me as comical when people tell me that something they wanted didn't work out. They have merely desired or longed for something, not willed it. He who really wills something attains his goal." He had dramatized this theory in *Emperor and Galilean*. "Self-realization," he declared, "is man's highest task and greatest happiness." One of the tragedies of women, he thought, was that their will-power tended to remain undeveloped. This was to be very much the theme of *Hedda Gabler*. "What is healthy is the happiness one acquires through one's own will."

On 19 March Helene took a small oil-painting she had done, apparently an imaginary portrait of Solveig in *Peer Gynt*, to Suzannah and asked her to give it to Ibsen on the following day (his birthday,), as she herself would be away then. Suzannah thanked her but did not want to unwrap the present, saying: "He must do that himself." Helene feared the paper might stick to the paint, which was not yet quite dry, so Suzannah unwrapped it, liked the painting greatly, and said: "I am quite sad to have seen it first—that pleasure should have been his." She repeated this several times. When, on 31 March, Helene saw Ibsen and told him of Suzannah's remark, "he seemed quite surprised, and said 'Oh. She doesn't say such things to *me*.' Then he was silent for a long time."[5]

His new play, *Hedda* (as he at first entitled it) was making the most painful progress. The character he was attempting to portray was of a complexity unprecedented even in Ibsen's work; it was a curious amalgam of himself and the young girl in Vienna to whom he had made such extravagant and unkept promises, and it involved the most searching and agonizing self-analysis.

Promising news reached him in April from Moritz Prozor, his French translator, who wrote that his version of *A Doll's House* was to be performed at the Théâtre de l'Odeon; also, less enthusiastically, that André Antoine was proposing to stage *Ghosts* at his Théâtre Libre, but in another version by Rodolphe Darzens. Since Ibsen had granted Prozor the French rights to the two plays, the latter asked Ibsen to intervene; but this he refused to do. Antoine later told Halvdan Koht that Prozor's translation was not sufficiently speakable,[6] and word of this may have reached Ibsen. He knew from experience how much his plays could be crippled by bad translation, and it is remarkable, considering the quality of most of the versions used, that they achieved the success they did.

[5] Letter from Helene Raff to Julius Elias, 26 June 1907, quoted in C.E., XIX, 534.
[6] *Loc. cit.*

The *Doll's House* project came to nothing (the play had to wait another four years before its first French production), but *Ghosts* was duly staged by Antoine at the tiny Théâtre des Menus Plaisirs—"a dark corner, deep hidden in a passage, and beyond this passage some ten feet of gallery," as George Moore described it—for two performances, on 29 and 30 May. Moore, who managed to get in ("Once the doors are opened, a thousand pounds would fail to procure you a seat. But M. Antoine is always anxious to oblige a *confrère*") thought Mlle. Barny excellent as Mrs. Alving and Antoine himself "wonderful" as Oswald, and declared the production to be the Théâtre Libre's greatest triumph since they had presented Tolstoy's *The Power of Darkness* two years previously, six years before it was allowed to be performed in Russia. Of the final scene of *Ghosts*, Moore wrote: "Most assuredly nothing finer was ever written by man or god. Its blank simplicity strikes upon the brain, until the brain reels, even as poor Oswald's brain is reeling.[7] The young Aurélien Lugné-Pœ, shortly to establish himself as Ibsen's most assiduous champion in France, wrote of the occasion that it was "a thunderbolt in French theatrical history. It can never be described how stunned and shaken we were that day."[8] Antoine toured his production around France, presenting it for over two hundred performances.

As if Ibsen had not enough guilt on his conscience concerning women that summer, Laura Kieler now dramatically re-entered his life. Two years earlier she had sent him a play she had written called *Men of Honour*. As he had shown in the case of her autobiographical novel, he could be severe on work he did not like, but of this play he had written to her (23 July 1888) that he had read it "with *keen* interest, and I think that *all* our theatres should *hasten* to perform it." Poor Laura's luck, however, continued as bad as ever. Dagmars Theatre in Copenhagen accepted it but went bankrupt before they could stage it, and although the Casino Theatre in Copenhagen put it on in 1890 and the Christiania Theatre in 1891, it failed on both occasions. It was keenly and eloquently defended by Bjørnson, and brought her a number of grateful letters from young people; but the pleasure this gave her was more than countered by a vicious article from the pen of (alas) Georg Brandes who, reviewing J. B. Halvorsen's *Dictionary of Biography* (which contained a long section on Ibsen) went out of his way to assert that the original of Nora had committed her crime for reasons much less idealistic than those which had inspired Ibsen's heroine.[9] Laura wrote to Ibsen's friend in Stockholm,

---

[7] George Moore, *Impressions and Opinions* (London, 1914), pp. 162–67.

[8] Lugné-Pœ, p. 11.

[9] As late as 1917 Brandes was still asserting that Laura got the money "not in order to save her husband's life but to beautify her home." Cf. his article "Henrik Ibsen: Personal Reminiscences and Remarks about his Plays," in *Century Magazine*, New York, February 1917, p. 543.

Fredrika Limnell, begging her to ask Ibsen to deny this and the other rumours that were circulating about her; and Fru Limnell wrote to Ibsen on 10 June, enclosing various press cuttings to show that Laura's complaints were justified.[10]

Ibsen refused; and his reply to Fru Limnell of 1 July is difficult to defend. "I don't quite understand," he wrote, "what Laura Kieler really has in mind in trying to drag *me* into these squabbles. A statement from me such as she proposes, to the effect that 'she is not Nora,' would be both meaningless and absurd, since I have never suggested that she is. If untrue rumours have been spread in Copenhagen that something happened earlier in her life which bears a certain similarity to the business of the forged document in *A Doll's House*, then she herself or her husband, preferably both, are the only people able to kill these rumours by an open and emphatic denial. I cannot understand why Herr Kieler has not long since taken this course, which would immediately put an end to the gossip. I am genuinely sad that I cannot accede to your request to intervene. But I think that on considering the matter more closely . . . you will agree that I can best serve our mutual friend by remaining silent and not intervening."

Ibsen's attitude in this matter was as cowardly and hypocritical as his account to Julius Elias of his relationship with Emilie Bardach. Whether or not he had suggested that Laura was the original of Nora, she was, and many people knew it; and he could easily have written an open letter to a newspaper stating truthfully that her conduct had been deserving only of praise and flatly contradicting Brandes's assertion. Such as action would have established her as what she was, a figure no whit less heroic than Nora. Bjørnson would have done it; and was Ibsen so afraid of offending Brandes? But there was something of Pontius Pilate in him, as in Peer Gynt.

On 18 July there occurred in London an event that was ultimately to prove of great importance in the establishment of Ibsen's reputation. Bernard Shaw, then an unsuccessful novelist of thirty-four who had yet to complete his first play,[11] delivered a lecture on Ibsen to the Fabian Society at the St. James's Restaurant. Since it was from this lecture (mainly devoted to *A Doll's House*) that *The Quintessence of Ibsenism* grew, it is worth recalling the particular terms of reference within which it was written. As Shaw states in his original preface to the *Quintessence,* the Fabian Society had arranged a series of lectures under the general heading of Socialism in Contemporary Literature. "Sydney Olivier consented to 'take Zola'; I consented to 'take Ibsen' . . . and . . . purposely couched it in the most provocative terms."

[10] Kinck, p. 527.

[11] He had begun *Widowers' Houses* (at Archer's instigation) in 1884, but did not finish it until 1892.

[12] Cf. Bernard Shaw: *Collected Letters, 1874–1897,* pp. 257–58.

The Quintessence of Ibsenism, Shaw's first important book, was to perform a great service for Ibsen in drawing attention to his work; but it was one of the most misleading books about a great writer that can ever have been written. Had it been entitled *Ibsen Considered as a Socialist,* or *The Quintessence of Shavianism* (not that the word Shavianism had been coined then), one would have no quarrel with it.

As a result of Shaw's lecture, a correspondent of the London *Daily Chronicle* questioned Ibsen on 12 August concerning his views on socialism, and next day the *Chronicle* printed the following report:

> In consequence of the continuous efforts of the Social Democrats to represent Henrik Ibsen as one of their party, and specially on account of the abuse of Ibsen's name by certain moral philosophers in England ever since *A Doll's House* was performed in London, I interviewed Ibsen, who since his return from Italy resides with his family [*sic*] permanently in Munich. Ibsen was very pleased to receive me, and glad to converse on the subject I had called to see him about. He declared that he had never at any time belonged to the Social Democratic Party. He never had studied the Social Democratic question, nor does he intend to join the Social Democratic Party at a future date. In fact, he declared he never was nor ever would be a Social Democrat. He was surprised to find his name used as a means for the propagation of Social Democratic dogmas. If a mere accidental coincidence of certain tendencies or principles involved in his book *Nora* with regard to the matrimonial and woman question are [*sic*] identical with or cover certain planks of the Social Democratic platform, his *Nora* is not, he explained, an abstract hypothesis conceived to demonstrate certain party dogmas, but was taken from life. Nora existed; but he never intended to lay down a hard and fast rule that all women in a similar position to Nora should or must act like Nora.

This report grossly distorted what Ibsen had in fact said to the reporter. He had no intention of being used as a stick to beat the socialists in any country, and on 18 August he addressed the following letter to H. L. Brækstad, the Norwegian bookseller who had first introduced his works to Edmund Gosse in Trondhjem seventeen years earlier, and who had for the past ten years been living in London, where he was Norwegian consul:

Dear Herr Brækstad,

Since an article from Berlin concerning me in the *Daily Chronicle* of 13 August strikes me as likely to be misinterpreted in several respects, as has already happened in Norwegian newspapers, I should like, for your sake and that of my other British friends, to correct some of the remarks attributed to me. I feel that what I said was not in all instances reported quite clearly or fully.

I did not say that I have never studied the question of Social Democracy. On the contrary, I have, as far as I was able and could spare the time, sought with keen curiosity to understand it. What I said was that I have never found time to study the great mass of literature on the subject dealing with the different socialist systems.

When the reporter quotes me as saying that I did not belong to the Social Democrat Party I would prefer that he had not omitted to mention what I added on the subject, namely, that I had never belonged and probably never would belong to any party.

In other words, it has become a necessity for me to operate as a complete independent.

The reporter's statement that I was astonished at seeing my name used as a means of spreading Social Democratic doctrines is likely to be especially misleading.

What I in fact expressed was my surprise that I, who had made it my principal task to portray human characters and human destinies, had, on certain issues—without having consciously or deliberately so intended—arrived at the same conclusion as that reached by the Social Democrat moral philosophers through scientific research.

This surprise—and, I may add, pleasure—I expressed as the result of the reporter telling me how someone, or some people, had given lectures in London which, according to his account, had been largely devoted to *A Doll's House.* . . .

Your affectionate and bounden
Henrik Ibsen

This letter was published in the *Daily Chronicle* on 28 August, and must have given considerable satisfaction to all good socialists.

A few days after Ibsen had written the above, William Archer visited him, en route for Oberammergau. He described the meeting in a letter to his brother:

His fame in England is, as he says, "a fairy tale" to him. . . . He is obviously older, but looks very well and is quite alert and cheerful. He trotted me round a vast exhibition of modern pictures, where there is a portrait of himself by a Norwegian named Smith—a vivid enough but far from flattering one. He won't go into the room where it hangs, but waited round the corner. Just as I discovered it, an Englishman and his wife were standing before it. The man looked up his catalogue and said: "Oh, that's Ibsen, the Norwegian poet," to which the lady replied with the greatest interest: "Oh, is it? Well, now, that's just what I would have expected him to look like." I was tempted to tell them that they need only step into the next room to see the original; but instead, I reported their conversation to the "Old Man," who was amused. . . .

You would see from Shaw's letter which I sent you that Ibsen was supposed to be infuriated at being classed as a Socialist by G.B.S. He explained to me, however, that his rage existed only in the imagination of the *Daily Chronicle* interviewer. What he really said was that he never had belonged, and probably never would belong, to any party whatsoever; but he expressed himself as pleasantly surprised that English Socialists, working on scientific lines, had arrived at conclusions similar to his. This the *Chronicle* interviewer . . . twisted into an expression of unpleasant surprise that anyone should have the audacity to make use of his name in Socialist propaganda. The Old Man was quite put out about this, for the thing had got into the German and Danish papers too. While I was with him he received a letter from Wollmar, one of the Socialist leaders in the Reichstag, asking him what the devil he meant by this seemingly contemptuous disclaimer, not only of Socialism but of all sympathy with Socialism. Ibsen had already written a letter to Brækstad, intended for the English papers; and he forthwith sat down to write a German translation of this letter for Wollmar.

Fru Ibsen and he had an amusing little scene apropos of this incident. She said: "I warned you when that man came from Berlin that you would put your foot in it. You should have let me see him; women are much more cautious than men in what they say." Whereupon the Old Man smiled grimly and said that wasn't generally supposed to be the strong point of the sex; adding that since the interviewer was going to lie about what he said, it didn't much matter whether he was cautious or not. Then Fru Ibsen suggested that he ought not to have seen him at all, and I closed the discussion by assuring her that in that case he would have made up the interview entirely from his own consciousness.[13]

Archer found the rooms in Maximilianstrasse no more homely than the apartment in the Capo le Case: "lofty and handsome, but still, to my thinking, unattractive."

Ibsen's unwillingness to commit himself to any political party has often been criticised; but he was not the only man of progressive sympathies who has felt unable to identify himself with the left-wing party in his country. He once said to Laura Kieler: "I sympathize with all my heart with the cause of the left, in both Norway and Denmark. I am a man of the left, in so far as the left fights against what is conservative. But if they do not also make the workers' cause their own, then the left has shirked its task; I am no longer one of them."[14]

The cause of the controversy in the *Daily Chronicle* himself almost met Ibsen that summer. Bernard Shaw was in Munich at the beginning of August, on a trip with Sidney Webb to see (like Archer) the Passion Play at Oberammergau; but "my total ignorance of Norwegian" (he wrote to Archer on 17 August) "prevented my calling on him during my stay . . . to explain his plays to him."[15] The two could have conversed in German, and one wonders why Shaw did not make the effort; perhaps he felt

[13] William Archer, "Ibsen as I Knew Him," pp. 14–15.
[14] Laura Kieler, *Silhouetter* (Odense, 1887), p. 13.
[15] Bernard Shaw, *Collected Letters, 1874–1897*, p. 258.

he would make a dull impression on his hero in any language but his own. The two were never to meet.

Meanwhile, Ibsen had continued to make heavy weather of *Hedda Gabler*. On 29 June he had written to Snoilsky that he would probably have to sacrifice his summer holiday, since "I shan't leave Munich before I have completed the first draft, and there is little or no prospect that I shall get that far during July." He did not even begin his first draft of Act Two until 13 August, and in the next three weeks he wrote only the opening stage directions (the scene was to take place in Hedda's garden) and three lines of dialogue (or if he wrote more, he destroyed it). There was obviously some deep technical or (more probably) psychological block. "I am not likely to get out into the country this summer," he wrote sadly to Nils Lund on 24 August. "I sit here fully occupied with my new work, and anyway the weather this year is not inviting for a country holiday. It is cold and rainy, with occasional days of intolerable heat and closeness." On 6 September he started a new draft of Act Two, and at last the play began to move. Nine days later, the act was ready; the third act took him only twelve days, and the fourth and final act a week.

The play was at this stage still entitled simply *Hedda;* and the differences between this draft and the play as we know it are numerous and revealing. Apart from changing Tesman from an ordinary bourgeois husband into a ninny spoiled (like Hjalmar Ekdal) by loving aunts, he improved him morally, for he originally intended that Tesman should suggest hiding Løvborg's manuscript "to frighten him"; and Hedda tells him to burn it "to see if I have any power over you. . . . I know I have over him." Miss Tesman's important account to Bertha in Act One of Hedda's life with her father was an afterthought; so were Mademoiselle Danielle, Mrs. Elvsted's abundant hair and Hedda's jealousy of it, the image of the vine-leaves, and Hedda's threat (before the play opens) to shoot Løvborg. Thea knows that the "other woman" who stands between her and Løvborg is Hedda; and Act One ends much less strongly than in the final version, with no mention of Hedda's disappointed hopes (the bay mare, etc.), or of the pistols. Tesman, like Thea, knows of Hedda's former close relationship with Løvborg; and Miss Tesman's role is much less rich than in the final version—she does not realize in Act One that Hedda is going to have a baby, and has a far less, effective scene with Hedda in Act Four. Indeed, there is no clear suggestion that Hedda is pregnant at all. The conversation between Hedda, Løvborg and Tesman over the photograph album about the honeymoon contains a direct reference to Gossensass, subsequently deleted (no doubt for reasons private to Ibsen). And Brack, in a passage which one is rather sorry to lose, describes sadly to Hedda how three "triangles" of which he was a part have been broken up during the past six months—not, as Hedda guesses, by other bachelors, but by intruders far more destructive to extra-marital relationships—children. Finally, one may note two remarks which Ibsen originally put into Hedda's mouth but subsequently deleted: (1) "I can't understand how anyone could fall in love with a man who isn't married—or engaged—or at least in love with someone else"; (2) "To take someone from someone else—I think that must be so wonderful!" He saved these thoughts for a character, already created in miniature in *The Lady from the Sea,* to whom he was to allot the principal female role in his next play two years later—Hilde Wangel in *The Master Builder.*

On 18 September, while wrestling with his draft, he had briefly broken his silence towards Emilie to write her a letter of commiseration on the death of her father; but, apart from some news of himself and his family, he said nothing more, avoiding the emotionally evocative tone of his earlier letters to her. All this time he was continuing his meetings with Helene. While fair-copying his final draft, on 30 October, he took time off to write an affectionate note to an old acquaintance from his student days. Karl Hals had, with his brother, started a piano factory in Christiania in 1847, three years before Ibsen's arrival there. The factory was about to celebrate the manufacture of its ten thousandth piano, and Hals invited Ibsen, for old friendship's sake, to attend the celebrations. The invitation obviously stirred warm memories, for Ibsen (though unable to accept) sent an unusually affectionate reply:

> . . . I should like to send you my warmest congratulations for the occasion. I dare not claim that I saw you working on piano no. 1. But one of the first of the long line must have been that on which you and your brother Peter were busy when we first met. It was in the autumn of 1850, and it was Ole Schulerud who brought me along. You and your brother were then living in the Cappelin building, where you had a little workshop. I remember well that you both actively partook in the work. As an assistant you had Thorman, who later appeared as an actor at the Christiania Theatre.
>
> I was very fond of your brother Peter. He died, of course, many years ago. But I still remember vividly what a fine man he was.
>
> So it is now forty years since we first met. Neither of us had much of the good things of life then. Not I, anyway. But since then the two of us have both done quite well, each in his own way.
>
> You learned to love work early in life. The joy of work was not revealed to me until later. But then I learned to prize it richly and with a vengeance.
>
> Now I sit down here, buried in a new play. I have not had a free hour for several months. For I receive an overwhelming mass of cor-

respondence, and that has to be taken care of too. But none of this shall prevent my thoughts from being with you in your festive circle on the evening of 3 November.

> Yours in sincere friendship
> Henrik Ibsen

On 16 November, after nearly six weeks of revision, he at last finished fair-copying *Hedda Gabler* (as he had re-entitled it, as though to underline the fact that, though officially Hedda Tesman, she was her father's child, a general's daughter who should have been born a boy). Two days later, late indeed for a Christmas book (and how badly he needed those Christmas sales), he posted the manuscript to Copenhagen. "It leaves me with a strange feeling of emptiness," he wrote to Moritz Prozor on 20 November. "But I am glad to be done with it. Living incessantly with these imagined characters was beginning to make me more than a little nervous."

That month the increasing English interest in Ibsen was marked by the publication of Clara Bell's translation of Jæger's biography; and he received sad news from Georg Brandes of the death of the latter's small daughter. "Your little girl lives in my memory in song," he wrote Brandes on 26 November. "The last time we were at your home she sang for us. I think I still hear that beautiful child's voice, and I shall always remember it."

The next day he himself had sad tidings to convey to Julius Elias about their mutual friend Julius Hoffory, who had been living up to the character of Ejlert Løvborg which (unknown to him) Ibsen had just modelled on him:

> He came here from Weimar about two weeks ago and settled in at the Hotel Roth, where he still is. Almost as soon as he arrived it struck me that his thought and speech were impaired. He had difficulty in finding words, and particularly in remembering the names of various people, even those close to him.
>
> This condition of his has worsened daily. Dr. Brahm saw him and spoke with him several days ago and will be able to tell you about that. I can only add that since Brahm's departure things have continued to go downhill with Hoffory. Yesterday I tried earnestly to persuade him to return at once to Berlin. But unhappily in vain. He made a pathetic pretext about some love affair which kept him here and which he had to settle before he could leave. I think his will is so broken that he cannot take the decision to pack his bag, ask for his hotel bill or go to the railway station. I think too that he is quite incapable of looking after his money. Both last night and the night

before I saw him at the Café Maximilian try repeatedly to pay his bill after he had already done so.

Under these circumstances it seems to me obvious that he must get away from here. But how this is to be done I don't quite know. I beg you to discuss this with Eric Schmidt, who lives quite near you and for whom Hoffory has especial respect. Possibly an earnest insistence from him might persuade H. to return and put himself in the care of doctors who know the history of his illness. That is absolutely essential. Here he has no one whose advice he can, or will, ask. So he gets worse and worse every day.

I know from my own experience how ready you are to sacrifice your time and endeavours in the cause of friendship. That is why, in this sad history, I am turning to you. A man's life, or at least his future, is at stake.

Hoffory, who was only thirty-five, was removed to a sanatorium before the end of the month. He was later released, but never fully recovered. The following year he sent Ibsen a deed of gift bequeathing to him all his possessions—a dreadfully ironic situation to arise between Løvborg and his creator. He was to die insane at the age of forty-two.

On 4 December Ibsen asked Hegel to invest as much as 12,000 crowns in securities for him; and the same day he stressed in a letter to Moritz Prozor: "I have not tried in this play to deal with so-called problems. My main object was to portray human beings, human moods, and human destinies, as conditioned by certain relevant social conditions and attitudes." Though happy to be reckoned a socialist, he was tired of being branded a sociologist, a reputation which Bernard Shaw's lecture, and the controversy it had aroused, had considerably fostered.

The English publisher William Heinemann, impressed by the constant publicity that was now being accorded to Ibsen in England—apart from the *Doll's House* production, Shaw's lecture, and the appearance of Jæger's biography, the first four volumes of the collected edition under Archer's editorship had appeared that November—had offered Ibsen £150 for the rights of *Hedda Gabler,* provided the proof-sheets could be sent direct from Gyldendal to Edmund Gosse (who was to translate it) as they came off the press. Ibsen happily accepted this windfall, telling Gosse (29 November) that he felt "much bounden to Mr. Heinemann for so liberal an honorarium" and expressing his "deep joy and satisfaction at seeing how my writings increasingly win an entry into the immense territory of the English-speaking peoples, in which a foreign author generally has such difficulty in establishing a foothold".[16] To secure his copyright Heinemann, then only twenty-seven and in his first year as a

[16] This letter, not in the Centenary Edition, was first published in Bredsdorff, pp. 43–44.

publisher, issued an edition of twelve copies of the play in Norwegian on 11 December, five days before the Gyldendal edition—a procedure he was to adopt with Ibsen's subsequent plays. On 16 December the Gyldendal edition appeared, in a printing of 10,000 copies.

Hedda Gabler received the worst press notices of any of Ibsen's mature plays, not excluding *Rosmersholm*. Bredo Morgenstierne, who had written a front-page tribute to Ibsen on his sixtieth birthday, regretted in *Aftenposten* (20 and 21 December) that, after the "cleaner air and brighter perspectives of *The Lady from the Sea*," Ibsen had now reverted to the unpleasant thematic matter of *Ghosts* and *Rosmersholm*—"and the obscurity, the eccentric and abnormal psychology, the empty and desolate impression which that whole way of life leaves, is here stronger than ever. . . . With the best will in the world one has difficulty in following the master's thought. We do not understand Hedda Gabler, nor believe in her. She is not related to anyone we know." Alfred Sinding-Larsen in *Morgenbladet* (21 December) described Hedda as "a horrid miscarriage of the imagination, a monster in female form to whom no parallel can be found in real life . . . far from likely to cause any joy or much admiration." Harald Hansen, reviewing the year's drama in *Samtiden* (1891, p. 312), dismissed it in a sentence as "an ungrateful play which hardly any of the participants will remember with real satisfaction."

Even some of Ibsen's warmest supporters were disappointed. Gerhard Gran wrote sadly in *Samtiden* (1891, pp. 75–77) that the play "awoke my curiosity without capturing my interest. . . . It is a law, or anyway has until now been a law, that drama, in its present state of technical development, can only present comparatively simple characters. . . . Everything that should make this curious being intelligible to us, her development, her secret thoughts, her half-sensed misgivings and all that vast region of the human mind which lies between the conscious and the unconscious—all this the dramatist can no more than indicate. For that reason, I think a novel about Hedda Gabler could be extremely interesting, while the play leaves us with a sense of emptiness and betrayal." Gran's remarks explain why people who accepted Emma Bovary, Anna Karenina and Dorothea Brooke were baffled by Ellida Wangel, Rebecca West and Hedda Gabler. Neither actors nor audiences, nor even those who bought the play in book form, were able to read between the lines of dialogue as we can today.

Nor did the Swedes and Danes appreciate it. *Fædrelandet* thought the book should not be found on the table of any decent family. C. D. af Wirsen wrote in *Post och Inrikes-Tidning:* "One doubts whether reality can provide an example of Hedda Gabler. Certain traits are perhaps truthfully portrayed, but the psychological combination of these traits is without logic. And a dramatist should make his play intelligible as a whole, not unintelligible. . . . Here and there things appear which strike us as very true, but they do not add up to anything which, taken as a whole, gives us the impress of truth. Still . . . we have no doubt that even with this play there will be many who will praise the emperor's non-existent new clothes, and will pretend to discover in this *camera obscura* an infinitude of subtleties that do not exist."[17] Georg Göthe in *Nordisk Tidskrift* (1891, pp. 171–75) complained: "The whole characterisation of the play is obscure. . . . They are alive, but only to a degree; deep inside them there is something abstract, cold, dead."

Some of the critics were embarrassed that the first Norwegian author to gain widespread international recognition should give such a gloomy picture of their country's way of life and morals. Alfred Sinding-Larsen, in the *Morgenbladet* review quoted above, suspected him of pandering to contemporary European fashion. "Ibsen is *fin-de-siècle*," he declared. ". . . As long as his works were healthy they remained unnoticed [abroad]. But . . . once his plays had the right tinge of darkness and comfortlessness, the right undertone of pessimism, Godlessness and despair, they were fitted to satisfy the contemporary craving for sensation and titillation. . . . The fact that Ibsen has become fashionable does not mean that the works with which he has achieved this will have any real permanence or significance. . . . Ibsen's modern drama is the drama of abnormality. His main characters have nothing human about them save the flesh in which they are clothed."

Almost the only critics to appreciate what Ibsen was trying to do in *Hedda Gabler* were Henrik Jæger in Norway and Edvard Brandes in Denmark. Jæger, who had come a long way since he had stumped the country lecturing against *Ghosts,* wrote a late review of the play in *Dagbladet* on 4 February, and after lambasting the other critics for their treatment of the play, he declared: "Bigness and pettiness are so blended in Hedda's character that she belongs neither to hell nor heaven but to earth. She is neither a monster nor a saint . . . simply a tragic character who is destroyed by the unharmonious and irreconcilable contrasts in her own character. . . . Tragedy is not very popular in Norway just now. People do not want to see tragedies on the stage. . . . So naturally the play is 'foul,' 'contemptible,' and 'immoral.' " And Edvard Brandes, reviewing the Copenhagen premiere in *Politiken* on 26 February, wrote:

> Ibsen's latest play is being debated round the world. There are today two or three writers who set people's minds in motion when a work leaves their desk—Tolstoy, Zola—but a novel does not nag at the mind and *demand* an answer like a play. Whether *Hedda Gabler* is in the top rank of Ibsen's works is difficult to decide. For people who are interested in things of the mind, Ibsen's plays are milestones in their development; people have *thought* differently in Scandinavia since *Ghosts* and *Rosmersholm*. . . . *The Lady from the Sea* did not have quite the same impact, and *Hedda*

17 Wirsen, p. 108.

Gabler too will scarcely have a significance comparable to that of *Ghosts.* Many will rejoice that the supernatural element is absent from *Hedda Gabler.* No white horses ride here, no Stranger rides to Hedda Gabler by night.

Brandes found Hedda like the heroines of Russian novels—cold, scornful, ambitious to win men and oust other women, blasé, and eager for excitement. Though doubtful whether she would have killed herself, he found the play "gripping and powerful," and concluded: "One may read it again and again and find new things to marvel at."

One suspects, too, that, as with *Ghosts* (and, for that matter, *Rosmersholm* and *The Lady from the Sea*), there were many young men and women whose views were inadequately represented by the main body of printed criticism. Carl Georgsson Fleetwood was probably speaking for many of his generation when he noted in his diary his amazement that anyone should be puzzled by the psychology of Hedda or think her unreal.[18]

Herman Bang, one of Ibsen's most eloquent Danish admirers, also saw the point. "Most of Ibsen's plays," he declared perceptively in a lecture delivered in Christiania on 14 November 1891,[19] "had been about egotistical men and selfless women; but here was a play about an egotistical *woman,* and whereas a man's egotism may at least often cause him to accomplish much, a woman's merely drives her into isolation and self-adoration. Hedda has no source of richness in herself and must constantly seek it in others, so that her life becomes a pursuit of sensation and experiment; and her hatred of bearing a child is the ultimate expression of her egotism, the sickness that brings death."

Hedda Gabler is, today, perhaps the most universally admired of Ibsen's plays, the most frequently performed (in England, at any rate), and certainly one of the easiest for an average audience to appreciate. Why did it so baffle its contemporaries? Partly because, as stated, people who could comprehend a complex character in a novel, with the aid of narrative explanation and the character's reflections, were often helpless when faced with the same character expressed only through dialogue. And partly, too, because Ibsen was using a new technique, though it has since become so much a part of common practice in play-writing that it is difficult for us to realize that it can ever have been new. Several times in contemporary criticisms of *Hedda Gabler* one comes across the comment that here, for the first time, Ibsen has virtually dispensed with long speeches, that he has written the play almost entirely in short exchanges of two or three sentences per character, a kind of dramatic shorthand. "No concession is made to the general public to help it to understand," wrote Henrik Jæger in the review quoted above. "No explanations by other characters, no self-characterization to excuse or de-

18 Fleetwood, II, 1127 ff. and 1217.
19 Printed in *Tilskueren* (October–November 1892), pp. 827–38.

fend herself, even a minimum of information about events that have gone before—Ibsen has scorned all this as the quackery of salesmanship. Nor is that all. He has so striven to make the dialogue natural and life-like that everything is chiselled out in very short lines, usually no more than a few words, seldom more than one or two lines." And Edmund Gosse, reviewing the play in the *Fortnightly Review* on 1 January 1891, remarked:

> In the whole of the new play there is not one speech which would require thirty seconds for its enunciation. I will dare to say that I think in this instance Ibsen has gone perilously far in his desire for rapid and concise expression. The *sticomythia* of the Greek and French tragedians was lengthy in comparsion with this unceasing display of hissing conversational fireworks, fragments of sentences without verbs, clauses that come to nothing, adverbial exclamations and cryptic interrogations. It would add, I cannot but think, to the lucidity of the play if some one character were permitted occasionally to express himself at moderate length, as Nora does in *A Doll's House,* and as Mrs. Alving in *Ghosts. . . .* On the stage, no doubt, this rigid broken utterance will give an extraordinary sense of reality.

But with actors and actresses looking less for reality than for big theatrical moments, it didn't.

As with most of Ibsen's plays, elements in *Hedda Gabler* can be traced to incidents in the lives of people whom he knew personally or had heard or read about. On his visit to Norway in 1885 he must have heard of the marriage the previous winter between a famous beauty named Sophie Magelssen and the philologist Peter Groth. Groth had married her on a research grant which he had won in competition with Hjalmar Falk, whom many thought the better scholar of the two (and who gets a consolatory mention in the play as the dead Cabinet Minister who had previously owned the Tesmans' villa). Neither Tesman nor Løvborg, however, was modelled on either of these two. Ibsen told his son Sigurd[20] that he had based Tesman on Julius Elias, the young German literary historian whom he had got to know in Munich. Elias's great passion was for "putting other people's papers in order" (which Tesman describes as his speciality); later he became a distinguished man of letters, and ironically it fell to him to put Ibsen's own papers in order when he shared with Halvdan Koht the task of editing the dramatist's literary remains.[21] Løvborg was, as previously stated, closely modelled on Julius Hoffory, the Dane who had translated *The Lady from the Sea* into German and was Professor of Scandinavian Philology and Phonetics in Berlin; he

[20] Cf. Halvdan Koht's introduction to *Hedda Gabler* in C.E., XI, 279.

[21] In fairness to Elias, one should add that Tesman is a much less ridiculous character in the draft of the play than Ibsen subsequently made him. His maddening repetition of nursery phrases such as "Fancy that!" was added during revision.

mixed freely with women of low repute and had once lost the manuscript of a book during a nocturnal orgy. He recognised himself delightedly when *Hedda Gabler* appeared, and thereafter adopted Løvborg as his pseudonym.

At the same time, it has been convincingly argued[22] that Løvborg and Tesman both represent aspects of Ibsen's own self: Løvborg an idealised portrait of himself as he had been in the wild days of his youth, Tesman a *reductio ad absurdum* of what he had chosen to become; in other words, Løvborg stands for his emotional self, Tesman for his intellectual self. Ibsen was haunted throughout the latter half of his life by the feeling that he had stifled his emotional self and that only his bourgeois and slightly ludicrous intellectual self had lived on; and although he had persuaded himself to accept this state of affairs, the encounter with Emilie must have reminded him forcibly of his self-betrayal.

Miss Tesman, George's aunt, was based on an old lady from Trondhjem named Elise Holck. Ibsen had met her a number of times during the early seventies in Dresden, where she tended a sick sister for three years until the latter died. He wrote a charming poem in tribute to her in 1874. She is the only character, as far as is known, who was based on a Norwegian original, and this may have influenced early critics who wrote that *Hedda Gabler* was the least Norwegian of Ibsen's plays and that the town (unnamed as usual) in which the action takes place was less suggestive of Christiania than of a continental capital (though William Archer, who knew Christiania well, felt sure that Ibsen had that city in mind).

Three further incidents which came to Ibsen's notice found their way into the play. While he was actually working on it, a young married couple came to seek his advice; their happiness, they said, had been ruined because the husband had been hypnotized by another woman. Then there was the unfortunate case of the Norwegian composer Johan Svendsen, whose wife Sally, in a fit of rage at discovering a letter from another woman hidden in a bouquet of flowers, burned the score of a symphony which he had just composed. Finally, he heard of the even more unfortunate incident of the Norwegian lady whose husband had cured himself of drink and had resolved never to touch it again. To see how much power she had over him, she rolled a keg of brandy into his room as a birthday present, and before the day was over he was dead drunk. All these episodes are reflected in *Hedda Gabler*.

What of Hedda herself? She has been rather glibly assumed by some critics to be a portrait of Emilie, on the grounds that both were beautiful and aristocratic and did not know what to do with their lives, and that Ibsen's description of Hedda (aristocratic face, fine complexion, veiled expression in the eyes, etc.) corresponds to early photographs of

[22] By Arne Duve, *Symbolikken i Henrik Ibsens skuespill* (Oslo, 1945), pp. 315–26.

Emilie. The same characteristics could, however, be found in the photograph of almost any well-born young lady of the period (the description would apply equally to Queen Alexandra), and few women of Ibsen's time, let alone girls of eighteen, knew what to do with their lives. In any case, the idea of creating such a character had been at the back of Ibsen's mind long before he met Emilie, for his rough notes for *Rosmersholm* in 1886 contain a sketch of a girl, intended as Rosmer's elder daughter (though he finally decided not to include her in the play), who "is in danger of succumbing to inactivity and loneliness. She has rich talents which are lying unused."

On the other hand, Emilie must certainly have been at the back of his mind when he was writing *Hedda Gabler,* and it is possible that Hedda may be a portrait, conscious or unconscious, of what Ibsen felt Emilie might become in ten years if she did not marry the right man or find a fixed purpose in life. If so, it was a prophecy that came uncomfortably near the truth, for Emilie, though she lived to be eighty-three—she died on 1 November 1955—accomplished nothing and never married.

But a Norwegian psychologist, Dr. Arne Duve, has persuasively argued that Hedda is in fact a self-portrait, and that she represents his own repressed and crippled emotional life. Hedda longs to be like Løvborg, but lacks the courage; she is repelled by the reality of sex, as (can we doubt?) Ibsen was (what man not frightened of sex would be shy about exposing his sexual organs to his own doctor?); she prefers to experience it vicariously by encouraging Løvborg to describe his experiences to her. Two emotions are dominant in her, the fear of scandal and the fear of ridicule, and we know that Ibsen, though willing to trail his coat in print, was privately dominated by these emotions. But if Hedda is a self-portrait, it is almost certainly an unconscious one—not that that makes it any the less truthful; rather the reverse.

One contemporary who particularly hated *Hedda Gabler* was August Strindberg, now fast approaching his "Inferno" crisis when he hovered on, if he did not indeed cross, the brink of madness. He was convinced that Ibsen had based Ejlert Løvborg on him (as, six years previously, he had believed himself to be the original of Hjalmar Ekdal in *The Wild Duck*). He had, he explained to Karl Nordström on 4 March 1891, revealed some secrets about his private life to friends, and:

> *Hedda Gabler* is based on this! And it's obvious that Ibsen has just patched this together from gossip, not observed it at first-hand. . . . How can a man of talent be "destroyed" because he gets drunk, whores, and fights with the police? It seems to me that Ibsen realizes that I shall inherit the crown when he's finished. (He hates me mortally and had the impertinence to refuse to contribute to Jacobsen's tombstone unless my name was struck off the list). And now the decrepit old troll seems to hand me the revolver a

second time! But his shit will rebound on him. For I shall survive him and many others, and the day *The Father* kills *Hedda Gabler* I shall stick that gun in the old troll's neck![23]

Strindberg repeated the accusation in another letter four days later, to the poet Ola Hansson, adding the charge that "Hedda Gabler is a bastard of Laura in *The Father* and Tekla in *Creditors*"; and, querying whether Løvborg could have been destroyed by a night's drinking, he added irrelevantly, "For my part, I have always felt refreshed by a good debauch!"[24] On 10 March, he wrote to Birger Mörner: "Do you now see that my seed has fallen into Ibsen's brainpan—and fertilized! Now he carries my seed and is my uterus!"[25]

The German publisher S. Fischer had bought the German rights of *Hedda Gabler* for the ungenerous sum of 300 marks, exactly one-tenth of what William Heinemann had paid. He also wanted to serialize the play in one of his magazines, but Ibsen refused him permission. "If Herr Fischer really believes that my play will mean so much to his magazine," he wrote to Julius Elias on 17 December, "he need only print a much bigger edition of the book and advertise that he will give a free copy as a Christmas present to every subscriber." He added that he had promised his German translator, Emma Klingenfeld, half of any fees he might get from German productions of the play, an extraordinarily generous arrangement, adding that "on my table lies a mass of written requests from German theatre directors, including several from Berlin, begging for copies of the play so that they may stage it."

Ibsen was having a little trouble with Fischer. "A few days ago," he wrote Elias the next day, "he explained in a letter that he could not possibly have the book out before the New Year. Now he thinks he can have it ready by Monday. A few days ago he assured me that I need not worry about competition. Now he seems almost distraught at the thought of Fru v. Borch. But never mind." Fischer printed an edition of 3,000 copies, Ibsen's return from which works out at about two cents a copy.

Still, 1890 had been quite a good year financially, by Ibsen's standards. German payments totalled 3,386 crowns, not much, but something; and even England had provided £75 (Heinemann's fee for *Hedda Gabler* did not arrive until he published the English edition in January, and then only after two sharp letters from Ibsen asking why he had not fulfilled his contract). But Ibsen must, as he looked down his list of earnings for the year, have noted sombrely how little his earlier plays were bringing him. He had received nothing at all from Norway or Denmark, apart from

[23] *August Strindbergs brev,* VIII, 198–99. The accusation about Ibsen and the tombstone was, of course, completely untrue.

[24] *Ibid.,* p. 201.

[25] *Ibid.,* p. 205.

Gyldendal's fee for *Hedda Gabler*—there had been no performances of his plays in either country, and no reprints. No wonder that, although he had 110,310 crowns locked away in securities, he invested a further 15,000 crowns during the next three months.

	crowns
Fee for one performance of *The Pillars of Society* at Mannheim	27
Misc. royalties from Berlin from previous year, via Felix Bloch (agent)	305
Misc. royalties from Munich Hoftheater for previous year (*The Pillars of Society, A Doll's House, An Enemy of the People*)	528
Fee from Walter Scott (London) for collected edition	906
Royalties from Bloch for unspecified German performances of *The Vikings at Helgeland, The Pillars of Society, A Doll's House* and *An Enemy of the People*	627
Fee from August Lindberg for Swedish rights of *Love's Comedy*	250
Misc. German royalties for *The Pillars of Society* and *A Doll's House*	228
Fee from Royal Theatre, Stockholm, for *Love's Comedy*	250
Fee from Royal Theatre, Stockholm, for two performances of *A Doll's House*	24
Royalties from Bloch for German performances of *The Vikings at Helgeland* and *The Pillars of Society*	96
Royalties from Munich Hoftheater for *The Pillars of Society*	167
Misc. unspecified royalties from Munich Hoftheater	252
Fee from Philippe Reclam, Leipzig publisher, for various of Ibsen's plays published by him	889
Fee from Walter Scott and William Archer for *Emperor and Galilean* and *Hedda Gabler*	450
Fee from Gyldendal for 1st edn. of *Hedda Gabler*	9,000
Fee from S. Fischer for German edn. of *Hedda Gabler*	267
	14,266 £791

28

The End of an Exile

1891

1891 opened with a tremendous row between Ibsen's two British champions, Edmund Gosse and William Archer, in which Ibsen found himself an unwilling and embarrassed participant.

William Heinemann had offered Ibsen £150 for (as Ibsen supposed) first publication rights of *Hedda Gabler*. But Gosse did not send Ibsen the formal contract until 2 January, and it then became clear that Heinemann was demanding not merely the first, but the exclusive English rights, which would debar Archer from publishing his translation of the play in the collected edition which he was editing for Walter Scott. Archer, who had waived his rights in the matter to oblige Gosse, not unnaturally complained to Ibsen, and on 8 January Ibsen wrote to Gosse expressing the hope that Heinemann would withdraw his veto and regretting that "through an excess of trust I may have helped to frustrate Mr. Archer's intentions—something that his gentlemanly conduct towards me has in no way deserved, and which lay very far from my own intentions. The fee which Mr. Archer has sent me from Walter Scott for *Hedda Gabler* I have of course returned. But the great collected edition will thus be incomplete, and this I deeply regret."[1]

This request was ignored. Gosse's translation of *Hedda Gabler* appeared on 20 January, and was the subject, three days later, of an uncharacteristically violent attack in the *Pall Mall Gazette* by Archer, normally the mildest of men. Archer described it as "one of the very worst translations on record," which "reproduces the terse and nervous original about as faithfully as a fourth form schoolboy, translating at sight, might be expected to reproduce a page of Tacitus." Pointing out that "'some months ago I waived in Mr. Gosse's favour a position of advantage which I held in regard to *Hedda Gabler* . . . on the explicit under-

[1] Cf. Bredsdorff, pp. 44–45.

standing that the privilege I thus transferred to him could not and would not be used to impede Mr. Walter Scott in completing his edition of Ibsen's Prose Dramas under my editorship," Archer concluded: "To find a parallel for Mr. Gosse's conduct in this matter, I need go no further than the play itself. Yet the parallel is not exact. It was by chance, not through an act of courtesy, that Hedda became possessed of Løvborg's manuscript; and having become possessed of it, she did not deface, stultify, and publish it—and then claim copyright. She did a much less cruel thing—she burned it."

Could any friendship survive such a betrayal on the one side, and such a public denunciation on the other? Amazingly, it did. Not only did Archer's translation of *Hedda* appear later that year, both independently and as Volume 5 of the Walter Scott Collected Edition; Gosse even included it, in preference to his own, in the Collected Ibsen which he himself was editing for Lowell's of New York. Indeed, as Archer's brother points out, "the incident had the happy result of bringing Archer into relations with the firm [Heinemann] which was eventually to publish, under his editorship, the complete standard [English] edition of the poet's works."[2]

So that unpleasant matter was settled; and the first six months of 1891 saw an unprecedented number of productions of Ibsen's plays, as the following list shows:

27 January	*A Doll's House* in London (single matinee)
31 January	World premiere of *Hedda Gabler* in Munich
6 February	*Hedda Gabler* in Helsinki
9 February	*A Doll's House* in Milan
10 February	*Hedda Gabler* in Berlin
19 February	*Hedda Gabler* in Stockholm
23 February	*Rosmersholm* in London
25 February	*Hedda Gabler* in Copenhagen
26 February	*Hedda Gabler* in Christiania
13 March	*Ghosts* in London
30 March	*Hedda Gabler* in Gothenburg
11 April	*The Pretenders* in Vienna
15 April	*An Enemy of the People* in Vienna
16 April	*The Wild Duck* in Vienna
20 April	*Hedda Gabler* in London
20 April	*A Doll's House* in Budapest
28 April	*The Wild Duck* in Paris
10 May	*The Pretenders* in Berlin
11 May	*The Lady from the Sea* in London
late May	*A Doll's House* in Paris (private performance)
2 June	*A Doll's House* in London (new production)

[2] Charles Archer, p. 175. Two years later, Gosse and Archer translated *The Master Builder* together!

Before January was out, *A Doll's House* was published in Italian, in a Rome theatrical magazine, *Carra di Tespi* (surprisingly, it did not appear in book form in Italy before 1895); and on 27 January it was performed in a new production in London, albeit only for a single performance. An actress named Marie Fraser, who had played the part a few months earlier in Edinburgh, acted Nora; Bernard Shaw thought her "desperately in earnest and desperately bad,"[3] but the *Athenæum* (31 January) observed: "Whatever may be the character of Ibsen's work . . , that its influence is growing day by day is one of the things that he who runs may read." *Dagbladet* in Christiania (2 February) offered the interesting tidbit that "there is talk that the famous Mrs. Langtry intends to play Hedda Gabler at the earliest opportunity." Had this happened, Ibsen would doubtless have had the gratifying experience of having one of his plays attended by royalty, with one wonders what effect on the anti-Ibsen movement in England; but sadly (or perhaps, from an artistic viewpoint, fortunately) Mrs. Langtry found other fish to fry.

On 31 January *Hedda Gabler* received its world premiere at the Residenztheater in Munich; but it was not well done, and Ibsen, who was present, was much displeased at the declamatory manner of Marie Ramlo in the title role. The audience was as baffled as the critics had been when the play was published. Ibsen took a call, and bowed to those who clapped; but there was a good deal of hissing and whistling. When someone commiserated with him afterwards, Ibsen shrugged his shoulders and murmured: "The public likes to laugh."[4]

On 9 February an Ibsen play was acted in Italy for the first time; Eleonora Duse, then thirty-one, acted Nora at the Teatro di Filodrammatici in Milan. Her translator, the novelist Luigi Capuana, Pirandello's mentor, had asked Moritz Prozor (from whose French version he had presumably made his own) for permission to change the last act so as to provide a happy ending; but a copyright agreement had recently been signed between Norway and Italy, which put Ibsen, at last, in a position to say No, and he did so. "I can almost say," he wrote to Prozor on 23 January, "that the whole play was written just for the sake of that final scene. And I think Herr Capuana is wrong in fearing that the Italian public would not be able to appreciate or understand my work if staged in its original form." In Germany, he reminded Prozor, "the play did not remain long in the repertory with the altered ending. But in its original form, it is still performed."

The day after the Italian premiere of *A Doll's House*, *Hedda Gabler* was staged at the Lessingtheater in Berlin. Ibsen went up for the occasion, but although the performance was better than in Munich it was not really a success. Even the critics normally friendly towards him found the

[3] Letter to Charles Charrington, 30 March 1891 (Bernard Shaw, *Collected Letters, 1874–1897*, p. 287).

[4] Koht, II, 234.

play illogical, and the liberal journalist Theodor Wolff wrote a parody in *Berliner Tageblatt:* "Wie Röschen Müller in Schönheit starb." A Swedish producer, Adolf Paul, who was present, noted how Ibsen "took a curtain call after each act, his face copper-red, and returned without the slightest change of expression to his box."[5] The Danish novelist Henrik Pontoppidan, who was there too, thought that "Ibsen cut a wretched figure. He looked like a troll that had been hauled up by the hair from the prompter's box."[6] Ibsen gave a party for his friends before leaving the city, in a private room at the fashionable Dressel Restaurant; the guests included Otto Brahm, Paul Schlenther, Paul Marx (the editor of *Der Tag*), Leo Berg, and Ejlert Løvborg himself in the person of poor Julius Hoffory, now released from his asylum but a broken man, in dark glasses and black gloves. Ibsen moved among them, a genial host, constantly refilling their glasses with champagne.[7]

On 23 February *Rosmersholm* was staged for the first time in England, for two matinees at the Vaudeville Theatre in the Strand. Frank Benson, then a rising Shakespearean actor of thirty-one, played Rosmer, with Florence Farr as Rebecca; but it was evidently a far from satisfactory production. "Archer was so disheartened by the rehearsals," wrote Bernard Shaw to Charles Charrington in Australia on 30 March, "that I had the greatest difficulty in inducing him to come. . . . Rebecca . . . got through by dint of brains and a certain fascination and dimly visible originality. . . . Benson . . . forced his playing; but he did not distinctly fail except in the last act, which did not get for a moment on to the plane on which alone the catastrophe is credible." At the second performance "a sort of dim photograph of the play as it was meant to be was arrived at."[8] "Being ill produced and on the whole poorly acted," comments Charles Archer, "[it] gave the anti-Ibsenites a plausible excuse to say 'Aha!.'"[9] His brother William collected some specimens of press reaction:

[5] Adolf Paul, *Profiler* (Helsingfors, 1937), p. 114.

[6] Letter from Pontoppidan to Henri Nathansen, quoted in Elias Bredsdorff, *Henrik Pontoppidan og Georg Brandes* (Copenhagen, 1964), II, 135.

[7] Elias, "Ibsenminne af hans tyske oversætter," pp. 405–6.

[8] Bernard Shaw, *Collected Letters, 1874–1897*, pp. 287–88.

[9] Charles Archer, p. 173. The main reason why the Vaudeville was so often chosen for early Ibsen productions seems to have been that it was regarded as an "unlucky" theatre, and so was cheap and easy to hire. "Who does not know" asked the *Academy* on 23 March 1901, "the forlorn and furtive enterprises undertaken at 'unlucky' theatres, with afternoon sunlight coming in through the side windows, at which Ibsen's masterpieces have been exposed to the admiration of the few and the laughter of the many?" Sir Lewis Casson, who as a young man attended several of these occasions, told me when he was over ninety that both William Archer and Elizabeth Robins imparted to the proceedings an atmosphere of puritanism to which Archer's translations also contributed, and that he thought this one reason why the tradition of presenting Ibsen's plays as totally humourless has, until very recently, survived in England.

A handful of disagreeable and somewhat enigmatical personages . . . Ibsen is a local or provincial dramatist.

The Times

Impossible people do wild things for no apparent reason. . . . Those portions of the play which are comprehensible are utterly preposterous. . . . Ibsen is neither dramatist, poet, philosopher, moralist, teacher, reformer—nothing but a compiler of rather disagreeable eccentricities.

Standard

A singularly gloomy and ineffectual function was that undergone at the Vaudeville on Monday afternoon.

Observer

The stuff that Ibsen strings together in the shape of plays must nauseate any properly constituted person.

Mirror

Ibsen's gruesome play. . . . His repulsive drama. . . . Greeted with the silence of contempt when the curtain finally fell.

The People

The whole affair is provincial and quite contemptible.

Saturday Review

To judge it seriously either as literature or as drama is impossible.

St. James's Gazette

These Ibsen creatures are "neither men nor women, they are ghouls," vile, unlovable, unnatural, morbid monsters, and it were well indeed for society if all such went and drowned themselves at once.

The Gentlewoman

Rosmersholm is not very dramatic. It is hardly at all literary. . . . It is without beauty, without poetry, without sense of vista. It is not even dextrously doctrinaire. . . . The farce is almost played out.

Mr. F. Wedmore in *The Academy*

There are certain dishes composed of such things as frogs and snails, stews in which oil and garlic reek, and dreadful compounds which we taste out of sheer curiosity, and which, if we expressed our honest, candid opinion, we should pronounce to be nasty and unpleasant. . . . *Rosmersholm* is beyond me.

Topical Times

To descant upon such morbid, impracticable rubbish would be an insult to the understanding of every reader, except an Ibsenite. . . . If Herr Ibsen were well smothered in mud with his two creations [*A Doll's House* and *Rosmersholm*] and with every copy of his plays, the world would be all the better for it.

Licensed Victuallers' Gazette

"Alas, poor Ibsen!" commented Archer. "It is well that he does not read English, else who knows but the disesteem of the *Licensed Victuallers' Gazette* might drive him into his mausoleum in good earnest!"[10]

That last week in February was a bad one for Ibsen, or anyway for the theatres presenting his works. Two days after the *Rosmersholm* premiere in London, *Hedda Gabler* opened at the Royal Theatre in Copenhagen, and had the worst reception of any of his plays in Denmark. "The public received *Hedda Gabler* coolly this evening," wrote Edvard Brandes in *Politiken* (26 February). "Some hissed, a few even whistled; though there was also warm and loud applause. . . . After the close of the play the rival noises continued until the gong sounded. . . . The opposition to the play was not æsthetic. . . . People feel compelled to forbid authors to treat of the ugly side of life." He admired Betty Hennings as Hedda, Emil Poulsen as Løvborg and Karl Manzius as Brack, but thought that "the play will not prove a financial success," and was right, for it was withdrawn after only five performances.

In Bergen it managed only three; and when it was given in Christiania on 26 February the reception was again tepid. "There was no real enthusiasm," reported Henrik Jæger in *Dagbladet* the next morning. ". . . The applause weakened as the play progressed. . . . The net result was a success, but not one of those decisive successes we have grown used to when a new work by Ibsen or Bjørnson is performed." The reason, Jæger concluded, was that Ibsen "has treated the psychological conflicts portrayed here as Pasteur and Koch treat bacteria. The whole thing takes place in an abstract realm in which the public is not accustomed to moving." Nor, the previous week, had the play fared better in Stockholm. "No dramatic talent can make a character as obscurely complex as Hedda Gabler really clear and dramatically consistent," wrote Georg Göthe in *Ny Svensk Tidskrift* (1891, p. 175), and even Ibsen's champion J. A. Runström complained in *Ny Illustrerad Tidning* (14 March) of the obscurity which "surrounds the central character like a thick fog."

While Ibsen's latest play was baffling the Scandinavians, the ones he had written a decade earlier continued to be belatedly discovered abroad; and on Friday, 13 March 1891, there occurred one of the most famous of all theatrical occasions, as controversial and epoch-making as the first nights of Victor Hugo's *Hernani* or Synge's *Playboy of the Western World:* the London premiere of *Ghosts*.

Inspired by the example of Antoine's Théâtre Libre in Paris and the Freie Bühne in Berlin, a twenty-nine-year-old Dutchman named Jacob T. Grein, working for a tea merchant in Mincing Lane at £180 a year, had resolved to found a similar venture in London, to stage plays from which the larger theatres shrank and which the censor would forbid. The era of the little theatres had begun, and it was from these that the new

[10] William Archer, "The Mausoleum of Ibsen," in the *Fortnightly Review*, July 1893, pp. 79–80.

dramatists were to emerge; without the Moscow Arts there would have been no Chekhov as we know him, without the Dublin Abbey no Synge or O'Casey; in the following decade Strindberg was to found his own Intimate Theatre to perform his chamber plays. The next fifty years belonged not to the state- or city-subsidised theatres, still less to the commercial theatre, but to the little theatres, often possessing no locale of their own but performing in whatever halls or rooms they could afford to hire. They all lost money consistently and, except where saved by private patronage, ended by going bankrupt, as good theatres do.

The previous year Grein had produced Pinero and Henry Arthur Jones in his native Holland, and their plays had proved so successful that the Amsterdam Theatre sent him £50, to be used "in the interest of art in England." Thus, by a stroke of irony of which Ibsen would surely have approved, Jones, who had been chiefly responsible for the travesty *Breaking a Butterfly,* and was to be one of Ibsen's most vehement opponents in England, was also largely responsible for getting *Ghosts* on to the English stage. For it was principally with *Ghosts* in mind, since that play would obviously stand no chance with the Lord Chamberlain, that Grein added to his £50 another £30 which he had received for translating a play and founded, with Thomas Hardy, George Meredith and Henry James among its first members, the Independent Theatre Society, "a modest organization [as Charles Archer described it][11] of most slender resources, intended to give the non-commercial drama, both native and foreign, a chance upon the stage, by means of occasional subscription performances in theatres hired for the purpose. Since no money was to be taken at the doors, the performances would be technically private."

The Society, then, opened its first season, as the Freie Bühne had opened its, with a single performance of *Ghosts,*[12] at the Royalty Theatre in Dean Street, Soho. Of the reception by the British press, William Archer noted: "The shriek of execration with which this performance was received by the newspapers of the day has scarcely its counterpart in the history of criticism." Three weeks after the performance, on 8 April 1891, he published in the *Pall Mall Gazette* an anthology of the choicest comments, worth quoting in full, for they show how Ibsen got under people's skin, whether they approved or disapproved of him:

"GHOSTS" AND GIBBERINGS
DESCRIPTIONS OF THE PLAY

An open drain; a loathsome sore unbandaged; a dirty act done publicly; a lazar-house with all its doors and windows open. . . . Candid foulness. . . . Offensive cynicism. . . . Ibsen's melancholy and malodorous world. . . . Ab-

---

[11] Charles Archer, p. 173.

[12] Plus a public dress rehearsal to hold the overflow. For a full account of the circumstances surrounding this production, see *Ghosts,* translated by Michael Meyer (London, 1962), pp. 95 ff.

solutely loathsome and fetid. . . . Gross, almost putrid indecorum—*Daily Telegraph* (leading article). This mass of vulgarity, egotism, coarseness and absurdity—*Daily Telegraph* (criticism). Unutterably offensive. . . . Prosecution under Lord Campbell's Act. . . . Abominable piece. . . . Scandalous —*Standard*. Naked loathsomeness. . . . Most dismal and repulsive production—*Daily News*. Revoltingly suggestive and blasphemous. . . . Characters either contradictory in themselves, uninteresting or abhorrent—*Daily Chronicle*. A repulsive and degrading work—*Queen*. Morbid, unhealthy, unwholesome and disgusting story. . . . A piece to bring the stage into disrepute and dishonour with every right-thinking man and woman—*Lloyd's*. Merely dull dirt long drawn out—*Hawk*. Morbid horrors of the hideous tale. . . . Ponderous dullness of the didactic talk. . . . If any repetition of this outrage be attempted, the authorities will doubtless wake from their lethargy—*Sporting and Dramatic News*. Just a wicked nightmare—*The Gentlewoman*. Lugubrious diagnosis of sordid impropriety. . . . Characters are prigs, pedants, and profligates. . . . Morbid caricatures. . . . Maunderings of nook-shotten Norwegians. . . . It is no more of a play than the average Gaiety burlesque—*Black and White*. Most loathsome of all Ibsen's plays. . . . Garbage and offal—*Truth*. Ibsen's putrid play called *Ghosts*. . . . So loathsome an enterprise—*Academy*. As foul and filthy a concoction as has ever been allowed to disgrace the boards of an English theatre. . . . Dull and disgusting. . . . Nastiness and malodorousness laid on thickly as with a trowel— *Era*. Noisome corruption—*Stage*.

DESCRIPTIONS OF IBSEN

An egotist and a bungler—*Daily Telegraph*. A crazy fanatic. . . . A crazy, cranky being. . . . Not only consistently dirty but deplorably dull—*Truth*. The Norwegian pessimist *in petto* [*sic*]—*Black* and *White*. Ugly, nasty, discordant and downright dull. . . . A gloomy sort of ghoul, bent on groping for horrors by night, and blinking like a stupid old owl when the warm sunlight of the best of life dances into his wrinkled eyes—*The Gentlewoman*. A teacher of the æstheticism of the Lock Hospital—*Saturday Review*.

DESCRIPTIONS OF IBSEN'S ADMIRERS

Lovers of prurience and dabblers in impropriety who are eager to gratify their illicit tastes under the pretence of art—*Evening Standard*. Ninety-seven per cent of the people who go to see *Ghosts* are nasty-minded people who find the discussion of nasty subjects to their taste in exact proportion to their nastiness—*Sporting and Dramatic News*. The sexless. . . . The unwomanly woman, the unsexed females, the whole army of unprepossessing cranks in petticoats. . . . Educated and muck-ferreting dogs. . . . Effeminate men and male women. . . . They all of them—men and women alike—know that they are doing not only a nasty but an illegal thing. . . . The Lord Chamberlain left them alone to wallow in *Ghosts*. . . . Outside a silly clique, there is not the slightest interest in the Scandinavian humbug or all his works. . . . A wave of human folly—*Truth*.[13]

[13] The *Truth* article was by Clement Scott, who also wrote the *Daily Telegraph* review and leader.

One of the few English critics courageous enough to defend the play was A. B. Walkley. Writing in the *Star* (over the pseudonym of "Spectator"), he asked:

> Do these people really find nothing in *Ghosts* but a mere hospital-ward play? Is it really for them nothing but a painful study of disease? Have they no eyes for what stares them in the face: the plain, simple fact that *Ghosts* is a great spiritual drama? Like nearly all other great masterpieces of the stage, it is a drama of revolt—the revolt of the "joy of life" against the gloom of hide-bound, conventional morality, the revolt of the natural man against the law-made, law-bound puppet, the revolt of the individual against the oppression of social prejudice. . . . This is the spiritual drama which I see in *Ghosts*.

Bernard Shaw did not review this production (he had not yet a regular dramatic column), but he described the audience's reaction in a letter to Charles Charrington (in Australia with *A Doll's House*) a fortnight later. "The play was a most terrible success. After the first act the applause was immense. After the second, a third of the applauders were startled into silence. After the third four-fifths of them were awe-struck. When Grein came out, very nervous, to make his speech, a lady in the stalls said naively: 'Oh, is that Ibsen?', throwing her neighbours into confusion. Then a man in the gallery cried out to Grein: 'It's *too* horrible,' and was instantly met with a sarcastic shout of 'Why don't you go to the Adelphi?' "[14]

The 1889 production of *A Doll's House* had established Ibsen as a force in the English theatre. The 1891 performance of *Ghosts* made his name a household word even among those Englishmen who never went to the theatre or opened a book. It elicited over five hundred printed articles. "Behind the times indeed," writes a historian of the period, "was the journal that omitted its daily column or so on Ibsen's iniquities. By the end of 1891 Ibsen was a name known to every reader of a London newspaper."[15] In the November issue of the *Fortnightly Review* William Archer wrote:

> I can call to mind no other case in literary history of a dramatist attaining such sudden and widespread notoriety in a foreign country. His name is in every newspaper and magazine, his rankling phrases—call them catchwords if you will—are in every mouth. An allusion to Nora Helmer will be as commonly understood as an allusion to Jane Eyre. Hedda Gabler . . . is now as well known as Becky Sharp. . . . This is the first time for half a century (to keep well within the mark) that a serious literary interest has also been primarily a theatrical interest.

The following January a London critic was to declare: "To contest the influence of Ibsen upon this country would be needless. . . . It may be

[14] Bernard Shaw, *Collected Letters, 1874–1897,* p. 289.
[15] Franc, pp. 88 and 120.

said of Ibsen's influence, as Napoleon said of the French Republic, that it is as obvious as the Sun in Heaven, and asks for no recognition."[16]

One wishes that the people who imagined Ibsen as a "crazy fanatic" and a "gloomy sort of ghoul" could have seen the target of their abuse on his walks in Munich, with his top hat, umbrella and order ribbons. On the day of the *Ghosts* premiere in London Ibsen was, in fact, occupied in writing a long letter to his sister Hedvig, his first to her in many years. She had written from Skien to inform him that a new civic centre was to be opened in the town and to convey an invitation from the committee to attend the inauguration ceremony. The thought of returning in triumph as an honoured guest to the town which he had last visited as a beggar must have tempted him; but Skien was always to remain the forbidden place. His conflicting emotions appear clearly in his reply:

Munich, 13 March 1891

My dear Sister,

I thank you most warmly for your letter, which I received last month and to which I must no longer postpone a reply.

It was with much pleasure that I learned that Skien, too, is now to have a civic centre. This will, I am sure, be both large and handsome, and no doubt modernly equipped in every respect, as befits the town and its present size.

And you tell me that this centre is shortly to be inaugurated with a series of celebrations.

Would indeed that I could have been present on that day! I suppose I would have met very few of those people I knew as a child. I would have found myself in the midst of a new and, to me, foreign generation. Yet perhaps, after all, not completely foreign. In all my many years of absence I have always felt that I still belonged to the town of my birth.

Had these festivities occurred a few years earlier, and had I known of them, I would have written a song or a poem and sent it home. I hope and believe that people there would have received it in friendship.

But I no longer write poems and songs of that kind. So there can be no talk of that. And yet I would very gladly be with you all in some way or other.

So you must tell people of this letter so that they shall all know that I am with you in my thoughts at your celebrations, just as I have so often been with you in my thoughts both in your afflictions, and in your confidence of happier days to come.

It was in 1850 that I was last at home in Skien. Not long after-

[16] Justin Huntly McCarthy in *The Gentlemen's Magazine,* January 1892.

wards a time of spiritual tempest began to sweep the city and spread thence into wider circles.

I have always liked storms. And I was with you in this storm—though absent. That I was with you, a deal of my writing testifies.

Then great tragedies struck the town and harried it repeatedly. The house where I was born and spent my first childhood years, the church, the old church with its baptismal angel under the roof, were burned. Everything that my earliest memories could cling to—it was all burned.

How could I but feel, with all of you, deeply and personally touched by the blows which smote our mutual home town?

But you can also imagine with what vivid joy I read accounts of how our town raised itself again in beauty and splendour—how it has grown and how it has progressed in various fields of endeavour.

I think you must all feel happy and hopeful when you reflect upon our town's future.

Would that I could have said this to you all personally—and more. But I am there among you all the same, in my way.

And should I, as I hope, some time come up to Norway—yes, then I should like to see home again—the old and yet the new home.

This, my dear Hedvig, is what I wish to tell you today—I will do my best to see that you hear more from me later. Best wishes! My greetings to your husband and children, and to the rest of the family.

Your affectionate brother
Henrik Ibsen

The inhibited and semi-formal style, even allowing for the fact that he probably intended it to be read out at the celebrations, is that of a deeply divided man. They celebrated his birthday in Skien a week later, and sent him a telegram, to which he replied in an exceedingly formal letter of one sentence containing fifty-eight words.

On 31 March August Lindberg staged *Hedda Gabler* in Gothenburg, with his bright new star Julia Håkonsson (fresh from attempting Hjørdis in *The Vikings at Helgeland* and Svanhild in *Love's Comedy*) as Hedda and himself as Brack. It seems (as one would expect) to have been the most successful production of the play to that date; Karl Warburg, writing in *Handelstidningen,* though he felt that the play itself "could scarcely arouse any enthusiasm," found the ensemble playing "a brilliant triumph." Julia Håkonsson's performance he thought "among the finest that our audiences have had the chance to see during the past decade," and Lindberg's interpretation of Brack he found "magisterially executed."[17]

That spring the Freie Bühne in Berlin planned a party, and a member

[17] Per Lindberg, p. 308.

who was a waxwork artist conceived the idea of making a model of Ibsen to serve as a kind of patron saint to the proceedings. The man wrote to Ibsen asking if he would lend one of his old suits to dress the model in; but clothes, like religion, were a sacrosanct subject as far as Ibsen was concerned. "Be so good as to tell this gentleman," he informed Julius Elias, "that I do not wear 'old suits,' nor do I wish a wax model of myself to be clothed in an 'old suit.' Obviously I cannot give him a new one, and I therefore suggest that he order one from my tailor, Herr Fries, of Maximilianstrasse, Munich."[18] Whether they solved the problem with a costume, or whether they dropped the idea, is not on record.

There was an Ibsen festival in Vienna that April, with productions (at different theatres) of *The Pretenders, An Enemy of the People* and *The Wild Duck.* Ibsen was invited to attend, and accepted; it was the first time he had been there since the Exhibition of 1873. The productions were, like those in London and Berlin earlier in the year, a mixture of success and failure. *The Pretenders* on 11 April went splendidly. Ibsen was called after each act, and at the banquet which followed at the Kaiserhof, where the guests were mostly young enthusiasts for the "new naturalism" which Ibsen had long since left behind him, he was acclaimed in both verse and prose. He replied in two lengthy Germanic sentences, saying that when anything made him happy and moved him it "became a poem," and that he thought that this occasion too would "become a poem." (There is no evidence that it ever did; the "joy of life" appears in his last works only as something never achieved or, if achieved, lost.) Later that evening a radical Member of Parliament expressed his amazement that a fellow-radical should sit covered in medals. Ibsen replied: "I like to wear these orders which I have received from my king when I am with younger friends who I anticipate may continue celebrating into the small hours. It reminds me that I need to keep within certain limits"—evidence, as Halvdan Koht remarks, of the division between Ibsen and the Ibsenites.[19]

Radicals of every kind were claiming Ibsen as their champion. Some Viennese ladies, predictably, came to thank him for the pioneering he had done on behalf of their sex, and to name him an honorary member of the Society for Extended Female Education. It was in vain for him to protest that *A Doll's House* was not specifically about women's rights but about the rights of humanity in general, and he doubtless deemed it discourteous to point out that the play represented a phase in his work which he had now left behind him. A Freie Bühne was founded while he was in the city, on the model of the one in Berlin (another had been established in Munich likewise), and they elected him to honorary membership. *An Enemy of the People* went well on 15 April; but evidence that his more recent plays were less admired came the following evening when the newly-

[18] Elias, "Ibsenminne af hans tyske oversætter," p. 404.
[19] Koht, II, 235.

founded Deutsches Volkstheater opened its doors with a production of *The Wild Duck*, with Friedrich Mitterwurzer (who had toured *Ghosts* through the United States) as Hjalmar Ekdal. The play at first went well, and Ibsen was called after the second act; but thereafter it evoked increasing disapproval, expressed in whistles. At the final curtain his supporters countered with applause, and the hubbub of the rival factions did not cease until Ibsen, waving his hat at those who were applauding, left the theatre. Although the premiere had been sold out, so few people came afterwards that the production had to close after three performances. The director remarked that he had felt it a duty to open his theatre with an Ibsen play, but that it had cost him money.

On 18 April Ibsen's stay in Vienna was concluded with a final banquet at the Hotel Continental, given by the writers and journalists of the city. Many speeches were made, and the actor Max Devrient greeted him as the great liberator who had given mankind an "inner freedom," banished ghosts, and had the courage to admit daylight into corners that had previously been kept in darkness. Ibsen, as before, replied briefly ("I am no speaker," he declared), thanking the city both for the "warm understanding" they had showed him, and also for the "honourable opposition" which some had felt bound to express.

His return home, which he had hoped to make two days earlier, was further postponed, for he was persuaded to go on from Vienna to Budapest, where on 20 April the National Theatre gave a special performance of *A Doll's House* in his honour. Ibsen's reception here exceeded anything that he had yet experienced. When he took his call on the stage, and made a short speech of thanks in German, the cheering was such that, according to a newspaper report, he "made huge eyes through his even huger spectacles." The enthusiasm was not confined to the theatre, but followed him out into the street, where the students so mobbed him that he had to take refuge in a carriage. Two banquets were held for him. The first was official, with members of Parliament, distinguished scientists and men of letters, and the press; the second, much more to his taste, was given by the students, two of whom made speeches of welcome in Norwegian. In his reply, Ibsen recalled that as a young man (at Grimstad) he had written a poem in honour of the Magyar freedom fighters.[20]

Ibsen's stay in Budapest was an unqualified triumph. The Hungarian press interviewed him on every possible subject, and German journalists who were present noted with amusement how passionately they questioned him and how little Ibsen answered. Strindberg, in the process of divorcing Siri von Essen, read of Ibsen's imperial progress with indignation. "The 'Lonely One,'" he wrote to Ola Hansson on 12 May, "has degenerated into a touring prima donna . . . a self-styled aristocrat who greets the new

[20] *Ibid.*, pp. 236–37, C.E., **XIX**, 453–54.

aristocracy in the shape of women and artisans. . . . Farewell Ibsen, my youth's ideal!"[21]

Ibsen returned to Munich in the last days of April. While he had been away, two highly controversial premieres of his plays had taken place. On 20 April, the night that Ibsen was mobbed in Budapest, *Hedda Gabler* was performed at the Vaudeville Theatre in London, thanks to the enthusiasm of two American actresses resident there, both ardent feminists, Elizabeth Robins and Marion Lea. Such unkind comments as had been passed on the play by the Scandinavian and German critics paled before the abuse poured forth by the English press:

> It was like a visit to the Morgue. . . . There they all lay on their copper couches, fronting us, and waiting to be owned. . . . There they all were, false men, wicked women, deceitful friends, sensualists, egotists, piled up in a heap behind this screen of glass, which we were thankful for. . . . What a horrible story! What a hideous play!
>
> Clement Scott in the *Daily Telegraph*

> Hideous nightmare of pessimism . . . the play is simply a bad escape of moral sewage-gas. . . . Hedda's soul is a-crawl with the foulest passions of humanity.
>
> *Pictorial World*

> Tedious turmoil of knaves and fools.
>
> *The People*

> Mean and sordid philosophy. . . . Insidious nastiness of photographic studies of vice and morbidity.
>
> *Saturday Review*

> Funereal clown [i.e., Ibsen]. . . . For sheer unadulterated stupidity, for inherent meanness and vulgarity, for pretentious triviality . . . no Bostonian novel or London penny novelette has surpassed *Hedda Gabler*.
>
> Robert Buchanan in *Illustrated London News*[22]

For the Ibsen enthusiasts, however, it was a great occasion, for this was plainly an unusually perceptive and powerful production. William Archer, who never allowed his passion for the cause to blind his eyes to bad acting, wrote in *The World*: "In rapidity and subtlety of intellect, I find it hard to think of a woman in the whole range of the drama who can rival Hedda Gabler; and Miss Robins makes us feel throughout that her own mind could work as rapidly as Hedda's. She played upon her victims with the crisp certainty of touch of the consummate virtuoso. Behind every speech we felt the swift intellectual process that gave it birth. . . . Miss Robins never forgot that Hedda is neither a hypocrite nor a fiend. I do not hesitate to call her performance in the last act the finest piece of modern

---

[21] *August Strindbergs brev,* VIII, 266–67.

[22] William Archer, "The Mausoleum of Ibsen," pp. 81–82.

tragedy within my recollection. Sarah Bernhardt could not have done it better; and it is long since Sarah attempted a scene so well worth doing." Bernard Shaw, who saw the performance from the back of the pit "in company with a large and intelligent contingent of Fabians,"[23] wrote to Elizabeth Robins that same evening: "You may safely accept all the compliments you get about the play and the part. I never had a more tremendous sensation in a theatre than that which began when everybody saw that the pistol shot was coming at the end. . . . You were sympathetically unsympathetic, which was the exact solution of the central difficulty of playing Hedda."[24] Thomas Hardy (who the previous Easter had noted in his diary that "Ibsen's edifying is too obvious") went, and was sufficiently impressed to pay a second visit when it was revived in 1893. Oscar Wilde admired it too. "I felt pity and terror," he wrote to Lord Lytton, son of the novelist, "as though the play had been Greek."[25]

The production made at least one important convert. Henry James had been trying for two years to appreciate "the northern Henry," as he called him, and had failed. "How provincial all these Dear Norsefolk," he had written to Edmund Gosse in 1890. "They all affect me like intensely domestic fowl plucking behind a hedge—the big bristling hedge of Germany." He saw the bad Marie Fraser production of A Doll's House, which did not help; Rosmersholm he found dreary, and Ghosts shocked him. By April 1891 he was still unconvinced. "Must I think these things works of skill?" he asked Gosse, dismissing them as "moral tales in dialogue—without the objectivity, the visibility of the drama."[26] But Elizabeth Robins's performance as Hedda won him over; six weeks later, after sitting through three performances, he wrote an essay on the play, which appeared that June in the New Review.

James's feelings towards Ibsen remained ambivalent. The plays still seemed to him (as to Yeats) grey and parochial, even ugly; yet what contemporary writer had probed so deeply into the depths of the human, and especially the feminine mind, and how could one forget those awkward questions which he was forever asking? How unlike James's own settings were "the ugly interior on which his curtain inexorably rises, and which, to be honest, I like for the queer associations it has taught us to respect; the hideous carpet and wall-paper and curtains (one may answer for them), the conspicuous stove, the lonely centre table, the 'lamps with green shades,' as in the sumptuous first act of The Wild Duck, the pervasive air of small interests and standards, the sign of limited local life!" And yet, James reflected, "the oddest thing happens in connection with this effect— the oddest extension of sympathy or relaxation of prejudice. What happens is that we feel that whereas, if Ibsen were weak or stupid or vulgar, this

[23] Bernard Shaw, Collected Letters, 1874–1897, p. 291.
[24] Ibid., p. 292.
[25] The Letters of Oscar Wilde, ed. Rupert Hart-Davis (London, 1962), p. 293.
[26] Leon Edel, Henry James, The Treacherous Years (London, 1969), pp. 23 ff.

parochial or suburban stamp would only be a stick to beat him with, it acts, as the case stands, and in the light of his singular masculinity, as a sort of substitute—a little clumsy, if you like—for charm." He went on to praise Ibsen's "remarkable art, his admirable talent for producing an intensity of interest by means incorruptibly quiet, by that almost demure preservation of the appearance of the usual in which we see him juggle with difficulty and danger and which constitutes, as it were, his only coquetry. There are people who are indifferent to these mild prodigies; there are others for whom they will always remain the most charming privilege of art. . . . His recurrent ugliness of surface, as it were, is a sort of proof of his fidelity to the real, in a spare, strenuous, democratic community; just as the same peculiarity is one of the sources of his charmless fascination—a touching vision of strong forces struggling with a poverty, a bare provinciality, of life. . . . He deals with a homely and unæsthetic society, he harps on the string of conduct, and he actually talks of stockings and legs, in addition to other improprieties. He is not pleasant enough nor casual enough; he is too far from Piccadilly and our glorious standards." In a shrewd and memorable phrase, he summed up Ibsen's peculiar magic as "the operation of talent without glamour." The plays which James himself was about to write owe an obvious debt to Ibsen (*The Other House* carries clear echoes of both *Hedda Gabler* and *Little Eyolf*) ; but the most important lessons which Ibsen had to teach him as a dramatist James sadly failed to learn.

Hedda Gabler, originally presented only for five matinées, did well enough at the Vaudeville for the manager of the theatre to transfer it to the evening bill, where it ran for five weeks and was taken off at the height of its success. Archer seems to have sent Ibsen a somewhat coloured account of the whole business, for Ibsen, sending him two signed photographs for Elizabeth Robins and Marion Lea ("I have, as you will see, written the inscription in Norwegian and beg you to be so kind as to append an English translation underneath"), expressed (29 April) his delight at Archer's information that *Hedda Gabler* "has enjoyed a good and uncontested [!] reception on its performance in London."

A week after the London premiere of *Hedda Gabler,* on 28 April, Paris had its first chance to see *The Wild Duck,* when André Antoine presented it at the Théâtre Libre, with himself as Hjalmar Ekdal—the first production of any Ibsen play in France apart from the same theatre's *Ghosts* eleven months earlier. It had a very mixed reception; some of the spectators showed their displeasure by quacking like the bird of the title, and it is indicative of how little the play was understood that Francisque Sarcey, writing in *Le Temps* (4 May), thought that Hedvig had shot herself out of grief because the wild duck was dead. *"La pièce est obscure,"* he concluded. *"Elle est incohérente; elle est insupportable."* Yet again, it excited a sizeable minority, especially among the young and the avant-garde.

"Ibsen's fame," wrote Georges Viollat in the *Revue Blanche* (1891, pp. 222 ff.), "increases daily. It already equals that of Tolstoy"; and Edmond de Goncourt, whose efforts at play-writing had brought him nothing but failure, complained in his diary that to be noticed in the French theatre one needed to be a Scandinavian. The unconverted included Romain Rolland, who wrote to Lugné-Poe that November: "I am sorry that all his works are getting into France; what have they to do with us? He is a man; but he is not of our race; let him stay in his fjords, the barbarian!"[27]

The flood of Ibsen productions continued. On 10 May *The Pretenders* was staged by Max Grübe at the Schauspielhaus in Berlin, and was a big success. The next evening Londoners had their first chance to see *The Lady from the Sea*, presented (for the usual five matinees) at Terry's Theatre in Eleanor Marx-Aveling's translation, and directed by her shady husband, Dr. Edward Aveling (using the inappropriate pseudonym of Nelson). William Archer thought it "an inadequate production," and Bernard Shaw, in a letter to Ellen Terry a year later, recalled how he "went into an afternoon performance and found a poor ungifted, dowdy, charmless young woman [Rose Meller] struggling pathetically with Ibsen's *Lady from the Sea*. She was doing her best; and I thanked my stars that I was not a dramatic critic, and had not to go home and tell her that after all her study and toil she had done far more harm than good."[28] *The Times* dismissed the play with contempt: "It offers no opportunity for powerful acting, while its general analysis of character is shallow and its dialogue commonplace. . . . Studies in morbid heredity are very well in a scientific treatise. On the stage, put forward as a public entertainment, they tend to perplex, irritate and repel, besides being useless for any practical purpose."

Some time at the end of May *A Doll's House* had its first performance in France, privately at the salon of Madame Aubernon de Nerville, the part-original of Proust's Madame Verdurin.[29] "*Malheureusement*," Ibsen wrote to her on 22 May (though the French wording was probably Sigurd's, since the letter is in his hand except for Ibsen's signature): "*il m'est impossible de quitter Munich, et je le regrette infiniment, car j'aurais été enchanté d'assister à la representation de Maison de Poupée.*" A few days later the same play was revived for yet another single matinee in London, at the Criterion Theatre, with Rose Norreys as Nora.

As he was not writing a play this year, Ibsen decided to take a summer holiday. On 8 May he had written to Nils Lund that he was "vaguely thinking of taking a trip north." On 17 May, he told Julius Hoffory, who was threatening to descend on him in Munich, that he was "considering going away for a longish time." Suzannah was planning to revisit her

---

[27] *Correspondance: Romain Rolland, Lugné-Poe, 1894–1901,* ed. Jacques Robichez (Paris, 1957), p. 17.

[28] Bernard Shaw, *Collected Letters, 1874–1897,* p. 348.

[29] Unfortunately Proust was not at the performance. He did not join her circle until a few months later.

relatives in Norway, but Ibsen seems to have been thinking only in terms of Denmark. "It is still uncertain whether I myself shall come as far as Norway," he wrote to Didrik Grønvold on 6 June. "I am for the moment tired and sated with travelling, of which I have had so much this year, first in Berlin and then in Austria and Hungary. I should like best to settle for a while by the beautiful Sound, which I so love and where I can see hundreds of ships sail in and out."

On 11 June he thanked Jacob Hegel for sending him 3,000 crowns and for the news that an eighth edition of *Peer Gynt* and a sixth edition of *Love's Comedy* were in the press (a third edition of *Catiline* had appeared earlier in the year). At the end of the month *The Vikings at Helgeland* was revived in Munich at the Residenztheater, and Ibsen attended it. Early in July he left for the north, leaving his furniture, paintings and other possessions in the apartment at Maximilianstrasse. He would have been surprised, possibly incredulous, if anyone had suggested to him that he would never return to Germany again, and that he was to spend the remaining fifteen years of his life in Norway, broken only by two brief visits to Denmark and Sweden. His twenty-seven years of self-imposed exile were over.

PART SIX

The Top of a Cold Mountain

29

A Lion at Evening

1891

Ibsen returned to Christiania on 16 July. Reporters from the two left-wing dailies, *Dagbladet* and *Verdens Gang,* greeted him at the quayside as he disembarked from the SS *Melchior,* and *Dagbladet* welcomed him on behalf of "all liberal-minded Norwegian men and women." Embarrassingly, the right-wing papers welcomed him too, as a possible counterweight to Bjørnson. "Our great and celebrated author," wrote *Aftenposten* on the day after his arrival, in language reminiscent of Dr. Rørlund in the final act of *The Pillars of Society,* "is now visiting his fatherland after several years absence. His stay will, again, be brief; but we must express the hope that it may be long enough for him to assure himself that his compatriots, too, are able to appreciate the fame he has acquired by his distinguished works, and the honour he has thereby helped to bestow upon his country. As our readers will be aware, we do not share Ibsen's view of life or of social conditions; but we are well able to perceive and admire the mighty poetic power which his country has fostered in him— and we would wish that Herr Ibsen could emancipate himself from the bitter feelings which have for so long caused him to prefer other countries to his fatherland. For, after all, it is from the spiritual soil of his homeland that Henrik Ibsen has drawn his best strength and, should he decide to settle permanently among his fellow-countrymen, his sharp pen and acute critical mind would soon find worthy subjects here, where vulgarity still dominates the intellectual scene, and where superficiality and dilettantism hold sway under Bjørnson's leadership."

The words could scarcely have been more calculated to make Ibsen catch the next ship back to Germany.

He stayed in fact only a day or two in Christiania; the main purpose of his visit was to make the sea voyage up the west coast to the North Cape. He had never been farther north than Trondhjem, and by the time he returned his oft-expressed yearning for the open sea must have been amply satisfied. There are few more spectacular landscapes in the world than the west coast of Norway viewed from offshore, and one suspects that this voyage may considerably have influenced his subsequent decision to remain. Suzannah did not accompany him. Some commentators have adduced this as evidence that they had quarrelled, but a more likely reason is that her by now crippling gout and rheumatism would have made the journey, with its continual climbing and descending of narrow stairways, agony for her; and she had seen it before.

He returned to Christiania on 7 August, and spent the next ten days at the Grand Hotel. He had already decided to remain for some months; on 11 August, thanking August Lindberg for inviting him to attend a performance at Gothenburg "on my projected return to Germany," he explained: "I am not planning to go south just yet, but intend to spend the winter here."

Georg Brandes was also staying at the Grand. After the suspicions and estrangements of recent years, they were now friends again, and on 15 August Brandes gave a dinner for him. Ibsen was at first reluctant to attend, agreed only on the understanding that it would be limited to a few friends, and was much disturbed when he discovered that a number of left-wing writers, artists, and journalists had been invited. The resultant occasion was anything but happy. "Yesterday," wrote Brandes to Alexander Kielland the next day, "we had a small dinner of about twenty persons which I arranged for the Troll King, H.I., and which failed most comically when he found all the praise that was showered upon him insufficient, and behaved most coarsely and ill-temperedly."[1] The painter Erik Werenskiold, who was present, has left a fuller account:

Well, the evening arrived, and we were around 30–40 [sic] people. I was fortunately placed so as to be able to see and hear everything. I had Fru Augusta Sinding to table; Ibsen, who liked young ladies, had Fru Kitty Kielland—not exactly beautiful nor young, but a well-known painter and hard-boiled bluestocking. He was clearly not much pleased. After a while Brandes rose and said: "He who comes at the eleventh hour is just as good as he who comes at the seventh or ninth hour; but there is a difference, none the less; we of the North have come at the seventh hour; we understood Ibsen earlier than others." Then Ibsen began to shake his heavy grey head. Brandes was somewhat taken aback and began a long explanation to show how we had understood him before the rest, but the more he explained the more Ibsen shook his head; and when we finally stood to drink Ibsen's health he merely half-rose from his chair and said: "One could say much about that speech"—but did not enlarge further.

The atmosphere was oppressive. Then O. Thommessen [the editor of *Verdens Gang*], who had Constance Bruun to table, thanked Ibsen on behalf of the

[1] *Brandes Brevveksling*, IV, 368.

actors for all the great roles he had written for them. "I have not written roles for actors and actresses," snorted Ibsen. "I have written to portray human beings, not to create roles."

Then Kitty Kielland began to talk earnestly to Ibsen. She said she thought everything worthwhile in Norway had been accomplished by people from the west coast. "You are from the west, are you not?" she asked. "I am Norwegian," replied Ibsen, "but I understand that you are from Stavanger [in the south-west]." A little later they were discussing *Hedda Gabler*. Kitty said she could not stand Mrs. Elvsted—"those women who sacrifice themselves for men." "I write to portray people," said Ibsen, "and I am completely indifferent to what fanatical bluestockings like or do not like."

Whew! At last dinner was finished. But then Ibsen got hold of my wife, whom he knew well from Munich, took her under one arm and her sister under the other, and strolled up and down the room with them in the most sparkling humour.

Later that evening Thommessen mentioned to Ibsen that Brandes was going to apply for the professorship after Skavlan. "Well," said Ibsen, "then he'd better not talk about Norwegian literature, because he doesn't know anything about it." It became rumoured that Thommessen repeated this to Brandes later, when they were having a drink in the café. This may just have been gossip. But the next day Brandes returned to Copenhagen. What a party![2]

Ibsen disliked big gatherings. Johannes Steen, who became Prime Minister that year, invited him and Bjørnson to an official reception. "So the animals are to be put on show," commented Ibsen; but he accepted. There was a buffet supper, occupying several rooms. "In one stood Bjørnson, the centre of a large circle of admiring guests; in another stood Ibsen, alone, holding his plate and facing a corner containing a tiled stove, presenting an unapproachable back to the company."[3] On the other hand, he enjoyed small, select parties, especially if he was given an attractive young lady to take to the table, and then he could talk charmingly and rewardingly. He disliked the custom of paying thank-you visits after a party, and would send a visiting-card on which he had written beneath his name: "Active member of the Anti-Visit Society."[4]

On 17 August Ibsen and Suzannah leased (though they did not move in until October) an apartment at 7^B (later 13^B) Viktoria Terrasse, yet another corner-house, situated in the centre of Christiania, only a few minutes from the palace and the theatre. He saw two plays during the next couple of weeks. One was Strindberg's *The Father*, performed at the Tivoli Theatre by a Danish touring company under Hans Riber Hunderup, who had directed and played the lead in the original production of the play four years earlier at his Casino Theatre in Copenhagen. It was a tre-

---

[2] Bergliot Ibsen, pp. 147–49.
[3] Bull, *Tradisjoner og minner*, p. 99.
[4] *Ibid.*, p. 101.

mendously hot evening, no less than 102° Fahrenheit, and the little theatre was almost empty (the night's takings were only 33 crowns). Ibsen —records one of the actors—sat by himself in a box almost on the stage, "staring at us in lonely majesty." After the interval following the final curtain, when there was to have been a French farce to round off the proceedings, Ibsen and the other spectators had gone, and the theatre was completely empty; one old lady returned as the actors stood bewildered on the stage, but explained that she had only come to collect her programme; then she went home and so did the actors.[5] Ibsen's opinion of the performance is, sadly, not on record.

On 28 August he attended the Christiania Theatre, for the first time since 1874 when they had given *Love's Comedy* and *The League of Youth* for him on the occasion of his first return to Norway. Now they offered *Hedda Gabler*, and Ibsen sat in the place of honour, in the stage box. He was greeted with applause as soon as he was seen, after each act and, thunderously, after the final curtain.

By this time, Ibsen had decided to make Norway his base. "We do not of course intend to stay here all the year round," he wrote Hegel on 5 September, "but to travel as hitherto. So it is just our starting-point which has altered. But we shall stay the winter and I have planned a big new dramatic work which I intend under all circumstances to complete up here. I have not for a long time felt in such good spirits as this summer. The voyage to the North Cape was quite glorious, and my wife has enjoyed the mountain air up at Valders. So my dream of spending a few months by my beloved Sound must be forgotten for this year; but henceforth it will be much easier for me to get down there." He was not in fact to leave Norway for another six years.

On 14 September he was at the theatre again, for the hundredth performance of *The League of Youth*—a figure which none of his other plays had reached. He sat in the stalls, wearing his full panoply of medals, and again was greeted with tumultuous applause, which he acknowledged by rising from his seat and bowing; though, contrary to his custom in Germany, he refused to take a call from the stage. After the performance there was a banquet at the Tivoli Restaurant, at which a speech in Ibsen's honour was made by Schrøder, the man who still steadfastly refused to allow *Ghosts* to be staged at his theatre. Ibsen, to the delight of many present and the discomfiture of a few, devoted his reply to demanding that something should be done, and done quickly, about the building of the new National Theatre, which had so long been promised. He reminded his hearers that shares in the new theatre had been offered to the public as long as sixteen or seventeen years ago, yet no action had been taken. *Aftenposten* reported his speech:

[5] Vilhelm Petersen, *Foran og bag Kulisserne* (Copenhagen, 1931), pp. 57–58.

Were the speaker a member of the building committee, had he the power
and authority of the building committee, he would commit himself to raising a
million *reichsmarks* within a month. Had he total authority, he would undertake to start building within two years. (*Laughter*). "Yes, you may laugh";
but he, the speaker, would not sit and wait for contributions from rich men,
for such contributions did not flow richly. He would go to the State Wine
and Spirits Monopoly and . . . undertake to raise on such-and-such conditions a million at four or five per cent. He was a business man, as (he
trusted) he had shown. . . . He would ask Oskar Blumenthal how he had
erected his beautiful Lessingtheater [in Berlin] in a single year. He would
go to Ludwig Barnay and ask how he had built his fine Berliner Theater,
then to Vienna to ask the director of the Volkstheater how he had raised two
to three millions in eighteen months, then to Zurich, where eighteen months
ago the theatre had been burned down but where they were not going to wait
sixteen or seventeen years to lay a new foundation stone. . . . He had a
dream of a new occasion for celebration. This evening had been the
hundredth performance of his play, a banquet of celebration for 18 October
1869, but if our city was to take its place among the capitals of Europe
there must be a banquet to celebrate the laying of the foundation stone of the
new theatre. . . . This speaker concluded by thanking his listeners for the
kindness they had shown him this evening and expressing the hope that
he would see them again on the occasion of the laying of the new foundation
stone this day two years hence.

The speech, like so many of Ibsen's best, seems to have been spontaneous
(he had opened by explaining that when accepting the invitation to
attend he had made it a condition that he would not have to speak), and
it reminds one how eloquently he could hold forth when he felt deeply about
an issue, as opposed to conventional after-dinner speaking when people
expected nothing but flattery and facile wit.

Most of his listeners that evening were establishment figures; but three
days later he was equally feted by his radical admirers. August Lindberg
and his Swedish company were playing in Christiania that month, at the
Tivoli Theatre, and Ibsen (possibly, one suspects, to needle Schrøder)
expressed a desire to see their production of *Ghosts*. It was some time
since the play had been in their repertory, but Lindberg managed to assemble the original cast; and so at last Ibsen saw it as it had first been
staged in Europe. The audience, mainly young and left-wing, acclaimed
him as their champion. Nor did he only attend their production of *Ghosts*.
The company included a young singer named Sigrid Arnoldson; every
time she sang, he came to the theatre, and when she left Christiania he
was at the railway station with flowers and a portrait of himself.[6]

Yet while both political parties strove to make him their own, there
were still many of the extreme right who regarded him as a pariah, and

[6] Per Lindberg, p. 315.

these included some of his old Holland friends. Christiania was by now full of people who regarded themselves as the originals of various characters in his plays; even the elderly Camilla Collett had improbably claimed to be the inspiration of Ellida in *The Lady from the Sea*. Professor L. L. Daæ, who had been a friend of Ibsen's for years, was convinced that he was the original of Dr. Kroll, the bigoted pedagogue of *Rosmersholm,* and cut Ibsen publicly in the street. More worrying was the number of people who claimed him as a brother-in-arms; he cannot have been pleased when the right-wing poet Kristofer Randers dedicated an aggressive volume to "Henrik Ibsen, the poet of individualism, in deep gratitude for what he has taught me: to write verse and despise the masses."

Suzannah's gout was proving so troublesome that she had gone south with Sigurd to take the cure at Salo on Lake Garda, leaving Ibsen to make the arrangements for moving into their new apartment. He was not, however, alone. He had found a new companion to replace Emilie and Helene. On his return from the North Cape in August he had renewed the acquaintance he had struck up in 1874 with Annette Andersen, the daughter of his old Bergen landlady, Helene Sontum, and her daughter Hildur. Hildur, now twenty-seven, had fulfilled the musical promise of her youth, and was maturing into a distinguished concert pianist. A close and warm friendship quickly developed between her and Ibsen. When he first met her this year she had just returned from a holiday in the mountains, bronzed and fresh—exactly like Hilde Wangel at the latter's first entrance in the play which he was about to write.

In Suzannah's absence Hildur became his constant companion on walks and visits to art galleries and theatres. She even got him to an occasional concert, and helped him with the furnishing of his new apartment. The date 19 September held some particular significance for Ibsen in connection with their relationship, for he subsequently gave her a diamond ring with the date engraved on it, and referred to it in other letters and dedicatory inscriptions. Was it the date of their first meeting in 1874, or their first meeting this year, or did something particular once happen between them on that day? We do not know, just as we do not know whether anything happened on that same date two years earlier between him and Emilie Bardach.[7]

On 7 October they attended a lecture together at the Brothers Hals's Concert Hall, owned by his old friend the piano-maker. It was a notable occasion. The lecturer was a thirty-two-year-old working-class man named Knut Hamsun, who the previous year had caused a sensation with his first novel, the grim autobiographical *Hunger.* The advertised subjects of his three lectures, of which this was the first, were Norwegian Literature,

[7] For a full account of the relationship between Ibsen and Hildur Andersen, see Francis Bull, "Hildur Andersen og Henrik Ibsen" in *Edda* (1957), pp. 47–54.

Psychological Literature, and The Literature of Fashion. It was known, for he had already delivered them in other Norwegian towns, that they contained an attack on both Ibsen and Bjørnson. Hamsun had boldly invited Ibsen to attend and, to the general amazement, up he turned, and sat in seat number one in the front row with Hildur beside him.

Hamsun pulled no punches. "This evening," he began, "I shall be as aggressive, as destructive as possible." He attacked Ibsen, extraordinary as it now seems, for over-simplifying his characters and making them mere mouthpieces. For this, Hamsun largely blamed the literary form which Ibsen had chosen. "A play," he declared, "must always be easy for the gallery as well as the stalls to follow . . . Molière's Miser is only miserly, Shakespeare's Othello only jealous, Iago only a scoundrel, and Rosmer in *Rosmersholm* only noble. . . . I suggest that any psychology which is sufficiently clear, that is to say sufficiently shallow, to be understood and enjoyed in the theatre, is to an indefensible degree a coarse and false psychology."

Hamsun went on to deliver a particular attack on the character of Rosmer. "There is no more strength in his noble body than could be contained in my fist. He crumples aristocratically at the first hint of opposition . . . an exceedingly bourgeois conception of the meaning of aristocracy." One reason for the inadequacy of Ibsen's psychology, he asserted, was "the inherent stiffness and poverty of his emotional life"; and he attacked him for writing too much in "fully-rounded, typical speeches instead of, at least occasionally, in fragments. . . . There has never yet lived a dramatist on this earth who has been a sensitive psychologist. Not as a dramatist. We have grown so accustomed to believe everything the Germans say about Ibsen that we read him pre-conditioned to find wisdom there, determined to find everything good. . . . If anything strikes us as odd, it is not the author's fault that we do not understand him." Ibsen was too often wilfully obscure, as in *The Lady from the Sea*—"a book for Germans. I read and read and . . . cry in despair: 'Damn you, man, talk clearly!' . . . But if I have in any way suggested that Ibsen is a small writer, that he has not earned his fame, that he is not worth much . . . then I have said something I did not intend, and I take it back, take it back most humbly. Ibsen's interest circles continuously around problems; that is his calling as a writer, and it is a sufficient calling. . . . Let Ibsen write about problems and questions, it enriches our literature and occupies our minds; we must naturally be interested in what a man like Ibsen thinks about this and that. . . . I say, too, that more than any other man Ibsen has raised our literature from being the literature of little Norway to the status of world literature, and that only a man of his mighty powers could have achieved this. But I say too, for it is a fact, that his writing is the literature of social questions, and that his personages are characters and types. I say this not in blame, but to state a fact."[8]

Hamsun's contempt for the drama as a literary form, and even his disparagement of Shakespeare as a psychologist, were, one must remember, widely shared by nineteenth-century men of letters; and his condemnation of Ibsen as a man who wrote mainly about social problems has been echoed by many critics since. Bernard Shaw's *Quintessence of Ibsenism*, expanded from his Fabian lecture and published a couple of months before Hamsun's Christiania lectures, widely encouraged this view. To most people then, as (alas) now, he was the author of *The Pillars of Society*, *A Doll's House*, *Ghosts* and *An Enemy of the People*. If it seems incredible now that the author of *Brand*, *Peer Gynt*, *The Lady from the Sea* and *Hedda Gabler* should still have been regarded primarily as a social commentator, we must remember that in these plays, too, he viewed man as a creature at the mercy of social as well as of inner psychological forces—as a thing, in other words, influenced by outward as well as by inward pressures. Today, the outward pressures have changed, the inward pressures remain the same; and *A Doll's House*, *Ghosts* and the rest survive because we are still conscious of those inward pressures. It is odd that Hamsun, who the previous year had published an essay entitled "From the unconscious life of the mind"[9] in which he demanded that writers should investigate the dark and inexplicable powers that haunt and motivate us, should have failed to perceive the true significance of *Rosmersholm*, *The Lady from the Sea* and *Hedda Gabler*. Yet his indictment expressed the irritation of many people with Ibsen then; and his condemnation of him for making his characters speak too roundly, instead of in a broken and fragmentary style, would have been echoed by Strindberg, whose characters jump illogically (as Joyce's and Virginia Woolf's were to) from thought to thought, in a manner which many actors at first find disturbing, but which gradually imposes its own remorseless logic on them and their listeners.

Ibsen, we are told, "sat quiet and serious, with unmoved countenance. . . . His strong blue eyes did not leave the speaker for a minute." Two days later he said to Hildur: "Well, tonight we must go to Herr Hamsun's second lecture." "You don't mean," said she, "that you want to listen to that impudent fellow again?" to which Ibsen replied: "Surely you realize we must go and learn how we are to write."[10] And they attended both that lecture and the third three evenings later. Ibsen is not likely to have bothered over-much about Hamsun's suggestion that he over-simplified his characters; but he must surely have found confirmation in the young man's words of the conviction he himself had already reached that a writer must explore the uncharted waters of the unconscious.

[8] Knut Hamsun, *Paa Turné* (Oslo, 1960), pp. 31–38.
[9] In *Samtiden*, 1890, pp. 325 ff.
[10] Bull, "Hildur Andersen og Henrik Ibsen," pp. 49–50.

Hamsun's lectures held a further interest for Ibsen; they were revealing of something that increasingly intrigued him in his old age—the views of the young. Lugné-Poe, his youthful French champion, records (quoting an unnamed source) that Ibsen, during this first year after his return to Norway, showed an almost obsessive interest in the rising generation, and went out of his way to get to know the new artists and writers of Norway, as though afraid lest he might lose touch with the people who understood his plays most clearly.[11] His interest in Strindberg, a portrait of whom he was about to buy and hang in his study, is further evidence of this; and his next play was to present a confrontation between his own generation and theirs.

On 21 October Ibsen moved into Viktoria Terrasse, and the following month he wrote Hegel asking for a further 2,000 crowns to cover furnishing expenses (he had requested 6,000 on 5 October). Suzannah was still in Italy; and he now initiated the ritual, which was to become so famous, of his daily walk across to the university, where he would check his watch (a "frightful old Waterbury with no chain,"[12] curiously out of keeping with his smart clothes) by the university clock, and down Carl Johan gade to the Grand Hotel. This ritual has been described by many observers; Edvard Brandes noted that as he walked

> he kept his eyes to himself, so that one felt unwilling to greet him even if one knew him, and he was certainly not insulted if you avoided forcing him into a brief acknowledgement of your presence. . . . At the hotel . . . he had a kind of reading-room to himself which in the nineties lay separate from both hotel and restaurant. [The café which he was later to frequent had not yet been built.] But one could visit him there, more conveniently than at his home, if one had an errand to him or some topic of conversation that interested him. And it might happen that he became so interested that he would invite his visitor to take a glass with him. He always expressed his opinions in an individual and stylish form. The great master of dialogue chiselled and hammered out his words in short sentences, well considered, carefully shaped, and anyone who heard his slightly crackling voice and still retains the memory of it must regret not having noted at the time the sharp and forceful observations which emerged from those narrow lips.[13]

Brandes adds the shrewd and probably correct surmise that the Grand Hotel somehow represented "abroad" to him in the same way that the loft in *The Wild Duck* represented the forests of Højdal to Lieutenant Ekdal;

[11] Lugné-Poe, p. 74.

[12] Johnsen, p. 17.

[13] Edvard Brandes, "Henrik Ibsens personlighed," in *Politiken,* 20 March 1928, reprinted in Brandes's *Litterære Tendenser* (Copenhagen, 1968), pp. 231–38. Kristian Glœrsen (pp. 348–49) says that they kept a large armchair for him in his room, with his name on a plaque at the back.

and that had Ibsen been a poet instead of a dramatist no one would have been surprised at his unapproachability.

That November a ghost appeared from the past to prick his conscience. Laura Kieler arrived in Christiania, and wrote Ibsen a letter. One might have expected him to avoid a further meeting with that sad and emotional lady. But her letter must have touched him, for he replied at once:

Dear Laura Kieler!

I received you letter late yesterday evening. Today I am invited out and cannot meet you. But come tomorrow at 2:30, so that we can dine together and talk undisturbed about these things. Note the address: 7ᴮ. You will be most welcome.

Your affectionate
Henrik Ibsen

As an old woman, Laura remembered how they had talked for four hours. She told him her whole story. When she spoke of her hatred of illusion and her determination to look reality in the face, he replied, "You and I are the same kind." He was so moved he wept. She said he must, even at this late stage, tell Georg Brandes the truth, to which he replied: "No, I can't. That's impossible." She said he must think it over and she would return the next day for his answer. He said: "Oh, Laura, Laura, I can't let you go—but you mustn't come tomorrow. No, no, I can't do it. I can't. It's impossible."[14] They never met or corresponded again. Did this really happen, or was it the confused and coloured fantasy of an old lady whose life had been a protracted tragedy? One suspects the latter; but Laura may not have been wrong in supposing that she had given something at least to the character of another cruelly treated model, the deranged Irene in *When We Dead Awaken*.

The same month, Herman Bang, the young Danish writer whom Ibsen had known in Munich, sent him tickets for two lectures he was to give in Christiania, one on Guy de Maupassant and one on *Hedda Gabler*. Ibsen came to both, on 10 and 11 November. At the first, on de Maupassant, Bang thought he had never seen so indifferent a listener. Ibsen "sat staring incessantly into the bottom of his silk hat, as though into the depths of a well." But when Bang spoke of the story, *Une Vie,* in which the heroine is locked in a room with a fly which she cannot catch, and from which she cannot escape, symbolizing the thought of death, Bang suddenly looked at Ibsen. Ibsen had raised his head and was staring at Bang. Such a look, Bang says, he had never seen except at the zoo, when a huge lion, before settling down to sleep at dusk, suddenly, with an indescribable emptiness of spirit, shot a glance from its half-closed eyes at the disappearing daylight. Such a glance Bang now saw in Ibsen's eyes, and

[14] Kinck, pp. 528–31.

the thought went through his mind: "Yes, you should have guessed. He has lived and has achieved everything. Now he has only death awaiting him."

The next evening Bang spoke of *Hedda Gabler*. The hall was full, largely (says Bang) because people wanted to see Ibsen listening to criticisms of himself. It was a perceptive lecture; Bang compared Hedda to the woman in Maupassant's *Notre cœur* who owned a triptych mirror and shut herself up inside it every day for several hours. Ibsen again kept his eyes fixed on the bottom of his hat, so that it was impossible to know whether the lecture was interesting him. The following day Bang met Ibsen in the street. After a sly reference to Hamsun, Ibsen said: "But you were kind to me." Then, giving him a sidelong glance, he added, "At least you read the stage directions." He made no reference to Maupassant and the fly.[15]

On 17 December occurred the first attempt to stage Ibsen commercially in France. Albert Carré, the young director of the Théâtre Vaudeville, impressed by Ibsen's growing reputation in artistic circles, decided to try out *Hedda Gabler* as a matinee piece in the hope of transferring it to the evening bill should it prove a success. It did not. Marthe Brandes, a fashionable actress who was cast as Hedda, made no secret of the fact that she did not understand the play. "People laughed," records Lugné-Poe. "There were smiles at this curious specimen of Scandinavian literature"; and he describes the production as "a crushing failure." Francisque Sarcey wrote in *Le Temps:* "In spite of everything, I am glad this play has been performed. Perhaps after this effort we shall be left in peace. Ibsen is now dead in France."[16]

Despite the failure of *Hedda Gabler* on the stages of Scandinavia, 1891 had, thanks mainly to payments from German and Austrian theatres and various reprints, been a good year financially—Ibsen's best, indeed, since 1880:

	crowns
Royalties for *An Enemy of the People* at Wien Burgtheater	2,259
Fee for *The Pillars of Society* at Munich Hoftheater	123
Fee from Heinemann for English edn. of *Hedda Gabler*	2,720
Fee for *Hedda Gabler* at Svenska Teater,[17] Stockholm	500
Royalties for *A Doll's House* in Milan	88
Fee for *Hedda Gabler* at Christiania Theatre	2,500
Fee for *Hedda Gabler* at Svenska Teatern,[17] Stockholm	250

[15] Herman Bang, "Hedda Gabler," in *Tilskueren*, October–November 1892, pp. 827–38; Lugné-Pœ, pp. 91–93. Bang's lecture includes a reference to "a London journalist, almost unknown," who claims that he has often taken Hedda Gabler in to dinner. This obscure figure was Bernard Shaw.

[16] Nyholm, pp. 51–55; Lugné-Pœ, pp. 23–27.

[17] Formerly Nya Teater; the name had been changed in 1888.

	crowns
Fees from August Lindberg for *A Doll's House* and *The Vikings at Helgeland*	250
English monies from William Archer	57
Royalties for *An Enemy of the People* at Wien Burgtheater (extra perf.)	160
Royalties for *An Enemy of the People* and *Hedda Gabler* at Munich Hoftheater	420
3rd edn. of *Catiline*	540
8th edn. of *Peer Gynt*	1,815
6th edn. of *Love's Comedy*	800
Unspecified royalties from Royal Theatre, Copenhagen	772
Further monies from William Archer	90
Unspecified royalties from Wien Burgtheater	1,548
Royalties for *The Vikings at Helgeland* at Munich Hoftheater (1 perf.)	96
3rd edn. of *Lady Inger of Østraat*	747
6th edn. of *Poems*	1,020
Unspecified royalties from Munich Hoftheater	296
Fee for *Ghosts* at Bergen	160
Fee for Danish tour of *Hedda Gabler*	40
Royalties for *The Pillars of Society* at Mannheim Hoftheater (2 perfs.)	53
Royalties from Giacomo Brizzi, Milan	39
Unspecified royalties from Felix Bloch (German agent)	2,120
	19,463 £1,081

Thus, at the age of sixty-three, Ibsen, for the second time in his career, earned over a thousand pounds in one year. The fact that he received no payments for Norwegian productions of any of his earlier plays (apart from a few performances of *Ghosts* at Bergen) does not, of course, mean that none of them was staged. On the contrary, the 1890–91 season at the Christiania Theatre included revivals of *The League of Youth, A Doll's House, The Lady from the Sea, The Vikings at Helgeland* and *Hedda Gabler*. But as the theatre had paid him in each case a lump sum for the rights, these extra performances brought him nothing. He was as dependent as ever on book sales and German theatre royalties.

30

The Master Builder

1892

On one occasion when visiting the Andersens, Ibsen met Hildur's cousin, a young doctor named Christian Sontum. The two became good friends, and one of Dr. Sontum's children, Bolette, who later settled in America, vividly recalled (in English) her first impression of Ibsen during that winter of 1891–92:

> Ibsen came a great deal to our house, and I remember well the first time we children were allowed to see him. We were at my uncle's. My little brother and I were to play a duet sonata by Beethoven for the famous guest. We were both very frightened. I can still feel my fingers getting cold as they touched the keys. When we rose I sent a timid, beseeching glance at the old man standing in the doorway, in his long black frock coat with the broad lapels, which he always wore with the pride of a dandy. He came over to us at once and said: "How wonderful! How wonderful!" so kindly that our dread for the great silent old man disappeared at once. To him the simplest accomplishment of a child was always a wonder. No doubt it was our complete self-possession that awed him. Ibsen's real knowledge of the music was little better than our own.
>
> He had no idea of how to treat children and addressed one by the formal "De" (You) instead of the familiar "Du" (Thou), when I was only eight years old. That winter he came often to our house for dinner with a few other friends. He was always very prompt. . . . I remember once we children went to speak to him while he was in the drawing-room. My mother was called out and my father was still busy with his patients; no other guests arrived, so we felt it our own duty to entertain our guest. My younger sister promptly asked: "Would you like to play dolls with us?" Ibsen wrinkled his heavy white eyebrows, but in a moment was ready, looking at though he were going to do a serious job, but meant to do it well. She trotted out of the room and soon came back loaded with dolls, dolls of all sizes and in all conditions, dolls with heads and without. She placed them all in his lap, and

told him all their names, giving him a maternal account of their rag and bisque tragedies.

One specimen, the doll Mette, who was perhaps worse-looking than any, had once been a great beauty in a wonderful red and white dress. Now she was headless and legless and of course my sister's pet. Mette had to have an honorary position on Ibsen's knee. My father opened the door just as the master of the Great Doll's House was taking all our dolls for a ride.[1]

Another affectionate recollection of Ibsen that winter comes from a young actress, Elisabeth Dybwad. The actors of Christiania were holding a celebration at Tivoli to raise money for their building fund, and a bookseller had presented a complete bound set of Ibsen's works to be put up for auction. Elisabeth Dybwad was chosen to go up to Ibsen's apartment and ask him to write a few words in, or at any rate sign, one of the volumes, so that they would fetch a better price. On 21 February she went along with five volumes, and was duly admitted to the presence.

> He was very friendly and asked if all his works were contained in those five volumes.
>
> "No," I replied. "Each of the nineteen plays has a volume to itself."
>
> "What!" he said. "Have I written nineteen plays? That's many too many for one man, you must agree. What shall I write?" he asked.
>
> "I think it'd be enough if you wrote your name in one of the volumes— say, *Catiline*."
>
> "No, I must write a verse," he said. "But must you have it at once? I can't write poetry by artificial light."
>
> "No," I replied. "There's no hurry. Perhaps I might come back in a day or two?"
>
> "You can collect it tomorrow," said Ibsen.
>
> Next day, in the morning, I collected the book. In *Catiline* he had written a verse which, that same day, was telegraphed around the world—the postscript to "Burned Ships":

> At long last he dismounted,
> Found open every door.
> Might not this homeless wanderer
> Have come somewhat before?[2]

This verse, as Elisabeth Dybwad says, received wide publicity, not only in Norway, and was taken as a sign that Ibsen now felt totally at home in Christiania. And indeed, his letters of this year refer repeatedly to an unexpected sense of peace and euphoria. The set of signed volumes fetched over 400 crowns.

On 14 January *The Vikings at Helgeland* had been performed at the Moscow Little Theatre—the first Ibsen play to be staged in Russia since

[1] Bolette Sontum, "Personal Recollections of Ibsen," in the *Bookman*, XXXVII (New York, 1913), 247–56.

[2] Elisabeth Dybwad, "Et Ibsen-minde," in *Urd, Ibsen-nummer* (Oslo, 1928), p. 158.

A Doll's House eight years earlier. Several of his later plays had apparently offended the Tsar's censor, but they seem to have enjoyed a kind of underground circulation.

That February, Hildur went to Vienna to pursue her music studies. Possibly her parents felt that, platonic as her relationship with Ibsen was, they were seeing a little too much of each other. The tongues of Christiania had begun to gossip. He corresponded frequently with her while she was away, by both letter and telegram. Hildur, who lived to be ninety-two, kept these letters almost—not, alas, quite—until her death.

On 7 March he attended the dress rehearsal of a new production of *Peer Gynt* at the Christiania Theatre—the first time he had seen the play staged—and two evenings later he was at the premiere. Bjørn Bjørnson played Peer, and a young actress named Johanne Dybwad was Solveig; she was later to be perhaps the greatest of all Aases. The production drew full houses for fifty performances.

Despite his abandonment of verse as a medium for public self-expression, Ibsen had developed the habit, when preparing a play, of composing a short poem to enshrine the theme, and on 16 March he wrote such a poem relating to the play that was taking shape in his head. It is the only one of these poems which has survived:

> They dwelt, those two, in so cosy a house
> In autumn and winter weather.
> Then came the fire—and the house was gone.
> They must search the ashes together.
>
> For down in the ashes a jewel lies hid
> Whose brightness the flames could not smother,
> And search they but faithfully, he and she,
> 'Twill be found by one or the other.
>
> But e'en though they find it, the gem they lost,
> The enduring jewel they cherished—
> She ne'er will recover her vanished faith,
> Nor he the joy that has perished.[3]

On 30 March, in the intervals of writing to Hildur, he sent a long and warm letter (in Norwegian, which she had now learned) to Helene Raff in Munich:

Dearest Frøken Raff,

Allow me to send you my warmest, my most heartfelt thanks for your dear letter, which reached me on my birthday, and for your wonderfully beautiful picture, which I had the inexpressible joy to

---

[3] A. G. Chater's translation. Ibsen incorporated this poem, with one alteration ("peace" instead of "faith" in the penultimate line) in his first draft of *Little Eyolf* two years later. But he deleted the poem in revision.

receive some days ago. It now hangs in a good place in my study, so that I can have it constantly before my eyes, and constantly feed my sight with that prospect of the wide open sea—and long even more to see again the dear, dear, enchanting young girl who has created this exquisite little work of art. And who, while creating it, has been thinking of me, far away. Ah, if only I could have the chance to thank you personally, face to face—thank you as I would most wish to! I love the sea. Your painting takes my thoughts and my mood to the thing I love. Yes—you have indeed enriched me for life with your gift. Now little Solveig [the painting she had done for his birthday two years earlier] shall hang beside the painting of the sea. Thus I shall have you collected and complete before me—and within me—

My memories of Munich arose so powerfully in me when I received these greetings from you in words and colours. How happy I would be to be there again! I feel so deeply at home there. But there is so much in life which blocks and frustrates our wishes and longings.

You have achieved an extraordinary fluency in Norwegian. Do you never think of taking a summer holiday up here? Of dreaming a bright, fleeting summer night's dream among the mountains or out at sea?

Answer me this, dearest Frøken Raff. Would you like to? It would give me inexpressible pleasure—should you have the time and the opportunity—to receive some further lines from you.

> Your affectionate and grateful
> Henrik Ibsen

But she does not seem to have written to him again; or if she did, he did not reply.

Ibsen had seen little if anything of Bjørnson since his return to Norway. Sigurd, however, had put himself very much in Bjørnson's good books by his polemics against the union with Sweden, and Bjørnson invited him to stay at Aulestad. He paid several visits there and, as Ibsen had forecast on his return from Schwaz seven years earlier, fell in love with Bjørnson's young daughter, Bergliot. They became engaged; Bergliot has left a pretty account of how it happened:

Much had been written and said of Sigurd, and we young ones were greatly excited at the prospect of his visit. One night I dreamed we were engaged, and was foolish enough to tell my brothers and sisters. They so teased me about it that I did not dare to show myself when he arrived, but hid behind a curtain. I didn't see much of him the first few days; he spent most of the time talking with Father. They had long conversations up in his study. Sigurd was very serious, and I didn't altogether like him. But one day he was standing with Father on the upstairs verandah and I was standing on the one below.

Then suddenly Sigurd smiled and looked down at me with his beautiful eyes, and from that day I loved him, as I have loved him ever since . . .

We were very different. He was a true Ibsen, I a true Bjørnson, and a bigger contrast could not be imagined. Sigurd was by nature very melancholic; but how many times did I not succeed in making him laugh! When we got engaged he wanted to give me a ring, but I asked him instead to give me a concertina, as I did not much like ornaments. Sigurd could never forget this; it made him laugh even when he was old. But I got my concertina, and no girl ever received a more beautiful engagement gift. It was silver-plated, and sounded like a full orchestra. I still love to play it [she wrote in 1947] and then I remember the days at Aulestad when I used to play for him. The sun shone, the sky was blue, and I sat out in the fields with my concertina and sang, while Sigurd lay in the grass beside me and laughed till there were tears in his eyes.[4]

The Bjørnsons were delighted, the Ibsens (according to Bergliot) less so. Certain "so-called friends who were opposed to the engagement did their best to sustain Ibsen's distrust. . . . When Father and Mother came to Christiania they were not received with open arms as they had expected, and Father's enthusiasm and happiness changed. He became furious with Ibsen."[5] Bergliot adds that her father's extremes of mood must always have had an unsettling effect on Ibsen, and that Ibsen consequently avoided him on his return to Norway because "he knew what emotional explosions Father could arouse in him." On his return to Aulestad, Bjørnson wrote characteristically to his daughter:

Aulestad, 21 March 1892

Dear Bergliot,

You are much too young to understand all the *evil* Ibsen has done to me. It could all have been forgotten. But he came back to Norway without sending me a greeting. . . . He even disavowed the engagement. He did this repeatedly and to all kinds of people. . . . He wants nothing more to do with us. Very well! But then I shall be as free and shall say what I think about him and his writings and personality. . . .

Your father and friend, B.B.[6]

Whom is one to believe? Bergliot says that Ibsen received her "amiably but formally," and that the gossips of Christiania soon set to work, especially when Sigurd went off again to Italy with Suzannah, which they took to be the first sign that the engagement was short-lived. But they were wrong; and on 2 May Ibsen wrote affectionately in Bergliot's album: "Always be yourself, as you are now. I know no better destiny I could wish you."[7]

[4] Bergliot Ibsen, pp. 126–28.
[5] *Ibid.*, p. 129.
[6] *Ibid.*, pp. 129–30.
[7] *Ibid.*, p. 133.

By now Ibsen was working busily on his new play, although since his preliminary notes and first draft have disappeared we cannot, as with his other plays (except *An Enemy of the People*), trace its first beginnings. On 4 May he wrote to Jacob Hegel that it "now occupies me completely and, as usual, takes all my time and all my thoughts. I should gladly like to spend the summer somewhere in Jutland. But alas, I dare not think of it; for I work best here in my own apartment and at my own desk. I have made my study up here very (to my mind), pleasant, comfortable, and good for work, and can sit here undisturbed. I couldn't do that in Munich, and often felt creatively inhibited down there. So this summer I shan't leave Christiania."

Suzannah had by now returned from Italy. They saw a few friends; the Dietrichsons, with whom Ibsen had now patched things up, were invited to dine "very plainly, at three," on 11 May; and he renewed one of his oldest friendships, with Christopher Due, his companion from Grimstad days, now a retired customs officer. The meeting was evidently a success, for we find a note from Ibsen on 9 May telling Due: "I should be delighted if you could look in again; I am usually to be found here between 11 and 12 of a morning." Yet even with so old a friend he retained an extreme formality. It was an ancient custom, but one scarcely observed among old friends, that the senior of any two walked on the right. Due records that one day

> Ibsen was walking at his measured pace along Drammensveien when I happened to see him, caught up with him on his left side and greeted him. After a friendly response, a to me incomprehensible restlessness seemed to overcome him, and he shifted around me in a manner which I sought in vain to interpret, until I realized that he wanted to walk on my left. "No," I said, "you cannot expect me to walk on the right of one who holds the Grand Cross of St. Olaf." "Certainly," replied Ibsen. "You are the elder."[8]

When Due remarked that Ibsen took his time over each play, since two years always elapsed before the next one appeared, Ibsen said: "And yet I work hard each day." "But not just at your plays?" "Yes, mostly on them. I spend at least five hours each day on creative work." Due comments: "Seeing Ibsen live this lonely life, I could not but think of him as a young man, when he was always so keen to have friends around him. Had life and humanity brought him so much disappointment that he had felt compelled to isolate himself and speak merely through his works?"[9]

On 5 June, a hundred miles to the south, an event occurred of which Ibsen probably never heard, since it was not of sufficient interest to appear in any newspaper. An old blind pauper woman died, aged seventy-four: Else Sofie Jensdatter, who had borne him a son nearly half a century before. It may have been around now (the year is not recorded, and

[8] Due, p. 53.
[9] *Ibid.*, pp. 51–52.

indeed the whole incident is based upon hearsay, though Professor Francis Bull, who is usually right in such matters, believes it to be true) that, for the first and last time, Ibsen met that son, Hans Jacob Henriksen, now a ne'er-do-well of forty-six. The story goes that Hans Jacob, penniless as always, knocked one day on the door of his father's apartment, revealed his identity and asked for financial help; to which Ibsen is said to have responded by handing him five crowns with the comment: "This is what I gave your mother. It should be enough for you," and shut the door in his face. But there was so much malicious gossip about Ibsen in Christiania that there may be no truth in the story.

What is sure is that some of Ibsen's acquaintances, led by Christen Collin (later a professor at London University), hit on the idea of a fearful prank—to dress Hans Jacob, who in build and general appearance much resembled his father, in clothes such as Ibsen wore, and, having paid him a small sum to secure his willingness, to sit him in Ibsen's chair at the Grand to see what would happen when Ibsen himself walked through the door. But either they or Hans Jacob lost courage, and this macabre jest remained a thing of the imagination.[10]

Ibsen kept in touch with his sister Hedvig, and grew fond of her daughter Anna. A touching little note to his niece has survived from this summer, begging her to look him up before leaving town and not to be afraid of disturbing him. Once he even attended a largish family party given in Christiania by one of his Paus half-uncles, and agreed, if only momentarily, to revisit Telemark. Among the guests at the party, relates Francis Bull (who had it from one of the Pauses present), was a gentleman named Løvenskiold who owned a large estate at Fossum, no distance from Venstøp, where Ibsen had spent so much of his childhood. Løvenskiold invited Ibsen to come and stay with him there, suggesting that it might amuse him to look over his old haunts. "Ibsen," continues Bull, "was clearly pleased at the invitation and said that he would gladly come. It is easy to imagine how as a child he must have gazed longingly at the great house which a bankrupt's son could never hope to enter, and that the invitation must at first have seemed like the fulfilment of a childhood dream. But later in the evening Ibsen came back to Løvenskiold, very depressed and in a totally different mood. He had thought over the matter, he said, and regretted that he felt bound to refuse the invitation to Fossum, for he realized that once he came there he would inevitably be forced to revisit the town of his birth and revive old memories and acquaintances which he preferred to keep at a distance."[11]

Bull also tells that at another party around this time Ibsen, on being presented to an attractive young lady, turned away in embarrassment on hearing her name. It transpired that her father, a lawyer, had been

---

[10] Information from Professor Francis Bull.

[11] Bull, *Tradisjoner og minner*, pp. 100–1.

approached by Ibsen in 1862 for a loan. Ibsen had with him his manuscript of *Love's Comedy* as evidence that he would soon be in better financial conditions and be able to repay the money. "The lawyer asked to read the play before deciding and, having done so, said that one passage offended him and that he would only lend the money on condition that Ibsen deleted it. Ibsen accepted the condition and took the money, but never forgot the humiliation and never repaid the loan, although the lawyer lived for several years after Ibsen's return to Christiania in 1891. They lived near each other, and when Ibsen saw him he would cross to the far pavement."[12]

Christian Sontum had by now become Ibsen's doctor. He was working that summer at a sanatorium at Grefsen, a short way outside Christiania, and Ibsen several times allowed himself the luxury of driving out to visit him. Little Bolette Sontum was there and remembered his visits:

> Nothing could be a better advertisement of the tonic air of Grefsen than this fact, that Ibsen actually drove out to inhale it. His fear of driving was a by-word in Christiania. However, only one particular horse and driver were trusted. Certainly he had little to fear from their energies. As the funny little rig came creeping up the valley slowly and laboriously, like a very tired snail, it creaked and swayed with the roughness of the roads. Then the whole grotesque little outfit took up the motion—the old horse nodding from his ears to his tail, the fat lazy little coachman droning in his half-sleep, the reins lax in his podgy hands, his cap with its silver band tick-tocking like a pendulum. And behind on the soft, worn cushions sat Ibsen, conjuring up every accident possible to unrestrained speed. . . .
>
> I used to run down to meet our old friend. "Welcome to Grefsen!" I would call out, very cautious with my best muslin dress and my most ceremonial curtsey. "*Goddag, goddag*" [Good day, Good day] he would call back, his whole face lighted up with smiles. Promptly, he would open the low door— "You will drive the rest of the way, my little friend?" Then I would spring up to the back seat more respectfully than timidly. "No, no, right here beside me," Ibsen would urge, and I, trembling with happiness, quickly obeyed, murmuring, "No, no, perhaps I had better not." "Grunt-grunt," he would reply. Each time he came we had our little comedy.[13]

The political strife between the conservatives and liberals reached a pitch of particular bitterness that summer in Norway. "The party newspapers outbid each other in abuse and accusations," Ibsen wrote to Jacob Hegel on 5 July. "Speeches, processions and torchlights displays are held, and other demonstrations are being prepared. Today a big procession of the conservatives is to go to the palace to greet the king. The conservatives are in a decisive majority here in Christiania. . . . It interests me to observe all this at close quarters. But I don't involve myself in these

[12] *Ibid.*, p. 100.
[13] Sontum, p. 250.

conflicts personally; that would be against my nature. And this attitude of mine is respected up here. Since my return last year I am in the happy position of knowing, and daily experiencing, that I have both the right and the left behind me. I can therefore work with undisturbed peace of mind at my new play, and I do so daily. So I shall probably not leave town this summer. But the air here I find healthy and invigorating. I have not for a long time felt as well in myself as I do up here."

All that summer of 1892 he was writing regularly to Hildur Andersen in Vienna, and she to him. Professor Francis Bull, who knew Hildur well, gathered from conversations with her that he discussed the progress of his play in detail in these letters. She promised to let Bull have them after her death; but most unfortunately for posterity, around the age of ninety in the late nineteen-fifties, she underwent a change of heart and burned them. Ibsen is usually assumed to have destroyed his notes and first draft during the spring or early summer; but since, according to the date on the manuscript, he did not begin his final draft until 9 August, it seems likely that he spent the summer writing a second draft and destroyed that too. *The Master Builder* was to be the most personal and revealing of all his plays, or at any rate the most consciously revealing, though *Hedda Gabler* possibly tells us more about him.

The final draft of the play went swiftly. Act One took him from 9 to 20 August, Act Two from 23 August to 6 September, and Act Three from 7 to 19 September—six weeks in all. On 4 October he wrote Hegel that he was busy on the fair copy and hoped to let him have it soon after the middle of the month. In fact, due to a brief illness, he did not post it off until the end of the month.

On 11 October Sigurd Ibsen and Bergliot Bjørnson got married at Aulestad. Bjørnson, still offended at Ibsen's supposed coolness towards him, issued a frostily-worded invitation:

Aulestad, 3 September 1892

Dear Friend,

The wedding is now arranged for 11 October, and it is an honour and pleasure for Karoline and me to invite you to attend.

You will reach Lillehammer in the evening and can stay the night there or carry on and arrive here between 9 and 9:30. In that case you would need to have a carriage waiting at the quayside (telegraph the Victoria Hotel to book one). If you are very busy you could return to Lillehammer the same day as the wedding (scarcely twelve miles) and be in Christiania the following day.

Questions will be asked if you don't come and for the sake of the young couple only good questions should be asked. Moreover, since I (and probably Karoline) shan't attend the church ceremony, since we know it to be as much humbug for them as it is for us, you, who expressed the wish that it should take place, ought to be there, so that they won't be altogether parentless for the

occasion, by which you set such store. For company on the journey I presume
you will have Thoresen and my brother.

No one except close relatives will be there. We shall do our best to make
things pleasant for you. I could of course meet you on the quayside at Lillehammer, but it would only be a bother for both of us. Apart from that we
shall try to arrange everything for you as comfortably as possible. Karoline
sends her best wishes to your wife, and I too beg you to convey my most respectful greetings and warmest thanks for our last visit to you.

Everyone here is well and happy.
Your friend,
Bjørnst. Bjørnson[14]

A church ceremony would in fact have been far from humbug as
far as Bergliot was concerned. "I have always been a believer," she
comments, referring to the above letter. ". . . But it was useless to try
to explain this to Father; he was so fanatical on this point that one dared
not for the sake of one's life mention the subject of religion,"[15] As things
turned out, when the day for the wedding came Ibsen was ill and could
not come, so to please Bjørnson Sigurd and Bergliot got married in his
study. Suzannah, despite her gout, made the long journey with her brother,
Judge Herman Thoresen. The predictions of the gossips who declared that
for an Ibsen to marry a Bjørnson was asking for trouble were confounded.
It was a profoundly happy and successful marriage, though relations
between the two fathers remained distant for some time. When the
important occasion of Bjørnson's sixtieth birthday occurred on 6 December that year, Ibsen sent him the coldest of congratulatory telegrams.
It comprised, in Norwegian, seven words: "Henrik Ibsen sends good wishes
for your birthday."

In Berlin, meanwhile, the unfortunate Julius Hoffory had gone rapidly
downhill. "I am afraid he must be regarded as incurable," Ibsen had
written Rudolf Schmidt on 31 August; and on 1 November he told
Julius Elias: "He continually sends me old, paid hotel bills, private letters
and the like, with no indication of what he expects me to do with them."
Next year, he added, he might take a trip south to meet all his German
friends. Hegel sent word that a twelfth edition of *Brand* was in the press;
and this news reminded Ibsen of an old promise. "Twenty years ago," he
wrote Hegel on 10 November, "when the sixth edition of *Brand* was about
to appear, we and the Falsens [Suzannah's younger sister, Dorothea, and
her husband] were living in Dresden. I did not then dream that I should
ever live to see a *twelfth* edition of the poem, and I promised Dorothea
that if such a thing ever happened she should have half my fee for it.
Now it has happened; and she has turned up here and, like Hilde in my

new play, demands that I keep my promise. May I therefore beg you to be so kind as to send her the sum in question?"

On 6 December, six days before *The Master Builder* was published in Scandinavia, William Heinemann issued an edition of twelve copies in Norwegian to safeguard his copyright; and the following morning, at 10 A.M., as a further safeguard, the play was read in Norwegian at the Theatre Royal, Haymarket. Edmund Gosse, who read Dr. Herdal, described this strange occasion:

> Yesterday we had a curious little excitement. The new Ibsen play had to be nominally performed here to save copyright, it not having yet been played or published even in its own country. So Heinemann rented the Haymarket Theatre, put a bill outside, and inside, with an audience of 4 persons, we read the play in Norwegian. I send you the bill (of which 12 copies only were printed); it marks my solitary appearance as an actor! It was odd to think that all this could go on in the very heart of London, where everybody thirsts for something new, and yet totally escape the newspapers. One journalist did discover the bill and wanted to make "copy" of the affair, but was promptly nobbled.[16]

Consul H. L. (misprinted on the bill as R. L.) Bræstad, appropriately for the man who had introduced Gosse to Ibsen's work, read Solness, and his wife, Kaja. Elizabeth Robins and William Heinemann, who seem to have learned some Norwegian between them, took Hilde and Knut Brovik, and Amy Haldane was Mrs. Solness.

Gyldendal published *The Master Builder* on 12 December in Christiania and two days later in Copenhagen, in a printing of 10,000 copies. Although many of the critics were bewildered, it got, over-all, a better press in Scandinavia than any other play Ibsen had written since *A Doll's House*. Professor Bredo Morgenstierne predictably disliked it. "It represents a step backwards," he lamented in *Aftenposten* (5 January 1893). "The people we meet in it have little reality, or at best make a curiously airy and unreal impression. . . . Solness and Hilde seem to belong to another world than the one we inhabit. . . . We have difficulty in believing and understanding them. And the whole plot consists of a long string of improbabilities." But Henrik Jæger in *Dagbladet* (27 and 30 December), after remarking that what was inhibited in Rebecca and Ellida was uninhibited and free in Hilde, concluded: "The play is really a dialogue between Solness and Hilde, but a dialogue so powerful and brilliant that it is more gripping than the most exciting 'scene.' A poet who can write a play like *The Master Builder* has no reason to fear youth. . . . His play is one long pæan of praise to youth and the future." Christian Brinckmann, in *Nyt Tidsskrift* (1892–93, pp. 272–81),

[16] Bredsdorff, *Sir Edmund Gosse's Correspondence with Scandinavian Writers,* p. 48.

also wrote admiringly of the play, in which "despair resounds like jubilation and madness sounds like wisdom."

In Sweden, opinions were similarly divided. Georg Göthe, in *Nordisk Tidskrift* (1893, pp. 153-57) found it "essentially negative. . . . It can be amusing to guess riddles; but when the riddles are so complex that one suspects that even the riddler himself does not really know the answer, the game ceases to be amusing. . . . What are all these precious and pretentious abstract grandiloquencies which he has used so continuously since *The Lady from the Sea*? . . . Is it strange if some foreign observers find us Scandinavians abnormal?" The poet Gustav Fröding, however, praised the play in *Karlstads-Tidning* (4 February 1893), deploring "the hateful attacks which the young have made on him" (presumably a reference to Hamsun); and Edvin Alkman reviewed it perceptively in *Svensk Tidskrift* (1893, pp. 138-52). Ibsen, he wrote, "does not shrink from treating of phenomena which science has as yet barely and feebly started to illuminate, and which a few years ago were regarded by educated men as credulous and superstitious nonsense—such phenomena as hypnosis and telepathy"; and he shrewdly observed that the true subject of the play was "self-love . . . and that curious power which men call God and which the egotist cannot endure because it sets bounds to his ego."

Both the Brandes brothers praised it hugely. "It is a masterpiece," wrote Edvard in *Politiken* (22 December). "Only this man, already advanced in years and belonging to a small nation, could write such a play, in which supreme craftsmanship is allied to characteristic profundity. . . . A work of genius." And Georg, in *Verdens Gang* (28 December)—the first review he had written of an Ibsen play on publication since *Ghosts* eleven years previously—thought it his best yet. "The piece," he wrote, "echoes in the mind long after one has read it. And when one has read it, one reads it again with increasing admiration. Technically faultless, profound and precise in its symbolism . . . Ibsen's new play is at the same time enthralling and liberating. Never has there existed a more perfect dramatic technique; never has dialogue been written like this." Brandes's only regret, and it is a fair one, was that Ibsen had not made Solness more of an artist and established him more clearly as genuinely creative, a genius and not a mere tycoon. He concluded: "Since Ibsen abandoned the matter and manner of his early plays, we have seen him acclaimed and attacked as a so-called 'naturalist.' Recently the so-called 'symbolists' started a feud against 'naturalism.' That kind of catchword seldom means much, and all such are least applicable to Ibsen. For twenty years or more naturalism and symbolism have been harmonious partners in his work. . . . Although both as a man and as a writer he loves reality, he is poet and thinker enough constantly to underlay the reality he portrays with a deeper interpretation."

Great arguments developed as to the meaning of the play, and some extraordinary theories were advanced. Solness was variously taken to represent Ibsen himself, Bjørnson, the conservative party, the liberal party, Man rebelling against God and, seriously, Bismarck (with Ragnar Brovik as the young Kaiser).[17]

Ibsen never ceased to be amazed at the meanings people tried to read into his plays. Ernst Motzfeldt records a conversation he had with him shortly after the publication of *The Master Builder:*

> Ibsen said: "It's extraordinary what profundities and symbols they ascribe to me. I have received letters which ask if the nine dolls [of Mrs. Solness] signify the Nine Muses, and the dead twins Scandinavianism and my own happiness. They have even asked if the dolls are connected with something in some Epistle of St. Paul which I don't even know, or something in the Book of Revelation. Can't people just read what I write? I only write about people. I don't write symbolically. Just about people's inner life as I know it—psychology, if you like. . . . I draw real, living people. Any considerable person will naturally be to some degree representative of the generality, of the thoughts and ideas of the age, so that the portrayal of such a person's inner life may seem symbolic. And I create such people. And with good reason. I have often walked with Hedda Gabler in the Munich arcades. And have undergone somewhat of the same experience myself.
>
> "Solness and his wife are worthy people who don't suit each other and so aren't happy in their life together. They don't become what, being the people they are, they could and should have become—despite the fact that they aren't actually miserable, and despite their consideration for each other and a kind of tenderness and love. They keep each other down, cramp each other. . . . Their worst characteristics are brought out, and they brood perpetually, because each goes his own way mentally and doesn't share with the other. Contrast Hilde and Solness. They are not portrayed as extraordinary persons, it is just that they feel spiritually akin, strongly attracted to each other, feel that they belong together and that life together would be immeasurably richer than it would otherwise be, and also that they themselves would be better people (Hilde immediately makes him do for Brovik what he wasn't willing to do before—did his wife ever try to make him do that?)—and that their relationship would elevate instead of debasing them, and give their lives greater meaning. Then the collision comes—when one still has a zest for life, a need for happiness, and feels unable to live without joy in subdued resignation. And so they decide to build a castle in the air and to live together in spirit. This lifts him up higher than before, to do things he had not been able to do for a

[17] An anonymous critic in the London *Saturday Review* (4 March 1893, pp. 241–42) commented on these theories: "We would undertake ourselves to get out of it a criticism on Mr. Gladstone's Home Rule Bill, a system of phallic worship, a refutation of evolution and a diatribe against the Institution of British Architects. . . . The fact of course is that it is of the essence of a fantasy piece to admit of almost any number of interpretations. And it is of the essence of the intelligent reader of a fantasy-piece not to insist upon any." But the reviewer summed up *The Master Builder* as "an impossible play. . . . It will not stand examining."

long time (symbolically). But he stakes his life on it—and is killed. But was it so mad if it cost him his life, if he did it for his own happiness and only then, for the first time, achieved it?"

During our conversation he said it was wrong to think of unhappy love as when two people who love each other don't get each other. "No, unhappy love is when two people who love each other get married and feel they don't suit each other and cannot live happily together."[18]

Despite the generally favourable reviews it received on publication, *The Master Builder* at first failed almost everywhere when staged. In Christiania it achieved only fifteen performances that season, and thirteen the next. In Copenhagen, it managed no more than eleven. In retrospect, this is not surprising. More than any play Ibsen had yet written, it demanded the kind of acting between the lines of which very few actors then were capable; and, like *The Lady from the Sea, The Father* and *Othello,* it needs a very particular kind of player in the leading role—an actor, as Yngvar Brun remarked when reviewing the Christiania production in *Morgenbladet* on 19 March 1893, "as dazzlingly beautiful as love, as hideous as disease or egotism, as doubting and tormented as an evil conscience." Another reason for its early failures on the stage was that in Scandinavia (then as now), and in Germany also, leading female roles tended to be awarded according to seniority rather than suitability. Edvard Brandes complained of the Copenhagen production (*Politiken,* 9 March 1893) that Betty Hennings was twenty years too old for Hilde.

Although today Hilde is usually played by actresses younger than Betty Hennings (then in her mid-forties), the age difference between her and Solness is still often under-emphasized. The Hilde too frequently looks thirty, the Solness a bare fifty or even less. For such a pair to become lovers strikes nobody as incongruous. Ibsen does not specify Solness's age—he merely called him "aging," probably to avoid too close an identification with himself— but he should surely be at least approaching sixty. Hilde is twenty-three; in other words, there should be not twenty, but nearly forty years between them; he should be old enough to be not merely her father but her grandfather. The theme of the play is an old man's fear of, and yearning for youth:

HILDE. What do you want from me?
SOLNESS. Your youth, Hilde.
HILDE. Youth, which you are so frightened of?
SOLNESS (*nods slowly*). And which, in my heart, I long for.

[18] Ernst Motzfeldt, "Af samtaler med Henrik Ibsen," in *Aftenposten,* 23 April 1911 (also published as an offprint, Christiania, 1911).

"Oh, high and painful joy—to struggle for the unattainable!" Ibsen had written in Emilie's album three years earlier in Gossensass. But if we see a handsome man of fifty wooing a girl of thirty, the point is lost. Even when Solness is played by an actor who is in fact sixty, one has too often seen him age himself down to forty-five.

Another fault too often committed by actors playing Solness is a tendency to push him up the social scale. Solness has fought his way up; his way of speaking is rough, not the language of one socially sure of himself. He is socially inferior not merely to his wife, but also to Hilde (whose language, by contrast is immensely self-assured). Of course it is possible to argue that the son of "pious, country people" (as Solness describes himself) need not be, or feel, socially inferior to the daughter of a country doctor; what is certain is that the play gains immeasurably if the social difference is there, between Solness and Hilde as well as between Solness and Aline. And he must be played sensually; one has seen Solnesses who behaved as though they would have not have known what to do if Hilde had started to take her clothes off.

The character of Solness was the nearest thing to a deliberate self-portrait that Ibsen had yet attempted (though he was to follow it with two equally merciless likenesses in *John Gabriel Borkman* and *When We Dead Awaken*). He admitted in an address to the students of Christiania six years later that Solness was "a man somewhat akin to me"; they shared an arrogancy and ruthlessness, a readiness to sacrifice the happiness of those close to them in order to further their ambitions, and that longing for and fear of youth. The sensuality was Ibsen's, too, inhibited though he was about giving rein to it. Edvard Brandes noted that "in his later years there lurked a strong sensuality in his bearing and speech."[19]

Ibsen had, moreover, long regarded himself as a builder and his plays as works of architecture. In his youthful poem "Building Plans" he had compared the artist to a master builder; and when the painter Erik Werenskiold, seeing him looking at some new buildings in Christiania, asked: "You are interested in architecture?" Ibsen replied, "Yes; it is, as you know, my own trade."[20] And Ibsen, like Solness, had always had a fear of looking down from a great height or into a chasm, and this had become worse as he had grown older.

[19] Edvard Brandes, "Henrik Ibsens Personlighed," in *Litterære Tendenser* (Copenhagen, 1968), p. 231. Gunnar Heiberg describes how Ibsen looked at a girl he introduced to him. "I presented her and Ibsen looked emotionally at her face and cast a quick, admiring glance at her figure. He said nothing but his lips trembled. 'She's very pretty, isn't she?' I said. Suddenly a smile flickered across his mouth. 'She is,' he said quietly and unwillingly, and his smile grew so that it illuminated his whole face. 'Yes, she is,' he repeated in a clear voice, this time directly to the young lady, as though in thanks." (*Salt og sukker*, pp. 60–61.) This took place in Christiania in the nineties.

[20] Interview with Erik Werenskiold in *Dagbladet*, 20 March 1928.

It has been argued by several commentators that Solness's development as a builder corresponds precisely, if one reads between the lines, with Ibsen's career as a dramatist. "The churches which Solness sets out by building," suggested William Archer, "doubtless represent Ibsen's early romantic plays, the 'homes for human beings' his social dramas, while the houses with high towers, merging into 'castles in the air,' stand for those spiritual dramas, with a wide outlook over the metaphysical environment of humanity, on which he was henceforth to be engaged."[21] The theory may at first seem fanciful, of the kind that Ibsen himself derided; but the more one ponders it, the more truthfully it rings, whether the analogy was conscious or not. And one interesting variant between his extant draft and the final version of the play reveals how closely he identified himself with Solness. In the second act, when Solness is telling Hilde how success came to him, Ibsen originally made him conclude with the words: "And now, at last, they have begun to talk of me abroad," which was exactly Ibsen's situation when he began work on the play. But he deleted the sentence in revision, doubtless because he felt that it made the identification too obvious.

Ibsen's interest in hypnosis, and the power that one human being could gain over the mind of another, has already been noted; and he carried it further in *The Master Builder* even than in his three preceding plays, concentrating here especially on how unexpressed wishes could sometimes translate themselves into actions. But if Solness is to be identified with Ibsen, Hilde is not to be identified with Emilie, Helene or Hildur. Was it from the needs of the play that Ibsen made her a harpy, or was it, remembering Elias's account of his maliciously untruthful description of Emilie, from a sense of guilt towards her and frustration with himself? Whatever the reason, from the time that Ibsen's letters to Emilie and Elias's story were published, both within a few months of Ibsen's death, everyone identified Emilie with Hilde, and for the remaining forty-eight years of her long life she was regarded as a predatory little monster. The play brought her as little joy as *A Doll's House* had brought to Laura Kieler.[22]

Nor was Emilie the only person to whom *The Master Builder* caused distress. The grim relationship between Solness and his wife was generally assumed, at any rate in Norway, to be a picture of the Ibsens' own marriage. Things seem to have been getting difficult between Ibsen and Suzannah around this time (as we shall shortly see); and Magdalene

[21] Koht, II, 257.

[22] "I didn't see myself," Emilie said, on seeing the play for the first time in 1908, "but I saw him. There is something of me in Hilde; but in Solness, there is little that is not Ibsen." Some commentators have suggested that Hildur Andersen was the original of Hilde. But he would hardly have modelled so unsympathetic a character on someone of whom he was so deeply fond, and he had originally created Hilde three years before he became interested in Hildur.

Thoresen described their situation a couple of years later in words which precisely reflect the Solness marriage: "They live in grand style, all most elegant, but in a suburban silence; for they are two lonely people—each for himself—each wholly for himself."[23] The gossips of Christiania must have had a field day. And Francis Bull tells how a lady of his acquaintance who had known Ibsen in Munich was surprised, when Ibsen returned to Norway, to receive several invitations from him to dine out at restaurants. He seemed eager for her company and conversation until, suddenly, he stopped seeing her. She could not understand why until *The Master Builder* appeared. Then she recognised herself unmistakably in the character of Kaja Fosli, and realized that it was only as a model, not as a human being, that Ibsen was interested in her.[24]

Shortly before Ibsen had left Munich two years earlier (on 22 April 1890, according to her diary), Helene Raff had mentioned to him the legend of the master builder who had built St. Michael's Church there and had thrown himself down from the tower because he was afraid the roof would not hold. Ibsen remarked that he thought the legend must have originated in Scandinavia, since he had heard it there, and when Helene observed that every famous cathedral in Germany had the same legend he replied that this must be because people felt instinctively that a man could not build so high without paying the penalty for his hubris. Did he perhaps feel that his plays, taken as a whole, were now approaching the size and seeming permanence of a cathedral, or that in some way he was challenging God? Of the repeated imagery of spires, which make an old man feel dizzy and a young girl hear harps in the air, the significance scarcely needs underlining; and I do not think it is reading too much into the play to assume that when Hilde, at the age of thirteen, saw Solness standing dangerously at the top of the tower in Lysanger, she had her first sexual orgasm, and that she drives him to the top of another tower in order to repeat it. Of their first meeting alone, when she says he kissed her and he denies it, we never know whether he wanted it so much that she thought it had happened, or *she* wanted it so much that she thought it had happened, or whether it did in fact happen and either a sense of guilt or mere forgetfulness caused him to forget. There is a close analogy with the film, *Last Year in Marienbad,* in which a similar situation occurs; and in both instances, part of the fascination lies in the fact that neither the people involved, nor we, ever know the truth.

A few days after the publication of *The Master Builder,* on 16 December, there was a seemingly unimportant and almost unnoticed performance of an Ibsen play in Paris. The young Lugné-Poe presented *The Lady from the Sea* under the humble auspices of a theatre club which he had founded

23 Magdalene Thoresen, *Breve, 1855–1901,* ed. J. Clausen and P. F. Rist (Copenhagen, 1919), p. 240.

24 Bull, *Tradisjoner og minner,* pp. 101–2.

while still at school, Les Echoliers. He had lectured on the new dramatist of the north to his fellow-pupils, who included an awkward youth named Marcel Proust. The actors were all very young—Lugné-Pœ himself played Dr. Wangel—and it seems to have been a very bad production. Herman Bang, who saw it, declared that had Ibsen been present he would have "wept blood or stared into his hat."

The symbolist movement in poetry and art was then at its peak in Paris—Paul Fort had founded his Théâtre de l'Art, the first symbolist theatre, in 1890, with Mæterlinck as his idol—and it was as a symbolist, not as a realist, that the French welcomed Ibsen. They drew delighted parallels between his plays and those of Mæterlinck, whose work Ibsen detested (Lugné-Pœ records that he even refused to read *Pelleas et Mélisande* to the end, and that when Bang told him how in Paris they played Mæterlinck behind a transparent veil, Ibsen exclaimed violently: "Why? What does it mean? I don't understand that kind of thing!").[25] Moreover, they had borrowed the worst methods that the Germans had been applying to Ibsen. "In the German theatre," wrote Francisque Sarcey, "it has become a tradition . . . when they play Ibsen, that they strive to make the audience forget that these are real people of flesh and blood whom they see treading the boards. They move but little, use almost no hand gestures and, when they do, make them broad, almost sacerdotal. Their whole recitation is characterized by a slow recitation, which seems to emanate from supernatural and symbolic lips."

Lugné-Pœ confirms that "faced with the difficulty of doing [Ibsen's plays] they hit on this monotonous, religious intonation, which we in our turn yielded to and plagued others with," and adds that Ibsen, "when he heard of my friendly relations with his German interpreters and directors, took pains to urge me above all to avoid them." But this contact between Lugné-Pœ and Ibsen did not happen until later, so that *The Lady from the Sea* was practically a model of how Ibsen ought not to be acted—and yet it was a success among everybody enamoured of symbolism. Avant-garde magazines such as *Mecure de France, l'Ermitage,* and *l'Académie Française* praised it glowingly, and its imagined obscurities were for months a talking-point in the cafés.[26] And the occasion marked the beginning of an important partnership. Lugné-Pœ was to do more for Ibsen than any

---

[25] Mæterlinck, ironically, appreciated better than most of his contemporaries what Ibsen was trying to do, especially his use of sub-text ("dialogue du second degré"). *Le Trésor des humbles* (Paris, 1897, pp. 176–80) contains a penetrating section on *The Master Builder:* "Hilde et Solness sont, je pense, les premiers héros qui se sentent vivre un instant dans l'atmosphère de l'âme, et cette vie essentielle qu'ils ont découverte en eux, par delà leur vie ordinaire, les épouvante. . . . Leurs propos ne ressemblent à rien de ce que nous avons entendu jusqu'ici, parce que le poète a tenté de mêler dans une même expression le dialogue intérieur et extérieur. Il règne dans ce drame somnambulique je ne sais quelles puissances nouvelles."

[26] Cf. Nyholm, pp. 38–39; Lugné-Pœ, pp. 91–93.

other Frenchman, before or since; and within eighteen months, at the age of twenty-four, he was to be the first actor to succeed in the role of Master Builder Solness.

"A voice within me cries for you!" Ibsen wrote in the copy of *The Master Builder* which he sent to Helene Raff in Munich that New Year's Eve. He had not found any companion to replace Hildur Andersen. But he gave Hildur the manuscript of *The Master Builder;* also a copy of *Ghosts* inscribed with the lines from *Peer Gynt:*

> And the game can never be played again.
> Oh, here was my empire and my crown![27]

His earnings for 1892 had been as follows:

	crowns
6th edn. of *Poems* (supplementary fee)	20
Unspecified German royalties from Felix Bloch	47
Unspecified royalties from Wien Burgtheater	540
Unspecified royalties from Munich Hoftheater	176
Fee for provincial tour of *Hedda Gabler* by the Royal Opera, Stockholm	150
4th edn. of *Emperor and Galilean*	1,600
Unspecified royalties from Wien Burgtheater	265
Unspecified royalties from Felix Bloch	121
Unspecified royalties from Munich Hoftheater	83
Royalties for *The Wild Duck* from Royal Theatre, Copenhagen (14th–20th perfs.)	1,848
Unspecified royalties from Felix Bloch	1,058
Unspecified royalties from Munich Hoftheater	52
12th edn. of *Brand*	1,360
Fee for illustrated edition of "Terje Vigen"	250
Unspecified royalties from Felix Bloch	313
Fee from French publisher, Savine, for vols. 2 and 3 of Prozor's translations of the plays (250 francs)	180
Royalties from Munich Hoftheater	138
Fee for 1st edn. of *The Master Builder*	8,550
Fee for German edn. of *The Master Builder* (S. Fischer)	533
Fee from L. Dorsch and E. Zachrison for Swedish rights of *The Vikings at Helgeland*	50
Fee from Dorsch and Zachrison for Swedish rights of *The Master Builder* for one year	1,000
Fee from Wm. Petersen for Norwegian provincial rights of *The Master Builder* for one year	1,000
Royalties from Royal Theatre, Copenhagen, for 21st perf. of *The Wild Duck*	123
	19,457 £1,086

[27] Bull, "Hildur Andersen and Henrik Ibsen," p. 49.

31

"Dull, Mysterious, Unchaste"

1893

The Master Builder had two world premieres simultaneously on 19 January 1893—at the Lessingtheater in Berlin (with Emmanuel Reicher as Solness), and in the little north Norwegian town of Trondhjem, under the humble auspices of William Petersen's travelling company, which had acquired the provincial rights. One might have expected the play to appeal to German taste, but it failed disastrously; the Berlin production had to be removed from the repertory after three performances. A touring Swedish company staged it in both Åbo (in Finland) and Helsinki that month; but, as with *Hedda Gabler,* the first successful production of the play took place in London, again thanks to the American actress Elizabeth Robins.

England was beginning to atone for its long neglect of Ibsen. Thanks very largely to him, the theatre was again beginning to attract men of letters; the previous year had seen the dramatic debuts of Oscar Wilde, Bernard Shaw and J. M. Barrie (to say nothing of *Charley's Aunt*), and the literary world of London awaited Ibsen's new play with immense expectation. Elizabeth Robins recalled the pre-publication fever:

> Months before *The Master Builder* reached these shores, the excitement that was set up by mere anticipation will never be credited in these times. . . . Impatience for the play to come was exacerbated by the darkness that shrouded it. . . . Neither the man who had committed himself to publishing it [William Heinemann] nor anybody else had even now the faintest idea what the play would be about. People lived on supposition, and were as hot over it as though they knew what they were contending for.[1]

Among the enthusiasts who visited Miss Robins "up those seventy-four steps" (as she described it) for news of the play were Henry James, Sidney Colvin, Sir Frederick Pollock, Mrs. Humphry Ward, Rhoda Brough-

[1] Elizabeth Robins, *Theatre and Friendship* (London, 1932), pp. 75 ff.

ton, Bernard Shaw, Gertrude Bell the explorer, Herbert Beerbohm Tree, R. B. Haldane, Hubert Crackanthorpe, W. T. Stead, Arthur Symons and Oscar Wilde. The play arrived in instalments during November 1892, as each batch of proofs emerged from Gyldendal's presses—"in small, in very small, violently agitating spurts—or, as one might say, in volts, projected across the North Sea in a series of electric shocks."[2]

But as the pattern of the plot emerged even the most ardent Ibsenites began to have qualms. "More in the dark than ever," wrote Miss Robins to Florence Bell on 12 November. "Think the old man's stark mad." A few days later she reported that Archer himself "is a good deal puzzled; but he says the 1st Act is powerful and fascinating though he can't 'see it' on the English stage. I am desolate." As the second act came in "W.A. seems less hopeful. . . . He writes: 'The interest certainly hangs fire, etc. etc.' *I* fear the thing is hopeless!" Henry James also found the first instalments unpromising. "I have kindly been favoured with the communication of most of it," he wrote to Florence Bell on 16 November, "and am utterly bewildered and mystified. . . . It is all most strange, most curious, most vague, most horrid, most 'middle-classy' in the peculiar ugly Ibsen sense— and alas most *un*promising for Miss Elizabeth or for any *woman*. What is already clear is that a *man* is the central figure . . . and the man, alas, an elderly white-haired architect, or Baumeister, is, although a strange and interesting, a fearfully *charmless* creature."[3]

Miss Elizabeth tried several of the established theatres; but her enthusiasm for Ibsen was not shared by the managements. "I was told *The Master Builder* was simply unintelligible. Oh, it was wild! It was irritatingly obscure. It was dull, it was mad, it would lose money."[4] She tried reading it to Herbert Beerbohm Tree, who "was swept away by Solness, wants to play it"; but it transpired that before doing so he demanded "amazing alterations" (including making all the characters English and Solness a sculptor), to which Heinemann and Archer refused to agree. Eventually Herbert Waring, who had acted Helmer to Janet Achurch's Nora in 1889, agreed to play Solness on Ibsen's terms, and on 20 February *The Master Builder* was presented (for the usual five matinees) at the Trafalgar Square Theatre in St Martin's Lane (now the Duke of York's).

Henry James tried to encourage intelligent appreciation of the play by an article in the *Pall Mall Gazette* three days before the premiere, in which he praised Ibsen's "independence, his perversity, his intensity, his vividness, the hard compulsion of his strangely inscrutable art . . . [and] his peculiar blessedness to actors. . . . No dramatist of our time has had more the secret, and has kept it better, of making their work interesting

[2] *Ibid.*, p. 78
[3] *Ibid.*, pp. 82–84.
[4] Elizabeth Robins, *Ibsen and the Actress* (London, 1928), p. 39.

to them. The subtlety with which he puts them into relation to it eludes analysis, but operates none the less strongly as an incitement." But this plug had little effect on the London dramatic critics, who greeted the play, like its predecessors, with a chorus of vituperation:

> Dense mist enshrouds characters, words, actions, and motives. . . . One may compare it . . . to the sensations of a man who witnesses a play written, rehearsed and acted by lunatics.
>
> *Daily Telegraph*

> Platitudes and inanities. . . . The play is hopeless and indefensible.
>
> *Globe*

> A feast of dull dialogue and acute dementia. . . . The most dreary and purposeless drivel we have ever heard in an English theatre. . . . A pointless, incoherent and absolutely silly piece.
>
> *Evening News*

> Assuredly no one may fathom the mysteries of the play, so far as it can be called a play. . . . It is not for a moment to be understood that we personally recommend anyone to go and see it.
>
> *Standard*

> Rigmarole of an Oracle Delphic in obscurity and Gamp-like in garrulity. . . . Pulseless and purposeless play, which has idiocy written on every lineament. . . . Three acts of gibberish.
>
> *Stage*

> A distracting jumble of incoherent elements. There is no story; the characters are impossible, and the motives a nightmare of perverted finger-posts.
>
> *Saturday Review*

> Sensuality . . . irreverence . . . unwholesome . . . simply blasphemous.
>
> *Morning Post*
>
> Dull, mysterious, unchaste.
>
> *Daily Graphic*[5]

On the day after the opening performance Henry James wrote to Elizabeth Robins:

> I have looked at the papers, and there is little edification in them of course. They are stupid, angry and mean. The weaknesses of the play do indeed come out strongly in representation, but it would have been only honest in them to acknowledge also its *hold*, the odd baffling spell it works and the remarkable

[5] William Archer, "The Mausoleum of Ibsen," pp. 85–86.
Her Majesty's Censor (a Mr. Pigott) shared these opinions. "I have studied Ibsen's plays pretty carefully," he had declared in 1892, "and all the characters appear to me to be morally deranged. All the heroines are dissatisfied spinsters who look on marriage as a monopoly or dissatisfied married women in a chronic state of rebellion . . . and as for the men, they are all rascals or imbeciles." (Quoted by Charles Archer, p. 178 note.)

spell of the interpretation. . . . I thought Waring *extremely* good—various and interesting, intelligent and coloured: BUT distinctly not loud enough. You were—keep it up, *up*, UP.[6]

However, when he revisited the theatre for a subsequent performance James noted to his amazement that "the house . . . was *full*."[7] Intelligent opinion had decided to ignore the critics. George Moore wrote to Elizabeth Robins: "I thank God I came a second time. It has grown upon me. I understand."[8] Indeed, he came a third time. Oscar Wilde attended the final performance and was greatly impressed; and Bernard Shaw wrote to Elizabeth Robins after the first matinee: "There is no saying what the papers will come out with tomorrow morning; so I had better send you my certificate of the perfect success of the play as far as I am concerned. It held me and moved me from beginning to end.[9]

Unfortunately, very few of Ibsen's supporters ran a dramatic column. "The New Critics are to the Old Critics," William Archer had written in the *Fortnightly Review* the preceding August, "in number as one to ten, in opportunities for disseminating their views as one to ten thousand." And even two of the most prominent of these New Critics, sad to relate, disliked *The Master Builder*. A. B. Walkley, who had praised *Hedda Gabler* as "a masterpiece of piquant subtlety, delicate observation and tragic intensity,"[10] felt compelled to write coolly of *The Master Builder* in the *Fortnightly Review* that April, saying that he disliked symbolism on the stage; and Justin Huntly McCarthy, who had regarded both *A Doll's House* and *Hedda Gabler* as major plays, declared of *The Master Builder* in the *Gentlemen's Magazine:* "A great man can blunder, and this great man has blundered." Yet the play did well enough to be transferred on 6 March to the evening bill at the Vaudeville Theatre, where it continued until the end of the month.

A fortnight after the London premiere, on 8 March, *The Master Builder* was staged simultaneously in Christiania and Copenhagen; and in both cities it failed. On 23 March August Lindberg presented it in Gothenburg, with himself as Solness and another new discovery of his, Hilda Borgström, as Hilde; but although the production received splendid notices, it achieved only five performances, and the takings were so poor that Lindberg could not pay Ibsen the 1,000 crowns he owed him. Ibsen had demanded 2,000 crowns for the Gothenburg and Stockholm rights, half in advance and half after the fifth performance, and refused to allow Lindberg any grace, informing him (13 February) that "last week I sent a large sum of money to Copenhagen to buy shares and

---

[6] Robins, *Theatre and Friendship*, pp. 101–2.

[7] *Ibid.*, p. 103.

[8] *Ibid.*, p. 107.

[9] Bernard Shaw, *Collected Letters, 1874–1897*, p. 382.

[10] A. B. Walkley, *Playhouse Impressions* (London, 1892), p. 62.

have practically no money left," and even wiring him on 3 April forbidding him to present his production in Stockholm until the money had been paid—churlish treatment, one might think, towards the man who had done more than any other actor-manager for his plays in the theatre. Fortunately, Lindberg managed to find a Norwegian friend (a chief of police, of all things) to lend him the money, and so was able to open in Stockholm (where again the production was acclaimed) and to tour it for a month; though when he asked to take it to Copenhagen, where Dagmars Theatre wished to present it, Ibsen and the Royal Theatre of Copenhagen prevented him from doing so.[11]

All this while, Sigurd was going through a very difficult time. Since leaving the diplomatic service in 1889 he had been without a permanent job, and was to remain so until 1899. Despite his outstanding ability and unquestioned patriotism, he was finding everywhere a resistance similar to that which his father had so often encountered in his field. Ibsen was so furious with the authorities for their ostracism of his son that he again seriously considered giving up his Norwegian citizenship, as witness the following extract from a letter to Sigurd (now living with Bergliot in the country near her parents) on 8 February 1893:

On Sunday we had a visit from O. Arvesen [a member of Parliament] and his wife, and I took the opportunity to have a talk with him, the gist of which was this. He began by saying that he had recently seen you and had suggested that you should come down here for a talk about your position vis-à-vis the foreign service. I then took occasion quietly but forcibly to express my personal opinion of the government's conduct towards you. I said that for a long time now you had placed yourself at their disposal, but that all their promises to you had remained unfulfilled. I told him that Steen [the Prime Minister] had, without my raising the subject, told me that it had been decided to create a political department within the Home Office in the near future. But I said that as far as I knew no steps had yet been taken and that I had therefore lost all confidence and trust in the government's promises. I ended by telling him slowly, coldly and forcibly that I was now considering giving up Norwegian citizenship and leaving the country next autumn to become naturalized in Bavaria, and that I would counsel you to do likewise.

This announcement appeared greatly to disconcert Arvesen, and his wife no less. Both begged me most earnestly to pause before taking any final step. He said he would use this statement of mine in a way that would, he hoped, quickly precipitate a decision that would be satisfactory to both you and me. I assured him repeatedly that

[11] Per Lindberg, pp. 339–44. Bergliot Ibsen (pp. 175–76) defends Ibsen's conduct towards Lindberg, but not very convincingly.

you knew nothing of what I had in mind; so my remarks cannot harm your case. Whether it will assist it and your prospects I cannot yet say.

Ibsen's efforts on behalf of his son were unavailing. Sigurd's campaign to rally opinion against the union with Sweden had antagonised the Conservative government which had been in office since 1889, and he cotinued to be regarded as a political pariah, dependent on his pen to earn a living. He pamphleteered energetically for the cause that lay so near his heart; he insisted that his book, *The Union,* should be priced as cheaply as eight øre (about 2 cents) so that it should be within the reach of every pocket, and continued the fight in a further series of articles which formed the basis of another book, *Men and Powers.* Yet he found surprisingly little support among his countrymen. The apathy which his father had denounced in *Brand* remained. But Ibsen did not carry out his threat to leave Norway. Sigurd was determined to stay there to continue the fight, and Ibsen was more than ever, as he grew older, reluctant to be far from him. And he had, after all, withdrawn from the political battle; politics and current affairs were to play no further part in his writing.

In London, the Ibsen fever continued. From 29 May to 10 June *Rosmersholm, Hedda Gabler* and *The Master Builder* (together with Act Four of *Brand*) were presented in repertory at the Opera Comique in the Strand. Elizabeth Robins played Hedda and Hilde as before, and also Rebecca West, with Lewis Waller as Løvborg, Solness and Rosmer; William Archer wrote in the *World* that he thought her Rebecca West "the largest, finest, most poetic thing [she] has yet done." Thomas Hardy visited all three productions within a week, and was impressed; the doubts he had felt on reading Ibsen were, like Henry James's, dispelled when he saw the plays staged. His companion to *The Master Builder,* Florence Henniker, was "so excited by the play as not to be able to sleep all night,"[12] and the final scene must curiously have reminded Hardy of his own first published novel, *Desperate Remedies* (1871), which begins with a master builder falling from one of his own towers. On 9 June Eleonora Duse opened a season of *A Doll's House* in Italian at the Lyric Theatre, and on 14 June Herbert Beerbohm Tree presented *An Enemy of the People* at the Theatre Royal, Haymarket, with himself as Dr. Stockmann. Archer found the text "monstrously mutilated" and noted that "the first actor-manager performance of Ibsen, despite the excellent talents employed, was distinctly below the level of the so-called 'scratch' performances to which we have become accustomed"; and Bernard Shaw thought that Tree's performance "though humorous and entertaining in its way, was, as a

[12] Florence Emily Hardy, *The Life of Thomas Hardy,* 2nd edn. (London, 1965), p. 256.

character creation, the polar opposite of Ibsen's Stockmann." But the play was a success, and Tree, who had originally presented it for seven performances only, made it a regular item in his repertory. Ibsen's reward from this expensive production came to approximately five guineas a performance; one wonders how many guineas Tree was getting.

In July William Archer published in the *Fortnightly Review* the article already cited, "The Mausoleum of Ibsen," in which he surveyed Ibsen's progress in England since the breakthrough of 1889. Admitting that there had been a good deal of sane and competent criticism, and even some that had been extravagantly enthusiastic, Archer observed sadly that "both in bulk and influence the favourable, or even the temperate criticism has been as nothing beside the angrily or scornfully hostile. All the great morning papers, the leading illustrated weeklies, the critical weeklies with one exception, and the theatrical trade papers, have been bitterly de-nunciatory." And yet (he continued) the volume incorporating *The Pillars of Society, Ghosts* and *An Enemy of the People* which Walter Scott had published in the Camelot Classics at a shilling (25 cents) had, in less than four years (to the end of 1892) sold 14,367 copies, plus 16,834 copies of the five-volume edition published by Scott in 1891–92 at 3s.6d. (85 cents). Additionally, only publishers had issued single-volume editions of *A Doll's House, Rosmersholm, Ghosts, The Lady from the Sea, Hedda Gabler* and *The Master Builder*.

Thus, I think, we are well within the mark in estimating that 100,000 prose dramas by Ibsen have been bought by the English-speaking public in the course of the past four years. Is there a parallel in the history of publishing for such a result in the case of translated plays? . . . The publishers to whom I proposed a collected edition of the Prose Dramas before Mr. Walter Scott undertook it, dismissed the idea as visionary, roundly declaring that no modern plays could ever "sell" in England. . . . For fifty years or more, the English public had lost the habit of reading plays . . . yet the fact remains that 100,000 of his plays are at this moment in the hands of the reading public. . . .

Except in omnivorous Germany, have translated plays ever been known to take very deep root on a foreign stage? In adaptation there has for centuries been a brisk international trade . . . but translations have been few and far between. In England least of all have we shown any appetite for them. Even of Molière we have made, for the stage, only crude and now almost forgotten adaptations. Since, then, Ibsen—translated, not adapted—has met with some acceptance in the English theatre, that fact is in itself practically unique. If he had indeed been "impossible" on the English stage, he would have had as companions in impossibility Corneille, Racine, Molière, Marivaux, Lessing, Goethe, Schiller, Lope and Calderon; no such despicable fraternity. As a matter of fact, and in the face of the unexampled tempest of obloquy in the press, seven of his plays—not adapted, but faithfully translated—have been placed on the English stage. If our theatrical history presents any parallel to this, I shall be glad to hear of it: I certainly can think of none.

Archer goes on to point out that of the seven Ibsen plays so far produced in London (excluding *The Lady from the Sea,* of which he knew no details, and *Ghosts,* which did not charge for its two performances), the receipts for *The Pillars of Society* (one matinee) and *Rosmersholm* (in 1891, two matinees) totalled £276. The three remaining plays—*A Doll's House, Hedda Gabler* and *The Master Builder*—took £4,600. *Hedda Gabler* made a profit, after paying all expenses, of £281 on its ten matinees. Yet he concluded with the surprisingly pessimistic forecast that "It is scarcely to be expected . . . that they [Ibsen's plays] should take deep and permanent hold on the English stage," and expressed the hope that English successors to Ibsen would emerge and be played instead. He would have been happy to know that, over three-quarters of a century later, around twenty professional productions a year of those plays would regularly be mounted on the English theatre, television, and radio.

The enemies of Ibsen, naturally, continued to fulminate. In the prologue to his play *The Tempter,* written this year, Henry Arthur Jones exhorted his audience to

> Shun the crude present with vain problems rife.
> Nor join the bleak Norwegian's barren quest
> For deathless beauty's self and holy zest
> Of rapturous martyrdom, in some base strife
> Of petty dullards, soused in native filth.[13]

On 11 July Sigurd and Bergliot had their first child, a boy. Mercifully rejecting the suggestion of their landlord that he should be called Bjørnstjerne (how could any child or man have lived up to the name of Bjørnstjerne Ibsen?) they christened him Tancred, a Norman name (writes Bergliot) so as to symbolize the union between the north and the south, between Scandinavia and the Mediterranean. Soon after he was born they moved to Christiania, and came to Ibsen to show him his first grandchild.

"I can still see Ibsen [recalled Bergliot] drifting with his short steps around his wife as she sat in the centre of the room with Tancred on her lap. Each time he passed he bent down and looked at him, childishly gentle and happy because it was a boy." They had him baptized by Christopher Bruun, the part-original of Brand; he wore the robe in which his grandfather had been baptized, and Suzannah carried him to the font. Ibsen was very nervous lest any accident should befall the child, and as Suzannah

---

[13] Two years later, in an essay entitled "The Renascence of English Drama," Jones declared: "A strong, dirty man has written plays, and now every feeble dirty person thinks himself a dramatist." But in 1913, in *Foundations of a National Drama,* Jones recanted, and spoke of himself as one of "those whom his shattering genius has at length conquered," referring to him in the same volume as "a great destroyer; a great creator; a great poet; a great liberator. . . . There is no serious modern dramatist who has not been directly or indirectly influenced by him."

approached the font he rose, crossed over to Bergliot, took her arm and whispered "Do you think she'll drop him?" At the dinner afterwards in Viktoria Terrasse Ibsen made a speech thanking Bruun for everything he had meant to him, and Bruun replied with the eloquence which Ibsen had so admired in him in Rome.

For the first time, Bergliot was now seeing her parents-in-law regularly.

It was a new and strange world. The Ibsens' home was as quiet as Aulestad had been full of fun and life. Few people visited them. . . . There was one thing I could not understand at all. I came from the company of my own family, from Father, who believed in everything and everyone, the good that people told him and the bad; believed in people; both those who told the truth and those who lied; and then I came to the Ibsens, to Henrik Ibsen, who believed no one and nothing that anyone told him. I remember I would come up from town full of news which I enthusiastically recounted to them. Ibsen would sit and listen attentively, and when I had finished he would say: "Don't believe a word of it, it's all untrue." I had to hide my disappointment; but what surprised me most was that he was nearly always right.

The strange thing about Ibsen was that he seemed so slow at grasping things. One always had to tell him a story twice. First he listened, the second time he always asked very searchingly for details which lay very far from my Bjørnson nature. But he would insist. He took note of every detail; one could literally see him absorbing them. When anything particularly interested him, he would raise one eyebrow like Sigurd, and one of his eyes seemed much bigger than the other. But soon after he would go into his room; he was always occupied with his work.[14]

That summer Ibsen renewed a friendship, which had been allowed to lapse, with the only other Norwegian whose name was as internationally famous as his own. Edvard Grieg had recently returned from Germany in a state of poor health and extreme nervous exhaustion, and had gone to the sanatorium at Grefsen to recuperate. One Sunday in July Ibsen was visiting Christian Sontum and his family there, and Grieg walked over to join them. Bolette Sontum was present and, in her awkward English, recalled the occasion:

Ibsen sat brooding, solemn and relentless. But suddenly his face lighted up radiantly as Grieg, light-hearted and buoyant as a sunbeam, tripped up the steps. The two masters clasped hands. They had not met for years, and there was a shot of questions and answers as between two boys, Ibsen's deep basso vibrating thunders to Grieg's piping Bergen soprano. Half-serious, half-jesting, they discussed the plan of Grieg's setting *The Vikings at Helgeland* to music. . . . . After dinner at the Sanatorium we induced Ibsen, in behalf of the balmy summer afternoon, to walk with us to the "Little Outlook," a particularly choice viewpoint on the Grefsen plateau, which commands an excellent

[14] Bergliot Ibsen, pp. 143–44.

perspective of Christiania miles below in the valley. Ibsen walked very slowly, his shoulders stooped, one hand against his back, the other clasping the gold head of his walnut stick. This stick was as personally associated with him as his big gold-rimmed spectacles. These he had twisted so that the left eye always seemed larger and more drooping than the right, and really exaggerated the severity of his piercing gaze. The stick itself was a necessary complement to the glasses, as his near-sightedness made him helpless one step beyond his immediate vision.

We walked very slowly on his account, especially when climbing the last steep round of the mountain. Finally, we came up breathless but rewarded with the inspiring view of the fjord. Ibsen sat down heavily on a rustic bench under one distinctly black fir, whose branches cut appealing grotesques against the blue sky.[15]

Ibsen was to remember this place, and the view of the distant city with its factories, three years later when writing the final scene of *John Gabriel Borkman*. But he was to write another play before that, and on 18 September he informed Jacob Hegel that he had begun to plan it, and "intend to complete it next summer."

He seems to have kept largely to himself for the rest of that year; with Hildur still abroad, he paid fewer visits to theatres and none to lectures or concerts. Among his infrequent visitors was Jonas Lie's youngest daughter Johanne, then at the start of her career as an actress. Ibsen, with her father, attended her debut at the Christiania Theatre, and asked her to come and read to him at Viktoria Terrasse. When she arrived, Suzannah admitted her with the daunting welcome, "Dr. Ibsen is expecting you," and showed her into his "very small study."

Ibsen wanted to chat. And I got the feeling that this great writer was no cold satirist but a man of strong and lasting passions. He was not taciturn nor coldly curt; indeed, there was something confidential about his manner of talking. Suddenly there would be a flash of lightning under those bushy eyebrows, and one felt that this man could see right through one. I rose to leave, certain that he had forgotten about the reading. "No, now you must read for me." . . . I read him scenes [from *Love's Comedy*]. Dr. Ibsen rose. "You shall play that part." And the amazing thing was that he actually wrote to Schrøder, the head of the theatre, and I did play Svanhild.[16]

But she remembered how cold he could be to people he did not like, or who were over-familiar.

I see Dr. Ibsen standing in a doorway at a big party at Dr. Bœck's at Munkedammen, looking straight ahead as though in a dream. A gentleman claps him on the shoulder. "Come on, Henrik, let's have a drink. Don't stand there brooding." Ibsen did not reply, but a motion of the hand dismissed the

[15] Sontum, pp. 250–51.
[16] Johanne Lie's reminiscences of Ibsen were published in *Urd, Ibsen-nummer* (Oslo, 1928), pp. 150–51.

speaker mercilessly, like a feather that one blows away. . . . He worked all
the time, at home, on the street, in cafés. . . . He was not especially afraid
of death—only, when he was working on a play he would fear he might be
taken away before he had said what he had to say to the world. And he did
not want to die abroad.

Once Johanne introduced another young girl to him as he was checking
his watch by the university clock. "Later that young girl often visited
him at his home. She interested him." Who this girl was we do not know,
nor whether he used her in any of the three plays he had still to write.
Like so many men who cannot fulfil themselves sexually for one reason
or another (and I think there is little doubt that he could not, at any
rate in old age), he needed a variety of attractive companions.

A Danish schoolboy, too, met Ibsen for the first time this year, and
carried away an unusual impression. Jacob Hegel's son, named Frederik
after his grandfather, was in the capital and had been told by his father
to pay his respects. Aged thirteen, he arrived without warning.

> I rang; and Fru Ibsen warily opened the front door. When I told her who I
> was, she let me in, and Ibsen, who had been lying on the sofa with a rug over
> him, unwrapped himself slowly and came to greet me. . . . He began to
> talk and talk of Denmark. What Denmark had meant to him. He spoke
> warmly, not grandly but humbly, softly and with deep emotion. He took
> me out on to the balcony and looked over Oslo [sic] as he spoke, and became
> more and more moved. Remarkable to relate, this lonely man opened his
> heart completely to the youth from Denmark who he scarcely knew, and wept.
> He laid his head on my shoulder and wept. . . . Fru Ibsen gave me an
> angry glance as I left. She sensed that something had happened.[17]

No wonder she gave young Hegel a resentful look. Although he does not
say so, and may not have realized it, Ibsen only behaved this way when he
was drunk, and Suzannah must have wondered what story the boy would
take back to his father in Copenhagen.

1893 was, as we have seen, an important year for Ibsen in England, and
it was to prove equally so in France. That autumn Lugné-Pœ founded,
together with Edouard Vuillard and Camille Mauclair, a "little theatre"
on the lines of Antoine's Théâtre Libre and Paul Fort's short-lived
Théâtre de l'Art, (in which Lugné-Pœ himself had played the Old Blind
Man in Mæterlinck's *L'Intruse*). They called their new enterprise Le
Théâtre de l'Oeuvre, and opened it on 6 October with *Rosmersholm*.
Vuillard did the decor and designed the programme and posters; Lugné-
Pœ played Rosmer and Berthe Bady, Rebecca. The production was much
better than that of *The Lady from the Sea* the previous year, for Ibsen,
on hearing about the latter effort from Herman Bang, had asked Bang
to advise Lugné-Pœ on the way his plays ought to be done: realistically, as
opposed to ritualistically, and above all quickly. Antoine had had the right

[17] Frederik Hegel, *Erindringer*, I (Copenhagen, 1946), 115.

naturalistic approach, but lacked any background of Scandinavian knowledge, and especially of Norwegian manners. Bang was able to provide this. The case was similar to that of Chekhov in England; he was never fully understood until Theodor Komisarjevsky, in the nineteen-twenties, was able to explain that what had been assumed to be eccentric and symbolic was far more effective if played with the simplest realism.

On 10 November the Théâtre de l'Oeuvre followed *Rosmersholm* with *An Enemy of the People,* as though to underline Ibsen's expressed hostility to overt symbolism in drama. Yet here again Ibsen showed his gift for reflecting topical issues anywhere and at any time, for the premiere occurred on a day when there were fierce anarchical demonstrations in the streets of Paris, and Dr. Stockmann's hard words about the mob won an enthusiastic response from the young poets and artists who formed a large part of the audience and, odd as it may seem today, regarded themselves as an elite and dissociated themselves from the rioters outside.

The dress rehearsal itself turned into a riot. It was preceded by a lecture, ostensibly about the play, by Laurent Tailhade "which [writes Archer] consisted not so much of an exposition of the play as of a violent attack upon all the 'leading men' in French literature and politics. Beside it, Dr. Stockmann's harangue in the fourth act seems moderate and almost mealy-mouthed." Among the writers attacked were several who were present, including Sarcey; and Tailhade compared Dr. Stockmann to the prophet Elijah. Archer continues: "The audience listened, not without protest, to M. Tailhade's diatribe, until he thought fit to describe the recent Franco-Russian fêtes as an act of collective insanity. At this point a storm of indignation burst forth, which lasted without pause for a quarter of an hour, and was not allayed by an attempt at intervention on the part of M. Lugné-Pœ. The lecture closed amid wild confusion, and altogether the preliminary scene in the auditorium was like a spirited rehearsal of the meeting at Captain Horster's."[18]

Thus Ibsen found himself simultaneously acclaimed as the opponent and the champion of anarchy. Clemenceau felt that the occasion recalled the brave days of 1830; the Théâtre de l'Oeuvre came to be regarded as a centre of anarchy, and was the subject of a debate in the French Parliament; and a young anarchist named Auguste Vaillant who had been arrested for an attempt to set off a dynamite explosion named among the writers who had inspired him Darwin, Herbert Spencer and Ibsen, three singularly law-abiding men. But the play received tepid reviews. Apart from Henri Bauer in *Echo de Paris,* the French critics found it ill-constructed (which it certainly is not).[19]

One would like to be able to record the German productions of Ibsen

[18] William Archer, Introduction to *An Enemy of the People* (London, 1901), pp. xv–xvi.

[19] Nyholm, pp. 42–44.

that took place this year; but most of his royalties from that country were now coming through his agent, Felix Bloch, and are not separately itemized in his accounts, and the history of Ibsen on the German stage is lamentably ill-documented. W. H. Eller, in his book *Ibsen in Germany* (Boston, 1918), lists no new productions in 1892 and none in 1893 save the Berlin *Master Builder;* but although Ibsen's royalties from Block were down to 1,353 crowns in 1893, compared with 1,539 in 1892 and 2,120 in 1891 (an outstanding year), one doubts whether those sums can refer only to repeats of old performances. Even if they do, the figures show that, contrary to some supposition, he was still being frequently performed there. A windfall of £200 from Heinemann for the English edition of *The Master Builder* made 1893 a fair year for one in which Ibsen had written no new play:

	crowns	
Royalties from Bloch	204	
Fee from Heinemann for English edition of *The Master Builder*	3,628	
Fee for English edition of *Peer Gynt*	242	
Fee from Christiania Theatre for *The Master Builder*	3,000	
Fee from August Lindberg for Stockholm and Gothenburg rights of *The Master Builder*	1,000	
Royalties from Bloch	750	
3rd edn. of *The Pillars of Society*	700	
Royalties for *The Master Builder* at Royal Theatre, Copenhagen (1st–5th perfs.)	1,775	
Royalties from Société des Auteurs Dramatiques (810 fr.)	577	
Royalties from H. Beerbohm Tree for 1st and 2nd perfs. of *An Enemy of the People* in London (£11–7–0)	205	
Royalties from Bloch	204	
Royalties from Wien Burgtheater for *An Enemy of the People*	120	
Royalties from Tree for 3rd–7th perfs. of *An Enemy of the People* in London (£25–5–0)	458	
Royalties for *The Pillars of Society* at Munich Hoftheater	135	
Royalties from Opera Comique, London, for *Rosmersholm,* etc. (£12–10–0)	227	
Royalties for *The Master Builder* at Royal Theatre, Copenhagen (6th–11th perfs.)	1,095	
Royalties from Bloch	195	
7th edn. of *The Vikings at Helgeland*	406	
9th edn. of *Peer Gynt*	1,815	
Royalties for *The Pillars of Society* and *A Doll's House* at Munich Hoftheater	456	
	17,192	£955

32

Little Eyolf

1894

Lugné-Pœ's enthusiasm for Ibsen continued unabated into 1894. On 3 April he directed and acted *The Master Builder* for his Théâtre de l'Oeuvre at the Bouffes du Nord. The production was received with derision. Gunnar Heiberg records that the audience shouted their own answers to Hilde's questions to Solness; the business about the crack in the chimney-pipe was greeted with roars of laughter; and whenever (as happens several times in the play) any character said, "I don't understand this," the audience echoed, "Neither do we." Yet again, the mockery of the first-night audience represented only one view. Heiberg, reporting on a revival of the production five years later, comments: "The general public liked neither the play nor the performance, but the young, the supporters of Ibsen and l'Oeuvre loved both. 'God, what a play!' exclaimed one young man with long hair." But despite Herman Bang's coaching, Heiberg still noted with regret the tendency of the French to intone Ibsen like a mass and surround his plays with a kind of mystique, even (indeed, especially) when having to express everyday sentiments; and he felt that Lugné-Pœ acted Solness "tastefully and intelligently, but without suggesting a living person."[1]

Yet two more distinguished judges than Heiberg found both the production and Lugné-Pœ's performance powerful and moving. When the company visited London the following year, Bernard Shaw wrote:

> Comparing the performance with what we have achieved in England, it must be admitted that neither Mr. Waring nor Mr. Waller were in a position to play Solness as M. Lugné-Pœ played him. They would never have got another engagement in genteel comedy if they had worn those vulgar trousers,

---

[1] Gunnar Heiberg, *Ibsen og Bjørnson på scenen*, pp. 81–86. At the dress rehearsal of the 1898 production a disaster occurred in the final act when the dummy figure that was to drop from the flies (showing Solness's fall from his tower) burst and showered its contents over the front stalls.

painted that red eruption on their faces, and given life to that portrait which, in every stroke, from its domineering energy, talent and covetousness, to its half-witted egoism and crazy philandering sentiment, is so amazingly true to life. Mr. Waring and Mr. Waller failed because they were under the spell of Ibsen's fame as a dramatic magician, and grasped at his poetic treatment of the man instead of at the man himself. M. Lugné-Pœ succeeded because he recognized Solness as a person he had met a dozen times in ordinary life, and just reddened his nose and played him without preoccupation.[2]

How much better Shaw wrote about Ibsen when reviewing productions of his plays than in the *Quintessence!* The other authority who set the seal of his approval on the production and performance was, as we shall see, Ibsen himself.

A fortnight after *The Master Builder* opening, on 20 April, Paris enjoyed another and more fashionable Ibsen premiere when Gabrielle Réjane played Nora at the Théâtre Vaudeville. Ibsen sent her a telegram thanking her for fulfilling his "dearest dream, in creating Nora in Paris." She enjoyed a great triumph in the role, thanks largely to Herman Bang, who advised on this production as he had on Lugné-Pœ's. "If I succeeded in overcoming the many difficulties in the part of Nora," Réjane wrote to Lugné-Pœ, "I owe it to Herman Bang"; and she added that she had never met a director who exuded so strong a personality in the theatre. The production provided Ibsen with his first popular success in France, and even the critics who were usually hostile to him found something to praise. Sarcey himself declared *A Doll's House* to be the best constructed and most interesting foreign play yet performed in France, though he felt that it showed an obvious debt to Scribe and Sardou, and could not believe in Nora's abandonment of her husband and children. He summed it up as "an enjoyable comedy, apart from its dénouement." Nora's final action struck many observers as typifying the difference between Scandinavian and French manners. Edmond de Goncourt wrote in his diary that "this naïvety, sophism and emotional perversion is characteristic of Scandinavian women," and Ernst Tissot thought it showed that Norwegian women read too much, with the result that "a kind of intellectual hysteria forces itself into minds ill-equipped to think."[3]

Numerous tributes reached Réjane from Norway; the artist Fritz Thaulow sent her a painting, Jonas Lie a poem and Edvard Grieg a piece of music. The success of *A Doll's House* and the interest created by the l'Oeuvre productions opened the way for Strindberg in Paris. His *Creditors* was produced by the L'Oeuvre that June and *The Father* in December, the latter play being especially acclaimed. The consciousness of his debt

[2] *Saturday Review,* 30 March 1895, p. 413.

[3] Nyholm, pp. 55–59. Goncourt's diary (6 May 1894) shows how wildly Ibsen's contemporaries speculated about his literary ancestry: "Zola declares Ibsen to have sprung from French Romanticism, especially George Sand, while Léon Daudet says he sprang from the German Romantics."

to Ibsen annoyed Strindberg. *"Pourquoi servirai-je comme chien de chasse à Ibsen?"* he wrote to Lugné-Pœ on 16 December 1894. *"J'ai été sa victime depuis dix ans,"*[4] and he repeated his complaint that *Hedda Gabler* was a crib of *The Father.*

On 4 May London, for the first time, saw *The Wild Duck,* produced by J. T. Grein for his Independent Theatre Society at the Royalty in Soho, with Laurence Irving, the son of Henry Irving, as Relling. William Archer, who had been disappointed with the play on reading it, confessed himself "utterly mistaken. The play now proved itself scenic in the highest degree. . . . Hardly ever before, as it seemed to me, had I seen so much of the very quintessence of life concentrated in the brief traffic of the stage." Not all the critics were enthusiastic; Clement Scott wrote that "to call such an eccentricity as this a masterpiece, to classify it at all as dramatic literature, or to make a fuss about so feeble a production, is to insult dramatic literature and outrage common sense."

The previous winter steps had been taken in Christiania to found an Authors' Society, for the protection of literary rights. Ibsen readily agreed to join, signed the invitations to the inaugural meeting on 7 May, and attended himself; but it was the last time he did so. Three days before the meeting an article by a young writer named Gabriel Finne appeared in *Dagbladet* attacking the project on the grounds that such a society would inevitably be controlled by old men, and that the old hated everything that was young, fresh and alive. He specifically excepted Ibsen from this generalisation; but at the supper following the meeting another young writer, Nils Kjær, jumped to his feet and delivered a violent denunciation of "the old writers who have never been able to portray women but have always obstructed the ambitions of youth." He did not name Ibsen but (despite the peculiar inapplicability of the words to him) aimed his speech at the table where the latter was sitting, and ended: "We hate you! But your time is past! If you want to see the poet of Norway's future, here he sits!" So saying, he placed his hand on the shoulder of Gabriel Finne, who had fallen asleep with his head on the table. As Ibsen left, he said to Dietrichson: "That was the most unpleasant occasion I have ever been present at. I shall never set foot in this society again." Next day, Nils Kjær came to apologise to him, and received the immortal snub: "Young man, the secret of drinking is never to drink less the day after."[5]

Meanwhile, his new play had been maturing in his mind, and on 15 June he wrote Bergliot: "Tomorrow I shall start writing the dialogue in earnest." A week later he wrote Gerda Brandes that he was well under way, and by 10 July he had completed Act One. The next day he began Act Two, and a fortnight later, on 25 July, was able to inform Jacob

---

[4] *August Strindbergs brev,* X, 332.

[5] Koht, II, 251–52; Dietrichson, IV, 416–17; Georg Brochmann, *Den norske forfatterforening gjennem 50 år* (Oslo, 1952), pp. 27–33.

Hegel: "Yesterday I completed the second act of my new play, and have already today begun work on the third and last act. So I hope to have the final version finished in good time. This of course means that I cannot think of taking any summer holiday this year. But I don't need one. I am very content here, and happiest when I am working at my desk." The third act he completed on 7 August, also in a fortnight. But he then revised the play so thoroughly that over two months elapsed before he was ready, on 13 October, to send *Little Eyolf* to the printers.

As William Archer commented: "Revision amounted almost to re-invention; and it was the re-invention that determined the poetic value of the play. The poet's original idea . . . was simply to study a rather commonplace wife's jealousy of a rather commonplace child. The lameness of Eyolf proves to have been an afterthought: and as Eyolf is not lame, it follows that the terrible cry of 'The crutch is floating!' was also an afterthought, as well as the almost intolerable scene of recrimination between Allmers and Rita as to the accident which caused his lameness. We find, in fact, that nearly everything that gives the play its depth, its horror and its elevation came as an afterthought. . . . In no case, perhaps, did revision work such a transfiguration as in *Little Eyolf*."[6]

Georg Brandes was in Christiania again that August with his family, and Ibsen took especial delight in the company of Brandes's young daughter Edith. "This evening," he wrote in her album on 15 August, "two little girls sang so beautifully for me. Thank you for the song, Edith! I often think I hear it still."[7] She lived, like so many of the girls whom Ibsen liked, to a great age, and must have been one of the very few people who personally knew both Ibsen and Brecht.

On 3 October, while Ibsen was fair-copying *Little Eyolf*, Aurélien Lugné-Pœ and his company from the Théâtre de l'Oeuvre arrived in Christiania to give guest performances of *Rosmersholm* and *The Master Builder*. They were a very young group—"ten players," recalled Lugné-Pœ in his memoirs, "whose total ages came to less than two hundred years." He himself, one may repeat, was only twenty-four. Their first morning they went to the Grand Hotel to catch a glimpse of their author. At the stroke of twelve, Ibsen made his ritual entry.

We stood waiting for him, and recognized him immediately. As he walked through the hotel to the dining-room he reminded me of a doctor on the way to visit his patients. . . . He paced with careful steps to seclude himself in a corner of the large restaurant. Berthe Bady . . . begged Hammer to present her to him. . . . Ibsen was exactly as I had often heard described. He rose and adjusted his gold spectacles, then amiably and smilingly said a few words in a low voice and sat down again. Then he took out a small comb and smoothed his hair where it had been crimped by his hat. At first glance his ap-

[6] William Archer, *From Ibsen's Workshop* (London, 1912), p. 18.
[7] Gerda Brandes, "Prinsessans Album" in *Svenska Dagbladet*, 9 May 1965.

pearance struck me as correct and somewhat diffident, his face luminous above
a high white cravat. . . . I would like to have had the extraordinary gaze of
this man. Indeed, I have never been able to forget his eyes, which only the
painter Edvard Munch once succeeded in reproducing. One eye, half-closed,
seemed to reflect and ponder, while the other observed Bady sharply and with
intense and surprising animation and warmth. The indeterminate colour of
those eyes behind the spectacles seemed to shine with an unusual brilliance.
His brow was unique, proclaiming intelligence, discipline and distinction, its
breadth and proportions perfectly matched. Bady wept. At last she let Ibsen
bury himself in his newspaper and disappear behind it. We had imagined
Ibsen to be gruff and unapproachable, but after their conversation Bady told
everyone: "He is charming and his face is quite pink—and his eyes are so
gentle and good—and how young his voice is!"

They were to play in the Carl Johan Theatre, "a kind of large barn in
the old Tivoli Gardens . . . neither pleasant nor elegant." Ibsen came to
the first night of *Rosmersholm*. "During the whole performance Ibsen
remained motionless. He seemed to wish to restrain the audience from
demonstrating in any way. Only at the end of every act did he applaud,
without manifesting pleasure. After the final act he rose, bowed to us actors,
then to the audience who were applauding him. That was all."
At eleven the next morning Herman Bang took Lugné-Pœ to visit Ibsen
at Viktoria Terrasse.

He received us, as before, with that exceptional amiability which I have
often remarked in him, like a doctor receiving a patient. . . . Dare I say
without lack of respect that that morning Ibsen was *"dans le décor"*? . . .
Very *soigné*, his hair and beard shaggy yet combed in a curiously fastidious
style, his glasses on his nose, just as I had seen him in the Grand Hotel. From
time to time Bang came to my assistance. I felt so tall that the furniture, the
knick-knacks, the paintings on the wall, even my host himself, all made me
feel gauche and clumsy. I waited for Ibsen to indicate that I might sit. He,
somewhat small compared with me, seemed visibly ill at ease. His eyes bored
deeply into mine as though exploring me.

Bang explained that Lugné-Pœ understood German, and Ibsen said he
was grateful for the performance of *Rosmersholm* but was particularly
looking forward to their interpretation of *The Master Builder*.

He was not surly as we had been led to expect, nor seemed distrustful, but
almost immediately made that remark in German which I subsequently repeated in Paris and which helped me greatly the following evening [when acting *The Master Builder*]: "French actors are more suited than many others to
act my plays. People have not fully appreciated that a passionate writer needs
to be acted with passion, and not otherwise." . . . As he saw us to the door
he added something which I could not understand, but I heard two or three

8 For these and following details of Lugné-Pœ's visit to Christiania, cf. his *Ibsen*,
pp. 75 ff.

times the name Ulric Brendel. When we left the Master after a reception that had been friendly and courteous, but nothing more, I expressed my amazement to Herman Bang that he had said nothing about the previous evening's performance of *Rosmersholm*. "Well," said Bang, "he was a little upset because in the last scene Brendel's entrance was lit by electricity. He doesn't want to have any stupid mysticism in his plays."

Ibsen came to their opening performance of *The Master Builder* on 5 October and Herman Bang remembered his reaction:

> By general agreement, this strange play had not succeeded in the Scandinavian theatres. . . . Ibsen took his place in his box. As usual he sat motionless throughout the first act. . . . Towards the end of the act it was as though something had been awakened in him. In the second act Ibsen rose to his feet and leaned against the wall of his box. His eyes followed every movement of the actors, and the Master's eyes dwelling on them seemed to increase their power and magic. . . . In the third act Ibsen leaned out over the balustrade of the box. . . . When I went to the Grand that night Ibsen came to greet me. Only once have I seen him moved, and that was on this occasion. He stretched out both his hands to me; they were ice-cold, as though his excitement had drawn all the warmth from them. "This," he said, "was the resurrection of my play."[9]

Ibsen used his influence to recommend that Lugné-Pœ should be awarded a medal, which the latter received soon after his return to France and which proved useful in a way that neither Ibsen nor King Oscar can have foreseen. "Shall I confess," Lugné-Pœ writes, "that that medal rescued many a performance? Every time we found ourselves short of money for a new production, off it went to the pawnbroker, and Ibsen never learned what a service he had done us."

The Swedish actor-manager Albert Ranft was in Christiania at this time, anxious if possible to obtain Ibsen's forthcoming play before the bigger Stockholm theatres. He put up at the Grand Hotel and, having unpacked his bags, went down to the reading-room, and was about to enter when he was stopped by a waiter with the words: "You can't go in there. The Doctor's there and mustn't be disturbed." "What doctor?" asked Ranft. "Is someone ill?" "No, it's Dr. Ibsen. He's reading the newspapers." Ranft bribed the waiter with a tip and went in. Ibsen gave him a look as though to say: "Who's this who dares to enter while I am here?" But when he learned who Ranft was and why he had come, he treated him with kindness and courtesy. Ranft asked if he might read *Little Eyolf* before publication "to see if we can play it, and if so, buy it."

> Ibsen said: "So you want to read it first and buy it later?" He stared at me in such astonishment that I feared I had said the wrong thing.

9 *Ibid.*, p. 82. Bang originally recorded his memories of Ibsen in *Die Neue Rundschau* (1906), pp. 1498–99.

"Well—." "I see, you want to read it first. Everyone else has wanted to buy it first and read it later. You shall have the play." And he shook my hand and said: "Won't you have a drink?"

But when, later, Ranft began to question him about the play, he found Ibsen accommodating but totally unhelpful. "Can't this line be interpreted thus, and spoken thus?" asked Ranft. "Oh, yes." "But how do you think it should be said?" "Oh, my dear fellow," replied Ibsen. "You say it how you please, it's all the same to me."[10] Similar evidence of Ibsen's indifference to how actors spoke his lines is given by Helena Nyblom, quoting the great Danish actor Emil Poulsen. Poulsen told her that after Ibsen had attended a performance of *The Wild Duck* in Copenhagen the cast waited expectantly for his comments. "But it seemed as though he no longer knew what he had meant by the play. He went around asking us actors, as though we should know better."[11]

At the beginning of December Suzannah, accompanied by Sigurd, went south again to escape the worst of the winter, and on 11 December Ibsen wrote to her one of those touchingly Darby-and-Joan letters which they exchanged when parted:

Dear Suzannah!
I have received your telegrams, and now your letter. How happy and relieved I am to learn that everything has so far gone so well! I hope it will continue so! Here all is well. Frøken Blehr's[12] cooking suits me excellently. And there is plenty of it, so that we have ample left for supper should I want any. But I usually just have herring then, with the most beautiful boiled potatoes which Lina [their maid] prepares in the new machine. She does everything for me most attentively. Bergliot had dinner with me on Sunday. Otherwise, no one has been here. The evenings are lonely, of course; but then I sit and read at the dinner table. In the morning I drink coffee, which I have brought to my bedroom at eight o'clock sharp. Indeed, everything goes like clockwork, just as if you were here. Every morning Augusta brings me a little tray with crumbs for the birds. Lina is good to her and gives her some of all the food that gets left over. My new play is being published today, both here and in Berlin and London. I got the fee from Heinemann yesterday, and am having Hegel invest 10,000 crowns for us. And later I hope a further 4,000 without having to leave ourselves short. I am overwhelmed with correspondence, as you can imagine. But I answer it all in as few words as I can—and so manage. Give Sigurd my warmest regards. I shall soon see his new book [*Men and Powers*] to which I greatly look forward. Greet also the Grønvolds, Frøken Klingenfeld, and Frøken Raff—not to forget

10 Albert Ranft, *Memoarer*, I (Stockholm, 1928), 151–52.
11 Helena Nyblom, *Mina levnadsminne*, I (Stockholm, 1922), 236.
12 A lady who ran a domestic science school in the same street.

Clemence if she is still in Munich, and thank both the last-named deeply for the beautiful pictures! I wish you and Sigurd the happiest of times in our old haunts! Write soon again.

Your affectionate
H.I.

William Heinemann having safeguarded his copyright by a public reading at the Haymarket Theatre on 3 December, *Little Eyolf* was, as Ibsen stated, published simultaneously in Copenhagen, Christiania, London and Berlin on 11 December 1894—though it almost missed being on sale in Christiania that day, for a fog prevented the steamer from Copenhagen containing the copies from arriving until the late afternoon, to the vexation of prospective purchasers who had been waiting in the bookshops since early morning.

Surprisingly, for it is one of Ibsen's subtlest and most elusive plays, it received an almost unanimously favourable (if somewhat bemused) reception from the Scandinavian press. "A new triumph," wrote the penitent Nils Kjær (who had so insulted Ibsen at the Authors' Society, but who was embarking on what was to be a distinguished career as a dramatic critic) in *Dagbladet* on 12 December. "He has conjured forth another of those monumental dramas the architectonic perfection and severely symmetrical beauty of which will be enough to ensure the continuing admiration of the world"—though he suspected that "for the latest vintage of Ibsen's admirers the play may disappoint because it is less symbolic and more realistic."

Kristofer Randers, who had severely criticized several of Ibsen's recent plays, praised this one highly in *Aftenposten* (13 December): "Has our old poet become young again? Does he wish to put our younger writers to shame, so youthful he is here, so fresh, immediate and powerful?" An anonymous reviewer in *Verdens Gang* (12 December), after remarking on "the feverish interest with which the famous poet's new play is awaited," thought it "fully worthy of this attention; the view of life it expresses will arouse bitter opposition, but the play will live."

Georg Brandes, in an open letter to the same paper three days later, observed: "There has always existed a duality in Ibsen; he advocates the cause of Nature, and he rebukes it. . . . Now Nature has the voice over Morality, now the reverse. In *The Master Builder*, as in *Ghosts*, the advocate of Nature was dominant; here, as in *Brand* and *The Wild Duck*, he is the chastener." By now, Brandes concluded, it was impertinent to criticize such a giant as Ibsen; one could merely thank him. Edvard Brandes, who that year had been appointed director of the Royal Theatre in Copenhagen, also praised the play, remarking (*Politiken*, 14 December) that it would not give rise to the violent debates and differing interpretations which had greeted most of Ibsen's works. "Here no riddles are posed without solutions, no mighty questions which are not answered. Neither those who defend the social system nor those who have declared war on it will be able to use this play as ammunition."

Nils Vogt in *Morgenbladet* (15 December) found the third act weak but praised the play as a whole; and on 20 December Just Bing wrote a perceptive article pointing out that the play has a concealed meaning as well as its obvious one, and that, like Solness and Hilde, the Allmers are people through whom other powers speak. "Ibsen's characters are at home in only one place—in Ibsen's plays. But there, they are totally at home. At the peak of crisis . . . they can breathe and move in their rightful atmosphere."

Among the few dissident voices the leading one was, as usual, C. D. af Wirsen. "As in *The Master Builder*," he protested (*Kritiker,* pp. 115–17), "the symbolism over-reaches itself, the action is thin, we do not believe in the characters' change of heart. . . . A real decadence is revealed in these three plays, *Hedda Gabler, The Master Builder* and *Little Eyolf.* Where is the author of *The Pretenders* and *The Vikings at Helgeland?*"

Commercially, *Little Eyolf* was an immense success. The first edition of 10,000 copies sold out almost at once; a second edition of 2,000 appeared on 21 December, and a third of 1,250 on 20 January. A surprising proportion of these were sold outside Scandinavia. *Morgenbladet's* Copenhagen correspondent reported on 15 December that, apart from the Scandinavian bookshops in America taking large quantities, "there is scarcely anywhere in the world where people do not want to read Ibsen in the original and as quickly as possible. As soon as a new work by him is announced, orders begin to pour in to the publishers, not merely—indeed, perhaps least—from foreign booksellers, but from private individuals—in Germany, France, England, Russia, Rumania, Turkey, Greece, Italy. . . . And these orders, as their language proves, do not come merely from Scandinavians. It is no exaggeration to say that myriads of people in foreign countries all over the world have learned Norwegian in order to read Ibsen's works in the original tongue."

The reporter added that on the day of publication P. A. Rosenberg, the director of Dagmars Theatre in Copenhagen, had given a public reading of the play in the Concert Palace, and that another theatre director named Neergaard had given another public reading a couple of days later —news which cannot have pleased Ibsen, remembering his strictures on Andreas Isachsen for doing the same thing with *Emperor and Galilean* twenty years earlier. But Rosenberg's reading, at least, was poorly attended, with only a few hundred people scattered around an auditorium holding three thousand. Most people evidently preferred to read it for themselves or wait until it was performed.

These were not the only irritations Ibsen suffered in Denmark in connection with *Little Eyolf;* the plot had been leaked to the press before publication, something he so dreaded that he always requested Gyldendal to print the title page and list of characters last, lest any of the compositors or employees should feel tempted to turn a dishonest penny. The novelist Thomas Krag had accidentally been sent the proofs of *Little Eyolf* instead of some proofs of his own (or, according to another account, had purloined them). He told a journalist what they contained, as a result of which an inaccurate résumé of the first two acts appeared in *Politiken* on 14 November and was copied by many other newspapers. Ibsen was furious; but it is an old adage among publishers that any publicity is good publicity, and the brouhaha probably helped the sales.

Ibsen's fame in England was by now such that *Little Eyolf* was widely reviewed in the London press, though the reception was predictably mixed. The *Daily Chronicle* welcomed it, describing Ibsen as "incomparably the most powerful influence in contemporary literature"; but the *Daily Graphic* thought the play exemplified his weaknesses as well as his strengths, and the *Daily News* found it wholly undramatic, the characters mere abstractions and the dialogue obscure and pointless.

Ibsen lost no time in informing Suzannah and Sigurd of the book's success. "This has been a busy time for me, as you may imagine," he wrote them on 20 December. ". . . It has aroused a storm of enthusiasm, unanimous as never before. The first edition is sold out and a second is appearing tomorrow. Director Ranft has bought the Swedish theatre rights and paid 3,000 crowns for them. The Christiania Theatre ditto. My English fee has been paid. I am straightway investing *seventeen thousand* crowns, which yet leaves a good deal over for us. The play has been accepted by the Royal Theatre in Copenhagen. And the Burgtheater [in Vienna] and the Deutsches Theater [in Berlin]. And doubtless by many other German theatres I don't yet know about."

Bergliot came to spend Christmas Eve with him. Christmas had always meant a lot to Ibsen; Fru Werenskiold, the wife of the artist Erik Werenskiold, once visited him in Munich shortly before Christmas and was surprised to find him occupied in cutting out paper decorations for the tree, which "he did very skilfully," as in his childhood when old Mother Maren had sold his products at her stall in the market place in Skien.

> Now [writes Bergliot] he no longer cut out paper decorations. Lina, the maid, had decorated the tree as Fru Ibsen liked it, just with candles and white cotton wool on the branches. We went in to the Christmas tree. Ibsen had a terror of fire, and was very worried about all the candles on the tree. Still, I had to light them, and a few moments later had to go out into the passage to fetch something. When I came back I saw to my astonishment Ibsen kneeling on the floor blowing the candles out, one after the other. The tree was on the floor and was not big. I can still see Ibsen's profile, and how his nose disappeared each time he blew.

As we sat chatting afterwards, Ibsen told me he had discovered there were a lot of mice in the apartment. But he had his own way of keeping them at a distance. He said: "In the evening I take a glass of milk and some biscuits into my room. I put a little in a saucer for the mice and leave it in the next room, and then they don't come into mine."[13]

On 28 December Ibsen wrote to Suzannah:

Bergliot . . . has been up to me several times and has been very helpful with the Christmas things, which you prepared before you left; or rather, she did it all for me. . . . I have bought you two pretty gifts, which are at present in the drawing-room. And a couple of landscapes from Lofoten. . . . I have been invited out once or twice. . . . Otherwise I sit at home in the evenings and read. Hegel has sent me several new books, and when I know where you are staying for the winter I will forward some to you.   29. 12. I was interrupted at this point yesterday, first by the designer and then by the producer. They are painting new decor for the play and rehearsals are in progress. . . . I have received many flowers and cards . . . even from America. If only I were through with answering them all! The most welcome and useful present was from Bergliot. She gave me an enormous bath sponge, with which I wash and rub myself morning and evening; it suits me splendidly. Don't write your letters criss-cross. I have such difficulty with my eyes in deciphering it. . . .

With the two editions of *Little Eyolf,* various sales of the performing rights, reprints of (at last) *Ghosts* and *The Pretenders* and a miscellany of small royalties and honoraria, 1894 had been a bumper year for Ibsen, though it would have seemed nearly disastrous to an author of comparable stature in England, France, Germany or America. He had earned over 24,000 crowns, more even than in his previous best year, 1800:

	crowns
German royalties from Felix Bloch	155
Unspecified fee from Wien Burgtheater	108
Unspecified royalties from Munich Hoftheater	182
Fee for *The Master Builder* from P. Reclam (Leipzig publisher) (300 marks)	266
Royalties from Agence Roger, Paris (422 francs)	300
Royalties from Bloch	201
Royalties from Walter Scott and William Archer	49
Unspecified theatre royalties from Wm. Heinemann (£15)	272
Royalties from Munich Hoftheater	58

[13] Bergliot Ibsen, p. 153.

	crowns	
8th edn. of *The Pretenders*	1,200	
Fees owed by Bergen Theatre	760	
Royalties from Bloch	324	
Royalties from H. Beerbohm Tree (8 gns.)	152	
Royalties from Munich Hoftheater	203	
Royalties from Bloch	245	
2nd edn. of *Ghosts*	666	
Royalties from Munich Hoftheater	124	
Royalties from H. Beerbohm Tree and Walter Scott (£21–2–4)	416	
Royalties for *Ghosts* at Lessingtheater, Berlin (3 perfs.)	101	
1st edn. of *Little Eyolf*	7,200	
English edn. of *Little Eyolf* (Heinemann, £150)	2,700	
Fees owed by M. Savine, Paris publisher	215	
German edn. of Little Eyolf (S. Fischer)	885	
Fee for *Little Eyolf* at Christiania Theatre	3,000	
Fee for *Little Eyolf* at Bergen Theatre	400	
Fee for Swedish performing rights of *Little Eyolf* (2 years) from Albert Ranft	3,000	
2nd edn. of *Little Eyolf*	1,440	
	24,622	£1,368

As with *The Master Builder,* proofs of *Little Eyolf* had been sent to London as they came off the Gyldendal presses, in order that the translation might proceed without delay. Henry James persuaded William Heinemann to let him have an advance look at the English version, and on 22 November he wrote to Elizabeth Robins:

> Heinemann has lent me the proofs of the 2 first acts of the Play—the ineffable Play—and I can't stay my hand from waving wildly to you! It is indeed immense—indeed and indeed. It is of a rare perfection—and if 3 keeps up the tremendous pitch of 1 and 2 it will distinctly stand at the tiptop of his achievement. It's a masterpiece and a marvel; and it *must* leap upon the stage. . . . The inherent difficulties are there, but they are not insurmountable. They are on the contrary manageable—they are a matter of tact and emphasis—of art and discretion. The thing will be a big *profane* (i.e., Ibsen and non-Ibsen *both*) success. The part—*the* part— is Asta—unless it be the Rat-hound in the Bag! What an old woman—and what a Young!

But three days later, in a letter of apology for having talked indiscreetly about the play "in the despair of a dull dinner—or after-dinner," he wrote to Miss Robins:

> I fear, in truth, no harm can be done equal to the harm done to the play by its own most disappointing third act. It came to me last night—and has been, to me, a subject of depressed reflection. It seems to me a singular

and almost inexplicable drop—dramatically, *representably* speaking. . . . The worst of it is that it goes back, as it were, on what precedes, and gives a meagreness to that too—makes it less interesting and less significant. . . . I don't see the meaning or effect of Borghejm—I don't see the value or final *function* of Asta. . . . I find the solution too simple, too immediate, too much a harking back, and too productive of the sense that there might have been a stronger one. . . . My idea that Asta was to become an active, *the* active agent, is of course blighted.

However, he admitted: "Really uttered, *done,* in the gathered northern twilight, with the flag flown and the lights coming out across the fjord, the scene might have a real solemnity of beauty—and perhaps that's all that's required!" But, he concluded: "I fear Allmers will never be thought an actor-manager's part."

James's objections to the third act of *Little Eyolf* have been shared by many readers; yet, if properly understood and intelligently interpreted, this act is by no means meagre, nor the solution, as James supposed, simple. The great mistake is to imagine that Ibsen envisaged the ending as happy.[14] Surely it is obvious that devoting themselves to charity, sharing their "gold and their green forests" with the poor, will not ultimately provide the answer and the peace which Alfred and Rita are seeking. They have reached rock-bottom; but unless they can prove that they have undergone a genuine change of heart, and are prepared to grapple with the realities of life, this will be no solution but merely another, more plausible but equally insidious "life-lie." They are only at the beginning of their long climb to salvation.

My own belief is that the third act of *Little Eyolf,* like the two that precede it, is among the greatest that Ibsen ever wrote, and that in it he achieved exactly what he set out to achieve, namely, to reveal the interior of what, in *Brand,* thirty years before, he had called "the Ice Church"—the interior of a human soul in which love has died—so that, in Rita's words, all that is left to her and Alfred is to "try to fill that emptiness with something. Something resembling love." In Michael Elliott's delicate production of the play at the 1963 Edinburgh Festival, the two characters spoke the final lines of the play (after Alfred has hoisted the flag to the top of the mast), not facing, but half-turned away from each other, so that the effect was not of facile optimism, but of fear and uncertainty.

Yet James was right in one thing at least—the reluctance of actors of the "actor-manager" type to play Alfred. Like John Rosmer, and Torvald Helmer in *A Doll's House,* Alfred Allmers is weaker than the woman with whom he is in love, and leading actors tend to be conscious of what is nowadays called their image (which means the kind of man their fans mistakenly imagine them to be). "How," asked Bernard Shaw

[14] Witness his own remark to Caroline Sontum, p. 730 below.

in his review of the first English production of the play in 1896, "could he recommend himself to spectators who saw in him everything they are ashamed of in themselves?"

Allmers is usually, in practice, either romanticized or (as with Rosmer) played as sexless; and a sexless or romanticized Allmers and a happy ending are burdens that no production of *Little Eyolf* can hope to survive. *A Doll's House, Ghosts* and *Hedda Gabler* are robust plays; they can be ill-cast, ill-directed, ill-acted, and yet make a goodish evening. *Little Eyolf,* like *The Lady from the Sea* and *When We Dead Awaken,* is fragile; if it is not done well, one would rather it had not been done at all; performed as it was written to be performed, it is a haunting and memorable experience. Nowhere else does Ibsen probe so mercilessly into the complexities of human minds and relationships; it is like a long, sustained and terrifying operation. On the occasion of the first English production William Archer wrote: "I rank the play beside, if not above, the very greatest of Ibsen's works, and am only doubtful whether its soul-searching be not too terrible for human endurance in the theatre."

33

John Gabriel Borkman

1895–1896

Suzannah stayed abroad for nearly a year. It was the longest time they had been separated during their marriage. She spent the winter at Meran in the southern Tyrol, and he wrote to her regularly and at length, enquiring solicitously after her health, warning her against this or that possible excess and giving her dull little pieces of news and local or family gossip; his letters are more than ever those of a man to whom correspondence is an agony. He was "overwhelmed" with preparations for the Christiania production of *Little Eyolf*, which in fact can have made little demand on him, and "bombarded" with requests that he visit Berlin for the German premiere, "which is of course an impossibility." Suzannah's niece, Magdalena Falsen, meeting him on the street and suggesting that she visit him, received the reply that "I was so occupied with business matters that I could not receive anyone." Bergliot came to dine with him on Sundays; no one had filled the gap left by Hildur's absence.

The world premiere of *Little Eyolf* took place on 12 January at the Deutsches Theater in Berlin, with Emmanuel Reicher as Allmers and Agnes Sorma as Rita; it was a measure of the international fame which Ibsen now enjoyed that critics (or at least reporters) from all over the world attended. It was not a success, any more than *The Master Builder* had been in Germany, and, like the latter play, it does not seem to have been performed for several years in any other German town. Ibsen's social dramas were continually revived (his royalties from Bloch were considerably up this year), but his recent plays struck the Germans as less realistic and topical, and therefore less interesting.

In Christiania, by contrast, *Little Eyolf* proved such a success that it was performed thirty-six times that year, compared with eighteen performances for *Hedda Gabler* and fifteen for *The Master Builder* during their first seasons. Ibsen attended the premiere on 15 January, together with Christian and Caroline Sontum and young Bolette:

> Ibsen was very anxious about the reception. He kept saying to my mother, who sat next to him: "Do let's get out before the curtain comes down." It was always a torture to him to see his own plays. . . . *Little Eyolf* was received with great enthusiasm, and there were many curtain calls, but, persistently as they clapped, the audience could not persuade the author to take a bow. Finally, the stage manager promised to convey their congratulations personally to him.
>
> Ibsen, meanwhile, was driving to the Grand Hotel in a shabby little sleigh as fast as the plodding horse could carry him through the streets. It was snowing heavily. . . . When Ibsen reached the Grand, he was much overcome by the performance and exceedingly nervous. He begged my mother to order the supper for him, and seemed like a child asking for protection. The heavy food and some good wine soon raised his spirits. When my mother, still full of the play, said: "Poor Rita, now she has to go to work with all those mischievous boys," Ibsen replied: "Do you really believe so? Don't you rather think it was more of a Sunday mood with her?" . . . The only other remark I can recall him ever making on his own plays was in discussing *Love's Comedy* with my mother. "But Svanhild should not have engaged herself to Guldstad," she said. "Console yourself, dear friend," he replied. "The next day she will have a rendezvous with Falk."[1]

Before the end of January, *Little Eyolf* was also staged in Bergen, Helsinki and Gothenburg; Milan and Vienna saw it in February. On 3 February he had another Russian premiere, when (of all plays) *The Feast at Solhaug* was performed in prose—only the third of his plays to be seen in that country.

At the beginning of February Sigurd returned to Norway, leaving his mother at Meran. He had published a caustic article on Swedish liberalism in the December number of the Stockholm magazine *Nyt Tidskrift,* extracts from which had been quoted in the Christiania press. Ibsen proudly wrote to Suzannah on 6 February that the piece "has excited much attention, and not only in Norway; as have his articles on the consular question." With equal pride he added: "Can you guess how much I have already invested of the royalties that have come in? No less than 20,000 crowns! And I hope in the near future to be able to put by another 4,000 crowns, without our having to pinch in any way." The winter in Norway, he told her, was the coldest for years; not merely shipping, but even railways were at a standstill; but "the air is brilliantly clear and clean." Sigurd looked in only occasionally; otherwise "I sit by myself and read the newspapers, and am quite content." He was economizing as much as ever as regards food. His lunch was being sent in; and for

---

[1] Sontum, pp. 251–52.

his evening meal "I have hot soup and fish or meat left over from lunch, so that we hardly ever have to send out for anything."

Georg Brandes sent him an essay he had written about the young Marianne von Willemer's infatuation with Gœthe when the latter was sixty-six, and its stimulating effect on the poetry of Gœthe's old age. He could scarcely have chosen a subject closer to Ibsen's heart.[2] "I cannot forbear," wrote Ibsen to him on 11 February, "to send you especial thanks for your 'Gœthe and Marianne von Willemer.' I didn't know anything about the episode you describe in it. I may have read about it years ago in Lewes's book, but if so I had forgotten it, because at that time the affair held no particular interest for me. But now things are somewhat different. When I think of the quality which characterizes Gœthe's work during that period, I mean the sense of renewed youth, I ought to have guessed that he must have been graced with some such revelation, some such reassurance of beauty, as his meeting with Marianne von Willemer. Fate, Providence, Chance, can be genial and benevolent powers now and then." Ibsen must have been comforted to know that other great writers had become emotionally involved with girls forty years their junior; and certainly his own last five plays, after his meeting with Emilie, have, like the aged writings of a young poet just then emerging into fame, W. B. Yeats, all the vigour and sharpness of youth.

Camilla Collett died in March at the age of eighty-two. "I met her son Robert almost daily in the street," Ibsen wrote to Suzannah on 12 March, "and he said she lay there talking ceaselessly of Welhaven and us, and of her time with us abroad." Ibsen went to her funeral service. "Upon the coffin, beside the queen's wreath, lay a large and handsome wreath from you, with long white ribbons and gold letters saying: 'To Camilla Collett, greetings from Suzannah Ibsen.' I sent a big laurel wreath with ribbons in the national colours."

His sixty-seventh birthday was looming, but any hope he might have had that it could be allowed to slip by peacefully in Suzannah's absence had been knocked on the head. "For the dreadful day, 20 March," he continued in this same letter of 12 March, "Bergliot must manage as best she can, since you will have it so. And I shall receive everyone, even the spies, as politely as I can. I hope Falsen [his brother-in-law, a *generalkonsul* married to Suzannah's sister Dorothea] won't be able to come. Dorothea and Magdalena [her daughter] have influenza; so they won't be able to. Incidentally, I hear they have moved to Parkveien. Herman has twisted his foot and can't go out. Then I must tell you that a

---

[2] Brandes may already have heard about Emilie and Hildur. In his "Third Impression" of Ibsen, written in 1898, he suggests that the real meaning of *The Master Builder* is: "It must not be possible for anyone to say with justice that my poet in his life cannot rise to the height of the ideals which he proclaims in his books." (*Henrik Ibsen*, pp. 166–67. Muir-Archer translation).

third edition of *Little Eyolf* is printing and will probably be out next week. The day after tomorrow the play will open in Copenhagen. Hegel has commissioned a big portrait of me from Eilif Peterssen, and I am now sitting to him. There is a very widespread epidemic of influenza in the city. But so far I haven't noticed any signs. On Sunday evening there was a fire upstairs in Fru Bjørn's boarding-house. They had overfilled a lamp, which of course exploded. The fire brigade arrived, and there was a great scene, with screaming on the stairs; but the fire was soon put out. At the exhibition I bought a fine painting by Chr. Krohg. It is actually a portrait of Strindberg; but Sigurd calls it 'The Revolution,' and I call it 'Insanity Emergent.' Sigurd urged me to buy it, for the ridiculously cheap price of 500 crowns. Sigurd and his family are well. Bergliot has been so good as to give me some *gammelost* and pickled herring and a splendid joint of roast pork, which I enjoy in the evenings. I hope you are having a good time down there."

Ibsen hung the painting of Strindberg (a very large one) on the wall of his study; it helped him, he explained to astonished enquirers, to work with "that madman staring down at me." He especially liked the "demonic eyes," and once remarked: "He is my mortal enemy, and shall hang there and watch while I write."[3] August Lindberg, who knew Strindberg, relates how Ibsen once asked him if it was a good likeness and, "in a whisper that he perhaps did not intend to be heard, muttered, 'A remarkable man!'"[4] As with his visits to the Hamsun lectures, it seemed as if Ibsen wished to remind himself of the younger generation challenging and threatening him. Some writers are enervated by competition and hostility; Ibsen thrived on it. Bergliot recalls that once when Bjørnson was so ill that he was not expected to live, but recovered, Ibsen, on being gently taunted by Sigurd, declared with deep feeling: "It would not have been easy to lose one's only rival."[5]

He was (he told Suzannah on 3 April) sitting each day to Eilif Peterssen; otherwise "everything is as usual except that we have begun to cook meals here. Frøken Blehr's food got worse from day to day until it was practically uneatable. Lina, on the other hand, cooks quite excellently, just the kind of food she knows I like; a lot of fish, and excellent potatoes." Ten days later he informed her proudly that he had invested 24,000 crowns' worth of royalties and hoped soon to be able to invest a further 6,000, and that his total investments now totalled 166,000 crowns [about 40,000 dollars] "which I venture to say is not bad." Far from indulging in any luxuries, apart from the Strindberg painting, he boasted a few weeks later (2 July) that his household expenses over the

[3] Koht, II, 250.
[4] Per Lindberg, p. 308.
[5] Bergliot Ibsen, p. 191.

past quarter had averaged 116 crowns [less than 30 dollars] a *month*—"including laundry and everything."

He did a lot of modelling that spring, for as soon as Peterssen had finished his portrait Erik Werenskiold moved in to paint another. "This puts me somewhat behind in my work, I mean my correspondence," he confessed to Suzannah on 27 April. "But I find it an agreeable distraction, and a change, and it doesn't greatly inconvenience me since it all takes place in my study. After Werenskiold, Sinding is coming to model the statue for the new theatre."

Both Erik Werenskiold and Stephan Sinding recorded their impressions of Ibsen. Werenskiold remembered him as an excellent model, who "stood still as a pillar . . . stood happily for a couple of hours on end, he was so immensely strong. Even the last time I saw him, he was as round and firm as a rolling pin." He found Ibsen "extraordinarily winning, delightfully agreeable and full of jokes." Before he started to paint, Ibsen liked to sit and chat, and "was exceptionally curious, asking question after question; he was especially interested about women. Whenever I was able to tell him about some unusual woman he would sit there like a bird of prey and would not let me stop until I had told him everything I knew." He remembered that Ibsen once used the phrase "the terrain of the face," and rightly comments that "it wasn't a phrase *anyone* would use." Impressed by the size of Ibsen's forehead, he asked if anyone had ever measured his brain-pan; Ibsen replied that a German professor had, and had told him it was the largest he had ever come across. Werenskiold also recalled that every Saturday some little boys from a school in the street would come to Ibsen's apartment, and that he would give them each 25 øre (6 cents). When his charlady complained that they dirtied his floors and would only spend the money on cakes, Ibsen replied, "Why shouldn't they buy cakes?"[6]

Stephan Sinding found Ibsen equally courteous and patient but (through no fault of his) a most awkward subject to model.

> I worked and worked and couldn't get it right. I discarded one effort after another. While I was working on the sixth it occurred to me to ask Ibsen to take his spectacles off. He laid them aside and looked at me. I have never seen two eyes like those. One was large, I might almost say horrible—so it seemed to me—and deeply mystical; the other much smaller, rather pinched up, cold and clear and calmly probing. I stood speechless for a few seconds and stared at those eyes, and spoke the thought that flashed into my mind: "I wouldn't like to have you as an enemy!" Then his eyes and his whole body seemed to blaze, and I thought instinctively of the troll in the fairy tale who pops out of his hole and roars: "Who's chopping trees in *my* forest?"[7]

[6] *Dagbladet,* 20 March 1928.

[7] Kristofer Visted, "Henrik Ibsen i karikaturen," in *Boken om bøger,* II (Oslo, 1927), 145–47.

Werenskiold made no fewer than six portraits of Ibsen during the first six months of that year,[8] including one delightful one painted from memory entitled "The Laughing Ibsen." It is the only laughing painting or photograph of him in existence; Werenskiold notes at the foot of the portrait that it was a remark of Ibsen's own that put him into this good humour. Recalling a bad portrait that a Norwegian artist named Ole H. B. Olrik had painted of him in Rome in 1879, Ibsen said to Werenskiold: "For a long time he had been painting nothing but saints, so I wasn't a very suitable subject for him."[9]

Peterssen, Werenskiold, and Sinding were not the only artists to portray Ibsen that winter and spring. Edvard Munch had done the first of his lithographs of Ibsen just before the turn of the year, and Hans Heyerdahl and Christian Krohg painted him too. A contemporary Danish caricature by Alfred Schmidt shows Ibsen surrounded by Norwegian artists trying to capture his likeness.

Hildur Andersen had by now returned to Christiania, and Ibsen had been seeing a good deal of her. Their frequent appearances in public together had, naturally, Christiania being what it was, led to a good deal of gossip; the rumour had spread that Ibsen was considering divorcing Suzannah, and her stepmother, Magdalene Thoresen, thought fit to write to Suzannah and tell her of this. Suzannah, still in Meran, wrote to Ibsen asking him if there was any truth in the gossip, an action which is, perhaps, less surprising when one remembers that they had, for the first time in nearly forty years, been separated for six months. Ibsen replied on 7 May in a letter which one is surprised, though grateful, that she kept:

Dear Suzannah,

It hurt me deeply to read your last letter, dated 1 May. And I hope that, on closer reflection, you will regret having sent it. So your stepmother, that damned old sinner, has been at work again, trying to cause trouble by setting us against each other. But it's easy to guess who is behind that poor twisted woman. It is of course her good daughter, who is still wandering around the streets here and is doubtless angry with me because whenever I see her I slip into a side-street, which I have done once or twice. And now she is trying to take her revenge. And you can let yourself be fooled by that!

I don't understand your stepmother's hysterical utterances and sham profundities. I never have understood them. But when she writes this rubbish about my "wanting freedom at any price"—then I can most solemnly and sacredly assure you that I have never seriously thought or intended any such thing and that I never shall think or intend it. What I may have blurted out in a temper when

8 Reproduced in C.E., XX, 235-53.
9 Ibid., p. 247.

your moods and humours drove me to a temporary despair is something quite different to which no weight should be attached. But my earnest advice is that if you wish to retain the peace of mind necessary if you are to be cured you should break off all correspondence with your mentally confused stepmother. It is possible that she means well. But that woman's intervention in any matter or situation has always proved disastrous. If you don't want to tell her this yourself, I will. But I must have your consent first. Enough of this for today.

And now I come to the next main point in your letter. You beg me to lease a new apartment. And of course, since you so positively demand it, I shall do this. But in your letter you reproach me for taking our present apartment without consulting you. (At that time you were in Valdres and in no frame of mind for me to consider asking your advice.) Now when you come home and find this new apartment leased and furnished, you must remember that I have acted in accordance with your expressed wishes and that on this occasion, too, I have been unable to consult your opinion. And the task of finding something that will suit you in every respect is one that I shall indeed not find easy. Remember how Sigurd and Bergliot had to search and search before they at last and at great expense found something suitable. Our difficulties will be even greater. You don't want to live on the ground floor because the floors will be cold, and you won't or can't live higher up because of the stairs. But, as I say, your demand will be met. A new apartment will be leased.

I neither can nor wish to write about other matters today. Nor have I anything to say as regards myself. Werenskiold is here every morning and paints for an hour, otherwise the household routine remains unchanged. I presume Sigurd and the newspapers keep you in touch with political events.

And let me soon receive a calm, and calming, letter from you. And above all, keep these damned witches out of your life! That is the best advice and the best wishes that I can send you. Warmest regards,

> Your affectionate
> H.I.

On 21 June he wrote again to Suzannah, by now in Monsummano, a spa near Pisa with a natural steam-bath in a grotto:

Well, I have now terminated our lease of Viktoria Terrasse and taken the first-floor apartment in a new house which the brothers Hoff are building on the corner of Arbins gade and Drammensveien.

It was Sigurd and Bergliot who suggested this, and I think you will be happy with it. I have a big study with a door direct to the hall, so that people visiting me will not have to enter any other room in the apartment. You will have for your exclusive use a large corner room with a balcony and, next to it, an almost equally large drawing-room leading into the dining-room, which will hold 20–22 people and has an alcove for a sideboard, which I shall get. The dining-room leads straight into a large library and thence into your bedroom, which is much bigger than your one here. My bedroom is next to it and has a balcony. You won't need to use the corridor except when you want to go to the bathroom. There is also of course a big, light kitchen, a pantry and a servery, and many built-in wall-cupboards. As I say I think you will be pleased.

It was to be the last of their many apartments, and both Ibsen and Suzannah were to die there.

William Archer, enclosing a couple of money drafts from Beerbohm Tree that summer, seems to have suggested to Ibsen that he should visit England to meet his many and distinguished admirers there. What a gathering that would have been! But Ibsen was as timid as ever of visiting a country where he could not speak the language. "More and more do I feel it a painful deficiency," he replied on 27 June, "that I did not in time learn to speak English. Now it is too late! Had I mastered the language I would now come at once to London. Or rather, I would have been there long ago. I have been thinking over many things, recently, and now feel sure that my Scottish ancestry has left deep marks in me. But this is just an idea—possibly the wish is father to the thought." And indeed it must have been, for his only Scottish ancestor had been seven generations earlier, in the seventeenth century. There seems to have been something of a conspiracy to get him to England this year, for Georg Brandes also wrote (on 16 December), but got the same reply.

By now, Ibsen had become a kind of tourist attraction in Christiania. Foreigners gathered at the Grand to see him make his entry. Among them was the English poet Richard le Gallienne:

The large café was crowded, but we found a good table on the aisle, not far from the door. We had not long to wait, for punctually on the stroke of one, there, entering the doorway, was the dour and bristling presence known to all the world in caricature—caricatures which were no exaggerations but as in the case of Swinburne, just the man himself. The great ruff of white whisker, ferociously standing out all round his sallow, bilious face as if dangerously charged with electricity, the immaculate silk hat, the white tie, the frock-coated martinet's figure dressed from top to toe in old-fashioned black broadcloth, at once funereal and professional, the trousers concertinaed, apparently with dandaical design, at the ankles, over his highly polished boots, the carefully folded umbrella—all was there, apparitionally before me; a forbidding, disgruntled, tight-lipped presence, starchily dignified, straight as a ramrod; there he was, as I hinted, with a touch of grim dandyism about him, but with no touch of human kindness about his parchment skin or fierce badger eyes. He might have been a Scotch elder entering the kirk.

As he entered and proceeded with precision tread to the table reserved in perpetuity for him, which no one else would have dreamed of occupying, a thing new and delightful—to me a mere Anglo-Saxon—suddenly happened. As one man, the whole café was on its feet in an attitude of salute, and a stranger standing near me who evidently spoke English and who recognized my nationality, said to me in a loud but reverent aside: "That is our great poet, Henrik Ibsen." All remained standing till he had taken his seat, as in the presence of a king, and I marvelled greatly at a people that thus did homage to their great men.[10]

A granddaughter of Queen Victoria, the lively young Princess Marie Louise, was intrigued to note that he carried a small mirror in the crown of his hat and used it like a woman when combing his hair.[11] Foreigners did their best to obtain introductions; that summer he was visited by a Russian Count Galitzin, who (he wrote to Suzannah on 2 July) "has been General in the Caucasus and has seen all the Russian borderlands touching India, Tibet and China, and the whole of the north coast of Siberia." The Hungarian novelist Giula Pekar visited him too, as did his French translator Count Prozor and a Serbian Prince, Bojidar Karageorgevitch, "whose father ruled until the present regime came into power." On one occasion "a group of forty to fifty tourists cheered me loudly outside the Grand Hotel, led by an Austrian Lieutenant-Field Marshal"; indeed, he was (he complained) "properly plagued" by tourists, one of whom, an American, gained entry to his apartment and, as Ibsen glared at him, slid round him into his study, seized a pencil from the desk and disappeared with it through the door. All this, except the last incident,[12] he reported to Suzannah and Sigurd in his letters of that summer, urging Sigurd not to let Suzannah hurry home since "I manage excellently alone." Apart from two dinners, he told Suzannah (22 September), he had not been outside the city all summer.

Lugné-Poe was in Christiania again, after his theatrical triumph of the previous autumn (which he had repeated in London that spring).

[10] Richard le Gallienne, *The Romantic Nineties* (London, 1926), pp. 59–60. Le Gallienne's daughter, Eva, became a distinguished interpreter of Ibsen on the American stage.

[11] H.R.H. Princess Marie Louise, *My Memories of Six Reigns* (London, 1956), pp. 213–14.

[12] Bergliot Ibsen, p. 150.

He had staged *Little Eyolf* and *Brand* in Paris that summer, evoking the usual violently mixed reactions. On 10 August a dinner was given for him, which Ibsen attended—"I cannot avoid going, little as I feel inclined to" he grumbled to Suzannah the previous day. However, he seems to have enjoyed himself, for Lugné-Poe notes that he stayed until one in the morning, joined in a game of cards, and kept saying to him: "I am so happy for your sake."[13]

On 15 October he moved with Bergliot's help into the new apartment at Arbins gade. Despite the pride with which he had written of it to Suzannah, it was to be as cheerless and unindividual as Viktoria Terrasse, or any of the furnished apartments they had inhabited abroad. "Here he lodged for the eleven years that remained to him," writes Gerhard Gran. "I say 'lodged' deliberately, for these rooms never acquired the character of a home. They seemed cold and unlived-in, as regards not merely ordinary comfort and intimacy, but every personal stamp or in- dividuality of taste. The only room which possessed a little of this was his study."[14] A young child who lived in the flat below and occasionally visited Ibsen's kitchen for titbits from their maid Lina remembered it as drab and icy-cold; she also recalled the incessant sound above her head, when she was in her own room, of footsteps pacing back and forth, back and forth.[15] King Oscar gave Ibsen a key to a private section of the palace grounds known as the Queen's Park, so that he could walk there undisturbed.

August Lindberg, who had taken his productions of *Peer Gynt* and *Little Eyolf* to St. Petersburg that March, was in Christiania in October preparing a production of *Brand,* and asked Ibsen if he could meet him to discuss it.

> He agreed to see me one evening at the Grand Hotel. The room where we were to meet was out of the way and quiet, lit only by a couple of candelabra. I was a few minutes late, and he was already seated when I arrived. He sat with his back to the door, and the powerful head seemed even bigger in the large, dark room with its curious lighting. Quietly I closed the door behind me and went forward to greet him. He was in a brilliant humour, so I cried: "I'm sure you must have some mischief cooking, to judge from your smile." "Yes," he replied. "Some of those little imps are flocking around me, and I only have to put them in order." I thought he looked like an old wizard, and felt that the men who long ago had created the old sculptures in the great cathedral up at Nidaros [Trondhjem] must have looked like him.

> Ibsen asked whom Lindberg had in mind to provide the music.

[13] Lugné-Poe, pp. 85–86.
[14] Gran, II, 330.
[15] Told by Fru Signe Meyer, née Hansen, to Herr Gordon Hølmebakk, who told me.

"I'd thought of Grieg, naturally."

"Why Grieg?"

"Well, he wrote the music for *Peer Gynt*."

"Oh," said Ibsen. "You think that's good, do you?"

They wrangled about the price. Ibsen asked three thousand crowns, but Lindberg managed to beat him down to a thousand, and on 21 October his production opened at the Eldorado Theatre in Christiania, the first time *Brand* had ever been seen in Norway. The actors were all Swedish and, the question of the union being a subject of more than usual controversy just then (thanks not least to Sigurd's pamphleteering), Swedes were less than popular in Norway; but Lindberg's performance overcame chauvinistic feelings, and the production proved a great success. He toured it, in repertory with *Peer Gynt,* to Bergen and Trondhjem, where he played to full houses for nearly a month; his company, containing as it did several young players who were to be the great names of the future, was better than the resident companies at the big theatres in any of the Scandinavian capitals.[16]

1895 had been an important year for Ibsen in America. Although there is no record of any native performances, apart from a *Little Eyolf* in Chicago in the spring, New Yorkers had had the opportunity to see three European productions: Janet Achurch in *A Doll's House,* Gabrielle Réjane in the same play, and Tree's *An Enemy of the People.* Of this last production, Lucy Monroe wrote in the magazine *Critic:* "With a singular lack of faith in the discretion of the public, it was reserved for the close of the engagement and put on then, apparently more as an experiment than with any expectation of success. But the enthusiasm was of a kind not easily provoked in an American audience. The house was keenly appreciative throughout, and after the third act it fairly rose to the play, shouting and cheering."[17] By the following year, an American was to write: "Ibsen has become so familiar to the American public that one need scarcely touch upon the incidents of his career."[18]

It had been another fair year financially. New editions of *Brand, Little Eyolf, Love's Comedy* and *The League of Youth* had brought him 4,610 crowns, but this represented only about one-fifth of his income; the rest came from performing rights. His German and Austrian royalties aggregated 9,067 crowns, his French royalties 2,947 crowns, his Danish royalties 3,420 crowns. His English royalties (from Tree's *Enemy of the People*) were only £17–10–0; and for Norwegian performing rights he received no more than 580 crowns, made up of 80 crowns owed him from Bergen for the previous year and 500 crowns for the touring rights of *Little Eyolf.*

[16] Per Lindberg, pp. 372–78.

[17] *Critic*, nr. 26 (1895), 208–9.

[18] Edgar O. Achorn, "Ibsen at Home," in *New England Magazine,* nr. 13 (1896), 737–48.

		crowns
German royalties from Felix Bloch		333
Royalties from Lessingtheater, Berlin		82
Fees from Bergen for previous season		80
Fees for *Little Eyolf* at Svenska Teater, Helsinki, and Finska Teater, Helsinki		359
Royalties for *The Pillars of Society* at Wien Burgtheater		2,413
13th edn. of *Brand*		1,870
Royalties for *The Pillars of Society, A Doll's House* and *An Enemy of the People* at Munich Hoftheater		546
Fee for provincial rights in Norway of *Little Eyolf* (excluding Christiania and Bergen) (Olaus Olsen)		500
3rd edn. of *Little Eyolf*		780
French royalties from Société des Auteurs Dramatiques		2,947
German royalties from Bloch		1,726
Royalties for *The Pretenders, The Pillars of Society* and *Little Eyolf* from Wien Burgtheater		1,790
Unspecified royalties from Munich Hoftheater		84
Royalties from H. Beerbohm Tree for *An Enemy of the People* (£17–10–0)		317
Fee from Oda Nielsen for *Little Eyolf*		600
Royalties from Bloch		930
Unspecified royalties from Wien Burgtheater		805
7th edn. of *Love's Comedy*		800
6th edn. of *The League of Youth*		1,160
Royalties from Royal Theatre, Copenhagen, for *The Wild Duck* (21st–26th perfs.)		595
Ditto for *Little Eyolf* (1st–7th perfs.)		1,625
Fee for *Lady Inger of Østraat* at Dagmars Theatre, Copenhagen		600
Royalties from Bloch		85
Royalties from Wien Burgtheater		123
Fee for *Brand* from August Lindberg		1,000
Royalties from Munich Hoftheater		150
		22,300 £1,239

Suzannah had returned home during the autumn, to settle for the first time in their new apartment; so he wrote no more letters to her, and few to anyone that have survived from 1896. Edvard Brandes visited him that winter and was amused to see how he "enjoyed studying the harrowed and embittered face of his adversary" hanging on the study wall. The Strindberg portrait seemed to Brandes to provide the sole example of individuality in the furnishing of Arbins gade. When he remarked on it, Ibsen half-closed his eyes and said, "I like to look at that face."[19]

Ibsen spent the first months of the year brooding on his new play, getting his "little imps" into order. "I am busy with preparations for

[19] Edvard Brandes, "Henrik Ibsens Personlighed," p. 235.

a big new work," he wrote to Georg Brandes on 24 April, "and don't want to put it off for longer than I need. I could so easily have a tile fall on my head before I had 'managed to write the last verse.' And what then?" On 11 July he began his draft, and on 27 July was able to inform Jacob Hegel that it was "progressing quickly and easily, despite the more than southerly warmth we are having up here this summer." It went smoothly indeed, for by 26 August he had finished his draft.

As he was revising it, in September, the great explorer Fridtjof Nansen returned from his Greenland voyage, and practically the whole population of Christiania flocked to the quayside to greet him. Edvard Brandes, who was in the city, tells how he was walking through the deserted streets when, near the Post Office, he encountered Ibsen. The two stood facing each other, seemingly alone in Christiania. "You here, Herr Doctor, and not at the reception?" asked Brandes. "Ibsen's face stiffened. 'No,' he replied, almost angrily. 'This is an Indian deed to be celebrated with an Indian dance, at which I don't belong.' And he walked on."[20] Brandes surmises that to Ibsen Nansen's voyage was an athletic feat which hardly deserved "the acclamation of a nation," but that seems a cynical and unjustified comment. Returning heroes, like coronations, are not to everyone's taste.

On 3 October Ibsen thanked Georg Brandes for sending him his "great monumental book on Shakespeare," which "I have not merely read but have buried myself in, as I have done with scarcely any other book." One wonders if he recalled the youthful lecture he had given on Shakespeare in Bergen forty-one years before to the week. A week later he wrote again to Brandes, this time to deny (as so often before) various supposed influences upon his own writing. The French dramatist and critic Jules Lemaître, in an article on the influence of Scandinavian literature in France,[21] had suggested that Ibsen had said and done nothing that George Sand and Dumas *fils* had not said and done before him. Brandes put this to Ibsen, who replied (11 October): "I hereby swear on my honour and conscience that I have never in my whole life, neither in my youth nor later, read a single book by George Sand. I once began *Consuelo* in translation, but put it aside as soon as I realized it was the work of a dilettante philosopher and not of a writer. But I read only a few pages, so I may be mistaken in this. . . . I owe Alexandre Dumas nothing whatever in respect to dramatic form—except that I have learned from his plays to avoid certain gross faults and misconceptions of which he is not infrequently guilty."[22]

[20] *Ibid.*, pp. 237–38.

[21] Reprinted in Lemaître's *Les Contemporains*, VI (Paris, 1896), 225–70. Brandes's reply, "Henrik Ibsen in France," appeared in *Cosmopolis*, January 1897, pp. 112–24. Cf. Sprinchorn, p. 322.

[22] Dumas, however, apparently admired Ibsen (cf. Jules Claretie's account of a conversation with Ibsen in *Figaro*, 20 July 1897, reprinted in *Morgenbladet*, 24 July 1897, and in C.E., XIX, 208–11).

On 18 October he finished fair-copying his new play—he had spent eight full weeks polishing it—and two days later he posted it off to Hegel with the prophecy: "I think we shall both have joy from it."

Happy with his English publisher, William Heinemann, Ibsen was less content with S. Fischer in Germany. "I am afraid," he wrote on 1 November to Julius Elias, who was handling his book rights there, "I am not rich enough to go on using Herr Fischer as a publisher, which more or less amounts to giving him my books gratis. I have had to pay most of the translation fees myself, since I have had to grant the translators half my theatre royalties while Herr Fischer himself has paid the merest trifle for their labours. My fee last time was 1,000 marks [887 crowns]; and in a letter I received at the same time as your telegram he very generously offers to pay me a full 200 marks more! Now, when the work is protected by the Berne Convention! . . . By comparison, let me tell you how Herr Albert Langen of Munich feels able to pay for my new book without any compulsion to talk of sacrifices. Herr Langen is paying me 5,000 marks as author's fee, and all theatre royalties will come to me, since Herr Langen is paying for the translation. Bearing this in mind, I hope you will appreciate that I cannot continue to carry the financial burden of having Herr Fischer as my publisher. As a further example for comparison with Herr Fischer's offer I may tell you that my English publisher, Mr. W. Heinemann, London, has paid me the same fee as Herr Langen for each of my last two plays and, now that I am protected by the Convention, will pay me even more."[23]

Ibsen's threat worked. Fischer, unwilling to lose so profitable an author, matched Langen's terms—and was well rewarded, for by his own statement he published 40,000 copies of the German collected edition (and according to the widow of Julius Elias, who co-edited, he in fact published twice that number).[24]

In France, Lugné-Pœ had presented *The Pillars of Society* that June; and on 12 November, greatly daring, he followed it with the French premiere of *Peer Gynt*. Bernard Shaw went over to Paris for the performance, and found it disappointing. "The characteristic Northern hard-headed, hard-fisted humour, the Northern power of presenting the deepest truths in the most homely grotesques, was missed," he wrote in the *Saturday Review* (21 November). "M. Lugné-Pœ, with all his realism, could no more help presenting the play sentimentally and sublimely than M. Lamoureux can help conducting the overture to *Tannhäuser* as if it were the 'Marseillaise'; but the universality of Ibsen makes his plays come home to all nations; and Peer Gynt is as good a Frenchman as he is a Norwegian, just as Dr. Stockmann is as intelligible in Bermond-

---

[23] Heinemann's fee for *John Gabriel Borkman* was in fact £200, compared with Langen's £245.

[24] Bergliot Ibsen, p. 177.

sey or Bournemouth as he is in his native town. . . . Peer Gynt will finally smash anti-Ibsenism in Europe, because Peer is everybody's hero. He has the same effect on the imagination that Hamlet, Faust and Mozart's Don Juan have had." Yet the press (according to Bjørn Bjørnson, who was also there) was surprisingly good, and Shaw records that the play aroused such interest in Paris that Prozor's translation "was sold out immediately after the performance." The Old Man of the Mountains was played by a twenty-three-year-old actor who was the secretary of the Théâtre de l'Oeuvre—Alfred Jarry (appearing under the pseudonym of Hemgé), whose play *Ubu roi*, written for marionettes when Jarry was a schoolboy of fifteen, had been performed by the l'Oeuvre that year, with Bonnard, Vuillard and Toulouse-Lautrec among the designers of scenery and masks.

On 23 November *Little Eyolf* was staged in England for the first time, at the Avenue Theatre (later the Playhouse) behind Charing Cross station. The cast was the strongest that had yet been assembled in England for an Ibsen play. Not only were Janet Achurch and Elizabeth Robins paired together for the first time, as Rita and Asta; Allmers was played by Courtenay Thorpe, who had been a remarkable Oswald in New York in 1894, and a West End star, Stella Patrick Campbell, who had burst into fame as Pinero's Mrs. Tanqueray in 1893, was secured for the part of the Rat-Wife. Bernard Shaw in the *Saturday Review* (28 November) commented:

> The performance was, of course, a very remarkable one. When, in a cast of five, you have the three best yet discovered actresses of their generation, you naturally look for something extraordinary. . . . Miss Achurch was more than equal to the occasion. Her power seemed to grow with its own expenditure. . . . As Rita she produced almost every sound that a big human voice can, from a creak like the opening of a rusty canal lock to a melodious tenor note that the most robust Siegfried might have envied. She looked at one moment like a young, well-dressed, very pretty woman; at another she was like a desperate creature just fished dripping out of the river by the Thames Police. Yet another moment, and she was the incarnation of impetuous, ungovernable strength. . . . It is encouraging to see that the performances are to be continued next week, the five matinees—all crowded, by the way—having by no means exhausted the demand for places.

The production was such a success that it was transferred to the evening bill; but in the hope of ensuring a commercial success the new backers removed Janet Achurch from the part of Rita and replaced her with Mrs. Patrick Campbell who (according to Shaw in the *Saturday Review*, 12 December) "succeeded wonderfully in removing all unpleasantness from the play," and thereby ruined it. It was not to be the last time that an Ibsen production was to be spoiled by the replacement of the right player by a supposedly more magnetic star[25] (though in the next century Mrs. Campbell was to be a memorable Hedda Gabler and Mrs. Alving, with the young John Gielgud as Oswald).

Not all the critics, naturally, admired the play. *The Theatre* called it "dull, wordy, unpleasant and prodigiously tiresome," and *The Times* wrote: "Gloom, depression and a sense of the remoteness of the action from all living human interests overcome the spectator, whose abiding impression of the play is that of having seen in a dream the patients of a madhouse exercising in their yard."

On 5 December *Emperor and Galilean* was staged for the first time, in a shortened form, at the Leipzig Stadttheater, and the same month *Love's Comedy* also received its German premiere, at the Belle-Alliance Theatre in Berlin—the first performance of that play outside Scandinavia. But neither was a great success.

On 15 December *John Gabriel Borkman* was published, in, thanks to the success of *Little Eyolf*, the unprecedently large edition of 12,000 copies. Even this proved insufficient; the demand was such that Hegel had to reprint another 3,000 before publication. It was even better received than *Little Eyolf*—not surprisingly, the critics found it less obscure. "Ibsen has never climbed so high as a dramatic master builder," wrote Nils Vogt in *Morgenbladet* (24 December), and he thought the play "fascinating and exciting." Georg Brandes, in *Verdens Gang* (19 December) found it magnificently constructed "as though built of iron on a foundation of granite. The play moves with the speed of youth, but the voice is that of age and wisdom, a stern wisdom"—and yet, too, of "a deep sympathy for human suffering which yet has not retracted a single one of its demands." Carl Nærup, reviewing the play again in the same newspaper on 21 December, also spoke of "the breath of youth," and found the characters "bigger, stronger—not the centre-less, crumbling characters of his earlier plays, at the mercy of every emotional wind and weather. They choose for themselves." In Sweden J. A. Runström, in *Ny Illustrerad Tidning* (27 February 1897), wrote that it was "in the opinion of many people the author's finest play since the days of *An Enemy of the People* and *The Wild Duck*. The much debated obscurity which has enveloped Ibsen's latest creations is here dispelled. . . . *John Gabriel Borkman* is a mighty play." The Danish magazine *The Corsair* printed a cartoon, humorously entitled "A Disappointment," showing Ibsen offering a bowl marked "No Problems" to a forlorn gathering of critics.

Naturally, there were dissidents, most of whom reacted against the play's apparent pessimism. Kristofer Randers, in *Aftenposten* (20 December), found it "a curious play, dark and obscure, full of bitter contempt

---

[25] Lugné-Poe (p. 22) tells that Ibsen hated to hear of any actor doing a play "for his own sake," and that when told that Le Bargy was thinking of doing Oswald, Ibsen exploded: "Of course, like that Italian actor who acts the whole play!" (He was referring to Ermete Zaccone.)

for humanity. . . . This is the blackest and most comfortless play Ibsen has yet written. . . . *Vanitas vanitatum,* the poet seems to cry, all is emptiness. Empty the ambitious dreams of power, empty the belief in the happiness of marriage. . . . Only one thing is true—the love of a steadfast woman—but that is seldom found, and when found it is shamed or betrayed. Shall this philosophy be the aged master's last words as the twilight shadows gather? We must hope not." C. D. af Wirsen similarly complained: "These are lofty heights onto which Ibsen leads us through the whirling snow. But they are cold and empty. However brilliant this play may be, it is unlikely to warm or rejoice a single human heart."[26] And an anonymous reviewer in *Nordisk Tidskrift* (1897, pp. 160–62) wrote, perhaps rather wishfully: "Undoubtedly the tight phalanx of Ibsen's admirers has been thinned by this work. . . . The whole play makes an empty and hollow impression, and we turn disappointed to the author and ask: 'Why?' . . . His technique is failing him." But the Ayes had it. *John Gabriel Borkman* was acclaimed as none of his plays had been since *A Doll's House.*

John Gabriel Borkman tells the story of a miner's son who becomes a financier and, for idealistic reasons, embezzles and is sent to prison. Released after eight years, he lives alone in an upstairs room of his house refusing to see his wife, visited only by an old clerk and waiting in the conviction that the people will demand that he emerge to save them. As a young man he had married not for love but to get his foot on the ladder; now his wife's twin sister, whom he had loved and rejected, comes to reproach him and to beg that she be given charge of his son, and that this son, Erhart, should take her name. Borkman agrees, but his wife, who overhears their conversation, refuses; as the two women argue, Erhart arrives to announce that he is leaving with a woman nearly twice his age. Borkman wanders out and dies on the mountainside.

The plot is based on a story Ibsen had heard in his student days. In 1851 a high-ranking army officer had been charged with embezzlement. At first he denied the charge but then, like Old Ekdal in *The Wild Duck,* he unsuccessfully tried to shoot himself. He was sentenced to four years penal servitude and, when released, shortly before Ibsen returned to Christiania to run the Møllergaden theatre, shut himself up in his house and spent the rest of his life brooding in solitude, unable even to speak to his wife. Later, in the eighteen-eighties, a great scandal had occurred at Arendal; a bank director speculated and embezzled his clients' money, and was sent to prison.

After the obsessive references to bankruptcy in his earlier plays Ibsen

[26] Wirsen, p. 120.

had not touched on the subject since *The Wild Duck* twelve years before; and in several other ways, *John Gabriel Borkman* marks a curious return to the past. His youthful poem "The Miner," written when he was twenty-three in the year the officer was charged, perfectly crystallizes the theme of the play:

> . . . Here in the darkness there is peace.
> Peace and rest for eternity.
> Heavy hammer, break me the way
> To the heart-chamber of what lies hidden there . . .

> When I first entered here
> I thought in my innocence:
> "The spirits of the dark will solve for me
> Life's obscure riddles."

> No spirit has yet taught me that strange answer.
> No ray has shone from the depths.

> Was I wrong? Does this path
> Not lead to the light?
> But the light blinds my eyes
> If I seek it in the mountains.

> No, I must go down into the dark.
> Eternal peace lies there.
> Heavy hammer, break me the way
> To the heart-chamber of what lies hidden there.

> So blow follows blow
> Till he sinks weak and tired.
> No ray of morning shines.
> No sun of hope rises.

As a young man, Ibsen had had a friend named Vilhelm Foss, an old copying clerk who had once published a collection of verses and still lived in the hope that he might some day achieve poetic fame. He had remembered Foss when planning *The Lady from the Sea,* in the notes of which Foss makes a phantom appearance. Ibsen discarded him from that play, but he kept him in mind, and at last Foss achieved immortality as Vilhelm Foldal, the clerk who spends his life polishing a youthful play which he dreams he may one day see acted.

The gossips of Christiania, naturally, took the loveless marriage of the Borkmans to be a picture of Ibsen's relationship with Suzannah, especially now that Hildur Andersen was back in town.[27] It is hardly that; yet,

[27] As an example of the malicious rumours that circulated in Christiania about Ibsen and Suzannah, William Archer tells that "my brother was one day going to call

despite Ibsen's demand that we should treat his plays as pure fiction, one may be forgiven for suggesting that *John Gabriel Borkman* does in fact represent a sad survey of the dramatist's bleak emotional life. The Ibsens were not precisely the Borkmans; the immense tie that bound Henrik and Suzannah together is absent from the marriage in the play; a kind of love, perhaps the most profound and lasting kind, existed between the Ibsens, but it was not, and never had been, romantic love, the kind that Ella Rentheim represents. Ibsen, like Borkman, had turned his back on romantic love for a woman who could enable him to achieve his ambitions, and Emilie Bardach, Helene Raff and Hildur Andersen were living symbols of what he had rejected. By choosing, and remorselessly pursuing, the career of an author he had sacrificed his chance of that other kind of happiness; and he may have felt that to some extent he had sacrificed Suzannah's chances too. The recent quarrel with Suzannah about his supposed intention to divorce her must have helped to make *John Gabriel Borkman* the guilt-ridden play it is. In a sense the play is about what Ibsen's marriage might have been like had he failed as a writer; in another sense, it is about emotional bankruptcy, the buried treasures of the heart that lie unmined; how a man may gain the whole world and lose his soul. Edvard Munch called *John Gabriel Borkman* "the most powerful winter landscape in Scandinavian art."

Formally, the last act of *Borkman* marks a return to the epic and poetic symbolism of *Brand* and *Peer Gynt*. As we have seen, Ibsen had deliberately suppressed the poet in him while writing the "social" plays, from *The Pillars of Society* to *The Wild Duck;* there are no moments of poetry in them, save perhaps Mrs. Alving's speech about the ghosts that "lie as thick as grains of sand." But in every play he had written since *Rosmersholm*, with the solitary exception of *Hedda Gabler* (and was the laconic short-hand of that play the result of a desire not to let his hidden feelings break the surface?), there are times when we are aware of the buried river. A writer who delves into the dark unconscious, as Ibsen had done in these last plays, cannot wholly suppress the poet within him, far less the symbolist. But it is not, I think, until the final act of *John Gabriel Borkman* that we find the writer of realistic dialogue being edged aside by the symbolist and the poet:

BORKMAN (*stops by the precipice*). Come, Ella, and I shall show you.
ELLA. What will you show me, John?

---

upon him in Christiania and remarked to a friend resident in the town that if Ibsen was not at home he hoped he might see Fru Ibsen. 'Oh, no,' said his friend. 'You won't see her. She hasn't been able to live with him for years.' My brother paid his call and the first person he saw on crossing the threshold was Fru Ibsen. The incident was typical." ("Ibsen as I Knew Him," p. 10.)

BORKMAN (*points*). See how the country stretches out before us, open and free—far, far away.

ELLA. We used to sit on that seat, and stare into the distance.

BORKMAN. It was a country of dreams we gazed into.

ELLA. The country of our dreams, yes. Now it is covered with snow. And the old tree is dead.

BORKMAN (*not listening to her*). Can you see the smoke from the great steamers out on the fjord?

ELLA. No.

BORKMAN. I can. They come and go. They create a sense of fellowship throughout the world. They bring light and warmth to the hearts of men in many thousands of homes. That is what I dreamed of creating.

ELLA. But it remained a dream.

BORKMAN. Yes. It remained a dream. (*Listens*). Listen. Down there by the river the factories hum. My factories. Listen how they hum. The night shifts are working. They work both night and day. Listen, listen! The wheels whirl and the pistons thud, round and round, in and out. Can't you hear them, Ella?

ELLA. No.

BORKMAN. I hear them.

ELLA (*frightened*). No, John, you can't.

BORKMAN. Ah, but these are only the outworks surrounding my kingdom.

ELLA. What kingdom?

BORKMAN. My kingdom. The kingdom I was about to take possession of when I died.

ELLA. Oh, John, John.

BORKMAN. And there it lies, defenceless, masterless, abandoned to thieves and robbers. Ella! Do you see those mountains far away? Range beyond range, rising and rising? That is my infinite and inexhaustible kingdom.

ELLA. Ah, but it's a cold wind that blows from that kingdom, John.

BORKMAN. To me it is the breath of life. It is a greeting from the spirits that serve me. I feel them, those buried millions. I see those veins of iron ore, stretching their twisting, branching, enticing arms towards me. I've seen you all before, like shadows brought to life—that night when I stood in the vaults of the bank with the lantern in my hand. You wanted to be freed. And I tried to free you. But I failed. Your treasure sank back into the darkness. But let me whisper this to you now, in the stillness of the night. I love you where you lie like the dead, deep down in the dark. I love you, treasures that crave for life, with your bright retinue of power and glory. I love you, love you, love you.

That is the voice of the young Ibsen, the author of *Brand*. In his next play, the movement away from realism, or rather from the realism of prose towards the realism of poetry, was to be carried a stage further. In *When We Dead Awaken,* as in *Brand* and *Peer Gynt,* Ibsen seems to be writing for a theatre of the mind—though, like them, *When We Dead Awaken* works powerfully on the stage, given the right quality of imagination in the staging.

As though to underline the message of *John Gabriel Borkman,* that the quest for material success may lead to emotional bankruptcy, 1896 had proved, in terms of money, Ibsen's richest year yet:

	crowns	
German royalties from Felix Bloch	50	
Royalties from Wien Burgtheater	225	
Fee from Bergen Theatre for previous year	360	
Fee for *Love's Comedy* at Folketeatret, Copenhagen	1,200	
Royalties from Munich Hoftheater	98	
Fee for *Little Eyolf* at Royal Theatre, Copenhagen (8th–13th perfs.)	1,276	
4th edn. of *A Doll's House*	675	
7th edn. of *The Pretenders*	1,020	
French royalties from Société des Auteurs Dramatiques	144	
Royalties from Bloch	145	
Royalties from English book sales (Archer) (£2–7–1)	43	
Royalties from Wien Burgtheater	448	
10th edn. of *Peer Gynt*	1,815	
1st German edn. of *Catiline* (A. Langen of Munich)	400	
Fee from August Lindberg for 3 perfs. of *Brand* at Folketeatret in Copenhagen	300	
Royalties from Bloch	75	
Royalties from Wien Burgtheater	120	
Royalties from Munich Hoftheater	83	
Royalties from Bloch	26	
Royalties from Munich Hoftheater	52	
1st edn. of *John Gabriel Borkman*	11,160	
1st German edn. of *John Gabriel Borkman*	4,444	
Balance on German edn. of *Little Eyolf*	444	
2nd edn. of *John Gabriel Borkman*	2,790	
English edn. of *John Gabriel Borkman* (£200)	3,600	
Swedish performance rights for two years of *John Gabriel Borkman* (Albert Ranft)	3,000	
Fee from August Lindberg for Norwegian provincial rights of *John Gabriel Borkman* (2 years)	1,000	
	34,993	£1,944

34

Irritations

1897

1897 opened with a row with an Englishman. Robert Harborough Sherard, the friend (and later biographer) of Oscar Wilde and a great-grandson of William Wordsworth, had visited Norway the previous summer and autumn, and on 3 January he published in the New York magazine *The Humanitarian* a purported interview with Ibsen at the latter's home. In this article Sherard attributed to Ibsen several outspoken remarks about Norwegian manners—*inter alia,* that Christiania was "the most immoral city in Europe," and that one of the reasons for his living there was that "there is nowhere else where a student of social life can find better subjects. One can, for example, say that marriage in a practical sense no longer exists here." One cause, he allegedly added, was that the suppression by the police of licensed prostitution "throws young people into their neighbours' arms. . . . *Ménages à trois* flourish and, thanks to the present equality of the sexes, the third party is often a woman."

The publication of these remarks naturally caused a sensation in Norway, and Ibsen immediately issued a refutation in *Aftenposten,* declaring that "partly because of the Grüttefien affair [a German journalist of that name had printed supposed interviews with Bjørnson and King Oscar the previous summer, which turned out to have been faked], partly because the gentleman in question [Sherard] gave the impression of being untrustworthy," he had refused to receive him and had merely conversed with him for a couple of minutes in public without discussing Christiania or Norway at all; "there is not a true word in what the Englishman writes." Sherard sent a telegram to *Aftenposten* which appeared on 8 January standing by his article, to which Ibsen replied (in the same issue) that a journalist who tells a lie always pretends it is true.

If Frank Harris had written the article, one would have no doubts as to what had happened; but Sherard was a rather guileless man, not given to falsification. Ibsen is hardly likely to have uttered the above remarks to a journalist, or directly to a stranger; yet they are precisely the kind of things he might have said over a glass to friends, and a sneaking suspicion remains—would an intelligent and quite reputable writer like Sherard, the friend and biographer not merely of Wilde but of Zola, Daudet and Maupassant, have invented such a tissue of lies? Sherard, in his telegram to *Aftenposten* on 8 January, referred to friends in Christiania as witnesses; did he perhaps sit in on a conversation in which Ibsen was indiscreet, perhaps not realizing that Sherard was a journalist as well as an author of books? We shall never know (if there were such friends present they would scarcely have risked their friendship with Ibsen by supporting Sherard's story); but I do not think Ibsen's denial should be accepted without a certain reserve. Grüttefien had published fake interviews, but Sherard was not a fake.

John Gabriel Borkman received two simultaneous premieres, on 10 January in Helsinki, when both the Finnish and Swedish theatres staged it. On 16 January it was performed at Frankfurt-am-Main. The German censor had ordered the excision of two passages which he found offensive, Ella's line in Act Two about "the sin for which there is no forgiveness" (to murder love in a human being), and Mrs. Wilton's remark in Act Four about the advisability of Erhart having another girl to fall back on if he should tire of her, or she of him. Here, as in Helsinki, the play was a success. Three days later it received its Norwegian premiere, under bizarre circumstances. August Lindberg had secured from Ibsen the rights to present it in the Norwegian provinces, and managed to stage it at the little town of Drammen, a bare thirty miles from Christiania, six days before the Christiania Theatre was ready with its production. He enterprisingly ran special trains from the capital to Drammen and so drew off a proportion of the Christiania Theatre's public, which probably caused Ibsen no displeasure (as he had received a fixed fee for both productions, it did not matter to him which one people attended). The provincial production got much the better reviews.

Lindberg had one or two meetings with Ibsen while preparing the production, to ask him about various points, "but he always answered briefly and evasively." Lindberg thought his attitude towards his plays was like what, as an apothecary, he must have felt towards his medicines; once he had mixed them, there was an end to it. "I had to console myself with the thought that we actors were as air to him."

One day Ibsen invited him to lunch at the Grand Hotel at noon.

> I met him in the foyer and saw how he took out a small girl's comb and combed his hair meticulously, surveying himself in a small mirror in the crown of his hat. When we arrived at the table reserved for him there stood on it nothing but a carafe of schnapps and a bottle of light brown ale.

The head waiter came, and was commanded to lay another place. Immediately there arrived another carafe of schnapps and bottle of beer. Ibsen helped himself and bade me do likewise. Then he raised his schnapps glass and said; "Skaal!" I repeated the word but did not drink. He continued; "What I like about this schnapps is that it's a healthy drink and a native one. I don't order Hungarian wine in Bavaria or Bavarian lager in Hungary. One should do as the natives do, and since schnapps is the only wine this country produces one must enjoy it as such. Skaal!"

"But what about something to eat?" I asked squarely and without thinking.

"You want something to eat?"

"Well, I'm sorry," I said. "But didn't you invite me to lunch?"

"Are you hungry at this hour?"

"I must at least have a sandwich."

He rang for the head waiter and ordered him to bring "a sandwich for the director."[1]

Before the end of January, *John Gabriel Borkman* had also been staged in Stockholm, Berlin (where Hermann Nissen played the title role with a make-up suggesting both Ibsen and Bjørnson), and Copenhagen (where Emil Poulsen clearly identified the character with the author). The play proved a greater success in the theatres than any Ibsen had written since *A Doll's House*. No one could find this obscure, or politically or morally offensive—though Edvard Brandes, seated beside Ibsen at the Christiania dress rehearsal, noted his misery at the actors' failure to give the play life.[2] In London Ellen Terry tried to interest Henry Irving in the role. He was ill, and she took advantage of his enforced immobility by reading him the first two acts; he read the third to her. "What a play!" he commented, with an inflection that left no doubt of his opinion. To his notebook Irving confided: "Threadworms and leeches are an interesting study; but they have no interest to me."[3]

If Irving found *Borkman* uninteresting, Henry James did not. In a London Letter to *Harper's Weekly* of New York, dated 15 January and published on 6 February, James declared:

> The author who, at the age of seventy, a provincial of provincials, turns out *John Gabriel* is frankly for me so much one of the peculiar pleasures of the day, one of the current strong sensations that, erect as he seems still to stand, I deplore his extreme maturity and, thinking of what shall happen, look round in vain for any other possible source of the same kind of emotion. For Ibsen strikes me as an extraordinary curiosity, and every time he sounds his note the miracle, to my perception, is renewed. I call it a miracle because it is the result of so dry a view of life. . . . There is a positive odour of spiritual paraffin. The author nevertheless arrives

[1] Per Lindberg, pp. 384–86.
[2] Edvard Brandes, "Henrik Ibsens Personlighed," pp. 236–37.
[3] Laurence Irving, p. 601.

at the dramatist's great goal—he arrives for all his meagreness at intensity.
The meagreness, which is after all but an unconscious, an admirable economy,
never interferes with that; it plays straight into the hands of his rare
mastery of form. The contrast between this form—so difficult to have reached,
so civilized, so "evolved"—and the bareness and bleakness of his little northern
democracy is the source of half the hard frugal charm that he puts forth.
In the cold fixed light of it the notes that we speak of as deficiencies
take a sharp value in the picture. There is no small-talk, there are scarcely
any manners. On the other hand there is so little vulgarity that this of itself
has almost the effect of a deeper, a more lonely provincialism. The background
at any rate is the sunset over the ice. Well in the very front of the scene
lunges with extraordinary length of arm the Ego against the Ego, and rocks
in a rigour of passion the soul against the soul—a spectacle, a movement,
as definite as the relief of silhouettes in black paper or a train of Eskimo
dogs on the snow. Down from that desolation the sturdy symbolist comes
this time with a supreme example of his method. It is a high wonder and
pleasure to welcome such splendid fruit from sap that might by now have
shown something of the chill of age. Never has he juggled more gallantly
with difficulty and danger than in this really prodigious *John Gabriel,* in
which a great span of tragedy is taken between three or four persons—a
trio of the grim and grizzled—in the two or three hours of a winter's evening;
in which the whole thing throbs with an actability that fairly shakes us
as we read; and in which, as the very flower of his artistic triumph, he
has given us for the most beautiful and touching of his heroines a sad old maid
of sixty.[4]

Sadly, when it was staged in London at the Strand Theatre on 3 May,
it was very inadequately done. "Mr. Vernon's Borkman was not ill acted,"
commented Bernard Shaw, "Only, as it was not Ibsen's Borkman, but the
very reverse and negation of him, the better Mr. Vernon acted, the worse
it was for the play"—a statement which could be applied to many subsequent Ibsen performances by this actor or that. Shaw also denounced the
poverty of the sets, which seem to have been dire even for an experimental
production. "I beg the New Century Theatre,"[5] he wrote, "when the next
Ibsen play is ready for mounting, to apply to me for assistance. If I have
a ten pound note, they shall have it; if not, I can at least lend them a
couple of decent chairs."[6]

After the quiet of the previous year, when only *Little Eyolf* of Ibsen's
plays had been staged in London, the summer of 1897 saw a renewed
flurry of activity. A week after the *Borkman* opening, *A Doll's House* was
revived for a series of matinées at the Globe Theatre, with Janet Achurch
in her old part and Courtenay Thorpe (who was playing Hamlet in the

[4] *The Scenic Art,* pp. 291–94.
[5] A private subscription society founded by Elizabeth Robins, William Archer,
H. W. Massingham and Alfred Sutro, and patterned on Grein's Independent Theatre Society, which was about to close after six brave years.
[6] *Our Theatres in the Nineties,* rev. edn. (London, 1954), III, 123.

evenings) as Helmer. "He plays Helmer with passion," wrote Bernard
Shaw. "It is the first time we have seen this done; and the effect is overwhelming. We no longer study an object-lesson in lord-of-creationism,
appealing to our sociological interest only. We see a fellow-creature blindly
wrecking his happiness and losing his 'love-life,' and are touched dramatically."[7]

On 17 May *The Wild Duck* followed at the same theatre (likewise for
five matinées), and on 24 June *Ghosts* was revived at the Queen's Gate
Hall for three performances, with Mrs. Theodore Wright (who had
played Mrs. Alving in the first London production) and Courtenay
Thorpe as Oswald, the role in which he had startled New York. The
production coincided with Queen Victoria's Diamond Jubilee, which led
Bernard Shaw to draw an irreverent comparison:

> On the one hand, the Queen and the Archbishop of Canterbury; on the other,
> Mrs. Alving and Pastor Manders. Stupendous contrast! . . . Suppose the Queen
> were to turn upon us in the midst of our jubilation and say: "My Lords and
> Gentlemen! You have been good enough to describe at great length the changes
> made during the last sixty years in science, art, politics, dress, sport, locomo-
> tion, newspapers and everything else that men chatter about. But you have not
> a word to say about the change that comes home most closely to me? I
> mean the change in the number, the character and the intensity of the
> lies a woman must either believe or pretend to believe before she can
> graduate in polite society as a well-brought-up lady." If Her Majesty could
> be persuaded to give a list of these lies, what a document it would be! . . .
> Depend upon it, seventy-eight years cannot be lived through without finding
> out things that queens do not mention in Adelphi melodramas. Granted that
> the Queen's consort was not a Chamberlain Alving . . . it is possible to
> have better luck than Mrs. Alving without missing all her conclusions.[8]

In Norway, meanwhile, the spring of 1897 had brought a bitter personal
disappointment to Ibsen. Three years previously Sigurd had proposed,
in a series of articles, that a new chair of sociology be established at
Christiania University. There was opposition to the scheme in the Storthing,
which compromised by granting sufficient money for a series of lectures to
be held during the autumn of 1896, leaving the question of the professorship open. (According to Sigurd's wife Bergliot, several of his colleagues
in the Liberal Party disliked the idea of his becoming too important.)
At all events, Sigurd delivered his lectures that autumn, with a panel of
five professors present; the attendances were very large, and there was an
atmosphere of great excitement. But on 29 April 1897 the panel published

---

[7] *Ibid.*, pp. 131–32.

[8] *Ibid.*, pp. 177–78. This passage has given rise to a curious myth among Ibsen
commentators that Queen Victoria saw *Ghosts* performed (e.g., Koht, II, 224; Ollén,
p. 104).

its verdict that: "Dr. Ibsen has not in his lectures succeeded in demonstrating such qualities that one could confidently at the present juncture entrust him with a university teaching post in sociology."

Sigurd immediately left for Italy. "Never since I left the diplomatic service," he wrote to Bergliot, "have I been as angry as I am this week. . . . It looks as though they have all conspired to make it impossible for me to live in Norway." His father was, if possible, even more outraged. He had attended all Sigurd's lectures with immense pride; and when the university invited him to a banquet he replied curtly: "I shall never enter those doors again." Suzannah wrote to Bergliot from Monsummano: "The truth is that Sigurd's talent, with his European viewpoint, does not suit their academic outlook. It is foreign and unpleasing to them, as his father's was, which they only accepted when the world acclaimed him. We owe nothing to Norway, and all the humbug and mean-mindedness we have experienced there makes me weep. They are trying to bar every road to Sigurd."

Indignation was widespread in Christiania. "It was clear to everyone," writes Bergliot, "that Sigurd did not lack the qualifications. But they were afraid of his liberal views and of his consequent influence on the young." The university tried to compromise by offering him a new series of lectures with a different panel of judges, but Sigurd refused. "I dread the prospect of returning to Christiania," he wrote to Bergliot from Monsummano on 17 July.[9]

The affair caused Ibsen to think seriously again of finally abandoning Norway. "Can you guess," he wrote to Georg Brandes on 3 June, "what I am dreaming and planning, and picturing to myself as so delightful? It is to settle by the Sound, between Copenhagen and Elsinore, in a free, open place, where I shall be able to see all the deep-sea ships coming from afar and going afar. Here I can't do that. Here every sound is locked (in both senses); every channel of understanding is stopped. Oh, my dear Brandes, one does not live for twenty-seven years out in the great, free, liberating world of culture for nothing. Here among the fjords is my native land. But—but—but—where shall I find my home? The sea is what draws me most. I live here alone and plan some new dramatic work. But I can't yet see clearly what shape it will take." Twelve days later, thanking Bjørnson for a note of condolence about Sigurd's treatment, he wrote: "If all roads are barred to Sigurd in Norway, I do not see that I have anything more to do here. And I have other places I could go to. I have lived long enough in Munich to acquire Bavarian nationality, and I can be sure I would be welcomed there. In Italy too. I must say, Norway is a difficult country to have as a fatherland."

Yet he stayed. Suzannah, no doubt, would have found Munich or Italy

[9] Cf. Bergliot Ibsen, pp. 156 ff.

more convenient for her gout cures. But Ibsen, at sixty-nine, was reluctant to uproot himself. His letters to Suzannah that summer are full of touching little domestic details.

The hydrangea has begun to show its buds again as abundantly as last year. I have had to order a dozen new dress-shirts, for the ones I had from Munich are now quite worn out. As regards food, I have been eating very much to my taste: smoked mutton, scrambled eggs, a lot of salmon done different ways, spiced-beer soup, and other good, wholesome summer dishes. So I am very content—and in my solitude I have begun to hatch and germinate plans for a new play. I already sense the general theme; but as yet I see only one of the characters clearly. Well, the others will come too.

Thus on 13 June; and on 2 July:

Last week there was a great to-do here; my study was springcleaned from ceiling to floor. The paintings have been taken down for cleaning, and now glitter and shine so that it is a joy to see them. The curtains have been washed and the walls also. The floor was scoured and then lacquered, so that you would not recognize it. It took six days to dry, during which time the furniture had to stand in the yard and got a thorough going-over. I used the red room while this was happening. Now it is the turn of the blue room, the floor of which is likewise to be lacquered, as is that of the dining-room. I can eat in the library; it is lucky we have enough rooms, and Mina [the new maid] is very good; she has had the charlady to help her for a couple of days. I am now busy with correspondence about the German collected edition, which is to fill nine thick volumes. There are already masses of tourists here, and yesterday a flock of journalists arrived from the congress in Stockholm; most of them have left their cards or spoken with me here and at the hotel. I am really very content, and don't think I could be more so anywhere now that it is summer. And I have begun to think about a new play! To that purpose I have extended my walks, and start each day by strolling to Skillebæk and back, and then down into town; and find this very contenting. But the most important thing is how the steam cure is suiting you this year. The iodine tincture which you found painful in Labers you must of course throw away and get a new bottle down there. Let me know how everything is with Sigurd . . . I sent Bergliot a telegram on 16 June. That is her birthday, isn't it? . . . Well, I have rambled on; but I felt I had to write to you today. We have the most wonderful summer weather; it is lovely to breathe.

Lugné-Pœ revisited Christiania later that summer. He had courageously followed his production of *Peer Gynt* with one of *Love's Comedy* on 23 June. Gunnar Heiberg attended the public dress rehearsal in Paris and, imperfect though the performance was, found the electricity and driving power of the young company stimulating; and "a better, or anyway a more responsive public, no theatre, actor, or dramatist could wish for. They are artists, writers, joyful malcontents of every profession. . . . They are young, these Frenchmen, as I have never seen young people in Norway or anywhere else. . . . They shout with joy. They rejoice and cry Bravo and think life is full of meaning and beauty when such men as Ibsen are around."[10] At the premiere next evening, however, the play was less successful—not surprisingly, the general public found it small beer after the works of Ibsen's maturity.

Lugné-Pœ brought to Christiania his young actress-wife Suzanne Desprès, who had replaced Berthe Bady as Hilde in his *Master Builder*, and had played Solveig in *Peer Gynt*. They met Ibsen at the Grand Hotel; Ibsen expressed the desire to hear some of her Solveig, so they got hold of Henrik Klausen, who had played Peer in the original production of 1876, and together they read all the great scenes between the two characters, Klausen in Norwegian, Suzanne in French. Ibsen also persuaded her to read some scenes from *The Master Builder*, and praised her warmly.[11]

Ibsen's letters that autumn show him in a peppery mood; perhaps it was the change of the year, perhaps his loneliness was beginning to weigh on him. On 19 September he wrote a discourteously irritable note to the faithful Julius Elias forbidding him to include *St. John's Night* in the German collected edition which Elias was preparing with Georg Brandes and Paul Schlenther (though for some reason he allowed them to use the much inferior *Warrior's Barrow*).[12] He wrote so rudely, indeed, that a fortnight later he sent Elias an apology for "my unseemly way of expressing myself." Then the Christiania Theatre annoyed him by arranging a revival of *The Feast at Solhaug* without informing him, so that he first heard through a third party. When Schrøder penitently invited him to attend rehearsals and the premiere, he replied curtly (3 December): "Dr. Ibsen is grateful for the information but will not attend rehearsals and does not wish to have tickets for the performance." And when Paul Clemenceau, brother of the statesman, raised his hat to him on Drammensveien and began: *"Cher maître! Permettez-moi de vous exprimer ma profonde admiration—"* Ibsen replied: *"Je ne parle pas français,"* and walked on.[13]

In a kindlier mood, he wrote (18 October) a charming little note of

[10] Heiberg, *Ibsen og Bjørnson på scenen,* pp. 71–79.
[11] Lugné-Pœ, p. 88.
[12] Cf. p. 98 above.
[13] Bull, *Tradisjoner og minner,* p. 99.

congratulation to his doctor's wife, Caroline Sontum, on the birth of a new child; and when the young poet Sigurd Obstfelder, lately released from an asylum and shortly to die of consumption, sent him a volume of his poems, Ibsen thanked him (10 December) with the assurance that he had "already begun to read the book, which fascinates and interests me."

Despite the absence of any reprints, except a small fourth edition of *An Enemy of the People,* Ibsen's income again exceeded £1,000 in 1897. Over two-thirds of this came from Germany and Austria, where his performing rights totalled as much as 7,902 crowns, and where Fischer gave him a not very generous flat fee of 8,000 crowns for the collected edition, from which that firm was to make immense sums over the next fifty years. From England he got only £18–6–0 for the Independent Theatre Society productions of *The Wild Duck* and *A Doll's House,* and £2–15–11 from the book sales of *Peer Gynt* in the translation by the Archer brothers. France did a little better by him with £40 for the publication of *John Gabriel Borkman* in the *Revue de Paris* and £11 in performing rights. The Russians had done *The Pillars of Society* on 24 September, but of course he got nothing for that; and from Norway he received nothing but £167 for the Christiania production of *Borkman* and £32 from Bergen:

	crowns
German fees and royalties from Felix Bloch	5,119
Royalties from Wien Burgtheater	2,295
Royalties from Munich Hoftheater	403
Royalties from Leipzig Stadttheater	85
Fee from S. Fischer for German collected edition	8,000
Fee for *John Gabriel Borkman* at Christiania Theatre	3,000
Fee from Bergen for 1 perf. of *John Gabriel Borkman*	400
Fees from Bergen for performances in 1896	180
Fee for *John Gabriel Borkman* in Helsinki	300
Fee for *Ghosts* at Dagmars Theatre, Copenhagen	600
Fee for *Little Eyolf* at Royal Theatre, Copenhagen (13th–16th perfs.)	434
4th edn. of *An Enemy of the People*	899
French royalties from Société des Auteurs Dramatiques	202
Fee from *Revue de Paris* for publication of *Borkman* (1,000 fr.)	725
Fee for London productions of *The Wild Duck* and *A Doll's House* (£18–6–0)	332
Share of English book sales of *Peer Gynt* (£2–5–11)	50
	23,024 £1,279

During 1897 he had invested as much as 34,000 crowns (nearly £1,900) in securities, representing almost his entire earnings of the preceding year.

35

The Wrong Side of the Medal

1898

In normal circumstances, Ibsen would have spent the first months of 1898 hatching his new play, so as to be ready to write it in the summer and autumn. But this was the year of his seventieth birthday, always an occasion of special celebration in Scandinavia, and in Ibsen's case it involved a series of distractions not merely in Norway, but in Denmark and Sweden too. Moreover, the proofs of the German collected edition had now begun to arrive, several thousand pages of them. For the first time since *The Pillars of Society* in 1877, there was to be a three-year gap between one play and the next.

Jacob Hegel sent him the good news in January that he was proposing to issue a cheap popular edition of the plays. Ibsen was delighted; as he said in his reply of 16 January, it would bring them "into strata of society where the more expensive editions have difficulty in gaining entry." He went on: "Where do I intend to spend my birthday this year? Well, I don't yet know. If the choice were mine alone I would escape up to the mountains somewhere or other, where I could be beautifully alone. But that time of year is unsuited to such a recreation, so I suppose I shall stay where I am. But I hope this won't exclude the possibility that I may later be able to fulfil my favourite dream, which is to see again the Sound and my Danish friends."

As his birthday approached, the messages began to arrive. Among the earliest was a telegram of congratulations from Emilie Bardach, the first contact between the two for seven years. His reply of 13 March has already been quoted.[1] On the day itself, telegrams, flowers and gifts of every kind poured in from all over the world One of the first gifts to come was a handsome set of silver from his British admirers, comprising a loving-

[1] See p. 626 above.

cup (a facsimile of one executed for King George II in 1730) and an original ladle and small cup of the same period, the three pieces being fitted into a case of polished oak. The contributors included Thomas Hardy, Henry James, Bernard Shaw, J. M. Barrie, William Archer, Edmund Gosse, Richard Garnett, A. C. Bradley, Gilbert Murray, A. W. Pinero, Elizabeth Robins, Herbert Beerbohm Tree, and the future Prime Minister, H. H. Asquith. Since none of these was able to make the journey, Karl Keilhau, the editor of *Norske Intelligenssedler*, presented the gift, together with a vellum address and a list of the subscribers' names. Keilhau reported to Gosse and Archer:

> He was obviously very much moved. While we were standing in front of the oak case and admiring, visitors began to arrive—a deputation from the Storthing, headed by the leader of the House, deputations representing the University, the Christiania theatres, etc., etc. Ibsen then asked me to translate the address, and I took out of my pocket a translation of it, which I read to him and to the others. He then himself read out all the names of the subscribers from the flyleaf. Ibsen repeated again and again that it was a splendid present, and all the afternoon he was occupied in taking his hundreds of visitors, in parties, up to the case, showing them the objects and explaining their origin.[2]

Performances to celebrate Ibsen's birthday were given that evening in many countries: at two theatres in Christiania, two in Copenhagen, three in Stockholm, four in Vienna and six in Berlin. In London, surprisingly, there were none—indeed, there were no Ibsen productions there in 1898, 1899, or 1900. The Christiania Theatre gave *The Feast at Solhaug*, with selected scenes from *Peer Gynt*, and Centraltheatret did *Ghosts*. For the following evening a gala performance of *The Master Builder* was planned, and Bergliot records that when a deputation came from the theatre to ask Ibsen and Suzannah to honour them with their presence Suzannah thanked them but asked that he and she should each sit in a separate box. "Ibsen must sit alone," she said. "This is your evening, and I have nothing to do there." And, despite his protests, so it was. Similarly, when the students came to honour him with a torchlight procession:

> I can still see Ibsen walk over to her with his short steps, and hear him say: "Won't you come with me to the window?" But she replied: "No, you must stand there alone." . . . She never bothered to borrow the reflected glory of his fame. She cared only about him, and that his work should succeed.[3]

[2] Bredsdorff, *Gosse's Correspondence with Scandinavian Writers*, pp. 48 ff. and 180 ff. The appeal was not launched publicly, but by private approach. Forty subscribers contributed £50–8–0 between them. Several of those not approached, including J. T. Grein, voiced their discontent, and Shaw, though among the subscribers, criticized in the *Saturday Review* of 26 March the way the thing had been done.

[3] Bergliot Ibsen, p. 171.

A *festskrift* had, naturally, been arranged, headed by a tribute from King Oscar, and containing contributions from, amongst others, Snoilsky (whose poem is one of the best things in the book) and two future Nobel Prize winners, Verner von Heidenstam and Selma Lagerlöf. Two unexpected names in the list are those of John Paulsen and Nils Kjær, who had both so insulted him; Kjær, since that unfortunate drunken outburst, seems to have undergone a remarkable change of heart. Old friends such as Georg Brandes and Jonas Lie reminisced affectionately, and August Lindberg and Emil Poulsen spoke for the acting profession. But what an opportunity was wasted by not inviting foreign admirers to contribute! Hardy, Henry James, Shaw, Hauptmann—other admirers such as Freud, Rilke, Pirandello and Joyce were scarcely if at all known, and Tolstoy[4] would not have contributed, but Chekhov and Zola might have. Strindberg nearly did. In a letter to Gustaf af Geijerstam later that year asking him to send Ibsen a copy of *To Damascus*, Strindberg told him to tell Ibsen that: "Strindberg is ashamed that as a prominent Swedish author he did not join in the homage to the Master, from whom he learned much. But he was in a state of depression and did not think his homage could honour or gladden anyone." Fearful lest this might be taken to imply a modification of his antagonism to Ibsen's general view of life, he assured Geijerstam that his homage would have been to "the master of dramatic art, not the philosopher."[5]

On 23 March the city of Christiania gave an official banquet for Ibsen. In his reply, Ibsen, after a conventional paragraph of thanks, asked:

Were you perhaps expecting that I should speak about my books? That I could not do, for then I should have to bring in my whole life. And that alone would make a very thick book. And talking of that, I am indeed just now thinking of writing such a book—a book which will knit my life and my work together into an integral and explanatory whole. For I think I have now reached a sufficiently mature age to permit myself a short breathing-space—take a year's holiday; for such a book would be a holiday task compared with the nagging and exhausting work of dramatic composition. And I have not had a real holiday since I left Norway thirty-four years ago. I think I could do with one now. But, ladies and gentlemen, you must not therefore suppose that I intend to lay down my pen as a dramatist for good. No, I intend to take it up again and to cling tightly to it until the end. For I still have a few lunacies in my locker which I

[4] The day before his birthday *Ørebladet* printed an interview in which Ibsen, after praising *Anna Karenina*, described Tolstoy as "a great man when he isn't being crazy. . . . Tolstoy . . . spends his life abusing me. . . . But that is natural in view of his beliefs." (C.E., XIX, 214.)

[5] Sten Linder, *Ibsen, Strindberg och andra* (Stockholm, 1936), p. 95.

have not yet found the opportunity to express. Only when I have got them off my chest will it be time for me to stop. And how easy would it not be to stop then, in contrast to the time when I was still a beginner! What a silence and emptiness surrounded one then! One's fellow-combatants were scattered, isolated and apart. It often seemed to me, after I had gone away, as though I had never been here. Nor my work, neither.

But now! Now the place where I stood is crowded. Young forces have arisen, confident of victory. They need no longer write for a tiny circle. *They* have a public to speak to, an entire people to whom to address their thoughts and feelings. Whether they meet with opposition or acceptance does not really matter. What destroys a writer is indifference and rejection. That is what I encountered.

I regret deeply that I have come into so little contact with many of those who are to continue my work in this country. Not because I would have wished to influence them, but so that I myself might achieve a deeper understanding. And I would especially have used this closer contact to dispel a misconception which has in many ways been a hindrance to me—I mean, the idea that unqualified happiness is a necessary consequence of the rare and saga-like fate which has befallen me, of winning fame in many foreign lands. I have, too, won friendship and understanding in those countries. That is the most important thing of all.

But true, inward happiness does not fall from heaven. It must be earned at a price which may often seem heavy. For the point is this: that he who has won a home in many foreign lands feels in his heart of hearts nowhere truly at home—scarcely even in the country of his birth.

But perhaps this may happen yet. And I should like to think of this evening as a starting-point.

For here I see something that resembles an entity. Here every viewpoint, every divergent opinion, has been assembled with a single purpose. I have no longer the painful sense of being regarded as the spokesman of a party. This party or that party. A writer must have all his people around him, whether they agree with him or whether they oppose him. And then the idea of unity can march forward, to higher goals and grander ambitions. That is my hope and my belief.

And so, ladies and gentlemen, I ask you to accept my warmest thanks for all your goodness and kindness towards me.[6]

The book he was considering writing—"A Dramatist's Apology," he might have entitled it—had, as we have seen, been in his thoughts for years; only the opposition of his old publisher and counsellor Frederik

[6] C.E., XV, 412-14.

Hegel had discouraged him from attempting it earlier. Yet he was fated never to write it; though in some ways, the theme was to be that of his next and final play.

Meanwhile, there were other capitals besides Christiania waiting to acclaim him, and on 29 March he left for Copenhagen to attend the celebrations which had been prepared there. It was the first time he had left Norway since his return eight years earlier. The editor of *Morgenbladet*, Nils Vogt, accompanied him on the journey, by train through south-west Sweden and across the Sound. Vogt later recalled that Ibsen was a little feeble on his feet, the first evidence we have that age was beginning to tell on him; the Swedish railways courteously arranged that food should be brought to his carriage at the various stops, to save him the trouble of getting out. When they reached Gothenburg Ibsen found a telegram awaiting him from Peter Hansen, who had been his companion on the trip to Egypt and was now head of the Royal Theatre in Copenhagen, telling him that he had been awarded his most impressive medal yet, the Grand Cross of the Danish Order of Dannebrog. Ibsen was hugely gratified. "I can recall many Norwegians," he said proudly to Vogt, "who are Knights or Commanders of Dannebrog, but none who has the Grand Cross" (a statement which was not quite accurate but which Vogt prudently refrained from correcting). As they approached Denmark on 31 March Ibsen sat long at the window staring silently out across the water. Suddenly he said: "Do you know, when I come from Norway to the Sound I feel as though I were emerging from a tunnel into the sunshine." Then, after a pause, he added: "But please don't tell them that in Norway, at any rate until I am dead."[7]

Jacob Hegel and Peter Hansen met him on his arrival in Copenhagen, and took him to the Hotel Angleterre, where the royal suite had been placed at his disposal and the Norwegian flag was flying in his honour. As they entered the suite the first thing that met their eyes was a small box on the table. Ibsen opened it and there, resplendent, lay the Grand Cross. He gazed at it. "How beautiful!" he exclaimed. "This is indeed a great honour. No Scandinavian writer since Oehlenschläger has received so high a Danish decoration." Suddenly his expression changed. "But what is this?" he cried. "This is no medal! It is papier-maché!" Hegel and Hansen were as amazed as he; on enquiry, however, they learned that it was the custom for the recipient of this great honour to buy the medal himself from the court jeweller, only a papier-maché copy being provided by the state.

Hegel gave a small lunch for Ibsen that day, the only other guests being Vogt and the Norwegian poet and novelist Alexander Kielland,

[7] For the details of Ibsen's visit to Copenhagen, cf. Nils Vogt, "Paa reise med Henrik Ibsen," in *Samtiden* (1906), pp. 329 ff., and Peter Nansen in *Aftenposten*, 4, 7 and 11 March 1917.

who happened to be in town. In the evening, the Royal Theatre gave a gala performance of *The Wild Duck*. It was not the most inspired of choices, for Ibsen had already seen this production twice with the same cast, and Betty Hennings, the country's leading actress, was now, at forty-eight, more than ever too old for the role of Hedvig. But the theatre had omitted to do anything about arranging a new production of any of Ibsen's plays until it was too late. Still, the performance was royally attended, for not only were the King and Queen of Denmark there, but also their daughters, Princess Alexandra of Wales and the Tsarina of Russia, all in the royal box with Ibsen seated majestically alone in the box opposite.

The unfortunate Peter Hansen, already under fire for not having remembered to arrange a new production, was to have a bad evening. His troubles began immediately after the performance when, in his tactless way, he issued a military-sounding directive that the actors were to be ready to be presented to Ibsen immediately after the performance. They were so offended at being thus commanded that they refused in a body. Hansen was desperate. Among other things, this refusal meant that Ibsen got no refreshment during the long interval, for Peter Nansen of Gyldendal (not to be confused with Hansen) records that when he mentioned the matter to Hansen the latter replied: "I really have no time to think about refreshments," and Ibsen had to go thirsty.

When the performance ended, at first all went well. The entire audience, including the crowned heads, rose and bowed to Ibsen in his box, applauding, while he bowed aristocratically back. He then waited for the company to be presented; but the company held to their refusal, and all Hansen could rustle up was a few of the younger actors who were sufficiently frightened of him to obey. With some presence of mind he presented them as "my most promising actor," and "my most promising dancer," and so partially saved the situation.

But Hansen's troubles were by no means over. The students of Copenhagen decided to greet Ibsen with a torchlight procession before he left the theatre. He stood on the theatre balcony acknowledging their applause; meanwhile, Hansen went on to the hotel, where he found Kielland waiting. As they chatted, there was a fearful noise outside, and Ibsen shot in "like a cannonball from a gun, dazed, his coat torn, his top hat at the back of his head and his medal dangling outside his overcoat," with a mob of students pushing and cheering him, so that "it was a miracle that the helpless little old man survived unharmed." Peter Hansen, however, seemed by now to have forgotten his famous guest. Not only had his company mutinied against him; that same evening one of his star actors, Karl Mantzius, had given notice because his wife had not been re-engaged. So Ibsen stood dishevelled and forgotten in a corner.

His fellow-Norwegian, Alexander Kielland, was furious. "God Almighty, how typically Danish!" he cried. "Typical bloody Danish! The Royal Theatre has the most famous author in Scandinavia as its guest and doesn't even hire a carriage to take him home! He ought to have been driven across the square in a bridal carriage with white horses and the director of the theatre as postilion, and a proper dinner awaiting him. Instead of which the old man has to fight his way through a mob on foot and no one even bothers to ask whether he's hungry or thirsty!"

Nansen said to Hansen, "Ibsen would like to have something to eat."

The distraught Hansen turned to Ibsen. "You want something to eat?"

"Yes, please."

"Waiter! Bring a sandwich menu. Thank you. Now [to Ibsen] just tick off what you'd like. Steak, sausage, salmon, anything you like. Perhaps you'd like a drink too?"

"Yes, please."

"A beer for Dr. Ibsen. Do you want a schnapps too?"

Ibsen said yes. So he got three sandwiches, a schnapps and a glass of beer, and thus his first day in Copenhagen ended.

The next day, which was 1 April, began no more promisingly and ended even more disastrously. Nils Vogt and Peter Hansen, the latter no doubt anxious to redeem himself after his showing of the previous evening, had the pleasant idea of going out first thing to the court jeweller to buy Ibsen his expensive Grand Cross of Dannebrog. They bore this to Ibsen in his suite at the Angleterre but, as they entered, were much embarrassed to see one already lying in its box on the table. Ibsen, an inveterate early riser, had been to the jeweller before them. As the three stood there in confusion, the Minister of Culture was announced, and entered carrying a third Grand Cross as a personal gift from the king. The other two were silently removed and returned with apologies to the jeweller.

That evening a gala banquet was held for Ibsen at the Angleterre. Unusual difficulty had been experienced by the organizers in securing appropriate people to make the speeches of welcome. Georg Brandes was away. His brother Edvard was suggested but (says Nansen) he was "as hated then as he was beloved later," and anyway was editor of the radical newspaper *Politiken,* so that for him to have made the principal speech would have offended the conservatives present. Eventually they chose the professor of philosophy, Kroman, with Peter Hansen following as the second speaker and Professor Sophus Schandorph as number three. So that was settled; but now the organizers learned that several of the invited guests considered the price of a ticket for the dinner (25 crowns, $6.75) excessive. (Nansen admits that it was "a then unheard-of price.") Among the objectors was Betty Hennings, whose husband had just become deeply religious. She declared it to be immoral to spend so much on a dinner, and could not be persuaded to attend.

The banquet was an almost total disaster. At two o'clock Professor Kroman, the principal speaker, sent word that he was too ill to come (Nansen suspected it was an attack of nerves). Five hours was not enough to find a substitute, and as Kroman had been going to make the formal speech, to be followed by Hansen in lighter vein, they had to compromise by persuading Hansen to introduce serious matter into a set comic speech of his which had been successful on previous occasions and which Ibsen had not heard. But Hansen found the time at his disposal insufficient to make the adaptation, so that his speech turned out an unhappy mixture of jokes and formality. Among other gaffes, he referred to Ibsen as "one of our leading dramatists" and thanked him for the "many full houses" he had brought the Royal Theatre.

A profound embarrassment settled on the company, and Ibsen, who had clearly prepared a speech on the assumption that it would be in response to the usual courteously formal welcome, made the briefest reply. "Professor Hansen's speech has confounded me, and rendered inappropriate the reply I had intended to make. . . . I must therefore improvise, and ask your indulgence. Today is 1 April. This same day in 1864 I visited Copenhagen for the first time. That is now thirty-four years ago. Mark well the date and the year! I travelled south, through Germany and Austria, and crossed the Alps on 9 May." He went on to describe his first sight of Italy, in words already quoted,[8] and concluded: "This feeling of being released from darkness into light, of emerging from mists through a tunnel into the sunshine—this feeling I had again now, as I gazed along the Sound. . . . I felt that these two journeys had some hidden connection, and I therefore give you my most grateful thanks."

As usual when Ibsen improvised, the result was almost certainly more interesting than what he had prepared. That crisis, then, seemed to have been bridged; but the troubles of the evening were by no means over. Professor Sophus Schandorph, who rose to speak next, proved to be so drunk that he had to support himself on the shoulders of his two neighbours, a count and a bishop. The guests, already embarrassed, began to titter and interrupt, at which Schandorph, clutching the bishop closer to him, thundered what can most faithfully be translated as: "Shut your fucking mouths while I speak!"

He was allowed to finish, and a cantata, specially composed by Holger Drachmann, partially restored order, as did two tactful and appropriate speeches by younger guests, Professor Vilhelm Andersen and Dr. Poul Levin. But now a new unrest developed as several of the guests began to complain about the food. The German proprietor of the hotel, one Heene, anxious to celebrate the occasion in style, had composed a gas-

8 See p. 215.

tronome's menu of real turtle soup, duckling, and out-of-season asparagus. The Danes, who had come expecting the enormous steak that was customarily served on such occasions, were now feeling hungry. "If we'd charged twelve crowns and given them a piece of fish, a steak, cheese and an ice," said Heene to Nansen, "they'd have been happy. That's what they're used to." Heene was so disillusioned by the whole business that he left the Angleterre shortly afterwards.

When the meal ended Ibsen rose and made his way to the door, escorted by the count and the bishop who had supported Schandorph. Suddenly an old painter named Thorvald Niss, in a flush of, among other things, enthusiasm, rushed from his place, embraced Ibsen, shook him backwards and forwards and cried: *"Du er kraft steile mig en gut! Tak for alt, gamle dreng!"* (something like: "You're a right lad! Thanks for everything, old cock"). Ibsen stared in horror and murmured, "Take this man away."

As he sat drinking his coffee, Peter Nansen presented some young writers to him. He was courteous and affable to them until Nansen introduced a popular playwright of intellectual pretensions. "I don't know, Dr. Ibsen," said Nansen, "if you have heard of Sven Lange," to which Ibsen in his silkiest tones replied: "Of course I know of Sven Lange, the Scribe of Denmark." Nansen tells that he did not dare to look at the unfortunate man (who had contributed a vapid article on "Henrik Ibsen and the Young Europe" to the *festskrift*).

So, as they say in the sagas, that day ended.

The next morning, Saturday 2 April, Ibsen was received by King Christian to be formally handed his medal, and was presented to the Tsarina of Russia and the Princess of Wales. Ibsen's impression of the meeting is not on record but King Christian's, surprisingly, is. Not long afterwards the Speaker of the Storthing, Hegsbro, was received by the king and, on the latter's enquiring after his health, replied: "Well, Your Majesty, one notices that one's getting old." "You should talk about growing old," said the king. "I'm several years older than you, and I don't notice any weakness. I felt rather proud some while ago. I had to receive the Norwegian writer, Henrik Ibsen. He was seventy, and I was ten years older. I thought: 'It won't be easy to make conversation with such a genius. What is one to say to him?' But I must honestly confess I thought he seemed much older than me. He was really most timid and unhelpful. I had to keep nudging him along."

By contrast, when, later that day, a young girl came to Ibsen's suite to offer him flowers and found herself speechless, Ibsen sat her down and put her at her ease with the greatest charm. After she had left, he said to Nansen: "How pretty the young ladies of Copenhagen are!" Nansen adds that Ibsen would sometimes fantasise to young girls of what he would do if he were very rich—how he would buy the finest ship in the world, engage a gipsy orchestra and sail to some tropical island with a few good friends and "the most beautiful young women in the world"— very much as Solness must have spoken to Hilde Wangel during their first encounter at Lysanger.

They kept him busy in Copenhagen, for he attended two receptions that same afternoon and evening, one given by the Women's Literary Guild and one by the Students' Union. At the latter, Valdemar Vedel (another contributor to the *festskrift,* on "Ibsen and Denmark"), began his speech of welcome with the familiar second person singular (*"Mester, Du—"*) which Ibsen so detested. Accounts vary as to what happened next. According to some, Ibsen immediately rose and left the room.[9] Peter Nansen simply says that he left without replying to the speech; and Nils Vogt, who accompanied him to the dinner as to everything else on this trip, reports merely that he left early, and remarked to Vogt on the way downstairs: "Vedel's a good fellow, but I can't remember having drunk *Du*'s with him." Georg Brandes's daughter Edith, who accompanied Ibsen to the dinner in a carriage (and recalled that he was much annoyed on arrival to find that he was not sitting next to her, as he had assumed, but to the much less youthful and attractive suffragette Amalie Skram, to whom he did not address a word all evening) writes that he said simply "Thank you" after the speeches of Vedel and Harald Høffding, made no speech himself, but, although he had ordered a carriage for 10:30, did not leave till 11.[10] What is sure is that as he left (whenever it was) some wit recited Ibsen's own poem "Gone," substituting "he" for "she":

> He was but a guest
> And now he is gone.

which was greeted with laughter and cheers.

The next day, Sunday 3 April, the privately owned Dagmars Theatre, now under solvent management, gave a gala performance of *Brand*. It was a new production, the company was young, and Nansen wondered with some trepidation how Ibsen would survive a performance lasting five hours or more. But against all expectations, the evening turned out to be the peak event of Ibsen's visit. Martinius Nielsen, the head of the theatre, who was acting the title role, had, with more foresight than Peter Hansen at the Royal Theatre, supplied the royal box in which Ibsen sat with an excellent cold collation, accompanied by "champagne, beer, whisky, coffee, liqueurs, and flowers." Nansen records: "It was a

[9] Cf. letters from Bengt Zinglersen, Otto Zahle and Valdemar Petersen in *Politiken*, 14, 16 and 18 January 1966. My attention was drawn to these letters by Dr. Elias Bredsdorff.

[10] "Prinsessans Album" (Gerda Brandes's memories) in *Svenska Dagbladet*, 9 May 1965.

young people's performance, and he liked it far better than *The Wild Duck.*" He clapped loudly at the fall of each curtain and showed no signs of tiredness.

It was the first time Ibsen had seen *Brand* played, and another observer, P. A. Rosenberg, reports that "he seemed moved and several times dried the tears from his cheeks during the fourth act. 'Don't blubber! [*Ikke tude!*]' he muttered to himself."[11] He said to Nielsen's wife Oda, who sat next to him: "This moves me. This is—my youth. I haven't thought about *Brand* for thirty years." At the end he led the applause, which the audience then directed towards him. Although the performance lasted until midnight he did not return home, but stayed at a party which the actors improvised for him, and did not leave until 3 A.M. He was very lively and talked continuously. Of Nielsen's performance, he said: "That is *my* Brand. That's how I saw him." "You haven't cut much," he said to Rosenberg, and when told that they had in fact cut a third of the play he asked to see the prompt book and, as he leafed through it, seeing page after page deleted, murmured: "I'll be damned. Yes, I suppose I've forgotten most of it."

As they at last broke up, at three o'clock, Ibsen said: "I must go home now. I must be at my desk at 7." "Not *this* morning?" exclaimed Rosenberg. "Yes," he replied. "Come and see. I'll be there at 7." "But you won't have had enough sleep," said Nielsen. "Yes, I will," said Ibsen. "Under such circumstances I sleep more energetically. Thank you for tonight. It has been a good night." As a favour he asked that his two companions at table, Fru Nielsen and Fru Rosenberg (who had played Agnes), should accompany him home in the carriage, declaring: "Their husbands can manage without them for a few minutes."

Yet (we are told) he did not sleep, but lay awake most of that night.[12] As he lay there he may have remembered that thirty years before, just after *Brand* had brought him the recognition he had longed for, he had remarked to Georg Brandes (26 June 1869) that Brand "could as well have been a sculptor or a politician as a priest." The chief character in his new play was to be a sculptor, of the same uncompromising ruthlessness as Brand; and, like Brand, he was to die in an avalanche near the top of a mountain, his pride crushed, with a Latin blessing cried out to him as though from a forgiving deity at the moment of death.

The next day, luckily, was a rest day; and on 5 April, his last day in Copenhagen—the last that he was ever to spend there—Jacob Hegel gave a farewell dinner for him at his villa, Skovgaard. According to Vogt, Ibsen enjoyed himself, but the evening was spoilt by Sophus

---

[11] For the details of this evening, cf. Nansen in *Aftenposten*, 11 March 1917; Rosenberg in *Nationaltidende*, 28 July 1926 (reprinted in C.E., XIX, 215-20); Kinck, p. 537.

[12] A. Fibiger, *Henrik Ibsen* (Copenhagen, 1928), p. 14.

Schandorph, who had delivered the drunken speech at the Angleterre and now, in a fit of remorse and enthusiasm, attempted to kiss Ibsen on the cheek, causing him to leave early. However, on the way home with Vogt, in a carriage drawn by two white horses (like the ones in *Rosmersholm*, reflected Vogt, though he was tactful enough not to mention it), Ibsen thawed again. Speaking of a classical scholar of rigid conservative views, he said: "He has no idea of what real classicism and humanism are. He has read some books in Latin and Greek which I, for good reason, have not. But I have lived myself into its spirit by studying its buildings and art, as you may possibly have gathered from *Emperor and Galilean*. X's æsthetic and intellectual horizon stops at Lübeck and Greiswald."

Ibsen particularly disliked the narrower type of academic mind, especially after the treatment Sigurd had received from the professors of Christiania. Once during this visit to Copenhagen he asked Vogt: "Can't you help to get Georg Brandes a professorship in Norway? Never mind that he's unreliable on odd details, and to many people personally antipathetic—he makes people think, and forces us to be aware of the intellectual currents of our time, and how many of our professors do that?"

On 6 April Ibsen left Copenhagen by train for a further round of celebrations in Stockholm. They installed him in the best suite at the Hotel Rydberg in Gustav Adolfs Torg and gave him a couple of days to recover his breath; then, on 9 April, he was received at the palace by King Oscar and given another medal to add to his collection, the Grand Cross of the Northern Star. The king, during the conversation, graciously employed the phrase "we two kings," and spoke with some apprehension about Sigurd. The Norwegian government was considering setting up its own Foreign Office, something that Sigurd had urged ever since he had been a young attaché, and they had in mind to appoint him head. King Oscar expressed gloomy doubts. "He doesn't want me as King of Norway," he said to Ibsen. "But let that pass. As long as that wife of his doesn't make him too much of a radical and an agitator!"

The combination of the leading pamphleteer against the union and Bjørnson's daughter in joint charge of Norwegian affairs must have been an alarming prospect to that conservative monarch. Ibsen assured him that Bergliot's views were not as extreme as her father's. That evening, the king gave a banquet for Ibsen at the palace; among the guests was the explorer Sven Hedin, whom he had met on the Göta Canal eleven years previously, and whom he afterwards took back to his hotel and proudly showed his medals, carefully arranged on a table in little red and black boxes.[13]

During the meal the king said to his guest of honour: "But you shouldn't have written *Ghosts*, Ibsen. That's not a good play. Now, *Lady*

[13] Bergliot Ibsen, pp. 183–84; Hedin, p. 79.

Inger of Østraat—there's a good play." Ibsen was embarrassed and remained silent. Queen Sophie tried to rescue him by speaking of other things; but after a long pause, Ibsen exclaimed: "Your Majesty, I *had* to write *Ghosts!*"[14]

Two days later, the Swedish Society of Authors gave a dinner for Ibsen at Hasselbacken Restaurant on Skansen. "I'm not very curious about him," wrote the poet Oscar Levertin to a friend that morning. "Great men are best appreciated at a distance, and every utterance that the Sphinx has delivered during these past weeks of divine revelation seems to me about as empty as the usual wisdom of Sphinxes." And the evening indeed was not a great success. Carl Snoilsky, who took the chair, had promised that there would be no speeches, but unfortunately Gustaf af Geijerstam improvised one, full of Ibsen quotations, and at the end of the evening Levertin, despite his lack of enthusiasm for Ibsen, made another. Ibsen replied (untruthfully) that he did not think he had ever belonged to any Society and that this was the first time he had attended one. "I am pretty sure there is a Society in Christiania of the same name as this, but I am a member of that only for appearance's sake and for various reasons never partake in its meetings." (He had still not forgotten how he had been insulted at the inaugural meeting.) He went on: "A Society is not a thing for me. And in a way it might seem that a Society is least of all appropriate for authors, for they must go their own wild ways—yes, as wild as they wish, if they are to fulfil their life's calling." (Loud applause). However, he granted that such a Society might serve to protect writers "which can often be very necessary," and concluded by expressing the hope that it might also encourage Scandinavians to read each other in the original language and not in translation—a hope which has hardly been fulfilled. To a foreigner, it is amazing how reluctant Scandinavians are to read each other in the original, despite the close similarity of Norwegian, Danish and Swedish.

After dinner, the Swedish writer and artist Albert Engström sang some Swedish country songs, which Ibsen, despite the view he had just expressed, was unable to understand; and (records a lady who was there) "despite being primed with punch and other stimulants, he remained stiff and unapproachable. No amount of effort could provoke any Ibsenian profundities, far less any witty conversation. At last he turned to a lady seated near him and began: 'Can you tell me—?' The lady in question adopted an expression of deep concentration. 'Can you tell me if I can go direct to Christiania by the night train, or if I have to change at Laxå?' "[15]

Engström himself describes how Ibsen spent the second half of the evening surrounded by elderly authoresses, from whom he tried repeatedly

[14] Bull, Introduction to *Ghosts,* C.E., IX, 13.
[15] Gurli Linder, pp. 129–33.

to rescue him by saying; "May I drink with you, Doctor?" for which Ibsen was grateful.

At last it grew late and the ladies departed, accompanied by some of the gentlemen. I had rescued Ibsen at least ten times during the evening. And now, when there were only a few young people left, he became a new man. He joked and toasted us continuously. It was just midnight when he declared that his age no longer allowed him to exceed a certain limit. So we gathered around him and he said a few words, very simply, rather shyly; but I think that we who heard them will remember them and the mood of that moment. He clasped our hands in farewell. To me he said: "Do you know how many brandies you've made me drink tonight, my dear Engström? I've lost count."[16]

Next evening, 12 April, he attended a performance at Vasa Teatern of *The Pretenders,* with a distinguished cast: Emil Hillberg (the original Brand) as Bishop Nicholas, Tore Svennberg as Skule, and a new young star, Anders de Wahl, as Haakon. Harald Molander directed. Ibsen sat in a box with Gustaf af Geijerstam and, towards the end of his long life, de Wahl recalled:

I had received a flower arrangement in the form of a long, tall Viking ship, and the thought occurred to me that I ought to present these flowers to the author. . . . I noted that the gentlemen had put this ship on the edge of their box so that they were invisible to us and the audience. During one of the intervals I was summoned to pay my respects. . . . I was determined to have every sense alert so as to memorise every word the great man might utter, note every glance, engrave every nuance of the occasion on my memory and, at some future date, tell the world of this great meeting. Thus prepared, I entered the box on trembling legs. There he sat, the great man, beside my Viking ship, at a small table covered with glasses and bottles. "What, what, what . . . . what d'you want?" In a word, he was drunk. As I came closer he pointed at me and said: "You're dolled up. Do you think Haakon was a dandy?"[17]

On 13 April the city gave an official banquet for Ibsen at the Grand Hotel, and in reply to Snoilsky's speech of welcome Ibsen said that his life had been "a long, long Passion Week" which, however, had now

[16] Albert Engström, *At Häklefjäll* (Stockholm, 1914), pp. 13 ff.
Strindberg was unfortunately in Paris, though one doubts whether he could have been persuaded to attend. On being asked during this visit by a Swedish journalist what he thought of Strindberg, Ibsen described him as "a very great talent. I don't know him personally—our paths have never crossed—but I have read his work with *great* interest. Not least, his last book *Inferno* [written the previous year] has made a powerful impression on me." (Interview in *Aftonbladet,* 13 April 1898, reprinted in C.E., XV, 429–32).

[17] Per Lindberg and Sten af Geijerstam, *Anders de Wahl* (Stockholm, 1944), pp. 40–41.

been "transformed into a poem, a fairy tale . . . a midsummer night's dream."[18] Next day a deputation of students from Upsala brought him greetings; and in the evening the Royal Theatre gave *Lady Inger of Østraat,* that play of which King Oscar approved and which he now graced with his presence. 15 April seems to have been a rest day, but on the 16th Ibsen, who so disliked the company of elderly bluestockings, found himself the guest at Skansen of the two women's societies of Stockholm: Nya Idun and the Fredrika Bremer Society. The officials of these two formidable bodies, indignant that the dinners arranged for Ibsen had been mainly male affairs, had managed to persuade him to stay an extra day in Stockholm to meet their members. When they put the idea to him "Ibsen became nervous, waved his arms and exclaimed: 'No, no, I shall be like Carl XII, I shall be carried across the frontier a corpse!' "[19] But a historian present reminded him that when Carl XII had crossed the frontier from Sweden to Norway, he had been very much alive (he had been killed on the other side of the border at Frederikshall in 1718); so Ibsen accepted.

Perhaps he hoped that he might have at least one reasonably youthful and attractive lady to table. But as usual on these occasions, he found himself flanked by dragons, in this instance the presidents of the two societies, Ellen Key and a Fru Anckarsvärd; nor did Ellen Key help matters by beginning her speech: *"Du . . . ,"* as Valdemar Vedel had done in Copenhagen. She thanked him for his "new religion, under which every human being will obey his or her own laws without being daunted by a sense of guilt, and self-fulfilment shall be deemed as justifiable and meaningful as self-sacrifice."

To entertain their guest the ladies had arranged an exhibition of folk dancing, and here at least there were some young faces. One, twenty-six years old, especially attracted his attention. Her name was Rosa Fitinghoff, the daughter of a well-known popular author, Laura Fitinghoff (whose *The Children from Frostmoor Mountain* is still one of the most read children's books in Sweden). Ibsen spoke to Rosa several times during the evening, expressing particular admiration of her long and beautiful hair, and asked her to see him off at the station next day. She was to be the last of his dream girls, following in the footsteps of Emilie, Helene and Hildur.

Ibsen's rather pathetic longing for young girls was demonstrated several times during these days in Stockholm. Gurli Linder reports that he received several in his hotel room, gave them signed photographs of himself, said: "You are just like my Hilde," and kissed them; and that when a lady at one of the receptions told him that she had once been in the same town as he in Norway and had only with difficulty

18 C.E., XV, 432–33.
19 For the account of this dinner, cf. Gurli Linder, pp. 130–32.

restrained herself from running up to him, seizing his hand and saying: "Thank you!" he replied: "Do you know what I would have done if you had? I would have hugged you to my breast and kissed you many times"—precisely as Hilde Wangel claimed Solness had done to her.[20]

On 17 April he returned to Christiania. He had been away for over a fortnight of almost unbroken celebration, but his constitution seemed unimpaired. "I am always well," he had told an interviewer on 13 March. "I have never been ill, not for a single day in my life. I have never consulted a doctor. I have never used a prescription. Despite the fact that I have often lived in feverish atmospheres and exposed myself to illnesses."[21] It was not quite true; he had been ill in 1861, 1889 and 1892; but even then he had probably not consulted a doctor, though the period of his immunity was almost past.

Eight days after his return he sent a photograph of himself to Rosa Fitinghoff, with an accompanying letter:

Dearest Miss Fitinghoff!

When I received your beautiful postcard yesterday it was as though you had entered my house yourself with a spring greeting to warm my heart. There was music and dance in what you wrote; and it was through dance and music that we met. That is the happy part of the story. The sad part is that we did not meet until my last evening. Parties are often like life; people do not meet until they have to say goodbye. But go on writing to me. Write of everything you wish to, and can—and make happy

Your affectionate
Henrik Ibsen

On 26 May he had another formidable body of ladies to face. The Norwegian Society for Women's Rights gave a banquet for him in Christiania. Suzannah, appropriately for one who had for so long been a champion of that cause, for once attended with him. In his reply to the toast Ibsen said something that must have disconcerted his hearers, and that every dramatic critic ought to learn by heart before reviewing any production of A Doll's House:

I have been more of a poet and less of a social philosopher than people generally tend to suppose. I thank you for your toast, but must disclaim the honour of having consciously worked for women's rights. I am not even quite sure what women's rights really are. To

[20] Ibid., pp. 130–31.
[21] Interview with Hans Tostrup in Ørebladet, 19 March 1898 (reprinted in C.E., XIX, 211–15).

me it has been a question of human rights. And if you read my books carefully you will realize that. Of course it is incidentally desirable to solve the problem of women; but that has not been my whole object. My task has been the portrayal of human beings.

On 29 May he informed Julius Elias that, owing to the distractions occasioned by his birthday celebrations, it was doubtful if he would be able to finish his projected new play that year, adding "I have never planned to complete my so-called 'Memoirs' in the immediate future." (He presumably regarded the childhood memories which Jæger had incorporated in his biography as the foundation.) On 26 June he wrote again to Rosa Fitinghoff thanking her for a profile photograph of herself "so that now I can sit each day and look at you from the side without your knowing. And when I want to look into your eyes I take out the big group photograph. There you sit so still and thoughtful, as though you were dreaming and had no idea that anyone was looking at you. . . . Your letters can never be too long for me. But I must, alas, limit myself to telegraphic brevity. But do not think ill of me for this. What I do not write I say to your photograph." On 8 July he wrote suggesting that she should visit him in Christiania on her way back to Stockholm from her holiday with her mother on the Swedish west coast. This visit did not materialize, but she wrote to him twice from Lysekil and continued the correspondence on her return to Stockholm.

Gustaf af Geijerstam visited him in Christiania that August; so did William Archer, who was somewhat surprised to see "holding a very prominent position in his study, a bright corner-room looking out upon the palace park, a huge gilt-edged and brass-clasped family Bible. 'You keep this close at hand?' I said, pointing at it. 'Oh, yes,' he replied. 'I often read in it—for the sake of the language.'" (Bolette Sontum likewise records that she heard him assure people, "gazing fiercely at them," that he read it only for the language. "But we knew him to be a faithful reader of the Bible, as the worn pages of his own huge copy testify.") On Archer's expressing further surprise at seeing the portrait of Strindberg, Ibsen replied: "I think he looks so delightfully mad."[22] The same month Ibsen received news from Hegel that they had decided to increase the first printing of the popular edition of his collected works to 15,000—the more gratifying since Bjørnson's works in the same series were being printed in an edition of only 4,000.

In September he received his first letter for over a year from Georg Brandes. Brandes had been gravely ill and, quarrelsome as ever, had apparently rebuked Ibsen for not writing. "You know how much I owe you," Ibsen replied on 30 September, "recently as well as of old, and

[22] "Ibsen as I Knew Him," p. 16; Sontum, p. 253.

that I gratefully acknowledge this. And if you doubt it, would a written assurance help? Good God, you know how easy it is to put together a French-general-staff kind of letter. I can therefore not feel that the crime of silence is sufficient to justify your addressing a friend of many years standing as 'Respected Sir.' I don't think it worthy of you to take this attitude because of a couple of unwritten letters—especially from someone whose main passion is certainly not correspondence, even with his best and dearest friends." Of Ibsen, Bjørnson and Brandes, which was the most difficult to remain friends with? Yet somehow, against the odds, the friendships survived.

On 3 October Ibsen sent a photograph of himself to his sister Hedvig with a tender little note: "I think we two have been close to each other. And so it will continue." In a similar mood he inscribed a copy of *Peer Gynt* that Christmas for a two-year-old boy, Odd Arstal:

To little Odd!
   You shall have this book for Christmas. But you won't read it till you've grown into a big boy. And then, please remember the man who wrote this book.

                                                                      H. Ibsen

On 29 December he wrote to Bjørnson that he was asking the National Theatre (it was now nearing completion, and the old contracts with the Christiania Theatre would not apply to it) to pay him ten per cent of the gross intake instead of the flat fees he had opted for since the failure of *Rosmersholm*. It is a sad comment on the position of dramatists then that he felt compelled to add in his letter to Bjørnson that "according to the law . . . copyright continues until fifty years after the author's death." The copyright position of dramatists was (despite the Berne Convention) by no means watertight. Bernard Shaw had written to the publisher T. Fisher Unwin on 11 February that it was by no means clear whether a play could be "performed from the printed copies without illegal copying. . . . For instance, all Ibsen's stage rights are voided here except those which Heinemann so ingeniously secured by his performance of the last two or three plays in Norwegian at the Haymarket before they were translated."[23] As Ibsen's account books show, some of the productions in London and other English cities (and all American productions) still brought him nothing.

Thanks to the 75,000 crowns for the popular edition of his works, Ibsen earned over three times as much in 1898 as in any previous year. Without this windfall, however, his earnings would have fallen well below £1,000:

[23] Bernard Shaw, *Collected Letters, 1874–1897,* p. 595.

	crowns	
German royalties from Felix Bloch	2,821	
Royalties from Munich Hoftheater	538	
Royalties from Wien Burgtheater	1,909	
Swedish rights from Albert Ranft for 5 years of *The Pretenders, The Vikings at Helgeland* and *A Doll's House*	2,000	
Fee from Royal Theatre, Stockholm, for 1 perf. of *Ghosts*	55	
Fees from Dagmars Theatre, Copenhagen, for *Brand, Love's Comedy,* and *Rosmersholm*	3,000	
Fee for *The Wild Duck* from Helsengren	300	
Old fees from Royal Theatre, Copenhagen	950	
English book sales (£1–16–5)	32	
French royalties via G. Roger	925	
Extra fee from Philippe Reclam (Leipzig publisher)	880	
Fee from Gyldendal for popular edition of Collected Works	75,000	
	88,410	£4,912

It is ironical to note that for most of the birthday performances in Scandinavia he received nothing, thanks to the fixed fee system which gave a theatre rights to a play in perpetuity.

36

The Top of a Cold Mountain

1899

During the first weeks of 1899 Ibsen at last got down to work on his new play. On 13 February he wrote Hegel that he had "now begun to grapple with it in earnest," and on 20 February he made his first notes. Two days later he began to write the dialogue, giving the play the provisional title of *The Day of Resurrection*. But spring came, and summer, and still he, who normally wrote so rapidly, had not finished the first act. No doubt the theme was partly to blame: this play was to be about an artist's final reckoning with himself. Perhaps, too, he found it difficult to adapt himself to the unusual task of writing in winter instead of, as had for so long been his habit, during the summer or autumn.

On 19 February an important event (though Ibsen would not have realized its significance, and received no money from it) occurred in Russia. The Moscow Arts Theatre staged their first Ibsen production— *Hedda Gabler*, with Konstantin Stanislavsky as Løvborg. They were to perform seven more of his plays during the next nine years: *An Enemy of the People, When We Dead Awaken, The Wild Duck, The Pillars of Society, Ghosts, Brand* and *Rosmersholm*. Surprisingly, only *An Enemy of the People* and *Brand* were complete successes. One would have expected plays such as *Ghosts* and *The Wild Duck* to have been perfectly suited to the Stanislavsky method, but the company seem to have found as much difficulty in comprehending their realism as other countries at first did with Chekhov. "More's the pity I was not a Scandinavian," mourned Stanislavsky, "and never saw how Ibsen was played in Scandinavia. Those who have been there tell me that he is interpreted as simply, as true to life, as we play Chekhov."[1]

In March Ibsen wrote to Edvard Brandes, asking him to look after

---

[1] Stanislavsky, p. 345.

Hildur Andersen who was visiting Copenhagen to play in a concert. He was still seeing much of her, and corresponding with Rosa Fitinghoff. On 17 April he wrote to Rosa thanking her for sending him a little blue flower—"*die blaue Blume,*' which signifies so much and is so seldom found. And thank you for thinking of me and of 11 April last year. I shall never forget that day. Be assured of that! Your letters live in a special little place in my desk and when I go to my work in the morning I always look into that little drawer and greet my Rosa." His memory had slipped; it had been on 16 April that the had first met her; 11 April had been the date of the Society of Authors banquet in Stockholm.

On 15 June he attended the last performance of the Christiania Theatre, which was to close its doors after seventy-two years to make way for the National Theatre. The play was *The Pillars of Society*, with Lucie Wolf, who had worked under Ibsen as a young actress at Bergen, in her old role of Lona Hessel, which she had played in the original production twenty-one years before. As Øyvind Anker has written,[2] it must have been a moving occasion for Ibsen; this was the theatre which had rejected his early work and had employed him at a starvation wage, and the demolition of which he had so long advocated. He had first written for it as a young rebel; now he sat himself among the pillars of society, loudly cheered from both the auditorium and the stage.

His play still eluded him; but July brought good news for the family. Sigurd was appointed head of the new Foreign Office; after eight years in the wilderness, he was to return to active politics. "At last, at last!" he wrote to Bergliot, adding, "My parents were transported with joy."[3] He was a tremendous success in his new post, far-sighted, able and popular; importantly, too, he and Bergliot established an admirable relationship with the suspicious old king. Sigurd would have made a great prime minister; but his cosmopolitan and independent outlook and lack of chauvinism were always, as hitherto, to make him an object of distrust in political circles, a kind of Norwegian Churchill.

Rosa at last visited Christiania that month, with her mother (inevitably) in tow. They met Ibsen at the Grand Hotel, where the three drank champagne on the verandah. Thirty years later she remembered how he had spoken of "the emptiness of Christmas." He invited them back to his home, and told her how he kept small pieces of paper, each bearing the name of a character in the play he was writing, on a string in front of his desk. When a character died, he pulled off that piece of paper and tore it up. "One doesn't want too many bits of paper in front of one's nose," he explained. She remembered his alternations of deep brooding and urchin merriment. "Sometimes," he said, "all these characters I have

[2] Anker, *Henrik Ibsens brevveksling med Christiania Theater, 1878–1899,* pp. 67–68.

[3] Bergliot Ibsen, p. 181.

imagined weary me with their squabbles and griefs and lovings and hatings, and when I get really tired I pull out the drawer of my desk and look into this little box." He showed it to her; it contained her letters. "Then I sit and talk with you and after a little while I can carry on with the people I'm writing about." He spoke of the play he was writing. "If only my powers last! But they must, they must! This play will be the best and the biggest I have ever written."[4] On her departure, on 26 July, he gave her a photograph of his study with the inscription: "In memory of a summer meeting in Christiania, 1899."

Rosa's visit may have helped to thaw his inspiration, for on 31 July he finished the first act. On 2 August he began the second act, and finished it on 23 August; and on 25 August he started the third and final act, completing it on 21 September. By this time he had altered the title from *The Day of Resurrection* to *When the [sic] Dead Awaken.*

On 1 September the National Theatre was formally opened. Bjørnson's son, Bjørn, had been appointed director, and faced the ticklish problem of which dramatist should be performed on the first night. Clearly, it had to be a Norwegian writer, and to have performed either Ibsen or Bjørnson would have mortally offended the other; and although Bjørnson had written half-length plays, Ibsen had not, so that there could be no question of sharing the evening between them. Ibsen reminded Bjørn that he was the senior of the two. Bjørn replied: "There is a Norwegian dramatist who is senior to both of you," and diplomatically solved the question by presenting an evening of extracts from Holberg. When the day came statues of Ibsen and Bjørnson were unveiled in front of the theatre, Ibsen staring pensively at his feet, Bjørnson, as Ibsen uncharitably but accurately observed, looking as though he were competing in a spitting contest. At the performance, they sat in the centre of the dress circle in separate boxes, tactfully segregated by a vast garland of red and white roses. "They were the objects of universal attention," noted Edmund Gosse, who was there, "and the King never seemed to have done smiling and bowing to the two most famous of his Norwegian subjects."[5] Bolette Sontum, who was also present, says that "the whole house cheered as they entered. Bjørnson stood and bowed gracefully to each salute, while Ibsen sat rigid, looking straight at the curtain, nervously tapping his chair."[6]

Earlier that day Gosse had met Ibsen for the first time, twenty-seven years after having first introduced his name to the English reading public. Being the man of letters that he was, Gosse was a little shocked at seeing in his apartment "no books at all, except the large Bible which lay always at his side"—referring presumably to Ibsen's own study; he cannot have seen the room they proudly called the library, which was full of books.

4 *Nya Dagligt Allehanda* (Stockholm), 4 March 1928.
5 Edmund Gosse, *Ibsen,* p. 221.
6 Sontum, p. 253.

Gosse mentioned Tolstoy, and Ibsen exclaimed: " 'Tolstoy! He is mad!' —with a screwing up of the features such as a child makes at the thought of a black draught." Gosse adds that Ibsen had read of Tolstoy "with contemptuous disapproval, only some of the polemical pamphlets"— another inaccurate observation, for we know that Ibsen admired *Anna Karenina*.[7] He also remarked to Gosse that "it was almost useless for actors nowadays to try to perform the comedies of Holberg, because there were no stage directions and the tradition was lost," an observation which doubtless sprang from his own frequent productions of the plays in earlier years.[8]

Gosse noted "the smallness of his extremities" in contrast to his burly figure and huge head of hair. "His little hands were always folded away as he tripped upon his tiny feet. . . . His voice was uniform, slow and quiet. The bitter things he said seemed the bitterer for his gentle way of saying them. . . . His movements were slow and distrait." Some time that day or the next, presumably at the theatre or at one of the receptions afterwards, Gosse witnessed "his *sang-froid* under distressing circumstances. Ibsen was descending a polished staircase when his feet slipped and he fell swiftly, precipitately, downward. He must have injured himself severely, he might have been killed, if two young gentlemen had not darted forward below and caught him in their arms. Once more set the right way up, Ibsen softly thanked his saviours with much frugality of phrase—'*Tak, mine Herrer*'—tenderly touched an abraded surface of his top-hat and marched forth homeward, unperturbed."[9]

The following evening, 2 September, the National Theatre performed *An Enemy of the People*. Gosse describes the scene:

He occupied, alone, the manager's box. A poem in his honour, by Nils Collett Vogt, was recited by the leading actor, who retired, and then rushed down the empty stage, with his arms extended, shouting: 'Long live Henrik Ibsen!' The immense audience started to its feet and repeated the words over and over again with deafening fervour. The poet appeared to be almost overwhelmed with emotion and pleasure; at length, with a gesture which was quite pathetic, smiling through his tears, he seemed to beg his friends to spare him, and the plaudits slowly ceased. *An Enemy of the People* was then admirably performed. At the close of every act Ibsen was called to the front of his box, and when the performance was over, and the actors had been thanked, the audience turned to him again with a sort of affectionate ferocity. Ibsen was found to have stolen from his box, but he was waylaid and forcibly carried back to it. On his reappearance, the whole theatre rose in a roar of welcome, and it was with difficulty that the aged poet, now painfully exhausted from the strain of an evening of such

[7] Interview in *Ørebladet*, 19 March 1898 (C.E., XIX, 214).
[8] Gosse, *Ibsen*, pp. 238, 243, 263.
[9] *Ibid.*, pp. 238–39.

prolonged excitement, could persuade the public to allow him to withdraw. At length he left the theatre, walking slowly, bowing and smiling, down a lane cleared for him, far into the street, through the dense crowd of his admirers. This astonishing night, September 2, 1899, was the climax of Ibsen's career.[10]

No wonder that the next day, refusing an invitation from J. B. Halvorsen, he wrote: "The interruptions during these past few days of my normal routine have much affected my strength, and now I must catch up on almost a whole week's neglected work." But in less than three weeks, on 21 September, he had finished his draft. He took a full two months revising it; but on 20 November he was able to telegraph Gyldendal that *When We Dead Awaken* was ready. On 19 December Heinemann published the now customary London edition of twelve copies in Norwegian to cover general copyright,[11] and on 22 December the Gyldendal edition appeared. Hegel printed 12,000 copies, the same as he had for *John Gabriel Borkman*, and again he had to reprint a further 2,000 before publication.

The press reaction in Scandinavia was, predictably, respectful, despite the obvious problems that the play presented. "The work the aged dramatist has now completed," wrote an anonymous reviewer in *Morgenbladet* (21 December), "is superior rather than inferior to its predecessors." Kristofer Randers, who had been critical of so many of the earlier plays, described it in *Aftenposten* (22 December) as "less a truthful and objective picture of life than a personal expression of his own needs and feelings —a confession from the heart, a desperate cry of doubt, an apotheosis of love. It is as though the aging poet wishes to say: 'Let everything in life fail, woman will not fail; let everything in life break, the power of love will hold.' And never has he proclaimed this gospel more beautifully and powerfully than here". Carl Nærup in *Verdens Gand* (21 December) spoke admiringly of "an extraordinary lyricism stronger than in any of his earlier plays" in this "apocalyptic tragedy of an artist." Georg Brandes, in the same paper on 28 December, wrote: "This work is born of no happy view of art, any more than Zola's *Lœuvre*. . . . With sad bitterness he dwells, as in *The Master Builder,* on what Art and Genius cost the artist and, especially, what they cost others. . . . It speaks as every artist, even the greatest, speaks in the moments of despair and bitterness. . . . Whatever [Ibsen's plays] say, they always keep something in reserve. . . . One

---

[10] *Ibid.*, pp. 221–22.

[11] There was a row with Heinemann about the English edition. Heinemann demanded that the Gyldendal edition be postponed on some obscure copyright ground. Ibsen refused. Heinemann wired Gyldendal: "In that case inform Ibsen I only pay half fee." Ibsen wrote Archer on 16 December: "Let him keep the whole fee on condition I am freed from all future commitment to him." Eventually they compromised on a fee of £120, only two-thirds of what Heinemann had paid for *John Gabriel Borkman*. (Tysdahl, pp. 255–57.)

is never finished with any Ibsen play, but always feels the need to take it up again and study it afresh. So, in general, one does not fully understand or assess a new play by Ibsen until several years after it has appeared. One's first immediate verdict on it is totally inadequate. . . . Ibsen's plays are like certain human beings; they improve with the years." And Edvard Brandes, in *Politiken* (20 December) declared: "The deeper one digs into the play, the better one is able to appreciate its greatness."

When We Dead Awaken tells of an aged sculptor, Arnold Rubek, who has achieved fame at the expense of personal happiness. His marriage with a much younger wife, Maja, is a failure. Returning to Norway after a long absence, he meets a former model, Irene, who had loved him but in whom he had been interested only as an artist. She is now deranged. She accuses him of destroying her life (as Ella had accused John Gabriel Borkman); together, painfully, they dredge up the past; then she asks him to climb with her to the top of the mountain on different levels of which the action of the play takes place. They climb together, and near the top meet Maja and a huntsman, Ulfhejm, with whom she has become enamoured. As a storm rises, Maja and Ulfhejm go down the mountain to safety, while Rubek and Irene continue towards the top where, like Brand, they are killed by an avalanche. In other words, Maja and Ulfhejm return to what they think is life but what Rubek and Irene regard as death, while Rubek and Irene climb upwards to what the others regard as death but they regard as life. As long as people remain imprisoned in flesh, Ibsen seems to say, they are dead; it is only when the body dies that the dead awaken.

It is a very short play, much the shortest Ibsen ever wrote; in performance, it lasts under two hours (unless one is foolish enough to have two intervals, of which more anon). The third and final act occupies only a quarter of an hour. This brevity is curious; and so is the language in which the play is written. In the last act of *John Gabriel Borkman,* Ibsen had moved into a heightened prose very near to poetry; in *When We Dead Awaken,* he uses this heightened prose a great deal more—for most, indeed, of the dialogues between Rubek and Irene. I well remember that when I translated this play I found myself continually feeling how much easier my task would have been if he had written it in poetry. There is a certain kind of abstract high-flown writing which in any prose sounds grandiose, even windy (when I translated *Brand* I tried at first to put it into prose, and found exactly this result). I cannot but feel that *When We Dead Awaken* would have been a much greater play if he had written it in poetry— as he nearly did. He told C. H. Herford, a Welshman who translated *Brand* into English, that he would probably write his last play in verse "if only one knew which play would be the last."[12] To have done this with *When We Dead Awaken* would have been tantamount to an acceptance that he would never write any more. Yet the straining is clearly there.

The shortness of the last act is a mystery; not merely its shortness but its (to my mind) inadequacy. It is the only less-than-great final act that Ibsen wrote after *The Pillars of Society* (whatever objections may be raised against the endings of *The Lady from the Sea* and *Little Eyolf*, they both work wonderfully well if—to borrow Henry James's phrase—really *done*). There are, I think, two possible explanations. One is physical exhaustion; he was within a few weeks of his first stroke, and there are hints of weakness that summer and autumn—his remark to Rosa: "If only my powers last! But they must, they must!"; his remaining seated at the theatre as the audience applauded, while Bjørnson stood; his fall down the steps; his words to Halvorsen about his strength being "much affected"; Gosse's observation that his movements were "slow and distrait." He may have sensed that he had not an indefinite time left, and perhaps felt unequal to the immense strain of executing an appropriate final act, especially to so self-searching a play.

But it is also possible that he felt some strange compulsion to leave it as a fragment. Another sculptor, Henry Moore, once remarked:

> There is a fact, and for me a strange fact, about the really great artists of the past; in some way their late works become simplified and fragmentary, become imperfect and unfinished. The artists stop caring about beauty and such things, and yet their works get greater.[13]

This is one way to assess *When We Dead Awaken*, as a marvellous and flawed fragment, like those unfinished statues of Michelangelo's old age which Ibsen may have seen, and drawn inspiration from, on his way to Rome thirty-five years before. Many admirers of Ibsen dislike and even dismiss it; but on some it has always exercised a peculiar fascination. "His magic is nowhere more potent," wrote Bernard Shaw. "It is shorter than usual. That is all."[14] And the young James Joyce proclaimed: "On the whole, *When We Dead Awaken* may rank with the greatest of the author's work—if indeed it be not the greatest."

It is not the greatest; but he is at his greatest in it, and in some ways it is a more moving memorial to him than if it had been a perfected whole. As Michael Elliott, who staged the play memorably at the 1968 Edinburgh Festival, has written, "Like the last quartets of Beethoven, *When We Dead Awaken* has all the intensity of the master at the height of his powers. . . . It too is a quartet. At times it may see impossible to rise to the music, but the score itself can only be regarded with wonder."[15]

[12] William Archer, "Ibsen as I Knew Him," p. 7.
[13] *Sunday Times* (London) colour magazine, 16 February 1964.
[14] Shaw, *The Quintessence of Ibsenism*, 3rd edn. (London, 1922), p. 147.
[15] In the programme note to that production.

It needs gigantic yet delicate acting: a Rubek who can suggest genius, an Irene who can suggest madness without alienating our sympathy. Rubek is sometimes played soft on the excuse that Irene accuses him of being "soft and self-indulgent, and so ready to forgive all your own sins." But it should come as a shock to us when she says that he should seem a figure of granite, a Sibelius, a Hemingway. Like *Brand* and *The Master Builder* and *John Gabriel Borkman*, *When We Dead Awaken* has to be played big or it had better not be played at all. It is no place for gentlemanly or lady-like understatement; Rubek and Irene are the shadows of mighty arche-typal creatures moving near the sun. And the way to solve the briefness of that last act is to have no interval between Acts Two and Three. The scene-change, from one level of the mountain to another, can easily be made dur-ing a brief blackout.

It is significant that *When We Dead Awaken* should have so appealed to Joyce, for although Ibsen sub-titled it "A Dramatic Epilogue," he took pains to make it clear that he intended it, not as his final work, but as a declaration that he had now finished with the realistic type of drama through which he had won international recognition, and was intending to break out into new and experimental fields. When, a few days before the publication of the play, the Danish newspaper *Politiken* assumed from the subtitle that "with this play the author will have said his last word, and will thereby have written *finis* to his dramatic work," the correspondent of *Verdens Gang* asked Ibsen if this were true. Ibsen replied:

> No, that conclusion has been too hastily reached. The word "Epi-logue" was not meant by me to have any such implications. Whether I write any more is another question, but all I meant by "Epilogue" in this context was that the play forms an epilogue to the series of plays which began with *A Doll's House* and which now ends with *When We Dead Awaken*. . . . It completes the cycle, and makes of it an entity, and now I am finished with it. If I write anything more, it will be in quite another context; perhaps, too, in another form.[16]

On 5 March 1900 he wrote to Moritz Prozor: "If it be granted to me to retain the strength of body and spirit which I still enjoy, I shall not be able to absent myself long from the old battlefields. But if I return, I shall come forward with new weapons, and with new equipment."

I do not think there is much doubt that, by these remarks, Ibsen meant that he was finished with orthodox realism and was intending to move, as Strindberg had recently done, back towards poetry and symbolism. In 1898 Strindberg had sent Ibsen the first two parts of his highly symbolic drama, *To Damascus*, and it is known that he read both volumes. One can only speculate on what Ibsen would have written if illness had not struck him down and rendered him helpless; but *When We Dead Awaken* gives us

[16] *Verdens Gang*, 12 December 1899.

a hint, and one may speculate on its possible influence on Joyce, who was to make the same decision to abandon realism in favour of symbolism barely a dozen years later.

Ibsen had been planning to write an autobiographical book which would relate his life to his work. Did he perhaps, before starting *When We Dead Awaken,* decide to write that book in dramatic form? For the play certainly covers that ground; it is Ibsen's final account with himself. He had portrayed different facets of himself in most of his plays: the unsatisfactory husband preoccupied with his work (Tesman in *Hedda Gabler,* Allmers in *Little Eyolf*), the uncompromising idealist who brings unhappiness to those he loves most (Brand, Gregers Werle, Dr. Stockmann), the egotistic artist (Ejnar in *Brand,* Hjalmar Ekdal, Lyngstrand in *The Lady from the Sea*), the ruthless old man who despises the world and neglects his wife (Solness, Borkman). But nowhere do we find so complete and merciless a self-portrait as the character of Arnold Rubek. The ageing artist, restless in his married life, restless in the homeland to which he has returned after a long sojourn abroad, restless in his art, shocked, like Brand, near the top of a mountain, into the realization that to reject love is to reject life; such is Ibsen's Portrait of the Dramatist as an Old Man, painted at the age of seventy-one.

When We Dead Awaken received its premiere at Stuttgart on 26 January 1900, and within the next few weeks was performed in Copenhagen, Helsinki, Christiania, Stockholm and Berlin. Despite the acclaim with which it had been received on publication, it failed everywhere (in Christiania it achieved only eleven performances that season), for the same reason that *The Master Builder* had failed; it was beyond the range of any of the actors who tackled it. "The play is good enough, big enough," wrote Edvard Brandes on the occasion of the Copenhagen premiere (*Politiken,* 29 January 1900). "The actors were too small."

Ibsen's earnings for 1899 had been as follows:

	crowns
German royalties from Felix Bloch	1,664
Royalties from Wien Burgtheater	699
Royalties from Munich Hoftheater	570
Fee from S. Fischer for German edn. of *When We Dead Awaken*	4,444
Fee from Gyldendal for 1st edn. of *When We Dead Awaken*	9,360
Fee from Gyldendal for 2nd. edn.	1,560
14th edn. of *Brand*	1,870
8th edn. of *The Vikings at Helgeland*	520
9th edn. of *The Pretenders*	1,200
Swedish performing rights of *When We Dead Awaken* (Albert Ranft)	3,000

	crowns
Royalties from Royal Theatre, Copenhagen, for *The Lady from the Sea* (12th–14th perfs.) and *The Pillars of Society* (26th perf.)	1,460
Fee for *Rosmersholm* from Dagmars Theatre, Copenhagen	600
Unspecified fees from Bergen Theatre	260
Extra fee from Christiania Theatre following 50th perf. of *A Doll's House*	220
Fee from Olaus Olsen for 1 perf. of *Lady Inger of Østraat*	100
Fee for Danish provincial rights of *The Pretenders*	500
Fee for Danish provincial rights of *The League of Youth*	400
French royalties from Société des Auteurs	1,024
Unspecified fees from Mr. Perrin and M. Prozor	279
	29,730 £1,651

He invested more than this amount during the year in gilt-edged securities—34,000 crowns.

37

The Running Demon

1900–1906

> O friend, if you should venture to that country,
> Pass guardedly, be unseduced
> By its too subtle promises of peace.
> Its quiet is of a kind you should not seek . . .
> This is a very ancient land indeed;
> Aiaia formerly or Cythera
> Or Celidon the hollow forest called;
> This is the country Ulysses and Hermod
> Entered afraid; by aging poets sought,
> Where lives no love nor any kind of flower—
> Only the running demon, thought.
>
> Sidney Keyes, Sour Land

The new century dawned, and Ibsen, though approaching seventy-two and at last showing signs of physical fallibility, seemed as intellectually vigorous as ever. Ernst Motzfeldt visited him on New Year's Day:

> He was then already weakened by illness, but said that when he had taken a short rest and settled a few business matters, he would start on a new play. "Then your last play, which you have described as an Epilogue, is not your final work?" I asked. "No, it is only a phase which is now completed. Now I want to start on a new one." When I asked him if he would not publish some guide to the meaning of this "recently completed phase," about which there was so much speculation, Ibsen said: "No. Just as I myself claim complete freedom as far as the public is concerned in my choice and treatment of material, so the public too must have complete freedom in interpreting my writings as they choose. I have no right to deny the public that freedom." And I did not question him further.[1]

[1] Ernst Motzfeldt, "Af samtaler med Henrik Ibsen," in *Aftenposten*, 23 April 1911.

That he had at last had cause to break his proud record of never having consulted a doctor is evidenced by a letter he addressed to Christian Sontum three days later:

Dear Dr. Sontum,

I can no longer permit myself to parade in your files as an unreliable debtor from the last century. And since you take no steps to secure what is due to you, I must take the matter into my own hands, and presume to send you the enclosed trifle as compensation for your trouble and time. The rejuvenation you have caused I could not repay with its weight in gold. A Happy New Year to you and yours.

Your most grateful friend
Henrik Ibsen

On 15 January he wrote to Jonas Lie, who had likewise returned to live in Norway, that he was thinking of giving himself a holiday that summer, the first since his trip to the North Cape nine years previously, and that "it would be delightful if we could chat about all things as we did in Berchtesgaden twenty years ago." He was well able to afford it; on 6 February he asked August Larsen of Gyldendals to invest a further 32,000 crowns in gilts, a sum which a decade earlier would have represented three years' normal earnings. Yet that same evening he did not attend the premiere of *When We Dead Awaken* at the National Theatre, and it is not easy to imagine what other cause but illness could have prevented him.

On 5 March he wrote to Moritz Prozor that he still enjoyed intellectual and physical strength; but within a few days his health had deteriorated badly. "I have been very poorly since the day after the palace ball," he confessed to Nils Vogt on 2 April, and on 30 April he had to tell August Larsen: "I have been sick (though not bedridden) since the beginning of March, and my doctor has forbidden me the use of pen and ink. But now that is over, and I have leave to write short letters to my closest friends." It seems likely that he had suffered his first stroke,[2] resulting in a partial paralysis of his right side, and he was never to be a fully fit man again.

On 1 April the *Fortnightly Review* in London published a review of *When We Dead Awaken* by an eighteen-year-old Dublin student, the first example of the young man's work to appear in print outside school and university magazines. The student's name was James Augustus Joyce; his enthusiasm for Ibsen, which was to last throughout his life, had probably been fired by his fellow-Irishman Shaw's *Quintessence,* a book which Joyce is known to have read as a boy, though unlike Shaw Joyce

[2] Thus Francis Bull (*Norsk litteratur-historie,* IV, 463–64). Koht (p. 294) dates Ibsen's first stroke as coming the following year, but a lesser illness would hardly have caused him to be forbidden to use a pen.

admired Ibsen not for his sociological iconoclasm so much as for what, in the *Portrait of the Artist as a Young Man,* he called "a spirit of wayward boyish beauty" that blew through him "like a keen wind." At first he read him only in translation, drinking him, as Yeats unkindly put it, through William Archer's hygienic bottle (though his opinion of *When We Dead Awaken* was based on a reading of the French translation). On 20 January Joyce had read an essay in the Physics Theatre of University College on "Drama and Life," in which he had praised Ibsen for the way he put real life on the stage—life "as we see it before our eyes, men and women as we meet them in the real world, not as we apprehend them in the world of færy. . . . *Ghosts,* the action of which passes in a common parlour, is of universal import—a deep-set branch on the tree Igdrasil, whose roots are struck in earth but through whose higher leafage the stars of heaven are glowing and astir." He had concluded this essay by quoting Lona Hessel's line from *The Pillars of Society:* I will let in fresh air, Pastor."[3]

Joyce had written to the editor of the *Fortnightly,* a confirmed anti-Ibsenite Oxford don named W. L. Courtney, asking if he would consider a general article on Ibsen's work. Courtney had rejected this idea, but had suggested that Joyce review *When We Dead Awaken.* His letter reached Joyce on the morning he was to read the essay in the Physics Theatre. For this article, Joyce received the then handsome sum of twelve guineas.

It is an extraordinary eulogy. "It must be questioned," declared Joyce, "whether any man has held so firm an empire over the thinking world in modern times. Not Rousseau; not Emerson; not Carlyle; not any of those giants of whom almost all have passed out of human ken. . . . His genius as an artist faces all, shirks nothing." After a detailed appreciation of the play, Joyce expresses particular admiration of Ibsen's understanding of women, and perceptively observes: "If one may say so of an eminently virile man, there is a curious admixture of the woman in his nature. His marvellous accuracy, his faint traces of femininity, his delicacy of swift touch, are perhaps attributable to this admixture. But that he knows women is an incontrovertible fact. He appears to have sounded them to almost unfathomable depths. Beside his portraits the psychological studies of Hardy and Turgenieff, or the exhaustive elaborations of Meredith, seem no more than sciolism. With a deft stroke, in a phrase, in a word, he does what costs them chapters, and does it better." He also shrewdly notes (and one must remember that this is a boy of eighteen writing): "One cannot but observe in Ibsen's later work a tendency to get out of closed rooms. Since *Hedda Gabler* this tendency is most marked. The last act of *The Master Builder* and the last act of *John Gabriel Borkman* take

---

[3] Richard Ellmann, *James Joyce* (London, 1959), pp. 54–55, 72–75.

place in the open air. But in this play the three acts are *al fresco*. . . . And this feature, which is so prominent, does not seem to me altogether without its significance."[4] The article concludes:

Henrik Ibsen is one of the world's great men before whom criticism can make but feeble show. Appreciation, hearkening, is the only true criticism. Further, that species of criticism which calls itself dramatic criticism is a needless adjunct to his plays. When the art of a dramatist is perfect the critic is superfluous. Life is not to be criticized, but to be faced and lived. Again, if any plays demand a stage they are the plays of Ibsen. . . . At some chance expression the mind is tortured with some question, and in a flash long reaches of life are opened up in vista. . . . In this play, Ibsen has given us very nearly the best of himself. . . . On the whole, *When We Dead Awaken* may rank with the greatest of the author's work—if, indeed, it be not the greatest. It is described as the last of the series which began with *A Doll's House*—a grand epilogue to its ten predecessors. Than these dramas, excellent alike in dramaturgic skill, characterization and supreme interest, the long roll of drama, ancient or modern, has few things better to show.

This article, over eight thousand words long, came to Ibsen's attention and, despite his faulty command of English, he took the trouble to send his new admirer a personal message of thanks via William Archer.

Christiania, 16 April 1900

Dear Mr. William Archer,

I should long ago have thanked you for *Wehn* [sic] *We Dead Awaken*, but I have been ill for five weeks and my doctor has forbidden me to write during all that time.

The English edition looks handsome and in every way distinguished, and I have found it quite easy to read and understand most of it; though I am sure the book has been difficult to translate.

I have also read—or rather, spelt out—a review by Mr. James Joyce in "Fortnightly Review," which is very benevolent and for which I should greatly like to thank the author, if only I had sufficient knowledge of the language . . .

Your ever affectionate and grateful
Henrik Ibsen

[4] The six plays from *The Pillars of Society* to *Rosmersholm* are all set entirely indoors. By contrast, four out of five acts of the "optimistic" *Lady from the Sea* take place out of doors. Then followed the meeting with Emilie and the darkly pessimistic *Hedda Gabler*, again set totally indoors. But the last act of *The Master Builder*, the last two acts of *Little Eyolf*, the last act of *Borkman* and all of *When We Dead Awaken* are out of doors; surely, as Joyce observed, not without significance.

Archer relayed Ibsen's message to Joyce on 23 April. Five days later Joyce replied:

13, Richmond Avenue,
Fairview, Dublin
April 28, 1900

Dear Sir,

I wish to thank you for your kindness in writing to me. I am a young Irishman, eighteen years old, and the words of Ibsen I shall keep in my heart all my life.

Faithfully yours,
Jas. A. Joyce

William Archer, Esq.
Southampton Row
London

Joyce's biographer, Richard Ellmann, comments: "Before Ibsen's letter Joyce was an Irishman; after it he was a European."[5] A few months later, in one of the prose poems which he called "Epiphanies," Joyce, describing a dream which he interpreted as being about Ibsen, wrote:

> But here he is himself in a coat with tails and an old-fashioned high hat . . . He walks along with tiny steps, jutting out the tails of his coat . . . My goodness! how small he is! He must be very old and vain . . . But then he's the greatest man on earth.[6]

Within a year, Joyce was to write a passionate letter of admiration to Ibsen himself, an admiration he was never to lose. Both *Ulysses* and *Finnegans Wake* are full of references to and echoes of Ibsen.[7]

Dr. Sontum was working at Sandefjord, a watering-place on the Christiania fjord, that summer, and Ibsen, anxious to be near him in case he should suffer another stroke, went there on 8 June. Suzannah, after several months back in Norway, was about to leave again for Italy, and on 13 June Ibsen wrote what was to be his last letter to her:

[5] Ellmann, p. 78.

[6] *Ibid.*, p. 89.

[7] For example, from *Finnegans Wake:* "For peers and gints, quaysirs and galleyliers, fresk letties from the say and stale headygabblers, gaingangers and dudder wagoners, pullars off societies and pushers on rothmere's homes." (Cf. J. S. Atherton, *The Books at the Wake: A Study of Some Literary Allusions in James Joyce's* Finnegans Wake [London, 1959], pp. 152–57 and 257–58). *Kejser og Galilæer, Gengangere,* and *Naar Vi Dode Vaagner* are the Norwegian titles of *Emperor and Galilean, Ghosts,* and *When We Dead Awaken. Peer Gynt, The Lady from the Sea, Hedda Gabler, The Pillars of Society* and *Rosmersholm* are the other plays punned upon in this passage. Atherton lists over sixty such examples of puns on Ibsen's plays (or his name) in *Finnegans Wake.*

Dear Suzannah!

Thank you for your letter, which I have just received. Every-thing goes excellently. Sleep well. Appetite ravenous at every mealtime. I have massage daily, and it does me remarkable good. No trace of pain. I can already walk as far as I wish without my foot feeling tired.

This is the last time I shall write to you before you leave. I received Sigurd's letter yesterday.

The room must not be locked without Helga [their maid] hav-ing access to the key. This is because of the insurance. Be sure to remember this! Otherwise I shall not have an hour's peace down here.

Well, I wish you with all my heart a good and successful trip. I shall at least celebrate the red-letter days 18 and 26 June[8] quietly here. May you receive as much benefit from the grotto as I from the massage. My best wishes to Sigurd.

Your affectionate

H.I.

According to Bolette Sontum, he had had Sandefjord in mind when describing the setting for the first act of *When We Dead Awaken*. Iron-ically, he found himself attended, like Irene in that play, by a nun. Soon after his arrival, erysipelas developed in his right foot, and the attack was sufficiently critical for Suzannah to be summoned back from Italy. But he recovered rapidly. A beautiful old house, Hjertnes hovedgaard, was secured as a retreat for him where he could enjoy privacy, and he ate many of his meals with the Sontums. Bolette remembered:

> While he was ill, we were allowed to pay him short visits. My youngest sister was only three years old, and a very popular little pet among the patients. She had heard so much about the Great Man, and was anxious to see him. One day when my mother went to take tea with Mrs. Ibsen she brought little Ellen with her. While Mrs. Ibsen and my mother were chatting, Ibsen was busy in his study with some letters, and as the little girl thought the teatime very long and tedious, she left them to hunt for the Great Man herself. Ibsen was just stepping out on the verandah with his nurse when little Ellen came peeping in the door. When she saw him she stopped short, opened her baby lips round and said: "Oh, are you the Great Man?" Her little face showed how disappointed she was that any Great Man was not a Great Big One.
>
> Ibsen was much amused and winked at the nurse. To make up for her disappointment he took her around to his study, and as he never knew how to treat children or what to give them, he offered her some claret. Shortly afterwards she came tripping in to her mother, her eyes shining from the wine. "I have had such a good time with a little, kind man in there!" she said. . . .

[8] Their wedding anniversary and Suzannah's birthday.

Since his illness my father had ordered a special shoe for him, flat and broad. He did not like these, as they were not nearly as neat as his own patent leathers, but he was partially consoled when my father told him he could have them tan.[9]

Bolette wanted to photograph him, and as she was about to click the shutter Ellen came running down the street. Ibsen tried to catch her and asked why she was in such a hurry. "It's dinnertime," she replied. "Papa says I must get there early today because the old doctor is coming." As he paused a moment, his hand on her shoulder, Bolette snapped them together—one of the very few occasions when Ibsen was photographed off his guard.

He was as regular in his routine on the promenade at Hjertnes as on his walks down Carl Johan in Christiania. Bolette recalled:

When my sister said one day: "The old doctor is my clock," it so pleased Ibsen that he told my father that he thought his little daughter was extremely intelligent. The last day of our summer vacation he gave a special dinner for us, as my mother too was going to the city. He slyly gave us children champagne when our parents were not looking. In a little speech he thanked us for the pleasant summer and hoped we would study hard and please our teachers.[10]

On 11 August he wrote to his niece, Anna Stousland:

My dear little Anna,
    Thank you for your kind and dear letter. It warmed my heart to read it, and I wished I had you here with me. You may certainly continue to call me your "Sun God." All the fire of my youth still burns in me.
    I am almost completely well again and take long walks on the roads.

Your "Sun God"

But during the autumn his health began to fail again.

I went to see him a couple of times [writes Bolette], and he looked pale and thin, but was still interested in everything. . . . One day when my father made his daily call at noon Ibsen handed him a parcel, saying that his brother-in-law had brought something for him, if my father would give it to me on my Confirmation Day. It was a beautiful brooch with a large amethyst in an exquisite setting.[11]

[9] Sontum, p. 254.
[10] *Ibid.*, p. 255.
[11] *Loc. cit.*

It must have been this 19 September, nine years since their meeting, that he sent Hildur Andersen a bouquet of roses with a card:

Nine red roses for you, nine rose-red years for me. Take the roses as thanks for the years.

H.I.

He also sent her, probably this year or the next (it must have been after the appearance of *When We Dead Awaken* and before he became unable to write) a set of his collected works, twenty-four plays plus the *Poems,* bearing the dedication:

Hildur!
These twenty-five twins are all ours. Before I found you I wrote seeking, groping. I knew you were somewhere in the world, and once I had found you I wrote only of princesses in varying forms.
H.I.[12]

On 4 November he sent Dr. Sontum a photograph of himself with an inscribed message of thanks, and the children were amused to see that he had ruled pencil lines so as to be able to write straight—a sad sign of how shaky that iron hand had become.[13] But three weeks later he felt well enough to allow himself to be interviewed, by Hans Tostrup for the newspaper *Ørebladet.* He declared that he was in excellent health save that "perhaps my left leg is not quite as it should be; but that is a trifle. . . . I do most of my walking now on my home ground—the handsome pavements out here on Drammensveien." He was, he said, mooting a new play and doing a bit of groundwork for it; but this year, being the one following that in which he had produced a work, he would regard as a rest year, as was his custom.

[12] Neither the card nor the dedication exist; shortly before her death Hildur destroyed not merely Ibsen's letters to her but also several pages bearing dedicatory inscriptions. Her servant remembered these two items, however, and told Francis Bull (cf. his "Hildur Andersen og Henrik Ibsen," pp. 44, 48).
On 14 August 1962 the provincial newspaper *Halden Arbeiderblad* reported that two letters and two visiting cards in Ibsen's hand had been found in a house previously occupied by Hildur's housekeeper, Valborg Ottersen. These were: (1) a letter dated 7 January 1893 addressed to "My wild forest bird" and signed: "Your, your master builder"; (2) a visiting card dated 5 October 1893 addressed: "To the princess"; (3) a letter dated 22 October 1893 addressed to: "My own dearest, most beautiful princess"; and (4) a visiting card inscribed: "19 September 1891–1895. Thank you for everything, everything in these four crowded years. A thousand greetings!" But no more has been heard of these items, and it has proved impossible to discover whether there is any substance in the report. A veil of silence has descended, and one can only presume, eight years later, that the report proved to be unfounded.
[13] Sontum, p. 255.

Tostrup asked Ibsen's opinion of Nietzsche, who had died in Weimar that August. Ibsen replied that he "did not know so much about him," but that he was "a rare talent who, because of his philosophy, could not be popular in our democratic age." When Tostrup remarked that some people regarded Nietzsche as "a spirit of darkness, a Satan," Ibsen cut in: "No, he wasn't that." And when asked about the Bœr War, which had been in progress for just over a year, he surprised his interviewer, and no doubt many who read the interview, by saying that his sympathy for the Bœrs was somewhat divided. "Remember that the Bœrs themselves took possession of the country illegally by driving out the original inhabitants. And they came only as a half-civilized people, not with the purpose of spreading civilization. And now a more civilized people, the British, come and force their way in. That is no worse than—indeed, it is not as bad as—what the Bœrs have done. The British are simply taking what the Bœrs themselves have stolen."[14]

These remarks naturally offended the Dutch, and a young journalist, Cornelius Karel Elout, editor of the Amsterdam *Algemeen Handelsblad*, attacked Ibsen's attitude in the Copenhagen newspaper *Politiken* on 7 December. Ibsen defended his viewpoint with dignity in an open letter to *Algemeen Handelsblad* on 9 December, saying: "I owe a deep personal debt of gratitude to your country. But you cannot ask me to repay part of this debt by denying my convictions."[15] It was the last public appearance that he was to make in print.

Thanks mainly to performing rights, especially German and Danish, the first year of the new century had been a good one. German royalties and fees alone had amounted to nearly £800.

	crowns
Royalties for *An Enemy of the People* at National Theatre, Christiania	2,950
Unspecified royalties from Wien Burgtheater	535
Fee for *The Pillars of Society* at Mannheim Hoftheater	80
German royalties from Felix Bloch	13,479
Additional royalties from National Theatre, Christiania	3,106
French fees from Société des Auteurs	1,869
Fee from *Revue de Paris*	725
11th edn. of *Peer Gynt*	1,815
8th edn. of *Love's Comedy*	625
English edn. of *When We Dead Awaken* (Heinemann)	2,160
Extra fee from Archer for book sales	24
Royalties from Royal Theatre, Copenhagen:	
The League of Youth (25th–31st perfs.)	1,299
The Lady from the Sea (15th–18th perfs.)	1,035

[14] C.E., XV, 435–36.
[15] *Ibid.*, p. 383.

	crowns	
The Pretenders (20th–28th perfs.)	2,224	
The League of Youth (32nd–35th perfs.)	451	
The Lady from the Sea (19th–23rd perfs.)	489	
Swedish rights of *The League of Youth* and *The Pillars*		
of *Society* (A. Ranft)	1,600	
Unspecified rights from Danish director, Stephensen	300	
	34,766	£1,931

On 1 January 1901 he received 1,836 crowns from the National Theatre and 2,460 crowns from Felix Bloch. These are the last entries in his account book, apart from a note on 21 January that he had bought 5,000 crowns' worth of shares in the Sundsvall Cellulose Company, bringing his total investments to 338,310 crowns, or £18,795. Over half of this amount, 171,000 crowns, he had purchased in the past four years—34,000 in 1897, 25,000 in 1898, 34,000 in 1899, 73,000 in 1900, and this last purchase of 5,000 in January 1901.

Ibsen's optimism about his health proved sadly false. He was very ill that winter, with repeated small apoplectic fits, and Bolette Sontum remembered how "we were all very anxious every time the night telephone rang and my father was called out."[16] These fits paralysed his right arm and leg and the right side of his face, left his speech slurred and occasionally caused hallucinations.[17] Henceforth his health showed little change. Occasionally there were small improvements. The newspapers prepared their obituaries; but his strength carried him through, and he even spoke confidently of writing a new play. It was, he told Christian Michelsen (later to become Prime Minister), to deal, like *John Gabriel Borkman*, with the conflict between love and the desire for power, a conflict finally to be resolved by a third driving passion, envy.[18] But this he was never to begin.

One hopes he was well enough to appreciate a remarkable letter of tribute which arrived for his seventy-third birthday that March from his young Irish admirer, James Joyce. Joyce wrote it in Norwegian, which he had begun to teach himself so as to be able to read his idol in the original;[19] this letter has not survived, but luckily Joyce drafted it in English first, and the draft remains:

8, Royal Terrace,
Fairview, Dublin
March 1901

Honoured Sir,

I write to give you greeting on your seventy-third birthday and to join my voice with those of your well-wishers in all lands. You may remember that shortly after the publication of your latest play, "When We Dead

16 Sontum, p. 255.
17 Gran, II, 339, quoting information given him by Dr. Edvard Bull.
18 Bull, "Henrik Ibsen" in *Norsk litteratur-historie*, IV, 463.
19 As did Thomas Mann and Stefan George.

Awaken," an appreciation of it appeared in one of the English reviews—The Fortnightly Review—over my name. I know that you have seen it because some short time afterwards Mr. William Archer wrote to me and told me that in a letter he had from you some days before, you had written: "I have read or rather spelt out a review in the 'Fortnightly Review' by Mr. James Joyce which is very benevolent and for which I should greatly like to thank the author if only I had sufficient knowledge of the language." (My own knowledge of your language is not, as you see, great but I trust you will be able to decipher my meaning). I can hardly tell you how moved I was by your message. I am a young, a very young man, and perhaps the telling of such tricks of the nerves will make you smile. But I am sure if you go back along your own life to the time when you were an undergraduate at the University as I am, and if you think what it would have meant to you to have earned a word from one who held as high a place in your esteem as you hold in mine, you will understand my feeling. One thing only I regret, namely, that an immature and hasty article should have met your eye, rather than something better and worthier of your praise. There may not have been any wilful stupidity in it, but truly I can say no more. It may annoy you to have your work at the mercy of striplings, but I am sure you prefer even hot-headedness to nerveless and "cultured" paradoxes.

What shall I say more? I have sounded your name defiantly through a college where it was either unknown or known faintly and darkly. I have claimed for you your rightful place in the history of the drama. I have shown what, as it seemed to me, was your highest excellence—your lofty impersonal power. Your minor claims—your satire, your technique and orchestral harmony—these, too, I advanced. Do not think me a hero-worshipper. I am not so. And when I spoke of you, in debating-societies, and so forth, I enforced attention by no futile ranting.

But we always keep the dearest things to ourselves. I did not tell *them* what bound me closest to you. I did not say how what I could discern dimly of your life was my pride to see, how your battles inspired me—not the obvious material battles but those that were fought and won behind your forehead—how your wilful resolution to wrest the secret from life gave me heart, and how in your absolute indifference to public canons of art, friends and shibboleths you walked in the light of your inward heroism. And this is what I write to you of now. Your work on earth draws to a close and you are near the silence. It is growing dark for you. Many write of such things, but they do not know. You have only opened the way—though you have gone as far as you could upon it—to the end of "John Gabriel Borkman" and its spiritual truth—for your last play stands, I take it, apart. But I am sure that higher and holier enlightenment lies—onward.

As one of the young generation for whom you have spoken I give you greeting—not humbly, because I am obscure and you in the glare, not sadly because you are an old man and I a young man, not presumptuously, nor sentimentally—but joyfully, with hope and love, I give you greeting.

Faithfully yours,

James A. Joyce

Mr. Henrik Ibsen
Arbiens Gade 2
Kristiania

A second stroke in the summer of 1901 left Ibsen virtually unable to walk; though occasionally he would obstinately struggle out for a few painful paces. An observer recalled one such occasion as he crossed Drammensveien on his way from Arbins gade to the Queen's Park twenty yards from his door.

> A young man held him firmly under one arm while he struggled forward with short, dragging steps, his body heavily slouched, his head bowed, his eyes on the ground. His mouth, which had always looked like a line, had acquired an underlip.[20]

That summer of 1901 Dr. Christian Sontum himself became afflicted by an illness which in a few months was to prove fatal. He and his family had to return from Sandefjord to Christiania. Bolette records:

> [Ibsen] called every day at our house to hear how the patient was. I usually went down to his carriage. . . . He was so kind and sympathetic to us all in our sorrow. . . . He was so touching when one day he asked me if he might go in and see my father for the last time. "I cannot walk, you know, but they can carry me." My father was too ill to see anybody so Ibsen asked me to take his card in to him. On it was written in pencil and with a trembling hand the word *"Tak"* [Thanks] . . . . After my father's death Ibsen called again and when I came down to his carriage he took my hand and his voice quivered as he said: "How are you all? I am thinking about you all the time. I, too, have lost my best friend."[21]

Dr. Sontum's successor as Ibsen's private physician was an eminent professor of medicine at the university, but his unpunctuality greatly annoyed Ibsen; and when, on one occasion, he arrived an hour late, Ibsen, sitting up in bed with a sweater up to his neck, ordered him from the house and swore he would never consult him again. He asked his friends if there was a good doctor in the capital who could be relied on to arrive in time, and was recommended Edvard Bull, a Bergenser aged fifty-six. An appointment was fixed for two o'clock and, as the hour of Dr. Bull's appearance approached, Ibsen sat waiting with his watch in his hand. From five to two, Ibsen glanced cynically every minute at Dr. Bull's recommender, who was sitting with him. As the clock struck two, Ibsen opened his mouth triumphantly, but before he could speak the doorbell rang.[22] Edvard Bull remained Ibsen's doctor until the writer's death.

Ibsen took the air daily in his carriage, accompanied either by Dr.

[20] Peter Egge, *Minder fra nord og syd* (Oslo, 1952), pp. 26–27.
[21] Sontum, p. 255.
[22] Information from Dr. Bull's son, Professor Francis Bull.

Bull or by the masseur who now attended him, Arnt Delhi. He would make the coachman stop before the university clock, so that he could set his watch by it as he had been wont to do on his walks down Carl Johan to the Grand Hotel, and he was now as familiar a sight on his rides as he had been during those walks, a top hat on his head in summer, a round fur hat covering his ears in winter. The great muff of white hair that had surrounded his neck for the past few years was now shaven at the front of the chin. Once he decided that instead of riding he would take a walk. By now he had a nurse permanently in attendance; she helped him down the stairs and no sooner had they reached the street than Ibsen commanded her to disappear. When she hesitated (Suzannah told Bergliot), "Ibsen swung his stick at her so that she fled back into the house. And all the way down the street Ibsen kept turning to see if she was still there." Bergliot had never heard Suzannah laugh so as when she told this story. "She was always amused when Ibsen got angry. He always jutted out his underlip, showing his lower teeth. He hated being ill. He never addressed a barber who visited him each day, except once, when he suddenly hissed at him: 'Ugly devil!' "[23]

Exaggerated reports of his state of health were printed from time to time in most western countries, and in August the New York *Critic* published a long letter purporting to be from Georg Brandes which stated that Ibsen could not possibly live beyond the autumn. Brandes denied authorship, pointing out that so far from having been at Ibsen's side, as the letter claimed, he had not been in Christiania since 1893. But similar rumours continued to appear over the next five years.

That autumn the first Nobel Prize for Literature was awarded. The world speculated which living writer would be the first to receive this honour: Tolstoy, Ibsen, Zola, Chekhov, Hardy? But the Swedish Academy chose the French poet Sully-Prudhomme, the first of many curious decisions which that body was to make over the years. Incredible as it seems, none of the five great writers named above ever received it, though Ibsen was to live another five years, Chekhov three, Tolstoy nine, and Hardy twenty-seven. Nor did Strindberg, Gorki, Proust, Henry James, Joseph Conrad, H. G. Wells, or James Joyce. Bjørnson was to be awarded it in 1903, in Ibsen's lifetime; but Ibsen enjoyed one small piece of revenge. When Bjørnson went to Stockholm to receive the prize, he tried to enter the palace through a side door but found his way barred by a sentry. "My good man," Bjørnson informed him. "I am Norway's greatest writer." "Oh," said the sentry, making way. "I beg your pardon, Herr Ibsen."[24]

[23] Bergliot Ibsen, pp. 212–13
[24] Told by Bjørnson's son Bjørn, in *Hjemmet og vennerne* (Oslo, 1932), pp. 191–92.

On 10 September Ibsen's second grandchild was born. Sigurd and Berg-liot named her Irene, after the heroine of *When We Dead Awaken*. Ibsen became very devoted to her, and called her "my little princess," as he had called the young girls who had been the dream images of his old age, from Emilie Bardach to Rosa Fitinghoff. "Little Irene is beauti-ful," he once said to Suzannah. "But my Irene was also beautiful." He greatly missed Sigurd, who was able to make only infrequent visits from Stockholm. On one such visit "as soon as he caught sight of Sigurd, he raised both arms towards him and cried despairingly: 'Oh, I have been so sick—so sick.' He took Sigurd's hand between his and so they stood."[25]

Yet on 24 November he felt well enough to give another interview to Hans Tostrup of *Ørebladet*. "Dr. Henrik Ibsen [wrote Tostrup] sits in his black morning coat with a pocket watch before him at the corner window of his apartment. . . . He looks well, and his complexion is healthy. His eyes shine with the same sharpness as before. Only his hair has grown somewhat whiter than when we saw him last. We asked how he was and Ibsen replied: 'Thank you, better than I have been for a long while. But I cannot walk easily nowadays. To drag myself through the streets would cause me such difficulty that I have to drive. My head is all right. That is fine. But I get tired easily, and my doctor has for-bidden me to work very much.' He spoke of his hope of completing a new play once he had regained his full health, and even of travelling abroad, though not in the immediate future, since 'I would then have to take a masseur and a servant with me, and it would be no fun to travel with such an army.'" He managed to accompany his interviewer through three large rooms to the front door.[26]

On 8 December 1902 Bjørnson celebrated his seventieth birthday, and surprised Ibsen with a visit. Both Ibsen and Suzannah were much moved that he should have come on such a day, and Suzannah left them alone together in Ibsen's study. On returning home, Bjørnson told his family that Ibsen had said to him: "When I think back—I can't think ahead, I'm too ill for that—when I think back, my dear Bjørnson, in spite of every-thing it's you who have been closest to my heart all these years. And in that play, you know—the one about the doctor at the baths—" "The doctor at the baths?" asked Bjørnson, puzzled. "The one about those microbes. You know." "No." They both pondered. "*The* [sic] *Enemy of the People*," said Ibsen eventually. "I was thinking of you when I wrote it. Partly. Of course, you're not a bourgeois like him. But it's you all the same." When Bjørnson finally rose to leave, Ibsen suddenly gripped his hand tightly and would not let it go. They remained thus for a long

[25] Bergliot Ibsen, p. 205.
[26] Reprinted in C.E., XV, 439–41.

time. At last Ibsen said: "You are the dearest of all men to me." It was the last time they met.[27]

About this time Georg Brandes saw him for the last time. "His mind," he recalled, "was as brilliant as ever. An extraordinary mildness pervaded his manner, supplanting his former sternness. His charm had grown, while his distinction of manner was as great as ever. Yet the general impression was one of weakness." And Brandes remembered Oswald's terrible cry in *Ghosts:* "Never to be able to work again! To be dead, yet alive! Can you imagine anything more horrible?"[28]

On 19 February 1903 he granted Hans Tostrup a last interview:

> As we crossed Drammensveien yesterday morning we caught a glimpse behind the corner window on Arbins gade of a handsome, white-bearded and white-haired old head, staring with a friendly and gentle expression, half-dreaming, half-observing, down the street towards the wintry trees of the palace park.
>
> "Well, Henrik Ibsen looks brisk and well!" we thought, so we go up and visit him. It is long since any word was heard from him. . . . We announced ourselves and were received.
>
> "I don't usually receive anyone now. I don't feel really strong in the daytime, and conversations, much as I'd like them—no, no, do sit down."
>
> So we sat beside him in the corner window, enquired after his health, and the old poet was friendliness and kindness itself.[29]

Unfortunately, the interview dealt only with the question of closer co-operation between the Scandinavian kingdoms, and Ibsen's views on the subject, that small nations could achieve more by co-operation than by squabbling—a useful reminder at a time when squabbling was the order of the day, but one would have liked to have learned his views on something less parochial as he moved, in Joyce's phrase, near the silence.

On 28 March Magdalene Thoresen died at the age of eighty-three; luckier than her stepson, she had retained her physical and mental vigour to the last. That spring Ibsen had another stroke. He tried to learn to write with his left hand, practising every day; he sadly remarked to Suzannah: "Strange that I, who was once quite a dramatist, now have to learn to write the alphabet."[30] Yet on 17 August he let the sculptor Gustav Vigeland, who had made busts of him in 1901 and 1902, make sketches for a new one. These sketches show a sad change, the mouth slack, the

---

[27] Bjørn Bjørnson, *Hjemmet og vennerne,* pp. 257–58; *Fra barndommens dage,* p. 11.

[28] Georg Brandes, "Henrik Ibsen," in *Century Magazine* (New York), February 1917, pp. 541 and 546. Brandes adds that "he no longer spoke with bitterness of Norway, but merely complained about its slow development. Norwegian ideas and theories seemed old-fashioned and out of date to him."

[29] C.E., XV, 442–43.

[30] Bergliot Ibsen, p. 214.

expression almost vacant.[31] Gunnar Heiberg, who was present on one of these occasions, says that Ibsen "complained that there was a limit to how long he could sit in that cold room; his health would not stand it, and anyway he had not promised to give so many sittings. Vigeland gave him a look but said nothing. Ibsen glanced at the clock and said he was expecting someone." Heiberg said he had to go; Ibsen accompanied him to the next room, where he stumbled and had to grasp a chair. "I asked if he would like to lean on my arm. No, he replied, there was nothing wrong. His face was stern and splendid; he looked like a Jupiter betrayed." As they got to the door Heiberg asked who was the visitor he was expecting, and Ibsen gave a little smile and replied: "The tailor." Heiberg remembered that Ibsen was bitter because he felt that the National Theatre, under Bjørn Bjørnson's direction, was playing too much of Bjørnson's work and too little of his own.[32]

On 14 February 1904 Ibsen wrote the last word we have from his hand: *"Tak,"* shakily pencilled on a card to Dr. Bull, who told his son that it took Ibsen three days to write it.[33] On 19 March he granted his last interview, to *Verdens Gang:*

> Tomorrow the poet celebrates his seventy-sixth birthday. One of our colleagues who visited him yesterday reports that Dr. Ibsen is comparatively well and has in general been in quite satisfactory health all winter.
>
> "There is nothing much wrong with me just now," said the poet. "I just have to be careful, and Dr. Bull says that March with its changeable weather could be dangerous for me. I find walking a little difficult, but as soon as the air becomes milder I shall try to take a stroll outside. I am allowed to enjoy myself in the Queen's Park, which gives me great pleasure." Our colleague extended his best wishes to the poet for his birthday and asked if he was receiving any visitors. "No," he replied. "It is so difficult to speak with so many people that I am not receiving anyone."[34]

Halvdan Koht, who had recently edited Ibsen's letters, visited him during the autumn of 1904.

> He had difficulty with his speech and forgot his words, sometimes using the wrong ones, e.g., "lexicon" instead of "letters." [Arnt Delhi was present at the meeting to interpret his meaning when the right words would not come.] One could see how it pained him. His eyes were dull and had lost their colour. But they could still sparkle. It happened twice during our conversation, once when I greeted him from old German friends of his whom I had recently seen, and again when I mentioned that I knew his sister, Hedvig Stousland of Skien. Both times his eyes suddenly went steel-blue and shot like a flash at me.[35]

[31] They are reproduced in C.E., XX, 429–35.
[32] *Aftenposten*, 16 April 1911, reprinted in Heiberg's *Salt og sukker,* pp. 45–46.
[33] Bull, *Tradisjoner og minner,* p. 97.
[34] C.E., XIX, 227.
[35] Koht, II, 294–95.

That same autumn Bolette Sontum saw him for the last time, before going to America to study at the Carnegie Library School in Pittsburgh:

> He was very much changed, so thin and white and, oh, so little. His shoulders, always so proudly erect, had shrunken pathetically, and his lion head had grown so small that it was only the intense fire of his eyes that quickened it. It seemed to pain him that he did not have the strength to keep up a conversation. Yet he recognized me, and smiled when I came in, and in a few minutes he regained his interest and asked about all my America plans. Mrs. Ibsen had told him that I was sailing for New York and had come to say goodbye. We talked about the happy days at Grefsen and my father. Then he said: "And now you are going to America. Are you going to write books?" "Oh, no," I laughingly answered. "I am going to learn how to put them correctly on the shelves." He said: "Yes, their libraries are famous," and then he sat thinking. "It must be a great country with many chances," he repeated slowly, twice. "But it seems so far away. You must be careful with yourself. My son says, beware of the iced water and the hot bread." Mrs. Ibsen also asked me not to have too many of those American dishes. Chivalrous as always, despite his absolute frailty, Ibsen wanted to see me to the door, but asked me to excuse him, adding he was so tired. He kissed my hand and I left him. When I was out on the street I looked up to his window where he was standing in his black frock coat, and I waved my last goodbye to "the old Doctor."[36]

Hildur Andersen does not seem to have visited him during these years of sickness; presumably Suzannah, despite Ibsen's protestations of innocence, still took their relationship seriously. Nor, being unable to go out alone, did he visit her. One winter's day, driving in his carriage, he saw her on the pavement. Raising his hand, he called weakly, "Bless you! Bless you!" It was the last time they saw each other.[37]

Yet the old man lived on. One January night in 1905 he was heard to cry in his sleep: "I'm writing! And it's going splendidly!"[38] Dreams, too, brought him occasional comfort and joy. He, who had always been so taciturn and self-contained, was now pathetically grateful for someone to talk to him, provided it was someone he knew. Jens Wang, the artist, paid him several visits to show him his designs for new decor and costumes, and he especially enjoyed these occasions. He even allowed an American photographer to take two portraits of him, rigid-faced and clutching the arm of his chair.[39] But his helplessness increased; that spring another visitor noticed that he sat with a piece of paper in his hand wishing to put it on the table but unable to do so. His guest did it for him and

36 Sontum, pp. 255–56.
37 Bull, "Hildur Andersen og Henrik Ibsen," p. 54.
38 Bull, "Henrik Ibsen," in *Norsk litteratur-historie*, IV, 464.
39 Reproduced in C.E., XX, 199–201.

received a grateful glance.[40] A frequent visitor at this time was Christopher Bruun, who half a century earlier had helped to inspire Ibsen with the character of Brand. One day he tentatively brought up the question of Ibsen's relationship with God. Ibsen "went red in the face with anger and said: 'Leave that to me!' "[41]

Sigurd, meanwhile, had run into trouble over the question of dissolving the union with Sweden. His skilful diplomacy in Stockholm, where he had taken up residence in 1903, and especially the trust and friendship he had inspired in King Oscar, had achieved what a few years earlier had seemed impossible. The king (who, on Sigurd's first mentioning the question of dissolution soon after taking office, had replied: "If anyone suggests that to me I shall shoot him with my own hand"), now seemed not totally to reject the idea, and several Swedish newspapers began actively to support it. Unfortunately, this produced a reaction, and a new and chauvinistic Swedish Prime Minister, E. C. Boström, enraged Norwegian opinion by closing down on the proposals for a separate consular service. The Norwegian government resigned and the new Prime Minister, Christian Michelsen, wanted Sigurd to remain in charge of foreign affairs, but Sigurd believed that the Treaty of Union should be dissolved legally by changing the constitution and not violently by a coup d'état, and refused. As a result, he was suspected by jealous circles in Norway of having played a double game, and felt compelled to resign. "I am one of those," he commented to Bergliot, "who work for eleven hours of the day and at the twelfth hour have to look on while others gather the fruits of my labour."[42]

At least this meant that for the last year of his life Ibsen had Sigurd constantly with him in Christiania. Bergliot relates that when Sigurd returned, Ibsen "not only was no worse; he was up again, and followed Sigurd's account of the latest developments in Stockholm with great interest. Fru Ibsen listened silently while Ibsen asked question after question. The conversation continued through dinner. I can still see Ibsen as he sat there, his hands far apart gripping the table edge. He looked like some powerful judge. When Sigurd had finished Ibsen suddenly rose and said loudly and firmly: 'Sigurd shall give up politics. He shall continue my life's work.' "[43] Sigurd was beginning to write a philosophical work called *The Quintessence of Man*, which was to take him several years; and one day when he asked his father about one of his plays which had just been revived with great success, Ibsen waved his hands and said: "Don't talk about my things, I'm only interested in what you write."[44]

[40] "Da Henrik Ibsen døde," anonymous article in *Morgenbladet*, 23 May 1931.
[41] Bergliot Ibsen, p. 214.
[42] *Ibid.*, p. 209.
[43] *Ibid.*, pp. 211–12.
[44] *Ibid.*, p. 212.

That summer Sigurd arranged the outright sale of his father's Danish and Norwegian copyrights for a lump sum of 150,000 crowns (£8,333), of which 20,000 crowns were to be paid forthwith, 10,000 annually for the next eight years and 5,000 annually for the following ten. Sigurd signed the contract on his father's behalf on 3 June. It seems a terribly bad bargain from the point of view of Ibsen's grandchildren; but the news galvanized Bjørnson into demanding 200,000 crowns from Gyldendal for the outright purchase of his copyrights. "Ibsen is a rich man and I a poor one," he told Peter Nansen, who negotiated on behalf of Gyldendal, "and who knows whether my work won't last longer than Ibsen's?" He got the sum he asked, spread over twenty years.[45]

On 7 June Michelsen's government, by a coup d'état, dissolved the union with Sweden. Dr. Edvard Bull told Ibsen that people now referred to a famous restaurant called The Queen as "Fru Michelsen," and was able to report to his family that the joke had made Ibsen smile, something Dr. Bull had seldom seen.[46] His difficulty in speaking had, however, now worsened, though his other senses remained sharp. He liked to sit hour after hour at his corner window gazing out, and tourists would stand in the street below to catch a glimpse of him, just as (noted Peter Nansen) a few years earlier the old Kaiser Wilhelm had been exhibited like a mummy in a window of his palace in Berlin.[47] His only pleasure was when Sigurd came; he would sit with his watch before him, waiting for the visit.[48]

In 1906 Sigurd and Bergliot had their third child, another girl.

She was only a few weeks old when Sigurd and I took her up to the Ibsens. Ibsen was sitting in an armchair at the table in the library when we came in. I showed him the baby, and he looked at her for a long time. Then I asked him if we could call her Eleonora. He became very moved, so that he could only slowly reply: "Yes." Then he turned towards me and added: "God bless you, Bergliot." He was happy to see his family grow. When we had gone he said to Fru Ibsen: "My Nora was also called Eleonora."

That was one of the last times Sigurd and I saw him up. Afterwards, Ibsen lay mostly in his bed. His wife was the only person whom he allowed to give him food; and when he was up he only wanted to eat in her bedroom, which lay next to his.

He lived in a permanent fear lest she should die before him. He said: "If you die before me, I shall die five minutes later." Toward the end he had difficulty in speaking and always called her *"Fruen"* [Ma'am]; it was easier to say, and he always heard the nurse call her that.

Once I was sitting with him—it was the last time. He lay holding my hand, and his eyes and face shone with kindness as he spoke many loving

[45] Harald Grieg, pp. 156 ff.
[46] Bull, *Tradisjoner og minner*, p. 97.
[47] Interview in *Aftenposten*, 4 March 1917.
[48] Bergliot Ibsen, p. 214.

words to me. It is a beautiful memory. Sigurd was with his father every day. One evening his father said to him: "Soon I shall go into the great darkness."[49]

That February another Eleonora came to Christiania. Duse was visiting Norway for the first time, largely in the hope of meeting the dramatist who had provided her with her greatest triumphs. On her arrival she sent a letter and flowers to Ibsen asking if she might call merely to say "Thank you." Suzannah, however, telephoned that Ibsen was too ill to receive anyone. Lugné-Pœ, who was with Duse at the time, tells what followed:

> I remember very well that morning when she had just received this sad message. I went in to her and found her swathed in the long white *palan-drane* which she loved to wear. She sat fearful, annihilated, hollow-cheeked, her face tired and lined as though life was abandoning her. She asked me: "What shall I do? Please, what shall I do?" . . . What could I do for her? I had hoped so much, for her sake. . . . Next morning around noon Duse and I found ourselves outside Henrik Ibsen's house. She had bought Norwegian boots, for she wished to go there on foot. We walked round the left of the palace, and at the stroke of twelve we stood beneath the corner window, where, every day at this time, people could see Dr. Ibsen in person, sometimes with a secretary or someone at his side. Duse stood there waiting in the cold and snow. Who, even thirty years later, would not be shaken by the memory of having been present at that sad and silent meeting? Eleonora Duse on the pavement, looking for the old poet's silhouette behind the big window?[50]

His seventy-eighth birthday passed, and still death would not come to relieve him. Suzannah, herself in almost constant pain, sat by his side. "I could not do without her greatness," he told Bergliot; and the nurse told her that she heard him say to Suzannah: "You have been my guiding star. You were the eagle that showed me the way to the summit."[51] Occasionally, little spurts of strength seemed partially to revive him. Once when Dr. Bull asked the masseur how Ibsen was, Delhi replied: "Not too bad. He's sworn a couple of times."

From 16 May he was too weak to stand, and lay in a coma, occasionally muttering a word or two indistinctly and incoherently. At noon on 22 May he opened his eyes, pressed Dr. Bull's hand and murmured, "Thank God!" A little later, the nurse said to the others who were in the room that he seemed to be a little better. From the bed came the single word: *"Tvertimod!"* ("On the contrary!"). It was the last word Ibsen ever

[49] *Ibid.*, pp. 216–17. Ibsen enjoyed stressing that "Nora" in *A Doll's House* was the kind of affectionate abbreviation that one uses to a child, and that Helmer employed it as Nora's father had done, her real name being Eleonora.

[50] Lugné-Pœ, pp. 95–97.

[51] Bergliot Ibsen, p. 238.

spoke;[52] and it came appropriately from one who had devoted his life to the correction of lies.

He died at 2:30 P.M. on 23 May 1906. Bergliot was present:

One morning our telephone rang and we were told we must come at once. We came in to Ibsen, who lay calm and beautiful with closed eyes. Fru Ibsen sat crying in the next room. We went in to her. It was so strange to see her cry. Most people distort their faces when they cry, but not she. Tear after tear simply streamed down her cheeks. I can still see her large, clear face as she sat and spoke of the one she loved and must now lose. The nurse came and asked us to go in to Ibsen, since she thought the end was near. We went quickly in, but Fru Ibsen, who had difficulty in walking, came slowly after. Death brings with it a sublime stillness, and in this stillness we heard her approach with very short steps. First the stick was heard, then her foot which she dragged after her. It seemed an eternity. I can still see her as she stood as though lost above his bed. Now it was finished.

There was a majestic peace and greatness about Henrik Ibsen's departure from this world. We remained with him a long time and then went and sat down in the library. There she told us very emotionally that the previous night,[53] before falling into a doze, his last words to her had been: "My dear, dear wife, how good and kind you have been to me." This had made her happy. After a while she rose, and said: "Now I must go. Ibsen liked me to look after the house." In this sad atmosphere we again heard her small steps and the sound of the stick growing weaker and weaker until at last they were gone.

Before he was taken away from Arbins gade we gathered for the last time around his open coffin. His face was transfigured in death; all the tightness and severity that had marked it in life were smoothed away. It was as though for the first time I saw how beautiful he was; the mighty brow lay smoothly serene, and the chiselled features stood classically forth.[54]

The Norwegian government granted him a state funeral, and this took place on 1 June at Trinity Church. Bolette Sontum, now back from America, was among the mourners:

For the last time he was dressed in his black frock coat with the broad lapels and laid out in state. . . . The day before the funeral people flocked to the church and thousands stood outside waiting for their turn to pay their last respects to him. In the choir the coffin stood loaded with flowers and

---

[52] Some deny this, but cf. Dr. Edvard Bull's journal, quoted in Lis Jacobsen's "Ibsens sidste ord," in *Ibsen-Årbok, 1957–1959*, p. 81. There is a legend that in his last moments Ibsen cried: "No!," but this seems to be without reliable foundation.

[53] But Dr. Bull's journal states that he was in a coma from the afternoon of 22 May. Bergliot recorded her memories over forty years later, and may have misremembered Suzannah's exact wording; or she may have been right and Dr. Bull wrong. It hardly seems to matter.

[54] Bergliot Ibsen, pp. 217–18.

around it the students of the university kept a guard of honour. The organ
played softly and the crowd [estimated at 12,000] filed past the coffin. There
was nothing in the white little Ibsen that awed them now. The task of the
fiery judge was done.[55]

Suzannah was forbidden by Dr. Bull to attend the ceremony, and remained alone in the apartment at Arbins gade. Afterwards, Bergliot and
Sigurd returned there. "There seemed an enormous emptiness in all the
rooms. I sat and watched Sigurd and his mother as they talked together.
Now those three had become one."[56] A column was erected over Ibsen's
grave bearing the simple and appropriate symbol of a hammer.

[55] Sontum, p. 256.
[56] Bergliot Ibsen, p. 219.

Epilogue

Suzannah lived on for eight years at Arbins gade; she died there on 3 April 1914. Only once during that time did she leave the apartment, when she had herself carried down the stairs and driven to see her husband's grave. Despite her condition, she would never let anyone else dust the paintings which Ibsen had brought so proudly back from Italy. Twice a month she would have steps brought in, send her maid out of the room and painfully climb up to wipe the dust off each picture. Dr. Bull once suggested to her that her discomfort would be eased if he designed a special chair for her to sit in; and she thanked him, moved that anyone should think of her, who had always lived in the shadow of her husband. But the next time he came, and showed her the drawing, she asked what it would cost, and when he replied: "About a hundred crowns," she declared that having managed for so long without such a luxury, she could continue for the short time that was left to her. Dr. Bull's son Francis once visited her with his mother and remembered that, before she rang the bell, his mother told him to take a deep breath so as to have fresh air in his lungs, since the atmosphere in the closed apartment was so suffocating. "I remember that I was shocked at how unbeautiful Fru Ibsen was, and how lacking in any kind of feminine charm; but when she spoke of the old days, she became alive."[1]

A few days before she died she spoke to Bergliot about the early years of her marriage. "With great difficulty she said: 'When we were young, many so-called friends came to Ibsen, but I sent them away.' After a long pause: 'I had many unkind words for it, but I didn't care. He had to have peace for his work.' After another long pause: 'Ibsen had no steel in his character—but I gave it to him.' Finally she said: 'I have never spent a day in bed in my life, and I don't want to die there. I want to die standing or sitting.' "[2] She died in her armchair early one morning.

[1] Bull, *Tradisjoner og minner*, pp. 102–4.
[2] Bergliot Ibsen, p. 237.

Sigurd never returned to politics. The year after his father's death he settled in Italy, but three years later, at Suzannah's request and with the greatest reluctance, came back to Norway. Despite his gifts, he remained unwanted there and could obtain no permanent post, even in journalism or teaching. His philosophical work, *The Quintessence of Man,* was translated into many languages and was especially successful in America; Eugene O'Neill, in his autobiographical play *Ah, Wilderness!,* made his hero name it as one of the influential progressive books of his youth. In 1913 he published an interesting play, *Robert Frank,* about the conflict between the proletariat and the Old World; it was translated into English, French and German, but was as viciously attacked in Norway as his father's early works had been. After Suzannah's death he resettled in Italy, and died in 1930. Bergliot lived on until 1953. Their son, Tancred, became a pioneer aviator and a distinguished film director; he and Ibsen's other grandchildren, Irene and Eleonora, are still alive at the time of writing, and there are many great- and great-great-grandchildren.

Jonas Lie and Edvard Grieg died within a year of Ibsen, and Bjørnson in 1910, in a Paris hotel. Bergliot was at her father's deathbed, as she had been at Ibsen's, and noted that where Ibsen had said: "Soon I shall enter the great darkness," Bjørnson spoke of ascending into "the great whiteness." Strindberg died of cancer in 1912, aged 63; Georg Brandes in 1927, aged 85.

The young girls whom Ibsen loved in his last years all lived to a ripe age. Helene Raff achieved some success as a painter and novelist, and died in Munich in 1942 at the age of 77. Emilie Bardach survived until 1 November 1955. By good fortune she left Vienna for Switzerland before Hitler's invasion and settled in Berne; during the second World War she was called before Hitler's Austrian representatives there and (being a Jewess) stood in danger of being returned to her native country, but (writes Basil King's daughter, Mrs. Reginald Orcutt, whose husband was instrumental in persuading the Swiss authorities to let her remain) "she was too old and dotty to travel and obviously harmless. . . . She was sweet and kind up to the last."[3] So she escaped the gas chambers. She died a spinster.

Hildur Andersen lived even longer; she died in December 1956 at the age of 92. She, too, never married; nor did Rosa Fitinghoff, who died on 27 March 1949, aged 76. Rosa wrote several novels and children's books of moderate quality, and a trivial autobiography, *Minnenas kavalkad,* which contains no reference to her friendship with Ibsen. Her Swedish publisher, Dr. Ragnar Svanström of Norstedts, remembers her as "a rather eccentric little old lady always accompanied by about ten poodles." During the Second World War she turned up in Oslo at the offices of Cappelin

[3] Letter to the author, 14 February 1969.

and asked if they would be interested in publishing a book about poodles. On being asked: "Would you not consider writing something about Ibsen?" she left without reply.

Ibsen's contribution to the theatre was threefold, and in each respect the drama owes more to him than to any other dramatist since Shakespeare. Firstly, he broke down the social barriers which had previously bounded it. He was the first man to show that high tragedy could be written about ordinary people and in ordinary everyday prose, and the importance of that seemingly simple achievement can hardly be exaggerated. Soon after his work had been introduced to England, W. L. Courtney, that Oxford don who edited the *Fortnightly Review* and also wrote dramatic and literary criticism for the *Daily Telegraph,* complained that Ibsen's plays were "singularly mean, commonplace, parochial . . . as if Apollo, who once entered the house of Admetus, were now told to take up his habitation in a back parlour in South Hampstead. There may be tragedies in South Hampstead, although experience does not consistently testify to the fact; but, at all events from the historical and traditional standpoint, tragedy is more likely to concern itself with Glamis Castle, Melrose Abbey, Carisbrooke or even Carlton House Terrace."[4] In other words, as William Archer commented, Ibsen's characters were not what the Victorians called "carriage people." Before Ibsen, tragedy had (always excluding Büchner) concerned itself with kings and queens, princes and princesses or, at the lowest, Montagus and Capulets. Ibsen showed that high tragedy could and did take place at least as frequently in back parlours as in castles and palaces. He was, of course, not the first dramatist to attempt this, any more than the Wright brothers were the first people to build an æroplane; they were the first to build one that got off the ground, and *Ghosts* is, after *Woyzeck* and *Danton's Death,* the first tragedy about back parlour people that gets off the ground.

His second great contribution was technical. He threw out the old artificialities of plot which are usually associated with the name of Scribe, but of which Shakespeare and Schiller were also guilty: mistaken identities, overheard conversations, intercepted letters, and the like. It was a slow and painful process to rid himself of these; something of the old machinery is still there as late as *A Doll's House;* but his last ten plays are free of it. As A. B. Walkley noted as early as 1891: "Whatever we learn we learn at first-hand, from the characters themselves, not from a Dumasian commentator or *raisonneur*."[5] Equally important, he developed

---

[4] Quoted by William Archer, "The Real Ibsen," in *The International,* February 1901, p. 196.

[5] A. B. Walkley, *Playhouse Impressions* (London, 1892), p. 56.

the art of prose dialogue to a degree of refinement which has never been surpassed; not merely the different way people talk, and the different language they use under differing circumstances, but that double-density dialogue which is his peculiar legacy, the sub-text, the meaning behind the meaning. Through this he was able to create characters as complex as the most complex characters of Flaubert or Henry James, without the aid of explanatory narration or monologues. And this demanded, and opened the way for, a new kind of acting, analytical, penetrating, self-effacing and sensitive. There was no place in his plays for the old operatics.

What nowadays seem technical limitations, such as the over-exposition in the opening scenes, the excessive and sometimes repetitive planting of information needful to the audience, was dictated by the limitations of those audiences; as we have seen, when he tried in *Hedda Gabler* to reduce his exposition to a modern minimum, the reaction was almost total bewilderment. (Even Henry James on reading it was left "muddled and mystified."[6]) It is no coincidence that this, the least popular of his mature plays in his own time, is the one most frequently performed today and for which fewest allowances have to be made.

But none of these technical contributions explains the continued life of Ibsen's plays on the stage today; and one regrets the (very natural) tendency of the compilers of programme notes to stress his importance as an innovator. Few things put an audience off a play as much as reading beforehand that its author was the first man to do this or that; it is like being asked to sit for three hours in the first armchair, or in the first house to have been equipped with central heating. Ibsen's enduring greatness as a dramatist is due not to his technical innovations, but to the depth and subtlety of his understanding of human character (especially feminine character), and, which is rarer, of human relationships.

None of the great novelists, Stendhal and Flaubert included, created more memorably observed women than Agnes, Nora, Helen Alving, Rebecca West, Ellida Wangel, Rita Allmers or Ella Rentheim. And he created a succession of male characters of a size and strength that represent a challenge to any actor equal to that of Hamlet or Lear—Brand, Peer Gynt, Oswald Alving, Thomas Stockmann, Halvard Solness, John Gabriel Borkman, Arnold Rubek—characters which defy shallow or "clever" acting, but which, worthily interpreted, offer as rewarding experiences as it is possible to receive in a theatre. Yet so delicate was Ibsen's understanding of human relationships that a selfish actor can only partially succeed in these roles. Unless the relationships with the other characters are right, the performance fails. And it can never be sufficiently stressed that, as Ibsen himself insisted, his leading characters are almost without exception passionate characters, even when those passions are inhibited. They are never sexless (though how often has one not seen them played so!).

[6] *The Scenic Art*, p. 246.

It would be an exaggeration, perhaps, to say that Ibsen's plays are about sex, for they are about so much besides; but there is none of his plays, except *Brand* and *An Enemy of the People,* in which sex is not a major and decisive element.

Ibsen's uniqueness among dramatists as a contributor to the social debate has been noted, but one must underline an essential difference in this respect between him and his great contemporaries. A major writer's biography is only partly the story of his life; perhaps more importantly, it is the story of a series of explosions which he causes in places he has never seen and among people he has never met. With a poet, a novelist, or a philosopher, these explosions occur in myriads of individuals reading in their homes. But this was only partially true of Ibsen. Unlike Tolstoy or Zola, Mill, Nietzsche, Freud or even Marx, unlike, indeed, any writer before him, more like a preacher, a Savonarola or a Wesley, he wrought his effect most powerfully on crowds, gathered together not in a market place or a church or chapel, but in a theatre. It is a commonplace that a man may more easily be converted in a crowd than alone, and it is not the least of Ibsen's numerous contributions to the theatre that he turned it from a place of entertainment and occasional catharsis into a place from which men emerged compelled to re-think basic principles which they had never before seriously questioned. Euripides had done this, but no dramatist since—or anyway not on the same scale. Shakespeare never questioned the established tenets and beliefs of his time as Ibsen did. There were more social abuses in Shakespeare's England than in Ibsen's Norway, but Shakespeare never challenged one of them. Who ever walked out of a Shakespeare play, in his time or since, feeling compelled to re-think their basic concepts of life? Yet that was the effect of Ibsen's "social" plays on his contemporaries, like reading Darwin or Marx or Freud. Nowadays we tend to regard his later plays, less appreciated in his time, as his greater. But because Ibsen's supreme quality was his understanding of human mind and his ability to portray its depths and nuances (so that no actor or actress can ever honestly say that he or she has totally explored or filled that character), and because he did this as surely in the "social" plays as in everything else he wrote, *A Doll's House* and *Ghosts* and *An Enemy of the People* remain as hypnotic today as when it was their messages rather than their psychology that buzzed like a caged fly in the minds of their audiences. As Desmond MacCarthy wrote: "Ibsen's theatre is the theatre of the soul. Important as he was, and is, as a social reformer, it is that which makes him even more important as an artist. Society changes quickly, the mind hardly at all; it is that which makes his work permanent."[7]

Ibsen's two great successors in the realm of tragedy explored fields that

[7] *New Statesman,* 26 May 1917.

he did not. Strindberg, like no writer before him, mapped that no-man's-land where reality and fantasy, sanity and insanity abut; and he wrote of sex with a frankness which Ibsen, being Ibsen, could not match, especially of sex divorced from love and riding hand-in-hand with contempt or hatred. The only other dramatist since Ibsen who is his peer in stature is Chekhov, and to argue whether he or Ibsen is the greater is like arguing whether Bach is superior to Beethoven. Chekhov's feelings about Ibsen were as mixed as Strindberg's. He read him, we must remember, in bad translation (by non-Russians), and Stanislavsky remembered only his frequent expressions of distaste for Ibsen's work. "I recall A. Chekhov once being present at rehearsals of *The Wild Duck*. He looked bored. He did not like Ibsen. He said: 'Look here, Ibsen does not know life. In life it does not happen like that.'" "Just as much as Chekhov disliked Ibsen's plays, he liked Hauptmann's." "At a rehearsal of *Hedda Gabler* at the Moscow Arts, Chekhov said: 'Look here, Ibsen is not a playwright.'" And in his autobiography Stanislavsky summed up: "Chekhov did not like Ibsen as a dramatist, although he placed Ibsen's talents very high. He thought him dry, cold, a man of reason." But this may have been due to the bad translations and the unrealistic way in which Ibsen was played in Russia. Towards the end of his life, however, Chekhov's attitude seems to have been changed. On 30 October 1903, when planning to visit Moscow, he wrote to Stanislavsky: "I haven't yet seen *The Lower Depths, The Pillars of Society,* or *Emperor and Galilean.* I very much want to see all three"; and a week later, on 7 November, he wrote to A. L. Vishensky: "You know Ibsen is my favourite writer."[8]

Pirandello and O'Neill had none of Chekhov's doubts. "After Shakespeare," declared Pirandello, "I unhesitatingly place Ibsen first";[9] and O'Neill found him "much nearer to me than Shakespeare."

O'Neill said that people are too apt to think of Ibsen as merely dreadful and deep. "He's deep, all right," O'Neill continued, "and sometimes dreadful, like life itself, but he's also intensely human and understandable. I needed no professor to tell me that Ibsen as a dramatist knew whereof he spoke.

[8] Cf. Stanislavsky, p. 345; *Chekhov: Literary and Theatrical Reminiscences,* tr. and ed. S. S. Koteliansky (London, 1927), pp. 156, 161–62; *Life and Letters of Anton Chekhov,* tr. and ed. S. S. Koteliansky and Philip Tomlinson (London, 1925), p. 293. Martin Nag (*op. cit.,* p. 111) argues persuasively that *The Wild Duck,* which had been translated into Russian in 1892, four years before Chekhov wrote *The Seagull,* may well have influenced the latter play, which likewise has a dead (or about to be killed) bird as its central symbol. But we must remember Ibsen's warning against confusing parallelisms with influence. It is interesting to note that the Theatre Literary Committee of St. Petersburg approved *The Seagull* for performance only after much criticism, condemning, in the words of the report, "its symbolism, or more correctly, its Ibsenism" as ineffective and unnecessary (Ernest J. Simmons, *Chekkov* [London, 1963], p. 365).

[9] Quoted by Zucker (title page), and in several other books about Ibsen.

I found him for myself outside college grounds and hours. If I had met him inside, I might still be a stranger to Ibsen."[10]

A reaction against Ibsen's work inevitably set in, even before his death. In 1902 Max Beerbohm, reviewing a production of *The Lady from the Sea,* noted with dismay that Ibsen already seemed old-fashioned.

> "Byron is dead"—can that message have fallen with a more awful suddenness on our grandfathers than "Ibsen is old-fashioned" falls on us? . . . But Time is a cyclist. The things of the day before yesterday are nearer to us than the things of yesterday, and nearer still are the things of the day before the day before. Ellida and the rest, creatures of yesterday, will grow gradually younger, and will doubtless be much admired at the close of the century.[11]

Beerbohm was right as far as England is concerned. It has not been the same in all countries; in the Mediterranean lands (because they and their ways of acting are southern, or because they are Catholic?) he is not often played, and then usually in the wrong way for the wrong melodramatic reasons. To the French Ibsen is still, as Georg Brandes wrote in 1902, a Protestant who protests too much.[12] In Germany he is, as he was until recently in England, still regarded primarily as a social commentator, and is in urgent need of reassessment. But in England his reputation stands higher than ever, he is performed with annually increasing frequency, and it is difficult to imagine that other western countries will not soon follow suit. As a Swedish critic has written, Ibsen is the Rome of modern drama. All roads ultimately lead from him and to him.[13]

Ibsen was a poet who used prose as other poets have used the sonnet, as a medium which, by its strict confinement, intensifies and liberates. Let the last word on him be spoken by a poet. Four years after Ibsen's death, Rainer Maria Rilke addressed to him, in *The Notebook of Malte Laurids Brigge,* one of the most eloquent and penetrative tributes ever paid by one great writer to another:[14]

> Loneliest of men, withdrawn from all, how rapidly have they overtaken you by means of your fame! But lately they were fundamentally opposed to you, and now they treat you as their equal. And they carry your words about with them in the cages of their presumption, and exhibit them in the streets and excite them a little from their own safe distance: all those wild beasts of yours.
> When I first read you, they broke loose on me and assailed me in my wilderness—your desperate words—desperate, as you yourself became in the end, you whose course is wrongly traced on every chart. Like a fissure it

[10] Croswell Bowen, *The Curse of the Misbegotten* (London, 1960), p. 125.
[11] Max Beerbohm, *Around Theatres* (London, 1953), pp. 207–8.
[12] Georg Brandes, "Henrik Ibsen i frankrig," in *Norden* (1902), pp. 29–47.
[13] Martin Lamm, *Det moderna dramat,* paperback edn. (Stockholm, 1964), p. 83.
[14] *The Notebook of Malte Laurids Brigge,* tr. John Linton, 2nd edn. (London, 1950), pp. 76–79. It is one of the great English translations of this century.

crosses the heavens, this hopeless hyperbola of your path, that only once curves towards us and draws off again in terror. What mattered it to you whether a woman stays or goes, whether one is seized with vertigo and another with madness, whether the dead live, and the living appear to be dead: what mattered it? It was all so natural to you; you passed through it, as one might cross a vestibule, and did not stop. But yonder, within, you remained stooped, where our destiny seethes and settles and changes colour, farther in than anyone has yet been. A door had sprung open before you, and now you were among the alembics in the firelight. Yonder where, mistrustful, you took no one with you, yonder you sat and discerned processes of change. And there, since your blood drove you to reveal and not to fashion or to speak, there you conceived the vast project of magnifying single-handed these minutiæ, which you yourself first perceived only in test-tubes, so that they should be seen of thousands, immense, before all eyes. Then your theatre came into being. You could not wait until this almost spaceless life, condensed into fine drops by the weight of centuries, should be discovered by the other arts, and gradually made visible to the few who, little by little, come together in their understanding and finally demand to see the general confirmation of these extraordinary rumours in the semblance of the scene opened before them. For this you could not wait. You were there, and you had to determine and record the almost immeasurable: the rise of half a degree in a feeling; the angle of refraction, read off at close quarters, in a will depressed by an almost infinitesimal weight; the slight cloudiness in a drop of desire, and the well-nigh imperceptible change of colour in an atom of confidence. All these: for of just such processes life now consisted, our life, which had slipped into us and had drawn so deeply in that it was scarcely possible even to conjecture about it any more.

Given as you were to revelation, a timeless tragic poet, you had to translate this fine-spun activity at one stroke into the most convincing gestures, into the most present things. Then you set about that unexampled act of violence in your work, which sought ever more impatiently, ever more desperately, equivalents among things that are seen to the inward vision. There was a rabbit, a garret, a room where someone paced to and fro; there was the clatter of glass in a neighbouring apartment, a fire outside the windows; there was the sun. There was a church and a rock-strewn valley that was like a church. But that did not suffice; towers had ultimately to be brought in; and whole mountain ranges; and the avalanches that bury landscapes destroyed the stage, overladen with things tangible used for the sake of expressing the intangible. And now you could do no more. The two extremities that you had bent together, sprang apart; your mad strength escaped from the flexible shaft, and your work was as nothing.

Who should understand, otherwise, why in the end you would not leave the window, headstrong as you always were? You wanted to see the passers-by; for the thought had occurred to you that some day one might make something out of them, if one decided to begin.

London—Stockholm—Oslo. January 1965–March 1970.

Select Bibliography

AGERHOLM, EDVARD. "Henrik Ibsen og Det Kongelige Teater," in *Gads Danske Magasin* (Copenhagen), 1910–11.

AMDAM, PER. "Ibsen og Molde," in *Edda* (Oslo), 1952.

ANDERSEN, ANNETTE. "Ibsen in America," in *Scandinavian Notes and Studies* (Menasha, Wis.), 1935–37.

ANDERSEN, HANS CHRISTIAN. *Brevveksling med Edvard og Henriette Collin,* ed. C. Behrend and H. Topsøe-Jensen, I–VI. Copenhagen, 1933–37.

———*Dagbøger og Breve, 1868–1875,* ed. Jonas Collin. Copenhagen, 1906.

ANDERSON, RASMUS B. *My Life Story.* Madison, 1915.

ANKER, ØYVIND. *Christiania Theaters Repertoire, 1827–1899.* Oslo, 1956.

———*Henrik Ibsens brevveksling med Christiania Theater, 1878–1899.* Oslo, 1965.

———*Kristiania Norske Theaters Repertoire, 1852–1863.* Oslo, 1956.

ARCHER, CHARLES. *William Archer.* London, 1931.

ARCHER, WILLIAM. "Ibsen as I Knew Him," in *Monthly Review* (London), June 1906.

———Introductions to *The Collected Works of Henrik Ibsen,* revised and edited by William Archer, I–XII. London, 1906 ff.

———"The Mausoleum of Ibsen," in *Fortnightly Review* (London), July 1893.

———*The Theatrical 'World' of 1893, 1894, 1895, 1896, 1897.* London, 1894 ff.

ARVESEN, O. *Oplevelser og erindringer.* Christiania, 1921.

BANG, HERMAN. *Teatret.* Copenhagen, 1892.

———*Ti Aar.* Copenhagen, 1891.

BERGGRAV, EIVIND, AND BULL, FRANCIS. *Ibsens sjelelige kriser.* Oslo, 1937.

BERGMAN, GÖSTA M. *Den moderna teaterns genombrott, 1890–1925.* Stockholm, 1966.

BERGSØE, VILHELM. *Henrik Ibsen på Ischia og 'Fra Piazza del Popolo.'* Copenhagen and Christiania, 1907.

BEYER, HARALD. *Søren Kierkegaard i Norge.* Christiania, 1924.

BJÖRKLUND-BEXELL, INGEBORG. "Ibsens *Vildanden,* en studie." Unpublished thesis, 1962.

BJØRNSON, BJØRN. *Bare ungdom.* Oslo, 1934.

———*Fra barndommens dage.* Christiania, 1922.

———*Hjemmet og vennerne.* Oslo, 1932.

BJØRNSON, BJØRNSTJERNE. *Breve til Karoline, 1858–1907,* ed. Dagny Bjørnson-Sautreau. Oslo, 1957.

———*Brevveksling med danske, 1875–1910,* ed. Øyvind Anker, Francis Bull, and Torben Nielsen, I–III. Copenhagen and Oslo, 1953.

———*Brevveksling med svenske, 1858–1909,* ed. Øyvind Anker, Francis Bull, and Örjan Lindberger, I–III. Oslo, 1960–61.

————*Brytnings-aar (brev fra aarene 1871–1878)*, ed. Halvdan Koht, I, II. Christiania, 1921.

————*Gro-tid (brev fra aarene 1857–1870)*, ed. Halvdan Koht, I, II. Christiania, 1912.

————*Kamp-tid (brev fra aarene 1879–1884)*, ed. Halvdan Koht, I, II. Oslo, 1932.

BLANC, T. *Christiania Theaters historie, 1827–1877*. Christiania, 1899.

————*Norges første nationale scene*. Christiania, 1884.

BLYTT, PETER. *Minder fra den første norske scene i Bergen*. Bergen, 1894.

BOTTEN HANSEN, PAUL. "Henrik Ibsen," in *Illustreret Nyhedsblad* (Christiania), 19 July 1863.

BRANDES, EDVARD. *Litterære Tendenser*. Copenhagen, 1968.

————*Om Teater*. Copenhagen, 1947.

————and BRANDES, GEORG. *Brevveksling med nordiske Forfattere og Videnskabs-mænd*, ed. Morten Borup, Francis Bull, and John Landquist, I–VII. Copenhagen, 1939–42.

BRANDES, GEORG. *Henrik Ibsen*. Copenhagen, 1898.

————"Henrik Ibsen i Frankrig," in *Norden* (Stockholm), 1902.

————"Henrik Ibsen og hans Skole i Tyskland," in *Tilskueren* (Copenhagen), June 1890.

————"Henrik Ibsen: Personal Reminiscences and Remarks about His Plays," in *Century Magazine* (New York), February 1917.

————*Levned*, I–III. Copenhagen, 1905–8.

BREDSDORFF, ELIAS. *Sir Edmund Gosse's Correspondence with Scandinavian Writers*. Copenhagen, 1960.

BULL, FRANCIS. *Essays i utvalg*. Oslo, 1964.

————"Henrik Ibsen," in *Norsk litteratur-historie*, ed. Francis Bull, Fredrik Paasche, A. H. Winsnes, and Philip Houm, IV. Oslo, 1960.

————"Hildur Andersen og Henrik Ibsen," in *Edda* (Oslo), 1957.

————Introductions to *Catiline, The Warrior's Barrow, Norma, St. John's Night, The Feast at Solhaug, Olaf Liljekrans, The Vikings at Helgeland, Love's Comedy, Peer Gynt, Ghosts, The Wild Duck, Rosmersholm* and *The Lady from the Sea* in *Henrik Ibsen, Samlede verker, hundreårsutgave*, q.v.

————*Nordisk kunsterliv i Rom*. Oslo, 1960.

————*Tradisjoner og minner*, 3rd edn. Oslo, 1963.

————*Vildanden, og andre essays*. Oslo, 1966.

BULL, MARIE. *Minder fra Bergens første nationale scene*. Bergen, 1905.

CHESNAIS, P. G. LA. Introductions to *Oeuvres complètes d'Henrik Ibsen, traduites par P. G. la Chesnais*, I–XVI. Paris, 1914–45.

COLLIN, CHRISTEN. *Bjørnstjerne Bjørnson, hans barndom og ungdom*, I, II. Christiania, 1902, 1907.

DAÆ, LUDVIG. "Paul Botten Hansen," in *Vidar* (Copenhagen), 1888.

DARDEL, FRITZ VON. *Dagboksanteckningar, 1873–1876*. Stockholm, 1916.

————*Dagboksanteckningar, 1881–1885*. Stockholm, 1920.

DERRY, T. K. *A Short History of Norway*. London, 1957.

DIETRICHSON, LORENTZ. *Svundne tider*, I–IV. Christiania, 1894–1917.

DOWNS, BRIAN W. *Ibsen: the Intellectual Background*. Cambridge, 1946.

DUE, CHRISTOPHER. *Erindringer fra Henrik Ibsens ungdomsaar*. Copenhagen, 1909.

DUVE, ARNE. *Symbolikken i Henrik Ibsens skuespill*. Oslo, 1945.

EITREM, HANS. *Ibsen og Grimstad*. Oslo, 1940.

ELIAS, JULIUS. "Ibsenminne af hans tyske oversætter," in *Samtiden* (Oslo), 1940.

ELLER, W. H. *Ibsen in Germany, 1870–1900*. Boston, 1918.

ELLMANN, RICHARD. *James Joyce*. London, 1959.

FENGER, HENNING. *Georg Brandes Læreår*. Copenhagen, 1955.

————"Ibsen og Georg Brandes indtil 1872," in *Edda* (Oslo), 1964.

FLEETWOOD, CARL GEORGSSON. *Från studieår och diplomattjänst*, I, II. Stockholm, 1968.

FORESTER, THOMAS. *Norway in 1848 and 1849*. London, 1850.

FRANC, MIRIAM. *Ibsen in England*. Boston, 1919.

GEORGE, DAVID E. R. *Henrik Ibsen in Deutschland: Rezeption und Revision*. Göttingen, 1968.

GLÆRSEN, KRISTIAN. "Henrik Ibsen: minder fra mit samvær med ham i utlandet," in *Kringsjaa* (Christiania), 1906.

GOSSE, EDMUND. *Ibsen*. London, 1907.

————*Two Visits to Denmark, 1872, 1874*. London, 1911.

GRAN, GERHARD. *Henrik Ibsen: liv og verker*, I, II. Christiania, 1918.

————ed. *Henrik Ibsen: festskrift i anledning of hans 70de fødselsdag*. Bergen, Stockholm, and Copenhagen, 1898.

GRANVILLE BARKER, HARLEY. "The Coming of Ibsen," in *The Eighteen-Eighties*, ed. Walter de la Mare. Cambridge, 1930.

GREGERSEN, H. *Ibsen in Spain*. Cambridge, Mass., 1936.

GRIEG, HARALD. *En dansk forlegger og fire norske diktere*. Oslo, 1955.

GRØNVOLD, DIDRIK. *Diktere og musikere*. Oslo, 1945.

GRØNVOLD, MARCUS. *Fra Ulrikken til Alperne*. Oslo, 1925.

HALVORSEN, J. B. "Henrik Ibsen," in *Norsk forfatter-lexicon, 1814–1880*, III. Christiania, 1892.

HAMMER, S. C. *Kristianias historie*, IV. Christiania, 1923.

HAMRE, KARI. *Clemens Petersen og hans forhold til norsk litteratur i aarene 1856–1869*. Oslo, 1945.

HAMSUN, KNUT. *Paa turné*. Oslo, 1960.

HEDIN, SVEN. *Stormän och kungar*. Stockholm, 1950.

HEIBERG, GUNNAR. *Ibsen og Bjørnson på scenen*. Christiania, 1918.

————*Salt og sukker*. Christiania, 1924.

HEIBERG, JOHAN LUDVIG. *Om Vaudeville og dens Betydning paa den danske Skueplads*. Copenhagen, 1826.

HEIBERG, JOHANNE LUISE. *Et Liv gjenoplevet i Erindringen*, III. Copenhagen, 1892.

HØST, ELSE. *Hedda Gabler. En monografi*. Oslo, 1958.

HØST, SIGURD. *Ibsens diktning og Ibsen selv*. Oslo, 1927.

IBSEN, BERGLIOT. *De tre*. Oslo, 1948.

IBSEN, HENRIK. *Efterladte skrifter*, ed. Halvdan Koht and Julius Elias, I–III. Christiania and Copenhagen, 1909.

IBSEN, HENRIK. *Samlede verker, hundreårsutgave* (The Centenary Edition, abbr. C.E.), ed. Halvdan Koht, Francis Bull, and Didrik Arup Seip, I–XXI. Oslo, 1928–58.

JÆGER, HENRIK. *Henrik Ibsen: et livsbillede*. Christiania, 1888.

JAMES, HENRY. *The Scenic Art*. London, 1949.

JANSON, KRISTOFER. *Hvad jeg har oplevet*. Christiania, 1913.

JOHNSEN, P. ROSENKRANTZ. *Om og omkring Henrik Ibsen og Suzannah Ibsen*. Oslo, 1928.

JOSEPHSON, LUDVIG. *Ett och annat om Henrik Ibsen och Kristiania Teater*. Stockholm, 1898.

KIELER, LAURA. *Silhouetter*. Odense, 1887.

KINCK, B. M. "Henrik Ibsen og Laura Kieler," in *Edda* (Oslo), 1935.

KING, BASIL. "Ibsen and Emilie Bardach," in *Century Magazine* (New York), October and November 1917.

KNORRING, OSCAR VON. *Två månader i Egypten*. Stockholm, 1873.

KNUDTZON, FREDERIK G. *Ungdomsdage*. Copenhagen, 1927.

KOHT, HALVDAN. *Henrik Ibsen: eit diktarliv*, rev. edn., I, II. Oslo, 1954.

————Introductions to *The Pretenders, Brand, The League of Youth, Emperor and Galilean, The Pillars of Society, A Doll's House, An Enemy of the People* and *Hedda Gabler,* in *Henrik Ibsen, Samlede verker, hundreårsutgave,* q.v.

KOMMANDANTVOLD, K. M. *Ibsen og Sverige.* Oslo, 1956.

LAMM, MARTIN. *Det moderna dramat.* Stockholm, 1948.

LEFFLER, ANNE CHARLOTTE. *En sjävlbiografi* (Stockholm, 1922).

LIE, ERIK. *Erindringer fra et dikterhjem.* Oslo, 1928.

————*Jonas Lie, oplevelser, fortalt af Erik Lie.* Christiania and Copenhagen, 1908.

LINDBERG, PER. *August Lindberg.* Stockholm, 1943.

LINDER, GURLI. *Sällskapsliv i Stockholm under 1880- och 1890-talen.* Stockholm, 1918.

LINDER, STEN. *Ibsen, Strindberg och andra.* Stockholm, 1936.

LINDSTRÖM, GÖRAN. *Strindberg contra Ibsen,* in *Ibsen-Årbok, 1955–1956.* Skien, 1956.

LUGNÉ-POE, AURÉLIEN. *Ibsen.* Paris, 1936.

LUND, AUDHILD. *Henrik Ibsen og Christiania Norske Theater, 1857–1863.* Oslo, 1925.

McFARLANE, J. W., ed. *The Oxford Ibsen,* II, IV–VII. London, 1962–66.

MEYER, MICHAEL. Introductions to and Stage Histories of *Brand, The Lady from the Sea, The Master Builder, John Gabriel Borkman, When We Dead Awaken, The Pillars of Society, The Wild Duck, Hedda Gabler, Little Eyolf, Peer Gynt, A Doll's House, Ghosts, An Enemy of the People, Rosmersholm,* translated by Michael Meyer. New York, 1960–66.

————The same, with the addition of *The Pretenders.* London, 1960–66.

MIDBØE, HANS. *Streiflys over Ibsen.* Oslo, 1960.

MOHR, OTTO LOUS. *Henrik Ibsen som maler.* Oslo, 1953.

MOSFJELD, OSKAR. *Henrik Ibsen og Skien.* Oslo, 1949.

NAG, MARTIN. *Ibsen i russisk åndsliv.* Oslo, 1967.

NEHENDAM, ROBERT. *Gjennem mange Aar.* Copenhagen, 1933.

————*Mennesker bag Masker.* Copenhagen, 1931.

NIELSEN, L. C. *Frederik V. Hegel: et Mindeskrift,* I, II. Copenhagen, 1909.

NIELSEN, YNGVAR. *En Kristianiensers erindringer fra 1850- og 1860-aarene.* Christiania and Copenhagen, 1910.

NYHOLM, KELA. "Henrik Ibsen på den franske scene," in *Ibsen-Årbok, 1957–1959.* Skien, 1959.

OLLÉN, GUNNAR. *Ibsens dramatik.* Stockholm, 1955.

ORDING, FREDERIK. *Henrik Ibsens vennekreds: Det lærde Holland.* Oslo, 1927.

ØSTVEDT, EINAR. *Henrik Ibsen.* Oslo, 1968.

————*Henrik Ibsen og la bella Italia.* Skien, 1965.

PAULI, GEORG. *Mina romerska år.* Stockholm, 1924.

PAULSEN, JOHN. *Erindringer. Siste samling.* Copenhagen, 1903.

————*Mine Erindringer.* Copenhagen, 1900.

————*Nye Erindringer.* Copenhagen, 1901.

————*Samliv med Ibsen,* I, II. Copenhagen and Christiania, 1906, 1913.

PETTERSEN, HJALMAR. *Henrik Ibsen 1828–1928, bedømt af Samtid og Eftertid.* Oslo, 1928.

ROBINS, ELIZABETH. *Theatre and Friendship.* London, 1932.

RUDLER, RODERICK. "Scenebilledkunsten i Norge for 100 år siden," in *Kunst og kultur* (Oslo), 1961.

SCHINDLER, PETER. *En Ungdom.* Copenhagen, 1942.

SCHNEIDER, J. A. *Fra det gamle Skien,* III. Skien, 1924.

SEIP, DIDRIK ARUP. "Henrik Ibsen og K. Knudsen: Det sproglige gjennembrud hos Ibsen," in *Edda* (Christiania), 1914.

————Introductions to *Poems, The Master Builder, Little Eyolf, John Gabriel Borkman,* and *When We Dead Awaken,* in *Henrik Ibsen, Samlede verker, hundreårsutgave,* q.v.

SHAW, GEORGE BERNARD. *Collected Letters, 1874–1897,* ed. Dan H. Laurence. London, 1965.

———*Our Theatres in the Nineties,* rev. edn., I–III. London, 1954.

———*The Quintessence of Ibsenism,* 3rd edn. London, 1922.

SKAVLAN, EINAR. *Gunnar Heiberg.* Oslo, 1960.

SONTUM, BOLETTE. "Personal Recollections of Henrik Ibsen," in *The Bookman,* XXXVII (New York), 1913.

SPRINCHORN, EVERT, ed. *Ibsen: Letters and Speeches.* New York, 1964.

STANISLAVSKY, KONSTANTIN. *My Life in Art,* translated by J. J. Robbins. London, 1924.

STEINER, GEORGE. *The Death of Tragedy.* London, 1961.

STRINDBERG, AUGUST. *August Strindbergs brev,* ed. Torsten Eklund, I–XI. Stockholm, 1948 ff.

———"Konstakademiens utställning, 1877," in *Kulturhistoriske studier.* Stockholm, 1881.

———"Den litterära reaktionen i Sverige sedan 1865," in *Tilskueren* (Copenhagen), May 1886.

TEDFORD, INGRID. *Ibsen Bibliography, 1928–1957.* Oslo, 1961.

THORESEN, MAGDALENE. *Breve, 1855–1901,* ed. J. Clausen and P. F. Rist. Copenhagen, 1919.

———"Om Henrik Ibsen og hans hustru," in *Juleroser* (Copenhagen), 1901.

VISTED, KRISTOFER. "Henrik Ibsen i karikaturen," in *Boken om bøger,* II. Oslo, 1927.

WIESENER, A. M. *Henrik Ibsen og det norske theater i Bergen, 1851–1857.* Bergen, 1928.

WIRSEN, C. D. AF. *Kritiker.* Stockholm, 1901.

WOLF, LUCIE. *Mine livserindringer.* Christiania, 1898.

ZUCKER, A. E. *Ibsen, the Master Builder.* London, 1929.

NEWSPAPERS AND PERIODICALS

Aftenbladet	Christiania	*London Figaro*	
Aftenposten	Christiania	*Morgenbladet*	Christiania
Aftonbladet	Stockholm	*Morgenbladet*	Copenhagen
Bergenske Blade		*Nationen*	Christiania
Bergens-Posten		*Nordisk Tidskrift*	Stockholm
Bergens Tidende		*Ny Illustrerad Tidning*	Stockholm
Christiania-Posten		*Ny Illustreret Tidende*	Copenhagen
Dagbladet	Christiania	*Nya Dagligt Allehanda*	Stockholm
Dagbladet	Copenhagen	*Nyt Tidsskrift*	Christiania
Dagens Nyheder	Copenhagen	*Ord och Bild*	Stockholm
Dagens Nyheter	Stockholm	*Pall Mall Gazette*	London
Dansk Maanedsskrift	Copenhagen	*Politiken*	Copenhagen
Dølen	Christiania	*Samtiden*	Oslo
Edda	Christiania	*Saturday Review*	London
Fædrelandet	Copenhagen	*Spectator*	London
Fortnightly Review	London	*Sunday Times*	London
Illustreret Nyhedsblad	Christiania	*Tilskueren*	Copenhagen
Illustreret Tidende	Copenhagen	*The Times*	London
Illustrated London News		*Urd*	Oslo
Juleroser	Copenhagen	*Verdens Gang*	Christiania
Kunst og kultur	Oslo	*Vikingen*	Christiania

Index

Works by Ibsen are printed in small capitals. For the convenience of readers unacquainted with the Scandinavian alphabet, æ, ä and å have been listed under a, and œ, ö and ø under o

561, 611, 630, 673, 706n, 706, 717,
721, 731, 735–36, 754–55, 756, 760,
779, 800
Ibsen, Birgitta, 3
Ibsen, Eleonora, 806, 811
Ibsen, Hedvig, 5, 14, 19, 21, 23, 51–53,
164; 294–95, 399, 439, 540, 553, 590,
660–61, 689, 776, 803
Ibsen, Henrich Petersen (grandfather),
4
Ibsen, Henrik Johan
  Skien (1828–43)
    ancestry, 3–4; childhood, 7ff.; father
    ruined, 13; move to Venstøp, 13;
    supposed illegitimacy, 14–16; school-
    ing, 16, 18–20, 23; early appearance,
    17; love of puppets and conjuring,
    17–18; takes art lessons, 20; early
    character, 20–21; moves to Snipe-
    torp, 23; leaves for Grimstad, 24
  Grimstad (1844–50)
    first impressions, 25–26; work at
    apothecary's, 28–29, 32–34, 37–38;
    remembered by Due, 28–29, 36–40;
    by Marie Thomsen, 28–29, 33–34;
    by Eriksens, 29–30, 33; adolescent
    appearance, 29–30; early reading,
    29; fathers illegitimate child, 31;
    painting, 32–33; debt to Elizabeth
    Crawfurd, 35–36; early poems, 35–
    36; "On Self-Knowledge," 36; early
    views on marriage, 37; as caricatur-
    ist, 37; toughness, poverty, meets
    Schulerud, 38; reaction to 1848 revo-
    lutions, 39; revisits Skien, 40; revo-
    lutionary poems, 41–42; writes CATI-
    LINE, 42–44; possible literary in-
    fluences, 42–43; first poem published,
    45; infatuation with Clara Ebbell,
    48; physical timidity, 48; mixed
    views on dancing, 48–49; leaves
    Grimstad, 51; revisits Skien, 51–53
  Christiania (1850–51)
    Heltberg's "student factory," 55–56;
    CATILINE published, 56–58; meets
    Botten Hansen, Vinje, etc., 58; takes
    part in political demonstration, 59;
    meets Bjørnson, 59; writes THE WAR-
    RIOR'S BARROW, 60–61; and THE
    PTARMIGAN OF JUSTEDAL, 61–62;
    continued poverty, 63; fails matricu-
    lation, 63; more poems, 65–70;
    journalism and drama criticisms, 69–
    73; political commentaries, 73–76;
    name printed for first time, 77; es-
    capes arrest for sedition, 78; doubts

about career, 79; engaged by Old
Bull for Bergen Theatre, 82–83
  Bergen (1851–57)
    tasks at theatre, 86–89; visits Copen-
    hagen, meets Heiberg and Hans An-
    dersen, sees Shakespeare acted for
    first time, reads Hettner's *Das Mod-
    erne Drama*, 90–97; visits Dresden,
    97–98; writes ST. JOHN'S NIGHT,
    98–100; it is staged and fails, 102;
    isolation from good drama, 102–3;
    stage conditions at Bergen, 103–6; I.
    as a director, 106–8; falls in love
    with Rikke Holst, 109–11; chased
    away by her father, 110; rebuked
    by board, 112–13; offers LADY INGER
    anonymously, 114–15; it fails, too,
    117; smartness of dress, 118–19; dis-
    covers sagas and mediaeval ballads,
    120–22; writes THE FEAST AT SOL-
    HAUG, 122–23; directs *As You Like
    It*, 123; FEAST AT SOLHAUG is a suc-
    cess, 124–25; lectures on Shake-
    speare, 123; meets Magdalene and
    Suzannah Thoresen, 124–25; Suzan-
    nah accepts him, 126; compared by
    Magdalene with Kierkegaard. 127–
    28; takes company to Trondhjem,
    128–29; prepares command perform-
    ance for Prince Napoleon, 130–32;
    writes OLAF LILJEKRANS, 132–33; it
    fails, 134; writes essay on the Heroic
    Ballad, 135–38; leaves for new the-
    atre in Christiania, 139–42
  Christiania (1857–64)
    first productions in Christiania, 146;
    castigates public for lack of taste and
    condemns photographic realism, 146–
    47; on proper use of symbolism, 148;
    completes THE VIKINGS AT HELGE-
    LAND, 149–51; is condemned by
    Bjørnson as derivative, 153; I. on his
    own character, 154; attacks "Danish"
    Christiania Theatre, 155; directs
    dreadful plays, 156–57; marries, 158;
    stages THE VIKINGS, 159–61; defends
    policy in annual report, 162–63; re-
    visits Skien to borrow money, 164; is
    attacked for incompetence, 166–68;
    helps to found Norwegian Society,
    169; his marriage described, 170; son
    born, 170; frequents "The Learned
    Holland," 171–73; writes ON THE
    HEIGHTS, 174–75; I. and Kierke-
    gaard, 175–77; last visit to Skien,
    178; appeals unsuccessfully for travel
    grant, 178–79; writes hack poetry,
    180; is attacked by Knud Knudsen,

206; I. thanks for this notice, 207; criticises BRAND, 249; introduces G. Brandes to I.'s work, 250n; Bj. writes to about BRAND, 251; condemns PEER GYNT, 269; I.'s rage at this notice, 270–71; Bj. defends Petersen to I., 271; contrasted with G. Brandes, 284; involved in homosexual scandal, 287; sees GHOSTS in Chicago, 590; condemns THE WILD DUCK in Chicago paper, 602; keeps up attacks on I., 602n; also 290, 344, 422

Petersen, Frederik, 455

Petersen, Julius, 559

Petersen, Laura, see Kieler, Laura

Petersen, Margrethe, 434

Petersen, Morten Smith, 434–35

Petersen, N. M., 120–22, 135, 149

Petersen, Otto, 522

Petersen, Richard, 155; 226, 227

Petersen, Valdemar, 768n

Petersen, Vilhelm, 674n

Petersen, William, 701, 702

Peterssen, Eilif, 419, 732–33, 734

Petrograd, 508–9

Pettie, John, 373

Pharo, 27, 33

Phelps, Samuel, 179

Philippi, Felix, 561

Photographic realism, I. attacks, 147

Photography, 147; 270, 794, 804

Physical appearance, I.'s, 15–17, 21, 29–30, 34, 60, 63, 92, 106–7, 118–19, 127–28, 134, 139–40, 153–54, 161, 164, 172, 176; 254, 292, 317n, 344, 361, 372, 374–75, 376, 415, 429–30, 450, 451, 462, 468, 469, 493, 494, 515–16, 552–53, 558, 559–60, 573, 579, 581, 585–86, 595–96, 654, 660, 678, 680–81, 683–84, 710–11, 718–19, 733–34, 736–37, 738, 781, 795, 799, 800, 802, 803, 804–5, 808–9

Pigott, W. S., 704n

Pilgrim, H. von, 577

PILLARS OF SOCIETY, THE, Skien and, 11n; Grimstad and, 27–28, 34; difficult gestation of, 317, 318, 366, 377, 406, 425; possible debt to G. Brandes, 363, 364; counterblast to THE LEAGUE OF YOUTH, 390, 510; its significance for I.'s future work, 418, 437; mutilated title leaked, 430; publication and reception, 430–32, 456–57; in Germany, 418, 430, 440, 441–42, 495, 511, 571, 577, 595, 607, 608, 630–31, 650, 681–82, 714, 740, 796; summary and analysis, 432–37; effect on the young, 435–

36; first productions of, 437–38; compared with A DOLL'S HOUSE, 454, 455–56; in England, 442–43, 470, 493, 495, 524, 525, 604, 607; Archer translates, 443, 470–71, 493; style compared with GHOSTS, 490; in America, 502, 629n; in Russia, 628, 758, 778, 815; in France, 742; I. sees, 779; Joyce quotes, 790; in *Finnegans Wake,* 792n; Chekhov wishes to see, 815; also 15, 100, 199; 248, 296 404, 426, 427n, 428, 453n, 453, 458, 483, 488, 496, 534, 570, 574, 593, 599, 628, 671, 678, 708, 709, 714, 747, 758, 759, 784, 787, 791n

Pingel V., 442n

Pinero, Sir Arthur Wing, 472, 657, 743, 760

Pirandello, Luigi, 761, 815

Pirenne, Henri, 576n

Pisa, 39

Pius IX, Pope, 219, 224, 480

Planché, James Robinson, 179, 182

Playboy of the Western World, The, 656

Plesner, Johanne Cathrine, 4

Plimsoll, Samuel, 435

Poe, Edgar Allan, 520

Poel, William, 547

POEMS, I.'s Collected, I. prepares, 275, 319, 328, 335–40; publication, 340; reception, 340–41, 348–50, 354; also 342–43, 351–52, 394, 407, 450, 458, 507, 508, 682, 701, 795; see also under titles of individual poems

Poland, 59; 236, 406, 495, 523, 546, 594

Political Tinker, The, 69

Politics, I. and, 39–42, 58–59, 69, 73–79, 109–10, 173, 212–15; 296, 313–14, 329–31, 338–39, 343, 357, 360, 361–62, 390–91, 457, 480, 485–86, 498–99, 503, 510, 515, 525–26, 557–58, 570, 579–80, 583, 595, 598–99, 635–38, 642, 671, 675, 690–91, 707

Pollock, Sir Frederick, 702

Politiken, 536, 545, 564, 602, 605, 644, 656, 679n, 694, 696, 722, 724, 765, 768n, 783, 785, 786, 796

Pompeii, 198; 266, 311, 316

Ponsard, Francis, 88

Pontius Pilate, 635

Pontoppidan, Henri, 654

Pope, Alexander, 200; 252

Potter County, 87

Poulsen, Emil, 325, 333, 456n, 547, 656, 721, 752, 761

Poverty, I.'s, 12–14, 20–22, 25, 29, 31, 38, 49, 57, 62, 93–94, 110, 164–65,